THE OXFORD HANDBOOK OF
SLAVIC AND EAST EUROPEAN FOLKLORE

THE OXFORD HANDBOOK OF

SLAVIC AND EAST EUROPEAN FOLKLORE

Edited by
MARGARET HIEBERT BEISSINGER

OXFORD
UNIVERSITY PRESS

Oxford University Press is a department of the University of Oxford. It furthers
the University's objective of excellence in research, scholarship, and education
by publishing worldwide. Oxford is a registered trade mark of Oxford University
Press in the UK and certain other countries.

Published in the United States of America by Oxford University Press
198 Madison Avenue, New York, NY 10016, United States of America.

© Oxford University Press 2025

All rights reserved. No part of this publication may be reproduced, stored in
a retrieval system, or transmitted, in any form or by any means, without the
prior permission in writing of Oxford University Press, or as expressly permitted
by law, by license, or under terms agreed with the appropriate reproduction
rights organization. Inquiries concerning reproduction outside the scope of the
above should be sent to the Rights Department, Oxford University Press, at the
address above.

You must not circulate this work in any other form
and you must impose this same condition on any acquirer.

CIP data is on file at the Library of Congress

ISBN 978-0-19-008077-8

DOI: 10.1093/oxfordhb/9780190080778.001.0001

Printed by Marquis Book Printing, Canada

To the memory of my loving parents

Contents

Acknowledgments	xiii
About the Editor	xv
List of Contributors	xvii
A Note about the Play Symbol	xxi
Introduction	xxiii
Margaret Hiebert Beissinger	

PART I. LIFE-CYCLE FOLKLORE

Weddings   3

1. Ukrainian Wedding Rituals   5
   Natalie Kononenko

2. Russian Wedding Songs   30
   Olga Levaniouk

3. Serbian Wedding Practices in Postwar Kosovo   60
   Sanja Zlatanović

4. *Tambura* Bands and Sonic Flag Rituals in Croatian Weddings   83
   Ian MacMillen

5. Marriage and Wedding Traditions among the *Cortorar* Roma in Romania   108
   Cătălina Tesăr

Childbirth   137

6. Estonian Runosongs on Childcare, Pregnancy, Birth, and Intimacy   139
   Mari Väina

7. The Folklore of Childbirth in Russia   168
   Jeanmarie Rouhier-Willoughby

Death Rites — 191

8. Greek Death Rituals and Lament — 193
   GAIL HOLST-WARHAFT

9. Customary Practices of Death and Mourning in Albania — 216
   BLEDAR KONDI

10. Death Rites and Laments in Russia — 240
    ELIZABETH WARNER

PART II. THE TRADITIONAL CALENDAR, MAGIC, AND FOLK BELIEF

Folklore of the Seasonal Cycle — 273

11. Baltic Calendrical Folklore — 275
    ELO-HANNA SELJAMAA

12. Seasonal Rituals, Traditional Dance, and Ethnochoreology in Serbia — 295
    SELENA RAKOČEVIĆ

13. Folklore of the Seasonal Cycle in Croatia: The Lastovo Carnival — 311
    IVA NIEMČIĆ

14. Dance in Calendrical Community Celebrations in Romania — 335
    LIZ MELLISH

Magic and the Power of Words — 361

15. Magic in Hungary: Verbal Charms, Benedictions, and Exorcisms — 363
    DÁNIEL BÁRTH

16. Inverted Behavior in South Slavic Ritual and Magic — 385
    MARIA VIVOD

Varieties of Folk Belief — 401

17. Eschatology and Peasant Visions in Moldovan Folk Religion — 403
    JAMES A. KAPALÓ

18. Songs, Rites, and Identity in the Religious Folklore of Latvia and Lithuania   430
    MICHAEL STRMISKA, GATIS OZOLIŅŠ, ODETA RUDLING, AND DIGNE ŪDRE

19. Folk Belief and Religion in Ukraine: Creating the Charisma of Place   459
    MARIYA LESIV

PART III. ORAL TRADITIONAL NARRATIVE

Poetry: Epic and Ballad   485

20. *Byliny*: Russian Folk Epic   487
    NATALIE KONONENKO

21. *Dumy*: Ukrainian Folk Epic   513
    NATALIE KONONENKO

22. South Slavic Epic and the Philology of the Border   541
    DAVID F. ELMER

23. South Slavic Women's Ballads   576
    AIDA VIDAN

Prose: Folktale and Legend   603

24. Folk Tales in Greece   605
    MARIA KALIAMBOU

25. Slovak Tales and the Collections of Pavol Dobšinský   628
    JANA PIROŠČÁKOVÁ

26. Vladimir Propp and Russian Wondertales   655
    SIBELAN FORRESTER

27. Supernatural Legends in the Western Balkans   675
    DORIAN JURIĆ

28. Polish Urban Legends as a Folklore Genre   698
    MARTA WÓJCICKA

PART IV. MUSIC, SONG, IDENTITY, AND PERFORMANCE

Ethnoreligious Identity: Music and Song — 721

29. The *Sevdalinka* as Traditional Bosnian Love Song — 723
    NIRHA EFENDIĆ

30. The Traditional Yiddish Folk Song — 741
    MICHAEL LUKIN

31. Klezmer Music in Eastern Europe and America — 769
    WALTER ZEV FELDMAN

Balkan Romani Music Traditions — 789

32. Romani (Gypsy) Music in Bulgaria and Macedonia — 791
    LOZANKA PEYCHEVA

33. The Music of Urban *Lăutari* in Southern Romania — 817
    SPERANȚA RĂDULESCU AND MARGARET HIEBERT BEISSINGER

34. Romani Musical Labor and Cultural Politics in Southeastern Serbia — 845
    ALEXANDER MARKOVIĆ

Folk and Popular Music in Post-communist Eastern Europe — 869

35. Bluegrass as *Folk* Music in the Czech Republic — 871
    LEE BIDGOOD

36. *Folktron*: Folklore Influences in Contemporary Bulgarian Popular Music — 895
    ASYA DRAGANOVA

37. Albanian-Language *Etnopop* and the Emergence of a "Balkan" Regional Music Sphere — 918
    JANE C. SUGARMAN

PART V. THE FOLKLORE OF EVERYDAY LIFE

Folk Wit, Wisdom, and the Spoken Word   951

38. *Chastushki*   953
    LAURA J. OLSON AND SVETLANA ADONYEVA

39. Wise and Humorous Words: Hungarian Proverbs, Riddles, and Jokes   985
    ANNA T. LITOVKINA, KATALIN VARGHA, PÉTER BARTA, AND HRISZTALINA HRISZTOVA-GOTTHARDT

Material Culture   1011

40. Tradition and Adaptation in Russian Folk Art   1013
    ALISON HILTON

41. Folk Art Reassessed: Entangled Material Culture in Rural Romania   1036
    ALEXANDRA URDEA AND MAGDALENA BUCHCZYK

42. Foodways in Moldova   1055
    JENNIFER R. CASH

Index   1085

Acknowledgments

I wish, first of all, to thank the many authors who have contributed to this exciting handbook. They have all brought original and intriguing perspectives to a diverse set of topics in the field of Slavic and east European folklore. Their expertise, insights, and dedication are present on every page of this volume. I am also grateful to the editors at Oxford University Press, who have been a joy to work with. I am indebted to Elda Granata for originally inviting me, on behalf of the Press, to edit this handbook. I am likewise thankful to Holly Mitchell, who was the first project editor to work with me in this capacity. Katie Lowry cheerfully took over as acquisitions editor about halfway through this journey, and I thank her warmly for her sustained encouragement, good humor, and understanding. More recently Olivia Kier joined the team as my second project editor, fitting right in as she generously and thoughtfully responded to all my inquiries.

I can never adequately express my gratitude to my colleagues, friends, and students, many of whom have contributed to this volume and who, over the years, have furthered this project in ways big and small: a list of all of their names would continue for pages! So I convey my sincere appreciation to them collectively for discussions we have had, emails we have exchanged, books and essays that they have written, and in general for opening my mind to so many new and illuminating perspectives. I would like, however, to single out a few whose knowledge and suggestions have been especially helpful. They include Natalie Kononenko, Mariya Lesiv, Susan Niditch, Simon Bronner, Barbara Kirshenblatt-Gimblett, Galit Hasan-Rokem, Mirjam Fried, Victor Friedman, Thomas Keenan, Tsering Wangyal Shawa, and Joshua Velasquez.

I am deeply saddened to relay that there are two contributors to this volume who are no longer with us. It is with profound sorrow and a sense of loss that I acknowledge the passing of my dear friend and colleague, the ethnomusicologist Speranța Rădulescu, who left us in 2022. During my many trips to Romania after the revolution, Speranța and her husband Lali were perpetually there waiting for me with open arms, sharing with me their home, generosity, and many lively exchanges, not to mention the endless cups of coffee in their cozy kitchen as we talked shop. The year 2022 also brought the loss of my gracious and buoyant colleague and friend, the ethnochoreologist Selena Rakočević.

My family has been a constant source of love and encouragement during this project. I fondly acknowledge my sister Cathy and brother Tom, who have been loyal, caring, and always there for me during the years of "the handbook"; their ongoing support has been invaluable. My children Jonathan and Rebecca forever inspire me with their spirit and love. As always, Jon has been strong, comforting, and "chill," and Becca—sweet and blessed with an inimitable sense of humor—cheered me on many a long day of editing.

She also expertly produced the photograph for the cover of this volume. To Mark I express my deepest affection and gratitude for his steadfast love and encouragement, patience, and advice. His devoted companionship and delicious pots of cabbage soup heartily sustained me. Finally, I tenderly thank my late parents, who enthusiastically supported my dreams and to whose memory (and with cherished memories) I dedicate this volume. Their hearts and home were always filled with love, warmth, laughter, joy, and celebration. I sorely miss them still.

About the Editor

Margaret Hiebert Beissinger is a research scholar and lecturer in the Department of Slavic Languages and Literatures at Princeton University. Before teaching at Princeton, she was on the faculty of the Slavic Department and the Folklore Program at the University of Wisconsin–Madison. Her research and publications focus on Slavic and east European folklore, oral epic, and Romani culture and music-making. She has authored numerous articles and chapters as well as *The Art of the Lăutar: The Epic Tradition of Romania*; she has also co-edited *Epic Traditions in the Contemporary World* and *Manele in Romania: Cultural Expression and Social Meaning in Balkan Popular Music*.

Contributors

Svetlana Adonyeva, Director of non-profit organization The Propp Centre: Humanitarian Studies in the Sphere of Traditional Culture

Péter Barta, Department of Translation and Interpreting, Institute of Language Mediation, Faculty of Humanities, Eötvös Loránd University

Dániel Bárth, Professor of folkloristics, Department of Folklore, Eötvös Loránd University

Margaret Hiebert Beissinger, Research scholar and lecturer, Department of Slavic Languages and Literatures, Princeton University

Lee Bidgood, Professor of Bluegrass, Old-Time, and Roots Music Studies, Department of Appalachian Studies, East Tennessee State University

Magdalena Buchczyk, Junior professor of social anthropology, Humboldt-Universität zu Berlin

Jennifer R. Cash, Lecturer, Department of History, Nanyang Technological University

Asya Draganova, Senior lecturer in popular music culture, Birmingham City University

Nirha Efendić, Curator for oral poetry, Department of Ethnology, National Museum of Bosnia and Herzegovina, University of Sarajevo

David F. Elmer, Eliot Professor of Greek Literature, Department of the Classics, Harvard University

Walter Zev Feldman, Former professor of music, New York University Abu Dhabi

Sibelan Forrester, Susan W. Lippincott Professor of Modern and Classical Languages and Russian, Swarthmore College

Alison Hilton, Wright Family Professor of Art History, emerita, Georgetown University

Gail Holst-Warhaft, Adjunct professor, comparative literature, Cornell University

Hrisztalina Hrisztova-Gotthardt, Foreign Language Center, University of Pécs

Dorian Jurić, Visiting assistant professor, Indiana University Bloomington

Maria Kaliambou, Senior lector II, Hellenic Studies Program, Yale University

James A. Kapaló, Senior lecturer, Study of Religions Department, University College Cork

Bledar Kondi, Senior researcher and assistant professor, Department for Ethnomusicology, Martin-Luther-University, Institute for Music, Media Studies and Linguistics

Natalie Kononenko, Kule Chair of Ukrainian Ethnography, emerita, Department of Modern Languages and Cultural Studies, University of Alberta

Mariya Lesiv, Associate professor, Department of Folklore, Memorial University of Newfoundland and Labrador

Olga Levaniouk, Professor of classics, Department of Classics, University of Washington

Anna T. Litovkina, Department of English Language and Literature, J. Selye University

Michael Lukin, Research fellow, Jewish Music Research Centre, The Hebrew University

Ian MacMillen, Lecturer in Russian, East European, and Eurasian Studies and in Music, Yale University

Alexander Marković, Independent researcher

Liz Mellish, Independent academic researcher

Iva Niemčić, Senior research associate, director of the Institute of Ethnology and Folklore Research, Institute of Ethnology and Folklore Research

Laura J. Olson, Professor of Russian, East European, and Eurasian Studies, University of Colorado, Boulder

Gatis Ozoliņš, Senior researcher, Institute of Literature, Folklore and Art, University of Latvia

Lozanka Peycheva, Professor of ethnomusicology, Institute of Ethnology and Folklore Studies with Ethnographic Museum, Bulgarian Academy of Sciences

Jana Piroščáková, Senior researcher, Institute of Slovak Literature of the Slovak Academy of Sciences

Speranța Rădulescu[†], Former associate professor of ethnomusicology, National University of Music

Selena Rakočević[†], Former associate professor of ethnochoreology, Department of Ethnomusicology, Faculty of Music, University of Arts

Jeanmarie Rouhier-Willoughby, Professor of Russian, folklore, and linguistics, Department of Modern and Classical Languages, Literatures and Cultures, University of Kentucky

Odeta Rudling, Researcher, History Department, Lund University

Mari Väina, Senior researcher, Estonian Folklore Archives, Estonian Literary Museum

Elo-Hanna Seljamaa, Associate professor of Estonian and comparative folklore, Institute of Cultural Research, University of Tartu

Michael Strmiska, Professor of world history, Global Studies Department, Orange County Community College

Jane C. Sugarman, Professor emerita of music, The Graduate Center, City University of New York

Cătălina Tesăr, Researcher, Department of Ethnological Studies, National Museum of the Romanian Peasant

Digne Ūdre, PhD candidate, Department of Estonian and comparative Folklore, University of Tartu

Alexandra Urdea, Independent researcher

Katalin Vargha, Senior research fellow, Department of Folklore Studies, Institute of Ethnology, HUN-REN Research Centre for the Humanities

Aida Vidan, Director of studies, International Literary and Cultural Studies, Tufts University

Maria Vivod, Freelance scientific researcher

Elizabeth Warner, Former professor of Russian, head of Russian Department, University of Durham

Marta Wójcicka, Professor, Department of Media Communication, Institute of Social Communication and Media Sciences, Maria Skłodowska Curie University

Sanja Zlatanović, Senior research fellow, Institute of Political Science, Slovak Academy of Sciences

A Note about the Play Symbol

All audio and video examples referenced in-text with the symbol ▶ are available in the chapters online on Oxford Academic and on YouTube.

Introduction

MARGARET HIEBERT BEISSINGER

FOLKLORE historically has played and continues to play a fundamental role in all of the national, ethnic, racial, religious, linguistic, and cultural communities of the Slavic and east European world. These lands—loosely connected by circumstances of geography, history, culture, and politics—are spread over a massive area, extending from the eastern zones of Russia to the western borders of the Czech Republic and from Estonia along the Baltic Sea to Greece at the southern tip of the Balkan Peninsula.[1] Occupying the easternmost territories of this broad expanse are the East Slavs (Russians, Ukrainians, and Belarusians). Moving westward are the Baltic states and central European countries: Estonia, Latvia, and Lithuania (which border on the Baltic Sea and are situated to the west of Russia and north of Belarus), along with the West Slavic nations of Poland, Slovakia, and the Czech Republic (now also called "Czechia"), as well as Hungary. Located below central Europe is southeastern Europe, of which Slovenia, Croatia, Serbia, Bosnia-Herzegovina, Montenegro, North Macedonia, and Bulgaria are South Slavic, while Romania, Moldova, Kosovo, Albania, and Greece belong to the rest of the Balkans (Figure 1). Viewed in terms of geography, the Slavic and east European regions form one contiguous space. Yet political and national borders in this part of the world, names of countries or cities, and people(s) who reside in them have repeatedly changed over time, reflecting complicated and shifting histories. In other words, ethnic, linguistic, religious, and/or cultural identities of the various communities who inhabit these lands frequently do not correspond neatly with the various boundaries of nation-states, empires, or geographic features.

This broadly defined territory includes a wide variety of distinctive cultures. Many of the languages spoken are Slavic, including East Slavic (Russian, Ukrainian, and Belarusian), West Slavic (Polish, Czech, and Slovak), and South Slavic (Slovenian, Croatian, Serbian, Bosnian, Montenegrin, Macedonian, and Bulgarian). But many are not Slavic, including Finno-Ugric (Estonian and Hungarian), Baltic (Latvian and Lithuanian), East Romance (Romanian), Albanic (Albanian), Hellenic (Greek), Indic (Romani), and Germanic (Yiddish). Moreover, religious identities in the region range from Christianity, Islam, and Judaism to pockets of neo-paganism reflecting pre-Christian beliefs and folklore. The majority of Slavs and east Europeans are Christian (Cooperman and Sahgal 2017:20).[2] Orthodox Christians are the most

FIG. 1. Contemporary eastern Europe.

(*Source*: "Political Europe" (2021).)

numerous among them and are predominantly East Slavs and southeast Europeans.[3] By contrast, Roman Catholicism has traditionally been practiced chiefly by central Europeans and the westernmost South Slavs, whose lands form the western edge of eastern Europe.[4] Protestant Christians are located in smaller numbers mainly in central Europe, while over the twentieth and twenty-first centuries Neo-Protestants have found converts throughout the area. Islam was adopted in the Balkans during the early years of Ottoman rule, especially in Bosnia, Albania, and Kosovo.[5] Roma in eastern Europe are Orthodox Christians, Muslims, and Catholics.[6] Judaism—virtually non-existent in the region since the Holocaust—was professed by communities of Ashkenazim who had emigrated from western Europe starting in the sixteenth century; they settled primarily in the East Slavic zones, central Europe, Romania, and Moldova. Finally, neo-pagan beliefs and practices have been espoused by small groups—mainly in the Baltic countries, Russia, and Ukraine—especially since the fall of communism.

The Oxford Handbook of Slavic and East European Folklore is about the many diverse communities of people in the region—living in different lands, experiencing different histories, speaking different languages, and observing different faiths—and how they mark the life cycle and the calendar year, tell stories and jokes, make music, dance, celebrate, and feast, among a variety of other things, in traditional ways that are meaningful to them. It is about the abundant array of folklore—both the very traditional as well as the very contemporary—experienced by the many men, women, and children who have been and are part of the Slavic and east European world.

The chapters are written by an international team of specialists. They are locals, "outsiders," and those in-between: east European, west European, and North American folklorists, ethnographers, scholars of oral traditions, ethnomusicologists, ethnochoreologists, and historians. While many of the authors employ archival and/or historical research in their discussions, the majority of the chapters are based, at least in part, on fieldwork, thus giving the authors' findings a resonant immediacy. Indeed, the field of Slavic and east European folklore offers such rich and exciting possibilities for research precisely because the oral traditions there have remained vital and dynamic so much longer than elsewhere in Europe and, as a result, continue to provide abundant opportunities for fieldwork. As will be evident in the pages ahead, a wide variety of methodological and theoretical approaches are employed by the authors, representing a rich diversity of scholarship.

The term "folklore" was coined in 1846. While the British antiquary William Thoms is credited with this word invention (Dundes 1965:1), variant forms of the term had been around well before the mid-nineteenth century, and certainly the materials of folklore had long before been collected and examined (Bronner 2018:17–18). The "folk" may be said to "refer to *any group of people whatsoever* who share at least one common factor" (Dundes 1965:2).[7] The "lore" covers a vast array of fluid and ever-evolving traditions. It encompasses verbal genres, music, dance, customs, rituals, practices, celebrations, beliefs, material culture, and folklife. The designation "folklore" quickly became not only a quotidian term in mid-nineteenth-century anglophone circles but an international idiom, adopted all over Europe as the study of oral traditions took root and flourished, including in the lands and communities discussed in this handbook. Its cognates, whether in the Latin or Cyrillic alphabet, are used throughout the Slavic and east European languages, with the exception of Greek, which employs *laografía* or "study of the people" (see Holst-Warhaft, Chapter 8).

The major forms of Slavic and east European folklore (and *laografía*) include the rituals, practices, songs, music, dances, and celebrations of the life cycle and calendrical cycle; oral narrative poetry and prose; lyric songs; traditional, "folk," as well as contemporary popular music; and short verbal constructions: charms and related forms meant to effect magic, as well as proverbs, riddles, jokes, and humorous rhymes. It also includes folk belief and religion, as well as folklife and material culture (folk art and architecture, crafts, and foodways).[8]

Folklore Scholarship in the Slavic and East European World

Little is known about the folklore of the pre-Christian world of the Slavs and neighboring cultural groups. When the early Slavic communities converted to Christianity in the ninth and tenth centuries, the Church appropriated the rich, symbolic frameworks and verbal genres that permeated preliterate and pre-Christian society—traditional "systems" that helped make sense of the cyclical life and seasonal events that shaped existence. The clashes between pre-Christian cultures and the emergent Church were typically resolved by the clergy's adopting early folklore and blending it with Christian beliefs and practices, thus serving to bolster religious teachings and institutions (Kononenko 2007:4–7). How peasants perceived life (and death) and the world around them were long dependent on the deeply rooted oral traditional culture that surrounded them, combined with the Church's influence, what is often termed *dvoeverie*, meaning "two faiths" or "dual belief" (Kononenko 2007:6). The Slavic and east European peoples remained predominantly rural and non-literate for centuries. Folklore was central to their lives and was embedded in everyday outlooks and activities, as well as in familiar rituals and genres.

Already in the seventeenth and eighteenth centuries, before the rise of indigenous "folklorists" in the Slavic and east European world, foreign travelers from western Europe explored "exotic" lands of the "East," such as Ukraine and Greece, where some of them engaged in collecting "curiosities" (see Kononenko, Chapter 1; Kaliambou, Chapter 24). It was not until the nineteenth century, however, that a desire by native Ukrainians, Greeks, Serbs, Croats, Russians, and many others in the region to collect and preserve local folklore emerged. This was stirred primarily by the Romantic nationalism that was sweeping through western Europe, inspired by the great German Romantic philosopher and poet of the Enlightenment, Johann Gottfried von Herder, who had promoted the notion that it was the spirit of the common people (*das Volk*), as heard in the local epic and lyric songs, tales, proverbs, and so on, that expressed the real "soul of the nation" (see Elmer, Chapter 22; Vidan, Chapter 23). Members of the educated elite throughout the area became fascinated by the folklore of the peasantry and enthusiastically explored and collected it. They were impassioned intellectuals moved by a strong sense of the "nation" and its "truest" expression, the folk,[9] as well as a yearning for independence from imperial domination: Ottoman, Habsburg (later Austro-Hungarian), or Russian.[10] Throughout the nineteenth century, local folklore, and particularly verbal genres, kindled and empowered the pursuit of national-cultural identity, nationhood, freedom, and self-determination.

Oral epic poetry, viewed as a noble genre of distinction among Europe's peoples, represented a powerful means to legitimize culture and nation-building in largely non-literate societies. East Slavic *byliny*—narrative songs, literally, "of former times"—glorified and validated Russia's heroic past (see Kononenko, Chapter 20), while Ukrainian *dumy* (some of which were quasi-historical songs) established a strong sense of Ukrainian national identity (see Kononenko, Chapter 21). In the Balkans, the recognition of oral epic as a strong national voice of resistance to imperial hegemony reinforced a desire for liberation, especially from Ottoman rule. Heroic epic songs were eagerly collected by South Slavs such as Vuk Stefanović Karadžić (1787–1864), the leading cultural figure in nineteenth-century Serbia, as well as others (see Elmer, Chapter 22; Vidan, Chapter 23). The genre ignited and emboldened Balkan subjects yearning for liberation from the Porte.

The renowned German collectors of folk tales Jakob and Wilhelm Grimm inspired numerous Slavic and east European scholars and folklore enthusiasts to locate and record prose narrative. Aleksandr Afanas'ev (1826–1871) was the foremost collector of traditional Russian wonder tales; he published hundreds of them, which formed the Russian folk tale "canon" (see Forrester, Chapter 26). The Romantic poet and intellectual Pavol Dobšinský (1828–1885) collected tales in Slovakia (in the Habsburg Empire), some of which were viewed as allegories for the Slovak national cause (see Piroščáková, Chapter 25). And in nineteenth-century Greece, folk tales gathered from storytellers were likewise an important part of modern Hellenic identity: narratives that continued a local tradition established in ancient Greece (see Kaliambou, Chapter 24).

Other productive verbal genres were also collected and published by local scholars and folklorists at the time. They included lyric song (see Levaniouk, Chapter 2; Sarv, Chapter 6; Efendić, Chapter 29; Lukin, Chapter 30), legends (see Jurić, Chapter 27), as well as proverbs, riddles, and jokes (see Litovkina et al., Chapter 39).

Folklorists in the region continued to gather oral traditions in the twentieth century. But scholarship was adopting a more theoretical character, perhaps most notably in the study of oral poetic and prose narrative. These genres became key as structure, composition, and meaning in sung and spoken tales learned and perpetuated without the aid of memorization or literacy were examined. Indeed, some of the most significant research in the discipline of folklore worldwide is based on Slavic oral literary models. This includes the 1928 work of the Russian formalist Vladimir Propp (1895–1970), who set forth a seminal structural analysis of Russian wonder tales, *The Morphology of the Folktale*, based on a selection from the Afanas'ev collection (see Forrester, Chapter 26). Moreover, pioneering work on oral composition in traditional epic poetry was grounded in fieldwork undertaken among South Slavic and Albanian epic singers in the 1930s by the American classicists Milman Parry (1902–1935) and Albert B. Lord (1912–1991). This resulted in Lord's pivotal *Singer of Tales* (1960), in which the theory of oral-formulaic composition was elegantly laid out (see Elmer, Chapter 22; Vidan, Chapter 23).

Also influential in international folkloristics at the time were a number of notable local scholars who likewise explored the rich folklore of the region. They included the Slovene Matija Murko (1861–1952), whose ethnographic expeditions among South Slavic Muslim female ballad singers broke new ground (see Vidan, Chapter 23). Ethnomusicologists also exploited the living laboratories of the fertile Slavic and east European field. Béla Bartók (1881–1945) collected and analyzed traditional music and song not only in his native Hungary but in Romania and Yugoslavia as well (see Rădulescu and Beissinger, Chapter 33; Marković, Chapter 34; Vidan, Chapter 23). Moreover, numerous folklore institutes and ethnographic museums (including open-air exhibits) were set up during the twentieth century in cities and towns everywhere, reflecting the significant roles that folklore and ethnography played (and play) in these societies (see Hilton, Chapter 40; Urdea and Buchczyk, Chapter 41).

In the meantime, among the many critical historical events of the twentieth century, the imposition of repressive communist rule took place throughout most of the Slavic and east European lands. In 1917, the Russian Revolution spawned the Soviet Empire, while in the mid- to late 1940s, communist regimes were implemented in the countries of eastern Europe (except for Greece), an outcome of World War II. Brutal governments took control of all aspects of life. Freedom of speech and religion, as well as travel beyond the "Iron Curtain," were outlawed, while shortages of basic food and goods were commonplace. Religious practices were secularized or banned, while verbal texts were purged of politically "subversive," "bourgeois," or "offensive" content. State directives were imposed, among them invented genres that celebrated communism, Lenin and other local party heads, the proletariat, factories, industrial accomplishments, and so on (Kononenko 2007:127–135). Minority musicians (Romani and/or Muslim) were ostracized and their identities denied; repertoires were banned.

Scholarship on oral traditions suffered as well since communist dogma dictated research (see Rădulescu and Beissinger, Chapter 33). Folklore topics that were "worthy" of study were enforced from above. Considerations of religious or spiritual elements and meanings in life-cycle and calendrical-cycle traditions were suppressed. Atheism was prescribed in both the Soviet Union (see Rouhier-Willoughby, Chapter 7; Warner, Chapter 10; Seljamaa, Chapter 11) as well as elsewhere in eastern Europe (see Kondi, Chapter 9; Rakočević, Chapter 12). The study of topics considered "bourgeois" or "vulgar" was banned. In short, communist doctrine closely controlled what scholars could and should research and how (see Rakočević, Chapter 12; Forrester, Chapter 26; Rădulescu and Beissinger, Chapter 33). Due to the many restrictions, genre classifications and typological studies often provided comparatively "safe" research areas. Virtually everything became centrally planned, including folklore and research on it.

As the twentieth century drew to a close, momentous political and historical changes occurred in the region once again. The communist governments of eastern Europe were overthrown in remarkable succession in 1989 (and in Albania in 1991). In Yugoslavia, the end of communist rule took place in the early 1990s, although matters were also complicated by the various wars of secession that raged there from 1991 to 2001. In 1991, the Soviet Union folded as well. These monumental changes have deeply informed folklore itself in the Slavic and east European world, as well as the study of folklore there, not to mention the character of virtually every chapter in this handbook.

Post-communism and the Twenty-First Century

The collapse of communism and the ensuing political changes that occurred in the late twentieth century and the first decades of the new millennium were huge and effected economic, social, and cultural transformations. Overall, the post-communist period brought about a tremendous loosening of restrictions and controls surrounding the performance, practice, and study of traditional genres, beliefs, and folklife. Liberated of political controls, religious faith, political humor, erotic folklore, and so on became publicly acceptable (see Lesiv, Chapter 19). Almost overnight, previously forbidden subjects could be openly expressed—such as in urban legends, jokes, proverbs, riddles, and *chastushki* (short comic rhymes) (see Wójcicka, Chapter 28; Litovkina et al., Chapter 39; Olson and Adonyeva, Chapter 38). Contemporary popular urban song genres, including *chalga* (pop-folk) and other pan-Balkan ethno-pop styles that had been banned (as "foreign" and "uncivilized") were suddenly permitted, including genres in the repertoires of Romani musicians (see Draganova, Chapter 36; Rădulescu and Beissinger, Chapter 33). Neo-pagan adherents could openly observe, celebrate, and "worship" without repression in Latvia and Lithuania (see Strmiska et al., Chapter 18) as well as Ukraine and Russia (Kononenko 2007:136). Local folklore also gradually began to mirror social change within the realm of gender and sexuality, such as who can love whom in the public celebration of weddings (see MacMillen, Chapter 4).

Folklore scholarship in the region likewise has evolved since the 1990s. Intellectual inquiry into oral traditions and culture that for much or most of the twentieth century had not been allowed to "breathe" was resuscitated and fortified virtually instantaneously. Archives that had been off limits for decades were unlocked and provided new opportunities for scholars to explore and write openly about genres that had been viewed as subversive or offensive (see Sarv, Chapter 6). Literature, especially from the West, became available, opening the door to decades of previously forbidden scholarly perspectives. Liberated from the embedded raft of communist-period political and social controls, scholars focused on a new range of topics, engaging in explicit discussions of issues that previously had been prohibited or discouraged, such as folklore and religion (see Kondi, Chapter 9; Warner, Chapter 10; Rakočević, Chapter 12; Lesiv, Chapter 19), erotic genres (see Sarv, Chapter 6; Wójcicka, Chapter 28), Romani folklore (see Tesăr, Chapter 5; Peycheva, Chapter 32; Rădulescu and Beissinger, Chapter

33), urban folklore (see Rouhier-Willoughby, Chapter 7; Mellish, Chapter 14; Cash, Chapter 42), and gender (see Niemčić, Chapter 13; Sugarman, Chapter 37). While local scholarship has generally expanded intellectually since the 1990s, this trend is moving alarmingly in the opposite direction in Russia. For well over a decade by now, longtime president Vladimir Putin has been tightening his grip on freedom of expression, the effects of which, in the field of folklore, remain to be seen.

Twenty-first-century folklore has reflected not only present conditions but contemporary social, national, and political crises as well. Disease, violent conflict, and war vividly illustrate how current realities of all sorts have informed the folklore of the region. The COVID-19 pandemic impinged on (or, on occasion, promoted) folklore in various ways as restrictions on public and private rituals, customs, and performances not only challenged age-old traditions and social mingling but also sometimes provided fodder for new jokes and other genres (see Tesăr, Chapter 5; Rouhier-Willoughby, Chapter 7; Rakočević, Chapter 12; Niemčić, Chapter 13; Litovkina et al., Chapter 39). Furthermore, the interethnic conflicts of the 1990s in Yugoslavia were mirrored, even up until recently, in traditional weddings: in songs and customs in Kosovo (see Zlatanović, Chapter 3), as well as displays (sometimes violent) of nationalism in Croatia (see MacMillen, Chapter 4). Finally, the unprovoked war in Ukraine that Putin launched in February 2022, an attack on national sovereignty that has devastated people and places, has also both influenced and generated folklore. Much folklore has been destroyed or forever changed. At the same time, various verbal genres, such as Ukrainian jokes on the war, along with humorous memes and other forms of digital and social media, now circulate.[11] They provide levity in one sense, yet in another they serve, through familiar genres, to help locals process and cope with the cruel and terrible gravity of this war. In all of these references, folklore reflects reality; it conveys what is happening in the moment, what is important, what we fear, and what we treasure.

The Organization of the Handbook

This handbook is divided into five broad thematic sections: I. Life-Cycle Folklore; II. The Traditional Calendar, Magic, and Folk Belief; III. Oral Traditional Narrative; IV. Music, Song, Identity, and Performance; and V. The Folklore of Everyday Life. The chapters are genre-based. Yet each chapter also organically addresses other forms and genres that intersect and overlap, creating a network of meaningful junctures and correlations that bear witness to the profound interconnectedness of folklore.

Due to the universal centrality of the rites of passage, the volume begins, in Part I, with "Life-Cycle Folklore" and its major thresholds: wedding, childbirth, and death. The chapters deal with the songs, laments, dance forms, rituals, and customs that celebrate or commemorate these fundamental transitions. The most vibrant and ritually marked life-cycle event and the social celebration par excellence throughout the Slavic and east European world is the traditional wedding. This is presented in the first five chapters of Part I, with a focus on East Slavic and Balkan weddings, including Romani nuptial traditions. The next two chapters, on songs (including lullabies) and practices related to childbirth, are from Estonian and Russian folklore, while the chapters that treat death rites and laments reflect distinctive, age-old funerary customs in the Balkan and Russian traditions.

The chapters on life-cycle folklore comprise the initial section of the entire volume for a number of reasons. Most significantly, the traditions that articulate the life cycle underlie Slavic and east European folklore as a whole and are essential to an understanding of it. Rituals that mark and express the life cycle are vital for an appreciation of all of folklore and especially the traditional oral narratives that humans have felt the need to communicate and perpetuate for millennia. These are traditional stories about the critical events of our own lives: birth, initiation/matrimony, and death. Birth and death of the hero and other protagonists form the framework of much of oral storytelling. But it is the experiences, in particular, of coming of age and marriage (often intimately linked in traditional story patterns) that comprise countless narratives of epic, folk tale, and ballad—not only of heroes but also of other archetypal figures (both male and female). The meanings of these life-cycle events and the characters who live them have inspired traditional society since ancient times.

The chapters in Part II, "The Traditional Calendar, Magic, and Folk Belief," address three main topics: the folklore of the seasonal cycle, magic and the power of words, and varieties of folk belief. The first pertains to the other main "cycle" in the traditional world, the annual sequence of agrarian events that happens year in and year out. The chapters reflect folklore and scholarship from the Baltics and southeastern Europe, with accents on how yearly customs and dance forms mark the seasons. The folklore of the calendrical cycle is comprised of traditions that focus on the agricultural year as the backdrop for the planting, growing, and harvesting of crops that formerly occupied most inhabitants of the Slavic and east European lands. Calendrical folklore is intimately linked to magic as people traditionally attempted to ensure—through ritual and words—the ample production of crops and welfare of animals, and thus prosperity and survival in the human realm. Christian holidays overlap with folklore rooted in the passage of the seasons, including traditions that originally belonged to pre-Christian society. These topics, in many cases, became taboo during the communist period due to their incompatibility with the rigid and oppressive state ideologies (atheism and the prohibition of folklore that related to belief in magic). Yet there has been a post-communist return of annual agricultural folklore, especially in dance and celebration that invoke the seasons, although in the twenty-first century, the meanings are often more symbolic.

The second group of chapters in Part II relates to magic and various verbal formulas in the Hungarian and South Slavic traditions. Words are fundamental to the efficacy of magic, such as in folk healing; and charms, benedictions, and exorcisms have long been believed to function in powerful ways. Magic is also revealed through inverted verbal forms and behavior in efforts to offset evil forces. Finally, folk belief and religion are discussed in three distinct contexts (in Moldova, the Baltics, and Ukraine). These branches of folklore (including the role of magic in society and folk religion), which had been vigorous before the twentieth-century impositions of communist rule, have undergone significant revivals since the disintegration of local political regimes. Scholars now openly explore how belief-based expressive culture has re-emerged among rural but also urban folk since the end of the twentieth century and into the twenty-first.

Part III, "Oral Traditional Narrative," is devoted to the "classic" poetic and prose story genres that formed so many of the nineteenth- and twentieth-century collections of oral literature. The first group of chapters addresses epic and ballad and covers the East Slavic (Russian *byliny* and Ukrainian *dumy*) and South Slavic traditions: epic as a genre "of the border" and ballads as narrative songs by Muslim women, both of which intersect with the work of Lord and Parry. The second subsection in Part III treats the rich Slavic and east European oral narrative prose traditions—both magic tale and legend (a still-vibrant genre that illustrates the robust state of stories believed "to have really happened"). The theoretical contributions to the study of folk tale offered by Propp are considered as well. Altogether, these nine chapters center on the oral narrative "canon" (poetic and prose), as well as the theoretical templates that the study of these genres have generated.

Part IV, "Music, Song, Identity, and Performance," explores music-making by individuals who represent minority and subaltern communities and/or who have adopted now-globalized genres in places where they previously were not performed. They include ethnoreligious identity in music and song, focusing on the traditional Bosnian Muslim lyric *sevdalinka*, Yiddish traditional folk song, and local klezmer music (later introduced in North America). Moreover, several chapters are concerned with Balkan Romani music-making, including a retrospective of professional musicians in Bulgaria and North Macedonia, urban Romani genres in Romania, and musical labor among Serbian Roma. The last cluster of chapters considers folk and popular music in post-communist eastern Europe. It reports on bluegrass in the Czech Republic and contemporary pop and ethno-pop music in the Balkans. The chapters in Part IV are informed by reflections on ethnoreligious and racial identity, globalization, and modernity.

Part V is designated "The Folklore of Everyday Life." The first chapter takes up verbal constructions: Russian, Ukrainian, and Belarusian *chastushki*, followed by a discussion of Hungarian proverbs, anti-proverbs, riddles, and jokes, including the role of the internet as a medium for the transmission and circulation of these genres. The final chapters, on material culture and folklife, cover Russian folk art and architecture, the contexts and uses of rural artifacts in Romania, and foodways in Moldova. Altogether, these chapters present vivid portraits of everyday life and the folklore that represents it.

This handbook brings together a wide range of oral traditions from a variety of Slavic and east European communities. Despite the multiplicity of ways of conveying what is significant and meaningful to each "folk" group, this broad world area represents a rich and multi-layered cultural continuum. It reveals astounding similarities and connections between verbal genres throughout the region, forms of music, the yearly sequence of seasonal events, how and why stories are told, and why celebration and commemoration are so fundamental to life's journey. Although the immensity and variety of folklore represented in this handbook are undeniable, there clearly are also profound connections and intersections, as well as collective meanings that, it is hoped, readers will discover, explore, and appreciate.

Notes

1. The English-language names of countries in contemporary eastern Europe are used here; see the current map in Figure 1.
2. See Cooperman and Sahgal (2017) on current religious affiliations and national identities in eastern Europe.
3. In the Balkans they are Greeks, Bulgarians, North Macedonians, Serbs, Montenegrins, Romanians, Moldovans, and Roma; sizable minorities also reside in Bosnia and Estonia, while in Latvia they comprise a small majority (Cooperman and Sahgal 2017:20).
4. Lithuania, Poland, the Czech Republic, Slovakia, Hungary, Slovenia, and Croatia comprise this area. A small but historically important number of Ukrainians are Greek Catholic (Uniate).
5. Minority populations of Muslims also reside in North Macedonia and Montenegro.
6. Roma migrated from India circa 1000, settling in eastern Europe by the fourteenth century.
7. The emphasis is in the original.
8. See also the classic survey article, "Slavic Folklore," by Svatava Pirková Jakobson (1950).
9. In Slavic languages, *narod* (and other cognates) in general means both people and nation.
10. Borders frequently changed over the centuries of imperial rule, but in general terms, the Ottoman Empire dominated most of southeastern Europe from the late fourteenth to the early twentieth centuries; the Habsburg (later, Austro-Hungarian) monarchy extended over much of central Europe from 1526 to 1918; and the Russian Empire, in existence between 1721 and 1917, was spread over an enormous landmass, from the eastern shores of Siberia to eastern Poland (in the nineteenth and early twentieth centuries).
11. I thank Mariya Lesiv for guiding me to valuable materials on this topic as well as Natalie Kononenko for her thoughts on how various forms of Ukrainian folklore mirror "unofficial" resistance in the face of oppression, not to mention her reminder of how *dumy* have traditionally reflected (and may well continue to reflect) momentous events in Ukrainian history.

Works Cited

Bronner, Simon. 2018. *The Oxford Handbook of American Folklore and Folklife Studies*. New York: Oxford University Press.

Cooperman, Alan, and Neha Sahgal. 2017. "Religious Belief and National Belonging in Central and Eastern Europe: National and religious identities converge in a region once dominated by atheist regimes." Pew Research Center. https://assets.pewresearch.org/wp-content/uploads/sites/11/2017/05/15120244/CEUP-FULL-REPORT.pdf. Accessed July 31, 2024.

Dundes, Alan. 1965. "What Is Folklore?" In *The Study of Folklore*, ed. Alan Dundes, 1–3. Englewood Cliffs, NJ: Prentice-Hall.

Jakobson, Svatava Pirková. 1950. "Slavic Folklore." In *Funk & Wagnalls Standard Dictionary of Folklore, Mythology, and Legend*, ed. Maria Leach, 1019–1025. New York: Funk & Wagnalls Company.

Kononenko, Natalie. 2007. *Slavic Folklore: A Handbook*. Westport, CT: Greenwood Press.
Lord, Albert B. 1960. *The Singer of Tales*. Cambridge, MA: Harvard University Press.
"Political Europe." *The World Factbook 2021*. Washington, DC: Central Intelligence Agency, 2021. https://www.cia.gov/the-world-factbook/static/aa4062d5389be0558f0e7f745580cd1d/europe_pol-1.jpg.
Propp, Vladimir. 1958. *Morphology of the Folktale*, trans. Laurence Scott, Introduction by Svatava Pirková-Jakobson. Bloomington, IN: Indiana University Research Center in Anthropology, Folklore and Linguistics.

PART I
LIFE-CYCLE FOLKLORE

Weddings

CHAPTER 1

UKRAINIAN WEDDING RITUALS

NATALIE KONONENKO

The earliest known account of Ukrainian wedding rites was written by Guillaume Levasseur de Beauplan and published in 1651. Serving in the Polish army, de Beauplan went to Ukraine, where he charted maps and wrote a description of Ukrainian life (de Beauplan 1993), including weddings. Extensive documentation of weddings did not come until the second half of the nineteenth century when interest in ethnography produced accounts of weddings, among other depictions of village life. The most extensive was the work of Pavlo Chubinskii (1877) who, with the support of the Russian Imperial Geographical Society, collected wedding descriptions across multiple regions. Smaller nineteenth-century works also appeared and were assembled and published in two volumes by the Ryl's'kyi Institute of Folk Art, Folklore, and Ethnography, Ukrainian Academy of Science (Shubravs'ka and Pravdiuk 1970). In addition to scholarship, the Soviet era produced prescriptive handbooks that instructed civic officials on proper Soviet Socialist marriage rites (Zakovych et al. 1986:295–315). These contained illustrated suggestions for decorating the wedding palace with portraits of Lenin, step-by-step instructions on how to run the rite, and examples of text with proper Soviet values for officials to recite. Current rituals are a combination of traditional actions, similar to those in nineteenth-century accounts, and those aspects of Soviet rite that had become meaningful. What follows is a description of Ukrainian weddings drawn from my fieldwork in the villages of central Ukraine conducted from 1998 to 2019 (Fig. 1.1).[1] Using fieldwork (interviews and participant observation) offers the immediacy that published sources cannot provide. Furthermore, the period close to the collapse of the Soviet Union and the declaration of Ukrainian independence, the beginning years of my fieldwork, was an extraordinary time when Ukrainians were trying to discover what was truly Ukrainian. Soviet practices were not instituted in villages until the relative prosperity of the Brezhnev era provided the finances that made this possible. Traditional practices continued, and all of my older respondents had participated in pre-Soviet-style practices and were eager to describe these.

FIG. 1.1. An interview session in Krut'ky, 1998. The folklorist in the back is Halyna Kornienko.
(All of the photos courtesy of Natalie Kononenko)

Village and Family Life Shape Ukrainian Weddings

Traditional Ukrainian weddings, as described in published sources, are complex rituals that affect not only the couple getting married but also their respective families and the entire village. In villages, these traditional practices largely hold true today. While focus has typically been on the bridal pair and their rite of passage to married status and adulthood, attention to the specifics of village life is essential to understanding the actions that occur during a Ukrainian wedding. In Ukrainian villages, people live in very close proximity to one another. Under such circumstances, conflicts between neighbors and friction among in-laws can arise. These can lead to quarrels and even witchcraft accusations (Dysa 2020:96–113, 122–133). Weddings, as ritual events, provide an arena where village and familial tensions can be openly expressed. Because weddings are circumscribed in time and space, the overt manifestation of antagonisms that occurs during the ritual allows release of tension and helps maintain stability and balance. The wedding ritual places special emphasis on the bride because she is the one person who changes domiciles at marriage. It also focuses on the bride's mother and mother-in-law because the bride must sever her connections to her birth family and become an integral part of her husband's household, where she will come under the authority of his mother (Fig. 1.2). The marriage impacts the entire village, and that impact extends beyond the

FIG. 1.2. The mother of the bride leads the couple out of the house and into a car on the way to the marriage ceremony—Krut'ky, 1998.

creation of another family unit. The ritual itself serves to mitigate the tensions inherent in Ukrainian village life, a most important but understudied effect.

The layout of Ukrainian villages is typically a cluster of houses built close together, either in ribbon formation, along a river or a road, or in a circle surrounding a market area. Each house has an adjacent kitchen garden. The large fields where crops are raised fan away from the inhabited center. A household is not surrounded by the land that a family owns, a pattern that separates neighbors. Instead, Ukrainians live close enough to each other to have intimate knowledge of what goes on in each other's homes. This works well when villagers need to cooperate, whether while farming or when threatened by disaster. But close proximity and knowledge of the details of neighbors' lives can breed resentment, and when things go wrong, jealous neighbors are suspect. In an interview conducted in Kropivne in 1998, my respondent blamed her daughter's troubled marriage on a neighbor. She was convinced that the fact that she served store-bought pastries, a luxury item, instead of traditional homemade *kysyl'*, a thin fruit pudding, at the daughter's wedding, made the neighbor jealous, whereupon she cursed the marriage. As proof she cited the fact that she found cherries, a fruit often used in *kysyl'*, on her doorstep the morning after the marriage ceremony.

Fear of jealousy is great. Children are warned not to show off any toy or clothing that is nicer than what belongs to others. Sickness is often attributed to the evil eye caused by jealousy of one's possessions, accomplishments, or happiness. Furthermore, a person can cast the evil eye unwittingly. Envy alone can cause damage, and people are advised to give away any object that another praises because this is indicative of potentially destructive desire. With the possibility of resentment between neighbors, weddings are very public affairs: they include the whole village to ensure that everyone is favorably disposed toward the couple. Temporary theft of property is allowed, and jealousy is mitigated by allowing damage to the possessions of the groom's family, the ones who gain most from the marriage.

In Ukrainian villages, brides join the household of the groom's family and are expected to sever connections with their birth family. To facilitate this drastic transition, weddings allow the bride's family to express their pain at losing a beloved member and important worker. Within the groom's family, there can be tension between the bride and her mother-in-law. The groom's mother may be discomforted by a new person in her home who needs to be taught how things are done. She may feel that the bride does not work hard enough or be jealous if she feels her son has excessive affection for his bride. Weddings contain ritual acts and songs to aid this transition also. Because the bride's mother must sever connection with her daughter, while her mother-in-law must accept her own successor, the role of women in the wedding is of utmost importance. While Soviet-era works (Shubravs'ka and Pravdiuk 1970) interpret this as a remnant of matriarchy, I believe that living patterns are central here also. With men out in the fields, the household is run by the matriarch. The home is the domain of women, and the wedding is the acquisition of a future matriarch.[2]

The dynamics of female life are expressed in verbal as well as ritual lore. Ukrainian ballads sing of conflicts between the bride and her mother-in-law, conflicts that may end in the death of the young woman and her child. In a ballad about Halia published by Dei et al. (1988:237–243),[3] the mother-in-law considers Halia lazy. Even worse, she makes her reap on Sunday and then milk the cows. When Halia is done with her chores and has a moment to think, she realizes that she left her infant in the fields. She rushes back but is too late: she finds the child dead and being devoured by ravens. Halia impales herself on a knife, and, as she dies, she blames her mother-in-law for her own death, her child's, and the sin of working on Sunday.

> Оце, мати, аж три гріхи маєш:
> Один же гріх—в неділеньку жати,
> Другий же гріх—дитина малая,
> Третій же гріх—Галя молодая.
>
> Well, mother [addressed to the mother-in-law], now you have three sins,
> The first sin is that you sent me to reap on Sunday,
> And the second sin is [the death of] my small child,
> And the third sin is [the death of] me, young Halia.

Some ballads sing of the mother-in-law trying to poison her bride. Tragedy follows because the unsuspecting groom drinks from his beloved's cup and dies with her (Dei et al. 1988:255–260). In real life, most brides do get along well with their mothers-in-law, and

I believe that part of the reason is the structure of the wedding which openly expresses potential tensions and mitigates them.

Part of the bride's task of smoothly joining her household of marriage is severing connections with her birth family. Lyric songs, epics, ballads, and folktales express the pain of this requirement. Numerous epics (*dumy*) end with praise of blood kin and state that only they can be counted on in bad times as well as good (Kononenko 2019:267–278, see chapter 18). Ballads tell of a desire to go home to the birth family. In one, the young wife yearns for her childhood home so intensely that she turns into a bird and flies there. Unfortunately, her brother does not recognize her and prepares to shoot what he takes to be a strange bird (Dei et al. 1988:302–310). The ballad begins with the young woman speaking:

> Отдала мене матінка за далекії гори
> Та наказала мні не приходити в гостиноньку ніколи.
> Не була рочок, не була другий, на третій заскучила;
> Щоб мені крильця з самого злотка, полетіла б в гостину . . . .
> Ой сяду, впаду в вишневім саду, на черешеньку стану,
> Буду кувати ще й промовляти, чи не почує мати.
> Сидить матінка край віконечка, вона все теє чує,
> Ходить братічок по нових сінцях, все стрельбоньку готує.
> —Ой мій синоньку, мій голубоньку, не стріляй зозуленки,
> Бо тій зозульці, як нашій дочці на чужій сторононьці.

> My mother gave me away in marriage into a land beyond the distant mountains,
> And she told me never to come back to visit.
> I did not come back for a year and for two, and in the third year I began to pine,
> If I had wings of gold I would fly and pay a visit . . . .
> I will alight, I will fall in the cherry orchard, I will perch on a cherry tree,
> I will coo and I will murmur and perhaps my mother will hear me.
> My mother sits by the window, and she hears all this,
> And my brother walks in the new entryway getting his arrows ready.
> "Oh, my son, my dear one, don't shoot the cuckoo,
> For her plight is like that of our daughter in a faraway land."

The separation of the bride from her birth family is dramatic and final, even when she marries within her own village. Weddings allow the bride and her family to express their sorrows and fears.[4]

Traditional Ukrainian village weddings developed over time to allow expression of tensions which are otherwise kept secret for the sake of family and village harmony. They articulate the fears of the bride, her family, and the groom's relatives as they enter this most crucial union. They serve to make all residents of the village positively predisposed toward the couple. They contain a wealth of symbols that wish the couple health, reproductive success, and financial prosperity. Because weddings are so important to the entire village, as well as the couple and the families involved, they are accompanied by magic acts, mini-rituals aimed at marital success. Divinations and omens to predict what will happen to the couple in their married life abound.

COURTSHIP: *VECHORNYTSI, DOSVITKY, VULYTSIA*

In Ukraine, the wedding was preceded by formal courtship. Until the Brezhnev era when there were sufficient funds to institute government-run village clubs that showed films and played music, providing opportunities for young people to meet, villages held semi-organized events designed to acquaint young people with members of the opposite sex. All of the older people I interviewed had participated in such events, practices similar to those attested in published sources. The references to religious holidays come from pre-Soviet material. There were two types of rites: winter courtship events were called *vechornytsi* (evening parties) or *dosvitky* (parties until first light), which took place in a rented house, and summer rites, which took place outdoors and were called *vulytsia* (street).

For *vechornytsi*, a group of unmarried women living in a particular neighborhood would rent a house. The renter was usually a poorer villager, often a widow, and payment was typically work that was needed such as harvesting, fence-mending, or house repair. In October, once the crops were harvested, unmarried women gathered at the rented home. They brought handiwork such as spinning or embroidery and food to share among themselves and with the homeowner. After they had worked for a while, young men would join them. The young men brought no work. Their contribution was treats such as sweets and nuts and entertainment such as music. If the men did bring musical instruments, those present would sing songs that were currently popular. After the singing, the young people played games. The games were traditional and were described by both the people I interviewed and in published sources (Hnatiuk 1919). They included a version of musical chairs, only without music. The "leader" of the game walked around and dropped a handkerchief behind a person who lost their place. All then ran around trying to claim a seat. There were kissing games such as "Postman" where the person playing postman entered and announced that they had a letter for a particular person. The group then said how many stamps were on the letter, and that was the number of kisses that the recipient gave the postman. The recipient then assumed the role of postman, and the game would repeat. Accounts of *vechornytsi* often include tales of pranks played on the people in the rented house by boys too young to be included in the *hromada*, the group of courting men (Ripets'kyi 1919).

After the entertainment was over, the young women and men spent the night in the rented house. If a young man and a woman were interested in each other, they could sleep together. Typically, the man asked the woman for permission to sleep at her side, and she conferred or denied consent. Those who had not formed couples slept alone. All participants in the *dosvitka* or *vechornytsia* slept in one room, with the owner sleeping on the stove (*pich*) in the same room to ensure chastity. To what extent chastity was preserved is much debated, with some commentators claiming that everything was innocent and others insisting that few brides were virgins on their wedding day (Ripets'kyi 1919; Hnatiuk 1919). My respondents insisted that the encounters were innocent, with Olha Basans'ka of Iavorivka contrasting the chaste play of the courtship parties that she attended as a young woman in the 1960s with the amoral behavior of today's youth. Ukrainian ballads, like ballads recorded in Great Britain and elsewhere, tell of girls who acquiesced to sex, became pregnant, and were abandoned by their lovers. In one, the jilted girl kills her illegitimate child. As she is taken to be executed, she warns her mother not to let her younger siblings attend courtship parties lest they suffer a similar fate (Hnatiuk 1919:261).

> Всі дівоньки-паненоньки ой пют, гуляют,
> Молодую Марисеньку в Дунай пускают.
> Молодая Марисенька як потопала
> Тай на свою матір пальцем кивала:
> Мати моя старенька, маєш дочок пять,
> Не пускай їх на вечірки, нехай дома сплять.
> На вечірках чужа хата, на земли спати,
> Там си може межи ними причина стати.
> Мати моя старенька, маєш дочок сім,
> Не давай їм розпустоньки, як дала мені.
> Мені дала розпустоньку, як в день, так в ночи,
> Тепер мине молодую в Дунай тонучи.

> All of the girls, the young maidens, drink and make merry,
> And they throw young Marysenka into the Danube River.
> Young Marysenka, as she was drowning,
> She shook her finger at her mother:
> My mother, my elderly one, you have five daughters,
> Don't let them go to *verchirki*; let them sleep at home.
> At the *verchirki* you are at a strange house and you have to sleep on the ground,
> There, something can happen between them.
> Mother, my elderly one, you have seven daughters,
> Don't let them engage in loose behavior, the way you let me.
> You let me engage in loose behavior at nighttime, as well as during the day,
> Now I, a young one, have to drown in the Danube.

Vechornytsi/dosvitky lasted until Great Lent, typically with a break for the pre-Christmas fast and Christmas. After the fast, a special event called a *skladka*, a meal to which all contributed substantial amounts of food, took place. People normally excluded from *vechornytsi* and *dosvitky*, such as young married couples and teenagers, were allowed to participate. The attraction of participating in courtship-like events shows that they were indeed entertaining. In fact, Hanna Martynenko of Topyl'ne, whom I met in 1998 when she was in her fifties, said that she had so much fun at *vechornytsi* that she "sang away" her opportunity to marry. In other words, she had such a good time that she neglected the serious business of finding a husband.

Vulytsia events began after spring planting and lasted until harvest. Young men dug a doughnut-shaped trench at a highly traveled location such as crossroads. The center of the circle served as a table, while the outside provided seating. The other option was to use logs as benches. No handicrafts were brought to this event, and it began later in the day because of the work that needed to be done in summertime. Young people brought nuts, pumpkin and sunflower seeds, and other snacks. They sang popular songs and partied into the evening. *Vulytsia* events, unlike winter courtship parties, were unstructured, and the descriptions of them are limited, with respondents like Vasyl' Latysh of Iavorivka saying things like "the whole village would resound with song."

If a couple formed during the *vulytsia*, they would go to the young woman's house and spend the night in the barn, the shed, or the *komora* (underground cellar); they did not enter the house. It was the young man's responsibility to leave before daybreak to keep the tryst secret, and, with no older person to supervise, it was the couple's responsibility to ensure that the woman remained a virgin, avoiding the consequences described in ballads.

Summer *vulytsi*, unlike *vechornytsi/dosvitky*, were not confined within a building. With several *vulytsi* likely going on in any village and people free to go from one event to another, organizers did their best to attract the greatest number of participants to their particular event. Men could tar the gates at the home of any woman who failed to participate, thus shaming her into joining the group. Women used more subtle means. To attract the largest possible number of eligible men, women used road magic, acts based on the importance of territorial passage in Ukrainian belief. They would pierce their shoe with a needle attached to red thread, remove the needle, and walk through the village dragging the red thread. This would "drag" young people from all over the village to their *vulytsia*. A number of people told me that, if a young woman fancied a particular young man, she could practice road magic, specifically, she could dig up dirt with an imprint of his shoe and place it in the *pich* to make the man burn with desire or "dry up" with longing. The road back from the *vulytsia* was as magical as travel to the event. Respondents report being followed by animals or objects when they returned home from *vulytsia* events. These animals or objects, they feared, were witches in disguise. Motria Perepechai of Ploske, a woman whom I have visited numerous times since 2000, told a number of stories about supernatural attacks (Fig. 1.3). One was about a wheel that followed her and her friends as they walked home from a *vulytsia*. They knew this wheel was a witch because it did not lose momentum or fall over like an ordinary wheel.[5] The stories of witchcraft and magic enhanced the thrill of summer courtship.

FIG. 1.3. Motria Andriivna Perepechai—Ploske, 2000.

BETROTHAL

Courtship is the one time in the marriage process when the young have initiative and freedom of choice. Once a man and a woman decide to marry, they, and especially the groom, are passive participants in rituals that are conducted by their families and involve the entire village. The formal request for the bride, *svatannia*, is made by a delegation arranged by the prospective groom's family. The family approaches two mature men of good repute, called *starosty* or *svaty*. Being articulate is a desirable characteristic of a *svat*, and Mykhailo Koval of Velykii Khutir, a retired schoolteacher whom I have known since 1998, told me recently that his ability to speak well meant that he has served as *svat* many, many times. The *starosty* or *svaty* accompany the groom to the bride's home and enter, leaving the groom outside. They address the bride's family in cryptic language, asking for the bride's hand without stating their purpose outright, pretending, for example, that they are chasing a lost animal. Thus, they would say that they had lost a ram and heard that the family whose house they had entered had a ewe. Would the ram have wandered here by any chance? While the presentation by the *starosty/svaty* is in progress, the bride must display modesty and hide. After the cryptic request, the men state their mission, and the father calls his daughter and asks if she consents. She signals her acceptance by draping a *rushnyk* (ritual towel), preferably one that she has embroidered herself, over the shoulder of each of the *starosty*, tying it like a sash. The groom is then summoned, and all sit down to a meal. *Svatannia* is still regularly practiced, especially in rural areas, and my respondents said that this was so in their villages. One recent modification to *svatannia*, one that enhances the status of the groom, is driving to the bride's house by car instead of walking. A number of my respondents objected to this since a car can make it difficult to see who is courting whom. This underscores the fact that the formation of couples is of concern to the entire village.

Traditionally, if the bride rejects a marriage proposal, she can offer the groom's *starosty* a pumpkin. The pumpkin is more metaphor than fact because the couple agrees to wed in advance of formal matchmaking. Rejected proposals do occur, and one was described to me in Iablunivka in the 1990s. About ten years earlier, I was told, a young man courted a girl, and they agreed to wed. The parents, however, did not accept the young man's proposal. Their older daughter was still single, and the parents insisted that she marry first. There was no pumpkin given, but the parents did stand firm when it came to the proper order for daughters to marry. The young man agreed and married the older sister, and, according to my respondents, this marriage worked out well.

A second meeting between the bride and groom's parents, called *zmovyny* or *domovyny*, occurs several days after the *svatannia*. This is a practical rather than ritual event. The bride's parents visit the home of the groom and discuss matters such as who will cover which part of the wedding costs. Since the bride goes to live with the groom's family, this is her family's chance to make sure that the household she will join is a good one in terms of both family relations and economic prosperity.

Wedding Preparations

The wedding comes one week to one month after the *zmovyny*, and celebrations occur in the homes of both the bride and the groom.[6] Preparations begin on Thursday with the baking of the wedding bread (*korovai*). The mothers of the bride and groom summon women to act as bakers (*korovainytsi*). They must be happily married women to ensure the success of the marriage; even widows who had been happily married are not acceptable. *Korovainytsi* dress in festive clothing and bring a gift or a *korovai* ingredient. Their job is a big one. In addition to the *korovai*, an ornate bread consisting of an underlayer, a middle loaf, and decorations, *korovainytsi* make many smaller breads, the most important being *shyshky*, pinecone-shaped loaves. The baking is accompanied by ritual acts, songs, and magic objects. Coins or eggs are placed inside the *korovai*, and, like its decorations, they are meant to promote the couple's wealth and fertility. What happens during the preparation of the *korovai* and to the bread itself foretells the future of the marriage. To ensure the couple's happiness, the *korovainytsi* sing happy, joking songs. The *korovai* is baked in a traditional oven called a *pich*, a large, clay structure that takes up approximately one-quarter of the room. It is used for cooking and to heat the house and has a sleeping alcove for the elderly and infirm. To heat the *pich*, a fire is built inside. When it burns down and the walls of the stove are hot, the ashes are swept out, and food is placed inside. The *korovainytsi* call a virile young man to do the sweeping so that the couple about to marry will have strong children. They sing him songs of praise to support the efficacy of his magic. While the bread bakes, the *korovainytsi* carry the dough trough thrice around the house to protect the *korovai* and make it round and solid, predicting a sound marriage. How the bread turns out is indicative of the future, and any cracks are bad omens.

On Friday the bride's *skrynia* is ceremonially transported to the groom's house. The traditional *skrynia*, an object I saw in every home I visited, is an elaborately hand-painted wooden wedding chest containing the bride's dowry. Until the recent past, the bride filled it with her handiwork. Girls started working on their *skrynia* at age ten or twelve. They embroidered festive clothing for themselves and their future husband and made items for the home, including bed linens and tablecloths. They embroidered *rushnyky* to use during the wedding and to hang over icons and family portraits. Making both *rushnyky* and bed linens is very time-consuming if they are well executed. People sleep on plain sheets, but each bed has an embroidered skirt and is piled high with embroidered pillows. Today embroidery is still highly valued, and high schools such as the one in Velykii Khutir offer embroidery classes. Many *skrynia* items, however, are now store-bought.

To fetch the bride's *skrynia*, the groom assembles his *prychet*, his entourage of friends and relatives. They eat a meal and walk to the bride's home, where they must "buy" the *skrynia* and sometimes the bride herself. Payment is *horilka*, a distilled spirit similar to vodka; and when it is received, the *prychet* is treated to a meal. The transport of the *skrynia* to the groom's house displays to the whole village the bride's industriousness and her potential to become a good wife. For this reason, the bride's family makes sure that the contents show. These days not all brides have a *skrynia*. They do, however, have a dowry of linens, clothing, and household items that are ceremonially transported to the house where the bride will live. Whether or not there is a *skrynia*, and even if the bride's dowry is driven to the groom's house by car, the *prychet* still walks beside it, singing songs that praise the bride and her ability as a homemaker.

Because everyone in the village knows that a wedding is about to take place, invitations can be issued as late as Saturday and typically are. The bride dresses in her finest clothing, with traditional folk costumes, called *ukrains'ke*, preferred by many. Particularly important is a woven red and white *krolevets rushnyk*[7] tied under the bosom with the ends covering the bride's abdomen to protect her ability to bear children from the evil eye that may be cast by jealous girls who have not received marriage proposals.

The bride summons her friends, or *druzhky*, and they walk from house to house carrying *shyshky* tied in a kerchief. At each home, the group enters, and the bride leaves a *shyshka* on the table and utters a verbal invitation. The groom, in the company of his best man, or *boiaryn*, also issues invitations. If a parent of either the bride or the groom is deceased, they are nonetheless invited by placing a *shyshka* on the grave. Kin are an integral part of life, and parents play such an important role in the wedding that they must be included, even if they are no longer among the living. Many omens are associated with issuing invitations, and running into one's prospective spouse or into another group carrying invitations is considered inauspicious. During the Soviet period, under pressure to modernize, postcards with photographs of the bride and groom became popular. These could be mailed but were often delivered by hand. Today many people seek to revive pre-Soviet traditions, considering them genuinely Ukrainian, and many brides and grooms hand-deliver *shyshky*.

On Saturday the bride's friends and female relatives gather at her home for the *divych vechir* (girls' evening). In some areas, the groom and *boiaryn* are also invited. The group sits down to a meal and sings sad songs intended to make the bride cry so that she can release the fear she may have about the upcoming transition in her life, along with the sadness of leaving her parents' home. For older women, this is an occasion to express their own losses and sorrows, and they are often the main singers. One example of a sad song that I recorded during a wedding in the village of Krut'ky in 1998 goes as follows:

> Там поміж дружками, тай поміж боярами,
> Там поміж Турками, тай поміж Татарами,
> Там молода дівчина наряджається,
> До свого батька по поради звертається.
> Ой не йди поміж чужими жити.
> Там ти будеш ся журити.
> Там свекруха наровиста,
> Вона тобі свої нрави покаже,
> Вона тобі правди не скаже.

> There among the *druzhky* and among the *boiary*,[8]
> There among the Turks and among the Tatars,
> There a young girl dons her clothing,
> And she turns to her father for advice.
> [He answers:]
> Don't go to live among strange people,
> For there you will experience sorrow.
> There the mother-in-law has strong opinions;
> She will show you her ways,
> She will not tell you the truth.

This song expresses the potential tensions between the new bride and her mother-in-law in the hope that they will occur in song only.

After the meal, the group makes a wedding tree (*hil'tse*), typically the top of a pine sapling or a fruit tree branch provided by the *boiaryn*. It is decorated with candy, ribbons, and artificial flowers made by all present at the *divych vechir*. The flowers are made out of rye stalks and rowan berries to ensure the fertility and longevity of the couple because rye is called *zhyto*, which sounds like *zhyttia* (life), while rowan berries produce red juice and are associated with virginity. After the meal, the *hil'tse* is thrown on top of the bride's house to mark it as the location of the wedding, or the *boiaryn* (probably in a hint at defloration) thrusts it into a loaf of bread with a single stroke and carries it in the wedding procession the next day.

The Marriage Ceremony

On Sunday morning the bride's senior *druzhka* (maid of honor) and her other *druzhky* help her dress, making her look beautiful and wealthy. In the past, wealth was necklaces of coral and mother-of-pearl, plus ducats. Unlike the other items that she brings to her marriage, jewelry remains the bride's property, providing insurance should things go wrong. With the financial hardships of the Second World War, precious jewelry was replaced by glass beads, but recent growing prosperity allows people to secure real items again. During the Soviet period, the bride wore a Western-style white dress, an erasure of national identity mandated as a mark of modernity by Soviet policy. Because white wedding dresses were not part of local tradition, old photographs show that brides wore them to official ceremonies only, changing into *ukrains'ke* for those events that took place in the home, something Halyna Kapas of Iavorivka did when she married in 1985. The independence of Ukraine (1991) allowed people to wear *urkains'ke* for all wedding functions if they chose. Particularly nationalistic women, such as Liudmyla Sokolova (née Bezvikonna), married in 1991, made their own wedding costumes following traditional patterns (Fig. 1.4).

The groom comes to the bride's home, and the bride's parents bless the couple with paired icons, typically Mary Mother of God and either Christ the Savior or St. Nicholas. The couple takes these icons and goes to church, where they hold them during the wedding service. The icons become part of the couple's household and hang either in the couple's bedroom or in the main room of the home. In Soviet times, a ceremony in the village *klub*, or civic center, replaced the church wedding and was followed by an obligatory visit to a monument for war dead. The civil ceremony is retained in many areas, in which case the couple has two wedding ceremonies: a civil one on Saturday and a church service on Sunday, as I witnessed in Mryn in 2000 (Figs. 1.5 and 1.6). The civil and/or church services constitute the official aspect of the wedding, after which the groom escorts the bride to her home and leaves her there so that the folk part of the wedding, the part handed down through tradition rather than dictated by officialdom, can begin. For villagers, the part held in the homes of the bride and groom is the most important aspect of the wedding, the set of acts that seals the marriage.

FIG. 1.4. Liudmyla Sokolova modeling the wedding outfit she made.

The traditional part of the wedding begins with the groom and bride each having a meal with their own family. Afterward, the groom's party sets out in a procession called a *poizd* (train). The *poizd* consists of the groom, his *boiaryn*, the *starosty* who led the matchmaking, a female relative called a *svitilka*, and at least one other woman called a *svashka*. The *svitilka* carries a bouquet of flowers with two candles, one representing the

FIG. 1.5. Civil ceremony held in the village *klub*—Mryn, 2000.

bride and the other the groom. The *svashka* bears small gifts for the bride's family. The *poizd* has the appearance of a raiding party, with the *starosty* carrying sturdy staffs or cudgels, perhaps as a remnant of the bride capture practices described by de Beauplan. As they exit the gate, the groom's mother showers them with rye, small coins, and candy to protect them. The *poizd* faces mock impediments on its path to the bride's home, barriers set up by young men who demand *horilka* as payment (Fig. 1.7).

The meal at the bride's home is accompanied by more sad songs to help the bride and her family deal with imminent separation. When the groom's party arrives, it is stopped at the gate with demands for payment called *voritne* (from *vorota*, gate). At the wedding in Mryn in 2000, the bride's *druzhka* came outside and demanded money before she would let the groom's party inside. The *boiaryn* paid on behalf of the groom and

FIG. 1.6. Church ceremony held in Mryn, 2000.

FIG. 1.7. A photo from Krut'ky, 1998, showing the *poizd* with *starosty* at the head, protecting the groom. They are going to the bride's home.

offered *hryvny*, the Ukrainian national currency. The *hryvny* were rejected. He then offered American play money, and this too was rejected. When he paid in American dollars, the groom's *poizd* was allowed entry. Once inside, the *svashka* hands out gifts to the members of the bride's family. In some areas, the bride's younger sister sews a flower made of rye stalks and rowan berries onto the groom's lapel. In Mryn, this was done by the *druzhka*. The bride does not participate in the action at the gate but sits behind the table on a fur coat, an object designed to represent the hope for future wealth. On the table before her is the *korovai* plus "paired" items such as two bottles of champagne and two spoons tied with a ribbon. The *svitilka* can add her two candles to these paired items. I was told that the candles would be lit and that the candle that burned down first would predict which spouse would die first. I have never seen this done, although possibly this happened after guests had left.

The younger brother of the bride often acts as intermediary between his sister and the groom, and at the table, he demands money for the seat next to his sister. In Krut'ky, the boy was so young that he was held on his grandmother's lap. Once the groom joins the bride, the other guests are also seated, and the bride's entourage taunts the groom's *poizd* with mocking songs that express the tension of joining not just the couple but two families. An exchange of mocking songs is followed by songs of praise and toasts to the couple and their parents. Examples of songs sung by the bride's girlfriends are as follows:

Їли бояри, їли,
Цілого вола з'їли.
На столі не рісочки,
Під столом не кісточки.

The *boiary* ate and ate,
They ate an entire ox.
There is not a crumb left on the table,
And there is not a bone left under the table.

Ви бояри чужесторонці,
Не берить по повной ложці.
А берить по половину
Щоб хватило на родину.

You *boiary* are strangers,
Don't take entire spoonfuls,
Take just half,
So that enough will be left for the family.

Наш боярин красний,
А другий без носа,

> А третій без вуха,
> Хай цью пісню слуха.

> Our *boiaryn* (best man) is handsome,
> And the other one has no nose,
> And the third one is missing an ear.
> Let him listen to our song.

The groom's male friends can counter with

> Старша дужка як шпилька,
> А друга як матужка,
> А третя як лопата,
> Бреше як собака.

> The senior *druzhka* is as thin as a pin,
> And the next one is like a hank of linen,
> And the third one is like a shovel,
> And she barks like a dog.

Or

> На припічку кружка стояла,
> А в ту кружку кицька насцала,
> Дайте мені кружку,
> Напоїти старшу дружку.

> On the shelf by the stove there stood a cup.
> A cat peed into that cup.
> Give me the cup, please,
> So that I can give the senior *druzhka* a drink.

After the taunting songs, the two sides make up. I was not able to record during the wedding, and we held a special recording session in Krut'ky several days after the wedding took place. Even here, people had too much fun singing insults, and I was not able to collect songs of reconciliation. I did record a reconciliation song in Velyka Burimka, which goes as follows:

> Хай чужинці відійдуть,
> Хай родина в перед йдуть,
> Хай батько за молодих випиває,
> Їм щастя здоров'я бажає.

> Let the strangers step aside,
> Let the relatives step forward,

Let the father toast the couple,
Let him wish them luck and good health.

After the two parties "reconcile," the *korovai* is cut by either the *boiaryn* or one of the *starosty* and served to the guests by the bride. She approaches each guest with a glass of *horilka* and a piece of *korovai* on a plate. The guest accepts the food and thanks the bride, placing money on the plate or giving the couple a gift while singing ribald ditties, such as "I give you a pistol so that (his) prick will stand (erect) for one hundred years" (Я дарую пістолет, щоби хуй стояв на сто лет). The gift given with this verse was not a firearm but a household appliance. Off-color verses create a sexually charged atmosphere and encourage the couple to consummate the marriage. They also allow villagers to say things that would not otherwise pass their lips.

After the meal, the couple departs for the groom's house. As they leave, the bride's mother ties their hands together with a *rushnyk* and blesses them with bread the way that she and her husband had earlier blessed them with icons. She gives them what is left of the *korovai*, crumbs included, so that the bride will take everything that is hers with her and not return. The mother, holding on to the *rushnyk*, then leads the couple outside the gate. As she is considered to have the strongest bond to her daughter, so she must be the one to relinquish her child.

The trip to the groom's house is considered the most dangerous part of the wedding. This is the point where the bride makes her final break from her birth family. Because this is such an irrevocable transition, the bride and groom are considered vulnerable and are guarded by both the groom's *prychet* and the bride's *prydane*, her group of friends. They face impediments such as straw fires which force the groom to pick up his bride and carry her, demonstrating that he will protect her from all threats.

When she arrives at the groom's home, the bride hands his mother a *shyshka*, a sprig of rowan, and what is left of the *korovai* (Fig. 1.8). The mother reciprocates by welcoming her into the family. The passage from the bride's home to the groom's is accompanied by songs which speak on behalf of the two mothers, expressing the bride's mother's sorrow at parting with her child and warning the groom's mother to treat her new family member kindly. A song I recorded in Moshny in 1998 and addressed to the bride's mother-in-law follows:

> Прилетіла тетеречка
> Не учора а теперечка,
> І не бийте її
> І не лайте її
> Не хай вона привикає
> Тай до дома не тікає.

> The little grouse flew on over,
> Not yesterday, but just now.

> Do not beat her,
> And do not scold her.
> Let her get used (to our family),
> So that she will not flee on home.

At the groom's home the couple is treated to another meal and another round of gift-giving. This is followed by rebraiding and covering of the bride's hair, a ceremony that signals her new status as a married woman. In all areas, the groom's female relatives participate in this ceremony, and, in some, the bride's younger brother is again the one to surrender his sister to her marital kin. The role of the younger brother as intermediary may be based on his having the least claim to his family's inheritance and, thus, to his sister. It may also serve as a counterweight to the mother's ties to her daughter. The hair ceremony is important because hair marks status, and married women, whether they wear a cap covered by a kerchief or a kerchief alone, are not supposed to go bare-headed. As Odarka Panchenko of Domantovo explained, in the past, a single woman who bore a child out of wedlock was subjected to a similar hair ceremony and received the name *pokrytka* (covered one), a mark of shame.

After the hair ceremony, the bride is undressed by the same *druzhka* who earlier helped her dress, and the couple is escorted to their marriage bed. Their nuptial night is

FIG. 1.8. The groom's parents welcome the newly married couple with breads held on *rushnyky*—Krutky, 1998.

followed by an announcement of the bride's virginity, either a verbal proclamation by the groom or the display of a red object such as a ribbon or kerchief. In Soviet times, the red Soviet flag was hoisted above the groom's house. As noted earlier, many commentators presume that premarital sexual contact was common and led to the loss of virginity. Since producing progeny is central to marriage, the proclamation of virginity on the morning after the wedding has less to do with actual virginity than with signaling that the groom's family accepts any children that their daughter-in-law may bear as their own. This particular action belongs to the groom and, along with what he does in the marriage bed, is his one active role.

Post-Wedding Events

On Monday, the day after the wedding, rituals begin in the morning with the bride's parents visiting the groom's house. They are offered trick foods, items that look appetizing but taste disgusting, such as *varenyky* (perogies) stuffed with raw beets. The trick foods are another expression of potential tension between the two families. But, as with the taunting songs between the bride's entourage and the groom's men, teasing soon turns to actual celebration; and the two families share a meal, both contributing food. Many other "jokes" are possible on Monday. The bride can be asked to perform her tasks as a new member of the household, only to be forced to sweep trash deliberately thrown on the floor. Finally, coins are thrown under her broom for her to keep. The "teasing" prepares her for the subordinate position that she will hold until she begins to bear children, eventually assuming the position of matriarch. It both forces her to endure mockery and rewards her for doing so. The groom's parents are also made to suffer. Uninvited guests show up at their home and tally the gifts the bridal couple received by writing the list of presents on the whitewashed walls. The "guests" then "clean up" the mess, splashing water and mud everywhere as they "work." The groom's family, the household that gains a new member, is the envy of its neighbors; and here the villagers get to put the lucky family in their place.

A widely practiced carnivalesque post-wedding event is the *tsyhanshchyna* (Gypsy fest). People dress as Gypsies (*tsyhane*) and engage in pranks. They steal chickens, bring them to the groom's house, and cook them so that the feasting can continue. Cross-dressing is part of the rite, and the groom's parents are forced to wear opposite-sex clothing with "body parts" made out of fruits and vegetables. Melons are inserted into the shirt worn by the father, and a large squash is stuck into the mother's pants. The parents are seated on a cart and paraded around the village, then dunked in a body of water like a pond or a stream. "Gypsies" can capture the groom's godparents and force them to buy drinks and treats for the wedding "guests." These are acts that allow violation of neighbors' property and disrespect of elders, the inverse of proper behavior. Villagers express any resentment they may feel to the family that has gained a

FIG. 1.9. Tyshanshchyna in Hrechkivka, 1998.

new member, and such expression in the confines of ritual mitigates against tensions in subsequent daily life. Human sexuality is on display, and cross-dressing, which extends to many male attendees, negates the reproductive capacity of all but the couple (Fig. 1.9). In the *tsyhanshchyna*, the wedding extends beyond fellow villagers to all of nature. I was told on several occasions that the bride can have a favorable influence on the weather, and if there is a drought, the bride sprinkles water as she walks in the *tsyhanshchyna* procession to make rains come. With the conclusion of *tsyhanshchyna*, life returns to normal, and the now-married couple assumes their roles within the groom's family.

Conclusion: The Power of Tradition

Soviet practices had little impact on weddings in villages. The club/*klub* did successfully replace *vechornytsi/dosvitky* and *vulytsia* and, in post-Soviet times, has itself been recently replaced by nightclubs. The actual wedding, however, has remained largely untouched. One reason is that many Soviet modifications to the wedding were based on tradition. For example, in Soviet times male members of the wedding party wore red sashes. These are clearly a modification of the *rushnyky* draped over the shoulders of *starosty* and other male wedding party members. Thus, when the Soviet Union collapsed, *rushnyky* were easily brought back. Today's *rushnyky* are not always hand-embroidered, but they are towels nonetheless. Certain Soviet modifications were kept as add-ons. During the Soviet period brides wore white wedding gowns as a sign of internationalism and modernity. Now almost all brides wear white, at least for the civil ceremony. Church weddings were actively discouraged, and the ceremonial part of the Soviet wedding was the signing of the marriage contract. This additional ceremony continues and is widely observed, even as the church wedding has returned. In many places both ceremonies occur.

Where Soviet modifications have taken hold is in cities. One reason is that urban Soviet weddings provided the pomp desired by many (Fig. 1.10). While the civil ceremony in villages took, and still takes, place in the modest *klub*, in cities weddings take place in ornate palaces, a most attractive venue. Driving around in specially decorated cars, first introduced as the economy improved after the Second World War, is now virtually a must in urban weddings. Receptions are held in restaurants, not in the home, and include the very Soviet addition of the *tamada*. This is a master of ceremonies whose job is to toast the couple and provide entertainment for the wedding guests. During the Soviet period, when the various nationalities of the Soviet Union were encouraged to interact and become one people, there was borrowing from culture to culture. Hiring a *tamada* is a Georgian custom now observed by Ukrainians and many other post-Soviet peoples, including non-Slavs.

The reason that Soviet practices have taken hold in cities is, in my opinion, connected to living patterns. Urban dwellers live isolated lives. They are not privy to what goes on in their neighbors' apartments the way villagers know about the lives of their fellows. Young couples do not join the groom's family but set up their own household. The need to separate the bride from her mother and place her under the authority of her mother-in-law does not exist. Similarly, because knowledge of neighbors' lives is greatly reduced, mitigating potential jealousies is not urgent. In villages old living patterns continue. Houses are still adjacent to one another, and brides join the household of the groom. As living patterns continue, so do the wedding practices developed over centuries, practices which express and mitigate tensions between neighbors and resentments between the family of the bride and that of the groom. Tradition remains a powerful force because it meets the needs of the people who observe it.

FIG. 1.10. Urban wedding of Oleksii and Olena Prokopenko—Kyiv, 2003.

Modernization in villages is very practical, and brides contribute housewares rather than the results of their craftsmanship when they join their new family. The *skrynia* is often replaced by the *garderob*, a wall unit with built-in closets and drawers. This is transported much as the *skrynia* was in the past. Some of my favorite modifications go unnoticed. In Pidhaitsi in 2006, a tradition-minded woman invited *korovainytsi* to prepare for her daughter's wedding. They sang songs and performed ritual acts. And, when the *korovai* was done, they decorated it with white and pink icing and plastic swans. Modifications that do not affect the core functions of ritual are not perceived as such.

Notes

1. My Ukrainian sound files can be accessed at http://www.artsrn.ualberta.ca/UkraineAudio/.
2. The oldest son typically stays with his parents, and his wife eventually becomes the household head. Younger sons inherit a parcel of land split from the parents' property. If this is not possible, they take jobs either in the village or in urban centers.

3. Page numbers for ballads include all songs published on a single topic.
4. Ballads, like weddings, express potential rather than reality. By singing of the worst things that could possibly be, they allow expression of fears and thus help real life function more smoothly.
5. Similar stories were published by Hnatiuk (1904, 1912).
6. Older sources (Chubinskii 1877) state that the groom moved in with the bride during this period, a practice that no longer exists.
7. Krolevets is a city known for its weaving of red and white, intricately patterned *rushnyky* often with fertility symbols such as birds and vegetation.
8. *Druzhky* (singular *druzhka*) references the bride's female friends who comprise her entourage during the wedding ceremony. *Boiary* (singular *boiaryn*) are the groom's male friends who make up his entourage.

Works Cited

Chubinskii, P. P. 1877. *Obriady: Rodiny, krestiny, svad'ba, pokhorony, Trudy etnograficheskostatisticheskoi ekspeditsii v zapadno-russkii krai*, Vol. IV, Imperatorskoe russkoe geograficheskoe obshchestvo. St. Petersburg: Tipografiia Kirshbauma.

de Beauplan, Guillaume Le Vasseur. 1993. *A Description of Ukraine*, trans. and ed. Andrew B. Pernal and Dennis F. Essar. Cambridge, MA: Harvard University Press.

Dei, O. I., A. Yu. Yasenchuk, and A. I. Ivanyts'kyi. 1988. *Balady: Rodynno-pobutovi stosunki*. Kyiv: Naukova Dumka.

Dysa, Kateryna. 2020. *Ukrainian Witchcraft Trials: Volhynia, Podolia, and Ruthenia, 17th–18th Centuries*. Budapest–New York: Central European University Press.

Hnatiuk, Volodymyr. 1904. *Znadoby do Halyts'ko-Rus'koi demonolohii*, Vol. XV. In *Etnografichnyi zbirnyk, vydae Naukove Tovarystvo im. Shevchenka*. L'viv.

Hnatiuk, Volodymyr. 1912. *Znadoby do ukraiins'koi demonologii*, Vol. XXXIII, part 1, and Vol. XXXIV, part 2. In *Etnografichnyi zbirnyk, vydae Naukove Tovarystvo im. Shevchenka*. L'viv.

Hnatiuk, Volodymyr. 1919. "Pisnia pro pokrytku, shcho vtopyla dytynu." In *Materiialy do Ukraiins'koii etnolohii, vydae etnografichna komisiia naukoho tovarystva im. Shevchenka*, Vol. XIX–XX. L'viv.

Kononenko, Natalie. 2019. *Ukrainian Epic and Historical Song: Folklore in Context*. Toronto: University of Toronto Press.

Ripets'kyi, Oleksa. 1919. "Parubochi i divochi zvyzhaii." In *Materialy do ukraiins'koi etnol'ogii, Naukove tovarystvo im. Shevchenka*, Vol. XIX–XX. L'viv.

Shubravs'ka, M. M., and O. A. Pravdiuk. 1970. *Vesillia u dvokh tomakh*. Kyiv: Naukova Dumka.

Zakovych, N. M., P. I. Kosukha, and V. A. Perunov. 1986. *Sosialisticheskaia obriadnost'*. Kyiv: Vyshcha Shkola.

CHAPTER 2

RUSSIAN WEDDING SONGS

OLGA LEVANIOUK

THE traditional Russian wedding, as attested primarily in the nineteenth and early twentieth centuries (this chapter is based on records taken between the 1850s and the 1990s), is diverse yet stable in its outline. It begins with some contact between the two families, followed by a betrothal, and then by a variable number of steps—gift exchanges and games, the presentation or "leading out" of the bride, the viewing of the groom's house, the sewing and singing gatherings of the youth, the baking of wedding breads, the bridal bath, etc. The list of events differs by region and diminishes over time, as does the "cast" of characters, which could be very large. The most important participants—two families, the *tysiatskiĭ* (master of ceremonies), *druzhki* (male agents), and *svakhi* ("matchmakers," or female agents)—on both sides often had some hierarchy among them and specific songs. Young women, the peers of the bride, would act and sing collectively, often in her voice.

The decisive moment of the wedding comes when the groom's party arrives to take the bride, her hair is dressed in the way of a married woman, there is a festive meal, and the wedding cortege takes her to her new family, where another celebratory meal lasts until late on the bridal night. Depending on the region, various events happen the next morning and for several days afterward, for example, the "awakening" and housework tests for the newlyweds. The church ceremony (the "crowning") in effect breaks up the procession to the groom's house: the wedding party goes to the church and then continues on its way.

Every event in this sequence is accompanied by songs, long and short, fixed or variable, wedding-specific or not. Their sheer number is striking, especially in regions where laments were practiced. Some rituals involved multiple actors with their sung or spoken "parts," traditional postures, and gestures. In records from Siberia, the groomsman says something in verse almost constantly (Potanina et al. 2002:185–208). In the early nineteenth century, Snegirev described the wedding as "a folk drama, or, more precisely, opera-vaudeville" (1839:119).

The mood and tone of this opera modulate over the course of it—lyrical, dramatic, playful, celebratory, and bawdy. There are songs of praise aiming to promote the prosperity, fertility, and health of the new family (Kulagina and Ivanov 2001:16). There are songs of blame and teasing, usually humorous and sometimes obscene. The mockery is frequently tied to an occasion—the arrival of the groom's party or the newlyweds' departure for bed—and it is possible to discern a ritual significance in the blame—the acted-out resistance of the bride or the fertilizing magic of obscenity. Short songs of praise often demand a reward and can turn to blame to extort a better one. Such songs occur at multiple points during the wedding, as do erotic songs.

The agonistic aspect of the wedding is fully reflected in song. Each side praises their protagonist and disparages the other. The mutual visits and gift exchanges are staged as conflicts—the groom's party, for example, may be barred from the bride's house, only to buy their way in, all the while responding to mockery and teasing. Quick repartee is a demand of the genre, and both sides would have to find representatives with well-hung tongues.

There are songs tied to ritual—the undoing of the bride's braid, the bath, or the baking of the bread. Such songs are usually choral even if they are in the voice of a single protagonist—the bride's party voices her role; the groom's voices his. Solo singing is absent, but solo performance, called причет (translated here, imperfectly, as "lament"), was common in several regions, especially in the north (Arkhangel'sk, Vologda, and shores of the White Sea and Onega) and parts of Siberia.

The Drama of the Bride

The unmarried young women, friends of the bride, often do most of the singing, bewailing or resisting her departure from their midst, teasing the groom's party, praising the bride and, eventually, the groom. The bride sings with them or laments alongside them, and fieldwork records contain many exchanges in song and lament between the bride and her parents, her brother, or her friends.

The story of the bride—her initial resistance and eventual resignation to the loss of her maidenhood—is the central plot line that stands out against the background of the wedding. This loss is irreversible and dramatic in its finality, and even the happiest weddings involve songs expressing the bride's complaint. In some regions, this drama of the bride could take the form of a week of public laments. In regions to the south and west of Moscow, the wedding seems less dramatic, the bride (in song, at least) is more cheerful. Yet even here there are songs with familiar themes: the loss of youthful beauty and freedom, blame of the bride's parents for giving her away, and separation from her peers.

Laments are distinct from songs in meter, music, and manner of composition; solo laments are composed in performance by each lamenter. She would use traditional diction and express traditional themes; but there was no set text, and a talented lamenter could expand and vary her performances, adding similes, metaphors, and description. Group laments either followed a text known to all or relied on traditional diction: it was enough for the leader to start a verse, and the group would step in to finish it. Solo and group laments could be performed simultaneously in dialogue and competition, like a dissimilar duet in opera. For example, a choral song representing the bride's words could accompany a solo lament of her mother (Potanina et al. 2002:37–38).

Several features of lament are suited for composition in performance: stichic form, repetition of syntactical patterns, and abundance of traditional expressions. Laments share these features with other oral traditional poetry including epic tales (Gerd 1997:609), and it is no accident that the most expansive laments are attested in the regions where epic poetry flourished the longest (Kuznetsova 1993:6). In their size, variety, and richness of narrative elements, the famous laments of Irina Fedosova can compete with epics. Her lament of the bride, recorded by Barsov in 1867–1869, is 1,070 verses long and answered by the mother's lament of 514 verses (Chistova and Chistov 1997:277–312).

The wedding also has many points of contact with fairy (magic) tales. In wedding songs, the groom finds his bride by shooting an arrow, traverses impassable forests and mountains to find her, and has to pick her out among identically veiled figures, while the bride shapeshifts to avoid marriage, or turns into a swan, all elements attested in folk tales (Potanina et al. 2002:129–130, 213; Gura 2012:608, 683). The tale of the Frog Princess (ATU 402 "The Animal Bride"[1]) can be read as a script of the wedding and a collection of attendant beliefs (Barber 2013:153–232).

Although there are many songs on the groom's side of the wedding, the repertoire is richer on the bride's side. The *devishnik*, the gathering of the bride's friends, was an especially lyrical moment where songs about the bride's loss of maidenhood predominated (Kulagina and Ivanov 2000:13–14). The bride is the prima donna of the wedding opera, and the reasons are not difficult to see. She alone undergoes an irreversible transition, ceasing forever to be a girl, free and playful and cherished by her parents and friends (or such is the depiction of maidenhood in wedding songs). She enters a transitional and altered state marked by changes in her dress, the way she moves, where she can be within the house (Kuznetsova 1993:15–20; Balashov et al. 1985:33–35). Where laments were sung, the bride would, in her altered state, communicate almost entirely through lament—everyday speech was reduced to a minimum (Baĭburin 1993:66). In the end, the bride emerges from this state as if from a chrysalis, irrevocably changed. The endpoint of her transformation is childbearing, and so the bride's ability to produce new life is central to the wedding, which is permeated everywhere by fertility magic (Barber 2013:152).

The Green Orchard

One of the most widespread wedding themes is that of the bride's "green garden," the association between her maidenhood and flowers or green trees. The betrothal lament by Fedosova contains an expanded description of the "green orchard" full of flowers and birds, which suddenly begins to wither—the flourishing of maidenhood is over:

> И вдруг поблёкли тут цветочики лазуревы,
> И вдруг позябли тут сахарни деревиночки;
> И малы птиченьки—чего они спугалися—
> Из зелёна сада соловьи розлетались! (Chistova and Chistov 1997:285)

> And suddenly the sky-blue flowers faded,
> And the sugar-sweet trees were bitten by frost,
> And the little birds—who knows what scared them—
> All the nightingales flew away from the green orchard![2]

The same theme is present in songs recorded at different times in different places—for example, in this song from Kaluga sung by the friends of the bride while she lamented alongside:

> Остался мой зелен сад без мене,
> Заблёкнут в саду цветики алые. (Kulagina and Ivanov 2000:386–387, no. 261)

> My green orchard is left without me,
> The scarlet flowers will fade in it.

The bride then asks her father (or mother, in other versions) to water the garden:

> Утренней, вечернею зарёю,
> И сверх того горючею слезою. (Kulagina and Ivanov 2000:386–387, no. 261)

> At sunrise and at sunset,
> and also with your warm tears.

The garden, field, or forest is a verdant landscape where the maidens play, dance, and sing, their hair decorated with ribbons and flowers. Until now, the bride was one of them, enjoying her *volia* ("freedom"), *nega* ("tender care"), and *dev'ia krásota* ("maidenly beauty"). Now the bride is taken out, absent from the playful group of girls, as in the following lament, addressed to her mother:

> Погляди-ка ты родимая
> Кого теперь в толпе-то нет?
> Уж как нет в толпе чада милого,
> Уж как нет чада любимого! (Shapovalova and Lavrentieva 1985:109)

> Look, my dear mother
> Who is absent in the crowd?
> Your dear child is not in the crowd,
> Your beloved child is absent!

The Bride's Parents

In songs belonging to the early stages of the wedding, the bride reproaches her father for selling her or "drinking her away" (a reference to a betrothal custom), and the notions of betrayal, deception, and being married too young are prominent. The bride might complain about being chased away like a wild animal or that her father is selling her for a pittance. In a lament from the Kokshen'ga Basin, the bride recalls her father's past pity for her, a contrast to his present cruelty:

> Мой корминец ты батюшко,
> Дак ты возьми меня на руки,
> Пожалей меня, батюшко,
> Старопрежней-то жалостью. (Balashov et al. 1985:37)
>
> My father, you brought me up,
> So take me up in your arms,
> Have pity on me,
> That old pity, like you used to.

The bride as a child, too young to marry, is a common trope in laments. In one lament by a mother, all the other girls are still playing with dolls and sticks, only her child "sits under a storm cloud" (Chistova and Chistov 1997:302).

In regions where the bride laments, her mother does likewise—in fact, she may persist in lamenting even after everyone else stops. In her laments, the mother often echoes the bride, as in this one, sung on the day of the bride's departure:

> Уж ты яблонька, ты кудрявая,
> Я садила тебя, насадила себя,
> Поливала-укрывала,
> От мороза берегла;
> Я на яблоньке цветика не видывала,
> Я сахарного яблочка не кушивала. (Koskina 1997:214–215)
>
> Oh my apple tree, my curly apple tree,
> I planted you, I planted you,
> I watered you, covered you,
> Protected you from frost,
> I have not seen flowers on the apple tree,
> I have not tried its sugar-sweet apples.

The implication is that someone else (the family of the groom) will eat the apples from this cherished tree. The beauty of trees and flowers in these songs is either unproductive, as here, or untouched by agriculture. Maidenhood is associated with growth and flowering rather than fruit and harvest, and the bride may complain that she is "ungrown grass" (Balashov et al. 1985:37) or her friends may reproach her for marrying too early, calling her an "unripe berry in the field," to which she responds that it is not her will (Potanina et al. 2002:84). To the mother's lament above the bride responds, threatening never to come to visit if her married life is unhappy.

Competing claims about the bride's "betrayal" may be voiced in dramatic, sung dialogue. In one such dialogue from the Pinega Basin, the bride laments that her parents are selling her to an utter stranger (Kolpakova 1928:122), while the maidens contradict her in a choral song, saying that she deceived them and invited in the "young prince":

> Паладья обманщица,
> Обманула своих подружек;
> Сама-то большой росла,
> Сама вину сделала:
> Молодого князя в сеницу звала,
> Со сеней в нову горенку. (Kolpakova 1928:122)
>
> Paladia is a liar,
> She deceived her friends,
> She grew up tall,
> She herself is at fault:
> She invited a young prince into the hallway,[3]
> From the hallway into the room.

In Pinega, the bride might conclude by lamenting in her mother's arms, asking what she did wrong (was I not obedient? did I not do my work?), describing the hardships that await her, the suddenness of the change (Kolpakova 1928:124). Such interactions between different actors of the wedding drama were both ritualized, requiring certain gestures and postures (such as holding an apron or kerchief to her eyes), and highly emotional. In Zauralye, the mother might kneel before her daughter and, rocking back and forth with emotion, *vyt'* ("howl") a lament:

> Да и, родимое ты мое дитятко,
> В эту ночку-ноченьку,
> Да и спалось тебе малешенько.
> Не видала ли ты сон,
> Свою девью красоту? (Fedorova 1997:3.4.2)
>
> And now, my dear child,
> In this night, this night,
> You slept so little,
> Did you see a dream—
> Your maidenly *krásota*?

The *Krásota*

The bride's *krásota*, a symbolic object that embodies maidenhood and freedom, has a prominent place in the wedding. In practice, it could be the bride's wreath, ribbons, branches of a tree, or a small cut tree decorated with ribbons, beads, and flowers. The loss of her *krásota* corresponds to a change in the bride's hair, the undoing of her braid. By the end of the wedding, her hair is bound or covered, the ribbons given away, and the little tree, if present, denuded of its decorations.

The green landscape from which the bride is excluded is also the one into which her *krásota* escapes, though the escape is never a happy one. In a Siberian song, the *krásota* clings to a dry tree, a symbol of the irrevocable loss of maidenhood:

> Пошла дивья красота
> Во зелёные луга,
> Во дремучие леса,
> Привилась дивья красота
> К сухому этому дереву,
> Не бувать ему зелену.
> Тебе, Анна Ивановна,
> В красных девушках не бывать,
> Весёлых песен не певать,
> С нами, с подружками, не гулять! (Shapovalova and Lavrentieva 1985:159, no. 855)

> The maidenly *krásota* has gone
> To the green meadows,
> To the forest thickets,
> It has grafted itself
> To a dead tree.
> This tree will not be green,
> And you, Anna Ivanovna,
> Will not be a maiden,
> Will not sing joyful songs,
> Will not play with us, your friends!

In some songs, the bride looks for a place to put her *krásota*, a place where it would turn into flowers (Potanina et al. 2002:132). Yet nothing will save her *krásota*—it is taken to a beautiful meadow, only to be destroyed by grass-cutters:

> "Да унесу я дивью красоту,
> Да во чисто поле, на травинку,
> Да под кусточек ракитовый,
> Да под цветочек лазоревый!"
> Да тут и шли сенокоснички,

Да мужики деревенские,
Да подкосили девью красоту,
Да подкосили и подрезали,
Да матушку дивью красоту! (Shapovalova and Lavrentieva 1985:188, no. 904)

"I will take my maidenly *krásota*
To the open field, to a blade of grass,
And put it under a bush of broom,
And under a sky-blue flower."
But then some hay-cutters were passing by,
Peasants from a village,
They mowed the maidenly *krásota*,
They mowed it and they cut it,
The mother, the maidenly *krásota*!

The *krásota* is often personified and voiced by the bride's friends as a chorus or actually impersonated by one of them (Potanina et al. 2002:127), being variously depicted as offended or abandoned by the bride, crying, and begging to be picked up (Shapovalova and Lavrentieva 1985:187, no. 902).

In regions where a visit to the bathhouse was practiced, this is often the moment when the *krásota* is lost. In a lament from Mezen', the bride says she washed off her maidenly *krásota* and asks her sister to fetch it from the bathhouse; but the sister opens the door too wide, and the *krásota* escapes. It flies into the "wide field," perches on top of an aspen, and "howls like an animal, and whistles like a nightingale." Still lamenting, the bride asks her brother to cut down the aspen and retrieve her *krásota*, to which the brother responds, in everyday speech, "I went, but there was nothing there, I missed it, that's it. It flew away! A maiden's *krásota* is not coming back, no way!" (Kulagina and Ivanov 2000:143, no. 13).

In parts of Siberia, the removal of the bride's *krásota* (symbolized by her wreath and ribbons) took the form of a dramatic act with several family members taking off some part of it. For each participant, the bride's friends would sing a request, in her voice, to take off her *krásota* because не приладилась по старому, не приладилась по прежнему ("it does not sit as it used to") (Potanina et al. 2002:126).

The equation of the bride's *krásota* and her headdress is common, and her separation from peers is often expressed in terms of hair, as in the following example, which is also typical in depicting the bride as the only sad one in a crowd of joyful maidens:

Из саду, сада,
Из сада-вишенья
Там и шли-пришли
Весёлых девушек толпа.
Они все девушки,
Они все красныя,
Да все весёлыя идуть!

Буйны головы у их учёсаны,
Косы русые у их уплётены.
Ленты алые да в косах ввязаны,
Шёлковым платком они повязаны.
Только одна Леночка
Невесёлая идет.
Буйная голова у ней не учёсана,
Русая коса у ей не уплётена,
Лента алая в косы не вплётена,
Шёлковым платком не подвязана. (Shapovalova and Lavrentieva 1985:181, no. 889)

From the orchard, orchard,
From the orchard, the cherry orchard
There was coming, arriving
A crowd of joyful maidens.
They are all maidens,
They are all pretty,
They are all joyful as they walk along!
Their luxuriant hair is combed,
Their blond braids are made,
Their silk ribbons are braided in,
They are covered with silk shawls.
Lenochka alone
Is sad as she walks along.
Her luxuriant hair is not combed,
Her blond braid is not made,
Her red ribbon is not braided in,
Nor tied with a silk shawl.

The head of a maiden is often described by the adjective *buĭnyĭ* ("tempestuous"), applied also to epic heroes and referring to willful thoughts as well as hair (Dal' 1981: under *buĭnyĭ*). The luxurious and brightly decorated hair of a young woman is an expression of her "potential energy," her burgeoning but as yet unspent fertility, and her *volîa* ("freedom")—qualities lost in marriage.

When the bride's braid was made for the last time, it was often made especially tightly and with knotted ribbons. In songs, the bride asks her helpers to make it in such a way that the groom's agent, *svakha* or godmother, will not undo it; for example, she may ask her mother to put knives and sabers into her braid:

Заплети-ко кормилица
Ты в мою русу косу
Два ножа, да два булатные,
Две сабельки острые,
Две иголочки колючие! (Shapovalova and Lavrentieva 1985:135, no. 755)

Braid, mother,
Into my long braid,
Two knives, two damask knives,
And two sharp sabers,
And two prickly needles!

Once undone, the braid is divided into two (or more) parts, which were usually wound around the bride's head under her new headdress. The conventional cruelty of the "godmother" who "tears" the braid dramatizes the bride's resistance and the dark vision of the groom's family that often prevails before crowning:

Приехали свашеньки немилосливы,
Немилосливы.
Стали её косаньку всю рвать-порывать,
Всю рвать-порывать.
Стали её русую на две разделять,
На две разделять. (Potanina et al. 2002:299, no. 291)

The pitiless *svakhi* arrived,
The pitiless ones,
They began to tear and rend the braid,
To tear and rend,
They began to divide it, the blond one, in two,
To divide it in two.

Violence, Hunt, and the White Swan

The sexuality and violence implicit in the image of the torn braid are persistent themes in wedding songs. In an image that echoes torn hair, the bride is depicted as a bird whose feathers are pulled out. In a song recorded in Arkhangel'sk, the falcon finds a mate, but she asks to be released, to return to her own "warm nest." The falcon responds:

Я тогда тебя спущу, ой рано рано да
Крылья-перья ощиплю, ой рано рано да
Право крылышко уломлю, ой рано рано да.[4] (Kulagina and Ivanov 2001:114, no. 375)

Here's when I'll let you go—oh, early, early, yes
Once I pluck your wings and feathers—oh, early, early, yes
Once I break your right wing—oh, early, early, yes.

In a song from the Kursk region, the bride is a "sparrow-cuckoo" who begs the falcon to let her go *sy vorobkami popyrkhat'* ("to flutter about with other sparrows"), but he responds that he will let her go only once he plucks out her крылья-перышки ("wings and feathers") (Kulagina and Ivanov 2001:114, no. 376). In a song from the Sevskii district, it is a swan that has her wing broken (Slavianina 1978:59, no.99). The story then repeats on the human plane, with the bride's undone braid (*kosatku raspleli*) corresponding to the broken wing.

The bride can be a sparrow or cuckoo, a dove, or a jackdaw, while the groom is often the nightingale or falcon. Songs about the nightingale looking for his cuckoo are especially widespread to the south of Moscow. Most often, however, the bride is a *belaîa lebëdushka* ("white she-swan"), presumably because swans are especially associated with abundance and fertility (Barber 2013:181–183). In a group lament from Mezen', the bride is the only wounded swan in the flock:

> Как во стаде да лебедином у
> Есть одна только лебедь подстрелена,
> Как во кругу, роду девьем
> Красна девушка есть запоручена. (Kulagina and Ivanov 2000:193, no. 67)

> In the flock of swans,
> there is one swan who is shot,
> In the circle, in the family of maidens,
> There is one maiden beauty betrothed.

In their laments, the brides sometimes sing about being unable to walk up the stairs or to see clearly, as if they were bodily hampered in their altered state, physically unable to run and dance with the other girls, like a wounded swan who cannot fly with the others (Balashov et al. 1985:36; Kuznetsova 1993:79–81). Separated from her flock, the swan-bride finds herself in a flock of geese, who begin to peck at her, a metaphor for her change of family.

> Отставала да лебедь белая,
> Как што от стада да лебединово,
> Дак приставала да лебедь белая
> Ко стаду—серым гусям. (Balashov et al. 1985:243)

> A white swan fell behind,
> Separated from the swan flock,
> A white swan joined
> A flock—of gray geese.

In a widespread folk tale, "The Swan Maiden" (ATU 400, "The Man on a Quest for His Lost Wife"), swan-maidens dance on the shores of a lake and are spied by a hunter. He steals the feathers or dress of one of them, and she becomes his wife but eventually regains her dress and flies away (Barber 2013:13–27, 202–207; Hatto 1961:331–333). These swan-women are allied with other dancing groups of girls in nature—the *vily*, *rusalki*, and other "nymphs." These "dancing goddesses," to use Barber's term, are figures of fertility and have many points of contact with the bride, herself such a figure. A belief that the brides who died before consummating their marriages became *rusalki* or *samodivy* was widespread (Gura 2012:677). The swan and hunter meet again in wedding songs but with a different outcome. In Mezen', when the party of the groom arrives at the bride's house, they are told that she has disappeared. One of the excuses given is the following:

> Она ранним утром вышла на взвоз,
> Обвернулась белой лебедью
> И улетела по поднебесью.
> Вот вы там, надь, дак ей и ловите. (Kulagina and Ivanov 2001:279, no. 538)

> Early in the morning she came out to the porch,
> Turned into a swan,
> And flew away in the sky.
> So, go catch her there.

Sometimes, the bride also turns into a pike, another egg-laying creature associated with fertility. But the bride, of course, will not escape her wedding; and in the dialogue from Mezen', the groomsmen respond:

> У нашего князя молодого Степана Матвеевича
> Есть собаки порато гонкие,
> Охотники ловкие,
> Ружья наши шибко меткие,
> И мы, как об этом узнали,
> И сразу же её догнали.
> И не стреляли, не ранили
> И в полной сохранности сюда ей доставили.
> И здесь она находится. (Kulagina and Ivanov 2001:280, no. 538)

> Our prince young Stepan, son of Matvei,
> Has very swift dogs,
> Agile hunters,
> And our guns have very good aim.
> As soon as we learned about it [that the bride turned into a swan]
> We caught up with her right away.
> We did not shoot or wound her,
> But brought her here completely safe and sound,
> And that's where she is.

The groom himself is frequently a hunter, while the bride is his prey. He might be urged to "hunt the marten" (an animal standing for the bride) (Kulagina and Ivanov 2000:252, no. 128), or his party might be on the trail of a *kunitsa-lisitsa* ("marten-fox") (Kulagina and Ivanov 2001:272, no. 535). Often, the instrument of the groom's hunt is the unmistakably sexual arrow, just as it is in the folk tale of the Frog Princess (Afanasiev 1855–1864:no. 267–269). In a song from the region of Onega, the groom is described in a near-epic way as a young hero sailing on a ship. He walks on deck and combs his curls so that they spread down his white neck. Then he takes out his bow and aims his arrow with the following prayer:

> Уж ты стрелка, ты стрелка моя, да,
> Да калёна да муравлёная да,
> Полети, моя калёная стрела да,
> Высоко вверх под облако,
> Да далёко во чисто полё да,
> Застрели, моя калёная стрела да,
> Черна ворона под тучею,
> Ясна сокола во полуволоку,
> Да белу лебедь на перелети да,
> Серу утицу на заводи да,
> Красну девицу в высоком терему да
> Да Анну-от Ивановну. (Kulagina and Ivanov 2001:342)

> My arrow, my arrow,
> My tempered, slender arrow,
> Fly, my tempered arrow,
> High up under a cloud,
> Far away into the open field,
> Hit, my tempered arrow,
> A black raven under a dark cloud,
> A bright falcon under a light cloud,
> A white swan in flight,
> A grey duck on water,
> A pretty maiden in her high bower,
> Anna Ivanovna.

The bride asks him not to shoot, and the groom dismounts from his horse (the boat being, apparently, forgotten), lowers his arrow, and gets congratulated. In some songs, he does let the arrow fly—and in all cases, he gets the bride.

Water

Water birds, boats, and riverbanks are elements of another theme in wedding lyric, that of water, and especially rivers with their vivifying powers. The bride and groom meet by the water, where he waters his horse and she washes clothes (Kulagina and Ivanov

2000:311, no. 182), and riverbanks are the favorite haunts of the maidens. Whatever the local river may be, in wedding songs it is often the mythologized "Danube," the river of maidenhood and marriage (Ivanov and Toporov 1995:172) or else "Jordan" (Fedorova 1997:3.2). Fedorova describes an old custom of choosing the brides "by the water": on a day in January, young women, dressed in their best, would arrive in sleighs at the river and line up "by the Jordan," to be seen by potential grooms and matchmakers.

Wind and water also mark the manner of the bride's transition to her new life (Gura 2012:638–645). The morning of the crowning day often features songs about black clouds and storms that fell forests and disturb lakes, a metaphor for the force that compels the bride (Yamaguchi 2020). It is often this storm that separates the one swan from her flock (Kulagina and Ivanov 2000:338, no. 211), while the arrival of the groom's party is described as wind:

Не было ветру—да ветры дунули, да ветры дунули, эх,
Не было гостей—гости наехали, гости наехали, да. (Potanina et al. 2002:241, no. 222)

There was no wind—and then the wind picked up, then the wind picked up, eh,
There were no guests—and then the guests arrived, then the guests arrived, yes.

In harmony with this mood, the bride reports a terrifying dream when she is woken up by her mother on the crowning day, the content of the dream being as traditional as its occurrence and often involving fast rivers or floods:

И приснился мне, родна матушка, страшный сон:
Речка быстрая и в этой речке быстрой
Я купалася,
Предо мною, родна матушка,
Сильная волна колыхалася,
А я, родна матушка,
Её напугалася. (Koskina 1997:235, no. 42)

And I saw, dear mother, a terrifying dream:
A swift river, and in that swift river
I was bathing,
In front of me, dear mother,
A big wave rose up,
And I, dear mother,
Was afraid of it.

In a lament from the Povetluzhie, the bride, carried away by water, tries in vain to hold on to a "white birch tree" and, at last, grasps two plants that are painful to touch—the cutting sedge and the prickly shepita. The white birch, the last verses explain, is her mother, the sedge her future mother-in-law, and the shepita her future father-in-law (Lobanov et al. 1998:111).

In other songs of the crowning morning, the mother calls out to her daughter to return because she has forgotten her "golden keys." The bride responds that she will not return; it is not her keys but her maidenhood that she has forgotten:

> Позабыла я, матушка,
> Всю волюшку батюшкину
> И всю негу матушкину,
> Всю красу свою девичью (Snegirev 1839:175, no. 9)

> I forgot, my mother,
> All the freedom of my father,
> All the tender care of my mother,
> All my own maidenly beauty.

The Work of the Bride

Neither the *krásota* nor "the keys" exhausts the list of the bride's losses: the songs speak also about the loss of her handiwork. The bride's peers are still filling up their wedding chests, sewing shirts and embroidering the towels they will distribute as gifts; but the bride's chest is now being emptied. Near Sevsk, the two families would gather on the eve of crowning and exchange gifts. One of the songs sung on this occasion was the following:

> Плакала Маринушка,
> Плакала Гавриловна,
> К сундуку привпадала,
> К сундуку привпадала:
> —Я не год не два пряла,
> Я не год не два пряла,
> Не неделюшку ткала,
> Не неделюшку ткала,
> Не лето белила,
> Не лето белила,
> А за час раздарила. (Slavianina 1978:32, no. 34)

> Marinushka was crying,
> Gavriolvna was crying,
> She was falling on her chest,
> She was falling on her chest:
> —I spun not for one year only, not for two
> I spun not for one year only, not for two
> I wove not for one week only

> I wove not for one week only,
> I bleached not for one summer only,
> I bleached not for one summer only,
> But I gave it all away in one hour.

There are also songs about her family's loss of the bride as a worker. In a song about two fathers, the father of the bride complains: she will no longer be there to help in the fields or to clean the house or to honor her parents; the father of the groom rejoices: now it is he who will reap these benefits (Kulagina and Ivanov 2000:358–360, no. 232, 233).

The Bride and the Two Families

The undoing of the braid was often also the moment for the bride to receive blessings from her family, and, at this point especially, the completeness of the family seems to have a magical significance, a prediction, perhaps, of future good fortune. An orphan bride was a special case, and for her there were separate "orphan" songs, in which she often asks a relative to ring the big church bell and to wake up her parents:

> Не расступится ли мать сыра земля?
> Не расколется ли дубова доска?
> Не услышит ли родна маменька?
> Не придёт ли благословить меня? (Kulagina and Ivanov 2000:397, no. 271)
>
> Perhaps the dank earth will part for my mother?
> Perhaps the oak board [of the coffin] will split?
> Perhaps my dear mother will hear me?
> Perhaps she will come to bless me?

Sometimes orphan brides would go to the cemetery to perform such songs (Teplova 2017).

At this point in the wedding, the songs begin to persuade the bride to accept her fate. Prior to this moment, the bride's future in-laws appear in her songs as strange, foreign, and harsh, her future life as unending work, poverty, and oppression (Balashov et al. 1985:51–52). But eventually the bride must acquiesce, and the songs speak of her "reasonableness" and give her advice on how to live in the "foreign land" of her future husband:

> Ты не плачь-ка, наша умница,
> Не тужи, наша разумница,
> Мы тебя ведь не в полон даём,
> Мы тебя ведь замуж выдаём.
> Брат сестрицу уговаривал,

Брат сестричушке наказывал:
—Ты сестрицюшка родимая
Туды выйти надо навеки,
Жить-то надо там умеючи,
Носить злата там, не снашивать,
Терпеть горя, не рассказывать. (Kuznetsova and Loginov 2001:221)

Do not cry, our sensible one,
Do not cry, our intelligent one,
We are not giving you away into captivity,
We are giving you away in marriage.
The brother was persuading his sister,
The brother was instructing his sister:
—My dear sister,
You have to go there forever,
You have to know how to live there,
There you have to wear gold and never wear it out,
You have to tolerate grief and never tell it.

Such songs about brotherly persuasion often end with the bride's objections, such as this one, in which the bride paints a dire picture of her future life:

Ведь мне будет настояться
У жернова, у ступы-ти,
Вот поганого корыта,
Ведь не будет допроситься
Рабодатного кусочка. (Kulagina and Ivanov 2000:431, no. 304)

I am sure I'll get my fill of standing
by the mill or by the mortar
or by the refuse trough.
I am sure I'll keep asking in vain
for a piece of bread for all my work.

Such grim visions are sometimes expressed in song even during the journey to the groom's house.

Just as there is only one possible outcome to the bride's resistance in the wedding script, so there is only one way for the "foolish white swan" to become "reasonable" and "intelligent"—to accept her fate without complaint (Chistova and Chistov 1997:302.38; Shapovalova and Lavrentieva 1985:105). A song about how the bride who "was sitting tallest of all, bent her head lowest of all" to think about marriage occurs in several regions:

Сама она садилася—была выше всех,
Склонила головушку—стала ниже всех.

—Подумайте, девочки, подумайте мне: (twice)
Как же мине быть, как замуж идти?⁵ (Potanina et al. 2002:93, no. 40)

She sat down—she was taller than all,
She bent her head—she became lower than all.
—Think, girls, think for me: (twice)
What should I do, how should I marry?

The song concludes with the bride's decision to call her parents-in-law "mother" and "father."

"Do not give me away" is perhaps the most dominant theme in the laments before crowning. The following song, which enacts a dialogue between a daughter and her father, exists in many variants, often with the mother rather than the father as the bride's addressee:

—Тятенька родимый, тятенька родимый,
Колокольчики звенят, да колокольчики звенят.
—Мила моя дочь, да мила моя дочь, да
Не убойся—не отдам, да не убойся—не отдам.
—Тятенька родимый, тятенька родимый,
Женихи-то у ворот, да женихи-то у ворот
—Мила моя дочь, да мила моя дочь, да
Не убойся—не отдам, да не убойся—не отдам. (Potanina et al. 2002:182 no. 151)

—Dear daddy, dear daddy,
The bells are ringing, the bells are ringing!
—My dear daughter, my dear daughter,
Don't fear—I will not give you away, don't fear—I will not give you away.
—Dear daddy, dear daddy,
But the groom's party is at the gates, the groom's party is at the gates!
—My dear daughter, my dear daughter,
Don't fear—I will not give you away, don't fear—I will not give you away.

In this way, the song continues step by step, with the groom opening the door, entering the house, and finally taking the bride by the hand, at which point the father says:

—Мила моя дочь, да мила моя дочь, да
Теперь воля не моя, да воля Сашина

—My dear daughter, my dear daughter,
Now it's not my will, it's Sasha's [the groom's] will.

The sudden reversal of this song is iconic and matches the reversal at the core of the wedding, which is often expressed by paradoxical wording, as in the song about a falcon summoning a dove from her "green orchard"—she does not want to go, but then she just does.

> Она не хотела, она не хотела, да,
> Вот и за им полетела, да. (Kulagina and Ivanov 2000:342, no. 214)

> She did not want to, she did not want to,
> And so she flew with him.

The Crowning and the Songs of the Groom

The day of the crowning is one of the occasions for songs claiming that only the groom can do something at which everyone else fails and that is why he gets the bride. It is the conceit of the wedding that the bride is the best of the maidens—the most beautiful, the best singer, and the leader (Balashov et al. 1985:226)—and when they lose her it is as if a tree is losing not just a branch but its very top:

> Да на тебе ли, ёлка-сосенка,
> Да много сучьев, много отраслей,
> Да одного сучочка нетутко,
> Да что сучка, самой вершиночки. (Shapovalova and Lavrentieva 1985:194)

> You, our fir-tree-pine,
> Have many branches, many twigs,
> But one branch is missing,
> And not even just a branch, the very top.

Songs about the groom participate in the same system of metaphors and follow the same logic, only here the inaccessibility of the bride is transformed into an exceptional quality of the groom, who alone can find or catch or save her. In a song from Pomorye, the bride is hiding behind exactly the kind of tree that elsewhere stands for the bride—a green, "curly," and flourishing tree atop a tall mountain. She boasts that no one will find her, but the groom hears her and promises:

> Я один тебя повысмотрю,
> Я повысмотрю, повыгляжу. (Kulagina and Ivanov 2000:310, no. 180)

> I alone will spy you,
> I will spy you and notice you.

In a song from Kaluga, the bride is unable to cross a river, standing on a "white stone," crying, and looking at the "steep banks." Her father does not have enough pity to help her, nor does her mother, but the groom does.

> У Ванюшки жалости побольше,
> Он снял меня с камушка с белого. (Kulagina and Ivanov 2001:51, no. 330)

> Vanyushka had more pity,
> He picked me off the white stone.

In a song from the vicinity of Sevsk, the bride is weaving and will not come out to the guests. Her father asks her, then her mother, and she sets her conditions, but still does not come:

> Сметайте дворы—я пойду,
> Стелите ковры—я сяду,
> Наливайте чару—я выпью.
> Сметали дворы—не пошла,
> Стелили ковры—не села.
> Наливали чару—не пила. (Slavianina 1978:77–78, no. 139)

> Sweep the yard—and I will come,
> Spread the carpets—and I will sit down,
> Fill my cup—and I will drink it.
> They swept the yard—she did not come,
> They spread the carpets—she did not sit down,
> They poured her cup—she did not drink.

Finally, the groom asks her, and she comes out. These songs dramatize the bride's resistance but also shift the focus from her "unfreedom" to the suitability of the groom and the willingness of the bride to come to him.

The Journey and the Feast

As the bride's momentous departure approaches, the mood of the wedding shifts. The laments decrease and finally cease, replaced by songs of praise. The transition is often a gradual one. In the Kokshen'ga Basin, for example, the bride would still lament as she was led out by her father for the last time. She had to turn back three times—to say goodbye to her "green orchard," to "part with her *krásota*," or "because she forgot her friends"; but once the father hands her over to the groom, saying, "I have given my daughter to you," a decisive break occurs in the mood: the maidens gradually switch to songs of praise, and, once this happens, the bride's laments also cease (Balashov et al. 1985:219). Balashov and colleagues describe the transition: "For some time these two elements (the laments and the praise-songs) struggle with each other, overlapping in a peculiar way, and then the joyful element wins over: soon it is time for the crowning" (1985:220). From now on, joyful songs overtake the wedding, and themes that so far were sung primarily on the groom's territory begin to dominate. In some regions, this stage of the wedding is full of jokes and humorous teasing. Near Sevsk, for example, the table was first occupied by a fake bride, who was eventually rejected by the groom's party. Then the girls, here called *igritsy* ("players"), sang insulting little songs about the groomsman and his party (Slavianina 1978:83, no. 153), who responded in kind. The main agents on both sides would be subjected to personal mockery (the groomsman has a frog on his nose, the *svakha*'s cap is moving because of lice underneath, etc.). One frequent caricature is that someone is extremely big and heavy—the benches groan underneath them, and the *svakha* is so heavy that seven horses cannot pull her (Kulagina and Ivanov 2001:61–62, no. 337). Eventually, the groomsman would suggest reconciliation, offer wine and money to the girls, and they would cede the table.

The actual journey to the groom's house was seen as the most dangerous and precarious moment of the wedding, and precautions were taken (the ground swept for the bride to walk on, salt placed in various places, and needles stuck in the hem of her dress). There are tales about whole wedding companies turned into animals, bears, or wolves (Balashov et al. 1985:289). In song, the bride's mother describes her daughter's journey as going "beyond the tall mountains, beyond the swift rivers, beyond the dark forests."[6] Some spell-like songs ask the horse not to stumble or ask the "noblemen" to be careful on the way (Kulagina and Ivanov 2001:266, no. 519, 520; Kolpakova 1973:141, no. 273). Sometimes, choral songs were sung on the way, for example, ones about the bride walking in a meadow and coming across a smithy where her golden ring is being made (Slavianina 1978:53–53, no. 81).

The arrival of the bride and the festive meal at the groom's house were events full of praise: in Zaonezhye, this meal was called *khvalenie* ("praise") (Kuznetsova and Loginov 2001:236). The father-in-law would "open" the bride—pick up her shawl and three times circle the heads of the newlyweds with it. At this moment, the *svakha* exclaims, *khvalite moloduîu!* ("Praise the young (wife)!"), and everyone shouts, *khorosha, khorosha molodaîa!* ("Fair, fair is the young wife!") (Balashov et al. 1985:295). Fertility magic is abundant at this stage—sitting on furs, being showered with grain and hops, the bride being given a child to hold in her lap, etc.—and the songs also display the exuberant imagery of fertility and productivity. The ungrown grass and trampled flowers of the bride's laments are replaced by flourishing grapes, red apples, and ripe berries. From the beginning, "grape trees," and roses are mentioned in the groom's songs, but now they come to dominate. The following song is typical:

> Виноград в саду цветет,
> Виноград в саду цветет,
> А ягода, а ягода созревает,

> А ягода, а ягода созревает.
> Виноград-то—Иван сударь,
> Виноград-то—Иван сударь,
> А ягода, а ягода—свет Прасковья его,
> А ягода, а ягода—свет Прасковья его. (Kolpakova 1973:158, no. 312)

> A grapevine blooms in the orchard
> A grapevine blooms in the orchard
> And a berry, a berry ripens
> And a berry, a berry ripens.
> The grapevine is master Ivan
> The grapevine is master Ivan,
> And the berry, and the berry—his Praskovia,
> And the berry, and the berry—his Praskovia.

Vinogradië krasno-zelënoe ("Red–green grapevine") is a frequent refrain in such songs, as is *roza, roza, roza—alye tsvety* ("rose, rose, rose—red flowers") or *sladko îablochko nalivchato* ("sweet apple full of juice") (Kolpakova 1973:158, no. 313).

Some of the themes familiar from the bride's songs and laments persist throughout but appear in happier variations. A song that could be sung almost at any point during the wedding features familiar themes: the bride washes clothes in a river, the groom walks on the banks, he aims his arrow at a swan:

> Он и хоча бить бела лебедя на воде,
> Он и хоча взять вот Шурочку за себе. (Kulagina and Ivanov 2001:104, no. 366)

> And he wants to hit the white swan on the water,
> And he wants to take Shurochka to be his wife.

In this song, however, there are no broken wings, lonely swans, or pecking geese. Instead, at the end we have a happy pair:

> Да у лебедя лебёдушка под крылом,
> Да у Колечки вот Шурочка под бочком

> A he-swan has a she-swan under his wing,
> Kolechka has Shurochka under his side.

Even "green orchard" appears in a new guise. In one of the плясовые ("dancing") songs for the concluding feast, the young wife wakes up her husband and tells him that his "raven horse" broke free and got into his green orchard:

> Заскочил конь во зелёный сад,
> В сад со калиной, со малиной,
> С чёрной ягодой смородиною. (Kulagina and Ivanov 2001:128, no. 380;
>   cf. 379, 381, 382)

> The horse jumped into the green orchard,
> The orchard with viburnum and raspberries,
> With black currant berries.

This orchard is filled not with pretty flowers but with ripe berries, and when the horse tramples the garden, no tears are shed. Instead, the young husband consoles his bride—they'll grow a green orchard together:

> Не печалься, красна девица душа,
> Наживём с тобой зелёный сад
>
> Don't be sad, pretty maiden, my soul:
> You and I will grow a green orchard.

Songs about the groom come to the fore now, and in them he rides up to the bride on his "raven-colored" horse, whip in hand. In one song, the groom is going to church: he puts on his boots, washes his face, puts on a marten fur coat and a black hat, "crosses himself as it is written, bows in a learned way" (Kulagina and Ivanov 2001:83, no. 354). His most impressive attribute—most frequently mentioned in all regions—are his curls, no doubt a sign of his youthful virility, corresponding to the bride's "tempestuous" hair. His curls are usually gold:

> На главе-то золоты кудри свиваютсе,
> В три ряды его кудри да завиваютсе. (Kulagina and Ivanov 2001:83, no. 354)
>
> On his head the golden curls are rolling
> His curls are curling three rows deep.

All the "noblemen" wonder whether perhaps such a brave and handsome youth has the moon for his father and the dawn for his mother, a typical praise for the groom:

> Не светёл ли месяц-батюшко взосеял молодца?
> Не заря ли тебя да спородила молодца?
>
> Was it perhaps the bright father-moon that sired such a lad?
> Was it perhaps dawn that gave birth to you, such a lad?

The groom responds by naming his father and mother and adds that it was his sister that curled his hair.

Hair is so important in the lexicon of the wedding that sometimes it can stand metonymically for the newlyweds, as in the following song from Zaonezhye, performed after the bride's hair was done up in the fashion of a married woman. The groom puts his hand on the bride's hair, turns the bride around three times, and then kisses her as the maidens sing:

Жёлтые кудри за стол пошли,
      за стол пошли
Русую косаньку вслед повели,
      ой, вслед повели. (Kuznetsova and
 Loginov 2001:231, no. 151)

Yellow curls went to the table,
      went to the table
They led the blond braid after them,
      oi, after them.

The symmetry of this song belies a difference between the hair of the bride and that of the groom: nothing happens to the groom's curls; they are as golden and flowery as ever at the concluding feast, in contrast to the bride's maidenly hair, which is celebrated and then undone.

The loss of the bride's *krásota*, however, is now firmly in the past. In songs, she chooses the groom, waits for him, and desires him (Kolpakova 1973:145, no. 284). A typical example is a much-varied song beginning with the question *Kto u nas khoroshiĭ, kto u nas prigozhiĭ?* ("Who here is good, who here is handsome?"). The answer is, of course, the groom, depicted as mounting his horse and arriving at the bride's bower to be welcomed by her:

Долго я тебя ждала,
Долго дожидала,
Со скуки пропадала,
Со скуки пропадала да,
С горя помирала. (Kulagina and Ivanov 2001:90, no. 359)

How long I waited for you,
how long I waited,
I was perishing from boredom,
Perishing from boredom, yes,
Dying of grief.

The groom, for his part, is also free and chooses for himself the best bride among many:

Перебор, перебор,
Часты звёздушки,
Перебрал, перебрал,
Часты звёздочки!
Выбрал себе, выбрал себе
Да заряночку!
Маленьку, маленьку,
Да ясненьку! (Shapovalova and Lavrentieva 1985:280, no. 1292)

Looking through, looking through
The countless stars,
He chose among, he chose among,
The countless stars!
He chose for himself, he chose for himself
The dawn star!
A little one, a little one,
But a bright one!

Songs of praise celebrate the bride's beauty and ornate dress (Kulagina and Ivanov 2001:93, no. 361) but also the future work she will do for her new family. The mother of the groom is depicted rejoicing at the help she will get:

А взрадовалася Иванова матушка: А теперь у меня и топлёная горенка,
А теперь у меня и метёные сенюшки. (Kulagina and Ivanov 2001:103, no. 365)

Ivan's mother rejoiced:
Now my main room is warm,
Now my entrance way is swept.

The idea that the groom's family acquires another daughter is often expressed though the contrast between the two children—their first child is born (*Pervoe ditë rozhënoe*), but their second child—the bride—is fate-given (*A vtoroe suzhënoe*) (Kulagina and Ivanov 2001:141, no. 385). A widespread song contrasts the "three griefs" of the bride's mother and the "three joys" of the groom's mother. The former cries when she gives birth to her daughter, brings her up, and gives her away in marriage. The latter rejoices when she gives birth to her son, brings him up, and sees him married (Kulagina and Ivanov 2001:146, no. 390).

It was not all praise for the bride, however. If the groom received his fair share of mockery earlier, now it is the bride's turn. Blame songs for the bride are not as frequent as those for the groom and especially for his party, the main butt of attacks; but when she is blamed the themes of her songs are transmogrified. Instead of lyrical laments about being too young, now it is the mother of the groom who complains:

Ты куда, дитя, ездило?
Ты кого, дитя, привезло?
Она худым да худёшенька,
[Она] малым да малёшенька. (Kulagina and Ivanov 2001:209, no. 445)

Where did you go, child?
Whom did you bring, child?
She is so thin,
She is so small.

At issue is the bride's ability to work. Most often, however, the bride is blamed for her pride: she is гордёна ("the prideful one"), who refuses to go into the groom's house because it is not up to her standards—the rooms are dirty and dark, full of flies and mosquitoes. The bride's earlier fears of hardship and poverty are echoed in these songs, but now she gets little sympathy:

Да горденушка горлива,
Да молодушка ломлива. (Kulagina and Ivanov 2001:208, no. 442)

This prideful one is proud,
This young wife is demanding.

These songs are a vivid reminder of the women's hardships since the remedy for the bride's pride is found at once, and it is a whip. A song from the region of Kaluga laconically states:

На эти-то мухи—листвяной веник,
На эту гордёну—шелковую плетку! (Kulagina and Ivanov 2001:209, no. 444)

For these flies—a broom with green leaves,
For this proud one—a silken whip!

As with the groomsman earlier, blame for the bride can turn into praise, depending on her response. In a report from Vyatsk, as soon as the newlyweds entered the house people from the village would start to blame the bride, comparing her body parts to various household implements (the technique often used on the groom's party). Then she would stand up and bow to the singers, and the song, to the same tune, would change:

Учёная дитя, учёная дитя,
Она выучена, она выучена, ой,
Выучена, выучена,
В люди вывезена, в люди вывезена, ой
Умиет она, умиет она
На резвые ножки встать, на резвые ножки встать, ой
Умиет она, умиет она
Поклон воздать, да поклон воздать. (Kulagina and Ivanov 2001:211–212, no. 446)

She is an educated child, an educated child,
She is well brought up, she is well brought up,
Well brought up, well brought up
She's been taken out, taken out to show the people, oy
She knows how to, she knows how to
Stand on her swift feet, stand on her swift feet, oy,
She knows how to, she knows how to,
Bow respectfully, bow respectfully.

The blame turns to praise, but it is clear what is expected of the bride: modesty, resignation, and hard work. Songs advising the bride to bow politely are very common (Slavianina 1978:232).

Sexual Songs

Songs on either side of the nuptial night often have transparent sexual overtones, and sending the newlyweds off to bed was the prime occasion for obscene songs, plentiful in the wedding (Kolpakova 1928:157; Varagova 1995:150–151). In a song attested in numerous variations, the noblemen ride along and see a cunt atop a tall haystack (*shakshu na zarode*). They don't know how to get it down until the groom comes to the rescue, giving the familiar "top of the tree" and "only the groom" tropes a bawdy twist:

Как мы будем доставати,
                         доставати?
Да вилами доставати, дак проколешь,
                         дак проколешь,
А граблями доставать—расцарапашь,
                         расцарапашь,
Да у нас ведь Сергей-то догадлив,
                         да догадлив,
Он ведь праву полу загибает,
                         загибает,
Толстый хер из штаны вытягает,
                         вытягает,
Да с зароду шакшу он снимает,
                         да снимает. (Kulagina and Ivanov 2000:302–303, no. 174)

How will we get it,
will we get it?
If we get it with a pitchfork, we'll pierce it,
we'll pierce it,
If we get it with a rake, we'll scratch it,
we'll scratch it.
But our Sergei is quick thinker,
yes, quick thinker,
He lifts, he lifts the right flap of his coat,
                         lifts it up,
He takes out, he takes out his thick dick,
                         takes it out,
And he takes down the cunt from the haystack,
                         yes, takes it down.

According to some reports, sexually explicit songs were sung by old women, who take on a disparaging role in other ways as well—for example, in songs about the bride's future work (Ivanova and Kliaus 1995:167).

The joking mood would often return the next morning, when the bride's party would come back to look for their "lost heifer," sometimes even with jesters in costume (*rîazhenye*) (Kulagina and Ivanov 2000:84–85; Kulagina 1995:174). Around Sevsk, songs similar to the ones above could be sung at festivities after the first night (Slavianina 1978:102–110). The newlyweds would usually visit the bride's family the next day (Balashov et al. 1985:298). The songs on that occasion, however, were already outside the wedding "libretto"—the "opera-vaudeville" was over.

Conclusion

This is a superficial picture: behind the generalizations and simplifications of this chapter lies an astonishing complexity of available material. A look at the laments, for example, of the White Sea region reveals subregions with different melodies and meters (Efimenkova 2008); and similar complexity is to be found in Siberia, where the songs of the bride and the groom were musically different and local traditions more distinct musically than in genre, plot, or themes (Potanina et al. 2002:39, 45). The music of the wedding song requires a separate chapter.

Questions remain about the antiquity and spread of this type of wedding. Many of its elements find parallels in ancient Greece, for example—including the laments of the bride, her interrupted weaving, trampled flowers, meeting by the river, girls dancing in groups in a flowering landscape, the inaccessible bride, humorous songs about the size of the wedding participants, the bride's luxurious hair, and the groom's tight curls. This points to the systemic and diachronic persistence of wedding poetics of similar magic and ritual logic across time and space.

The fieldwork on the Russian wedding contains a treasure trove of interviews with the singers, a glimpse into the ways people related to the traditional wedding. There is no ready-made category for describing what the bride does when she performs her laments. Is she acting? To some extent yes, since she is supposed to lament and cry even if she feels quite happy. As one respondent commented,

Хоть пошла за любого, так людей-то стыдно—охота не охота, а реви! (Balashov et al. 1985:33)

Although I married for love, still, you feel shame in front of people—whether you want to or not, you have to cry!

Is the bride expressing her personal emotions? This is also true, and many former brides recall the passion and sincerity of their laments and the emotional responses of their families. There are reports of the brides fainting from strain and emotion, of mothers "falling as if dead" at the sound of their daughters' laments (Kuznetsova and Loginov 2001:43), of a father so moved by his daughter's lament that he stopped leading her, announcing "I can't do this! Go on your own!" (Balashov et al. 1985:219). When the bride was forced to marry against her will, her resistance could be in earnest. As Shmelyova remarks, the bride's laments are "like monologues of the wedding's main actor" and express both her emotion and the wedding "script" (1980:111–112). The language of laments is traditional but fluid, the degree of play-acting and self-expression in each performance is unique. It would be facile to say that such performances are a mixture of the personal and the traditional: the two elements are never separated in the first place. The wedding follows a traditional scenario, and in it the bride plays the bride, acting her own self within the world of the wedding. Her words reflect both deep and more recent traditions of song, tale, and ritual, just as they reflect human life shaped by agriculture and, in particular, life in Russian villages of different times and places. In the case of solo laments, they reflect the creativity, personalities, and emotions of individual performers. None of this is easy to disentangle, but the possibilities for future study are immense.

Notes

1. The Aarne-Thompson-Uther (ATU) Tale-Type Index is an international catalogue of folk tales.
2. Translations here and subsequently are my own.
3. In the language of the wedding, the groom is always a *князь* ("prince"), the bride a princess, and the other participants *бояре* ("noblemen").
4. The refrain, translated here literally as "oh, early, early, yes," is, in effect, a musical feature.
5. Potanina et al. (2002:93, no. 40). The authors (p. 74) hypothesize that this song belonged to the ritual of *posad* "seating" (no longer practiced at the time of recording) in which the bride and the groom would be brought (seated) together.
6. See Gura (2012:672) on mountains in the wedding.

Works Cited

Afanasiev, A. 1855–1864. *Народные русские сказки*, 8 vols. Moscow: Publishing House of K. Soldatenkov.

Baĭburin, A. 1993. *Ритуал в традиционной культуре. Структурно-семантический анализ восточнославянских обрядов*. St. Petersburg: Nauka.

Balashov, D., I. Marchenko, and N. Kalmykova. 1985. *Русская свадьба. Свадебный обряд на верхней и средней кокшеньге и на уфтюге (Тарногский район вологодской области)*. Moscow: Sovremennik.

Barber, E. 2013. *The Dancing Goddesses: Folklore, Archaeology, and the Origins of European Dance*. New York: W. W. Norton.

Chistova, B., and K. Chistov eds. 1997. *Причитания северного края собранные, Е.В. Барсовым*. St. Petersburg: Nauka.

Dal', V. 1981. *Толковый словарь живого великорусского языка*, 4 vols. Moscow: Russkiĭ Iazyk.

Efimenkova, B. 2008. *Восточнославянская свадьба и ее музыкальное наполнение: Введение в проблематику*. Moscow: Rossiĭskaia Akademia Musyki imeni Gnesinykh.

Fedorova, P. 1997. *Свадьба в системе календарных и семейных обычаев старообрядцев Южного Зауралья*. Kurgan: Kurganskiĭ Gosudarstvennyĭ Universitet.

Gerd, A. 1997. "Язык причитаний северного края." In *Причитания северного края собранные, Е.В. Барсовым*, eds. B. Chistova and K. Chistov, 603–618. St. Petersburg: Nauka.

Gura, A. 2012. *Брак и свадьба в славянской народной культуре: Семантика и символика*. Moscow: Indrik.

Hatto, A. 1961. "The Swan Maiden: A Folk-Tale of North Eurasian Origin." *Bulletin of the School or Oriental and African Studies*, 24:326–352.

Ivanov, V., and V. Toporov. 1995. "Дунай." In *Славянская мифология. энциклопедический словарь*, eds. V. Petrukhin, T. Agapkina, L. Vinogradova, S. Tolstaia, 171–173. Moscow: Ėllis Lak.

Ivanova, A., and B. Kliaus. 1995. "Фрагменты пинежской свадьбы." In *Русский эротический фольклор*, ed. A. Toporkov, 165–169. Moscow: Ladomir.

Kolpakova, N. 1928. "Свадебный обряд на р. Пинеге." In *Крестьянское искусство СССР II: Искусство Севера: Пинежско-Мезенская Экспедиция*, 117–176. Leningrad: Academia.

Kolpakova, N. 1973. *Лирика русской свадьбы*. Leningrad: Nauka.

Koskina, V. 1997. *Русская свадьба. По материалам, собранным во владимирской области*. Vladimir: Kaleĭdoskop.

Kulagina, A. 1995. "Эпизоды чухломской свадьбы." In *Русский эротический фольклор*, ed. A. Toporkov, 173–175. Moscow: Ladomir.

Kulagina, A., and A. Ivanov. 2000. *Русская свадьба*, Vol. 1. Moscow: Gosudarstvennyĭ Respublikanskiĭ Tsentr Russkogo Fol'klora.

Kulagina, A., and A. Ivanov. 2001. *Русская свадьба*, Vol. 2. Moscow: Gosudarstvennyĭ Respublikanskiĭ Tsentr Russkogo fol'klora.

Kuznetsova, V. 1993. *Причитания в северно-русском свадебном обряде*. Петрозаводск: Karel'skiĭ Nauchnyĭ Tsentr RAN.

Kuznetsova, V., and K. Loginov. 2001. *Русская свадьба заонежья* (конец XIX–начало XX века). Petrozavodsk: Petrozavodskiĭ Gosudarstvennyĭ Universitet.

Lobanov, M., K. Korepova, and A. Nekrylova. 1998. *Нижегородская свадьба: Пушкинские места, нижегородское поволжье, ветлужский край*. St. Petersburg: Kul'tInformPress.

Potanina, R., N. Leonova, and L. Fetisova. 2002. *Русский семейно-обрядовый фольклор сибири и дальнего востока: Свадебная поэзия. Похоронная причеть*. Novosibirsk: Nauka.

Shapovalova, G., and L. Lavrentieva. 1985. *Традиционные обряды и обрядовый фольклор русских поволжья*. Leningrad: Nauka.

Shmelyova, T. 1980. "Причитания." In *Обрядовая поэзия пинежья*, ed. N. Savushkina, 111–116. Moscow: Izdatel'stvo Moskovskogo Gosudarstvennogo Universiteta.

Slavianina, O. 1978. *Старинная севская свадьба*. Moscow: Izdatel'stvo Moskovskogo Gosudarstvennogo Universiteta.

Snegirev, I. 1839. *Русские простонародные праздники и суеверные обряды*. Moscow: v Universitetskoi Tipografii.

Teplova, A. 2017. "О феномене сиротства в русском фольклоре на примера свадебных песен и причитаний." *Научный вестник московской консерватории*, 3/30:94–115.

Varagova, V. 1995. "Сексуальное в свадебном обряде." In *Русский эротический фольклор*, ed. A. Toporkov, 149–157. Moscow: Ladomir.

Yamaguchi, R. 2020. "Образ ветра с любовных заговорах и свадебной лирике." *Scientific Notes of Orel State University*, 87/20:122–125.

CHAPTER 3

SERBIAN WEDDING PRACTICES IN POSTWAR KOSOVO

SANJA ZLATANOVIĆ

THIS chapter is based on extensive multi-sited fieldwork conducted among members of the Serbian community in southeast Kosovo (part of the Kosovo Pomoravlje region or the Morava River basin), including towns and villages in the Gornja (Upper) and Donja (Lower) Morava.[1] The research also involved displaced people from this area in several towns in Serbia. Fieldwork was undertaken between 2003 and 2006, shortly after the war of 1998–1999 and the establishment of the United Nations (UN) administration in Kosovo in June 1999.[2] It was my intention to elucidate understandings of ethnicity and other forms of collective identification (religious, regional, local, gender) within the Serbian community in this postwar region marked by radically altered political and social conditions. My interests were focused on the subjective dimensions of war and life in a postconflict region, the interpretation and construction of inter-ethnic and intra-ethnic relations and boundaries on the part of my interlocutors, the viewpoints of individuals, and local knowledge.

I wanted to find out how the wide and complex political and social processes at work at the end of the twentieth and beginning of the twenty-first century were manifested in the discourse of so-called ordinary people and reflected in their social interactions in the course of their everyday and ritual practices. My research involved both their identity discourse and narrations as well as their concrete practices. As I observed in my fieldwork, processes of identification in the Serbian community of southeast Kosovo were clearly reflected in their nuptial celebrations. In other words, weddings provided a fundamental key to understanding identity. Weddings as a theme was raised in virtually all of the interviews that I conducted. During our conversations in the homes of my interlocutors we often watched video recordings and viewed wedding photographs from various periods in the twentieth century. This documentary testimony allowed me to form an impression of how the celebration of marriage had changed over time (cf.

Beňušková 2020). I also used participant-observation methods at weddings in the village of Šilovo (2 km from town of Gnjilane)[3] during the summer of 2006.

Weddings are the most important ritual in the life cycle of the researched community, not to mention the most multifaceted and richest in content. They are complex rituals because, among other things, they entail a large number of transitions (van Genep [1909] 1960:116, 144) and lead to all-encompassing changes in status and associated roles. The solemnization of marriage between two people establishes relations of kinship between members of their families of origin and the wider community of relatives. Weddings reflect, in condensed form, social reality—family, kinship, and gender relations; religious beliefs; and economic conditions—and constitute a paradigmatic event in the culture of members of the community (Zlatanović 2003:7; Zlatanović 2012:90). The wedding represents "a 'total social phenomenon' in the way that it touches upon all aspects of social life"—if we follow Leutloff-Grandits's (2014:137) paraphrasing of Marcel Mauss. Due to their form, content, and significance, weddings are particularly well suited for the expression of various types of collective identification (ethnic, religious, local, gender, etc.). They are private family rituals, but they also involve a great many participants (with different roles and status), as well as activities which, at certain points, are performed in public (the procession of the guests from the house of the groom to that of the bride, then from the bride's house to the church, the marriage ceremony in the church, and the wedding feast at the restaurant). Weddings are long in the planning and preparation; in form, content, and significance they lend themselves to association with tradition, that unquestioned yet protected concept which connotes the past, ancestors, the handing-down of values from generation to generation, and continuity. During my fieldwork in the region under investigation, weddings, like fine-tuned seismographs, registered and expressed deep social processes and "shocks" or tectonic tremors of a social nature.

A Paroxysm of Ethnicization

Kosovo is a very complex area historically, politically, socially, and culturally. Within the Socialist Federal Republic of Yugoslavia, it had the status of an autonomous province of the Republic of Serbia. The first hints at a deeper crisis in the federation appeared in Kosovo in the early 1980s, and by the late 1980s, the Kosovo Albanians had called for the separation of Kosovo from Serbia. Clashes between the paramilitary Kosovo Liberation Army and Serbia and the Yugoslav military, police, and paramilitary forces escalated in 1998 and 1999. In June 1999 the UN administration in Kosovo was established, and the Serbian and Yugoslav military, police, and paramilitaries withdrew from the region. With them left convoys of displaced Serbs and Roma, particularly from ethnically mixed parts of the province.

At the time that my research was conducted, a few years after the war, the Serbian community in southeast Kosovo was an ethnic, religious, and linguistic minority in an environment that was predominantly Albanian. Everyday life was marked by violence, insecurity, chaos, and limited freedom of movement, all amid a new legal framework established by the international administration, the mass migrations of the Serbian and Romani populations, and the sale of property to Albanians. For the remaining Serbian population, the situation varied drastically from place to place. Life in the enclaves (in Vitina and several nearby villages and in a small urban enclave in Gnjilane) was far less favorable than in the large and ethnically homogenous Serbian villages around Gnjilane, such as Šilovo and Pasjane. Though the war was formally over, it felt very much as if it was still underway.[4]

At that time, Kosovo was conspicuously ethnicized. The need to draw and reinforce ethnic boundaries had been brought to paroxysm. Ethnonational symbols had flooded both public and private space. Beginning in the late 1980s, the ethnicization of the area had intensified with time, becoming firmly established during and after the war. The dominant Albanian population displayed ethnonational symbols publically—there were a multitude of newly erected monuments to members of the paramilitary Kosovo Liberation Army where the national flag was on prominent display, as it was on all larger apartment buildings, on houses, and in cemeteries. The Albanian national flag was omnipresent. At a noisy procession of Albanian wedding guests in the center of Vitina in 2003, the flag was waving from almost every automobile. The postwar "industry" producing Albanian ethnonational symbols was working at maximum capacity. At a specialized outlet in the center of Gnjilane they were even selling carpets and cushions with the same design as the national flag (a black, two-headed eagle on a red background). The graffiti UÇK, the acronym of the Kosovo Liberation Army, had been scrawled on the walls of many buildings in ethnically mixed neighborhoods; and dumpsters bore the number 1244, which was intended to imply that the UN resolution of that number was garbage.

The Serbs ethnicized their spaces more discreetly in the postwar period but with no less fervor: in every house there was a large number of icons and other Orthodox paraphernalia (religious and ethnic identification were amalgamated; see Zlatanović 2018:172–198). And in 2003 the *kafana* (pub) Car Lazar[5] in the village of Grnčar was plastered with pictures of Serbian Orthodox Church saints and national heroes. In 2005 at the textile shop in Vrbovac, a larger village with a Serbian population, there were T-shirts on sale with pictures of the Hague war criminals and defendants Ratko Mladić and Radovan Karadžić; and the Serbian flag was flying from the roof of the tallest house in the center of the village.[6]

At the time of my research both the Serbian and the Albanian communities were—albeit from different perspectives—in a liminal state of waiting for the final resolution of the status of Kosovo and uncertainty as to what that solution would be. Both communities had a need to materialize the presence of their own national states but also to assert dominance over the other. The ubiquity of the Albanian national flag, but also other symbols of both groups in interaction (in the public or hidden domain), offered "material evidence for a postulated imagined community" (Eriksen 2007:9). As Thomas Hylland Eriksen explains,

Flags representing modern nation-states have an *emotional* and an *instrumental* pole in their range of signification. The emotional pole attaches the individual to an abstract collective entity, a metaphoric kin group. The instrumental pole may be political or commercial, intended to mobilise for conflict or to integrate peacefully. Symbols of unity, flags nevertheless always have divisive potential within the group and outwards, and the less ambivalent and multivocal a flag becomes in political practice, the higher its conflict potential. Ambiguity tends to go away at relational boundary markers.

(2007:10, italics in original)

The choice of symbols plays a key role in the processes of nation-building. As Anthony Cohen remarks, concepts such as justice, patriotism, responsibility, and loyalty defy simple definition. However, their wide spectrum of meaning can be expressed through generally accepted symbols into which members of the community can read their own understandings. They can have a shared symbol, which need not necessarily have the same meaning for all (Cohen 1985:15). The need to express, emphasize, and confirm ethnonational identification through chosen symbols is characteristic to both groups in interaction. It is exactly these processes of "placarding" ethnicity (Putinja and Stref-Fenar [1995] 1997:189) that show how much importance it is given, subordinating all other forms of belonging. Miroslav Hroch explains how the visualization of the nation through selected symbols (images, monuments, and, in the example considered here, the national flag) plays a significant role in its construction and constant affirmation and confirmation. He also points out how the nation is built by narrative and performative means (Hroch [2005] 2015), and for this purpose the wedding is an ideal social event.

Before 1999 national flags were obligatory at weddings in Kosovo, be they Serbian or Albanian. According to one interlocutor, this was the practice so that it could be seen from afar whose wedding it was. Even at that time, the national flag was the symbol chosen to profile the boundary between *us* and *them*. After the war the Serbs only displayed their flag above the entrance into the yard of the groom's home and carried it at the front of the procession of wedding guests in ethnically homogenous villages such as Šilovo (Figs. 3.1 and 3.2). In ethnically mixed villages during the postwar period of heightened tensions, everything that might attract attention at weddings was avoided, even the decoration of cars with flowers. The ethnomusicologists Mirjana Zakić and Sanja Ranković (2020:421–422), who conducted research in the township of Gračanica in central Kosovo in 2015, write that a girl with a Serbian flag in her right hand led the *kolo* circle-dance before the guests left for the marriage ceremony at the church and that after the ceremony a man led the dance with a flag in his hand in front of the monastery of Gračanica. It is the use of the national flag which indicates that weddings are not *only* a private, family event. A middle-aged female interlocutor from Šilovo explained the flag displayed at a wedding with the following statement: "It's a sign that we're Serbs. . . . The Serbian flag is carried because it's a sign that Serbia is still here." The flags displayed over the gateway into the groom's courtyard and at the front of the procession of wedding guests that passes through the village on the way to the marriage ceremony at the

FIG. 3.1. A national flag displayed over the gateway to the courtyard of the groom's house. Women dressed in traditional costumes dance in the yard. The village of Šilovo, 2006.

(Photo by Sanja Zlatanović.)

church give weddings a political dimension. The conclusion reached by Robert Pichler (2009:225–226) in connection with the display of national flags at Albanian weddings in North Macedonia—"Wedding ceremonies thus can turn into political events. . . . The public space thus becomes a stage where social polarization is expressed in ethnic categories"—applies just as completely to southeast Kosovo.[7] Richard Jenkins's explanation may be of assistance in understanding the use of national flags at weddings which are in essence private rituals:

> The ritual symbolization of identity—in *rites de passage*, but in many other ritual observances, too—is an effective way to make collective identities matter to individuals, affectively and cognitively. Through participation in ritual, people may come to identify themselves in a manner, and with a degree of commitment and enthusiasm, that amounts to something altogether greater than the sum of its parts.
>
> (2008:126–127, italics in original)

National affiliation and the presence of the national state are visualized, but they are also constructed by other means, one of these frequently being through narrative.

FIG. 3.2. A national flag at the head of the procession of wedding guests on their way to the church. The village of Šilovo, 2006.

(Photo by Sanja Zlatanović.)

During the segment of the ritual known as *zaigruvanje*, when the mother of the groom opens the wedding celebrations with the *svekrvino kolo* (mother-in-law's dance), about which more will be said below, it is customary to sing traditional folk songs.[8] These usually have romantic and family-related themes, with the frequent use of metaphors drawn from nature (cf. Beissinger 2020). One of the best-loved songs begins with the verse "Ne plači, Stano mori, ne žali" ("Don't Cry, Stana Dear, Don't Lament"). This song is sung a number of times (in Gnjilane and surrounding villages it has been recorded in different variants: Vasiljević 1950:no. 130; Zlatanović 2007:no. 79 and 80). Songs taking Kosovo as their theme are very common at weddings, among which the most popular are the folk song "Gusta mi magla padnala na toj mi ramno Kosovo" ("A Thick Fog Has Fallen over the Plains of Kosovo") (Vasiljević 1950:no. 268). Even though this song does not deal explicitly with national themes, it stands out as a kind of anthem for the Serbs of Kosovo. The word "Kosovo" is sung with deep feelings of sadness and belonging. At weddings the newly composed song "Vidovdan"[9] ("St. Vitus's Day"), written at the end of the 1980s by Milutin Popović Zahar, is sung many times. This song speaks of the deep connection that members of the Serbian community feel for Kosovo and is sung with great emotion. The song has the line, *K'o večni plamen u našim srcima, Kosovskog boja ostaje istina* ("Like an eternal flame in our hearts, the Battle of Kosovo will always remain the truth"). And the chorus, which is repeated many times, is *Kud god da krenem tebi se vraćam ponovo. Ko da mi otme iz moje duše Kosovo?* ("Wherever I go, to you I will always return. Who can wrest Kosovo from my soul?"). At the part of the wedding celebration which takes place in the enclosed space of the restaurant, marquee, or home, songs with national and/or nationalistic themes are frequently sung. One of the most popular is "Srpska se truba s Kosova čuje" ("The Serbian Trumpet Sounds from Kosovo"), the chorus of which is *Trubite, braćo, silnije, bolje/opet je srpsko Kosovo Polje* ("Blow brothers stronger and better/Kosovo Polje is Serbian again"). The song ends with the words *Sve nas je srpska rodila majka* ("We were all born to a Serbian mother"). Women—as is common in ethnonationalistic discourse—are virtually always mentioned in the role of mother, the one who gives birth to members of the nation.[10] Songs play a central part in this discourse because they express, affirm, and confirm ethnonational affiliation with equal strength, both through the narrative they establish and in performance.

Ethnicity is an important dimension of social identification, and its significance can vary from person to person within the same group, as well as from situation to situation. As Eriksen explains,

> Ethnic symbolism referring to the ancient language, religion, kinship system or way of life is crucial for the maintenance of ethnic identity through periods of change. Generally speaking, social identity becomes most important the moment it seems threatened. Several factors may constitute such a perceived threat, but they are always related to some kind of change. . . . Conspicuous forms of boundary maintenance become important when the boundaries are under pressure. Ethnic identities, which embody a perceived continuity with the past, may in this way function in a psychologically reassuring way for the individual in times of upheaval.
>
> (2002:68)

It is exactly at periods of change and crisis that ethnicity is expressed most forcefully (Eriksen 2002:33), as can be seen from weddings held in the Serbian community of southeast Kosovo.

Overview of Weddings in the Second Half of the Twentieth Century

Among Serbs in south-east Kosovo in the mid-twentieth century, weddings involved a long series of customs before, during, and after the marriage itself. The complete process, from the conversation between the groom's and the bride's fathers to the first visit of the married daughter to her parents, could last from three to six months or longer. The wedding events lasted a week and began with what my older interlocutors called *činimo žito* ("we do the wheat"), using the first-person plural verb. Members of the community (relations and neighbors) would bring a certain quantity of wheat to the groom's home, where they would be entertained with music and refreshments. After that, the collected wheat would be taken to the mill to be ground into flour for the bread to be served at the wedding feast. This part of the wedding ritual indicates the close connections and solidarity between members of the rural community, where bread was a highly valued staple as well as a ritual requisite (in addition to weddings, on feast days and at other social gatherings). From the early 1970s, however, and at an accelerated pace through the 1980s, weddings were gradually shortened. Some segments were omitted, others blended together so that, by the turn of the twentieth century, the ceremonials had been significantly simplified. The segment *činimo žito*, which was described with a strong sense of community, had been wholly abandoned. The wedding proper consisted of *zamesuvanje* (on Thursday, when preparation of the wedding breads began), *zaigruvanje* (on Saturday, when the groom's mother opened the celebrations with the mother-in-law's *kolo* circle-dance), and on Sunday, when the procession of the guests to collect the bride from her parents' house, the marriage ceremony itself, and the return of the groom with his bride to his house for the wedding feast took place. The wedding night had great significance, and even at the turn of the millennium the groom's mother would inspect the bed linen (to be sure the bride was a virgin) and, on the following Tuesday, host a celebration of the bride's honor known as the *blaga rakija* ("gentle brandy"), inviting only the married women among her relations and neighbors to drink mulled brandy with her.

Although it underwent significant modifications during the second half of the twentieth century, the wedding remained patriarchal and patrilocal in fundamental character. Almost the whole procedure took place at the groom's home, and the bride's parents and relations did not attend either the marriage or the feast that followed it. Nonetheless, with time, certain deep-rooted patriarchal norms softened somewhat under the influence of the modernization that socialist Yugoslavia was working to bring about. After the early 1980s, for example, the custom in which the bride would kiss the hand of the *kum* (chief witness) and all her husband's kin at the wedding, including the groom himself, as a mark of respect and subordination, began to be seen as inappropriate and was omitted. The bride traditionally wore a hand-made nuptial costume at her wedding; but as of the 1970s, early pioneers began to adopt the white bridal gown, and by the 1980s this had become the norm. This change in the attire of the principal ritual figure of the wedding is indicative of the influences that had begun to shift established practices.

Sudden Changes in Custom Practices since 1999

The year 1999 was a reference point in Kosovo that divided past from present, a "temporal marker of the border" (Ćirković 2012:9, 83, 188). For a number of years after the war, weddings were not organized. The young man would simply bring his girlfriend into the parental home, and his parents would ask their closest relatives to join them for coffee and snacks. With that the community would accept that the marriage had taken place, and the young couple would be married in church at a later date. At the time of my research this manner of marrying was still the most common. In ethnically mixed areas where Serbs represent the minority, weddings were not held at all. The postwar period of heightened tensions made it extremely risky to gather a large number of people for festivities. Certain families from ethnically mixed villages around Gnjilane held weddings in a shortened form in the village of Šilovo, which had a restaurant with a capacity for larger gatherings. During my fieldwork, weddings were rare. Their structure had changed, and certain elements had either been shortened or abandoned completely.

The practice whereby a young man would bring his girlfriend into the family home and the family would put on a small celebration for their closest friends and kin became an established way to get married. In the community this was considered sufficient for the marriage to be recognized. A wedding celebration might take place a few months later or be omitted altogether. It would begin on a Thursday with making the loaves. With loaves in hand, the father-in-law would personally invite the most honored guests. They included the *kum* (principal witness), *stari svat* (traditionally the second witness), and *dever* (his role being to take the bride from her parents' house and take care of her during the wedding; in the researched area his role in the ceremonies was taken by the groom's mother's brother). The local term for this part of the nuptials is *zamesuvanje*—the beginning of the kneading. On Thursday morning the bridegroom's mother would invite relations and neighbors to the *zamesuvanje*, and the women assembled would be served the first-baked loaf.

The Mother-in-Law's Dance

On the day of the wedding a wide circle of relations, neighbors, and friends gather at the home of the groom's parents. Relations who have moved to Serbia also make the journey back to Kosovo to attend. The celebrations are opened by the mother-in-law (groom's mother) with the *svekrvino kolo* (mother-in-law's dance). This particular *kolo* is of the

FIG. 3.3. Before the wedding the groom's mother shows the gifts and sieve with which she will dance the mother-in-law's dance. The village of Šilovo, 2006.

(Photo by Sanja Zlatanović.)

open type, moving in a curve to the right; it is danced slowly and lasts for a long time.[11] The mother-in-law leads the *kolo*, dancing with the decorated sieve in her right hand (Figs. 3.3–3.5). In the sieve there are sweets, and at the end of the dance she scatters them as if sowing seeds. It is believed that, in this way, she is sowing the seeds of a sweet and fruitful marriage. Beside the mother-in-law her sisters-in-law dance, followed by other female relations (husband's sisters, sisters, and so on); and at the end of the line, ideally, is the mother-in-law's mother-in-law (i.e., the groom's paternal grandmother) with a round loaf in hand (Fig. 3.6). There should be an odd number of dancers (usually from three to eleven).[12] This is how this *kolo* is danced in Šilovo. In the area covered by my research there are other more or less pronounced variations from the one described here. All the dancers must be married women, and they are known collectively as "mothers-in-law"—the groom's mothers.

After the groom's mother has danced three rounds, the sieve is taken from her by a male child. The boy takes his place at the front of the line of mothers-in-law, and then he leads the dance with sieve in hand. After the dance led by the boy, the sieve and lead position are taken by the wives of the principal guests (*stari svat*, *kum*, and *dever*) in

FIG. 3.4. The mother-in-law's *kolo*. The village of Šilovo, 2006.

(Photo by Sanja Zlatanović.)

FIG. 3.5. The mother-in-law's *kolo*. The village of Šilovo, 2006.

(Photo by Sanja Zlatanović.)

FIG. 3.6. The mother-in-law's *kolo*: the mother-in-law (the groom's mother) leads the dance with sieve in hand. At the end of the line is the mother-in-law's mother-in-law (groom's paternal grandmother) holding a loaf. The village of Šilovo, 2006.

(Photo by Sanja Zlatanović.)

succession and then by other relations who were not in the mother-in-law's *kolo* but who joined from outside. The mothers-in-law (the groom's mother, her sisters-in-law, and other relations) remain together in the line until the end of this part of the festivities. No one leaves the dance; rather, the women take turns at its head according to age and degree of kinship. While only married women can take part in the mother-in-law's *kolo* (the dance led by the groom's mother), the dances that follow can be led by unmarried girls to tunes of their own choosing.

This part of the wedding celebration is known locally as *zaigruvanje*; today, it lasts from two to four hours and is considered the most significant, festive, and exciting part of the nuptials. The *zaigruvanje* is a special social occasion, held in the open air with musical accompaniment. But it is either omitted entirely in ethnically mixed environments or, in some villages, reduced to a short form. A mother-in-law from the mixed village of Cernica, where tensions between the Albanian and Serbian population were very strong, danced her *kolo* inside at a restaurant in Šilovo, an event that my interlocutors spoke of regretfully. It is believed that the mother-in-law must dance her *kolo* in the yard of her house and, with its symbolism, ensure the fertility of the newlyweds and the continuity of the family.

Women's Attire in Identity Discourse

At Serbian weddings in Kosovo, the women wear their traditional costumes, the appearance and preservation of which the community is still very proud. Various forms of identification (ethnic, regional, local, and gender) intersect in the discourse over traditional women's costume, so I describe it here in some detail. The traditional women's costume of the Serbian inhabitants of the Kosovo Pomoravlje has a considerable number of elements and is characterized by multiple layers and rich decoration. In its most basic form it survives to this day, although it underwent significant modification during the second half of the twentieth century (cf. Urošević 1935:123–125; Đekić 1989). Over time the materials out of which it is made have changed (hemp and wool making way for cotton), as has the way it is decorated. Certain elements have fallen out of use, while others have been adapted to new trends. In general, vibrant colors and bold patterns have been replaced with shades of white and smaller decorations in pastel colors. The costumes vary considerably from place to place. While in the latter half of the twentieth century certain elements of the costume became increasingly less common, the *bošča* (a type of apron)[13] stands out among other items by virtue of its significance and is still made to this day. The *bošča* varies widely in its style of ornamentation and color as well as its purpose and usage. Until the 1960s and 1970s it was an integral part of everyday, formal, and even bridal attire. By the beginning of the twenty-first century, however, the *bošča* had been reduced in its functions to the two parts of the wedding celebration: the *zamesuvanje* (in which the mother-in-law wears a traditional costume with a *bošča*) and the *zaigruvanje* (in which the mother-in-law and her relatives in traditional dress, with a *bošča*, open the wedding celebrations with the mother-in-law's dance).[14]

The *bošča* is an item of clothing, an apron that protects the woman's attire as she works; but it is also a decorative element on the female body, an essential component in the complex system of wedding gifts, a valuable piece of craftwork that is carefully preserved and handed down from generation to generation, a rug, and much more. The framed *bošča* which hung on the wall like a painting at the refugee center in Vranjska Banja represented a window onto the homeland left behind (Fig. 3.7). In the context of its role in community life the *bošča* has a significance that goes far beyond that of a simple garment. It is a complex social and cultural artifact, a metaphor that summarizes the traditional culture of the people of the Kosovo Pomoravlje and stands in a sense as its emblem. Some families owned collections of over a hundred of these items, and the older women in the refugee centers had taken parts of their traditional costumes, including these aprons, with them among their essential belongings. Part of life in UN-administered Kosovo was the sale of *bošča* aprons to soldiers of the Kosovo Force (KFOR, a NATO-led force in Kosovo) who showed a great interest in them as a form of traditional craftwork.

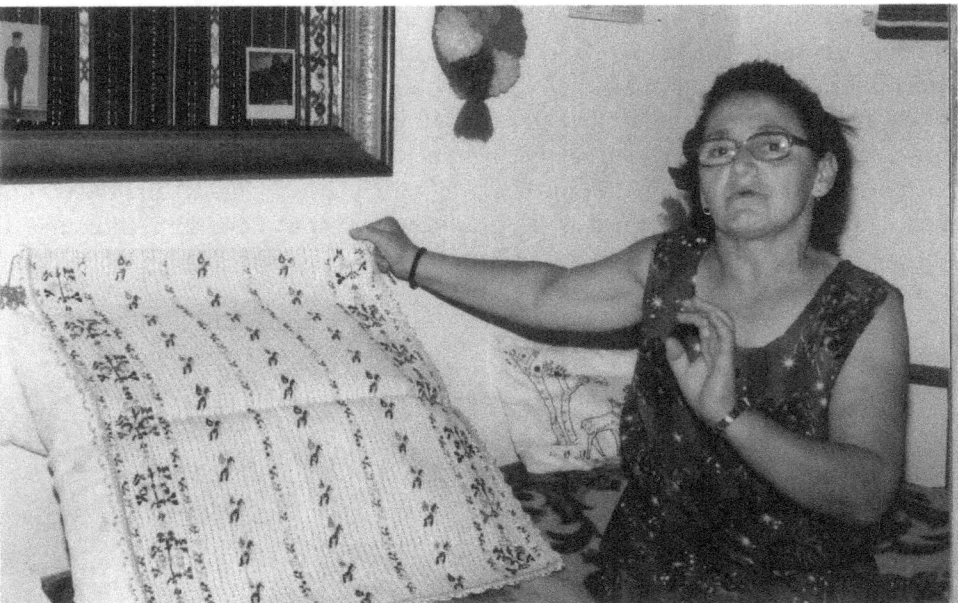

FIG. 3.7. An interlocutor from a refugee center displaying a *bošča*. On the wall above her is a framed *bošča* with added family photographs. The township of Vranjska Banja, 2005.

(Photo by Sanja Zlatanović.)

Traditional women's costumes are treated as jewelry and preserved with particular care. The women I interviewed spoke with great emotion of how they were made, stored, maintained, and worn; and women dressed in these costumes were described as "adorned." Traditional dress is seen as so important that many women are portrayed in it on their gravestones, and women who did not possess such attire felt themselves handicapped, in a sense, and lamented this fact in my conversations with them.

The discourse around the preserved female costumes (now limited in use to ritual functions) revealed community members' pride and densely interwoven layers of different forms of identification. At one of the weddings I attended an elderly man told me, "Look! This is the Old Serbia,"[15] adding that it was easy to be a Serb in Serbia, but that in mixed surroundings it was more difficult, yet they had succeeded in preserving the old Serbian dress and customs. At other weddings too, while I was watching the women in the mother-in-law's *kolo*, the men expressed their pride in the beauty of the costumes and the women's dancing, weaving this into an identity discourse on ancient Serbian culture and the old Serbian customs that had been preserved. At a wedding among displaced Serbs in the town of Smederevo (in Serbia, some 45 km from Belgrade) I asked the mother-in-law's sister to explain why she felt the need to be dressed in this way. "We may have left Kosovo," she explained, "but not our customs. We've brought our customs with us." National identity is a category which seeks constant affirmation, and visualization with the aid of certain symbols is one of the main tools to achieve this (Hroch [2005] 2015). The ceremonial aspect of women's costumes and social gatherings such as weddings provides an ideal opportunity for this. Traditional women's attire (particularly the *bošča*) and the part of the wedding celebrations known as *zaigruvanje* were synonymous in the discourse of my interlocutors with the tradition and "rootedness" of the Serbian population of the Kosovo Pomoravlje.

Collective Identification and the Symbolic Role of Women

Collective identification and festival days are mutually connected and conditioned phenomena. The community selects and proclaims certain days to be holidays, enclosing them within what it categorizes as its identity and protecting them with the unquestioned notion of tradition. Furthermore, festival days involve gatherings of the group and consolidation through the use of symbols. For the members of the Serbian community of southeast Kosovo the holidays of the Orthodox Church are of great importance for the integration of the community and its symbolization, particularly in the postwar situation. However, the ritual which most completely condenses the symbolization of collective identity is the wedding, particularly the segment known as the *zaigruvanje*. The wedding is indeed a private ritual, but it is nonetheless performed on a wider social stage. The mother-in-law's dance is witnessed by the whole village gathered together, not just by members of the kinship group. In other segments too (the procession of the wedding guests that makes its way on foot to the church) the wedding involves the wider social community in a variety of ways. Bearing in mind the specificities of the local context and family and kinship organization as well as the dense and multiple connections that bind together members of the community (Zlatanović 2011; Zlatanović 2022), it is clear that weddings bring together a large number of people emphasizing kinship ties and belonging. The wedding includes the marriage in the Orthodox church, the carrying of the flag, the singing of particular songs, etc.; and through its form and content it is a very convenient and opportune vehicle for the condensed expression of various types of collective identification.

Weddings place women—the mother(s)-in-law—in the first rank and procreation as the meaning of marriage, into which the community injects a distillation of many symbols of and discourses on identity. In an area with a marked patriarchal culture, it is the mother-in-law (a woman) who takes the most prominent role in the nuptials. She opens the celebrations with her *kolo*, which is today viewed as the most important moment in the proceedings. In the patriarchal family the mother, through her male child, has established her position. With her dance at the wedding she experiences promotion to the position of mother-in-law—the highest possible status for a woman in a patriarchal community (Malešević 1986:106–107). The maternal role of the woman, as mother of a son, is emphasized and celebrated in this ritual. This is further stressed by the fact that all the women who dance with her are also said to be mothers-in-law. Their important role and mutual connection are further accentuated by their formal (ritual) attire. The mother-in-law's dance demonstrates the deep-rootedness of the value norms of the extended patriarchal family organization, as well as these women's need to emphasize and maintain them (see the statement of an interlocutor in Zlatanović 2011:238–239). The line of dancers led by the groom's mother is completed by her own mother-in-law, the groom's paternal grandmother, which further underlines continuity, reproduction, and affirmation of the patriarchal family and the roles assigned to the women within it.

Variations in the traditional women's attire is one of the load-bearing pillars of regional and a multitude of local (village) and subgroup identifications, for example, the Lower and Upper Morava. The existence and emphasis of local permutations in women's customs and in the mother-in-law's dance show that they have spent their lives enclosed within a tight family, kinship, and village circle. Even today, women are guided toward the circle of family and relations, and this has become further accentuated in ethnically mixed areas after the war. Functioning in a limited social space, women direct their attention (and are directed) toward the production and reproduction of traditional values, and therefore toward craftwork (sewing, embroidery), as well as toward—for them—appropriate areas of self-expression. In the donning of their traditional dress for occasions such as weddings, the women are expressing their commitment to traditional gender roles and values in general (Zlatanović 2012).

While other segments of the wedding celebration in the new, postwar context are being omitted or shortened and simplified, the *zaigruvanje* is still maintained in what appears to be the same form. Nonetheless, while the text of the ritual may remain the same over time, its significance shifts foundationally with the nature of the context (Cannadine 1995:105). Through its symbolism the wedding subtly expresses the need of the community for continuity at a time of discontinuity and the need for family and kinship gathering and stresses the role of the mother-in-law, the mother of a son, within the patriarchal family whose foundations have become unstable. Following the migration of part of the community and a radical change in context, the extended family has undergone a process of nuclearization. The processes underway within the family—the re-patriarchalization and simultaneous liberalization of relations—are accompanied by conflicts and ambivalence (Zlatanović 2022).

The Bride between Serbian Community Traditionalism and the Influences of Globalization

While the mothers-in-law dance, the bride prepares herself in her room in the groom's house, where she will have been brought earlier and has resided for months before the wedding. When the *zaigruvanje* has finished, the *dever* enters the room and leads her outside. In the yard of the groom's house, the wedding gifts are exchanged, and the festivity proceeds to the marriage at the church. Before 1999 in Serbian communities in Kosovo, the wedding procession would go from the groom's house to that of the bride's parents and from there to the church. In the postwar period, however, the excursion to the home of the bride's parents was discontinued since movement between certain villages (if the bride's parents were from a different place) could be hazardous. The omission of this important part of the nuptial proceedings—the fetching of the bride—is a clear indication of the degree to which the events of 1999 had impacted the life of the community.

Marriage in a Serbian Orthodox church is obligatory since ethnic and religious identification blend together entirely. Members of the Serbian community perceive the Orthodox Church as the only Serbian institution that has stood by them through the hard times in Kosovo since the withdrawal of the Serbian military and political forces in 1999. The Orthodox Church takes an explicit political position on the Kosovo question: Kosovo is the "Serbian Holy Land" and an inalienable part of Serbia, explained in large part by the "historical right" to the territory by referring to the period before the Ottoman conquest of the Balkans. Indeed, the marriage ceremony at a wedding I attended was followed by a sermon from the priest on the theme of procreation as the meaning of marriage and hence its importance in the biological preservation of the Serbian nation (see priest's sermon in Zlatanović 2022:12). The marriage of two people in church is not simply a religious rite but takes on a political connotation.

After the marriage ceremony at the church, a feast would be held in a marquee set up in the groom's courtyard or at the restaurant in Šilovo since other villages did not have the space to host such events. The idea of holding the wedding feast at a restaurant was new and characteristic only of Šilovo and the villages in its immediate vicinity. But it was the subject of some disagreement in the community. Some of my older interlocutors took a critical stance toward this novel trend of organizing weddings at a restaurant. This is because the groom's house would be empty at the time, and the merrymaking would happen in a "non-place" (Augé [1992] 1995; cf. a similar view in the Albanian community in Leutloff-Grandits 2023:180).

With reference to concepts of gender, it is worth examining the fact that, as in earlier times, the bride's parents and relations are still entirely excluded from the nuptials: they

FIG. 3.8. The mother-in-law presents the bride with a traditional costume. The village of Šilovo, 2006.

(Photo by Sanja Zlatanović.)

do not attend the marriage ceremony at the church or the banquet and merrymaking at the restaurant or the groom's house (cf. the situation in the Albanian community in Leutloff-Grandits 2023:162, 180). Rather, the bride's parents and a small number of their close relations arrive at the groom's house or the restaurant during the festivities to bring her the craftwork and gifts that they have prepared for their daughter. Excluding the bride's parents and family from the key moments of the wedding ceremony (marriage at the church and feast) emphasizes the profoundly patriarchal and patrilocal family, kinship, and gender roles embedded in the nuptial rituals.

The bride wears a fashionable white wedding dress, and about her gather elements of glamor and romance—representing the world that she desires and materializes in her appearance. The wedding is filmed, and at the restaurant the guests are served multilayered wedding cake and champagne. Nonetheless, the mother-in-law will still present the bride with part of or even an entire handmade traditional costume, thus sending her a clear message about the values that she should adhere to (Figs. 3.8 and 3.9). Weddings among the Serbs of southeastern Kosovo in the postwar context offer a richly nuanced picture of the fusion between the global and the local into *glocal*. As faithful reflections of the social reality in which they occur, the intersection of many of the wedding traditions, innovations, and symbols exhibits significant ambivalence.

FIG. 3.9. Traditional costume wrapped as the mother-in-law's gift to the bride. The village of Šilovo, 2006.

(Photo by Sanja Zlatanović.)

Concluding Remarks: The Wedding as a Fine-Tuned Seismograph of Social Processes

The wedding is a multidimensional ritual. In itself, in its condensed form, it expresses the social reality as well as various forms of collective identification and their interrelation. In a postwar region and a minority enclave situation, ethnicity is the dominant, all-consuming form of identification (Zlatanović 2018:324). In form, content, and significance, the wedding is an opportune occasion for the expression, confirmation, and assertion of ethnonational belonging. Hroch's work on the sources and elements used in nation-building, its affirmation, and reaffirmation by narrative, visual, and performative means (Hroch [2005] 2015) is instructive in this analysis. By means of narrative (songs with national and/or nationalistic themes, the priest's sermon, the meanings embedded in the women's dances), visualizations (the display of the Serbian national flag, traditional women's costume reduced to its ritual form), and its inherently performative nature, the wedding has become increasingly politicized. In the postwar region the wedding also has a distinctly cohesive function. The celebrations are attended by kin-members who have moved to Serbia and thus affirm and reaffirm belonging to the family, kinship, local groups, and ultimately the far wider—national—community. Also expressed in the discourse of weddings, the re-patriarchalization of the family runs parallel with the liberalization of relations and roles within it. Indeed, the inevitable tensions which arise as a result of these dynamics are reflected in the contrasts between the ritual attire of the bride and her mother-in-law (global vs. traditional) as well as in other aspects of change and stability in the ritual procedures and customs.

The sudden and radical political and social changes in the immediate aftermath of the war and establishment of the UN administration in 1999 have fundamentally impacted daily and customary behavior and routines in the community, and like a sensitive seismograph, wedding practices have registered and expressed this fact. The structure of the nuptial observances has changed, as have the ways they are performed. The ambiguous elements within the wedding as a whole express the social reality of the Serbian community members in postwar Kosovo.

Acknowledgment

The study was supported by VEGA scientific grant agency of the Ministry of Education, Research, Development and Youth of the Slovak Republic and of Slovak Academy of Sciences, grant no. 2/0068/23: "Forms and Mechanisms of Differentiation and Reconfiguration of Public and Political Life. Collective Actions and Political Attitudes" conducted at the Institute of Political Science, Slovak Academy of Sciences.

Notes

1. They included the town of Gnjilane/Gjilan (the regional center) and the surrounding villages of Šilovo/Shillova, Gornji Livoč/Livoç i Epërm, Gornje Kusce/Kuske e Eperme, Parteš/Partesh, and Pasjane/Pasjan as well as the township of Vitina/Viti and the neighboring villages of Vrbovac/Vërboc, Grnčar/Gërnçar, Binač/Binçë, Mogila/Mogillë, and Klokot/Kllokot. Additional field sites were provided by the villages of Letnica/Letnicë and Draganac/Dragancë because of their religious significance. Although place names are presented here in both Serbian and Albanian, from this point onward, the names of the localities are given in the Serbian variant only since the research was conducted within the Serbian community.
2. For more details on my research methodology, see Zlatanović (2018:19–39) and Zlatanović (2022:2–3).
3. See the map in Zlatanović (2017:149).
4. For more on life in postwar southeast Kosovo, see Zlatanović (2011:232–237) and Zlatanović (2022:4–7).
5. Lazar Hrebeljanović was the Serbian ruler who died in combat against the Ottoman army at the legendary Battle of Kosovo in 1389. Lazar Hrebeljanović had the title *knez* ("prince"). He is called *car* ("tsar") only in folk narratives.

6. The emphasis on the ethnic, which reached the absurd on both sides, is clearly portrayed in the documentary film *UNMIK Titanic*, by Boris Mitić (2004), made in Priština, the capital city of Kosovo, on New Year's Eve 2003. In the city even the New Year's balloons bore the Albanian national symbol of a black two-headed eagle on a red field. The children sitting on Santa's lap held Albanian flags along with their presents, and calendars, T-shirts, and emblems were on sale that bore the images of fighters and ethnic and military insignia. The remaining hundred Serbs in Priština were living in one apartment building. There, the song "Kosovo je srpsko, srpsko ostaće" ("Kosovo Is Serbian and Serbian It Will Stay") was softly playing on the radio. On the night of New Year's Eve, as inhibitions waned, a few young men in front of the apartment building started loudly singing a song with a nationalist theme. An older relative called down a warning to them from the windows above, and one of the young men shouted back, "Who asked you anything? Is this Serbia or not?"
7. After the unilateral declaration of independence of Kosovo in 2008, the Kosovo parliament adopted multiethnic symbols of statehood: an anthem without words and a blue flag bearing a map of Kosovo in gold, above which there are six stars symbolizing the six officially recognized ethnic communities living within it (Albanians, Serbs, Bosniaks, Turks, Gorani, and Roma, with Ashkali and Egyptians). Kosovo's state symbolism does not derive from national or regional traditions. At the celebration of the anniversary of the declaration of independence of Kosovo, this flag simply hangs on public buildings, while the majority Albanian population waves with heated emotion the Albanian national flag of a black two-headed eagle on a red field. The Albanian flag is also waved at other public and private social gatherings. The Serbs do not recognize the independence of Kosovo and therefore wave the Serbian national flag at weddings and other social gatherings within the ethnically homogeneous Serbian environment. Michael Billig makes a distinction between waved and unwaved flags: "The reproduction of nation-states depends upon a dialectic of collective remembering and forgetting, and of imagination and unimaginative repetition. The unwaved flag, which is so forgettable, is at least as important as the memorable moments of flag waving" (1995:10). And "The familiar patterns of the patriotic flag are being waved" (1995:103).
8. On the musical component to Serbian wedding ceremonials at Gračanica, see Zakić and Ranković (2020). On multiculturalism of Kosovo and Metohija in the 1950s and 1960s in traditional music, see Lajić Mihajlović and Jovanović (2018).
9. Vidovdan (June 28) is the day on which, according to legend, the Battle of Kosovo took place in 1389 between an army led by the Serbian Prince Lazar Hrebeljanović and an invading army of the Ottoman Empire. In the Orthodox calendar the day is sacred to St. Lazar and the sainted Serbian martyrs who died at the Battle of Kosovo.
10. The lyrics of the song were written by the teacher Mihajlo Zastavniković (1879–1927), who fought in the First World War. It is sung in several variations.
11. For the mother-in-law's dance (*svekrvino kolo*) and other folk dances of the Gnjilane region including patterns and analysis, see Janković and Janković (1951:47–142).
12. In traditional Serbian culture, odd numbers are used in rituals intended for the living, while even numbers are practiced in posthumous rituals.
13. The *bošča* is a feminine noun of Persian derivation, a Balkan Turkism; it is a rectangular cloth wrapping, tablecloth, or apron (Škaljić [1965] 1979:149).
14. On the *bošča* from the perspective of a community member, see Maksimović (2011).
15. *Stara Srbija* (Old Serbia) is a geopolitical term which emerged in the nineteenth century, corresponding to the territories that made up the medieval Serbian state.

Works Cited

Augé, Marc. 1995. *Non-places: Introduction to an Anthropology of Supermodernity*, trans. John Howe. London–New York: Verso. First published 1992.

Beissinger, Margaret H. 2020. "Nature as Metaphor in Romanian and Slavic Ritual Wedding Poetry." *Philologica Jassyensia*, 31/1:187–204.

Beňušková, Zuzana. 2020. *Už sa chystá svadba istá. Svadobné obyčaje slovom a obrazom*. Bratislava: Ústav etnológie a sociálnej antropológie Slovenskej akadémie vied & VEDA.

Billig, Michael. 1995. *Banal Nationalism*. London: SAGE Publications.

Cannadine, David. 1995. "The Context, Performance and Meaning of Ritual: The British Monarchy and Invention of Tradition, c. 1820–1977." In *The Invention of Tradition*, eds. Eric Hobsbawm and Terence Ranger, 101–164. Cambridge: Cambridge University Press.

Ćirković, Svetlana. 2012. *Stereotip vremena u diskursu raseljenih lica sa Kosova i Metohije*. Belgrade: Balkanološki institut SANU.

Cohen, Anthony P. 1985. *The Symbolic Construction of Community*. Chichester: Ellis Horwood.

Đekić, Mirjana. 1989. *Srpska narodna nošnja Kosova—Gnjilane*. Zagreb: Kulturno-prosvjetni sabor Hrvatske.

Eriksen, Thomas Hylland. 2002. *Ethnicity and Nationalism*. London: Pluto Press.

Eriksen, Thomas Hylland. 2007. "Some Questions about Flags." In *Flag, Nation and Symbolism in Europe and America*, eds. Thomas Hylland Eriksen and Richard Jenkins, 1–13. London and New York: Routledge.

Hroch, Miroslav. 2015. *European Nations: Explaining Their Formation*. London–New York: Verso. First published 2005.

Janković, Ljubica S., and Danica S. Janković. 1951. *Narodne igre*, Vol. VI. Belgrade: Prosveta.

Jenkins, Richard. 2008. *Rethinking Ethnicity: Arguments and Explorations*. Los Angeles, CA–London–New Delhi–Singapore: SAGE Publications.

Lajić Mihajlović, Danka, and Jelena Jovanović. 2018. "Multiculturalism of Kosovo and Metohija in the 1950s and 1960s Expressed in Traditional Music." In *Kosovo and Metohija: A Musical Image of Multiculturalism in the 1950s and 1960s*, eds. Danka Lajić Mihajlović and Jelena Jovanović, 137–161. Belgrade: Institute of Musicology SASA.

Leutloff-Grandits, Carolin. 2014. "The 'Social Glue' of Wedding Festivals in Kosovo's South: Linking the Village to Migration and Reshaping Gender and Social Relations." In *Albanian Transitions from Contemporary and Historical Perspectives*, ed. Robert Pichler, 135–162. Münster: Lit. S.

Leutloff-Grandits, Carolin. 2023. *Translocal Care across Kosovo's Borders: Reconfiguring Kinship along Gender and Generational Lines*. New York and Oxford: Berghahn Books.

Maksimović, Zoran. 2011. *Bošče Kosovskog Pomoravlja—Beleg tradicije*. Belgrade: "Naša Srbija."

Malešević, Miroslava. 1986. "Ritualizacija socijalnog razvoja žene—Tradicionalno selo zapadne Srbije." Belgrade: Zbornik radova Etnografskog instituta SANU, 19:9–11.

Mitić, Boris, director. 2004. *UNMIK Titanic*. Documentary film, produced by Dribbling Pictures, 56 minutes. YouTube video, October 30, 2010. https://www.youtube.com/playlist?list=PLD55575075748541F.

Pichler, Robert. 2009. "Migration, Ritual and Ethnic Conflict. A Study of Wedding Ceremonies of Albanian Transmigrants from the Republic of Macedonia." *Ethnologia Balkanica*, 13:211–229.

Putinja, Filip, and Žoslin Stref-Fenar. 1997. *Teorije o etnicitetu*, trans. Aljoša Mimica. Belgrade: Biblioteka XX vek. First published 1995.

Škaljić, Abdulah. 1979. *Turcizmi u srpskohrvatskom jeziku*. Sarajevo: Svjetlost. First published 1965.

Urošević, Atanasije. 1935. "Gornja Morava i Izmornik." In *Naselja i poreklo stanovništva*, Vol. 28, 3–242. Srpski etnografski zbornik LI. Belgrade: Srpska kraljevska akademija.

van Gennep, Arnold. 1960. *The Rites of Passage*, trans. Monika B. Vizedom and Gabriella L. Caffee. Chicago: University of Chicago Press. First published 1909.

Vasiljević, Miodrag A. 1950. *Narodne melodije koje se pevaju na Kosmetu*. Belgrade: Prosveta.

Zakić, Mirjana S., and Sanja Ranković. 2020. "Zvučna semantika u savremenoj svadbenoj procesualnosti Srba u Gračanici." *Baština*, 52:419–428. https://doi.org/10.5937/bastina30-29130

Zlatanović, Momčilo. 2007. *Narodne pesme i basme iz Kosovskog Pomoravlja*. Vranje: Vranjske knjige.

Zlatanović, Sanja. 2003. *Svadba—priča o identitetu: Vranje i okolina*. Belgrade: Etnografski institut SANU.

Zlatanović, Sanja. 2011. "Family in the Post-War Context: The Serbian Community of Southeast Kosovo." *Ethnologia Balkanica*, 15:227–250.

Zlatanović, Sanja. 2012. "Svadba, tradicionalni ženski kostim i identitetski diskursi srpske zajednice jugoistočnog Kosova." *Glasnik Etnografskog instituta SANU*, 60/2:89–105. https://doi.org/10.2298/GEI1202089Z

Zlatanović, Sanja. 2017. "Approaching Preferred Identity: 'Serbian Gypsies' in Post-War Kosovo." *Romani Studies*, 27/2:147–172. https://doi.org/10.3828/rs.2017.9

Zlatanović, Sanja. 2018. *Etnička identifikacija na posleratnom području: Srpska zajednica jugoistočnog Kosova*. Belgrade: Etnografski institut SANU.

Zlatanović, Sanja. 2022. "Everyday Practices of Gender in the Serbian Community of Post-War South-East Kosovo." *Genealogy*, 6/78:1–19. Special issue *The Balkan Family in the 20th Century*, eds. Petko Hristov and Maria Todorova. https://doi.org/10.3390/genealogy6040078

CHAPTER 4

TAMBURA BANDS AND SONIC FLAG RITUALS IN CROATIAN WEDDINGS

IAN MACMILLEN

Musical rituals involving the wild, at times violent, parading of Croatian flags with *tambura* music and honking cars at weddings have become significant patriotic rites in Croatia, particularly since 1991. Upon the Republic of Croatia's secession from Yugoslavia in that year, the "new" flag that it adopted—with the red, white, and blue bars of previous Croatian flags and the formerly forbidden red and white–checkered coat of arms that the 1971 "Croatian Spring" had used in its own project for autonomy from Yugoslav governance—became a profuse and affectively charged index of Croatian independence. As ethnologist Maja Povrzanović wrote at the time, "the Croatian coat of arms, the new flag, and new songs, as well as the old 'nationalistic' ones" were "symbolic characteristics of Croatian identity" that "[f]ollowing forty-five years of repression and proscription . . . 'exploded' in national euphoria" (1993:127). This explosion coincided with the at times spectacular re-emergence into common view of religious weddings, which along with displays of ethnic nationalism had largely been ostracized from the public sphere under state socialism before Croatia's violent separation from officially multinational and atheistic Yugoslavia. The use of Croatian musical and visual symbols by young men, especially among the friends and kin of a groom and his best man, became especially prominent in weddings of Catholics, which were the dominant religious persuasion of the new nation-state's nominal ethnic group.[1] Yet, as I show in this chapter, they have also overlapped, if sometimes uneasily, with secularized as well as religious practices of minority groups, including Bosnian Croat and Muslim Bosniak refugees fleeing the war in Bosnia.[2] Such symbols' functionality has become far more versatile than initially suggested in conventional wartime interpretations, which read the flag and music as indexes of the militarized, ready, and ultimately sovereign nation-state.

References to the flag and coat of arms commonly feature in new patriotic songs played at weddings by musicians or by DJs spinning recordings released over the first

FIG. 4.1. *Tambura* players, flag-bearer, and guests at a 2013 wedding in Osijek.

(Credit: Ian MacMillen.)

three decades of Croatian independence by Croatian and Croatian-diaspora pop stars, rock groups, and popular *tambura* bands. The latter ensembles perform on an eponymous string instrument family, spanning from the small lute-like *bisernica* up to the double bass–sized *berde* (both are pictured in Fig. 4.1) and including several midrange, guitar-shaped *tamburas*. These chordophones have been mobilized as Croatia's "national" instruments since the mid-nineteenth century (March 2013). The *tambura*, however, was introduced as a solo instrument by Ottoman forces several centuries ago and is played by many ethnicities in the region, including Orthodox Christian Serbs, Roma of various faiths, and Muslim Bosniaks (*Bošnjaci*, historically referred to as *Muslimani*). While women have become increasingly prominent in amateur and even some professional Croatian *tambura* ensembles (MacMillen 2019:188–195, 202–220), it is largely men of these ethnic backgrounds who play in the professional bands that couples engage for performance at their wedding.

During the 2009–2010 academic year and for several shorter stints in 2008, 2011, 2013, and 2015, I conducted intensive ethnographic research in Croatia's eastern Slavonia region, working with female and male musicians of various ethnic backgrounds but attending weddings always at the invitation of male Croat players, who are in high demand for the heavily masculine activities that the groom, best man (*kum*), and their entourage lead and that commandeer the flag for much of the wedding day. I focused on this region's most populous cities of Osijek and Slavonski Brod, which, though never occupied by the Yugoslav People's Army, are located near the borders with Serbia and Bosnia, respectively, and were heavily affected by the war. As my fieldwork with *tamburaši* ("*tambura* musicians," sg. *tamburaš*) in the Croatian cities of Osijek and Slavonski Brod attests, Croatia's flag, hymn, and popular patriotic music are prominent in the country's nationally oriented religious rites, of which the weddings that I describe here are the most widespread and public examples. Yet they also function as sites of interethnic and interreligious encounter, contestation, and reconciliation, there as well as in regions of ethnoreligious diversity elsewhere in the former Yugoslavia and in the Croatian diaspora (which has become an important second source of new *tambura* songs).

The patriotic ritual in which these symbols and practices are often most prominently deployed together in weddings is the parading of the flag by cars and motorcycles that honk and blast music as they transport people between the day's various sites and events. In Catholic Croat weddings these processions typically connect several important sites and customs of contemporary Slavonian weddings, at which the groom's party first gathers for a small celebration and then advances with the flag while singing and playing traditional songs to the house of the best man (*kum*). After celebrating with the best man, the latter might return with the groom, guests, band, and flag to the location of the groom's initial party before setting out for the bride's house; or else everyone would depart directly from the best man's house to the bride's. In either case, they are met there by the bride's family, who negotiate a bride price and then present first a false bride (usually a man or an older woman disguised as a bride to humorous effect) and then, finally, the bride. After more celebration there with food and alcohol, the flag, the male flag-bearers, and the band (men again) proceed with the bride, groom, and their parties on to the church; later greet the newly married couple, family, and guests for singing and dancing immediately after the wedding ceremony; and accompany everyone to the wedding hall, where the banner and the musicians are prominent in the day's final celebrations. Under communism (1945–1991), weddings sometimes included both state and church ceremonies, and processions in between the various sites often raised not Yugoslavia's banner but the Socialist Republic of Croatia's flag (see Dunin 2013:145–156). In the 1990s, this long-standing ritual took on the zeal of revolutionary separation from

Yugoslavia, expressed overtly in combinations of the new flag; flares lit around the flag, wedding party, and musicians (Fig. 4.2); reckless, high-speed driving of vehicles; and new *domoljubne tamburaške pjesme*, or "patriotic *tambura* songs," with quick tremolos and rich, offbeat harmonies played by bands and on car stereos.

As Croatia's 1990s nation-building project connected with wealthy North American diaspora organizations and saw thousands of Croats resettle in the newly independent homeland via population exchanges with Serbia and influxes of Bosniak/Bosnian Croat refugees, weddings became key sites for musically navigating diverse displacements, attachments, and differences in religious, flag, and song customs. In the harried realignments of wartime and early postwar networks, the new "symbolic characteristics" that Povrzanović cites were quickly devised and given significance yet soon reinterpreted again or even forgotten. While in most other situations my interlocutors brought up the war frequently, weddings proved to be one of the few contexts in which it did not overdetermine the significations and interpretations of *tambura* music that they presented to me.[3] What has endured instead is a set of gestures and feelings, an archive that, following Ann Cvetkovich (2003), Gayle Wald (2015), and Deborah Thomas (2019), we can identify as more affective than lexical, preserving much of the feeling and

FIG. 4.2. White-shirted *tambura* band (bottom left), cars, flares, and Croatian flag (bottom far right) at a 2010 wedding in the Slavonian city of Đakovo.

(Credit: Ian MacMillen.)

aesthetic, if not the higher-level semiotics, of wartime rituals, even those involving the complex signifiers of musical and cultural texts which upon their introduction through recordings released in the 1990s people interpreted as referring specifically to the war and to the presence of Serbian and Yugoslav soldiers. Using participant observation as an access point to such archives, this chapter examines musical rituals of the flag at weddings and the displacement and violence that they restructure in an affective, non-memorial fashion.

There is a long-standing tradition of folklorists noting the forgotten meanings of wedding rituals in Yugoslavia and its successor states, particularly with regard to the magical capacities of processions (Čulinović-Konstantinović 1983:191–192; Vitez 2003:183) and sounds (Rihtman 1982:262; Talam 2013:35, 214–215) for driving away evil spirits when the young couple are in a liminal status on the cusp of marriage and are therefore most susceptible. This chapter connects such forgotten, archaic meanings to the wartime re-emergence and adaptation of magically tinged rituals such as winding processions and to the forgetting, in turn, of wedding rituals' wartime signification. It thereby demonstrates why such forgetting is so common and how it nonetheless produces archives that sidestep the requirements of more standard forms of cultural memory, which typically involve conscious forms of remembrance. The chapter argues ultimately for ethnographic consideration of who does and does not attend to cultural texts in the context of folkloric practice, highlighting a mode of musical forgetting that participants enact as they adopt ritual aesthetics introduced during the war but in a manner inattentive to the significations (and sometimes to the phenomena altogether) that these practices once implied. This forgetting is facilitated by embodied, affective, and sonic archives that sustain violent deployments of music, other sounds, the flag, and vehicles past living memory into generations who did not experience the conflicts.

SONGS AND FLAGS

Povrzanović's observation that music and flags operate in coordination as symbols is borne out in many studies of nationalism, though ethnomusicological analyses tend to see significatory capacities as more fixed for visual emblems than for song. Such analyses place musical texts in their performance contexts and read them as processes rather than products, granting to song an ontological flexibility between function and representation—that is, a capacity to affect people (and to gain social standing as a tradition) through its temporal, oral, participatory dimensions and not only through top-down systems of official symbolism. Carol Muller and Philip Bohlman draw attention to, respectively, (1) the South African anthem's pluralistic interweaving of national singing practices in parallel with the forming of the democratic nation out of multiple constituencies (that the anthem's performers dress in robes fashioned after the flag, however, "symbolizes the [state's] protection" instead of paralleling it) and (2) the shifting "ritual functions" of "God Bless America," an "unofficial national anthem" that "in the United States after September 11, 2001 . . . was more widely sung than 'The Star Spangled Banner'" (which anthem, along with its namesake, remained entrenched in the "top-down sanction to represent the nation beyond its borders"[4]) (Muller 2008:23; Bohlman [2004] 2011:111).

Thomas Turino reads such difference through representational semiotics, arguing that in the North during the American Civil War the unofficial Confederate anthem "Dixie," but not the Confederate flag, was embraced because the latter "was an index for the Confederate state" while the song had a "more complex" history, being "an index for the people themselves" (2008:190).[5] Though writing earlier and calling for a consideration of desires and intensities altogether outside of the correspondences of representation, Gilles Deleuze and Felix Guattari nonetheless similarly argued that "music (drums, trumpets) draws people and armies into a race that can go all the way to the abyss (much more so than banners and flags, which are paintings, means of classification and rallying)"; this results from music's "much stronger deterritorializing force" in comparison to the territorial mark of the flag ([1980] 1987:333).

Such claims also pertain to a certain extent to the mobilization of flags and musical/sonic performance during the conflicts between the Yugoslav People's Army (later joined and/or paralleled by Serb militias) and the armed forces of first Slovenia and Croatia and later Bosnia-Herzegovina as these republics declared independence from Yugoslavia in 1991 and 1992. The period's most infamous wedding and flag procession was a March 1992 event that many cite as the provocation for the war's outbreak in Bosnia a month afterward, although, as Mladen Ančić notes, antagonisms were already deeply rooted and had "many possible triggers" (2004:356). Members of an ethnic Serb wedding party processing with a Serbian flag after the wedding ceremony at a church on the other side of Sarajevo parked their cars with the usual "honking of car horns and discharging firearms" and prepared to continue on foot to a meal celebrating their wedding at Sarajevo's oldest Orthodox church in the traditionally Muslim quarter of Baščaršija; "the noise drew many onlookers," among them a man (presumably a Bosniak) who fatally shot the groom's father in an altercation after the latter "got out of the lead car and, as was customary, started waving the Serbian flag he was carrying" (Ančić 2004:356). In Ančić's interpretation, sound again plays the more ambiguous role, attracting "onlookers" to whom honking could signify any of Bosnia's three main faiths and who approach in order to *look on* the scene for further signs of who is coming, while the flag affords that visual clarification in a territorializing fashion that "was evidently perceived as a provocation" (Ančić 2004:356). Yet this tragic event also suggests that flags, and not only music, can draw people into volatile, even violent, abysses via gestures that make them more than means of classification (the procession bore several "national and religious symbols" classifying it as "Serbian," yet the father's "actions" with the flag drew the murderous response [Ančić 2004:356]). My fieldwork at recent weddings suggests that as wartime associations have faded from memory, flags' capacity to slip beyond a fixed symbolic and territorializing function has equaled and even surpassed that of weddings' sonic traditions.

My aim here is to extend to flags some of the ontological flexibility between dynamic functionality and top-down representation that Ančić, Bohlman, Muller, and Turino ascribe to ritual sound. Acknowledging music's important power in such processes (which is, mostly, these scholars' focus), I argue that weddings' musical flag rituals—particularly the embodied attention and participation of men and women from various lands and diasporas as singers and standard-bearers—challenge standard theories of the emblems' respective affective capacities. In the fading wake of wartime violence, the material, multisensory impact of pulsating sounds and fabrics has outlasted the context that once overdetermined its significance.

In addition to highlighting flags' dynamic, musical lives, I seek to do ethnographic justice—that is, to pay long-warranted yet lacking scholarly attention—to forms of forgetting, enabled through inattention to signifiers, that I have observed in the field. Several factors suggest that the overt semiosis between the euphoric parading of the flag by the wedding's standard-bearer (*barjaktar* or *zastavnik*) and the "national euphoria" of the revolutionary moment that inspired the transformation of the older ritual's aesthetics in the 1990s is itself fading. Many couples, musicians, and flag-bearers are now too young to recall the battles of 1991. Also, significant numbers of wedding participants in Slavonia are immigrants who arrived after those wartime scenes that inspired the revised tradition had subsided, and they brought other sonic and visual wedding symbols from their native Bosnia or Serbia. That immigrants participate in the same revisions of older, widely spread wedding rituals as locally born Croats (and that locals participate in them without conceiving of concrete wartime origins or meanings) suggests the effective dispersion of what Pierre Bourdieu identified as *habitus*: "systems of durable, transposable dispositions, structured structures predisposed to function as structuring structures ... collectively orchestrated without being the product of the orchestrating action of a conductor" (1977:72). In this instance, it specifically involves an embodied feeling for practices shared across generational and regional difference that elides or transcends contextual cultivation.

Yet many older natives of Croatia who secured its independence and celebrated it with the new national symbols are less than euphoric about the procession, despite its patriotism. This suggests further splits between remembering the war's meaning (for many soldiers a safe, independent, often patriarchal, and ethnically Croatian country) and practicing wild rituals that imitate wartime scenes yet facilitate cultural forgetting. It seems that the irritation of older onlookers and of state institutions targets the rowdiness of the young men who participate and views it not as a continuation of the revolutionary parading of the flag from the early days of independence but rather as an unjustified disturbance. A leading Croatian newspaper's 2013 article alluded in its title ("Police at War with Weddings") to the recontextualization of the tradition as finalized in the 1990s into a somewhat more trivial and internal societal conflict and stated that: "At the procession's front are sometimes *tambura* players, horse-drawn carriages, a standard-bearer or a private automobile with an attached rotating [light] that regulates traffic on its own and stops all other vehicles. They call him *Čajo*![6] The procession is loud, merry, true Slavonian. Of course there is drinking. However" (Novak 2013; my translation). It elaborates that although this is an old regional tradition, police in Slavonia's Vukovar-Srijem district have curtailed the activity due to complaints over drunk drivers, cars with illegal flashing police lights, and vehicles that speed through red traffic signals. Negative reactions to the flag's ritual parading with the groom's party are symptomatic of a broader array of tensions over such weddings and the meaning of patriotism itself. While on any given Saturday in the summer one can encounter multiple such visibly patriotic wedding processions, and although weddings also often fulfill the secessionist government's dream of Croats returning from abroad by cementing or enticing their resettlement as they marry into Croatian families, these events and rituals do not proceed with unchecked approval.

Indeed, tensions arise largely *because of* the noisy, even violent nature of the processions and the diversity of religious, ethnic, and national backgrounds and perspectives of the people involved. Gay and lesbian weddings have become somewhat common following the passing of Croatia's 2014 Life-Partnership Act, and the public use of rainbow Pride flags and involvement of non-Croatian partners and legal systems in high-profile same-sex weddings has brought attention to the fact that not all such processions uphold patriarchal and patriotic norms (see ATV 2015). One gay groom, addressing his and his partner's decision to out themselves by name in the media as wed and legally joined, recently stated, "Wedding ceremonies are by definition a public event—why do we drive through the entire village/city in a column that honks and wave flags? In order to notify as many people as possible that it's a wedding" (Posavec, as quoted in Tomečić 2018; my translation). Yet even in the much more common instances of heterosexual and ostensibly Catholic weddings visible in Croatian cities and newspapers, what such columns of cars announce may be diversely interpreted and received, even among participants, and the sounds of cars and musicians are central in emerging tensions regarding differences in custom and background.

A Croatian–Bosnian Wedding

A 2010 wedding near Slavonski Brod between a Croatian-born bride and a Croat immigrant groom whose family and best man are originally from Bosnia illuminates these tensions. The bride's brothers played in a *tambura* band, but as they were obligated to participate as family members rather than as performers, they recruited replacements to play with their bandmates at the wedding from 1 p.m. until 4 a.m. the next day. I heard grumbles throughout the day, however, from the groom's and best man's guests (including both Bosnian Croats and Bosniaks) that the families should have recognized that this was a Bosnian wedding and hired a Bosnian accordionist. The brothers also play in the city *tambura* orchestra, and their family has a long history in Slavonia; but a good number of guests were from Slavonski Brod's large Bosnian Croat and Bosniak populations, who came as refugees from nearby Bosnian towns across the Sava River during the 1990s. Although officially welcomed, they sometimes encountered hostility due to cultural differences and job competition during the wartime and recent recessional economies. Many Croats in Bosnia-Herzegovina, particularly in the country's south (Herzegovina), were at this time enthusiastically hiring Croatian *tambura* bands for weddings; but unlike them, Slavonski Brod's Bosnian Croats had spent much of the war in Croatia during the music's rise to national prominence and generally were not fans of the music.

This suggests what Timothy Rommen (2006) calls music's "negotiation of proximity," involving the desire to hear that which fulfills a longing for distant places and which distance promises (perhaps falsely) are the places where one could become what one ought to be. In this instance, many of the guests desired accordion music, which was still popular in Bosnia (if less so at the weddings of Croats, who hired *tambura* bands from Croatia). Their distance from accordion music was both geographic and sociopolitical as 1990s Croatian media had associated accordions with Bosnian and Serbian folk music and painted them as a threat to the *tambura* and its Croat proponents (Pettan 1998).

The distinction extends beyond instruments to harmonic/melodic organization: Croatia's "neotraditional" (Bonifačić 1998) *tambura* music has mostly abandoned the modal folk music construction and nineteenth-century harmonization style that still dominate in Serbian and Bosnian newly composed folk music.[7] Croatian neotraditional *tambura* music uses functional tonal harmony typical of central European art music instead. Recognizably Croatian music was audible throughout the weddings, even at events led by Bosnians. Although I heard griping about instrumentation and repertoire, the central men and several younger Bosnians, who included members of both Muslim and Catholic immigrant families from the same Bosnian towns, reveled in the sounds of this music at key moments. As I will argue, this happens at points in the rituals when music no longer serves to turn attention to the regional symbolism and themes of religious, ethnic, or gendered identity in its lyrics but rather re-emerges alongside the flag as a deterritorializing force.

I helped the band set up the wedding hall before setting off for the best man's village in Slavonski Brod's foothills. They stood outside the door to a tent by the town hall where the groom's family was preparing food and drinks (Fig. 4.3). As one band member remarked, they would play *od kapije* ("from the gate"), a reference to the threshold's importance in rituals of movement that chart the liminality of the wedding process upon local geography. They immediately played a *bećarac*, a Bosnian/Croatian/Serbian reveler's song in which guests take turns semi-improvising humorous, rhyming, decasyllabic couplets:

> Mladoženjo ovo često čutćeš
> Ideš pišat', žena pita kud'ćeš
>
> Groom, you'll often hear this [when you're wedded][8]
> Go to piss, the wife asks where you're headed

FIG. 4.3. *Tambura* band and groom's family outside the *kapija* ("gate") with motorcycle and flag at a 2010 wedding near Slavonski Brod.

(Credit: Ian MacMillen.)

A distinct genre, *bećarac* belongs to the same overarching tradition as *pjevanje u kolu* (singing in a circle dance, which soon followed at this party), and singers often repurpose verses from that genre or other decasyllabic traditions. In contrast to new *tambura* ballads, which I detail shortly, these songs draw close attention as guests listen for clever cross-genre borrowings, intertextual references, and humorous punchlines and double entendres. Similarly, during circle dances, the flag-bearer and other male authorities in the processions would historically "sit still and watch the dancers with respect as if they were judges" (Černelić 1991:185; citing Sušić 1970:96). The hosts paid particular attention to the musicians at the wedding near Slavonski Brod: as guests emerged from the tent's gate, the groom's father gave each *tamburaš* 100 *kuna* (roughly $20 at the time). Others emerged, including the groom, giving more tips and beckoning the band inside to play.

After thirty minutes, we started processing to the best man's house, with one young man bringing the Croatian flag from the initial reception space and others bearing smaller ones (Fig. 4.4). The band and Croatian and Bosnian guests alike joined in the *bećarac*, whose modal organization and harmonization mediate between Croatian and Bosnian styles. As we neared the house, people began singing best man–themed verses:

FIG. 4.4. *Tambura* band, groom's party, and flag-bearer approach the best man's house.
(Credit: Ian MacMillen.)

> Jedi, kume, i mesa i sosa
> Samo nemoj umočiti nosa
>
> Eat, best man, of both the meats and sauces
> Just be sure you don't dunk your proboscis

We entered the yard and the band continued to play as the best man came out to greet the groom. A man had come up the hill driving a miniature motorcycle in front of us, and the best man took it and rode it around the yard and street, weaving between the guests (Fig. 4.5). After drinking again and eating more meats and cheeses (with some of the Muslim attendees abstaining from the alcohol), we headed back down the hill. The best man and the groom went ahead of us on a second, larger motorcycle wearing shiny, black, World War II–era helmets (cf. Fig. 4.3). *Bećarac* verses accompanied our return to the party tent for more food and music.

One of the band members had introduced me to young male friends of the best man, and they asked me to eat with them and then ride with them to the bride's house. Processions between various wedding sites/rituals involve both male and female participants of many generations, but parading the flag is within the purview of young men on the groom's side and in this sense involves the patriarchal passing of "patriotic"

FIG. 4.5. *Tambura* band, flag-bearer, and motorcyclist on their way to the best man's house. (Credit: Ian MacMillen.)

traditions (the adjective *domoljubni* lacks the gendered etymology of its English equivalent "patriotic" but here similarly has clear masculine associations regarding the *običaji*, or "traditions," it modifies, as well as who guards them and how). Joining through a connection on the bride's side, I would not normally have been able to play such a central role, but my status as a foreign guest warranted their enthusiastic hospitality. One man got in the back of a small car and stood up through the sunroof holding a large Croatian flag. I crawled into the back seat beside him while another sat on the other side of his legs and others got in the front. The driver remarked of the Bosnian melismatic singing and accordion on the stereo, "I don't want *narodne*" (new "folk" recordings) and inserted a CD of hit *tambura* songs by Miroslav Škoro, one of the leading *tambura* singer-songwriters to emerge during Croatia's war of independence. The tracks that we listened to from the CD included *Ne dirajte mi ravnicu* ("Don't Touch My Plain"—Croatia's unofficial wartime anthem) and other popular wartime collaborations that the Slavonian Croat singer had recorded with Croatian American *tamburaš* Jerry Grcevich. With the hired *tambura* band several vehicles behind us, the driver could have blasted his well-loved Bosnian hits; but, for reasons that I detail in the following section, he selected patriotic *tambura* songs popularized during the war as the accompaniment proper to our car's procession of the flag along the roads to the bride's family's home.

Perception and Attention in Vehicles

Accompaniment (*pratnja*) is the operative term here, for music quickly fades from attention in such rituals. The verb *pratiti* means "to accompany" but also more generally "to follow," and *tambura* bands traditionally walk behind processions on foot, accompanying *singing* as the focal point of musical concentration but also frequently giving up the spotlight to other sonic and visual stimuli, such as roaring lead vehicles, the waving flag, and the groom's and family members' shouts and laughter. In car convoys (which at more curtailed weddings comprise the sole processions), the band follows in an automobile far behind the banner-bearing car. In our lead vehicle, *tambura* music *was* blasting, but it, too, soon began to accompany/follow us rather than occupy our attention. In this state of lower attention, in which music was but one of many auditory and other stimuli (and no one seemed to be listening to or singing along with the lyrics), *tambura* music's tremoloing vibrations and its ready association as sonic background to Slavonian weddings were acceptable and even preferable to those who at other parts of the wedding had longed for Bosnian song with which to sing along.

Studies of music and cars emphasize how sound devices "make the automobile more 'habitable'" and "the driver feel even more at 'home,'" with cars "represented as safe technological zones protecting the driver from the road" (Bull 2001:187, 2005:174). Motorized vehicles' historical associations with prolonged, attentive focus date back at least to the early decades of train travel (cf. Ong, 2018, on Anna Karenina reading on a train). Cars in particular provide closed, interior spaces from which "the highway might well be the site of radio's most captive audiences" (Loktev 1993:203). Yet in Croatian wedding processions, audition is not individualized and isolated from the outside but part of cacophonous, spectacular, intervehicular assemblages. Such perception approaches what submarine ethnographer Stefan Helmreich calls "transductive" attention: a sensorially, materially dynamic process in which listening does not produce objectifying, interiorized subjects but envelops one in "the modulating relations that produce insides and outsides, subjects and objects, sensation and sense data" (2007:623). In Croatia such contorted liminality persists from the swerving of non-enclosed motorcycles (with *tambura* bands in pursuit) on to the veering of cars with closed doors but flag-bearers hanging out of windows (and music accompanying, if not securing their active listening).

Such inattention contrasts with close listening to decasyllabic *bećarac* verses or, during the war, to ballads. The Škoro/Grcevich recordings playing in our lead car had been mobilized by politicians and state-sponsored *tambura* bands in the 1990s *because* the lyrics were ambiguous, with vague references from which specific connotations could be coaxed through strategic, attentive deployment. In particular, "Don't Touch My Plain" became the war's poignant refrain of victimhood, with listeners interpreting the line "my fields are calling me" (*mene zovu moja polja*) as a longing for the flatlands occupied by Yugoslav forces. Yet Škoro wrote it about missing his mother and home as he dwelt with his Croatian American wife in Pittsburgh years before the war in 1989. It never mentions violence, and its wartime meaning required attentive, creative interpretation.

Tambura songs written *during* the war do allude to dangers and perpetrators of violence but usually ambiguously or in allegories of demons, the referents again left open to interpretation and reinterpretation. For instance, *Istinu svijetu o Baranji reci* ("Tell the World the Truth about Baranja") by Slavonski Bećari, one of the most influential bands to carry over from the Yugoslav era, names the *Šokci* (a subgroup of the Croat ethnic group) as the protagonists of this song about Croatia's occupation but only states with regard to the enemy that "an evildoer is within you" (*zlotvor je u tebi*) (see Baker 2010:29; MacMillen 2019:58–59). The use of pronouns and general terms like "evildoer" in the lyrics, rather than specific mention of enemies by name, ethnicity, or nationality, suggests something of the collective post-socialist (here also post-Yugoslav) trauma that Albena Lutzkanova-Vassileva sees in post-modern poetry, which similarly resists cognitive semantics in testimony to overwhelming experiences of post-socialist transition and media saturation (2015). They contributed to a trauma culture that in Cvetkovich's (2003) formulation straddled the binary between acting out and working through trauma, accumulating a musical archive of the feelings pervading public life. Referencing without naming enemies emphasized male Croats as the sole agents and authors of heroic stories while casting these narratives in the internationally useful media frame of Croatia as victim (aggressor neither in the trenches nor in the media). Many, of course, remember the songs' implications of Yugoslav forces and Serb militias; but their texts' ambiguous referents allow songs to serve different patriotic functions in today's Croatian public sphere, where minorities are more closely integrated and younger generations who play the songs did not experience the war. Those different patriotic functions involve moments of textually inattentive listening in which masculine fervor, not ethnic nationalism, frames the target affective atmosphere, with which the participants in the flag convoy aim to suspend more specific worldly concerns as they transport the flag and the wedding couple in between their childhood homes and the spaces (the church and banquet hall) where they will celebrate completing their journey through this life-cycle event. Provocative textual references would only hinder this, and I have never heard more specifically nationalistic songs used in the processions or receptions.

Multisensory Stimuli and Perception in Motion

Our driver honked the horn the entire way. Whenever the road went straight, he drove in an "S" formation, snaking back and forth across the centerline, our cramped bodies swinging side to side against doors and the flag-bearer's legs. Of our first foray into the oncoming lane, he noted driving in the reversed "English way." His veering mirrored the motorcycle route of the best man, whose military appearance in the army helmet had similarly set a martial tone that was initially important to yet also quickly overshadowed by their driving maneuvers.

The bride's town was several kilometers away, and we drove in this loud, ostentatious fashion for fifteen minutes. The band followed us to the bride's home, entered the inner courtyard, and began playing as we enjoyed more food and drinks. We then walked down the street to the church entrance, where the band stopped. This point, when the flag-bearer and musicians set up on the church steps or yard and the guests and participants process past them into the building, is momentous, signaling the couple's arrival at the church and the transference of the ceremony to the priest's hands for the Catholic rite of marriage. On this day the bride's home was close to the church, so we proceeded there on foot; but often a line of cars would reassemble, and the flag would move to the church at the head of another fast, sometimes reckless and dangerous column of speeding vehicles. At this point, the car bearing the wedding couple often offers a calmer, more contemplative, and less overtly masculine space where the bride and groom can pay attention to one another and to any music that they may have selected for the occasion; and this is also the case with the final procession from the church to the wedding hall, where the bride knows that the band will play the song that she has chosen for the first dance (at this particular wedding the newlyweds' car was notably quieter, though the din of the other cars' horns must have still been audible within). However, the young men in the now larger convoy of cars from both the groom's and the bride's parties/guests still do their best to dominate sonically and typically succeed in drawing the attention of onlookers in the public space—something that the bride usually does only relatively briefly in liminal moments when she and her groom are exiting the church or car doors.

At the church, it is common to light flares, framing the flag and wedding pair with smoke and red light, often as the sun begins to set (a motorcycle or car burnout, in which the spinning of tires on the road produces smoke through friction, is a popular alternative). This event may supersede the musicians' activity if their role is more minor. At a 2009 wedding that I witnessed in Osijek, a *tambura* trio playing for tips outside the cathedral soon drifted away from one another, joining the guests around the flag and its bearer (Fig. 4.6). The latter led the crowd in singing songs, then placed the standard prominently before the church doors and held it there in the light and smoke of the flares. At weddings where the families have hired bands to facilitate all such events, however, the musicians set up directly on the steps—often in between the doors and the flares and flags that guests pass as they near the church (cf. Fig. 4.2).

One Croatian wedding manual calls pyrotechnics "an excellent addition and a marvelous event in the wedding night. With . . . fireworks, flares, crackers, sprayers and other pyrotechnic aids you make your 'great day' unforgettable and effective" (Vrbanus 2004:37; my translation). The author suggests one "consult with an expert" and "leave the realization to the professionals" (37). Yet as news reports suggest, caution and official procedures are not hallmarks of the processions, nor are flares mere additions that are

FIG. 4.6. *Tambura* bassist (sixth from left), flag, and flares at a 2009 wedding in Osijek.
(Credit: Ian MacMillen.)

easily eliminated if one cannot afford to hire professionals—a pressing concern since the great recession.

As Mirko Delibašić, a Serb *tambura* musician and folklorist from Vukovar, Croatia, told me in 2013, the flares seem to have replaced older traditions among Croats, Bosniaks, and Serbs of firing rifles near flags at important points along the procession. Zorica Vitez has documented this practice at Croatian weddings back through the nineteenth century, when it accompanied the departures of brides from their family homes (2003:55). The shooting of guns in conjunction with patriotic music and dispelling evil spirits at weddings is a practice widely documented throughout the folklore of southern Europe and its diasporas (cf. Sugarman on firearms and heroic songs at Prespa Albanian diasporic weddings [1997:164–165], Brayer on southern European beliefs in guns and fireworks as driving off evil spirits [1986:31], and Monger on gunfire's broad use against malevolent forces [2004:xi]).

Of firearms and noise-making in Croatia's urban weddings, Vitez writes,

> processions set off in automobiles, regardless of the distance, and honking accompanies their movement. That din can be set off in connection with the shooting of firearms with which village weddings used to announce important moments of

the pre-wedding and wedding customs, as well as the completion of the church ceremony and the bringing of the bride into the new home. . . . Honking, with respect to making noise at weddings, has deep magical roots little known today: it was once believed to chase off evil powers and influences. (2003:183; my translation)

Just as flares replaced firearms, honking replaced bells to ward off evil, a change that in some parts transpired through an intermediary step in which bells—banned as Christian implements during the early years of Ottoman rule—were first replaced with resonant wooden clappers and hammers that could "protect guests at the wedding from bad spirits" (Talam 2013:214–215). Tone Bringa also writes that, in Bosniak weddings, car horns replaced firearms (1995:128), while Mark Forry documented Croat and Serb *tambura* players humorously imitating gunshots (by causing a bass *tambura* string to crack forcefully into the instrument's finger board) in order to scare wedding guests (1990:247). The various substitutions for firearms in south Slavic folklore suggest an interchangeability between not only the specific instruments used but also auditory and visual perception. What is necessary, evidently, is a sudden, shocking sensory overload, whether of the ears or of the eyes.[9]

None of my interlocutors who performed at weddings or were married during socialism recalled seeing flares or the newer tradition before 1991. Delibašić posited that new technology and growing interest in Italian fireworks had prompted the postwar transformation. Ethnologists have documented guns (often old, ramrod pistols) at weddings in Croatia since the 1990s (see Zebec 1993; Dunin 2013), but in my fieldwork I never heard gunshots and found flares to be far more common, though was told that both practices continue. Two factors might elucidate flares' effectiveness and development into a common tradition: unlike gunshots, they do not sonically overpower the hired musicians (whose music mixes with the loud but not overwhelming din of car horns); and the atmosphere that they help to create in tandem with patriotic singing and the waving of the Croatian flag is of a decidedly warlike and perhaps revolutionary character, even if the specific war of 1991 is no longer the referent (which it could traumatically be for gunshots in the case of war veterans).

Neither flares nor gunshots accompanied our car in Slavonski Brod, and the honking and blaring of Škoro and Grcevich's songs announced such important moments as our arrival at the bride's house and church. After the wedding ceremony, we emerged from the church and again joined the *tambura* band and flag, which the standard-bearer left outside, for an immediate celebration with dancing and photographs with members of the wedding party and the flag. At several weddings that I observed, various young men would take up the flag, waving it vigorously around the band and guests or holding it above the wedding family for a photograph. The photographer would motion for the guests and band to assemble before the church with the bride, groom, and wedding party. The flag would be raised behind and above us for a portrait, bringing the collective Croatian family of locals, Croats from the diaspora, and both Croats and Bosniaks (whom Croatians widely view as Croats converted to Islam) from neighboring republics under its fold. Such moments did not fully resolve or eliminate differences in tastes and expectations between these diverse participants. Guests at the wedding near Slavonski Brod, especially men born in Bosnia, continued to grumble about the repertoire well into the evening. Instead, such moments created contexts in which *tambura* music was effective not as representing region or identity but as a part of a broader, multisensory, affective atmosphere.

Flags and songs have undoubtedly served as Croatian national symbols, perhaps never so urgently as during the war and events that commemorate it. At this level of deliberate semiotics, they have often functioned as indexes of the state and its people. In Croatia's case, however, the flag has come to be associated as much with Croatia the nation as with Croatia the state. I know from my interlocutors and from online wedding videos that Croats in Bosnia-Herzegovina use the Croatian flag for weddings at which musicians from Croatia perform, while Serbs in Croatia now raise the Serbian national standard (though doing so during the war was risky). Croat weddings in Bosnia and in North America also combine the Croatian flag with the Bosnian, American, and/or Canadian flags (standards of state rather than ethnic belonging); and Croatian *tambura* bands who play for ceremonies abroad typically perform the Croatian as well as the local state anthems.

Deterritorialized Becomings

Deleuze and Guattari proposed moving beyond the analysis of such music's representations (its top-down, official systems of signification on behalf of a particular nation) to consider the intensities, the "relations of movement and rest," the material processes of affecting and being affected through which humans and objects draw into closer proximity as music drives them to transform, to become something more than they were previously ([1980] 1987:259, 274). The two writers are interested more in flags' "means of classification and rallying" (333) and the territorial signature that engenders the "formation of a domain" (349) than in banners' potential to symbolize through formal representation or to recall through the neat alignment of reference and reference point in what they call the "point-system of memory" (294).[10] Yet, as I have stated, they, too, grant flags a more limited capacity to excite humans than music. Music's "collective fascination," its "potentiality of [a] 'fascist' danger" to carry collectives into the "abyss" of warfare, is due to its "much stronger deterritorializing force, at once more intense and much more collective, and the voice['s] much greater power of deterritorialization" (333). As I conclude and connect back to several points relating to music and rituals that bring together under the flag participants with diverse claims on Slavonian wedding customs, I will also reconsider this appraisal.

Deleuze and Guattari link the idea of becoming to deeper, non-representational relations between a subject and that which it simulates. Music's deterritorializing power is an affective capacity to enact becomings: the becoming of the war machine, of a racial or other minoritarian term. In their famous example of the tarantella dance, the afflicted does not imitate or identify with a tarantula: "the victim . . . becomes a dancing spider only to the extent that the spider itself is supposed to become a pure silhouette, pure color and pure sound to which the person dances" (305). Both patient and spider are musically deterritorialized from their stable identities.

A similar relation joins the procession leader and the flag he carries, indeed the banner and the entire convoy. In weaving in and out of street lanes in cars and motorcycles, in contorting their bodies through sunroofs, in raising the flag and making it course over family and friends to the music's beat, they wave themselves as much as they do the flag, entering into relation with its movement and rest. The standard-bearer's deterritorialization, his becoming the flag, transpires only to the extent that the flag itself is supposed to become a pulse, a rhythmic flickering in the smoke and the red light of the flares and pistols, the burnouts and hazard lights. Becoming, write Deleuze and Guattari, "is affect in itself, the drive in person, and represents nothing," meaning that significance here is not abstracted into higher-level symbols but operates through the musical indexing of refrain and movement to territory (Tomlinson 2016:168). The contemporary flag ritual seems to have developed out of an older tradition in which a *barjaktar* led the procession with a special wedding flag (*svatovska zastava*) made of multiple strips of differently patterned, multicolored, rippling fabrics (Vondraček-Mesar 2003:19). The use of state flags today expands on this meaning by indexing people and territory yet preserves the relationship of pulsating motion that connects bearer to flag in a more-than-symbolic fashion. This relationship's affective dimension, the investment of movements with drive and intensity, is critical.

The pulse in which participants move has acquired a specific set of sounds, including canonized Croatian and diasporic patriotic songs mobilized during the war but also sounds produced by neither band nor stereo: horns, screeching tires, roaring engines, sirens, yells, laughter. Music facilitates the procession, but the broader sounds and stimuli make the flag more than a symbol or means of rallying. As Jacques Attali notes, "[a]mong sounds, music as an autonomous production is a recent invention"; in other periods, and still in many parts of the world, "it was effectively submerged within a larger totality" ([1977] 1985:3). In Croatian wedding processions this submergence is vigorously re-enacted within broader fields of noise, slipping in and out of what Anahid Kassabian calls "ubiquitous" forms of listening at "lower levels of attention" (2013:xii–xiii).

Timothy Ingold argues that "the eyes and ears should not be understood as separate keyboards for the registration of sensation but as organs of the body as a whole, in whose movement, within an environment, the activity of perception consists" (2000:268). Following this, we can recognize how, for whole sensing bodies, distinctions blur between sight, sound, even haptic and olfactory sensations. The flag's waving to *tambura* wedding music involves layered rhythms of pulsation that merge (in various combinations): blinking/rotating lights; blaring horns and sirens; swerving cars; waving, flag-bearing bodies; rippling flags; quickly alternating plectra tremoloing across instrument strings; vibrating engines; wafting smoke (intermittently obscuring sight, smell, feeling); and chanting voices. The differences between music and flags that scholars note thus seem to be differences of context, with moments of higher cognitive attention actively overproducing these dimensions' autonomy. Unsurprisingly, these fade as flags are lifted out of their static, two-dimensional, monosensorial lives as paintings and are multisensorially activated in rituals. Participation and investments in the flag's continuing life by former refugees and emigrants help extend the rituals' urgency for reproducing pulsations of wartime patriotism as explicit memories of war also fade. Loosed from their referents, ritualized actions externalize past acts of violence into embodied social memory, which "took shape first as *memory archived* in the form of patterned gesture, transmitted from one body to another" (Tomlinson 2015:75, emphasis in original).

Weddings' musical flag rituals begin among the groom's and best man's young male kin and friends, and unequal participation divides first along lines not of nationality or religion but of gender. It is young, local, but not necessarily locally born men on the groom's side who take charge of the flag, flares, and music, selecting *tambura* recordings or shouting out *bećarac* verses and song requests. Their actions often curry disfavor among wedding attendees and onlookers who are distanced from the ritual by virtue of gender, nationality, age, or membership in the bride's party. Yet these men also re-create among the new generation the passion, bravado, and risk-taking of the war that established their territories' security, their banner's officialdom, and their music's popularity. This transpires not through the point system of representation or even of memory but in a process of becoming: an open becoming of a geographically, culturally disparate extended family assembled for the rite of marriage and familial reconstitution.

Despite the often devoutly Catholic nature of these events and the loss of knowledge of certain traditions' pagan origins, magic is not altogether absent from these rituals. Vesna Čulinović-Konstantinović argued that a related village ritual of processing with a plough or cart to the groom's house was being upheld "today without awareness of the symbolism of the magic circle which is *recalled* also by the dancing of the 'crooked reel' . . . with which wedding participants wind through the village in an open 'single file'" (1983:192; my translation and emphasis). This suggests a tension within folklore's embodied archive of gesture and habitus between lost symbolic awareness and preserved capacity for recalling. Similarly, flares, a form of modern technology, do not memorialize the war's fires, bombs, or other material violence or recall the gunshots of earlier weddings so much as generate a pulsating atmosphere of light and smoke in which the flag, wedding participants, and musicians (heard/seen as they themselves wind back and forth within the layered rhythms of pulses) can properly vanquish any evil accompanying them on the liminal procession to the church's threshold. This atmosphere is largely affective, assembling desires and stimulations that coalesce in and around moving vehicles as bodies swerve back and forth at high speeds, bombarded with pulsations of *tamburas*, engines, lights, flags.

This is a materially dangerous practice but one that confronts both the dangerous liminality of bride and groom, as they move toward married life from maidenhood and bachelorhood, and certain dangerous immaterial (and potential physical) presences. At the moment of official canonization of the flag and of Croatia's new wave of patriotic *tambura* songs during the war, "evil" was located aurally, visually, affectively, and discursively in the incursion into Croatian territories of socialist Yugoslavs and orthodox Serbs, who were often named only through references to demons and evildoers (Čolović 1994:133; Baker 2010:24, 96). This trend paralleled the branding as "witches" of Croatian feminists who spoke out against Croatian soldiers' and politicians' roles in wartime misogyny and sexual violence (MacMillen 2019:195, 203). Such enemies were positioned against patriotic heroes in what Lada Čale Feldman calls a "manichaean struggle of absolute good and absolute evil" for which were summoned "elements of the magical" (1993:18). In Croatian popular music lyrics, these elements often re-emerged from Yugoslav secularization alongside Catholic symbolism in what Catherine Baker calls "a semi-historical, semi-magical narrative" involving "a syncretic treaty of mutual assistance" between protective figures such as the *Vila* of Velebit (a supernatural feminine being who guards Croats in the Dinaric Alps) and the Virgin Mary (Baker 2010:113; cf. Schäuble 2014:218). Some aspects of magical discourse have been preserved in folklore; and in liminal periods such as wars of independence, and much briefer moments such as wedding processions, these reinforce the reactivation of a magical imaginary that is fostered also by the para-religious nature of the ritual, even as the vagueness of such expressions (which are more about meaning as felt and indexed than about the higher-level symbolism of sacred dogma and secular discourse) allows the momentary referents of songs and customs to slip out of attention as these practices pass on through patterned gesture and multisensory stimulation. By finding new uses for such rites' habitus and aesthetics, participants could, in ways that broke significant new ground within sites where my interlocutors were usually quick to mention ethnic conflict, forget disputes over matters ranging widely from music selection to territorial sovereignty.

Ingold has called on ethnographers to overcome the ideological baggage of Western subjectivity and its theorizing of sight as distant and active (and audition as intimate and passive) in order to recognize how both senses interpenetrate and are employed from various subjectivities. Not just audition but sight, too, involves the subject intimately in the sensorial generation of the cosmos and affords the subject a means of summoning the magical to face (or create) danger and sorcery (2000:250–254). Making the flag pulsate in layers of sonic and visual rhythms, and just as importantly hearing and seeing these rhythms, confronts a number of potential dangers, past and present.

The flag procession simultaneously facilitates an affective non-memorial of past dangers. Eschewing constructing or sensing a Serb/Yugoslav presence as evil, the musical rituals of flags and flares summon wedding participants from the core national territory and its foreign enclaves to connect and celebrate the forging of family relations and the creation and defense of the broader collective. To the extent that the rituals are challenged by neighbors' shifting concerns—from unrestrained patriotism to preventing noise, light, and smoke pollution, from resisting active enemies to warding off dangers posed by the processions themselves—the role of magic is again ceding some of its power to the political, and the specific politics of post-Yugoslav south Slavic fraternity and its admission of national symbols widely vary. Yet the residue of feeling retained outside of conscious memorialization in the magic of *tambura* bands, smoke, and lights physically shores up gender and age hierarchies while eliding interreligious and interethnic distinctions and representational politics. Equalization of investment, if not power, between local and foreign-born participants involves just this affective purpose: to sense danger at the moment of a new union and address it with the musical, material, and sensorial resources at hand.

Notes

1. In this chapter, I refer to such weddings as "Croat weddings." I use "Croatian" to refer more generally to weddings, flags, and other entities/events that occur within or come from the country of Croatia.
2. This is particularly the case in Slavonski Brod ("Slavonian Ford"), a city positioned at a historically important crossing and, later, bridge on the Sava River (the border with Bosnia and Herzegovina). The Bosnian war between Serb, Croat, and Bosniak forces that would continue until December 1995 had commenced farther to the south in spring 1992; and Slavonski Brod was a key entry point for thousands of Bosniaks and Croats fleeing to Croatia up until October 1992 when, on the opposite side of the Sava, Serb militias took the twin city of Bosnanski Brod from combined Muslim–Croat forces (soon thereafter, the bridge was destroyed).
3. I quickly grew accustomed to people turning my attention constantly to bullet holes in the buildings around us, but this was not done at weddings, even those performed in buildings damaged during the war.
4. Reactions to Colin Kaepernick and other American football players kneeling during the pre-game anthem in protest of police killings of African Americans show the close relationship between a flag and an official anthem ("The Star Spangled Banner" is *about* the flag and is typically expected *to occasion standing for* the flag); they also show the strict expectations for the use of an anthem connected so directly to the flag through lyrics and ritual practice, whereas unofficial anthems can sometimes be used more flexibly.
5. In this regard we might note that Muller's distinction is between what she seems to read as the iconic resemblance of the song to the democratic nation and the indexical and symbolic significations of state protection interpretable in the choir's flag robes.
6. The *čajo* (or *čauš*, *čavuš*, or *čavo*) oversees the wedding guests' entertainment and often leads the procession alongside the *barjaktar*.
7. Newly composed folk music is a genre of songwriting that peaked commercially in the 1980s and that is characterized by the combination of aspects of several local musical styles and the incorporation of elements considered foreign and more "Eastern."
8. I have added "when you're wedded" to the otherwise faithful translation in order to preserve the rhyme scheme and syllable count. Improvisation in this line takes the form of replacing *mladoženjo* ("Oh groom") with the groom's name(s).
9. My sense from communicating with young men involved in these customs is that today they no longer conceive of the threats addressed with such actions as taking the form of evil spirits but rather locate them in social constraints on masculine enjoyment and bachelorhood (on which the wedding of one of their own puts a further damper). That said, belief in more abstract metaphysical forces is widespread among *tambura* players in Slavonia (MacMillen 2019:199–231), and most young men line up to receive sprigs of rosemary to augment virility and fertility upon arriving at the church for the wedding ceremony; thus,

pre-Christian powers do still exert themselves in such contexts and encourage young men to court their influences, and certainly the idea of negative energy persists as something to be dispelled through the rowdy actions of young men.

10. As Deleuze and Guattari argue, "the point-system of memory" is opposed to the "line-system (or block-system) of becoming. . . . Becoming is the movement by which the line frees itself from the point, and renders points indiscernible" ([1980] 1987:294).

Works Cited

Ančić, Mladen. 2004. "Society, Ethnicity, and Politics in Bosnia-Herzegovina." *Časopis za suvremenu povijest*, 36/1:331–359.

Attali, Jacques. 1985. *Noise: The Political Economy of Music*, trans. Brian Massumi. Manchester: Manchester University Press. First published 1977.

ATV. 2015. "Gej vjenčanje Srbina i Hrvata, ovo je njihova ispovijest!" March 11. https://www.atvbl.com/gej-vjencanje-srbina-hrvata-ovo-je-njihova-ispovijest. Accessed June 15, 2020.

Baker, Catherine. 2010. *Sounds of the Borderland: Popular Music, War and Nationalism in Croatia since 1991*. Farnham: Ashgate.

Bohlman, Philip. 2011. *Focus: Music, Nationalism, and the Making of the New Europe*, 2nd ed. London: Routledge. First published 2004.

Bonifačić, Ruža. 1998. "Regional and National Aspects of Tamburica Tradition: The Case of the Zlatni Dukati Neotraditional Ensemble." In *Music, Politics, and War: Views from Croatia*, ed. Svanibor Pettan, 131–149. Zagreb: Institute of Ethnology and Folklore Research.

Bourdieu, Pierre. 1977. *Outline of a Theory of Practice*, trans. Richard Nice. Cambridge: Cambridge University Press.

Brayer, Menachem M. 1986. *The Jewish Woman in Rabbinic Literature: A Psychohistorical Perspective*. Hoboken, NJ: Ktav Publishing House.

Bringa, Tone. 1995. *Being Muslim the Bosnian Way: Identity and Community in a Central Bosnian Village*. Princeton, NJ: Princeton University Press.

Bull, Michael. 2001. "Soundscapes of the Car: A Critical Study of Automobile Habitation." In *Car Cultures*, ed. Daniel Miller, 185–202. Oxford: Berg.

Bull, Michael. 2005. "The Intimate Sounds of Urban Experience: An Auditory Epistemology of Everyday Mobility." In *A Sense of Place: The Global and the Local in Mobile Communication*, ed. János Kristóf Nyíri, 169–178. Vienna: Passen Verlag.

Čale Feldman, Lada. 1993. "The Theatralisation of Reality: Political Rituals." In *Fear, Death and Resistance: An Ethnography of War, Croatia 1991–1992*, eds. Lada Čale Feldman, Ines Prica, and Reana Senjković, 5–23. Zagreb: Institute of Ethnology and Folklore Research, Matrix Croatica X-Press.

Černelić, Milana. 1991. "Role of the *Starješina Svatova* among the Bunjevci." *Studia Ethnologica*, 3:181–191.

Čolović, Ivan. 1994. *Bordel Ratnika: Folklor, Politika i Rat*. Belgrade: Biblioteka XX. Vek.

Čulinović-Konstantinović, Vesna. 1983. "Promjene seoske porodice i običajnog ponašanja pri sklapanju braka." *Sociologija i prostor*, 21/82:183–197.

Cvetkovich, Ann. 2003. *An Archive of Feelings: Trauma, Sexuality, and Lesbian Public Cultures*. Durham, NC: Duke University Press.

Deleuze, Gilles, and Félix Guattari. 1987. *A Thousand Plateaus: Capitalism and Schizophrenia*, trans. Brian Massumi. Minneapolis: University of Minnesota Press. First published 1980.

Dunin, Elsie Ivancich. 2013. *Prošlost u Sadašnjosti: Svadbe u Dubrovačkom Primorju/Past into the Present: Weddings of the Dubrovako Primorje*. Dubrovnik: Matica Hrvatska–Ogranak Dubrovnik.

Forry, M. 1990. "The Mediation of 'Tradition' and 'Culture' in the Tamburica Music of Vojvodina (Yugoslavia)." PhD dissertation, University of California Los Angeles.

Helmreich, Stefan. 2007. "An Anthropologist Underwater: Immersive Soundscapes, Submarine Cyborgs, and Transductive Ethnography." *American Ethnologist*, 34/4:621–641.

Ingold, Timothy. 2000. *The Perception of the Environment: Essays on Livelihood, Dwelling and Skill*. London: Routledge.

Kassabian, Anahid. 2013. *Ubiquitous Listening: Affect, Attention, and Distributed Subjectivity*. Berkeley: University of California Press.

Loktev, J. 1993. "Static Motion, or the Confessions of a Compulsive Radio Driver." *Semiotexte* 6/1:204–208.

Lutzkanova-Vassileva, Albena. 2015. *The Testimonies of Russian and American Postmodern Poetry: Reference, Trauma, and History*. London: Bloomsbury Academic.

MacMillen, Ian. 2019. *Playing It Dangerously: Tambura Bands, Race, and Affective Block in Croatia and Its Intimates*. Middletown, CT: Wesleyan University Press.

March, Richard. 2013. *The Tamburitza Tradition: From the Balkans to the American Midwest*. Madison: University of Wisconsin Press.

Monger, George. 2004. *Marriage Customs of the World: From Henna to Honeymoons*. Santa Barbara, CA: ABC-CLIO.

Muller, Carol. 2008. *Focus: Music of South Africa*, 2nd ed. New York: Routledge.

Novak, Tomislav. 2013. "Slavonska policija u ratu sa svatovima." *Jutarnji List*, June 12, 2013.

Ong, Yi-Ping. 2018. "Anna Karenina Reads on the Train: Readerly Subjectivity and the Poetics of the Novel." *PMLA*, 133/5:1083–1098.

Pettan, Svanibor. 1998. "Music, Politics, and War in Croatia in the 1990s: An Introduction." In *Music, Politics, and War: Views from Croatia*, ed. Svanibor Pettan, 9–27. Zagreb: Institute of Ethnology and Folklore Research.

Povrzanović, Maja. 1993. "Culture and Fear: Everyday Life in Wartime." In *Fear, Death and Resistance: An Ethnography of War, Croatia 1991–1992*, eds. Lada Čale Feldman, Ines Prica, and Reana Senjković, 119–150. Zagreb: Institute of Ethnology and Folklore Research, Matrix Croatica X-Press.

Rihtman, Cvjetko. 1982. "O stvaraocima i prenosiocima u oblasti narodne muzičke tradicije." In *Rad 27. Kongresa saveza udruženja folklorista Jugoslavije*, ed. Cvjetko Rihtman, 261–266. Banja Vrućica, Bosnia and Herzegovina: Udruženje folklorista Bosne i Hercegovine.

Rommen, Timothy. 2006. "Protestant Vibrations? Reggae, Rastafari, and Conscious Evangelicals." *Popular Music*, 25/2:258–263.

Schäuble, Michaela. 2014. *Narrating Victimhood: Gender, Religion and the Making of Place in Post-War Croatia*. Oxford: Berghahn.

Sugarman, Jane. 1997. *Engendering Song: Singing and Subjectivity at Prespa Albanian Weddings*. Chicago: University of Chicago Press.

Sušić, Zvonimir. 1970. "Valvasor o Istranima." *Dometi*, 3/5:87–99.

Talam, Jasmina. 2013. *Folk Musical Instruments in Bosnia and Herzegovina*. Newcastle upon Tyne: Cambridge Scholars Publishing.

Thomas, Deborah. 2019. *Political Life in the Wake of the Plantation: Sovereignty, Witnessing, Repair*. Durham, NC: Duke University Press.

Tomečić, Iva. 2018. "Ivan i Stjepan: Naše vjenčanje iz snova u engleskom dvorcu." *CroL*, September 25. https://www.crol.hr/index.php/zivot/9415-ivan-i-stjepan-nase-vjencanje-iz-snova-u-engleskom-dvorcu. Accessed June 15, 2020.

Tomlinson, Gary. 2015. *A Million Years of Music: The Emergence of Human Modernity*. Brooklyn, NY: Zone Books.

Tomlinson, Gary. 2016. "Sign, Affect, and Musicking before the Human." *boundary 2*, 43/1:143–172.

Turino, Thomas. 2008. *Music as Social Life: The Politics of Participation*. Chicago: University of Chicago Press.

Vitez, Zorica. 2003. *Hrvatski svadbeni običaji*. Zagreb: Golden Marketing–Tehnička knjiga.

Vondraček-Mesar, Jagoda. 2003. *Svadbeni običaji sesvetskog prigorja: Katalog u publikaciji*. Zagreb: Nacionalna i sveučilišna knjižnica.

Vrbanus, Ratko. 2004. *Vjenčanja: Mali svadbeni priručnik*. Sisak, Croatia: Aura.

Wald, Gayle. 2015. *It's Been Beautiful: Soul! and Black Power Television*. Durham, NC: Duke University Press.

Zebec, Tvrtko. 1993. *Suvremena svadba u Posavini, Hrašće, Bukevje, 2.10.1993*. IEF video 485. Zagreb: Institut za Etnologiju i Folkloristiku.

CHAPTER 5

MARRIAGE AND WEDDING TRADITIONS AMONG THE *CORTORAR* ROMA IN ROMANIA

CĂTĂLINA TESĂR

As I begin writing this chapter, Romania has just come out of the lockdown due to the spring 2020 COVID-19 pandemic. Among the restrictions enforced during the lockdown was limiting the number of persons attending funerals and weddings—customarily large-scale ceremonies—to merely eight. While most of the ethnic Romanians I knew or heard of postponed their wedding ceremonies previously scheduled to take place during the unexpected pandemic, my Cortorar Romani acquaintances thought little both of the epidemiological consequences of large gatherings of people who did not observe social distancing and the governmental measures enforced and carried on with their customary weddings, which are occasions for almost the entire community to come together. Coincidentally the peak of the pandemic in Romania overlapped with the peak of Cortorar Romani wedding season, which occurs imperturbably at Orthodox Easter. Around that time the Facebook pages of my Cortorar acquaintances were flooded with live videos of their wedding parties in the teeth of all official bans on large gatherings at life-cycle events. In a phone conversation, a male Cortorar friend breathlessly and proudly recounted a police raid meant to stop a wedding party that he was attending. Once the police entered the courtyard with the intention of fining the wedding attendees and putting an end to the ceremony, the crowd scattered in all directions and hid in several neighboring houses. Their quick wits brought them through, and people continued to celebrate the wedding in the multiple locations to which they had sneaked away.

I find this story about the obduracy with which Cortorari (sg. Cortorar), a Romani-speaking population from Transylvania, do not give up on their wedding celebrations irrespective of any external thwarting forces to be illustrative of the centrality of the institution of marriage, and the ritual acts that communicate it, to their social and cultural life. Writing about the Parisian Rom, Patrick Williams (1984) contends that the ceremonial manifestations of marriage are of interest to the whole community because they enact the moral and social order of the notional community (cf. Gay y Blasco 1999). For Cortorari to live a meaningful life means to arrange the marriage of one's children and see them bringing forth children in wedlock and to arrange the latters' marriage(s). The social order prescribed by the wedding ritual is that girls marry away, leave the parental house, and go to live with their spouses and the latters' parents, produce offspring, and be incorporated into their marital families. Marriage is mandatory and tantamount to conceiving offspring, and those who do not succeed in this pursuit are symbolically denied belonging. Because they do not fulfill the imaginaries of the local categories of relatedness, they are treated almost as outsiders. People harness all their energy and money to celebrate agreements, contracts, and weddings; make and break marital arrangements; and pay dowries and enable successful marriages for future generations. Marriage-making is bound here to tradition, continuity, and permanence and, as illustrated by the above vignette, resists change and denies creative significance to history.

One of the reasons for the unchanging nature of marriage-making not only among Cortorari but also among other "traditional" Romani populations worldwide is that their institution of marriage does not fall under the regulations of the state and is concluded outside the canonical rites of the church. In Western societies marriage is a realm where the public, in the form of state and law, meets up with the private and emotional life of individuals. Here, the state and its laws are the source of innovation and change in marriage (Carsten et al 2021). Contrariwise, marriages among Roma are private affairs, in the sense that they are confined to the community and lack a public facet. They bridge the person and the community, while keeping the state at bay. Living amidst populations whose marriages have for a long time been regulated by civil and religious laws, the Roma have preserved their marital practices untinged by the *Gadge*[1] (Piasere 2015:11). Thus, Romani marital practices, those of Cortorari included, have a series of specificities that scandalize the Western liberal mind: they are concluded between cousins of different degrees, arranged by parents as opposed to the widespread practice of marriage by free choice, occur at early ages, and require marriage payments and that brides be virgins (see Gay y Blasco 1999; Gropper 1975; Sutherland 1975; Okely 1983; Hașdeu 2007). In the absence of written contracts that establish marriages, the wedding and betrothal rituals are the only instances that acknowledge unions.

As for other Roma, for Cortorari too marriage-making is key to both the fulfillment of personal ethical projects and the enabling of a notion of themselves as a collective. Illustratively, Romani-speaking populations, including Cortorari, identify themselves as *ame, al Roma*[2] (we, the Roms) (see Gropper 1975; Olivera 2012; Tesăr 2013), namely a collection of married people (Hașdeu 2007). *Al Roma* is the plural of the noun *rom* that designates a man married to a woman (*romni*)—at least for Cortorari, who produce offspring inside wedlock (Tesăr 2012).

Yet, seemingly paradoxically, among Cortorari the achievement of marriage is fraught with difficulties. Beginning with their ceremonial manifestations that are organized almost impromptu and are prone to halt at any time of their deployment and carried through the cohabitation of spouses, marriages are tenuous ventures. Marital ties are fragile and unstable, subject to individuals' spontaneous emotions and affects, their economic potentialities and political abilities, and, above all, their bodies' procreative capacities. Despite their centrality to the social life of Cortorari, marriages are constantly under threat of dissolution; and it is only the birth of a son that makes them endure.

To offset the tendency toward dissolution, Cortorari place at the core of their marriages ancient chalices (*taxtaja*[3]), putative objects inherited from their forebears. Male heirlooms that are passed from father to the youngest son when the latter begets a son of his own, chalices are circulated in marriages as a way to secure unions, as I endeavor to show.

Based on the data that I collected among Cortorari in villages in Transylvania during the eighteen months of fieldwork for my PhD in anthropology (from 2008 to 2010 and during subsequent visits), this chapter gives an ethnographic account of Cortorar marriages and their ceremonial celebrations, teasing out the coexistence of the centrality of marriage with its tenuous nature.

Introducing Cortorari

The Cortorari are a conspicuously "traditional" Romani population residing in several villages scattered across Transylvania in central Romania. Before 1944, the advent of communism in Romania, they led an itinerant lifestyle, of which only the denomination of "Cortorari," literally tent-dwellers, given by the Romanian population in whose midst they live, remains. Cortorari come to preeminence by means of their attire: women wear colorful ankle-length, pleated, flowery skirts and red scarves on their heads to signal their marital status, while men sport velour black hats (Fig. 5.1). They are a kin-based, non-hierarchical population of autonomous individuals who display great gender sensitivity and have always lived outside waged labor relations (see Tesăr 2015; cf. Tauber 2008). At present they derive their livelihood from a combination of economic activities, such as agriculture, manufacturing of and commerce with copper artifacts, and begging in countries of western and northern Europe (see Tesăr 2015).

Seemingly contrary to other Romani people who are uninterested in the material world around them and whose attitudes toward time are informed by a presentist orientation (Gay y Blasco 1999; Stewart 1997; Kaprow 1982; Day et al. 1999), Cortorari convey a strong commitment to the possession of specific material items, chalices (*taxtaja*), and relatedly, a strong interest in their past. Cortorari believe themselves to be all descendants of a common generative source, and they intermarry. They express relatedness through the local category of *neamo*,[4] aggregates of people both dead and alive, connected in multiple ways, through kinship and marriage, characterized by unboundedness. Webs of relatedness overlap across different *neamo* groups in such a way that a person can claim belonging in more than one at the same time. *Neamo* is a marker of

FIG. 5.1. A Cortorar couple dancing in the village street on Easter.

(Photo by Cătălina Tesăr, 2008.)

concurrently shared identity and difference, and one's acknowledgment of belonging to one *neamo* or another is a matter of negotiable and shifting individual claims.

A *neamo* is either good (*lašo*) or bad (*žungalo*), according to the fame and honor of the people associated with it. Those belonging to a good *neamo* are rich (*barvale*), while those belonging to a bad or weak *neamo* are *čora*, poor or fortuneless. As a matter of fact, the economic status of a person is not important in acknowledging their belonging to a *neamo*. Rather, one's breadth and depth of relatedness, that is, knowledge about the ancestors and people related to them, is tantamount to affluence. More often than not, *neamo* extraction is qualified in relation to possession of chalices.

Cortorari consider chalices to be their wealth (Rou. *avere*) and in their talk contrast them with other kinds of affluence, such as houses or money. Although they have been keen on raising villa-type houses as of late, Cortorari believe nonetheless wealth in houses to be of a transient nature, given that buildings are subject to the vagaries of the weather. Contrariwise, chalices last in time. They are concealed from sight and kept in the custody of ethnic Romanian neighbors. Chalices are limited in number and distributed among a handful of families, on whom they bestow aristocratic qualities. In people's talk, chalices appear ranked, yet they are idiosyncratically valued: age, volume, material, or decorations are variables that contextually weigh in the evaluation of a chalice. As a matter of fact, the value of chalices resides in the stories told about them by their possessors and the power of the stories to circulate and reach far in space and time.

Marriages, Gender, and the Social Order

The arrangement of marriages is the most salient preoccupation of Cortorari, given much emphasis both in everyday politicking and in ritual elaborations, and even suffusing children's games and their socialization. Marriages are not merely yes or no propositions or agreements between two partners: arranged by parents and grandparents, they are constituted by a series of economic exchanges and political arrangements between the extended families of the couple and sexual obligations inside the couple. Moreover, marriages are not events. They are processes that start with the removal of the bride from her parental household and her relocation to the house of the groom's parents (proceedings that are symbolically elaborated in the wedding ritual), are carried through cohabitation and the production of children, and are completed with the replacement of generations within the house (Tesăr 2018).

Cortorari do not have a word for marriage: they give (*den*) and take (*len*) daughters, and in so doing, the two parties *penden pes* (tie up, unite, make a commitment). Marital alliances entail the formation of *xanamika* (co-parents-in-law) relationships—or what the parents of one of the two partners are for the parents of the other. As suggested by the above wording that marks the initiation of the marriage process, residence is patrilocal among Cortorari. The bride goes to live with her spouse's parents—she arrives there as a stranger (Rou. *străină*)—and needs to learn the habits of the household in which she will gradually be incorporated, a pursuit that is approximated by the language of kinship. The bride is expected to address her mother- and father-in-law as "mother" and "father," respectively. Moreover, as we shall see later, the lyrics of the bride's song that is part of the central ceremonial sequence of the wedding ritual persuade her to assimilate new affinal relations, to kinship.

To intimate that daughters marry away at early ages, Cortorari have a saying: "The girls are not ours, they belong to strangers" (*al cheja n-ai amarendar, von san avrendar*). Conversely, boys stay with their parents, look after them in old age, and arrange and sponsor their funerals. Yet a girl, once she becomes a maiden (*chej bari*), meaning that she has had her first menses and is still a virgin, is expected to be severed from her parental home. The transition from childhood to marriageable age at the outset of puberty is signaled by the clothing of the girl who will forsake wearing pants forever and dress in long, colorful pleated skirts. She will nonetheless still differentiate herself from the fold of married women by her head that has yet to be covered with a scarf (Fig. 5.2).

The process of incorporation of a daughter-in-law (*bori*) in her marital house is lengthy and uneasy, and for several years she lives in-between her parents and in-laws. On the one hand, she maintains strong connections with her parental family, who may even provide for her daily expenses, look after her if she falls ill, and offer solace when she is mistreated by her parents-in-law. On the other hand, in her marital abode she is expected to do the bulk of the domestic chores and be subservient to her mother-in-law,

FIG. 5.2. A marriageable Cortorar girl wearing her best dress and a little Cortorar girl wearing trousers.

(Photo by Cătălina Tesăr, 2009.)

while being excluded from commensality. Inclusion and exclusion from commensality publicize the closeness of the bonds of relatedness. As in almost all societies, eating and drinking together removes social distance and contributes to the creation of sameness (Bloch 2005). Of all the people living in a house, usually three generations with accretions, the daughter-in-law (*bori*) alone does not participate in commensality: she prepares the meals and serves them yet is not supposed to sit at the same table with her parents-in-law or other kin who might happen to join them for the meal. Only when her son gets married and brings his own bride into the parental house does a daughter-in-law join her spouse's parents at the table. Her participation in commensality symbolically communicates her incorporation into her marital family.

Women marry with dowry (Rou. *zestre*), marriage payment tendered by their parents to the groom's parents, which consists in both cash and a trousseau. Because daughters are born with the prospect for their parents to pay big cash dowries to marry them off, they are not desired as offspring. Reminiscent of the meanings attached to marriage payment in agricultural societies, for Cortorari, dowry is an expression of parental care for daughters because—their way of reasoning runs—it is meant to alleviate the misery of a bride in her marital household. Additionally, the amount of the cash dowry that a bride receives gives the measure of her father's and grandfather's honor in the eyes of the community (cf. Goody 1990:442).

Underpinning the processual incorporation of the bride in her marital household, dowry is tendered gradually. The cash dowry is paid in installments, the first usually requested by the wife-takers once a girl is born to their bride. In contradistinction with agricultural societies where cash dowry is used as an endowment of the bride, here the cash dowry is withheld from the sphere of everyday consumption and is circulated to pay dowries for daughters in the next generation or for the sisters of the groom, if any, and even debts incurred by the wife-takers in the community. Irrespective of the terms of the initial agreement, once the process of the alliance is underway, new claims are laid for dowries, or old claims might be written off, depending on the families' economic dispositions at one time or another. Recently, Cortorari have started to brandish lump sums of money as big as 50,000 euros[5] as dowries at weddings. Yet this money does not belong to one single family. On the contrary, it circulates as dowry, compensation money, bails, etc. among a pool of related families. Smaller amounts of money, 5,000–10,000 euros, might be saved by a family and circulated as dowry.

Besides cash, dowry also consists in a trousseau. Mothers of daughters, and to a lesser degree their fathers, save money to invest in items of clothing and bedding, carpets, and curtains that they store in a wardrobe in the best room,[6] with a view to passing them on to their daughters. These new items add up to those that the women inherited from their own mothers. When a girl is married off and leaves her parental house, she is endowed with one set of bedding, several textile objects to decorate the conjugal room, and probably an extra outfit. The rest of the trousseau is kept in her parents' house until her marriage is secured by the birth of a son (Fig. 5.3). Until then, if she needs to change her everyday clothes, she goes to her parents' to do so—and likewise if she needs her best attire for a special occasion.

The process of marriage may be halted at any time. From its inception until its accomplishment, a marriage is always under threat of dissolution for different reasons. If a bride fails to acclimate to the habits and demands of her marital household, her parents may take her back home and arrange a new marriage for her. Misunderstandings between the spouses' parents triggered by economic cooperation or disagreements over the size and content of the marriage payment may also lead to the dissolution of a marriage. Yet the most recurrent reason for a marriage to break off is postponement of offspring conception, which may be caused by different contingencies that relate or not to the procreative capacities of the spouses' bodies. It is only the birth of a son to the new couple that secures a marriage and guarantees its successful completion.

Cortorari conclude two kinds of alliances: Rou. *tocmeala pe schimbate* (marriage through exchange [of daughters], namely a reciprocal exchange of brides between two families with a similar composition, i.e. with a son and a daughter) and Rou. *tocmeala în particular* (discrete or side marriage). The latter evinces a one-way flow of the bride and of the marriage payment.

Parents of daughters are particularly willing to contract a marriage exchange for several reasons. First, such an alliance should ideally entail the writing off of the cash

FIG. 5.3. Part of a girl's trousseau.
(Still from documentary *The Chalice: Of Sons and Daughters* [2022] by Cătălina Tesăr and Dana Bunescu.)

dowry. Second, it should place the two parties involved in the exchange on equal footing and, third, ensure an equally good treatment for the two brides in their respective marital households. Moreover, the dissolution of one of the unions should trigger the dissolution of the other, at least so Cortorari say. It could easily be inferred that the idiom of reciprocity underpins this kind of exchange. Writing about the Parisian Roms' preference for marriage exchanges, Williams (1984) contends that reciprocity intimated their ethos of egalitarianism. In a Cortorar marriage that is not concluded by exchange of women, wife-givers find themselves in an inferior position vis-à-vis wife-takers, given the greater symbolic value placed on boys compared to girls. Therefore, the marriage exchange should counterbalance the general tendency of marriages to introduce hierarchical elements in an otherwise egalitarian society (see Olivera 2020).

Yet only seldom is the ideal of reciprocity enacted in everyday social life. I recall here the negotiation of the cash dowry in a marriage exchange. One of the parties persuaded the other to pay dowry on grounds that not only were the latter of lower birth extraction (*neamo*) but they also possessed a less valuable chalice. Later on, I witnessed how the two brides were treated in their respective marital households. Rather than enable the enactment of equally good treatment expectations for the two brides, the reciprocity embedded in the exchange took the form of retaliation. Should one of the two brides suffer ill treatment, her parents revenged her by mistreating their daughter-in-law. Furthermore, the bride married with dowry strove for several years to bring forth a son. All this time her parents-in-law threatened to release her from the marital union should she not conceive an heir. Her own parents retorted that they would forsake their own daughter-in-law, though the prospect was very unlikely given that she had already given birth to a son. The chances for the two parties being on equal footing in the event that one of the wedlock would dissolve were thus null.

Chalices in Marital Arrangements

If asked, Cortorari locate their strong desire for chalices and obduracy not to part with them in the heirloom qualities of these items. Cups made of gilded silver, footed or not, the chalices were manufactured by the Transylvanian craft guilds during the Middle Ages (Fig. 5.4). They were initially in the possession of the privileged classes, the Saxon and Hungarian Transylvanian nobility.[7] Though Cortorari purchased the chalices found in their possession either from the *Gadge* or from the Gabor Roma only several generations ago, when asked, most do not remember the precise date of the acquisition, locating the origin of these precious objects "at the beginning of the world."

Chalices are normally passed on from father to the youngest son when the latter begets a son. If he has brothers, they expect to be compensated with shares (Rou. *parte*) in money from the inheritance. The chalice does not actually change hands as it is permanently kept tucked away in the houses and granaries of Romanian peasants. Therefore, the lexicon of possessorship of the chalice abounds in sensory expressions: one is entitled to see one's chalice, touch it, or hold it in one's hand. Moreover, one is entitled to bring out and display one's chalice, and this happens on life-cycle occasions, such as marriages or funerals. It is generally the oldest man among the living possessors of a chalice who is entitled to do so, that is, the grandfather who has the final say in the orchestration and distribution of rights in a chalice.

Although circulated vertically as heirlooms, chalices are of chief importance to marriages. First, because they are an endowment of the groom, they are much sought after by the parents of future brides. Thus, families with chalices stand more chances to find a bride on the marital market than families without chalices. Second, the size of the cash dowry tendered by the bride's family to the groom's is negotiated in relation to the value attributed to the groom's chalice. Last but not least, in marital arrangements the groom's chalice is entrusted to the bride's family until the new couple brings forth a son; and, as such, it contributes to the endurance of marriage.

We have seen that dissolution is the one thing that constantly looms over a marriage. The bride's side is normally in an inferior position in respect to the groom's, and the potential breaking off of a marriage would bring more harm to the former than to the latter. Were a bride released from marriage after losing her virginity, she would

FIG. 5.4. An old Cortorar man shows a picture of a renowned chalice.

(Photo by Cătălina Tesăr, 2013.)

theoretically be less likely to remarry successfully unless her parents would be willing to pay a bigger dowry. To prevent any of these misfortunes from happening, the wife-givers usually ask to get hold of the groom's chalice as guarantee for the endurance of their daughter's marriage. The chalice is pledged (Rou. *lăsat zălog*) for the daughter-in law. "I gave a chalice and took a daughter-in-law" (*dom taxtaj thaj lom bori*), as the wife-takers gloss the transaction. On such occasions, the chalice is retrieved from its guardians and placed with Romanian hosts chosen by the wife-givers. As temporary possessors, the wife-givers cannot use it to arrange marriages, and they cannot display it as they please. Conversely, divested of their chalice, often not even being allowed to see it, the groom's side is not able to arrange new marriages; their actions and agency are suspended. Temporary possession of a chalice ends with the birth of a son to the new couple as the ultimate guarantee of the matrimonial bond against any threats of dissolution and the promise of a new generational cycle. Should the alliances concluded through the pledging of a chalice dissolve before the new couple brings forth a son, the groom's family redeems their chalice in exchange for a sum of money which might be provided by new wife-givers.

It thus becomes obvious that much as Cortorari praise chalices for their heirloom qualities and for endorsing a patriarchal bias of their kinship, the value of these objects resides in their potential not only to make a marriage possible but also to make it endure. It was only toward the end of fieldwork dedicated among other things to thoroughly tracing the circulation of chalices that a Cortorar man in his twenties told me, "You know, Cătălina, what a chalice is good for? It brings [its possessor] a daughter-in law [*anel bori*] and binds the co-parents-in-law [*pandel al xanamikuri*]"—and this is no small feat, given the centrality of marriage and its tenuous nature among Cortorari.

Marital alliances are publicized through two different types of ritual statements: *tocmeala* (negotiations, contract, and the celebration of these) and *abiav* (wedding), prefaced by the agreement (Rou. *înțelegerea*). *Tocmeala* and *abiav* are similar in their ceremonial expressions, being celebrations with live music, dancing, and prodigious feasts attended by almost the entire community. Sometimes collapsed into only one ceremony, *tocmeala* and *abiav* are differentiated by the participation of the spouses in the latter and their absence from the former.

Marriage Arrangement Rituals

The Agreement: Înțelegerea

Often, the discussions that lead to negotiations for marital unions start at the inebriated end of a life-cycle event such as a wedding, funeral, or baptism. While drunk, men who have marriageable children or (great-) grandchildren leverage their energy and gestures toward the unions of their offspring. Other instances when marital negotiations are likely to be initiated are the horse fairs organized locally or the monastery processions on the Assumption of Mary, August 15.[8] These are all opportunities for people who live in different villages or even in the same one but ordinarily mind their own business or who might have been on the move abroad for economic reasons to meet up. On these occasions, men commence talk, either loud and racing or, on the contrary, low and slow-paced, about possible unions, while women assemble behind clusters of men, parading their daughters, who sport their best attire, to be seen and "chosen" by potential in-laws. This occurs at such major Orthodox holidays as Easter, Christmas, and the Assumption of Mary, when money brought from abroad is plentiful and adds up to the money earned at the local animal fairs, feeding commensality and, more broadly, sociality and buoyancy. On other occasions, a family in search of a daughter- or son-in-law might just pay a visit to potential in-laws living in the same or a more distant village (cf. Olivera 2012:254ff.; Olivera 2020:29ff.).

Once discussion about a possible match sparks either in secrecy (by means of furtive visits) or within earshot of others, the two parties dare to communicate their intentions by means of public rituals, what is known as *înțelegerea* (the agreement). The family of the groom usually sends a messenger(s) to the family of the bride to make sure that their demand for her will not be turned down publicly, which would be debasing. If the messengers bring back positive signals, then the groom's extended family, accompanied by people who will give their support in the negotiations, pays a visit to the family of the bride to ask for a daughter-in-law (*mangel bori*), establish the terms of the exchange, and seal the agreement. This can take place either in the confines of the groom's house or courtyard or outside his family's courtyard, along the roadside ditch. Irrespective of the private or public character of the premises of a particular *înțelegere*, people other than the two extended families, neighbors, and close kin alike, participate in it; and the terms of the agreement reach beyond the walls or fence surrounding a house. Actually, both parties are willing to gather external witnesses to their agreement who will be called upon in the event that arguments arise between them later on (Fig. 5.5).

The two parties now stage the terms of their agreement, and they do so as if there has been no prior negotiation, through impressive gesturing and loud speech, with the audience cheering them on. The terms for the marital union are now negotiated, such as the amount of the cash dowry and the conditions under which it should be tendered, as well as the timing of the bride's relocation from her parental household into the groom's. Public negotiations can last for hours, lead to fights, and be followed by reconciliations; and successful agreement depends upon both the determination of the two parties and the support or, on the contrary, malicious involvement from the

FIG. 5.5. An agreement preceding *tocmeala* unfolding in front of the bride's parents' house.
(Photo by Cătălina Tesăr, 2013.)

audience. The agreement is sealed by the spouses' fathers and paternal grandfathers shaking hands, while alcohol flows freely. The Cortorari involved put on quite a performance in the negotiations: the assembly drifts from one place to another, it disperses only to come together again, voices are raised, bodies are gesturing. There are many hypothetical and conditional scenarios left open to amendments in the future. I recall one negotiation when the family of the groom was fairly reluctant to discuss and establish the amount of the cash dowry on grounds that should one of the two sisters of the groom have a daughter (though one sister was not even married while the other was struggling to conceive), they would marry her off to the bride's brother (who was about one year old at the time of the negotiations). Needless to say, the age gap between the future spouses was so big that chances for the union to materialize in the future were slight. While the boy was thirteen years old, the girl was only a toddler, in her mother's arms during the negotiations. Not only are the terms agreed on for the conclusion of the union generally left open-ended, but in the likelihood that the marriage process starts, they are renegotiated and reinterpreted countless times. They might provide grounds for dismantling the union or only reflect tensions characterizing it.

The negotiations glossed as *înțelegerea* ideally lead straightaway to the organization of the ceremony of *tocmeala*. Yet I witnessed instances when the agreement fell apart immediately after its sealing by means of shaking hands. The reasons for breaking *înțelegerea* are numerous and diverse. For example, the unavailability of the musicians might trigger the postponement of the feast, which might be later canceled altogether on grounds that the two parties changed their minds. Alternatively, when sobering up in the morning, the men agree with their spouses that they did not choose the best in-laws, counting here either birth extraction or everyday bearing. Or yet again, a more common scenario is that a third party interferes offering a bigger cash dowry.

The Contract: Tocmeala

Tocmeala designates the negotiation, the spoken contract between the parties, and the ceremony that celebrates it. It intimates the creation of the *xanamika* (what the two pairs of parents-in-law are in relation to each other), who from now on will cooperate in economic activities, participate in commensality, and lend each other a hand when in need. There is a yearning among Cortorari for organizing *tocmeala* for young children, allegedly motivated by the (grand-)parents' wish to secure a future marriage for their (grand-)children. When challenged, Cortorari acknowledge nonetheless that it is unlikely for *tocmeala* arranged for children with an age gap of seven years or more to be seen through to completion (i.e. to produce two actual spouses). Rather than marital promises (and we will see that the promised spouses do not feature as main actors in the celebrations), *tocmeala* is a political affair meant to create loyalties and bonds between the two parties, social capital that is needed in a kinship-based economy. These bonds are as variable and versatile as politics is, meaning that allegiances change in accordance with circumstances. Cortorari conclude and break off *tocmeala* almost on a whim, and in so doing, they continuously create opportunities to manifest as *roma* (i.e., people with a proclivity for dance, pork, alcohol, speech, and bargaining and, above all, people who constitute themselves through marital bonds). In the majority of cases, *tocmeala* does not result in an actual union, and the spouses-to-be have usually several of them arranged and broken off before any of them actually engages in the process of marriage.

Tocmeala as a ceremony might take place either at the house of the promised bride's parents, where her hand was asked for, or at the house of the promised groom's parents, depending on the financial standing of the two. It usually lasts for twenty-four hours and is followed by a feast at the house of the other party that only the organizers' close kin attend. At the time of my fieldwork, the costs of such a ceremony reached an average of about ten thousand euros, either split between the two parties or contributed to by only one of them, depending on their financial situations and the terms of the agreement. Should the agreement be broken off later on (*pitardol pes*), the costs of *tocmeala* would be either split between the two parties, if the dissolution was agreed to by both, or borne entirely by the party who initiated the dissolution of the betrothal.

In contradistinction to the populations in whose midst they live, who plan in advance and prepare for the public enactment of marriage in weddings and betrothals, Cortorari, as well as other Romani-speaking populations (cf. Williams 1984:205), make no preparations for the celebration of *tocmeala*. This is only one instantiation of the ethos of living in the present, with no thought for the future, specific to Romani people (Day et al. 1999; Stewart 1997). Once two Cortorar families reach an agreement, they hasten to throw the party. They hustle and bustle to fetch the alcohol and slaughter a pig for the feast. Today, when some of the young Cortorari have drivers' licenses, they drive the male representatives of the two parties accompanied by a few close male kin to a discount retailer in the nearby town. At the time of my fieldwork, they would have called several taxis to pick them up, drive them to town, wait for them to do the shopping, and bring them back to the village. Depending on the time of day and the working hours of the shops in town, the alcohol can be bought in a petrol station open 24 hours. No matter how expensive the drink might be in a petrol station, Cortorari do not postpone the shopping and consequently *tocmeala* for the next day, fearing that a postponement might put their agreement at risk to fall apart. The several men invited by *xanamika* to assist with the shopping and acknowledge the quality and quantity of items bought are offered gifts of the most expensive drinks in the shop, such as whiskey or other types of liquor. During the trip to town, the men also call on the musicians who will perform at the party.[9] *Tocmeala* is a party with live music and dancing, where huge quantities of alcohol and meat are consumed. A long table is cobbled together in the middle of the courtyard, on the porch, or even inside if the weather is bad and is heaped with crates of beer and bottles of wine and brandy. A pig (or two) is slaughtered, barbequed, and served with bread. Because of the high value Cortorari attach to meat, and especially pork, they avoid serving vegetables or cooked dishes at their feasts.

The Ritual Oath: Colax

In order to reinforce the terms of the agreement, as well as the commitment to the endurance of *tocmeala* and hence to the completion of the union, the two parties might resolve to take the ritual oath (*colax*) (see also Sutherland 1975; Fosztó, 2008)—a practice that is also enacted on other occasions when mistrust permeates relationships. The ritual might be performed either during the celebration of *tocmeala* or at a later time when one of the parties might suspect the other of hidden intentions to break off the agreement. To ask one party to take the ritual oath (*mangel colax*) is a sign of circumspection. The party demanding the oath might take it as well to underscore their willingness to safeguard the contract. One or more members of the extended families involved in negotiations might take the oath, and when they do so, they do it as members of a wide kin group that will potentially bear the consequences in case of oath-breaching or perjury. The ritual is performed at symbolic places dense with meaning. It is held at a crossroads since for Christians the cross is replete with meanings suggestive of the atonement of Jesus and more broadly of death; at the village limit, as a reminder of the stalemate reached by the parties; or near a well, which might be seen as a source of life as well as death (such as accidental drownings). On rare occasions, the two parties involved in *tocmeala* take the ritual oath in church, before a priest; this kind of oath-taking is deemed the most sacred and, in case of perjury, would be followed by the worst consequences such as supernatural punishment. Public oath-taking is the most common among Cortorari, and it entails communal emotional arousal. Its performance necessitates stage props such as one or two two-foot-high lit candles, salt and bread, and the presence of outside witnesses, the Gabor Roma who specialize in oath-giving (*del colax*). Virtually the entire community attends such public oath-taking ceremonies, with the people standing in a wide, open circle in order not to be touched by the power of the *colax*. As such, public oath-taking communicates the strengthening, through conjuring a metaphysical force, of the bond between the two parties: wife-takers and wife-givers.

The following is an excerpt of an oath taken by the wife-givers at a *tocmeală* that I witnessed (in 2010). The lines in italics were uttered by the Gabor Rom and reproduced by the bride's parents:

> *O Del te marel tume*
> O Del te marel ame
> *P-al droma*
> P-amare droma
> *P-al cărări*
> P-amara cărări
> *O bibaxt te marel tume*
> O bibaxt te marel ame
> *Te n-aven tume pacea*
> Te n-aven ame pacea
> *Te roven tume*

Te roven ame
Te târân tume
Te târân ame
Pa-l droma kaj jas tume
P-al droma kaj jan ame
Te schimonosin tumara muja
Te schimonosin amare muja
O Beng k-al dešuduj a răt
O beng k-al dešuduj a răt
Te sucil tumare šera
Te sucil amara šera
Tumara thaj tumara chave
Tumara thaj tumara chave
Daka ci jas p-o čačimos
Daka ci jan p-o čačimos
Te das tumare chej
Te dan bori
Pe jekh, p-o duj
Pe jeck, p-o duj
P-o trin vanghelii
P-o trin vanghelii
P-o štar
P-o štar
P-al enja
P-al enja
P-al enja šela thaj enja vardeš thaj enja
P-al enja šela thaj enja vardeš thaj enja
Al vanghelii sa te meren tume
Al vanghelii sa te maren ame
Daka pîtras o colax
Daka pîtran o colax

Let God smite you
Let God smite us
On your roads
On our roads
On your paths
On our paths
May ill luck pursue you
May ill luck pursue us
May you have no peace
May we have no peace
May you weep
May we weep
May you crawl
May we crawl
Down the road you will travel

Down the road we will travel
May your faces be disfigured
May our faces be disfigured
May the Devil at midnight
May the Devil at midnight
Twist your heads
Twist our heads
Both yours and your children's
Both ours and our children's
If you do not tell the truth
If we do not tell the truth
That you will give your daughter as a daughter-in-law
That we will give our daughter as a daughter-in-law
By one, by two
By one, by two
By three gospels
By three gospels
By four gospels
By four gospels
By nine
By nine
By nine hundred and ninety-nine
By nine hundred and ninety-nine
May all the gospels smite you
May all the gospels smite us
If you break your oath
If we break our oath

When the new couple reaches marriageable age, a wedding (*abiav*) is organized that takes place at both the bride's and the groom's parents' houses. A wedding might be planned in advance, following *tocmeala*, or might stand alone (not as a sequel of *tocmeala*), and in this case might be thrown impromptu. In contradistinction to *tocmeala* where the spouses-to-be play no role in the ceremony, the wedding features the groom and the bride as the main actors in the ritual elaboration. The wedding ceremony symbolically enacts the relocation of the bride from her parental family and her incorporation into the family of the groom.

The Wedding: Abiav

In their ceremonial elaboration, Cortorar weddings follow the main sequences of a traditional Romanian wedding (see Marian 1995; Kligman 1988). The major difference between the latter and the weddings of Cortorari and other Roma is that they lack both the civil and religious ceremonies. Even though the ritual manifestation varies in terms of performativity from wedding to wedding, I shall depict here the primary ceremonial sequences of an ideal typical wedding. Similar to what I described for *tocmeala* ceremonies, there are usually no preparations for a wedding prior to its unfolding.

A wedding starts at the groom's house with the adornment of the flag (Rou. *steag*), at any time of the day. The groom's mother accompanied by several close female relatives prepares the flag in the best room. They tie a handful of colorful scarves to the top of a wooden pole, together with a bunch of plastic flowers. Carrying the flag is the responsibility of a bachelor—and in several weddings that I witnessed he happened to be the groom's unmarried paternal cousin—who raises it during the most spectacular sequences of the ritual. Once the flag is adorned, the live music starts and a first dance is performed, with the flag bearer brandishing the flag. There will be several more dances and a feast, before the groom's cortege leaves for the bride's house. If the bride lives in the same village, the cortege proceeds along the main road, led by the flag bearer, the groom, the groom's family, and the musicians (Fig. 5.6). If the bride lives in a different village, the gathering gets into several cars—some of which are taxis—and drives to the bride's parental home. Depending on the financial standing of the bride's family and their willingness to cultivate their reputation by means of conspicuously offering drinks and food, the celebration might unfold at the family of the bride for the day and coming night.

Ideally at sunrise, and not later than midday, the central sequence of the wedding ritual unfolds: Rou. *gogitul miresei* (approximately the bride's farewell). The bride is at the center of this ceremonial sequence that dramatizes her leaving of the fold of (unmarried) girls and alienation from her parental home, as well as her changing status

FIG. 5.6. A wedding cortege led by the flag bearer leaving the groom's parental house.

(Photo by Eric Roset, 2007.)

from a girl (*chej*) to a married woman (*romni*). As the name of this ceremonial sequence suggests (Rou. *gogitul* < Rou. *a gogi* means both to take out of the shell, to peel and to languish, to lose vigor without any obvious symptoms, to long for something), it is filled with the sorrow, grief, and affliction that the bride experiences as she leaves her parental household. The ritual is held in the best room, where only women are allowed, together with the groom (who might be accompanied by one or two of his peers). The women gathered chant an assortment of verselets that enthuse about the spouses or their families. I reproduce here verselets shouted in Romanian, recorded in 2018:

> Soacră mică să trăiești,
> Fete mici ca să mai crești.
> Că i-ai dat pită cu sare
> Și-ai făcut-o fată mare
> Și-ai măritat-o la avere mare.

> Mother of the bride, may you live long
> To raise more little girls.
> You fed the bride on bread and salt
> And grew her into a maiden,
> And married her off to a wealthy family.

> Soacră mare și voioasă,
> Ți-ai luat noră frumoasă.
> Se duce la Timișoara
> Și-aduce banii cu poala.

> Mother of the groom, be merry;
> You've taken a beautiful bride.
> She travels to Timișoara[10]
> And she brings back good money.

> Mireasă frumoasă ești
> Parcă ești din București.
> Și mirele tot așa,
> Parcă-i din America

> What a beautiful bride you are,
> Like women in Bucharest.
> And the groom, [so handsome] as well,
> Like men in America.

The mother readies the bride. She starts by braiding her hair in two braids, then dresses her in her best attire, either items of clothing passed down from previous female generations or new garments, according to their taste. There is not a consensus regarding how a bride should be dressed, and women gathered for the event advise her mother while ransacking through the piles of skirts and blouses taken out of the wardrobe where the mother keeps and displays her trousseau. In recent years in villages with a smaller concentration of Cortorari, where the influence of Romanian ways of doing things is greater than in villages where Cortorari live in larger numbers, the white veil has been introduced as a garment of the bride. Irrespective of the fashion that dictates the bride's attire, it is compulsory that she wear a bright new white underskirt (*poghea*) usually made of cotton with lace (Fig. 5.7). This is the piece of clothing that should be stained with blood on the occasion of the couple's first sexual intercourse at the closing of the wedding, proving the girl's virginity. A layer of colorful skirts covers the underskirt.

Once dressed, the bride kneels on two big pillows and is surrounded by all women present. The eldest women hold a big round bread on which a pinch of salt is placed and a bottle of wine above the bride's head (Fig. 5.8). Bread, salt, and wine are symbols of fertility. All other women, who are lined up in rows behind them, participate in the ritual by holding on to the backs or arms of the eldest women. They all sing the "bride's song" (Rou. *cântecul miresei*) that depicts the easy, carefree life that a daughter leads in her parents' home in stark contrast with the cheerless, burdensome life that she

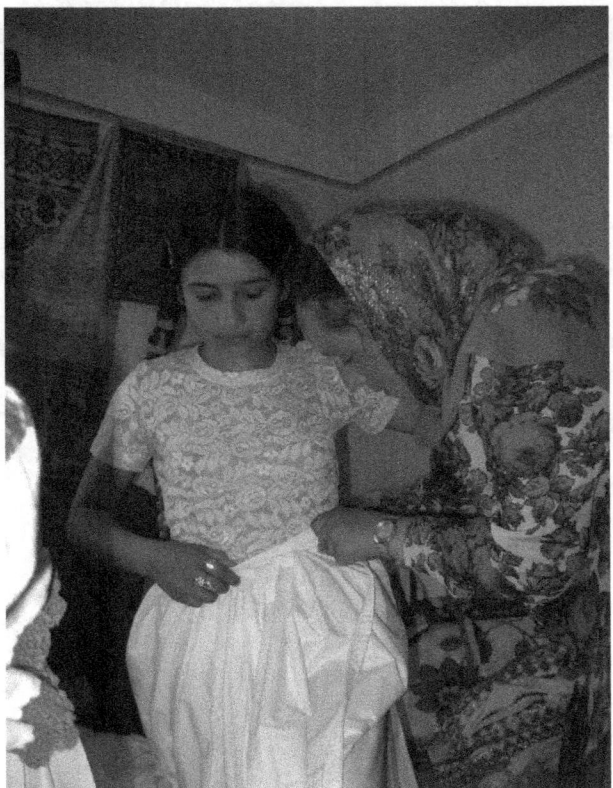

FIG. 5.7. A bride's mother readies her.

(Photo by Cătălina Tesăr, 2009.)

FIG. 5.8. A bride's farewell.

(Photo by Cătălina Tesăr, 2009.)

will experience in her parents-in-law's house. The song opens with the bride's bidding farewell to her parents and, combined with the symbols of fertility present, suggests the transfer of the bride's procreative capacities from her parental family to her husband's family. She is advised to assimilate her mother-in-law and her father-in-law to her mother and father, respectively. The bride is typically moved to tears by the lyrics, such as the following, chanted in Romanian, from 2005:

>Rozmarin în capul mesii,
>Rosemary at the head of the table,
>
>Cum plângea ochii miresii.
>Look at the bride's tears.
>
>Las să plângă cât de mult,
>Let her lament all she likes
>
>Binele care-a avut.
>The good that she had [before].

Las să plângă cât de tare,
Let her lament as loudly as she likes

Binele măcuței sale.
The good of her mama.

Ia-ți mireasă ziua bună
Bid, oh bride, farewell

De la tată,
To your father,

De la mumă.
To your mother,

De la frați, de la surori,
To your brothers, to your sisters,

De la grădina cu flori.
To your garden full of flowers.

Astăzi ești cu fetele,
Today you are with the maidens,

Mâine cu nevestele.
Tomorrow with the wives.

Ia-ți, mireasă, ziua bună
Bid, oh bride, farewell

De la fir de busuioc.
To the basil leaf.

Și când o vezi pe soacră-ta,
And when you see your mother-in-law,

Mireasă, mireasă,
Bride, bride,

Să gândești că-i mumă-ta,
Think of her as your mother,

Mireasă, mireasă.
Bride, bride.

> Şi când îl vezi pe socru-tău,
> And when you see your father-in-law,
>
> Mireasă, mireasă,
> Bride, bride,
>
> Să gândeşti că-i tată-tău,
> Think of him as your father,
>
> Mireasă, mireasă.
> Bride, bride!

On the closing stanza of the song, the eldest women take the bride by her arms and sit her down. Concomitantly, they tear up the bread and divide it among all those present: there is quite a fight over the pieces of bread, which are much longed for. The eldest women who participated in the ritual entreat the bride's mother and grandmother for money, as a compensation for their performance meant to initiate the bride into her marital life. They usually receive ten to twenty euros per person in local currency. Meanwhile the group gathered outside the door, comprising the men on the bride's side and the family of the groom, rushes into the room. The bride's father makes a speech and offers the hand of his daughter to his son-in-law. The groom's father pledges that his family will look after the bride and treat her like their own daughter. They resume the terms of their agreement, the value and the timing of the dowry payment, the entrusting of the chalice, if any, etc. The speech can be made outside the house and, as I witnessed recently, involve the use of a microphone, in front of a large assembly in the courtyard. The groom, who until now has been a silent witness to the entire ritual, is called to tie a scarf on the head of the bride—which signifies her and her family's consent to consummate the union. However, if the two families have consented to the couple's deferring sexual intercourse to an agreed time in the future, the groom drapes the scarf on the back of the bride—a sign that she is married yet will keep her virginity for a while. A dance follows, performed by the bride and groom, their close families, and the flag bearer, with other attendees slowly joining in. Next, food is served, and the bride, who was not allowed to eat anything until the ceremony that publicized her new status as a married woman was accomplished, eats now her first meal of the day. Her refraining from food prior to her engagement might be read both as fasting meant to enhance her premarital purity and as a symbolic dissociation from her parental family. As mentioned earlier, commensality is for Cortorari a sign of belonging or incorporation. The bride's having her first meal of the day publicly, in the company of the groom's kin, indexes thus her inclusion into her spouse's family.

After the feast the crowd slowly makes its way back to the groom's house. This time the bride and groom holding hands lead the cortege through the village, in the company of the flag bearer and their parents who hold bottles of alcohol in their hands. On its way, the suite encounters several obstacles: neighbors and kin hold ropes across the road, sometimes with a carpet hanging on them, which are meant to prevent the progression of the train toward the groom's parents' house. They also bring buckets of water to splash on the two families, protagonists of the wedding. These are all symbolic attempts at stalling the suite and thus the marriage altogether. The parents of the new couple offer gifts of money and alcohol to those who raise the obstacles, who will easily bargain the hindrances away (Fig. 5.9). The party will continue at the groom's house, only to fade away at dusk, when the musicians make their way home.

Recently, in areas where the influence of Romanian ways of doing things is greater, the wedding ritual has been condensed into only one day: the adornment of the flag early in the morning, followed by the procession to the bride's house where her farewell is performed, and lastly the suite's proceeding to a restaurant or the local culture house, where the party will unfold. Here, several courses are served: appetizers, soup, grilled meat, finishing with dessert. In-between courses, Cortorari frenetically dance to the live music.

The wedding comes to a close with the consummation of the union, which ideally takes place at night, after the attendees have left to their homes. Several women, close kin of the bride's and groom's mothers and grandmothers, accompany the new couple to their room. Exhilarated by the event, they advise the bride to be docile and the groom

FIG. 5.9. Obstacle raised to halt a wedding cortege advancing through the village.

(Photo by Cătălina Tesăr, 2009.)

FIG. 5.10. The bride's honor. A mother-in-law showing her bride's underskirt stained with blood.
(Photo by Cătălina Tesăr, 2009.)

to sip some red wine, which should help him get aroused. The groom's mother brings a wash basin for the couple to clean their feet. Early the next morning, she checks the bride's underskirt for stains of blood, the sign of the latter's lost virginity. If the union was consummated and the bride was a virgin, the mother-in-law comes out of the room brandishing this item of clothing among a fold of women including the bride's mother and offers them brandy. Called the "bride's honor" (Rou. *cinstea miresei*), the ritual is meant to publicize the qualities of the two families. The bride's virginity indexes the respectfulness of the groom's family for having received an honorable bride and the pride of her family for having raised an honorable daughter (Fig. 5.10).

Conclusions

The rituals that dramatize the marriage alliance, the contract (*tocmeala*), and the wedding (*abiav*) communicate an ideal social order that Cortorari endeavor to reproduce. First, the negotiations for an alliance and the words given in the agreement, as well as the energy and resources invested in the feast of *tocmeala*, all substantiate the desire of the two parties to conclude a marriage project. Then, the ritual sequences of the wedding that communicate the severance of the bride from her parental family and the transfer of her reproductive capacities from her family to the groom's provide the terms in which Cortorari understand and organize gender differences, economic exchanges, residence patterns, and the reproduction of generations.

Similar to other "traditional" Romani populations, for Cortorari, marriage is central not only to the fulfillment of personhood by means of effecting an internal ethical project but also to definitions of *roma* in respect to the others. *Ame al roma* (we, the Roms) are an aggregate of married people, and therefore the marital project is crucial for the collective self. Yet marriages are neither a yes or no proposition nor up to the couple. Conversely, marriages are the business of extended families who enter a contract replete with economic, political, and sexual obligations. Moreover, marriages are not merely events; they are processes that begin with the relocation of the bride from her parental home into the parental home of the groom, are carried through by cohabitation and the production of children, and are completed with the birth of a son to the new couple. Marriage alliances, which are subject to individual emotions and affects, involve several people, each of them pursuing their own project, both in the economic realm and in political life. Furthermore, because marital unions rely for their completion on the reproductive capacities of bodies, they are always threatened with dissolution. In other words, the unchanging scenarios that Cortorari imagine for the reproduction of each family and *neamo* are subject to changes and instability. To offset the tendency toward dissolution that characterizes marital unions, Cortorari place at the core of their alliances chalices, ancient objects inherited from their ancestors and passed on to future generations. When given as a pledge by the parents of the groom to the parents of the bride on the occasion of a marital contract, chalices should ensure the endurance of the alliance: they bind the *xanamika* (co-parents-in-law), Cortorari assert.

The nonchalance, invoked in the opening of this chapter, with which Cortorari performed their weddings during the 2020 COVID-19 pandemic when a ban on gatherings of more than eight people was enforced should now be easily understood in light of the importance attached to the process of marriage.

Notes

1. The denomination given by the Roma to non-Roma, the significant other in relation to whom the Roma define themselves.
2. Throughout this chapter I use native Romani words and expressions in italics. Where Romanian words are used by Cortorari for native notions, I flag their first occurrence with "Rou." (< Romanian). For the Romani language, I use the transcription system of the Romani Linguistics Project at the University of Manchester.
3. The Gabor Roma who are culturally akin to Cortorari hold dear chalices as well (Berta 2007, 2019; Olivera 2012). In contradistinction to Cortorari who reside in areas that had a significant population of Saxons in the past, the Gabor reside in areas with big Hungarian populations, whose language they speak.

4. Though it may convey different meanings, this category of relatedness (spelled *neam*) is also common among Romanian Transylvanian peasants (Kligman 1988:31). It occurs among Transylvanian Gabor Roma (Olivera 2012:191ff.) as well and bears similarities with the category of *vici/vitsa* found among Roma elsewhere (Williams 1984; Sutherland 1975; Gropper 1975).
5. Most Cortorar savings are in euros rather than the national currency (RON) both because they are derived from earnings outside the country, in western Europe (see Tesăr 2015), and because the euro is considered stronger than the national currency.
6. A room in any house that is not used on a daily basis, where fancy trinkets and trousseau dowries are displayed. Its doors are opened for ritual events such as funeral wakes and wedding rituals, as well as for special guests.
7. Medieval Transylvania was part of the Kingdom of Hungary. The Transylvanian feudal system comprised three "nations"—Hungarian nobility, Saxon patrician class, and the free military Székelys—and excluded commoners (peasants, irrespective of their ethnic origin).
8. Orthodox Roma consider St. Mary their guardian.
9. These are local Romani musicians who live in nearby small towns and cater to the Cortorari when called upon, with no prior booking. When they play at Romanian weddings, they are hired in advance.
10. City in western Romania.

Works Cited

Berta, Péter. 2007. "Ethnicisation of Value–the Value of Ethnicity: The Prestige-Item Economy as a Performance of Ethnic Identity among the Gabors of Transylvania (Rumania)." *Romani Studies*, 17/1:31–65.

Berta, Péter. 2019. *Materializing Difference: Consumer Culture, Politics, and Ethnicity among Romanian Roma*. Toronto: University of Toronto Press.

Bloch, Maurice. 2005. "Commensality and Poisoning." In *Essays on Cultural Transmission*, 45–61. Oxford: Berg Publishers.

Carsten, Janet, Hsiao-Chiao Chiu, Siobhan Magee, Eirini Papadaki, and Koreen M. Reece. 2021. "Introduction." In *Marriage in Past, Present and Future Tense*, eds. Janet Carsten, Hsiao-Chiao Chiu, Siobhan Magee, Eirini Papadaki, and Koreen M. Reece, 1–33. London: UCL Press.

Day, Sophie, Evthymios Papataxiarchēs, and Micheal Stewart, eds. 1999. *Lilies of the Field: Marginal People Who Live for the Moment*. Boulder, CO; Oxford: Westview Press.

Fosztó, László. 2008. "Taking the Oath: Religious Aspects of Moral Personhood among the Romungre." In *Roma/Zigeunerkulturen in neuen perspektiven/Roma/Gypsy Cultures in New Perspectives*, eds. Fabian Jacobs and Johannes Ries, 119–133. Leipzig: Veröffentlichungen des Instituts für Ethnologie der Universität Leipzig.

Gay y Blasco, Paloma. 1999. *Gypsies in Madrid: Sex, Gender and the Performance of Identity*. Oxford: Berg.

Goody, Jack. 1990. *The Oriental, the Ancient, and the Primitive: Systems of Marriage and the Family in the Pre-Industrial Societies of Eurasia*. Cambridge; New York: Cambridge University Press.

Gropper, Rena C. 1975. *Gypsies in the City: Culture Patterns and Survival*. Princeton, NJ: Darwin Press.

Hașdeu, Iulia. 2007. "Bori, R(r)omni et Faraoance. Genre et ethnicité chez les Roms dans trois villages de Roumanie." PhD dissertation, Université de Neuchâtel, Neuchâtel, Switzerland.

Kaprow, Miriam Lee. 1982. "Resisting Respectability: Gypsies in Saragossa." *Urban Anthropology*, 11/3–4:339–431.

Kligman, Gail. 1988. *The Wedding of the Dead: Ritual, Poetics, and Popular Culture in Transylvania*. Berkeley: University of California Press.

Marian, Simion Florea. 1995. *Nunta la români: Studiu istorico-etnografic comparativ*. Bucharest: Editura Grai și Suflet, Cultura Națională.

Okely, Judith. 1983. *The Traveller-Gypsies*. Cambridge and New York: Cambridge University Press.

Olivera, Martin. 2012. *La tradition de l'intégration. Une ethnologie des Roms Gabori dans les années 2000*. Paris: Edition Petra.

Olivera, Martin. 2020. "Entre idéologie nobiliaire, utopie égalitaire et circonstances singulières: Le 'bon mariage' chez les Roms Gabori." *Martor: The Museum of the Romanian Peasant Anthropology Journal*, 25:17–37.

Piasere, Leonardo. 2015. *Mariage Romanes. Une esquisse comparative*. Florence: Seid Editori.

Stewart, Michael. 1997. *The Time of the Gypsies*. Boulder, CO: Westview Press.

Sutherland, Anne. 1975. *Gypsies: The Hidden Americans*. New York: Free Press.

Tauber, Elisabeth. 2008. "Do You Remember the Time We Went Begging and Selling"—The Ethnography of Transformations in Female Economic Activities and Its Narrative in the Context of Memory and Respect among Sinti in North Italy." In *Roma/Zigeunerkulturen in neuen perspektiven/Roma/Gypsy Cultures in New Perspectives*, eds. Fabian Jacobs and Johannes Ries, 155–177. Leipzig: Veröffentlichungen des Instituts für Ethnologie der Universität Leipzig.

Tesăr, Cătălina. 2012. "Becoming Rom (Male), Becoming Romni (Female) among Romanian Cortorari Roma: On Body and Gender." *Romani Studies*, 22/2:13–40.

Tesăr, Cătălina. 2013. "'Women Married off to Chalices': Gender, Kinship and Wealth among Romanian Cortorari Gypsies." PhD dissertation, University College London, London.

Tesăr, Cătălina. 2015. "Begging: Between Charity and Profession. Reflections on Romanian Roma's Begging Activities in Italy." In *The Public Value of Anthropology: Engaging Critical Social Issues through Ethnography*, eds. Elisabeth Tauber and Dorothy Zinn, 83–111. Bolzano: Bolzano University Press.

Tesăr, Cătălina. 2018. "Mariages, richesse et générations chez les Roms Cortorari de Roumanie. Notes sur une parenté tournée vers l'avenir." *Ethnologie française*, no. 172:613–622.

Williams, Patrick. 1984. *Mariage tsigane: Une cérémonie de fiançailles chez les Roms de Paris*. Paris: L'Harmattan: SELAF.

Childbirth

CHAPTER 6

ESTONIAN RUNOSONGS ON CHILDCARE, PREGNANCY, BIRTH, AND INTIMACY

MARI VÄINA

SINGING is and has been a cultural practice that is common to the whole of humankind. In different cultures and different historical and societal conditions, it has acquired very diverse forms and functions. Most of the Finnic peoples,[1] including the Estonians, share a common archaic poetic-musical tradition, the runosong, which is considered to have evolved in the late Proto-Finnic language stage approximately two thousand years ago and spread further together with the Finnic languages (Korhonen 1994; Frog 2019).[2] The main common features of runosongs are (1) a trochaic syllabic meter with four stresses and specific rules on placement of short and long, stressed and unstressed syllables that vary slightly across the area (Sarv 2015, Sarv et al. 2021); (2) the use of highly regular, intertwined, but not compulsory alliteration and parallelism (single lines without any parallel lines and lines without alliteration also occur); (3) stichic diction with no rhymes or stanzas; (4) song texts that are not fixed (singers have the freedom to compose songs on the basis of known plots, motifs, and poetic formulae); (5) group singing in which the verses sung by the lead singer are often repeated by the choir (in solo singing repetition is not necessary); and (6) a runosong poetic form that extends outside of the singing tradition and may be occasionally used in ordinary speech or prose genres of folklore as well as in sayings, proverbs, and riddles. The details on the content, thematic foci, and poetic form of songs, performance style, and uses of singing vary across tradition regions and linguistic subregions.

The runosong tradition with its communal and expressive functions clearly originated in pre-modern society. By and large, it can be considered to have been used with the aim to support, and sometimes magically impact, the sustainability of communities and to transmit knowledge of selected aspects of the functioning of the world, sometimes along with respective rituals. The communal focus is strikingly explicit when comparing the content of the texts, for example, with the European ballad tradition and with newer layers of rhymed folk songs in Estonia, in which the thematic focus is more on individual feelings, experiences, and behavior (see Sarv 2009).

Especially in Estonia, but also in several other Finnic traditions, the dominant viewpoint of the runosong is lyric—most of the songs represent plots through the eyes of "me," be it in narrative mode (descriptions of what happened to "me") or in communicative mode (singing as live interaction with human or non-human participants, for example, during the wedding ritual or during healing when a healer uses charms in poetic form to talk to the cause of the illness). The most prominent characters in Estonian runosongs besides "me" and "you" are family members: mother, father, daughter, son, and in-laws—but also boy and girl. The content of the songs reflects various aspects of Estonian peasants' daily life and has accumulated their worldview, beliefs, experiences, and attitudes from various time periods within the poetic texts. The thematics of the songs cover family life, work, environment, and relations within village communities, especially among youth, but also attitudes toward the Germans, colonizers who formed the upper class in Estonia from the invasion under the aegis of the Crusades in the thirteenth century to the establishment of independence in 1918 (Merilai and Talviste 2019). The actions of the songs usually take place at home, in village landscapes, in the woods, or at the seashore. The mythological topics are often also set in familiar environments and happen either with "me" (or "me" as a witness) or "my" family members. For example, a song about creating the sun, moon, and stone can be set in "our backyard." Traditionally, the songs and singing have often been related to certain times or situations, the most important being weddings, work, and calendar events, for example, swinging in the springtime, when songs about the creation of the world, among others, were sung.

On the cusp of modern society and emerging nationhood in the second half of the nineteenth century, the regular use of runosongs in family and community life was gradually fading away due to the implications of modern, literary, and "cultured" society. Among the leaders of the Estonian national movement, attitudes toward runosongs were ambiguous. On the one hand, the image of a cultured nation was mainly adopted from the Baltic Germans.[3] Estonians of this time aimed to reach the cultural level of Germans in order to prove that they deserved the title of "nation." The singing of runosongs, which sounded "non-harmonious" as per the standards of Western culture, was seen as an uncultured form of expression that, according to the cultural patterns adopted from the Germans, should be abandoned as quickly as possible. Instead, the German style of singing was propagated to develop the culture suitable for a "proper nation." Runosongs were also resented due to their content and performance situations—singing related to mundane life and traditional (pagan) beliefs was derogated and frowned upon on educational grounds by clergymen (who were predominantly German). Moreover, uncontrollable singing at traditional feasts and in pubs (often along with drinking) was not associated with cultured behavior and was seen as a habit that Estonians should free themselves of as quickly as possible (Laugaste 1963:178). On the other hand, the knowledge and poetic expression stored in the songs were perceived as valuable sources which could be used to access the "pure nature" of the nation in a Herderian[4] sense and as a base on which to build a new national culture. The latter direction, however, did not aim to preserve the living tradition or to perpetuate the singing of the songs as they were. Folk songs were collected to be used in further artistic reworkings that would bring them to a higher, cultured level (Särg 2012). Under German rule, Estonians had had very limited access to higher education, and almost all of the early writings about their life and culture were made by foreigners and local Germans and depicted them from a distance, through the eyes of outsiders. Therefore, recordings of folklore, especially runosongs, were widely perceived as a more authentic access to the mindset of early Estonians. Both attitudes toward runosongs—rejecting and adopting them—have been present and persist in Estonian society up until today. During the last few decades new tendencies of reintroducing the singing of runosongs in community interactions have emerged and thrived (Särg and Oras 2021).

Estonian runosongs have been extensively recorded since the 1880s, first, as a nationwide crowdsourcing project inviting everyone to save the ancient knowledge initiated by pastor Jakob Hurt (1839–1907), followed shortly by a similar campaign by Mattias Johann Eisen (1857–1934), also a pastor and in 1920–1927 a professor of folkloristics at the University of Tartu. In 1904–1916 Oskar Kallas (1868–1946), the first Estonian doctor of folkloristics, organized a collecting campaign of folk melodies with the help of students at the conservatory of St. Petersburg with skills in musical notation. In the 1920s, students and folklorists from both the newly established Department of Folkloristics at Tartu University as well as the Estonian Folklore Archives stepped into action to save the remnants of the runosong tradition before it completely faded. All of the largest Estonian folklore collections (and thus most of the knowledge that we have on the Estonian runosong tradition) have been gathered into the Estonian Folklore Archives (established in 1927). It has been estimated that there are altogether 150,000 Estonian runosong texts recorded. In addition, there are notations of melodies, audio and video recordings, and some information on the use, performance, singers, etc., in the archives, all of which is today by and large accessible online. As a rule, the recordings are provided with metadata on singers and the exact locations of the recordings, but there are only a few or no comments on the uses of the songs: on what occasion and for what reason the songs were traditionally sung.

From Tradition to the Public Domain

In traditional societies with oral culture, poetic text often functions as a major way to store knowledge, experiences, and attitudes for the future. Compared to the functions of music and poetic text in modern or contemporary society, in traditional society important functions of songs and singing have also been securing community sustainability along with various customs and rituals as well as managing and easing uncontrollable situations with various acts of magic (see also Ong 1982). Runosongs were composed and performed to fulfill the needs of the communities and individuals who used the songs, but not all of the occasions of singing were meant for wider audiences.

Folklore collecting clearly reframed this body of knowledge, transferring the habits, actions, and performances into texts and bringing the songs from personal and community use into the public domain (cf. Anttonen 2005, 2012). The campaigns by Hurt and his successors invited Estonians to create a folklore collection explicitly for the sake of the emerging Estonian nation (Hurt [1888] 1963). With the establishment of a state-funded institution, the Estonian Folklore Archives, the collections officially became public property that should serve the public interest, "cultural heritage." The songs that once were part of the people's way of life were now detached from their original context, decontextualized (Briggs and Bauman 1999), and started to serve new kinds of aims and needs. Not all of the types of songs proved to be equally suitable for fulfilling the new tasks, such as those including topics considered inappropriate to expose in public or attitudes that clashed with modern morals and as such were not considered suitable to use for representing the nation's mindset.

Since the very start of large folklore collecting activities in the late nineteenth century, the organizers stated the need to document the tradition in all its directness, to preserve the "ugly" next to the "beautiful" (Kalkun and Sarv 2014). The moral and ideological attitudes of collectors and singers, however, had an impact on what kinds of songs were perceived as valuable, decent, and appropriate to share outside of one's closest community as well as which were worthy of building the "national treasury." The selections made in the course of the collecting process and in further disseminating the content of collections created a shifted, somewhat glorified, and purified picture of the whole tradition that left out expressions and references that were considered unsuitable or improper for various reasons.

To observe more closely the discrepancy between popular modes of expression and their uses as cultural heritage, we will examine three groups of Estonian runosongs that relate to topics that in modern society have been considered as belonging predominantly to the private spheres of life: (1) taking care of newborn babies, (2) pregnancy and childbirth, and (3) sexual matters. The content and main characteristics of the selected song groups will be introduced, their historical background outlined, and the attitudes affecting their reuse analyzed.

Although we can glimpse remotely the mindset of pre-modern Estonians through runosongs, we must always keep in mind that the songs that were performed were regularly reconfigured and adapted until the moment of recording, filtered by the singers and collectors before reaching the archives, and that, in the end, we view these texts through our own contemporary prisms. We have no sufficient objective data on what was considered private, unsuitable, or normal in pre-modern peasant society. Some information can be found in the writings of local Germans, occasional travelogues, and court records; but as mentioned previously, these were, as a rule, written by outsiders and reflect the situation from their perspective. The habits, beliefs, moral attitudes, social relations, and life conditions have gone through considerable changes with the transition to modernity and beyond.

Lullabies and Other Songs about Newborns

The runosongs related to taking care of infants are expressed predominantly through the eyes of their main caretakers, mothers, or other family members.

Lullabies

The lullabies focus mostly on the future of the child; the words call upon the infant to grow and gain weight and dream of the child-to-be helping out in the household.

> Sussu, sussu suuremaks,
> kasva, kasva kangemaks
> etel takukedrajaks
> ja tatal taarilaskijaks.
> Maka, kasva, kasva suureks,
> emal ernekiskujaks
> ja taadil aoraiujaks.
>
> E 70693 (3)

> Rock, rock bigger,[5]
> grow, grow, stronger,
> to be your mother's spinner,
> and the one to bring mead to your father.
> Sleep, grow, grow big,
> to be a pea weeder for your mother,
> and a hacker of branches for your father.

In the initial period of folklore collecting, when there were many other songs with more elaborate plots circulating among the people, folk song collectors did not turn much of their attention to the lullabies, probably because of their improvisational nature. Lullabies are not sung in public but are meant to soothe small children and put them to sleep. Traditionally, lullabies were performed solo; the text consisted of many repetitions and lulling words and was partly improvised on-site by the singer.

> Äiu, äiu, kussu, kussu!
> Tsuu, tsuu tsuuremasse,
> kasva, latse, karjatsesse,
> esä-emä pikutsesse.
> Tsuu, tsuu, tsuka jalga,
> kiigu, kiigu, kinnas kätte!
>
> ERA II 78, 387 (4)

> Rock, rock, shush, shush!
> Sleep, sleep, [grow] bigger,
> grow, child, to [be] a shepherd,
> as tall as your mother and father.
> Sleep, sleep, stockings on,
> rock, rock, mittens on!

In the second half of the twentieth century, however, when the runosong tradition had already degraded to remnants, lullabies were among the few types of songs that were still in use, evidently because of their practical function, and could still be audio- and video-recorded (Sarv 2013).

Despite their original intimate nature, informed by the interaction between a mother and her child(ren), lullabies have been widely used in reinterpretations by composers, musicians, etc., on public stages, on radio broadcasts, and at folk dance festivals. Motherhood and taking care of children have been universally perceived as constituting a positive and even heroic role, and thus, in general, lullabies have fit perfectly to represent national culture.

Among the lullabies, however, there are also songs that suggest that the child be gently rocked to death.

> Su'u lasta surma poole,
> kanna lasta kalme poole.
> Kiiluvad kirikuuksed,
> karjuvad kalmeväravad,
> ussi suuda ootelleb,
> mao suuda matsatelleb.
> Ootvad toorest toodanekse,
> värsket veetanekse.
>
> H II 20, 670 (42)

> Hush a baby toward death,
> bring the child toward its grave!
> Church doors are whining,
> the gates of a grave are shouting,

a worm is waiting for food,
a snake is munching with its mouth.
They are waiting for raw [meat] to be brought,
fresh [meat] to be dragged.

There has always been a certain perplexity among researchers as to why mothers would have sung their children to death. It has been suggested that this kind of song might have been sung by nannies who had already been overwhelmed by taking care of a moody child (Tedre et al. 1974:334) or by midwives to diagnose the condition of a newborn (Sarv 2013). In modern society death has become a topic avoided in public discussions and left to be handled by medical facilities and specialists with respective training (Foucault 1978). Accordingly, lullabies wishing for an infant's death have usually been considered too awkward for reuse; as the pastor and pastoral counselor Naatan Haamer (2019:101) has reflected, "Nowadays we try not to remember these lullabies." However, infant mortality was considerably higher in earlier times, and children's deaths needed to be processed by families. These songs might have functioned as a support to accept this reality.

The Burdens of Mothers

A specific type of runosong describes the burden of mothers' breastfeeding and taking care of their small and often ill infants.

> Millal maksan memme vaeva,
> ea ema piimavaeva,
> noore ema nutuvaeva?
> Ei lõppend tuli toasta,
> säde ei sängisamba'asta.
> Naine noor jäi riietesse,
> obu alli rakke'esse.
> Otsis lapse lausujada,
> Noore valu võttijada.
> Andis lamba lausujale,
> kitse keelepeksijale,
> tuhkru ruuna tuusijale.
> Mina aga kiusta kiljatasin,
> soota suuda maigutasin.

H II 46, 333/4 (33)

> When will I repay my mother's work,
> my good mother's suckling,
> my young mother's solacing?

> Light was never turned off in the chamber,
> sparkling at the bedpost.
> My young mother had always her clothes on,
> and a gray horse harness ready to go out.
> She was looking for someone who could cast healing spells,
> who could take away pain from the young one.
> She gave a sheep to the one who cast the spells,
> a goat to the one who used their tongue,
> a pale gelding to a witch.
> I still whimsically screamed,
> and just moved my mouth.

The songs stress the boldness and endurance of mothers and the debt of children to reward this hard work and are widely known, found in schoolbooks and used in numerous reinterpretations. The main verse of the song "Millal maksan memme vaeva" ("When Will I Repay My Mother's Work") is considered one of the most representative and beautiful expressions in Estonian (Liivamägi 2008).

Another well-known motif of infant care in runosongs tells of a mother taking her newborn child along to work outside and leaving the baby in the care of birds, which teach their singing skills to the future good singer.

> Ega ei olõ ma tummast suusta,
> kalõ naase kannõtusta!
> Minno kande naane kallis,
> imä illos imetelli,
> vei mu rüpün rüü mano,
> põllega vei põllu mano,
> tegi kiigu kesä pääle,
> paino palo nuka pääle,
> kutse partsi painutama,
> suvelindu liigutama.
> Säält sai latsi laululine,
> imätütar iloline,
> iloline, naläline.
> Kos ol' mäke, sääl ol' nalja,
> kos ol' luhta, sääl ol' lusti.
>
> EÜS IX 1511/2 (103)

> I am not from a dumb family,
> borne not by a careless woman.
> I was carried by a dear woman,
> a beautiful mother was breastfeeding me,
> in her lap she brought me to a rye field,

in her apron she carried me to the field,
she made a cradle for me at the hayland,
a swing at forest edge.
She invited a duck to rock me,
a summer bird to move me.
That's how the child learned to sing,
the mother's daughter became cheerful,
cheerful and joyful.
Where there was a hill [on their way], there was lots of joy,
where there was a meadow, there was lots of fun.

In the spirit of romanticism these songs have likewise been interpreted as positive and endearing childhood memories (rather than pictures of negligence and solitude) and have become popular subjects of reinterpretation by composers and musicians from the very early stages of Estonian classical music.

The Unwanted Child

Among the songs about newborns are some plots that deal with unwanted children. A well-known song type tells about the mother of "me," the singer who presents the song. Usually, the family or other community members express their expectation for a boy to be born.

> Emakene memmekene,
> tundsid mind ilma tuleva,
> tundsid sülle sündivada,
> isa oot obustepoissi,
> vennad tahtsid tallipoissi,
> sõsar ootis sõidupoissi.
>
> H, Kolga-Jaani 2, 192/3 (119)

> Mother, my mum,
> when you felt that I would come to the world,
> when you felt that I would be born into your lap,
> my father was waiting for a horse herder boy,
> my brothers wanted help at the stable,
> my sister waited for someone to ride her around.

When the child is born, the people around ask whether it is a girl or a boy and, in the latter case, invite the mother to bring her newborn baby into a chamber. Should the baby be a girl, then the mother is told to throw her into the water.

> Kui on poega tuu tubaje,
> mähi poega mähkemie,
> sidu siidirätikuie!
> Pojast saab tuba tegija,
> tuba nuka nummerdaja,
> tuba lael lassu lüöjä.
> One tütar vii vesile,
> kanna kaevutii radule!
>
> ERM 5, 35/6

> If it is a boy, bring him to the chamber,
> wrap him in a nappy,
> tie him in a silken cloth!
> A boy will build new chambers,
> will make nice corners,
> will hit the wooden chips for the roof.
> If it is a girl, bring her to the water,
> carry her to a well!

The mother sits down to take care of her infant and makes up her mind to resist the suggestion of her family, sometimes listing the future benefits of the girl's help in the household. Due to the references to the sacrifice of silver or money in some of these song texts, archeologist Pikne Kama (2017:102) refers to the possibility that these songs are reminiscences of the custom of human sacrifice that was admittedly known among Estonians, according to medieval chronicles, and confined to child sacrifices in the final phase of this practice, the last known case being described by Pastor Gutslaff in 1644 (Valk 2014:17). The content of such songs sounds unrealistic as killing a newborn had been considered a hard crime already for centuries, and no one would consider it a valid option for family planning or discuss it openly. It is evident from the popularity of the song throughout Estonia, though, that the topic of gender preference has long been relevant for the singers.

Estonian runosongs encompass a distinct group of ballad-like songs that by their features are close to the west European medieval ballad tradition. These songs usually tell true, often scandalous, stories related to particular higher-class people, and individuals' emotions are brought to the forefront (Asplund 1994). Atypically of the Estonian runosong tradition in general, the characters in these songs usually have proper names. Among this group of songs is one story that describes the conception, birth, and abandonment of an illegitimate child.

> Mareta kõreta neido,
> see jäi naeseks naitematta.
> See läks mängides mäele,
> lehte lüües lepikuie.
> Annus saare saksa poega,
> see läks Mareta järele

pistis penningid pihuje,
kulda naastud alla kurgu,
hõbe naastud alla hõlma,
vaski naastud alla vammuse.
Hakkas siis magatamaie,
magatas salo seessa,
salo keero keske'ella.

H II 55, 815/25 (14)

Mareta, a slender maiden
could not get married.
One day she went on the hill,
and into the alder wood.
Annus, the son of a nobleman,
he went after Mareta,
put pennies in her hand,
golden garments below her neck,
silver plaques under her coat edge,
copper plates under her jacket.
Started to sleep with her,
slept with her in a grove,
in the middle of a grove thicket.

The song focuses on detecting the true parents of the discovered newborn. In some versions of the song one of the parents reveals the truth.

Annus saare saksa poega
hakkas Maretil ütlema:
"Maret piiga, neitsikene,
eks sina seda mäleta
kui mina sinu magasin
taga tamme aavikussa,
lehtedessa lepikussa,
laia luadide vahella!"

E 7949/50 (11)

Annus, the son of a nobleman,
started to tell Maret:
"Maret, maiden, dear girl,
don't you remember
when I slept with you
in the aspen wood behind the oak tree,
among the leaves in the alder forest,
within the cloth of your large skirt!"

In other versions of the song the infant acquires the skill of speaking and reveals who its parents are, or clairvoyants recognize the parents. In some versions the parents who have previously denied that the child is theirs cannot stand the threats to the child.

> Madli, madal neiukene
> võttis see lapse sülesse,
> pidi viskama tulesse.
> Mis seal tule eessa oli?
> Mareta punane palakas.
> Võttis see lapse sülesse,
> pidi viskama vedeje.
> Mis seal vee eessa oli?
> Annukse sinine särki.
>
> EÜS X 2691/2 (263)

> Madli, a humble girl
> took the child in her lap,
> started to throw it into the fire.
> What was in front of the fire?
> Mareta's red shawl.
> [Madli] took the child in her lap,
> started to throw it into the water.
> What was in front of the water?
> Annus's blue shirt.

The story of a higher-class father made to acknowledge his offspring is known in various countries (Jürgenson 1998). Folklorist Ingrid Rüütel (2017:45) considers the origin of this late-medieval song to be in Scandinavia or Finland.

Both of the aforementioned plots have found their way into compositions and reinterpretations in the twentieth and twenty-first centuries. The song "Child of Mareta" belongs to one of the best-known twentieth-century runosong-based classical compositions by the well-known Estonian composer Veljo Tormis, the cantata-ballet "Estonian Ballads" (1980). From the contemporary viewpoint, the idea of inflicting such cruelty on newborns seems unimaginable but can be distanced when singing or listening to the story. At the same time, the issues of gender preference and unwanted children are still germane.

Songs about Pregnancy and Childbirth

Pregnancy and childbirth form a natural and significant part of a woman's life cycle in traditional society. There are a number of runosong motifs that either mention or focus on pregnancy and childbirth. These events are only rarely expressed through the eyes of pregnant or delivering women.

Pregnancy of the Singer's Mother

Songs that describe the pregnancy of the singer's mother and its implications comprise one group of runosongs. The behavior of the mother during pregnancy was believed to leave its impact on the child's constitution and outlook. In the runosongs that describe the pregnancy of the singer's mother, she often acts in tandem and together with the father as if his behavior would have a similar impact as well.

> Kui iks ime minnu olli,
> kallis ime minnu kandi,
> oisõ uman süämen,
> kasvi uma kandli all ...
> imä jõi pik´äst pihlõõst,
> esä orsikõtsõst uiuõst,
> imä uik´i uiuõn,
> esä viilis´k vislapuin.
>
> H II 36, 158/9 (203)

> When my mother was pregnant with me,
> dear mother was bearing me,
> she kept me within her heart,
> grew me under her armpit ...
> my mother drank from a tall rowan tree,
> my father from a slender apple tree,
> my mother shouted from an apple tree,
> my father whistled from a cherry tree.

Most often the parents' behavior is related to the ability to sing well.

> Kui emä minuda olli,
> naene kallis kan´d kanada,
> emä jõie lõo lõõri,
> esä jõie kure kurgu,
> säält ma siis latsi laululine,
> tõine sõsar sõnuline.
>
> H II 25, 773/4 (51)

> When my mother was pregnant with me,
> the dear woman was bearing a hen,

> my mother drank the gorge of a swallow,
> my father drank the throat of a crane,
> therefore I am a singer child,
> another sister is a poet as well.

Another motif that is used in various contexts recalls the mother's care during pregnancy from the singer's viewpoint.

> Eide maksus ma magasin,
> eide kopsus ma kosusin,
> sõin aga eide südamesooni,
> purin aga eide puusaluida,
> närisin eide nänninahku.
>
> ERA II 111, 58/59 (23)

> I was sleeping in my mother's liver,
> I was growing in my mother's lung,
> I was eating my mother's heart vessels,
> I was gnawing my mother's hip bones,
> I was eating my mother's breast skin.

The Discovery of Pregnancy

Another, larger group of songs describes the discovery of pregnancy by a seemingly ignorant observer, most often a bewildered new husband who, after a year of marriage, wonders why his young wife is not able to work properly anymore. The troubles of a pregnant woman might be enumerated in great detail.

> ... hakkas jalgu ta põdema,
> sääremarju ta magama,
> õlanukke oigamaie,
> käevarsi kaebamaie,
> silmakulmu kolletama,
> põllepaelast paisumaie,
> suurest varbast valu kaebama,
> ei ta tahtnud tangupudru,
> ei ta võtnud võida-leiba,
> ei söönud sealihada,
> ei katsund kanamunada,
> ega mekkind meekooki.
>
> H II 11, 314/8 (84)

> ... her legs started to ache,
> her calves gave her trouble,
> she started to complain about her shoulder tips,
> and about her forearms,
> her eyebrows started to turn yellow,
> and her apron strings appeared to be too tight,
> her big toe gave her pain,
> she did not want to eat porridge
> nor would she have bread and butter,
> she would not eat pork
> nor have eggs,
> did not taste honeycake.

Subsequently, either the pregnant wife, the parents of the young man, or the village people tell him to bring a midwife and to start to prepare beer to celebrate the birth of the baby. Sometimes the reason for this "illness" is recalled and described in detail.

Childbirth

The third group of songs is related to childbirth. The songs describe the labor pains and how the woman tries to manage the agony and get help either from (even sometimes talking to) the corners and walls of the chamber or from nature. In this group of songs the singer seems to be mostly just an observer whose connection, atypical to the runosong, with the woman in pain remains unexpressed. In some variants the delicacy of the situation is mentioned: the young woman does not want to wake up her family members—her husband and in-laws or young men are turned away from the situation of pain they would not be able to understand. In other variants the distressed and fearful family members are mentioned.

> ... lapsed nutsid laua all,
> pere nuttis pingi all,
> oma kaasa kamberis.
>
> EÜS VIII 92 (44)

> ... the children were crying under the table,
> the family under the bench,
> her own husband in the chamber.

The songs of childbirth sometimes also refer to the possibility or fear of death during labor.

Although runosongs in general do not rely on the concepts of Christianity, the labor of childbirth is often mentioned as solved and relieved by God, Jesus, or St. Mary. In the song texts they close again "the doors of the grave, the cover of the tomb"—a poetic reference to the liminality of the situation—and after their intervention, there are "two heads at the head of the bed, and four legs at the foot of the bed" (*kats pääd sai pähütsehe, neli jalga jalotsehe*—E 80728/30 [3]). There are also charms in runosong form that were used to promote the labor. In these charms St. Mary or other Christian saints are invited to help.

> ... lõika valud, lõika vaevad,
> lõika niid lõngad punased, ...
> tee lahti luised uksed,
> kisu kinnitud värävid.
> E 56377/8 (6)

> ... cut off the pains, cut off the troubles,
> cut these red cords ...
> open the bone doors,
> drag open the shut gates.

In other charms the body of the woman is called to let out the head.

> Tee teed ja raiu rada,
> peasta peakene
> ja aruta ingekene!
>
> KKI 1, 179 (190)

> Make the way, cut the path,
> let out the head,
> and untangle the soul.

Pregnancy and childbirth were obviously far more frequent and usual events in traditional society than they are in the modern world. Women had more children on average, which was necessary for the quick recovery of population during intermittent wars and deadly contagions, and they usually spent a large part of their adult fertile life either being pregnant or breastfeeding. Demographic transitions along with the decrease of the birth rate started in Estonia comparatively early, in the 1850s–1860s (Katus and Puur 2006:493). The changes in family planning and sexual behavior formed part of the general modernization of society, overlapping with the end of the restrictions on movement of the Estonian peasantry, increasing access to higher education, and rising national awakening.

Along with modernization, discussing the human body and its functioning became taboo in public spheres. Similar to death, pregnancy and childbirth were transferred from the home sphere to the control of medical institutions (cf. Foucault 1978). Nevertheless, it is known from recordings of traditional beliefs and customs that pregnancy was not displayed openly in order to avoid possible harm from the "evil eye." It was preferable to experience the liminal period of pregnancy as well as childbirth in the privacy of one's home (Salu 1990; Mikkor 2000). The songs suggest that both pregnancy as well as childbirth might not have been explicitly discussed even within the family.

Songs about pregnancy and childbirth have been included in academic publications of runosongs. But given that the topic was for such a long time not discussed or reflected on in public, the songs have by and large not found a place in modern public compositions or performances.

Songs about Sexual Matters

Runosongs in general do not recognize or express romantic love, intense personal feelings toward a loved one, missing, longing, flirting, jealousy, or infidelity, topics that are well known in the newer layer of rhymed folk songs. When runosongs concern the relations of men and women, they are more frequently about practicalities of life, both good and bad, including private parts and having sex. Often the songs develop into expressions of pure joy of expressing poetic images and figurative language:

> Iidu-tiidu till on pikka,
> minu munn on muidu pikka,
> piiga on pikka voodiessa,
> kala on pikka kaldaessa,
> angerjas meressa pikka,
> madu on maassa pikka.
>
> H II 9, 432 (33)

> Hiddle-diddle, a dick is long,
> and my cock is simply long,
> a maiden is long in bed,
> and a fish is long on the shore,
> an eel is long in the sea,
> and a snake is long on the ground.

Despite this, the language is quite direct rather than euphemistic, following the general poetic structure of parallelism in runosong, where the first line in a group of parallel lines gives more or less directly the main idea of what is said, and the successive lines repeat the idea, adding to the poeticism euphonically as well as figuratively.

The songs about sexual matters form a blunt collection of loose motifs and longer plots. The shorter motifs can be freely combined into longer wholes should they fit together and be suitable for the occasion of singing. The longer plots with fixed structure can be either lyric or narrative. One of the typical narrative schemas of Estonian runosongs is the so-called repetition song, which describes an accident happening to "me," a young person, who then goes home and complains to "my" parents (or occasionally to villagers, an old wise woman, etc.) about what has happened—the singer repeats the whole story word by word—and then the parents usually comfort "me," approve "my" behavior, and find a good solution to the problem.

Private Parts

The songs and song motifs about private parts include purely poetic yet graphic, bawdy descriptions.

> Oo, türa, teravikene,
> otsast kui oravikene,
> keskelt keeruveeruline,
> tagant kui taprivarrekene!
>
> H II 9, 432 (33)

> Oh, sharp dickie,
> the tip like a squirrel,
> curvy in the middle,
> the back-end like an ax-handle!

> Homikul oli oravakarva,
> karukarva kaste'ella,
> lõhekarva lõune'ella,
> muu pääval mudisekarva.
>
> H II 37, 434 (15)

> [A cunt] ... was in the morning the color of a squirrel,
> in the morning dew the color of a bear,
> in the midday the color of a salmon,
> on another day the color of a goby fish.

Or they contain concerns about their qualities and functioning. The size of male genitals seems to be a feature of social status and could be openly discussed in songs and serve as a sign of a man's desirability (or not) as a partner or husband. In wedding songs, as a part of the wedding ritual, the groom might be praised for his big and beautiful genitals.

> Mis viga mu vellele tulla,
> mu vellel vereva türä,
> kurõmunasõ kotiku:
> küünüse maha kükäten,
> üle aia hüpäten.
>
> H II 32, 240 (14)

> You have nothing to worry about if you marry my brother,
> my brother has a red dick,
> balls like stork eggs:
> they reach the ground when he squats,
> or jumps over the fence.

The songs contain grotesque images of big or huge male genitals, so heavy that they must be dragged on one's back or so long that they get in the way when walking around in the woods. Private parts can acquire fantastic properties; they can be easily separated from the body, stolen, left at home when they are too much trouble to drag along, put somewhere to dry or warm up, replaced by artificial ones, or repaired by a blacksmith. Depending on the situation, a penis can be called a "stick of women's pleasure" or a "tool of shame."

In some cases, male and female genitals are personified and act as independent characters who can have discussions and fights with each other or travel around. According to the general animistic worldview of runosongs, similar to other things and phenomena (including body parts), private parts can be, if not conversed with, then at least addressed by their owner (*Keki, keki kellikene, muki, muki munnikene/*"Up, up, my dear dick, swell, swell, my cock"—EKS 41, 20 [19]) or even put to work.

> Ennem panen vitu vihtu tegema,
> putsi puida raiuma,
> ennem kui annan ullu kätte,
> pistan pööratse peusse.
>
> H II 16, 644 (9)

> I'd rather tell my cunt to gather branches,
> my pussy to hack wood,
> than to give it to a lunatic
> or leave it in the hands of a crazy one.

Sexual Desire and Resentment

Runosongs also tell about sexual desire and resentment, concerns and pleasures, and the social implications of sexual relations. There are numerous songs and song motifs that most often directly, although sometimes indirectly or figuratively, refer to the desire to have sex. In songs, the attraction to the genitals of the opposite sex or the desire to have sex is expressed by both sexes.

> Oleks aga putsi puusse luodud,
> türa tammeje tautud,
> palumata saaksid poisid,
> nurumata nuored mihed.
>
> EÜS X 1624 (190)

> What if cunts had been wooden,
> the dicks had been oaken!
> then the lads could get it without asking,
> the boys without pleading.

More often than not, desire seems to be characteristic to women's behavior. Men sometimes express their disappointment in not being chosen by girls as their future husbands not because of their work but because of their genitals.

> Neitsikene, noorukene,
> kirjapihta peenikene,
> miks ep mullu mulle tulnud,
> tunamullu kui toutid,
> kui käisid käsud järele,
> viied viinad ja kuued kosjad?
> Läksid teisele mehele,
> kel oli küünar kürva pika,
> kaks vaaksa kara jämeda.
>
> H II 9, 803/4 (86)

> Dear girl, young one,
> slender one with the nice waist,
> why did you not marry me last year,
> two years ago when you promised me,
> when I invited you,
> when I proposed to you six times and sent you brandy five times?
> You married another man,
> who has a dick one ell long,

a cock as large as two spans.

Unmarried girls' having sex or too many partners as well as having children before marriage were looked down upon. These matters were checked by the kin of the groom at weddings through songs.

> Las mi kae, las mi katsu,
> kas om näiu poissest puhas,
> poissest puhas latsist lake.
>
> H II 31, 828 (4)

> Let us look, let us see,
> whether the bride is pure of boys,
> free of children.

Wedding songs also mocked the bride and bridegroom as well as their kin, especially the lead singers, for either having sex with many partners or with animals. The bride is sometimes accused in song by in-laws of seducing the groom and inviting him to sleep with her in the woods or the meadow. Sexual relations with Germans who were of a higher class were also viewed negatively and warned about in runosongs.

The songs also express doubts, rejection, or regrets for having sex. As for boys, they voice their resentment toward "half-used" girls, sometimes as a negative response to a girl's invitation to go to bed with her.

> Aiu-raiu ratastega,
> ennem mina mängin mätastega,
> kargan kasekändudega,
> ennem kui nende neidistega,
> mis olid pooleli peetud,
> enneaegu armastatud,
> poiste käed olid käperdanud,
> poiste munnid musserdanud.
>
> EKS 1 (44)

> Hey-hoo with wheels,
> I'd rather play with sods,
> dance with birch stumps,
> than with those girls,
> who were half-used,
> made love with too early.
> The boys' hands had groped around,
> the boys' dicks browsed around.

Sometimes boys complain about overly aggressive girls who want to unfasten their pants when they sleep alongside them. Girls are often warned of, or themselves express their distrust toward, boys' promises. Sometimes the warnings allude to the possibility of being shamed or bringing shame to the family by an unwanted child and teach girls to confront malevolent intruders.

> Tütär, lilli, linnukene,
> memme mesimarjakene,
> mängi sina kõik mäe,
> tandsi sina kõik tare,
> oia iks kivi peona!
> Kui lääp poisi puutumaie,
> ahkasärki haaramaie,
> lüü purus poisi pää,
> eritse igä löhendä,
> ennembä kui au annat,
> au annat, häbi kannat,
> üles panet häbi hälli,
> pallet partsi hällitämä,
> suvilindu liigutämä.
>
> H II 31, 506 (6)

> My dear daughter, my flower, my bird,
> honeyberry of your mother!
> Play on all the hills,
> dance in all the houses,
> still keep a stone in your hand.
> If a boy comes to grab you,
> a gray shirt to touch you,
> then break the head of this boy,
> shorten the age of the evil one,
> rather than giving away your dignity, and
> bear the shame,
> put up the cradle of shame
> and ask the duck to swing it,
> the summer bird to rock it.

Sexual Intercourse

The songs also contain direct descriptions of or references to sexual intercourse. Some of them are quite pornographic and describe personal experiences. There are also songs about singers' imagined memories of how they were conceived; they sometimes simply describe their mother and father having sex. Sometimes the occasion may acquire fantastic dimensions.

Olgõ terve mu tegijä,
raha saagu mu tsagaja,
ke mu tegi tervel aol,
koputasi kuival aol,
tuhat titti minnu tei,
sada vembä vemmeldi.

H II 36, 283/4 (459)

Be healthy [you] who made me,
be healthy and wealthy,
[you] who made me in good times,
who knocked me with dry weather,
a thousand dicks were making me,
a hundred cudgels were clubbing at it.

Others describe sexual encounters through the eyes of an observer or listener. Often, sexual activities are conveyed in songs through an aural picture; since the extended families used to live together, the living room, especially in winter time, usually accommodated several couples. Thus, it was not uncommon to be a witness of other people having sex in an audible vicinity.

Eit lääb taadiga magama,
vend lääb noore noorikuga,
mina üksi ühtepuhku. . . .
Tuleb see õnnis õhtuke,
kallis kaasa mängi aega,
kes läävad sängi ja teevad mängi:
liikvad linad ja paukvad padjad
ja nõtkuvad nõdrad voodilauad,
ägisevad äärelauad,
põgisevad põhjalauad.
Ma lään sängi, ma muretsen.

EÜS X 662/3 (113)

My mom is going to sleep with my dad,
my brother with his newlywed wife,
I always go alone. . . .
When the evening approaches,
the time for playing with one's spouse comes,
they are going to bed and are going to play:
the sheets are moving,
the pillows are banging,
the thin bed planks are flexing,
the board planks are groaning,

the bottom planks are rumbling.
When I go to bed, I feel sad.

Although most of the descriptions of sexual encounters are expressed in positive or neutral tones, as something to be awaited and enjoyed or just part of everyday life, there is a group of songs in which someone having sex is presented disapprovingly, sometimes to demean the person in question.

> Küll mina nägin siegi aja,
> kui sinu koplis koinitie,
> pingi nurgas pistetie,
> paju alla painatie . . .
> Küll mina nägin siegi aja,
> kui sinu au aeti,
> särki säärile vieti
> tua taga tapuajassa,
> kuue kutsari vahella,
> poiss oli alla, poiss oli päälla,
> ise kierid keske'ella.
>
> EÜS X 1544/6 (89)

> I saw this time,
> when you were fucked in the paddock,
> stuck on the bench corner,
> pressed down under the willow . . .
> I saw this time,
> when your dignity was lost,
> your blouse was lifted up,
> in the hop-garden behind the house,
> in between six coachmen,
> there was a boy on top of you, a boy under you,
> and you yourself swirled in between them.

There are also longer repetition songs about a violent intruder(s) whom the female "me" encounters in the woods or in the bog. In some cases, the girl confronts the attacker, stabs him with a knife, and eventually kills him; in others, she is robbed and sometimes raped by a man or group of men.

> Ma läksin mööda pikut' sooda,
> poiss tuli vasta põigit' sooda,
> sai mo kätte käänapilla,
> viis mu alla viderikku,
> kandis alla kadanikku.
> Hullu ussi nõelas minda,

> pime ussi pistis minda,
> madu musta mõetis minda! . . .
> See oli paha paistetama,
> kena kõhtu kergitama!
>
> E 11027/8 (a)

> I walked along the marsh,
> the boy went across the marsh,
> caught me up at the turn,
> brought me in between the bushes,
> in the middle of the junipers.
> The mad snake stung me,
> the blind snake stuck me,
> the black viper measured me! . . .
> This made me swell badly,
> made my belly nicely higher.

Typical to the songs with a repetition structure, the parents, after having heard the whole story, console their daughter, approve her behavior, and/or offer a solution to the problem.

As we can see, songs about sexual matters form a diverse group of graphically explicit runosongs, which clearly demonstrates that the topic of human sexuality was not avoided or silenced but openly expressed and discussed as an inevitable part of human life. We have no data concerning if and how much these topics were avoided in Estonian traditional society or what the occasions or channels were when it would have been appropriate to discuss them. What was considered shameful or improper could be and probably was very different in pre-modern peasant society compared to modern or current moral ideas.

We only have limited knowledge on sexuality among pre-modern Estonians that might help us explain the meanings and attitudes behind the recorded song texts (Metsvahi 2016). Perhaps the most striking difference between runosongs and the general morals of modern European society is the open discussion of sexuality and especially the acceptance of female sexuality and desires. However, some of the songs directly express the unacceptability of unmarried young people (or only girls) having sexual encounters, especially leading to offspring. The songs reflect the clash within a society in which fertility was a blessing and absolutely necessary for securing the sustainability of the population yet could cause problems that should be kept under strict control. There are some references that in traditional communities, singing could be used to talk about topics and issues that usually were not appropriate to comment on or discuss in public (Virtanen 1987).

The stigmatization of sexuality in keeping with European morals has had implications in terms of the collecting, research, and reuse of runosongs. Although it was stated from the outset of collecting activities that all kinds of songs should be collected, we still can find instances of moral conflict among collectors expressed in their letters concerning the songs that were considered improper in the framework of modern literary culture. Early correspondents have expressed their doubts as to whether such songs were suitable for the "treasury of Estonian culture." We may only guess at how many such songs were left unrecorded or unsent to collectors or archives because of these doubts. Considering the questionable reputation of runosongs among clergymen and educated people and even considering the whole genre of runosongs as indecent and suitable "only for drunkards," it is probable that the share of songs related to sexual matters circulating in oral tradition was considerably higher than documented.

Discussing sexuality was even more strictly tabooed under the Soviet regime. In the 1950s the Estonian Folklore Archive collections were censored, and, along with ideological issues, folklore on sexual matters was also either cut out or redacted (Kulasalu 2013). In the archival systems the songs considered improper were mostly left untypologized, labeled only as "rubbish." In academic discussions the topic of sexuality in Estonian runosongs was never closely examined until 2014 (Kalkun and Sarv 2014). The songs about sexual matters were sometimes issued in a separate section of academic runosong publications, and only a few examples have been printed in text anthologies meant for wider audiences, not to mention in schoolbooks for students. These songs have not made it into the compositions, pop music, or the repertoire of folklore ensembles. In their article "Inappropriate," on Finnish runosong tradition, Heidi Henriika Mäkelä and Lotte Tarkka (2022) note that the songs about sexual matters were removed or excluded from the body of national cultural heritage in Finland for a long period, regaining attention only along with the wave of sexual liberation in the 1960s. In Estonia, the last few decades have seen the growth of runosong use in informal situations such as organized events or occasional singing. The songs about sexual matters have found their way into more private singing events that often are for men or women only, offering cultural support to participants' gendered bodily experiences.

Cultural Heritage or Not?

Although singing in itself is a culturally accepted means of bringing personal experiences to a wider audience, the analysis of the backgrounds, reception, and reuse of three selected song groups demonstrates clear differences in the functioning of those songs as cultural heritage. While lullabies and songs about taking care of newborns were in general considered positive examples of Estonians' culture, the songs about pregnancy and childbirth, and especially the songs about sexual matters, have not always been considered appropriate to represent the "imagined community" of the nation in public.

In general, we have no information on how singers interpreted the content of various songs, whether they considered the songs "beautiful" or "ugly," proper or improper, intimate or public. On the basis of the handful of clues that we have about the songs and the knowledge of Estonian peasants' everyday life, we may suppose that they had different perceptions regarding what to consider private or improper and what not. Entire extended families lived in close proximity, and the worries and sounds of having sex or giving birth belonged to everyday life.

Attitudes toward sex and sexuality as well as desire and lust form a part of a complex system related to economic sustainability, power relations, and proprietary circumstances in society. The concepts of privacy and indecency have definitely changed along with the modernization of living conditions and societal formations. Moral attitudes toward the content and thematics of the songs have influenced their validity to represent "the culture of Estonians." The norms and morals of modern society had their impact already on the selection of the songs that were considered worthwhile and appropriate during the collecting of songs for the sake of the "Estonian nation" or suitable to represent one's immediate community or family in esteemed folklore collections. Furthermore, they have also impacted the research on and mediation of runosongs to the public, creating a picture of Estonian peasant culture that was more suitable to contemporary morals and closer to the expectations of modern people than what the culture of "our ancestors" might have been. What is considered immoral according to current standards has been excluded from dissemination and public access. While motherhood has been seen as positive and, in a sense, a heroic effort, and songs on taking care of children were widely known and reused, songs related to bodily aspects of motherhood—pregnancy and childbirth—have mostly not entered into modern or pop interpretations. Indeed, songs about sexual topics have been sabotaged even in archival systems and research. The reintroduction of private singing occasions in recent decades has also brought into reuse the songs that concern more private themes and are not suitable for the public stage according to common morals.

History has shown that attitudes are subject to change, and parts of the heritage that were once left aside can acquire new meanings and uses over the course of time. On the one hand, the content of archives is formed as a result of selective processes determined by contemporary value assessments and ideologies; on the other, the archives still have an amount of silent power to preserve the materials intact for long periods independent of temporary fluctuations and to open up their doors when the right time arrives.

Acknowledgments

This research was funded by the Estonian Research Agency [project PRG1288] and the Estonian Ministry of Education and Research [project EKKD126].

Notes

1. The Finnic peoples include the Finns, Estonians, Karelians, Ingrians (Izhorians), Votes, Livonians, and Veps. The two last-mentioned peoples do not have known runosongs.
2. On the various names of this song tradition used in different languages and academic traditions, see Kallio et al. (2017).

3. This is a common term for the Germans who were living in Estonia and Latvia from the Middle Ages up to 1939.
4. Johann Gottfried Herder (1744–1803) was instrumental in laying the groundwork for interpreting folklore as a symbol of the nation.
5. This and all subsequent translations are mine.

Works Cited

Anttonen, Pertti. 2005. *Tradition through Modernity—Postmodernism and the Nation-State in Folklore Scholarship*. Helsinki: Finnish Literature Society.

Anttonen, Pertti. 2012. "Oral Traditions and the Making of the Finnish Nation." In *Folklore and Nationalism in Europe during the Long Nineteenth Century*, eds. T. Baycroft and D. Hopkin, 325–350. Leiden–Boston: Brill.

Asplund, Anneli. 1994. *Balladeja ja arkkiveisuja: Suomalaisia kertomalauluja*. Helsinki: Suomalaisen Kirjallisuuden Seura.

Briggs, Charles, and Richard Bauman. 1999. "The Foundation of All Future Researches; Franz Boas, Native American Texts, and the Construction of Modernity." *American Quarterly*, 51/3:479–528.

Foucault, Michel. 1978. *The History of Sexuality*, trans. Robert Hurley. New York: Pantheon Books.

Frog. 2019. "The Finnic Tetrameter—A Creolization of Poetic Form?" *Studia Metrica et Poetica*, 6/1:20–78. https://ojs.utlib.ee/index.php/smp/article/view/smp.2019.6.1.02/10407.

Haamer, Naatan. 2019. "Sinu riik tulgu." *Teater, muusika, kino*, 4:98–104.

Hurt, Jakob. 1963. "Paar palvid Eesti ärksamaile poegadele ja tütardele." In *Eesti rahvaluuleteaduse ajalugu. Valitud tekste ja pilte*, ed. Eduard Laugaste, 202–210. Tallinn: Eesti Riiklik Kirjastus. First published 1888.

Jürgenson, Aivar. 1998. "Tapetud laps ja lapsetapmine pärimuses sotsiokultuurilisel taustal." *Mäetagused* 8:28–57.

Kalkun, Andreas, and Mari Sarv. 2014. "Seks ja poeetika: Regilaulu peidus pool." *Vikerkaar*, 4–5:91–108.

Kallio, Kati, Frog, and Mari Sarv. 2017. "What to Call the Poetic Form: Kalevala-Meter or Kalevalaic Verse, regivärss, Runosong, the Finnic Tetrameter, Finnic Alliterative Verse or Something Else?" *RMN Newsletter*, 12–13:139–161.

Kama, Pikne. 2017. *Arheoloogiliste ja folkloorsete allikate kooskasutusvõimalused: Inimjäänused märgaladel/Combining Archaeological and Folkloristic Sources: Human Remains in Wetlands*. Tartu: Tartu Ülikooli Kirjastus.

Katus, Kalev, and Allan Puur. 2006. "Eesti rahvastikuarengu pöördepunktid." *Akadeemia*, 18:259–286, 491–523.

Korhonen, Mikko. 1994. "The Early History of the Kalevala Metre." In *Songs beyond the Kalevala. Transformations of Oral Poetry*, eds. Anna-Leena Siikala and Sinikka Vakimo, 75–87. Studia Fennica Folkloristica 2. Helsinki: Finnish Literature Society.

Kulasalu, Kaisa. 2013. "Immoral Obscenity: Censorship of Folklore Manuscript Collections in Late Stalinist Estonia." *Journal of Ethnology and Folkloristics* 7/1:65–81.

Laugaste, Eduard. 1963. *Eesti rahvaluuleteaduse ajalugu. Valitud tekste ja pilte*. Vol. I. Tallinn: Eesti Riiklik Kirjastus.

Liivamägi, Toomas. 2008. "Ütle üks kaunis eestikeelne lause . . ." *Oma Keel*, 2:60–68.

Mäkelä, Heidi Henriika, and Lotte Tarkka. 2022. "Sopimatonta: Seksuaalisuuteen liittyvien kalevalamittaisten runojen perinnöllistäminen Suomessa 1818–1997." *Elore*, 29/2:34–58. https://doi.org/10.30666/elore.121473.
Merilai, Arne, and Katre Talviste. 2019. "A Small Literature in the Service of Nation-Building: The Estonian Case." *Interlitteraria*, 24/1:247–260.
Metsvahi, Merili. 2016. "Description of the Peasants' Sexual Behaviour in August Wilhelm Hupel's Topographical Messages in the Context of the History of the Estonian Family." *Journal of Baltic Studies*, 47:301–323.
Mikkor, Marika. 2000. "Sünnikombestikust linnas ja maal." *Akadeemia*, 12:806–847, 1017–1044.
Ong, Walter J. 1982. *Orality and Literacy: The Technologizing of the Word*. London–New York: Routledge.
Rüütel, Ingrid. 2017. "Rahvalaulud ja rahvamuusika Virumaal." *Mäetagused*, 67/2:41–74.
Salu, Edith. 1990. "Rasedusega seotud uskumused ja kombed eestlastel." *Eesti Rahva Muuseumi aastaraamat*, 38:105–139.
Särg, Taive. 2012. "Eesti regilauluviisid ja rahvamuusika 20. sajandi alguse haritlaste vaates." *Eesti Rahvaluule Arhiivi toimetused*, 29:71–142.
Särg, Taive, and Janika Oras. 2021. "Regilaulu eripära ja elujõud." *Horisont*, 6:54–57.
Sarv, Mari. 2009. "Stichic and Stanzaic Poetic Form in Estonian Tradition and in Europe." *Traditiones*, 38/1:161–171.
Sarv, Mari. 2013. "Traditional Estonian Lullabies. A Tentative Overview." In *Estonia and Poland: Creativity and Tradition in Cultural Communication*. Vol. 2, *Perspectives on National and Regional Identity*, eds. Liisi Laineste, Dorota Brzozowska, and Władysław Chłopicki, 161–176. Tartu: EKM Teaduskirjastus.
Sarv, Mari. 2015. "Regional Variation in Folkloric Meter: The Case of Estonian Runosong." *RMN Newsletter*, 9:6–17.
Sarv, Mari, Kati Kallio, Maciej Janicki, and Eetu Mäkelä. 2021. "Metric Variation in the Finnic Runosong Tradition: A Rough Computational Analysis of the Multilingual Corpus." In *Tackling the Toolkit: Plotting Poetry through Computational Literary Studies*, eds. Petr Plecháč, Robert Kolár, Anne-Sophie Bories, and Jakub Říha, 131–150. Prague: Institute of Czech Literature CAS. https://doi.org/10.51305/ICL.CZ.9788076580336.09.
Tedre, Ülo, Aino Koemets, Eduard Laugaste, Ruth Mirov, Urmas Mägi, Juhan Peegel, and Veera Pino, eds. 1974. *Eesti rahvalaulud: Antoloogia IV*. Tallinn: Eesti Raamat.
Valk, Heiki. 2014. "Püha Võhandu rahvausundis ja pärimuses." *Õpetatud Eesti Seltsi aastaraamat*, 2013:9–51.
Virtanen, Leea. 1987. "Setukaiset kertovat lauluistaan." In *Viron veräjät. Näkökulmia folkloreen*, ed. Leea Virtanen, 161–194. Tietolipas 105. Helsinki: Suomalaisen Kirjallisuuden Seura.

Archival Collections at the Estonian Folklore Archives of the Estonian Literary Museum

E—Folklore collection of Matthias Johann Eisen (1880–1934)
EKS—Folklore collection of the Estonian Literature Society (1872–1924)
ERA—Folklore collection of the Estonian Folklore Archives (1927–1944)
ERM—Folklore collection of the Estonian National Museum (1915–1925)
EÜS—Folklore collection of the Estonian Students' Society (1875–1917)
H—Folklore collection of Jakob Hurt (1860–1906)
KKI—Folklore collection of the Institute of Estonian Language and Literature (1941–1984)

CHAPTER 7

THE FOLKLORE OF CHILDBIRTH IN RUSSIA

JEANMARIE ROUHIER-WILLOUGHBY

The rituals of the life cycle have been the subject of countless articles and monographs by folklorists, ethnographers, and anthropologists since the nineteenth century. The classic work by Arnold van Gennep, *Les rites de passage* (1909), set the stage for future scholarship in all these disciplines. Van Gennep's approach to birth, initiation, marriage, and death rites was based on an elegant analysis of the tripartite system of separation (departure from the old category), transition (the liminal phase), and incorporation (formal introduction into the new category). He outlined the characteristics of each stage, arguing for a common thread that defines rituals across cultures of all kinds. While this structuralist approach provides a framework for rites of passage, it is actually only a starting point for ritual analysis. The rites themselves are extremely complex events that engage with cultural and social beliefs and individual and group identity in a myriad of ways.

Rites require us to consider the perspective of the people undergoing the transition and the point of view of the social group to which they belong. As such, the experience can vary significantly even within a small social group. Therefore, it is hard to establish a single narrative for any rite. That is not to say that scholars have not attempted to do so for decades. As Russian folklorist and anthropologist Albert Baiburin (1993:31–33) outlines, rites might serve multiple functions, including socialization of an individual, integration into a group, reinforcement of cultural values, psychological comfort, licensing of sexual reproduction, and adaptation to external circumstances (e.g., aging). Baiburin (p. 35) concludes that this variety raises the inevitable question about whether ritual is in fact multifunctional or whether it allows for the possibility of many interpretations. For that reason, other theorists have focused on its symbolic and expressive nature, as a type of artistic language (Firth 1964; Beattie 1966). This theoretical approach, in turn, resulted in a series of dissents from scholars who objected to the unitary reading of ritual symbols by the participants (see Bourdieu 1991; Humphrey and Laidlaw 1994; Bell 1997; Ortner 1989). These proponents of "practice theory" (a term coined by Bourdieu 1977) argue that participants are more agentive in rituals than had been assumed in earlier scholarship and that position results in more individualized interpretations of a rite than the celebrants may have intended (or scholars may have posited). This chapter will outline the challenges faced by researchers on childbirth in the East Slavic context and discuss major studies in this area from the twentieth and twenty-first centuries. We will examine the gap in folklore scholarship on childbirth (at least among the Russian populace) from 2010 on, when the study of childbirth was ceded to social scientists and gender studies. However, I will argue that folklorists bring an important perspective to the table that scholars in these fields often overlook, which is essential to an understanding of the cultural resonance of childbirth practices.

The Challenges of Research on Birth Rites

Regardless of the theoretical approach, the core purpose of life-cycle rituals is to introduce a person into a new social status. During the rite, the community likewise acknowledges this change in an individual's social status and, as a result, the change in the group's composition. While the person undergoing the rite has often been the focus in the scholarship, it is essential to recognize that the community as a whole must come to terms with the results of the ritual as well. Of the four life-cycle ties (birth, death, marriage, and initiation into adulthood), birth is distinctive in that it results in two very different statuses for the participants rather than a unitary outcome. That is, funerals ensure that the soul of the dead passes safely to the afterlife, marriage creates a new family unit for the bride and groom, and initiation ushers children into the responsibilities of adulthood. However, childbirth rites perform two distinct and disparate functions: (1) to make a newborn "human" by incorporating it into the community and (2) to indoctrinate parents into their new roles. The latter is more important for women in the traditional East Slavic context. While the father of the child does play some role in the ritual, the main focus is on the mother and her transition into a new social status, particularly as a result of her first delivery. As a result, birth rites contain a diverse set of practices that vary significantly for the two main participants, which makes it distinctive among life-cycle rites.[1]

An additional complication of childbirth rites, at least in the east European context, is that they have been much less widely documented than funerary and marriage rites. The reasons for this lacuna are threefold. First, childbirth rites were kept largely secret in nineteenth-century East Slavic villages. Secrecy served two purposes. It ensured protection from evil forces for both the mother and the child. As a result, it was difficult for ethnographers to document the rite at all, given that it was hidden from view, even from those close to the mother and child. In addition, since childbirth was associated with sexuality, it was not appropriate to discuss the topic with outsiders, especially with men.

Since most early ethnographers and folklorists were male, this fact created a gulf between the interviewers and locals regarding this topic. This reluctance extended into the Soviet era as well, when reticence about openly discussing sexual practices and, as a result, birth persisted. Second, childbirth rites in the Russian vernacular tradition lack the rich oral heritage of weddings and funerals. Both weddings and funerals had an intricate tradition of laments (for the bride and for the deceased). In addition, the wedding featured dance songs, joking songs (during the buying of the bride, for example), and an elaborate cycle sung by the bride's attendants throughout the process. Aside from the charms that a midwife would cite during labor and after the birth (largely in private), there were few ritual texts to document. Folkloristics was a nascent discipline in the nineteenth century when these traditional practices were documented, focused primarily on the oral tradition of songs and stories. Since birth rites lacked both of these genres, they were often given short shrift in early studies. Finally, the one place where ritual texts existed was during the baptism and the subsequent meal. Since church rites were considered to be outside the purview of folklore by early collectors, such texts were also not collected or were given only summary treatment in the scholarship. This tendency was also complicated by the anti-religious attitudes of the Soviet era as well. While such texts may have been collected, they could not be published. As a result, early studies of life-cycle rituals and, indeed, twentieth-century publications included only a cursory treatment (if that) when compared to weddings and funerals, at least until the collapse of the Soviet Union.[2]

An additional complication for documenting this rite was the medicalization of childbirth. This process had already begun in the nineteenth century, as Tuve (1984:60) documents, with the passage of a law that allowed women to become medical midwives in an effort to reduce infant and maternal mortality. The Soviet government continued this push to turn birth into an entirely medical and "rational" process through rigid controls on the woman's body (Issoupova 2000:34). Medical authorities were dedicated to combatting "old wives' tales" and vernacular practices promoted by female relatives (Shening-Parshina and Shibaeva 1967:148). They strove to establish the maternity hospital as the only appropriate and safe place to give birth, which they accomplished by the 1950s (Ransel 2000; Shening-Parshina and Shibaeva 1967:143). Since folkloristics is dedicated to the study of unofficial culture, a medical procedure was beyond the purview of the discipline, like the religious practices noted above. In sum, contemporary birth practices were not considered to be part of the vernacular tradition at all among Soviet folklorists through much of the twentieth century.

Scholarly Approaches to Childbirth Ritual in Post-Socialist Russia in the 1990s to 2010

The fall of the USSR in 1991 opened the door onto a more comprehensive study of life-cycle rituals broadly and childbirth more specifically. No longer did scholars need to censor the religious elements, for example; and access to a broader range of scholarship in folkloristics and cultural anthropology ushered in new approaches to the material. At the time, the trend in Russian folkloristics was to view the rituals as a symbolic whole. This approach was facilitated by the access to complete data on life-cycle rituals (including religious practices and psycho-social effects). We can find examples of this approach from the late 1980s through the early 2000s in works by folklorists and anthropologists in Russia and in the United States. Of particular note are studies by Svetlana Adon'ieva, Galina Kabakova, and Albert Baiburin. Adon'ieva (1998) focuses on life-cycle rites in the Russian north, particularly on the role of women within those rites. As such, she studies how the woman's roles at various stages were established and shifted over time, lending support to the analysis of life-cycle rituals as a coherent and connected system. Her research on this topic culminated in the coauthored book with Laura J. Olson (Olson and Adonyeva 2012) on village women's lives and folk practices. Olson and Adon'ieva trace women's ritual experiences and folk expression (both songs and stories) to illustrate the coherence of their (often neglected) lived experiences in Russian villages today. Kabakova's work (2001) examines the treatment of the woman's body within traditional life-cycle rituals. Attitudes toward the body, she argues, demonstrate the coherence of the three rites in the Slavic worldview as well as how social status (wife, mother, widow/deceased) is inscribed on the bodies of women as they move through their lives. Both of these works also represent the disappearance of the taboo on discussing sexuality and the body that hindered a comprehensive treatment of childbirth rites. Both works are likewise noteworthy in that they draw on a larger scope of material than the rites alone (Olson and Adon'ieva emphasize oral folk genres, as mentioned above, while Kabakova studies girlhood and menstruation as well as women's sex and work lives). This broader context is the hallmark of contemporary folkloristics, which strives to demonstrate not just the coherent sweep of folk practices in human lives but also the range of sources (traditional and otherwise) that make up a vernacular understanding of the world.

The most comprehensive study of East Slavic life-cycle rites from this period is Baiburin's Ritual v traditsinnoi kul'ture (1993). Baiburin focuses on the coherence among the three rites (weddings, funerals, and birth) within the context of life as a biological and social journey marked by ritual transitions. In order to demonstrate the coherent symbolic practices, Baiburin highlights four distinctions that lie at the heart of each ritual: person/non-person, married/unmarried, young/old, and living/dead. In the context of birth, Baiburin (pp. 41–42) argues that the child is "defined" as a person as part of the rite, while the mother, in particular, undergoes a death of sorts to be reborn into a new status.[3] These categories, in his view, form a coherent system of ritual practice, even in holiday celebrations, within the East Slavic worldview. Of particular import in all three of these studies is the psycho-social approach that was not characteristic of Soviet folkloristics. These authors not only explore the coherence of ritual practices at three different life stages but consider the emotional and social effects of the shift from one stage to another, especially for women, who are the primary focus of life-cycle rites in the East Slavic tradition.[4] The latter is also innovative, at least in the context of Soviet-era folkloristics, where the focus was on the structural elements of a rite, not on the psycho-social effects on the initiate and the community.[5]

The acceptance of religious texts within rites produced a plethora of studies on the midwife and the spiritual practices and religious texts they recited during birth rites, including Listova (1989, 1992, 2003a, 2003b), Naumenko (2001), and Pankeev (1998). Similarly, scholars began to explore the nature of family and religious life (in villages as well as in cities) and thus expanded on the limited offerings from the Soviet period that had viewed the village family as a flawed and backward entity (Bernshtam 2007; Razumova 2001; Lipinskaia 1996). Razumova's study on the contemporary family was evidence of yet another shift in the field: the study of urban folklore. The earliest (and still thriving) efforts in this area of scholarship emerged from the folklore program directed by Sergei Nekliudov at the Russian State University of the Humanities. Under his auspices, urban folkloristics, including the study of both practices and oral genres, was introduced into Russian folklore scholarship. He and his colleagues produced two seminal works centered around urban folk practices (including those related to medicalized childbirth): *Rodiny, deti, povitukhi v traditsiiakh narodnoi kul'tury* (Belousova and Nekliudov 2001) and *Sovremennyi gorodskoi fol'klor* (Belousov et al. 2003). Ekaterina Belousova (1998, 1999, 2002, 2003) emerged from this group as the primary representative of a new wave of folklorists willing to explore urban birth as a vernacular rite. Her studies of the folklore of the maternity hospital and nascent home birth communities in post-socialist Russia were the first of their kind. Belousova argued, like Western scholars such as Davis-Floyd (1992), that medical birth functioned like a rite of passage in van Gennep's terms and included a set of folk practices no different from those in the rural villages of past centuries. My own research on births, weddings, and funerals in contemporary Russian cities (Rouhier-Willoughby 2008) drew on the unified approach to life-cycle rites seen in Adon'ieva, Kabakova, and Baiburin as well as the work of folklorists and anthropologists, in Russia and elsewhere, studying urban rites as an example of vernacular practice.

Scholarly Approaches to Childbirth Ritual in Russia from 2010 to the Present

We can describe this period of the first two decades after the fall of the USSR as the heyday of scholarship on childbirth in Russia. By the middle of the first decade of the 2000s, the landscape of Russian folkloristics had changed significantly, and research on birth rituals by folklorists fell off considerably (the one exception being Olson and Adon'ieva's 2012 book, although they devote little attention to the rite itself and more to the psychological and social consequences of it). There has been no other major publication by a folklorist on Russian childbirth rites since the first decade of the twenty-first century. It is almost as though, having demonstrated that medicalized childbirth could be classified as a vernacular rite, folklorists abandoned the study of this ritual (at least among the Russian populace) entirely. We are thus faced with a situation rather similar to that of the nineteenth century, when attention was focused on other rites and their ritual texts. Folklorists studying the urban landscape in Russia today collect material on yearly-cycle holidays and on oral lore (especially legends, memorates, and rumors) but not on childbirth. In rural contexts, collectors focus on weddings, funerals, and calendar rites and their songs as well as on vernacular prose genres (for example, there has been a boom in the collection and publication of memorates and legends on supernatural themes).

However, folklorists studying minority populations in Russia have taken up the gauntlet. Publications on this material began to appear in earnest in the second decade of the twenty-first century. They explore childbirth traditions of non-Russian ethnicities from across the country, including Jews, Nenets, Siberian Tatars, Mordvins, Komi, Karelians, Mongols, the peoples of the Northern Caucasus, Bashkirs, Kalmyks, the Altaic peoples, Yakuts, and the peoples of the Lower Amur Basin.[6] In addition, some studies document how rites demonstrate influence from various ethnic groups living together in the same area or who share a cultural heritage (see Bunina and Popovicheva [2013] comparing Russian and Mordvin practices in the Tambov region and Sapalova [2010] on the commonalities between Yakut and Kyrgyz childbirth rites). Since the focus of much of the Soviet-era folklore collection among the non-Russian ethnicities was on oral lore, these pieces provide invaluable data on the ritual practices of the diverse ethnicities in the territory of Russia. Given that village culture was seen as "backward" from the perspective of Soviet authorities, minorities' traditional ways of life were even more suspect. As a result, much of this material has never been published. These works attest not only to the diversity of the nation (a fact often obscured in scholarship as well as in media reports about Russia) but also to the interest in folk practices that has risen across the country since the fall of the USSR in 1991. The general perception among the populace (true or not) is that the Soviet government and its cultural policies altered traditional ways of life and "destroyed" folklore as a result. These works represent an attempt to reclaim the past and emerge out of pride in local practices and ethnic heritage. They also demonstrate, as is the case with folkloristics related to the Russian populace, how the attitude toward religion has changed the field since the collapse of the USSR. These peoples represent Judaism, Islam, Buddhism, and agrarian religious traditions, which are necessarily involved in childbirth practices as well as in the way the child's role in society is conceived. While sources studying influences among different ethnic traditions are fewer in number, they also represent a rare acknowledgment of Russia's diversity as well as the recognition that "pure" traditions have never existed, despite the idealization that we find historically in the discipline of folkloristics.

In essence, childbirth practices among the Russian populace, whether urban or rural, have largely become the purview of gender theorists, medical anthropologists, and sociologists. Folklorists (at least those studying Russians/East Slavs) are largely absent from the academic conversation today. The medical anthropologist Anna Ozhiganova

(2009, 2011a, 2011b, 2012, 2016, 2017, 2019) researches alternative birth methods (natural childbirth, water birth, and home birth). Following on the work done by Belousova in the early 2000s, Ozhiganova documents unofficial cultures of childbirth that represent a rejection of the Russian medical system. This development represents a significant change in attitudes among the Russian populace since the first decade after the collapse of the Soviet Union. By contrast, in her works, the American medical anthropologist Michele Rivkin-Fish (2005, 2010, 2013, 2018) studies the culture of official Russian reproductive policies (including the maternity hospital, abortion, familial support systems, and pronatalism). Her study with the sociologist Anna Temkina (Temkina and Rivkin-Fish 2020), "Creating Health Care Consumers," documents the shift (at least for those with the financial wherewithal) to a new model of childbirth, where pregnant women choose (and pay for) a personal doctor. A rise in consumerist attitudes in healthcare that have emerged since the middle of the first decade of the 2000s has allowed for this option. The authors explore the social resonance of official and unofficial payments (or gifts) to doctors and patient attitudes as conveyed by these payments. In addition, Temkina and Rivkin-Fish track the legacy of Soviet (and immediate post-Soviet) healthcare culture even in this context, including "medical paternalism" and lack of participation in decisions by the patients. Another scholar, the feminist sociologist Ekaterina Borozdina (2014a, 2014b, 2016, 2019), has researched both "unofficial" and "official" birth practices in contemporary urban Russia. Her work explores how women and their (typically female) doctors negotiate social power through the process of childbirth. The one exception in this regard is Tatiana Kuksa, a folklorist and anthropologist (and a practicing lawyer), who has recently begun studying birth in the urban Russian context (2018, 2020a, 2020b, 2021a, 2021b, 2022). Her work focuses on discourses of childbirth as well as shifting attitudes toward birth fostered by doulas and midwives in urban Russia since the 2010s.

While these theorists approach the questions from a different disciplinary point of view, they provide important ethnographic data to folklorists working on childbirth. However, the perspective of folklorists is crucial in scholarly approaches to childbirth. Their absence from this conversation results in the omission of the three major contributions of the discipline: (1) the role of unofficial, traditional culture in daily life; (2) the structure and function of narratives; and (3) consideration of people's voices in broader contexts (e.g., in urban and rural settings, the latter of which are often overlooked by anthropologists, sociologists, and gender specialists of Russia).

David Hufford, a folklorist who has spent his career working with medical doctors at the University of Pennsylvania Medical School, researches the power of folk belief (and indeed folk practices that emerge from it). His investigation of the cultural aspects of medical experiences (and narratives about them) demonstrates how critical it is to consider vernacular systems to understand patients and to design medical care. By all rights, according to Hufford (1995:16–18), based on scholarly arguments about the demise of superstition in the face of science, these beliefs and practices should have disappeared long ago. However, they persist, and Hufford argues that they do so because they are based on both our experience of living in this world as well as interaction with cultural traditions. Hufford (p. 22) defines folk beliefs as "unofficial beliefs . . . that develop and operate outside powerful structures." While Hufford argues (p. 25) these beliefs are often stigmatized in the face of these powerful structures, "folk tradition has served as a repository of the cultural knowledge acquired from day-to-day living." The studies of Russian childbirth by folklorists discussed above demonstrate this exact relationship; medical authorities have challenged the traditions of Russian childbirth practices (in some cases with great success).

My own research among urban[7] Russian women between 1996 and 2004 could serve as an exemplar for Hufford's claims. Beginning already in the nineteenth century, Russian physicians were attempting to medicalize birth, even opening a school for female obstetricians (Ramer 1992). Mothers, especially in rural areas, resisted these shifts toward medicalization in birth. First, because birth, as noted above, was a secret process, to have an outsider, even a woman, attend at birth was potentially dangerous. Second, physicians would not necessarily perform the charms and prayers necessary for a successful delivery. Nor would they enter into the household, as the midwife did, to help with the child during the isolation period and introduce it formally to the community at the baptism. In other words, birth is not solely a medical process, even today, but a ritual act that incorporates significant cultural messages and serves to indoctrinate the participants in their roles. Institutional medicine largely overlooks these facts. However, participants may find them valuable touchstones that help guide their experience of childbirth. For example, Temkina and Rivkin-Fish (2020) discuss how midwives today receive gifts from mothers after delivery even though they have already paid for medical treatment. As a folklorist, I immediately recognized that this behavior carries a multilayered cultural resonance, related to the Soviet vernacular economy as well as to village practices of giving gifts (rather than money) to the midwife. The families in my study typically brought food and drink to the midwives upon the mother and child's release from the maternity hospital (Rouhier-Willoughby 2008:85–86). In a striking parallel to the traditional birth system, they were expected to acknowledge the child at a meal, like the village midwife did, to welcome it to the community. Even medical midwives have a spiritual power, reflected in the minor magical rite of toasting their health. Awareness of folk practices is central to an understanding of how childbirth is conceived of as a type of ritual exchange by the participants and argues for the importance of the consideration of unofficial cultural traditions in these studies.

Childbirth had largely become a medical process by the 1950s (Ransel 2000). Mothers (and their families) had also largely accepted the primacy of medicalized birth, but they did not eliminate vernacular elements completely. In fact, as I have documented in my research on urban childbirth, essential elements that were not antithetical to medical practice became the norm for medical institutions. Examples include the isolation of the mother and child (Rouhier-Willoughby 2008:82–83) as well as the persistent exclusion of men from childbirth (pp. 74–78). In the village, the mother and child remained in the bathhouse for several days and then in the house until the fortieth day,[8] when the mother was purified in a ritual at the church. Isolation protected them from ill-wishers, who could give them the evil eye. In twentieth- and twenty-first-century urban Russia, women also isolated their children from outsiders for the same period. For a week, they were kept in the maternity hospital (visitors were not allowed at all so that family members would speak to mothers through the windows, yelling up from the street). When out for daily walks with their children, they also hid them from the view of strangers and even from acquaintances for another month. They also did not invite guests during this time. While medical personnel argue that isolation prevents infection—and mothers may certainly agree with this claim—nearly to a person, they said that isolating the infant from view protected it from the evil eye.

It is also clear that the woman's transition to motherhood is the focus of all these works on birth practices, regardless of discipline. In keeping with gender norms found in Russian society at the time of the Bolshevik Revolution, women were perceived to be "more suited" to medical fields than men, particularly, but not exclusively, in obstetrics (see Ramer 1990; Goldman 2002; Tuve 1984 for a discussion of the feminization of the Russian and Soviet medical systems). As a result, 91% of medical personal in the Soviet Union by 1970 were women (Sacks 1976:97). In fact, it was a conversation with a young male intern, who referred to obstetrics as "women's work," that began my interest in this research. If the bulk of doctors were women, I thought, even in the 1990s when this conversation took place, why would obstetrics be singled out? Even today, while men may be present at the birth, their status as fathers is rarely the object of study. As noted above, within the traditional Russian childbirth ritual, it is the mother who is the focus of the rite. This attitude persists in contemporary Russia, even after the medicalization of birth and the adoption of a new attitude toward men's roles (at least to some extent) in the process. As Olson and Adon'ieva document (2012:195), in Russian villages even today, women who have given birth are referred to by a distinct term from those who have not; but there is no parallel form for men who have become fathers. While this terminology is not used in the urban settings I studied, even young women who gave birth in the early 2000s, when the father was allowed to be a birth partner, did not want him to be present; medical personnel I interviewed agreed with this decision since men were not prepared mentally to withstand the delivery experience (Rouhier-Willoughby 2008:244–245). In other words, medicalized childbirth in twenty-first-century Russia is largely consonant with the traditional focus on women as primary actors, on mothers and on female midwives who control the process. My research shows that, even in the face of scientific changes (and attacks), vernacular beliefs and practices can persist and even form the model for medical processes themselves. While my study on life-cycle rites focused on Soviet Russia and the first fifteen years of post-socialism, Kuksa (2022:7) has documented that, since that time, there has been a shift among educated, upper (middle)–class women, who are more likely to want the father (or some female friend or family member) to serve as a birth partner. Nevertheless, the independent medical midwives and doulas she interviewed were all women. They also describe how the (female) medical personnel at maternity hospitals are still not in favor of this option. For example, they took advantage of COVID-19 restrictions to eliminate birth partners of all kinds, even the father of the child, which is guaranteed by federal law (2022:6, 19).

Even after COVID-19 restrictions were lifted, birth partners were still not allowed back into many Moscow hospitals (2022:22).

The child also makes a transition into the status of "human" during this rite. Within the village context of traditional birth rites, the events surrounding the delivery and the actions of the midwife can have a profound effect on the child's fate (Vlaskina 1998:17; Dobrovol'skaia 2001:95). As Belousova documents (1998:25), the same is true within the context of the medical system in contemporary Russia. If a medical midwife pronounces the child to be "defective" in some way, this early diagnosis persists as the child grows and affects perceptions of the family toward the child (I documented [Rouhier-Willoughby 2008:98] similar attitudes among some mothers, who attributed their child's problems to a problem during pregnancy or birth, brought about by midwives and later commented on by medical personnel). In sum, an awareness of folk practices can reveal vernacular assumptions about daily life and status conferred by rituals, even those that take place in medical institutions. As a result, it is particularly important that folklorists return to the consideration of birth rites not only in the maternity hospitals but also within the alternative birthing community. Folklorists can provide a more comprehensive understanding of how traditional practices are understood in the contemporary period and indeed why they persist. As Hufford discusses (1995:23), these choices between official and unofficial cultures are not binary. Rather, these systems overlap and interact in complex ways. For example, isolation of the mother and child has both a medical and a vernacular basis; both aim to protect the vulnerable child but from two different types of threats—physical (viral infection) and supernatural (evil eye). Similarly, the female centrality in birth, resulting in limits on the participation of men, fits both village beliefs and ideas about gender derived from these conceptions as reflected in Soviet official policy. The people in my study incorporated elements from both official dogma and unofficial aspects of cultures. In some cases, they were consonant with each other, such as the importance of swaddling for infants to ensure that their limbs grow properly, while other vernacular practices resisted or contradicted official policies, for example, the importance of grandmotherly wisdom in how to care for a child and a new mother by stimulating breastmilk production with folk medicine or secret baptism by grandmothers (Rouhier-Willoughby 2008:113). Therefore, to ignore the role of vernacular practice is to relegate core belief systems in people's cultural identity to the wayside and, according to Hufford (1995:24), stigmatizes their value as an interpretive system, a particular concern for a folklorist working within the context of a medical school and indeed for cultural theorists broadly who study these practices.

Folk Narrative Genres in Childbirth

Contemporary ritual practices are not alone in drawing on traditional folk material. The structure of narratives, typically the source of the data analyzed by both humanists and social scientists, is also heavily influenced by forms of oral folklore. Folklorists are thus uniquely positioned among specialists in all these fields to understand how and why a narrative is constructed by an interlocutor. Diane Goldstein (2004, 2015), a folklorist who has published on narratives in both medical and legal contexts, documents how stories told by patients conform to traditional patterns. Particularly within the context of trauma and medical experiences, the way a narrative is constructed can convey a great deal about the teller's attitude and cultural assumptions. Skultans (1998), for example, demonstrated how narrative helped to re-establish meaning and identity among Latvians who been exiled to the Gulag. She (p. 26) contends that "narrators attempt to compensate for biographical disruption by restoring unity and coherence to narrated lives. The breakdown of the everyday structures of living creates a need to reconstitute meaning in storytelling." Of particular import is the fact that these narratives are characterized by formulas typical of folk genres (tales and legend). Skultans (1998:49) noted that, "a reading of the narratives suggests the notion of prefabricated discourse. This consists of 'verbal formulas—conventional phrases, idiomatic expressions, even whole sentences—that we have heard and used many times before.'" My own research (Rouhier-Willoughby 2008) revealed similar patterns in interviews with women who gave birth in maternity hospitals between the 1950s and the early 2000s. They used formulaic phrases to describe birth that were indicative of a shared vernacular experience of narrative structures. The most common was the description of the birth process as a конвейер ("conveyor"), indicating that the doctors viewed the women (and their bodies) as machines. Their descriptions of their experience contain aspects of both a folk tale and of a lament (see Ries [1997] and Kuksa [2022] for additional discussion of narratives of suffering, aka laments, in the Russian tradition). While a folk tale may seem an odd parallel for a narrative about childbirth, in fact the stories contain a similar pattern. Like tale heroes, the women I interviewed (from cities in European Russia, the Urals, Siberia, and the Far East) faced significant trials to give birth in the face of maternity home restrictions. Women were isolated from their family, feeling alone and in pain; they were treated by medical personnel who were seemingly more interested in moving the process along quickly than responding to patient needs. As one mother, who gave birth to her first child in 1984, told me,

> Грубо разговаривали, это конечно сразу убивало. Такое чувство, будто ты что-то делал плохое. Во-вторых это мокро, холодно, помещение неуютное. Там холодно, тебе больно, ты раздетый, страшный какой-то, рубахи, постели, всё это было так неуютно что роды не связывались с какой-то радостью или ожиданием чего-то хорошего, никто к тебе не подходит, не успокаивает. Это у меня так было.

> They spoke rudely to me, and that, of course, killed me right away. It felt as though you had done something bad. Second, it was wet, cold, an uncomfortable place. It's cold there, you are in pain, you are undressed, it's sort of terrible, the gowns, the beds, everything was so uncomfortable, that the delivery was not associated with any kind of joy or expectation of something good, no one comes to check on you, does not reassure you. That's how it was with me.

(Novosibirsk, 2001)

Her description of the cold and uncomfortable environment exacerbated by the rudeness and inattention of the medical personnel was a common refrain in women's narratives about the delivery experience. In this sense, they conform to the trials of a tale hero, who faces similar physical and mental tests of endurance. In the end, of course, as in a tale, these women triumphed over adversity. The happy ending, needless to say, is successful delivery and taking the child home to the family circle (Fig. 7.1). A Novosibirsk mother who gave birth in 1993 described it as follows:

> Я тогда чуть не расплакалась, потому что пять дней никого из них толком не видела, только в окно и по телефону разговаривали. Это было такое замечательное ощущение что всё, домой. Почему-то казалось, что в этом роддоме я провела не пять дней, а так долго времени. И когда ты прижимаешь к себе этого ребёночка, везёшь его домой, то это счастливый момент.

> I almost cried, because for five days I hadn't seen any of them [her family] at all, we had only talked on the phone. It was such a marvelous feeling, it's over, [we're going] home. For some reason, it seemed that I had spent not five days in the maternity hospital, but a very long time. And when you take that little child into your arms, take him home, that's a happy moment.

(Novosibirsk 2001)

FIG. 7.1. *Vstrecha* (meeting) in 2004 at a Novosibirsk maternity hospital.

(Photo by the author.)

An additional trial was spending most of the time in the hospital apart from their newborns, who were kept in the nursery and only brought in for feedings. Several mothers remarked that they were at a loss about how to swaddle the child upon their release because nurses had handled this procedure, which caused them anxiety and feelings of inadequacy (Rouhier-Willoughby 2008:108–109). They relied on their mothers to teach them proper techniques, thereby strengthening the family's role in childcare and undermining state control of the process (Fig. 7.2). These narrative patterns rely on story types that themselves perform a social function—the magic tale's victorious hero but also the litany of suffering and endurance brought about by the medical institutions. As Ries (1997:59) also documents, the tale and narrative of suffering center around a *podvig* (feat) of endurance and overcoming adversity in the face of a system designed to make people powerless. While certainly each woman had a distinct experience, the common features of the narratives they told me revealed cultural tropes that convey important cultural attitudes toward societal institutions and women's roles within them.

In addition, folklorists are adept at narrative analysis broadly that can reveal patients' unofficial cultural assumptions. For example, in her article "'When Ovaries Retire': Contrasting Women's Experiences with Feminist and Medical Models of Menopause,"

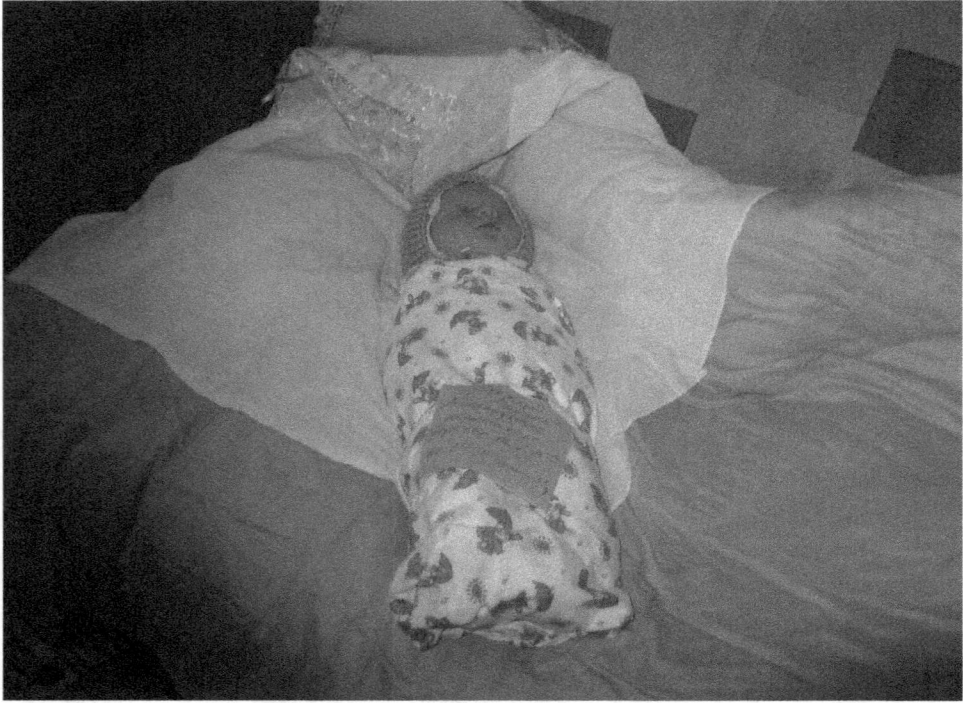

FIG. 7.2. First unswaddling after release from maternity hospital, 2004.

(Photo by the author.)

Goldstein (2000) explores how narratives in internet self-help groups are constructed to oppose both medical authority and feminist interpretations regarding menopause. She demonstrates (p. 315) that these narratives create a vernacular theory of menopause that allows participants to (1) create authority based on their own experience (cf. Hufford's conclusions discussed above), (2) establish patterns to define a "health theory" of menopause, (3) promote local control of the narrative that helps to negotiate experiences beyond the group, and (4) provide "an experientially based, alternative construction of illness which while subjugated in terms of medical authority, is likely to address the actual daily concerns and worldview of those coping with illness . . . it . . . makes its fullest sense in the cultural context out of which it arises." As discussed above, Russian mothers created similar narrative patterns about their own experiences, based on two traditional narrative forms, the tale and the lament. These patterns indicate a common folk belief in women's strength in the face of adversity and their ability to manage a critical medical situation, when medical personnel seem indifferent or even antagonistic. Not surprisingly, most of the women I interviewed, whether medical professionals or mothers, did not want a man to be present at the birth. Men were perceived as psychologically unprepared to deal with childbirth and likely to faint and to interfere with the process, rather than provide support. While Kuksa (2022) demonstrates that this attitude is changing among educated professionals, it has not totally disappeared even in contemporary Russia. In other words, within the context of a vernacular construction of health and illness for women (whether during childbirth or menopause), dismissal of these narratives by medical authorities is infuriating (as anthropologists also document). However, if scholars overlook their coherence as vernacular narratives and how they are structured, they also undermine their power to convey essential cultural beliefs.

Folkloristics in the Urban Setting

While the study of folklore in the urban setting only became accepted by the field of folkloristics in Russia after the fall of the Soviet Union, it would appear that the opposite is true of social scientists working on childbirth in today's Russia. Seemingly, outside of Saint Petersburg and Moscow, women do not give birth at all, at least based on the material in contemporary works on this topic. These analyses do not even include data from larger cities in the Urals or Siberia, such as Ekaterinburg and Novosibirsk. By contrast, folklorists gather data in rural regions as well as in urban centers outside of the two largest. As I mentioned above, the data for my study on life-cycle rites relied on middle-class women from cities of various sizes across Russia and in some former Soviet republics (not surprisingly, the folklorist Tatiana Kuksa also collects from a similar range of locations). If we hope to get a sense of practices broadly among the peoples in Russia, scholars in the social sciences must emulate folklorists by expanding the geographic range of their studies, whether urban or rural. Similarly, folklorists themselves must once again take up research on childbirth to fill in the gaps since the boom of publications on this topic ceased in the first decade of the 2000s. The rituals themselves can and do change, even in the context of medical establishments. Childbirth practices must be documented as they exist now, be they home births or those in private clinics. Likewise, it is important to record the narratives of parents about their experiences (and their children's) to ascertain what messages the institutions are sending about motherhood (or indeed fatherhood and personhood, in the case of the child) and how those messages are perceived. In my study on life-cycle rituals in urban Russia (Rouhier-Willoughby 2008:105–110), I demonstrated how the vernacular practices could be at odds with official messages and resist them. The prime example was that the Soviet government attempted to become the provider to families, sending the message that it (not blood relatives) would provide for the mother and child. However, the USSR never actually provided the material goods to live up to this promise. As a result, the family had to rely on its own resources and initiative to support the mother and newborn. In this context, grandmothers became central to the process, both in providing childcare and in passing along wisdom about childrearing, including religious elements necessary for the proper acculturation (e.g., baptism in Christian families and circumcision in Muslim ones). M. M. Shening-Parshina and A. N. Shibaeva (1967:50, 137, 143, 148), in their writings in the Soviet period on proper behavior during pregnancy and for a new mother, lament the lack of control over a family and the "danger" that a grandmother represents when she passes on folk remedies. New mothers persisted, however, in trusting the older generation, who provided more support than the medical system that had treated them as less than human. Nevertheless, the two systems could also be in harmony in many cases, as discussed above regarding isolation of the mother and child and the preeminence of women in the process even today. As Kuksa (2022) has documented, situations of resistance and acceptance persist, regardless of whether a child is born in a state hospital, in a natural birth center, or at home. While urban practices may once have been beyond the purview of our field, they are central to an understanding of the birth rite in contemporary Russia and complement the work done in rural areas by providing a more complete picture of the ritual process.

Conclusion

Study of the Russian childbirth rite presents a number of challenges to scholars. First and foremost has been the medicalization of birth in the twentieth century, which removed it from the purview of folk culture in the classical sense of our discipline. However, folklorists have demonstrated that medicalization, even in urban settings, does not eliminate the ritual processes characteristic of birth rites in vernacular contexts. In addition, limited access to medical institutions and the traditional secrecy surrounding childbirth create obstacles for the researcher. Nevertheless, as we have seen, the field of folkloristics has produced some of the most insightful works on this topic since 2001.

Folklorists have revealed the persistence of cultural norms from East Slavic traditions within the medical system. They have explored the way mothers and their families negotiate institutional and vernacular systems to create meaning in the process and establish new social roles. We are best placed to evaluate these questions of overlap among official and unofficial discourses and practices. All in all, more should rejoin the conversation to ensure that the discipline is at the forefront of important questions regarding the beginning of life in Russia.

Notes

1. It could be argued that birth is parallel to funerals in this case, which involve both mourners and the deceased. However, the person undergoing the life-cycle rite is, in fact, only the deceased. The mourners are part of the community that adjusts to the new social conditions as a result of the rite. In the case of birth, two people are indoctrinated into different social roles by the same ritual. While weddings also initiate two participants, their social status is parallel as a married couple, which is not the case with birth rites.
2. That is not to say that there were no data at all on childbirth, but they were eclipsed by the other two rites in ethnography and folklore collections of the time. See, for example, Firsov and Kiseleva (1993), Tian-Shanskaia (1993) and Zelenin ([1927] 1991) for discussion of childbirth rites in the nineteenth century that were collected during that time.
3. The symbolic death of an initiate can be seen in all three Russian life-cycle rites. While this is obvious in the case of the funeral, the transition from one stage to another, as Baiburn demonstrates, is conceived of as death. For example, during the traditional village wedding, a woman underwent a symbolic funeral. She "died" to her own family and was reborn into her husband's. See also Olson and Adonyeva (2012) and Rouhier-Willoughby (2003) for a discussion of this conception in the rites.
4. The one exception was funerals; a man's funeral was typically much more elaborate than a woman's in the Russian village. Women, who had already passed through two symbolic deaths during wedding and childbirth, required less intense ritual preparation for the passage to the afterlife than men in the traditional East Slavic context. However, women were central to the safe passage of men's souls to the other world. They prepared the body for burial, maintained the necessary vigils for the three days before burial, and sang the ritual laments for the deceased.
5. As with the religious elements in rites, the psychological ramifications of the transition (and even the discipline of psychology itself) were considered bourgeois and thus inappropriate topics for Soviet-era folklore studies.
6. See Amosova and Nikolaeva (2008) on Jewish childbirth practices; Serpivo (2012) on Nenets; Bakieva (2015), Liliavina (2016), and Aminova and Moskvina (2016) on Siberian Tatars; Shchankina (2011), Trofimova (2010), Kandrina (2011), and Shigurova (2011) on Mordvins; Boiko (2009) on Komi; Litvin (2016) on Karelians; Sodnompilova and Nanzatov (2015) on Mongols; Musaeva and Khasbulatova (2012), Tekaeva (2015), and Iakh"iaeva et al. (2014) on the Northern Caucasus (including the Chechens and Ossentians, among others); Kagarmanova (2012), Fattakhova (2012), and Abdulgazina (2011) on Bashkirs; Boldyreva (2009) on Kalmyks; Tadysheva (2019) on Altaic peoples; Iakovleva (2017) on Yakuts; and Fadeeva (2019) on the peoples of the Lower Amur Basin.

7. I conducted interviews with residents of Moscow, Saint Petersburg, Novosibirsk, Khabarovsk, Krasnodar, Chebeksary, Chita, Samara, Perm', Voronezh, Vladimir, Sergeev Posad, Kazan', Ufa, Suzdal', Ekaterinburg, Tver', Tomsk, Noril'sk, and Nizhnii Novgorod. Some interlocutors had also lived in cities in former Soviet republics, such as Gomel', Tashkent, Semipalatinsk, and Ashkhabad before returning to Russia.
8. The christening and subsequent meal may have occurred during this period of isolation, often on the third or the eighth day after birth. Aside from that public event in the context of a Christian rite, the child was shielded from those outside the family for at least forty days.

Works Cited

Abdulgazina, Gul'sasak Vaisovna. 2011. "Zapretyi okhranitel'nye obychai v sisteme dorodovykh obriadov bashkir Cheliabinskoi oblasti." *Magistra Vitae*, 238/23:144–146.

Adon'ieva, Svetlana B. 1998. "O ritual'noi funktcii zhenshchiny v russkoi traditsii." *Zhivaia starina*, 1:26–28.

Aminova, E. G., and V. A. Moskvina. 2016. "Beremennost' i rody v sovremennykh predstavleniiakh tatar bol'sherechenskogo raiona omskoi oblasti." In *Narodnaia kul'tura Sibiri*, ed. Tat'iana G. Leonova, 90–98. Omsk: Omskii gostudarstvennyi pedagogicheskii universtitet.

Amosova, S. N., and S. N. Nikolaeva. 2008. "'Chelovek rodilsia': Zametki o evreiskom rodil'nom obriade." In *Shtetl, XXI Vek. Polevye issledovaniia. Sbornik statei*, eds. V. Dymshits, A. L'vov, and A. Sokolova, 83–98. St. Petersburg: European University of Saint Petersburg Press.

Baiburin, Al'bert Kashfullovich. 1993. *Ritual v traditsinnoi kul'ture. Strukturno-semanticheskii analiz vostochnoslavianskikh obriadov*. St. Petersburg: Nauka.

Bakieva, Gul'sifa Takiiollovna. 2015. "Obriady i rituadly, sviazannye s rozhdeniem rebenka u sibirskikh tatar iuga Tiumenskoi oblasti." *Vestnik arkheologii, antropologii i etnografii*, 28/1:125–132.

Beattie, John. 1966. "Ritual and Social Change." *Man*, 1/1:60–74.

Bell, Catherine. 1997. *Ritual: Perspectives and Dimensions*. New York: Oxford University Press.

Belousov, A. F., I. S. Veselova, and S. Iu. Nekliudov, eds. 2003. *Sovremennyi gorodskoi fol'klor*. Moscow: Russian State Humanities University.

Belousova, Ekaterina A. 1998. "Nash malysh: Sotsializatsiia novorozhdennogo v sovremennoi gorodskoi kul'ture." *Zhivaia starina*, 2:24–25.

Belousova, Ekaterina A. 1999. "Predstavleniia i verovaniia, sviazannye s rozhdeniem rebenka: sovremennaia gorodskaia kul'tura." Kandidatskaia [Ph.D.] dissertatsiia, Russian State Humanities University.

Belousova, Ekaterina A. 2002. "Preservation of National Childbirth Traditions in the Russian Homebirth Community." *Slavic and East European Folklore Journal*, 7/2:50–77.

Belousova, Ekaterina A. 2003. "Sredstva i sposoby sotsializatsii materi v rodil'nom dome." In *Sovremennyi gorodskoi fol'klor*, eds. A. F. Belousov, I. S. Veselova, and S. Iu. Nekliudov, 340–369. Moscow: Russian State Humanities University.

Belousova, Ekaterina A., and Sergei Iu. Nekliudov, eds. 2001. *Rodiny, deti, povitukhi v traditsiiakh narodnoi kul'tury*. Moscow: Russian State Humanities University.

Bernshtam, T. A. 2007. *Prikhodskaia zhizn' russkoi derevni*. Saint Petersburg: Kunstkamera.

Boiko, Iuliia Ivanovna. 2009. "Rodil'naia obriadnost' lokal'noi gruppy letskikh komi v sovremennykh zapisiakh." *Izvestiia Rossiiskogo gostudarstvennogo pedagogicheskogo universiteta im. A.I. Gertsena*, 93:42–46.

Boldyreva, V. M. 2009. "Traditsionnaia rodil'naia obriadnost' erketenevskikh kalmykov." *Vestnik Instituta kompleksnykh issledoovannii aricnykh territorii*, 18/1:135–139.

Borozdina, Ekaterina A. 2014a. "Sotsial'naia organizatsiia estestvennykh rodov (sluchai tsentra akusherskogo ukhoda)." *Zhurnal issledovanii sotsial'noi politiki*, 12/3:413–428.

Borozdina, Ekaterina A. 2014b. "'Iazyk nauki i iazyk liubvi': Legitimatsiia nezavisimoi akusherskoi praktiki v Rossii." *Laboratorium*, 6/1:30–59.

Borozdina, Ekaterina A. 2016. "Zabota v rodovspomozhenii: Vygody i izderzhki professionalov." *Zhurnal issledovanii sotsial'noi politiki*, 14/4:479–492.

Borozdina, Ekaterina A. 2019. "Sozdavaia estestvennost': Modeli estestvennykh rodov v sovremennoi Rossii." In *Kriticheskaia sotsiologiia zabota: Perekrestki sotsial'nogo neravenstva*, eds. Ekaterina Borozdina, Elena Zdravomyslova, and Anna Temkina, 117–139. St. Petersburg: European University of Saint Petersburg Press.

Bourdieu, Pierre. 1991. *Language and Symbolic Power*, ed. John Thompson, trans. Gino Raymond and Matthew Adamson. Cambridge, MA: Harvard University Press.

Bourdieu, Pierre. 1977. *Outline of a Theory of Practice*, trans. Richard Nice. Cambridge: Cambridge University Press.

Bunina, M. A., and I. V. Popovicheva. 2013. "Traditsionnaia kul'tura Tambovskogo kraia: Regional'naia spetsifika obriadov rodil'nogo tsikla." *Molodoi uchenyi*, 59/12:739–743.

Davis-Floyd, Robbie. 1992. *Birth as an American Rite of Passage*. Berkeley: University of California.

Dobrovol'skaia, V. E. 2001. "Institut povival'nix babok i rodil'no-krestil'naia obriadnost'." In *Rodiny, deti, povitukhi v traditsiiakh narodnoi kul'tury*, eds. Ekaterina A. Belousova and Sergei Iu. Nekliudov, 92–106. Moscow: Russian State Humanities University.

Fadeeva, Elena Viktorovna. 2019. "Zhenshchina v traditsionnoi rodil'noi obriadnosti korennyx narodov nizhnego amura." *Izvestiia vostorchnogo institute*, 42/2:39–47.

Fattakhova, Tamara Daianovna. 2012. "Traditsionnye rodil'nye obriady u satrotovskikh bashkir." *Vestnik Cheliabinskogo gosudartvennogo universiteta*, 261/7:13–20.

Firsov, B. M., and I. G. Kiseleva, eds. 1993. *Byt velikorusskikh krest'ian-zemlepashtsev. Opisanie materialov etnograficheskogo biuro kniazia V. N. Tenisheva*. St. Petersburg: Izdatel'stvo Evropeiskogo doma.

Firth, Raymond. 1964. *Essays on Social Organization and Values*. Monographs in Social Anthropology No. 28. London: London School of Economics.

Goldman, Wendy. 2002. *Women at the Gates: Gender and Industry in Stalin's Russia*. Cambridge: Cambridge University Press.

Goldstein, Diane E. 2000. "'When Ovaries Retire': Contrasting Women's Experiences with Feminist and Medical Models of Menopause." *Health*, 4/3:309–323.

Goldstein, Diane E. 2004. *Once upon a Virus: AIDS Legends and Vernacular Risk Perception*. Logan: Utah State University Press.

Goldstein, Diane E. 2015. "Vernacular Turns: Narrative, Local Knowledge, and the Changed Context of Folklore." *The Journal of American Folklore*, 128/508:125–145.

Hufford, David J. 1995. "Beings without Bodies: An Experience-Centered Theory of the Belief in Spirits." In *Out of the Ordinary: Folklore and the Supernatural*, ed. Barbara Walker, 11–45. Logan: Utah State University Press.

Humphrey, Caroline, and James Laidlaw. 1994. *The Archetypal Actions of Ritual*. Oxford: Clarendon; Logan: Utah State University Press.

Iakh"iaeva, Z. I., Kh. M. Bataev, and L. I. Iusupova. 2014. "Kharakteristika obychaev i rodil'nykh obriadov, sviazannykh s rozhdeniem rebenka u narodov severnogo kavkaza." *Vestnik Chechenskogo gosudarstvennogo universtiteta*, 1:82–86.

Iakovleva, Kapitolina Maksimova. 2017. "Rodil'nye obriady iakutov: Traditsii i sovremennost." *Nauchno-prakticheskii elektronnyi zhurnal Alleia Nauki*, 15:41–46.

Issoupova, Olga. 2000. "From Duty to Pleasure? Motherhood in Soviet and Post-Soviet Russia." In *Gender, State and Society in Soviet and Post-Soviet Russia*, ed. Sarah Ashwin, 30–54. London: Routledge.

Kabakova, Galina I. 2001. *Antropologiia zhenskogo tela v slavianskoi traditsii*. Moscow: Ladomir.

Kagarmanova, Iuliia Valitovna. 2012. "Rodil'nye obriady permskikh bashkir." *Istoricheskaiai sotsial'no-obrazovatel'naia mysl'*, 4:38–39.

Kandrina, Irina Alekseevna. 2011. "Narodnye znaniia i opty v obriadakh detorozhdeniia mordvy Respubliki Mordoviia." *Vestnik Tambovskogo gostudarstvennogo tekhnieheskogo universtiteta*, 17/3:884–894.

Kuksa, Tatiana. 2018. *Rasskazy o rodakh i rodovspomozhenii v soremennoi gorodskoi kul'ture*. Master's thesis, Russian State University for the Humanities, Moscow.

Kuksa, Tatiana. 2020a. "Biopoliticheskie resheniia i pravozashchitnyi aktivizm v period rasprostranenia COVID-19 v Rossii: Ogranicheniii sub"ektnosti i novye granitsy vzaimozavisimosti." *Medical Anthropology and Bioethics*, 1/19:67–99.

Kuksa, Tatiana. 2020b. "'Strashilki' dlia rozhenits: Konstruirovanie i preodelnie strakha v rodakh." *Urban Folklore & Anthropology*, 3/1–2:166–187.

Kuksa, Tatiana. 2021a. "Doul'skoe soprovozhdenie rodov: Genesis, diskursy i praktiki emotsional'noi i fizicheskoi nemeditsinskoi zaboty." *Monitoring obshchestvennogo mneniia: Ekonomicheskie i sotsial'nye peremeny*, 3/163:226–249.

Kuksa, Tatiana. 2021b. "Partner-Accompanied and Individual Care Providers in the Setting of COVID-19 Pandemic: Power Decisions, Practices and Discourses." *Etnograficheskoe obozrenie*, 6:294–313.

Kuksa, Tatiana. 2022. "Activism and Patient Vulnerability: Resistance to Medical Authority and Regulation in Russia." *Folklorica*, 26:1–33.

Liliavina, E. V. 2016. "Evolutsiia rodil'noi obriadnosti tomskikh tatar v XX-XXI vv." *Vestnik antropologii*, 34/2:167–184.

Lipinskaia, V. A. 1996. *Starozhili i pereselentsy*. Moscow: Nauka.

Listova, Tatiana A. 1989. "Russkie obriady, obychai i pover'ia sviazannye s povival'noi babkoi (vtoraia polovina XIX-20-e gody XX v.)." In *Russkie: Semeinyi i obshchestvennyi byt*, eds. M. M. Gromyko and T. A. Listova, 142–171. Moscow: Nauka.

Listova, Tatiana A. 1992. "Russian Rituals, Customs, and Beliefs Associated with the Midwife (1850–1930)." In *Russian Traditional Culture*, ed. Marjorie Mandelstam Balzer, 122–145. Armonk, NY: M. E. Sharpe.

Listova, Tatiana A. 2003a. "Narodnaia religioznaia kontseptsiia zarozhdeniia i nachala zhizni." In *Russkie*, eds. V. A. Aleksandrov, I. V. Vlasova, and N. S. Polishchuk, 685–701. Moscow: Nauka.

Listova, Tatiana A. 2003b. "Obriady i obychai, sviazannye s rozhdeniem detei. Pervyi god zhizni." In *Russkie*, eds. V. A. Aleksandrov, I. V. Vlasova, and N. S. Polishchuk, 685–701. Moscow: Nauka.

Litvin, Iu. V. 2016. "Rodil'naia obriadnost' i institute materinstva v karel'skoi kul'ture (vtoraia polovina XIX–nachalo XX v.)." In *Vepsy, karely i russkie Karelii i sopredel'nykh oblastei: Issledovaniia i materialy k kompletksnomu opisaniu etnosov*, ed. I. Iu. Vinokurova, 113–123. Petrozavodsk: Karel'skii nauchnyi tsentr.

Musaeva, M. K., and Z. I. Khasbulatova. 2012. "Nekotorye traditsionnye obychai i obriady chechentsev i narodov Dagestana, sviazannye s rodami." *Izvestiia vysshikh uchebnykh zavedenii. Severno-Kavskazskii region. Obshchestvennye nauki*, 4:35–42.

Naumenko, G. M. 2001. *Narodnaia mudrost' i znaniia o rebenke*. Moscow: Tsentrpoligraf.

Olson, Laura J., and Svetlana B. Adonyeva. 2012. *The Worlds of Russian Village Women: Transgression, Tradition, Compromise*. Madison: University of Wisconsin Press.

Ortner, Sherry B. 1989. *High Religion: A Cultural and Political History of Sherpa Buddhism*. Princeton, NJ: Princeton University Press.

Ozhiganova, A. A. 2009. "Sovremennye perinatal'nye kul'tury: Traditsionnaia i al'ternativnaia modeli." *Polevye issledovaniia IEA RAN*, :63–83.

Ozhiganova, A. A. 2011a. "Antropologiia i meditsina: Perspektivy vzaimodeistviia (diskussiia 1980-kh–2000-kh godov)." *Etnograficheskoe obozrenie*, 3:10–21.

Ozhiganova, A. A. 2011b. "Rozhdenie 'novogo cheloveka': Utopicheskii proekt dvizheniia za estestvennye rody." In *Konstruiruia detskoe (filologiia, istoriia, antropologiia)*, eds. M. R. Balina, V. G. Bezrogov, S. T. Maslinskaia, K. A. Maslinskii, and M. V. Tendriakova, 444–460. St. Petersburg: Azmyt.

Ozhiganova, A. A. 2012. "Formirovanie tela mladentsa v sovremennykh meditsinskikh i al'ternativnykh ozdorovitel'nykh praktikakh." In *"Vsia istoriia napolnena detsvom": Nasledie F. Ar'esa I novye podkhody k istorii destsva*, eds. V. G. Bezrogov and M. V. Tendriakova, 434–446. Moscow: Rossiiskii gostudarstvennyi gumanitarnyi universitet.

Ozhiganova, A. A. 2016. "Domashnie rody: Strategii individual'nogo." In *Materinstvo i ottsovstvo skvoz'prizmu vremeni i kul'tur*, eds. N. L. Pushkareva and N. A. Mitsiuk, 277–279. Moscow: IEA RAN.

Ozhiganova, A. A. 2017. "Domashniaia akusherka kak sovremennyi kul'turnyi geroi." In *Sila slabykh: Gendernye aspekty vzaimopomoshchi i liderstva v proshlom i nastoiashchem*, eds. H. L. Pushkareva and T. I. Troshina, 268–271. Moscow: IEA RAN.

Ozhiganova, A. A. 2019. "Zabota o sebe, zabota o drugikh: Praktiki vzaimodeistviia zhenshchin i akusherok v domashnikh rodakh." In *Kriticheskaia sotsiologiia zabota: Perekrestki sotsial'nogo neravenstva*, eds. E. Borozdina, E. Zdravomyslova, and A. Temkina, 139–168. Saint Petersburg: Izdatel'stvo EUSPb.

Pankeev, Ivan. 1998. *Ot krestin do pominok. Obychai, obriady, molitvy*. Moscow: Iauza.

Ramer, Samuel. 1990. "Feldshers and Rural Health Care in the Early Soviet Period." In *Health and Society in Revolutionary Russia*, eds. Solomon, Susan Gross, and John F. Hutchinson, 121–145. Bloomington, IN: Indiana University Press.

Ramer, Samuel. 1992. "Childbirth and Culture: Midwifery in the 19th-Century Russian Countryside." In *Russian Peasant Women*, eds. Beatrice Farnsworth and Lynne Viola, 107–120. New York: Oxford University Press.

Ransel, David. 2000. *Village Mothers. Three Generations of Change in Russia and Tataria*. Bloomington: Indiana University Press.

Razumova, I. A. 2001. *Potaennoe znanie sovremennoi russkoi sem'i*. Moscow: Indrik.

Ries, Nancy. 1997. *Russian Talk: Culture and Conversation during Perestroika*. Ithaca, NY: Cornell University Press.

Rivkin-Fish, Michele. 2005. *Women's Health in Post-Soviet Russia: The Politics of Intervention.* Bloomington: Indiana University Press.

Rivkin-Fish, Michele. 2010. "Pronatalism, Gender Politics, and the Renewal of Family Support in Russia: Towards a Feminist Anthropology of 'Maternity Capital.'" *Slavic Review*, 69/3:701–724.

Rivkin-Fish, Michele. 2013. "Conceptualizing Feminist Strategies for Russian Reproductive Politics: Abortion, Surrogate Motherhood, and Family Support after Socialism." *SIGNS*, 38/3:569–593.

Rivkin-Fish, Michele. 2018. "'Fight Abortion, not Women': The Moral Economy Underlying Russian Feminist Advocacy." *Anthropological Journal of European Cultures*, 27/2:22–44.

Rouhier-Willoughby, Jeanmarie. 2003. "'Ne posylai menia na chuzhuiu storonu': Traurnye aspekty severno-russkoi svad'by glazami amerikanskogo issledovatelia (po zapisiam 19-ogo veka)." *Sibirskii filologicheskii zhurnal*, 2:13–23.

Rouhier-Willoughby, Jeanmarie. 2008. *Village Values: Negotiating Identity, Gender, and Resistance in Urban Russian Life-Cycle Rites.* Bloomington, IN: Slavica.

Sacks, Michael Paul. *Women's Work in Soviet Russia: Continuity in the Midst of Change.* New York: Praeger, 1976.

Sapalova, Dariia Usenova. 2010. "Traditsionnaia rodil'naia obriadnost' iakutov i kyryzov." *Oikumena. Regionovedchekie issledovaniia*, 13/2:72–77.

Serpivo, S. E. 2012. "Ob osobennostiakh ispol'zovaniia narodnoi meditsiny v rodil'noi obriadnosti nentsev." *Nauchnyi vestnik Iamalo-Nenetskogo avtonomnogo okruga (IaNAO)*, 74/1:22–25.

Shchankina, Liubov' Nikolaevna. 2011. "Rodil'nye obriady mordvy Sibiri." *Vestnik Tomskogo gosudarstevennogo universiteta. Istoriia*, 14/2:168–174.

Shening-Parshina, M. M., and A. N. Shibaeva. 1967. *Sanitarnoe prosveshchenie po okhrane zdorov'ia zhenshchin.* Moscow: Central Scientific-Research Institute for Sanitary Enlightenment.

Shigurova, Tat'iana Alekseevna. 2011. "Odezhda v rodil'nom ritual mordvy." *Vestnik Chuvashskogo universiteta*, 4:117–122.

Skultans, Vieda. 1998. *The Testimony of Lives: Narrative and Memory in Post-Soviet Latvia.* London: Routledge.

Sodnompilova, Marina M., and Bair Z. Nanzatov. 2015. "Narodnaia ginekologiia mongol'skikh narodov: Perinatal'nyi period, rody i lechenie besplodiia." *Vestnik Buriatskogo nauchnogo tsentra Sibirskogo otedeleniia Rossiiskoi akademii nauk*, 18/2:39–54.

Tadysheva, N. O. 2019. "Rodil'nyi obriad i rituraly detskogo tsikla. Etnograficheskoe opisanie." In *Obriadnost' v traditsionnoi kul'ture altaitsev*, eds. A. A. Konunov and N. O. Tadysheva, 409–420. Gorno-Altaisk: Nauchno-issledovatel'skii institute altaistiki.

Tekaeva, A. M. 2015. "Rodil'nye obriady i poeziia osetin." *Severo-Osetinskii institute gumanitarnykh i sotsial'nykh issledovanii im V.I. Abaeva*, 13:159–165.

Temkina, Anna, and Michele Rivkin-Fish. 2020. "Creating Health Care Consumers: The Negotiation of Un/Official Payments, Power and Trust in Russian Maternity Care." *Social Theory & Health*, 18:340–357.

Tian-Shanskaia, Olga Semyonova. 1993. *Village Life in Late Tsarist Russia*, ed. David L. Ransel. Bloomington: Indiana University Press.

Trofimova, O. Iu. 2010. "Mordovskie rodil'nye obriady Cheliabinskoi oblasti." *Aktual'nye problem gumanitarniykh i estestvennykh nauk*, 11:385–386.

Tuve, Jeannette E. 1984. *The First Russian Women Physicians.* Newtonville, MA: Oriental Research Partners.

van Gennep, Arnold. 1909. *Les rites de passage.* Paris: Emile Nourry.

Vlaskina, T. Iu. 1998. "Donskie bylichki o povitukhakh." *Zhivaia Starina*, 2:15–17.

Zelenin, D. K. 1991. *Vostochnoslavianskaia etnografiia*, ed. K. V. Chistov, trans. K. D. Tsivina. Moscow: Nauka. First published 1927.

Death Rites

CHAPTER 8

GREEK DEATH RITUALS AND LAMENT

GAIL HOLST-WARHAFT

DESPITE differences in death rituals in the countries and regions of the Balkans, there are common threads that researchers have noted among them, especially in countries that follow the Greek or Russian Orthodox traditions. Laments for the dead were once common to many countries in the region but are gradually disappearing except in remote villages. Before they disappear entirely, anthropologists and ethnographers are anxious to document them. Greek laments, in particular, have been studied by a number of scholars, especially from the 1980s. Besides the common interest of modern researchers in folk beliefs and death rituals, Greek rituals and beliefs have been studied by classicists and literary scholars because of their so-called continuity with ancient Greece. The approaches have been varied and the field sometimes fraught, but the study of Greek death rituals continues to attract an unusually broad range of scholarship.

CONTINUITY, NATIONALISM, AND THE SPECIAL CASE OF MODERN GREECE

Although it is a question that has been argued and discussed for more than a century, and has perhaps exhausted its importance, it is impossible to omit any mention of the issue of continuity of modern Greek customs, rituals, and folklore with those of ancient Greece. Greece is unique among Balkan countries in occupying the same territory and speaking a modified version of the same language as the ancient Greeks. In their struggle to achieve independence from Ottoman rule, Greeks relied heavily on the assistance of Philhellenes, who idealized Hellenic culture and were prepared to lay down their lives in defense of what they saw as an affront to Western civilization: the repression of the Christian descendants of Plato and Aristotle by Muslim overlords. Conscious that European assistance was invaluable not only to the revolution but to the development of an independent nation, Greek politicians and intellectuals strove to strengthen the case for continuity and the special treatment they thought they deserved as the heirs of a glorious past. Folklore, including the rituals surrounding death, was enlisted as an important source of evidence for a continuous tradition, and not only by the Greeks. Foreign scholars steeped in ancient Greek literature, like John Lawson (1910), sought to find continuities, not in order to establish the legitimacy of modern Greek claims to be heirs of the ancients but to throw light on classical texts and practices. Pointing out the similarities of modern Greek wedding and funeral practices and without making any comparative study of other Balkan traditions, Lawson found evidence for a direct line of continuity between ancient and modern Greek beliefs about death and the afterlife. He noted that women tore their hair and lacerated their breasts at modern Greek funerals and that there were professional or semi-professional lament singers who lamented not only the individual whose funeral they attended but their own dead (1910:346).

In his important study of the relationship between modern Greek folklorists and early Greek nationalism *Ours Once More: Folklore, Ideology, and the Making of Modern Greece* (1982), Michael Herzfeld describes how folklore became the primary tool for legitimizing the new Greek state and for establishing the country's special status in the Balkans. Before the revolution of 1821, there were no systematic studies of folklore. After it, *laografia*, literally "study of the people," became an ideological and political project of the utmost importance to the formation of the new Greek state.[1] Unlike their European counterparts, Greek intellectuals, as well as political leaders, were anxious not only to stress the parallels between modern and ancient folklore and rituals but to combine the legacy of the ancient world with that of the Byzantine Empire. This involved some intellectual juggling but was soon knitted into a nationalist garment that Greek nationalist leaders have donned on frequent occasions ever since.

In an address to the National Assembly that met in Athens in 1844 to draft the constitution of the new state, one of the early Greek leaders, Ioannis Kolettas, expressed the mood of the gathering succinctly: "Each of us," he announced, "has in himself a sense of his splendid Greek origin. . . . Contemporary Greece, united as she is in one state, one purpose, one power, one religion, should therefore inspire great expectations in the world" (quoted in Kitromilides 1979:14).[2] "One religion" is the key phrase here—the central position of the Orthodox Church in the Greek state and its emerging nationalist thinking had an impact on the study of Greek rituals and ethnography, particularly on the study of popular beliefs about death and the afterworld. It was difficult not to recognize the contradictions between the teachings of the church about paradise and hell and the folk tradition in which death is seen as an injustice, an evil that befalls the family and the community, and where the personification of death is Charos—not Charon the boatman of antiquity, although he is occasionally portrayed as a ferryman, but a rider on a black horse who carries the dead to his dark underworld kingdom. We will see that some scholars have addressed that challenge and argued for an accommodation between orthodoxy and popular belief.

What distinguished early studies of Greek laments and death rituals, beginning in the second half of the nineteenth century and continuing through much of the twentieth, was a preoccupation with the similarities of contemporary tradition and ancient practices. While it is impossible to deny some similarities between the ancient and modern Greek imaginary worlds, the insistence on continuity between them biased research and excluded aspects of the tradition that drew on later influences. It also stood in the way of any comparative study of Balkan death rituals. Researchers are all creatures of their time and place, and the first studies of Greek folklore were made by foreign, or foreign-educated, scholars who were influenced by European currents of thought, especially those of the Enlightenment. For most inhabitants of the new Greek nation, however, the issue of continuity with an ancient past was less significant than the fact that they were Orthodox Christians. What had sustained them through centuries of Ottoman domination was their Christian faith and the considerable power given to religious leaders by the Ottomans through the system of self-governing, religious millets. As Greek folklorists joined foreign scholars in their search for ancient survivals, they felt the necessity of integrating the legacy of Byzantium and orthodox belief with their determination to excavate traces of an ancient Greek heritage.[3]

Not all studies of continuity in Greek tradition had a nationalist bias. Margaret Alexiou's classic study *The Ritual Lament in Greek Tradition* (1974) discussed continuity as a way not to bolster the special status of Greece but to illuminate both modern and ancient traditions, using her thorough knowledge of classical and Byzantine Greek literature to examine laments from Homer to the present. Alexiou notes, from the sixth century BCE in Athens and later in a number of city-states, a dramatic change in what were otherwise among the most stable rituals of ancient Greece. Legislation was introduced by Solon to restrict the singing of laments by women as a corpse was carried through the streets of Athens. Only kinswomen were allowed to mourn; there was to be no lacerating of flesh and no reciting of "set dirges" or lamenting of one person at the funeral of another (Alexiou 1974:110; Holst-Warhaft 1992:114–115). Alexiou suggests a possible explanation for the limitations on women's behavior at funerals in the link between mourning and rights of inheritance; women may have had at least some behind-the-scenes influence on decisions about property. She also thought the establishment of the two major state festivals in which women played a dominant role, the Thesmophoria and the Eleusinian Mystery Cults, may have been a way of providing a state-sanctioned forum for women to exercise their authority rather than at private funerals. There is also the possibility, and this seems to me the most likely explanation, that women's loud and extravagant displays of mourning may have posed a danger to society by stirring up a desire for revenge. This was Plutarch's view. He said the laws were passed by Solon on the advice of Epimenides of Crete, who had suffered the effects of civil feuding at Phaistos (Alexiou 1974:14–22). After looking at the texts of the so-called revenge laments of the Mani, an area in which blood feuds continued until after World War II, it is difficult to avoid the conclusion that laments were a powerful means of inspiring violent action and had their desired effect.[4]

Modernization and the View from the Margins

Any discussion of death rituals in Greece and elsewhere in the Balkans must deal with the problem of modernization, loss of tradition, and the cultural context we are referring to when we describe these rituals. Most Greeks now live in urban centers where many of the practices discussed in this chapter are no longer maintained or are preserved in a diluted form. Does this mean these rituals should no longer be studied in the rural setting where the rites surrounding death are still adhered to and where they fit into the ritual structures that once marked village life from birth to death? There are obvious reasons why most studies we have of Greek death rituals are of rural communities. One is a fascination with what is disappearing in such societies and an understandable eagerness to record dying customs, songs, and laments before they disappear entirely. The other is the attraction of an exoticism that is far removed from the culture of the observer and at the same time appears like a vision of their own society as it might once have been—a simpler, more organic version of social organization. Greek death rituals and the laments that play a central role in them are particularly remote from modern urban societies where death is institutionalized, sanitized, and subsumed into a narrative of consolation created partly by the Christian church and by the quasi-medical assumption of expertise by professional grief counselors. But by studying laments in their village context, are we in danger of privileging what is to the outside observer an exotic or "primitive" form of social organization over a more sophisticated or Europeanized urban one? Are Greek urban dwellers who have ceased to observe nightlong vigils around the body of their deceased relatives or to lament them with loud cries and formal sung poetry more representative of Greek culture than the inhabitants of a village in the mountains of Epirus?

This is a question Herzfeld (1987) addressed provocatively more than thirty years ago, arguing that "Avoiding the study of remote communities simply displaces the problem itself (of how modern ethnographies shed light on national images), and still further trivializes the voice of the already much neglected rural population" (p. 188). Similarly, Nadia Seremetakis, in her study of death rituals and lament in Inner Mani, argues for "the empowering poetics of the periphery," which, she argues, "is always concerned with the imaginary dimension of material worlds, of things and persons made and unmade" (1991:1). Like the mountain villages of Epirus, those of Inner Mani may be a "detached fragment of global modernity" (Seremetakis 1991:1); nevertheless, they are not isolated from the urban world where many Maniates now live, maintaining strong ties with communities of their region. Repression, marginalization, and emigration have been the fate of poor rural societies in Greece at least since the Byzantine Empire. What has survived of traditional ritual practices, especially those dominated by women, may appear fragmented and doomed to disappear; but Seremetakis argues that only through the study of these survivals in their social context can we understand the complex emotional, creative, social, and political milieu where traditional rituals, including lament, were created.

Modern Greece is a country that moved from rural tradition, based on generations of continuous occupation of the same lands and villages, to urbanity in a single generation. That did not mean that former villagers broke all ties to their rural past. The cultural traditions that developed on islands or in mountain villages depended on a continuous relationship with a place, a *topos*, that dictated all aspects of life including death. Without it, Greeks often felt rootless, which is why so many Athenians go back to their parents' or grandparents' villages to celebrate Easter or other festivals of the calendar year. There is a nostalgia for the traditional and unique rituals associated with village life, even for the pitiless rhetoric of the laments, that draws urban dwellers to return. A musician I know from Epirus who works in Athens told me in 2009 that when he returned to his village for his mother's funeral, he sat up all night with the mourners who sang laments around her open coffin. "I didn't cry all night," he said, "but in the morning I went out for a cigarette and I cried like a baby. That's what laments do. The more you dig, the more you find—like water in a well."

Laments, like folk songs, dances, tales, embroidery, cuisine, and other village creations that developed slowly into a cultural tradition, were never static creations—there was space for improvisation—but they were artistic creations, judged by the community for their emotional power and poetic skill. They endured not because they were endlessly repeated but because they developed and evolved over centuries. It is important, then, to consider them not only from a cultural–anthropological perspective but also from a creative one. It may be that laments lose their ritual force outside the context of village life, but the poetry of lament remains timeless.

Fieldwork and Anthropology and the Semiotics of Death Rituals

Despite the fact that Herzfeld was an anthropologist who did his fieldwork in Rhodes, Crete, and other rural Greek settings (1977, 1981, 1985), his writings about the nationalist agenda of Greek folklore studies (1985) were wide-ranging, historical, and philosophical, addressing the nature of the disciplines of anthropology and folklore themselves as they pertained to Greece. I have highlighted their importance not because death rituals were a special focus of his research but because he establishes the unique problems of Greek anthropology and folklore studies, noting that from the earliest studies of its folklore Greece was regarded by researchers, politicians, writers, and eventually the population at large as a unique case in the Balkans. Researchers less concerned with the history of Greek folklore studies avoided this issue. Loring Danforth's *Death Rituals of Rural Greece* (1982), accompanied by the striking photographs of Alexander Tsiaris, was an anthropological study of rural death rituals based on his fieldwork and not complicated by issues of continuity or nationalist sentiment. Danforth carried out his study in a village in Thessaly, close to Mt. Olympus. He saw Greek death rituals as an "attempt to mediate the opposition between life and death" (1982:32). This may be true for all death rituals, but in countries like Greece, where exhumation and reburial of the bones are practiced, the dramatic unearthing of the bones and their placement in an ossuary provided graphic evidence of the finality of bodily life (Fig. 8.1). For Danforth, laments were a special example of the mediating nature of death rituals. Drawing on van Gennep's (1909) classic analysis of rites of passage and on Robert Hertz's (1960) study of secondary burial, Danforth considered the death rites in the Greek village to be not only a mediation between life and death but one dependent on a religious perspective.

One of the most interesting features of the language of Greek laments is that it strains the boundaries of Christian faith. Greek villagers may all be believers in the Orthodox Church, but the contrast between the teachings of Christianity and the images of the afterlife presented in the laments is so striking that a "religious perspective" is difficult to maintain. The laments refuse the comforting Christian belief in an afterlife that will reward the dead for their piety in their earthly existence. It can be argued that the dark vision of an underworld kingdom ruled by Charos is simply a parallel form of religion, but reconciling the two visions into a consistent philosophical or religious system is not easy. Can it be that death, especially premature death, is such an obvious injustice, so

FIG. 8.1. Cemetery in the village of Richia, Peloponnese, showing boxes containing disinterred bones.
(Photo by Laurie Kain Hart.)

inimical to the mothers, sisters, wives of the deceased, that the official teachings of religion are rejected in favor of what seems a comfortless and bleak acceptance of reality? Before we consider this question in more detail, it may be useful to summarize what takes place when someone dies in a Greek village.

Death and Its Immediate Aftermath

Death does not just happen in rural villages. Usually it is preceded by a warning—in Mani this can take the form of a "death bird" (usually a carnivorous bird) that may hover over a house or come repeatedly to visit a relative. It may also take the form of a prophetic dream or an apparition that makes threatening noises as it circles a house (Seremetakis 1991:50–63). The immediate behavior induced by a death is a flurry of household activities prescribed by custom, all of which have to do with the correct management of death and all of which are performed by women. Coins are sometimes placed on the eyes of the body, and the mouth is closed. The body must be washed with wine or vinegar and all orifices closed. The hands, feet, and jaw of the corpse are tied with ribbon and a narrow sheet-like garment, or *savano*, is placed on the corpse before it is dressed in clothes that have been saved for the burial. Then the body is placed on the floor or another surface with feet facing east.

Relatives and members of the household must also change their clothes. Floors are washed, and walls are often whitewashed. Mirrors are covered or turned to the wall, some say because they are orifices to a spectral world (Seremetakis 1991:67). Candles are placed around the body, and a long, flexible candle made by the women of the household and measured to match the length of the corpse is coiled round on itself and placed on the navel. The direction in which the candle is wound is critical. It must burn in a right-hand direction—as the villagers say, "like the dance."[5] One-third of its length will be burned each night for three nights. The candle, or *isou*, is said to be related to the journey of the dead to the other world.

This journey, often quite inconsistent with what will be said in the laments, involves an angel accompanying the soul of the deceased to various places where it lived as well as to heaven and hell, before it comes to God for judgment. After the pollution of death has been washed away from the house and the household members, community members are invited to enter. Corn may be scattered on the floor and incense swung in right-hand circles around the room, but nothing can "cross" the body. It is believed that if someone were to pass anything over the corpse, it could turn into a vampire. The first twenty-four hours after a death are fraught with danger, as Guy Saunier (1999:235) notes. The villagers are confronted by the possibility of their own death and take care to observe the rituals expected of bereaved relatives.

When the church bell announces a death, people may call at the house, returning in the evening to sit all night beside the body. Offerings of flowers or fruit may be made, and some visitors may ask that these offerings or messages be conveyed to their own dead. This suggests that the dead are gathered together in a common place, although where that is, is far from certain. At the house, those who are not closely related to the dead may chat and make general remarks, but the relatives and women who lament over the dead confine themselves to mourning.

At the same time as the bell informs the broader community that a death has occurred in the village, the chief lamenter, or *moirologistria*, organizes the laments, summoning other women to join her. Usually mothers and wives do not lament their dead immediately following a death; other women do it on their behalf. The only qualification for leading and performing the lament is the personal experience of grief. If you are experienced in pain, if you wear black because you have lost a father or husband, you have the right to weep on behalf of another person. This does not mean that poetic or musical artistry are ignored, but they are secondary to the emotional intensity required in a lament. The verb μοιρολογώ (*mirologo*) means to speak of fate. Laments for the dead speak of the fate of the community, of the dead person, and sometimes of all people. Death, in the laments, is the ultimate evil. As Saunier remarks, "For the Greek people, faithful . . . to a tradition that looks back to Homeric poetry, death is the heaviest and most complete form of evil" (1999:9). In the folk tradition, there is no idea of original sin. It is death and its personification as Charos that is cruel, implacable, and the epitome of evil. Charos rules over the underworld with his wife, sometimes feasting on the bodies of children. Although he bears the name of the ancient ferryman of dead souls, he is much more than that in the modern tradition. A sinister figure, often portrayed as riding a black horse, he snatches up the dead, carrying the children in front of him on his saddle. Even the heroes of the folk ballads who wrestle with Charos on a marble threshing floor and appear to be defeating him will ultimately be defeated by some trick he plays.[6]

Death cuts off everything that the dead crave—family, the beauty of nature, and, above all, light. The dead go to a dark place where they cannot see. Yet in the laments they remain emotionally tied to the world above, capable of communicating, through lament, with their mourners and lamenting their own situation in a dark and isolated underworld:

> Καλημέρα σ' Ανατολή, καλημέρα σου Δύση,
> Καλημέρα σου μαύρη γη, μ' ούλους τα' αποθαμένους.
> Κ' εκείνος απογήθηκε με το καημένο χείλι:
> Την καλημέραν έχετε εις τον απάνω κόσμο,
> Που περπατείτε με δροσιά, που φέγγετε με λύχνο.
> Κ'εγώ το βαρυορίζικο στη γη πολλά καημένο,
> Χωρίς νερό βρεγμένο 'μαι, χωρίς φωτιά καημένο,
> Χωρίς μαχαίρια και σπαθιά, σπαθοκονταρεμένο.
>
> Good morning to you East, good morning West,
> good morning black earth where the buried lie.
> And he reported with his poor lips;
> you have good morning in the upper world
> you who walk in the cool, with lamps to light you,

and I, wretched among the wretched
with no water to refresh me, without fire, poor me,
without knives and with swords all ruined.

(quoted in Saunier 1999:180, my translation)

In the aftermath of a death, the lamenter not only expresses sorrow and anger. She becomes the mouthpiece of the dead person. Through her, the dead person may ask for messages to take to other dead members of the family. They may also encourage the mourners to weep until the procession begins. During the placing of the body in its wooden coffin, which has previously been decorated to receive it, the lamenter introduces the theme of farewell. In these ritual farewells, sung in rhyming couplets in many parts of Greece, the dead person bids farewell not only to their family but to the upper world with its beautiful nature and sunlight.

Ἔχετε γειά ψηλά βουνά και δέντρα με τους ίσκιους
στον ίσκιο σας δεν κάθομαι μάϊδε και στη δροσιά σας
κατέβηκα στη μαύρη γης στον πικραμένο Άδη.

Health to you high mountains, and trees with your shade,
I don't sit in your shade, nor in your freshness,
I went down into the black earth, into bitter Hades.

(Saunier 1999:40)

Women, Feminism, and Lament

The prominence of women's voices in ancient and modern Greek death rituals made lament a natural subject for women scholars to research. Following Alexiou, studies by, among others, Caraveli-Chaves (1981), Caraveli (1986), Auerbach (1987), Seremetakis (1991), Holst-Warhaft (1992, 2000), Du Boulay (2009), and Håland (2014) stress the importance of women in death rituals. Written by female scholars from diverse disciplines, these studies all stress the centrality of women's role in lament and, more broadly, in mourning and remembering the dead. Auerbach's research was unusual in concentrating on the musical aspects of lament. Basing her analysis on fieldwork carried out in the Konitsa district of Epirus, she argued that the laments women composed were not necessarily different in terms of their melodies or even their lyrics from songs sung on other occasions except that they were delivered in a particular tone of voice, sometimes with falsetto exclamations, setting them apart from songs performed in a different context.

In the Mani, this type of high-voiced articulation is described as "screaming the dead" (Seremetakis 1991:72), a process that transfers sound from the inner world of the

FIG. 8.2. Woman informant known for her lament skills. Mani, Greece.

(Photo by Gail Holst-Warhaft.)

household to the community and mimics the disorder of death. High-pitched shrieks may also punctuate the otherwise normally pitched narrative of a lament (Holst-Warhaft 1992:69), alternating with sobs, sighs, and exclamations and acting as intensifiers. In the complex mixture of sounds at a wake, a partly improvised lament may be punctuated by "screaming" but not by uncontrolled weeping. The immediate next of kin are not those who lead the lament because they are regarded as too affected to create a satisfactory lament. Those who disrupt the lament by excessive weeping may be led away from the lament circle until they compose themselves (Fig. 8.2).

Women who are immediately affected by a death may draw their black scarves across their heads or pull them off entirely as they tear their hair or scratch their cheeks and beat their breasts in a universal gesture of grief. Such extreme gestures may be rare today, but women remember when it was common to see the streets covered in women's hair and to hear their voices hoarse from screaming (Seremetakis 1991:73). The intensity of women's bodily movements is accompanied by the violence of their anger against whoever or whatever was considered responsible for the death. That included God.

Α ρε Θεέ από ψηλά
που δε σε φτάνει ούτε γκρας,
δε κατεβαίνεις χαμπηλά
να πούμε δικαιώματα;
Τα πλέα τάχομε εμείς
πο' μείναμε χωρίς παιδί.

> Hey, you, God, from high above
> where the gun can't reach you
> why don't you descend below
> to talk about rights!
> We have the most [rights]
> because we're left without a child.[7]

From the time women gather around the dead body to when the men join them at the house or funeral, the hierarchies of mourning are expressed by physical proximity to the body and by bodily gestures. The intensity of mourning reflects a hierarchical structure, where a young man, especially one who is well educated or particularly brave and popular in the village, is at the apex, followed by an elderly man who is similarly regarded, followed by a young woman, an elderly man, a young child, an old woman, a handicapped person, or an infant (Kassis 1980:271). Seremetakis (1991:86–87) argues that the rigid hierarchy of kin, gender, and age presented by Kassis may be broken by mourners who enter the ceremony, greeting those to whom they may not be related by blood with more general salutations such as "brother," "sister," or "child."

Still, there is a pecking order in lament, and the women will sometimes argue over their right to lament based not only on kinship but on being raised in the same village. Laments for the dead are sung not exclusively but predominantly by women all over the world. In some parts of Greece, men may sing women's laments that have become popular (Fig. 8.3). Kyriakos Kassis, who has made the most extensive anthology we have of laments from the Mani, describes working in the summer in an olive press where the men sang laments as they worked. He insists (contra Auerbach, Herzfeld, and Seremetakis) that the *moiroloi* (lament) is in fact the *tragoudhi* (song) of the Mani (1979:78). In November 2019, I interviewed a lament singer, Glykeria Fyli, in the village of Veltsista near Ioannina and asked her why instrumental pieces called *moiroloyia* were played at weddings and at festivals. She said, "In this village we have known nothing but pain. Everything we sing is a lament. We don't have any other songs."[8]

Glykeria Fylis's account accords well with Seremetakis's view of the centrality of pain (*ponos*) to the legitimacy of discourse in lament and to the "truth-claiming strategies of Maniat women when in conflict with various aspects of the social structure" (1991:3). The pain of death is only one of the great losses women face in such villages. Marriage, which entails the separation of a bride from her parental household and her integration into the groom's family, is likewise a terrible loss for mothers and their daughters. At the exhumation of a young woman's body that he observed in Thessaly, Danforth noted that a number of the laments could be sung with slight modification at either an exhumation or a wedding, and he concluded that marriage was "a kind of half death" (1982:83). He quotes a wedding lament of a type common not only to other regions of Greece but to many cultures from China to the Balkans, one that parallels the music and lyrics of a lament for the dead:

FIG. 8.3. Polyphonic singers from the village of Ktismata, Epirus, practicing laments.

(Photo by Gail Holst Warhaft.)

> Τώρα κίνησα, τώρα θα φύγω
> Απ' το σπίτι μου κι απ' τα γλυκά μ' αδέλφια
> Ν' όλοι με διώχνουν κι όλοι με λένε:–Φεύγα.
> Ν' ως κι η μάνα μου με διώχνει, δε με θέλει.
> Κι ο πατέρας μου, κι αυτός μου λέει:--Φεύγα.
> Φεύγω κλαίγοντας και παραπονεμένη.
>
> Now I have set out. Now I am about to depart
> From my home and from my dear brothers and sisters.
> Everyone is driving me away; everyone is telling me to leave.
> Even my mother is driving me away, she doesn't want me.
> And my father too, even he tells me to leave.
> I am leaving with tears and with a heavy heart.
>
> (1982:87)

A third loss commonly faced in poor areas of Greece such as the Mani, Epirus, and on many of the Greek islands is emigration. In a village culture where women were largely illiterate, the emigration of a son, fiancé, or husband for economic reasons was regarded as a loss comparable to death. Nowadays, as communication has been transformed and women not only visit their urban-dwelling compatriots but may travel to Greek communities abroad in Melbourne, Chicago, Toronto, and New York, the pain of emigration has lessened; but the laments created out of that pain are still part of the repertoire of lament that endures. One of the most popular songs in the repertoire of island songs call *nisiotika* to this day is a mother's lament for a son lost to emigration:

Αχ! Πανάθεμά σε ξενιτιά, τζιβαέρι μου
εσέ και το καλό σου, σιγανά, σιγανά, σιγανά και ταπεινά.
Αχ! Που πήρες το παιδάκι μου, τζιβαέρι μου
και το 'κανες δικό σου, σιγανά πατώ στη γη.

Ach! A curse on foreign lands, my treasure
and your virtue, softly. Softly, softly, softly and humbly
Ach! You took my child, my treasure
and you made him your own, softly, softly, softly I tread the earth.

If pain is what qualifies a woman to lead the lament, there are also artistic and performative qualifications that single out an exceptional lamenter. Her personal pain is a necessary stimulus, but she will also be judged by the way she improvises the words of a lament, combining traditional formulas with personal reflections or imaginative details, like the lament of a woman who says she will take her pain to the goldsmith and have it gold-plated and made into a talisman, a ring, and a cross so that she can wear it forever (Saunier 1999:124). There is a reason why certain laments last. They are remembered for their art and their emotional impact. Like the leader of an ancient chorus, the woman soloist who leads the lament is called a *korifea*. She may "pass" the lament to another soloist, but she must be supported by a chorus of women who reinforce her performance with antiphonal responses, sometimes repeating the last line of what she has just sung or adding a short refrain, sometimes sobbing or exclaiming. Seremetakis (1991) developed an elaborate argument about the nature of antiphony in Maniat laments. She ascribes a number of essential functions to the technique including the fact that it is "a prescribed technique for witnessing, for the production/reception of jural discourse, and for the cultural transmission of truth . . . and a political strategy that organizes the relation of women to male-dominated institutions" (1991:100).

The leader of the lament customarily invites her chorus of fellow mourners to come close and share the "truth" of their discourse. Seremetakis quotes a lament by a woman for her sister who died and was not properly mourned by her husband. Instead, he remarried before the customary forty days of mourning were over. In her lament the sister described saying to the husband,

Δε να πούμε τίποτα
Να τίνε μαρτυρίσουμε?

Are we not going to say anything
to witness her, to suffer for her?

(1991:104)

As Seremetakis interprets this lament, it addresses the improper behavior of the husband by bearing witness to his wife's death. In the time before World War II, when blood feuds were still common in the Mani, lament was not only a way of bearing witness, speaking the truth that comes from pain, and passing judgment but also the means of stirring up revenge. The long revenge laments of Mani were chilling narrative ballads that became popular with men as well as women. One of the best known is the nineteenth-century lament for Kalopothos Sakkakos. Not only did his sister compose a lament for her murdered brother; she explained, in her lament, how she avenged her brother's death at the hands of her husband and brothers-in-law. She describes buying rat poison and serving it to the killers in an omelet. As they breathe their last she tells them,

> Μα τόνε δίκηωσα καλά
> Με κριάρι με παχύ σφαχτό
> Κι όχι με παλαιζύγουρο.
> Έκαμα ότι εκάματε
> κι' εκτέλεσα το χρέο μου
> με τόκο και κεφάλαιο.
>
> I avenged him well
> with a ram, with a fat slaughter
> and didn't weigh him short.
> I did just what you did
> and carried out my duty
> with interest and capital besides.
>
> (Kassis 1979; Holst-Warhaft 1992:81)

The lament is carefully crafted and has no doubt been reworked over the many years since it was composed. Nothing could illustrate more clearly the discrepancy between Christian and folk beliefs than this lament that begins at Easter with the narrator/lamenter preparing the traditional Easter foods to take to her brother and ends with her proud and merciless description of avenging her brother's death, not merely with an eye for an eye but "with interest," that is, by killing the three murderers—her husband and brothers-in-law—together. The text of the lament, with its Christian symbolism (the brother slain like a lamb among his flock, the Easter foods that refuse to bake) and pagan references to sacrifice and revenge, illustrates the problems of interpreting Greek laments through a single lens. The same women who sing such laments live in villages where the year is regulated by a Christian calendar of festivals and observances. How they deal with the incompatibility of their belief systems is an issue few researchers have addressed.

Accommodation

Two women anthropologists who have not taken a feminist approach to Greek death rituals but have simply observed the important role women play in them are Laurie Kain

Hart (1992) and Juliet Du Boulay (2009). Both scholars approach the study of death rituals as part of a broader observation of traditional village life, one that takes into account the central role of the Orthodox Church. Their accounts of village life pay attention to the simultaneous and apparently contradictory beliefs expressed in Christian teaching and folk laments. Hart's summary of the centrality of death (and resurrection) to Christian belief reminds us that although the congregation may believe in Christ's resurrection, they are not convinced by the promise of personal salvation after death: "while they use the theoretical and ritual apparatus of the church in dealing with death, they do not therefore passively surrender the discussion ... they struggle with tensions inherent in the complex doctrine of the church, as well as with other sources of thought" (Hart 1992:130). Death, as we have seen in the lament texts, is a punishment, a calamity, an injustice:

> Ανάθεμά σε Χάροντα και πολυτραϊτούρο,
> της μάνας παίρνεις τα παιδιά, των αδερφών τ' αδέρφια,
> χωρίζεις και τ' αντρόγυνα τα δυο στεφανωμένα ...
>
> Curse you Death, terrible traitor,
> you take children from their mother, brothers from brothers
> and you separate wedded couples
>
> (Lament from Kefalonia. Saunier 1999:346)

In laments, women rail at God, Charos, or Fate about the unjust death of a relative, but Hart argues that religious thought in Greece "bears a 'popular' character and that even the most 'intellectual' of the categories of Orthodoxy have been formed in a dialectic with 'popular thought'" (1992:133). This nuanced view of the contradictions between popular beliefs as reflected in women's lamentation and the teachings of Christianity is thought-provoking. Whereas women's laments were condemned and successfully eliminated across Europe by the Protestant and Catholic Churches (Holst-Warhaft 1992:32–40), the Orthodox Church, at least at the village level, has come to some compromise with the practice and with the bleak, comfortless beliefs about death expressed in the songs. How was such an accommodation arrived at? By necessity? By the contradictions inherent in death? Or is it that death throws the world of the bereaved into such disorder that a temporary license is granted to them to flout the teachings of religion?

Juliet Du Boulay has reflected thoughtfully on this question after long years of fieldwork in Greece, noting that death "provides one of the clearest examples of how village symbolism and the Orthodox liturgy can express the view from the world of the fall and the view from the divine world at the same time. ... Village laments at the wake about the black earth which covers the face of the dead are followed by verses chanted before and during the last kiss in the church which make the same uncompromising statement" (2009:385–386). In Du Boulay's view, both the language of the Orthodox Church and the village imagination expressed in lament draw on "tragic,

FIG. 8.4. Mourning women circling a freshly dug grave.
(Photo by Alexander Tsiaras, courtesy of Princeton University Press. Source: Danforth 1982.)

skeptical, pre-Christian thought" (2009:386). In the church's case, according to Du Boulay, this imagery is Jewish in origin and drawn from the poetry of the psalms, although Du Boulay admits that even the most desolate of psalms "are tinged more deeply with repentance; and in both Christian and Jewish tradition it is repentance that is the chief pathway from the world of the fall to the divine world" (2009:386). Du Boulay's argument is informed by her deep knowledge of Orthodox Christianity and the symbolism of religious thought that overlaps with and accommodates village symbolism. One of the central symbolisms of the church and popular Greek belief is the right-hand movement of the dance that marks each rite of passage in village life from baptism to mourning (Fig. 8.4). The church may come into conflict with villagers over such practices as divination, spells, traditional cures for illnesses, and the inevitability of fate; but beyond this, Du Boulay maintains, are underlying beliefs in a cosmos that involves the upper and lower worlds, good and evil. The recently dead, according to this cosmic belief, inhabit an underworld that represents darkness and evil. The exhumed bones, however, are brought back into the world of light, and the souls of the dead are freed to go to a higher region. Laments sung at exhumations reflect this optimism. As a lament recorded by Danforth expressed it,

Τώρα κίνησα, τώρα θα φύγω
απ' τη μαύρη γης κι απ' τ'αραχνιασμένη.

Now I have set out. Now I am about to depart
from the black and cobwebbed earth.

(1982:86)

What observers like Hart and Du Boulay offer to the study of Greek death rituals is a perspective that those who focus exclusively on death rituals and lament often lack. What Du Boulay calls "the dance of life" reminds us that in all transitional periods of village life, especially baptism, marriage, and death, a complicated dance is being enacted in which the forces of good and evil are in precarious balance. Greek village life, especially in the mountains, in the arid Mani peninsula, or on infertile Aegean islands, was precarious, its resources limited. If both men's struggle for existence and women's subordination in marriage can be linked to the biblical fall from grace, they can be at least understood, if not always accepted. Death, however, takes away the meaning of a life. A human being may struggle against nature and succeed or raise children who offer hope of a better future; against death they are powerless. Defiance of death is the ultimate dance. Images of the struggle on a threshing floor where a hero wrestles with Charos or of a dance staged in defiance of death are common in Greek folk song. They are also thrillingly defiant. Death may win in the end, but before he does, he is trampled underfoot by the spirit of a human life lived to the full.[9]

Lament Revival and Lament as Therapy: A Post-Modern Phenomenon?

Lament may be disappearing in Greek villages or reappearing in the suburbs of Athens, but it is far from dead. Indeed, one of the most fascinating phenomena of the twenty-first century for scholars of lament is the revival, teaching, and co-option of lament as therapeutic practice in Finland and other countries. James Wilce's provocative 2009 study of lament not only reminds us that features of "traditional" lament, such as the alternation between soloist and chorus or the interjection of loud cries and weeping, were not unique to certain areas but remarkably widespread. The "death" of these traditional features and the concomitant "shame" associated with displays of extreme grief are also common twenty-first-century phenomena (Wilce 2009:4). And yet, in one way or another, lament has been revived. As Wilce argues, it can be co-opted in the service of ultra-nationalism, as we saw when historic ballads lamenting Serbian defeat at the hands of the Turks were revived by Milošević's forces during the Balkan wars, or may be used as a therapeutic practice that is not limited to the local practitioners but can be shared and taught to strangers (2009:209–214).

Many of us who studied lament in the Balkan context were concerned about the loss of tradition. In that, we were, if Wilce's argument is correct, representatives of modernism itself, a movement he and others regard as obsessed with loss.[10] Now, in what could be characterized as the post-modern period, rather than lament their loss, some scholars are embracing what can be transmitted. The best-known example of this is the Finnish revival movement. Wilce, who participated in a lament revival class, disputes critics who say that without the traditional context of village life such revivals are inauthentic. In Greece, while there is nothing like the Finnish lament movement, there are lament studies by young scholars who appreciate the therapeutic value of lament. Mitsi Akoyunoglou, for example, describes herself as an "ethnomusicological therapist"; she is also a post-doctoral researcher at the Music Department of the Ionian University. She recently published a study of lament based on her fieldwork on the island of Chios. Although she is not dealing with a revival of tradition, her approach to lament is rather different from earlier studies in that she focuses on the therapeutic benefits of performing laments, especially for village women on the island but not excluding men. The circle of lamentation, in her view, can be seen as "a potentially therapeutic self-help group, offering socially-constructed support based on social unity" (2020:313). Her subjects were old women, but as a therapist, Akoyunoglou is investigating the beneficial aspects of lament as a communal activity and a form of emotional catharsis. One of her informants spoke about the relief of lament for the bereaved: "maybe someone wants to break out . . . the weeping isn't enough; she wants to say words, to tell her pain with the lament, to say something to the dead" (2020:326). Another woman, who no longer laments, said, "We felt a lightening, that we were thanking the dead person who was listening to it . . . we said them so beautifully that it was moving to hear them" (2020:326).

The women Akoyunoglou spoke to all felt the decline of lament performance in the villages to be a significant loss. They complained that these days the body was taken from the house and placed in a "freezer." The absence of the body robbed the lament of focus. The "foreigners" from Athens, they said, do not even go to the grave any more or wear black as a sign of mourning. It is clear that the therapist/researcher sympathizes with the loss of what she sees was once a valuable means of confronting the pain of loss. What is not clear is how she can incorporate this knowledge in her work.

One of the strangest contemporary examples of what might be termed "lament revival" was a show entitled *An Occupation of Loss* orchestrated by the New York–based artist Taryn Simon and first performed at the New York Armory in 2016 and repeated two years later in London. It consisted of lamenters from all over the world performing in a dozen concrete towers. Greece was represented by a trio of singers from Epirus performing the polyphonic laments that are unique to five villages in Epirus near the border of Albania (Figs. 8.5 and 8.6).

I talked to the Greeks after the performance and months later in Athens. They were at a loss to know what the artist had in mind when she commissioned them, but, never having been to the United States, they were pleased to have the opportunity to travel. Simon's introduction to the show indicates she was aware of the problems inherent in staging lament away from its usual context but said that lament was, in any

GREEK DEATH RITUALS AND LAMENT 211

FIG. 8.5. Three polyphonic singers from Epirus performing laments for *An Occupation of Loss*, New York Armory. Nota Kaltsouni, Vangelis Kotsos, Nikos Menoudakis.

(Photographer unknown, supplied by singers.)

FIG. 8.6. Setting for *An Occupation of Loss*.

(See Fig. 8.5.)

case, "publicly performed" and acknowledged "the tension between authentic and staged emotion, memory and invention, spontaneity and script." *An Occupation of Loss* investigated "the intangible authority of these performers in negotiating the boundaries of grief: between the living and the dead, the past and the present, the performer and the viewer" (Simon 2016).

Death and the Post-Modern

Just when we think something is disappearing, it appears in another form. Greece may not have a "lament revival" going on; but the complex and musically difficult polyphonic laments of northern Epirus are being taught to young people in Athens, and young Greek scholars are studying the therapeutic benefits of lament. Have we arrived at an age of less preoccupation with loss of tradition and more focus on sustaining what is left? Does revival preserve tradition or, but by removing it from its context, destroy it? Is it only when a tradition is dying that its benefits are realized? These are questions that apply across the Balkans and beyond. Greece's death rituals have received more attention in recent years than they ever did when they were taken for granted as part of village life. Nostalgia may be one reason for the interest, feminism another. What has largely disappeared from contemporary research is the preoccupation with an ancient past. Does this mean the study of traditional death rituals has entered a post-modern phase? Or are we entering a post-post-modern age where the fragments of tradition can be adopted, rearranged, and put to new uses?

The rituals surrounding death, including lament, may be theatrical; but so long as they are still performed in a ritual context, they have a meaning that is shared by performers and audience, bereaved and sympathizers. That context may be shifted to a new location, such as an urban community of ex-patriots; but when a ritual is performed in a gallery exhibition or taught in a music conservatory, it is no longer a ritual act. It is a fragment of what was once a whole, a circle, a dance. It may be beautiful to listen to or therapeutic to perform, but it becomes an art. How can a foreign observer relate to a woman who tells her the village has known "nothing but pain?" This is the challenge of studying laments and death rituals. We can listen to what is left, describe beliefs about the underworld, appreciate the therapeutic benefits of laments; but wherever we tread, we come up against the knowledge that we are not insiders. Rituals evolve slowly in a particular historical, geographical, and political context that excludes us. Our analysis will always be only partially informed, but the more we know about context, the more likely we are to discover new insights into Greek rituals and the beliefs that underlie them. Knowing more about the context means expanding our gaze to the countries surrounding Greece, to Romania, Bulgaria, Albania, Serbia, and other countries that were once part of the Ottoman Empire or the Byzantine Empire, countries that shared a common belief in the Orthodox Church combined with an underlayer of older popular beliefs. Comparative studies of lament are still a relatively rare phenomenon and offer rich possibilities to students of Greek death rituals. It is important to understand the particular and the shared, the unique and the common features of these practices as they fade and change.

Notes

1. The Greek revolution, usually dated as beginning in 1821, was inspired largely by Greeks living outside the borders of modern Greece. An effective means of attracting support for the Greek cause was to link modern Greeks to their illustrious forebears. Since the literature available in the language spoken by contemporary Greeks took the form of folk tales and songs, these manifestations of popular culture were used as evidence of a continuous tradition between ancient and modern Greece. After the revolution, the most influential figure in the new discipline of *laografia*, or folklore, was Nikolaos Politis (1852–1921), who undertook a vast project of collecting folk song texts, focusing on those that mentioned historical events and heroic figures.
2. This sort of rhetoric was responsible for the nationalist project of recovering what the Greeks saw as the lost lands of the Byzantine Empire, a dream that ended tragically with the Turco–Greek War of 1920–1922.
3. The attempt to reconcile these two strands of Greek tradition was a complicated juggling act. Constantine Paparrigopoulos, together with the folklorist and historian Spyridon Zambelios, created a vision of the new Greece as a repository of ancient influences that had passed through the prism of Byzantium to create a uniquely rich civilization.
4. See the lament texts collected by Kyriakos Kassis and translated into English in Holst-Warhaft (1992:75–97).
5. All Greek circle dances begin with the lead dancer stepping to the right and moving in an anti-clockwise direction. The same is true of the circles performed by bride and groom at a wedding or of mourners around a coffin. Failure to observe this rule is thought to bring misfortune.
6. It is interesting that Charos, the personification of death, is masculine—one might say ultra-masculine—in the Greek folk tradition. It may be because the word for death (*thanatos*) is masculine in Greek, while in Romanian *moarte* is feminine, as it is in other Romance languages; and personifications of death in other Balkan folklore are mostly female. It is also because of Charos's association with the male figure of Charon, the boatman of ancient mythology who ferried the souls of the dead across the Styx.
7. Lament quoted by Seremetakis (1991:75).
8. Interview with Glykeria Fyli in Veltsista, November 26, 2019. My fieldwork in Greece began when I recorded a lament singer from Epirus in Athens in 1979. It was not until 1988 that I was able to return to Greece and talk to lament singers in Athens, the Mani, and Epirus, where I recorded polyphonic laments in the village of Ktismata three miles from the Albanian border. I revisited the Epirus to interview Glykeria Fyli in the village of Veltsista in 2019 and recorded her laments.
9. I have necessarily simplified Du Boulay's detailed analysis of the relationship between village beliefs and orthodoxy.
10. Wilce's study is a wide-ranging and important reflection on the subject (2009:156–169).

Works Cited

Akoyunoglou, Mitsi. 2020. "Το μοιρολόι τα νεώτερα χρόνια σε χωριά της Χίου (μια διαχρονικά συλλογική τέχνη απέναντι στο θάνατο)." In *Μουσικές κοινότητες στηνΕλλάδα του 21ου αιώνα: Εθνογραφικές ματιές και ακροάσεις*, eds. E. Kallimopoulou and A. Theodosiou, 313–338. Athens: Pedio.

Alexiou, Margaret. 1974. *The Ritual Lament in Greek Tradition*. Cambridge: Cambridge University Press.

Auerbach, Susan. 1987. "From Singing to Lamenting: Women's Musical Role in a Greek Village." In *Women and Music in Cross-Cultural Perspective*, ed. Ellen Koskoff, 25–44. New York: Greenwood Press.

Caraveli, Anna. 1986. "The Bitter Wounding: The Lament as Social Protest in Rural Greece." In *Gender and Power in Rural Greece*, ed. Jill Dubisch, 169–194. Princeton, NJ: Princeton University Press.

Caraveli-Chaves, Anna. 1981. "Bridge between Worlds: The Greek Women's Lament as Communicative Event." *Journal of American Folklore*, 94:129–157.

Danforth, Loring. 1982. *The Death Rituals of Rural Greece*. Princeton, NJ: Princeton University Press.

Du Boulay, Juliet. 2009. *Cosmos, Life, and Liturgy in a Greek Orthodox Village*. Limni: Denise Harvey.

Håland, Evy Johanne. 2014. *Rituals of Death and Dying in Modern and Ancient Greece: Writing History from a Female Perspective*. Newcastle upon Tyne: Cambridge Scholars Publishing.

Hart, Laurie Kain. 1992. *Time, Religion, and Social Experience in Rural Greece*. Lanham, MD: Rowman and Littlefield.

Hertz, Robert. 1960. *Death and the Right Hand*. Glencoe, IL: Free Press.

Herzfeld, Michael. 1977. "Ritual and Textual Structures in Rural Greece." In *Text and Context: The Social Anthropology of Tradition*, ed. Ravindra K. Jain. ASA Essays in Social Anthropology, Vol. 2, 29–50. Philadelphia, PA: Institute for the Study of Human Issues.

Herzfeld, Michael. 1981. "Performative Categories and Symbols of Passage in Rural Greece." *Journal of American Folklore*, 94:44–57.

Herzfeld, Michael. 1982. *Ours Once More: Folklore, Ideology, and the Making of Modern Greece*. Austin: University of Texas Press.

Herzfeld, Michael. 1985. *The Poetics of Manhood: Contest and Identity in a Cretan Mountain Village*. Princeton, NJ: Princeton University Press.

Herzfeld, Michael. 1987. *Anthropology through the Looking-Glass: Critical Ethnography in the Margins of Europe*. Cambridge: Cambridge University Press.

Holst-Warhaft, Gail. 1992. *Dangerous Voices: Women's Laments and Greek Literature*. London: Routledge.

Holst-Warhaft, Gail. 2000. *The Cue for Passion: Grief and Its Political Uses*. Cambridge, MA: Harvard University Press.

Kassis, Kyriakos. 1979. *Μοιρολόγια της μέσα μάνης Α'*. Athens (author's publication).

Kassis, Kyriakos. 1980. *Μοιρολόγια της μέσα μάνης Β'*. Athens (author's publication).

Kitromilides, Paschalis. 1979. "The Dialectic of Intolerance." *Journal of the Hellenic Diaspora*, 6/4:5–30.

Lawson, John C. 1910. *Modern Greek Folklore and Ancient Greek Religion*. Cambridge: Cambridge University Press.

Politis, Nikos. 1914. *Δημοτικά Τραγούδια. Ἐκλογαι από τα τραγούδια του Ελληνικού λαού*. Athens: Estia.
Saunier, Guy. 1999. *Ελληνικά δημοτικά τραγούδια. Τα Μοιρολόγια*. Athens: Nefeli.
Seremetakis, Nadia C. 1991. *The Last Word: Women, Death, and Divination in Inner Mani*. Chicago, IL: University of Chicago Press.
Simon, Taryn. 2016. *An Occupation of Loss*. http://tarynsimon.com/works/occupation_of_loss/#1.
van Gennep, Arnold. 1909. *Les rites de passage*. Paris: Emile Nourry.
Wilce, James M. 2009. *Crying Shame: Metaculture, Modernity, and the Exaggerated Death of Lament*. Chichester: Wiley-Blackwell.

CHAPTER 9

CUSTOMARY PRACTICES OF DEATH AND MOURNING IN ALBANIA

BLEDAR KONDI

How to understand the meaning of death? Death insights are the result of a deeply affected perceptual activity that requires that something must exist before it becomes an object of perception. As long as death is not lived through, all cultural conceptualizations of death cannot be true representations of its imagined reality. Radical constructivism emphasizes that humans can know only what humans can experience and construct in their own minds.[1] Seen from this perspective, cultural constructions of death do not visualize death as it really is or reveal a preexisting, inaccessible, mysterious reality in itself and for itself; but they do show how human beings organize their own experiential world, how they orient themselves in it and fit into it. In short, "death reveals to us only ourselves" (Sartre 1969:682). The essential difference between limit and boundary penetrates and illuminates the fundamental concepts of death, emotional responses, and funeral celebrations in a transcultural context. Death as limit signifies an absolute negation of human existence—it is a catastrophe—whereas death as boundary presupposes an existential continuity beyond a certain definite time and space—it is a crisis.

This chapter examines cultural attitudes to death and bereavement in Albania, with a special focus on local funeral traditions of southern and northern areas. Albania, the small enigmatic land of the living past, has been historically positioned between cross and crescent, East and West. Two thousand years of Christianity, five hundred years of Islam, approximately fifty years of communist dictatorship, and thirty years of postcommunist crisis and painful transition have shaped, influenced, and colored Albanian cultural life.[2] When common Albanians talk about death in a funeral ceremony, one has the feeling that their reflections are nothing but thrown filters after having smoked a cigarette. And the task of a researcher is precisely to gather these thrown filters in order to delineate their affective apprehension of death.[3]

Studies on Death and Mourning in Albania

Since the beginning of the fifteenth century, European scholars, diplomats, missionaries, journalists, and travelers who visited a land as unknown as the heart of Africa would pay attention to cultural particularities imprinted on death practices, the daily routine of mourning, and folk belief in postmortem beings. Anton Berisha and Anton Çeta were the first to summarize chronologically Albanological literature, research topics, and findings about death and lament from a historical-ethnographic perspective (1987:3–28; see Kondi 2012:42–43). Franciscan priests in northern Albania established a fruitful tradition of ethnographic research in the first part of the twentieth century, but their "trend-setting" contribution remained ideologically repressed or anonymously (mis)used during the communist period (1944–1991). The Franciscan priest Shtjefën Konstandin Gjeçovi (1874–1929) set a cornerstone with his emblematic publication *The Code of Lek Dukagjini*, which functioned as a stock of cultural knowledge and customary law in the northern Albanian mountains. He gave a powerful impetus to the exploration of the sociocultural norms of death, mourning, and burial in Malësia e Dukagjinit, an isolated mountainous region in northern Albania that was historically composed of free, stateless, self-contained communities belonging to the Roman Catholic faith. For the first time, male collective crying (*gjama*), the lack of female songs, and burial ceremonies at midnight appeared as unique cases in Albanian cultural history. A ninety-two-year-old man from Dukagjini Highland, interviewed by Bogdani in 1972, told him that "We have never danced. There was no drum anywhere in Dukagjini. The women have neither played frame-drum nor sung. The women have only lamented at death events. If a woman would sing, she would be immediately divorced" (Bogdani 1997:161).[4]

Even the bride leaving her parents' house after sunset was accompanied only by the collective laments of her kinswomen—as if she were a dead person—and not with wedding songs, joyous dances, and instrumental music, as is common in Albanian tradition. After World War II, the Albanian communist dictator Enver Hoxha (1908–1985) installed a new nationalist-socialist system, in which ideology appeared as the substance of culture and culture as the form of ideology. The communist regime militated against the projection of mythological consciousness, magical beliefs, and religious attitudes of Albanian rural society and imposed the anti-historical "language of one-dimensional thought," which identifies a thing with its function (Marcuse 2002:98, 104–106) (Figs. 9.1 and 9.2). A (pseudo)-Marxist worldview was authoritatively subjected, transformed, and ritualized into a closed, anti-critical, anti-dialectical, post-Stalinist language that could not explain but only established facts, communicated commands, and became an instrument of control. The ideological character of descriptive analysis did not render the facts recognizable as they really were; it concealed the factors behind the facts and at the same time expressed a repressive reduction of thought trying to understand

Posters of anti-religious propaganda in communist Albania. Atheist Museum in Shkodër, 1980.

FIG. 9.1. Muslim woman in southern Albania.

(Photo by Robert Çollaku.)

FIG. 9.2. Catholic woman in northern Albania.

(Photo by Robert Çollaku.)

the antagonistic structure of reality. Self-limitation, practiced as a habit of thought, assumed a larger significance within the imposed one-dimensional reality and alienated existence.

To build a bridge between scientific and political interests, it seemed necessary to explore the (r)evolution from old to new traditional culture through concrete evidence and dogmatic interpretations, preferably in Marxist style. In the unpublished booklet *Guidelines for Folk Research*, devised by the Institute for Ethnography in Tirana in 1968, one year after the abolition of religious institutions in Albania, one reads the following:

> In various cases, the populace has become an unconscious carrier of . . . backward thoughts. . . . Such thoughts, together with many customs, constitute the negative [part] of the broad folk heritage. . . . A new materialist, Marxist–Leninist worldview is born under the conditions of socialist construction. . . . During our field research, we have to clearly explain to the masses the war against backward religious prejudices [i.e., worldviews] and customary practices.
>
> (*Udhëzues për kërkime folklorike* 1968:14–15)[5]

In another updated version of guidelines for researching "family customs," a questionnaire about death is unmistakably transformed into an ideological investigation in the field:

> - Do people *today* believe in foretelling signs of someone's death? . . .
> - Does the populace believe that the spirit leaves the body in death? . . .
> - Do you believe in such superstitions today? . . .
> - Is it still a custom to cry with one's voice . . . with wails or words? . . .
> - What about burials? . . . Do they bring flowers instead of candles [a religious symbol]? . . . Is there [still] any difference between burials for Christians and Muslims?
> - Do they have any custom to commemorate the dead on the third day, in a week, in 9 days, in 40 days, in six months, in a year, etc.? . . . Are the worthless remnants (*mbeturina*) from these customs still kept alive? . . .
> - How do the parents of a [dead socialist] martyr behave? Do they cry, do they keep mourning? . . . What about the role of the [political] social organizations? . . . Do they create songs for the socialist martyrs? . . . Do they send letters to the Central Committee of the Party and to Comrade Enver [Hoxha]? What kind of ceremonies are held when they send letters and when they receive an answer?
>
> (*Doke Familjare. Vdekja [pyetsor]* 1973:4–18)

Within this repressive frame of reference, the essential meaning is not elicited from the fact, but it is imposed on it. A few Albanian researchers in Albania, Kosovo, Montenegro, and Macedonia have done careful ethnographic studies of death customs under the cover of ideologically certified explanations, thus providing a solid base for a critical anthropology of death that remains within the frame it attempts to break (Zojzi 1953, 1956; Mitrushi 1974; Tuda 1978; Vinca 1978; Ahmeti 1986). In addition, the network of village teachers and local cooperators has been an invaluable source of detailed historical-ethnographic accounts about mortuary practices and folk beliefs. Thanks to their firsthand data, it is possible for the researcher today to find the lost meanings of lost practices.[6] Unfortunately, Albanian ethnography did not have sufficient theoretical and methodological potentialities to explore human thought and cultural idioms encapsulated in local customs. As a consequence, it could not constitute any model for future studies beyond its empirical approaches.

New anthropological and ethnomusicological contributions have highlighted diverse aspects referring to the revival of customary law and practice after the collapse of the Albanian communist dictatorship (Pichler 1995; Schwandner-Sievers 2002), Albanian death rites (Kondi 2012, 2020), and the modern culture of migration (Pistrick 2015). Eckehard Pistrick writes that "in local discourses . . . migration itself is understood as a metaphoric extension of death." Therefore, "performing a lament and singing a migration song can be seen as two cultural responses to . . . [a] community that lives with a feeling of loss and absence" (2015:60, 189, 93). Traditional multipart songs of pain and longing constitute a sonic chronicle of dramatic sociocultural changes in a devastated country wherefrom the Albanian migrants "cross the sea on foot" toward Europe (interview, Brahimaj 2016).

Religious and Political Ideologies against Mourning

The church, mosque, and, later, Communist Party all permanently opposed violent forms of public crying and mourning as well as expensive funerals that generally ruined the economic situation of the population. According to the customary law of the northern Albanian mountains that was in effect until World War II, "anyone who lacerates himself during a funeral lament or *gjamë* must pay 1000 grosh [Albanian coins] to the Church and 1000 grosh and 10 sheep to the chieftains" (Gjeçovi 1989:§246). A "Regulation for [both Muslim and Catholic] citizens of Shkodër in the event of weddings, circumcisions, death events, etc." as well as "for the simplification of burial ceremonies" (1930) approved by the Municipality of Shkodër, under the rule of Albanian King Zog I (1895–1961), reads as follows:

> The funeral meal, coffee, and tobacco offered at death events are prohibited to both women and men. The consolation visits (*vizitat për kryeshdnoshje*) should be made within three days for both women and men. Mourning (*jazi*) is strictly prohibited in every respect. . . .
> [T]he coffin must be simple, built with ornamented wood and painted with only one color. . . . The dead body should not be accompanied to the graveyard by playing a double-headed drum (*daulle*).[7]
>
> (*Shkodra në shekuj* 2000:322, 325)

Islamic authorities took harsh measures against female public lamenting among the Albanian communities in Macedonia and Kosovo but without success: "the women continue to lament even during [the Islamic feasts of] Lesser Bayram and Greater Bayram," reports Shpresa Tuda (1978:160, 166). When religious norms ran counter to Albanian ways of thinking and living, the destitute people preferred to pay a fine or change their religion, and for that reason, they have historically been a thorn in the side of all their spiritual pastors. Avni Bejkova, a ninety-year-old former political prisoner, reconfirms this historical truth: "I believe in God. But we have never been attached to religious institutions. ... [W]e believe in the humanness of the people who preach, because religion is just a dogma" (interview, Bejkova 2016). Beneath the observable side of customary practices shaped by religious norms, a truly original form of magical life has always been present in Albanian tradition; hallucinatory transfigurations and a certain cosmic manifestation have been the objective basis for religious feeling and thought. According to a naturist belief in the region of Lumi i Vlorës in southern Albania, "the sun belongs to the Christians and the moon to the Muslims." As long as religious practices were not uprooted by the communist system, the Orthodox village women of Dardhë in southeastern Albania used to "make the sign of the cross towards the rising sun (*bëjnë kryq nga lint djelli*)" and then bid their last farewell to the dead (Zdruli 1962:1) because the "sun is the beam of God" (*dielli á rrezja e Zotit*)—such is the mixed credo of Catholic communities in Malësia e Dukagjinit.

As soon as the communists came to power in 1944, they unleashed attacks on everything traditional that did not suit their worldview. They aimed to transform the historical consciousness from a shepherd of tradition into a *musée imaginaire* of the past. Collectivization produced a new peasantry, a new mode of life, and a new tradition; but the insoluble core and petrified structure of many customary practices and values resisted violent cultural transformations. The uprooting of old religious practices and sacralization of new atheistic roles would reconfigure the traditional burial scene in socialist Albania, especially for the World War II veterans and political authorities. In these cases, party activists, Heroes of Socialist Labor, and members of the Organization of Youth had to pay homage and put floral wreaths at the grave of prominent figures (a new ideological symbol for the new national heroes). At the same time, the comrades of the Organization of the Democratic Front started to hold dithyrambic speeches at the graveyard or read "farewell letters" on behalf of the community to the dead and his family. "The folk approved such an activity and called it a 'great beauty,'" reports Fadil Mehmeti (1978:356). This repressive framework did not allow much room for counteraction; as a consequence, the ethnographer had to sacrifice the truth for the sake of ideological beauty.

The Situation in the Field

The shared life-world and cultural tradition of a community form the background for every emotional, expressive, and communicative interaction between individual members in a death event. Cultural meanings of death are generally located within the existential domain of the group, and for that reason, they do not claim universality as do norms of ritual action. When a researcher enters the presence of grief-stricken people in a funeral ceremony, they have to discover the basic facts of the situation: the dead, the bereaved family, participants in the funeral ceremony, cultural patterns of ritual crying, and so on. The active presence of an observing–participating subject, who is gathering sonic and verbal data surrounded by mourners, unavoidably influences the original scene. All researchers live, observe, realize, and interpret only their own situations as an organized totality of being there. Neither the sum of total impressions, which the dead and the mourners make on us, nor the affected apprehension of particular emotional states can illuminate a disturbing situation. Moreover, we cannot observe, measure, and interrogate immediately the factors in the facts. So, how can we uncover the unperceivable reality behind the appearances? Erving Goffman has clearly showed how we approach and focus on a concrete situation:

> To uncover fully the factual nature of the situation, it would be necessary for the individual to know all the relevant social data about the others. It would also be necessary for the individual to know the actual outcome or end-product of the activity of the others during the interaction, as well as their innermost feelings concerning him. Full information of this order is rarely available; in its absence, the individual tends to employ substitutes—cues, tests, hints, expressive gestures, status symbols, etc.—as predictive devices. In short, since the reality that the individual is concerned with is unperceivable at the moment, appearances must be relied upon in its stead. And, paradoxically, the more the individual is concerned with the reality that is not available to perception, the more must he concentrate his attention on appearances. (1956:160–161)

Various descriptions of funeral performances are generally concentrated on performed roles as basic units of socialization, but life stories and the meaning of interactions objectified in a collective mourning remain inaccessible to an outsider. "Understanding meaning is a mode of experience" only for the members of a community, who share a common life-world and have a privileged access to it (Habermas 1984:111). Therefore, the researcher has to focus on the life-world and relevant social data of the targeted participants to understand the truly concrete context because "context makes the facts and determines their function" (Marcuse 2002:195).

Instead of waiting for naturally occurring death situations, a researcher hurries to record a subject out of the funeral context and, in a few cases, tries to reconstruct the original circumstances necessary for studying the ritual performance. Can a bereaved woman cry for her lost beloved person one, five, ten, twenty years later with the same emotional intensity as on the day of death and burial? In order to give an informed answer, we would need to compare audiovisual recordings, systematic observations, and detailed descriptions of one individual in different times and settings. To my knowledge, no one has conducted such systematic research; therefore, the statements are generally based on personal intuition. Although it is difficult to derive general conclusions from single case studies, they can be a valuable source for hypotheses and conjectures about grief experience and funeral crying. Nikolai and Dimitrina Kaufman claim that a Bulgarian "lamenter falls into the *same* emotional state—she weeps and gives up herself entirely to her grief" anywhere and anytime (1988:386, my emphasis). Anna Caraveli adds that widows in rural Greece have the "ability to recall effortlessly almost the original intensity of one's grief over the loss of a beloved person who has been dead for a considerable length of time" (1986:173).

Based on my fieldwork, I can confirm that re-experiencing a loss cannot be an exact repetition of the unique moment of death but an emotionally distanced act in the continuum of mourning. When a woman is asked to lament for her own beloved dead, her lament leads to deeply hurtful memories and piecemeal distressing ideas; her sighs are gradually increased, associated with exaggerated movements of the torso to and fro, and then the woman is sufficiently excited to burst into tears or break off the recording session. The presence of the dead determines the intensity of the discharged emotions on the spot. Old Albanian women in rural areas participate in a death ceremony to console the grief-stricken family and to cry for their own dead or their own self. In this way, every funeral ceremony transcends the fresh loss of a member and unfolds itself as a great rite of crying for all the dead of the village. Dostoyevsky keenly observed the long-suffering sorrow of Russian peasant women, and his psychological insight is worth quoting as a confirmation:

> There is silent and long-suffering sorrow to be met with among the peasantry. It withdraws into itself and is still. But there is a grief that breaks out, and from that minute it bursts into tears and finds vent in wailing. This is particularly common with women. But it is no lighter a grief than the silent. Lamentations comfort only by lacerating the heart still more. Such grief does not desire consolation. It feeds on the sense of its hopelessness. Lamentations spring only from the constant craving to re-open the wound. (1912:47)

THINKING DEATH IN IMAGES, SIGNS, COUNTERMEASURES

Albanian ethnographic research on death rites generally has left the reader with a stubbornly wordless silence regarding the essential question: What is death for Albanians? A cursory survey of Albanian traditional worldviews reveals life and death as two radical opposites that belong together as day and night. Kolë Kamsi was among the few Albanian ethnographers who collected folk aphorisms about death in pre-communist Albania (*Folklorë Nr.* 9 1943:19–21), and some of them are worth quoting and explaining:

- *Hall të rrosh e gjyq të vdesësh*, "Life is trouble; death is a punishment," i.e., it is hard to live, and even harder to die.

- *Me dijtë nieri se kur des i a bân vorrin vedit*, "If a man had known before when he is going to die, then he would bury himself alive," i.e., being-toward-death is natural, but waiting for death is self-destructive.
- *Njeriu është biri i vdekjes*, "Man is the son of death," i.e., death is unavoidable, and this fact can be internalized and humanized through the consoling image of a mother–child reunification.[8]
- *Deka e njenit gjella e tjetrit*, "One's death is someone's meal" (or "Your death is my meal"). This economic justification of death with "cannibalistic" overtones dictates "Make room for the others!"
- *Kuleta e të vdekurit kthehet përmbys*, "The purse of the dead is turned upside down," i.e., death overthrows the order of things and dispossesses people from life and property.
- *Me e pa vedin të dekun, des mortja*, "If you see yourself dead [in a dream], your death dies." Our death can die *like* us and *instead* of us, and this magical belief is the source of self-transcendence and immortality.

According to local folk beliefs, the beyond and the underworld constitute a singular mental picture embracing all deaths and the dead within. In a few cases, affective intuition of after-death mediates a concrete experience, which "goes behind" the known facts or events. Here, the spirits of the dead *appear* clearly as those who they really were in their essential qualities and former existence. Josif Nika, a resident from the village of Strëmbec, Përmeti area, southern Albania, recalls his unconscious experience in the gray area between here and beyond:

> I lapsed into a coma. Suddenly I saw all the dead people of the village, who were singing and dancing under the music of *saze* [traditional ensemble] on the other side of the Vjosa shore. One of them, an old friend of mine who had died some years ago, called me by name, gave me a sign with his hand, and said to me: "stay some more time there, and then come to join us!" Then I opened my eyes, and I saw that I had come out of my coma.
>
> (Interview, 2002)

Such near-death experiences affirm the potentiality of human consciousness to transcend itself and provide a basic insight into death as an existential continuity of this life. Despite that, it is not easy to convert subjective unconscious appearances into substantial evidence of the unknowable. Death announces itself without showing itself; therefore, Albanians have been always focused on the mysterious signs (*shenja*) that point to the anxious, unavoidable end of a human life. The rich repertoire of visible and audible bad omens encountered in folk beliefs and sayings generally encapsulates the image of death as a destructive force: "When stones roll down a mountain and crash into a village-quarter, a member of that quarter is going to die" (Berati area, southern Albania). "When a little child digs a hole in the ground, then somebody in that family is going to die" (Korça area, southeastern Albania). "When a mirror is broken at home without a cause, someone in that house will die" (city of Himara, southern Albania). Other folk beliefs, ominous signs, and magical countermeasures mirror the inverted world of death, pulsating within itself, shaken to its depth, breaking asunder. In the Myzeqeja[9] plain, situated in southwestern Albania, it is believed that "if a hen sings like a cock she must be slaughtered immediately" in order to prevent death at home (Mitrushi 1974:257). In the Orthodox villages around Himara, it was customary that, when a mother lost several children one after the other, she changed their names from Christian to Muslim in order to protect them from death (Gjidede 1970:26). The poetic imagination of mourning women in Lumi i Vlorës states that whenever a great man is born and dies, the natural order of things changes, "the river flows upward." And the fabulous vision of the dark underworld reaffirms the violent triumph of a primordial disorder where "the dogs eat grass, and the horses eat bones" (Frashëri 1936:234).

One of the most significant ritual practices of burial ceremonies in the villages of Skrapar, southern Albania, reads, "Those who are [economically] unable to make a sacrifice break a cup at the headstone" (*ata që nuk bëjnë dot kurban, thyejnë një filxhan te koka*) (Cakaj 1972:68). The first encoded message of this symbolic magical act refers to the emotional discharge of painful anger in death: "if you don't kill someone, then destroy something!" In addition to that, the raw meat of a slaughtered ram was shared with burial participants for the spirit of the deceased—a practice prohibited by the communist system—whereas a cup or pot was symbolically broken "on the head of death" to prevent other deaths in that house and community. This powerful ritual protest against human finitude commands, "Kill the death!" Given that magical countermeasures and desperate heroism could not help the anxious spirits avoid the unavoidable, the Çam people in northwestern Greece and southern Albania "would dig their own graves to prolong their life" (*çamët i hapnin varrin vetes për të rrojtur gjatë*) (Zojzi 1953:6).

The Dying, the Spirit, the Dead

Closed traditional worldviews unified by myth and colored by animism and naturalism have permeated the life-practice of northern Albanian mountain people and explained the origin, place, and value of everything within its imagined order. Mountain dwellers in Malësia e Dukagjinit believe that "every human being has his own Hour (*Orë*), like a shadow, like his own body wandering in the blossomed plains." This mythical being represents existential time and protects one's fortune. "When the Hour of a person is going to die, she shouts in the ear of God and falls into the Drin River and drowns." "You cannot die before your Hour dies," said an old resident from the village of Nikaj (interview, Papleka 2011; see also Kondi 2012:196–197). In a few cases, a man can outlive his prescribed lifetime for two to three years after the death of his Hour. Mountain dwellers used to attribute thunderous shouting to the "black hour of death," who performs *gjamë* (male funeral crying) and rolls stones on sinister rocks. This highly pregnant notion unifies the mental image of death as "catastrophe" and "unbearable suffering" with the natural "thunderclap" and explosive "shouting" of men. Every shout is a carrier of preverbal meaning; it temporalizes its energy through the superimposed structure of basic emotions in the face of death.

Basic contours of funeral crying
(direction, character, symbolism)

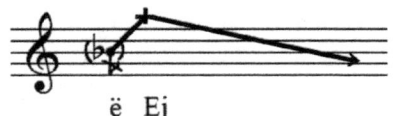 

brima – male shouting
thunderclap
north
descending
passive

kuja – female shouting
wolf's howl
south
ascending
active

Death consciousness, traditional knowledge, and a mythical horizon are objectified in male collective *gjamë*, whose practice enacts at the same time a supernatural form of crying and a foretelling sign of death.

In some villages of the Berati area, southern Albania, it is told that when a sick person was suffering for a long time, village dwellers used to sacrifice a sheep to hasten that person's end, while uttering a spell to death: "Choose one of two ways!" (*Nga dy udhët njëra!*; i.e., "Either take the sick with you or let him recover from illness!"). The emotional display of crying and imploring of family members impedes the dying from giving up their souls; it prolongs their agony and lets them hang "neither on this side, nor on the other." Therefore, the relatives have to remind the bewildered family members of the customary imperative: the dying person "must not be implored, otherwise the spirit turns back and toils hard" (*Nuk duhet thirrur se i kthejet shpirti dhe mundojet*). In a few unique cases, provisional mourning for the dying helps their conscience to look death in the face, to overcome their own mortality, to experience a postmortem pleasure of survival, to celebrate triumph over death. Fatos M. Rrapaj reports that a well-known man from the village of Tërbaç, southern Albania, lying on his deathbed, demanded that his sister cry upon him as if he were dead. Although funeral "crying with words" in the presence of the dying is strictly prohibited in Albanian tradition, the sister had to fulfill the last wish of her dying brother and improvised her symbolic verses, in which she glorified and reproached him (Rrapaj 1991:561):

> O Lulo Abaz Mehmeti,
> pamporri që shkon nga deti.
> O Lulo Abaz me alle,
> dash me këmborë të madhe,
> si e hoqe,
> kujt ja vare,
> e flake në një përralle.

> O Lulo Abaz Mehmeti,
> O steamship sailing toward the [open] sea.
> O Lulo Abaz charged with many troubles,
> O Ram with a big bell [man of great power and authority],
> How did you dare to take it off [why are you leaving us]?
> On whose neck did you hang it [who can replace you]?
> You threw it on a streamlet [who will care for us afterward?]

The people of the Lab area[10] (in southwestern Albania) and Malësia e Dukagjinit in the north have always praised the virile and dignified attitude toward death. Traditional ethics of the mountains declared, "The men who know how to die should not be lamented, no, but only the survivors" (*Burrat që dijnë me dekë s'duhen vajtue, jo, por të gjallët*). This stoic norm of mourning in northern Albania is nothing but a customary consolation formula that is echoed in the female "crying with recount" of the area (Kondi 2012:152):

> Nuk po kjaj se kush ka dekë
> Por të mjerët qi kanë metë
>
> I am not crying for the one who has died
> But for the poor ones who have survived.

Once the heart has stopped, the spirit will not return. The departed spirit has ceased to present any picture to the minds of modern Albanians—it has become a mere last breath lost in nothingness. By contrast, among the old generation in rural and urban areas, the soul is imagined as a vital breath, a clear wind, an evanescent shadow, a smoke-like silhouette invested with the name and personality of the departed in their immaterial materiality. Zef Harapi, a local ethnographer from northern Albania, describes a unique folk belief in survived shadows among the people of the northern Albanian Alps:

> After death, every man leaves his shadow (*hije*) on earth. This belongs neither to the spirit nor to the body. His shadow goes on searching through the fields and mountains. It traces back in a certain way the line of life that the deceased used to follow in this world. (1961:280)

According to a prevalent belief in southern Albania, the butterfly still represents the transmigrated spirit of the deceased, who visits their house for forty days during the mourning period or intends to take one of the living members of the family to the underworld.[11] When Lab women would see a butterfly circulating in the room, they would immediately take three embers from the fire of the hearth and throw them toward the door, while blessing the butterfly: "May you find forgiveness and travel to Heaven!" (*Gjeçi rahmet e shkofshi në xhenet!*) (Rrapaj 1974:47).[12] This ancient Mediterranean belief in butterflies as a symbol of resurrection mixed with Christian and Islamic elements of blissful afterlife is poetically expressed in sad female songs of central Albania:

> Ky Haliti kaq i bukur,
> në xhenet po shkon si flutur.
>
> Halit, such a beautiful guy,
> is going to Heaven like a butterfly.

"The snake of the house" (*gjarpri i shtëpisë*) has been widely regarded as one of the reincarnated dead spirits of the family, and for that reason it was always honored and never killed. Aqif Tartari reports that the village women of Bolena in southern Albania used to address the snake of the house in a lovely manner, as if it were a little child: "Who are you my dear that have come to meet me? I see, my dear, you are unable to speak, because God has turned you into a snake" (*E kush je ti a të keqen që ke ardhë të më takosh? E shof a të keqen që nuk ke gojë të flasësh, zoti të ka bërë gjarpër*) (1982:120).[13] By contrast, the weasel was believed to be the reincarnation of a dead young bride, hence the significant name *nuselala*, from *nusja e lalës*, "the bride of the brother." She represented the "fortune of the house" and was honored as a "sacred animal," and the village women caressed her and recited several times the incantation "with distaff and spindle!" (*me furkë e me bosht!*) (Tartari 1982:120).[14] When a child resembles a dead member of the family, it is believed that the soul of the departed has entered into the body of the newborn infant and, in this way, the deceased is reborn and ensures the biosocial continuity in the lifeblood of the family.

Albanians refer to the dead in both vernacular and Islamic terms: (a) *i vdekuri* (south), *i vdekmi* (central), *i dekuni* (north); (b) *xhenaze* (from Turkish *cenaze*, "burial") and *meiti* (from Arabic *al-mayt*, الميت, "dead," "departed person"). Death is a destructive punishment that expiates every guilty wrongdoing of a human being; therefore, the deceased is generally called "the absolved" (*i ndjerë* or *rahmet pastë*). Unlike in Western societies, Albanians still keep their own dead from twelve to twenty-four hours at home, in both urban and rural areas. The dead person is abruptly experienced as a painful, venerable, mysterious object that violently enters into the survivors. These experiential facts constitute the affective texture of bereavement, reveal the socially conferred meaning of *being in death*, and darken the whole postmortem future of the dead (Figs. 9.3 and 9.4). The jaw of the corpse is tied with a ribbon by a female relative during the funeral ceremony and is untied shortly before the burial by the same female relative. It is widely believed that the open mouth of the dead represents the gaping jaws of death that threaten to devour the survived family members; hence, a tied jaw holds death at a safer distance. Southern Albanian custom explains that "the handkerchief that ties the jaw of the deceased is further used to shut the mouth of the opponent[15] in the next world." The emotional attitude of the community against an abhorrent dead person displays a great moral power beyond the ambivalent conflict: "One can hate the dead but not the grave" (*i vdekuri urrehet, varri s'urrehet*) (interview, Brahimaj 2016). This ethical principle dictates that the grave is sacred and should never be violated even when the deceased is nothing but a criminal.[16]

FIG. 9.3. Death ceremony (*mort*) for a murdered officer of the Albanian army during the state anarchy in 1997. Men performing collective *gjamë* in the village of Kajvall, Malësia e Dukagjinit.

(Photo by Rhodri Jones.)

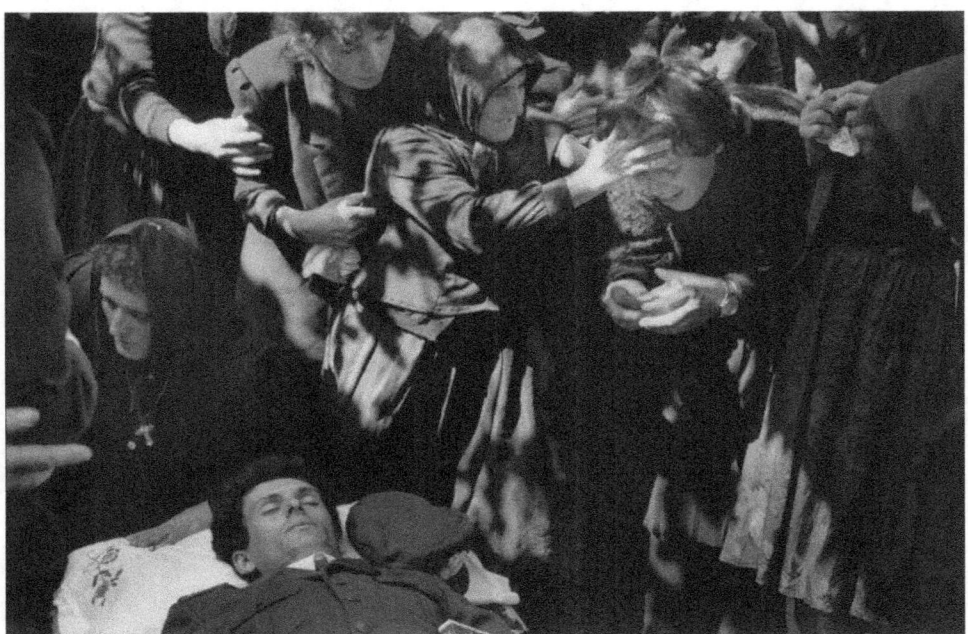

FIG. 9.4. Stupor, grief crisis, and convulsive discharges are common among the kinswomen of the dead. This emotional sphere of death event is called *trazim* (perturbation).

(Photo by Rhodri Jones.)

Cultural Practices of Crying for the Dead

The collected ethnographic data and observational studies of different societies around the globe point to both similarities in core responses and extremely diverse cultural patterning of grief and mourning. Is ritualistic crying indicative of grief? Are the bereaved individuals feeling grief or simply playacting according to strictly prescribed norms? Ask psychologists Wolfgang and Margaret Stroebe (1994:177, 188–189). If social norms and culturally constituted patterns dictate the rules of feeling, then there is no room for a deeply authentic, uncontrollable emotion to run its own free course until it exhausts itself. Albanian traditional culture produces a strong social awareness of "we." It incorporates the irreplaceable uniqueness of every bereaved person into a role to be played without repressing the deepest personal emotions behind social obligation. The immediate death-stricken woman has the right to discharge her emotions as a form of debt toward her beloved dead. And the dead counts the tears of the truly grief-stricken mourners. A true feeling of loss must agree with its expression; that is, what is contained inwardly in the heart must necessarily be one with the emotional experiences and cultural responses to death. When a village family has undergone many painful losses of its members, a dweller of Lumi i Vlorës says, sighing, "my family had many wailings" (*familja ime ka patur shumë kuje*). The premature departure of the only male member is still considered the most devastating blow in a patrilocal society. A father without a son is called "the uprooted one" (*rrënjëdalë*), whereas the unfortunate mother calls herself "nun" (*murga*) or "cuckoo" (*qiqe*), wears black clothes, and keeps mourning for the rest of her life. Pavlo Gjidede noted down the "crying with words" of a sonless mother from the coastal town of Himarë, in southern Albania, whose house was closed forever (1970:99) (Fig. 9.5):

> U derëzeza o djalë!
> mbenë motrat vardharë.
> Pse s'mejtove për ta?
> U derëzeza o djalë!
> M'i vure gurë shtëpisë
> u derëzeza o djalë!
> Shove farë e shove fis,
> u derëzeza o djalë!
> M'i vure llozin shtëpisë
> u derëzeza o djalë!
>
> Oh me, the unlucky, o my son!
> Your sisters will remain unmarried.
> Why didn't you think about them?
> Oh me, the unlucky, o my son!
> You buried our house under the stones
> Oh me, the unlucky, o my son!
> You extinguished the clan forever,

Oh me, the unlucky, o my son!
You barred the door of our house forever,
Oh me, the unlucky, o my son!

FIG. 9.5. A deserted house, Gjirokastër, southern Albania, 1956.

(Photo by Wilfried Fiedler.)

The broken biosocial continuity of a family without a male inheritor leaves a burning pain, lifelong mourning, and a deserted house behind, especially when the young widow has to depart too:

Ç'u këput kulmi e ra
Mbetnë vajzat pa baba
Dhe Hasafi pa vëlla.
Ngreu Bastri, thuaj një fjalë,
Mbae nusen mos të dalë,
i shuat e rrënjëdalë,
që s'të dha zoti një djalë!

> The top beam of the roof is broken down,
> and the daughters remained orphans, without a father,
> And even Hasaf without a brother.
> Rise up, Bastri, speak a single word,
> Don't let your wife leave the house
> O extinguished and uprooted one,
> for God didn't give you a son!

This "crying with words" was improvised by a Christian Orthodox lamenting woman for a dead Muslim man, both from the city of Gjirokastër, who lost everything in death (Rrapaj 1991:595). When a wife lost her husband, the village women of Dukat, in the Lab area, used to take a peeled onion and strike the woman "poisoned by grief" with onion on the head in order to increase her tears and crying: "You had to swallow even this evil, o poor you!" (*E pate për të pirë edhe ktë qoqe anackël, a e mjera ti!*). In a harsh patriarchal society, where marriages have been generally arranged and women were treated as a "sack to endure" the hardships, it is extremely difficult to find and record any funeral crying of a wife for her dead husband. But in a few cases, the crying of a widow for her husband turns into a powerful accusation against divine will (Rrapaj 1991:585):

> Burri im ujk shënëndreu ...
> Allahu si buf kërceu,
> Ngjajti thonjtë e të rrëmbeu.
>
> My husband [was like] a wolf of Saint Andrea valley ...
> Allah jumped like an owl,
> extended his claws, caught you and flew away.

The old dwellers of Lumi i Vlorës, devastated by migration, are past-oriented in the description of their customs: "Every house used to sing, every house used to cry" (*Në çdo derë qahësh, në çdo derë këndohësh*). Every young village woman in the Lab area used to know about eight or nine funeral laments created for her own family members and in-laws, whereas the old talented lamenting women possessed about seventy funeral discourses (*ligjërime*).[17] Death laments of the Lab area in southwestern Albania are generally short, laconic, compact, from seven to eleven verses long, and mainly constructed upon local poetic formulas according to age, gender, and rank of the deceased. An experienced lamenting woman is called *vajticë, vajtuese*, or *ligjëruese*; and she usually participates at every "death event" (*vaki*) of the village. According to custom, the young brides are not allowed to "cry with words" but only "with tears" at death events of the other villagers in order not to take upon their families the *gjëmë* (misfortune) of others. As soon as they become mothers and accumulate creative experience, they can join the circle of old, authoritative lamenting women of the village, who are predominantly postmenopausal widows.

Every death ceremony in Albanian tradition is generally shaped by the funeral crying of the bereaved women. They are considered the "head of the labor" and are always aligned on the side of the dead body according to their "social status and degree of pain."

The grief-stricken kinswomen take off their scarfs and let their hair free as a symbol of emotional disorder, and for that reason, they are called "the ones with the untied hair" (*flokleshuar*). The simultaneous and consecutive "crying with words" constitutes a cure of talking *away* the unbearable, the unsufferable. Painful anguish imprints an irrepressible trembling upon the vocal style of the affected women. "We cry with all the desire of our belly, but our mind does not go mad" (*Ne qajmë me gjith dëshirën e barkut, edhe mëndja nuk shkallon*), said an old woman from the village of Dukat in southern Albania. The well-known folk singer from the village of Lapardha Nazif Çelaj, however, affirms the contrary: "My mother Mbete Çelaj, is a great lamenting woman, but we do not allow her to participate in death events because she cries until she loses her mind [*lajthitet*]" (interview, Çelaj 2016). The Lab tradition is concerned with the structures of an ideal crying situation full of emotional spontaneity as well as with the structures of a ritualized competition for better rhetorical arguments and logical interrelations. "There is a rivalry between affected women as to 'who cries better with words' (*kush ligjëron më bukur*), and the most distinguished lamenting woman is heard again at the end of the funeral ceremony," according to a resident from the village of Kotë, in Lumi i Vlorës.

In parallel with the female domain, even men "cry with voice" (*qajnë me zë*), "with words" (*me fjalë*), "with a howl" (*me ulurimë*) but only for hardly bearable deaths. According to the Lab custom, a lamenting man turns a shepherd's coat inside out as a sign of death disorder, covers his head and face to hide his tears, and then starts "to howl from inside the coat" (*ulërin te guna brënda*) at a distance of thirty to forty meters from the house while approaching the dead. This traditional pattern is called "crying with the coat over the head" (*e qarë me gun' në kuk'*), and it is usually performed by a father for his son, a brother for his brother, or a friend for his friend. Since the fall of the communist regime in 1991, this form of male ritual crying has been dying out even among the old generation in the Lab area. But a poet from Lapardha assured me that "when a good friend dies, a man still covers his head with a shepherd's coat and cries with words until he is saturated" (interview, Brahimaj 2016).

Unlike southern traditions, the institution of professional lamenting women (*vajtojce*) is culturally established in northern Albania, and their poetic virtuosity and kind-hearted contribution are highly appraised everywhere (Fig. 9.6). They are usually invited by friendship and community to lament for the dead without demanding any payment, except when a dead person had previously expressed such a wish and their last will must be fulfilled. A professional woman covers her face with a black or blue mourning scarf and starts to "recount" (*me njeh*) the life and deeds of the deceased according to improvised and adapted poetic patterns, whereas the women present around the dead punctuate her verses with sobbing, pants, sighs, or exclamations.

She can improvise very long poetic texts from thirty to three hundred verses without sobbing. A professional lamenting woman aims to console and cry on behalf of the bereaved members of the family (who have to stoically suppress and control their emotions according to custom), raise significant emotions in the crowd, and please the dead. The performative style of collective and individual lamenting refers to "walking" (*tuj ec*) toward the deceased and "sitting" (*ndejun*) next to the deceased. The ceremonial "lament between two village-quarters" (*vaj dy lagjesh*) constitutes an antiphonic exchange

FIG. 9.6. A professional lamenting woman "recounts" the life and deeds of the dead. Village of Balldre, Lezha district, northern Albania, 1990.

(Photo by Robert Çollaku.)

between two spatially separated groups of Christian and Muslim women walking toward the dead (Kurbin, Lezhë; the village of Kryezi, Pukë). Sometimes the talented professional lamenters do not spare their sharp irony to any unworthy member of community: "If you praise someone much more than he deserves, the lament turns into humor," notes a resident from Puka; and the bereaved members of the family accept the bitter truth in silence.

Mourning, Remembrance, Oblivion

When I asked a 60-year-old woman from the village of Lapardha to sing a song for me, she categorically refused to do so, explaining that "When I was 18 years old, my younger sister died in my arms, and I was totally unable to save her life. Since then I have never sung or danced."[18] In such cases, the sorrow, powerlessness, and sense of guilt transform the real loss of the beloved person into a morbid grief, a never-ending mourning. Seeking the dead establishes their absence. And pathological mourning aims to overcome this intolerable separation from the departed; it performs a great, desperate task which makes live in us that which does not exist, as the poet Paul Valéry aptly puts it (2014:70–72). So long as a mourning woman is deeply affected by the image of her own dead, she regards her lost beloved one as necessarily present in her mind, dreams, sense of presence, imaginary talks, and funeral crying (Fig. 9.7).

A village woman from Bisakë, Kukës, north Albania, lamented upon her dead cousin on behalf of his mother (Xhatufa 1972):

Po lizhron nana me ty,
Si me qen tuj t'pa me sy …
ku me marr ma t'madh gazep
me mlue nana gjaln e vet? …
Poj ty nana s'të harron,
Zemra e nanës nuk pushon …
Emni yt s'ka me u harrue,
kojka jote ka me u knue.

I, your mother, am talking with you,
as if you are in front of my eyes. …
Is there any greater misfortune,
than when a mother buries her own son? …
I, your mother, cannot forget you,
my heart as a mother will never stop [remembering you] …
Your name will be never forgotten,
a song for you will be always sung.

FIG. 9.7. Old mourning woman from the village of Shala, Malësia e Dukagjinit, northern Albania, 1995.

(Photo by Gabriele Ponisch.)

Every commemorative song is a protection against death that liquidates the past. When a "song is opened" (*hapet kënga*), the mourning period is closed.

In recent decades, Albanians have had to face for the first time the bureaucratic medicalization and dehumanized technologization of dying alone behind the curtain. Despite the invisible death of modernized society, the dignified dying of an old parent at home, surrounded by loving children, grandchildren, and relatives, is still a norm in rural and suburban Albania. On the other hand, many young women in urban areas do not know *how* to cry, they cannot express their emotions according to prescribed cultural patterns, and everything is reduced to a natural response of "crying with tears." The ancient tradition of funeral crying is gradually dying in Albania. After the Albanians destroyed the communist dictatorship and the first democratic state with an anarchic optimism, they started to lose progressively their understanding of values. The young generation neither knows the old meaning nor is interested in making a new sense of traditional practices. According to this pragmatic attitude, if life is a disturbed and irreversible energy process directed toward a perpetual state of rest that can never reestablish itself, then it is useless to cry, senseless to protest, and certainly irrational to ask why we have to die. The modern indifference toward the dead "makes the dead die again" (Sartre 1969:695).

Notes

1. Inner images of after-death and pre-rebirth in *The Tibetan Book of the Dead* reveal the natural life of the unconscious psyche as a great annulling factor of space and time. But "the results of cognitive activity can never be a replica of ontological structures," notes von Glasersfeld (2007:26, 93, 67).
2. The religious affiliations of the Albanian people were purposely excluded from any postwar statistics; therefore, many scholars refer to the Italian statistics of 1942. According to them, Albanians were 69.1 percent Muslim (Sunni and Bektashi orders), spread all over the country, with a higher density in central Albania; 20.6 percent were Christian Orthodox, mostly located in southern parts and less in central Albania; and 10.3 percent were Roman Catholic, concentrated in the northern area. Prior to national independence from the Ottoman Empire in 1912, all religious bodies held their services in Arabic, Greek, or Latin but not in Albanian. The assimilation strategies of these three religious faiths were harshly opposed by nationalists and later by communists. After the systematic execution and imprisonment of the clergy, the communist leader Enver Hoxha (who ruled from 1944 to his death in 1985) closed 740 mosques, 530 tekkes and turbes, 608 Orthodox churches, and 157 Catholic churches within a few months in atheist Albania (1967). In the second half of the twentieth century, the Albanian population tripled, and the postwar generation was shaped after a new political religion: "I believe in God, but God is an atheist" (as an Italian writer keenly encapsulated it). (On religious history in Albania, see Bartl 1993.) The fall of communism took place in 1991.
3. My interviews were conducted in the city of Shkodër and town of Pukë (northern Albania) in 2002 and 2011; in the villages of Lapardha, Kotë, and Kuç of the Lab area (southwestern Albania) in 2005, 2012, and 2016; in the cities of Përmet and Gjirokastër (southern Albania) in 2004 and 2008; as well as in Tirana (central Albania) in 2002, 2005, 2016, and 2017.
4. This and all subsequent translations are mine.

5. The general ideological guidelines were primarily compiled by the Department for Propaganda at the Central Committee of the Albanian Party of Labor, and each research institution had to adopt and apply them according to scientific disciplines.
6. Some village teachers started their reports with the formula "Once upon a time . . ." and then continued to describe the living customary practices; for example, "hands and burial tools have to be washed in order to prevent death entering the home" (*duart dhe veglat lahen që të mos hyjë më vdekja në shtëpi*). Taking into account the anti-religious worldview of the communist dictatorship, the teachers had to play with politically correct formulas: "today the population believes in science." "After the burial, participants wash their hands because they are dirty and not as a result of any superstition." This was an effective strategy to satisfy the censors and to offer ethnographic data about forbidden magico-religious practices of burial.
7. The *daulle* (drum) was loudly played by a news-caller (*tellall*) to attract the attention of the public and to announce events, activities, and ceremonies in the city. Its simple monorhythmic pattern had no musical intention.
8. Life (*jeta*) and death (*vdekja, mortja*) in Albanian language are both feminine.
9. The villages of the Myzeqeja plain are populated mostly by Albanians and partly by Aromanians. Unlike Aromanians who have a deeper affiliation to the Orthodox Church, the religious feelings of Albanian Muslims in this area are pragmatically liberal and adapted to their village life-world: they do not attend religious services but celebrate only the great Muslim feasts; men produce and consume alcohol and pork, while women do not wear the burka, and so on.
10. The Lab area (Albanian, Labëria) extends from the coast city of Vlora to the Greek border.
11. The butterfly (Alb. *flutur*) is a feminine noun (Frashëri 1936:48, 194). See also Mitrushi (1974:271), Cakaj (1972:65), Rrapaj (1974:47), and Pando (1970:108).
12. "The fire of the hearth" symbolizes the life of the house; hence, the magico-ritual practice with embers has a protective function.
13. Concerning the mythological narratives, magical practices, and symbolism of the snake in Albanian traditional culture, see Elsie (2002:191–192).
14. Every village woman used to spin with spindle and distaff anywhere and anytime to provide clothing for her family members. Therefore, the incantation "with spindle and distaff!" addressed to the weasel confirms the daily work of women and their belief in postmortem transmigration.
15. The "opponent" of the dead presupposes an enemy in life who speaks ill in the afterworld.
16. The grave of the Albanian communist dictator Enver Hoxha was permanently violated by anti-communist militants (1992–1997), but this "modern" phenomenon does not belong to Albanian traditional ethics (see Kondi 2020:137).
17. During the communist dictatorship, several male folk poets of the Lab area adopted the poetic creations of lamenting women (that were fixed in social memory) and turned them into multipart "songs of pain" (*këngë derti*) for the loss of the communist leader Enver Hoxha (see Kondi 2020:134).
18. See also *zija* (mourning) in Kondi (2012:183–186).

Works Cited

Ahmeti, Ali M. 1986. *Vajtimet dhe gjëmat shqiptare të Plavës dhe Gucisë*. Master's thesis, University of Titograd.

Bartl, Peter. 1993. "Religionsgemeinschaften und Kirchen." In *Albanien, Südosteuropa-Handbuch*, vol. 7, ed. Klaus-Detlev Grothusen, 587–614. Göttingen, Germany: Vandenhoeck & Ruprecht.

Berisha, Anton, and Anton Çeta. 1987. *Vajtime, Gjamë dhe Elegji*. Prishtina, Kosovo: Rilindja.

Bogdani, Ramazan. 1997. *Vallëzimi popullor shqiptar*. Tirana, Albania: Akademia e Shkencave.

Cakaj, Luman. 1972. "Mbi gjendje e familjes dje dhe sot dhe mbi problemet që lidhen me luftën kundër zakoneve prapanike në fshatin Potom të rrethit Skrapar," nr. 543/15. Arkivi i Etnografisë, Instituti i Antropologjisë, Tirana, Albania.

Caraveli, Anna. 1986. "The Bitter Wounding: the Greek Lament as Social Protest in Rural Greece." In *Gender and Power in Rural Greece*, ed. Jill Dubisch, 169–194. Princeton, NJ: Princeton University Press.

Doke Familjare. Vdekja (pyetsor). 1973. Tirana, Albania: Akademia e Shkencave e RPSH.

Dostoyevsky, Fyodor. 1912. *The Brothers Karamazov*, trans. Constance Garnett. New York: Lowell Press.

Elsie, Robert. 2002. *Handbuch zur albanischen Volkskultur*. Wiesbaden, Germany: Harrasowitz Verlag.

Folklorë Nr. 9. 1943. Permbledhje vrojtimesh permbi zakonet edhe giuhen popullore të botueme në rivisten "leka" nder 11 vjetët e para, Mbledhë nga Kolë Kamsi, Botim i Ministris S'Arsimit. Shkodër, Albania: Sh. "Zoja e Paperlyeme."

Frashëri, Stavro Th. 1936. *Folklor Shqiptar*. Durrës, Albania: Litho-tipografia "Stamles."

Gjeçovi, Shtjefën. 1989. *Kanuni i Lekë Dukagjinit/The Code of Lekë Dukagjini*, ed. Leonard Fox. New York: Gjonlekaj Publishing Company.

Gjidede, Pavlo. 1970. "Bregdeti i Himarës," nr. 411/45. Arkivi i Etnografisë, Instituti i Antropologjisë, Tirana, Albania.

Goffman, Erving. 1956. *The presentation of self in everyday life*. Edinburgh: University of Edinburgh Social Sciences Research Centre.

Habermas, Jürgen. 1984. *The theory of communicative action. Reason and the rationalization of society*. Boston: Beacon Press.

Harapi, Zef. 1961. *Etnografia e Dukagjinit*, unpublished study, nr. 301/52. Arkivi i Etnografisë, Instituti i Antropologjisë, Tirana, Albania.

Kaufman, Nikolai, and Dimitrina Kaufman. 1988. *Pogrebalni i drugi oplakivania v Bŭlgaria*. Sofia, Bulgaria: Bŭlgarska Akademia na Naukite.

Kondi, Bledar. 2012. *Death and Ritual Crying. An Anthropological Approach to Albanian Funeral Customs*. Berlin: Logos.

Kondi, Bledar. 2020. "Even the Gods Die . . . The State Funeral and National Mourning for the Albanian Communist Dictator Enver Hoxha." *Traditiones*, 49/2:123–140.

Marcuse, Herbert. 2002. *One-Dimensional Man. Studies in the Ideology of Advanced Industrial Society. With an Introduction by Douglas Kellner*. London–New York: Routledge Classics. First published 1964.

Mehmeti, Fadil. 1978. "Zakone, rite e besime vdekjeje në Kelmend." *Etnografia Shqiptare*, 9:333–356.

Mitrushi, Llambrini. 1974. "Zakone e rite të ceremonialit të vdekjes në Myzeqe." *Etnografia Shqiptare*, 5:257–274.

Pando, Stavro. 1970. "Hllomo, Gjirokastër," 411/45. Archive of Ethnography, Institute for Anthropology, Tirana, Albania.

Pichler, Robert. 1995. "Macht der Gewohnheit. Die Dukagjin-Stämme und ihr Gewohnheitsrecht." In *Albanien: Stammesleben zwischen tradition und moderne*, eds. Helmut Eberhardt and Karl Kaser, 65–83. Vienna: Böhlau Verlag.

Pistrick, Eckehard. 2015. *Performing Nostalgia. Migration Culture and Creativity in South Albania*, SOAS Musicology Series. Farnham: Ashgate.

Rrapaj, Fatos Mero. 1974. *Mitologji e besime ndër shqiptarë*, unpublished study, 808/92. Archive of Ethnography, Institute for Anthropology, Tirana, Albania.

Rrapaj, Fatos Mero. 1991. *Këngë popullore të Labërisë*. Tirana, Albania: Shtypshkronja e re.

Sartre, Jean-Paul. 1969. *Being and Nothingness—An Essay on Phenomenological Ontology*. New York: Washington Square Press. First published 1943.

Schwandner-Sievers, Stephanie. 2002. "Narratives of Power: Capacities of Myth in Albania." In *Albanian Identities—Myth and History*, eds. Stephanie Schwandner-Sievers and Bernd J. Fischer, 3–25. Bloomington, IN: Indiana University Press.

Shkodra në Shekuj. 2000. vol. 1. Shkodër, Albania: *Muzeu historik i Shkodrës*.

Stroebe, Wolfgang, and Margaret Stroebe. 1994. "Is Grief Universal? Cultural Variations in the Emotional Reaction to Loss." In *Death and Identity*, eds. Robert Fulton and Robert Bendiksen, 177–209. Philadelphia: Charles Press.

Tartari, Aqif. 1982. *"Bolena—Vështrim etnografiko-historik,"* unpublished study 503/24. Archive of Ethnography, Institute for Anthropology, Tirana, Albania.

Tuda, Shpresa. 1978. "Të dhëna për zakonet e vdekjes dhe vajtimet në Strugë e rrethinë." *Gjurmime Albanologjike*, 7:157–179.

Udhëzues për kërkime folklorike. 1968. Instituti i Folklorit, Arkivi i Etnografisë, Tirana, Albania.

Valéry, Paul. 2014. The Art of Poetry. Princeton, NJ: Princeton University Press.

Vinca, Nuhi. 1978. "Vajtimet në regjionin e Strugës." *Gjurmime Albanologjike*, 7:181–189.

von Glasersfeld, Ernst. 2007. *Key works in radical constructivism*, ed. Marie Larochelle. Rotterdam, the Netherlands: Sense Publishers.

Xhatufa, Osman. 1972. *"Field recording of a female funeral lament in the village of Bisakë, Kukës, North Albania,"* nr. 12259. Arkivi i Muzikës, Instituti i Antropologjisë, Tirana, Albania.

Zdruli, Koçi. 1962. "Zakone në vdekje." Unpublished accounts, 321/45. Archive of Ethnography, Institute for Anthropology, Tirana, Albania.

Zojzi, Rrok. 1953. *Ekspedita etnografike në Nikaj Mërtur*. Unpublished accounts. Archive of Ethnography, Institute for Anthropology, Tirana, Albania.

Zojzi, Rrok. 1956. *Materiale të mbledhura në Dukagjin, Nikaj–Mërtur etj*, vol. 10, unpublished accounts. Archive of Ethnography, Institute for Anthropology, Tirana, Albania.

Interviews

Bejkova, Avni. 2016. Ex-political prisoner, Tirana.

Brahimaj, Feti. 2016. Folk poet and singer of the folk vocal group of Lapardha, Vlorë, southern Albania.

Çelaj, Nazif. 2016. Principal singer of the folk vocal group of Lapardha, Vlorë, southern Albania.

Nika, Josif. 2002. Resident from the village of Strëmbec, Përmet, southern Albania.

Papleka, Noc. 2011. Ethnographer and resident from Lekbibaj, Tropojë, northern Albania.

CHAPTER 10

DEATH RITES AND LAMENTS IN RUSSIA

ELIZABETH WARNER

"The Russian people attach huge significance to the process of death itself. For them it must be accomplished with a solemnity commensurate to the importance of the moment. They need to have a funeral service, a proper send-off (*provody*) and farewells said to them before the grave" (Vinogradov 1923:271). These words, written over a century ago about the Russian settlers of Siberia, still have resonance today across Russia. During my fieldwork[1] the rituals of death and *memoria* have been a frequent topic of conversation with elderly villagers. Proudly shown photographs of grandchildren, weddings, trips to Leningrad, village festivals lead naturally to perusal of funeral albums charting the "send-off" for parents, husbands, and neighbors.

Vinogradov pinpoints an Orthodox funeral service as one of the standard components of funeral and memorial ritual in the first decade of the twentieth century, something which would come under increasing pressure during the following years of Soviet power. His other comments about a "proper send-off" and "farewells said to them before the grave" hint at customs and beliefs which may be only tenuously linked to Orthodoxy, or not at all, and which derive from the complexities of the spread of Christianity in Russia over many centuries (see Bernshtam 1989 and 1992 [English translation of the former] for the evolution of "folk" or "lived" orthodoxy).

The following commentary, which draws on material from the Folklore Archive of St. Petersburg State University[2] together with my own observations during fieldwork, illustrates the main elements of death rites as conducted today in rural Russia, drawing examples mostly from Vologda and Arkhangel'sk Provinces. It concentrates on what are often referred to as "traditional" funeral and memorial practices still widespread today in village communities across Russia. As will be seen, however, tradition here is not viewed as a unified schema of ritual transmitted down the ages. The precise details of funerary practice vary widely, even from village to village, and have always done so. They are also tied to the special circumstances of individuals. Nevertheless, certain aspects have remained immutable and are underpinned by intrinsic spiritual, psychological, and emotional needs. They still play a pivotal role in the conduct and moral imperatives of daily life and not exclusively in the villages. As will be seen, the outward forms of funeral practices in towns have changed in the course of the twentieth and twenty-first centuries for historical and other reasons; but in essence, care for the dead and remembering and honoring the "ancestors" (*roditeli*) retain their fundamental significance in the life-world of Russians. It is worth remembering that until the latter half of the twentieth century the greater part of Russia's population was in any case rural (Becker et al. 2012:1–22).

Preparations for Burial

Washing and Dressing

It is common practice still, unless the village is in close proximity to a town with funeral services, to keep the deceased at home, where they are made ready for burial. The corpse must first be washed, something which is not done immediately after the death. The recently dead, still regarded as sentient beings, are allowed around two hours in which to adjust to their new status. Washing, usually carried out while the deceased are seated, is made easier by binding their legs and arms, with hands crossed over the chest, right hand uppermost. These bindings must be removed before the coffin is lowered into the grave as the dead are not necessarily imagined as always prone and motionless.

Ideally, in order to avoid the polluting influence of death, the task of laying out the corpse is not done by close family members but by older women, past childbearing age, with a reputation in the locality for their experience in such matters, although today, with village populations in severe decline, the availability of such "professional" help is rare. Although most of the work necessary before burial has always been the prerogative of women, it was not unusual, indeed in some places it was the custom, for men to wash close male friends.

Over much of rural Russia it is still common for women to prepare their death-clothes in advance, what they term their "bundle" (*uzelok*). They speak about the inevitability of death in a matter-of-fact way that is alien to most cultures in the West. There comes a time in life when they seem to understand that death is no longer an abstract idea but an actual event for which they must prepare. Collecting the various garments and other necessary objects, such as material for a mattress and pillow, a pretty coverlet to lay over the body, or, for the devout, an Orthodox shroud, is done when a woman feels the time is right for her, such as after a serious illness (Fig. 10.1). Preparing clothing in advance has both utilitarian and aesthetic functions. If an elderly woman lives alone, for example, access to the bundle will ease the burden of relatives obliged to deal with the funeral. In northern territories there is also a risk that roads to the nearest town where items can be bought may be blocked at the time of a death because of heavy snowfalls or springtime

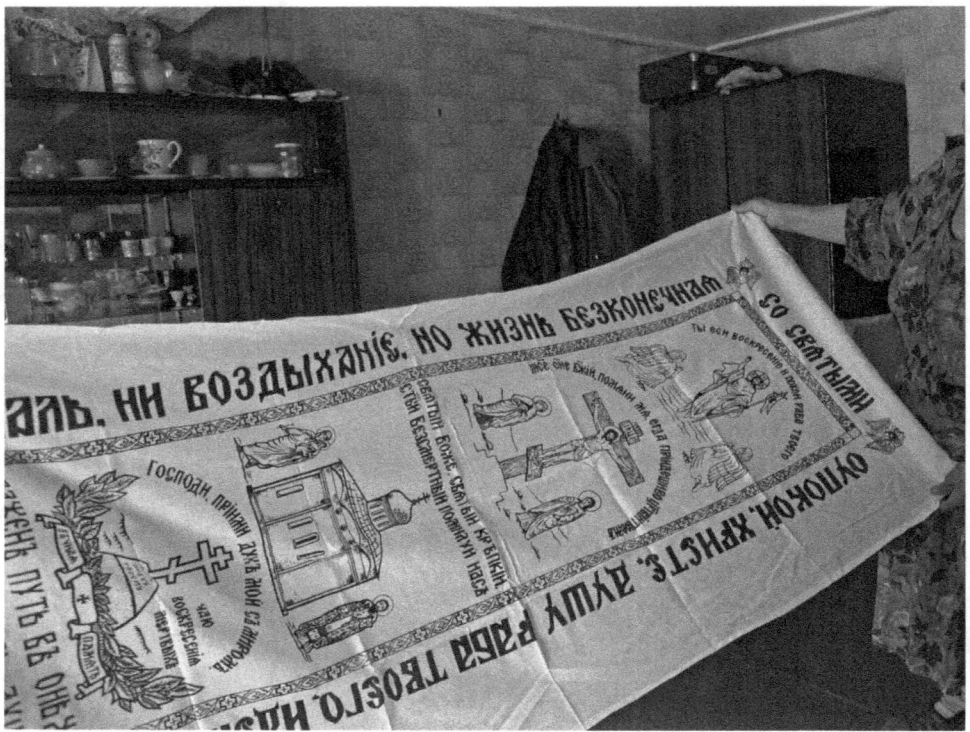

FIG. 10.1. The shroud from this woman's "bundle" proclaims the certainty of resurrection and the hope of life eternal. Kimzha, Arkhangel'sk Province, 2007.

(Photo by Elizabeth Warner.)

meltwater. Above all, however, women want to look their best in the "other world" (*tot svet*). "Where are you off to, all dressed up?" is a frequent question addressed to the dead in laments:

> Ty kudy da naryadilosi?
> Ty kudy tak snaryadilosi?
> Na slukhu da netu prazdnika,
> Na slukhu da netu veselogo.

> Where are you off to, all dressed up?
> Where are you off to, equipped like that?
> We have heard nothing about a festival,
> Nothing about a festive occasion.

(FA Bel 17a-2)

Clothing must be clean, if not actually new. Cleanliness, with regard to both washing and dressing, is a matter of simple hygiene, yet it also has many symbolic meanings.

Like the newborn infant, the deceased is washed before entering a new phase of existence. In Orthodox terms the washing of the body signifies "a desire that he shall present himself clean before the presence of God" (Hapgood 1906:609). Clothes, for both men and women, are chosen in accordance with their wishes and must be complete, as in the world of the living; otherwise, the deceased may be angry and voice their anger in dreams. If this happens, it is imperative that the situation is rectified. A missing item may, for example, be taken to the cemetery and buried alongside the person or hung on the grave-marker (Fig. 10.2). A garment unacceptable to the deceased may be exchanged for another by giving it away to someone else with the injunction that they wear it and "remember" the deceased. In the northern provinces it is not unusual to discover that the deceased has been dressed to reflect the harsh climate. Many times one hears that the deceased must be cold and need their warm gloves, hat, fur-lined boots, or winter

FIG. 10.2. Essential items, like this walking stick, may also be deposited on the grave. Rodoma, Arkhangel'sk Province, 2013.

(Photo by Elizabeth Warner.)

underwear. These conventions, like others in Russian funeral and memorial ritual, bear witness to a conviction not only that death is not an end but also that those who live this new life in their coffin-homes and their cemetery-villages have similar material requirements to the living.

Normally, the body lies at home for two days and is buried on the third, according to Orthodox tradition, and during this time it is never left alone. Family members take turns to sit with the corpse, even to sleep at its side on occasion. Orthodoxy again requires readings from the Psalter at this time, a custom which largely died out in the course of the Soviet era.

Providing for the Deceased

With candles lit around it, the coffin is laid on a bench or on the table in the living room with the deceased's head toward the "front" or icon corner, under the protective gaze of Christ, his mother, and the saints, and with feet pointing toward the door to discourage the possibility of return. Appropriate clothing is not the only item the deceased requires. A variety of grave goods—favorite possessions, children's toys, cigarettes and matches, a comb, spectacles, false teeth, and the deceased's medication at the time of death—are often placed in the coffin. Many times, in response to questions about actions involving the dead, one receives the answer "They see and hear everything." In Arkhangel'sk Province some people still chalk windows on the inside of coffins so that the deceased may see out. If spectacles are worn in this life, they will be needed in the next too. Since providing the dead with nourishment is one of the most significant of all funeral and memorial requirements, teeth too are necessary. Fear of the polluting influence of death means that many items used in the preparation of the dead person, such as wood-shavings, the washcloth, soap, and towel, are placed in the coffin and buried, while the water in which the corpse was washed is poured away in some unfrequented place.

THE BURIAL

The grave should be dug ready for the burial to take place by around 11 o'clock in the morning. This is one of many frequently heard prescriptions and interdictions concerning time in the presence of the dead. They should not be woken from their sleep too early; they should not be visited at lunchtime or after sunset: "You shouldn't disturb the deceased.... It's also not recommended to visit too often. Let them lie in peace" (FA Lesh 17-3).

Given the size of parishes in the Russian north, the small number of priests, and the difficulties of travel, it is unrealistic to expect the presence of a priest at most rural funerals, even if the family wishes it: "There's no priest here to conduct a burial service! Who is going to do it?" exclaimed an elderly woman interviewed in 2007 in Pogorelets,

FIG. 10.3. A burial in the village Bazhenovo, Nizhegorod Province, 1970.
(DPh14_Arch_Lesh_GalevYuA_1970_130_17. The Yurii A. Galev Photo-Archive, Propp Centre, St. Petersburg.)

a village inaccessible by road until quite recently, in the Mezen' region of Arkhangel'sk Province (FA Mez 17-8) (Fig. 10.3).

Among the more persistent vestiges of Orthodox behavior at burials and memorial events is the practice of censing the coffin, at home and during the interment (Fig. 10.4). Later, the grave mound is censed following the "path of the sun" (*po solntsu*). Little attention is paid to any religious or symbolic meaning of the act. Rather, the physical needs of the dead person are paramount: "Well, it's sort of warming them" (FA Mez 17-6). The other world of the dead is a world of cold and hunger, both of which must be reversed by the compassion of the bereaved.

From the above, it may be seen that the notion of a "send-off" referred to by Vinogradov has remained at the core of funeral ritual. The dead are prepared and clothed and provided with indispensable objects, as if they are setting off on a long journey. Vinogradov's "farewells before the grave" are not forgotten either. Relatives, friends, and neighbors all bid farewell to the dead person while the coffin is still at home, kissing a forehead, touching a hand. Before setting off for the cemetery a photograph is often taken of the relatives as they stand around the coffin, a concrete reminder of a last moment of family unity in this world, and goodbyes continue at the graveside (Fig. 10.5). Each stage of the ritual marks a point of departure and passage into a new state of being.

Many people are involved in the organization of a funeral and not only close family members. It is also a community event. There are clear gender divisions in the allocation

FIG. 10.4. Censing the grave is carried out by women who are highly respected and may be a hereditary privilege in some villages. Edoma, Arkhangel'sk Province, 2011.

(Photo by Elizabeth Warner.)

FIG. 10.5. Farewells before the funeral cortege sets off for the cemetery. Vozhgora, Arkhangel'sk Province 1974.

(DPh14_Arch_Lesh_GalevYuA_1974_418_13 from the Yurii A. Galev Photo-Archive, Propp Centre, St. Petersburg.)

of roles. Women are in charge of the more intimate details of washing, clothing, and providing for other needs of the deceased, a continuation of their usual role in the household. They prepare food for the post-funeral meal. Men deal with matters involving less close contact with the dead. They make coffins, dig graves, carry and load coffins onto transport, and in general carry out any heavy work involved. No one expects payment, although food and drink may be provided and women often receive a gift of cloth in the form of bed linen, towels, or a headscarf (see Krinichnaya 2004 for the symbolism of cloth in rites of passage).

Acts of Remembrance (*Pominki*)

Among the many ways of showing the deceased how they are cherished and included in the circle of their family and kin is "remembering," an action which goes well beyond the simple notions of memory. Formal remembering is regarded as obligatory on the third day after the death (i.e., at the post-funeral meal) and on the ninth and fortieth days, times associated with the requirements of the Orthodox Church. Remembrance is also common on certain calendar dates, such as at Easter, the second Tuesday after Easter (*radonitsa*), Troitsa (Trinity) Saturday, and Meatfast Saturday, which ushers in the week preceding Lent.[3] Many people will also visit cemeteries on the twentieth day after a death, on the anniversary, and on the deceased's birthday. In the twenty-first century family gatherings around the graves of ancestors at Troitsa have become a mass phenomenon in the search for national identity and family coherence broken by a history of war, repressions, and economic necessity (Fig. 10.6). Acts of remembrance are invariably associated with food consumed by the living and the dead together. The first memorial act takes place in the home with a meal after the funeral. It is assumed that the deceased, or the deceased's soul, is present, so a place is always laid for them. A token spoonful of each dish is usually given together with, if the deceased is male, a glass of vodka covered with a slice of black bread and, if female, a cup of tea or a small glass of sweet liqueur. The deceased's place may be indicated by a lit candle together with a photograph (Fig. 10.7). To safeguard the fragile soul, sharp cutlery is banned from the table, while the deceased may be given a spoon only. By contrast with other traditional forms of feasting, the guests do not clink glasses with each other. Along with a great variety of food, two traditional dishes are almost always served, *kut'ya* (a grain dish with dried fruits) and *kisel'*, a jelly-like, fruit-flavored dessert which marks the end of the meal (for more information on the ritual uses of these foods, see Valentsova 1999, 2004).

During the forty-day period following a death, the soul, it is believed, may visit its home. Gates and doors are left unlocked, and the flue on the stove chimney is opened. Food and drink are left out and refreshed every day, as if for a living person. At the end of the forty-day period, the soul is invited to a farewell meal, at the conclusion of which comes the final and, by now, emphatic "goodbye" as the soul is escorted from the house and back to the grave.

FIG. 10.6. A family gathering to commemorate a loved one. Leshukon'e, Arkhangel'sk Province, 2010.

(Photo by Elizabeth Warner.)

FIG. 10.7. The deceased's small portion at a funeral meal reflects their diminished requirements in the world of the living. Azopol'e, Arkhangel'sk Province 2008.

(Photo by Elizabeth Warner.)

Although prayers for the dead and requiems may be carried out in the church if there is one in the village, the cemetery, the new home of the dead, is the main venue for all the semi-formal acts of remembrance which take place in the course of the year. On these occasions food is consumed and shared with the dead as a matter of course. Indeed, it is unthinkable to enter a cemetery at any time empty-handed, even if only a sweet is laid on the grave. These cemetery visits maintain and emphasize the closeness of contact between the living and the dead. Some people knock on the grave markers as on a front door, some caress portraits on the grave markers, one-sided conversations take place, food is placed on the graves, vodka may be poured directly into the grave or a spoon pushed into the earth near the deceased's hands. Food offerings are not merely symbolic gestures. Although those who leave food are canny enough to understand that it will eventually be consumed by scavenging animals, they also know, at some deeper level of consciousness, that it will nourish their dead kinsmen who have passed on and that they will be grateful (Fig. 10.8).

Past generations of Russians would recognize many aspects of funeral and memorial practice today, particularly those which affirm the core belief that life continues after death, that living and dead coexist, ensuring the continuity of family, kin, and community down the ages. The immortal soul is envisaged largely in material terms. Providing for its needs through ritual attenuates loss and maintains a balance of mutual benefit to all.

FIG. 10.8. Food for the living and the dead arranged on a grave on the occasion of the deceased's birthday. Edoma, Arkhangel'sk Province 2011.

(Photo by Elizabeth Warner.)

There is an enduring tradition which upholds the duty of care to those who have become, through death, the honored ancestors; but there is no template for a "traditional" funeral. Every act is created anew for a single death and a single individual.

Rites of Death in the Soviet Period

The principles at the heart of funeral ritual came under pressure in the years of Soviet rule. There were concerted attempts to impose an alien ideology on life-cycle rituals in general and particular antagonism for any traditions with a spiritual dimension. Nevertheless, replacing religious festivals and rituals with corresponding secular ones was a slow process. During Khrushchev's leadership of the Soviet Union (1958–1964), ruthless suppression of lingering religious beliefs together with a more conciliatory attitude to folk customs eventually produced some elaborate, transformed calendar and life-cycle rituals. The grandiose new wedding palaces offered music, theater, and "bling" as an alternative to the traditional wedding and church ceremony; but funeral and memorial rituals remained without acceptable civil substitutes. Elena Zhidkova remarked on the difficulties for party members when faced with the death of parents who were believers and who had demanded a church funeral. In the absence of "priests, icons, prayers and a funeral service," there was nothing (Zhidkova 2012:416).

According to V. A. Rudnev, a civil ceremony for the conduct of funerals even remotely fit to replace the church one was only introduced in the late 1960s. As late as 1972, if we can accept his figures, 32 percent of the dead in Russia were still being buried according to religious ritual (Rudnev 1982:111). This must be a considerable underestimate as it does not include the significant number of funeral services conducted without the presence of the deceased in church, the process known as *zaochnoe otpevanie* (lit. an in absentia funeral service; cf. *zaochnoe obuchenie*, distance-learning, when a student's physical presence is not required at an institution).

Other writers of the mid-twentieth century are even more frank about the surprisingly slow demise of "religiosity" in the rural population in particular. G. A. Nosova, for example, in her monograph on what she terms the "everyday" Orthodoxy (*bytovoe pravoslavie*) or Orthodox paganism (*pravoslavnoe yazychestvo*) of Russian villagers, admits that rural communities retained a strong hold on the rituals accompanying the major events of the life cycle: "Burials according to church ritual still predominate over civil funerals" (1975:120). Given the widespread closure of churches under the Soviets, the removal of priests, and virulent anti-religious propaganda, one wonders how this was achieved and maintained. One important factor, according to Nosova (120–121), was the involvement of elderly, devout village women who remembered how funerals had been conducted in the past. This practice was quite widespread, and in some places it proved remarkably tenacious, as Elena Levkievskaya's research of 2012–2014 in a Ukrainian Orthodox enclave in Russia shows. Women born there during the Soviet period continued the tradition learned from their mothers and grandmothers of reading from the Psalms during the wake and were also capable of reciting excerpts from the funeral service in Old Church Slavonic. Their ministrations were extremely popular and still very much in demand in the second decade of the twenty-first century. The survival of this tradition, according to Levkievskaya, may be attributed to the attitude of party ideologues who regarded it as part of the local folk tradition rather than an overt expression of religiosity (Levkievskaya 2015:22).

Of particular relevance to the survival of religious elements was a form of funeral service known as *zaochnoe otpevanie*. Even before the revolution, the Church permitted this aberration, although reluctantly and in extreme circumstances—such as when a death occurred abroad and the body could not be recovered. During the Soviet period this practice increased as a more discreet way of adding a religious dimension to a funeral. A member of the family would travel to the nearest church to buy the necessary attributes for the burial—the band or chaplet for the deceased's forehead with the words "Holy God, Holy Mighty, Holy Immortal" from the Trisagion (Thrice Holy) prayer for the dead, the prayer of absolution, and a handful of earth blessed by the priest, which would later be scattered in the coffin in the shape of a cross (see Sokolova 2011:194 for more details). The priest would read an adapted version of the funeral service, although the family was not obliged to attend the service and the priest could avoid attending the burial.

Clearly, there was no uniform or sudden switch during the years of Soviet antireligious propaganda from "traditional" to civil funerals. A. D. Sokolova, addressing Russian urban ritual in the 1960s–1970s, has pointed out that there were significant differences in practice between towns and rural locations. Town dwellers, somewhat distanced from their village roots and living in completely different circumstances, were often more open to change. They were less likely, for example, to keep the deceased at home before the burial. She also notes that any interference in village funerals (apart from the absence of clergy) mainly affected peripheral details such as the color of material used to cover the outside of coffins[4] or disapproval of overindulgence at memorial meals, while the really significant aspects of ritual, especially the preparation of the deceased for burial, remained untouched within the domestic sphere (Sokolova 2011:190, 192–193).

During the whole of the Soviet period, the extreme importance to village people of family, kinship, and community bonds significantly bolstered their reluctance to abandon traditional ways of honoring their parents and forefathers. Since collective farmers were unwilling to dump bodies unceremoniously in the ground, the old ways were retained for want of an alternative (Nosova 1975:121). The new Soviet civil funerals were inadequate and unattractive, particularly for ordinary people in rural areas, although some attempts were made to introduce new aesthetic elements, like classical music appropriate for funerals (Nagirnyak et al. 1970:231–235). Music of some kind, particularly brass bands, eventually became an accepted part of the funeral procession, a feature which continued in places into the post-Soviet era. In villages, the funeral procession was sometimes accompanied by an accordionist playing a funeral march. A woman I interviewed in 1999 (Vologda Province) recollected how upset she was when the village council (*sel'sovet*) refused permission for music at the funeral of her son who committed suicide at the age of twenty-four and left a note asking for his friend to play the accordion. In Russian village culture suicide was widely condemned. For Orthodox believers it was a mortal sin, but, in general, to shorten one's own life was to deny the notion of the "good" death, achieved in the fullness of time when an individual's allotted time span ran out. Happily, however, the authorities eventually relented, and the friend was allowed to play a funeral march.

Some Soviet innovations, such as the inclusion of music, did not disturb the deeper levels of relationship with the dead. Others, however, were designed to divert attention from traditional rituals which celebrated belief in an afterlife, such as private remembering by the graves of ancestors. The Khrushchev era saw the introduction of mass civil commemoration ceremonies for the dead heroes of World War II on Victory Day (May 9). Held in cemeteries beside newly erected war memorials, they replaced remembrance of living souls with remembrance of sacrifice in the cause of socialism (for descriptions, see Nagirnyak et al. 1970:233–235). Similarly, a new form of Soviet morality was promoted, according to which the deceased did not face judgment as an individual soul before their maker but as a contributor to the collective and to Soviet society as a whole. Many cemeteries in Russia today contain war graves and commemorative obelisks and continue to host official remembrance ceremonies on Victory Day (Fig. 10.9).

FIG. 10.9. World War II gravesite and memorial constructed in 1957. The bench is covered with food offerings at Troitsa. Lykoshino Cemetery, Tver Province, 2016.

(Photo by Elizabeth Warner.)

There were other attempts to subvert deeply held principles. Burial plots in new cemeteries were allocated by the authorities rather than chosen by the bereaved, often destroying that closeness of kith and kin people desired to have in death as well as in life. Cremation was encouraged over traditional burial in earth, and autopsies, previously sanctioned only in extreme cases, became obligatory for deaths in hospital. These measures were an assault on the belief that the body must remain whole and must be buried in the soil of one's native place and in the location where families gather to be with their ancestors.[5]

THE POST-SOVIET PERIOD

It is ironic that, in some respects, the post-Soviet period, which ushered in freedom of choice in the way funeral and memorial ritual is organized, should be the cause of more radical change than the proscriptive Soviet era which preceded it. As was pointed out earlier, acceptance of change was more evident in the conduct of urban funerals, with preparation of the deceased for burial moving away from the home. People had access to funeral service bureaus, where they could order a limited choice of grave markers, coffins, wreaths, and suchlike. The trend toward depersonalizing contact with the deceased while at the same time personalizing the choice of other arrangements has been accelerating since the 1990s. The main cause of change has been the introduction of a free-market economy and the growth of consumerism, signs of which can easily be seen even in village cemeteries. There is a proliferation of new granite headstones with elaborate, laser-etched portraits and landscapes and of grandiose monuments that present an obvious contrast to the homely appearance of the cemeteries I encountered in the Russian far north in the 1990s and early 2000s, with their aging wooden crosses and their Soviet-era rusting wrought-iron crosses and obelisks. Village women may comment on the fact that funeral services are now "big business" and disparage the ostentatious flaunting of wealth. At the same time, they welcome the chance to beautify the graves and bring pleasure to the ancestors who occupy them. A conversation I had with staff at a funeral stonemason's workshop in the small town of Borovichi in Novgorod Province (2016) showed quite clearly both the importance to clients of freedom of choice after decades of restraint and the financial implications of the choices made. Granite was said to be more expensive than marble but was more durable, promising also the durability of memory.

Although the introduction of the market economy into the intimate sphere of death rituals has, for many people, lightened the burden of arranging a funeral, it has also introduced an element of conflict, particularly evident in rural areas. During the post-Soviet period, commercial organizations seeking to maximize profit in the funeral business have increasingly exploited the rural market. Sokolova has identified a power struggle between three groups with a vested interest in the conduct of funeral ritual—laywomen with knowledge of traditional practices and religious rites, recently reinstated

Orthodox clergy, and workers in the funeral industry. The Church, with no experience of operating in a market economy, has found itself in competition with businesses that also arrange for church funerals. Local ritual specialists are undermined by the intrusive innovations of external funeral planners who instruct relatives, subvert their traditional functions in the funeral process, and introduce new customs, previously unknown in the locality (Sokolova 2014:14–25). Although Sokolova's research concerns Vladimir Province, market pressures will have increasing consequences for traditional funeral ritual across the country.

The Lament: Art or Instrument?

One particular feature of funeral and memorial ritual in Russia targeted during the Soviet years was lamenting. Women were made to feel uncomfortable about overt, vocal outpourings of grief.

The lament (*prichitanie*, *plach*, *goloshenie*, etc.) is a quintessentially female genre of oral folk poetry, a reflection of the primary role of women in caring for the dying and the deceased. According to S. M. Tolstaya, for all Slavs the imperative to lament over the dead was even greater than the imperative for burial in earth (1999:136). At one time ubiquitous in both town and country, it gradually fell out of favor in the upper echelons of society. Peter the Great, a zealous reformer, put an effective end to it among the urban gentry in the eighteenth century, leading to its eventual disappearance in towns. His reforms, designed to modernize Russia along Western lines, targeted all aspects of Russian life, even extending to the personal appearance and dress of Russians; and he denounced many popular customs and beliefs as ignorant superstitions. When Mariya Matveevna, the widow of his half-brother Tsar Fedor Alekseevich, died in 1715, Peter ordered a funeral commensurate with her royal status but forbade traditional lamenting—not only for the tsaritsa but for all—denouncing the "indecent" wails and howls of lamenting women (Golikov 1788:105). In rural Russia, however, lamenting during both funerals and acts of remembrance continued to survive. Field recordings of laments in Vologda and Arkhangel'sk Provinces show that lamenting was still relatively widespread there in the 1960s and 1970s (see, e.g., Efimenkova 1980; Razova 1994; Savushkina 1980). My own experience in north Russia from the late 1990s to 2016 showed that only very elderly women still knew how to lament or could at least remember fragments, while younger women had only memories of the lamenters in action (Fig. 10.10). In reality, lamenting was rarely to be heard as an integral part of normal village life by then.

Lamenting accompanied every stage of the funeral process, although it did not always begin immediately after a death for fear of howling (*razrevit'/razrevet'*) the deceased back to life (Efimenkova 1980:16). Women lamented as the body, freshly washed and dressed, was laid in the open coffin. Lamenting continued while the deceased remained at home, during the removal of the coffin, on the way to the cemetery, as the coffin was lowered into the grave, and as the bereaved gathered around the grave after the burial.

FIG. 10.10. Women lamenting at a burial in the village Bazhenovo, Nizhegorod Province, 1970.
(DPh14_Arch_Lesh_GalevYuA_1970_130_14. Yurii A. Galev Photo-Archive, Propp Centre, St. Petersburg.)

Each stage of this process was reflected sequentially in the themes of the lament. On memorial days, especially on the ninth and fortieth days after the death, there was lamenting both at home and in the cemetery.

Considered as a form of folk poetry the verbal aesthetics of the lament can easily be appreciated; but the lament is more than text. It has musical characteristics and a rhythmic structure. It has performance elements and, most importantly, a very particular mode of articulation. It also has a precise functionality in the lives of ordinary people. As K. V. Chistov put it, the lament is "on the border between daily life and art" (1997:463). Unless heard and seen as part of an actual funeral or memorial event, it cannot be fully appreciated.

The Lamenter as Artist

The latter half of the nineteenth century witnessed the appearance of a groundbreaking publication of great significance for the study of lamenting in Russia. This was E. V. Barsov's collection of laments from northwest Russia, specifically from Olonets Province, now in the Republic of Karelia (Barsov 1872, 1997).

Before Barsov, scholars in Russia had paid little attention to the genre, although a few texts had already been published (see, e.g., Dashkov 1842; Rybnikov 1864). Barsov's work had a profound influence on how the lament form would be understood and studied until almost the end of the twentieth century. His attention was drawn to its poetic qualities, particularly as displayed by highly gifted lamenters such as Irina Andreevna Fedosova (1827–1899), whom he recorded in Petrozavodsk in 1865–1866. Fedosova became a celebrity, performing publicly in Petrozavodsk, St. Petersburg, Moscow, Nizhnii Novgorod, and Kazan'. She was a peasant woman who, in her childhood, had watched, listened to, and absorbed the culture and rituals of her village. From an early age she was invited to perform both funeral laments and bridal laments at weddings (Barsov 1997:254). Nevertheless, neither the laments she recorded for Barsov nor those she "sang" for educated audiences at musical soirees should be equated with the laments of women responding spontaneously in their villages to an acute existential crisis, although in the decades that followed it was precisely the poetic fabric, the text of the lament, and the skill of particular lamenters that mostly claimed the attention of researchers. Barsov's work also ensured that the laments of northern Russia, rather than the more lyrical laments of the south, would become the standard of comparison for all Russian laments.

During the Soviet period, because of the lament's associations with religious beliefs and practices, in particular notions about the soul and life after death, it remained in the background of folklore studies. Hobbled by the undesirability of delving into religious and metaphysical arguments, researchers, following Barsov, concentrated on discovering new folk "poetesses" and analyzing the verbal mechanisms by which they created their art. G. S. Vinogradov, for example, graded lamenters as good, average, or mediocre, extolling the "model" laments of the lamenter-artist (*placheya-khudozhnitsa*) over the lackluster efforts of the humdrum howler (*voplenitsa*) (1940:15). Laments were said to have a materialistic rather than spiritual worldview, reflecting the hard life of the pre-revolutionary peasantry, while non-materialistic beliefs about death and ideas about the afterlife were dismissed as artistic devices devoid of contemporary relevance. Such views on the nature of lamenters and lamenting were common in the first half of the twentieth century (see, e.g., Mikhailov 1940; Sokolov 1941; Chistov 1955).

Study of the lamenting tradition was divorced from study of the funeral. Funeral laments were to be categorized as oral folk art alongside other "elegiac improvisations" on tragic events in the lives of peasant women, rather than more narrowly as ritual folklore (Chistov 1955:450). Nevertheless, although some women were indeed renowned in their villages for the power and beauty of their laments, they relied, like all women, on the ability not only to improvise, drawing on a wealth of conventional symbols, phrases, and structures inherited from and endorsed by preceding generations, but also to enter, empathize with, and "speak out" another person's grief.

The Lamenter as Intermediary between the Living and the Dead

Basically, every village woman had the potential and indeed the duty to become a lamenter. About a hundred years before Barsov's book was published a correspondent of the poet Gavriil Derzhavin commented on the fact that learning to lament was, for village girls, as natural and necessary as learning to dance was for the young ladies of polite society: "'She doesn't know how to lament,' he wrote, "is almost as much of a slur as 'She doesn't know how to spin'" (Lotman 1960:146). There was no formal instruction however. As they grew up, girls assimilated the basic principles of funeral ritual and lamenting from listening to older women and made use of their knowledge when the time was right, that is, at the death of someone close to them—a parent, husband, or child. Women recorded in the 1990s and early 2000s in Vologda and Arkhangel'sk Provinces consistently repudiated the idea that lamenting or weeping in the ritual sense could be taught and learned. It came of its own accord as a vocal modality activated by grief. It is the voice of grief: "When there is grief, it comes from the heart. The soul weeps. Grief itself speaks. . . . All the same when you weep it pours out on its own. . . . I don't weep myself, grief weeps" (FA Mez 17a-5). The woman who experienced this grief for the first time became "a bona fide participant in all future funeral-memorial rituals, with the right to use the 'lamenting voice,'" a voice which permitted contact with the world of the dead (Adonyeva 2004:223, 225).

The Lament as Communication

Every lament deploys stock linguistic and poetic features, many of which it holds in common with other forms of verbal folklore. These may be used for artistic effect by a skilled lamenter, but their primary purpose is to establish contact between the living who speak and the dead who listen. Each lament has a precise addressee, reflects the unique relationship between lamenter and deceased, and conveys a message.

One of the characteristic features of the lament is the use of diminutive forms of address, so, for example, we find *mamon'ka, papushka, detochki, sestritsa*, in place of the more formal *mat'* (mother), *otets* (father), *deti* (children), *sestra* (sister), creating a sense of tenderness and sympathy. Diminutive suffixes are also applied to a wide range of objects—parts of the body (*ruchen'ka* for *ruka* [hand]), household objects (*lavochka* for *lavka* [bench]), the features of the natural world (*travon'ka* for *trava* [grass]), birds and animals (*ptashechka* for *ptitsa* [bird]), and so on. Even the grave and the sandy soil in which it has been dug acquire diminutive forms (*mogilushka, pesochiki*). Diminutives show the deceased that they are loved and that the living are sensitive to their plight. They soften the contours of the deceased's new reality.

Svetlana Adonyeva argues that through her initial experience of profound grief the lamenting woman acquired "mystical insight into the realm of death" (Warner and Adonyeva 2021:115). Through metaphor, her lament informs the deceased what to expect. It explains the nature of death and how it is experienced through attenuation and loss. For example, since the deceased is often symbolized as sun, moon, or stars, their death is often depicted as a setting or waning, a withdrawal of light:

> Zakatilos' da yasno solnyshko,
> Potukhla da svetla zoren'ka,
> Potemneli kosyashchety da okoshechki,
> Pocherneli blestyashchie da stekolyshka.
>
> The shining sun has set,
> The sunset light has dimmed,
> The casement windows have grown dark,
> The gleaming panes have turned black.
>
> (Savushkina 1980:144)

Here, light disappears from the world of both the dead and the living; but although the homestead may be dark and cheerless while the family grieves, the world of the living is normally a light world (*belyi svet*), while that of the dead remains dark. Standing beside her mother's coffin, a daughter explains,

> Oi, eto vot tebe, mamushka,
> Oi, vot tebe novaya gorenka,
> Oi, temnaya bez okolenok,
> Oi, da na veki na veshnye!
>
> Oi, mamushka, this is for you,
> Oi, here is your new abode,
> Oi, it is dark, without windows,
> Oi, for all eternity!
>
> (Efimenkova 1980:96)

The grieving wife exhorts her dead husband, the daughter her dead parent, to "open your bright eyes" for a final glimpse of loved ones, but they know the eyes will not open and that they are indeed sightless and darkened in this world.

Through the use of metaphor, the lamenter explains the transforming nature of death and introduces the deceased to the changed world they will soon inhabit and to the ambivalent beings they will become. This may be expressed through images drawn from the world of nature. Thus, in one lament from Vologda Province the deceased has become a hybrid bird–human, a white swan lying on her sickbed, a dove stretched out on her favorite bench. The lamenter exclaims,

> Oi, ty krylyshka iznarostila,
> Oi, ty peryshka iznavodila,
> Oi, dak uzh ty khochesh', golubushka,
> Oi, ty vsporkhnuti da ulititi,
> Oi, ty vo mogilu glubokuyu,
> Oi, ty vo zheltye pesochki!

> Oi, you have grown little wings,
> Oi, you have acquired little feathers,
> Oi, now you want, little dove, Oi, to soar up and fly away,
> Oi, into the deep grave,
> Oi, into the yellow sands!
>
> (Efimenkova 1980:112)

The notion that death is like setting off on a journey down a long road which links the worlds of the living and the dead provides one of the most constant metaphors to be found in the lament. It is one of its earliest elements, introduced when the deceased, laid out in the coffin, is asked where they are off to in their fine clothes, as if to some village festival no one has heard of. The deceased is forewarned of what lies ahead. Here, for example, a mother learns from her daughter's lament that as she travels down this road the natural world will close behind her, preventing her return. The road leads far away:

> Vo syry bory, da vo temny lesa,
> Uzh vo krepost'-to vo krepkuyu,
> Vo krepkuyu da vo glubokuyu.
> Uzh ne budet tebe ni vykhodu, ni vynosu,
> Uzh nikakoi ne budet ot tebya vestochki,
> Uzh ni vestochki, da ni gramotki . . .
> Zarastut tvoi sledochki
> Da travami-to shelkovymi,
> Da tsvetami lazurevymi.
> Kak po zime da kholodnoi
> Uzh zaneset tvoi dorozhen'ki
> Da snegami pushistami,
> Da nastami glubokimi.
>
> Into damp pine woods and into dark forests,
> Into an impregnable fortress,
> Impregnable and deep down.
> You will not walk, nor be carried forth from there.
> There will be no news from you,
> No news, no letter . . .
> Your little tracks will be overgrown
> With silky grasses,
> And azure flowers.
> In the cold winter
> The little paths you have trodden will disappear
> Under falls of fluffy snow,
> And deep snowdrifts.
>
> (Savushkina 1980:141)

Other poetic devices typical of the lament may be more concerned with composition, rhyme, and rhythm. There is frequent use of paired words (*put'–doroga* [path–road], *roditel'–batyushka* [parent–dad], synonyms, and repetitions of essentially the same phrases with many variations. Such devices may aid the rhythmic flow of the verse and, where there is also alliteration, create patterns of sound. Knowing how to repeat the same thing in different ways may act as an aide-memoire for the lamenter. Above all, however, the emotional effect of the lament may be intensified by repeating or offering variations of certain significant words, phrases and passages:

> Uzh bolee vesel'itsa u nas da ne budet.
> Uzh i radosti ne stanet.
>
> There will be no more joyfulness for us.
> Happiness will not come again.
>
> (Savushkina 1980:142)

Of particular relevance to the sensations of loss experienced by the deceased is the repeated use of negative forms. The body no longer functions properly:

> Uzh ne vzglyanut tvoi da ochi yasnye,
> Uzh ne progovoryat tvoi usta sakharnye.
>
> Your bright eyes will not behold,
> Your sweet lips will not speak out.
>
> (Savushkina 1980:151)

Similarly, actions that were familiar and normal have been curtailed. When the deceased's daughters and all her dear friends and neighbors arrive to bid farewell, she is unable to welcome them:

> A ty ne vstretish' ikh da ne vyidesh',
> Da ne otkroesh' tesovykh vorot,
> Da ne razmakhnesh' ty da ruk belykh,
> Da ne nakroesh' stoly-to dubovy.
>
> You will not go out to meet them,
> You will not open the plank gates,
> You will not wave your white hands,
> You will not set the oaken table.
>
> (FA Mez 17a-26)

Memorial laments were also addressed directly to the deceased, now lying underground in the cemetery. On the fortieth day the deceased was exhorted to awake, rise up, return home to eat with the family for one last time, and ultimately accept their incorporation into a new state of being:

> Oi, priletite dva angela!
> Oi, podynite, dva angela,
> Oi, da rodimuyu sestritsyu,
> Oi, da na rezvye nozhen'ki!
> Oi, ved' ty stan'-ko po- staromu,
> Oi, ty uzh mov-ko po-prezhnemu!
> Oi, ty poidem-ko toperechi,
> Oi, da vo gosti, vo gosteiki,
> Oi, ko serdeshnomu dityatku!
>
> Oi, fly down, two angels!
> Oi, raise up, two angels,
> Oi, my own dear sister,
> Oi, onto her swift feet!
> Oi, stand up as before,
> Oi, speak as you used to,
> Oi, let us go now,
> Oi, on a visit, as dear guests,
> Oi, to your beloved child!

Having thanked her son and his wife for their hospitality, the deceased promises to be seen no more and returns "to her own place" (*Oi, na svoe-to na mistechke*), that is, the cemetery (Efimenkova 1980:97, 99).

The Lamenting Voice and Performance

The lamenting voice is "like a 'connecting rod' between the earthly, human world and the world of the ancestors beyond the grave" (Tolstaya 1999:135). It produces a type of recitative with a unique and intensely emotional sound and psychologically disorienting form of articulation: "They used to weep [i.e., lamented]. It was horrendous, girls. It was like your heart was being wrung. All that is very terrifying. You would have to be a very poor-spirited person not to be affected" (FA Mez 17a-16).

The lamenting voice is an extraordinary voice full of sobs, groans, sighs, exclamations, and incomplete sentences; but it reaches the dead: "The soul flutters above the deceased. It hears how you speak out your grief. That means the deceased person's soul is pleased" (FA Mez 17a-7). Catching the attention of the dead and establishing contact between them and the living required more than sound. The lamenter would turn toward the deceased, touch the coffin, sit "near-right near, beside-alongside" (Razova 1994:171). She was obliged to look at the deceased while lamenting and might be censured, as was the case in the Pinega region of Arkhangel'sk Province, if she covered her face with her hands (Savushkina 1980:136). In eastern parts of Vologda Province, the lamenter was particularly mobile and expressive, flinging herself to the floor or onto the bench, her body racked with sobs (Efimenkova 1980:84). In the cemetery, lamenters would bow low over the grave or prostrate themselves upon it.

As an integral part of funeral ritual, lamenting was not performed in isolation. While the deceased remained at home people gathered both to observe and to participate. As one lamenter tired, another would take over: "The [invited] lamenters start off, then everyone begins to weep. It was like a sort of hypnosis affecting them" (FA Kir 17a-2).

THE STUDY OF DEATH RITES IN RUSSIA IN THE TWENTIETH AND TWENTY-FIRST CENTURIES: WORLDVIEW OR LIFE-WORLD?

For more than half the Soviet period very little of substance was written on funeral and memorial ritual because of its religious (in the widest sense) connotations and its association with "unenlightened" rural ways. The cult of ancestors in all its aspects was described and interpreted by followers of the Marxist historical-comparative or "stadial" method as predominantly relictual in nature (see, e.g., Propp 1963:18, 22–23), while lamenting was viewed as the product of poetic imagination. From the 1960s, however, developments in linguistics began to affect the way in which folklore and traditional culture generally were studied. New ethnolinguistic directions, posited on the notion of an invariant model, like a protolanguage, were given the task of reconstructing, through comparative- and structural-typological methods, the spiritual culture of the ancient Slavs, including funeral and memorial ritual. Structural and semiotic folkloristics viewed the ritual text, both verbal and actional, as a system of signs or semantic codes, not necessarily understood by its creators, but the interpretation of which by others would reveal how those creators viewed their world. The text itself was the instrument by which a worldview was communicated. Between the 1980s and the early 2000s this approach has been reflected in numerous works on funeral ritual and laments (see Nevskaya 1980, 1990; Tolstaya 2000; Sedakova 2004), and it is still current today.

The latter half of the twentieth century saw other developments as well in the study of ritual. During fieldwork more attention was paid to funeral ritual as an integral part of village life and to the lament within its proper context. One of the major publications of the 1980s was B. B. Efimenkova's *The North Russian Lament* (*Severnorusskaya prichet'*, 1980). This collection of laments—for weddings and the departure of army recruits as well as for funerals and memorial occasions—contains material from field expeditions carried out between 1967 and 1976 in the eastern part of Vologda Province. It remains one of the major sources for studying the lament in a twentieth-century setting. It is one of the few to illustrate the musical features of the lament and to shed light on performance, the kinetic dimensions and vocal peculiarities of the lament.

As early as 1923 Bronislaw Malinowski had stressed the essentially pragmatic nature of language, the idea that words must be understood within a context of actual situations and experiences, the idea that language was a "mode of behavior, an indispensable element of concerted human action" (1923:316). By the beginning of the twenty-first century the study of traditional practices associated with death in Russia had, to a greater or lesser degree, embraced the notion that context and functionality, as well as text (in its widest sense), are important to our understanding of the purpose and meaning of ritual. Pragmatics has informed the work on both ritual and lament of a number of researchers, including M. D. Alekseevskii (see, e.g., 2005) and S. B. Adonyeva (2004, 2019, Warner and Adonyeva 2021). The latter has played a particular role in promoting the study of ritual from the "inside": "Behind the actions of funeral and memorial ritual stand the feelings and values of concrete individuals. . . . By contrast with the notion of world-view, which is something like a map and a schema, life-world is a dynamic, multi-measure object, whose meanings are subject to constant negotiation in concrete time and space between people interacting with each other face to face" (Adonyeva 2019:304). Adonyeva also addresses funeral ritual as a complex form of social interaction which reallocates roles within the family—the deceased husband becomes an "ancestor," the wife he has left behind becomes a widow, children become orphans. Through bereavement women as well enter a state of symbolic "orphanhood" (*sirotstvo*) or deprivation (cf. "without its master a house is orphaned" [Dal' 1955:4]) and acquire the right to the "lamenting voice," the conduit to the world of the dead (Adonyeva 2004:216–222; Warner and Adonyeva 2021:109–116).

Russian death rituals are also discussed in three major English-language publications which exemplify the value of immersive fieldwork and acceptance of the worlds in which people negotiate and explain their own lives and deaths. Paxson (2005:191–211) is concerned with death in the wider context of village memory, while Olson and Adonyeva (2012:277–305) examine the role of women in maintaining the rites associated with caring for and memorializing the dead. Warner and Adonyeva's monograph *We Remember, We Love, We Grieve: Mortuary and Memorial Practice in Contemporary Russia* (2021) is a comprehensive study of funeral and memorial ritual in a predominantly rural setting and of those fundamental beliefs in personal immortality and family survival that inform them.

Change, Evolution, and New Directions

Through the lament the newly dead are made aware of their changed status, the daunting contours of their new homeland beyond the grave, and the loss of what was familiar and safe:

> Ty proshchaisya, lada milaya,
> So lugam da so zelenym,
> So polyam da so shirokim,
> So lesam da so dremuchim.
>
> Bid farewell, my dear one,
> To the green meadows,
> To the fields so wide,
> To the dense forest.
>
> (FA Bel 17-4)

A death introduced changes not only for the deceased. The village family was a network of interdependent individuals, each with their own function, status, rights, and obligations. The role of the matriarch (*bol'shukha*) in the household, for example, was clearly differentiated from that of her daughter-in-law, spinsters were treated differently from married women with children, and so on. When someone died the relative stability of these conventional familial relationships was destroyed and the shared life-world of the village community temporarily disrupted. For some individuals, the change of social status occasioned by a death was reflected in a change of title—wives became widows, children became orphans. The status of widows, however, especially with regard to inheritance rights, was extremely complex in pre-revolutionary Russia and determined by a mixture of civil law and common law based on local custom (Mukhina 2013:323). There were many subtle gradations in the reshaping of lives occasioned by the loss of family members. With the death of her mother, for example, a young girl lost her guide into womanhood, with all that entailed for future marriage prospects and family life:

> Oi, da ostavila mamushka,
> Oi, da menya, sirotinochku,
> Oi, ne v poru, ne vo vremechko,
> Oi, nedorosluyu travon'ku,
> Oi, nedotsvelogo tsvitika,
> Oi, nedozreluyu yagodku.
>
> Oi, mama, you left me an orphan,
> Oi, when the time was not right, it was too soon.
> Oi, I am the grass which has not grown long,
> Oi, the flower which has not blossomed,
> Oi, the berry which is not yet ripe.
>
> (Efimenkova 1980:90)

Left alone after the death of her husband, an elderly widow acknowledges the changed balance of dependency between herself and her now grown-up sons:

> Ne podbros'te, da ne pokin'te,
> Vy svoyu kormilitsu—mamen'ku,
> Vy teplom da obogreite,
> Khlebom-sol'yu da nakormite,
> Dobrym slovom da prizashchitite.
>
> Do not abandon, do not reject
> Your dear mother—childhood nourisher.
> Keep her warm with your warm heart,
> Feed her with your hospitality [lit. bread and salt].
> Protect her with your kind words.
>
> (Savushkina 1980:149)

A death upset the status quo of relationships within the family and the wider community. It affected gender and generational roles. It realigned the wielding of authority in the family unit. How this reshaping is reflected in funeral ritual offers fertile ground for further research and may provide a greater understanding of the dynamics of familial and social change within traditional societies.

Customs and beliefs are flexible, and funeral practices themselves have been subject to change over the years. The enforced remodeling of cultural, moral, and behavioral paradigms is particularly evident in the case of the lamenting tradition and not only in Russia.

In Ireland, the Catholic Church routinely denounced lamenting as "unchristian" and "unseemly" (Lysaght 1997:66). In Scotland, the Gaelic lament (*coronach*) was targeted by both Catholic and Protestant reformers, not only for religious reasons but in response to "new conceptions of emotional authenticity and propriety" (Stiùbhart 2019:128). In Russia after the revolution the Soviet authorities dismissed lamenting as an archaic rural practice, out of keeping with the new model of the Soviet woman. It had become an "invaluable historical document, allowing us to delve deeper into the past of the Russian people" (Chistov 1960:7). Some women born before the revolution or early in the twentieth century refused to abandon lamenting, in protest against the Soviet condemnation of "women's howling" and as a conscious "act of transgression" in the face of religious persecution (Adonyeva 2019:306). Women born later, however, had learned to moderate their behavior. In the village of Azopol'e (Arkhangel'sk Province) in 2008, we asked Ida, a woman born in 1939, if she knew how to lament. "The only women left who can lament", she replied, "are the very old, the over-eighties. We seventy-year-olds are not able to lament. We are modern women. We don't lament. Maybe we're just not used to doing it in front of others in public. It's the way we were brought up" (FA Mez 17a- 11).

The art of the lament is a female attainment, and the waning of its authority was bound up not only with the stereotypical views of organized religion or the implementation of new political orthodoxies but with expectations about women's place in society and the way they conducted themselves. The extreme and unsettling behavior of lamenting women and the very loudness of their cries undermined notions of restraint and moderation, were even "indecent," according to the modernizing tsar, Peter the Great. In the ongoing, wider debate about the silencing of women's voices, the silencing of the lamenting tradition surely deserves a place.

Notes

1. From 1997 to 2013 I participated in the annual folklore expeditions of St. Petersburg State University to Vologda and Arkhangel'sk Provinces in the Russian Northwest Region. Between 2014 and 2016 I carried out my own fieldwork in Pskov and Novgorod Provinces, also in the northwest, and in Tver Province closer to Moscow.
2. Quotations from the Folklore Archive of St. Petersburg State University are indicated by the letters FA followed by an abbreviated reference to the region (*raion*) where the interview was recorded. "Province" is used for the larger geographical unit *oblast'*.
FA Bel (Vologda Province, Belozersk region).
FA Kir (Vologda Province, Kirillov region).
FA Lesh (Arkhangel'sk Province, Leshukon'e region).
FA Mez (Arkhangel'sk Province, Mezen' region).
3. In the Orthodox Church Saturdays in general are days for remembrance of the dead. Troitsa corresponds in time to Pentecost in the Western church, although it evolved into a festival celebrating the fifteenth-century icon of the Trinity by Andrei Rublev. In orthodoxy, the descent of the Holy Spirit at Troitsa promises renewal for the dead as well as the living. Church services on Troitsa Saturday, therefore, are devoted to remembrance of all the Orthodox dead, excluding only those who died by their own hand. The Sunday following Meatfast Saturday was the Day of Judgment with its reminder to the faithful of the fate of souls. Troitsa Saturday and Meatfast Saturday were known in the church calendar as "universal ancestor Saturdays" (*vselenskie roditel'skie subboty*). For detailed analysis of the Troitsa festival, see Warner and Adonyeva (2021:174–218).
4. Red, for example, was commonly used for party members and blue for mariners.
5. For the English-speaking reader, further information on the funeral ritual during the Soviet period may be found in Rouhier-Willoughby (2008). Soviet attempts to reframe funeral ritual, redesign cemeteries, and encourage the use of crematoria are addressed by Merridale (2002: 125–141).

Works Cited

Adonyeva, S. B. 2004. *Pragmatika fol'klora*. St. Petersburg: St. Petersburg University Press and "Amfora."

Adonyeva, S. B. 2019. "Pokhoronnye plachi, struktury pamyati i osnovaniya zhiznennogo mira." In *IV Vserossiiskii kongress fol'kloristov, Tula, 1–5 marta 2018 g.: Sbornik nauchnykh statei*, Vol. 2, *Mnogoobrazie fol'klornykh traditsii: istoriya i sovremennost'*, comp. V. E. Dobrovol'skaya and A. B. Ippolitova, ed. A. B. Ippolitova, 304–315. Moscow: GRDNT imeni V. D. Polenova.

Alekseevskii, M. D. 2005. "Pominal'nye trapezy na Russkom Severe: Pishchevoi kod i zastol'nyi etiket." In *VI kongress etnografov i antropologov Rossii. Tezisy dokladov Sektsiya*

10: *Traditsionnye sistemy pitaniya*, ed. Yu. K. Chistov, 222–236. St. Petersburg: Muzei antropologii i etnografii im. Petra Velikogo (Kunstkamera) RAN.

Barsov, E. V. 1872. *Prichitan'ya Severnogo Kraya, sobrannye E. V. Barsovym*. 2 vols. Moscow: Tipografiya "Sovremennye Izvestiya." Vol. 1, *Plachi pokhoronnye, nadgrobnye i nadmogil'nye*.

Barsov, E. V. 1997. *Prichitan'ya Severnogo Kraya sobrannye E. V. Barsovym*, eds. B. E. Chistova and K. V. Chistov, 2 vols. St. Petersburg: Nauka. Reprint of the 1872 edition.

Becker, Charles, S. Joshua Mendelsohn, and Ksenya Benderskaya. 2012. "Russian Urbanization in the Soviet and Post-Soviet Eras." *International Institute for Environment and Development. United Nations Population Fund: Urbanization and Emerging Population Issues Working Paper 9*. https://pubs.iied.org/pdfs/10613IIED.pdf. Accessed April 19, 2022.

Bernshtam, T. A. 1989. "Russkaya narodnaya kul'tura i narodnaya religiya." *Sovetskaya etnografiya*, 1/January–February:91–100.

Bernshtam, T. A. 1992. "Russian Folk Culture and Folk Religion." In *Russian Traditional Culture: Religion, Gender and Customary Law*, ed. Marjorie Mandelstam Balzer, 34–47. Armonk, NY–London: M. E. Sharpe.

Chistov, K. V. 1955. "Prichitaniya." In *Russkoe narodnoe poeticheskoe tvorchestvo*, vol. 2, ed. D. S. Likhachev, 449–466. Moscow: Izdatel'stvo Akademii Nauk SSSR.

Chistov, K. V. 1960. "Russkaya prichet'." In *Prichitaniya*, eds. K. V. Chistov and B. E. Chistova, 5–46. Leningrad: Sovetskii pisatel'.

Chistov, K. V. 1997. "*Prichitan'ya Severnogo Kraya, sobrannye E. V. Barsovym* v istorii russkoi kul'tury." In Barsov, E. V. *Prichitan'ya Severnogo Kraya sobrannye E. V. Barsovym*, eds. B. E. Chistova and K. V. Chistov, 2 vols., 400–495. St. Petersburg: Nauka. Reprint of the 1872 edition.

Dal', Vladimir. 1955. *Tolkovyi slovar' zhivogo velikorusskogo yazyka*, vol. 3. Moscow: Gos. izd. inostrannykh i natsional'nykh slovarei. Reprint of the second edition, Moscow: M. O. Vol'f, 1880–1882.

Dashkov, V. A. 1842. *Opisanie Olonetskoi gubernii v istoricheskom, statisticheskom i etnograficheskom otnosheniyakh*. St. Petersburg: Tipografiya Ministerstva Vnutrennikh Del.

Efimenkova, B. B. 1980. *Severnorusskaya prichet'*. Moscow: Sovetskii kompozitor.

Golikov, I. I. 1788. *Deyaniya Petra Velikogo, mudrogo preobrazitelya Rossii, sobrannye iz dostovernykh istochnikov i raspolozhennye po godam*, vol. 5. Moscow: Universitetskaya tipografiya.

Hapgood, Isabel Florence, comp. and trans. 1906. *Service Book of the Holy Orthodox-Catholic Apostolic (Greco-Russian) Church*. Boston, MA–New York: Houghton, Mifflin and Company.

Krinichnaya, Neonila. 2004. *Russkaya mifologiya: Mir obrazov fol'klora*. Moscow: Akademicheskii proekt 'Gaudeamus'.

Levkievskaya, Elena. 2015. "'Narodnoe otpevanie' v Samoilovskom raione Saratovskoi oblasti." In *Momento mori: Pokhoronnye traditsii v sovremennoi kul'ture*, comp. A. D. Sokolova and A. B. Yudkina, 10–34. Moscow: Institut etnologii i antropologii RAN.

Lotman, Yu. N. 1960. "Zapisi narodnykh prichitanii nachala XIX v. iz arkhiva G. R. Derzhavina." *Russkaya literatura*, 3:145–150.

Lysaght, Patricia 1997. "*Caoieadh os Cionn Coirp*: The Lament for the Dead in Ireland." *Folklore*, 108:65–82.

Malinowski, B. 1923. "The Problem of Meaning in Primitive Languages." In *The Meaning of Meaning: A Study of the Influence of Language upon Thoughts and of the Science of Symbolism*, eds. C. K. Ogden and I. A. Richards, 296–336. London: Kegan Paul.

Merridale, Catherine. 2002. *Night of Stone: Death and Memory in Twentieth-Century Russia.* New York–London: Penguin Books.
Mikhailov, M. M. 1940. "Russkie plachi Karelii." In *Karel'skie plachi*, ed. M. K. Azadovskii, 21–50. Petrozavodsk: Gos. Izd. Karelo-Finskoi SSR.
Mukhina, Z. Z. 2013. "Vdova v russkoi krest'yanskoi srede: Traditsii i novatsii (vtoraya polovina XIX- nachalo XXv.)." *Politika i obshchestvo*, 3:322–329.
Nagirnyak, E. V., V. Ya. Petrova, and M. V. Rauzen. 1970. *Novye prazdniki i obryady.* Moscow: Sovetskaya Rossiya.
Nevskaya, L. G. 1980. "Semantika dorogi i smezhnykh predstavlenii v pogrebal'nom obryade." In *Struktura teksta*, ed. T. V. Tsivyan, 228–239. Moscow: Nauka.
Nevskaya, L. G. 1990. "Balto-slavyanskoe prichitanie: Rekonstruktsiya semanticheskoi struktury." In *Issledovaniya v oblasti balto-slavyanskoi dukhovnoi kul'tury: Pogrebal'nyi obryad*, eds. V. V. Ivanov and L. G. Nevskaya, 135–146. Moscow: Nauka.
Nosova, G. A. 1975. *Yazychestvo vo pravoslavii.* Moscow: Nauka.
Olson, Laura J., and Svetlana Adonyeva. 2012. *The Worlds of Russian Village Women: Tradition, Transgression, Compromise.* Madison: University of Wisconsin Press.
Paxson, Margaret. 2005. *Solovyovo: The Story of Memory in a Russian Village.* Bloomington: Indiana University Press.
Propp, V. Ya. 1963. *Russkie agrarnye prazdniki.* Leningrad: Izdatel'stvo Leningradskogo Universiteta.
Razova, I. I. 1994. "Pokhoronnyi obryad Belozerskogo raiona Vologodskoi oblasti." In *Belozer'e: Istoriko-literaturnyi al'manakh*, ed. Yu. S. Vasil'ev, 168–189. Vologda: Rus'.
Rouhier-Willoughby, Jeanmarie. 2008. *Village Values: Negotiating Identity, Gender and Resistance in Urban Russian Life-Cycle Rituals.* Bloomington, IN: Slavica Publishers.
Rudnev, V. A. 1982. *Obryady narodnye i obryady tserkovnye.* Leningrad: Lenizdat.
Rybnikov, P. N. 1864. *Pesni, sobrannye P. N. Rybnikovym*, vol. 3. Petrozavodsk: Olonetskaya gubernskaya, statisticheskaya komissiya.
Savushkina, N. I., ed. 1980. *Obryadovaya poeziya Pinezh'ya.* Moscow: Izdatel'stvo Moskovskogo Universiteta.
Sedakova, O. A. 2004. *Poetika obryada: Pogrebal'naya obryadnost' vostochnykh i yuzhnykh slavyan.* Moscow: Indrik.
Sokolov, Yu. M. 1941. *Russkii fol'klor.* Moscow: Gos. uchebno-pedagogicheskoe izdatel'stvo Narkomprosa RSFSR.
Sokolova, A. D. 2011. "Pokhorony bez pokoinika: Transformatsii traditsionnogo pokhoronnogo obryada." *Antropologicheskii forum*, 15:187–202.
Sokolova, A. D. 2014. "Kommertsializatsiya pokhoronnogo obryada i novye roli lokal'nykh ritual'nykh spetsialistov." *Etnograficheskoe obozrenie*, 2:14–25.
Stiùbhart, Dòmhnall Uilleam. 2019. "Keening in the Scottish Gàidhealtachd." In *Death in Scotland: Chapters from the Twelfth Century to the Twenty-First*, eds. Peter C. Jupp and Hilary J. Grainger, 127–146. Bern: Peter Lang.
Tolstaya, S. M. 1999. "Obryadovoe goloshenie: Leksika, semantika, pragmatika." In *Mir zvuchashchii i molchashchii: Semiotika zvuka i rechi v traditsionnoi kul'ture slavyan*, ed. S. M. Tolstaya, 135–148. Moscow: Indrik.
Tolstaya, S. M. 2000. "Slavyanskie mifologicheskie predstavleniya o dushe." In *Slavyanskii i balkanskii fol'klor: Narodnaya demonologiya*, ed. S. M. Tolstaya, 52–95. Moscow: Indrik.
Valentsova, M. M. 1999. "Kislyi-presnyi." In *Slavyanskie drevnosti*, vol. 2, ed. S. M. Tolstaya, 497–500. Moscow: Mezhdunarodnye otnosheniya.

Valentsova, M. M. 2004. "Kut'ya." In *Slavyanskie drevnosti*, vol. 3, ed. S. M. Tolstaya, 69–71. Moscow: Mezhdunarodnye otnosheniya.

Vinogradov, G. S. 1923. "Smert' i zagrobnaya zhizn' v vozzreniyakh russkogo starozhil'cheskogo naseleniya Sibiri." In *Sbornik trudov professorov i prepodavatelei Gos. Irkutskogo universiteta*, 261–345. Irkutsk: Tip. Gub.VPO.

Vinogradov, G. S. 1940. "Karel'skaya prichet' v novykh zapisyakh." In *Karel'skie plachi*, ed. M. K. Azadovskii, 4–20. Petrozavodsk: Gos. Izd. Karelo-Finskoi SSR.

Warner, Elizabeth, and Svetlana Adonyeva. 2021. *We Remember, We Love, We Grieve: Mortuary and Memorial Practice in Contemporary Russia*. Madison: University of Wisconsin Press.

Zhidkova, Elena. 2012. "Sovetskaya grazhdanskaya obryadnost' kak al'ternativa obryadnosti religioznoi." *Gosudarstvo. Religiya. Tserkov'*, 3–4/30:408–429.

PART II

THE TRADITIONAL CALENDAR, MAGIC, AND FOLK BELIEF

Folklore of the Seasonal Cycle

CHAPTER 11

BALTIC CALENDRICAL FOLKLORE

ELO-HANNA SELJAMAA

THE term "Baltic" has multiple meanings. Often, and in the context of this chapter, it is a geographical and political term referring to Estonia, Latvia, and Lithuania. Located on the eastern shores of the Baltic Sea, the Baltic countries share this arm of the Atlantic Ocean with Denmark, Finland, Germany, Poland, Sweden, and Russia. *Balteus* is the Latin word for belt, and the eleventh-century German chronicler Adam of Bremen is believed to have coined the Latin term *Mare Balticum* to describe the elongated belt-shaped sea. The Latin *balticus* was replaced by the German *baltisch* in the seventeenth century, and gradually this adjective came to be used for new ethnic, political, and scholarly purposes. German nobility coined the endonym *der Balte* around 1840 to distinguish themselves from the non-German (*Undeutsch*) population of Estonia and Latvia. It was around the same time that linguists proposed that Latvian and Lithuanian constituted the Baltic subfamily of the Indo-European language family (Bojtár 1999:6–12, 129). Estonian, however, was classified as a Finnic language belonging to the Finno-Ugric language family.

The concept "Baltic States" entered the global arena only in 1919 at the Paris Peace Conference, where the independence of Estonia, Latvia, and Lithuania received international recognition. Identification with the label "Baltic" does not come naturally to residents of the Baltic countries, and very few scholars in the world master all three languages (however, see Šmidchens 2014). Despite linguistic affinity between Latvian and Lithuanian, it is the Lutheran Estonia and Latvia that share much of the same past, while the history of Catholic Lithuania is intertwined with that of Poland. The historian Aldis Purs has characterized Latvia as "the glue that holds Estonia and Lithuania together" and noted that the term "Baltic" holds little value outside selected "thematic myopias" (2012:12) such as the Soviet occupations (1940–1941 and again from 1944 until the restoration of independence in 1990 [Lithuania] and 1991 [Estonia, Latvia]), defense policy, or, indeed, post-Soviet Women's Day celebrations (Bula 2021) and social organization of national memory by means of official holidays (Andrejevs 2020).

Unless used to encompass Latvian and Lithuanian traditions (e.g., Muktupāvela 2000; Vaicekauskas 2013), "Baltic calendrical folklore" is thus an artificial unit of analysis. As an outsiders' construct, it offers an intriguing, even inspiring angle from which to examine the Baltic region, calendrical folklore, and the study thereof. Because there exists no template for exploring Baltic calendrical folklore, this chapter carves out its own approach that is inspired by the region's multi-tiered history and how it is stratified into layers of holidays, while layers in calendrical customs themselves manifest interactions between local populations, their ambitions, and those of successive rulers. As anywhere else, there also are layers and strands of research that interact with the society at large, sometimes even leading the way in political and social change, as was the case with mass campaigns for collecting folklore in Estonia and Latvia in the late nineteenth century.

The chapter begins by discussing these layers of research and proceeds by elucidating the layers of rulers, regimes, and events that have shaped calendrical customs in the Baltics and continue to serve as important points of reference for Baltic scholars and the public alike. The earliest habitation of the region and the most recent past are oftentimes equally close by in these discussions, which is why this chapter crisscrosses time and space, moving from medieval times to the Soviet era and back, from the thirteenth-century Crusades to the present. Rather than compressing into overview form Estonian, Latvian, and Lithuanian calendrical customs, this discussion aims to contextualize and comment on such (re)constructions of annual holiday cycles and to reflect on their allure.

While this chapter lays itself open to criticisms of methodological nationalism by focusing on the three Baltic countries, it also hopes to challenge the notion of distinct ethnic cultures and calendars by approaching the Baltic as a region that is and has always been a meeting point marked by diversity and interaction. Poles, Belarusians, Russians, Jews, Karaims, Old Believers, Tatars, Swedes, and Roma as well as other historical and present-day minorities residing in these territories ought to be kept in mind when approaching Baltic calendrical traditions inclusively. An effort has been made to think outside the Estonian box that I am most familiar with, but this chapter remains aware of its limitations and encourages readers to delve deeper into research on calendrical folklore in the Baltic countries and especially into research by Baltic scholars.[1]

Layered Research on Layered Traditions

The study of calendrical customs pushes disciplinary boundaries because time reckoning and the beliefs and rituals related to it are of interest to a wide range of fields. The histories of folklore studies and ethnology, the main disciplines dealing with calendrical customs in the Baltics, are complicated by the split that emerged when many academics emigrated to the West during World War II and continued to work on Estonian, Latvian, and Lithuanian materials in exile, while their colleagues in the new Soviet republics (1944–1991) did the same but within the state-imposed paradigm of scientific atheism that discouraged the study of belief-related topics (Bubík and Hoffmann 2015). The research topic of calendrical customs hovered in Soviet academia between ethnography, what ethnology was called, and folklore studies, dedicated to the examination of material and immaterial culture, respectively. A recurrent theme in post-Soviet accounts of Soviet-era dealings with calendrical customs has been how the need to walk the line between official ideology and archival empirical data that represented an earlier society where vernacular holidays were intertwined with religious feasts informed scholarship. Supposed pre-Christian elements were emphasized at the expense of "matter-of-fact treatments of the syncretic belief system" characteristic of vernacular calendrical customs (Hiiemäe unpublished data; cf. Lielbārdis 2018; Šaknys 2014). Also foregrounded was the long history of interactions between Slavic peoples and the inhabitants of the Baltic territories (e.g., Tampere 1965).

Several Estonian and Latvian folklorists have in recent decades pointed out that there is a tendency since the emergence of intellectual interest in folklore in the latter half of the eighteenth century to deem any non-Lutheran phenomena pre-Christian, whereas a closer look suggests that they represent vernacular interpretations of medieval Catholicism rather than an ancient pagan worldview (Jonuks 2012; Lielbārdis 2018; Reidzāne 2008; Reidzāne and Laime 2018). It could be thus argued that researchers in Soviet Latvia and Estonia were drawing on materials and interpretations that were already prone to ignoring or concealing the presence of Christian elements in vernacular beliefs and customs. Atheist propaganda fed on and fed into notions of ethnic particularity that Soviet nationality policies both nurtured and suppressed. There was a high demand for accessible information on traditional calendrical customs in Soviet Estonia. "Folk calendar" (*rahvakalender*), as this area was and is referred to in Estonian, featured among the most popular lecture topics offered by the Knowledge Society, one of the main channels for atheist propaganda. It was largely in response to the public's great interest in this topic that the folklorists of the State Literary Museum set in the 1960s on the arduous task of compiling an anthology of Estonian folk calendar (Hiiemäe unpublished data).

Researchers in Soviet Lithuania interested in calendrical topics faced harsher restrictions because Catholicism and religious feasts played a more visible and discernible role there than Lutheran traditions did in Estonia and Latvia. If folklorists in Soviet Estonia could compile instructions for collecting calendrical folklore throughout the 1960s and 1970s, the first questionnaire in Soviet Lithuania dedicated solely to calendrical customs was launched only in 1982 (Šaknys 2014). Similarly, due to historical reasons to be discussed in this chapter, the pre-Soviet layer of collecting and studying calendrical customs was thinner in Lithuania than it was in Estonia and Latvia. Of great importance were the calls and instructions compiled in the 1930s by Jonas Balys (1909–2011), one of the founders of the Lithuanian Folklore Archive in 1935; but there also existed earlier initiatives inspired by instructions and questionnaires published in Latvia, among others (Lapinskienė 2003; Šaknys 2014; Venskienė 2014). Beliefs, spells, and customs featured in various calls and instructions for collecting folklore that circulated in the Russian Empire[2] in the late nineteenth and early twentieth centuries (e.g., Lapinskienė 2003:46–48). One topic worthy of further study is the extent to which campaigns for collecting folklore in Estonia, Latvia, and Lithuania were influenced by and comparable to similar initiatives in Russia where many first-generation Estonian, Latvian, and Lithuanian intellectuals were educated (cf. Lielbārdis 2017; Reidzāne and Laime 2018:100–105).

Countrywide campaigns for collecting folklore in late nineteenth-century Latvia and Estonia were simultaneously symptoms and engines of modernization, recruiting, as they did, Estonians and Latvians to collect folklore from among themselves. One must bear in mind that serfdom was abolished in present-day Estonia and Latvia only in 1816–1819 (in Latgale, today a part of Latvia, only in 1861) and that peasants could not buy land until the 1850s, which is also when the Estonian and Latvian national awakenings began. Newspapers in Estonian and Latvian that took off in the 1850s addressed their readers in profoundly new ways, as members of a community tied by descent, and facilitated new kinds of collective activities, such as countrywide initiatives for collecting folklore. Repeated pleas to record folklore and instructions for what and how to write it down were published in Estonian and Latvian almanacs and other periodicals, which were also used by collectors to communicate with their growing networks of collaborators. An important precondition for all of this was literacy, which in turn was linked to religion. According to the 1897 all-Russian census, 96 percent of Estonians and 93 percent of Latvians, both groups that were predominantly Lutheran, could read, whereas the literacy rate among Catholic Latvians in Latgale was 57 percent and in the predominantly Orthodox empire as a whole 28 percent (Raun 2017:66, 71–72). National awakening and modernization gained momentum slightly later in Catholic Lithuania, where peasants were liberated from serfdom only in 1861 when the general emancipation of serfs took place in the Russian Empire and where the literacy rates were lower. Between 1864 and 1904, it was forbidden to publish and possess Lithuanian-language publications in the Latin alphabet, and use of the Cyrillic alphabet was demanded instead by the imperial government. However, the press ban did not bring Lithuanians closer to Russia but was met with resistance and is today "considered one of the formative events of the Lithuanian national movement" (Sužiedėlis 2011:488). Of crucial importance in this process were the activities of Lithuanians living in German East Prussia or Lithuania Minor, the territory of present-day Kaliningrad and its surroundings, who would smuggle Lithuanian publications, including calendars of various kinds, into the Russian Empire (Kasekamp 2010:80–81, 88; Kaunas n.d.).

In Estonia, the 1888 call "A couple of requests to the most vigilant sons and daughters of Estonia" by the Lutheran pastor Jakob Hurt (1836–1907) (Jaago 2005) proved to be seminal. Hurt, who had started collecting folklore in the 1860s, identified six areas of interest, one of which was "old customs and habits": calendar and life-cycle customs, healing practices, children's games, tools, clothing, farm buildings, as well as customs and habits observed in daily life while doing various chores, by different professions (Hurt 1989:50–52). As regards the calendar, Hurt asked his readers to write down "customs and habits that used to exist or exist on sacred days and holidays" (Hurt 1989:51), such as *jõulud* (Christmas), *vana aasta lõpp* (New Year's Eve), *nääripäev* (New Year's Day), *vastlapäev* (Shrove Tuesday), *paast* (Lent), *lihavõtted* (Easter), *nelipühad* (Pentecost), *jaanipäev* (St. John's Day), *tõnisepäev* (St. Anthony's Day), *küünlapäev* (Candlemas), *tuhkapäev* (Ash Wednesday), *madisepäev* (St. Matthew's Day), *jüripäev* (St. George's Day), *nigulapäev* (St. Nicholas's Day), *peetripäev* (St. Peter's and St. Paul's Day), *jakobipäev* (St. Jacob's Day), *lauritsapäev* (St. Lawrence's Day), *pärtlipäev* (St. Bartholomew's Day), *maarjapäevad* (the many days dedicated to the Virgin Mary), *mihklipäev* (Michaelmas), *mardipäev* (Martinmas), and *kadripäev* (St. Catherine's Day).

The fact that Hurt listed the holidays without giving their dates or without providing readers with detailed instructions as to what to pay attention to suggests that he relied on them to have first-hand knowledge of these customs. The situation had changed by the late 1930s: asking its correspondents for contributions on specific holidays, the Estonian Folklore Archives deemed it necessary to provide background information, sample texts, and detailed questions on each of them (e.g., Kutti-Lätt 1937).

Songs are another important part and source of calendrical folklore in the Baltics because singing was for centuries constitutive of agrarian holidays, customs, and daily life. The first collection of Lithuanian folk songs or *dainos*[3] published in 1825 by Ludwig Rhesa was followed by several others throughout the nineteenth century (Sadauskienė 2021:87). In Latvia, of the 217,996 folk song texts systematized by Krišjānis Barons (1835–1923) for the six-volume collection *Latvju dainas* (1894–1915),[4] 15,115 are about annual holidays and festive days. The holiday represented with most song texts (4,556) and types (22) is *Jāņi*, the summer solstice celebrated on June 24. The collection also contains over sixteen hundred songs pertaining to *Ziemassvētki* (Christmas) as well as songs associated with *Lieldiena* (Easter), *Jurģi* or *Ūsiņš* (April 23), *Metenis* (Shrovetide), *Miķeļi* (Michaelmas), *Mārtiņi* (Martinmas), and *Katriņa* (St. Catherine's Day) (*Krišjāņa Barona Dainu skapis* ["Krišjānis Barons's Cabinet of Folksongs"] n.d.). The quantity of songs and song types is only vaguely indicative of actual practices, depending as it does on the various factors that shape folklore archives and their collections. But however (in)complete and (in)consistent, materials recorded in the nineteenth and during the first half of the twentieth centuries constitute the historic nuclei of Baltic folklore collections and continue to shape prevalent understandings of folk culture, also because lacunae in these collections came to guide the interests of later researchers and collectors.

Folk Calendar: A Calendar of One's Own

The Estonian term *rahvakalender* stands for folklore about time reckoning and holidays, including customs and beliefs, songs, proverbs, and legends. Possibly a translation from the German *Volkskalender* (coined in the eighteenth century to designate printed calendars with literary supplements), the *rahvakalender* has figured in Estonian folklore studies since at least the 1930s without prompting questions or critical scrutiny. Calendrical customs were one of the research foci of the Estonian Folklore Archives established in 1927 and, as was discussed above, were taken up again by its Soviet successor, the State Literary Museum. The German term *Volkskalender* has also been used to describe fifteenth-century manuscripts that contained instructions for chronological calculations, information on labors of the month, zodiac signs, unlucky days, and other bits and pieces of this kind (Brévart 1988). Closer to the concerns of early twentieth-century folklore scholars in Estonia would have been the German edition of Alexis Yermoloff's (1905) collection of agricultural proverbs, figures of speech, and phenological observations titled *Der landwirtschaftliche Volkskalender* or "agricultural folk calendar."

While I have not come across the term "folk calendar" in Latvian-language research and it is rarely used in the Lithuanian one (Gutautas 1991), there exists in all three countries a deeply ingrained scholarly and popular idea of a distinctively Estonian, Latvian, and Lithuanian calendar. In Latvian, the terms *latviskā gadskārta* ("Latvian year"), *gadskārtu ieražas* ("annual customs"; e.g., Olupe 1992), and *gadskārtu svētki* ("annual feasts") are used—especially in popularizing and educational contexts—to refer to the cycle of celebrations organizing time and structuring the year. At the core of this calendar and its equivalents in Lithuania and Estonia is the peasants' annual cycle (re)constructed with the help of songs, proverbs, riddles, legends, and descriptions of customs and beliefs recorded mostly in the nineteenth and early twentieth centuries but expected to contain much older layers. Included in this body of knowledge are the names and origins of holidays, their ties to farming and other means of livelihood, crafts, chores, related taboos, rituals, songs, proverbs, foodways, phenological observations, and names of months and weekdays. Attention is paid to regional particularities as well as to similarities with the traditions of neighboring peoples but without losing sight of the ethnonational core.

Excellent monographs and source publications in this vein include the four-volume collection Latvian Folk Beliefs (*Latviešu tautas ticējumi*) compiled by Pēteris Šmits (1869–1938) and published posthumously in 1940–1941 (Šmits n.d.; cf. Jansons 1933; Līdeks [1940–1941] 1991; Olupe 1992), the eight-volume anthology *Estonian Folk Calendar* started by Selma Lätt (1909–1969) and completed by Mall Hiiemäe (cf. Hiiemäe and Lätt 2015; cf. Hiiemäe 1998), and the collections of Lithuanian materials published in exile by Jonas Balys (Balys 1978; cf. Dundulienė 1991; Vaicekauskas 2014; Tautos menta n.d.[5]). One volume of the series *Lithuanian Folk Songs* (*Lietuvių liaudies dainynas*), which contains both song texts and melodies, is dedicated to songs of calendar rites of the winter period (Ūsaitytė and Žičkienė 2007; "'Lietuvių liaudies dainynas'" n.d.; cf. Tampere [1960] 2012 on Estonian calendar songs with melodies).

It would be difficult for present-day scholarship not to oscillate around this peasant core and explore changes to the agrarian annual cycle that once was. Folklorists study diachronic shifts in the contents of the annual cycle and of specific holidays (e.g., Hiiemäe 2003; Kõiva and Muhu 2020; Kruks 2012; Lielbārdis 2016; Šaknys 2015a; Viires 2002), previously understudied aspects of the ritual cycle and well-known holidays (e.g., Laime 2008; Laurinavičiūtė-Petrošienė 2015), and practices such as masks and mumming that are constitutive of various holidays (Rancāne 2009; Tedre 2015a; Tedre 2015b). Repeated regime changes in the twentieth century have been accompanied by changes in official calendars and customs. Of interest to scholars are the emergence, implementation, and reception of new holidays introduced from above to legitimate the (new) current rule (e.g., Kõiva 2014; Paukštytė-Šaknienė 2016; Treija 2019; Boldāne-Zeļenkova 2019) as well as holidays that have been borrowed from elsewhere, most notably Saint Valentine's Day and Halloween (Vesik 2016). Of growing importance is the study of minorities' and migrants' (transnational) calendrical customs (e.g., Motuzaitė 2019; Šaknys 2015b; Seljamaa 2010). Urban celebrations have received more and more systematic attention in Lithuania, especially in Vilnius (e.g., Paukštytė-Šaknienė et al. 2016; Šidiškienė 2019). Research conducted for the purposes of this chapter suggests that, on the whole, calendrical customs are of greater and more diverse interest to scholars in Lithuania than elsewhere in the Baltics; but it is an established area of research in all three countries, as evidenced also by Baltic scholars' active participation in the International Society for Ethnology and Folklore working group on The Ritual Year that was inaugurated in 2004.

From the Ancient Past to the Present and Back

The first settlers arrived on the eastern shores of the Baltic Sea around eleven thousand years ago, toward the end of the last great glacial period. By around 1800 BCE, it was arguably already possible to distinguish between speakers of Finnic and Baltic languages, who had settled north and south of the river Daugava, respectively. These early inhabitants were hunter–gatherers and transitioned to farming around 1800–500 BCE (Kasekamp 2010:4–7).

The shift to farming must have been accompanied by a calendar reform of sorts as the importance of the sun in measuring time grew, while that of the moon diminished but did not wither away. Solar, lunar, and phenological frames of reference coexisted as one's survival came to depend increasingly on the ability to forecast weather as well as to pass on the accumulated observations. Paleo-astronomical calculations have been used to suggest that some of the weather and farming proverbs recorded in Estonia in the early twentieth century could be up to three thousand years old because of the way they describe the rise of the Pleiades (Eelsalu 1985:43–44). Scholars have also drawn attention to the longevity of the tradition of observing moon phases in agriculture and procedures such as cutting one's nails or hair (e.g., Hiiemäe 1998:26–28; Klimka 2009). The early twentieth century saw the emergence of *Dievturība*, a form of neo-paganism that "strove to reconstruct the traditional religion of ancient Latvians" based on the study of Latvian folk songs and folk beliefs (Stašulāne and Ozoliņš 2017:236) and that included an elaborate time-reckoning system. Whatever the truth behind such estimates and interpretations, they show how ideas about time and calendrical customs are used to establish continuity in time, territory, nature, and language and how these interpretations may take on a life of their own.

Presumably "by 1100, Baltic societies were moving toward primitive states with established ruling classes and religious hierarchies that were increasingly involved in long-distance trade" (Purs 2012:25). The proto-Latvian tribes included the Selonians, Semigallians, Curonians, and Lettigallians or Latgalians, while the main proto-Lithuanian tribes were the Žemaitians or Samogitians and Aukštaitians. The names of many of the ancient tribes are inscribed in topography and continue to structure the ways in which culture and folklore are being studied and interpreted. Lithuania's five so-called ethnographic regions include Samogitia and Aukštaitija, besides Lithuania-Minor, Sudovia, and Dzūkija (cf. Ragauskaitė 2019). The Latvian Parliament adopted in 2021 a law that defines Latgale, Kurzeme, Zemgale, Sēlija, and Vidzeme as "historical Latvian lands." Drafted by Latvian president Egils Levits, the law aims to "address the issues of the cultural and historical identity and belonging of local communities" (Latvijas Republikas Saeima 2021).

Arguably, no tribes could be differentiated among proto-Estonians, but there were regional differences, also owing to contacts with different neighbors. Linguistically related to proto-Estonians but living on the shores of present-day Latvia were Livs.[6] By the end of the twelfth century, these peoples and the Baltic tribes could be described as Europe's last pagans, despite having been exposed to Orthodoxy and Catholicism by their neighbors east and north. The territories of modern-day Estonia and Latvia were conquered and Christianized by Germans and Danes between the late twelfth and thirteenth centuries (Kasekamp 2010:11–19). Contemporary Baltic nation states have established new days of importance whereby they claim these ancient struggles as their own. Latvia and Lithuania observe September 22 as Baltic Unity Day to commemorate the 1236 Battle of Šiauliai where pagan Baltic tribes, led by Samogitians, arguably beat the crusaders (Latvian Public Broadcasting 2018; Andrejevs 2020:1311). Since 2013, Estonia celebrates Veterans' Day on April 23, St. George's Day, which was an important agrarian spring feast and the name day of soldiers' patron saint. It also commemorates a mid-fourteenth-century conflict that was long interpreted, especially by Soviet historiography, as a peasant uprising against Danish and German rulers (Harro-Loit et al. 2020:315–316).

Unlike their neighbors, Lithuanian tribes joined forces under the leadership of Duke Mindaugas and proceeded with state formation. Mindaugas entered an alliance with crusaders and was baptized in 1251, obtaining papal approval of his coronation as king of Lithuania in 1253 (Sužiedėlis 2011:56–58). Most nobles did not stick to Christianity after his assassination in 1263, but the successors of Mindaugas did consolidate the state further and expanded its territory. Christianity was accepted voluntarily after Lithuania and Poland formed a dynastic union in 1386 (Kasekamp 2010:24–28). The multiethnic, multicultural, multireligious, and multilingual Grand Duchy of Lithuania was by the end of the fourteenth century the largest state in Europe, extending from the Baltic

Sea to the Black Sea. In 1569 Poland and Lithuania established the Polish–Lithuanian Commonwealth (*Rzeczpospolita*). The Lithuanian elite was increasingly motivated to adopt the Polish language and customs, and the society "underwent a long and gradual division into a Polish-speaking nobility and Lithuanian-speaking peasantry," the latter becoming enserfed over time (Sužiedėlis 2011:536).

Present-day Lithuania commemorates several victorious medieval battles and important dates of the Grand Duchy, even though its modern national identity in the nineteenth century came to rest "entirely on the rural, Catholic identity of serfs and peasants" (Purs 2012:35). The assumed coronation day of Mindaugas, July 6, is celebrated as Statehood Day, symbolizing "the continuity of the idea of the coronation" (Šaknys 2018:153). The coronation day of Vytautas the Great on September 8, 1430, was a state holiday between 1930 and 1940 and regained this status in 1991 when it came to be called Thanksgiving for Independence and Defending Lithuania's Freedom; also on this day is the Nativity of the Blessed Virgin Mary (Šaknys 2018). By referencing this period, the Lithuanian calendar creates "a distinct depth and density of national timeline that cannot be claimed by Latvia or Estonia" (Andrejevs 2020:1309). If Estonia and Latvia declared independence in 1918 and restored it in 1991, Lithuania restored independence first in 1918 and again in 1990.

Towns versus Countryside, Others and Us

Thirteenth-century crusaders referred to the present-day territories of Estonia and Latvia as "Livonia" and, in the hope of attracting new fighters, dedicated them to the Virgin Mary, whose cult peaked in Europe at that time (Mänd 2009:194–199). *Terra Mariana*, or the "Land of Mary," was divided between multiple rulers. Over the course of the next nearly three centuries, feudal relations were established, with the crusaders forming the new ruling classes and granting land to foreign nobles, who started establishing manors. Both exacted dues from the native peasants, most of whom became enserfed gradually (Kasekamp 2010:31–39).

The social structure of medieval Livonian towns was corporate, built around associations of merchants, artisan guilds, and other unions of this kind. Recent scholarship describes Riga and Tallinn (Reval) as "multi-lingual and multi-ethnic hub[s] where the Middle Low German urban merchant elites and artisan middle classes lived alongside the indigenous populations—Baltic Latvians, Finno-Ugric Livs, Estonians, and small minorities of Russians, Swedes, Finns, and Lithuanians" (Strenga 2021:61). Livonian towns interacted closely with other towns and trading centers along the shores of the Baltic Sea and have been said to have been "typically 'German' in terms of their administration, guild system, economic network, architecture, the domination of the Middle Low German language"—and in terms of their celebrations and customs (Mänd 2005:10).

The religious and the secular, religion and economy were intertwined and interdependent, with the church acting as "the most influential organizer" of medieval citizens' time (Kala 1996:104). Written sources about the annual cycle of holidays in medieval Livonia are scarce. The oldest calendar manuscripts and excerpts thereof date to the mid-fifteenth and early sixteenth centuries and the oldest calendars compiled and printed in Livonia to the late sixteenth century (Lukas et al. 2021:144–146). Historians have gleaned information about urban calendrical customs from associations' and city councils' financial accounts and other documents, pointing out that different sources lead to different calendars. A medieval urban association would have its own patron saint, take care of this saint's altar in some church, and celebrate the saint's day. Saints' cults followed the model of northern Germany, and no local saints emerged, arguably due to "insufficient political, cultural and devotional integration among the various social groups and the prevailing transregional identity of the elites" (Selart and Mänd 2018:122).

Celebrations of urban seasonal feasts of which there is more evidence include Christmas; Shrovetide; Pentecost; Easter; Corpus Christi; Assumption of the Virgin; the feasts of St. John, St. Michael, St. Martin, and St. Catherine; and All Souls' Day. Historians argue that since merchants constituted the upper strata of urban societies, their calendrical customs and norms influenced those of other social classes (Kala 1996; Mänd 2005). What it meant and whether the opposite is true—what, if anything, was adopted from the natives?—is open for speculation. An intriguing example is All Souls' Day (November 2) in Tallinn. November 2 became the official day for the commemoration of the faithful departed in 998. From at least the 1360s onward and until the mid-sixteenth century, All Souls' Day was celebrated as a secular feast in Tallinn but not Riga, where it remained a religious feast. It was also the only celebration in Tallinn that was referred to by its Estonian names (*hinkepeve, hinkepe, henkepeve*; in modern Estonian *hingedepäev*, lit. "day of souls"). *Hinkepe* appears to have been the third most important feast of the local city council, celebrated with a great variety of (luxury) foods and wine. Expenditure on candles suggests that the festival venue "must have been almost as brightly illuminated on All Souls' Day as at Christmas and Carnival" (Mänd 2005:179). The latest written records about secular *hinkepe* celebrations in Tallinn date from the 1550s, meaning that this tradition was not immediately affected by the Reformation's suppression of Catholic feasts (Mänd 2005:177–180).

Reasons for Tallinn's fondness for *hinkepe* are unknown. Among the peasant population of medieval Livonia, late fall was the time—a period of several days or even weeks—for worshipping deceased ancestors. The souls of ancestors were imagined to be returning home, waiting to be fed and hosted (e.g., Hiiemäe 1998:197–204). Though the historian Anu Mänd deems it "not likely" that "folk customs had any impact on the scenario of the annual feast of the German upper classes" (2005:178) and though folklorists have been reluctant to juxtapose urban and rural traditions, the very name of the celebration bespeaks awareness of some sort, diversity and shared time and space (cf. Strenga 2021).

The tourist industry is today doing its bit to carve out a place for medieval Livonian towns in national and international imaginaries. Tallinn and Riga have both claimed the honor of having been the first town ever to erect a public Christmas tree, basing their statements on written records of merchants' celebrations from the mid-fifteenth and early sixteenth centuries, respectively. Following a controversy dubbed the "fir war," Latvian and Estonian prime ministers reached an agreement in 2010 that the public Christmas tree originated neither in Latvia nor in Estonia but in medieval Livonia (Sillaots 2010).

Intersecting Regional and Religious Layers

Close and diverse ties to northern Germany made Livonian towns susceptible to the Protestant Reformation, which started spreading after 1517 and already by 1524 had "triumphed" (Kasekamp 2010:39) in major Livonian towns but not yet in the countryside. It took somewhat longer for the Protestant Reformation to reach Lithuania. By the late 1660s the Counter-Reformation had won, and Lithuania remained Catholic, while Estonia and Latvia share a Lutheran history.

Historians argue that "at least by the end of the Middle Ages, the daily life and religious activities of the peasants can be characterized as vernacularly Catholic," though "naturally" there occurred regional "deviations from the 'ideal' forms of Christian cult" (Selart and Mänd 2018:93). Folklorists, on the other hand, have described the sixteenth and seventeenth centuries as the most colorful ones in terms of vernacular beliefs and religious practices, characterized by syncretism of Catholic, Orthodox, and Protestant influences and pagan features. The spread and mixing of traditions were fueled by wars, waves of plague, and famine, which killed up to half of the population and led to internal migration (Hiiemäe 1998:16; Reidzāne and Laime 2018:110–111). This is also a period from which there are more written records: protocols of church visitations to parishes, court records of witch and werewolf trials, annual reports by Jesuits in Catholic parts of present-day Latvia. A major, if not the main, concern of compilers of these documents was peasants' adherence to non-Christian beliefs and practices. Latvian scholars Beatrise Reidzāne and Sandis Laime (2018:123) emphasize the pragmatic ethos of pastors' interest in peasants and their way of life: "language skills [were acquired] to promote Christianity, and the knowledge of folklore in order to eradicate previously held religious tenets, beliefs, and customs." At the same time, the emphasis placed by the Lutheran church on written vernaculars, reading, and education contributed to the spread of literacy, as did the activities of the Moravian Brethren in the eighteenth century (Raun 2017), which in turn paved the way for the national awakenings of the nineteenth century.

In 1558, Russia invaded Livonia; and between 1558 and 1795, several wars were waged on present-day Baltic territories between numerous European countries. *Terra Mariana* disintegrated. The Livonian War or the First Northern War (1558–1583) divided the bulk of medieval Livonia into two: territories in present-day northern Estonia constituted the province of Estonia ruled by Protestant Sweden, while the term "Livonia" came to denote today's southern Estonia and northern Latvia. Livonia was controlled by the Commonwealth and the Catholic Church until 1629 when Sweden took hold of most of it (Kasekamp 2010:43–47). The border between Estonia and Livonia stayed in place until the Russian Revolution of 1917, outliving multiple rulers and developing into a significant cultural boundary.

The treaty that ended the Great Northern War (1700–1721) transferred Estonia and Livonia to Russia. Latgale, the Catholic southeastern part of Latvia, remained part of the Commonwealth until 1772. Lithuanian lands, including Latgale, were incorporated into different Russian provinces when the weakened Polish–Lithuanian Commonwealth underwent three partitions between 1772 and 1795. While this brought almost all present-day territories of the Baltic States for the first time under a common ruler, the Russian tsar governed them differently (Kasekamp 2010:63–66). The German nobility in Estonia and Livonia strengthened its position, as it had done under the Swedish crown, and took serfdom to the extreme. Significantly from the point of view of folk customs, enserfed peasants had no freedom of movement. Lithuanian nobles had initially many of the same privileges as Russian ones, but their attempts in the nineteenth century to restore the Commonwealth were suppressed with harsh measures, including the press ban mentioned above. Greater freedoms were enjoyed by Lithuanians who lived in German East Prussia (Kasekamp 2010:72–75).

Folk customs, beliefs, and expressions started to receive more and more positive attention in the latter half of the eighteenth century when Enlightenment ideas trickled into the Baltic provinces. Johann Gottfried Herder (1744–1803) taught in Riga in the 1760s and while there collected Latvian, Lithuanian, and Estonian songs with the help of correspondents (e.g., Šmidchens 2014:47–95). Among Herder's correspondents was pastor August Wilhelm Hupel (1737–1819), whose encyclopedic series *Topographische Nachrichten von Lief- und Ehstland* (Topographical messages from Livonia and Estonia; 1774–1782) contained detailed descriptions of Livonian and Estonian peasant life, also of holidays and other calendar customs. Some of Hupel's contemporaries came to idealize pre-conquest natives as "noble savages" morally superior to the Catholic crusaders of the thirteenth century, said to have brought darkness, not light. It is not difficult to see how such ethos, articulated by the Lutheran clergy, would have led to interpretations that favor pre-Christian elements at the expense of vernacular Catholicism (cf. Jonuks 2012; Reidzāne and Laime 2018:90–100).

On the other hand, the Latvian religious scholar Jānis Priede argues that "the study of pagan pre-Christian religion has particular relevance in the Baltic region" because "pagan beliefs survived among the non-German populations for a long time" (2015:199). Sandis Laime (2008) has drawn on written sources, folk song texts, and other folklore materials from Vidzeme and Latgale to show how the cult of Ūsiņš, the Latvian god of light, blended with that of St. George and how Ūsiņš became a patron of horses. St. George's feast day on April 23 came to be observed as the herdsmen's first night watch and was celebrated in eastern Latvia with ritual activities based on the Ūsiņš cult until the mid-nineteenth century and even longer.

From Regional to (Inter)National and Back

The many layers of rulers and borders discussed in the previous section matter from the point of view of Baltic calendrical customs because they continue to flavor regional traditions, as manifested, among others, by Latvian cemetery festivals (*kapusvētki*). Held in Livonia since the 1830s, cemetery festivals or feasts gained momentum in Latvia in the aftermath of the 1905 Russian Revolution (Uzule and Zelče 2014:249–250). The authoritarian interwar regime of Kārlis Ulmanis made them obligatory in Catholic Latgale in an effort "to integrate this region into general Latvian traditions" (Uzule and Zelče 2014:252). However, to this day, celebrations in Latgale feature processions and various other elements of religious rituals that are missing from Lutheran cemetery celebrations in other parts of Latvia. The latter are associated with national, the former with religious identity. Soviet propaganda co-opted *kapusvētki* starting from 1959 to promote atheism, but the new secular cemetery festivals are said to have developed into occasions for strengthening familial and generational ties, creating "a public site for the national community in a manner that did not require any confrontation with the occupying regime" (Uzule and Zelče 2014:256).

Though Estonian cemetery feasts (*surnuaiapüha*) and Latvian *kapusvētki* share the same root, originating as they do in nineteenth-century Protestant Livonia, Estonian celebrations have retained their religious core and lack national connotations. As in Latvia, secular remembrance days were introduced in the Soviet era and coexisted alongside religious ones. An English-language booklet published in Soviet Estonia in 1985 boasted that secular remembrance days "take place at the cemeteries of all districts and towns, the number of mourners each year amounting to hundreds of thousands" (Leitsalu 1985:110). Even so, this chapter about the new secular "modern rites" could be dropped from the 1991 revised version of this book without needing to bridge it in any way (Tedre 1991). There was no gap. Childhood reminiscences of the Estonian folklorist Marju Kõivupuu (2012) suggest that religious and secular remembrance days in rural south Estonia merged into one on an experiential level: both revolved around similar practices, which in turn enwrapped participants in similar sensations and emotions that could not be determined from without.

Former borders within and in between contemporary nation states have gained new relevance when in recent decades the public and scholars alike have taken a new kind of interest in the local and the regional (e.g., Blockytė-Naujokė 2020; Hiiemäe 2006;

Hiiemäe 2018; Zabielienė 2012). Among the manifold, intertwined reasons for it is the emergence of the concept of intangible cultural heritage. As defined in the highly influential UNESCO Convention for the Safeguarding of the Intangible Cultural Heritage, intangible cultural heritage positions communities and groups as inheritors of "practices, representations, expressions, skills, knowledge" and artifacts that have been "transmitted from generation to generation" (UNESCO 2022). It has also created new kinds of opportunities for the local to interact with the national and international levels as well as regenerated relations between state bodies executing cultural policies, cultural workers and practitioners on the ground, and researchers. In Latvia, Aīda Rancāne (2009 and 2012) has been for years involved in and studying the reviving of local masking traditions that used to be constitutive of various seasonal festivities. Discussing the efforts of contemporary masking groups to reconstruct local traditions, she shows how scholars have since the times of Krišjānis Barons lumped together the names, structures, and activities of different masked processions in different parts of Latvia, making Shrovetide customs in Zemgale indistinguishable from Christmastime traditions in Latgale (cf. critique of the concept "Latvian mythology" in Reidzāne and Laime 2018:110).

The campaign "Let's go mumming!" (*Hakkame santima!* n.d.) for popularizing mumming traditions in Estonia that was launched in 2018 by the Estonian Folklore Council does not foreground regional or local traditions either and is very much centered on countrywide Martinmas and St. Catherine's Day traditions. One driving force behind it appears to be opposition to Halloween as an imported tradition that signifies Americanization and commercialization (cf. Grīnvalde unpublished data, on similar reactions among Latvian exiles after World War II).

Analyzing the transformations of the contents of the Lithuanian Shrovetide celebration, Žilvytis Šaknys (2015a) has shown how Užgavėnės (Shrove Tuesday, lit. "before Lent") has spread abroad and developed in polyethnic environments into a distinctively Lithuanian festival that creates "a temporary deterritorialised Lithuanian ethnic cultural space" (Šaknys 2015a:124). Slavic *Maslenitsa* ("Butter Week") celebrations in the week before Lent have fulfilled a similar function in Estonia (Seljamaa 2010) and presumably in many other places with a sizable Slavic population. In diverse societies, traditional holidays of this kind provide minorities with opportunities to put *their* culture on display and to give others, including representatives of the majority, a taste of it, sometimes in the literal sense of the word. In the context of the post-Soviet Baltics, *Maslenitsa* is a relatively safe and neutral means for claiming public space in comparison to occasions such as May 9 or Victory Day, which according to the Soviet/Russian historical narrative marks victory in the Great Patriotic War and over Nazism but in the Baltic States is associated with Soviet occupation. In Estonia it is the most controversial and polarizing holiday with strong ethnic connotations (Harro-Loit et al. 2020). Though observed by tens of thousands of people in Estonia, it has not been included in any of the folk calendar overviews (e.g., Hiiemäe 2018). As such, it differs from another major Soviet-era holiday, Women's Day on March 8, which has experienced a renaissance of sorts even if in Estonia, unlike in Lithuania and Latvia, it has not made its way back to the official holiday calendar. Dace Bula found in an article published in 2021 that the continued celebration of this "festival of gender" across the Baltics does not signify a failure of the de-Sovietization effort that has dominated the recent decades but "the selectivity of post-socialist change, its steady union with trends of preservation ... and the continuation of Soviet cultural practices in the post-socialist present" (2021:47). It remains to be seen how the war in Ukraine is going to change these practices as well as May 9 celebrations among the Russian-speaking population of the Baltics.

Conclusion

Holidays and calendrical customs are and have always been a means of both communication and control, aimed at molding the present and future. There seems to be no end to layers, especially in the Baltics, where the synchrony between official and vernacular holidays has been waxing and waning for close to a millennium. Strictly speaking, there exists no Baltic calendrical folklore, maybe also because it is not an established scholarly category. However, using it as a lens, it is possible to see commonalities where one has been taught to see distinctive Lithuanian, Latvian, or Estonian calendrical customs. It brings to the fore the lingering impacts of linguistic, religious, and political borders that emerged or were drawn centuries ago as well as those of the more recent Soviet decades. Furthermore, it elucidates the role of folklore collectors and researchers in nurturing certain kinds of continuities in time and space, while disregarding or even discouraging others. If UNESCO's concept of intangible cultural heritage feeds into popularized imaginaries of an ethnonational calendar with peasants' annual holiday cycle at its core, Baltic calendrical customs offer a vantage point from which to trace out transnational and translocal connections.

Notes

1. I thank Jūratė Šlekonytė and Digne Ūdre for their helpful comments on earlier versions of this chapter. Mall Hiiemäe generously shared with me her article "The Estonian Folklore Archives as a Knowledge Hub" forthcoming in *Folklore: Electronic Journal of Folklore* and Rita Grīnvalde kindly sent me her manuscript "Foreign Festivals: Latvian Perceptions of Inceptions," for which I am grateful. All mistakes are mine. The research work carried out to obtain the results has been funded by the EEA Financial Mechanism Baltic Research Programme in Estonia (EMP340).
2. The territory of present-day Estonia and parts of present-day Latvia was conquered by Russia in 1710; further Latvian territories and Lithuanian lands became part of the Russian Empire in 1795. All three countries declared independence in 1918.
3. Lithuanian *dainos* (sing. *dainà*) and Latvian folk songs share many features, being mostly lyrical and in trochaic or dactylic meter. While Latvian folk songs tend to be short quatrains, *dainos* can be longer. About ten thousand Lithuanian *dainos* with around fifty thousand variants have been recorded (Biezais 2005; Ūsaitytė n.d.).

4. The word *daina* was borrowed from Lithuanian and propagated, among others, by Henrijs Visendorfs (1861–1916), a merchant, amateur mythologist, and close collaborator of Krišjānis Barons. In general usage, *daina* became a synonym for Latvian folk song after the publication of the *Latvju dainas*. However, folk song research in Latvia tends to refrain from generalizations, preferring the term *tautasdziesma* ("folk song"). Thus, the complete academic edition of Latvian folk songs published since 1979 is titled *Latviešu tautasdziesmas* (Latvian folk songs) (Krogzeme-Mosgorda 2020; Vīksna 2015; United Nations Educational, Scientific and Cultural Organization [UNESCO] n.d.).
5. *Tautos menta* ("Spirit of the Nation") is a website that has a bibliography of major works on Lithuanian mythology and folklore as well as PDFs of many older publications, including those of Balys.
6. Livs or Livonians spoke Livonian, a Finnic language closely related to Estonian and Finnish, and were first mentioned in chronicles at the beginning of the twelfth century. Their culture is said to have flourished in the eleventh and twelfth centuries ("The Livonians in Ancient Times"). Today, Livs are considered indigenous peoples of Latvia, and their contributions to modern Latvian identity are recognized in the Constitution of the Republic of Latvia (Likumi n.d.).

Works Cited

Andrejevs, Dmitrijs. 2020. "Revisiting the Social Organisation of National Memory: A Look at the Calendars of Lithuania, Latvia, and Estonia." *Memory Studies*, 13/6:1305–1320. https://doi.org/10.1177/1750698018784116.

Balys, Jonas. 1978. *Lietuvių kalendorinės šventės: Tautosakinė medžiaga ir aiškinimai*. Silver Spring, MD: Lietuvių tautosakos leidykla.

Biezais, Haralds. 2005. "Dainas." In *Encyclopedia of Religion*, 2nd ed., ed. Lindsay Jones, Vol. 4, 2127–2128. Detroit, MI: Macmillan Reference USA.

Blockytė-Naujokė, Kristina. 2020. "Easter Egg Symbolism in Lithuania Minor." *Acta Humanitarica Universitatis Saulensis*, 27:225–241.

Bojtár, Endre. 1999. *Foreword to the Past: A Cultural History of the Baltic People*. Budapest–New York: Central European University Press.

Boldāne-Zeļenkova, Ilze. 2019. "The Role of Ethnographers in the Invention of Socialist Traditions in the Latvian Soviet Socialist Republic." *Journal of Ethnology and Folkloristics*, 13/2:33–47. https://doi.org/10.2478/jef-2019-0012.

Brévart, Francis B. 1988. "The German *Volkskalender* of the Fifteenth Century." *Speculum*, 63/2:312–342.

Bubík, Tomáš, and Henryk Hoffmann, eds. 2015. *Studying Religions with the Iron Curtain Closed and Opened: The Academic Study of Religion in Eastern Europe*. Leiden, the Netherlands–Boston: Brill.

Bula, Dace. 2021. "Celebrating March 8: A Failed Attempt at de-Sovietization?" *Journal of Baltic Studies*, 52/1:43–59. https://doi.org/10.1080/01629778.2020.1851276.

Dundulienė, Pranė. 1991. *Lietuvių šventės: Tradicijos, papročiai, apeigos*. Vilnius: Mintis.

Eelsalu, Heino. 1985. *Ajastult ajastule: Muinasastronoomia ja -kalendriloo uudsest käsitlusest*. Tallinn: Valgus.

Gutautas, Stasys. 1991. *Lietuvių liaudies kalendorius*. Vilnius: Vyturys.

Hakkame santima! n.d. https://hakkamesantima.ee.

Harro-Loit, Halliki, Triin Vihalemm, Kirsti Jõesalu, and Elo-Hanna Seljamaa. 2020. "Mapping Celebration Practices in Estonia: Which Days of Importance Actually Influence Societal Rhythms?" In *Interdisciplinary Approaches to Culture Theory*, eds. Anu Kannike, Katre Pärn, and Monika Tasa, 248–328. Tartu: University of Tartu Press.

Hiiemäe, Mall. 1998. *Der estnische Volkskalender*. FF Communications 268. Helsinki: Suomalainen Tiedeakatemia.

Hiiemäe, Mall. 2003. "Nõukogudeaegsed jõulud." In *Võim & kultuur: Artiklikogumik*, eds. Arvo Krikmann and Sirje Olesk, 339–384. Tartu: Eesti Kirjandusmuuseum.

Hiiemäe, Mall. 2006. *Päiv ei ole päiväle veli: Lõunaeesti kalendripärimus*. Tartu: Eesti Kirjandusmuuseum.

Hiiemäe, Mall. 2018. *Virumaa kalendripärimus*. Tartu: EKM Teaduskirjastus; Rakvere: Viru Instituut.

Hiiemäe, Mall, and Selma Lätt, eds. 2015. "Koguteose 'Eesti Rahvakalender' (1970–1999) uuendatud väljaanne." *Eesti Kirjandusmuuseumi Eesti Rahvaluule Arhiiv*. https://www.folklore.ee/erk/.

Hurt, Jakob. 1989. *Mida rahvamälestustest pidada*, ed. Ülo Tedre. Tallinn: Eesti Raamat.

Jaago, Tiiu. 2005. "Jakob Hurt: The Birth of Estonian-Language Folklore Research." In *Studies in Estonian Folkloristics and Ethnology: A Reader and Reflexive History*, eds. Kristin Kuutma and Tiiu Jaago, 45–64. Tartu: Tartu University Press.

Jansons, Jānis Alberts. 1933. *Die lettischen Maskenumzüge*. Riga: Author.

Jonuks, Tõnno. 2012. "Rahvuslus ja muinasusund: Religioon eestlase loojana." *Ajalooline Ajakiri/The Estonian Historical Journal*, 141–142/3–4:269–285.

Kala, Tiina. 1996. "The Church Calendar and Yearly Cycle in the Life of Medieval Reval." In *Quotidianum Estonicum. Aspects of Daily Life in Medieval Estonia*, eds. Jüri Kivimäe and Juhan Kreem, 103–110. Krems: Medium Aevum Quotidianum.

Kasekamp, Andres. 2010. *A History of the Baltic States*. Basingstoke–New York: Palgrave Macmillan.

Kaunas, Domas. n.d. "Kalendorius." *Visuotinės lietuvių enciklopedijos*. https://www.vle.lt/straipsnis/kalendorius-1/.

Klimka, Libertas. 2009. *Tradicinių kalendorinių švenčių semantika*. Vilnius: Vilniaus Pedagoginio Universiteto Leidykla.

Kõiva, Mare. 2014. "Calendar Feasts: Politics of Adoption and Reinstatement." In *Through the Ages II. Time, Space, and Eternity*, ed. Liisa Vesik, 7–40. Tartu: ELM Scholarly Press.

Kõiva, Mare, and Kristina Muhu. 2020. "Changes in Estonian School Calendar Holidays in 1992–2018." *The Yearbook of Balkan and Baltic Studies*, 3/1:183–212. https://doi.org/10.7592/YBBS3.09.

Kõivupuu, Marju. 2012. "Surnuaiapüha." *Kirik & Teoloogia*, June 15. https://kjt.ee/2012/06/surnuaiapuha/.

Krišjāņa Barona Dainu skapis. n.d. http://dainuskapis.lv/katalogs.

Krogzeme-Mosgorda, Baiba. 2020. "Songs about Social Classes and Their Presentation in Two Largest Latvian Folksong Editions." *Tautosakos darbai*, 59:229–251. https://doi.org/10.51554/TD.2020.28376.

Kruks, Sergejs. 2012. "Tradīcijas robežas: Vasaras saulgriežu svētku pārveidošana 1960–2010 gadā." *Letonica*, 24/3:32–48.

Kutti-Lätt, Selma. 1937. "Küsimusi rahvakalendri alalt." *Rahvapärimuste selgitaja* 3:88–90.

Laime, Sandis. 2008. "Pirmās piegulas nakts svinēšana un Ūsiņa kulta vietas Austrumlatvijā." *Letonica*, 18:135–159.

Lapinskienė, Lionė. 2003. "Petro Būtėno 'Lietuvių tautotyros žinių ir senienų rinkimo programa.'" *Liaudies kultūra*, 88/1:44–53.

Latvian Public Broadcasting. 2018. "Latvians, Lithuanians Remember Victory over Crusaders." September 22. https://eng.lsm.lv/article/society/society/latvians-lithuanians-remember-victory-over-crusaders.a293297/.

Latvijas Republikas Saeima. 2021. "Saeima Adopts the Historical Latvian Lands Law." June 16. https://www.saeima.lv/en/news/saeima-news/29942-saeima-adopts-the-historical-latvian-lands-law.

Laurinavičiūtė-Petrošienė, Lina. 2015. *Žanro virsmas: Žemaitijos Užgavėnių dainos*. Klaipėda: Humanitarinių mokslų fakultetas. Baltistikos centras.

Leitsalu, Inna. 1985. "Modern Traditions." In *From Ancient Estonian Customs to Modern Rites*, ed. Ülo Tedre, 90–112. Tallinn: Perioodika.

Līdeks, Osvalds. 1991. *Latviešu svētki. Latviešu svinamās dienas*. Riga: Scientia. First published 1940–1941.

Lielbārdis, Aigars. 2016. "The Tradition of May Devotions to the Virgin Mary in Latgale (Latvia): From the Past to the Present." *Revista Română de Sociologie*, 27/1–2:111–124.

Lielbārdis, Aigars. 2017. "Fricis Brīvzemnieks at the Very Origins of the Latvian Folkloristics: An Example of Research on Charm Traditions." In *Mapping the History of Folklore Studies. Centres, Borderlands and Shared Spaces*, eds. Dace Bula and Sandis Laime, 193–206. Newcastle upon Tyne: Cambridge Scholars Publishing.

Lielbārdis, Aigars. 2018. "Latviešu kalendārs un kristietības ietekme." *Letonica*, 38:177–188.

"'Lietuvių liaudies dainynas.'" n.d. *Visuotinės lietuvių enciklopedijos*. https://www.vle.lt/straipsnis/lietuviu-liaudies-dainynas/.

Likumi. n.d. "The Constitution of the Republic of Latvia." https://likumi.lv/ta/en/en/id/57980.

"The Livonians in Ancient Times." n.d. Livones.net. http://www.livones.net/en/vesture/the-livonians-in-ancient-times.

Lukas, Liina, Vahur Aabrams, Meelis Friedenthal, Tiina-Erika Friedenthal, Katre Kaju, Tiina Kala, et al. 2021. *Balti kirjakultuuri ajalugu 1: Keskused ja kandjad*. Tartu: Tartu Ülikooli Kirjastus.

Mänd, Anu. 2005. *Urban Carnival: Festive Culture in the Hanseatic Cities of the Eastern Baltic, 1350–1550*. Turnhout: Brepols Publishers.

Mänd, Anu. 2009. "Saints' Cults in Medieval Livonia." In *The Clash of Cultures on the Medieval Baltic Frontier*, ed. Alain V. Murray, 191–222. Farnham–Burlington, VT: Ashgate.

Motuzaitė, Akvilė. 2019. "Calendar Festivals as a Form of Transnationalism and Cultural Strategy in the Mixed Finnish–Lithuanian and Greek–Lithuanian Families." *The Yearbook of Balkan and Baltic Studies*, 2/1:25–36. https://doi.org/10.7592/YBBS2.02.

Muktupāvela, Rūta. 2000. "Ziemas cikla masku gājieni Lietuvā un Latvijā." *Letonica*, 1/5:83–96.

Olupe, Edīte. 1992. *Latviešu gadskārtu ieražas*. Riga: Avots.

Paukštytė-Šaknienė, Rasa. 2016. "Šeima ir kalendorinės šventės sovietinėje Lietuvoje." *Lietuvos etnologija: Socialinės antropologijos ir etnologijos studijos*, 16/25:9–34.

Paukštytė-Šaknienė, Rasa, Jonas Mardosa, Žilvytis Šaknys, and Irma Šidiškienė. 2016. *Šventės šiuolaikinėje vilniečių šeimoje*. Vilnius: Lietuvos Istorijos Institutas.

Priede, Jānis. 2015. "Development of the Study of Religion in Latvia in the 20th Century." In *Studying Religions with the Iron Curtain Closed and Opened: The Academic Study of Religion in Eastern Europe*, eds. Tomáš Bubík and Henryk Hoffmann, 199–238. Leiden, the Netherlands–Boston: Brill.

Purs, Aldis. 2012. *Baltic Facades: Estonia, Latvia and Lithuania since 1945*. London: Reaktion Books.
Ragauskaitė, Alma. 2019. "Ethnocultural Regionalization of Lithuania or All the Truth about Our Regions." *Acta Museologica Lithuanica*, 4:162–168.
Rancāne, Aīda. 2009. *Maskas un maskošanās Latvijā*. Riga: LU Filozofijas un socioloģijas institūts.
Rancāne, Aīda. 2012. "Revival of Local Masking Traditions in Latvia as the Result of Cooperation between Performers and Researchers." *Traditiones*, 41/1:209–225. https://doi.org/10.3986/Traditio2012410118.
Raun, Toivo U. 2017. "Literacy in the Russian Empire in the Late 19th Century: The Striking Case of the Baltic Provinces." *Acta Historica Tallinnensia*, 23/1:65–77. https://doi.org/10.3176/hist.2017.1.06.
Reidzāne, Beatrise. 2008. "Latviešu svētku un svinamo dienu nosaukumu etimoloģijas, to problemātika." *Letonica*, 18:232–246.
Reidzāne, Beatrise, and Sandis Laime. 2018. "Latvian Folklore Studies and Mythology." In *Latvia and Latvians: Collection of Scholarly Articles*, eds. Jānis Stradiņš and Eduards Bruno Deksnis, 89–125. Riga: Latvian Academy of Sciences.
Sadauskienė, Jurga. 2021. "The Concept of Lithuanian Folk Song in Lithuanian Folklore 1800–1940." In *Literary Canon Formation as Nation-Building in Central Europe and the Baltics: 19th to Early 20th Century*, eds. Aistė Kučinskienė, Viktorija Šeina, and Brigita Speičytė, 86–106. Leiden, the Netherlands–Boston: Brill.
Šaknys, Žilvytis. 2014. "Tradicinių kalendorinių papročių tyrimai sovietinėje Lietuvoje." *Etnografija*, 20:92–106.
Šaknys, Žilvytis. 2015a. "Užgavėnės: A Rural and Urban, Religious, Socialist, and Lithuanian Festival of Shrovetide." *Folklore: Electronic Journal of Folklore*, 60:105–128. https://doi.org/10.7592/FEJF2015.60.shaknys.
Šaknys, Žilvytis. 2015b. "Karaimų kalendorinės šventės valstybinių švenčių aspektu." *Lietuvos etnologija: Socialinės antropologijos ir etnologijos studijos*, 15/24:99–128.
Šaknys, Žilvytis. 2018. "Valstybės (tautos) švenčių formavimo ypatumai 1918–1940 m. Lietuvoje." *Lietuvos etnologija: Socialinės antropologijos ir etnologijos studijos*, 18/27:129–154.
Selart, Anti, and Anu Mänd. 2018. "Livonia—A Region without Local Saints?" In *Symbolic Identity and the Cultural Memory of Saints*, eds. Nils Holger Petersen, Anu Mänd, Sebastián Salvadó, and Tracey R. Sands, 91–122. Newcastle upon Tyne: Cambridge Scholars Publishing.
Seljamaa, Elo-Hanna. 2010. "'Kui pidu korraldatakse, on järelikult seda kellelegi vaja': Vene vastlapühade tähistamisest Tallinnas." *Keel ja Kirjandus*, 53/8–9:671–686.
Šidiškienė, Irma. 2019. "Šventės ir bendradarbių kultūra Vilniuje bei jo apylinkėse." *Res Humanitariae*, 25:77–94. https://doi.org/10.15181/rh.v25i0.1975.
Sillaots, Marge. 2010. "Eesti ja Läti peaminister sõlmisid kuusesõjas rahu." *Õhtuleht*, November 12. https://www.ohtuleht.ee/406273/eesti-ja-lati-peaminister-solmisid-kuusesojas-rahu.
Šmidchens, Guntis. 2014. *The Power of Song: Nonviolent National Culture in the Baltic Singing Revolution*. Seattle–London: University of Washington Press; Copenhagen: Museum Tusculanum Press.
Šmits, Pēteris. n.d. *Latviešu tautas ticējumi*. http://valoda.ailab.lv/folklora/ticejumi/.
Stašulāne, Anita, and Gatis Ozoliņš. 2017. "Transformations of Neopaganism in Latvia: From Survival to Revival." *Open Theology*, 3:235–248. https://doi.org/10.1515/opth-2017-0019.

Strenga, Gustavs. 2021. "Turning Transport Workers into Latvians? Ethnicity and Transport Workers' Guilds in Riga before and after the Reformation." *Journal of Baltic Studies*, 52/1:61–83. https://doi.org/10.1080/01629778.2020.1863238.

Sužiedėlis, Saulius. 2011. *Historical Dictionary of Lithuania*, 2nd ed. Lanham, MD: Scarecrow Press.

Tampere, Herbert. 1965. "Kirde-Eesti rahvakalendri iseärasusi. (Kommentaare J. Truusmanni üleskirjutustele Iisakust 1886. a)." In *Slaavi-läänemeresoome suhete ajaloost I*, eds. Harri Moora and Lembit Jaanits, 205–262. Tallinn: Eesti Raamat.

Tampere, Herbert. 2012. *Eesti rahvalaule viisidega II. Kalendriliste ja perekondlike pühade laulud*. Tartu: EKM Teaduskirjastus. First published 1960. https://www.folklore.ee/pubte/eraamat/tampere/tampere2/index.html.

Tautos menta. n.d. http://tautosmenta.lt/.

Tedre, Ülo, ed. 1991. *Estonian Customs and Traditions*, 2nd ed. Tallinn: Perioodika.

Tedre, Ülo. 2015a. "Eesti jõuluaja sanditajad." *Mäetagused*, 61:19–68. https://doi.org/10.7592/MT2015.61.sanditajad.

Tedre, Ülo. 2015b. "Maskeerimisest." *Mäetagused*, 61:13–18. https://doi.org/10.7592/MT2015.61.mask.

Treija, Rita. 2019. "Baltā galdauta svētku sākotne." *Letonica*, 39:109–135.

UNESCO (United Nations Educational, Scientific and Cultural Organization). 2022. "Text of the Convention for the Safeguarding of the Intangible Cultural Heritage." https://ich.unesco.org/en/convention.

UNESCO (United Nations Educational, Scientific and Cultural Organization). n.d. "Cabinet of Folksongs." https://latvijasdargumi.unesco.lv/en/detailed-information/internationally-recognised-objects/cabinet-folksongs/.

Ūsaitytė, Jurgita. n.d. "Lietuvių liaudies dainos." *Visuotinės lietuvių enciklopedijos*. https://www.vle.lt/straipsnis/lietuviu-liaudies-dainos/.

Ūsaitytė, Jurgita, and Aušra Žičkienė, compilers. 2007. *Lietuvių liaudies dainynas*, t. XX: *Kalendorinių apeigų dainos 1: Advento-Kalėdų dainos*. Vilnius: Lietuvių literatūros ir tautosakos institutas.

Uzule, Laura, and Vita Zelče. 2014. *Latviešu kapusvētki: Identitātes rituāls*. Rīga: Mansards.

Vaicekauskas, Arūnas. 2013. "Carnival Culture in the Baltic Region: New Tendencies." In *The Ritual Year 5. The Power of the Mask*, ed. Arūnas Vaicekauskas, 48–54. Kaunas: Vytautas Magnus University.

Vaicekauskas, Arūnas. 2014. *Ancient Lithuanian Calendar Festivals*. Kaunas: Vytautas Magnus University.

Venskienė, Asta. 2014. "Etnografinės medžiagos rinkimo priemonių kalendorinių švenčių tema raidos tendencijos." *Litaunistica*, 4/98:252–273.

Vesik, Liisa. 2016. "The Evolution of Valentine's Day in Socialist and Post-Socialist Times." In *The Ritual Year 11. Traditions and Transformation*, eds. Guzel Stolyarova, Irina Sedakova, and Nina Vlaskina, 282–294. Moscow: Kazan.

Viires, Ants. 2002. *Meie jõulude lugu*. Tallinn: Eesti Entsüklopeediakirjastus.

Vīksna, Māra. 2015. "Krišjāņa Barona Dainu skapis, tā piepildīšana un liketeņgaitas." In *No Dainu skapja līdz "Latvju Dainām,"* ed. Rita Treija, 13–26. Riga: LU Literatūras, folkloras un mākslas institūts.

Yermoloff, Alexis. 1905. *Die landwirtschaftliche Volksweisheit in Sprichwörtern, Redensarten und Wetterregeln. Erster Band: Der landwirtschaftliche Volkskalender*. Leipzig: Brockhaus.

Zabielienė, Aušra. 2012. "Dzūkijos ir Suvalkijos folkloro ansambliai dabartinėse kalendorinėse šventėse." *Liaudies kultūra*, 142/1:46–55.

CHAPTER 12

SEASONAL RITUALS, TRADITIONAL DANCE, AND ETHNOCHOREOLOGY IN SERBIA

SELENA RAKOČEVIĆ

ALTHOUGH folklore research on dance in Serbia originated in the late 1800s, the beginning of ethnochoreology[1] as a scholarly discipline there dates back almost a century, to 1934, when the first of a total of eight volumes of *Narodne igre* (*Folk dances*; Janković and Janković 1934; Janković and Janković 1937; Janković and Janković 1939; Janković and Janković 1947; Janković and Janković 1949; Janković and Janković 1951; Janković and Janković 1952; Janković and Janković 1964), written by the sisters Ljubica and Danica Janković, was published (Rakočević 2013). These volumes, organized according to the various regions of Serbia and the former Yugoslavia, include detailed textual descriptions of some nine hundred dances, notations of their accompanying music, as well as general discussions of the ethnographic context in which the dances were performed. The ethnochoreological work of the Janković sisters generally belongs to an ethnographic research paradigm in which the cultural heritage of the peasantry is employed to establish national identity. This folkloristic perspective revolves around national identity as a primary cultural marker (Rakočević 2019).

One of the basic research tasks for dance folklorists was to collect the former, ethnically distinctive traditional dances and music of rural areas and to describe and interpret their functions in the life of agricultural village society. Indeed, the standard methodological path of ethnographers in the study of calendrical-cycle folklore up until 1945 involved research of village social events, which were organized according to the religious (Orthodox Christian) calendar and synchronized with the seasonal rhythms of nature. Viewed within this framework, the calendrical-cycle celebrations in traditional Serbia in which dance played the most significant role involved *koledari*, *lazarice*, *kraljice*, and *dodole*. They took place in winter and spring as key seasonal, agricultural moments of the year and the principal Orthodox Christian holidays (Christmas and Easter) converged. Coinciding with Christmas and New Year's, masked men and boys, or *koledari* (sg. *koledar*), paraded through the village, dancing in mock battles and circle-chain formations as they visited local households. *Lazarice* (sg. *lazarica*) were girls who performed dances with small, tapping steps one week before Orthodox Easter, while *kraljice* (sg. *kraljica*), similar to *lazarice*, performed on Pentecost (celebrated on the seventh Sunday after Easter). *Dodole* (sg. *dodola*) were young girls who danced for rain in dry periods of early summer.

This research paradigm no longer held after 1945, when the ideological platforms and sociopolitical objectives of socialist Yugoslavia were established. A repressive political system, complete with a centralized economy and official atheism, was imposed and continued into the 1990s. It profoundly affected the study of folklore and was interpreted for decades—according to state dictates—through a "socialist" lens. At this time, research was strictly controlled, and positivist and universalist approaches, in which folklore was regarded within a sociopolitical context, were implemented. The scholarly paradigm in Serbian ethnochoreology, as well as more broadly in the field of folklore, started to change only after 2000. This occurred when the turbulent breakup of the former Yugoslavia during the 1990s and the collapse of the socialist system caused radical, comprehensive cultural transformations including changes in prevailing ideologies of scholarly activities and interpretations (Rakočević 2020). Although the national perspective in dance research is still retained, the latest ethnochoreological explorations of ritual events in Serbia have moved toward more critical and reflexive readings and away from the doctrinaire universalism and positivism of previous folkloristics. Drawing, in part, from years of extensive fieldwork, I aim, in this chapter, to chart how theoretical interpretations of dance within traditional calendrical rituals have evolved over the past century. It begins with ethnographic descriptions of the key ritual-dance events, followed by how individual ethnochoreologists and broader trends within ethnochoreology have informed the study of them.

Seasonal Rituals and Ethnochoreological Narratives in Serbia

Koledari, lazarice, kraljice, and *dodole* refer to the participants of the principal Serbian seasonal rituals that traditionally involved dance and, in colloquial usage, the events themselves. These ritual-dance events were synchronized with Orthodox Christian holidays and were generally performed in southeastern Serbia until 1945. Short descriptions of them along with ethnochoreological interpretations provide a vivid picture of these traditional rural ritual practices from the central Balkans.

The singing of *kolede* (carols, sg. *koleda*) took place as processions of masked men and boys (*koledari*) went from house to house between January 2 (Saint Ignjat's Day) and January 19 (Orthodox Epiphany) but most often on January 6, the day before Orthodox Christmas. Their masks represented horned animals, and they were covered with inverted sheepskins, which were believed to represent "mythical creatures"—forest demons (*lesnici*) (Zečević 2008a; Zečević [1973] 2008b). In addition to the demons, two males were masked as "Grandpa" (*dedica*) and his pregnant "daughter-in-law" (*snaška*). In front of each house, the masked participants or *koledari* made noise and clutter. The demons jumped and fought with each other, performing dance movements imitating combat and constantly teasing the daughter-in-law with lascivious gestures. After a while, all of them, together with the hosts, joined in a round chain dance from their local repertoire encircling a set table. The ritual was repeated in front of each visited household. According to Zečević, it was important that the dances and dance movements that the *koledari* performed had a circular pathway, which, together with the dancers' high leaps, represented manifestations of the solar cult and the idea of universal fertility. He maintained that behind the name of the ritual—*koleda*—were vestiges of the fertility deity of the ancient Slavs.

The remaining rituals occurred in spring and early summer and were carried out by female dancers. *Lazarice* were processions of young girls who performed on Saint Lazar's Day, the Saturday one week before Orthodox Easter.[2] Actors were divided into different roles: *Lazar*, *Lazarče* (*Lazarče* is a diminutive of Lazar, most often the smallest girl), and singers. While singers performed ritual *lazaričke* songs, commissioned by the host, *lazarice* would perform various dances depending on the local tradition (Vasić 2004). In all cases, their dance consisted of small tapping steps. Zečević believed that this ritual was spread by the Greek Orthodox church in the Middle Ages, not only because memories of its performances are collected only in the area which was close to Greece (that is, the central Balkans)[3] but due to the fact that it belongs equally to the Greek, North Macedonian, and Bulgarian cultural heritages. This perspective was embraced by ethnochoreologist Olivera Vasić.

Kraljice (lit., queens) took part in female ritual processions very similar to those of the *lazarice*. *Kraljice*, however, performed most often on Pentecost, widespread over the broad geographical area from southern Serbia to Bačka, Banat, and Srem.[4] The roles of the female actors were *kralj* (king), *kraljica* (queen), *barjaktar* (standard-bearer), *dvorkinja* (charwoman), and singers. In this ritual, each of the main actors danced toward another: the king toward the queen and the standard-bearer toward the charwoman, similar to the dance performed by *lazarice*. Using small, tapping steps they would consecutively change places during the dance. For Serbian ethnochoreologists, the elaborate dance performed by the *kraljice* and accompanying actors represented the survival of an ancient agrarian Slavic ritual of ensuring annual fertility for the village communities.

Dodole were groups of youngsters who processed through villages in the dry season of early summer. One of them, usually the youngest girl (sometimes an orphan), was the main participant—the *dodola*. Her naked body was covered with greenery. While the other participants sang *dodolske* songs, the *dodola* danced in place, using small steps and turning herself around. Women from the visited households poured water on the young dancers (especially on the *dodola*), which was considered an act of imitative magic: the more water that was poured, the more that rain would fall. As for other rituals performed during the spring and early summer season by *lazarice* and *kraljice*, ethnochoreologists believed that within the dance ritual performed by the *dodole* were embedded the most ancient layers of the old Slavic religion based on imitative magic.

Early Serbian Ethnochoreologists: Ljubica and Danica Janković

The main seasonal rituals in Serbia depicted in scholarly literature in which traditional dance plays a constitutive part are the four winter and spring events in which *koledari*, *lazarice*, *kraljice*, and *dodole* perform. Ljubica (1894–1974) and Danica (1898–1960) Janković offered core theoretical explanations of these rituals as well as ethnochoreological interpretations of the structural-formal, functional, and semantic roles integral to the dances.

Along with monographs in which numerous comprehensive ethnographic accounts about calendrical dance events from individual geographic areas are incorporated, the Janković sisters published several books on specific aspects of traditional dance, one of which was *Prilog proučavanju ostataka orskih obrednih igara u Jugoslaviji* (*A Contribution to the Study of the Survival of Ritual Dances in Yugoslavia*; Janković and Janković 1957). In addition to noting examples of dances that were performed as part of seasonal-cycle (and life-cycle) village events during the course of their research and in earlier periods, the Janković sisters carefully sought, in this volume, to establish their theoretical standpoints about characteristics and meanings of ritual dances. Their methodology in this book did not include ethnographic descriptions of individual rituals. Rather, they focused on structural-formal and performance qualities of dance "components": kinetics, types of dance-step patterns, ways of dancing, formations of dancers, props and objects used in rituals, and times and places of performances. Their conceptual explorations were based on the fact that ritual village dance events had started to vanish rapidly from traditional cultural practice due to the social and economic transformations in Serbia and the former Yugoslavia which altered traditional ways of rural life even already before, but especially after, World War II. This explains their use of the word "survival" in the title of their 1957 publication. Considering the "survival" of ritual dances in the former Yugoslavia, they were explicit in stating that, for ethnochoreologists, "the most decisive task is to ascertain whether a dance has a ritualistic purpose or not," and they conclude that "as a matter of fact, it is *dancing* which is ritualistic or non-ritualistic," not a particular dance (Janković and Janković 1957:56).

Like other folklore research of their time, the methodology of the fieldwork undertaken by Janković and Janković was based on oral histories containing individuals' recollections of "previous" collective cultural practices—gleaned not only from the oldest rural inhabitants but also preferably from the remotest villages (Rakočević 2016a; Rakočević 2016b). Employing numerous descriptions by individuals from various geographical regions, the Janković sisters undertook to generalize characteristics of seasonal events within the theoretical concepts of *obred* ("rite") and *obredna igra* (lit., "ritual game"), diachronically separated according to "older" and "newer" practices corresponding to general chronological periods that divided Serbian history. The designated epochs were the mid-fourteenth-century medieval Serbian Empire, the subsequent Ottoman Empire (from the fourteenth to the nineteenth century), and the modern era, beginning with the establishment of the Serbian state in the late nineteenth century. This perspective—structuring the performance of certain collective village events through time—can be considered ahistorical since they miss explicit historical contextualization, which means that the exploration of particular socio- and geopolitical circumstances of conducting rituals in concrete situations within various geographical regions has not been included.

The Janković sisters conveyed strongly nationalist attitudes in their ethnochoreological research in Serbia. They avoided the old Slavic and Serbian expression *ples* (lit., "dance") in their publications because in everyday speech it signified a dance that was of "foreign" origin (though not perceived as ethnically specific) such as waltz, polka, tango, etc. Instead, focusing on nationally diverse dance forms, Janković and Janković established the usage, in Serbian ethnochoreology, of *narodna igra* (lit., "folk game") and *orska igra* (lit., "*oro* dance"), expressions conceived previously by the founder of Serbian ethnology, Tihomir Đorđević (1907). The local term *oro* ("hora," "circle dance") was used in the nineteenth century and earlier in southeastern Balkan village dialects of spoken Serbian (in today's southern and eastern Serbia, North Macedonia, and Montenegro). By using the emic expression *oro* for a chain dance in circular formation (Mladenović 1978) performed by the *narod* ("folk"), Đorđević situated dance research in Serbia from the very beginning within the domain of folkloristics or folklore studies. Janković and Janković pursued this theoretical perspective and consequently employed the expressions *narodna igra* and/or *obredna igra*[5] in their writings devoted to dance in calendrical village events. However, in their comprehensive "Summary" of the publication from 1957, which they wrote in English (by themselves), they used the term "dance" instead of "game" (Janković and Janković 1957:54).[6]

In addition to their influential research on dance as folklore, Janković and Janković contributed significantly to ethnomusicological research in Serbia (Zakić 2014). Their meticulous analyses of dance music were exemplary. Indeed, they observed dance kinetics right alongside its "musical accompaniment" and considered dance a syncretic union of dance movements and dance music. The 1957 volume by the Janković sisters provided especially important ethnomusicological examinations of the musical features of ritual dance. Analyzing more than one hundred ritual dance melodies,[7] they concluded that most of the melodies were vocal in 2/4 or 3/4 meter (although there were also those performed in the *parlando-rubato* style[8]). Moreover, they found that the melodies most frequently had a narrow ambitus and that they were often sung with special performance qualities such as taking a breath in the middle of a word, long exclamations on the vocal "e," etc.

Along with music, the Janković sisters focused on theoretical interpretations of structural-formal features of individual parameters of ritual dancing which were systematized according to their "complexity": from simpler to more intricate step patterns. This systematization was based on the evolutionist premise that simpler cultural forms precede complex ones and that they reveal the most ancient layers of dance traditions. Accordingly, all of the explorations by Janković and Janković were focused on defining the "magic" functions embedded in dance. For example, they interpreted both high leaps executed by *koledari* as well as tapping steps by *kraljice* and *lazarice* as movements of a "ritualistic nature" (1957:52). The function of leaps, they argued, is to imitate growth, and the purpose of tapping is to convey a message to the land to be fruitful in the following year. Along with specific leg movements, they believed that mimetic elements in dances, which were still in existence and could be recorded at the time of their research, revealed their undeniable ritual origins. "Ritual dances are usually performed in a solemn, quiet, reserved manner," wrote the Janković sisters (1957:53), claiming that they are most frequently performed in a circle, often around material objects (such as photographs, clothing, weapons, etc.), an animal, or a person, all of which, they maintained, reveal the indubitable magic and cult purposes of these dances.

Janković and Janković considered their standpoints incontestable—derived, they argued, a posteriori from analysis of the countless examples acquired exclusively from their own field experience and interpreted through reason and logic. These theoretical points of view, which they advocated for the rest of their lives and passed on to later researchers, represented the dominant positivistic approach of early folkloristics in Serbia. Regardless of subsequent critical assessments of the Janković sisters' interpretations of ritual dance, their contributions to the development of ethnochoreology in the former Yugoslavia and Serbia were immeasurable (Rakočević 2014). While theoretically they were, for the most part, in harmony with the prevailing approaches to folklore of their time, they were, in terms of ethnochoreological analysis, far ahead of them. They commanded immense authority and respect among their younger contemporaries, who represented the second generation of ethnochoreologists in Serbia (Rakočević 2013). Moreover, while the views put forth by Ljubica and Danica Janković have clearly been recognized by their successors, they have also been expanded and supplemented by subsequent scholars. Among the followers of the Janković sisters' theoretical interpretations of ritual dance were Olivera Mladenović and Slobodan Zečević and, a generation later, Olivera Vasić.

"Folklore on Stage": Seasonal Rituals and Dance in Southeastern Serbia after 1945

Establishing the socialist order in Yugoslavia in 1945 engendered broad political, economic, and cultural transformations of society based on the ideology of "brotherhood and unity" of all peoples of the country as well as modernization and emancipation of the labor class. All forms of religious and church activities were forbidden, and ethnically distinctive cultural forms were suppressed in favor of establishing notions of a shared Yugoslav heritage. An important aspect for achieving that overall goal of official policy was the establishing of folklore groups, dubbed "cultural-artistic societies" (*kulturno-umetnička društva*, or KUD) as amateur associations sponsored by the state. Their primary role was to bring together as many young people as possible presenting "scenic folklore" (*scenski folklor*), which meant traditional village dance and music on stage (Bajić Stojiljković 2019). Since shaping the repertoire policy of KUD was a part of the official socialist ideology, it was based on equal representation of dances from each of the six republics of the former Yugoslavia[9] within a theatrical form of "traditional dance choreography" reflecting generalized folklore heritage from broad geographical areas,[10] while local dance and music repertoires were ignored.

The ideology of the ultimate modernization for the "new society" was realized through intense industrialization, mass migration of the rural population to the cities, and the development of new forms of popular music. A contemporary genre called "newly composed folk music" (*novo-komponovana narodna muzika*), which emerged already in the 1950s, started to be widely accepted all over Yugoslavia (Rasmussen 2002; Nenić 2014). All of these processes contributed significantly to abandoning the practice of village calendrical rituals. Generally, it could be said that all participatory forms of traditional village dancing were neglected almost immediately after World War II. This was not only because of the essential changes of the rural lifestyle but also because the authorities in some areas of the former Yugoslavia (especially in Serbia) banned their performance as "decadent" and "obsolete" and severely punished those who participated in them. During field research in Banat (northeastern Serbia) as well as southeastern and eastern Serbia during the 1990s and early 2000s, I recorded numerous testimonies of older people about the suppression of any kind of activities connected with the Orthodox Church and "outdated" village rites based, as it was claimed, on superstitions.

Wanting to slow down the rampant migration from the villages by encouraging cultural activities of their inhabitants and, at the same time, trying to establish control over the unrestrained spreading of "newly composed folk music," the general official policies of the Serbian authorities toward rural culture started to change during the 1960s and early 1970s with the controlled establishment of new "folklore" manifestations, supervised by experts (ethnologists, ethnomusicologists, and ethnochoreologists) and sponsored by the Ministry of Culture. One of these manifestations, officially named "The Contest of Serbian Villages," was founded in 1973; it was called, colloquially, "village gatherings" (*susreti sela*). The supreme organizer at the state level was the Cultural-Educational Association (Kulturno-Prosvetna Zajednica), located in Belgrade; but the functioning of all activities was based on work of the local village KUD.[11] Advised, supervised, and judged by experts,[12] competitions consisted of short performances of traditional dance and music including condensed stage performances of calendrical rituals. Local versions put on by *koledari, kraljice, lazarice,* and *dodole* were revived for this purpose, most often executed by middle-aged participants who, based on their memories, devised short stage performances. These stage shows, presented within the "village gatherings," offered a unique opportunity for ethnochoreologists and dance researchers to see segments of calendrical rituals and archaic forms of ritual dances for the first time, albeit in a transformed performance context as short theatrical "pieces." It was believed that this was one of the only ways to preserve folklore from completely disappearing. Experts accordingly insisted that dance, music, and ritual actions be performed with minimal choreographic interventions.

In addition to the "village gatherings," the creation of several sponsored festivals for the participation of village groups was part of the affirmative official policy of the Serbian government toward rural culture during the 1960s and 1970s. The festivals were initiated as an attempt to mitigate the unrestrained development and "low aesthetic value" of the stylized staged folklore and were considered manifestations of great national significance.[13] Regardless of whether they were competitions or not, all of the festivals were designed and supervised by experts[14] who insisted that village KUD perform exclusively "authentic" local forms of music and dance, *izvorni folklor* ("folklore from the source"), as was also the case with the "village gatherings." Consequently, stage interpretations of the segments of calendrical rituals were a constant part of these big concert events as well.

Along with stage presentations, segments of calendrical rituals have also been the subject of many TV documentaries since the 1980s.[15] The screenwriters of these television programs were experts, including ethnochoreologists, who ensured that the magic functionality as well as the antiquity of calendrical rituals always be emphasized in the film narratives as a testimony to the continuity of Slavic culture in the Balkans.

The Second Generation of Serbian Ethnochoreologists: Mladenović and Zečević

Both Olivera Mladenović (1914–1988) and Slobodan Zečević (1918–1983) started their academic careers in the 1960s, at a time when the socialist system was already well established. With the intention of imposing general control over intellectuals and spreading unilateral ideological constraints of a "new" socialist order, cultural, educational, and scientific policies of early socialism in Yugoslavia were realized through the foundation of various institutions. Among them were the Ethnographic Institute (established in 1947) and the Musicological Institute (founded in 1948) at the Serbian Academy of Science and Arts.[16] As part of their professional commitment, neither Mladenović nor Zečević, like other contemporary scholars and intellectuals, was permitted to confront the prevailing ideology of the multinational makeup of socialist Yugoslavia. Consequently, the national (Serbian) character of ethnographic work was suppressed. This was one of the reasons why the universalist and evolutionist aspects of folklore-based interpretations of culture were embraced and emphasized. However, Mladenović and Zečević—in addition to the Janković sisters (whose work bridged the pre-socialist and socialist periods)—indirectly continued to maintain the theoretical distinctiveness of Serbian national culture in all of their scholarly writings, including in those devoted to calendrical rituals. They effected this by establishing Serbia's continuity within the Balkans as part of the wider Slavic cultural heritage.

Although Mladenović wrote a significant number of articles on various ethnochoreological topics, she devoted just two of them to "ritual-magic games" (*obredno-magijske igre*), as she called them. Both of them are extraordinary ethnographies. One treats dances at Carnival (*poklade*) in the village of Velika Ivanča in central Serbia (Mladenović 1954), while the other discusses a procession of *kraljice* in Dobra, a village in eastern Serbia (Mladenović 1970–1971). In the article on Carnival dances, Mladenović stays within the domain of ethnographic description without exploring the meanings of ritual actions. Later, however, obviously influenced by the Janković sisters' hypothetical evolutionary interpretations of rituals and ritual dances, Mladenović connects the female procession of *kraljice* to the tradition of organizing "closed women's societies, whose roots reach back to a matriarchal social system in which women played an extremely important role in production and cult life" (1970–1971:133).

Zečević was an ethnologist who was the first person to earn a doctoral degree in the field of ethnochoreology in Serbia. His dissertation, on pagan elements in Serbian ritual dance (Ilijin 1973:206), which he defended at the Faculty of Philosophy in Belgrade in 1962, is dedicated to a contemplative construction of the system of mythological beliefs and rural rituals in southeastern Serbia. Extending the Janković sisters' basic interpretations, Zečević was firmly convinced that it was possible to unravel the system of Serbian and South Slavic mythology and pagan religion through a comparative analysis of data from the literature as well as equally, if not more so, through the interpretation of personal recollections, descriptions of rituals, and demonstrations of ritual dancing collected in the field (Zečević 2008a; Zečević [1973] 2008b). He believed that ritual dance "conserved and preserved many motifs dating back to ancient times," which could help in the "reconstruction of our pagan religion" (Zečević [1973] 2008b:68, 69). Referring to "our," Zečević meant the Serbian people's as an integral part of the larger Slavic community.[17] Interpreting the role of dance in calendar rituals as a still-visible pagan and pre-Christian heritage, he considered ritual dance an important source of evidence for a continuous tradition of the Serbs from pre-Christian times. He was the first scholar in Serbia to provide general descriptions of the individual rituals from southeastern Serbia in the so-called ethnographic present. Yet it is not known whether Zečević attended any of the ritual events that he discussed (neither did the Janković sisters or later researchers) because most of those rituals were performed in local cultural practices only sporadically during the time of their research.

Folklore during the Breakup of Yugoslavia: The 1990s

The violent collapse of the former Yugoslavia during the 1990s, the Yugoslav Wars, and the huge economic crisis engendered radical changes in the approach to folklore-based activities in both participatory and presentational contexts in Serbia. Public displays such as folklore festivals were temporarily or permanently shut down, and villagers lost interest in reviving former local rituals. However, the economic and political situation was not the only factor contributing to the widespread discontent of the rural populace. The disappearance of locally specific cultural manifestations, including the "village gatherings" and various other festivals, which provided a sense of unity and cohesion within village communities during socialism, was equally important. As Gerald Creed observes with regard to Bulgaria, also a formerly communist country that has experienced economic and political crises during its post-communist transition, "Ritual decline is not simply a barometer of economic and political difficulty, but itself contributes to rural dissatisfactions and disappointment" (Creed 2002:70). In the Serbian context as well, the official post-socialist policies toward village communities were vague and unstable, generating disillusionment and malaise until well into the twenty-first century.

At the same time, as Tomislav Longinović (1992) points out, notions of ethnically and nationally specific Serbian cultural identity became prevalent in all official discourses especially during the 1990s. This reflected radical changes in the repertoire policy of KUD which, almost "overnight," rejected traditional dance choreographies that presented dances from other republics of the former Yugoslavia. The lack of choreographic pieces from Serbia in the previous period influenced the sudden blossoming of fieldwork through the creation of numerous new projects devoted to the "scenic" presentation of local Serbian traditions.

Subsequent Generations of Ethnochoreologists: Olivera Vasić and Her Legacy

As a passionate researcher of ritual dances, Olivera Vasić (1946–2015) turned her attention, in a great number of her articles, to their exploration, many of which have been published in *Ethnochoreology. Traces* (2004). Based on intense field research in numerous villages all over Serbia in the 1980s, Vasić devoted special attention to the ritual that *lazarice* performed, pointing to heterogeneous features of its kinetics and the special organization of *lazarica* dancing (Vasić 2004:66–72). As a great admirer of both the Janković sisters and Zečević, Vasić accepted wholesale their views and standpoints in her theoretical explorations, thus influencing the perpetuation of their folkloristic paradigm and promoting it among young ethnochoreologists. She used Zečević's writings for years as the main educational materials in the courses that she taught, as did many of her successors.

Vasić's legacy has been significant. She taught ethnology and ethnochoreology as integral parts of the ethnomusicological curriculum at the Faculty of Music in Belgrade from 1990 to 2014 as well as at the Academy of Arts in Novi Sad from 2000 to 2008 (Rakočević and Ranisavljević 2015). Moreover, with the goal of research and promotion of traditional dance heritage in the 1990s, she founded the Centre for Folk Dance Research of Serbia (Centar za proučavanje narodnih igara Srbije) at the Faculty of Music in Belgrade in 1990 as an independent professional association of ethnochoreologists and choreographers as well as dance instructors.[18] This association, led by Vasić, organized a large number of field research projects throughout Serbia and, along with ethnochoreologists, engaged many dance choreographers and folk dance instructors, both professionals and amateurs, as collectors. Focused exclusively on former village practices, the fieldwork methodology shaped by Vasić was based on recording oral histories of the oldest villagers who, during the 1990s and early 2000s, could still resurrect memories of traditional village rituals and describe and demonstrate dances from their youth.

Choreographers then used these collected oral histories about traditional village dances and their kinetic displays from various parts of Serbia to create a number of new choreographic pieces that, in presenting former village rituals, became popular and appreciated. The prevailing strategy of their "scenic" reinterpretations assumed a policy of "faithful" representation through the retention of dialectal features of Serbian in speech segments, the use of original traditional clothing, and the imperative retention of structural-formal and performing features of movement patterns. Indeed, the choreographic strategies of using stage space and varying formations of dancers developed greatly compared to those from the 1980s, depending on the creativity of individual choreographers. "Folklore on stage" in the last decade of the twentieth century became focused on national forms and was committed to "scenic" revivals of local archaic village cultural forms.

New Contexts, Old Dances: Ethnochoreological Research and Seasonal Rituals after 2000

Establishing democracy and a market economy in Serbia after 2000 was connected to the shift in the general ideological paradigms in which political models of Western societies became the quintessential paragons of social order. These radical changes led to the commencement of broad economic and cultural transformations, which are generally signified in the scholarly literature as post-socialist "transitions" (Hann 2002). Moreover, these processes inevitably affected the politics of academic education and scientific scholarship and consequently exerted an immediate influence on ethnochoreological research as well.

The idea of researching former village culture had been neither particularly supported nor disputed by the socialist officials. What can be said, however, is that folklore dance research had, during the socialist period, been marginalized in the mainstream narratives of official cultural and educational policies due to the radical changes that had been imposed such as broadening themes for investigation and fieldwork as well as the imperative to promote various interdisciplinary methodological orientations (Rakočević 2019:198–205; Rakočević 2020). The changes in official politics of scholarly work and the widening of research possibilities after 2000 were heightened by a global shift in the prevailing scholarly paradigm generally signified in cultural theory as the "interpretative turn." A new perspective in theoretical considerations of reality implied multiple interpretations based on critical and reflexive explications away from the positivism of scientifically oriented research. However, folklore-oriented themes focused on studies of collective forms of dance, and music transmitted orally stayed in focus in domestic ethnochoreology and ethnochoreological education as the very core of national disciplinary identification (Rakočević 2015). The basic changes that have led to this essential turn in the paradigm of ethnochoreological research relate to the terminology and methodology of fieldwork.

With the aim of the precise naming of the objects of ethnochoreological research, which should widen and "modernize" scholarly narratives about dance and at the same time would acknowledge its immanent interdisciplinary relationships with ethnomusicology, changes in terminology have led to a shift toward the use of the term "traditional dance" instead of folk/*oro* "game" (Rakočević 2011). The usage of the old Slavic expression *ples* has also expanded research possibilities considering dance genres and provided methodological consistency in ethnochoreological research.

On the other hand, these changes have affected fieldwork methodologies greatly. Field research aimed at the reconstruction of various forms of rural dance from the past has been expanded in the direction of examining individual dance events, which have become the primary focus of field research in Serbian ethnochoreology. The participant-observation method, which is at the core of all scholarly disciplines that are based on field research (Bernard 2006), has enabled direct social interaction between participants (dancers) and observers (scholars) and direct exchanges of knowledge between them. Conventional fieldwork methods such as writing up fieldnotes, interviews, and dance notation have been sustained but also certainly enriched by participation in dance performance together with mandatory filming and photography as well as making video and audio recordings.

Apart from the changes in the scholarly discourse of ethnochoreological research, broad political, economic, and cultural transformations in Serbian society have also influenced the remodeling of the organizations of calendrical village events. After the overthrow of the socialist government in 2000, but also already in the late 1990s, the activities of the Serbian Orthodox Church were no longer suppressed, and the faithful were given the opportunity to attend religious ceremonies freely. After 2000, the custom of celebrating rural holidays dedicated to village patron saints (*seoska slava* or *zavetina*) slowly began to be practiced again, having been stifled for more than fifty years. The village *zavetina* celebrations, which take place mainly during the summer, have been gathering huge numbers of people starting roughly in the 2010s as they take on the character of modern village rituals. The central components of the *zavetina* include the Orthodox liturgy as well as the consecration of a feast cake, a collective feast, and an obligatory dance event. My latest field research held on Saint Ilija's Day on August 2, 2021, in the village of Jastrebac (in the municipality of Vladičin Han in southeastern Serbia) confirms the vitality of these "new" calendrical celebrations. Despite the COVID-19 measures of social distancing and physical separation, the inhabitants—not only of Jastrebac but also of numerous other villages throughout Serbia—performed many traditional dances in round chain formation together, holding hands with each other.

Conclusion

The story of traditional dance and seasonal rituals in Serbia as well as how ethnochoreology and ethnochoreologists there adapted and adjusted to the ebb and flow of twentieth-century Serbian, then Yugoslav, followed again by Serbian historical, sociopolitical, economic, and intellectual circumstances has been eventful and momentous. Just as crises created by anomalies often lead, in unanticipated and consequential ways, to shifts of scholarly narratives, so too do unforeseen social realities produce the invention of novel traditions and the establishment of expressive new rituals.[19] A remodeled and modernized field of twenty-first-century Serbian ethnochoreology, with its new focus, open methodologies, and original interpretations, promises to keep enriching the field of today's ethnochoreology and folklore research.[20]

Notes

1. Ethnochoreology is the ethnographic, anthropological, and ethnomusicological study of dance.
2. The word *lazarice* is a female version in the plural of the male name Lazar.
3. Based on ethnographic literature, Zečević points to a much wider geographical spread of *lazarice* in the past.
4. Bačka, Banat, and Srem are regions located in the northernmost part of Serbia, in the province of Vojvodina.
5. *Narodni* and *obredni* are adjectives meaning "folk" and "ritual," respectively.

6. Both of the Janković sisters initially studied literature at the Faculty of Philology in Belgrade. They were fluent in English and French, which they continued to study abroad after graduation. Danica was in London and Oxford from 1922 to 1924, while Ljubica was in Austria, Germany, England, and France during 1922 and 1923. In subsequent years, they corresponded frequently with English researchers of their time, especially Maud Karpeles (Ivancich Dunin 2014; Rakočević 2014).
7. In other words, "About 114 melodies noted down simultaneously with other dance components have served as a basis for the study of their relation and conditionality to some rituals" (Janković and Janković 1957:54).
8. In the *parlando-rubato* vocal style, words are stressed in performance and are not bound by fixed metrical or rhythmic patterns.
9. The six Yugoslav republics were Serbia, Croatia, Bosnia-Hercegovina, Slovenia, Montenegro, and Macedonia.
10. These included choreographed dance suites such as *Igre iz Srbije* (*Dances from Serbia*) by Serbian choreographer Olga Skovran and *Podravski svati* (*Podravina Wedding Guests*) by Croatian ethnologist and ethnochoreographer Ivan Ivančan.
11. The competitions were organized at the four levels of the territorial governance: the local, municipal, regional, and republic (Hofman 2008).
12. Both Olivera Mladenović and Slobodan Zečević were very active in these contests for years.
13. Among the festivals were "Oplenačka berba" (Grape Harvest at Oplenac) in Topola (founded in 1963), "Crnorečje u igri i pesmi" (Crnorečje in Dance and Song) in Boljevac (founded in 1970), and "Sabor narodnog stvaralaštva" (A Gathering of Folk Creativity) in Leskovac (founded in 1972).
14. Among the experts were Mladenović and Zečević.
15. Such documentaries included "Putevima melografa" ("On the Paths of the Melograph") and "Trezor" ("Treasury"), produced by Radio Television of Serbia (Radio-Televizija Srbije).
16. Mladenović worked at the Musicological Institute from 1962 until her retirement, while Zečević worked at the Ethnographic Institute during 1965 and 1966, after which he would become the director of the Ethnographic Museum until he retired.
17. The title of the published version of Zečević's dissertation in Serbian is "Elementi naše mitologije u narodnim obredima uz igru" ("Elements of Our Mythology in Folk Rites Consisting of Dance," [1973] 2008b).
18. This ethnochoreological association would change its name to the Centre for Research and Safeguarding of Traditional Dances in Serbia (Centar za istraživanje i očuvanje tradicionalne igre u Srbiji, CIOTIS) in 2012. It has continued its activities since the death of Vasić in 2015.
19. See Kuhn ([1962] 1970) and Hobsbawm and Ranger (1983).
20. See, for example, Ranisavljević 2022.

Works Cited

Bajić Stojiljković, Vesna. 2019. *Scenska narodna igra i muzika*. Belgrade: Musicological Institute of the Serbian Academy of Science and Arts.

Bernard, H. Russell. 2006. *Research Methods in Anthropology: Quantitative and Qualitative Approaches*. Lanham, MD: Altamira Press.

Creed, Gerald W. 2002. "Economic Crisis and Ritual Decline in Eastern Europe." In *Postsocialism. Ideals, Ideologies and Practices in Eurasia*, ed. Chris M. Hann, 57–73. New York: Routledge.
Đorđević, Tihomir. 1907. "Srpske narodne igre." *Srpski etnološki zbornik*, IX:1–89.
Hann, Chris M., ed. 2002. *Postsocialism. Ideals, Ideologies and Practices in Eurasia*. New York: Routledge.
Hobsbawm, Eric, and Terence Ranger, eds. 1983. *The Invention of Tradition*. Cambridge: Cambridge University Press.
Hofman, Ana. 2008. "Performing Socialist 'Femininity': The Role of Public Manifestations in the Construction and Representation of Gender in Southeast Serbia." *Facta Universitatis: Philosophy, Sociology, Psychology and History*, 7/1:43–54.
Ilijin, Milica. 1973. "Razvoj etnokoreologije." In *Srpska muzika kroz vekove*, ed. Stana Đurić Klajn, 203–213. Belgrade: Galerija Srpske Akademija Nauka i Umetnosti.
Ivancich Dunin, Elsie. 2014. "Emergence of Ethnochoreology Internationally: The Janković Sisters, Maud Karpeles, and Gertrude Kurath." *Musicology* 17:197–217.
Janković, Ljubica, and Danica Janković. 1934. *Narodne igre*. Vol. I. Belgrade: Self-published.
Janković, Ljubica, and Danica Janković. 1937. *Narodne igre*. Vol. II. Belgrade: Self-published.
Janković, Ljubica, and Danica Janković. 1939. *Narodne igre*. Vol. III. Belgrade: Self-published.
Janković, Ljubica, and Danica Janković. 1947. *Narodne igre*. Vol. IV. Belgrade: Prosveta.
Janković, Ljubica, and Danica Janković. 1949. *Narodne igre*. Vol. V. Belgrade: Prosveta.
Janković, Ljubica, and Danica Janković. 1951. *Narodne igre*. Vol. VI. Belgrade: Prosveta.
Janković, Ljubica, and Danica Janković. 1952. *Narodne igre*. Vol. VII. Belgrade: Prosveta.
Janković, Ljubica, and Danica Janković. 1957. *Prilog proučavanju ostataka orskih obrednih igara u Jugoslaviji*, special edition, book CCLXXI, The Ethnographic Institute, Book 8. Belgrade: Serbian Academy of Science.
Janković, Ljubica, and Danica Janković. 1964. *Narodne igre*. Vol. VIII. Belgrade: Prosveta.
Kuhn, Thomas. 1970. *The Structure of Scientific Revolutions*, 2nd ed. Chicago: University of Chicago Press. First published 1962.
Longinović, Tomislav. 1992. "Music Wars: Blood and Song at the End of Yugoslavia." In *Music and the Racial Imagination*, eds. Ronald Radano and Philip V. Bohlman, 622–643. Chicago–London: University of Chicago Press.
Mladenović, Olivera. 1954. "Narodne igre na Bele poklade u Velikoj Ivanči." *Glasnik Etnografskog Muzeja*, XVII:91–96.
Mladenović, Olivera. 1970–1971. "Dobranske kraljice." *Glasnik Etnografskog Instituta*, XIX–XX:122–147.
Mladenović, Olivera. 1978. "Kolo i oro u našoj etnokoreološkoj terminologiji." In *Rad XVI Kongresa Saveza udruženja folklorista Jugoslavije*, 477–481. Cetinje (Igalo): Savez udruženja folklorista Jugoslavije.
Nenić, Iva. 2014. "'Folk' Behaving Badly: Newly Composed Folk Music as Popular Culture." In *Sweet Sixties: Specters and Spirits of a Parallel Avant-Garde*, eds. Georg Schöllhammer and Ruben Arevshatyan, 440–448. Berlin: Sternberg Press.
Rakočević, Selena. 2011. *Igre plesnih struktura. Tradicionalna igra i muzika za igru Srba u Banatu u svetlu uzajamnih uticaja*. Belgrade: Fakultet muzičke umetnosti.
Rakočević, Selena. 2013. "Tracing the Discipline: Eighty Years of Ethnochoreology in Serbia." *New Sound*, 41:58–86.
Rakočević, Selena. 2014. "Contribution of Ljubica and Danica Janković to Establishment of Ethnochoreology in Serbia as an Academic Scholarly Discipline." *Muzikologija*, 17:219–244.

Rakočević, Selena. 2015. "Ethnochoreology as an Interdiscipline in a Postdisciplinary Era: A Historiography of Dance Scholarship in Serbia." *Yearbook for Traditional Music*, 47:27–44.

Rakočević, Selena. 2016a. "Terenska istraživanja u etnokoreologiji u Srbiji i Bosni i Hercegovini: Fundiranje naučne discipline i potencijali njenog budućeg razvoja." In *Vlado S. Milošević: Etnomuzikolog, kompozitor i pedagog. Tradicija kao inspiracija*, ed. Dimitrije Golemović, 343–359. Banja Luka: Akademija umjetnosti univerziteta u Banjoj Luci, Akademija nauka i umjetnosti Republike srpske, Muzikološko društvo Republike srpske.

Rakočević, Selena. 2016b. "Teorijski aspekti etnokoreološko/etnomuzikoloških interpretacija svadbenog rituala u Srbiji." In *Zbornik radova sa naučnog i umetničkog simpozijuma "Muzika između teorije i prakse,"* ed. Vesna Ivkov, 78–90. Novi Sad: Akademija umetnosti.

Rakočević, Selena. 2019. "Practicing Ethnomusicology/Ethnochoreology within Post-socialist Realities: The Case of Serbia with Some Comparative Experiences from Former Yugoslav Republics." In *Ethnomusicology Matters: Influencing Social and Political Realities*, eds. Ursula Hemetek, Marko Kölbl, and Hande Sağlam, 191–214. Vienna: Böhlau Verlag.

Rakočević, Selena. 2020. "Political Complexities of Ethnochoreological Research. The Facets of Scholarly Work on Dance in the Countries of Former Yugoslavia." *Acta Ethnographica Hungarica*, 65/1:13–26.

Rakočević, Selena, and Zdravko Ranisavljević. 2015. "Olivera-Coka Vasić (18.VIII.1946, Gornja Badanja–28.X.2015, Beograd)." *Muzikologija*, 9:199–202.

Ranisavljević, Zdravko. 2022. "Kolo–tradicionalni ples u Srbiji. Kontekstualni i formalni aspekti." PhD dissertation. University of Arts, Belgrade.

Rasmussen, Ljerka Vidić. 2002. *Newly-Composed Folk Music from Yugoslavia*. New York: Routledge.

Vasić, Olivera. 2004. *Etnokoreologija. Tragovi*. Belgrade: Art grafik.

Zakić, Mirjana. 2014. "Delatnost Ljubice i Danice Janković na polju etnomuzikologije." *Muzikologija*, 17:245–258.

Zečević, Slobodan. 2008a. *Metodologija etnomitologije*. Belgrade: Službeni glasnik.

Zečević, Slobodan. 2008b. *Elementi naše mitologije u narodnim obredima uz igru*. Belgrade: Službeni glasnik. First published 1973.

CHAPTER 13

FOLKLORE OF THE SEASONAL CYCLE IN CROATIA
The Lastovo Carnival

IVA NIEMČIĆ

THE seasonally based customs that I address in this chapter, with a focus on Carnival, are connected to annual holidays in the traditional calendar, which include pre-Christian beliefs, rituals, and customs alongside Christian ones. In the Croatian case these customs are closely related to Catholic calendar holidays (Vitez 2001:310; Gavazzi [1939] 1988). Carnival events take place at the beginning of the year, between Catholic Christmas holidays and Lent, which ends on Easter Sunday.

In Croatian, Carnival is designated by multiple terms that, each in its own way, links it to the calendar period surrounded by Catholic holidays. *Poklade, maškare, mesopust, poklad, bušari, šafingari, fašnik, pust,* and *karneval,* among others, are used in different regions of Croatia to mark the period from the festival of Epiphany (Twelfth Night) until Holy (or Ash) Wednesday. Although it is not marked in the Catholic calendar, "Carnival is time-conditioned by Lent; the *worldly* is unequivocally bounded by the *sacred* as its opposite" (Lozica 1997:22). Apart from its time-wise positioning in the Christian calendar and its duration determined by the date of the most important Christian holiday, Easter, Carnival has no other contact points with Christianity (Vitez 2001:355). The church authorities never truly forbade or suppressed Carnival customs; neither did they protest against or condemn Carnival extravagance and intemperance because "they needed controlled and time-limited madness as a counterweight to the Christian way of life" (Lozica 1997:10). On the other hand, the transitional period between spring and winter, in which Carnival took place, was an important part of the agrarian year. For that reason, early ethnological interpretations linked Carnival events to protection and fertility-related magic. In modern Carnival, a more important and prominent element is social criticism (Lozica 1997:13). Carnival is a period of disguise: masks allow disguise, changes of identity, departure from everyday life, and critique of it with no consequences—madness without recognition, freedom without sin. Masks can intimidate or amuse; when hiding behind them, one is free of the constraints imposed by social norms. In addition to social criticism, modern carnivals are strongly characterized by an element of entertainment.

In light of contemporary theories, we distinguish between two types of Carnivals, named after the Roman festivities of Lupercalia and Saturnalia. The Lupercalian type of Carnival is more common in rural livestock-keeping areas and is associated with fertility magic. Masks represent animals, and costumes are made of animal skins, often with bells attached. The Carnival procession consists of men moving quickly and aggressively, making much noise with their bells and other noise-making props, with an aim of intimidating the onlookers. The Saturnalian type of Carnival is found mostly in urban areas but also in small towns and villages such as along the Dalmatian coast and on the islands. Besides parade-like masked processions, this type of Carnival is represented by a life-sized Carnival figure made of straw, typically called a "puppet," that takes upon itself the sins of the community in the past year. As a means of paying for the sins, the Carnival puppet is tried and then executed by fire, hanging, or drowning (Vitez 2001:356–357). Carnival processions are themed, often staging an event such as a wedding ceremony with a man disguised as a bride or featuring ethnic, professional, or social groups such as Roma, priests, soldiers, or grandparents.

Lastovski poklad (Lastovo Carnival) takes place on Lastovo, a small island in southern Dalmatia, in the eponymous village whose population is mostly engaged in agriculture (and, more recently, tourism). By its characteristics (urban processions and *Poklad*—the Carnival puppet), the *Lastovski poklad* belongs to a Saturnalian type of Carnival, although the village of Lastovo is not part of an urban area. This is not surprising given that an integral part of the carnival—the chain sword dance performed by the *pokladari* (male participants, sg. *pokladar*)—is thought to have arrived on the island from the city of Dubrovnik.

My original research centered on the chain sword dances of the islands of Lastovo and Korčula. Since the sword dances in this southern Dalmatian region are partly associated with the Carnival season, I extended my research focus to Carnival events. I became fascinated by the number of *pokladari* and *lijepe maškare* (pretty masks)—the male and female participants in the processions, their picturesque attire, and the passion with which they took part in the Carnival events. The *pokladari* are men from Lastovo (either born on the island or from at least one parent born on the island) who on Shrove Tuesday put on their traditional Carnival uniforms and become participants (*pokladari*), ready and willing to obey all the Carnival rules and follow their leaders (Fig. 13.1).[1] The procession of the *lijepe maškare* is mostly made up of women (and, to a lesser extent, children) who were born in Lastovo or are married to men from Lastovo and live there. The procession consists of pairs of women—two women, usually friends or cousins, dressed identically. Each pair designs and makes its own costumes, which are normally worn only once, on Shrove Tuesday. The *lijepe maškare* dress up as popular cartoon animal characters, mermaids, fairies, queens, Romani women, dancers, clowns, or unspecified individuals but always with very colorful masks that cover their eyes

FIG. 13.1. *Pokladari–pokladarsko kolo*.
(All of the photos were taken by Iva Niemčić during field research in 2009 in Lastovo.)

(Fig. 13.2). Since my first field trip (1999) and up to this day, I have kept returning to the Lastovo Carnival, observing it, researching it, and taking part in it.[2]

While preparing for my first encounter with the Lastovo Carnival, I was surprised by how little had been written about it. The available literature gave me a general idea about the custom and its continuity up to the present day. Information on dance and its structure during the Lastovo Carnival, however, was scarce. No one had written about it apart from Ivan Ivančan,[3] who compared the dances with the *kumpanija*[4] sword dances of the island of Korčula (1985:456, 46). With this in mind, upon my arrival in Lastovo[5] in 1999, I expected to see a dance similar to those I had just seen in Korčula. Taking part in the final days of Carnival, when the events reached their peak, I did witness the male chain sword dance, the structure of which indeed resembled the structure of the Korčula *kumpanija* dances. But I also observed, for the first time, the female chain dance.[6] Most researchers have focused on the customs related exclusively to the *pokladari*. It is true that some scholars have written in passing about women participating in Carnival as *lijepe maškare* alongside the *pokladari* (who are the bearers of the whole event), but that is as far as they go.

Notwithstanding the attention paid to the *pokladari* in the scholarship on Carnival, having seen and experienced the female dancing confirms for me that women are an

FIG. 13.2. *Lijepe maškare–lijepe maškare kolo.*

important and integral part of Lastovo's Carnival festivities. Indeed, it is critical to write about the role of women in these events because, as the *pokladari* themselves admit, Carnival is unimaginable without them. Moreover, to my knowledge, the chain dance of *lijepe maškare* is a unique example of a women's chain dance both in Croatia and beyond. The challenge for me was to emphasize the significance of *lijepe maškare*—women as a vital as well as both ethnologically and ethnochoreologically meaningful part of the Lastovo Carnival, worthy of serious attention (see Niemčić 2002; Niemčić 2005; Niemčić 2011).

In the pages that follow, this chapter includes historical and contemporary overviews of the Lastovo Carnival as well as discussions of the role of fieldwork methodology in research on Carnival, what Carnival means for the Lastovo community, how it has been challenged over time (most recently by the COVID-19 pandemic), and how the residents of Lastovo have loyally rallied to preserve their beloved annual Carnival traditions by conducting ethnographic fieldwork and sharing it with the outside world.

The Lastovo Carnival and Its Historical Influences

According to historian Stephen D. Corrsin, one of the most widespread dances in Europe in the last six centuries has been the chain sword dance. In his *Sword Dancing in*

Europe: A History (1997), however, he unfortunately fails to mention sword dances from Croatia, despite the fact that thirty years earlier, in his book *Narodni običaji korčulanskih kumpanija*, Ivančan (1967) had written about their diffusion in the former Yugoslavia, offering possible suggestions for the appearance of chain sword dancing on the island of Korčula. Ivančan believed that the sword dances typical of central Europe, especially of Germany, could have arrived in Croatia at the beginning of the fifteenth century, during the reign of the Hungarian–Croatian kings. At that time, sword dances were in full swing and were spreading from central Europe toward England, Spain, Italy, the Nordic countries, and probably even Dubrovnik. Since at that time the islands of Korčula and Lastovo belonged to Dubrovnik administration, many influences from Dubrovnik spread throughout the Dubrovnik Republic territory, especially to the island of Korčula. Lastovo had always belonged to the Diocese of Korčula, and the landholdings of Lastovo residents as well as marital relationships linked the residents of the two islands. Ivančan states these as reasons for the possible arrival and reception of the sword dance tradition from Dubrovnik via Korčula to the island of Lastovo (1967:149). Philologist Richard Wolfram likewise claimed that sword dancing had originated in urban encirclement (as a part of the European city-guild-center tradition) and spread to villages (Ivančan 1967:110–111). The case of Lastovo fits this theory. However, in addition to finding plausible the thesis that sword dances came to Dalmatia from central Europe, Ivančan allowed for the possibility that there was indirect influence from Spain and Italy (1967:138; Lozica 1990:188; Lozica 2002:118).

Historical events of that time as well as the division of power and territory further justify the hypothesis about sword dancing coming to Lastovo from Dubrovnik. Since Korčula and Lastovo then belonged to the Dubrovnik Republic, many influences from Dubrovnik went through the island of Korčula to Lastovo, which had always belonged to the Diocese of Korčula. Therefore, according to Ivančan, people from Lastovo could have taken over the sword dance from Dubrovnik via Korčula (1967:149).

Even while under French rule (1806–1813), English rule (1813–1815), and the Austro-Hungarian monarchy (until 1918), Lastovo was proclaimed a district belonging to the Dubrovnik region, thus continuing its centuries-old ties with Dubrovnik (Jurica 2001:159–160). During Austrian rule, with poor or almost non-existent traffic connections to the mainland, the remote island of Lastovo remained isolated and virtually unknown. Melko Lucijanović,[7] a native of Lastovo, was the only person who wrote about the richness of the island's customs at the time, informing the world about his hometown and island. He was the author of one of the oldest descriptions of the Lastovo Carnival, dating to 1877. In that text, Lucijanović describes the sword dance in detail, calling the Carnival circle dance a "magical folk dance" (Lozica 1984:169).

In 1918, the Italians arrived on Lastovo, to the utter surprise of the local people. The tradition of Lastovo Carnival was, however, preserved; and it continued to take place during Italian rule on the island, albeit with adaptations such as *pokladari* needing to sing in Italian. But in the written texts from that period there is no information as to whether women—*lijepe maškare*—took part in Carnival. There is only footage by František Pospíšil[8] from 1924 in which female participants, wearing folk costumes, dance together with *pokladari* around the donkey with the *Poklad* puppet. But this occurs outside of the context of Carnival since they are performing Carnival for Pospíšil and the other researchers who are filming.

The Italian capitulation to the Allies in World War II on September 8, 1943, marked the end of Italian rule on Lastovo. In what followed as Yugoslavia (1943–1991), the locals from Lastovo lived in a sort of isolation because the island was given to the JNA (Yugoslav National Army) and was controlled by it. Foreign tourists were not allowed on the island. Left to their own devices, the locals nurtured their customs. A number of texts about Carnival written by Croatian scholars date from that period. In his collection from 1960, the folklorist Nikola Bonifačić Rožin[9] mentions, for the first time, a group of *lijepe maškare* but does not write about them as something new and popular; he only states their existence and participation in Carnival. He also mentions a Carnival folk drama (an improvised play around the *Poklad* puppet) that has not been performed for many years now as well as numerous other fond memories of Carnival that the locals of Lastovo shared with him (Bonifačić Rožin 1960).

Many Carnival customs have been preserved until today. Carnival takes place every year, and it is an important part of Croatian identity among the people from Lastovo, especially after Yugoslavia disintegrated and the JNA left in 1991. Each year more and more foreign and domestic tourists come to discover the beauty and culture of this small, green island.

The Lastovo Carnival Today

In the 2021 census (https://podaci.dzs.hr/media/rqybclnx/popis_2021-stanovnistvo_po_naseljima.xlsx), the island of Lastovo had 748 inhabitants, of whom 309 lived in the village of Lastovo. There are a kindergarten, a primary school, a museum, a library, a cultural center, and a municipal building in the village. While the population is mainly engaged in agriculture and fishing, the island has seen a gradual development of tourism in recent years. In 2006, the island of Lastovo and its islets were declared a nature park.

On Lastovo, just as in countless other places, there are legends about the origins of local customs—stories that are told and retold many times and passed down from generation to generation. Each generation spices up the stories in its own way and tells its own versions of the origins of the Lastovo Carnival. The genesis of Carnival on Lastovo, or its recognizable contemporary variants, is linked to a historical event—the siege of Korčula by the Moors (Catalans) in 1483. The legend goes that in that year the Catalans sent their messenger to Lastovo with a request for a surrender without a fight. The messenger, however, was kept on the island. As he did not return, the Catalan army boarded its ships and set off for Lastovo with the intention of capturing and enslaving the inhabitants of the island. When the guard watching the sea from the hills above the village of Lastovo saw the Catalan fleet approaching from afar, he turned toward the village and shouted, "*Kukuriku* [Cock-a-doodle-doo], the upper village! *Kukuriku* [Cock-a-doodle-doo], the lower village! Here come the Catalans, and they will slay us all!" The villagers then left their homes and, together with their priest, climbed Hum, a hill on Lastovo, and came to the little church of St. George. There they prayed to God to save them as they watched the Catalan ships approaching the island. Then a storm arose and destroyed some of the ships, while the others turned back and returned to Korčula, never again attempting an attack on Lastovo. When the people of Lastovo saw what had happened and that the danger had passed, they returned to the village joyful and relieved. They seized the Catalan messenger, mounted him on a donkey, and took him through the village, treating him with scorn and ridicule. Then they made him slide down a stretched rope three times, brought him to Dolac Square (in the village), and sentenced him to death. The legend with its main protagonists—and antagonist—has lived on to this day, providing the local community with the foundation, interpretation, and meaning of their custom.

Carnival in today's Lastovo continues to be a vibrant event with great significance for the community. The following description, based on fieldwork, includes the most important Carnival events. The festivities start on St. Anthony's Day (January 17) and continue until Ash Wednesday (*Čista srijeda*), the first day of Lent. Carnival culminates on Shrove Tuesday (*Pokladni utorak*), the day before Ash Wednesday, when two organized processions, one male and one female, dressed in uniforms and costumes, tour the village. As part of the tour, they visit specific houses (agreed upon in advance), where they are welcomed by the hosts and offered food and drink. There they sing, dance, and entertain their hosts. The procession of men in costume (*pokladari*) follows a lyre (*lira*) player and the *Poklad* puppet riding a donkey. The *Poklad* puppet is made the day before according to certain rules and is dressed in its own distinctive costume.[10] After the rounds of the village are made, the *pokladari* send the *Poklad* puppet sliding down a rope from the top of the hill to the bottom of the village three times (Fig. 13.3). The sliding is accompanied by the explosions of bombs attached to the puppet. Finally, at dusk, the *pokladari* take off its clothes and burn it in front of all the Carnival participants as well as the spectators who have followed the day's events. These ritual practices with the *Poklad* puppet, which have remained virtually unchanged since the first written descriptions of the custom in the nineteenth century, find their foothold in the legend of the custom's origin. The *Poklad* puppet represents the Catalan messenger who needs to be punished publicly. Today, the puppet serves as a symbol of all the evil accumulated in the community in the past year. By punishing it and eventually executing it by fire, the community is freed from evil and ready for the beginning of a new agrarian year and the awakening of nature.

The Carnival season on Lastovo is marked by dance evenings—at which a *balo* (ball) takes place at the Hall (*sala*) once or twice a week. The first *balo* is held on St. Anthony's Day, regardless of the day of the week on which it falls. The Hall Master (*Kapo sale*)[11] welcomes the locals and special guests—the mayor, doctor, and priest—and announces the beginning of the Carnival festivities. From that evening on, the masked participants (*maškare*) are allowed to take part in all of the Carnival events.

FIG. 13.3. *Poklad* puppet.

In addition to the procession of the *pokladari*, their chain sword dance, and the procession of *lijepe maškare*, the *Poklad* puppet, donkey, rope (*uza*), and lyre, which provides the music for dancing, are indispensable to the Lastovo Carnival. There is no Carnival without the lyre. It provides a recognizable sound of Lastovo, and yet interestingly enough, it can be heard on the island only between Candlemas Day (February 2) and Ash Wednesday (the first day of Lent), that is, solely during the Carnival season. Other than that, the lyre is played only as an accompaniment to the Lastovo folklore association's performance of the Lastovo chain dance at various folklore festivals or as a promotional act for tourists.

Pretili ponedjeljak (Fat Monday)

While women finish their costumes and iron men's Carnival uniforms at home on Fat Monday, the *pokladari*—led by the *kapo sale*—depart to get the *sanatur* (lyre player), the donkey, and *prlina* (the soil dug at a specific location [opposite the cemetery] for filling the body of the *Poklad* puppet). They load the donkey with *prlina* and set off to get the tailor and the material needed for making the puppet. In the meantime, the bomb-maker and his assistants have already arrived at the Hall. From the moment the procession enters the Hall until lunch, the lyre is played constantly, and the musicians take turns. The bomb-maker makes bombs,[12] while the *Poklad* puppet-maker makes the puppet out of chaff and straw, filling the boots with *prlina*. They finish at the same time but not later than noon or just in time for lunch at the Hall, attended by all the *pokladari*.

In the afternoon hours, the so-called *grube maškare* (ugly masks)[13] divide into several groups, tour the village, and collect eggs, called *kupljenje jaja*. In contrast to the *lijepe maškare* of Shrove Tuesday, the ugly masks make a deliberate effort to look ludicrous and unsightly. They walk the same route that the *pokladari* and *lijepe maškare* will walk on the following day, and they enter only the houses that the *pokladari* and *lijepe maškare* will visit.

Pokladni utorak (Shrove Tuesday)

At 8 o'clock in the morning on Shrove Tuesday, the *kapo sale*, lyre player, and several male carnival participants (*pokladari*), accompanied by the sound of the lyre, depart to get the rope from the "host" (a Lastovo villager) who has been taking care of it the whole year (Fig. 13.4). The rope is then carried to *Novi put* (the main road leading to the village), where it is soaped so that the *Poklad* puppet will slide down it more easily. The lyre is played constantly. One end of the rope is carried to the top of the hill (*Pokladareva grža*), and the other is lowered to *Gornja luka*, or the village center. As soon as the rope is stretched out taut, the exclamation "Uvo!" is shouted three times.

At the same time, all around the village, the men dress as *pokladari* and the women as *lijepe maškare*. There are two processions touring the village: the women's *lijepe maškare* and the men's *pokladari*. The first and main procession, considered to be the backbone of the whole event, is the procession of *pokladari*, made up exclusively of the men of Lastovo. Another procession, of *lijepe maškare*, is a women's procession accompanied by several men dressed as officers.

On this day, the church clock strikes at 11:00 instead of noon, signaling that it is time for an early lunch. At 1 o'clock in the afternoon, the procession of *pokladari* starts its tour around the village. At the head of the procession is the flag bearer carrying the Croatian national flag, followed by a donkey carrying the *Poklad* puppet and a group of boys dressed in the same uniform as the *pokladari* (Fig. 13.5). Next come the lyre player, the *kapo sale*, a pair of ringleaders, and the rest of the procession in the order in which they have arrived at the Hall. At the very end are again boys. Accompanied by the lyre, but not singing yet, the procession goes to the mayor to ask permission to lower the *Poklad* puppet from the top to the bottom of the village (*culjanje*[14]) and then burn it. The mayor grants his permission with a short speech, thus allowing for public condemnation of and punishment for all the evil that has loomed over the community in the past year. This marks the beginning of the most ceremonious and important part of the Carnival custom. To the sound of the lyre and singing, the procession sets off on a tour around the village following a pre-arranged schedule. They dance on the terraces (*sulari*), and

FIG. 13.4. *Uza* and *lira*.

the hosts treat them to drinks, homemade desserts, prosciutto, and cheese (Figs. 13.6 and 13.7).

In the meantime, around thirty couples of *lijepe maškare* have gathered as well. In the processions, they stand in pairs, identically dressed and with an obligatory mask covering their eyes. Lagging behind the *pokladari*, the women's procession tours the village, following the strict rule that the two processions not meet. The *lijepe maškare*, who visit the same houses (chosen in advance) as the *pokladari*, are always at least one house behind them. The explanation for this may lie in the fact that women became actively involved in the carnival custom at a later date, when they formed their own independent procession modeled on that of the *pokladari*. This is why there are two parallel processions in the same custom. Although they faithfully imitate the practices of the *pokladari*, the *lijepe maškare* joined in for different reasons. As they themselves say, they also "wanted to have fun."

FIG. 13.5. *Poklad* and donkey.

FIG. 13.6. *Pokladari*.

FIG. 13.7. *Lijepe maškare* and *lira*.

The procession through the village continues until 2:30 in the afternoon, when the donkey carrying the *Poklad* puppet arrives at the bottom of the village—*Gornja luka*, which is the lower point for the puppet's descent. It is then carried to the top of the hill (*Pokladarova grža*), where it is met by the bomb-maker and his assistants. They fasten the puppet to the rope, together with the bombs that will detonate on the way down. At 3 o'clock sharp, the *Poklad* is ready to be lowered on the rope (*culjanje*). It is released and slides down the rope three times, accompanied by the explosions of the bombs hanging from it. Five bombs are set off on its way down the first time, seven bombs the second time, and nine the third time. The rope is then taken down and carried to the house, where it will wait for the next year's *culjanje*. The *Poklad* puppet is mounted on the donkey once more, while the *pokladari* perform their chain sword dance. Only then do the merry *lijepe maškare* arrive, after having watched the *culjanje* from the sidelines. When the *pokladari* have finished their chain sword dance, the *lijepe maškare* perform their chain dance with handkerchiefs (not swords).

After having danced and being photographed, both processions continue their tours through the village, which end at 6 o'clock in the afternoon with the arrival of the *pokladari* at Dolac Square (the space in the center of the village, between the church and the school).[15] Around fifty of them take their positions in the middle of the square and, at the ringleader's signal, start dancing the chain dance continuously accompanied by the lyre. This time too, the *lijepe maškare* lag behind at the last house, waiting for their turn to appear at Dolac Square. On this day only, the *pokladari* in their uniforms perform the entire male chain sword dance: all of its ten dance figures and their repetitions. The order in which the figures are repeated is decided solely by the ringleader and depends on his dancing abilities and mood. While the *pokladari* dance their dance at Dolac Square, the *lijepe maškare* are nearing the end of their procession through the village. The last terrace on which they dance overlooks Dolac Square. When the *pokladari* have repeated certain figures a few times and the *Poklad* puppet has been taken away to be undressed before it is burned, the *lijepe maškare* start heading for the square; but—as they themselves say—they are "late as always." The *pokladari* dance their dance alone, doing multiple repetitions until the arrival of the *lijepe maškare*. Once the *lijepe maškare* have arrived at Dolac Square, the *pokladari* do not stop dancing; instead, the groups dance their respective dances alongside each other. After a few repetitions of certain figures, a male ringleader indicates that the two chains—one of men and the other of women—should merge into one. At that moment, there are around one hundred or more performers at Dolac Square dancing together in a big chain dance (*kolo*). They repeat simple dance figures endlessly, almost running, which results in a nearly trance-like experience for the dancers. Although the dancers are reaching their limits, as it has been a very intense day for all of them, no one gives up; they have been living for this moment all year.

The Carnival events reach their peak when a stripped-down *Poklad* puppet is put on a stick, doused with paraffin, and set alight. The *kapo sale* goes around Dolac Square carrying the burning puppet, arrives at the center of the square, and holds the puppet there until it burns completely. With this act, the Lastovo villagers rid themselves of all the misfortunes that have befallen them in the past year. The *Poklad* puppet has been found guilty again, as he has been ever since the legend started. And a new agrarian year can begin. More recently, the climax of the events is rounded off by fireworks that are ordered especially for this occasion by the Lastovo Carnival Society. All the *pokladari* and *lijepe maškare* then gather, singing and rejoicing until the church bells ring, indicating that it is all over, that the eventful Tuesday, full of song and dance, has come to its end.

ČISTA SRIJEDA (ASH WEDNESDAY)

On Ash Wednesday morning, Lastovo is particularly peaceful. In the evening, the Carnival Society organizes the final gathering at the Hall. Everybody who took part in the dance evenings and Carnival events is invited to contribute to help cover the financial costs of Carnival. The Carnival Society members offer the guests homemade *prkle* (small deep-fried doughnuts) and hard-boiled eggs, the same ones that the ugly masks collected on Fat Monday. The Hall is then closed, and everyone goes home.

In addition to the fact that the Lastovo Carnival is held without exception every year in February or March (with 150 people taking part in it and around a hundred more following the culmination of the events) and is filmed by numerous cameras (television, researchers, onlookers), it is also thought, spoken, and written about, as well as researched, by the locals of Lastovo. All of this shows how important the Carnival custom is to the island's people. The spirit of *Lastovski poklad* is well exemplified by the Lastovo inhabitant Eduard Bačko, an avid lyre player, the leader of the local folklore society, and an active member of the Lastovo Carnival Society who also teaches primary school children to dance as well as play the lyre. He is an individual who never finds it difficult to do something for Carnival and the preservation of this custom in its entirety. Indeed, he is a flywheel who attracts young people to Lastovo, awakening and nurturing their love of tradition as well as organizing and motivating them by his own good example.

In addition to the Carnival season, the Lastovo Carnival lives on stage in the performances by members of the folklore society from Lastovo. They perform it for tourists in the summer and at folklore festivals in Croatia and abroad. The choreography of the Lastovo Carnival is in the permanent repertoire of LADO—the National Folk Dance Ensemble of Croatia—which testifies to its charm and distinction.

METHODOLOGICAL FRAMEWORKS FOR FIELDWORK

My fieldwork experience of the *Lastovski poklad* differed greatly from anything written about it until then. It was only during my second field trip (2000) that I realized and understood the importance and omnipresence of women—the *lijepe maškare* and their role in the Carnival chain dance (*pokladarsko kolo*). While I was observing all the activities taking place on Shrove Tuesday at that time, the question arose as to why, in the literature, the *lijepe maškare* were on the margins of that busy and picturesque event. The written sources did not indicate whether field researchers were participating in the main Carnival event or doing research at some other time of year. During my field trips I have met with different interpretations of the event, mostly informed by the *pokladari*. For them, the description of Carnival customs is always focused on the events that they take part in. This comes as no surprise because the male and female processions must not meet during their tours of the village, and so they are not interested in what happens with the other procession. And since the *pokladari* are the ones who *culjaju Poklad* (lower the puppet on the rope), which is the central part of the event, the story of carnival customs is naturally woven around them. Finding their part of the story more important, the *pokladari* tell it from their own perspective, mentioning the *lijepe maškare* only in passing. Although they are always present in their minds, the other participants are secondary, never important like them.

During my first visit to Lastovo (1999), I was introduced to potential informants, the people in charge of Carnival. Those were men from the procession of the *pokladari*. Our meetings were arranged and announced in advance. In keeping with the research "protocol" on the part of the locals, the informants had created their own idea about what I was interested in even before we met. They provided details of the Carnival custom events, giving me an in-depth account of the customs but only of the parts in which they participated. Adhering to the instructions furnished by the *pokladari*, I followed their procession since it is credited with Carnival's more representative moments, such as the tour around the village with the *Poklad* puppet on a donkey, *culjanje*, and, finally, Carnival's chain dance and setting *Poklad* alight. When I returned from the field trip and tried to turn my notes into a text, I realized that I had spent all of Tuesday running around the village after the *pokladari*, seeing the *lijepe maškare* only from afar since the two processions must never cross paths. Following the directions of the people from Lastovo who knew most about Carnival and its history and moving through the village according to their guidelines, I found out nothing about the *lijepe maškare*. At the end of that preparatory communication chain, it turned out that I had only focused on the procession and traditional practices of the *pokladari*. This is common practice in many fieldwork situations. On our first visits to the researched community, we often meet with the "professional informants." By that term, I do not mean paid informants, people who ask for a financial reward in exchange for their knowledge or skills (singing, dancing, or playing an instrument). "Professional informants" are the people whom the community sees as most knowledgeable about the subject of the research. They are usually prepared for a sequence of standard questions to which they have ready answers[16] since they are the ones who always present their community's customs and traditional practices to researchers and journalists. When it comes to the *Lastovski poklad*, the standard "professional informants" or interlocutors are the people in charge of organizing Carnival, the ringleaders, and the lyre players: the ones who supposedly have the most knowledge and experience in the Carnival customs and are in charge of the verbal presentation of Carnival (cf. Niemčić and Ćaleta 2011:67–68). I assume that the same thing had happened to the researchers who researched and wrote about this topic before me.

The next year (2000), I intentionally followed the procession of the *lijepe maškare*, and only then did I find out about the similarities and differences between their part in the custom and that of the *pokladari*. If I had not myself witnessed their parallel and ubiquitous existence in the event, I would have probably fallen into the same trap as other researchers concerning what the event represents and written only about the *pokladari* and their chain dance.

Fieldwork Research in Croatian Ethnology

In the decades-long tradition of Croatian ethnology, fieldwork has been one of its fundamental strongholds (Čapo Žmegač et al. 2006:8). Research practice is based on short field trips, participation in and observation of a particular event, and conversations between the interviewer and informants about the history of a researched tradition. Carnival events are a special challenge for a researcher since they reach their peak only one or two days during the year. If anything is left unclear or there are any dilemmas, the researcher needs to wait for the next annual cycle for a new field trip to verify or challenge information. Gaining an in-depth knowledge of the *Lastovski poklad* events took a decade of research and continually returning to the island in the middle of winter, when islands are left to themselves, stripped of tourists and cultural events, and it is difficult to find accommodations.[17] Research on the *Lastovski poklad* has given rise to some new research paradigms that can be linked to the essential principles of the beginnings of ethnology as a science in Croatia.

Antun Radić,[18] considered the founder of Croatian ethnology, defined ethnology as the science of the culture of *one's own*; he was primarily interested in the role of peasants in society. He was also the first to set parameters for fieldwork. He believed that peasant folk culture could be credibly and fully understood and consequently investigated and written about only by literate, educated people born into the researched communities, which would result in ethnographic material written down in the local dialect of the researched area (Čapo Žmegač et al. 2006:11). At the end of the nineteenth and beginning of the twentieth centuries, Radić started the fieldwork practice of "folk ethnographers": collectors of material about folk life who were primarily interested in the present (Čapo Žmegač et al. 2006:13). In the 1920s and 1930s, Radić's "folk ethnographers" were slowly replaced by professional ethnographers, with Milovan Gavazzi[19] at their head. They based their ethnological research on fieldwork, an approach still practiced today to some extent, with a focus on interviews with informants about the history of researched traditional practices.

In the 1970s, despite much stumbling and resistance from standard ethnological research practices, Dunja Rihtman-Auguštin[20] reintroduced the "present" as a relevant category in Croatian ethnological research (cf. Rihtman-Auguštin 1988:9; Gulin Zrnić 2004:7). The same paradigm was adopted in ethnochoreological practice. Ivančan collected data about dance with a focus on the past, interviewing numerous informants about how dance was once performed, while Stjepan Sremac introduced the present-based perspective in ethnochoreological research characterized by participant observation of a specific dance event (cf. Niemčić 2007:18). Since the 1980s, a small community of Croatian ethnochoreologists and ethnomusicologists at the Institute of Ethnology and Folklore Research (IEF) in Zagreb has based their fieldwork primarily on the participant observation of particular music and dance events, that is, on examining the performance context of the researched topic as a starting position. Structured in this way, the focus is primarily on monitoring contemporary music and dance practices and is supplemented by interviews with informants about both the past and the present. The first chosen to be interviewed are often "professional informants," who present, evaluate, and reflect on what they consider important in the tradition. But it is the participant observation of a researched event, including music and dance, that opens the door to new interpretations, scholarly reflection, and informants or interlocutors as well as marginalized elements of tradition.

With my long-term research presence on Lastovo, I have gained the community's trust and eventually made friends among the informants, so our conversations nowadays often "grow beyond mere questioning, turning communication into a mutually engaged dialogue" (Čapo Žmegač 2002:41; Čapo Žmegač et al. 2006:33). In recent years, we have gone a step further: besides being a committed researcher and academic promoter of the *Lastovski poklad*, I have also become a collaborator on many official statements about Carnival and the local government's projects.

Beyond Carnival, or How Carnival Lives Outside the Carnival Season

On January 17, 2008, the Ministry of Culture of the Republic of Croatia declared the Lastovo Carnival a protected intangible cultural heritage and listed it in the Registry of Cultural Goods of the Republic of Croatia. Ten years later, an idea was born among the people of Lastovo to submit the *Lastovski poklad* as the Croatian candidate for UNESCO's Representative List of the Intangible Cultural Heritage of Humanity. The local community, led by the mayor, the representatives of the Nature Park Lastovo Islands, and the Lastovo Carnival Society, invited Joško Ćaleta and me (both from the Zagreb IEF) to work with them to produce documentation for submission to UNESCO's list.

For us researcher-"outsiders," it presented an exciting challenge. After years of getting to know Carnival in depth using the methods of participant observation, an opportunity arose for us to expand our own research—mine in ethnochoreology and Ćaleta's in ethnomusicology—along with the voices of Radić's "folk ethnographers." With our help, local enthusiasts designed a project to collect ethnographic material on Carnival. The aim of the project was to gather as many stories as possible about Carnival and the changes it has undergone since its beginnings by talking to all the people in Lastovo who have participated in the tradition in one way or another. A list of potential informants was created, and they were divided into three age groups. The interviews were done by inhabitants of Lastovo themselves, guided by a series of questions that we came up with together. The locals also organized several storytelling events, where informants of the same generation tried to stimulate parts of the collective memory "buried" in recollections of the most unforgettable moments of twentieth-century Carnival events. Our participation in the first few storytelling events encouraged the young people of Lastovo to explore their community. They started with the oldest members on the island, whom they often visited individually at their homes where they recorded their conversations about Carnival. The "golden" generation was investigated individually to some extent but much more through storytelling events where together they recalled memories of events long gone, trying to reconstruct them in animated discussions. All the conversations were recorded and then transcribed. The transcriptions were made by young, educated residents of Lastovo who could best understand the local dialect, full of symbolic idioms that in most cases meant little to us outsiders. They also organized small Carnival-themed storytelling events for the youngest inhabitants of Lastovo as well as various activities in their school curriculum.

The collected and transcribed ethnographic material was archived in the Documentation Department of the IEF in Zagreb as a manuscript collection of interviews (Ćaleta and Niemčić 2022a; Ćaleta and Niemčić 2022b). The value of this initiative and project, not to mention the material collected, is significant. This is the first in-depth ethnographic study of Lastovo in which more than 20 percent of the local population of all generations was involved. All of the interviews were done face-to-face; there was no one-for-all questionnaire. They were conducted in environments that felt natural and comfortable for the informants such as their homes or community spaces and in the company of people whom they knew well, trusted, and could relax with. In these circumstances, the respondents shared exceptional knowledge of Carnival. Moreover, representational narratives about "ideal" traditional practices—that might be offered to strangers coming to the island guided by research curiosity—were avoided. Indeed, we heard some stories and interesting facts about Carnival that we had never heard before in the twenty years of field visits to the island. In these stories and memories of Carnival and its events, told by several generations, we experienced Radić's "dynamic conception of culture": the processes of adapting customs to changed life contexts as well as creativity in its sustainability.

The book that will emerge from this work will bring together in equal measure our ethnochoreological and ethnomusicological research of many years and the "voices" of the majority of the Carnival participants, the "builders of culture" on Lastovo, from the last half-century (Čapo Žmegač et al. 2006:33). Thus, we have come full circle in our research and fieldwork, starting as ethnologists using participant-observation methods as well as interviews with "professional informants." By actively participating in the most significant local traditional event, we gained the trust of the entire community and thus encouraged additional engagement of prominent individuals. The invaluable role of their initiative prompted a multitude of "insider voices"—"folk ethnographers"—to speak openly about their memories as well as their fears regarding their community's most important custom, the one that represents them to the outside world. The links between the local community and the annual Carnival festivities are indeed tenacious and provide a strong and vibrant sense of identity for the small southern Dalmatian island of Lastovo.

Epilogue: How Carnival Survived COVID-19

The overview of the history of the Lastovo Carnival in the first part of this chapter testifies to its almost uninterrupted continuity. Carnival was almost always held, even when it had to be performed on a reduced and adjusted scale. Indeed, an unprecedented challenge to Carnival surfaced in the form of the coronavirus just as the third decade of the twenty-first century unfolded. The epidemiological madness that began in 2020, with alternating periods of lockdown and relaxation measures, greatly changed everyday life by directing every segment of social existence to digital sociability. Physical distancing as one of the fundamental requirements of the pandemic age brought significant changes to the presentation, production, and even reception of all artistic and cultural formats, including traditional practices.

I was interested in the "new," COVID-restricted presentation of the Lastovo Carnival, different from the event which in the previous ten years had involved around 150 active performers and one hundred spectators—locals, journalists, researchers, and brave winter tourists. The 2020 Carnival was held just before the outbreak of the COVID-19 pandemic, when gatherings and celebrations involving large numbers of people were still a regular part of everyday life. The 2021 Carnival, however, took place in the "new normal," when everything that used to be regular and common was no longer so. At the same time, the 2021 *Lastovski poklad* was held at a time when the "second COVID-19 wave" was beginning to show signs of subsiding, which led to a moderate easing of lockdown measures. The "easing" enabled regular in-person school attendance and allowed gatherings of up to twenty-five people but with strict adherence to social distancing and the wearing of masks. In the meantime, the vaccination process had just started but was carried out only in nursing homes and among medical staff and senior government officials. In fact, due to its distance from the mainland and rare daily connections, Lastovo was for a long time COVID-free. But the very same isolation that enabled this also increased the feeling of fear of COVID-19 penetration on the island as a serious threat to the lives of the largely elderly population.

Yet despite the epidemiological measures and bans, the inhabitants of Lastovo never doubted whether the 2021 Carnival should be held or not. The only question was how they would adapt to the measures. They unanimously canceled all the parties and gatherings organized indoors throughout the Carnival period for the sake of safety yet fully intended to perform the outdoor events of the final day of Carnival in their entirety. In order to realize this, they negotiated with the authorities on the local, county, and national levels, all of whom had to reach a joint decision.

The first restriction referred to public gatherings of up to twenty-five people. It did not allow cultural events; the processions typical of the Lastovo Carnival, however, fit into what was permitted. In any case, the group of twenty-five *pokladari* would not have to abandon their procession. As a part of the "new normal," the names of all the *pokladari* and *lijepe maškare* taking part in the event were required, which is why the potential participants had to apply beforehand. A problem arose, however, when the submissions arrived: twenty pairs of *pokladari* and ten pairs of *lijepe maškare* had applied. It was clear that the maximum of twenty-five people was unacceptable to the community. One way of dealing with this was to choose a permissible number of "lucky" participants among those who applied. Another way was to include all who had applied, dividing them into three groups with a maximum of twenty-five people each. The first variant, consistent with the guidelines by the national and regional civil protection task force, was quickly rejected as it would displease and disappoint too many people. It was decided to fight not only for the preservation of the continuity of the custom but also for togetherness, joy, and a cheerful collective spirit of the island community.

A new request for at least one hundred participants was sent to the civil protection task force. They would strictly adhere to all COVID-19 preventive measures and be divided into smaller groups, each with a maximum of twenty-five people. The response was to reduce the number of participants to less than one hundred, without specifying the maximum number allowed. This is where the harmonious island community saw its chance to bring this "new normal" Shrove Tuesday as close as possible to all the jubilant and playful Shrove Tuesdays before it. Accordingly, the *pokladari*, who at Carnival typically wear only richly decorated hats on their heads, were also given red face masks that matched the color of their uniforms. Due to the large number of participants, the procession was divided into two smaller processions that followed each other but never went alongside or visited the same households. There was only one procession of *lijepe maškare* since fewer of them applied than in previous years. They also wore protective masks in addition to their characteristic Carnival eye masks.

Finally, the *Poklad* puppet was lowered on the rope accompanied by the explosion of bombs as the custom requires. But the *pokladari* and *lijepe maškare* did not merge and dance the chain dance together at the very end before the *Poklad* puppet was set alight as they normally would have. Instead, each procession danced its own chain dance, never exceeding the allowed number of twenty-five people. After the *Poklad* puppet burned out and the lyre player and donkey left, the participants and audience did not gather at the Hall to dance and enjoy themselves until morning. There were few people in the audience since expatriates did not return for Carnival in 2021, and neither did the Lastovo inhabitants who worked or went to school on the mainland. Rare queries from journalists and tourists asking whether it was worthwhile to visit the island and follow the events received the unanimous reply that the custom would take place on a modest scale and only within the community.

Instead of a Conclusion

The Lastovo Carnival is an excellent example of the preservation of a layered, multi-day event in a small, isolated community that has continued despite the change of rulers and vicissitudes of events throughout history. Based on the oral tradition of many generations of Lastovians, the custom finds its foothold and source in the legend of the defense of the island from Catalan attacks. The main actors and ritual practices, such as a tour of the village by a procession of *pokladari* and the *Poklad* puppet on a donkey, his *culjanje* down the rope, and his burning in front of the whole community, have remained unchanged for almost 150 years. On the other hand, we can follow the changes in customs and their adjustments to changes in political power (e.g., singing the *pokladari*'s song in Italian during Italian rule of the island), modern emancipatory achievements (such as the inclusion of the procession of *lijepe maškare* and their ongoing empowerment), and the epidemiological situation engendered by the coronavirus (the introduction of protective masks as part of carnival uniforms and costumes).

A Croatian proverb states, "The village may vanish but not the custom." The custom has survived, and the village has not vanished either; luckily, since the arrivals on the island were kept to a minimum, the coronavirus also failed to arrive. Long live the *Lastovski poklad*!

Notes

1. A *pokladar*'s uniform consists of a white shirt and classic-cut black trousers with a yellow side stripe called *kurdjela*, a red jacket (*koret*), and a black gilet (*dilet*) worn over the jacket. The so-called *Lastovo belt* (an approximately 5-cm-wide ribbon in several shades of yellow, variously decorated) is fastened around the waist and over the vest. Across their shoulders, chest, and back, the *pokladari* wear crossed ribbons called *korduni*, fastened at each hip. They wear a black bow tie called *farfala* around their necks and decorate their chests with family gold and corals. On their heads, they wear black bowler hats with a colorful ribbon band (*kanica*), the loose ends of which hang freely from the back of the hat. On the left side of the hat there is a festively decorated bouquet of artificial flowers and feathers, and on its front side there is a white wreath. Each *pokladar* carries a wooden sword in his hand.
2. Since 1999 I have visited the Lastovo Carnival fifteen times. During this twenty-three-year period I also conducted fieldwork several times on dance traditions in different seasons on the island of Lastovo.
3. Ivančan (1927–2006) was a Croatian ethnochoreologist and choreographer.
4. The *kumpanija* dances from the island of Korčula belong to a group of chain dances in which fencing is secondary or non-existent. Rather, the emphasis is on the connections between the dancers as each holds the tip of the sword of the dancer in front of or behind him. The dancers create a chain in which various dance figures alternate, intertwining and unraveling in different ways. Some of the figures are characteristic of almost all chain dances throughout Europe, while some are specific only to particular localities.
5. "In Lastovo" refers to the village, while "on Lastovo" refers to the island.
6. A chain dance with swords and handkerchiefs makes up an integral part of the Lastovo Carnival custom. It is executed by a group of male or female dancers who perform simple three-step dance moves, forming various geometrical shapes. The male participants' circle dance is a chain sword dance that is performed in its entirety exclusively on Shrove Tuesday by natives of Lastovo dressed as *pokladari*. They dance with wooden swords so that one holds the hilt of his sword in his right hand while the other holds the tip of the same sword in his left hand. Female dancers are mutually connected with handkerchiefs so that one dancer holds one end while the next holds the other end of a handkerchief. Dance theorists interpret handkerchiefs as substitutes for swords since there is a structural-spatial scheme of basic dance forms characteristic of all chain dances with swords. Chain dances, both with swords and with handkerchiefs, used to be guild dances, which is why they are mainly performed by men. According to Richard Wolfram, sword dances always belong to a society of men: "whether it be the miners with the rigid statutes or—in an urban milieu—the artisan guilds," they all have warlike as well as ritualistic functions (1932:39).

Lastovo's chain dance with handkerchiefs performed by *lijepe maškare* is unique for being exclusively female. It takes place on Shrove Tuesday only. It consists of four dance figures with repetitions. The figures are very similar to those of the male chain dance, but they are adjusted to a performance with handkerchiefs.

7. Lucijanović (1844–1929) was a Croatian historian and folklorist.
8. Pospíšil, a twentieth-century Czech ethnographer, was the first to record the sword dance of the *pokladari* on film. It is believed that Pospíšil spent some time on the islands of Korčula and Lastovo in 1924, when he filmed the *kumpanija* dance in the village of Blato (Korčula), the *moreška* (sword dance) in the town of Korčula, and the *pokladarsko kolo* (Carnival chain dance) and *balo pod liru* (ball under the lyre) dances in Lastovo.
9. Bonifačić Rožin (1913–1995), a Croatian writer and folklorist, was a longtime associate at the Institute of Ethnology and Folklore Research in Zagreb.
10. The *Poklad* puppet is dressed in a white shirt and red jacket (*koret*) with two ribbons (*kanice*) crossed on the chest. Around his neck he wears a black bow tie called *farfala*. Black boots called *šćuvale* are sewn to his pants and filled with fresh soil (*prlina*) taken from near the cemetery that morning. He wears a very short white skirt (*kotula*) and white gloves on his hands.
11. The *Kapo sale* is the person in charge of the organization of Carnival but not just at the Hall (*sala*) where dance evenings take place, as his title suggests. He is also responsible for maintaining order and discipline in general, and he ensures that the Carnival events follow in their regular order. He is assigned this role by the Lastovo Carnival Society (*Pokladarsko Društvo*), which consists of 100–150 members whose duty is to listen to, respect, and help him. The Hall Master (*Kapo sale*) is usually an elderly man, and it is a function for life or until he personally asks for a successor who will replace him.
12. Simultaneously with the making of the *Poklad* puppet, the bomb-maker makes bombs by wrapping a specific amount of gunpowder first in aluminum foil and then in packing paper together with fuses of different lengths. In front of the Hall, his assistants wrap up the bombs with a rope stretched between some trees to keep it taut. As soon as the first bomb is ready, they set it off in order to check the quality of both the gunpowder and the bomb-making.
13. *Grube maškare* consist of several groups of casually disguised Lastovians (who will participate in Carnival as *pokladari* or *lijepe maškare* the following day), dressed in old clothes and wearing excessive makeup. They are relaxed and have fun cheering up the locals who give them eggs.
14. *Culjanje* is the local term for lowering the *Poklad* puppet on the rope from the top to the bottom of the village, accompanied by the explosion of the bombs attached to it.
15. The term *Dolac* usually refers to a diminutive form of the noun *do*, meaning valley. Interestingly, in the case of Lastovo, the term *Dolac* stands for the main, most important square in the village (cf. Croatian *Placa*, *Pjaca*, *Trg*).
16. Typical "standard" questions include What are the leading roles in Carnival, and what are their customary obligations? Could you please describe the common practices?
17. The only hotel in Lastovo is closed in winter, and many private landlords do not work outside the summer tourist season.
18. Radić (1868–1919) was a Croatian ethnologist, politician, and writer.

19. Gavazzi (1895–1992), a nestor of Croatian and Slavic ethnology and the founder of ethnology as an academic discipline in Croatia, was the first to present a systematized account of annual customs among the Croats ([1939] 1988).
20. Rihtman-Auguštin (1926–2002) was a Croatian ethnologist.

Works Cited

Čapo Žmegač, Jasna. 2002. *Srijemski hrvati*. Zagreb: Durieux.
Čapo Žmegač, Jasna, Valentina Gulin Zrnić, and Goran Šantek. 2006. *Etnologija bliskoga. Poetika i politika suvremenih terenskih istraživanja*. Zagreb: Institut za etnologiju i folkloristiku and Naklada Jesenski i Turk.
Corrsin, Stephen D. 1997. *Sword Dancing in Europe: A History*. London: Hisarlik Press.
Gavazzi, Milovan. 1988. *Godina dana hrvatskih narodnih običaja*. Zagreb: Kulturno-prosvjetni sabor Hrvatske. First published 1939.
Gulin Zrnić, Valentina. 2004. "Urbana antropologija novozagrebačkog naselja. Kultura svakodnevice u Travnom." PhD thesis, Faculty of Philosophy, University of Philosophy, University Zagreb.
Ivančan, Ivan. 1967. *Narodni običaji korčulanskih kumpanija*. Zagreb: Institut za narodnu umjetnost.
Ivančan, Ivan. 1985. *Narodni plesni običaji južne Dalmacije*. Varaždin: Kulturno-prosvjetni sabor Hrvatske.
Jurica, Antun. 2001. *Lastovo kroz stoljeća*. Lastovo: Matica hrvatska Lastovo.
Lozica, Ivan. 1984. "Lastovski poklad 1981." In *Folklorni teatar u balkanskim podunavskim zemljama: Zbornik radova*, ed. D. Antonijević, 159–170. Belgrade: Srpska akademija nauka i umetnosti.
Lozica, Ivan. 1990. *Izvan teatra*. Zagreb: Hrvatsko društvo kazališnih kritičara i teatrologa.
Lozica, Ivan. 1997. *Hrvatski karnevali*. Zagreb: Golden Marketing.
Lozica, Ivan. 2002. *Poganska baština*. Zagreb: Golden Marketing.
Niemčić, Iva. 2002. "Tragom nevidljive plesačice." *Narodna umjetnost: Hrvatski časopis za etnologiju i folkloristiku / Croatian Journal of Ethnology and Folklore Research*, 39/2:77–92.
Niemčić, Iva. 2005. "The Invisible Female Dancers." In *Dance and Society*, eds. Elsie Ivancich Dunin, Anne von Bibra Wharton, and Laszlo Felfoldi, 117–123. Budapest: Akademiai Kiado, European Folklore Institute.
Niemčić, Iva. 2007. "Ples i rod." PhD thesis, Faculty of Philosophy, University of Philosophy, University Zagreb.
Niemčić, Iva. 2011. *Lastovski poklad. Plesno-etnološka studija*. Zagreb: Institut za etnologiju i folkloristiku.
Niemčić, Iva, and Joško Ćaleta. 2011. "Public Practice versus Personal Narratives—The Example of Music and Dance Traditions of Boka Kotorska." In *Proceedings of the Second Symposium of the ICTM Study Group on Music and Dance in Southeastern Europe*, eds. Elsie Ivancich Dunin and Mehmet Ocal Ozbilgin, 65–77. Izmir: Ege University State Conservatory of Turkish Music.
Rihtman-Auguštin, Dunja. 1988. *Etnologija naše svakodnevice*. Zagreb: Školska knjiga.
Vitez, Zorica. 2001. "Narodni običaji." In *Hrvatska tradicijska kultura na razmeđu svjetova i epoha*, eds. Zorica Vitez and Aleksandra Muraj, 309–381. Zagreb: Barbat, Galerija Klovićevi dvori, Institut za etnologiju i folkloristiku.
Wolfram, Richard. 1932. "Sword Dances and Secret Societies." *Journal of the English Folk Dance and Song Society*, 1/1:34–41.

Manuscript Collections at the Documentation Department of the Institute of Ethnology and Folklore Research, Zagreb

Bonifačić Rožin, Nikola. 1960. *Lastovski poklad god.* IEF manuscript, 340.

Ćaleta, Joško, and Iva Niemčić. 2022a. *Transkribirani razgovori o Lastovskom pokladu s lastovskim kazivačima 1.* IEF manuscript, 2493.

Ćaleta, Joško, and Iva Niemčić. 2022b. *Transkribirani razgovori o Lastovskom pokladu s lastovskim kazivačima 2.* IEF manuscript, 2494.

CHAPTER 14

DANCE IN CALENDRICAL COMMUNITY CELEBRATIONS IN ROMANIA

LIZ MELLISH

ROMANIA has a vast array of calendrical celebrations, customs, rituals, festivals, and traditions, some of which have been lost in history but many still take place today in similar or evolving forms. However, it is only a subset of these where dance plays an integral part. This chapter focuses on celebrations that include dancing and in particular those that have continued to take place rather than those that are nowadays rarely part of customary life in Romania.[1]

It is common to use certain basic criteria to group community celebrations. The broadest separation is into those that are associated with the life cycle of birth, coming of age, marriage, death, and what goes on in between and those that form part of the annual calendar, the latter being the subject of this chapter. These calendrical community celebrations can be divided into fixed date and variable date celebrations that are linked to the ecclesiastical calendar, the seasonal work cycle (including the interaction of the pastoral, agrarian, and viticulture calendars), or are annual secular (civil or state) organized commemorations of a particular historical event, person, or group of people.[2]

THE ANNUAL CALENDAR OF CELEBRATIONS IN ROMANIA

Calendrical celebrations can be grouped according to the time of year in which they take place linked to the four seasons. The midpoint of each season is marked by the winter and summer solstices and the spring and autumn equinoxes, and the passing of one season into the next is indicated approximately by the midpoint between the equinoxes (Fig. 14.1). This midpoint is often the focus of a bundle of calendrical celebrations, customs, traditions,

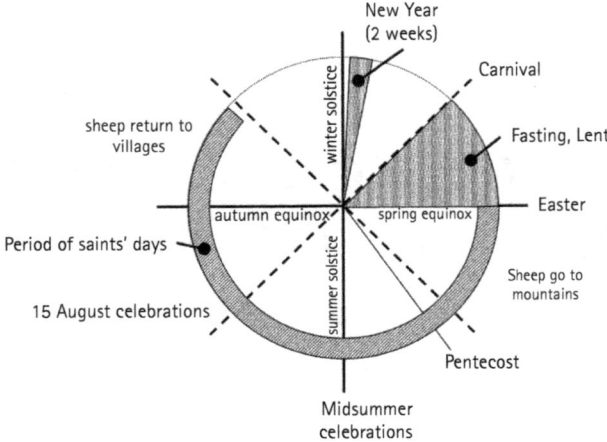

FIG. 14.1. Calendrical celebration calendar.

(Diagram: Liz Mellish.)

and rituals in folk terminology linked to a series of oppositions involving good/evil, ugly/beautiful, cold/hot, death/rebirth. It is also important to note that the timing of the fixed date celebrations among the majority Orthodox Christian church observers in Romania, as well as the Catholic minorities (Romanians, Hungarians, and Germans) is determined by the Gregorian calendar, except for Orthodox Easter and events linked to the timing of Easter. However, celebrations organized by Serbs and other Orthodox minorities living in Romania who continue to observe the Julian calendar take place thirteen days later (e.g., Christmas Day falls on January 7 and New Year's on January 14).[3]

In this chapter, I frame the discussion mainly according to the passage of the year starting with the calendrical celebrations around the end of winter that mark the arrival of spring and progress through the year to the New Year's customs that are renowned for their diversity and colorfulness, especially in the eastern part of Romania. This annual calendar of celebrations follows a similar trajectory to elsewhere, and parallels can be drawn between many of the events described in this chapter and celebrations throughout Europe and beyond. The final section of this chapter deals separately with the secular (civil or state) organized events that form part of the annual calendar in Romania. These dates are usually fixed. Some have long histories, such as Romania Day on December 1; others, including Children's Day, have only become a fixture in the Romanian annual calendar of celebrations since the turn of the millennium, following connections to the wider European calendar of secular celebrations.

Terminology and Meanings

Designating events as customs, rituals, or traditions can be confusing as the terminology employed depends on local use of language and translations. I mainly use the term "celebration" in this chapter, in preference to "custom," "tradition," or "ritual," in an attempt to avoid confusion around the meanings and usages of such words in both English and Romanian. In some cases, however, I revert to using "custom," "ritual," or "tradition" where these terms seem more appropriate in order to distinguish in more depth the type or origin of the event. Also, bearing in mind that the use of the word "celebration" in general terms can refer to any party, those discussed in this chapter are community celebrations held in Romania where participation includes those from the local area and beyond for larger-scale events but seldom from outside Romania or even from other regions of the country. Community celebrations can be festivals, but not all festivals are customary (regularly scheduled) events; they may be one-off occasions.

In Romanian *sărbătoare* can be translated as "celebration," "feast," or "holiday"—in other words, a day when an important event is commemorated or celebrated. It is used to designate days set aside as non-working days for religious or secular purposes or to mark an important event. *Sărbătoare* can also mean "festival," but "festival" can be translated as *festival, sărbătoare, serbare, petrecere* ("party" or "feast"), or *praznic* ("feast").

The English words "custom" and "tradition" (also "habit") can be translated in Romanian as *tradiție, datină,* or *obicei*; and these terms and corresponding translations are often used interchangeably. More anthropologically, "custom" is used to refer to something customary (regular, patterned behavior), but this can be either personal or community behavior or both. "Ritual" can also be considered as customary behavior, but again this term is used to represent a wide variety of situations.[4]

According to Victor Turner, celebrations are "'peak experiences' in social life which mark an occasion or an event with ceremony, ritual, or festivity" (1984:11–12). They are shared community occasions generally connected with planned cultural events linked to life-cycle events, the seasonal work cycle, religious observances, political connections, or social status. Turner continues by reflecting that "[s]easonal rituals and festivals do not therefore owe their persistence to the durability of their material expressions but to their connection with recurrent communal experiences and needs" (1984:27). This close link between calendrical celebrations and the local community is the reason that these annual events continue to take place despite the multiple changes in the local context and the surrounding worlds. Celebrations are not static events; they are dynamic and continuously evolving as new meanings are constructed with each repetition (see Guss 2000:7; Quinn 2009:18). However, within this the celebration retains the core "social function and symbolic meaning ... that the community recognizes as essential to its ideology and worldview, to its social identity, its historical continuity, and to its physical survival" (Falassi 1987:2).

Dancing within Community Celebrations in Romania

The majority of celebrations in Romania that I discuss are local events that have emerged over the years from specific folk beliefs, local histories, population movements, etc. These events include those organized by both Romanians and co-located ethnicities that live within the boundaries of modern-day Romania (Hungarians, Germans, Serbs, Croats, Ukrainians, Slovaks, Roma). In addition, many of these customs and traditions are shared with neighboring peoples beyond Romania's borders. What is customary in a certain location at a certain time of year is a cluster of elements each of which may have its own history, story of how it got there, and when and by whom it was introduced (see Mellish and Green 2020b; Mellish and Green 2022a). Dance is only one of these elements, as is its associated music (sound); in addition, there are costumes, words (sung or spoken), food, and many other elements that all change at different rates over time.

The most widespread format for local community celebrations is house-to-house visits through the village with the active participants providing some entertainment (dance, song, or folk theater) in return for gifts of money, eggs, and bottles of alcohol, usually wine or plum brandy. This format is similar to that found elsewhere in southeastern Europe and beyond. The "active participants" in certain of these customs in Romania are predominantly male, but for Carnival and New Year's customs the groups are mixed gender and age, especially when the participants are in disguise. However, the women also play an important role during the house-to-house visits by providing the hospitality, food, and drink and often join in the participatory dancing in the courtyard.

In Romania, these events conclude with an evening dance held in the village square in the summer or community center in the winter, attended by everyone from the village, with music (live or recorded), food, and alcohol. In the past, a Sunday dance event (*hora* or *jocul duminică*)[5] was held in most villages every week. These social events gradually died out during the 1980s and 1990s and have been replaced by evening dance events linked to specific calendrical celebrations.

The dance elements in these celebrations and customs can be broadly separated into two forms: firstly, presentational or participatory dancing,[6] which forms a fundamental part of the celebration itself (in these cases the celebration would not exist without the dance) and, secondly, social participatory dancing, which is included within the main part of the celebration and/or the community dance in the evening but is not fundamental to the celebration's "identity." This usually involves dances from the local social dance cycle which is familiar to people from the geographical area. This repertoire (and accompanying music) depends on the region of Romania. Within the borders of present-day Romania, north and to some extent east of the Carpathian Mountains, dancing in couples predominates, with connections to the central European couple dance genres. South and east of the Carpathians the emphasis is on chain dances of older strata that are more commonly linked to the pan-Balkan region. It is also important to note that although some celebrations have specific dances, most often the main dance is the generic community social dance (usually *hora* or *sârba*), which is used for opening customs and community events and for closing performative customs.[7]

Presentational dancing during celebrations in Romania can be structured group dances or unstructured, solo, or improvised movement. Unstructured movement is typical for dancers dressed as zoomorphic characters, either as a solo or in a group, and also where there is a solo role for a character within a larger performance with other characters. By contrast, structured group dances are generally dances for men, which are danced in unison. These can be in the *ceată* ("group") formation in a circle, line, or row without any physical connection between the dancers. In these dance forms it is common for a prop (stick, sword, or axe) to be held in the right hand while dancing. Although these props could be considered as weapons, in Romanian dances there are no percussive or fighting movements, and the prop appears to be purely a ceremonial item which is used in some figures as a support for the dancer.

In other group dances, the dancers are in a chain dance configuration where they are linked by holding their neighbors' shoulders or hands. These categories of men's dances also overlap with the social dance repertoire: the *ceată*-formation men's dances can also be the men's dance within the social dance cycle, the chain dances in the customs can be from the social repertoire, and dances from the social repertoire (including couple dances) can be adapted to be included in the men's dances during customs.

This presentational dance that forms the fundamental part of these celebrations can be either a formal performance intended for a seated audience or an informal performance in a courtyard or in the street during house-to-house customs, where the hosts are passive participants or even intended for a transcendent (invisible) audience. In all of these cases the "performance is an activity done by an individual or group in the presence of and for another individual or group" (Schechner 2004:22). All of these cases involve what Richard Schechner terms an "audience–performer interaction. Even where audiences do not exist as such . . . the function of the audience persists: part of the performing group watches . . . or, as in some rituals, the implied audience is God, or some transcendent Other(s)" (2004:22).

Formal performances for a seated audience are often nowadays included during local community celebrations. These can include a presentational performance by local children or mixed-age dance groups or, in the case of larger events, folk ensembles from nearby towns or cities. On some occasions there may also be social dancing in front of the stage by audience members.

Celebrations That Signal the End of Winter and the Coming of Spring

In the old calendar used until 45 BCE, the new year began on March 1, thus marking the death of winter and the arrival of spring (Pop and Zane [1976] 1999:44). This period is when the winter stocks of food have been depleted and the springtime agrarian work is just beginning, marking a lean period that lasts until the products from the new season are available. It also approximately coincides with the start of the Lenten period and pre-Easter fast (*postul Paștelui*), although the precise date varies from year to year and depends on the date of the Western or Orthodox Easter that is set by the cycles of the moon.

During this pre-Lenten period in Romania carnivalesque celebrations are organized mostly in Transylvania and Banat (southwest Romania) by the Catholic minorities, Germans, Hungarians, or Bulgarians who observe the Western dates for Easter, although in Banat Carnival is also celebrated among Orthodox Christians on the Orthodox date for the start of Lent. The most common name for these celebrations is *Fărşang* (also spelt *Făşanc* or *Făşang*), a term that has been adopted from the German word *Fasching*. In central Transylvania it is considered that the Hungarian community "borrowed" this celebration from the local Saxons (Strauti 2020). The same could apply in Banat—but it may also be the name given more recently to an already existing celebration of the end of winter that forms part of the annual agrarian calendar and involved older elements such as zoomorphic characters (Băcilă 2013:93). *Fărşang* in Romania involves a bundle of traditions connected to food, house-to-house visits by masked characters, mock weddings and funerals, burying or burning a straw doll, or satirical and humorous organized performances depending on the religion, ethnicity, and geographical location of the organizers.

For the Hungarians and Germans, *Fărşang* starts after January 6 (*Boboteaza*) and lasts until the beginning of the pre-Easter fasting period on Ash Wednesday (*Miercurea Cenuşii*). During this period various food-related events take place, including a celebration of making noodles (*Sărbătoarea tăițeilor*) or doughnuts (*Sărbătoarea gogoşilor*), which mostly end with an evening costume *bal* ("ball") that includes a fancy-dress and mask competition for children and participatory social dancing with mainly waltzes and polkas.

The "climax" of the period of *Fărşang* takes place in the two or three days (previously a week) immediately before the start of Lent. This period is known in Romania as *Lăsata secului* or *Zapostitul* (Shrovetide) and *Săptămâna nebunilor* (lit. "Crazy Week"). It is a period when everything is done in excess, full of allegory, involving overindulgence in food and drink and loud noises intended to drive away evil spirits before entering the new cycle of fasting. During these days, processions of rowdy masked characters with animals and carts decorated with various objects take place through villages, visiting houses and stopping at specific points such as crossroads and central squares. As the participants arrive at each house, they start to dance the local generic dance (in Banat a *hora*) as they enter (and exit). Inside courtyards, or in an open area along the road, they sometimes include other dances from the local social dance repertoire (such as *ardeleana* or *de doi*). The hosts from the houses reward the masked revelers with gifts of money, alcohol (beer or brandy), and food, including doughnuts and fresh eggs.

The masked revelers can be zoomorphic characters who wear animal masks or skins (e.g., bears in the village of Ciclova Montană in the Banat mountains). However, it is also common now for many real-life characters to appear in these parades, including brides, bridegrooms, doctors (sometimes dressed in white personal protective equipment), priests, modern topical figures such as migrants, even celebrities—for example, in 2019 Donald Trump was the "honored guest" during the masked parade in the Banat mountain village of Bănia.

The "progress" of the parade of masked revelers commonly mimics the local village life-cycle customs—baptisms, weddings, and funerals—the most common being the (inverted) wedding or funeral procession which includes all those expected to attend the village events; for the wedding this is the bridegroom and bride, the godfather (*naș*), priest, etc. In certain locations, such as villages in the Almăj Valley in Banat, this is an inverted wedding known as *nunta cornilor* in which all the participants are male.[8] In the Almăj village of Bănia the parade is accompanied by a brightly decorated pig (ready for the pig roast that follows) and the village brass band (*fanfara*). A *hora* is danced outside the "groom's" house; then the procession moves on to collect the "bride" at her house, where another *hora* is danced (Fig. 14.2), and continues through the village to the church or central square, where all present join in dancing the local suite of dances to the music of the *fanfară* (while the pig watches) (Mellish and Green 2020b).

The majority of *Fărșang* events end with a mock funeral, the symbolic burial of the *Fărșang* (*Înmormântarea Fărșangului*). The *Fărșang* is (often) a doll made of straw that is taken on its last journey through the village accompanied by various dubious characters, musicians, and even animals, although it can be a person who is very much alive and plays a role in the banter during the "funeral" procession. The *Fărșang* is placed in a "hearse" that can be a decorated cart, carnival float, wheelbarrow, or the back of an open truck. The hearse leads the procession through the roads of the village accompanied by the "sobbing" mourners, often the musicians from the night's ball, who perform party songs, with no connection to the moment. At the intersections, they stop so that the whole village is present at the final "burial" (Both 2013:22–23) (Fig. 14.3). The procession

FIG. 14.2. *Nunta cornilor* in Bănia, Caraș-Severin County, 2019, dancing outside "bride's" house.
(Credit: Nick Green.)

FIG. 14.3. *Fărşang*, 2017, Goruia, Caraş-Severin County.

(Credit: Nick Green.)

ends when the *Fărşang* is buried, drowned, or burned (if it is a straw effigy) on a bonfire in the center of the village or in a field on the edge of the village, which symbolizes the end of winter and the arrival of spring (death and rebirth), purification, and the banishing of evil spirits.

Masked Evening Balls

After the Carnival procession finishes, in the evening, the participants gather at the village hall for an indoor masked ball (*balul Fărşangului*). During these evening balls, unlike those held on other occasions, just people wearing masks join in the dancing, while others sit around the dance space and watch. Usually only the generic dance *hora* is danced, as during the processions through the village. At a certain point in the evening the dancers stop for the announcement of the winners of the competition for the "best" mask or group of masks.

On the Banat plain, in the west of Romania, during the period immediately before the start of Lent, the mostly urban Catholic communities of Germans, Hungarians, and Bulgarians organize *Fărşang* events that are presentational evening performances with satirical playlets and mask or fancy-dress competitions, mainly for children, followed by a communal meal, with music and social dancing. These events do not include the characteristic elements mentioned above that mark the passing of the seasons (see Mellish and Green 2020b).

Flower Saturday (Sâmbăta florilor)

The pre-Easter fasting period marks a gap of six weeks in events that involve dance. Toward the end of this period, on the Saturday before Easter known as "Flower Saturday" (*Sâmbăta florilor*), in villages in southeast Romania (in Tulcea, Constanța, Giurgiu, and Teleorman Counties and the village Brănești in Ilfov), and among the Bulgarian community in Banat (in Dudeștii Vechi), young girls ("Lăzărițele") in their traditional dress go from house to house dancing a simple *hora* (walking dance) while singing spring songs in a line arranged by height, with the tallest in front. The leader is called the *buianciu* (from the Bulgarian, *буенек*). The custom Lăzărelul' or Lăzărița is more widespread in Bulgaria, northern Greece, and North Macedonia (Popescu 1997:44a; Chiselev 2012; Chiselev 2014). At each house the girls exchange flowers for gifts of money, flour, and eggs in a basket. Afterward they return to the house of the *buianciu*, who divides the gifts and prepares a meal for the participants.

Spring and Summer Celebrations

Agrarian Festivals

The agrarian calendar starts from the time of preparing the soil, sowing seeds, and trimming the grapevines in February. The summer period is also framed by the pastoral cycle of taking the sheep to the higher pastures around the beginning of May and bringing them back down to the villages by the end of October and correspondingly the ploughing of the fields and the harvest. This seasonal work cycle guides the entire life of the villager, by the "seasons, weeks, days and even moments of the day" (Ghinoiu 1999:11). Specific moments in this calendar have been celebrated with festivals, customs, or rituals throughout history. In particular, the period between Easter and the end of October or mid-November is the time when outdoor celebrations (with or without dancing) take place that are linked to the agrarian, ecclesiastical, or secular calendar.

The spring festival linked to the custom of taking the sheep up to the hill pastures, *Sâmbra Oilor* (the shepherd's association or guild) (Giurchescu and Bloland 1995:49) and measuring the milk from the sheep (*Măsuratul Oilor*), takes place in all the pastoral areas of Romania in the period from around April 23 (St George's Day) until the beginning of June, with the exact date depending on the geographical location in Romania (April 23 in the southern Carpathians, June 1 in Maramureș in the northwest of Romania). The locals and their families gather at the sheepfold (*stâna*), where the amount of milk from each sheep is measured in order to determine the share of the cheese that each local receives for this season. This custom continues to be celebrated with a range of events from small village events that always include the flock of sheep, shepherds, milking the sheep, judges, cheese, a shared meal with caldrons of stew, with or without social dancing, to small hilltop festivals with musicians and informal dancing. Some of these are covered in local press reports (as in the Almăj Valley in Banat and the mountains around Petrila in Hunedoara[9]), whereas others are customary events that only locals know about.[10]

During and since the socialist period (1944–1989), in some locations a larger folk festival is organized to coincide with these events. These festivals mostly take place in an open field in the pastures and include a fair with market traders and food stalls and an area set aside for an organized performance of local dance and music. The event begins mid-morning with a formal opening ceremony and ends mid to late afternoon once the final group has performed and the participants depart for their homes. Social dancing is seldom included in the program, although sometimes the participants spontaneously dance in front of the stage while local singers are performing. One of the most prominent of these festivals is *Sâmbra Oilor* held the first Sunday in May on the Huta Pass, where the zones of Oaș and Maramureș meet. In this case the measuring of the milk custom forms part of the organized fair that includes performances by folk artists and dancers from both sides of the mountain pass.[11]

Saints' Days and Village Festivals

The celebration of the patron saint of the local church is observed in most Romanian villages during the summer period starting with the second day of Easter and ending mid to late October. These celebrations are similar to those in many other southeast European countries and beyond and have a long history, although the form of the celebrations has changed over the years. As Vassilis Nitsiakos observes, "[w]hen asked how old the community religious festival is, one could answer how old the community is . . . the worship of a common saint, to which the central church of the village is dedicated, [is] a central community symbol" (2010:241–244).

The most common days for these celebrations are the fixed saints' days on May 21 (St. Constantin and St. Elena), June 30 (St. Peter and St. Paul), July 21 (St. Ilie), August 15 (St. Maria the Great), and September 8 (St. Little Maria) and the variable dates: the second day of Easter, Ascension Day (forty days after Easter), and Pentecost or *Rusalii* (fifty days after Easter). In Romania these celebrations vary from just a church service to a daylong fair, often with presentational dance performances by a local group. In the evening there is social dancing usually with live music by local singers and musicians.

These events are known by various names depending on the region and local preference. The most general term is *hram* ("church"), which comes from Old Church Slavonic хрaмъ/*hramŭ* and can refer to the church itself, the church's saint, the church service, or the celebration in honor of the patron saint. In Transylvania, parts of Banat and western Oltenia, village saints' days are often called *Nedeile*; and in western and central Transylvania, the names, *Fiii satului* ("children of the village"), *Jocul/Danțul la șură*[12] ("the dance at the barn"), or *Jocul satului* ("the village dance") are used. In Banat the village saint's day celebration is typically called *ruga*, which is derived from "to pray" (*a ruga*). This term is also used by the majority of the co-located ethnicities and religious confessions in this region including Romanians, Serbs, Hungarians, Bulgarians, Slovaks, and Ukrainians for their saint's day celebrations, the only exception being the Swabian Germans who use the German term *Kirchweih*.[13] In addition, throughout Romania, secular village days are known as *zilele* ("the days"). These can coincide with the village saint's day or take place on a different day, but again usually during the summer months, and follow a similar pattern of a daylong fair, with organized presentational performances and sometimes participatory dancing.

The music and dance content of saint's day and village day celebrations nowadays varies according to the region of Romania, local funding, and preferences of the village mayor or politicians. The program for these days may include local music and dance, or they can be fairs with either no organized entertainment or only popular music. In cases where the emphasis is on the formal presentational performances within daytime slots, these start mid-morning or early afternoon and finish by the end of the afternoon or continue into the evening. In these cases, the dancing is mostly by organized dance groups from the region concerned, and if an evening event takes place, this is headlined by a pop artist.

Particularly in Banat the *ruga bal*, a participatory music and dance event, continues to take place in many localities, from late afternoon lasting until the early hours of the morning. Local mayors allocate money to book respected local singers and musicians in advance of the date. An area for dancing is set up, usually in the center of the village and bounded by stalls selling grilled meat and seats. A big fun fair, with an inflatable bouncy castle, and stalls selling other food, trinkets, and toys are set away from this space, usually along the main street of the village. Nowadays the formal opening of the *ruga* is often preceded by a short presentational dance performance by a local children's dance group, followed by a communal *hora* led by the priest and mayor, then the singer continues with melodies for the other dances in the local dance cycle. On the Banat plain this is mostly *ardeleana*, a dance with simple steps moving side to side, danced in a circle formation. In the Banat mountains it is *brâul bătrân*, which was originally a men's chain dance similar in structure to the local *hora*, followed by *ardeleana*, more often danced in couples, with the local dance cycle finishing with the fast couple dance, *de doi*, usually instrumental, or the Oltenian chain dance *sârba*, danced in a line with a leader commanding the direction (Fig. 14.4) (Mellish and Green 2020d; Mellish and Green 2022a).

Dancing for the Dead: Hora de pomană

In the southwest of Romania (Banat mountains, Mehedinți, Gorj, and Dolj Counties[14]), a custom of including a dance or dances to pay tribute in honor of a deceased person from the village often takes place within a participatory social event,

FIG. 14.4. *Ruga* in Foeni, Timiș County, 2015.

(Credit: Nick Green.)

especially the *ruga* held at Easter or *Rusalii*. This custom, known as *jocul* or *hora de pomană*, is usually arranged by the closest relative of the deceased person, who pays the musicians to play music for the slow dance from the region, usually *hora*, except in the Banat mountains, where it is *brâul*. The line of dancers is led by the closest relatives of the deceased, with other relatives at the end of the line and in the middle. The dancers hold lighted candles, wrapped in a scarf, or scarves. The close relatives also have bottles of plum brandy and ritual bread (*colac*), sweet cakes with nut paste (*colivă*), or plates of homemade cakes. The musicians start to play *hora* or *brâul*, and the dancers make three circuits of the dance space, then the music stops and the participants stand still while the singer sings a slow song (*doină*) and an announcement is made—"This is a *pomană* for [name of the person]"—and the cakes and brandy are offered to those dancing. This sequence of dancing *hora* or *brâul* followed by a *doină* is sometimes repeated twice more, followed by the dances from the local repertoire in the usual sequence of the dance cycle (see Mellish 2015; Țîrcomnicu 2021 with links to video examples).

Căluș *Village Ritual and Dances during* Rusalii

The Romanian *Căluș* ritual takes place at *Rusalii* (Pentecost, fifty days after Orthodox Easter) in certain villages in southern Romania. In the past *Rusalii* lasted for seven to nine days, but at the present time only two days are set aside as a national holiday. *Rusalii* is considered a liminal period[15] that marks the transition from spring to summer when, according to Romanian and south Slavic folklore, malevolent fairies, known as *iele*, are at their most active.[16] *Căluş* is a healing and fertility ritual intended to drive away these evil fairies and promote good health. It is performed by *căluşari*, groups of an uneven number of male dancers led by a *vătaf* (leader), who are bound together by a secret oath (*jurământ*) for the duration of *Rusalii*. Although the healing part of the ritual is seldom practiced now, the other elements of the ritual continue to take place during *Rusalii*, and locals still hold a strong belief in the ability of the magical powers of the *căluşari* to drive away evil spirits.

The village *Căluş* ritual commences early in the morning of the first day of *Rusalii* with the raising of the flag (*steag*) made of a wooden pole with a white cloth containing a bunch of wormwood and green garlic tied to its top[17] at a location outside the village. During the morning the *căluşari* go from house to house through the village performing the *Căluş* dances, which are an essential element of the *Căluş* ritual, together with elements of the ritual in the streets or in courtyards as required by the householders (Fig. 14.5). They are accompanied by one or more musicians, most often a violinist. At each designated location they start with the walking dance (*plimbarea*), moving anticlockwise in a circle. This is followed by a series of figures (*mişcări*) and dances that involve combinations of stamps, heel clicks, springs, and leg rotations performed in place, either in a circle, line, or column formation. The final dance is *sârba căluşarilor* (the *sârba* of the *căluşari*), after which the *căluşari* invite those watching to join them

FIG. 14.5. *Căluş* in village courtyard, Brâncoveni, Olt County, 2022.

(Credit: Nick Green.)

to dance *hora călușarilor* (the *hora* of the *călușari*). During this dance parents invite the *călușari* to hold their children in their arms as this is considered to bring good luck and good health to the children. On the final day of *Rusalii* the flag is taken down and buried at the place where the oath was taken. Once this is over, the *călușari* are released from their oath until the next year.

The *călușari* nowadays dance in various overlapping contexts: in their villages of origin during *Rusalii*, in formally organized parades such as *alaiul călușarilor* (the procession of the *călușari*) that is held annually on *Rusalii* Sunday in the city of Craiova, at festivals organized specifically for groups who dance *Căluș* in this period, and at other times of year at their village day celebrations. In addition, the *Căluș* dances have been adopted as the most spectacular dance suite for organized performance in the repertoire of folk ensembles throughout Romania and in the Republic of Moldova, and the *Căluș* ritual was included on the United Nations Educational, Scientific and Cultural Organization's (UNESCO's) List of Intangible Heritage in 2005 (UNESCO n.d.).

The summer solstice takes place soon after *Rusalii*. In Romania the traditional customs of *Sânziene* and *Drăgaică*, celebrated on the night of June 23–24, do not involve community dancing. On this night it is held in folk belief that the good fairies (*zâne*) pass through the air bringing health, well-being, and abundant harvest. However, recently this day has become part of the secular calendar as the "Day of the Romanian Blouse," which will be discussed in the last section of this chapter.

Countryside Celebrations, Inter-regional Fairs or Markets, and Girl Fairs

Nedeile, a term meaning village saint's day celebrations, is also more commonly used for inter-regional fairs not connected to the local church (although they may be held on fixed saints' days such as July 21). *Nedeile* that are inter-regional fairs have much in common with calendrically scheduled inter-regional produce markets called *târguri*, and both these occasions can also be grouped under the term *serbare câmpenească*, meaning "countryside celebration." These events have long histories, and many are held during the summer months on the tops of hills that formed the traditional meeting points between people from adjacent regions (Gălățan-Jieț 2021).[18] Historically, these were fairs where livestock, food products, and other goods were sold and exchanged. The people from each village brought their food and their musicians, and later in the day a party with music and social dancing took place. These occasions were important for meeting and sharing local dance repertoire in times before television or social media. As described by Anca Giurchescu,

> There may be two or more different *horas* going on simultaneously, each representing a specific local dance tradition. The opportunity to see dances and hear instrumental

groups from outside one's own community intensifies the process of circulation of both dance and melody. . . . In the past the dancing at these fairs also provided the rare chance for young people from distant villages to meet each other. The acquaintances established often resulted in courtships leading to engagement and marriage.

(Giurchescu and Bloland 1995:50–51)

Over time many of these markets and fairs moved location to take place within the villages or at lowland meeting points, often a road intersection (Gălățan-Jieț 2021:24), which are more accessible for those wishing to attend. As with the shepherds' meetings, during the communist period many of the larger *nedei* or *târguri* were appropriated as state-organized festivals, with presentational performances by local singers and dance groups taking place to replace or in addition to the social dancing. Many of these festivals continue to take place annually, some still on the hilltops, the most famous being *Târgul de fete* ("The Girl Fair"), held on Muntele Găina in the Apuseni Mountains on July 21, or *Hora la Prislop* ("Hora at Prislop"), held the first weekend in August on the pass between Maramureș and Suceava Counties. Others are arranged in lowland, more accessible locations, such as *Târgul cepelor* ("The Onion Fair"), which takes place in Asuaju de Sus, between Sălaj and Maramureș at the end of August. These events draw a large crowd; some come just for the market and fun fair, others specifically to watch the organized performances, and at times some people take part in participatory dancing in front of the stage.

The End of Summer

After the saint's day on September 8, there are few outdoor occasions with dancing, possibly because of the nights' drawing in or the cold damp autumn weather. The agrarian and pastoral events for this period include celebrations for the harvest, with fairs and organized festivals linked to produce such as plum brandy, wine, vegetables (*Roadele toamnei* ["The Fruits of Autumn"]), or specific produce (*Festivalul papricașului și vinului* ["The Paprika and Wine Festival"] in Buziaș, a town in western Romania), which often also include organized performances by local groups. In addition, there are customs linked to bringing the sheep down from the hills, which marks the end of the summer season. These pastoral festivals have various names including *Strânsul Oilor* ("The Gathering of the Sheep") and *Alesul Oilor* ("The Sorting of the Sheep") and take place on the fixed dates of September 22 or 26, October 14 (St. Paraschiva's Day), or October 26 (St. Dumitru's Day, the protector of shepherds). In the past these days were celebrated with parties and dancing (Giurchescu and Bloland 1995:50). However, nowadays dancing is less common, with only spontaneous dancing by small groups of locals[19]; and these are not generally occasions for organized festivals.

Also on the eve of St. Dumitru's Day, *Focul lui Sumedru* ("The Fire of Sumedru," the patron saint of the pastoral winter) is celebrated by shepherds' lighting fires in the pastures, which people from the local community gather around. They share food including pretzels (*covrigi*), nuts, and apples; social dancing takes place in a circle around the fire; and at a certain point toward the end of the evening, young people jump through the fires. These fires are considered to have the role of protection against the spirits by providing warmth and represent the death of nature and fertility for the coming season.

Christmas and New Year's Calendrical Celebrations

After the end of October, a period follows in which few celebrations take place. The pre-Christmas fasting season starts six weeks before Christmas on November 15. Although during a fasting period dancing does not generally take place, this is the time when the preparations for the Christmas and New Year's celebrations begin, the pig is sacrificed, and the men's groups are formed and start to rehearse carols (*colinde*), *căluşer* dances, and other elements of winter customs.

The winter custom celebrations in Romania mostly take place within the fifteen-day period between December 24 and January 7, thus marking the transition from the old to the new calendar year. The variety is especially rich north and east of the Carpathians. Mihai Pop divides the winter customs into traditional celebrations and those superimposed by the church from the late seventeenth and eighteenth centuries. The former include traditional caroling (by children and adults), folk theater, as well as many winter customs that incorporate dance, whereas the latter involves religious caroling, groups of children who walk while carrying a star (*umblă cu steaua*), and religious playlets (*vicleimuri*) (Pop and Zane [1976] 1999:45–46).

The most widespread winter custom is caroling (*colindatul*) that takes place in all regions of Romania between December 24 and 27 (Giurchescu and Bloland 1995:27). On these days, groups of men or children go from house to house in villages singing specific local songs. In many regions of Romania, *colindatul* is also often combined with other house-to-house customs that include dance, making music, drumming, or rowdy revelers resembling Carnival traditions. At each house they perform dances or playlets or sing carols according to the choice of their hosts, and their "performance" is paid for in food, drinks, and money that is used to fund the evening *bal* held inside the village hall (as winter nights are cold).

Winter customs are often done by organized men's groups, most commonly known as *cete* (sg. *ceată*). In Transylvania these groups are also called *juni*, *jieni*, or *căluşeri*,[20] or *dubaşi* (drummers) in western Romania (Arad County and the Făget subzone of Banat).

In Romanian Moldova (see Mellish and Green 2022b), these groups have characters with a military connection, including the *ofițeri* (officers) who often wear Romanian military uniform, the *arnăuți* named after the mercenary soldiers of mostly Albanian origin who came to Romania during the Phanariot ruling period (1711–1821), and in Bucovina, the *bumbieri* and *hurta* that imitate/parody the Austrian military and *irozi* who perform dances connected to the strata of Carpathian shepherds' dances. In central Moldova, in addition to the organized men's (unmasked) *cete*, groups of masked characters and zoomorphic characters (e.g., the bears from Bacău County) roam the streets during the winter holidays.

The *căiuți* (little horses) dominate in the northeast of Moldova in various forms. The dancers may hold a likeness of a horse's head in their hand, or the head is mounted at the dancer's waist (more like an English hobbyhorse), as well as more recent urban traditions. The Moldovan *căiuți* has become largely a dance for entertainment (Lavric 1976) especially in urban locations, which has resulted in the *căiuți* representing a wider repertoire of dances, including those related to the customs and additions from the local social dance repertoire.

New Year's customs without an associated organized form of dance include the *capră* (goat) zoomorphic tradition, which is found throughout Romania, and many versions of "folk theater." The *capră* generally performs an improvisational dance based on moving its head or knocking the pole that supports the head on the ground rhythmically, accompanied by the beat provided by a drummer (Fig. 14.6). In Iași County the *capră* is replaced by the stag (*cerb*), which is accompanied by a group of men or drummers who dance in a circle around it.

In addition to village events, during the Christmas period most regions organize colorful festivals of winter customs where local groups perform an arrangement of their own specific traditions shortened for a non-participatory audience. Many of these festivals start with an organized procession through the streets with some dancing along the route. This is followed by presentational performances in a designated space, usually a raised stage. One of the best known of these festivals, *Festivalul datinilor de iarnă* ("The Festival of Winter Customs"), is held in Sighetu Marmației, Maramureș, each January. Other comparable festivals take place in Moldova in Focșani, Piatra Neamț, and Iași; and in Transylvania, *Călușerul Transilvănean* ("The Transylvanian *Căluș*") is held in Orăștie in mid-December (Fig. 14.7).

Saint John's Day, also known as *Boboteaza* (Epiphany), is celebrated on January 6 and marks the end of the Christmas and New Year's celebrations. During the day many varied customs (without dance) connected to the baptism of St. John take place in numerous regions of Romania and honor those named John (Ion) (Băncescu 2006:73). In the evening a social dance known as *Bal de Boboteaza* ("The Epiphany Ball"), *Balul Ionilor* ("Johns' Ball"), or *Balul Sfântului Ioan* ("St. John's Ball") is held in villages in Transylvania and Banat.[21] In Transylvania (Sibiu, Brașov, and Mureș Counties), the announcement of the *bal* is made earlier in the day by young men, dressed in local costume, riding through the village on horseback, stopping at each

FIG. 14.6. The *capră*.

(Credit: Nick Green.)

household. People wearing traditional costumes from their village and surrounding locations gather in the village hall, where they dance until dawn. This is the final celebration until the Carnival period that signals the end of winter and the beginning of spring.

FIG. 14.7. *Festivalul Căluşerul Transilvănean*, Orăştie, Hunedoara County, 2019.

(Credit: Nick Green.)

Secular Calendrical Celebrations

The annual calendar of celebrations also includes secular events that celebrate a specific moment in Romanian history, are commemorations of a person or group of people, or mark Romania's participation in European or global celebrations. These ongoing commemorations are observed annually mostly in the main cities, with organized performances including dance, music, and song by Romanians and the co-located ethnicities, although recently they often also include an organized public participatory dance event at a town central square, shopping mall, or city park.[22] These commemorative events differ from the local calendrical celebrations discussed above in that they do not include house-to-house visits or social participatory dancing by the local community.

Romania Day on December 1 and Union Day on January 24 are formal calendrical celebrations that take place on the anniversaries of key events. Romania Day celebrates the unification of Romania with Transylvania in 1918 to form present-day Romania. It is a non-working day when military parades, official ceremonies, and organized performances of folk ensembles and famous popular (folk) singers take place in many of the major cities in Romania and are broadcast on television. This demonstration of belonging to Romania often also incorporates performances by groups from the co-located ethnicities. On January 24 the unification of the Romanian principalities of Wallachia and Moldova in 1859 is celebrated. Although not as "important" as December 1, commemorative events on Union Day are also organized including participatory dancing of the Union Hora (*Hora Unirii*) in city squares and evening performances by professional and amateur folk ensembles with Romanian dances, musical interludes, and singers who may incorporate certain patriotic songs into their program for the evening.

The annual calendar of events in Romania also includes many festivals commemorating a historical event, a famous person noted in Romanian history, or a famous singer or musician. These events do not take place on a specific date; instead, they are scheduled for a weekend date at approximately the same time each year. For example, the Festival of Hearts (*Festivalul Inimilor*) held in Timişoara during the first weekend in July in honor of those who died in Timişoara during the 1989 Romanian Revolution includes a ceremonial laying of a commemorative wreath by the monument in the central square of the city and presentational dance performances by groups from all areas of Romania, as well as the rest of the world (see Mellish 2013:178, 185).

Other calendrical secular celebrations honor a specific group of people, an aspect of heritage, or a concept. Most of these are European or global celebrations. Some date back to the communist period or before; others are newer "European" events. Children's Day on June 1 has been observed in many countries since 1950, although in Romania it has been marked by a national holiday only since 2017. On this day many cultural events and entertainments are organized for children in all regions of Romania. These include both presentational performances and organized participatory workshops with Romanian dance. On March 8, International Women's Day, it is the women's turn. Although there are some organized performances by urban-based folk ensembles, more often events are evening balls with social dancing and sometimes a short "cabaret" show with Romanian dancing. International Dance Day on April 29[23] is now celebrated each year in Romania and includes many activities involving all genres of dance. Romanian dance events are held in many city centers including dance workshops for children and adults, flash mobs, organized participatory dancing, and organized performances by adult and children's amateur dance groups. The International Day of the Romanian Blouse (*Ziua Internationalǎ a Iei*) was introduced into the Romanian annual calendar of celebrations in 2013 at the initiative of the online community *La Blouse Roumaine*. Its celebration on June 24 coincides with the summer solstice and the traditional Romanian customs of *Sânziene* and *Drǎgaicǎ*. This has led to tensions between the media and ethnologists who consider that this "new day of the blouse" subverts "the meanings of the traditional holiday" (Ţîrcomnicu 2022:17). However, the celebration of this day has become very popular throughout Romania and the Romanian diaspora, with many events including organized costume festivals, participatory dance, costume-making workshops, and costume displays.

Conclusion

This chapter has covered the main calendrical celebrations involving dance that take place annually in Romania in the early twenty-first century, although their precise order may vary because of the interrelationship between the fixed and variable date events. Celebrations linked to the seasonal calendar date back as far as memory allows, whereas many commemorative events have entered the annual calendar during the twentieth and twenty-first centuries.

Dancing that forms part of the calendrical events discussed in this chapter includes both presentational dance performances and social participatory dancing in both rural and urban areas. The dancing can be an integral part of a custom, with only the main participants involved, or part of the overall event, when members of the local community take part in social dancing. Presentational dancing can form part of house-to-house customs or is organized as formally arranged performances in a designated performance area, often a raised stage with a seated audience. Social participatory dancing can take place either as part of the house-to house customs or during social events, especially balls that form part of these celebrations.

As time passes, the events discussed in this chapter will continue to evolve, as many have done already for centuries, influenced by many other factors in their surrounding worlds. New community celebrations including participatory and/or presentational dance may be added to the annual calendar; the observance of some will become more prominent, while others may take a smaller role. However, as the calendrical calendar moves on from season to season and year to year, it seems likely that celebrations including dance will continue in some form for the foreseeable future.

Notes

1. I have undertaken long-term fieldwork throughout Romania for over twenty-five years, more recently focusing on the regions of Banat, Oltenia, and southwestern Transylvania.
2. Catherine Bell, in her work on rituals, also makes the distinction between calendrical rituals that form part of the seasonal calendar and those that have a commemorative role (1997:103).
3. Following a papal decree in 1582, the Gregorian calendar was eventually adopted in most parts of the world. However, the earlier Julian calendar, which dated from 45 BCE, continues to be used for religious holidays by Orthodox Christians in Serbia, Macedonia, and Russia, which has resulted in this discrepancy in dates for many calendrical celebrations.
4. As Bell observes, "there is no clear and widely shared explanation of what constitutes ritual or how to understand it. There are only various theories, opinions, or customary notions, all of which reflect the time and place in which they are formulated" (1997:x).
5. For discussion on the various names for the weekly Sunday dances, see Giurchescu and Bloland, 1995:45; Giurchescu 2015:30).

6. I am drawing on Nahachewsky's use of the terms "participatory" and "presentational dancing" (1995:1) and Turino's (2008:25) "participatory" and "presentational performance," taking the celebration as a form of performance (see also Mellish 2013:32).
7. *Hora* is generally a medium-tempo dance where the dancers hold hands at shoulder level and make walking steps, following the chain around the circle and moving forward and back from the center. *Sârba* is normally danced in low hand hold or, if only men, in a shoulder hold; it has a faster-tempo melody, which allows for more energetic steps, hops, and variations.
8. *Nunta cornilor* means the wedding of the *corn* trees. *Corn* is a local name for a tree that blooms too early in the spring so that its fruit is damaged by the frost (Băcilă 2013:240).
9. For example, https://www.infocs.ro/masuratul-oilor-smalsul-la-rudaria-traditia-merge-mai-departe-si-in-2021-video/ (accessed June 25, 2023) and https://povestea-locurilor.ro/2018/11/12/masuratul-oilor/ (accessed June 25, 2023).
10. While in the village of Svinița in April 2013 for fieldwork on Easter customs, we were only told about this event the following day as the locals did not consider it was of interest to the group of researchers.
11. See https://www.turism-taraoasului.ro/festivalul-sambra-oilor/ (accessed June 29, 2023).
12. The term *jocul la șură, jocul satului,* or *jocul duminică* was used in the past to refer to the weekly village Sunday dance. More recently, it refers to the annual village celebration (Poduț 2019:159).
13. The *Kirchweih* also includes a formal parade prior to the church service and organized dancing by the local German dance group outside the church after the service ends.
14. This custom is also found in villages in northeastern Serbia and northern Bulgaria along the Danube.
15. See Rapport and Overing (2000:229).
16. *Căluș* is found in villages in the counties of Dolj, Olt, Argeș, Teleorman, Giurgiu, and Vâlcea and in a few villages close to the banks of the Danube in northern Bulgaria. For further details of the southern Romanian *Căluș*, see Mellish and Green (2020a), Mellish and Green (2020c), Mellish (2006), and Mellish and Green (2013).
17. The wormwood is believed to cure all diseases and garlic to drive away evil spirits.
18. For a summary of the history of *nedeile,* see Gălățan-Jieț (2021:19–25).
19. See report by Adi Neagu: https://www.infocs.ro/raznitul-oilor-prilej-de-mare-sarbatoare-pe-dealurile-prigorului-video/ (accessed June 29, 2023).
20. In southwestern Transylvania, from the mid-nineteenth century, arrangements were made of dances performed by the *căluşer* groups during the winter customs for performances during public events in cities as a display of Romanian identity (Mureșianu 1901). These dances included *Romana* (given a patriotic name) and *Banu Mărăcine* (the latter from the suite of dances belonging to *căluşeri* of southwestern Transylvania (Giurchescu and Bloland 1995:29) that were subsequently retaught to the men's groups in Transylvanian villages.
21. See https://www.infocs.ro/video-balul-ionilor-din-tarnova-caras-severin/ (accessed June 29, 2023).
22. Organized participatory dancing differs from community social participatory dancing in certain ways, the main one of which is that the prime reason for attending is for dancing, not socializing. The participants are mostly members of hobby groups or cultural cohorts (Turino 2008:20), although members of the public also join in. It usually takes place at a

previously determined location and has an agreed start and finish time; dances are fixed length "tracks," usually prerecorded music but can be live music.
23. International Dance Day was created in 1982 under the auspices of UNESCO.

Works Cited

Băcilă, Daniela. 2013. *Istoria vieții folclorice în Banat de la începutul secolului al XX-lea până în prezent*. Timișoara, Romania: Editura Eurostampa.

Băncescu, Iuliana. 2006. *Obiceiuri tradiționale din România. Sărbători în imagini*. Colecția Tradiții. Bucharest: Centrul Național pentru Conservarea și Promovarea Culturii Tradiționale.

Bell, Catherine M. 1997. *Ritual: Perspectives and Dimensions*. Oxford: Oxford University Press.

Both, József. 2013. "Fărșang tradițional în casa dansului popular clujean 11 Februarie 2013." *Buletin informativ*, 67:21–25.

Chiselev, Alexandru. 2012. "Lăzărelul din Izvoarele—Județul Tulcea (7 Aprilie 2012)." *MEAP Tulcea—Un blog de muzeu prietenos*. https://meaptulcea.wordpress.com/2012/04/05/lazare lul-din-izvoarele-judetul-tulcea-7-aprilie-2012/.

Chiselev, Alexandru. 2014. "Sâmbăta floriilor: Lăzărelul din izvoarele, jud. Tulcea." *MEAP Tulcea—Un blog de muzeu prietenos*. https://meaptulcea.wordpress.com/2014/04/05/samb ata-floriilor-lazarelul-din-izvoarele-jud-tulcea/.

Falassi, Alessandro. 1987. "Festival: Definition and Morphology." In: *Time Out of Time: Essays on the Festival*, ed. Alessandro Falassi, 1–10. Albuquerque, NM: University of New Mexico Press.

Gălățan-Jieț, Dumitru. 2021. *Nedeia din poina muierii (1484–1947)*. Bucharest: Editura Etnologică.

Ghinoiu, Ion. 1999. *Calendarul țăranului român. Zile și mituri*. Bucharest: Editura Fundației.

Giurchescu, Anca. 2015. "Field Research in Svinica/Svinița, a Community Bridging Both Shores of the Danube: Comments across Four Decades." In *Dance, Field Research and Intercultural Perspectives: The Easter Customs in the Village of Svinița*, eds. Selena Rakočević and Liz Mellish, 23–46. Pančevo, Serbia: Kulturni centar Pančevo.

Giurchescu, Anca, and Sunni Bloland. 1995. *Romanian Traditional Dance: A Contextual and Structural Approach*. Mill Valley, CA: Wild Flower Press.

Guss, David M. 2000. *The Festive State: Race, Ethnicity, and Nationalism as Cultural Performance*. Berkeley, CA: University of California Press.

Lavric, Dumitru. 1976. *Folclor din județul Botoșani. Teatru popular*. Botoșani, Romania: Comitetul Județean de Cultură și Educație Socialistă.

Mellish, Elizabeth Sara. 2013. "Dancing through the City and Beyond: Lives, Movements and Performances in a Romanian Urban Folk Ensemble." PhD dissertation, University College London School of Slavonic and East European Studies, London.

Mellish, Liz. 2006. "The Romanian Căluș Tradition and Its Changing Symbolism as It Travels from the Village to the Global Platform." https://eliznik.me.uk/wp-content/uploads/artic les/The-Romanian-Calus-tradition-and-its-changing-symbolism-2006.pdf.

Mellish, Liz. 2015. "*Joc de pomană*: Dance for Commemorating the Dead in Svinița and Beyond." In *Dance, Field Research and Intercultural Perspectives: The Easter Customs in the Village of Svinița*, eds. Selena Rakočević and Liz Mellish, 61–90. Pančevo, Serbia: Kulturni centar Pančevo.

Mellish, Liz, and Nick Green. 2013. "Traditional Folk Dance Performance in the 21st Century: Romanian *Căluş* versus English Morris: Revivalist versus Ex-Communist?" In *Trapped in Folklore? Studies in Music and Dance Tradition and Their Contemporary Transformations*, eds. Drago Kunej and Urša Šivic, 81–99. Zurich: Lit Verlag.

Mellish, Liz, and Nick Green. 2020a. "The *Căluş* Ritual." *The Eliznik Pages*. https://eliznik.org.uk/the-calus-ritual/.

Mellish, Liz, and Nick Green. 2020b. "Crazy Week, the Disorganised and the Organised: *Fărşang* and 'Inverted' Weddings in the Banat Mountains." In *Music and Dance in Southeastern Europe: Migrations, Carnival, Sustainable Development*, eds. Tvrtko Zebec, Liz Mellish, and Nick Green, 132–144. Zagreb: International Council for Traditional Music Study Group on Music and Dance in Southeastern Europe, Institute of Ethnology and Folklore Research, ICTM Croatia National Committee.

Mellish, Liz, and Nick Green. 2020c. "Lower Danubian *Căluşari*." *The Eliznik Pages*. https://eliznik.org.uk/traditions-in-romania/traditional-dance/ceata-mens-group-dances/ritual-stick-dances/southern-romanian-calusari/.

Mellish, Liz, and Nick Green. 2020d. "Saints' Days Celebrations (*Ruga*) in Banat—Community Participation, Dance, Music and Good Times." *Acta Ethnografica Hungarica*, 65/1:395–410.

Mellish, Liz, and Nick Green. 2022a. "Saints' Days, and Village Days: Creating the Space for Community Events in Romanian Banat." In *Music and Dance in Southeastern Europe: Place, Space and Resistance. Seventh Symposium of the ICTM Study Group on Music and Dance in Southeastern Europe*, eds. Belma Oğul, Liz Mellish, and Nick Green, 169–177. Istanbul: Trabzon University State Conservatory, ICTM Study Group on Music and Dance in Southeastern Europe.

Mellish, Liz, and Nick Green. 2022b. "Men's Dances in Moldavian New Year Customs." *The Eliznik Pages*. https://eliznik.org.uk/traditions-in-romania/traditional-dance/ceata-mens-group-dances/ritual-stick-dances/mens-dances-in-moldavian-new-year-customs/.

Mureşianu, Iacob. 1901. "Romana." *Gazeta de Transilvania*, 64/22:1.

Nahachewsky, Andriy. 1995. "Participatory and Presentational Dance as Ethnochoreological Categories." *Dance Research Journal*, 27/1:1–15.

Nitsiakos, Vassilis. 2010. *On the Border: Transborder Mobility, Ethnic Groups and Boundaries along the Albanian–Greek Frontier*. Berlin: Lit Verlag.

Poduţ, Maria Mirela. 2019. "Obiceiuri din Valea Stejarului." *Memoria Ethnologică*, 72–73:148–161.

Pop, Mihai, and Rodica Zane. 1999. *Obiceiuri tradiţionale româneşti*. Bucharest: Editura Univers. First published 1976.

Popescu, Elena. 1997. *Brăneşti (sai) folclor*, Vol. 2. Bucharest: Comunitatea Bratstvo a Bulgarilor din România.

Quinn, Bernadette. 2009. "Festivals, Events and Tourism." *The SAGE Handbook of Tourism Studies*, eds. T. Jamal and M. Robinson, 483–583. London: Sage.

Rapport, Nigel, and Joanna Overing. 2000. *Social and Cultural Anthropology—The Key Concepts*. London: Routledge.

Schechner, Richard. 2004. *Performance Theory*. London: Routledge.

Strauti, Dan. 2020. "Fărşang apaţa." *La pas prin Braşov*. https://lapasprinbrasov.ro/farsang-apata/.

Ţîrcomnicu, Emil. 2021. *Inventarul naţional al elementelor vii de patrimoniu cultural imaterial—Hora de pomană*. Bucharest: Institutul naţional al patrimoniului. https://patrimoniu.ro/images/imaterial/pomana/hora-de-pomana.pdf. Accessed June 25, 2021.

Țîrcomnicu, Emil. 2022. *Inventarul național al elementelor vii de patrimoniu cultural imaterial—Practici culturale tradiționale asociate zilei de 24 Iunie: Sânzienele și Drăgaica.* Bucharest: Institutul național al patrimoniului. https://patrimoniu.ro/images/imaterial/sanzienele-dragaica/sanzienele-dragaica.pdf. Accessed June 29, 2022.

Turino, Thomas. 2008. *Music as Social Life: The Politics of Participation.* Chicago: University of Chicago Press.

Turner, Victor. 1984. *Celebration Studies in Festivity and Ritual.* Washington, DC: Smithsonian Institution Press.

UNESCO (United Nations Educational, Scientific and Cultural Organization). n.d. "The Căluș Ritual." https://ich.unesco.org/en/RL/clu-ritual-00090. Accessed June 14, 2022.

Magic and the Power of Words

CHAPTER 15

MAGIC IN HUNGARY
Verbal Charms, Benedictions, and Exorcisms

DÁNIEL BÁRTH

This chapter focuses on the textual and practice-based connections between church benedictions (prayers with the function of blessing), exorcisms (curse-type prayers serving to purge the object of a liturgical act of the influence of demonic powers), and peasant verbal charms (used for both positive and negative effects). It is based on manuscript and printed historical sources, ethnographic research, and my own fieldwork in the context of the Hungarian-language area. Among the diverse functions of verbal charms, benedictions, and exorcisms, I focus on their role in healing (mental and physical) illnesses. The aim of my analysis is to show the inseparability of historicity and the present, magic and religion, text and practice. I approach this topic in the pages ahead from a variety of different perspectives: history of science, historical anthropology, folklore, and the local sociocultural context.

HISTORICITY AND CONTEMPORARY RESEARCH IN HUNGARIAN FOLK BELIEFS AND POPULAR RELIGION

The research approach in this study, which interprets the historical context together with contemporary data at the level of a specific locality (village or town), is rather new in the field of ethnographic/folklore studies in central and eastern Europe. Even without a detailed overview of the history of science, it is evident that there are various interpretations and approaches to historicity in the Hungarian research tradition that are of particular interest here. The study of religious phenomena during the Romantic period in Hungary (1817–1872) was linked to the reconstruction of the Hungarian pagan "ancient religion" (i.e., before the adoption of Christianity in the eleventh century and its becoming the dominant religion). This "mythological" approach led researchers to see historicity in the folklore texts collected from the mid-nineteenth century onward as the unchanged, preserved, definitive imprints of the pagan Hungarian culture of a thousand years earlier. The history contained in the data of folk culture (in the absence of real medieval data) could only be placed in a relative chronology through analogies. Analogues have always been sought in the linguistic and cultural affinities of the Hungarian population identified during its Asian migrations (1200–896 BCE). Today, it is clear that the analogy approach of associating the "present" data of the so-called kindred peoples of the nineteenth century with the history and sociocultural characteristics of the Hungarian people a thousand years ago is a flawed one and is not viable in the absence of "hard" data. In addition, Géza Róheim, an influential scholar of psychoanalytic ethnology, who compared Hungarian folk beliefs and folk customs with those of the Balkan and neighboring Slavic and Germanic peoples, questioned the entire research concept in the first half of the twentieth century when he wrote, "It is no exaggeration to say, quite briefly, that Hungarian folk belief is Slavic folk belief" (1925:335). By this discovery, which surprised even the author at the time, he meant that the relevant data on Hungarian folklore were much more in line with the Slavic than with the Finno-Ugric and Turkish data, which were considered to be akin to the Hungarian people. The creation of constructs by scholars continued nonetheless and took spectacular forms, for instance, in the so-called parallels between the supposed ancient Hungarian shamanism and the present-day belief in the *táltos* (treasure-hunter and healer, born with special attributes and the gift of a trance technique) (cf. Pócs 2018).

At the same time, the documentary and interpretative investigations of contemporary phenomena of Hungarian popular belief and religion without the "mythological" agenda have been consolidated. A far greater emphasis than before is now laid on synchronic methods of investigation, meaning the broadest possible exploration of recent data using an analytic approach. Sample local investigations have been carried out in contemporary Hungary and, mostly after 1990, in ethnic Hungarian villages of the countries surrounding Hungary, primarily Romania (especially Transylvania and Moldavia) as well as parts of Ukraine, Slovakia, Serbia, Croatia, and Slovenia. This has proved particularly important because the Hungarian minority population living in neighboring countries has tended to preserve the archaic elements of its culture more than Hungarians living in Hungary. These regions represent ethnic peripheries of the Hungarian population, which constitute a kind of "cultural fossil" as modernizing tendencies which had gradually transformed traditional rural (peasant) culture in Hungary in the second half of the twentieth century often did not reach them until decades later. Similarly increased attention has been paid to exploring the folklore of Hungary's national and ethnic minorities.

It was in the form of texts arranged in archives that knowledge about traditional Hungarian popular belief reached the twenty-first century. A multitude of summaries and studies of particular areas were published based on this body of knowledge, which focused mostly on key issues of popular belief (worldview, supernatural beings, persons with supernatural abilities, space, and time) as well as on various aspects of popular medicine and popular "natural science." Owing to the systemic nature of popular belief, manifestations of magic occur in all areas of knowledge (separated by scholars as individual phenomena but closely intertwined in reality). This way, those who write about magic in the broader sense of the word with regard to a selected ethnic field find themselves facing an extremely complex and extensive problematic (Keszeg 2013).

As contemporary studies have gained ground, attitudes toward historicity have slowly changed. It was in the last decades of the twentieth century that scholars increasingly turned to ethnography, ethnology, and folklore studies that relied on genuine and authentic historical source data regarding the past thousand years of the Christian Hungarian population and interpreted them as part of the context of European cultural history.

The emphasis is therefore not on the reprojection of contemporary data but on the collection of real historical source data and its contextual analysis from a historical-anthropological perspective. Historical research is also committed to a local perspective: the sources show that the separation of fields of study by researchers is unjustifiable and unnecessary for the understanding of the historical reality of the past. The same is true of the forced separation of religion and magic (*religio, superstitio*) and religion and popular belief, which has always prevailed in the dominant discourses of power in historicity (mainly from a church-theological perspective) but is largely unintelligible in the subview of locality.

In both contemporary and historical studies of religion, the need to focus on locality has recently been growing. Borrowing primarily from cultural history studies (Christian 1981; Stewart 1991), the concept of local religion is used in a way that does not distinguish between subareas of formal religion, folk belief, popular religion, and ritual but rather examines them together at the focal point of local communities. In this way, the dimensions of magic and religion can be understood in the complexity of reality.

Magic in Hungary: General Historical Context

Although this chapter focuses on manifestations of popular/folk magic as they constitute a part of traditional culture, their development and overall system cannot be viewed independently, in a historical sense, from the manifestations of learned magic. Medieval source data testified primarily to the role of learned (elite) magic, while sources on folk magic did not become directly accessible until the transcripts of the witchcraft trials of the early modern period (sixteenth–eighteenth centuries). Works by the greatest figures of Renaissance Neo-Platonism were known mostly among the Hungarian aristocracy and higher nobility. For example, the English alchemist John Dee visited Hungary on several occasions. There is also evidence for the reception of Jesuits Martin del Rio and

Athanasius Kircher. One key area of learned magic concerned alchemy, divination from a ball, and magical healing practices. These were described and became widespread in manuscript form and, to a lesser extent, in printed books. Several verbal charms used by the peasantry in the early modern period originated in these texts on magic. Moreover, occultists of the eighteenth century and secret societies active in Hungary (the Rose Cross, the Freemasons, etc.) played a major part in inheriting the esoteric views of the latter Middle Ages (Szőnyi 2005; Szeghyova 2005; Wünsch 2006).

The other major area of learned magic was the "white magic" of the church, aimed toward positive results, which was present in practically all areas of human life in the Middle Ages. This form of magic was focused on help in farming (land cultivation, animal husbandry, fishing, hunting, and the handicrafts) as well as in the difficulties of the individual and collective life cycle (rites of passage, childbirth, disease, averting bewitchment, and fighting demonic possession). The magical aspect of folkloristic clerical practice, with its strong emphases on the agricultural lifestyle, manifests itself in the direct use of sacraments and sacramentals (cf. Thomas 1971; Scribner 1987). In the official, theological sense this wide array of blessings acts only indirectly, as a sign (*signa*), meaning that it is not the object (religious amulet) that helps but the divinity operating through the object. In practice, however, a whole line of religious amulets and sacramentals served direct magical purposes. In the sixteenth century, Protestantism (which was in Hungary relevant) attempted to make a sharp break with such practices. Certain known theories suggest that this gave rise to the emergence of rural "specialists," who in turn fell victim to anti-witchcraft persecution for the crime of practicing magic (*crimen magiae*). On the other hand, the persecution of witchcraft in itself pointed toward a wider goal of divesting the world of magic. Within the Roman Catholic Church, the spirit of the synodal decrees of Trento (1545–1563) gradually marginalized elements of medieval practice that were deemed superstitious. Nevertheless, the use of a broad range of sacramentals survived in the missionary activity of the monastic orders well into the sixteenth–seventeenth centuries and, indeed, in Hungary, went on into the mid-eighteenth century. A radical change in approach was brought about in this respect by the spirit of the Catholic Enlightenment in the second half of the eighteenth century (Bárth 2017; on the Catholic Enlightenment, see Lehner 2016).

Manifestations of lay and clerical magic naturally influenced rural ritual techniques and behaviors intended to influence the supernatural forces in service of a practical goal. Magic was mostly for positive effects, to promote success in agricultural and individual life (good fortune, prosperity, health). There are a few specific extant data testifying to the presence of malevolent (black) magic too (the Hungarian words *bű*, *báj*, and *bűbáj* come from pre-Christian times and probably referred to black magic.) One Byzantine historian recorded that in the twelfth century a Hungarian woman pointed her nude backside to the hostile Byzantine troops—which may be interpreted as an apotropaic gesture. Songs sung by the Hungarians with the intention of casting a spell on the enemy (*nefanda carmina*) probably also had a magical character. Early Hungarian graves contained pre-Christian protective amulets, and personal names from the tenth–twelfth centuries also preserve the remnants of several protective and taboo words of magic. The late Middle Ages are rather meager in data concerning popular magic. These mostly abound from the sixteenth century onward due to the proliferation of glossaries, Protestant pamphlets and sermons, and the documentation of witchcraft trials. The source material of witchcraft trials brings to life an entire hoard of village specialists and healers, along with a wide array of magical practices (analogous, sympathetic, rain magic, bewitchment and the aversion of bewitchment, binding and unbinding magic, etc.). Naturally, the most complete corpus on magic owes its origin to nineteenth–twentieth century collections of folk belief based on the work of systematizing Hungarian folk magic that was carried out (Dömötör 1982; Pócs 1990).

As regards certain areas of magic, alongside general collective knowledge and practice, particular importance is attached to the role of specialists who carried some kind of surplus knowledge and were seen as experts in one or another specific area. People with supernatural abilities constituted a communication channel between the spheres of this world and the other world. Even in the material of early modern witchcraft trials we see the emergence of a system of mediators within European practice (Pócs 1999). Within Hungarian research the two outstanding figures are the *táltos* and the witch, who often appear in the trials as each other's opponents. The male or female *táltos* is shown with positive attributes as his main functions in the early modern and modern periods were treasure-finding and healing (finding things hidden from humans, such as diseases). Their main characteristic is that they are born with certain special attributes (e.g., with teeth or in a sac) and possess the gift of a trance technique. The shamanic variants have obvious parallels among the south Slavs (*kresnik, zduhač*) and in northern Italy (*benandante*) (Klaniczay 1983). In Hungarian research, this figure was considered for a long time to be the relic of pagan shamanism. But constructs of this kind have come under increasing criticism in recent years (cf. Pócs 2018; Pócs 2019a). From the eighteenth century onward, data also start to appear testifying to the presence of village necromancers who often performed soul journeys to the other world using a trance technique (*rejtezés*) or in their dreams. In addition to them, village communities registered a line of other specialists (seers, clairvoyants, *garabonciás* or wizards, healers, midwives, sage shepherds, coach-drivers and hunters, rat-killing millers, etc.), whose figures are articulated in belief narratives (Pócs 1990). The healing aspect appears in the figures of the *táltos*, necromancer, and midwife alike.

Village healing specialists (*javas* [male healer], *javasasszony* [female healer]) carried the legacy of knowledge of the previous generations. In their healing they resorted to both magical and empirically based procedures and were acquainted with medicinal herbs, healing techniques (baths, steaming, smoking, rubbing, massage) as well as verbal charms. To promote healing they used various human secretions (saliva, mother's milk, urine, feces), animal substances (milk, butter, cobwebs from the stables, powdered animal bladder, dried frog, cantharis, or leeches), mineral and artificial materials (salt, rocks, incense, alcohol, gunpowder), as well as medicinal herbs. The healing practices of these specialists extended, in addition, to natural diseases, complaints, and illnesses caused by bewitchment (Hoppál 1990).

The other important negative figure of Hungarian folk belief is the witch (*boszorkány*). The real-life individuals (mostly women, sometimes men) who were the accused of sixteenth- to eighteenth-century witchcraft trials as a known part of European cultural history were victims of scapegoating mechanisms and stereotypical accusations. The historical *boszorkány* has demonic features (as a belief figure known for assaulting or "pressing" against people when they are sleeping at night) and powers of bewitchment. The figure of the witch is the amalgamation of several negative belief figures who existed earlier (e.g., the fairy [*tündér*], who has extensive parallels all over the Balkans, and the demons affecting women in childbed), which is how the witch became the most widespread representative of malevolent magic in the early modern period. It is a characteristic of Hungarian witchcraft trials that they are based primarily on a charge of bewitchment (*maleficium*), while the element of alliance with the devil, characteristic in other parts of Europe, is less apparent (Klaniczay and Pócs 2005; Klaniczay and Pócs 2006; Klaniczay and Pócs 2008; Klaniczay and Pócs 2017; Sz. Kristóf 2013).

Verbal Charms and Benedictions: Historical and Contemporary Contexts

The most important means of magic is the verbal charm (Kapaló et al. 2013; Pócs 2019b). The corpus of Hungarian verbal charms has recently been published in a two-volume modern, grand-scale edition (Pócs 2014; Ilyefalvi 2014). The verbal charm of the peasantry is mainly a traditional genre that is performed and transmitted orally.[1] The nineteenth- to twenty-first-century material has clear and obvious European parallels (Pócs 2019b). Éva Pócs arranges these texts into thirty-three groups, mostly on a functional basis. Using the magical and religious contexts as a basic frame of reference, she examines the textual connections shown between verbal charms (magical), prayers (religious), and clerical blessings and curses (magical-religious).

Moreover, Pócs establishes separate categories for the most widely known European epic charms (which include parallel stories as analogies about successful healings by Jesus and various saints) such as the text about the stumbling horse/donkey (second Merseburg charm, which was well known from the ninth century throughout Europe) or the encounter of the saint and the devil (2014). The former is mentioned in the earliest Hungarian record of verbal charms (Bagonya Charm, 1488) with the following text to heal *menyelés* (spraining of the horse's foot):

> Uronk Krisztus szamár hátán
> Jeruzsálemba ha ment,
> ő szamara megsántult vala.
> Azt meglátá Bódogasszony.

Az szót mondta vala:
"Fiam, Jézus Krisztus,
nám, megsántolt lovad."
Krisztus hallá,
az szót mondá:
"Én édes szilém-anyám,
megsántolt, mert lába kimenyelt."
"Én édes fiam, Jézus Krisztus,
poroncsolok te szent híreddel és te akaratodval,
hogy az te lovad megvigasszék." (Ilyefalvi 2014:41)

Our Lord Christ rode on a donkey
to Jerusalem
and his donkey went lame.
Our Lady saw this
and spoke these words:
"My son, Jesus Christ,
I see your mount has gone lame."
Christ heard this
and spoke these words:
"My dear mother,
it has gone lame, because it has sprained a foot."
"My dear son, Jesus Christ,
I can command by your holy reputation and by your will
your mount to recover."[2]

Texts from before 1850 have survived in various historical sources (e.g., healing books in the possession of aristocrats, witchcraft trial documentations, or anti-superstition texts). These testify to the mutual interaction between elite and popular cultures (Ilyefalvi 2014). A trait which historical and latter-day rural verbal charms share is that they aim to avert disease and to effect healing. Almost half of the Hungarian peasant charms have a clerical pre-formation in the Middle Ages (i.e., they closely parallel the textual stock of Latin benedictions and exorcisms).

Traces of the clerical practice of benedictions (which is part of the aforementioned "white magic") mostly survive in liturgical books (primarily books of rituals that were issued for priests). In the early modern period alongside the official books of rituals there were a number of semi-official books of benedictions in circulation. Some of these compilations had been published in Hungary, others abroad. Based on our sources, there emerges the use of a broad arsenal of benedictions in the clerical (and occasionally lay) practice of the sixteenth–eighteenth centuries. For the Middle Ages, however, the existence of the same can only be inferred from European analogies. Church benedictions offered assistance in the most varied areas of life, from farming due to natural disasters all the way to various diseases. The practice of benedictions was objectified in the form of the *sacramentalia*, whose varied use represents one of the best-known domains of popular religion (Bárth 2013).

The prayers of clerical benedictions were essentially of two types: besides prayers with the function of blessing (*benedictio*), equal importance was attributed to curse-type texts (*exorcismus*). This latter type of prayer mostly served to purge the object (goal) of a liturgical act (animals, plants, things, religious amulets, etc.) of the influence of demonic powers. Both types quoted biblical examples by way of reference. This way, blessings and curses complemented each other. Such "small exorcisms" were occasionally carried out on humans too, in cases of partial (*obsessio* or *circumsessio*) rather than general possession (*possessio*) or whenever a preventative act was required (Pócs 2001; Bárth 2010).

A model for the genetic interconnections between peasant verbal charms and clerical benedictions and exorcisms is elaborated in detail by Pócs, based on existing previous relevant scholarship over the 1980s (cf. Pócs 2002; Pócs 2013). For this endeavor Pócs relied on the widely known and acclaimed collection by Adolf Franz (1909), which presents the versatility of the medieval practice of benedictions using German and other western European sources. Obvious parallels between the texts demonstrate beyond a doubt the direction of these borrowings (from benedictions to later peasant verbal charms) but say little about the method and channels of this transmission.

Among the many convincing examples of the peasant use of the threefold structure of benedictions (which derives from the Holy Trinity) is a text of a verbal charm collected in 1962 in central Hungary (Zagyvarékas), which was recited during the baking of bread:

> Áldjon meg az Atyaisten,
> áldjon meg a Fiúisten,
> áldjon meg a Szentlélek Úristen.
> Süttessen meg az Atyaisten,
> süttessen meg a Fiúisten,
> süttessen meg a Szentlélek Úristen,
> hogy szép dombos legyél.
>
> May God the Father bless you,
> May God the Son bless you,
> May the Lord the Holy Ghost bless you.
> May God the Father bake you,
> May God the Son bake you,
> May the Lord the Holy Ghost bake you.
> So you come out risen nice and high.

Similarly, the textual link between storm-averting exorcisms and peasant verbal charms is striking. Also in Zagyvarékas, the following storm-averting verbal charm was collected:

> Oszlasson el az Atya,
> oszlasson el a Fiú,
> Oszlasson el a Szentlélek.

> May the Father disperse you,
> may the Son disperse you,
> may the Holy Ghost disperse you.
>
> (Pócs 2013:193)

The same reads in Latin in a 1697 manuscript of a book of Benedictine benedictions (Pannonhalma, Hungary) in an anti-storm ritual (*Exorcismus contra imminentem tempestatem fulgurum et grandinum*): *Destruat te Deus Pater+, destruat te Deus Filius+, destruat te Deus Spiritus Sanctus+* (Bárth 2010).

It is also common to send evil/harmful things (storms, disease, demons, etc.) to uninhabited, remote, and desolate places. The following is a Hungarian-language verbal charm collected in Gyimesközéplok (Harghita County, Romania) in the 1960s:

> Menj el, menj el te zápor jeges eső a kősziklára,
> ahol nem szántanak, nem vetnek,
> ahol a fekete kakasok nem kikerilnek,
> a fekete kutyák nem ugatnak,
> a fekete lovak nem nyeritnek,
> és ahol kovászos kenyérrel nem élnek.
>
> Go away, go away you storm and icy rain to the rocks
> where no one ploughs and no one sows,
> where no black cockerel crows,
> where no black dog barks,
> where no black horse neighs,
> where no leavened bread is eaten.
>
> (Pócs 2013:192)

Its parallel in the abovementioned late seventeenth-century Benedictine book of rituals for averting storms is *ut exeatis ab eis et eas dispergatis in locis sylvestribus et incultis, quatenus nocere non possint hominibus, animalibus, fructibus, herbis, arboribus, aut quibuscunque rebus humanis usibus deputatis* ("To leave them [i.e. you demons in the clouds] and send them [clouds] to the woods and desolate places, so that they cannot harm people, animals, fruits, plants, trees, or anything else that is of use to people") (Bárth 2010).

In order to gain clarity on the textual connections between verbal charms and clerical liturgical blessings and curses, it was necessary to explore the (official diocesan and particularly the semi-official monastic) source material of the intervening period (i.e., the sixteenth–eighteenth centuries). During this work I managed to isolate some 160 different orders of ritual with the purpose of benediction (*ordo*), which indicates that transmission (more accurately the translation from Latin to Hungarian) was still underway in this period (Bárth 2010). Particularly interesting for this subject area are the collections that were compiled with an expressly medical purpose, for example, the manuscript volume *Sacra arca benedictionum* held at the Benedictine monastery of Pannonhalma (1697), because they treated liturgical texts as a kind of medical prescription (Bárth 2019).

An example is the benediction against shivers (fever) from the Pannonhalma book of rituals:

> Contra febres
> Amygdala et nuccleos persicorum bene siccos conterat in pulveres. Deinde benedicat hoc modo.
> V. Adjutorium nostrum in nomine Domini R. Qui fecit coelum et terram V. Dominus vobiscum R. Et cum spiritu tuo
> Oremus
> Bene+dic Domine creaturam istam pulverum, ut sit remedium salutare generi humano, et praesta per invocationem sancti tui nominis, ut quicunque ex his pulveribus sumpserint vel gustaverint, liberentur a febribus tertianis, quartanis, quotidianis et continuis. Per Christum dominum nostrum. Amen.
> Aspergat aqua benedicta.
> Deinde dicat infirmo, ut in cuspide cultri (neque enim manu tangat) ter injiciat in poculum, bene comisceat in vino vel in aqua, quandoque febres invadunt, tunc summat bene se cooperiendo et se calide servando, schedulam febricitantem etiam collo alligando. (Bárth 2019)

> Against fever.
> Make a powder of crushed dry almonds and peach kernel. After that bless it in this way:
> Vers. Our helper in the name of the Lord. Resp. Who made heaven and earth. V. The Lord be with you. R. And with your spirit.
> Let us pray.
> Bless, O Lord, this creation of powders, that it may be a salutary remedy for the human race, and grant, through the invocation of your holy name, that whoever has taken or tasted of these powders may be freed from tertian, quartan, daily, and continuous fevers. Through Christ our Lord. Amen.
> Sprinkle the blessed water.
> Then tell the sick person to inject it three times into a cup with the point of a knife (for he must not touch it with his hand), mix it well in wine or water, sometimes fevers come on, then he sums up by covering himself well and keeping himself warm, also tying a card against fever around his neck.

Liturgical benediction is here mixed with the genre of the medical prescription book. The proper subject of the benediction against fever is a powder made of crushed dry almonds and peach kernel, upon which the priest asked God's blessing, so that the consumers of the powder be delivered of the "third day, fourth day, every day and continuous" fever. The priest had to explain to the patients to put, without making contact with their hands, three pinches of the powder in a cup, to mix with wine or water and, when the fever attacked, to drink of the liquid, under the covers and in the warmth, with the slip of paper to reduce fever placed around their neck. We know of numerous charms against the shivers and only slightly fewer benedictions with the same purpose. The prayer of the sixteenth-century Franciscan Saint Salvator of Horta (*Potentia Dei Patris + Sapientia Dei Filii + Virtus Spiritus + Sancti liberet te ab omni febre tertiana, quartana et continua, B. Salvatore orante pro te famulo suo, vel famula sua. + Dominus te N. benedicat, + ab infirmitate et ab omni malo te semper defendat, Amen.* "May the power of God the Father, the wisdom of God the Son, and the power of the Holy Spirit deliver you from every third, fourth, and continuous fever, Beatus Salvator praying for you his servant. May the Lord bless you, N., and protect you always from infirmity and from all evil, Amen.") was usually written on a slip of paper and hung around the neck of the patient. In terms of connections, it is most informative to mention the third-day, fourth-day, and daily fevers (cf. Pócs 2014:415). The importance of the medical function is enhanced by the fact that the majority of charms, analogous to benedictions and exorcisms, are texts aimed at expelling or cursing disease demons (while the other portion is related to driving away storms).

Another unique example is a set of eighteenth-century medicinal prayer formulas found in the registry books of a small southern Hungarian village along the Danube called Sükösd. Within the practice of benedictions used by the church to cure diseases from natural causes or bewitchment, an instructive and unique group of data is constituted by the prayer formulas from Sükösd. These were recorded in the registries of marriages and baptisms performed in the 1720s in this village (Sávai 1997). On the level of monographs and manuals, almost nothing is known about vicar Emericus Rády, who may well have been the first lay priest at the head of a parish originally established by the Franciscans. Although the Franciscan connection to these prayers is fairly obvious, the parish itself offers very little documentation for this period, nor do the sources of the Franciscan order provide us with sufficient information concerning the healing activities pursued here. From the registry itself it seems that Rády was parish priest at Sükösd between 1725 and 1728, so it must be in this interval that he committed these records to paper. Three relatively short prayers appear on the very last page of the first volume of the baptism registry of Sükösd (1711–1744), while the majority, another fourteen prayer formulas, are found in the second half of the first registry book of marriages (1720–1783).

Today it is hard to ascertain why the texts were preserved in these registry books. Possibly at this early date these were the only books available at a newly founded parish. If at this time a member of the clergy decided to record a text and wished to do so not on a slip of paper, which was a scarce and vulnerable article, but rather in a bound volume or *protocollum*, this must have been because he clearly wanted to preserve it for himself and for posterity. In such a case he even had to reckon with the disgrace of his clerical superiors possibly reprimanding him during their visit for irregular use of the volumes otherwise intended for registry purposes. In spite of all such seemingly plausible explanations, the remarkable and unusual position of these prayers remains suspicious. Quite recently, when I first held the originals of these volumes in my hands in the archives of the Archbishopric of Kalocsa, it was clearly visible that the texts in question had been inserted as extra leaves. The last page of the baptism registry had very clearly been glued in *post factum*, although it is hard to tell when. The prayers occupy the top of the page, while on the bottom we find registry entries with no dates. The three prayers included here may be found, in the same order, among the entries of the marital registry. Two sheets of paper of a noticeably different hue were glued in among the pages of a registry of marriages from 1777, and these four pages contain only prayers. Both of our sources were written with handwriting that shows great similarity with vicar Rády's own registry entries. My suspicion is that the formulas that Rády originally wrote on slips of paper or separate sheets were later incorporated into the registry book by himself or one of his successors.

Let us now take a closer look at the texts themselves. As regards their function, they mostly offer healing for common human ailments and diseases: cures for nosebleeds (*a fluxu sanguinis e naribus*), fever (*contra febres*), toothaches (*contra dolores dentium*), and headaches (*contra capitis dolores*). These everyday maladies are also regularly featured in medicinal literature. By contrast, texts against bewitchment (*contra maleficia*), rabies (*pro hominibus rabbiae infectis*), babies' crying (*contra fletum puerorum*), and the seduction of young women (*contra infestationem puellarum*) represent a separate domain.

One general characteristic of these records is that they are short—shorter than benediction (*ordo*) sequences tend to be. There is only one text that looks like an *ordo* of this kind: the prayer against headaches, which starts with the customary antiphony and *responsorium*.[3] If the practitioners considered these sections important in this case, why did they not feel the same way in other cases? This is probably because these texts were not used in the form of a blessing, in full priestly habit, as part of an official rite, but rather in the direct coercive (magical) form characteristic of verbal charms (cf. Pócs 2014). Although in the case of some texts the connection seems closer to some bygone (semi-official) clerical practice of benediction, on other occasions it is less obvious where the charms appear, with one exception: simplified texts taken from the context of the original *ordo* and shaped to be far more to the point. Among the three texts for reducing fever we find the above-mentioned St. Salvator of Horta prayer, which appears in a few books of benedictions with Franciscan ties as well as in a number of contemporary healing books (Sávai 1997:216; Ilyefalvi 2014:118). A much-simplified version with no reference to any specific saint offers an alternative solution to lower fever. Similar to the Salvator prayer, this contains the phrase "against three days', four days' and daily fever," which is known to survive through the transmission of peasant charms. Some close parallels to these two texts were also incorporated in the recently published textual corpus of Hungarian historic charms (Ilyefalvi 2014). The third text to reduce fever, on the other hand, remains without a parallel so far, even though the epic biblical beginning referring to Jesus's healing Simon and the act of repelling trouble by direct reference to this clearly show the character of a charm.

Contra febres. Surgens Jesus de Synagoga introivit in domum Simonis, socius (!)[4] autem Simonis tenebatur magnis febribus et rogaverunt illum pro eo (!) et stans super illum (!) imperavit febri et statim dimisit sic liberet te famulum N. per merita passionis Suae et B[eatae] M[ariaeg V[irginis] et beati patris nostri Adalberti. Amen.

Against fever. Rising from the Synagogue, Jesus entered the house of Simon, but Simon's fellow (mother-in-law) was seized with a great fever, and they begged him for him (her), and standing over him (her), he commanded the fever and immediately let him go. Thus may the servant N. free you through the merits of his passion and that of the Blessed Virgin Mary and of our blessed father Adalbert. Amen.

To render the mixed character of the text even more emphatic, they appended a clause to the end of the charm which refers to the suffering of Christ and the merits of the Virgin Mary and St. Adalbert. The text to counter nosebleeds found at the head of these records in the registry book also has parallels in the historical collection. The text to lessen toothache starts with an epic introduction about a conversation taking place at the gates of Jerusalem between Jesus and Peter, who has a toothache. The charm then goes on to refer to and emulate this in order to ameliorate the pains of the sufferer at hand.

Contra dolores dentium. Jesus in porta Jerusalem stabat Petrus et multum contristatus dentium in super veniens Jesus, dicitque Petro quid habes et Petrus respondens, D[omi]ne fluxu affligor dolore dentium, dicit ei Jesus, signa te Petre †. Signa tu D[omi]ne sicut signasti 5 panes in deserto rogo te D[omi]ne qui cumque hoc fecerit vel super se portaverit dolor dentium ei non noceat nec offendat. Et dixit ei Jesus, fiat sicut postulasti In nomine D[omi]ni † Amen.

Against toothaches. Jesus was standing at the gate of Jerusalem. Peter came up with a great deal of pain in his teeth. Jesus said to Peter, "What have you?" And Peter answers: "O Lord, I have a great pain of my tooth." Jesus said to him: "I sign you, Peter." Sign O Lord, as you signed the 5 breads in the desert, I beg you, O Lord, that whoever does this, or bears upon himself, the pain of his teeth may not harm him or offend him. And Jesus said to him, let it be done as you asked. In the name of the Lord. Amen.

In order to confirm the verbal charm nature of it, the following is a peasant verbal charm collected 250 years later (around 1980) in Doroszló (now in Serbia), which does not focus on a toothache but on pain in the lower back (in Hungarian, *szegedés*) in a similar epic framework:

> Mikor Jézus Krisztus a Jordán vize mellett járt,
> nagy sírás és jajgatás hallatszott a pusztába.
> Kérdi Jézus Pétertől:
> "Péter, micsoda sírás és rívás hallatszik?"
> Mondja Péter:

"Uram, Jézus Krisztus,
fájdalmak vannak az oldalukba,
azért sírnak, rínnak."
Akkó mondta Jézus:
"Eredj Péter, és tedd rá bűnös kezedet,
és leheld rá bűnös lelkedet,
hogy gyógyuljanak meg a Jézus, Mária, Szent József nevében!"

When Jesus Christ walked by the waters of the Jordan,
there was great weeping and wailing in the desert.
Jesus asks Peter:
"Peter, what is this weeping and wailing?"
Peter says:
"Lord Jesus Christ,
they have pains in their sides,
Therefore they weep and wail."
Jesus said:
"Go, Peter, and lay your sinful hands on them,
and breathe your sinful breath upon them,
that they may be healed in the name of Jesus, Mary, St. Joseph!"

(Pócs 2014:802)

The references of the prayer against bewitchment to the Franciscan saints (St. Francis of Assisi, St. Bonaventura, St. Anthony of Padova, and others) further strengthen the Franciscan ties to the entire collection, finally rendered indubitable by references in the text to St. Anthony and St. Salvator against seducing young women (Sávai 1997; Pócs 2014; Ilyefalvi 2014).

With regard to the Hungarian benedictions of the early modern period and the historic and contemporary corpuses of charms, we may safely declare that the Sükösd formulas represent a transitional genre from a number of points of view. They form a bridge between the "semi-official" benedictions reserved for priestly and monastic use and the prayers which can also be performed by laypeople. But they are likewise a halfway house between clerical liturgical texts (benedictions, orations) and the early modern charms used by several (elite and rural) sociocultural groups. We are aware that every one of the textual types mentioned has played a considerable part in the historical development of the peasant charms collected over the nineteenth and twentieth centuries. It has been a long-standing research question what the channels may have been that mediated the originally Latin text of benedictions and prayers to the vernacular practice of the lower strata of society. The present piece of eighteenth-century source data is particularly instructive in that here we see evidence of an originally liturgical body of text being used by the clergy, friars, and the lower priesthood and the transformation of its form and content still in the Latin language in the direction of charms (Pócs 2013; Pócs 2014; Bárth 2010).

Historical and Local Aspects of Exorcism

The more widely known type of exorcism is a liturgical act prevalent in both Western and Eastern Christianity, within which, following the New Testament example of Christ and the apostles, representatives of the clergy perform actions against possession by the devil. The practice of exorcism dates back to the very earliest decades of Christianity. From the third all the way to the late twentieth century, exorcism also played a distinguished part in the liturgy of baptism. The "grand" or "solemn" exorcism, which handles the demonic possession of humans, was carried out less frequently than benediction and only in the most justified cases during the early and middle parts of the modern period. The name indicates not only the number of exorcistic prayers and the length of the ritual but also the gravitas and significance of the job at hand. Interpretations of demonic possession were much disputed even in the late Middle Ages, while in the early modern period, after the onslaught of rationalism and the Enlightenment, the position of extreme skepticism also appeared on the scene. One point with which the clerical leadership was in accord throughout the period was that such ceremonies should only be carried out by the most competent priests, endowed with a sober lifestyle and staunchness of character. From the sixteenth century onward it became common practice in the Western church that exorcism should not be carried out except with the knowledge and approval of the leading clerical authorities (Pócs 2001; Bárth 2020).

As far as the liturgy of the solemn exorcism is concerned, sources are regrettably few and far between with regard to Hungary. We may assume on the basis of European monographs that readers of this kind may well have been in common circulation in Hungary, too, in the Middle Ages; but they seem not to have survived. The first regular *ordo* of exorcism was published in Hungary by primate Péter Pázmány in 1625 as the closing chapter to the Esztergom book of rituals (*Ritale Strigoniense*), which follows verbatim the text of the *Roman Ritual* published in 1614. The same was adopted later on by compilers of the books of rituals of other dioceses. Since the liturgy of exorcism underwent no particular change within even the *Roman Ritual* until as late as the end of the twentieth century, these regulations and prayer texts remained valid in Hungary for almost four centuries. In day-to-day practice, however, we find data testifying to the parallel use of several alternative manuals of exorcism (e.g., Girolamo Menghi's *Flagellum daemonum* and *Fustis daemonum*; see Mengus 1697a; Mengus 1697b). If printed copies of the famous sixteenth- to seventeenth-century Western European manuals did circulate in Hungary, then in the best of cases we find out about this from the book inventories of parishes and monasteries. Allusions also exist to manuscript books of exorcism circulating in handwritten copies. Naturally, all of this is closely related to the question of sources regarding the practice of "semi-official" clerical blessings and curses in the early modern period (Bárth 2020).

The literature of historical anthropology and the history of mentalities concerning the early modern period, in harmony with the relevant conclusions of clerical history, handles it as fact that cases of demonic possession peaked in terms of frequency in the sixteenth–seventeenth centuries, alongside the related instances of clerical exorcism (Almond 2004; Ferber 2004; de Waardt et al. 2005; Levack 2013; Young 2016). In western Europe the age of spectacular mass-scale exorcisms practically ended, with a few exceptions, before the eighteenth century set in. Close connections between possession by the devil and the witchcraft trials of the period have also been proven amply by sizable monographs (cf. Clark 1997). What we can point out so far based on Hungarian witchcraft trial documentation is that interconnections between witchcraft trials and concrete individual cases of exorcism can hardly be detected in the period. There are also no data testifying to mass-scale acts of exorcism in Hungary either in the sixteenth–seventeenth centuries or from the 18th century. There have been one or two microhistorical case studies based on the documentation of a few isolated cases (Bárth 2018; Bárth 2020).

Our sources speak little to this subject matter apart from seventeenth-century missions in Transylvania and the Turkish occupied territories. Franciscan and, particularly, Jesuit missions were more than willing to incorporate the weapon of one of their "miracles"—that of exorcism—into their arsenal of proselytizing and pastoral duty. Reports, letters, and annual records speak of a multitude of successful acts of exorcism. The faculty of carrying out exorcism functioned as an important means of converting Protestants and schismata and convincing the hesitant. The holy water and various holy icons and relics used for healing (St. Ignatius, St. Charles of Borrome) and Agnus Dei wax medals were highly popular even with the occupying Turks. Jesuits carried out exorcism not only in the seventeenth century but even in the eighteenth. Besides an extensive practice of benediction among the Jesuits, we have data from the eighteenth century which show that the fathers of the order of Jesus were often sought out as experts in the case of various instances of exorcism by the lay authorities (Bárth 2020).

After the spectacular exorcistic practice of the Middle Ages, tied in with saints and shrines, the early modern period brought along the emergence of a group of a select few specialists of exorcism endowed with unique capabilities, whose local popularity differed widely, and ever more widely during this period, given the way in which they were appraised by the higher clergy (Midelfort 2005). Such charismatic personalities occur in Hungarian sources, too. The life and activity of one Rochus Szmendrovich, a Croatian Franciscan who lived in the middle of the eighteenth century in Sombor, southern Hungary (now Serbia), has latterly become the subject of a separate monograph (Bárth 2020). His figure and history are particularly instructive because the conflict that emerged between him and the church leadership at the same time encapsulates the clash between the monastic practice which was medieval in character, close to the people, and ready to serve the demands of the believers (i.e., based on the frequent and successful use of an arsenal of benedictions with the purpose of healing), on the one hand, and the "Catholic Enlightenment," on the other. In his person, the "strong priest" (i.e., a true problem-solving specialist) was acting in opposition to the anomalies of the workings of the community (the "possessed" whom the lay legal system had failed to handle). Father Rochus extended his exorcistic services beyond the Catholic south Slavs to the Orthodox Christian Serbs because, driven by the hope for recovery, the latter sought out in great numbers the "strong priest" of another religion. What Szmendrovich expected in return for his services was that these possessed women and their families convert to the Roman Catholic faith. At this point we witness a kind of reciprocal antecedent to the practice prevalent in Transylvania in the late twentieth century and even today, when Catholic (and Protestant) Hungarians turn to Romanian *călugări* (orthodox monks) and priests so that they may resolve any bewitchment they are suffering from (Keszeg 2013). The notion of the strong priest and the practice of service that he provides emerge here in a reversed denominational structure.

In the nineteenth–twentieth centuries the Roman Catholic practice of exorcism retreated to continue within the walls of the monasteries and sacristies, and Hungarian sources reveal no further noisy scandals. Popular notions of possession gained ground and raised the attention in the subject area with folklore studies (Pócs 2003). Parallel to this, the last few years have also seen continued fieldwork aimed at exploring the witchcraft notions of a particular community (see Klaniczay and Pócs 2017; Pócs 2002). The basic forms of demonic possession recur in beliefs related to witchcraft. Incubus and succubus demons appear in the widespread form of the devil's lover known as a *lidérc*. Demonic (and divine) possession can be interpreted as a type of supernatural communication which is manifested in attaining an altered state of mind.

It is also a relevant part of the present-day context of exorcism that there are a number of neo-Protestant denominations where it still plays an outstanding role in religious practice. We have recently had particularly good analyses of the relationship between the Romanian, Romani, and Hungarian (Csángó) Pentecostal communities in Moldova and exorcism (Peti 2020). As far as Roman Catholics are concerned, its practice has intensified as a result of the charismatic movement, even if Hungary never experienced the kind of "renaissance of exorcism" that Italy, Poland, or certain communities in the United States saw in the early decades of the twenty-first century. In Hungary, the general public considers such practice medieval and relegates it to the world of horror movies (cf. Scala 2012). Nonetheless, each Catholic diocese has its own officially nominated exorcist priest, who carries out the ceremony, when necessary, relying on the official book of ritual issued by Pope John Paul II around the turn of the millennium. At the same time, the followers of the charismatic movement gather for occasions of "releasing prayer," where believers pray collectively for the bodily and mental recovery of their brother or sister standing in front of them (among them), through the departure of the possessing, harmful entities (demons causing disease, dependence, bad habits, homosexuality, etc.) (cf. Csordas 1994; Csordas 1997). Exploring such practices, some of which are also present in Hungary, is still a job waiting to be carried out.

Finally, I would like to summarize some observations on contemporary twenty-first-century forms of Roman Catholic purposeful prayer, rooted in the Catholic charismatic movements that gained strength in the last decades of the twentieth century.

I made my own observations at a so-called healing deliverance Mass in a monastic church in the Budapest area in 2017. Far be it from me to be anachronistic or ahistorical, but while writing my book on the exorcist of Sombor, attending these ceremonies and having several conversations (interviews) with the monk who invented, promoted, and ran the event, I noticed a whole series of parallels with pre-Enlightenment church practice. In addition to the purposefulness of the now two-decade-old local practice of free-attendance healing deliverance Masses on the third Friday of every month, the direct, effective, problem-focused, and problem-solving nature of the "informal" group prayer practice that followed, which lasted two to three times longer than the Mass and into the night, was particularly unexpected (and instructive) for me. The great difference of contemporary Catholic healing prayer compared to historical patterns is that the role of the priest is diminished (apart from celebrating Mass, it is limited to confession, communion, and, if necessary, non-public exorcism), and instead of the sidelined priest, the majority of the healing-deliverance "services" are provided by laypeople in the sanctuary or sacristy of the church. Believers seeking help come to a prayer group and quietly share their problems, and praying in groups of three or four increases the effectiveness of the prayer. Masses are also sometimes attended by modern Catholic lay religious leaders (popular targets for individual healing prayers as "strong men"), who give testimonies to the whole community before the small prayer group and after the Mass. The preacher invites those present to testify publicly whether they have felt any improvement in their physical problems or illnesses during the Mass. He says a long prayer, in which, one by one, he asks for the healing of the human organs and their deliverance from demonic powers (the evil spirits that cause sin). These prayers show a close textual correlation with the historical exorcism texts, which perform the same exorcism of bewitchments (*maleficia*) and possessing demons, one by one, body part by body part. I was present for the Eucharistic blessing (performed by a "strong" missionary guest priest), which is of course not officially part of the Catholic liturgy, especially not in this form, where the believers were blessed one by one, with the monstrance held near their heads, and some of them even leaned back ("filled with the Holy Spirit") and were caught by the helpers who were ordered behind each of them.

Among the main features of the healing deliverance Masses and prayer meetings, I see a significant difference from the historical examples in the freedom of the prayer texts, in their linguistic informality. The possibilities offered by the World Wide Web and social media have also led to the emergence of distance healing in this field, where prayer groups, bypassing physical contact, are virtually connected at a prearranged time and place, also for predetermined, concrete (healing) purposes. At the same time, I see a close parallel in the pathological approach to disease, which focuses on the medicinal importance of repentance and spiritual dialogue. In both the exorcist from Sombor and the modern charismatic group healing practice, the religious experience and practical application of the following flowcharts can be traced: sins → demons → disease; repentance → deliverance → healing (Bárth 2021).

Conclusion

The above analysis provides a clear demonstration of the close connection between historical and contemporary perspectives on the phenomena of magic and religion. The data available to ethnographers/folklorists through oral collections are rooted in complex and intricate historical processes. Focusing on the relationship between verbal charms as an oral instrument of magic and the practice of the clerical blessings and curses, this chapter uses historical anthropology to focus on the elemental human needs behind texts and practices. The "needs" of the believers and the church–secular "services" are reactivating what seem to be quick and effective solutions, regardless of the times. This is particularly true of the question of healing illnesses, for which even the texts of blessings (benedictions and exorcisms), which come in religious guise, contain the immediacy and magical coerciveness which characterize verbal charms. The blessing of the sick or of objects (religious medicines) that represent a cure for them, if the emphasis is on the role of the priest or layman who blesses and not on "divine grace," results in texts and practices of a similar character to those that exemplify verbal charms.

Notes

1. It is only recently that research publications on popular booklets have begun to appear containing verbal charms collected in Hungarian communities in Romania (cf. Takács 2018).
2. This and all subsequent translations (unless noted) are mine.
3. On the structure of benediction ceremonies, cf. Bárth 2010:91–100.
4. Instead of *socrus* (mother-in-law).

Works Cited

Almond, Philip C. 2004. *Demonic Possession and Exorcism in Early Modern England: Contemporary Texts and Their Cultural Contexts*. Cambridge: Cambridge University Press.

Bárth, Dániel. 2010. *Benedikció és exorcizmus a kora újkori Magyarországon*. Fontes Ethnologiae Hungaricae IX. Budapest–Pécs: L'Harmattan–PTE Néprajz-Kulturális Antropológia Tanszék.

Bárth, Dániel. 2013. "Benediction and Exorcism in Early Modern Hungary." In *The Power of Words: Studies on Charms and Charming in Europe*, eds. James Kapaló, Éva Pócs, and William Ryan, 199–209. Budapest–New York: CEU Press.

Bárth, Dániel. 2017. "Demonology and Catholic Enlightenment in Eighteenth-Century Hungary." In *Witchcraft and Demonology in Hungary and Transylvania*, eds. Gábor Klaniczay and Éva Pócs, 319–347. London: Palgrave Macmillan.

Bárth, Dániel. 2018. "Exorcism and Sexuality: The 'Thick Description' of an 18th-century Transylvanian Catholic Priest's Transgression." *Acta Ethnographica Hungarica* 63/1:107–128.

Bárth, Dániel. 2019. "Benedictions Serving Early Modern Benedictine Medicine." In *The Magical and Sacred Medical World*, ed. Éva Pócs, 246–264. Newcastle: Cambridge Scholars Publishing.

Bárth, Dániel. 2020. *The Exorcist of Sombor: The Mentality of an Eighteenth-Century Franciscan Friar*. New York–London: Routledge.

Bárth, Dániel. 2021. "Ráimádkozás pappal és pap nélkül. Történeti és jelenkori római katolikus alakzatok." In *Imák a népi és a populáris kultúrában: Tanulmányok Erdélyi Zsuzsanna születésének 100. évfordulója alkalmából*, eds. Krisztina Frauhammer, Sándor Horváth, and Ildikó Landgraf, 95–111. Budapest: BTK Néprajztudományi Intézet–Magyar Néprajzi Társaság.

Christian, William A. 1981. *Local Religion in Sixteenth-Century Spain*. Princeton, NJ: Princeton University Press.

Clark, Stuart. 1997. *Thinking with Demons: The Idea of Witchcraft in Early Modern Europe*. Oxford: Oxford University Press.

Csordas, Thomas J. 1994. *The Sacred Self: A Cultural Phenomenology of Charismatic Healing*. Berkeley, CA: University of California Press.

Csordas, Thomas J. 1997. *Language, Charisma, and Creativity: The Ritual Life of a Religious Movement*. Berkeley, CA: University of California Press.

de Waardt, Hans, Jürgen Michael Schmidt, H. C. Erik Midelfort, Sönke Lorenz, and Dieter R. Bauer, eds. 2005. *Dämonische Besessenheit: Zur Interpretation eines kulturhistorischen Phänomens*. Bielefeld: Verlag für Regionalgeschichte.

Dömötör, Tekla. 1982. *Hungarian Folk Beliefs*. Budapest: Corvina.

Ferber, Sarah. 2004. *Demonic Possession and Exorcism in Early Modern France*. London–New York: Routledge.

Franz, Adolph. 1909. *Die kirchlichen benediktionen im mittelalter I–II*. Freiburg im Breisgau: Herder.

Hoppál, Mihály. 1990. "Népi gyógyítás." In *Magyar néprajz*, ed. Tekla Dömötör, Vol. VII, 693–724. Budapest: Akadémiai Kiadó.

Ilyefalvi, Emese. 2014. *Ráolvasások: Gyűjtemény a történeti forrásokból (1488–1850)*. Budapest: Balassi Kiadó.

Kapaló, James, Éva Pócs, and William Ryan, eds. 2013. *The Power of Words: Studies on Charms and Charming in Europe*. Budapest–New York: CEU Press.

Keszeg, Vilmos. 2013. *Hiedelmek, narratívumok, startégiák*. Cluj-Napoca: Kriza János Néprajzi Társaság.

Klaniczay, Gábor. 1983. "Benandante–kresnik–zduhač–táltos. Samanizmus és boszorkányhit érintkezési pontjai Közép-Európában." *Ethnographia* 94:116–134.

Klaniczay, Gábor, and Éva Pócs, eds. 2005. *Communicating with the Spirits*. Demons, Spirits, Witches 1. Budapest–New York: CEU Press.

Klaniczay, Gábor, and Éva Pócs, eds. 2006. *Christian Demonology and Popular Mythology*. Demons, Spirits, Witches 2. Budapest–New York: CEU Press.

Klaniczay, Gábor, and Éva Pócs, eds. 2008. *Witchcraft Mythologies and Persecutions*. Demons, Spirits, Witches 3. Budapest–New York: CEU Press.

Klaniczay, Gábor, and Éva Pócs, eds. 2017. *Witchcraft and Demonology in Hungary and Transylvania*. Palgrave Historical Studies in Witchcraft and Magic. London: Palgrave Macmillan.

Lehner, Ulrich L. 2016. *The Catholic Enlightenment: The Forgotten History of a Global Movement*. Oxford: Oxford University Press.

Levack, Brian P. 2013. *The Devil within: Possession and Exorcism in the Christian West.* New Haven, CT–London: Yale University Press.
Mengus, Hieronymus. 1697a. *Flagellum daemonum, exorcismos terribiles, potentissimos et efficaces, remediaque probatissima, ac doctrinam singularem in malignos spiritus expellendos, facturasque et maleficia fuganda de obsessis corporibus complectens, cum suis benedictionibus, et omnibus requisitis ad eorum expulsionem. Accessit postremo pars secunda, quae Fustis daemonum inscribitur . . .* Venetiis: apud Paulum Balleonium.
Mengus, Hieronymus. 1697b. *Fustis daemonum, adjurationes formidabiles, potentissimas et efficaces in malignos spiritus fugandos de oppressis corporibus humanis. Ex sacrae apocalypsis fonte, variisque sanctorum patrum auctoritatibus haustus complectens . . .* Venetiis: apud Paulum Balleonium.
Midelfort, Eric H. C. 2005. *Exorcism and Enlightenment: Johann Joseph Gassner and the Demons of Eighteenth-Century Germany.* New Haven, CT–London: Yale University Press.
Peti, Lehel. 2020. *Krisztus ajándéka van bennünk: Pünkösdizmus moldvai román, roma és csángó közösségekben.* Budapest: Balassi.
Pócs, Éva. 1990. "Néphit." In *Magyar néprajz*, ed. Tekla Dömötör, Vol. VII, 527–692. Budapest: Akadémiai Kiadó.
Pócs, Éva. 1999. *Between the Living and the Dead: A Perspective on Witches and Seers in the Early Modern Age.* Budapest–New York: CEU Press.
Pócs, Éva. 2001. "Démoni megszállottság és ördögűzés a közép-kelet-európai népi hiedelemrendszerekben." In *Demonológia és boszorkányság Európában*, ed. Éva Pócs, 137–198. Studia ethnologica Hungarica 1. Budapest: L'Harmattan.
Pócs, Éva. 2002. *Magyar néphit közép- és kelet-Európa határán. Válogatott tanulmányok I.* Budapest: L'Harmattan.
Pócs, Éva. 2003. "Megszállottságjelenségek, megszállottságrendszerek. Néhány közép-kelet-európai példa." *Népi kultúra–Népi társadalom* 21:211–271.
Pócs, Éva. 2013. "Church Benedictions and Popular Charms in Hungary." In *The Power of Words: Studies on Charms and Charming in Europe*, eds. James Kapaló, Éva Pócs, and William Ryan, 165–197. Budapest–New York: CEU Press.
Pócs, Éva. 2014. *Ráolvasások: Gyűjtemény a legújabb korból (1851–2012).* Budapest: Balassi Kiadó.
Pócs, Éva. 2018. "The Hungarian Táltos and the Shamanism of Pagan Hungarians." *Acta Ethnographica Hungarica* 63:149–196.
Pócs, Éva. 2019a. "The Sieve and the Drum in the Labyrinth of Mythological Reconstructions." In *Present and Past in the Study of Religion and Magic*, eds. Ágnes Hesz and Éva Pócs, 197–212. Budapest: Balassi.
Pócs, Éva, ed. 2019b. *Charms and Charming: Studies on Magic in Everyday Life.* Ljubljana: ZRC SAZU.
Róheim, Géza. 1925. *Magyar néphit és népszokások.* Budapest: Athenaeum.
Sávai, János. 1997. *Missziók, mesterek, licenciátusok. Missziós dokumentumok Magyarországról és a hódoltságról II/I.* Szeged: Agapé.
Scala, Monika. 2012. *Der exorzismus in der Katholischen Kirche: Ein liturgisches ritual zwischen film, mythos und realität.* Regensburg: Verlag Friedrich Pustet.
Scribner, Robert W. 1987. *Popular Culture and Popular Movements in Reformation Germany.* London–Ronceverte, WV: Hambledon Press.
Stewart, Charles. 1991. *Demons and the Devil: Moral Imagination in Modern Greek Culture.* Princeton, NJ: Princeton University Press.

Szeghyova, Blanka, ed. 2005. *The Role of Magic in the Past: Learned and Popular Magic, Popular Beliefs and Diversity of Attitudes*. Bratislava: Pro Historia.

Sz. Kristóf, Ildikó. 2013. "Witch-Hunting in Early Modern Hungary." In *The Oxford Handbook of Witchcraft in Early Modern Europe and Colonial America*, ed. Brian P. Levack, 334–355. Oxford: Oxford University Press.

Szőnyi, György Endre. 2005. "The Occult Sciences in Early Modern Hungary in a Central European Context." In *The Role of Magic in the Past: Learned and Popular Magic, Popular Beliefs and Diversity of Attitudes*, ed. Blanka Szeghyova, 29–44. Bratislava: Pro Historia.

Takács, György. 2018. *Az én lelkemmel elfújlak. . . . A magyarcsügési ráolvasófüzetek*. Budapest: L'Harmattan.

Thomas, Keith. 1971. *Religion and the Decline of Magic*. New York: Scribner.

Wünsch, Thomas, ed. 2006. *Religion und magie in ostmitteleuropa. Spielräume theologischer normierungsprozesse in spätmittelalter und früher neuzeit*. Berlin: Lit Verlag.

Young, Francis. 2016. *A History of Exorcism in Catholic Christianity*. London: Palgrave Macmillan.

CHAPTER 16

INVERTED BEHAVIOR IN SOUTH SLAVIC RITUAL AND MAGIC

MARIA VIVOD

A black cat crosses the street, and in order to counteract the bad luck that this infers, passersby walk backward for a few steps: some take three steps, some just one; what is important is to take steps backward. Some people even spit once or twice on the side, making a loud sound when pronouncing "ppp!" ("p" being the onomatopoeic sound of spitting). Someone visits a newborn for the first time and, in awe, states that the little baby is so "ugly!" (Serbian[1]: *ružan, gadan*) or unfailingly insists that the newborn is "foul, foul, foul" *(ružan)* or even calls the baby "you little bastard, you!" *(gade mali!)*. During this whole scene the mother of the baby quietly acquiesces the "compliments," meant to bring good luck, with a big and agreeable smile. Or small children are spanked in jest so that "they grow some more" in size. Children get smacked on their behinds or cheeks while everyone present beams. Someone delivers a *čveger* (a flick of one's middle finger) on the forehead of someone who has just had a haircut so that the hair will grow back more vigorously. All individuals present approach one by one and deal a *čveger* to the head of the individual with the new haircut. It is a "must" to be given and a "must" to be "received." Someone sees someone else's domestic animal for the first time and utters with admiration and a smile that said pig or cow is "sooo ugly" *(ruuuužaaaan—* exaggerated pronunciation of the word *ružan)* or states that the animal looks just fine and then delightfully spits right next to it.

For those unfamiliar with such forms of behavior in the Balkans, these and other similar practices might seem strange. Some would quickly disregard them, calling them "superstitions." These examples and other little practices and vernacular formulae seem to be contrary to the usual forms of behavior considered "normal." However, some forms of behavior are more frequent in everyday life than others such as "knock on wood" *(da kucnem u drvo)* and less discernable to the unexperienced eye. Often, these forms are hidden in the language. For instance, a person who works a lot and is tired might answer the question "How are you doing?" with *živ nisam*. This vernacular expression can be loosely translated into English as "I am hardly alive"; however, it is an inverted form of the syntactically correct *nisam živ*, which has the opposite meaning ("I'm not alive" or rather "I'm dead"). The syntactic inversion shifts its sense, hence the meaning "I'm fine but tired/stressed out." Or the answer to the question as to whether someone is hungry might be *ma, jok, ti si* ("ah, I'm not, you are"), which is a definitive "yes."

For those unaccustomed to these modes of speaking and acting, such practices and others like them might seem illogical or, at best, examples of vernacular or dialect-related particularities. Some would quickly dismiss them, calling them "provincialisms." However, this form of behavior implies that a person will intentionally act out or say the opposite of what is normally or usually expected. People use such forms, as they readily admit, either as habitual expressions or in order to "prevent evil forces from causing harm" (*da zlo ne čuje*). It is always better to be safe than sorry. The belief that evil is very much present in the human world and is ready to hear the slightest compliment and unmercifully strike the object of our admiration or attention is widespread in almost all human cultures. The South Slavic world is no different. These and other formulae and forms of behavior are indeed fragments of ritualistic behaviors which were once abundant in southeastern Europe. Vuk Stefanović Karadžić's[2] *Srpski rječnik* (*Serbian Dictionary*), first published in 1818 in Vienna, provides sufficient evidence for this: the first edition of the dictionary contains 26,270 words and expressions, of which at least 10 percent refer to practices, customs, and beliefs which have to do with magic or ritual intended to avoid some harm or evil.

The aim of this chapter is to discuss a subcategory of ritual behavior that expresses opposite or inverted behavior: formulae and behaviors that are in opposition to what is desirable in the normal, usual course of events. Much scholarly work has been dedicated to the study of ritual and ritualistic forms of behavior, and categorizations of these forms of behaviors have been attempted many times; however, little attention has been directed to a special form of anti- or "counter-" behavior, which still persists in everyday practices of speaking and behaving.

Radenković and Inverted Behavior

In his masterpiece about South Slavic charming,[3] Ljubinko Radenković (1996) sets forth a classification of the forms of behavior during rituals of charming. These forms of behavior were and are still produced by charmers (*bajalice*, sg. *bajalica*)[4] while performing healing rituals (*bajanja*, sg. *bajanje*). Radenković introduces, under the concept of ritual behavior, a category that he calls *anti-ponašanje* (anti-behavior). In an article written twenty-three years later, in 2019, Radenković returns to an analysis of ritual behavior, this time from a more general perspective, and develops the concept of ritual behavior more broadly in Serbian popular culture. Here, he devotes a great part of his discussion to the same category, which he renames "inverted" or "counter-" behavior (*naopako ponašanje*). In his 1996 book, he does not mention any theoretical reference that inspired him in creating this subcategory; however, in the 2019 article he does relate it to the work of Boris Uspenski (1996) and examples of "anti-behavior" in the culture of old Russia.

In both the book as well as the article, Radenković provides subcategories and an abundance of examples for each form of what he considers anti- or inverted behavior in the ritual of charming and the broader field of symbolic behavior. Through a profusion of examples Radenković makes his case and successfully builds this subcategory, inverted behavior. While in his 1996 book, Radenković does not elaborate much on the characteristics of inverted behavior except for a one-sentence definition, "behavior oriented in the opposite sense of usual social behavior" (88), he does pay more attention to them in his 2019 article (125). For instance, Radenković abandons the term "anti-behavior" (*anti-ponašanje*) for a more powerful concept, *naopako ponašanje*.[5] His case is convincing; therefore, I suggest adopting an English translation that would convey this relatively new–old idea of "inverted behavior." Why not keep Uspenski's term, "anti-behavior," instead of proposing this one? Perhaps because the prefix "anti" has the connotation of opposing an activity and would mean in a literal sense a non-behavior, while the prefix "counter" (*naopako*) expresses the essence of this form of behavior: a behavior in an opposite direction. The goal of this chapter is to examine the validity of such a category, as suggested by Radenković, and to offer a critical assessment of this distinct model of ritual behavior. Ritual behavior per se in any culture is quite distant from usual, normative social behavior. So what is considered "magical behavior" could easily be interpreted as contrary to normal types of behavior. Ritual kissing or washing the body (hands, feet, chest, head, face) in places or social circumstances (a funeral or first visit to a newborn [*babinje*]) which are not intended for this type of activity (a graveyard or entrance of a house/threshold), or ritual nakedness, might fit in the category of an "unusual form of behavior." Further, it would be easier to label some of the "unusual" forms of behavior "anti"-behavior, in a literal sense of "anti-social" behavior, because such behavior is oriented against the usual social norms. Then again, putting on clothes inside out can be interpreted as ritualistic, but it takes some previous knowledge about what forms of ritual behavior are out there before one would be tempted to categorize them as "inverted."

Radenković's thinking on inverted behavior has advanced considerably in the twenty-three years from 1996 to 2019. The realization that the type of behavior that a charmer produces while charming can surely be applicable to other symbolic behavior in everyday life certainly had an impact on his choice to devote more attention to this subcategory and choose a more appropriate term for it. Additionally, Radenković introduces, in 2019, several other categories of behavior which he did not mention in his previous work. Given that the concept of inverted behavior exceeded its original frame as just one of many forms of ritual behavior during charming and that Radenković demonstrated that these forms were also present in the much broader "magical" behavior of everyday folklore, it became clear that the subcategory of inverted behavior deserves more attention. Therefore, another objective of this chapter is to develop the concept further by providing additional examples to the existing corpus and to argue for future directions in the general area of research of ritual behavior or behavior related to magic and ritual healing.

INVERTED BEHAVIOR AND CHARMERS

What were the categories of ritual behavior that Radenković used in his 1996 book to organize his classification of the forms of behavior of the South Slavic *bajalice*? For one thing, he organized the forms of behavior under the umbrella term "codified behavior" to establish communication with the forces of evil that brought harm to humans or the human world. He considered all ritual behavior non-verbal (as in non-verbal communication), made of symbolic acts and proceedings. Interestingly, he suggested that, although diverse, all of the subcategories he enumerated as forms of ritual behavior during charming could be reduced to one type of symbolic action. It is an action oriented toward ostensibly leaving the human world in order to get rid of the impure (evil) forces. This epitomizes what a charmer is supposed to do. Charmers are hence not only mere "communicators" or sacral mediators (Pócs 1997) between the human world and other worlds (worlds of demons). They are wayfarers between these worlds.

Radenković calls the symbolic action of the wayfarer *provlačenje* (loosely translated as "pulling" or "passing through"). This notion of "pulling through" or "being pulled through" figures first on his list of ritual behaviors and is a device, he argues, to remove the opposition between the relational axis humans–demons. The ritual behavior of *provlačenje* is an important category and a ritual per se that is a topic of many ethnological inquiries in the study of South Slavic folklore and elsewhere (Trebješanin 1991; Stajić and Pišev 2016; Frazer 1913; Eliade 1978; Kemp 1993). According to Radenković, this is also the type of ritual act to which some of the forms of inverted behavior belong.

The other type of ritual act is the creation of communication and the formulation of "requests" directed to the forces of evil, which are shaped by the charmer. It is the charmer who decides which request will be used to obtain the desirable result. Hence, the charmer plays the role of mediator.

For the sake of clarity, both types of actions are enumerated here. The types of ritual acts as forms of communication-creation/meditation are *pretnja* (threatening the evil spirits/demons), *ponuda* (offering to the malevolent demons/spirits), *očišćenje* (cleansing the house/body), *bratimljenje* (ritual fraternization with the malevolent spirit/demon), *odstranjivanje* (removal of the evil spirit/demon), and *pridobijanje* (winning over the malevolent spirit). The second type of action—whose goal is ostensibly leaving the human world/wayfaring—includes *promena imena* (changing names of the person who is "under attack" from a malevolent spirit), *oboravanje sela* (creating an enclosure around the village), *merenje* (measuring body parts), and forms of anti-behavior (defecating, spitting, nakedness). What are the types of inverted behavior during charming as enumerated by Radenković in 1996? They include *ćutanje* (being silent), *obrnuti govor* (inverted speech), *svlačenje* (taking off one's clothes), *oblačenje odela naopako* (getting dressed inside out), *okretanje stvari naopako* (turning things upside down), *pljuvanje* (spitting), *mokrenje* (urinating), and *žmurenje* (shutting one's eyes).

In his article (2019), Radenković keeps the above-mentioned subcategories and provides some more examples of them: *hodanje natraške* (walking backward), *pevanje umesto plakanja* (singing instead of crying), *ritualna kradja* (ritual stealing), and *maskiranje* (masking). The reason for adding these forms of behavior to the existing list is partially his concentration on ritual behaviors done by ordinary people, not solely charmers who perform them during special circumstances (Fig. 16.1).

The types of behavior that inspired Radenković to reorganize and further develop the notion of ritual behavior were from popular customs and the folklore of the human world: the life cycle (social cycle), annual customs (calendar cycle), legal (social-normative) customs, economic activity–related customs (farming, livestock, beekeeping, hunting, fishing, etc.), and occasional customs (protection from disease, hail, drought, vampires, witches, etc.). Radenković enumerates these ritual behaviors under the following subcategories: *pozivanje* (inviting people to a social event: wedding, christening, etc.), *pozdravljanje* (greeting kin), *ljubljenje/celivanje* (ritual kissing of newborn, new family members [wedding], etc.), *umivanje* (washing the face of the sick

Ritual behavior forms of a charmer (Radenković 1996)			
Forms of communication-creation/meditation	Leaving the human world/wayfaring		
pretnja (threatening), *ponuda* (offering), *očišćenje* (cleansing), *bratimljenje* (ritual fraternization), *odstranjivanje* (removal), *pridobijanje* (winning over)	*promena imena* * (changing names), *oboravanje sela* (creating an enclosure around the village), *merenje* (measuring)	Forms of inverted behavior	
		ćutanje (silence), *obrnuti govor* (inverted speech), *svlačenje* (taking off one's clothes), *oblačenje odela naopako* (wearing clothes inside out), *okretanje stvari naopako* (turning things upside down), *pljuvanje* (spitting), *mokrenje* (urinating), *žmurenje* (closing one's eyes)	

Ritual behavior in general (Radenković 2019)			
Forms of communication-creation/meditation		Leaving the human world/wayfaring	
By a charmer	*pretnja* (threatening), *ponuda* (offering), *očišćenje* (cleansing), *bratimljenje* (ritual fraternization), *odstranjivanje* (removal), *pridobijanje* (winning over)	*promena imena* (changing names), *oboravanje sela* (creating an enclosure around the village), *merenje* (measuring)	Forms of inverted behavior
			ćutanje (silence), *obrnuti govor* (inverted speech), *svlačenje* (taking off one's clothes), *oblačenje odela naopako* (wearing clothes inside out), *okretanje stvari naopako* (turning things upside down), *pljuvanje* (spitting), *mokrenje* (urinating), *žmurenje* (closing one's eyes)
By ordinary people	human existence: the human life cycles (social cycle), annual customs (calendar cycle), legal customs (social-normative), economic-activity related customs (farming, livestock, beekeeping, hunting, fishing, etc.), occasional customs (protection from disease, hail, drought, vampires, witches, etc.):		
	pozivanje (inviting), *pozdravljanje* (greeting), *ljubljenje/celivanje* (ritual kissing), *umivanje* (washing of the face), *darivanje* (giving gifts), *udaranje* (spanking/hitting), *obilaženje* (going around some object), *provlačenje* (passing through), *ljuljanje* (rocking), *vučenje* (pulling), *pucanje* (ritual shooting), *razbijanje sudova* (ritual breaking of dishes), *skakanje* (jumping), *kadjenje* (incensing).		

* suggested by the charmer, accomplished by the parents/kin of the child

FIG. 16.1. Taxonomy of ritual behaviors.

during incantation, of the deceased before burial, etc.), *darivanje* (giving gifts during ceremonies/rituals), *udaranje* (spanking/hitting), *obilaženje* (going around some object [house/yard/tree] during a ceremony), *provlačenje* (passing through as a part of a healing ritual), *ljuljanje* (rocking during an incantation ritual), *vučenje* (pulling during an incantation ritual), *pucanje* (ritual shooting during weddings, engagements, military draft [*vojničenje*]), *razbijanje sudova* (ritual breaking of dishes during wedding/funeral), *skakanje* (jumping during an incantation ritual/wedding), and *kadjenje* (incensing of the house or some other space during an incantation ritual). Of course, Radenković's list is not exhaustive, and he states that clearly too (Radenković 2019:101).

Radenković and Uspenski

In his article, Radenković refers theoretically to Uspenski's work on Old Russia (1996) and provides a short definition of what inverted behavior is: it is a replacement of the normative forms of usual behaviors. He writes,

> It represents the replacement of the normative forms of the everyday behavior of people with opposite forms of behavior: the right replaces the left, upper–lower, anterior–posterior, male–female, etc. That is, where it is seen that an action will be performed by the right hand—it is done with the left, objects are turned and placed on their head, clothes are put on inversely—instead of a man's clothes, a woman's clothes are put on, etc. Inverted behavior can likewise be expressed by using a special voice and speech but also through some actions such as ritual theft or ritual (imitative) holiness.
>
> (Radenković 2019:125, translation by M. Vivod)

Radenković refers to Uspenski's work when stating that forms of inverted behavior are accepted by the community only on special occasions, in special places, or at special times. He provides an example that is described by Uspenski: Archbishop Gennady of Novgorod expelled heretics from Novgorod in 1490. He ordered them to be put on their horses backward, turned toward the horses' tails, dressed in reversed clothing, with pointed caps made of birch-peel on their heads, adorned with feathers and wreaths of straw and hay, with the inscription "This is Satan's army" (Radenković 2019:125, from Uspenski 1996:460–461).

Indeed, Uspenski provided many historical examples of forms of anti-behavior. He even pointed out what was considered anti-behavior in the past:

> It should be borne in mind that any kind of masquerade or dressing up was inevitably thought of in early Russia as anti-behavior; i.e. a sinister, black magic significance was attributed to it in principle. This is quite plain from the example of the mummers of Yuletide, Shrovetide, St. John's Night and other festivals, who, it was

assumed (by participants in the masquerade as well as spectators!), depicted devils or unclean spirits; correspondingly, the dressing up was accompanied by extremes of disorderly behavior, often of an overtly blasphemous character.

(Uspenski and Zhivov 2012:127)

He was particularly interested in cases of imposture, which were forms per se of desacralization of the sacred, the inversion of what was considered beyond reach: "Dressing up in the Tsar's clothes should be seen in this context as a typical case of anti-behavior, to which, on the level of content, there corresponds the blasphemous attempt to procure sacred attributes through outer simulation" (Uspenski and Zhivov 2012:127). Uspenski did devote several studies to anti-behavior in Russia, although his analysis is from historical case studies (Uspenski and Zhivov 2012).

Ritual Behavior and the Ordinary

When examining the forms of ritual behavior executed not solely by the charmer but also by others, the "commoners," what jumps out are several possible inconsistencies. To begin with, most of the ritual behaviors are particular forms of behavior that are attention-grabbing. They are unusual. They are out of the ordinary. What makes them un-ordinary is the time, place, or circumstances in which the rituals are acted out or just how people do them: the number of kisses when greeting, which is often codified ("the Serbs kiss three times," *srbi se ljube tri puta*), or the kissing of someone's shoulder and then the palm of the hand (the traditional way that women greeted all men in central Serbia) or even a direct kiss on the mouth among men (in Montenegro). Even the ritual inviting to the *slava* (feast of the saint-protector of the family or kin), such as an invitation in person in the house of the potential guest with a ritual apple with coins pierced in the fruit, is not "normal" behavior sensu stricto. A linear symbolic meaning would be that the apple represents "health" (*zdrav k'o jabuka*) and the coins "wealth." Hence, the first and sole invitation for a *slava*—because one invitation lasts for a lifetime—is a desire to generate health and wealth in both houses and families: those who are invited and those who get invited.

What makes these behaviors ritualistic is the motivation behind them and their symbolic meaning, behind which is structured a cosmology of significations. However, among them there are also other forms of behavior that are notably un-ordinary: for instance, nakedness in times or places when or where nakedness is not accepted or urinating or spitting, forms of behavior usually considered "unclean." Behind these forms of behavior there is a lack of the usual linear symbolic meaning.

When examining further Radenković's subcategories of anti- and, subsequently, inverted behavior, a pattern that is common to them all can be established: they proceed in an opposite way from what is expected in a given situation. For instance, keeping obstinately silent when talking is expected, using negation in speech which does not make sense, putting on clothes inside out, walking backward, and so on are all forms of behavior that replace a form of "usual" behavior. Hence, there is a notion of "inversion" or "doing the opposite" of the normal course of action. However, there are a few forms of behavior that seem to be intruders when analyzing other forms of ritual behavior which are under the category of life-cycle customs (Radenković 2019). These forms of behavior do not entirely "fit" into the category. Let us examine ritual striking (*udaranje*). The rituals that are cyclical, according to Radenković, could easily figure under the subcategory of inverted behavior. When welcomed into this world, newborns were in the past traditionally kicked by their mothers at birth. It was believed that this was a symbolic act of separation between mother and child, and the children were treated as (falsely) "unwanted" or "unloved," which would protect them from evil spirits. Too much love, too much tenderness might have invoked or attracted evil spirits or the evil eye. Children coming home after their baptism would be ritually struck with a broomstick. When an adolescent girl had her first period, she was "greeted" with a ritual face slap by her mother. Newlywed couples were also ritually hit by their relatives when entering the house in which they were to live or just before entering the room in which their wedding night was to occur. A newlywed bride was hit by her husband's brother (*dever*) upon her arrival at the house: the brother-in-law smacked her head against the doorpost upon her entry to her new home. The deceased were slapped on their faces before burial in order to prevent them from becoming *vukodlaci* (werewolves, sg. *vukodlak*; Dalmatia). During burial, female relatives slapped themselves on the cheek or pulled out their hair to express grief. Little children were spanked by their mothers or relatives in order to foster their growth. The act of hitting or spanking is an act of symbolic separation, destruction with a goal to create some noise or inflict symbolic pain (Radenković 2019:111). Radenković considers the ritual act of hitting *normal* or rather *symbolically linear* (in opposition to the *inverted*). Correspondingly, *razbijanje sudova* (ritual breaking of dishes) figures also in the category of linear rituals. He argues that the breaking of dishes (usually porcelain or traditionally earthenware) is the symbolic creation of rupture between the past and the present, between what was and what is—it is symbolic of permanent change, for the dishes are never put back together; moreover, this ritual is mostly accomplished at weddings and funerals (Radenković 2019:122).

Ritual Violence

The two most interesting subcategories of inverted behavior are ritual striking or spanking and the ritual breaking of dishes. They both seem the opposite of what is considered desirable or normal behavior. Where is the symbolism in dishes being smashed? Is it the creation of a rupture, as Radenković states? Or is it against the evil eye, as people who practice it claim? Why is there so much ritual beating and hitting of the groom and the bride in South Slavic wedding rituals? Indeed, the ritual striking in wedding rituals across the Balkans makes the ceremony look more like a hazing than an act of celebration. Interestingly, the ritual striking is a common part of wedding and burial rituals—as if the creation of a new life (life of a couple: a wedding) and the ending of a life (burial) meet at the same ritualistic point, in which striking plays an important role, oriented to prevent evil forces.

Let us examine cases in which the ritual breaking of dishes and glasses is observed. Dishes are broken in the wedding ritual when the couple leaves the church. There is a person marching before the couple who drops plates in front of them as they march (Slovak minority of Vojvodina). Glasses from which the guests and couple have drunk are also broken. Dishes are broken when a new house is built. Coincidentally, it is believed that some sort of "blood sacrifice" is required when the building of a new house is completed. Thus, a chicken or some animal is sacrificed, and its blood is spilled on the foundation. It is believed that if the house/building does not obtain its sacrifice, it will "require" the life of someone from the household. There is also the custom of breaking some piece of pottery when the deceased were taken from their houses to the graveyard or at the graveyard itself. Interestingly, the intentional dropping of glasses in tap houses (*kafane*, sg. *kafana*) while getting drunk (*opijanje*) to express either uncontrollable joy or overwhelming sorrow is still a common thing in the Balkans. *Čaše lomim* ("I break glasses") is a common leitmotif of newly composed folk music such as in one of the great "classics" of the genre[6]—as if self-hurting and suffering would be inseparable parts of one's enjoyment. The ripping of one's clothes (usually a shirt) also takes place on such an occasion as an extreme expression of joy or sorrow. The ripping of one's shirt is likewise a custom for celebrating a newborn. Traditionally it was done when a male child was born; nowadays most firstborns are celebrated in this manner. The "new" father is greeted by his friends (male peer group) by each ripping off a little piece of his shirt when they approach him to congratulate him. This is done uniquely between males and uniquely when the first child is born.[7] The most likely explanation as to why the clothes of a new father are ripped off is related to the scarcity of clothes in ancient times, according to which the father's clothes that were ripped off were used to wrap up the newborn; this might also indicate the admission of paternity. However, the ripping of clothes can likewise be interpreted as a symbolic rite de passage. The young man is no more; a father is born. A more plausible explanation is that new clothes are needed which will mark his new social status. Clearly a ritual act, the ripping off of clothes appears to have some partial inverted meaning: something has to be destroyed for something new to take its place. In that same sense, the purposeful dropping of pottery or dishes, like the ripping of clothes, may indeed be interpreted as a ritual of breaking off from the past or marking a new beginning, a symbolic closing off of a chapter. Neither broken dishes nor ripped clothes can be repaired; hence, they are a convenient symbol to mark a moment in time. And although these practices bear the mark of the "inverted order"—because, after all, they do have the appearance of being the opposite of the usual order, of everyday life—they are in fact linear ritual behaviors with an aim to mark a certain moment in the linear passage of time. They are part of a "rite de passage."

What about the ritual act of spanking or hitting? Radenković considers hitting, spanking, or beating acts of separation, destruction, or pain (2019:111). Children are by far those who are spanked the most: at birth and baptism, when receiving a visit from a relative, when the first tooth appears, when first steps are taken. (Male) Children are hit on their face by their godfather when their hair is cut for the first time (*strižidba*). Incidentally, it is considered a bad omen if the child does not cry out loud at this time—perhaps because noise is a part of life, while silence is part of death and consequently evil forces. The first haircut is also often a moment when children get their first "real" clothes (traditionally, a three-piece outfit or *trodelno odelo*). Customarily, small children wore only a long white shirt. The end of breastfeeding is also considered a moment to ritually spank a child.

The ritual striking of a newlywed man by his group of peers just before heading off to his wedding night is also a remarkable one because this practice unites violence—even if it is symbolic—with joy and celebration. The newlyweds' stepping on each other's feet is also widespread. It is believed that the one who steps first on the feet of their spouse will be the one who will "command" (sometimes this results in an amusing scene of the newlyweds who, just after kissing each other, start "tap dancing" in front of the guests). The bride is also supposed to lift up a male child after the wedding ceremony; it is believed that the couple will ensure healthy (male) offspring by this act. When putting the child down she is expected to ritually spank him in some regions in Serbia, hence the expression *šljapenče* (the "spanked one") for such a child.

Ritual violence is present in other customary practices. The ritual striking in a group of peers is commonplace: for instance, in the game of "rotten mare" (*trula kobila* or *janjine*), which is usually played by adolescent boys, the one who makes a "mistake" by jumping aside or falling by accident will be spanked or hit by the other players.[8] The game of "scabies" (*šuga*) is also an example of a social game that usually ends with the player who makes an error being put in the middle and hit. The player with "scabies" is turned with his back to the other players; when he turns around, he has to guess who hit him on the back while he was not looking. It is a more or less controlled outburst of (male) violence in which one plays the "victim," while the others are "executioners."

The bride is the second most ritually slapped person after children. The ritual act of hitting a bride is probably the most widespread: depending on the region, she is hit on the back by the groom, brother-in-law, mother-in-law, or father-in-law. It was believed that the striking was important for her future health and fertility. The collective striking by all present guests of the couple, who are desperately running toward the exit, is also a common leitmotif. The ritual striking of visitors on Christmas Day or the first male visitor (*polaženik*) is also widespread. Ritual hitting and spanking are therefore very prevalent ritual acts in most stages of one's life.

Radenković explains ritual striking as an act of a rite de passage or an act to reaffirm the new situation and a change. However, ritual striking or spanking is far more common than just in transitional times in the life cycle, such as weddings or burials. Whether present in passages between life stages (birth, wedding, death) or during games, ritual violence functions as an act of stimulation of growth (of children, hair). It is an act of ensuring abundance and fertility. Hence the question, is this act a linear ritual behavior or a form of inverted behavior?

Other Forms of Inverted Behavior

In summary, Radenković (1996, 2019) considers the following forms of behavior as counter or inverted: *ćutanje* (silence), *obrnuti govor* (inverted speech), *svlačenje* (taking off one's clothes), *oblačenje odela naopako* (wearing clothes inside out), *okretanje stvari naopako* (turning things upside down), *pljuvanje* (spitting), *mokrenje* (urinating), *žmurenje* (shutting one's eyes), *hodanje natraške* (walking backward), *pevanje umesto plakanja* (singing instead crying), *ritualna kradja* (ritual stealing), and *maskiranje* (masking). While some of these forms are clearly already classified as inverted (as, e.g., masking by Uspenski), some are visibly inverted: such as walking backward, dressing up in clothes inside out, or putting things upside down. Other forms are less clearly categorized as inverted.

Let us examine some of these forms of behavior. Wearing clothes inside out is a "great classic" of inverted behavior. One wears clothes inside out—usually some piece of underwear—in order to protect oneself from the evil eye (*protiv uroka*). If it happens, by chance, that someone who is getting dressed inadvertently puts on a piece of clothing inside out, it is interpreted as a sign of some future "inverted" behavior. It means that a person who involuntarily puts on clothes inside out (say, underwear) will probably get drunk by the end of the day. An involuntarily "backward" action is a sign of what will happen. Wearing clothes inside out can also be "therapy": during the process of charming, the charmer might require that the patient wear a piece of clothing inside out—it is usually some piece of underwear, such as an undershirt—for a predetermined period of time (usually a week). Wearing clothes inside out is an efficient way to protect oneself against evil magic or a bad spell. In some wedding practices, the bride or both the bride and groom are required to wear some piece of clothing inside out. Wearing clothes backward has additional symbolism: it is a sign of someone's youth. A (male) person arguing that he is not "naive" or "childish" will state that he is not wearing his pants backward (or "he is not zipping up his pants backward"). Pants are a symbol of being male, while buttoning up pants "backward" (in back) means being a small child who is dressed by others. A sickly child believed to be suckled by a *mora* (a female nightly demon) was dressed in an adult male waistcoat, buttoned up in back (Lovrenčević in Radenković 1996).

Spitting is another form of inverted behavior. Usually considered an unclean practice, it is usually interpreted as an offense. Spitting next to others when arguing with them is a demonstrative act of contempt and disgust. However, in magical behavior it is abundantly present. Charmers spitting in the act of charming is interpreted by Radenković (1996:93) as the embodiment of the charmer's soul fighting with demonic forces. It was believed that spitting in the beak of a bird was an efficient way to get rid of some illness, after releasing it to fly away. Small children are often told that they should not pick up or take a strange object seen on the road: some evil spell might be attached to it. The best way to prevent an evil charm, when seeing such an object, is to spit next to it and pass it by. Spitting on small children—usually by the mother but also by female relatives—is also done in order to prevent the evil eye or a bad charm. A mother spitting in the mouth of a young child while saying "you ugly [thing]" (*gade*) was done to protect the child from harm (Radenković 1996:93). Likewise, making a desirable object less attractive by urinating on it figures on the list of inverted behaviors. Like spitting, urinating on things is an efficient way to protect against the evil eye. To sprinkle urine on domestic animals, especially cattle, is the safest way to protect the herd from an evil spirit or a demon who could sneak up in the stable during the night and take away the cow's milk. Places around the house that must be protected also require urine. A possible interpretation of spitting or urinating as a way to prevent harm is comparable to the binary clean/unclean. To make an object of our love or admiration less desirable, less close to the state of perfection, which can only be an attribute of the gods, is to symbolically "cut into it" or make it less perfect, less clean, and less desirable for the evil forces.

Therefore, I argue that some forms of ritual violence like spanking and hitting those who are present, especially at joyful occasions such as births or weddings, or dealing with "objects" that represent one's abundance and have a certain value (small children, domestic animals, and similar symbols of someone's "wealth") customarily entail the use of some form of inverted behavior. Making people and things less perfect, less desirable, and less clean is the safest way to protect them against the evil eye or some other malevolent force.

To that end I propose a non-exhaustive definition of inverted behavior as a form of ritual act: inverted behavior is purposeful magical/ritual conduct, practice, or speech that is linearly oriented in the opposite direction of the desirable goal of achieving abundance, increase of growth. Of course, not all ritual spanking belongs to the category of inverted behavior. Stepping on the foot of a newlywed spouse just after the ominous "yes" has the symbolic meaning of "control," and it is often interpreted as a joke. However, in all ritual behaviors where spanking and hitting are used to foster fertility (the "headbutt" of the bride by the *dever* as soon as she enters the house) or growth (spanking children after their baptism or at similar times), it certainly is a form of inverted behavior.

More nuanced forms of behavior are to be found in speech. Everyday vernacular constructions contain idioms which resemble in their form the usual formulae of charms (*basme*) (for more, see Radenković 1996). Saying the opposite of what one means when politeness prevents one from directly expressing a desire also belongs to the category of inverted behavior. A guest's asking for food is considered quite impolite; however, common civility and hospitality require the hosts' posing such a question. By answering a question as to whether one is hungry with *jok, ti si* ("ah, I'm not, you are"), the one who is offered provides leeway to the host. The vernacular expression *živ nisam* is another expression to avoid using an affirmative form of speaking which would directly invite the forces of evil—by stating that one is dead or barely alive—to pass into action. It is not a mere form of verbal mannerism. It is an expression of someone's condition by avoiding the uttering of a sinister parallel.

Like in the tradition of charmers, the speakers use short versions of negation or inverted speech in order to express their desires or wishes without being heard by the evil spirits. Some charms contain vernacular forms of negation, where the use of a negative prefix as a grammatical category does not make any sense (Radenković 1996:89–90), as in *O vilo, nevilo! Pošalji mi sito nesito po djetetu nedjetetu* (Vuletić Vuksanović in Radenković 1996; "Oh, fairy, non-fairy, send me a sifter, a non-sifter through a child, a non-child"; interestingly, the word *nesito* is both the negation of the word "sifter" and an adjective meaning "non-full-fed," i.e., "hungry"). In this charm the charmer uses negation in order to be heard by the fairies—or to have access to the world of fairies. Stating the opposite of what is meant, "ugly" when thinking about "beauty" or "sweetness," is a way to speak to the potentially malevolent forces who will either leave alone the object of our admiration or be satisfied by the use of negation.

In doing fieldwork about childrearing and birthing in the Balkans, what becomes most obvious is the fact that the presence of various forms of inverted behavior is tenacious. Not praising a child or the beauty of a little girl is almost an obsession (a young mother told me that she "actually became sick if someone praised the beauty of her little girl"—she just could not bear any praise of her spoken out loud). The obstinate reproducing of this practice is more than a socially controlled form of civility; it is a desirable and solely acceptable form of behavior.

Conclusion

The fragments or idioms of inverted speech is a topic which remains to be explored. There is, of course, a chance that only elderly people still use such kinds of speech. Possibly, inverted behavior in action and in practice is far more visible than that "hidden" in the language, which can be easily interpreted as a vernacular "particularity," slang, or even a mannerism. However, it is persistent in other areas of conversation that are considered important.[9]

Unarguably beside the above-mentioned forms of ritual behavior oriented toward preventing evil or harm there are plenty of other forms and vernacular expressions that are waiting to be explored for the purpose of solidifying the subcategory of ritual behavior, inverted behavior. I categorically find that Radenković's concept's English-language translation of "inverted behavior" is far more suitable than Uspenski's "anti-behavior," for it can be interpreted as a lack of action and not a symbolic ritual action oriented toward the opposite direction.

The Russian philologists Vyacheslav Ivanov and Vladimir Toporov reconstructed a mythical cosmology around several Slavic gods through the comparative study of various Indo-European mythologies and a large number of Slavic folk stories and songs. They brought forward, in that manner, the battle of Perun and Veles, which was, according to them, one of the basic myths of the Slavic pantheon. Ivanov and Toporov (1983) used the same methodology to reconstruct a mythical cosmology around other Slavic gods, such as the Goddess Mokosh. Their method, called the "basic myth" or "key myth" approach, involved engaging in the archive of beliefs and myths and attempting to recreate the basic features of at least a part of an ancient cosmogony of a once-coherent belief system. As a future investigation track, it would be interesting to gather and analyze other forms of ritual inverted behavior, which could possibly lead toward the uncovering of other remnants perhaps of an extinguished ancient belief system in which inverted behavior played a major role and might conceivably be traced back to basic or key myths.

Notes

1. This and all subsequent examples are in Serbian; all translations are mine.
2. Vuk Stefanović Karadžić (1787–1864) was a Serbian philologist, ethnographer, and linguist. In his efforts to reform the Serbian language, he standardized the Serbian Cyrillic alphabet and brought the literary language closer to common folk speech. His work resulted in the publication of the "*Serbian Dictionary*, paralleled with German and Latin words" (*Srpski rječnik istolkovan njemačkim i latinskim riječma*), published in Vienna in 1818. It also contains references to traditional customs and practices. In that sense, Vuk, as he is typically called, produced an ethnography of the Serbian-speaking people across the region that serves as a reference for most of the words, customs, and practices among South Slavs at that time.
3. The study of charms is a subdiscipline within folklore studies and cultural anthropology. This subdiscipline is well established and abundantly researched; see, for instance, Roper (2009) and Kapaló et al. (2013).
4. For more information about this practice and practitioners, see "Bajanje (Serbia and the Western Balkans)" in the Global Informality Project's online encyclopedia (https://archive.is/1yfJn).
5. The word *naopako* is often used in the vernacular Serbian as the idiom "God forbid" in English or *Astaghfirullah* in Arabic (*'astaġfiru llāha*, literally "I ask forgiveness from Allah"), denoting disapproval or hope that a bad thing will not happen. This vernacular expression not only expresses that something "took a wrong turn" but also in a way expresses the hope that it will not. Hence, Radenković really "strikes a chord" with this choice of word.
6. https://youtu.be/-1qJ5SdFwCU—https://archive.is/Xphwv. See also https://youtu.be/qDHNUiXh4sA/https://archive.is/dbGux.
7. See https://archive.is/xgP1i.
8. See the game: https://www.youtube.com/watch?v=zLAm4JLWoXQ/https://archive.is/JwbP2 or https://www.youtube.com/watch?v=YSa72qzq3Qs—https://archive.is/TllOg.
9. Analyzing narratives about Montenegro's joining the European Union as a part of research for a research project (INFORM: Closing the gap between formal and informal institutions in the Balkans), I was struck by the quantity of forms of inverted speech. I often wondered whether foreign researchers who were not trained enough in the nuances of the Serbo-Croatian-Montenegrin-Bosnian vernaculars would be equipped to interpret them.

Works Cited

Eliade, Mircea. 1978. *A History of Religious Ideas*. Vol. 1: *From the Stone Age to the Eleusinian Mysteries*. Chicago: University of Chicago Press.

Frazer, James George. 1913. *The Golden Bough. A Study in Magic and Religion*. Vol. II, Part VII. London: Macmillan & Co.

Ivanov, Vyacheslav Vsevolodovich, and Vladimir Nikolaievich Toporov. 1983. "K rekonstruktsii Mokosji kak zjenskogo personazja v slavjanskoj versii osnoyogo mifa." In *Balto-slavjanskije issledovanija*, ed. Vyacheslav Vsevolodovich Ivanov, 175–187. Moscow: Rossiîskaja akademija nauk. Institut slavjanovedenija i balkanistiki

Kapaló, James, Éva Pócs, and William Ryan, eds. 2013. *The Power of Words: Studies on Charms and Charming in Europe*. Budapest: Central European University Press.

Karadžić, Vuk Stefanović. 1818. *Srpski rječnik istolkovan njemačkim i latinskim riječma*. Vienna: Armeniera.

Kemp, Pejšns. 1993. *Slovenska magija*. Belgrade: Luta.

Pócs, Éva. 1997. *Élők és holtak, látók és boszorkányok. Mediàtori rendszerek a kra ùjkor forràsaiban*. Budapest: Akadémiai Kiadó.

Radenković, Ljubinko. 1996. *Narodna bajanja kod južnih Slovena*. Belgrade: Prosveta, Balkanološki, Institut SANU.

Radenković, Ljubinko. 2019. "O simbolici obrednog ponašanja u narodnoj kulturi Srba." In *Glas*, Vol. CDXXIX, book 31, 99–137. Belgrade: Srpska Akademija nauke i umetnosti. Odeljenje jezika i književnosti.

Roper, Jonathan, ed. 2009. *Charms, Charmers and Charming: International Research on Verbal Magic*. Basingstoke–New York: Palgrave Macmillan.

Stajić, Mladen, and Marko Pišev. 2016. "Provlačenje kroz 'Rupu': Magijski obred zaštite zdravlja dece." In *Antropologija: Časopis centra za etnološka i antropološka istraživanja (CEAI)*, Br. 16, sv. 3, 83–107. Belgrade: Univerzitet u Beogradu.

Trebješanin, Žarko. 1991. *Predstave o detetu u srpskoj kulturi*. Belgrade: SKZ.

Uspenski, Boris. 1996. *Semiotika istorii, semiotika kul'tury*. Moscow: Škola "Âzyki Russkoj Kul'tury."

Uspenski, Boris, and Victor Zhivov. 2012. *"Tsar and God" and Other Essays in Russian Cultural Semiotics*, trans. Marcus C. Levitt. Brighton, MA: Academic Studies Press.

Varieties of Folk Belief

CHAPTER 17

ESCHATOLOGY AND PEASANT VISIONS IN MOLDOVAN FOLK RELIGION

JAMES A. KAPALÓ

IN the worldview of traditional Orthodox societies, the cataclysmic events of the end of days framed the experience of time, of change, and of historical events. "Eschatology," the knowledge or study of the last things (from the Greek *eschata*), carries both positive and negative implications; on the one hand, it often infers the hope of rebirth or renewal, while, on the other hand, it presumes the destruction, often violent, of all that has gone before. Christianity's eschatological crisis, the continued failure of Christ to return, has ensured that eschatological ideas, rumors, and narratives that circulate in the modern world, from Siberia to the American Midwest, play a significant and enduring role in conditioning responses to change. Whether in relation to technological advances (Panchenko 2001; Lyubimova 2009), ecological disasters (Lookingbill 1994; Lyubimova 2016), the threat of nuclear destruction (Wojcik 1997), or dramatic political and economic events (Viola 1990; Smith 2006), eschatological narratives have animated diverse religious movements in the twentieth century. In general, so-called millenarian movements can be characterized by the close attention they pay to current events in the search for signs of the end times and the implications these events have for human agency in the present (see Schwartz 1987). The link between oral and literary folk cultures and sacred text formation among such millenarian movements in eastern Europe, however, remains relatively little studied (see Hammer and Rothstein 2012:114).

Popular protest characterized by apocalyptic prophecies and rumors increased markedly in Russia in the aftermath of the Bolshevik Revolution of 1917, especially during the Soviet collectivization campaigns that started in 1928 (see Viola 1990; Paert 2005; Smith 2006). In Bessarabia, which had until 1918 been under tsarist Russian rule, contemporary manifestations of apocalypticism also took shape in the form of popular eschatological movements led by peasant visionaries. With reference to the publications of two such visionaries, the brothers Alexandru (born 1886) and Grigore Culiac (born

1892)¹ (also spelled "Culeac" in some sources), in this chapter I illustrate how characters, images, and scenes from a number of familiar folk and apocryphal narratives were used to animate the events of the apocalypse and assert the truth of the return to earth of prophets and archangels wandering the Bessarabian countryside.² In contrast to the discursive centrality of the figure and identity of the Antichrist in both anti-tsarist and anti-Soviet popular dissent, which was largely the legacy of the Old Believers,³ in Bessarabia, in place of an embodied enemy, a cast of saintly and divine persons engaged in combating him instead took center stage in the unfolding eschatological drama in the here and now. Folk beliefs and narratives that were common among the Bessarabian peasantry gave birth to a local brand of existential eschatology (see Harrison 1979:228–229) that asserted that the end times were not merely close at hand but had actually commenced. My central argument in this chapter is that the folk textual and oral traditions the Culiac brothers had at hand reflected deeply held beliefs and that when we examine the folk narratives circulating at the time the Culiacs were experiencing their visions and composing their texts, we can understand how they resonated so powerfully among rural communities.

The significance of folklore in the emergence of new religious movements in post-Soviet and post-communist eastern Europe has been well charted with regard to so-called native faith or neo-pagan and shamanic groups, whose "unmasking" of Christian folklore motifs, narratives, and characters to reveal ancient pre-Christian beliefs, symbols, and deities has been central to the construction of a wide range of new, and often politically salient, religious identities (see Lesiv 2013; Povedák 2014; Povedák 2019). Indeed, classic folklore scholarship has contributed to this process through the analysis of the properties, symbolism, and functions of popular saints and holy persons such as Saint George, Saint Nicholas, the Archangel Michael, and the Prophet Elijah and their association with pre-Christian deities and mythic warriors (see, e.g., Ivanits 1992). Less attention, however, has been paid to other traditions of interpretation among new religions that are content to allow Elijah to remain in his role as God's Prophet and the Archangel Michael to maintain his Christian identity as commander of the heavenly host. In Russia, as Aleksandr Panchenko (2004) argues, alongside the use of elements of Slavic folklore, autochthonous new religious movements drew on two cultural currents, urban alternative "seeker" culture,⁴ including ufology, astrology, and eastern mysticism and the cultural legacy of the mystical and apocalyptic spirituality of Orthodox dissenters and the so-called catacomb church.⁵ In contemporary Moldova, the legacy of Orthodox dissent that stretches back into the early twentieth century and is associated with figures such as Inochentie of Balta, Ioan Zlotea (see Kapaló 2019:178–188), and the Culiac brothers continues as a strong folk-inspired apocalyptic current within contemporary orthodoxy.⁶ The texts discussed in this chapter, which represent part of this culture of Orthodox dissent, offer us a rare insight into the way in which folk narrative and motifs contributed to the processes of production of extra-canonical sacred texts in the formative period of a new religious movement (see Hammer and Rothstein 2012).

Just as the shock of the dramatic collapse of the Soviet Union encouraged the emergence of apocalyptic and messianic movements in the 1990s (Panchenko 2004), in the lead-up to and the aftermath of the Bolshevik Revolution, messianic movements took shape across the former Russian Empire, drawing on long-standing traditions of apocalyptic expectation, dissent, and schism within Russian orthodoxy. The Moldovan movements I discuss in this chapter emerged as popular religious revitalization movements during and in the wake of the Russian revolutionary period and continued their underground existence right through the Soviet era and into the present. The collapse of the Soviet Union and the ensuing economic and political turmoil inspired widespread belief in the imminence of the end times that found expression, for example, in the widespread rejection of the new barcoded Moldovan passports as a sign of the Antichrist (see Kapaló 2011:126) and in the enthusiastic circulation of apocalyptic rumors, apocryphal texts, and narratives.

In the first decades of the twentieth century, Moldova, or "Bessarabia" as it was known at the time, first as part of the Russian Empire (1812–1918) and then as a province of Romania (1918–1944), experienced an unprecedented series of political upheavals and religious turmoil, including the defeat in the Russo-Japanese War (1904–1905); the 1905 Revolution; the February Revolution of 1917, followed by the Russian Civil War (1917–1923); unification with Romania and the Romanian Orthodox Church; and finally, the 1924 introduction of the revised Julian calendar, which overturned the way that time itself was reckoned and experienced for Bessarabians.[7] These events gave traditional patterns of belief, especially those associated with the end of days, a new and powerful significance. The texts produced by Moldova's homegrown apocalyptic movements illustrate the entanglement of contemporary events with sacred time and the intersection of folklore and religious texts with national politics.

An appreciation of Moldova's geographical and political location on sensitive and unstable borderland can help explain how this came about. Moldova, whether it is viewed as a political or ethnographic territory, is difficult to define.[8] Situated on the southwestern borderlands of what was the Russian Empire while also representing the most easterly territories of the historical Romanian principalities, Moldova has been the home to a diverse population of Moldovans,[9] Ukrainians, Jews, and Roma and over the past two hundred fifty years has also received Russian, Bulgarian, Gagauz, and German settlers, among others. The province of Bessarabia, as it became known following its incorporation into the Russian Empire in the early nineteenth century, remained an imperial territory until 1918, when it was incorporated into Greater Romania until 1940–1941 when it was briefly occupied by the Soviet Union. In 1944 Bessarabia, officially named the Moldavian Soviet Socialist Republic (MSSR),[10] was reoccupied by Soviet forces and remained part of the Soviet Union until its collapse in 1991. Although multiethnic in character, Moldova is very largely Orthodox Christian in terms of culture, with both Russian and Romanian Orthodox traditions having influenced religious life in the region. Sustained cultural exchange and linguistic diversity, however, have resulted in an extremely rich mosaic of vernacular religious life. In many ways, Moldova can be considered a classic example of a borderland in the anthropological sense (Rosaldo 1989), a place where cultures overlap and where so-called hybrid populations are able to "appropriate and creolize" dominant cultural forms (Lavie and Swedenburg cited in Ballinger 2004:31). As a result, what "counts" as Moldovan, as opposed to Romanian, is contested, fluid, and difficult to define (see King 2000). The traffic of folk beliefs and practices across religious, ethnic, and linguistic divides in Moldova has been little studied (see Kapaló 2011; Kvilinkova 2012; Kvilinkova 2017); but the kind of creative work that relies on exchange, translation, and reinvention across boundaries, whether linguistic, religious, or political, characterizes both Moldovan folk religion and the grassroots religious movements that emerged in the twentieth century in the region.

Folk Religion and Eschatology in the Borderlands

Folk religion is a somewhat contested category among both religious studies and folklore scholars (see Primiano 1995; Bowman 2004; Primiano 2012; Kapaló 2013). The term has been critiqued from a number of perspectives not least in relation to the implied distinction between two discrete spheres of religious activity, sometimes shorthanded as the folk/elite or popular/elite distinction. The category of folk religion, therefore, may seem to underscore, among other things, a fundamental gulf between textual and oral traditions or between religious orthodoxy/orthopraxy and heresy or superstition (see Primiano 1995). As I have argued elsewhere (Kapaló 2013:4), when approached as a field of practice, the term "folk religion" can usefully signify "a site of struggle for legitimacy in religious life" that frequently becomes politically and culturally charged. Indeed, the stuff of classic "folk religion" is often targeted by representatives of "official" institutions, both religious and secular, as being the deposit of superstitious, heterodox, syncretistic, dangerous, and subversive practices or the result of a deficit in terms of doctrine, logic, and understanding. However, it is the very nature of this process of contestation between those who claim the power and authority to determine beliefs and practices and those who nevertheless choose to act differently or believe alternatively that makes the religion of the folk uniquely powerful and transformative in certain situations. Folk eschatology has been the source of numerous such struggles for authority and legitimacy in religious, and indeed political, life and constitutes a powerful resource for the mobilization of resistance. As such, folk eschatology, I argue, is indicative of the character of folk religion more generally.

As Leonid Heretz points out, among the Orthodox peasantry of eastern Europe, folk eschatology represented "the only possible model for history" (2008:102) and, as such, profoundly shaped religious responses to the unprecedented events that transformed traditional society in the first decades of the twentieth century. In Russian history, popular apocalypticism, starting with the Old Believers in the seventeenth century, has motivated extreme acts of resistance (Heretz 2008). During Soviet collectivization campaigns, the power of apocalyptic belief also galvanized mass acts of rebellion and subversion (Viola 1990). Critical for understanding the power of apocalyptic belief in

Russian religious history was the conviction that the end time was very near or indeed had already come. Some believed they were living in the final days and their actions, whether the self-immolation practiced by some Old Believers, the castration and mutilation among the Skoptsy[11] (Engelstein 1999:20–21), or the radical egalitarian practices of the Maliovantsy[12] (Zhuk 2004:370–395), can only be understood as a symptom of a "realized" (Clay 1988:41) or "existential" (see Harrison 1979) eschatology experienced and lived in the here and now. This brand of folk eschatology goes beyond mere expectation, or "folk hearsay," that is characteristic of most folk narratives of the end of the world (see Panchenko 2001:10).

The power of apocalyptic prophesy and folk eschatological narratives to mobilize peasant resistance in Moldova was noted in the 1920s and 1930s by some commentators on religion and traditional society. The Bessarabian theologian and Orthodox Church historian Nicolae Popovschi documented the apocalyptic oral narratives and prophecies in circulation among the followers of Inochentie of Balta[13] and the power of belief in the approaching apocalypse to motivate this Moldovan monk's followers to ignore the rulings and teachings of first the Russian and later the Romanian Orthodox Churches (see Popovschi 1926). Researchers from the influential Romanian sociological school headed by Dimitrie Gusti[14] also noted the power of popular eschatology in the course of a number of surveys conducted in Moldovan villages in the 1930s. One of Gusti's team, Henri Stahl (1931), in an interview with a village priest regarding his experience of meeting Inochentie of Balta, drew attention to aspects of popular demonology and the role of women in the movement, while Ernest Bernea (1997), through his interviews with peasants regarding their understanding of time and the calendar reform of 1924, grasped the apocalyptic implications of this change for ordinary believers (see Repciuc 2011). More recently, Eugene Clay (1998) and I (Kapaló 2019) have also explored the apocalyptic aspects of vernacular Moldovan religious movements.

Critical to understanding the power and enduring nature of eschatological belief in the Moldovan context is the relationship between the beliefs held by the people, as reflected in the works of Popovschi, Bernea, and Hasdeu (discussed below), and those transmitted and encouraged by representatives of the Orthodox Church. The lower clergy, and especially monastics, who acted as spiritual guides, healers, and exorcists for ordinary Moldovan peasants, were particularly close to the people culturally.[15] This cultural bridge ensured that ideas about the eschaton emanating from the Orthodox Church could be both polyvocal and polysemic. This sometimes "conflicted and not monolithic" messaging from religious authorities, as Primiano points out, is both characteristic and generative of religion as a lived phenomenon (see Primiano 2012:384).

The traffic of texts and beliefs between various layers of society with differing levels of literacy and diverse oral and textual cultures represents an important field of enquiry for scholars of lived religion in the region (see Crummey 1993; Lammel and Nagy 2005; Zayarnyuk 2006; Smith 2006; Jiga-Iliescu 2006), and this is especially the case with regard to folk eschatology (Panchenko 2001; Heretz 2008; Pokrovskii 2010; Kapaló 2011;

Kvilinkova 2012; Kvilinkova 2017). As Panchenko (2001:11) highlights with regard to Russian eschatological folklore, through "historical-genetic analysis" it is possible to establish "the fact of borrowing" and, in some cases, to determine the historical conditions under which it took place; but it is far more problematic to explain the reasons why or even to be certain in which direction the borrowings took place, from written to oral culture or vice versa.

As in other parts of the Orthodox world (Pokrovskii 2010:42), the folk eschatology of the Moldovan peasantry implicitly rejected the official church view that the exact date of the end of the world is unknowable and instead encouraged speculation and inquisitiveness as to "the physical, political, and religious signs of the world's impending end." However, following the 1905 Revolution in Russia, there was a distinct upturn in what Heretz (2008:104) refers to as "applied eschatology" on the part of members of the Orthodox Church who engaged in speculation about the unknowable in the hope of mobilizing the people in the defense of holy tsardom and "warning folk away from the forces of sedition." The fiery published sermons of Father John of Kronstadt in particular had a widespread influence on apocalyptic interpretations of contemporary Russian events (Heretz 2008; see also Kizenko 2000). The religious fervor at the heart of the empire found a perfect conduit to the Moldovan people in the shape of Inochentie of Balta, the Moldovan monk and priest, who after several years spent in some of the great spiritual centers of Russia, returned to Moldova with an acute appreciation of the impending apocalypse facing Russia (see Kapaló 2019).

The intense new messaging through various layers and channels within the Orthodox Church complemented an already rich collection of source texts circulating among the Moldovan people. Moldovan folk religion is rich with tales of supernatural and divine characters featured in the Slavonic and Romanian manuscript tradition of Orthodox monasteries, many of which were adapted and published in chapbooks. The appearance of popular books featuring apocryphal legends and the lives of saints contributed significantly to the appearance of theological themes more broadly in Romanian and Moldovan folklore as the boundaries between oral vernacular and written religious culture were particularly fluid (see Jiga Iliescu 2006:18–37; Kapaló 2011:117–153; Hasdeu 2017). The creative exchange between oral folklore and textual religious culture resulted in beliefs and narratives relating to the end of the world finding diverse modes of expression in a range of folklore genres (see Lammel and Nagy 2005:318–319). Consequently, the search for clues as to the approaching end of days drew little from biblical texts; the Book of Revelation, which was not read in the Orthodox liturgical cycle, played only a minor role in popular consciousness with the notable exception of Old Believer circles (Heretz 2008). Instead, the primary sources, as the examples given below illustrate, were drawn from a broad repertoire of folk legends, apocryphal apocalypses, charms, folk hymns or *colinde* (pl.) in Romanian, and so-called heavenly letters[16] that circulated orally and in manuscript and chapbook form. Often copied by hand and translated into local vernacular languages, these texts circulated widely in Moldova (see Kapaló 2011; Kvilinkova 2012;

Kapaló 2014; Kvilinkova 2017), supplying the key protagonists and events as well as revealing the critical signs of the end times. These same oral traditions, chapbooks, and manuscripts also provided the necessary arsenal of prayers, curses, and charms to thwart the enemy in any eventual encounter.

The use of these diverse materials by the Moldovan peasantry was nothing new, and in themselves—although not always approved of by some in the clergy—such texts did not represent a direct affront or challenge to Orthodox belief. However, the dramatic events that swept the region at the beginning of the twentieth century helped to bring the characters, stories, and events portrayed in these vernacular texts and oral traditions powerfully to life. As Primiano (2012:384) has highlighted, the challenge that religious creativity generated by oral tradition and ritual innovation presents to forms of power constitutes one of the central themes of critical scholarship on vernacular or folk religion. In the case of twentieth-century Moldova, the idiom of this creative contestation of political and religious developments was folk eschatological in character.

The Visionary Texts of the Culiac Brothers

The two texts I discuss in the chapter are the published accounts of the revelations and testimonies of two peasant visionaries, the brothers Alexandru and Grigore Culiac, the founders of the Archangelist movement. The brothers' writings synthesize short episodes from their encounters with the Romanian authorities, who were trying to put a stop to their movement as part of a broader assault on religious dissent and sectarianism in the Romanian countryside (see Kapaló, 2019:105–138; Clark 2021), with visionary episodes, mostly experienced while in detention in prison cells or in hiding in underground shelters. In their testimonies, the brothers recount their mystical experiences as evidence of divine election and proof of their status as incarnations of heavenly persons engaged in the final battle with the Antichrist. The legitimacy of the identities they take on and the authenticity of the imagery they employ in their visions texts are derived in very large part from vernacular textual and folk eschatological narratives that were in wide circulation among the rural population in Moldova.

Born into a large, poor peasant family in the north of Bessarabia, Alexandru and Grigore, together with their brother Ion, were among the most influential charismatic leaders who continued the lineage of the spiritual movement started by Inochentie of Balta, although they took Inochentism in markedly new directions (Kapaló 2019). Most significant of these innovations was the assumption by the brothers of heavenly or divine identities. Whereas Inochentie had been associated by his followers with the prophets Elijah and Enoch (discussed below) and with the Holy Spirit, Alexandru assumed the persona of the Archangel Michael, and his followers became known as *arhangeliștii*, or the Archangelists, a term that was later used to refer to all the networks associated with his siblings and their successors. Grigore became known as *Tătune*, a word that refers to a dear or wise father, and *Dumnezeul viu pe pământ*, the "living lord on earth." Ion, the eldest of the brothers, was referred to as *Tătunea Ion* by his followers and was considered the incarnation of John the Baptist. His followers became known as *Tătuniștii*, indicating they were followers of the father. Over time, the Soviet authorities began to refer to the groups as *inochentiști-arhangeliștii* and *inochentiști-tătuniștii* in an attempt to be more precise in their identification and analysis of the branches of the Inochentist sect. The religious networks associated with the Culiac brothers were repressed by the Romanian authorities in the interwar period, and following Bessarabia's reincorporation into the Soviet Union as the MSSR, they continued to be the target of anti-religious operations. Today, the small and secretive communities of Archangelists across the Republic of Moldova embrace the name given to them by their onetime detractors and oppressors (Kapaló 2019:247).

According to his published account, Alexandru's visionary career began in 1920 when he was 29 years old. He first published his visions in a Romanian-language thirty-six-page booklet in 1924 under the title *O vedenie ce s'a arătat în anul 1920* or *A Vision That Appeared in the Year 1920* (henceforth referred to as *A Vision* 1924). The booklet contains sixteen chapters, each recounting a visionary episode, with three hymns to the Archangel Michael, presumably composed by Alexandru or his close followers, at the end of the booklet. This publication was followed with a re-edited two-language Romanian and Russian version with the title *Lucrările care s'au lucrat în anul 1920* or *The Deeds That Were Done in the Year 1920* (henceforth, *The Deeds* [undated]) that included minor changes to the original text plus four additional chapters with new visions dated up to 1927 (Fig. 17.1).

The second vision-text discussed in this chapter is that of his younger brother Grigore, which was published under the title *Vedeniile lui Grigore Culiac și pătimirile lui pentru mărturisirea venirii a doua a domnului Isus Hristos* or *The Visions of Grigore Culiac and His Sufferings for the Confession of the Second Coming of Jesus Christ* (henceforth referred to as *The Visions of Grigore* [undated]). This publication states on the cover that it is a translation from Russian (see Fig. 17.2). Similar to Alexandru's text, Grigore recounts the visions he experienced in the course of the brothers' clashes with the Romanian gendarmerie. Neither brother is credited as the author of their respective texts, and indeed in later Soviet sources they are described as only partially literate in Cyrillic (Alexandrov 1958). The original editions of the brothers' texts are today extremely rare, but re-edited and expanded versions continue to be used by communities of believers in contemporary Moldova.

The Culiacs' texts are written in an idiomatic form of the local vernacular and generally lack precise detail in terms of events, context, and time frames. As the titles of the published texts suggest, the visions—*vedenia* (sg.), *vedenii* (pl.)—that the brothers "see" or that "appear" before them represent the central theme of the works. The texts, however, seemingly intentionally, blur the boundaries between lived reality, revelation, and

FIG. 17.1. The first page of Alexandru's bilingual edition of his visionary text entitled *The Deeds That Were Done in the Year 1920* (ANRM-TMC3A 738-1-6849).

(National Archive of the Republic of Moldova.)

sacred time (Kapaló, 2019:145) as familiar scenes from apocalyptic narratives and exorcism texts are creatively woven together with episodes from the brothers' clashes with the Romanian authorities and their visions of the eschaton. The events and characters of folk eschatology are made to come alive, creating a kind of "multitemporality" (Stewart

FIG. 17.2. The cover of Grigore Culiac's *Visions of Grigore Culiac and His Sufferings for the Confession of the Second Coming of Jesus Christ* (ANRM-TMC3A 738-1-6831).

(National Archive of the Republic of Moldova.)

2012:10–12) that situates the brothers and their followers in the very events of the apocalypse as it unfolds.

Folk Beliefs and Oral Narrative

We are fortunate that some well-known philologists and folklorists active at the end of the nineteenth and the beginning of the twentieth century recorded the apocalyptic sensibilities and oral traditions associated with the expectation of the end times. Among them was Bessarabian-born Romanian philologist and historian Bogdan Petriceicu-Hasdeu (1838–1907), who, in 1884, circulated a linguistic questionnaire across the whole of the Romanian-speaking territories that included a question on the end of the world (perhaps appropriately the final one on the questionnaire). This question solicited one of the largest numbers of responses, with 520 in total (Hasdeu 2017:6). The sometimes brief but at other times longer and more complex responses to Hasdeu's question open with expressions such as *poporul crede* (the people believe) or *despre vremea de apoi poporul zice* (about the end times [literally the "after" or the "next" times] the people say), indicating their origin as drawn from folk beliefs in circulation at the time. These narratives collected by Hasdeu are mirrored in the folk legends collected by one of the earliest collectors of Romanian folktales, Tudor Pamfile (1883–1921). Both Hasdeu's and Pamfile's collections illustrate the especially rich folk narrative tradition on the end times in the eastern territories of the Romanian-speaking world, in Bessarabia (today's Republic of Moldova), Bucovina (a region that sits astride the Romanian and Ukrainian border), and the Romanian province of Moldavia.

What was it about these narratives that encouraged people to believe that they were currently living in the end times? Among the most common signs of the approaching eschaton reported in the questionnaire echo the words ascribed to Jesus in the so-called little apocalypse in the Gospel of Mark (13:12–13). The overturning of the moral order, especially in relation to sexuality and inter-generational relations, with children turning against and beating their parents, young girls behaving immodestly or shamelessly, and the old marrying the young, are among some of the most characteristic of Romanian folklore relating to the end times. This motif appears as one of the two components of Romanian folk hymns or carols (sing. *colindă*, pl. *colinde*) that address the theme of the end of the world (Berindei 2015:159), as this extract from a *colindă* published by Cosmina-Maria Berindei (2015:135–136)[17] illustrates:

> Când e capul vacului,
> Sfârşitul pământului,
> Când o bate fiu pe tată,
> Fiică-sa
> Pe maică-sa,
> Fine-său

> Pe naşi-său.
> Cei mai mic pe cei mai mari.
> Atunci capul vacului,
> Sfârşitul pământului.
>
> When will come the end of time,
> The End of the Earth,
> When a son beats his father,
> A daughter
> Her mother,
> The godchildren,
> Their godparents.
> When the youngest beats the elder.
> Then will be the end of time,
> The End of the Earth.

The respondents who recounted the signs of the end of days for Hasdeu seemed convinced that these signs inscribed in folk knowledge "not only foretell the End of Days but also confirm that they were actually living in those final times" (Hasdeu 2017:6), or, as Berindei describes in relation to the apocalyptic mindset at the time, the changes brought about by the forces of modernity appeared in the consciousness of the people to be "equivalent to the apocalypse" (Berindei 2015:361).

The basic schema of the eschaton as revealed in the responses to the questionnaire present a range of themes that are indicative of folk beliefs and narratives that speak of the end times. As Ionel Oprişan summarizes (see Oprişan 2017:7–10), the turmoil of the end of the world begins with the confrontation between the forces of good and the Antichrist, "30 years after his [the Antichrist's] birth, when for three or three and a half years he attracts the world to believe in him through miracles and other means of recruitment." During this time there ensues a period of struggle between the forces of darkness and light. The Antichrist, who has caused a great drought and famine, attracts followers by offering them silver and gold or breadcrumbs soaked in water, which fail to quench their thirst or hunger. Divine and heavenly persons, on the other hand, including Jesus Christ; the Mother of God; angels; most significantly for this study, the archangels; and the three prophets who had been raised bodily to heaven, Elijah, Enoch, and John, also walk the earth, quenching the thirst and relieving the hunger of those they meet.

The Two Witnesses

In the Eastern Orthodox tradition, the significance of the appearance in the book of Revelation of the "two witnesses," also referred to as the "two lamp stands" or "two olive trees" (11:3–12), is reinforced by their naming in the Pseudo-Apocalypse of John the Theologian as the prophets Elijah and Enoch.[18] Revelation foretells that the two witnesses will prophesy for 1,260 days before being killed by the Beast from the Abyss and, after three days, rise up on a cloud to heaven. This episode, which appears numerous times in the replies to Hasdeu's questionnaire and is echoed in the folk legends collected by Pamfile (1997) and others (see Jiga Iliescu 2023), ends with the Antichrist killing the prophets and causing Elijah's fiery blood to reign down on earth, presaging the end of the world.

> At the End of Days iron birds will arise, and the Antichrist will arise and take up all the water from the face of the Earth, treasure will come out of the earth and people will run after them thinking it is water. The Antichrist will wander around with a barrel of water and with bread and will give it to the people and will mark those who drink from him. Then there will come three saints that were taken up to Heaven Saint Elijah, Saint John and Saint Enoch and they shall perish by the sword of the Antichrist and the blood that flows will ignite the world and [the flames] will burn up to 8 cubits [high]—then Christ and his 12 disciples will come and archangels who will blow the trumpet and the dead will rise and Christ will judge them everyone according to their deeds. Antichrist will take those who were deceived.
>
> (Hasdeu 2017:63)

This oral folk legend that places first Elijah and Enoch and then Christ and the Archangels on earth battling the Antichrist presented the Culiac brothers with the basic framework into which the characters of their vision-texts, whom they themselves personified, could perform the deeds that folk narrative foretold.

Chapbooks and Copybooks

This vision of the end of times captured in Hasdeu's and Pamfile's collections reveals a number of ideas absorbed from diverse sources including biblical or post-biblical Jewish scriptures and especially later Christian apocryphal apocalypses (see Gaster n.d.). These images and ideas found their way into Romanian folk belief through the Slavonic manuscript tradition of Orthodox monasteries of Moldavia and Wallachia and later through the publication of numerous chapbooks. The special significance of eschatological texts of Byzantine origin in the Romanian manuscript tradition is reflected by the large number of manuscripts that have survived, especially apocryphal apocalypses (Timotin 2002). These manuscripts were largely responsible for the appearance of theological, and specifically eschatological, themes in Romanian folklore and demonstrate the fact that the borders between oral vernacular and written religious culture were particularly fluid (see Jiga Iliescu 2006; Kapaló 2011).

The tradition of copying and translating apocryphal texts continued in rural Moldova throughout the twentieth and into the twenty-first century among Moldovans and the diverse ethnic communities who live alongside them (see Kapaló 2011; Kvilinkova 2012;

Kapaló 2014; Kvilinkova 2017). The sought-after nature and scarcity of print copies of religious themed chapbooks, or *cărți poporane* in Romanian, and the lack of spiritual literature in the mother tongue in the case of the Gagauz minority, contributed to a vibrant religious copybook culture in rural Moldova. Typically, the texts found in copybooks would include the most popular apocryphal legends, apocalypses, and prayers. Collections of texts were also kept specifically for healing and to ward off danger or evil. Copybooks might typically contain charms, curses, and exorcism texts alongside church prayers and heavenly letters, or so-called *epistolii* (pl.). While the Culiacs framed very closely their visions around the key events and images of the end times as transmitted in oral legend, the brothers' textual compositions also reference, cite, or otherwise incorporate elements of texts commonly found in the copybook tradition.

The copybook presented in this chapter and featured in Figs. 17.3 and 17.4 represents a particularly impressive example of this tradition. Meticulously copied with beautiful calligraphy, this example, which was gifted to me by a member of an Archangelist community in a village in the south of Moldova, contains a selection of texts, comprising a heavenly letter, an apocryphal apocalypse, a charm, and an exorcism text, that illustrate perfectly the range of vernacular apocryphal and folk texts that shaped the religious imaginary of the Culiac brothers and their communities of believers. The opening page

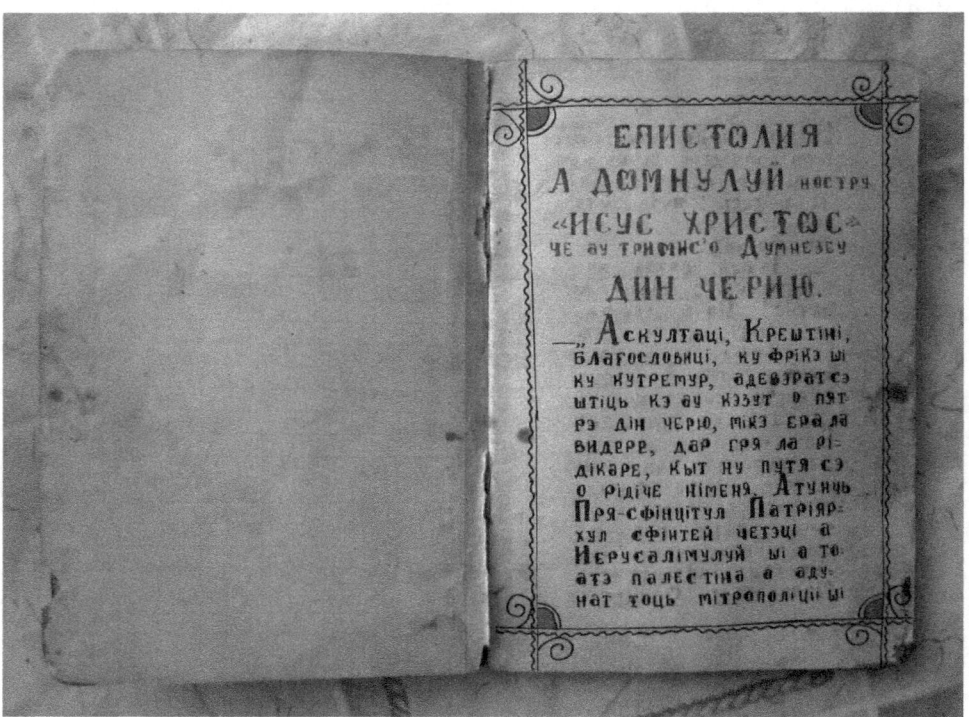

FIG. 17.3. Opening page of a copybook from southern Moldova containing diverse texts.

(Author's private collection.)

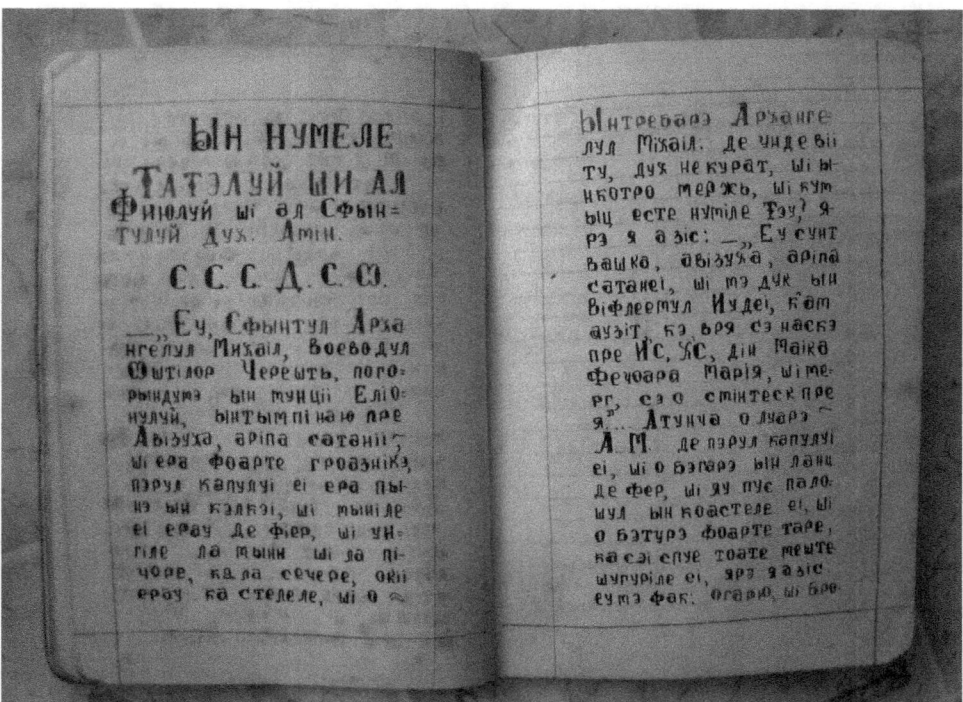

FIG. 17.4. The opening section of a charm against *Avestiță* from a copybook from southern Moldova.

(Author's private collection.)

of the copybook shown in Fig. 17.3 features a text entitled *Epistolia a Domnului nostru Isus Hristos ce au trimis-o Dumnezeu din ceriu* [sic], "The Epistle of Our Lord Jesus Christ Which Was Sent by God from Heaven," also commonly referred to as *Legenda Duminicii*, "Legend of the Sunday," in the Romanian tradition (Gaster n.d.:172). This text belongs to the so-called heavenly letter tradition and tells how a stone fell from heaven, very small in size but extremely heavy. The patriarch of Jerusalem calls a meeting of the church hierarchs to decide what to do with the stone, and while they are praying for guidance a voice from heaven instructs them to break open the stone, inside which they find a letter from Christ. The letter vilifies all those who do not respect Sundays according to Christian teachings. Those who follow Christ's instructions will be rewarded; those who do not heed his words shall be punished.[19] This opening text of the copybook contains the first reference to the Archangel Michael with the lines "This book was shown in front of the elders on the Mount of Olives in front of the Icon of the Saint Archangel Michael."

The Epistle of Christ is followed in the copybook by a text categorized by Schneemelcher (1992) as one of a group of "later apocalypses." The "Apocalypse of the Mother of God" featured in this copybook and another later apocalypse that frequently appears alongside it, the "Pseudo-Apocalypse of John the Theologian" (usually so named to avoid confusion with the book of Revelation), reflect very closely the version of events regarding the end of days found in canonical texts. Known in Romanian as *Călătoria Maicii Domnului la Iad*, or "The Journey of the Mother of God into Hell," this text first appears in Romanian manuscript form in the sixteenth century,[20] although it probably originates from around the eighth to ninth century and has been preserved in Greek and Old Slavonic variants. The text recounts how Mary, the Mother of God, prays to her son requesting that he reveal to her the sufferings of hell and the afterlife. The Archangel Michael then appears and takes her to the four directions showing her the torments of all those who suffer in hell. Finally, she pleads for all the saints to intercede on behalf of Christians everywhere, in answer to which her son, Jesus Christ, appears and grants the days of Pentecost as a period of respite to all those suffering the torments witnessed by his mother.

The final two texts in this example of a copybook are also extremely widespread in the tradition throughout Moldova, and significantly both feature the Archangel Michael as the main protagonist. Commonly copied as a pair of texts appearing one after the other, the first is a charm text, which, although often transmitted in written form, sits in close relation to the so-called verbal charm tradition of orally transmitted magical and healing practice (see Toporkov 2019), and the other is an exorcism or curse text. In the early twentieth century Pamfile (1999:171–173) gathered data on the significance of these special texts that were used for healing and to release one from the grip of the Devil or a demon. He notes that they would often include an image of the Archangel Michael, "Every household should have in their home a book of the grip [*o carte de strânsură*] with an image in which the Archangel Michael is seen piercing *Avestița*, the wing of Satan.[21] The book is bought or someone in the village makes it." The charm referred to here by Pamfile has been much studied in its various oral and written permutations (see Gaster 1900; Pócs 2002; Kapaló 2011:169–170, 221–223; Toporkov 2019). It recounts how the Archangel Michael, descending from the Mount of Olives, encounters *Avestița* and succeeds in preventing the demon from stealing the newborn baby Jesus by revealing the demon's nineteen names and thus also ensuring the salvation of humankind. This opening extract of the charm (taken from the manuscript copybook shown in Fig. 17.4) shows the archangel overpowering the demon and compelling her to reveal her malicious plot to steal the Christ child.

> In the name of the Father, and the Son and the Holy Spirit. Amen.
> S. S. S. D. S. O. H[22]
> I, the Archangel Michael, General of the Heavenly Host, descending from Mount of Olives came face to face with *Avizuhii*, the Wing of Satan, and She was very ugly, the hair of her head came down to her heels, her hands were of iron, her fingernails and her toenails, like a sickle, her eyes were like stars, and the Archangel Michael asked: Where are you coming from you unclean spirit, and where are you going, and what is your name? I'll say it again: "I am vashka, Avezuha, the Wing of Satan, and I am going to Bethlehem of the Jews, because I heard that Jesus Christ would be born

from the Virgin Mary, and I am going there to deceive her." Then Archangel Michael took her by the hair of her head, and stabbed her in the ribs with his sword, and beat her very hard in order that she tell him all her tricks, and again she said: "I will become a greyhound, and a frog, and a crow, and a pigeon and a fly and a spider."

This charm text is immediately followed in the copybook by *Afurisenile Arhangelului Mihail*, "The Curses of the Archangel Michael," that invoke the name of the Archangel Michael in a series of curses against Satan designed to banish him: *și te du în pământ pustiu, fără de apă, nelucrat unde om nu locuiește*, "and go to a desolate, waterless land where people do not live." In other copybooks, alongside these two texts featuring the Archangel Michael, we also find *Molitfele Sfântului Vasile*, the "Prayers of Saint Basil." These prayers form part of a canonical collection of prayers referred to as the *Molitfelnic* that are commonly used by Orthodox clergy in the performance of exorcisms. The prayers of Saint Basil are also read as part of the liturgy on the feast day of Saint Basil as a "ritual cleansing of the entire community" (Coțofană 2017).

The widely circulated texts briefly introduced here share certain common characteristics; notably, they affirm the central role and symbolism of the Archangel Michael in the struggle against Satan and in the salvation of humankind, and they foreground the impending final judgment and its consequences for those who ignore Christ's teachings. In this context, for the Culiac brothers the choice of the commander of the heavenly host as their leader and the decisive figure in the final battle against the Antichrist may appear to be an obvious one; but in order to assert that the Archangel Michael, John the Baptist, and Christ himself had appeared on earth in the persons of Alexandru and Grigore Culiac and their brothers and wives, they also needed to demonstrate that the necessary events leading up to the confrontation with the Antichrist had already taken place.

THE TIME OF THE ARCHANGELS

In framing their visions, Alexandru and Grigore drew on the folk legend tradition and the association that had already been made between Elijah and Enoch and their predecessors Inochentie of Balta, who had died in 1917 and whose followers they hoped to rally, and Father Feodosie Levițchi, an earlier charismatic leader and holy man who was the object of popular devotion in Moldova and the surrounding regions (see Kapaló 2019). In both Grigore's and Alexandru's texts, they place themselves at the critical juncture following the killing of the two witnesses or prophets, Elijah and Enoch of popular legend, when the Archangels are foretold to appear, as Grigore's opening lines from his vision show:

> Here is the vision that was brought to life with the presence on earth of Grigore Culiac. . . . For the true benefit of your souls believe that Father Inochentie was the prophet Elijah and that Saint Teodosie was Enoch. These two strong and great

prophets prophesied and showed the route to the Final Judgement. Christians, you heard the testimony of the Father and the Son and the Holy Spirit. The Archangel Michael and Gabriel in the flesh on earth.

(*The Visions of Grigore* [undated], 5-6)

Alexandru too situates himself in relation to the two prophets in a very similar way.

This vision was seen by Alexandru Culiac in Bessarabia, in the county Bălți, in Cornești, in the village of Todirești. And this is how it is said, the trumpet of the Final Judgement. As he sayeth, the Archangel Michael will come and will battle with the Antichrist, this he does now and this is the testimony of the 2 (the two prophets). As it was foretold 10 years ago by Father Inochentie and Saint Feodosie, which he has now done in Bessarabia. As he sayeth, the Holy Trinity has 3 (three) material forms, then [in the past] there were 2 (two) there was the Father and the Son and 3 (third) the Holy Spirit Archangel Michael.

(*A Vision* 1924:5)

Placing the prophecy of Grigore and Alexandru Culiacs' appearance as the Archangels Gabriel and Michael on the lips of Inochentie of Balta, who was already widely believed to have been the prophet Elijah come to herald the end times, allowed then to capitalize on the popularity of the recently deceased Inochentie as well as insert themselves perfectly into the role of the archangels according to the precise sequence of events in the Pseudo-Apocalypse of John, popular in the copybook tradition and in the folk eschatology of popular legend. In the apocalypse, the killing of Elijah and Enoch is immediately followed by the sending forth of the angelic host led by Michael and Gabriel sounding horns and awakening humanity. As Grigore's account affirms, the Archangels Michael and Gabriel have appeared in the flesh on earth to announce humankind's final opportunity for salvation.

Having situated themselves in the midst of the sacred drama by both affirming the prophesy of their coming and then announcing their own arrival, the brothers' texts then shift to the events leading up to their arrest sometime in 1920, the precise details of which are not given. During their time in the hands of gendarmerie and prison guards, they are mocked, beaten, and mistreated. According to Grigore's account, they were taken in "the deep snow, barefoot and naked" to Folești, the local town, and held captive in a freezing prison cell and denied food for three days; and it is at this point that Grigore begins to experience his visions: "They were all sleeping and Grigore woke from his sleep in the prison cell and a light appeared that illuminated the whole prison. And from the light came a great heat. But there was no candle or torch, it was a heavenly vision, [sent] for those Archangels, the great princes" (*The Visions of Grigore* [undated]:7).

In his vision, Alexandru describes how he was bound and mocked for the religious claims he was making. In parallel to the scene in the gospels where the Roman soldiers crown Jesus with thorns in mockery of his kingship (Matthew 27:29; Mark 15:17; John

19:2, 19:5), Alexandru's vision includes a scene where he is presented with symbols of his archangelic identity:

> and they came and men from the village took me to the Village Mayor and they tied me with my hands crossed and into one hand they placed a wheel and into the other a crutch and said that this is the Archangel Michael.
>
> (*A Vision* 1924:7)

In Alexandru's narrative, the crutch and wheel represent Michael's sword and shield, which, through this dramatic inversion, affirm rather than refute his archangelic identity. The several scenes in the texts that describe the brutality of their guards are instrumental in establishing the identities of Alexandru and Grigore as the archangels, the inference being that the Romanian authorities are the forces of the Antichrist, although this is not stated explicitly in the texts, and that through their sufferings their divine nature is revealed.

The narrative of Alexandru's text in particular leads us through many allusive twists and turns including his descent into hell, where he witnesses the sufferings of sinners reminiscent of scenes from "The Journey of the Mother of God into Hell," in which he accompanies the Mother of God into hell to show her humankind's torments. He also experiences an ascent to heaven and many battles with the Antichrist. In the course of one of these visionary battles, Alexandru encounters the demon *Avizuha* of the popular charm text found in copybooks, whom he sees "passing over the bodies searching for souls." This encounter with "her with 19 names," just as she is described in the charm text, comes immediately after his coronation alongside the Emperor of Heaven and before his realization that the final judgment has come. Alexandru also opens the "Great Hymn of the Archangel Michael," *Cântecul cel mare a* [sic] *lui Arhangelul Mihail*, which follows at the end of his vision, with the same legendary meeting in Bethlehem between Michael and *Avizuha*; but whereas in the charm Michael prevents him from abducting Jesus, in the hymn the archangel casts the demon down and releases Adam's soul from hell, an act that in Orthodox Christianity is associated with Jesus himself who descends to hell to rescue the souls of the righteous before the resurrection. In the closing lines of the hymn, in a poetic style reminiscent of popular folk charms and carols, the archangel presides at the final judgment.

> Și pe scara norului
> Șede scara raiului
> Și pe scara raiului
> Șade Arhangelul Mihail
> Cu toate vămile[23] în mână
> Și judecă toată lumea.
>
> And on the ladder of clouds
> Sits the ladder of Heaven

> And on the ladder of Heaven
> Sits the Archangel Michael
> With all the stations in his hand
> And judges all the world.

In his study of the cult of the archangels in Moldova, Vlad Bedros highlights that the rich tradition of the Archangel Michael in Moldavian orthodoxy is sometimes "inclined to practices, which from the point of view of Orthodox dogma, go to the verge of heterodoxy or heresy" (2011:96). Alexandru Culiac, inspired by the vernacular textual tradition available to him, was able to take on the identity of the archangel from the village chapbook tradition by writing himself into well-known episodes from apocryphal apocalypses and charm texts.

In contrast to Alexandru, Grigore casts himself more solidly in a Christ-like role, and instead of referencing the charm to legitimize claims, he draws on the power of "Prayers of Saint Vasile." Grigore prays alone late at night in captivity, perhaps an intentional parallel with Jesus's prayer in the garden of Gethsemane; and through the power of prayer his visions appear: "And behold here before us another vision that was shown to Grigore through the prayers of Saint Vasile" (*The Visions of Grigore* [undated]:18). The opening section of the "Prayers of Saint Vasile" is an invocation or summoning of God, and Grigore's reading of these words seems to trigger his visionary experiences and reinforce his message of divine election.

Conclusion

The examples from folk legend and from the copybook tradition presented in this chapter illustrate the intertextuality of the Culiac brothers' vision-texts while also highlighting the fluidity between oral and written traditions of folk eschatology that shaped their religious worldview and that were characteristic of folk religion in twentieth-century Moldova. The short examples presented here from the Culiacs' published visions illustrate how the brothers drew on a number of familiar texts and characters from narratives about the end of days in order to craft new texts in which they themselves were the main protagonists. The brothers' compositions illustrate the power of folk eschatology both to inspire repentance and to mobilize segments of the population to resist the reordering of social roles and religious life that was being promoted by the Romanian state and Orthodox Church in interwar Bessarabia. While peasants in Russia were using eschatological rumor as part of their widespread resistance to Soviet social and economic engineering, their compatriots in Bessarabia also found ways to resist the "civilizing" and "nationalizing" mission that was attempting to transform Moldovans in Greater Romania into loyal and trustworthy subjects of the new state (Dumitru and Negura 2014:3). Similar to the eschatology of Russian Old Believers before them, the folk-inspired eschatology of the Culiacs is projected not as an imminent event but rather as manifest in the present in their clashes and sufferings at the hands of the Romanian gendarmes in the 1920s. Theirs is a "realised eschatology" (see Clay 1998:256) that placed them directly within the apocalyptic narrative of the end times. Unlike the peasant rumors of the coming of the Antichrist that ran wild in Russia and Ukraine, however, in Bessarabia it was the power of the archangels to combat the forces of evil and realize the final judgment that took center stage. The Culiacs' texts tell us little about the identity of the Antichrist, a feature of Old Believer narratives where the tsar takes on the persona of the enemy, but reveal in great detail the attributes, deeds, and visions of the archangels.

From the perspective of folk narrative research, the Culiacs' vision-texts demonstrate that in the early twentieth century the characters of popular legend retained their saliency and that long established typological isomorphisms between figures such as Elijah and the Archangel Michael (Jiga Iliescu 2023:7) continued to serve as creative inspiration for vernacular religiosity to the extent that they could decisively shape a new religious movement that has survived into the twenty-first century. As Smith asserts, "the resources of peasant culture were manifold and contradictory, eminently capable of absorbing new elements" while also "revitalizing older elements that had lain dormant in order to cope with new tasks" (2006:317). The varied oral legends, charms, and texts of chapbooks and copybook traditions, which had formed the basis of folk ideas about evil, the Devil, and the eschaton for generations, leapt into life through the writings, deeds, and lives of the peasant visionaries introduced in this chapter.

Notes

1. It is difficult to establish with certainty the dates of birth of the brothers as Romanian and Soviet sources give conflicting information. The birth dates given here come from Alexandru Culiac's KGB personal investigation file (National Archive of the Republic of Moldova, R-3401, Inv. 2, file no. 4934, pp. 175–176). The dates of the deaths of the brothers are not given in any of the archival documents.
2. This chapter is based on ethnographic and archival research conducted in the Republic of Moldova between 2006 and 2015. The manuscript copybook presented forms part of my personal archive and was collected from members of the Archangelist movement. Archangelists do not form officially registered communities, and members remain secretive due to ongoing societal prejudice and vilification on the part of Orthodox Church clergy. For this reason, I do not give the location of the communities or the identity of individual informants.
3. Old Belief was a response to the reforms of Patriarch Nikon of Moscow, who served from 1652 to 1666. His liturgical reforms provoked mass resistance among clergy and believers alike and led to a lasting schism within the Russian Orthodox Church.
4. Seeker culture is a characteristic of twentieth-century spiritualities and is associated with the rise of the authority of the individual in forging one's own spiritual path. It is characterized by an openness toward diverse religions, ritual, and healing systems, with seekers often claiming to be "spiritual" rather than "religious."

5. In the eastern European context, the term "catacomb church" is used to refer mainly to communities of Orthodox believers and clergy who refused to accept the compromises demanded of the Orthodox Church by the Soviet state as well as to Greek Catholic communities that were forced underground when their church was banned and forcibly assimilated into the Orthodox Church in Russia, Ukraine, Romania, and elsewhere. Russian Orthodox members of the catacomb church were associated with the True Orthodoxy movement (see Vagramenko 2022).
6. The influence of the Moldovan figures listed here extended into neighboring Romania where an analogous blend of Orthodox mysticism, apocalypticism, and folklore gave birth in the early 1990s to an Orthodox revivalist movement referred to as "New Jerusalem" with many similar characteristics to Inochentism and its related offshoots (see Asavei 2020:137–148; Cloşcă 2009:331–337).
7. The revised Julian calendar was accepted by the Orthodox Churches of Constantinople, Alexandria, Antioch, Greece, Cyprus, Romania, Poland, and Bulgaria at a congress in Constantinople in May 1923 and was adopted in 1924. Russia along with Ukraine, Georgia, and Jerusalem rejected its introduction. The lunar part of the calendar, used for the calculation of Easter, was rejected by all Eastern Orthodox churches, which is why Easter is celebrated on the same day by all Orthodox churches, whereas fixed feasts such as Christmas differ between churches using the Julian calendar and those using the revised Julian calendar (which aligns with the Gregorian calendar used in Latin and Western Christianity). In this context, in Bessarabia long-established customs and practices clashed with a new form of official orthodoxy imposed from Bucharest. The adoption of the revised Julian calendar met fierce resistance in many rural communities and monasteries, giving birth to the illegal underground Old Calendarist movement.
8. The land that today we know as Moldova was incorporated into the Russian Empire in 1812 as the province of Bessarabia, having formerly formed part of the Principality of Moldavia, one of the two Romanian principalities that later formed the fledgling Romanian state. As part of its colonial imperial expansion, Russia invited settlers, primarily from the Balkans and German-speaking regions of Europe, to settle the relatively unpopulated portions of the new territory, creating an ethnic mosaic in the south of Moldova. The Moldovan cultural sphere, however, extends beyond Bessarabia into the neighboring formerly Russian provinces of Podolia and Kherson, today's Odesa region of Ukraine, which is home to a significant population of Moldovan descent.
9. Many Moldovans consider themselves part of the Romanian nation, although this is still contested by some. The language of Moldova was traditionally, and is still commonly, referred to as "Moldovan," or *limba moldovenească*. Its status as a distinct language separate from Romanian has been asserted as part of projects designed to assure Moldovan political independence and cultural distinctiveness from Romania (see King 2000).
10. During the Soviet period, Moldova was known, following Russian linguistic practice, as "Moldavia."
11. The Skoptsy (plural) broke with the Russian Orthodox Church in the eighteenth century convinced that the end times were near and that through the act of castration and sexual mutilation they could inaugurate the kingdom of heaven on earth.
12. Maliovantsy (plural), named after their founder Kondrat Maliovannyi, were Russian so-called spiritual Christians who rejected attempts to institutionalize their faith along the lines of the Baptist Church. In the 1890s, under the leadership of Kondrat Maliovannyi, they formed a millennial movement that believed that their leader was the incarnation of Christ who would ascend to heaven and then return to earth at the last judgment (Zhuk 2004:46–50).

13. Inochentie of Balta was a monk of Bessarabian peasant origin who, after having spent several years in monasteries across Russia and Ukraine, returned to the town of Balta close to his homeland of Bessarabia in what is today Odesa Oblast, Ukraine. There he encouraged the cult that had emerged around the relics of a local holy man, Feodosie Levitsky (1791–1845), and began preaching an intensely apocalyptic message of repentance. Balta became a site of mass pilgrimage under his influence before the local church leaders became concerned about his influence over the local, mainly Moldovan-speaking peasantry. In 1912, he was sent into internal exile to do penance in a monastery in the Russian far north. He was released in May 1917 and returned to Balta, where his followers had established a utopian community called the Garden of Paradise. He died there later the same year (see Kapaló 2019).
14. The sociological school of Bucharest, led by Dimitrie Gusti, pioneered the monographic research method of interdisciplinary, site-based, intensive fieldwork.
15. The territories that belonged to the historical principality of Moldavia have a strong monastic tradition. Moldavia was the center of a spiritual revival in Orthodoxy in the eighteenth century when the Ukrainian-born monk Paisii Velichkovskii was invited to lead a revival of monastic life by Prince Grigore III Ghica (1764–1767 and 1774–1777).
16. The tradition of heavenly letters has a long genealogy but probably became popular in eastern Europe under the influence of the flagellants from the fourteenth century onward. The miraculous letters, purportedly written by God or Christ, were inspired by the need for repentance in the expectation of the approaching final judgment and most commonly call on believers to observe Sundays and religious holidays. On the particular significance of the tradition of copying heavenly letters, see Smith (2006), Zayarnyuk (2006), and Kapaló (2011).
17. This and all subsequent translations into English are mine.
18. The tradition of associating the two witnesses with Elijah and Enoch is widespread from the Balkans to Russia and can be found in a plethora of sources (see, e.g., Heretz 2008; Pokrovskii 2010; Jiga Iliescu 2023). For a detailed account of the roots of the association of Enoch with the apocalypse, see Geller Badalanova (2010:22). These two Old Testament prophets are peculiarly powerful figures as they were carried up bodily into heaven without dying, giving them the power to return and intervene directly in human affairs. Also drawing on the biblical canon, and on Orthodox liturgical and patristic traditions, Elijah is expected to return twice as messenger or forebear; the first time in the person of John the Baptist (Matthew 17:10–13) and the second to herald Christ's second coming (Malachi 3:1) (Jiga Iliescu 2023).
19. The strict observance of the Sabbath as prescribed in the heavenly letter is one of the characteristics of Archangelist practice that differentiates its followers from their Orthodox neighbors and co-villagers.
20. Hasdeu published this version in his two-volume collection of Romanian popular literature in 1878–1881 (Hasdeu 1984:229–294).
21. The demon's name has several permutations. In the example given here she appears as *Avizuhii* but is also frequently given as *Avestița* and *Avizuha*.
22. These are the initial letters of the "Sanctus" or "Hymn of Victory" in Romanian, *Sfânt, Sfânt, Sfânt, Domnul Savaot*, or Holy, Holy, Holy, Lord of Hosts, with the final letter "O" representing the final syllable of *Savaot*. Elsewhere in the manuscript, *Savaot* appears as two words, *Sava Of*. The intention behind the placing of the "Hymn of Victory" before the charm text may be to emphasize Michael's role as commander of the heavenly host. Many thanks to Dumitru Lisnic for our discussions on abbreviations of liturgical prayers in Romanian.

23. *Vamă* (sg.), *vămi* (pl.) refers in Romanian popular belief to a series of stations or stops through which the soul has to pass after death in order to reach the kingdom of heaven.

Works Cited

Alexandrov, A. 1958. *Propovăduitorii obscurantismului (esența reacționară a sectelor religioase ale inochentiștilor, iehoviștilor și murașcoviților)*. Chișinău: Editura de Stat a Moldovei.

Asavei, Maria Alina. 2020. *Art, Religion and Resistance in (Post-)Communist Romania: Nostalgia for Paradise Lost*. London: Palgrave Macmillan.

Ballinger, Pamela. 2004. "'Authentic Hybrids' in the Balkan Borderlands." *Current Anthropology*, 54/1:31–60.

Bedros, Vlad. 2011. "Cultul Arhangelilor—Surse literare și iconografie. Moldova secolelor XV-XVI." In *Arhangeli și îngeri*. Stavropoleos, Bucharest: Deiesis.

Berindei, Cosmina-Maria. 2015. *Sfîrșitul lumii și destinul postum al sufletelor în imaginarul culturii tradiționale românești*. Cluj-Napoca: Editura Mega.

Bernea, Ernest. 1997. *Spațiu, timp și cauzalitate la poporul român*. Bucharest: Humanitas.

Bowman, Marion. 2004. "Phenomenology, Fieldwork and Folk Religion." In *Religion: Empirical Studies*, ed. Steven J. Sutcliffe, 3–18. Aldershot: Ashgate Publishing.

Clark, Roland. 2021. *Sectarianism and Renewal in 1920s Romania: The Limits of Orthodoxy and Nation-Building*. London: Bloomsbury.

Clay, J. Eugene. 1988. "The Theological Origins of the Christ-Faith [Khristovschina]." *Russian History*, 15/1:21–41.

Clay, J. Eugene. 1998. "Apocalypticism in the Russian Borderlands: Inochentie Levizor and His Moldovan Followers." *Religion, State and Society*, 26/3–4:251–263.

Cloșcă, Ciprian Marius. 2009. *Ortodoxia și Noile Mișcari Religioase*. Iași: Lumen.

Coțofană, Alexandra. 2017. "The Curse Prayers of Saint Vasile or How to 'Declare War on the Devil.'" In *Religion and Magic in Socialist and Post-Socialist Contexts: Historic and Ethnographic Case Studies of Orthodoxy, Heterodoxy, and Alternative Spirituality*, eds. Alexandra Cotofana and James M. Nyce, 99–118. Stuttgart: Ibidem Press.

Crummey, Robert O. 1993. "Old Belief as Popular Religion: New Approaches." *Slavic Review*, 52/4:700–712.

Dumitru, Diana, and Petru Negura. 2014. "Editorial: Moldova: A Borderland's Fluid History." *Euxeinos*, 15–16:3–8.

Engelstein, Laura. 1999. *Castration and the Heavenly Kingdom: A Russian Folktale*. Ithaca, NY: Cornell University Press.

Gaster, Mozes. 1900. "Two Thousand Years of a Charm against the Child-Stealing Witch." *Folklore: Transactions of the Folklore Society*, 11/11:129–162.

Gaster, Mozes. n.d. *Studii de folclor comparat*. Bucharest: Editura Saeculum I.O.

Geller Badalanova, Florentina. 2010. *2 (Slavonic Apocalypse of) Enoch: Text and Context*. Preprint 410. Berlin: Max Planck Institute for the History of Science.

Hammer, Olav, and Mikael Rothstein. 2012. "Canonical and Extracanonical Texts in New Religions." In *The Cambridge Companion to New Religious Movements*, eds. Olav Hammer and Mikael Rothstein, 113–129. Cambridge: Cambridge University Press.

Harrison, John F. C. 1979. *The Second Coming: Popular Millenarianism 1780–1850*. London: Routledge.

Hasdeu, Bogdan Petreceicu. 1984. *Cuvente den bătrîni*. Vol 2, *Cărţile poporane ale romînilor în secolul XVI în legătură cu literatura poporană nescrisă*. Bucureşti: Editura Didactică şi Pedagogică.

Hasdeu, Bogdan Petreceicu. 2017. *Lumea de apoi (sfîrşitul lumii):Ediţie critică, prefaţă şi anchetă mitologică contemporană, privitoare la sfîrşitul lumii de I. Oprişan*. Bucharest: Editura Saeculum I.O.

Heretz, Leonid. 2008. *Russia on the Eve of Modernity: Popular Religion and Traditional Culture under the Last Tsars*. Cambridge: University of Cambridge Press.

Ivanits, Linda J. 1992. *Russian Folk Belief*. New York: M. E. Sharpe.

Jiga Iliescu, Laura. 2006. *Răsplata paradisului: Filoane livreşti şi orale ale tradiţiilor despre blajini în spaţiul românesc*. Bucharest: Editura Academiei Române.

Jiga Iliescu, Laura. 2023. *Monografia tipologică a personalului legendar Sfântul Ilie. Tipologie, comentarii, corpus de texte*. Bucharest: Institutul de Etnografia şi Folclor Constantin Brăiloiu al Academiei Române.

Kapaló, James A. 2011. *Text, Context and Performance: Gagauz Folk Religion in Discourse and Practice*. Leiden: Brill.

Kapaló, James A. 2013. "Folk Religion in Discourse and Practice." *Journal of Ethnology and Folkloristics*, 7/1:3–18.

Kapaló, James A. 2014. "'She Read Me a Prayer and I Read It Back to Her': Gagauz Women, Miraculous Literacy and the Dreaming of Charms." *Religion and Gender*, 4/1:3–20.

Kapaló, James A. 2019. *Inochentism and Orthodox Christianity: Religious Dissent in the Russian and Romanian Borderlands*. London–New York: Routledge.

King, Charles. 2000. *The Moldovans: Romania, Russia and the Politics of Culture*. Stanford, CA: Stanford University Press.

Kizenko, Nadieszda. 2000. *A Prodigal Russian Saint: Father John of Kronstadt and the Russian People*. University Park, PA: Pennsylvania State University Press.

Kvilinkova, Elizaveta N. 2012. *Апокрифы в зеркале народной культуры гагаузов*. Kishinev and Blagoevgrad: Labirint.

Kvilinkova, Elizaveta N. 2017. "Gagauz Religious Manuscript Tradition in the Context of Moldavian Ethnic and Cultural Influence (on the Example of the Origin of the Gagauz Version of the Epistle on Sunday)." *Revista de Etnologie şi Culturologie*, 2:29–35.

Lammel, Annamária, and Ilona Nagy. 2005. *Parasztbiblia*. Budapest: Osiris Kiadó.

Lesiv, Mariya. 2013. "Ukrainian Paganism and Syncretism: 'This Is Indeed Ours!'" In *Modern Pagan and Native Faith Movements in Central and Eastern Europe*, eds. Kaarina Aitamurto and Scott Simpson, 128–145. Durham: Acumen.

Lookingbill, Brad. 1994. "'A God Forsaken Place': Folk Eschatology and the Dust Bowl." *Great Plains Quarterly*, 14/4:273–286.

Lucrările care s'au lucrat în anul 1920. n.d. Publisher unknown.

Lyubimova, Galina V. 2009. "'Technological Eschatology' in Modern Traditions of Popular Orthodoxy and among the Old Believers of Siberia." *Archaeology, Ethnology and Anthropology of Eurasia*, 37/3:119–127.

Lyubimova, Galina V. 2016. "Экологические аспекты религиозных воззрений и обрядовых практик сельского населения Сибири (1920-е гг.- начало xxi в.)." *The Soviet and Postsoviet Review*, 43:98–138.

Oprişan, Ionel. 2017. "Mitul sfârşitului lumii în viziunea poporului român şi a lui B. P. Hasdeu." In Lumea de apoi (sfîrşitul lumii):Ediţie critică, prefaţă şi anchetă mitologică contemporană,

privitoare la sfîrșitul lumii de I. Oprișan, ed. Bogdan Petreceicu Hasdeu, 5-10. Bucharest: Editura Saeculum I.O.
O vedenie ce s'a arătat în anul 1920. 1924. Iași: Institutul de Arta Grafice "Versuri și Proză."
Paert, Irina. 2005. "Preparing God's Harvest: Maksim Zalesskii, Millenarianism, and the Wanderers in Soviet Russia." *The Russian Review*, 64/1:44-61.
Pamfile, Tudor. 1997. *Sărbătorile la români*. Bucharest: Editura Saeculum I.O.
Pamfile, Tudor. 1999. *Boli și leacuri la oameni, vite și păsări după datinele și credințele poporului român*. Bucharest: Editura Saeculum I.O.
Panchenko, Aleksandr. 2001. "Eschatological Expectations in a Changing World: Narratives about the End of the World in Present Day Russian Folklore." *Folklorica: The Journal of the Slavic, East European, and Eurasian Folklore Association*, 6/1:10-25.
Panchenko, Alexandr. 2004. "New Religious Movements and the Study of Folklore: The Russian Case." *Folklore*, 28:111-128.
Pócs, Éva. 2002. "'Lilith és kísérete.' Gyermekágyas-démonoktól védő ráolvasások Délkelet-Európában és a Közel-Keleten." In *Magyar néphit Közép és Kelet-Európa határán*, vol. 1, ed. Éva Pócs, 213-238. Budapest: L'Harmattan.
Pokrovskii, N. N. 2010. "The Popular Eschatology of the *Gazette* of 1731." *Russian Studies in History*, 49/3:42-50.
Popovschi, Nicolae. 1926. *Mișcarea de la Balta sau inochentismul în Basarabia*. Chișinău: Tipografia Eparhială-"Cartea Românească."
Povedák, István. 2014. "Láthatatlan határok. A keresztény-újpogány szinkretizmus." In *Sámán sámán hátán. A kortárs pogányság multidiszciplináris elemzése*, eds. István Povedák and Réka Szilárdi, 55-77. Szeged: MTA-SZTE Vallási Kultúrakutató Csoport.
Povedák, István. 2019. "Keresztes újpogányok és életfás keresztények? Kísérlet a kortárs pogányság rítusainak elemzésére." *Pannonhalmi Szemle*, 3:51-65.
Primiano, Leonard N. 1995. "Vernacular Religion and the Search for Method in Religious Folklife." *Western Folklore*, 54/1:37-56.
Primiano, Leonard N. 2012. "Afterword: Manifestations of the Religious Vernacular: Ambiguity, Power, and Creativity." In *Vernacular Religion in Everyday Life: Expressions of Belief*, eds. Marion Bowman and Ülo Valk, 382-391. Bristol, CT: Equinox.
Repciuc, Ioana. 2011. "The Archaic Time Perception in the Modern Times: An Ethnological Approach towards a Religious Minority." *Journal for the Study of Religions and Ideologies*, 10/30:80-101.
Rosaldo, Renato. 1989. *Culture and Truth: The Remaking of Social Analysis*. Boston: Beacon.
Schneemelcher, W., ed. 1992. *New Testament Apocrypha*, Revised edition of the collection initiated by Edgar Hennecke, vol. 2. Cambridge: James Clark.
Schwartz, Hillel. 1987. "Millenarianism." In *Encyclopedia of Religion*, ed. Lindsay Jones, 2nd ed. 6028-6038. Detroit, MI: Macmillan.
Smith, Steve. 2006. "Heavenly Letters and Tales of the Forest: 'Superstition' against Bolshevism." *Forum for Anthropology and Culture*, 2:316-339.
Stahl, Henri H. 1931. "Despre inochentie și inochentism, fragment de convorbire cu părintele zamă, din satul cornova." *Arhiva Pentru Știința Și Reforma Socială*, 10/1-4:175-183.
Stewart, Charles. 2012. *Dreaming and Historical Consciousness in Island Greece*. Cambridge, MA: Harvard University Press.
Timotin, Andrei. 2002. "La littérature eschatologique Bizantine et post-Bizantine dans les manuscrits Roumains." *Revue des Études Sud-Est Européennes*, 1-4:151-166.

Toporkov, A. L. 2019. "St Sisinnius' Legend in Folklore and Handwritten Traditions of Eurasia and Africa (Outcomes and Perspectives of Research)." *Studia Litterarum*, 4/2:312–341.

Vagramenko, Tatiana. 2022. "Visualizing Invisible Dissent: Red-Dragonists, Conspiracy and the Soviet Secret Police." In *The Secret Police and the Religious Underground in Communist and Post-communist Eastern Europe*, eds. James A Kapaló and Kinga Povedák, 60–82. London–New York: Routledge.

Vedeniile lui Grigore Culiac și pătimirile lui pentru mărturisirea venirii a doua a domnului Isus Hristos. n.d. Iași: Viața Românească S.C.

Viola, Lynn. 1990. "The Peasant Nightmare: Visions of Apocalypse in the Soviet Countryside." *The Journal of Modern History*, 62/4:747–770.

Wojcik, Daniel. 1997. *The End of the World as We Know It: Faith, Fatalism, and Apocalypse in America*. New York: New York University Press.

Zayarnyuk, Andriy. 2006. "Letters from Heaven: An Encounter between the 'National Movement' and 'Popular Culture.'" In *Letters from Heaven: Popular Religion in Russia and Ukraine*, eds. John-Paul Himka and Andriy Zayarnyuk, 165–200. Toronto: Toronto University Press.

Zhuk, Sergei I. 2004. *Russia's Lost Reformation: Peasants, Millenialism, and Radical Sects in Southern Russia and Ukraine, 1830–1917*. Washington, DC: Johns Hopkins University Press.

CHAPTER 18

SONGS, RITES, AND IDENTITY IN THE RELIGIOUS FOLKLORE OF LATVIA AND LITHUANIA

MICHAEL STRMISKA, GATIS OZOLIŅŠ,
ODETA RUDLING, AND DIGNE ŪDRE

IN this chapter we examine the religious folklore of the Baltic region of northeastern Europe.)[1] Though there are three modern-day Baltic nation-states—Lithuania, Latvia, and Estonia (Fig. 18.1)—this discussion will be limited to Lithuania and Latvia, which possess a common Indo-European linguistic and cultural heritage not shared by Estonia, which has Finno-Ugric roots. With Christianity long the dominant religion in Europe, it might be assumed that European "religious folklore" expresses primarily Christian content. The Baltic region defies this expectation by having a great deal of folklore that either is rooted in pre-Christian, Pagan traditions; blends Christian and Pagan elements; or relabels Pagan contents as Christian (Balys 1972a, 1972b; Gimbutas 1963; Vaitkevičius 2009).

HISTORICAL OVERVIEW

Latvian and Lithuanian constitute the two surviving languages of the Baltic branch of the Indo-European language tree. A third Indo-European, Baltic language, Old Prussian, became extinct by the seventeenth century. The first Indo-Europeans, presumably the ancestors of the later Baltic peoples, are thought to have arrived in the Baltic region as early as 2500 BCE (Gimbutas 1997). Amber harvested from the Baltic Sea shores gave rise to a thriving trade that linked the Baltic peoples with the ancient Egyptians,

FIG. 18.1. Baltic States map from freeworldmaps.net.
(Accessed with permission from https://www.freeworldmaps.net/europe/baltic-states/baltic-states-map.jpg.
© www.freeworldmaps.net.)

Greeks, and Romans. Roman historian Tacitus describes an amber-gathering, goddess-worshipping Baltic tribe called the Aestii in his first-century work *Germania*.

By the late first millennium CE, the Baltic peoples had a fairly sophisticated Bronze Age lifestyle similar to other peoples in northern Europe at this time, with beautiful metalworking and thriving tribal communities centered around wooden hill forts. Viking raiding and trading in the tenth and eleventh centuries was followed by German crusader invasions from the twelfth through fifteenth centuries (Christiansen 1980).

Conquered by Christian knights by the end of the twelfth century, Latvia and Estonia, known together as "Livonia," became integrated into the German–Scandinavian world and the Hanseatic trade network (Kasekamp 2011). Lithuania maintained its Pagan traditions and resisted Christianization by transforming itself into the large and powerful, multiethnic and multireligious Grand Duchy of Lithuania, which encompassed much of modern-day Belarus and Ukraine and portions of western Russia in addition to Lithuania (Norkus 2018). A 1386 alliance with Poland to fend off German crusaders brought Catholicism and Polonization to Lithuania (Cruz 2014).

Latvia's and Lithuania's ethnic identities, including the Latvian and Lithuanian languages and Pagan religious traditions, were primarily preserved among the peasantry, with upper-class Latvians strongly influenced by German and Swedish ways, eventually including Lutheranism, and upper-class Lithuanians increasingly adopting Polish manners, including Catholicism. Clerics in both countries expressed consternation at the persistence of Pagan customs among the peasantry, despite the Church's increasingly dominant position. Pagan calendrical rites, solstice customs, and ancestor veneration endured, often relabeled as Christian observances without the original meanings ever being totally erased or replaced (Gimbutas 1963, 1997).

Both countries came under Russian tsarist rule in the eighteenth century. Influenced by Romanticism, Lithuanian and Latvian intellectuals, artists, and activists discovered great value and meaning in their ethnic folkways, though these had been scorned by the foreign-born elite. Scholars endeavored to collect and study folk songs and other folklore in both Latvia and Lithuania. This new appreciation of native languages, rural folklore, and Pagan traditions helped drive the nineteenth-century "national awakening" movements that came to fruition after World War I, when all three Baltic States became independent republics during the interwar period lasting from 1918 to 1940. A flowering of interest in rural customs and Pagan traditions was suppressed under Soviet rule after World War II, only to reassert itself in the more liberal, late Soviet era of 1980s *glasnost* and *perestroika* and reach its apex of enthusiasm in the second "national awakening" period of the late 1980s to early 1990s. The Baltic States threw off the Soviet yoke to become independent republics for the second time. Pagan religious associations, namely *Dievturi* in Latvia and *Romuva* in Lithuania, became established, legally recognized forms of religion in both countries, remaining active to the current time (Muktupāvels 2005; Nastevičs 2018a; Strmiska 2005; Strmiska and Dundzila 2005) (Fig. 18.2).

Pagan Elements in Latvian *Dainas*, Lithuanian *Dainos*, and Other Forms of Baltic Folklore

The type of Baltic folklore which most powerfully expresses pre-Christian, Pagan content is the genre of *daina* folk songs (Latvian plural form *dainas*, Lithuanian plural *dainos*). Both will be henceforth referred to as *dainas* for the sake of convenience now. Dainas may

FIG. 18.2. Romuva members singing at the beginning of a ritual. Krivis Hill, Vilnius, May 2015.
(Credit: Michael Strmiska.)

be sung with or without instrumental accompaniment, often provided by the zither-like Latvian *kokles* and its cousin the Lithuanian *kanklės* (Muktupāvels 2000). Dainas are rich in meaning and stand up quite well as Latvian and Lithuanian folk poems, even without the aid of music. Latvian dainas are generally brief and laconic, somewhat like Japanese haikus; but mythological dainas may display greater length and a multi-stanza structure. Lithuanian dainas exhibit a freer structure in general, with no limit on the number of stanzas. In the following Lithuanian *daina*, the sun and God referred to are more properly *Saulė*, the Lithuanian sun goddess, and *Dievas*, the Lithuanian sky god, whose name is also used for the Christian God. The Latvian equivalents are *Saule* and *Dievs*.

> Miela Saulyte, Dievo dukryte,
> Kur taip ilgai užtrukai,
> Kur taip ilgai gyvenai,
> Nuo mūs atstojus?

> O little Sun, God's daughter
> Where have you stayed so long?
> Where have you dwelt so long?
> Why have you left us all alone?

> Po jūrių, po marių
> Kavojau siratėles,
> Sušildžiau piemenaičius
>
> Beyond the seas and the hills
> I've shielded homeless orphans
> And kept the shepherds warm.
>
> Miela Saulyte, Dievo dukryte,
> Kas rytais vakarėliais?
> Prakūrė Tau ugnelę?
> Tau klojo patalėlį?
>
> O little Sun, God's daughter
> Who made your fire at dawning?
> Who made your fire at twilight?
> Who made your bed for you?
>
> Aušrinė, vakarinė:
> Aušrinė ugnį prakūrė,
> Vakarinė patalą klojo
> Daug mano giminėlės
> Daug mano dovanėlių.
>
> Morning Star and Evening Star
> The Morning Star my fire,
> The Evening Star my bed,
> I'm blessed with many kinsmen
> Many are my gifts.
>
> Rēzadainos (1958:282), Eng. trans., Katzenelenbogen
(1935:55, *daina* no. 6)

Dainas contain few sustained narratives, let alone any epics. They may, at first glance, seem little more than mundane reflections on nature and rural life with a bit of mythology sprinkled in for spice. This simplicity is deceptive, however, as many dainas skillfully juxtapose multiple levels of meaning including speculations on the order of the world, the activities of the gods, and the nature of the afterlife (Juzala 2012–2013; Vikis-Freibergs 1986, 1989). To cite a characteristic Latvian daina,

> Kalējs kala debesīs,
> Ogles bira Daugavā:
> Saules meitas saktu kala,
> Dieva dēli zobentiņu.
>
> Jāņu nakti nepazinu
> Kura sieva, kura meita:

I sievām, I meitām
Zaļš ozola vainadziņš.

Kalējs kala debesīs,
Ogles bira Daugavā:
Saules meitas saktu kala,
Dieva dēla zobentiņu.

The blacksmith hammers in the sky
Coals fall into the Daugava river:
He is forging a brooch for the sun goddess' daughter,
A sword for the sky god's son.

Dainas Bula et al. (2012:464, LD [*Latvian Dainas*] 33728)

Parallels between daina divinities and Indo-European mythology form a key argument for the antiquity of Lithuanian and Latvian Pagan heritage (Calin [1996] 2021; Chatterji 1968; Gimbutas 1963; Puhvel 1974, 1987). Scholars such as Endre Bojtár (1999) have expressed skepticism as to whether dainas actually mention gods at all, arguing that the Baltic "gods" may simply be metaphors for natural forces like sun, moon, and thunder that have been overinterpreted by excessively enthusiastic scholars, who imagine deities where none exist. With the existence of the gods summarily rejected, the Indo-European connections are likewise dismissed as fictitious. Such hyperskepticism is, however, a minority view, with most scholars continuing to regard dainas as preserving, however imperfectly, authentic traditions of pre-Christian Baltic deities with recognizable Indo-European features (Beresnevičius 2004; Biezais and Ankrava [1987] 2005; Greimas [1985] 1992; Paliepa 2011; Straižys and Klimka 1997; Vėlius 1989, 1996).

Latvian dainas first received serious scholarly attention from the German philosopher J. G. Herder, who encountered Latvian song traditions while a schoolmaster in Riga from 1764 to 1769 (Šmidchens 2014:24–29). Herder characterized folk songs such as dainas as expressions of each nation's distinctive "folk-soul," stimulating scholarly research into Latvian folk culture and kindling a new ethnic self-awareness (Jaremko-Porter 2008).

Under the leadership of Krišjānis Valdemars and others, folklore studies became both an academic pursuit and a political, nation-building process involving not only professional scholars but also lay enthusiasts and vernacular intellectuals. Nearly nine hundred correspondents representing different professional groups, generations, and levels of education assisted folklorist Krišjānis Barons in collecting song texts from across Latvia between 1894 and 1915, resulting in *Latvju dainas*, a six-volume compilation of some 217,996 Latvian *daina* folk song texts, with later additions (Barons, Visendforfs 1922). It remains the most prominent corpus of dainas in Latvia (Bula 2017).

Barons organized this collection into sections devoted to the life cycle of birth, childhood, marriage, farm and family, old age, and death, often including allusions to Pagan myths, beliefs, and practices, all in a pre-modern, rural context. Even Dievs, the high god of the Latvian pantheon, is portrayed as a hard-working farmer (Biezais and Ankrava 2005; Ogle 2012). Barons begins with a section of songs on the practice and significance of singing itself, emphasizing the importance of folk songs in Latvian traditional culture as something of a "school of song" for the rural population. This declaration of a distinctive Latvian culture possessing depth and beauty was a direct challenge to the old Baltic German aristocracy, which generally regarded the Latvians as culturally inferior, if not altogether lacking in culture, with Latvian Pagan traditions receiving particular scorn (Pūtelis 1997, 2003). It is, however, worth noting that the first to collect and comment on Latvian folklore were, in fact, Baltic Germans.

Latvian composers in the later nineteenth century created choral works that blended Latvian folk music with more contemporary European musical styles. These compositions became the mainstay of national singing festivals which were inaugurated in 1873 to rapturous public response, continuing today as extravagant quadrennial celebrations of Latvian song and dance in which thousands participate, with local groups practicing for years to compete at the national level (Smidchens 2014) (Fig. 18.3). Several of the most beloved Latvian national songs debuted at these festivals, including "Dievs, Svētī Latviju" ("God, Bless Latvia"), composed by Kārlis Baumanis, in 1873. It is now the Latvian national anthem. Such compositions were not "pure" folk songs but represented the fruitful grafting of Latvian folk traditions onto newer artistic forms.

The study of Lithuanian dainas followed a similar course, with nineteenth-century scholarly research into Lithuanian folk heritage, including its Pagan elements, inspiring new ethnic pride and a mass movement for national independence (Sadauskienė 2021). Collections of Lithuanian dainas were published by Liudvikas Rėza (Ludwig Rhesas) in 1825, Simonas Stanevičius in 1829, Antanas Juška in 1880–1882, and Adolfas Sabaliauskas and Augustas Niemis in 1911.

Historians such as Teodoras Narbutas (Teodor Narbutt; 1764–1864) and Simonas Daukantas (1793–1864) produced romanticized accounts of the Lithuanian Pagan past, further promoting Lithuanian pride in its ethnic culture and the pursuit of national independence (Krapauskas 2000). The first volume of Narbutas's nine-volume history of Lithuania was entirely devoted to Lithuanian Paganism. He took considerable poetic license, including inventing altogether new gods. The folklorist Jonas Basanavičius (1851–1927) became a leading figure in the independence movement and is now regarded as a founding father of the Lithuanian Republic.

Interest in Lithuanian Paganism received a boost from comparative Indo-European linguistics when the Lithuanian language was found to share archaic features with ancient Sanskrit, as was also true of Latvian (Calin [1996] 2021; Paliepa 2011). These affinities were found to also indicate mythological correspondences between Vedic-Hindu deities and pre-Christian Baltic gods. This Indo–Baltic link would become an important auxiliary theme in both Lithuanian and Latvian nationalistic discourses, making the small Baltic nations distant relatives of the much larger nation of India and

FIG. 18.3. Latvian Song and Dance Festival rehearsal. July 2018, Riga.
(Credit: Uģis Nastevičs. © Uģis Nastevičs.)

Baltic Paganism the long-lost cousin of ancient Hinduism. This theme would resurface in the Pagan revival movements of later times (Strmiska 2012b).

The pre-Christian religious milieu perceived in dainas and other folklore became a favored theme of Latvian and Lithuanian writers. In 1858, the Latvian philologist and author Juris Alunāns (1832–1864) applied much the same "creative" method as his Lithuanian counterpart Narbutas, "improving" the documented pantheon by inventing a number of new deities (Misāne 2011).

Alunāns's work inspired Andrejs Pumpurs (1841–1902) to craft a Latvian national epic, *Lāčplēsis* (The Bear-Slayer), first published in 1888, which also contained a number of newly minted "ancient" gods. Pumpurs envisioned Lāčplēsis as a medieval Latvian Pagan peasant hero defending the Latvian nation against German Christian invaders, with the Pagan gods looking on. In the 1980s, Pumpurs's epic would be repackaged as a "rock opera" in 1988 with libretto by Māra Zālīte and music by Zigmārs Liepiņš. At a moment when Latvians were on the verge of breaking free of the Soviet Union, a high-energy, rock-and-roll Lāčplēsis could not have been more welcome (Šmidchens 2014:246–248).

Rainis (Jānis Pliekšāns; 1865–1929), a revered Latvian poet of the early twentieth century, also utilized folkloric themes. Drawing on Alunāns as had Pumpurs, he featured Lāčplēsis as a character in his plays *Uguns un nakts* (*Fire and Night*) and *Rīgas ragana* (*The Witch of Riga*). The main character in the latter, the witch Dedze, daughter of Lāčplēsis, attempts to save Latvia from Russian invasion with Pagan magic.

The Lithuanian writers Vincas Krėvė-Mickevičius (1882–1954) and Vilhelmas Storosta (German name Wilhelm Storost, pen name Vydūnas; 1868–1953) similarly drew on dainas and folk traditions to glorify the Lithuanian Pagan past. Vydūnas was actively involved in the revival of summer solstice celebrations in Lithuania, and his trilogy of plays entitled *Amžina Ugnis* (*The Eternal Fire*) pays tribute to the fire altars of the Pagan Prussians, where, according to tradition, a constantly burning flame was maintained as a religious duty (Willeke 1990).

With Latvia and Lithuania reborn as independent republics after World War I, the 1920s–1930s saw intensified interest in dainas and other folklore as part of a renewed quest for national identity. In Latvia, there was a particular effort to foster "Latvian" styles in multiple spheres of society from art to architecture to seasonal celebrations (Ogle 2012). This promotion of ethnic culture and national identity came to a stop with the Soviet and Nazi invasions of World War II, followed by the Soviet occupation that would last until Latvia and Lithuania regained their independence in 1991 (Boldāne-Zeļenkova 2019).

A number of folklorists in this period investigated religious dimensions of Latvian folklore. Pēteris Šmits (1869–1938) published the first serious study of Latvian Pagan mythology in 1918 (Ķencis 2012; Šmits [1918] 2009). Šmits mapped out the academic terrain brilliantly, critiquing popular romantic ideas of a Latvian Pagan pantheon, noting how earlier scholars had at times crossed the line from investigating past beliefs and traditions to inventing them. Šmits thereby added a cautionary note to the study of Baltic Paganism no less relevant today than in his time. Šmits was also an Indo-European comparativist who saw the value of measuring Latvian mythological and religious phenomena against other Indo-European traditions, a path followed by later researchers such as Haralds Biezais (1909–1995) and Marija Gimbutas (1921–1994).

Other scholars also researched religious aspects of Latvian folklore in this period. Arveds Švābe examined the sacredness of oak trees in Latvian tradition, Mārtiņš Bruņenieks studied the relationship of the Pagan goddess Māra to the Christian Mary, Kārlis Straubergs researched folk magic and afterlife beliefs, and Ludvigs Adamovičs investigated Baltic funerary customs (Ķencis 2012; Kursīte 2005a, 2005b).

The 1920s also saw the formation of a Pagan religious movement firmly based in Latvian folklore, *Dievturība*, often shortened to *Dievturi*, a name loosely translating as "the keepers of God [*Dievs*]." As noted, Dievs means "God" in a general sense but more specifically indicates the Latvian sky god, with well-established Indo-European parallels. Dievturi also includes a Pagan trinity of Dievs and the goddesses *Māra* and *Laima*. This is a distinctly Dievturi trinitarianism not shared by *Romuva*, the major Pagan movement in Lithuania (Strmiska 2005). Dievturi's founder and main leader was the artist, folklorist, amateur archaeologist, and ardent nationalist Ernests Brastiņš (1892–1942) (Fig. 18.4).

FIG. 18.4. Ernests Brastiņš with Milda Apsīte and Alīne Bērziņa at the theatrical performance of "The Wedding of the Ancestors," Riga, January 12, 1935.
(Credit: Latvian State Archive of Audiovisual Documents. © Latvian State Archive of Audiovisual Documents.)

Though Dievturi partook of the extreme ethnonationalism and anti-Semitism common in its time (Misāne 2000, 2001; Stašulāne 2012), the movement established an enduring form of Pagan revival religion. Though it suffered repression in the Soviet period, Dievturi resurfaced after independence in 1991 to become an officially recognized Latvian religion centered on ethnic folk culture in which the dainas are regarded as something of a musical scripture (Ozoliņš 2013; Strmiska 2005). Dievturi has remained a small but significant force in Latvian society up to the present, constructing an impressive temple adorned with folk symbols and cosmological motifs on the Daugava River island of Lokstene in 2017 (Nastevičs 2018b; Ozoliņš and Stašulāne 2017) (Fig. 18.5).

Interwar Lithuania saw similar activity. Jonas Basanavičius continued to research Lithuanian mythology and other Pagan traditions. Jonas Beržanskis, who claimed to be a successor of the fourteenth-century Grand Duke Gediminas and was granted recognition of his Pagan faith by Russian tsarist officials in 1915, published a book in 1928

FIG. 18.5. Dievturi ritual inside the Lokstene shrine, with three members playing traditional Latvian folk instrument *kokles*, similar to a zither. Lokstene, Latvia, June 29, 2019.

(Credit: Uģis Nastevičs. © Uģis Nastevičs.)

listing a number of deities of the Baltic pantheon (Klimanskienė 2018; Trinkūnas 2009). Jonas Balys researched Baltic mythology, rites, and folk customs at Vytautas Magnus University from 1934 onward before emigrating to the United States after World War II, contributing significant essays on Lithuanian and Latvian mythology and folklore to *Funk & Wagnall's Standard Dictionary of Folklore*.

The Lithuanian parallel to Ernests Brastiņš' founding of Dievturi was the establishment by Domas Šidlauskas (1878–1944) of a Pagan revival movement that he called *Visuomybė* (Universalism), taking the name *Visuomis* for himself. Šidlauskas proclaimed his new religion in a book published in 1926—the same year Dievturi was launched. Šidlauskas attempted to reframe ancient Baltic Paganism in dualistic terms possibly derived from Zoroastrianism, with the force of good in our world identified with the Lithuanian Pagan deity Perkūnas and the force of evil with Pikulas, a deity mentioned in the scanty, garbled records of pre-Christian Baltic Prussian religion. The religion also contained a nationalistic glorification of Lithuania as a spiritually superior nation along with racist ideas about a hierarchy of human types that placed the fair-skinned Baltic peoples near the top (Dundzila 2007).

Šidlauskas established a sanctuary called *Romuva* in the town of Dusetos in northeastern Lithuania in 1930 where he led solstice rituals, fire offerings at sacred altars, and other activities. It was named for a legendary Pagan religious center in pre-Christian Old Prussia, today the Russian territory of Kaliningrad. Visuomybė attracted followers in both Lithuania and the United States among Lithuanian emigrants before fading into obscurity.

In the late 1960s, Jonas Trinkūnas (1939–2014) formed a folklore study association called *Ramuva* (Aleknaitė 2015; Čiubrinskas 2000:20–22; Pranskevičiūtė 2013:78; Rudling 2017:88; Savoniakaitė 2019). Like other folkloric and cultural movements in this period, Ramuva received support from Lithuanian authorities, as part of a Soviet strategy to foster alternative social movements that would pull people away from the Catholic Church, which remained the most potent source of opposition to Lithuanian communism (Cruz 2014; Narkutė 2002; Streikus 2017; Rudling 2017; Aleknaitė 2018). State support for Trinkūnas's Ramuva activities changed to suppression when it became clear that Trinkūnas and his associates were attempting to create an actual religious movement that might not so much weaken the Catholic Church as provide an additional, alternative form of anti-Soviet religious life (Strmiska and Dundzila 2005). Trinkūnas's increasingly religious Ramuva was shut down in the early 1970s and his academic career terminated. His group revived again in the more liberal atmosphere of *glasnost* at the end of the 1980s, openly proclaiming its religious character by taking the similar but significantly different name of *Romuva*, with its ancient Prussian and interwar Visuomybė associations. As Lithuania moved to independence in 1990–1991, Romuva offered a package of Lithuanian ethnic folklore, ancient religion, and enduring identity that suited the national mood extremely well. Romuva may have begun life under the tutelage of Soviet bureaucrats, but it would ultimately play an important part not in preserving Lithuanian communism but in burying it.

Like Dievturi in Latvia, Romuva became an officially recognized religious community in 1990s Lithuania. Trinkūnas received the Order of Gediminas from the president of Lithuania in 2013 for his contributions to ethnic culture. As with Dievturi, Romuva relies heavily on dainas as a sun form of scripture, with a well-regarded ensemble, Kūlgrinda, that records and performs updated versions of dainas dedicated to Lithuanian deities (Strmiska 2005, 2012a).

As of 2022, the current leader of both Romuva and *Kūlgrinda* is Jonas Trinkūnas's widow and successor, Inija Trinkūnienė (Fig. 18.6), a skilled singer of a distinctive genre of mesmerizing, polyphonic songs with intertwining, repetitive parts called *sutartinės*. Like dainas, sutartinės contain many references to Lithuanian Pagan gods and traditions. Unlike dainas, they are performed only by women. Sutartinės were granted the status of "intangible cultural heritage" by UNESCO in 2010. The antiquity of the genre is open to wide interpretation, with some claiming origins in the Paleolithic and others asserting a rather more recent provenance (Račiūnaitė-Vyčinienė 2002).

These differing views about the age of the sutartinės are of a piece with the varying estimations of the antiquity of many aspects of Baltic Pagan folklore. Such claims take on a polemical aspect because adherents of Pagan movements often assert the antiquity of their traditions as a measure of their value and authenticity, while critics of such claims assert that the lack of historical certainty about the actual age of Pagan traditions invalidates modern Paganism to a lesser or greater extent (Aleknaitė 2018; Nastevičs 2018a; Ozoliņš 2013). An excessive focus on slavishly reconstructing the religious forms of the past can be

FIG. 18.6. Inija Trinkūnienė, in front of a painting of Jonas Trinkūnas. Vilnius, July 2020.
(Credit: Michael Strmiska.)

stultifying for revivalist movements like Romuva or Dievturi, but the two movements have in recent times embraced greater flexibility and creativity, while still highly valuing the myths, songs, and other folkloric traditions of the past (Strmiska 2012a).

If Romuva has been distinguished by its leaders' involvement in folk music, Dievturi has had leaders accomplished in other art forms such as graphic design and kinetic art (Valdis Celms), poetry (Eva Mārtuža), and architecture (Andrejs Broks). While the Trinkūnases have dominated the national Romuva association in Vilnius, there are other local Romuva denominations with other leaders and tendencies in other parts of Lithuania (Aleknaitė 2018), just as there are other Pagan groups in Latvia besides Dievturi (Stašulāne 2009).

During the Soviet period, folklore research was stunted by Communist Party priorities. As religion could not be openly studied, most research into Baltic myth and religion in this period was carried out by émigré scholars such as the aforementioned archaeologist Marija Gimbutas, a Lithuanian who settled in the United States; the Latvian comparativist Haralds Biezais in Sweden; the Lithuanian semiotician Algirdas Julien Greimas (1917–1992) in France; and the Estonian émigré Indo-Europeanist Jaan Puhvel (b. 1932) in Canada. All relied on folklore as an important source for pre-Christian Baltic religion and Indo-European comparativism as a key framework of interpretation.

In the 1970s, Gimbutas proclaimed a controversial theory of a quasi-matriarchal "Old European" civilization supposedly preceding the later, male-oriented, war god–worshipping Indo-European culture that spread across Europe. Though Gimbutas's early studies like *The Balts* (1963) remain widely respected, the vision of a peaceful, egalitarian, pre-patriarchal society that Gimbutas put forward in such works as *The Civilization of the Goddess* (1991) received a more divided reaction, some dismissing it as consisting more of feminist fantasy than solid scholarship, others praising it for providing ideological inspiration to Lithuanian feminists in post-Soviet Lithuania and to others worldwide (Navickaitė 2019).

The reassertion of Lithuanian and Latvian ethnonational identity in the 1980s, culminating in the restoration of independence in the early 1990s, stimulated an upsurge in nationalistic appreciation for Baltic folklore, including the elevation of the Latvian and Lithuanian Pagan movements. The twenty-first century has seen a lessening of such nationalistic passions and a more critical assessment of Baltic history and folklore, including pre-Christian Paganism, which has affected Pagan revival movements as well. Uncritical and at times naive enthusiasm for recreating past traditions has been tempered by greater understanding of the difficulties involved in accurately reconstructing such traditions. This has opened the door to new creativity and new possibilities of adapting old Pagan traditions to contemporary tastes and conditions.

In post-Soviet Lithuania, the most influential researchers of Lithuanian Paganism have been Pranė Dundulienė (1910–1991), Norbertas Vėlius (1938–1996), and Gintaras Beresnevičius (1961–2006); more recently, Nijolė Laurinkienė (b. 1951), Dainius Razauskas (b. 1960), Vytautas Tumėnas (b. 1965), and Vykintas Vaitkevičius (b. 1974). In Latvia, the heirs of Haralds Biezais include the folklorists Janīna Kursīte (b. 1952) and Sandis Laime (b. 1982), the sociologist of religion Agita Misāne (b. 1965), and the linguist Didier Calin (b. 1968).

THE SUMMER SOLSTICE

Traditional celebrations of the summer solstice with singing, dancing, drinking, and feasting around communal bonfires were so deeply embedded in Latvian and Lithuanian culture that Christian authorities were more inclined to co-opt and relabel the celebrations as Christian than ban them altogether. The summer solstice practice in both countries of ritual bathing in a river or other body of water was linked to the rites of baptism performed by John the Baptist in the Bible, with the summer solstice renamed *Jāņi* in Latvia and *Joninės* in Lithuania, also known as *Līgo* in Latvia and *Rasos* in Lithuania (Anglickienė et al. 2014). The superficial nature of this relabeling is evident in the absence of much other Christian content and the abundance of Pagan symbolism, above all the songs sung to the sun goddess known as Saule in Latvia and Saulė in Lithuania, who is portrayed as dancing with her daughters in the sky (Vikis-Freibergs 2005).

In the late nineteenth century, the solstice festivals, having survived as local folkloric customs, were given a new validation as bearers of ancient pre-Christian religiosity and ethnic identity. Solstice celebrations were widely observed in the interwar period of independent republics, repressed as potential sources of ethnonational rebellion in the Soviet era, and, as with other forms of folklore, revived in the late and post-Soviet periods as expressions of renewed ethnic pride and national identity.

At the current time, the summer solstice is THE major holiday in both Latvia and Lithuania. To be in those countries in June is to see everything come to a stop in the middle of the month for the solstice celebrations. Despite the official, government-sanctioned date of the holiday being June 23 and 24, many people celebrate the festivities on the actual solstice date of June 20 or 21. Most businesses close, and cities like Riga and Vilnius become midsummer ghost towns as city dwellers seek out their country cousins to celebrate the solstice in more rural settings. A Latvian daina comments,

> Īsa, īsa Jāņu nakts
> Par visām naksniņām:
> Te satumsa, te izausa,
> Te saulīte kalniņā!
>
> Short, short, Midsummer [Jāņi] night
> Shorter than all other nights:
> Now it's twilight, now it's dawn
> Now the sun is high.
>
> Bula et al. (2012:446, LD 33200)

Though solstice celebrations have roots in pre-Christian, Pagan traditions, it should not be assumed that the solstice is a time of fervent Pagan religiosity for all Latvians or Lithuanians (Aleknaitė 2018). For most people, the solstice is mainly a fun and festive time to gather with family and friends, with the amount and degree of traditional activities being highly variable, as also the meanings attaching. Members of Dievturi, Romuva, or other Baltic Pagan associations may be highly conscious of the Pagan meanings of the songs they sing and other traditional activities; but for others, singing songs about a sun goddess and her daughters, dancing around a bonfire, rolling a burning wheel down a hillside, staying up all night to greet the dawning sun, or swimming in the sea as the sun rises may simply be fun traditions without any deeper meaning beyond having a rollicking good time being Latvian or Lithuanian (Figs. 18.7 and 18.8), as the following Latvian daina texts illustrate:

> Kas tos Jāņus ielīgoja?
> Mūsu pašu ciema ļaudis:
> Pirmie gani, pēc arāji
> Visupēc jaunas meitas.

> Who weaves the first song on Midsummer [Jāņi]?
> Our own village folk:
> First the cowherds, then the ploughmen
> Finally, the young girls [maidens].
>
> Bula et al. (2012:440, LD 32353)

> Jāņu nakti nepazinu
> Kura sieva, kura meita:
> I sievām, i meitām
> Zaļš ozala vainadziņš.

> On Midsummer night, I cannot tell
> Which one is a wife, which one a girl [maiden]:
> Both wives and girls
> Wear green oak wreaths.
>
> Bula et al. (2012:446, LD 33148)

FIG. 18.7. Ornaments set ablaze for Līgo/Jāņi, in the town Ērgļi, on the banks of the Ogre River, Vidzeme region, Latvia.

(Credit: Gatis Ozoliņš.)

FIG. 18.8. Midnight singing around the fire. Līgo/Jāņi at Vītolnieki farm museum in Kurzeme region, Latvia, June 20, 2020.

(Credit: Michael Strmiska.)

AUTUMNAL ANCESTOR VENERATION AND THE WINTER SOLSTICE

Latvia and Lithuania both possess a set of autumn-to-winter calendrical observances that flow into each other with overlapping meanings. The turning of the seasons shifts the region from the warm vitality, resplendent greenery, and natural abundance of the Baltic summer with its nearly eighteen hours of daylight at the peak of summer to the darker, dwindling days of autumn, with fragrant blossoms replaced by falling leaves. Rainy mists bear down on the land come October, setting the stage for the honoring of the dead and the fading of the year, which reaches its nadir at the time of the winter solstice with only seven hours of daylight. This is a season of contemplation and remembrance, of binding together and perseverance.

As with the summer solstice, we again find a Christian veneer over primarily Pagan content. The main Lithuanian day for the honoring of the dead is *Vėlinės*, "the day of the *vėlės*" (souls), celebrated on November 2, coinciding with the Christian All Souls Day reserved for the dead. Though the parallel feast honoring the dead in Latvia is typically observed on the last Sunday in November, the essential agreement in the two countries' ancestor traditions is evident in how in Latvian the autumnal period of honoring the dead is called *Veļu laiks*, a kindred term to Vėlinės.

In both countries, a key activity is tending to family graves, cleaning and sprucing them up, and then ornamenting them with flowers and lamps that burn through the night to light the way for the dead. In Lithuania this grave-tending takes place in the late October days leading up to Vėlinės, while in Latvia, Kapu svētki, which literally translates as "graveyard holy day," is observed in late August or early September (Muktupāvela 2005). This ancestral commemoration is one of the most important family gatherings each year for Latvians, bringing together not merely immediate relatives of the deceased but extended family as well.

A popular Lithuanian daina meditating on death and the memory of departed loved ones is "Seniai Buvau" ("So Long Ago").

>Seniai buvau, seniai buvau pas tėvulį kiemi
>Jau užaugo tie kelaliai pilkais akmenelais
>Aš tuos pilkais akmenėlius rankėlem prarisiu
>O aš del ta pas tevutį kemelin nuveisiu
>Seniai buvau, seniai buvau pas matutį kiemei
>Jau užaugo tie kelaliai pilkais baltais dobilėliais
>Aš tuos baltus dobilėlius po kojelie minsiu
>O aš del ta pas motulį kemelin nuveisiu
>Seniai buvau, seniai buvau pas brolalį kiemi
>Jau užaugo tie kelaliai pilkais žaliu beržyneliu
>Aš tuos žalius beržynėlius kirveliu pakirsiu
>O aš del ta pas brolalį kemelin nuveisiu
>Seniai buvau, seniai buvau pas sesutį kiemi
>Jau užaugo tie kelaliai žaliojom rūtytalam
>Aš tas žalias rūtytėlas rankelėm išskirsiu
>Tai aš del ta pas sesutį kemelin nuveisiu.

>So long ago, so long ago, I have been at my father's
>Those narrow paths have overgrown with stones so small and grey
>I will those stones so grey and small with my hands roll aside
>So this is how I'll take the road to my dear father's home
>So long ago, so long ago, I have been at my mother's
>Those narrow paths have overgrown with white and tiny clovers
>I will upon those clovers tread so lightly with my feet
>So this is how I'll take the road to my dear mother's home
>So long ago, so long ago, I have been at my brother's
>Those narrow paths have overgrown with birches oh so green
>I will those birches oh so green with my old ax chop down
>So this is how I'll take the road to my dear brother's home
>So long ago, so long ago, I have been at my sister's

> Those narrow paths have overgrown with greenest leaves of rue
> I will those leaves of rue so green with my hands brush aside
> So this is how I'll take the road to my dear sister's home
>
> Text and translation from Kūlgrinda CD *Rite of Fire* (2002)

In Lithuania, a secondary ancestral commemoration called *Kūčios* takes place in late December and is typically combined with Christmas Eve. This is a family feast of various traditional foods centering on *kūčia*, a special bread made with different grains and seeds. Portions of food and beer are offered to the ancestors. A Latvian echo of Lithuania's Kūčios is the *Kūķa* feast on Christmas Eve, when *kūķis* is served, a meal much the same as the Lithuanian kūčia. Traditional dainas may be sung as well as Christian ones. Except for the most committed Pagan revivalists, most Latvians and Lithuanians today do not sharply divide Pagan from Christian on these occasions.

Another practice observed in both countries during December is the display of handcrafted, house-like straw structures called *šiaudinis soda* ("straw gardens") in Lithuanian and *puzuri* in Latvian, which hang from the ceiling as mobiles, spinning and turning with the air currents around them. These mobile structures have been interpreted by some as an expression of a pre-Christian Baltic worldview, a model of a multilevel universe comprised of the underworld of chthonic spirits and the dead, the earthly world of the living, and the higher world of divine beings (Tumėnas 2013; Vaiskūnas 1992).

After the ancestral rites of November and December, the year concludes with joyful celebrations known as *Ziemassvētki* in Latvian and *Kalėdos* in Lithuanian. Originally solstice festivals, these events are now observed on December 25 to coincide with Christmas, rather than the actual 20–21 solstice date, owing to Christian influence. For many, these festivities are just amusing activities without deep meaning, but the Pagan undercurrent is perceptible to those who attend to it.

Masked processions involving mumming are other traditional activities of interest observed during the winter solstice period of Ziemassvētki and Kalėdos (Anglickienė et al. 2014; Janson [1933] 2010; Rancāne 2009; Vaicekauskas 2002). Participants would go door to door singing songs and behaving outlandishly, as these Latvian dainas suggest:

> Labvakari, nama māte
> Vai gaidīji budēlīšus?
> Ja gaidīji budēlīšus,
> Atver durvis līdz galam.
>
> Good evening, mistress of the house
> Were you expecting mummers?
> If you were expecting mummers
> Open the door wide.
>
> Bula et al. (2012:454, LD 33326)

> Zini pate, saimeniece
> Ko vajaga budēlim:

> Ceptas gaļas, baltas maizes,
> Jaunas meitas klātgulēt.
>
> You know yourself, mistress of the house
> What a mummer wants:
> Roast meat, white bread
> A young girl [maiden] to sleep with.
>
> Bula et al. (2012:456, LD 33433)

Masked revelers would act out animals like cranes, horses, bears, and goats; stereotyped human figures such as priests, doctors, millers, beggars, Roma (Gypsies), Jews, merchants, bear trainers, and witches; and other beings or concepts such as Death, Living Corpse, Luck, Misfortune, God, and the Devil. The following Latvian mumming daina refers to Roma:

> Iesam, bērni, čigānos
> Ziemas svētku vakarā:
> Dos mums ēst, dos mums dzert,
> Dos naksiņu pārgulēt.
>
> Let us play Gypsies, children
> On Yule eve:
> They'll give us food, they'll give us drink
> They'll give us shelter for the night.
>
> Bula et al. (2012:454, LD 33312.1)

Mumming and masking traditions were widespread in the nineteenth and early twentieth centuries in both Latvia and Lithuania. These boisterous activities may have originally been meant to awaken nature and energize the sun at the time when the cycle of the seasons is at its lowest and darkest ebb. They also served to reinforce social roles and mores through the performance of standard social types and behavior patterns. Masked processions and mumming became less popular in the interwar period of independent republics as well as the postwar Soviet period. They regained some popularity after 1991 as expressions of native ethnic culture but are nowadays mainly presented in primary schools as lessons in ethnic culture and performed by folklore groups, with much less frequent observation among the general population.

Pagan Folklore in Dialogue with Popular Culture

Ethnic folklore and, with it, Baltic Paganism enjoyed a surge of popularity in the early 1990s that abated in the early 2000s. Neither of the major Pagan associations, Dievturi or Romuva, has a membership exceeding 1 percent of their respective countries' populations. Their influence cannot, however, be measured in membership numbers

FIG. 18.9. Latvian singing group Tautumeitas (Daughters of the Folk) performing with Latvian neo-folk band Auļi at the Baltic culture festival Mėnuo Juodaragis (Moon of the Black Horn) at Dūburys Lake, Zarasai District, Lithuania, August 2017.

(Credit: Vincas Razma and Asta Skujytė-Razmienė. Accessed with permission from http://www.aesthastic.com/2017/08/menuo-juodaragis-xx-poperkunais.html. ©Vincas Razma and Asta Skujytė-Razmienė.)

alone as many names, motifs, and symbols associated with Baltic Paganism appear in Lithuanian and Latvian popular culture at various levels. Folk and rock music with Pagan themes from names of gods to historical events have become mainstays of Latvian and Lithuanian popular music and gatherings such as the annual *Mėnuo Juodaragis* festival in Lithuania (Fig. 18.9). These multiple, overlapping, and mutually reinforcing allusions to Pagan gods and myths in folk and popular music are constant reminders of the Pagan Baltic past (Strmiska 2012a).

Traditional Latvian and Lithuanian symbols once mainly found in textiles, jewelry, and folk art appear today in such diverse forms as fashion accessories, home furnishings, coffee mugs, bumper stickers, and refrigerator magnets, along with adorning more traditional items like mittens, woven belts, sashes, and knit caps. These symbols are commonly interpreted as expressions of a pre-Christian, Baltic Pagan worldview, an understanding dating back to the folk romanticism of the "National Awakening" in the nineteenth century and the heightened nationalism of the interwar period.

In 1923, Dievturi leader Ernests Brastiņš published the highly influential book *Latviešu ornamentika* (*Latvian Ornamentation*), which offered a systematic interpretation of various traditional ornamental patterns as signs of the chief Latvian Pagan deities. This has become known as the "mythological school of Latvian ornament"

(Ūdre 2019, Zemītis 2004). Brastiņš adapted the prevailing scholarly theories of the time to his own ethnonational purposes, viewing Latvian mythology as a living expression of the ancient Indo-European belief system. Analyzing archaeological materials and folk crafts, Brastiņš asserted that the true meanings of Latvian ornamental symbolism had been obscured by Christian influence, and he claimed to have recovered this lost pre-Christian significance. Brastiņš's interpretations of the mythological significance of traditional ornamental patterns found broad appeal with the general public, influencing popular ideas of Latvian symbols, myths, and deities down to the present time (Krūmiņa 2015). The associations Brastiņš drew between ornamental patterns and particular Pagan deities were also incorporated into the iconography of the Dievturi movement.

Lithuania has seen similar trends in the interpretation and usage of traditional symbols. With her 1958 work *Ancient Symbolism in Lithuanian Folk Art*, Marija Gimbutas began an investigation of the religious and cosmological meanings of ancient decorative markings and patterns that she would revisit in *The Language of the Goddess* (1989). Gimbutas's lifelong quest to systematize the meanings of ancient symbols has been continued by more recent Lithuanian scholars such as Vytautas Tumėnas (2008, 2009) and Vykintas Vaitkevičius (2009).

The interpretive schemes of Brastiņš, Gimbutas, and their successors are themselves open to widely differing interpretations of their validity. To those enchanted by the possibility of deep spiritual meaning in past folkloric tradition, such as the adherents of modern Pagan movements, such interpretations may be celebrated as holistic visions of ancient spirituality. For those who pride themselves on following the dictates of modern science, Brastiņš's and Gimbutas's ideas may be viewed as too speculative and unproven, indeed unprovable, to be taken as anything more than esoteric fantasy. It is therefore to be expected that both perspectives will continue to have their defenders and detractors (Meskell 1995).

One particular folkloric symbol found in contemporary Latvian textiles and elsewhere, the *auseklis* (morning star), aptly demonstrates the varying uses and interpretations and continuing popularity of such traditional symbols (Ūdre 2019). The morning star is, along with the sun and the moon, one of the three most frequently mentioned celestial deities in *daina* folk songs. It can be credibly traced back to Indo-European mythology, with analogues in Hindu Vedic myth and elsewhere (Biezais [1972] 1998). However, use of the auseklis as a visual symbol in folk ornamentation is strictly a twentieth-century phenomenon. Brastiņš and others promoted the representation of the morning star as an eight-pointed polygon, interpreting its meaning as the triumph of day over night, light over darkness. In this way, the visual symbol of the eight-pointed auseklis was inscribed with both ethnonational and religio-cosmological significance. Ironically, the eight-pointed polygon symbol is more likely of Estonian–Finno-Ugric origin than Latvian–Indo-European (Zemītis 2004) (Fig. 18.10).

The morning star also found its way into political applications of Latvian symbolism. After Kārlis Ulmanis (1877–1942) established an authoritarian regime in Latvia in 1934, the auseklis became the official symbol of the Latvian Guards Organization (*Latvijas Aizsargu organizācija*), a pro-regime paramilitary group. In the late Soviet period, the

FIG. 18.10. Morning star (*auseklis*) at the Park of Latvian Signs in Pūņas, Latvia.

(Credit: Digne Ūdre.)

auseklis took on a quite different meaning as a symbol of Latvia's peaceful struggle against the violence and repression of Soviet occupation, remaining a popular national symbol and decorative pattern in the post-Soviet era.

The Lithuanian morning star, the *aušrinė*, has been examined by Greimas (1992), Vaitkevičius (2018), and Tumėnas (2018). Greimas investigates the roles and meanings of aušrinė in a wide variety of myths and folktales, while Vaitkevičius and Tumėnas relate myths of the marriage of the goddess Aušrinė to Lithuanian wedding customs.

A more controversial symbol found in both Lithuanian and Latvian traditional culture is the swastika, which has a long history in the Baltic region, far predating the twentieth-century Nazi version of this symbol (Gimbutas 1958). The Lithuanian form of the swastika is known as the *sulaužtinis kryžiukas* (broken cross), and its Latvian equivalents are the *ugunskrusts* (fire cross) and the *perkonskrusts* (thunder cross, referring to the thunder god *Perkons*). Archaeologists and folklorists have found various swastika-like symbols on items such as pottery and jewelry dating back to the Bronze Age in Latvia, Lithuania, and Belarus (Dziarnovičius and Kviatkouskaya 1999). It should be noted that these swastikas were not solitary signs but part of a family of symbols constituting a coded visual language (Tumėnas 2008, 2014; Vaitkevičius 2019). Swastikas appear to have become more common in the thirteenth and fourteenth centuries, when Christian knights and missionaries were actively colonizing the Baltic region, suggesting that swastikas may have become associated with native resistance to foreign domination (Vaitkevičius 2020). Down to the present time, the native Lithuanian and Latvian versions of the swastika remain a common ornament on such items as scarves, woven sashes and belts, mittens, rings, and other jewelry (Ūdre 2018).

Contemporary usage of the swastika is inevitably complicated by worldwide identification of the swastika with Nazism since the time of Hitler. While Baltic folklore enthusiasts and Pagan revivalists may view the ancient Baltic forms of the swastika as legitimate ethnic and spiritual symbols far predating the Third Reich and entirely separate from Nazism, there are also ultranationalists and far right extremists who display the symbol in full awareness that it evokes the Nazi past. There is also the grim reality that in World War II a not inconsiderable number of Lithuanians and Latvians sided with the Nazis and actively participated in the killing of Latvian and Lithuanian Jews (Erzergailis 1996; Eidintas 2003; Reichelt 2015; Katz 2018). Given this constellation of factors, it is difficult today to separate the ancient Pagan associations of the swastika from the shadow of Nazism hanging over the symbol. Not surprisingly, efforts have been made to prohibit the display of the swastika as an instrument of Nazism, with champions of the retention of the symbol in its Latvian and Lithuanian forms arguing against any such ban. For the foreseeable future, the Baltic swastika will remain a contested symbol susceptible to widely varying readings.

"New Age" spirituality, with its eclectic mix of ideas and paraphernalia from crystals to karma to sacred trees to past lives, has also affected perceptions of Baltic religious folklore and its presumed functions and meanings (Ališauskienė 2012, 2017; Krūmiņa-Konkova 1999; Muktupāvela 2012). Pagan spiritual entrepreneurs with one foot in Latvian or Lithuanian folklore and the other in the cosmopolitan bricolage of the New Age, write books, run workshops, and offer spiritual teachings that link Baltic symbols, beliefs, and traditions with those of other peoples and places (Aleknaitė 2017; Stašulāne 2009). While some may criticize this as ill-founded amateurism that spoils the purity of the Baltic heritage, it could also be regarded as the natural evolution of Baltic religion—and, with it, Baltic religious folklore—in the globalized twenty-first century.

Note

1. This chapter is informed by fieldwork, interviews, and archival research as follows: Gatis Ozoliņš conducted observations and interviews of Dievturi groups in the Latvian regions of Vidzeme and Latgale and the capital city Rīga between 2006 and 2008; Odeta Rudling carried out research in government archives in Lithuania in 2014; Michael Strmiska observed and participated in summer solstice celebrations in Kernavė, Lithuania, in 1998 and in Vītolnieki, Latvia, in 2020; Digne Ūdre conducted ethnographic interviews in Rīga and other locations from 2017 to 2021.

Works Cited

Aleknaitė, Eglė. 2015. "Familiar or Exotic: Visions of the Singing Countryside in Lithuanian Folklore Ensembles." *Kultūras studijas*, 7:202–208.

Aleknaitė, Eglė. 2017. "Baltic Paganism in Lithuanian Neoshamanic Communities: Neoshamanic Interpretations of a Local Indo-European Religious Tradition." *Nova Religio: The Journal of Alternative and Emergent Religions*, 20/3:13–35.

Aleknaitė, Eglė. 2018. "Participation of Contemporary Pagans in Heritage Politics of Lithuania." *The Pomegranate: The International Journal of Pagan Studies*, 20/1:92–114.

Ališauskienė, Milda. 2012. "The New Age Milieu in Lithuania: Popular Catholicism or Religious Alternative?" In *Religious Diversity in Post-Soviet Society: Ethnographies of Catholic Hegemony and the New Pluralism in Lithuania*, eds. Milda Ališiauskienė and Ingo W. Schröder, 151–168. Burlington, VT: Ashgate.

Ališauskienė, Milda. 2017. "Introduction: New Religions in Eastern Europe, New Forms, Recent Developments." *Nova Religio: The Journal of Alternative and Emergent Religions*, 20/3:8–12.

Anglickienė, Laimutė, Giedrė Barskauskaitė, Dalia Senvaitytė, Arūnas Vaicekauskas, and Asta Venskienė. 2014. *Lietuvių šventinis kalendorius/Lithuanian Holy Calendar*. Kaunas: Vytauto Didžiojo universitetas; Vilnius: Versus Aureus.

Balys, Jonas. 1972a. "Latvian Mythology." In *Funk and Wagnalls Standard Dictionary of Folklore, Mythology, and Legend*, eds. Maria Leach and Jeremy Fried, 606–608. New York: Harper and Row.

Balys, Jonas. 1972b. "Lithuanian Mythology." In *Funk and Wagnalls Standard Dictionary of Folklore, Mythology, and Legend*, eds. Maria Leach and Jeremy Fried, 631–634. New York: Harper and Row.

Barons, Krišjānis, Henrijs Visendorfs, eds. 1922. *Latvju* dainas. 6 vols. Riga: Valters un Rapa.

Beresnevičius, Gintaras. 2004. *Lietuvių religija ir mitologija/Lithuanian Religion and Mythology*. Vilnius: Tyto Alba.

Biezais, Haralds. 1998. *Seno latviešu debesu dievu ģimene/The Latvian Family of Ancient Sky Gods*. Riga: Minerva. First published 1972 in German as *Die himmlische Gotterfamilie der alten Letten*. Stockholm: Almquist & Wiksell.

Biezais, Haralds, and Sigma Ankrava. 2005. "Baltic Religion—An Overview." In *Encyclopedia of Religion*, 2nd ed., Vol. 2, ed. Lindsay Jones, 756–762. New York: Macmillan Reference. First published 1987.

Bojtár, Endre. 1999. *Foreword to the Past: A Cultural History of the Baltic People*, trans. Szilvia Redey and Michael Webb. Budapest: CEU Press.

Boldāne-Zeļenkova, Ilze. 2019. "The Role of Ethnographers in the Invention of Socialist Traditions." *Journal of Ethnology and Folkloristics*, 13/2:33–47.

Bula, Dace. 2017. "A Complete Edition of an Oral Tradition: Text Selection: Practices in the History of Publishing Latvian Folk Songs." *Folklore*, 128/1:37–56.

Bula, Dace, Margita Gūtmane, Lauma Lapa, and Sanita Reinsone, eds. 2012. *Latvju* Dainas—*Latvian Folk Songs—Interlinear Translation*. Riga: Latvian Institute of Literature, Folklore and Art.

Calin, Didier. 1996. "Indo-European Poetics and the Latvian Folk Songs." MA thesis, Freie Universität Berlin. Revised edition published 2021. https://independent.academia.edu/DidierCalin. Accessed October 15, 2021.

Chatterji, Suniti Kumar. 1968. *Balts and Aryans in Their Indo-European Background*. Simla: Indian Institute of Advanced Study.

Christiansen, Eric. 1980. *The Northern Crusades: The Baltic and the Catholic Frontier 1100–1525*. London: Macmillan.

Čiubrinskas, Vytis. 2000. "Identity and the Revival of Tradition in Lithuania: An Insider's View." *Folk*, 42:19–40.

Cruz, Miranda Zapor. 2014. "The Role of Catholicism in the Development of Lithuanian National Identity." *Church History and Religious Culture*, 94/4:479–504.

Dundzila, Rudra. 2007, 1–4 November. "The 'Universalism?' of Domas Šidlauskas-Visuomis." Paper presented at the Collegium Association of Liberal Religious Studies annual meeting, Centerville, MD, USA.

Dziarnovičius, Alegas, and Ala Kviatkouskaya. 1999. "Svastika kaip kosmolginis simbolis ir etninis požymis/Swastika as cosmological symbol and ethnical sign." *Liaudies kultūra*, no. 3:49–53.

Eidintas, Alfonas. 2003. *Jews, Lithuanians and the Holocaust*. Vilnius: Versus Atreus.

Erzergailis, Andrew. 1996. *The Holocaust in Latvia, 1941–1944: The Missing Center*. Riga: Historical Institute of Latvia.

Gimbutas, Marija. 1958. *Ancient Symbolism in Lithuanian Folk Art*. Philadelphia, PA: Folklore Society.

Gimbutas, Marija. 1963. *The Balts*. London: Thames and Hudson.

Gimbutas, Marija. 1989. *The Language of the Goddess*. London: Thames and Hudson.

Gimbutas, Marija. 1991. *The Civilization of the Goddess*. San Francisco, CA: Harper.

Gimbutas, Marija. 1997. *The Kurgan Cultures and the Indo-Europeanization of Europe: Selected Articles from 1952–1993*, eds. Miriam Robbins-Dexter and Karlene Jones-Bley. Washington, DC: Institute for the Study of Man.

Greimas, Algirdas J. 1992. "Aušrine." In *Of Gods and Men: Studies in Lithuanian Mythology*, trans. Milda Newman, 64–111. Bloomington, IN: Indiana University Press. First published 1985.

Janson, J. Albert 2010. *Latviešu masku gājieni/Latvian Masked Processions*. Rīga: Zinātne. First published 1933 as *Die lettischen Maskenumzüge*. Riga: Selbstverlag.

Jaremko-Porter, Christine. 2008. "Johann Gottfried Herder and the Latvian Voice." PhD dissertation, University of Edinburgh.

Juzala, Gustaw. 2012–2013. "Folklore in the Modern Culture of Lithuania and Latvia." *Ethnologia Polona*, 33–34:185–195.

Kasekamp, Andres. 2011. "The New Order 1200–1500." In *A Concise History of the Baltic States*, 33–76. Cambridge: Cambridge University Press.

Katz, Dovid. 2018. "The Baltic Movement to Obfuscate the Holocaust." In *Mass Violence in Nazi-Occupied Europe*, eds. Alex J. Kay and David Stahel, 235–261. Bloomington, IN: Indiana University Press.

Katzenelenbogen, Uriah, trans. and ed. 1935. *The Daina: An Anthology of Lithuanian and Latvian Folk Songs*. Chicago: Lithuanian News Publishing Company.

Ķencis, Toms. 2012. "A Disciplinary History of Latvian Mythology." PhD dissertation. University of Tartu.

Klimanskienė, Natalija. 2018. "Kunigaikštis Jonas Gediminas Beržanskis-Klausutis." *Krantai*, 168/3:10–13.

Krapauskas, Virgil. 2000. *Nationalism and Historiography: The Case of Nineteenth Century Lithuanian Historicism*. East European Monographs No. DLIX. New York: Columbia University Press.

Krūmiņa, Inese. 2015. *Zīme, raksts, nozīme/Sign, Ornament, Meaning*. Riga: Zavaigne ABC.

Krūmiņa-Koņkova, Solveiga. 1999. "New Religions in Latvia." *Nova Religio: The Journal of Alternative and Emergent Religions*, 3/1:119–134.

Kūlgrinda. 2002. *Ugnies Apiegos/Rite of Fire*. Vilnius: Dangus Records, CD.

Kursīte, Janīna. 2005a. "Baltic Religion: History of Study." In *Encyclopedia of Religion*, ed. Lindsay Jones, 2nd ed., Vol. 2, 767–773. New York: Macmillan Reference.

Kursīte, Janīna. 2005b. "Mara (and Great Mothers)." In *Encyclopedia of Religion*, ed. Lindsay Jones, 2nd ed., Vol. 8, 5691–5694. New York: Macmillan Reference.

Meskell, Lynne. 1995. "Goddesses, Gimbutas and 'New Age' Archaeology." *Antiquity*, 69/262:74–86.
Misāne, Agita. 2000. "The Traditional Latvian Religion of Dievturība in the Discourse of Nationalism." *Religious Minorities in Latvia*, 4/29:32–52.
Misāne, Agita. 2001. "Inter-War Right-Wing Movements in the Baltic States and Their Religious Affiliation." *Acta Ethnographica Hungarica*, 46/1–2:75–87.
Misāne, Agita. 2011. "Senā reliģija un dzimstošais nacionālisms: Vēlreiz par Jura Alunāna mitoloģisko jaunradi/Ancient Religion and the Birth of Nationalism: Once Again, on the Mythological Creativity of Juris Alunāns." In *Kultūras identitātes dimensijas/Dimensions of Cultural Identity*, eds. Solveiga Krūmiņa-Koņkova and Māra Zirnīte, 99–114. Riga: University of Latvia, Institute of Philosophy and Sociology.
Muktupāvela, Rūta. 2005. "Ancestors: Baltic Cult of Ancestors." In *Encyclopedia of Religion*, ed. Lindsay Jones, 2nd ed., Vol. 1, 327–332. New York: Macmillan Reference.
Muktupāvela, Rūta. 2012. "The Mythology of Ethnic Identity and the Establishing of Modern Holy Places in Post-Soviet Latvia." *The Pomegranate: The International Journal of Pagan Studies*, 14/1:69–90.
Muktupāvels, Valdis. 2000. "On Some Relations between *Kokles* Styles and Contexts in the Twentieth Century." *Journal of Baltic Studies*, 31/4:388–405.
Muktupāvels, Valdis. 2005. "Baltic Religion: New Religious Movements." In *Encyclopedia of Religion*, ed. Lindsay Jones, 2nd ed., Vol. 1, 762–767. New York: Macmillan Reference.
Narkutė, Vilma. 2002. "The Chronicle of the Catholic Church in Lithuania in Defence of Religious Liberty (1972–1989)." *Lituanistika*, 7:159–180.
Nastevičs, Uģis. 2018a. "Latvian Religion—Dievturība?" *Reliģiski-Filozofiski Raksti*, 24:82–104.
Nastevičs, Uģis. 2018b. "Modern Holy Places of European Autochthonous Religions: The Sacred Space of Latvia and Dievturība." *Culture Crossroads*, 12:85–105.
Navickaitė, Rasa. 2019. "The Prehistoric Goddess of the Late Twentieth Century: Transnational Feminist Reception, Construction and Appropriation of Marija Gimbutas." PhD dissertation, Central European University, Budapest, Hungary.
Norkus, Zenonas. 2018. *An Unproclaimed Empire: The Grand Duchy of Lithuania from the Viewpoint of Comparative Sociology*, trans. Albina Strunga. London: Routledge.
Ogle, Kristīne. 2012. "Representations of Nature Spirits, Deities and Gods in Latvian Art in the First Half of the Twentieth Century." *The Pomegranate: The International Journal of Pagan Studies*, 14/1:47–68.
Ozoliņš, Gatis. 2013. "The Dievturi Movement in Latvia as Invention of Tradition." In *Modern Pagan and Native Faith Movements in Central and Eastern Europe*, eds. Kaarina Aitamurto and Scott Simpson, 94–111. Bristol, CT: Acumen.
Ozoliņš, Gatis, and Anita Stašulāne. 2017. "Transformations of NeoPaganism in Latvia: From Survival to Revival." *Open Theology*, 3:235–248.
Paliepa, Jānis Radvils. 2011. *The Origins of the Baltic and Vedic Languages: Baltic Mythology—Interdisciplinary Treatise*. Bloomington, IN: AuthorHouse.
Pranskevičiūtė, Rasa. 2013. "Contemporary Paganism in Lithuanian Context: Principal Beliefs and Practices of Romuva." In *Modern Pagan and Native Faith Movements in Central and Eastern Europe*, eds. Kaarina Aitamurto and Scott Simpson, 77–93. Bristol, CT: Acumen.
Puhvel, Jaan. 1974. "Indo-European Structure of the Baltic Pantheon." In *Myth in Indo-European Antiquity*, ed. Gerald Larson, 75–86. Berkeley, CA: University of California.
Puhvel, Jaan. 1987. *Comparative Mythology*. Baltimore, MD: Johns Hopkins University Press.
Pūtelis, Aldis. 1997. "Folklore and Identity: The Situation of Latvia." *Folklore*, 4:61–76.
Pūtelis, Aldis. 2003. "Historical Sources for the Study of Latvian Mythology." *Cosmos: The Journal of the Traditional Cosmology Society*, 19/1:63–92.

Račiūnaitė-Vyčinienė, Daiva. 2002. *Sutartinės: Lithuanian Polyphonic Songs*, trans. Vijole Arbė. Vilnius: Varga.
Rancāne, Aīda. 2009. *Maskas un maskošanās Latvijā/Masks and Disguise in Latvia*. Rīga: LU Filozofijas un socioloģijas institūts.
Reichelt, Katrin. 2015. "Between Initiative and Opportunism: The Role of Latvians in the Persecution of the Jews under Nazi Occupation." In *Konferenču un semināru Materiāli 2009-2014*, ed. Menaham Bakhan, 152–158. Riga: Biedriba Šamir.
Rėza, Liudvikas. 1958. *Lietuvių liaudies dainos/Lithuanian Folk Songs*, Vol. I. Vilnius: Valstybinė grožinės literatūros leidykla.
Rudling, Odeta. 2017. "The Cult of the Balts: Mythological Impulses and Neo-Pagan Practices in the Touristic Clubs of the Lithuanian SSR of the 1960s and 1970s." *Region: Regional Studies of Russia, Eastern Europe and Central Asia*, 6/1:87–108.
Sadauskienė, Jurga. 2021. "The Concept of Lithuanian Folk Song in Lithuanian Folklore 1800–1940." In *Literary Canon Formation as Nation-Building in Central Europe and the Baltics*, eds. Aistė Kučinskienė, Viktorija Šeina, and Brigita Speičytė, 86–106. Leiden, The Netherlands: E. J. Brill.
Savoniakaitė, Vida. 2019. "The Regional Studies Movement in Soviet Lithuania." *Journal of Ethnology and Folkloristics*, 13/2:71–89.
Smidchens, Guntis. 2014. *The Power of Song: Nonviolent National Culture in the Baltic Singing Revolution*. Seattle: University of Washington Press.
Šmits, Pēteris. 2009. *Latviešu mitoloģija/Latvian Mythology*, 3rd ed. Rīga: Eraksti. First published 1918.
Stašulāne, Anita. 2009. "New Religious Movements in Latvia." *Soter: Journal of Religious Science*, 32/60:107–124.
Stašulāne, Anita. 2012. "The Dievturi Movement in the Reports of the Latvian Political Police (1939–1940)." *The Pomegranate: The International Journal of Pagan Studies*, 14/1:31–46.
Straižys, Vytautas, and Libertas Klimka. 1997. "The Cosmology of the Ancient Balts." *Archaeo-Astronomy* (supplement to *Journal for the History of Astronomy*), 28:S57–S81.
Streikus, Arūnas. 2017. "Shifts in Religiosity in the Face of Soviet Type Urbanization: The Case of Lithuania." *Journal of Baltic Studies*, 48/2:235–249.
Strmiska, Michael. 2005. "The Music of the Past in Modern Baltic Paganism." *Nova Religio The Journal of Alternative and Emergent Religions*, 8/3:39–58.
Strmiska, Michael. 2012a. "Paganism-Inspired Folk Music, Folk Music–Inspired Paganism, and New Cultural Fusions in Lithuania and Latvia." In *Brill Handbook of New Religions and Cultural Productions*, eds. Carole M. Cusack and Alex Norman, 349–398. Leiden, The Netherlands: E. J. Brill.
Strmiska, Michael. 2012b. "Romuva Looks East: Indian Inspiration in Lithuanian Paganism." In *Religious Diversity in Post-Soviet Society: Ethnographies of Catholic Hegemony and the New Pluralism in Lithuania*, eds. Milda Ališauskienė and Ingo W. Schröder, 125–150. Farnham: Ashgate.
Strmiska, Michael, and Vilius Rudra Dundzila. 2005. "Romuva: Lithuanian Paganism in Lithuania and America." In *Modern Paganism in World Cultures: Comparative Perspectives*, ed. Michael Strmiska, 241–299. Santa Barbara, CA: ABC-CLIO.
Trinkūnas, Jonas. 2009. *Lietuvių senosios religijos kelias/The Way of the Old Lithuanian Religion*. Vilnius: Asveja.
Tumėnas, Vytautas. 2008. "The Visual and the Mythical-Poetic Interpretation of Sky Luminaries in Lithuanian Traditional Textiles." *Archaeologia Baltica*, 10:78–85.

Tumėnas, Vytautas. 2009. "The Connections between Old European Signs and Lithuanian Sash Ornamentation." In *Signs of Civilisation: Neolithic Symbol System of Southeast Europe*, eds. J. Marler and M. R. Dexter, 183–192. Sebastopol, CA: Institute of Archaeomythology.

Tumėnas, Vytautas. 2013. "Sakralioji šiaudinių 'sodų' simbolika regioniame ir platesniame tarpkultūrianame kontekste/Sacred Symbols of Straw Gardens in a Regional and Wider Intercultural Context." In *Tautodailės Metraštis/Folk Art Yearbook*. Vilnius: LMKA. https://lmka.lt/sakralioji-siaudiniu-sodu-simbolika-regioniniame-ir-platesniame-tarpkulturiniame-kontekste/.

Tumėnas, Vytautas. 2014. "Contemporary Social Art Festivals as Intertextual Manifestations of Postmodern Cultural Identity." *Lituanus*, 60/4. https://www.lituanus.org/2014/14_4_04 Tumenas.html. Accessed October 26, 2021.

Tumėnas, Vytautas. 2018. "Signs of morning star Aušrinė in the Baltic tradition: regional and intercultural features." *Mediterranean archaeology and archaeometry*, 18/4:377–388

Ūdre, Digne. 2018. "Ugunskrusts Latvijā strīdīga kultūras mantojuma kontekstā/The Latvian Fire-Cross in the Context of Controversial Cultural Heritage." *Letonica*, 38:123–142.

Ūdre, Digne. 2019. "The Symbol of the Morning Star during the Third Awakening in Latvia (1986–1991): From Cultural Opposition to Non-Violent Resistance." *Letonica*, 39:149–176.

Vaicekauskas, Arūnas. 2002, 16–22 August. "The Walking of the Maskers (in Lithuania)." Presented at the Traditional Masks and Mumming in Northern Europe conference, Turku, Finland. https://web.archive.org/web/20060617095737/http://www.hi.is/~terry/turku/Turku_ARUNAS_VAICEKAUSKAS.htm. Accessed October 15, 2021.

Vaiskūnas, Jonas. 1992. "Sodas ir Visatas/Straw Garden and Universe." *Liaudies Kultūra*, 4:26–32.

Vaitkevičius, Vykintas. 2009. "The Sacred Groves of the Balts: Lost History and Modern Research." *Folklore*, 42:81–94.

Vaitkevičius, Vykintas. 2018. "Signs of Morning Star Aušrinė in the Baltic Tradition: Regional and Intercultural Features." *Mediterranean Archaeology and Archaeometry*, 18/4:377–388.

Vaitkevičius, Vykintas. 2019. "Baltiškos svastikos savitumas/The Peculiarity of the Baltic Swastika." *Alkas*. https://alkas.lt/2019/12/27/v-vaitkevicius-baltiskos-svastikos-savitumas/?fbclid=IwAR2zDVeN6wbrU3zQCpMt2TGNmDinPlszJyp4PAKcSr3howIfDNWd1M7m3bE. Accessed October 21, 2021.

Vaitkevičius, Vykintas. 2020. "The Swastika in Lithuania: The Horizon of the 13th and 14th Centuries." *Archaeologia Baltica*, 27:104–119.

Vėlius, Norbertas. 1989. *The World Outlook of the Ancient Balts*. Vilnius: Mintis.

Vėlius, Norbertas. 1996. *Baltų religijos ir mitologojos šaltiniai/The Sources of Baltic Religion and Mythology*, Vol. I. Vilnius: Mokslo ir enciklopedijos leidybos institutas.

Viķis-Freibergs, Vaira. 1986. "The Lyrical and the Epical in Finnish and Latvian Folk Poetry." *Journal of Baltic Studies*, 17/2:98–107.

Viķis-Freibergs, Vaira. 1989. "Oral Tradition as Cultural History in the Lyrical World of the Latvian *Daina*." In *Linguistics and Poetics of Latvian Folk Songs*, ed. Vaira Viķis-Freibergs, 3–13. Montreal–Kingston: McGill-Queen's University Press.

Viķis-Freibergs, Vaira. 2005. "Saule." In *Encyclopedia of Religion*, ed. Lindsay Jones, 2nd ed., Vol. 12, 8131–8135. New York: Macmillan Reference.

Willeke, Audronė B. 1990. "Vydūnas' Dramas: A Ritual of National Salvation." *Journal of Baltic Studies*, 21/4:359–368.

Zemītis, Guntis. 2004. *Ornaments un simbols Latvijas aizvēsturē/Ornament and Symbol in the Prehistory of Latvia*. Riga: Latvian Institute of History.

CHAPTER 19

FOLK BELIEF AND RELIGION IN UKRAINE
Creating the Charisma of Place

MARIYA LESIV

IN the decades following the collapse of the Soviet regime, Ukraine experienced a great revival of established religions and created a favorable environment for new religious movements and expressions. This situation is often understood as a response to the Soviet atheist policies, when religion was officially banned and many faith communities were forced to operate underground (e.g., Bociurkiw 1996). In other words, the post-Soviet "spiritual renaissance" can be seen as a desire to taste "formerly forbidden fruit" (Kononenko 2006:46).

This chapter focuses on phenomena that fit the overall aura of post-Soviet religious awakening. I discuss supernatural apparitions of the Mother of God recently reported in many villages. They have generated attention from believers, tourists, curious passersby, and the commercial media and over time have developed into sacred sanctuaries. The latter reflect the global pattern of beliefs and practices surrounding Marian apparition sites, namely, locales associated with apparitions of the Mother of God (and, occasionally, other saints) that eventually have become pilgrimage centers. Themes of miraculous healing and supernatural protection associated with Marian centers elsewhere are also prominent in the Ukrainian context. Lingering post-Soviet political, economic, and social uncertainties reinforce such beliefs, leading people to search for alternative sources of help.

These themes of supernatural healing and protection appear to be important in the experiences of pilgrims and tourists and usually constitute the main focus of the related scholarly literature. My fieldwork, however, goes beyond this framework to discuss the significance of these sites in the lives of local residents. My findings reinforce what folklorists know well: creative cultural expressions often produce multiple contextually specific and dynamic meanings. I argue that, in addition to various other functions the sites may play in individual and community lives, they help to build and reinforce the charisma of place in localities that are otherwise marginalized. The "charisma of place" is the notion of a particular landscape, locale, or premises as special, distinct, significant, or powerful (e.g., Lindquist 2005; DeBernardi 2008). On the one hand, by becoming markers of a village's charisma, apparition sites perform a function that is beyond a strictly religious domain. On the other hand, it is precisely the close association with the firmly established understanding of religious power that allows these sites to communicate that non-religious function. It is the methodology of "vernacular" (Primiano 1995) or "lived" (Orsi 2003) religion that allows me to trace this symbolic meaning that, in turn, appears in a nuanced and indirect way.

I begin by briefly introducing the overall religious landscape in Ukraine to place my research and methodological approach in the larger context. I then describe the new Ukrainian apparitions, drawing contextual parallels between these and their more widely known counterparts, both in Ukraine and in other parts of the world. This is followed by a discussion of the charisma-building processes surrounding the sites as manifested in three overlapping expressive forms, namely, personal narrative, material culture, and ritual.

Religious Landscape in Ukraine

Ukraine is a religiously pluralistic society. Some scholars even regard it as a "model of religious pluralism among formerly socialist societies" (Wanner 2004:736; see also Long Ratajeski 2015:1557). The majority of Ukrainians have historically embraced Eastern Christianity, and the dominance of Byzantine Rite Christian churches is reflected in recent statistics: 12,437 communities of the Ukrainian Orthodox Church of Moscow Patriarchate, 5,363 units of the Ukrainian Orthodox Church of Kyiv Patriarchate, 3,470 communities of the Ukrainian Greek Catholic Church (UGCC), and 1,171 of those under the jurisdiction of the Ukrainian Autocephalous Orthodox Church were registered in the country as of January 1, 2019 (Religious Information Service of Ukraine 2019). On January 5, 2019, the Ukrainian Orthodox Church of Kyiv Patriarchate and the Ukrainian Autocephalous Orthodox Church were united and granted the Tomos of Autocephaly by the Ecumenical Patriarch of Constantinople, Bartholomew (*Kyiv Post* 2019).

Among various smaller denominations of Protestantism, the largest was the 2,484 communities of the All-Ukrainian Union of Churches of Evangelical Christian Baptists (Religious Information Service of Ukraine 2019). Other established world religions add to Ukraine's religious mosaic. For example, as of January 1, 2019, multiple branches of Judaism totaled 287 registered communities, while Islam and Buddhism were represented by 265 and 63 units, respectively. Among many organizations connected with new religious movements, the International Society for Krishna Consciousness consisted of 44 communities, while various forms of Modern Paganism and Native Faith embraced 144 units (Religious Information Service of Ukraine 2019).

Religion in Ukraine displays distinct regional differences. While 72 percent of Ukrainians declare themselves to be religious, the highest degree of religiosity is observed in the western parts of the country (Razumkov Center 2018:3). Another regional particularity is related specifically to the position of the UGCC. Its presence is significantly higher in western Ukraine than in the rest of the country; 40 percent of the region's population declares affiliation to this stream of Byzantine Christianity (Razumkov Center 2018:3). While Orthodox churches also experienced a boom in the post-Soviet time, the revival of the UGCC in western Ukraine is especially vibrant and dynamic, partly due to the fact that it was more severely persecuted during the Soviet era (see Bociurkiw 1996).

In addition to regional particularities, there is an urban–rural distinction. Village residents are known as bearers of especially complex belief systems historically shaped by multiple sources of influence. While many experiential dimensions of rural religiosity remain outside the scope of statistical studies, they can be revealed with the help of ethnographic methodologies. When traditional churches began to reinstate their influence in late Soviet and post-Soviet Ukrainian villages, they had to face a firmly established belief system. Some elements fit the prescribed institutional aspects of formal religions, while others were condemned by church authorities. For example, ethnographers continue to document beliefs in house, water, and field spirits; good and demonic forces; and other expressions among those who self-identify as Christians (e.g., Buiskykh 2018). Even though some of these beliefs may have pre-Christian origins, they produce present-day meanings and are, thus, viewed as current and functional in the context of everyday life (Buiskykh 2018:58–76). Soviet experiences added to the complexity of rural religiosity. Ukrainian villagers developed a distinct pattern of religious behavior during the time of state atheism. Due to the lack of priests, village residents, especially elderly women, learned to fulfill their communities' spiritual needs (such as conducting baptism or funeral rituals) independently and outside of the church (Kononenko 2006).[1] Women who held religious leadership roles in Soviet settings often experienced tensions with newly appointed clergy in the post-Soviet context (Kononenko 2010). Overall, rural religious traditions in Ukraine are especially complex, and the institutional aspects of Byzantine Rite Christianity constitute only one vector of influence in that multifaceted milieu. It is precisely this distinct form of rural religiosity that is most frequently referred to as "folk religion." The latter concept is widely used by both scholars and larger Ukrainian society, despite the recent Western scholarly trend to move beyond it.[2]

Methodological Approach

The present study is based on ethnographic fieldwork that took place in the rural contexts of western Ukraine between 2012 and 2019. It is also informed by my insider understanding of the country's internal political and cultural dynamics. While I have lived in Canada for the last two decades, I am a native of Ukraine. Since the time of my relocation, I have returned to Ukraine annually to both visit family and conduct fieldwork on a regular basis. I follow Leonard Primiano's methodological approach conveyed in his concept of "vernacular religion" (1995). Primiano's frequently cited definition of "vernacular religion" is that it is religion "as it is lived: as human beings encounter, understand, interpret, and practice it" (1995:44). Religious studies scholar Robert Orsi later introduced a very similar approach to the study of religion through the concept of "lived religion" (2003).

Primiano argues against the dichotomy of "folk" versus "official" religion that is often favored by scholars. In his opinion, these are outsider labels that endorse hierarchical understanding of religious dynamics, where "official" religion implies an institutional canon against which other spiritual expressions are measured (Primiano 1995:47). Moreover, such a dichotomy does not accurately reflect the complex ethnographic reality of everyday religious experiences. Anthropologist James Kapaló finds the scholarly move beyond the concept of "folk religion" to be somewhat misleading, specifically in European contexts. In his view, "[t]he term itself does not impose a dichotomy, rather the dichotomy is the result of a history of competing discursive practices that actually structure the 'field of practice' itself" (2013:8). Kapaló's fieldwork in rural Romania and Moldova reveals that the "folk religious field of practice" constitutes a distinct and prevalent entity that plays a competitive role in broader and shifting religious power-related struggles (2013:5). As described in the previous section, in Ukraine, the concept of "folk religion" is imparted with distinct historically loaded meanings and, in that respect, fully reflects Kapaló's remarks.

However, methodologically, I view "vernacular" or "lived" religion as a frame of understanding, somewhat in line with Erving Goffman's theory of "frame analysis" (1974).[3] This frame of view conveys the idea that any religious experience is vernacular, meaning contextually unique because it is lived in a particular moment and context (Primiano 1995:46). Applied to the case study of the recent supernatural apparitions in Ukraine, this frame shows that even "folk religion" as understood by Kapaló embraces diverse lived experiences that are often competitive and shifting within this category.

SUPERNATURAL APPARITIONS: ETHNOGRAPHIC SNAPSHOTS

My interest in what many believe to be supernatural apparitions was initially sparked by a news report over a decade ago. On December 3, 2009, the Television News Service (TSN) of the Ukrainian TV channel 1+1 focused attention on the central Ukrainian village of Vybli in the Chernihiv region (TSN 2009). According to the news report, an image of the Mother of God had recently appeared on an old linden tree near the local church.

There was a big windstorm in the village in 2007. As a result, the 130-year-old linden tree was cracked in half, creating a hollow in its center. Villagers had considered cutting down the remains of the old tree but never actually completed the task. Oleksandra Bulavko, an elderly woman, accidentally discovered an apparition in the hollow of the tree. She noticed an unusual image and exclaimed that it was Jesus Christ. Oleksandra showed her discovery to her neighbors. While some people also saw the image of Christ and others recognized it as the Mother of God, no one appeared to question the sacred nature of the apparition. According to the TSN report, many locals interpreted the apparition as the miraculous return of the seventeenth-century icon of the Sorrowful Mother of God that was stolen from the local church two years prior.

Shortly after this encounter, with news spreading by word of mouth, the village of Vybli became a major pilgrimage site, attracting people from all parts of Ukraine, including urban centers. Pilgrims leaned against the tree to pray and left offerings of flowers, food, and money. They took home pieces of the tree's branches or bark, believing in their miraculous powers. In particular, the TSN report mentioned belief in the healing properties of these items as well as their ability to protect households from robbery. By the time the TSN crew visited the village, there was no bark remaining, so pilgrims would instead collect handfuls of dirt from around the tree. Three female village activists, including Oleksandra, guarded the site at the time of the report.

In the summer of 2012, when I first decided to undertake an ethnographic study of supernatural apparitions, my primary residence was my parents' home in the city of Ivano-Frankivsk, in western Ukraine. I planned to begin my ethnographic endeavor by making a trip to the village of Vybli. This plan surprised my mother. She said, "Why do you need to go as far as central Ukraine? This also happened in Bryn." Bryn is a small village of slightly over 700 residents on the outskirts of Ivano-Frankivsk.

I went to Bryn. Since the apparition site was located on a side of the town's main road and was well known to every local resident, it was easy to find. My first consultants were the local children playing nearby. They told me a story very similar to that of the village of Vybli. In 2007, a local woman had noticed an unusual image in the hollow of an old linden tree. Even though the image had faded away by 2012, the children were still able to point out precisely where the eyes, the shoulders and the robe of the Mother of God had been. They also brought me photographs of the apparition that were sold in the village at the peak of pilgrimage activity immediately following the initial discovery. In the photographs, the image of the Mother of God that the children had indicated could be seen more clearly. The site was very well maintained. It was enclosed by a custom-made fence and gate and secured with a lock. Since the tree showed large bark-free patches, this was likely done to protect the site from further removal of the bark. The area immediately surrounding the tree inside and outside the fence was filled with fresh flowers planted both in the ground and in decorative planters. In addition, an elaborate new chapel was built behind the linden tree.

At the peak of its popularity, the site also brought many church authorities to the village of Bryn where they would conduct sacred services. By 2012, the site no longer attracted pilgrims on a large scale. Only the occasional passerby would stop to pray and drink water from a nearby spring that had been recently professionally landscaped. I revisited Bryn in the summer of 2019. The image of the apparition had faded further. However, the area was still well maintained, and the locals discussed it enthusiastically.

While searching for instances of similar phenomena elsewhere in Ukraine, I found another news report, produced on August 3, 2009, by a small-scale regional TV channel, NTK. It discussed an apparition in the village of Malyi Hvizdets (population of slightly over 1,600), Kolomyia County, also in the Ivano-Frankivsk region. In that village, a formation of moss on an old ash tree had drawn people's attention. The ash tree was growing by an old well that was believed to have healing powers. The news report featured Maria, a village schoolteacher, whose students had first noticed the miracle. According to Maria, moss had begun to grow on the tree at the end of May, 2009, but had not initially acquired any distinct shape. Near the end of June, the shape had begun to vaguely resemble a Byzantine-style icon of the Mother of God. Two weeks later, the image had become very clear (NTK 2009).

Shortly after this discovery, the village of Malyi Hvizdets also became a pilgrimage site attracting both rural and urban Ukrainians. Several pilgrims, including two women who had walked there from a neighboring village, were featured in the NTK report. The pilgrims unanimously said that they had come there to pray for good health for their families and friends. The site attracted not only pilgrims but also church authorities, who came there to conduct services on a regular basis. As in the case of Bryn, the apparition in Malyi Hvizdets evolved into a material shrine that was still well maintained in 2019 (NTK 2009).

While space allows me to focus on only a limited number of examples, the reported apparitions are not confined to these two villages in western Ukraine (see Pohliad.com 2015). I also visited other similar places in the village of Zhuravkiv and in the town of Stryi, both in the Lviv region, as well as a site in the town of Tlumach, Ivano-Frankivsk region.

Broader Context: Renowned Marian Apparition Sites

Intriguingly, these phenomena fit an old and familiar pattern connected with Marian apparition sites. Western Ukraine alone hosts a number of such places. While particular details of the initial apparitions differ, what unites them all is the idea of supernatural miracle. One of the most renowned recent examples is a spring called Dzhubryk in the Zakarpattia (Transcarpathia) region, where two young girls were reported to have met the Mother of God on August 27, 2002. This event and the subsequent apparitions of both the Mother of God and other biblical figures turned Dzhubryk into a very popular center of pilgrimage, which gradually filled with numerous buildings and statues (see Halemba 2015).

More historically distant examples include the Pohonia Monastery of the Dormition of the Mother of God in the Ivano-Frankivsk region. It is the home of the miraculous icon of the Mother of God of Pohonia.[4] The icon has a long history that dates back to the seventeenth century (Ukrainian Greek Catholic Church n.d.:32). It disappeared for decades during the Soviet era, only to miraculously reveal itself to Fr. Nykodym in 2001 (Lavreniuk 2018:26–29). The Pohonia monastery is one of many pilgrimage centers under the jurisdiction of the UGCC. Visitors to such sites may be impressed by their growing architectural landscapes and infrastructure. I will expand on this below (see "'Like the Holy Land': Sacred Materiality"), while addressing the Zarvanytsia Marian Center in the Ternopil region, perhaps the most popular site of this kind in western Ukraine.

Those familiar with Marian sites as a global phenomenon will recognize further parallels between the Ukrainian centers and their more widely known counterparts the world over. The most prominent examples include Our Lady of Fatima in Portugal associated with the Marian apparitions of 1917 (Ferreira 1996:233) and Our Lady of Lourdes in France whose history dates back to 1858 (Kaufman 2005:2). In addition to pilgrims and tourists, these and many other Marian sites have attracted a growing number of scholars. Notably, while exploring numerous theoretical issues, the majority of academics interested in experiential meaning-making aspects connected to the sites focus predominantly on pilgrim and tourist experiences.[5] This is understandable because, as anthropologist Agnieszka Halemba argues in the case of the Dzhubryk complex in Ukraine, apparition sites often acquire a life of their own, disconnected from initial apparition experiences (Halemba 2015:85).

While I had also planned to place pilgrimage at the center of my study, I was out of ethnographic luck. Since I had encountered these sites after their popularity had subsided, the only people I was able to converse with were local residents. This situation shifted my research questions: Why are the memories of the initial apparition encounters still cherished, and why are the actual sites still meticulously maintained? What meanings do the sites produce to the host villages and their residents?

Multiple Meanings, Dynamic Beliefs

Like any other folk expressions, the apparitions communicate multiple meanings, both collective and personal. Anthropologist Galina Lindquist would likely conceptualize these phenomena as a search for an "alternative form of hope" (2005:8). Lindquist coined this phrase to describe the years immediately following the fall of the Soviet Union, the collapse of state infrastructures, and the growing mistrust in institutions. While three decades have passed since the time of that major historical shift, post-Soviet political and economic uncertainties linger even so in Ukraine. In principle the judicial system is an independent body, but in reality, it is still closely linked to political powers and their interests, as is the law enforcement system. And while theoretically the country has a universal healthcare system, in actuality many medical institutions are underfunded and corrupt. Many people, especially those in rural areas, do not have access to and cannot afford the care that they need. Moreover, due to corruption in the educational system, there is often a lack of trust in medical doctors and their competence. The government's frequent failure to establish a transparent and functional state system stimulates people to search for alternative options in a time of need. From this perspective, it is understandable why a handful of dirt from the site of a perceived sacred apparition can be imparted with a meaning of hope, including healing and protective properties.

My recurrent visits to the recent apparition sites revealed that the meanings they communicate, especially on an individual level, are dynamic and often reflective of changing social and political realities. For example, while conversing with numerous residents of Malyi Hvizdets in 2012, I was under the impression that the apparition of the Mother of God was generally seen through a very optimistic lens. While positive interpretations still prevailed in 2019, there also was a noticeable shift. For instance, during my last visit, an elderly female resident told me that the apparition was "not for the greater good." She linked it to the ongoing Ukraine–Russia crisis that resulted in the military conflict in the Donbas region of Ukraine beginning in 2014. She interpreted the apparition as a supernatural warning about the impending turmoil in the country. A middle-aged woman residing in close proximity to the site drew a more personal connection. She shared the devastating experience of recently losing both her husband and her son. Since the apparition took place across the street from her home, the woman linked it to the tragic events in her family. Both women seemed to refer to the apparition as a harbinger of tragedy, whether on a country-wide or a personal level. Such references, of course, could not have taken place at the time of the initial apparition. Rather, they were retrospective reflections in light of the subsequent emotionally traumatic events. These examples illustrate that beliefs are dynamic entities that not only can rationally develop from physical experiences, as famously argued by folklorist David Hufford (1982), but can also be shaped by social, political, and emotional encounters.[6]

In the mosaic of beliefs and meanings surrounding recent supernatural phenomena, there is one distinct, persistent pattern that is indirectly related to their mysterious and miraculous nature. In particular, the apparitions and their surrounding folklore appear to play a significant role in what folklorists discuss as the creation of a sense of place (e.g., Ryden 1993; Pocius [1991] 2000; Banks Thomas 2015) and, more specifically, what some anthropologists would refer to as the charisma of place (Lindquist 2005; DeBernardi 2008).

Village as Place

In order to understand the said charisma-building strategies, it is necessary to place the sites into their larger social and economic contexts. The apparitions I have described occurred in remote rural settings. As mentioned, statistically, Ukrainian villages display a higher degree of religiosity than urban centers. They are also more frequently associated with supernatural beliefs and practices, a source of power that attracts many Ukrainians, especially considering the population's overall distrust in mainstream (medical) institutions. For example, village-based folk healers are often highly respected by both rural and even some urban residents. The interest the apparition sites have generated reflects the overall mystical and spiritual aura of Ukrainian villages.

Despite these favorable aspects of their reputation, on a hierarchical scale of settlements in Ukraine, villages occupy the most marginal economic, social, and political positions. In comparison to urban centers, many Ukrainian villagers have a more significantly limited access to resources. Even such essential necessities as running water and sewage systems, while gradually improving, are still frequently lacking in many rural areas. Moreover, limited resources and professional prospects result in the growing outmigration of the youth, leaving villages decreasing in size and with aging populations. These economic and social disadvantages have historically translated into cultural stereotypes. Ukrainian village dwellers are often the victims of what some social scientists have conceptualized as "placism."[7] Placism is a global phenomenon defined as a bias "or the discrimination against people based on where they live" (Jimerson 2005:211). In Ukraine, this form of discrimination against the rural way of life is often reflected in everyday speech. For example, the Ukrainian word *selo*, meaning "village" or "countryside," is often used in an insulting, albeit sometimes humorous, way similar to the English terms "bumpkin," "yokel," "hick," and "country cousin." The term is often applied by urbanites to their rural counterparts, whom they perceive as "backward" people unfamiliar with "progressive" urban life and not as intelligent as their city counterparts.

The recent apparitions appear to play a significant role in raising the status of the villages in which they occurred. They serve as symbolic markers that help to put small rural areas on the map and to overcome their inferior positions on the hierarchical scale of Ukrainian settlements. I focus next on how these charisma-building strategies manifest themselves in personal narratives, material culture, and ritual. These distinctions are provided exclusively for heuristic purposes. In real life, the boundaries are blurry, if existent at all.

"Something Told Me": Local Narratives about Apparitions

While some village residents were ambivalent about the miraculous nature of their local apparitions, the majority appeared to be strikingly confident that the apparitions were real. Their stories stood in opposition to supernatural narratives in the West. For example, while focusing on the mysterious encounters of elderly women in Manchester, England, folklorist Gillian Bennett shows that Westerners who encounter the paranormal are often very cautious when sharing their experiences and beliefs, especially with strangers. Their stories often illustrate the narrators' awareness of their larger sociocultural setting, where the voices of official institutions propagate rationalist views closely linked to science and logical reasoning. The narrators provide descriptions of not only actual experiences but also their exploration of evidence and attempts to defend themselves from the potential imagined judgment of rationalist audiences (1999:124–132).

In contrast, such self-defense motifs are not prominent in supernatural apparition narratives from contemporary rural Ukraine. One might expect that a belief in apparitions would need to be defended more aggressively than, for example, the personal sense of the presence of a deceased family member as shared by some of Bennett's respondents in Manchester. Unlike the private settings where individuals may claim to have had contact with the paranormal, apparition sites are public and easily accessible to skeptics who can suggest that the perceived miracles are merely naturally occurring mosses or hollows. In addition, the journalists and scholars who collected the apparition narratives addressed in this chapter, myself included, are all associated with "official" institutions that adhere to the rationalist paradigm of thinking.

Furthermore, not only do Ukrainian narrators not feel the need to defend and justify their supernaturalist trains of thought but they often reinforce the miraculous nature of the apparitions by adding a supernatural flavor to their description of events preceding the actual apparitions. For example, in 2012, Maria from the village of Malyi Hvizdets provided me with more details about the apparition on the tree than had been presented in the NTK news report. It turned out that this had actually been her own ash tree. Maria and her husband initially had twelve ash trees on their property. They had decided to cut them all down because one had fallen. They were worried that if another tree fell it could damage their electrical line. The ash tree that had been viewed as miraculous was the last one that they had planned to cut down. They had even hired a professional crew to do the job, but something caused Maria to stop. She said:

> Can you believe it, something told me, my inner intuition, and I said: "Let's not cut this ash tree down." . . . Some time later, students were coming back from school and said to me: " . . . did you see what is on your ash tree?" We looked, and saw the image. And I am telling you the image was so clear. You could see the contours of the moss very clearly.

It is precisely the "something told me" motifs in many Ukrainian apparition narratives that reinforce their supernatural characteristics, where "something" is implicitly connected to a supernatural force. The residents of Vybli featured in the TSN news report emphasized a similar aspect. They were going to cut the old linden tree down, but something prevented them; and they now felt that they understood why.

The confidence aspect of these supernatural narratives and the near absence of the self-defense motifs in them do not mean that Ukrainians, in contrast to their Western counterparts, do not strive for what is widely viewed as modern and progressive. Rather, due to numerous sociocultural, political, and religious factors rooted in pre-Soviet, Soviet, and early post-Soviet history, the supernatural occupies a more favorable position in Ukraine (and Russia) than it does in the West. In fact, it often serves as "a leading vehicle for communicating modernity, progress, and power" as viewed by many Ukrainians, both rural and urban (Lesiv 2018:47). One of the contributing factors is the role of Byzantine Christianity in post-Soviet Ukraine. While, according to Ukraine's constitution, church and state are separated, in reality Byzantine Christian institutions maintain a great degree of social and political authority, reinforced by an overall religious renaissance. Supernatural phenomena interpreted as God's miracles have historically constituted an important component of Byzantine Christianity. Many people understand certain supernatural encounters as being in line with the church rather than contradictory to it (Wigzell 2011:425–427; Lindquist 2005:30; Lesiv 2018:47).

Due to the reputable position of the supernatural, often reinforced by its direct link to established Christian concepts and imagery, my respondents elevate the status of their villages through their personal narratives. For example, in 2012, I asked a young woman in the village of Bryn whether she herself believed that a miraculous apparition had occurred in her village and if she knew of any miracles that had ensued as a result. The following was her answer:

> There is some kind of protection [of the village of Bryn by the apparition]. All these rains, storms, showers, hail [have been very severe in our region] lately, but passed over our village. Maybe you've heard that it was horrible what the weather has done in the neighboring village, Krylos. A severe storm tore apart the roofs on people's houses and washed away everything in their gardens [the main source of yearly food supply in many families]. But, thank God, it didn't touch us.

To provide another example, when I asked Maria (in 2012) if church authorities recognized the image on her ash tree as a miraculous apparition, she said that they did and quoted the bishop:

> The bishop did not object to that, but it was very striking to him that the apparition took place in such a small, poor place like the village of Malyi Hvizdets. He said: "It is interesting because it didn't appear in any palace." But it is not surprising because the Mother of God gave birth to Jesus in a small stable. Thus, it had to happen in such an inconspicuous place.

Discussing the relationship between narrative and place, cultural geographer and folklorist Kent Ryden points out,

> It is stories—narratives formal or informal, elaborate and detailed or offhand and telegraphic—of what happened to people in a place, of what they have done with the things that they found there, that best reveal the "real geography"—geography, that is, experienced and understood as place. (1993:46)

At first sight the two narratives presented above may appear unrelated. However, a closer look reveals that they are united by the common "my village is special" motif, adding an aura of significance to a narrator's place of residence. This motif reflects what historian Jelena Erdeljan embeds into the concept of "chosen places," drawing on the "identity of chosenness" famously formulated by historical sociologist Anthony Smith (Erdeljan 2017:7; Smith 2003). Bryn has special protection that other villages do not have. Malyi Hvizdets is symbolically linked to the place where Jesus was born because of the connection between the simple stable in Bethlehem and this inconspicuous village. This elevated status of Malyi Hvizdets potentially makes others jealous that the Mother of God had not chosen to appear in their own village. While the latter village may be considered an "inconspicuous place" from a mundane materialistic point of view, the chosenness manifested in the recent apparition puts it on the map and elevates its status to that of a spiritual center. In other words, personal narratives surrounding the recent apparitions contribute to the creation of the charisma of place in those localities where they occurred.

"Like the Holy Land": Sacred Materiality

In July 2019, while visiting family in the Ternopil region of western Ukraine, I asked Liuda, a relative of mine, whether she knew about similar apparitions in her area. She was not aware of anything recent but said that the residents of her village often made the pilgrimage to Zarvanytsia, a village in the Ternopil region known for a Marian apparition site (introduced above, see "Broader Context: Renowned Marian Apparition Sites"). Liuda implied that since there was such a prominent pilgrimage center in her region, there was no need to look for alternatives. With no further prompts, she enthusiastically expressed her admiration of the Zarvanytsia site, repeatedly emphasizing how "they made it look like the Holy Land."

Liuda's remark resonates with a global phenomenon that I call "comparative links," namely, symbolic connections between two places based on a certain degree of their (physical) resemblance. Usually a less culturally or politically prominent place is linked to a larger and more widely recognized counterpart. For example, while communicating their diverse senses of modernity via a daily promenade, residents of a small town in central Italy fondly refer to their place as "our little Paris" (Del Negro 2004:3, 157). Likewise, due to its prolonged history as part of the Austro-Hungarian Empire (resulting in many similarities of architectural styles), the city of Lviv, frequently regarded as the cultural capital of Ukraine, is often called "little Vienna." While such statements convey local pride, they also communicate, albeit implicitly, a degree of a preexisting sense of inferiority that the comparative links help to overcome. In the case of Lviv, a connection to the larger and more internationally known European city symbolically reinforces its status. Liuda displays a similar tendency in her description of Zarvanytsia. While it is an important site within Ukraine, Zarvanytsia is not widely known internationally. Liuda connects it symbolically with Jerusalem, elevating its significance. In general, the comparative links can be seen as distinct strategies that often play an active role in the construction of the charisma of place.

While referring to Zarvanytsia and symbolically connecting it with the most prominent center of Christianity, Liuda did not provide many specific details. Shortly after our conversation, I visited the site, and it became clear to me that she had been referring to the architectural ensemble and landscaping. It did not even vaguely resemble what I remembered from my own Easter-week pilgrimage to Zarvanytsia over two decades earlier. At that time, the area had not displayed any significant amount of site development and, since it had been a rainy day, the pilgrims' feet constantly sank in mud as they walked along the Stations of the Cross situated on a high hill. Present-day Zarvanytsia is a very different place. An impressive amount of expense, professional design work, and marketing thought are reflected in the site.

Leonard Primiano, while focusing on American Catholicism, draws our attention to the importance of the material dimensions of religious sites or what he labels "sacred materiality" (1999). The sacred materiality of Zarvanytsia ranges from spectacular architecture and landscaping to a great variety of souvenirs, printed literature, and religious paraphernalia sold in several stores. The site now embraces a very large material complex consisting of multiple religious structures and the Stations of the Cross, all connected by roads and paths, elaborately paved with concrete and professionally landscaped (Fig. 19.1).

Perhaps the most impressive component is represented by the most recent addition to the complex. In 2018, a four-year project—consisting of smaller replicas of seven biblical sites of Jerusalem, including the Tomb of Christ—was completed. A stone from the Holy Land was brought and placed at the site. Journalists frequently document the positive reactions of visitors to today's Zarvanytsia. For example, in 2018, a middle-aged male pilgrim conveyed his impressions to a regional news reporter in the following way: "There is a lot to see here. I did not expect that something like this could be raised here. There was nothing here two or three years ago, things were just getting started" (Espreso. TV 2018).

Church literature refers to the site as "one of the twenty best known Marian spiritual centers in the world" (e.g., Ukrainian Greek Catholic Church n.d.). The same literature labels it "Ukrainian Jerusalem," making it clear why Liuda, along with other believers, connects it to the Holy Land (Figs. 19.2 and 19.3). Further comparative links to Lourdes and Fatima can be encountered in media reports. The following example comes from Ukrinform, a multimedia national news platform in Ukraine:

> Among the Marian Centers recognized in the Christian world is a small Ukrainian village that one won't even find on every map. But thousands of believers of various denominations know their way here. They come to this locality year-round, like they do to French Lourdes or Portuguese Fatima. . . . And this is not just a "point

FIG. 19.1. A fragment of the Zarvanytsia Marian Center. July 2019.

(Photograph by author.)

on the map" of Ukraine. It is a miraculous place that has been inviting hundreds of thousands of Christians for 780 years.

(Snitovskyi 2018)

The origins of the site are obscure. According to legend, a Kyiv-based monk found refuge in the area at the time of the Mongol invasion in 1240. The Mother of God appeared to him in his sleep, comforting him. The monk then found an icon in a spring in a local valley. Astonishingly, the icon depicted an image of the Mother of God that was identical to that of his dream. The monk then constructed a chapel where the miraculous icon was placed. Soon after, a new church was built there and the village of Zarvanytsia was gradually established. Then followed centuries of recurring tragic military conflicts, including the relatively recent horrors of the First and Second World Wars as well as the Soviet regime, which affected the sacred site. The icon has miraculously survived. The site received the Catholic Church's institutional recognition in 1867, when Pope Pius IX crowned the icon and proclaimed Zarvanytsia to be a pilgrimage site (Bubnii, Hlubish, and Baliukh 2019). Although the site's history embraces many centuries, it is in the decades following the collapse of the Soviet regime that it experienced the peak of its popularity in Ukraine, attracting a growing number of pilgrims and tourists. Their donations help to reinforce the site's charisma by imparting it with abundant sacred materiality.

FIG. 19.2. "Ukrainian Jerusalem" in Zarvanytsia. October 2021.
(Photograph by Oleh Adrishak. Used with permission.)

It is a reported apparition of the Mother of God that has gradually put the small village of Zarvanytsia on the map. The apparition has acquired place-specific visual characteristics in the form of the miraculous icon of the Mother of God of Zarvanytsia, similar to the Mother of God of Pohonia mentioned above (see "Broader Context: Renowned Marian Apparition Sites") and the more widely known images of Our Lady of Fatima and Our Lady of Lourdes. The fact that the greater history of the present-day Zarvanytsia Spiritual Center began with a small-scale local event makes an intriguing parallel with the apparition phenomena at such places as Bryn and Malyi Hvizdets.

What initially were individual encounters with the mysterious gradually evolved into material sites that draw attention to the villages, reinforcing their charisma and local pride. For example, with the help of donations from pilgrims at the peak of its popularity, the apparition site in Malyi Hvizdets was turned into an attractive small material shrine. The actual image resembling a Byzantine-style icon of the Mother of God has faded away and is now barely noticeable. However, the stump of the ash tree on which it had emerged is well preserved. Decorative artificial flowers resembling a wreath are placed around the original image. Two strings of beads are arranged in the middle to help visitors visualize the original image. The tree stump and the miraculous old well are the main components of the site. The entire area is professionally landscaped and well

FIG. 19.3. The tomb of Christ in "Ukrainian Jerusalem." October 2021.

(Photograph by Oleh Adrishak. Used with permission.)

maintained. A small chapel was built around the well to one side of the stump, while a small bell tower is situated on the other side (Fig. 19.4).

Similarly, the image of the Mother of God on the old linden tree in Bryn was also turned into a material complex. The site embraces a landscaped spring and an elaborate new chapel built behind the linden tree (Fig. 19.5). Part of the complex is also a niche in the main facade in the old building featuring a statue of the Mother of God. The present-day niche is a revival of its original counterpart that had been walled up during Soviet times. It is adorned with planters with live flowers and a small, custom-made decorative roof. The residents were especially pleased that monetary offerings from numerous pilgrims helped fund this project. In 2019, a middle-aged woman who resides in close

FIG. 19.4. The Malyi Hvizdets apparition site. The original image of the apparition on the tree stump behind the chapel is marked with flowers resembling a wreath. June 2012.

(Photograph by author.)

proximity to the complex pointed out, "There was nothing here before. It's only now [in the years following the apparition] that they've made it fancy."

Similar to established Ukrainian religious sites, at which one can purchase copies of the icons of the Mother of God of Zarvanytsia or the Mother of God of Pohonia, pilgrims can acquire copies of the Mother of God of Bryn featuring photographs of the original apparition. For example, a folded four-page card produced by Bryn residents at the time of the original apparition in 2007 features a photograph of the apparition on the front page and an image of the local church on the back. The middle pages of the card include a prayer and a statement describing the apparition. The latter text begins in the following way:

> From now on, the village of Bryn is no longer just a brief historical mention in the rich history [of our region], but also a geographical point on the map of Prykarpattia [a geographical region at the foot of the eastern Carpathian Mountains, where the village is located] to which travelers from all over the region come day and night. The news of the Virgin Mary of Bryn has reached all the surrounding villages and towns of Prykarpattia.

It is easy to see striking similarities between this text and the one describing the village of Zarvanytsia. The residents of such places as Bryn and Malyi Hvizdets, whether

FIG. 19.5. The Bryn apparition (the silhouette formed by the barkless area of the linden tree). Part of the newly built chapel can be seen in the background. June 2012.

(Photograph by author.)

consciously or unconsciously, follow the trajectories of familiar established religious models like Zarvanytsia, while creating sacred materiality around their own sites. The materiality, in turn, fulfills a similar function to that of personal narratives. Physical objects, ranging from newly built chapels to small cards, mark the villages as "chosen places," putting them on the map and reinforcing their charisma.

"Even the Bishop Was Here": Church Rituals

In line with my initial view of the apparitions as "alternative forms of hope," I expected to hear many stories about miraculous encounters. However, while some individuals occasionally mentioned instances of miraculous healing, it was not a prominent theme. This may be related to timing as I visited the sites after the peak of their popularity had subsided. However, I did not have a single conversation where religious services officiated by clergy at the sites were not emphasized. These services reflect the defining characteristics of rituals as events that "have significance far beyond information transmitted" within the actual rituals (Mayerhoff 1977:200). Similar to personal narratives and sacred materiality, they reinforce both the importance of the sites and the charisma of the host villages.

A 2009 poster sold by the residents of Malyi Hvizdets features six images depicting a church service by the now famous ash tree. A Ukrainian Orthodox bishop accompanied by several priests conducted the service, with a large number of people in attendance. This is another example showing how this kind of marketing approach resonates with strategies developed at more established religious centers like Zarvanytsia. Numerous printed materials sold at Zarvanytsia highlight services conducted by the highest authorities of the UGCC, including the major archbishop. The fact that Pope John Paul II prayed in front of the icon of the Mother of God of Zarvanytsia during his visit to Ukraine in 2001 is perhaps the greatest highlight in such literature (e.g., Bubnii, Hlubish, and Baliukh 2019).

While the services in both Malyi Hvizdets and Bryn are not as frequent today as they had been during the peak of the sites' popularity, church authorities nonetheless continue to conduct rituals at the apparition sanctuaries at least once or twice a year on particular church holidays. In 2012, a middle-aged woman, while reflecting on my question of whether she believed in the miraculous nature of the Bryn apparition, sounded rather ambivalent but then added, "[Regardless of what it actually was], this place is already prayed-up [and, thus, powerful] because so many priests have been here and so many services have been conducted here."

Similar to religious dynamics in post-Soviet Russia (Rouhier-Willoughby and Filosofova 2015), the legitimization of the supernatural folk encounters by church authorities was not a one-directional hierarchical act. It was, rather, a complex negotiation process. An outside skeptic may wonder what would bring a bishop to a tree in a remote village and how church authorities can accept images that are likely nothing more than natural coincidences. However, the interpretations that dominated among the village residents and curious pilgrims from the surrounding regions were not skeptical. The self-sufficiency in religious behavior that rural residents had developed during Soviet times may have played a role. People were drawn to the sites. Subsequently, churches responded to these social impulses by accepting them and incorporating the sites into their institutional jurisdiction. Potential clerical skepticism would not have stopped the growing interest in pilgrimage at the time. Instead, it may have potentially created tension and turned the believers' attention away from churches.

Some Ukrainian priests were critical of the recent apparitions. For example, Fr. Volodymyr of the UGCC openly condemned this type of supernatural phenomenon in his town of Stryi, pointing out that there was no need to look for anything supernatural in natural things (Pohliad.com 2015). Similarly, Fr. Taras of the same church, while commenting on recent apparitions in both Stryi and Truskavets, emphasized that such encounters required a very careful examination on the part of church authorities, a process that could last for years and even decades (Pohliad.com 2015). Church authorities of Bryn and Malyi Hvizdets did not have decades at their disposal. They needed to respond to the folk impulses more promptly. This illustrates the complex lived relationship between such impulses and institutional religion. The discrepancies in clerical opinion in Ukraine clearly fit Primiano's argument that, in lived realities, official religion, as it is widely understood, does not exist since every leader must adjust to particular cultural situations and unique political conditions and, thus, practices in a lived, vernacular way (1995:46).

In light of the post-Soviet revival of churches and their authoritative positions, the lay village residents, on their part, sought institutional approval. Church services conducted by both local priests and visiting higher-ranked clergy provided such approval. The rituals also reinforced the charisma of the villages, imparting them with a larger-than-local sense of significance. A telling and somewhat humorous example comes from an informal conversation with Vasylyna, whose narrative, like those of my other consultants, included the distinct "my village is special" motif. Vasylyna is an elderly woman who took care of the apparition site in Malyi Hvizdets in 2012. She was proud that many priests from the city and even the bishop had come to this place to conduct services. (Her emphasis on the city is directly connected to the idea of placism. It is not only city people who often look down upon their village counterparts. Villagers are socialized into this mode of thinking and perceive the status of city dwellers to be higher than their own.) With an air of superiority and sarcasm in her voice, Vasylyna also pointed out that a priest from a neighboring village was not too happy that the apparition in Malyi Hvizdets had received a great amount of attention. He was upset that it had not occurred in his own village. If analyzed through the frame of "vernacular" or "lived" religion, it is not only institutional dimensions of religion that display complexity and diversity. What is understood in eastern Europe under the term "folk religion" is also complex, involving shifting and competitive dynamics within this very category.

Anthropologist Arjun Appadurai's discussion of the "center–periphery" dynamics in the context of cultural contacts can shed further light on the role of church rituals at the apparition sites. Appadurai argues that ideas and influences cross borders in complex multidimensional ways, not just from "centers" to the "peripheries," as previous thinkers often argued (1996:32). In line with the concept of placism, villages are traditionally seen as economic, political, and social "peripheries" of Ukraine. Moreover, they are also peripheral places in the context of institutional Christianity. Institutional religious centers such as eparchial headquarters are located in cities. The supernatural apparitions turn the host villages into spiritual "centers." With the help of the apparitions, these villages are empowered by attracting the attention of not only ordinary pilgrims but also church authorities. They obtain direct access to the kind of higher power that overcomes any political and economic dynamics in real life. From this perspective, the villages should no longer be perceived as marginal and backward-oriented. They become centers of spiritual progress because they have been chosen by the highest spiritual power.

Concluding Remarks

It is unlikely that the recent apparitions such as those in Malyi Hvizdets and Bryn, with their steadily decreasing number of pilgrims, will ever approach the scale of popularity that can be observed in Zarvanytsia and more widely known established Marian spiritual centers the world over. Nonetheless, the sites continue to produce meanings, playing important roles in the history of the villages as places. The dynamic and competitive folk expressions surrounding the recent apparitions, while drawing upon select models and strategies associated with established belief patterns and religious power, produce meanings that have little to do with religion per se. They contribute to the creation of the charisma of place, putting marginalized social units on the map and symbolically balancing power dynamics between different forms of settlement.

The present case sheds light on methodological and interpretative trajectories that can potentially be useful to folklorists and scholars of related disciplines who employ ethnographic methods in the study of religion. My focus in this chapter may appear to be "doubly marginal," to put it metaphorically. First, I have discussed relatively insignificant sites located in remote rural settings. Second, I examined these sites at a time when their popularity among pilgrims had already passed. This latter approach is somewhat counterintuitive as ethnographers of religion are often drawn to places characterized by a high degree of human action. My study shows that, at a closer look, this approach is not really marginal and is worth pursuing as small-scale daily realities shed light on important broader societal and political issues.

Notes

1. Jeanmarie Rouhier-Willoughby and Tatiana Filosofova observed similar dynamics in Russia (2015).
2. It is beyond the scope of this work to provide a detailed overview of the religious landscape in Ukraine. Among other studies, for a comprehensive survey focusing on Orthodox, Catholic, and Protestant Christianity as well as Islam in post-Soviet Ukraine, see Long Ratajeski (2015). For an in-depth anthropological analysis of complex forms of religiosity in the western parts of the country, with a particular focus on the UGCC, see Naumesku (2007). Among English-language monograph-length ethnographies exploring particular religions, see Wanner (2007) for a historically grounded study of evangelism and Lesiv (2013) for a discussion of Modern Paganism in post-Soviet Ukraine.
3. I am grateful to my colleague, Jillian Gould, for bringing Goffman's work to my attention during a personal conversation.
4. Miraculous icons, a widespread phenomenon in both Orthodox and Catholic Christianity, are associated with miracles such as faith healing.
5. Among numerous other works, see Kaufman (2005); Badone (2007); Hermkens, Jansen, and Notermans (2009); Halemba (2015); Bitel (2015); and Liutikas (2015).
6. I further develop this idea elsewhere (Lesiv 2017, 2019).
7. I benefited from a discussion of the concept of "placism" by Hazel T. Biana, Adrienne John Galang, and Jeremiah Joven Joaquin at the panel "Diaspora and Place" (Diasporas: An Inclusive Interdisciplinary Conference, December 2019, Prague).

Works Cited

Appadurai, Arjun. 1996. *Modernity at Large: Cultural Dimensions of Globalization*. Minneapolis: University of Minnesota.

Badone, Ellen. 2007. "Echoes from Kerizinen: Pilgrimage, Narrative, and the Construction of Sacred History at a Marian Shrine in Northwestern France." *Journal of the Royal Anthropological Institute*, 13:453–470.

Banks Thomas, Jeannie, ed. 2015. *Putting the Supernatural in Its Place: Folklore, the Hypermodern, and the Ethereal*. Salt Lake City: University of Utah Press.

Bennett, Gillian. 1999. *Alas, Poor Ghost!: Traditions of Belief in Story and Discourse*. Logan: Utah State University Press.

Bitel, Lisa. 2015. *Our Lady of the Rock: Vision and Pilgrimage in the Mojave Desert*. Ithaca, NY: Cornell University Press.

Bociurkiw, Bohdan. 1996. *The Ukrainian Greek Catholic Church and the Soviet State (1939–1950)*. Edmonton: Canadian Institute of Ukrainian Studies.

Bubnii, Petro, Orest Hlubish, and Vasyl Baliukh. 2019. *Зарваниця*. Lviv: FOP Vasylyk Andrii Ivanovych.

Buiskykh, Yulia. 2018. *Колись русалки по землі ходили: Жіночі образи української міфології*. Kharkiv: Клуб сімейного дозвілля.

DeBernardi, Jean. 2008. "Wudang Mountain: Staging Charisma and the Modernization of Daoism." In *Chenghuang Xinyang/City God Belief*, ed. Ning Ngui Ngi, 273–280. Singapore: Lorong Koo Chye Sheng Hong Temple Association.

Del Negro, Giovanna. 2004. *The Passeggiata and Popular Culture in an Italian Town: Folklore and the Performance of Modernity*. Montreal: McGill-Queen's University Press.

Erdeljan, Jelena. 2017. *Chosen Places: Constructing New Jerusalems in Slavia Orthodoxa*. Leiden: Brill.

Espreso.TV. 2018. "На Тернопільщині відкрили Український Єрусалим." YouTube video, 28 August. https://www.youtube.com/watch?reload=9&v=tPIYkvNvygo.

Ferreira, Celio. 1996. "Divine Grace, Gender and Reciprocity: The Cult of the Virgin Mary at Fatima." *Journal of Mediterranean Studies*, 6/2:233–246.

Goffman, Erving. 1974. *Frame Analysis: An Essay on the Organization of Experience*. Cambridge, MA: Harvard University Press.

Halemba, Agnieszka. 2015. *Negotiating Marian Apparitions: The Politics of Religion in Transcarpathian Ukraine*. Budapest: Central European University Press.

Hermkens, Anna-Karina, Willy Jansen, and Catrien Notermans, eds. 2009. *Moved by Mary: The Power of Pilgrimage in the Modern World*. Burlington, VT: Ashgate.

Hufford, David. 1982. *The Terror That Comes in the Night: An Experience-Centered Study of Supernatural Assault Traditions*. Philadelphia: University of Pennsylvania Press.

Jimerson, Lorna. 2005. "Placism in NCLB—How Rural Children Are Left Behind." *Equity & Excellence in Education*, 38:211–219.

Kapaló, James. 2013. "Folk Religion in Discourse and Practice." *Journal of Ethnology and Folkloristics*, 7/1:3–18.

Kaufman, Suzanne. 2005. *Consuming Visions: Mass Culture and the Lourdes Shrine*. Ithaca, NY: Cornell University Press.

Kononenko, Natalie. 2006. "Folk Orthodoxy: Popular Religion in Contemporary Ukraine." In *Letters from Heaven: Popular Religion in Russia and Ukraine*, eds. John-Paul Himka and Andriy Zayarnyuk, 46–75. Toronto: University of Toronto Press.

Kononenko, Natalie. 2010. "How God Paired Men and Women: Stories and Religious Revival in Post-Soviet Rural Ukraine." *Canadian–American Slavic Studies*, 44:118–150.

Kyiv Post. 2019. "Ukrainian Church's Autocephaly Tomos to Be Briefly Returned to Istanbul to Be Signed by Constantinople Patriarchate's Synod." 7 January. https://www.kyivpost.com/

ukraine-politics/ukrainian-churchs-autocephaly-tomos-to-be-briefly-returned-to-istanbul-to-be-signed-by-constantinople-patriarchates-synod.html.

Lavreniuk, Liliana. 2018. *Оповідки про навернення і зцілення за посередництвом молитов до Пречистої Діви Марії, яка прославилась у своєму чудотворному Образі в Погоні.* Ivano-Frankivsk, Ukraine: Nova Zoria.

Lesiv, Mariya. 2013. *The Return of Ancestral Gods: Modern Ukrainian as an Alternative Vision for a Nation.* Montreal: McGill-Queen's University Press.

Lesiv, Mariya. 2017. "Blood Brothers or Blood Enemies: Ukrainian Pagans' Beliefs and Responses to the Ukraine–Russia Crisis." In *Cosmopolitanism, Nationalism and Paganism*, ed. Kathryn Rountree, 133–155. London: Palgrave Macmillan.

Lesiv, Mariya. 2018. "Hope for Ukraine, Fall of America and Putin the Savior: The Supernatural in Ukrainian and Russian Media and Vernacular Contexts." *Journal of American Folklore*, 131/519:30–52.

Lesiv, Mariya. 2019. "'I Know History': Experience, Belief and Politics in the Post-Socialist Diaspora." *Western Folklore*, 78/2–3:119–150.

Lindquist, Galina. 2005. *Conjuring Hope: Healing and Magic in Contemporary Russia.* New York: Berghahn Books.

Liutikas, Darius. 2015. "In Search of Miracles: Pilgrimage to the Miraculous Places." *Tourism Review*, 70/3:197–213.

Long Ratajeski, Esther. 2015. "The Changing Religious Mosaic of Ukraine." In *The Changing World Religion Map: Sacred Places, Identities, Practices and Politics*, ed. Stanley D. Brunn, 1555–1576. Dordrecht: Springer.

Mayerhoff, Barbara. 1977. "We Don't Wrap Herring in a Printed Page: Fusion, Fictions, and Continuity in Secular Ritual." In *Secular Ritual*, eds. Sally Moore and Barbara Mayerhoff, 199–224. Amsterdam: Van Gorcum/Assen.

Naumesku, Vlad. 2007. *Modes of Religiosity in Eastern Christianity: Religious Processes and Social Change in Ukraine.* Berlin: Lit Verlag.

NTK. 2009. "На Коломийщині з'явилася Матір Божа." Телеканал НТК/NTK TV Channel. YouTube video, 3 August. https://www.youtube.com/watch?v=dOxg12UrvP0.

Orsi, Robert. 2003. "Is the Study of Lived Religion Irrelevant to the World We Live in?" *Journal for the Scientific Study of Religion*, 42/2:169–174.

Pocius, Gerald. 2000. *A Place to Belong: Community Order and Everyday Space in Calvert, Newfoundland.* Montreal: McGill-Queen's University Press. First published 1991.

Pohliad.com. 2015. "В Стрию об'явилась Матінка Божа." 18 September. https://provse.te.ua/2015/09/v-stryyu-obyavylas-matinka-bozha-foto-video/.

Primiano, Leonard. 1995. "Vernacular Religion and the Search for Method in Religious Folklife." *Western Folklore*, 54/1:37–56.

Primiano, Leonard. 1999. "Postmodern Sites of Catholic Sacred Materiality." In *Perspectives on American Religion and Culture*, ed. Peter W. Williams, 187–202. Oxford: Blackwell.

Razumkov Center. 2018. "Релігія і церква в українському суспільстві." In *Особливості релігійного і церковно-релігійного самовизначення українських громадян: Тенденції 2010–2018.* Kyiv: Razumkov Center.

Religious Information Service of Ukraine. 2019. "Religious Organizations in Ukraine as of January 1, 2019." https://risu.org.ua/ua/index/resources/statistics/ukr_2019/75410/.

Rouhier-Willoughby, Jeanmarie, and Tatiana V. Filosofova. 2015. "Back to the Future: Popular Belief in Russia Today." In *The Changing World Religion Map: Sacred Places, Identities, Practices and Politics*, ed. Stanley D. Brunn, 1531–1553. Dordrecht: Springer.

Ryden, Kent. 1993. *Mapping the Invisible Landscape: Folklore, Writing, and the Sense of Place.* Iowa City: University of Iowa Press.

Smith, Anthony. 2003. *Chosen Peoples: Sacred Sources of National Identity.* Oxford: Oxford University Press.

Snitovskyi, Oleh. 2018. "Зарваниця—український Лурд." Ukrinform, 14 June. https://www.ukrinform.ua/rubric-regions/2498343-zarvanica-ukrainskij-lurd.html.

TSN. 2009. ТСН: Телевізійна служба новин. "На Чернігівщині на дереві проявилася ікона Божої матері." Video, 3 December. https://tsn.ua/video/video-novini/chernigivska-ikona-bozhoyi-materi.html.

Ukrainian Greek Catholic Church. n.d. *Українська Греко-Католицька Церква: Паломницькі місця. Довідник.* Kyiv: Патріарший паломницький центр Української Греко-Католицької Церкви.

Wanner, Catherine. 2004. "Missionaries of Faith and Culture: Evangelical Encounters in Ukraine." *Slavic Review*, 63/4:732–755.

Wanner, Catherine. 2007. *Communities of the Converted: Ukrainians and Global Evangelism.* Ithaca, NY: Cornell University Press.

Wigzell, Faith. 2011. "The Orthodox Church and Commercial Fortune-telling and Magic in Russia." *Religion, State, and Society*, 39/4:420–442.

PART III
ORAL TRADITIONAL NARRATIVE

Poetry: Epic and Ballad

CHAPTER 20

BYLINY

Russian Folk Epic

NATALIE KONONENKO

Russian epic songs, *byliny* (sg. *bylina*), are THE folklore of Russia. When people in the West think of folklore, they think of classic folk tales. Russians do as well. But when they think of specifically Russian folklore, the characters that come to mind are Ilia Muromets, Dobrynia Nikitych, and Alesha Popovych, the heroes of traditional oral epic songs—*byliny*. *Byliny* are marvelous stories of high adventure and fierce combat. The heroes, called *bogatyri*, roughly translated as knights, battle-fearsome human adversaries, giants, dragons, and even elemental forces such as the passage of time. During the period of Romantic Nationalism, when manuscripts of epic songs recorded in earlier times, such as *Beowulf* and the *Nibelungenlied*, were receiving new and enthusiastic public attention, having an epic tradition was considered proof of a people's cultural awareness of itself as a nation and its advanced standing on the world stage. This was also the time when Russia was becoming increasingly engaged in world affairs and striving to be seen as a state on a par with European states. For Russia, having its own tradition of epic poetry was crucial proof that it was both modern and cosmopolitan.

From the time that they were first recorded, *byliny* and their heroes were seen as emblematic of the Russian soul and the Russian spirit. They have retained their position representing that which is truly Russian as times and political systems have changed. Originally part of an oral tradition that was alive in the late nineteenth and early twentieth centuries, *byliny* have lived on in popular culture into the present. Their heroes became the heroes of the Soviet period and were showcased in inspirational films. Soviet juvenile literature retold *bylina* narratives in child-friendly format to inspire desired traits in future generations. In the post-Soviet world, when Russia sought to create popular literature and culture that was uniquely native, *bylina* heroes were the choice again. The plots of the epics themselves were minimally retained, but select epic heroes went on to adventures, now in animated format, that dealt with contemporary issues and concerns.

Bylina Cycles

Epic came to widespread public attention in the period of Romantic Nationalism when concepts of identity and national awareness were closely linked to history. Epic is considered a historical genre, and, indeed, many epic poems, including Russian *byliny*, do refer to personages and events that can be connected to people and phenomena attested in sources such as chronicles and other records deemed historical. For this reason, *byliny* are often divided into cycles roughly corresponding to the time periods described in the texts. The group of songs considered the oldest are the mythological *byliny*. These cannot be connected to datable events, and their subject matter, while it does not contain the creation stories characteristic of myths, does deal with humans discovering the fundamental nature of the world; they tell of heroes learning the limits of the possible. Mikula Selianinovich tries to lift what seems to be an ordinary seed bag and cannot because it contains the weight of the earth. He races a seemingly decrepit nag only to find that his fine horse cannot outrun it because the bedraggled horse is time itself. Sviatogor, a superhuman warrior whose name translates as "holy mountain," is so huge that the earth cannot support his weight, forcing him to live on rocky, mountainous terrain, which gives him his name. Despite his enormous size and strength, Sviatogor discovers that even he cannot escape death. He befriends the more human Ilia Muromets, and the two ride the countryside together, coming upon a mysterious coffin in the mountains. Sviatogor orders Ilia to try the coffin on for size; it proves too big. Sviatogor then lies down in the coffin, and it fits him perfectly. In fact, the fit is so perfect that he cannot get out. He then tells Ilia to strike the coffin with his sword and break it. But each blow, instead of damaging the coffin, causes an iron brace to spring up over it, trapping Sviatogor all the more firmly. After three strikes, Sviatogor gives up and accepts his imminent death.

> Говорилъ-то Илья да таково слово:
> —«Да ты послушай—ко крестовой ты мой брателко!
> —Куды ударю—туды три обручи желѣзные»—
> Говорилъ-то Святогоръ да таково слово:
> «Ты послушай—ко крестовой ты мой брателко!
> Видно мнѣ-ка туто Богъ и смерть судилъ».
> Тутъ Святогоръ и помирать онъ сталъ,
> Да пошла изъ его да пѣна вонъ.
> Говорилъ Святогоръ да таково слово:
> «Ты послушай-ко крестовой ты мой брателко!
> Да лижи ты возьми вѣдь пѣну мою,
> Дакъ ты будешь ѣздить по Святымъ горамъ,
> А не будешь ты бояться богатырей,
> Ни какого сильного могучаго богатыря.»

Ilia spoke these words:
"Listen to me, my brother in God!
Where I strike—there are three iron hoops.—"
Sviatogor spoke these words:
"Listen to me, my little brother in God!
It appears that God willed that my death should be here."
Here Sviatogor, he began to die,
And a foam ran out of him.
Sviatogor spoke these words:
"Listen to me, my brother in God!
Go and lick this, my foam,
So that when you ride through the holy mountains,
You will not be afraid of bogatyrs,
(You will not fear) a single powerful bogatyr." (Fig. 20.1)

(Gil'ferding 1900:3:382–386; here and in the following examples,
the pages are for the *bylina* in its entirety)

This passage tells of another creation, namely that of the cycle of human heroes who will succeed men of superhuman stature like Sviatogor by taking on some of their strength. In other texts, Ilia's might is explained differently. Where his lowly origin, his peasant status, is emphasized, he is presented as a cripple who is endowed with special power by a group of pilgrims.

The next group of songs is the Kyivan cycle and centers around the court of Prince, or *Kniaz*, Vladimir (958–1015). These epics are the best-known texts and include heroes familiar to all Russians: Ilia Muromets, Dobrynia Nikitych, and Alesha Popovich (Fig. 20.2). In the oral tradition, a great many more heroes are associated with Kyiv, including Solovei Budimirovich, who sails to the city on magnificent ships to court a bride; Mikhailo Potyk, a man who keeps his vow to be buried with his deceased wife and resurrects her, only to have her betray him with another man; Vasilii Ignatiev, who behaves like a drunkard but manages to save Kyiv from attack; as well as other heroes. But most *bylina* heroes, even those from the Kyivan cycle, are not widely known.

There is some historical basis to the figures of the Kyivan cycle. Vladimir was a very important ruler who brought Christianity to Rus' in 988. Murom is a real city. A man named Dobrynia may have been a councilor at the royal court. While the characters about whom these texts sing may have some basis in fact, most of their adventures are hardly realistic: these are adventures on an epic scale. Dobrynia Nikitych is a dragon-slayer who violates his mother's injunction not to go to the Puchai River where the fearsome dragon Gorynishche dwells. He angers the dragon by trampling its young, then engages the beast in combat. The battle is a draw, and the Russian hero and his monster seal a pact of blood-brotherhood. The dragon soon violates this pact and attacks Russia, burning crops and even abducting Prince Vladimir's niece, Zabava Putiatichna, whereupon Vladimir summons Dobrynia and orders him to destroy the

FIG. 20.1. Ilia Muromets, Viktor Vasnetsov (1848–1926).
(*Source*: Vasnetsov, Viktor. *Knight's ride*. 1904. House-Museum of V. M. Vasnetsov, Moscow.)

dragon and free Zabava. This Dobrynia does, but only after nearly succumbing in the course of his second combat with the monster. Dobrynia then goes on to marry, not Zabava, but a huge, fearsome *polianitsa*, a female warrior whose ilk has disappeared from popular knowledge of *byliny*. Ilia Muromets and Alesha Popovich also battle the dragon-like monsters Idolishche and Tugarin Zmei (Tugarin the Dragon), respectively. These, more than the *bogatyri*, may be based on historical personages, with Tugarin possibly deriving from Tugar Khan, an eleventh-century Polovetsian ruler. Ilia must also overcome a peculiar being called Solovei Razboinik, the Nightingale Robber or Highwayman, who disables, and even kills, his opponents with his whistle. But, with the simplification that comes when oral literature becomes popular culture, the role of dragon-slayer has been assigned exclusively to Dobrynia Nikitych. While popular culture focuses on these three heroes, the oral, folk version of the Kyivan cycle is voluminous and complex with a great many songs and a variety of heroes. In this cycle, the action sometimes takes place in court, and the *bogatyri* brag and quarrel and engage in tests of military prowess. Sometimes the *bogatyri* are dispatched on missions, and sometimes they must defend the city of Kyiv from attack by enemies such as Kalin

FIG. 20.2. *The Three Bogatyrs: Dobrynia, Ilia, and Aliosha*, Viktor Vasnetsov (1848–1926).
(*Source*: Vasnetsov, Viktor. *The Three Bogatyrs: Dobrynia, Ilia, and Aliosha*. 1881, Tretiakov Gallery, Moscow.)

Tsar, another figure possibly based on a foreign ruler, in this case the Bulgarian Kaloian (r. 1197–1207) (Fig. 20.2).

The Halych cycle is sometimes distinguished from the Kyivan cycle and sometimes joined to it. Historically, a bitter and prolonged conflict between the principalities of Rus' began after the death of Iaroslav the Wise (r. 1019–1054). Kyiv lost its supremacy, and the Rostislavichi of Halych-Volyn' assumed pre-eminence for a time. The heroes of the Halych cycle are better known for their affluence and beauty than their skill as warriors. Diuk Stepanovich proves that the wealth of his city surpasses that of Kyiv, while Churilo Plenkovich is so handsome that he inadvertently seduces his host's wife, leading the cuckolded husband to kill them both. When Turko-Tatar enemies appear in these songs, they are distinctly human, unlike the almost formless monster Idolishche whom Ilia Muromets battles or Alesha Popovich's antagonist Tugarin who flies on dragon wings. Tsar Koshcheishche, the enemy in a number of texts, is human-sized and behaves as a man, seducing Ivan Godinovich's intended bride and leading the Russian *bogatyr* to brutally execute her by dismemberment. Partially because of its description of sexual relations and even more because of its emphasis on possessions and wealth rather than physical prowess, the epics of this cycle have not entered popular culture and are little known by non-specialists.

The last *bylina* cycle is associated with the Russian city of Novgorod rather than with places in what is now Ukraine and is said to be the newest cycle. No tsar or prince is present; rather, the songs tell of merchants of incredible wealth and arrogance who get their comeuppance and are punished by the forces of nature. This happens to Vasilii Buslaev, a young man who does not know his own strength and causes great physical damage to the citizens of Novgorod. In an adventure that takes place outside of Novgorod, he insults a skull only to meet his own death on the same hill where the skull lay. Sadko is a wealthy merchant who boasts excessively of his financial might. His ships are then magically immobilized by the sea king, forcing him to descend beneath the waves. Sadko's great weapon is, not his physical strength, but his skill as a musician who plays the *gusli*, a plucked and strummed zither held in the lap. It is his music that wins him the love of one of the sea king's daughters and his eventual release. While most heroes not characterized by physical might have not entered popular culture, Sadko, with his instrument, has become the subject of a recent animated feature produced in Ufa, Bashkortistan, one of the republics of the Russian Federation (Kononenko 2019a) (Figs. 20.3 and 20.4).

Byliny, when they were recorded in the late nineteenth century, were a vital, living genre, with each text existing in multiple variants. In the folk milieu, there were many songs that are currently known by folklorists only. Furthermore, the *bylina* singers' concept of genre differed from that of academic professionals. Many called their texts *stariny* (songs of olden times) and mixed historical songs about the tsar in Moscow in with songs that were about Kyiv and Novgorod. In a classic early collection compiled by Aleksandr Gil'ferding (1831–1872), most of the texts are indeed *byliny*, but the people who performed for this collector also sang about the rebels Ermak (1532–1585) and Sten'ka Razin (1630–1671). Razin and his exploits were a favorite topic of folk narratives, but the songs about him are not epics: they are best described as ballads, shorter, rhymed, and stanzaic narrative songs (Kononenko 1998). Several texts recorded by Gil'ferding are based on ballads that are not connected to historical figures. One example is the song about a sister and her highwayman brothers. The sister is married to a man in a distant land, and when she and her husband set out to visit her homeland, they are attacked by the robbers. The husband is killed, and the sister, not recognized by her brothers, is taken captive and, in some versions, raped. In a different ballad-like text, a hero battles an enemy only to discover that it is his brother, taken prisoner as a child and raised by Tatars. From the point of view of their original performers, *byliny/stariny* were songs of bygone times and extreme deeds; the genre purity that collectors tried to establish was not their concern.

COLLECTIONS AND PUBLICATIONS

The earliest Russian epic to be recorded is the *Lay of Igor's Campaign* (*Slovo o Polku Igoreve*) (Likhachev 1986). The events that it describes date to the twelfth century, but the poem was preserved in a fifteenth-century manuscript kept in the Spaso-Preobrazhenskii Monastery in Iaroslavl until it was discovered in the late eighteenth century and purchased by Aleksei Musin-Pushkin (1744–1817), a Russian statesman,

FIG. 20.3. Sadko in the underwater kingdom, Ilia Repin (1844–1930).
(*Source*: Repin, Ilia. *Sadko in the Underwater Kingdom*. 1876. Russian State Museum, St. Petersburg.)

FIG. 20.4. Screen capture from the 2018 Sadko film.
(*Source: The Underwater Adventures of Sadko.* 2018. Directed by Vitaly Mukhametzyanov, CTB Film and Cinema Foundation of Russia.)

historian, and art collector who served on the governing board of the Church of Russia. This manuscript was much like the manuscripts discovered in western Europe, and this proved to be both a blessing and a curse. It was a blessing in the sense that it set Russia on a par with the western European nations that had uncovered their own epic manuscripts. It was a curse because its original was destroyed in a fire and the only extant version was a copy that Musin-Pushkin made for Catherine the Great. This led to accusations of forgery, partially fueled by controversy surrounding James MacPherson's *Ossian* and partially based on the similarities between the *Slovo* and other texts that might have served as a model for its fabrication. The poetic narrative itself tells of the failed raid of Igor Sviatoslavich (1151–1202), prince of Novgorod/Seversk and later Chernihiv, on the Polovtsians (also known as the Kumans). It is a stirring text which not only speaks of tragic military conflict and heroic hubris but also contains a moving, poetic lament by Iaroslavna, Igor's wife, and interesting references to pagan, as well as Christian, deities.

It is indicative of epic that, while many of Igor's military forays were successful, the campaign that ended in his capture and the defeat of his troops was the one captured in song. The text is now accepted as genuine and is most likely an example of an early stage of epic, one performed at a time before the texts that are currently termed *byliny* came into existence (Mann 1989, 2005; Likhachev 1985).

The type of song that is now called a *bylina* is a narrative, usually about three hundred to five hundred lines long, focusing on a single dramatic incident. The verse lines are irregular, averaging eleven to fifteen syllables. The songs have ornamental features such as an optional opening section called a *zapev* that can be a description of nature unrelated to the plot of the narrative. Domna Surikova's *bylina* about Ilia Muromets and Kalin Tsar, for example, begins with the following *zapev* lines:

> Рѣки-то озера ко Новугороду,
> Мхи-то болота ко Бѣлоозыру,
> Широки роздолья ко Опскому,
> Темныя лѣса ко Смоленскому,
> Чисты поля къ Ерусололиму.

> The rivers and the lakes around Novgorod,
> The mosses and swamps around Beloozero,
> The wide expanses around Opsk,
> The dark forests around Smolensk,
> The open fields around Jerusalem.
>
> (Gil'ferding 1896:2:386–396)

The introduction to the narrative itself is called the *zachin*; it sets the scene for the action to follow and does so in an elaborate fashion, describing, for example, the feast at Vladimir's palace where all the *bogatyri* have gathered.[1] *Byliny* end with a conclusion, *kontsovka*, which gives the name of the hero one last time, sums up the action, winds down the plot, and thanks the audience for listening.[2] Ornamental features within the text may include exaggeration and negative antithesis such as a description of a wedding feast that says it spanned, not a short time, or a long time, but twelve days: Заводили они свадебку почестный пиръ, Не на мало не много на двѣнадцать денъ (Gil'ferding 1896:2:213). *Byliny*, like other oral compositions, have additive style, naming actions or objects, such as the items used to saddle a horse, one at a time, usually one item per verse line, thus slowing down the action and allowing the audience to enjoy elaborate, slow-paced description in a phenomenon called "epic retardation." Hyperbole, such as naming an impossible number of enemy combatants, is also a typical feature that adds to the richness of the texts. All of these traits contribute to a high, elegant style (Bailey and Ivanova 1998:xxiii–xxviii).

Bylina were first collected by Kirsha Danilov (1703–1776), perhaps at the behest of his employer, Prokopii A. Demidov. This collection was published in an abbreviated edition in 1804, and a full version was prepared by Nikolai Rumiantsev in 1818. A modern edition appeared in 1977 (Evgeneva and Putilov eds.). Suppositions are that Danilov was himself a performer, as well as a skilled tradesman, and that he wrote down *byliny* for Demidov. Danilov's work sparked interest in epic throughout the Slavic world and led to collection after collection. Piotr Kireevskii (1808–1856), along with his acquaintances, collected texts and an accessible version of this work was published in 1971 (Soimonov and Iazykov eds.). These texts are noteworthy because they include *byliny* from central Russia, a region which lost its oral tradition shortly thereafter. The best-known event is Pavel Rybnikov's (1831–1885) unexpected encounter with *bylina*-singing in the middle of the night, and his description of his experience is much quoted. Rybnikov was so moved by his discovery that he went on to record a number of texts. He was followed by Aleksandr Gil'ferding who was notable for collecting biographical information about his performers, along with their songs. Gil'ferding was a folk hero himself because he sacrificed his life for his fieldwork, contracting typhus on his second expedition and dying in Kargopol, a place where he could not receive proper medical attention. Important collectors who followed include A. V. Markov who produced a volume entitled *Belomoskiia byliny*, Vsevolod Miller who published new texts entitled *Byliny: Novoi i nedavnoi zapisi*, A. D. Grigorev who used phonograph recordings to produce *Arkhangel'skiia byliny i istoricheskie pesni s napevami*, and N. E. Onchukov—a dedicated fieldworker—who published *Pechorskiia byliny*. The Sokolov brothers (Iurii and Boris) also did collecting and Iurii Sokolov published *Onezhskie byliny* in 1948. The folklore center in Petrozavodsk on Lake Onega brought archival texts into print, including the unpublished texts of the expeditions undertaken by the two Sokolov brothers, *Neizdannye materiialy ekspeditsii B.M. i Iu.Sokolovykh*. With the turn of the century, women joined the ranks of collectors, notably Natal'ia P. Kolpakova (1902–1994) who produced *Novye zapisi bylin na Pechore*, among other works, and the prolific publisher of materials Anna M. Astakhova (1886–1971). Her work appeared in numerous collections including the multivolume *Bylina Severa* (Byliny of the North) and the specialized volume that focused on Riabinin-Andreev, Trokhim Riabinin's son and an important performer in his own right. Many important folklorists such as Onchukov suffered government persecution, and even Rybnikov ended up in the Russian north because he was accused of revolutionary activities and deported to Petrozavodsk. The relationship between the government and prominent folklorists is a topic that deserves further investigation (Fig. 20.5).

History of the Genre

The living tradition of *byliny* was attested in the Russian north from the time when they were first collected in the late nineteenth and up until the early twentieth century. The content of most of these songs, and certainly the best-known ones, refers to what is now Ukraine, far to the south, with Novgorod being the closest geographically to the locations where *byliny* were performed. It is impossible to determine with certainty why people in the north of Russia, the areas of Onega, Pechora, and Archangelsk where

FIG. 20.5. Aleksandr Gil'ferding, engraving from his collection of *byliny*, Vol. 1.
(*Source*: Gil'ferding, Aleksandr. Frontispiece in *Onezhskiia byliny, zapisannyia Aleksandrom Fedorovichem Gil'ferdingom letom*, Vol. 1, 1894.)

collectors did their fieldwork, sang about Kyiv. It is perhaps ironic that the heroes who have come to be emblematic of Russia performed their deeds outside this country.

One explanation may be that *byliny* originated in the south and then moved northward. Because the court plays a prominent role in many texts, scholars have speculated that *byliny* were first composed by bards in the royal service, presumably professional musicians who entertained the *kniaz* and his guests at the court in Kyiv by singing and playing the *gusli*, the instrument mentioned above in connection with Sadko (Oinas 1971, 1978). The fact that Kireevskii, an accessible version of whose work was published in 1971 by Soimonov and Iazykov, recorded epic singing in central Russia which disappeared shortly after his work supports this supposition. Russell Zguta (1978) argues that *skomorokhi* were the link between the putative place of origin and the place where *byliny* were found in the nineteenth century. *Skomorokhi* were a type of musician who might well have performed epic narrative and carried it to locations outside the capital city. The word *skomorokh* is of Indo-European derivation and refers to professional musician-entertainers. The fact that images of *skomorokhi* appear on the frescos of the St. Sophia Cathedral in Kyiv suggests that they did, in fact, exist on the territory of Ukraine. *Skomorokhi* were street entertainers who played musical instruments and sang; they wore costumes, staged little plays, and kept animals and performed with them. The eclectic nature of their repertory suggests that, even if they were not the original composers of epics, they may have picked up *byliny* from court bards. *Skomorokh* performances included songs with satirical elements, criticizing people in power. Such flaunting of authority led to the animosity of religious hierarchs and civil authorities toward them. Edicts were issued banning their art, their instruments were smashed, and they were generally persecuted. Zguta believes that they fled north, carrying their *byliny*, though not their instruments, with them. Those who stayed in the south stopped being *skomorokhi* and evolved into performers who eschewed any texts that might get them into trouble, limiting themselves to showing trained animals such as bears. By the nineteenth century *skomorokhi* as a cadre of professional entertainers who sang epics, along with other verbal genres, were no more. *Byliny* did live on but only in the Russian north where they were performed, not by professional entertainers, but by people who sang epics as something complementary to their other work.

A different, or additional, transmission from Ukraine to the Russian north were *kaliki*. A *kalika* could be either a religious pilgrim who traveled to holy sites or a beggar, typically a blind mendicant, who sang religious and other serious verses (Bezsonov 1861–1864). *Byliny* were in this serious poetry category, and, as wanderers, the *kaliki* sang them and could well have carried them northward. The mendicant *kaliki* might have been an evolution of an earlier type of performer that existed on the territory of what is now Ukraine, perhaps developing out of *gusli*-playing court minstrels. Support for this supposition comes in the form of Ukrainian professional beggar-musicians called *kobzari* and *lirnyki*. These minstrels were very similar to *kaliki*. They were mendicants who included epic songs (*dumy*) in their repertory (see Kononenko, "Dumy—Ukrainian Folk Epic," this volume). They also shared an instrument, the *lira*, with *kaliki*. It is tempting to suggest that the Russian and Ukrainian singers are both descendants of *gusli*-players who split, with *kaliki* preserving *byliny* and carrying them northward, while the repertory of the singers who stayed on Ukrainian territory evolved into *dumy*, epics which describe more recent times (Kononenko 2019b:45–55).

Further support for the role of *kaliki* in *bylina* transmission is the fact that they, along with *skomorokhi*, appear as characters in *bylina* texts. In the song entitled "Forty Pilgrims Plus One," the *kaliki* set out on a trip to Jerusalem. They encounter *Kniaz* Vladimir and ask him for alms. He demurs, saying that he has nothing with him because he is out hunting. He then sends the men to Kyiv where, he says, his wife Apraksiia will care for them. In Kyiv, the pilgrims, who are pictured as imposing, physically powerful men, are indeed wined and dined, and their leader, Kasian Mikhailovich, catches the eye of Apraksiia. She asks him to stay for a private meal, an invitation he refuses, saying that the pilgrims must be on their way. Enraged at being rejected, Apraksiia has a silver chalice planted on Kasian's person. She then arranges to have the chalice discovered, and, when this happens, Kasian is punished by burial up to his armpits. The pilgrims continue without Kasian, and Apraksiia falls ill. On their return, the pilgrims encounter Kasian who has miraculously survived. They stop by Kyiv again. Apraksiia's treachery is revealed, and Kasian heals her, leading to a happy ending. The *kaliki* in this *bylina* are as powerful and stalwart as any *bogatyr*, suggesting that these mendicants might have been singers of epic who wanted to present themselves as being on a par with military heroes.

THE SINGERS OF *BYLINY*

In the late nineteenth and early twentieth centuries, *bylina*-singing in the Russian north, specifically the Onega, Pechora, and Arkhangelsk regions, was a vibrant oral tradition that belonged to non-professional performers who sang unaccompanied. Anyone could sing *byliny*, women as well as men. While *byliny* were not a genre restricted to a particular social class, they tended to be learned and performed by the poor, not mendicants like *kaliki* but people who needed additional, paying work. The jobs that encouraged singing were those where people performed repetitive tasks that occupied the hands and freed the mind for long periods of time, such as net-mending. Trofim Riabinin (1791–1885), an outstanding *bylina* performer recorded by both Gil'ferding and Rybnikov, is an excellent example (Fig. 20.6). He was orphaned at a young age and raised as a ward of the community. He started mending nets to earn money. He learned *byliny* from the men alongside whom he worked, then picked up more songs while working for his uncle. Riabinin married a woman of some wealth and, through her, became a landowning peasant and broke free of his indigent status. He continued to perform nonetheless, presumably enamored of the art that he represented so well. Other singers about whom Gil'ferding provides biographical information include an elderly man dispossessed by his son, blind men, and cripples. Essentially it was the poor who became performers, singing for others who worked with them and for anyone else who would listen. Rybnikov's description of his discovery of *byliny* tells not of a repetitive task but of nighttime entertainment after a day of work, and Bailey and Ivanova (1998:xxxiv) say that fishing, hunting, and lumbering cooperatives called *artels* would hire singers for this purpose. Were the poor drawn to singing as a source of income? This is hard to determine from Gil'ferding and Rybnikov's descriptions. According to the biographical information provided by Gil'ferding, only one person, a blind man, sang for money. The singers who were hired earned a wage. Others were, presumably, rewarded at the pleasure of their audience.

Bylina-singing was typically a solo art because the songs were long and complex and composed in performance, the singer essentially retelling the narrative rather than repeating a memorized text. Yet there is at least one attestation of a joint performance: two women who sang together. Their typical venue was *posidelki*, courtship parties where young unmarried women would gather to work on a task such as spinning while socializing with young men and looking for potential marriage partners. *Bylina*-singing, at least at the time of Rybnikov and Gil'ferding, was a vital, living tradition. The situations in which *byliny* could be performed were many, and the circumstances

FIG. 20.6. Trokhim Grigorovich Riabinin, engraving from Gil'ferding's *bylina* collection, Vol. 2.
(*Source*: Gil'ferding, Aleksandr. *Trokhim Grigorovich Riabinin*. Engraving from *Onezhskiia byliny*, Vol. 2, p. 2, 1896.)

of performance could vary greatly. During performance, each singer sang their texts their own way, and comparison of Gil'ferding's collection with Rybnikov's shows variation from performance to performance. Each performer adjusted their text to suit the circumstances of narration.

Bylina Content

The *byliny* collected by Rybnikov, Gil'ferding, and the other folklorists who followed them are complex texts that treat real human issues. Their characters are often flawed.

Hubris is a central problem. From the mythological cycle on down through all of the cycles of *byliny*, heroes overrate their abilities and their strength and are convinced that they are invincible. In the mythological cycle, Sviatogor thinks he can escape death and Mikula Selianinovich overestimates his strength and that of his horse. Heroes repeatedly act in an arrogant manner, often to their own detriment and sometimes with tragic consequences. The valiant hero Dunai goes on a quest to fetch a bride for his *kniaz*. He secures the hand of Opraksiia, the younger daughter of the Lithuanian king, for his liege and himself encounters, battles, and then weds her sister, Nastasiia, a *polianitsa*, a skilled female warrior. At the feast celebrating the dual wedding, Dunai boasts of his wife's military prowess and challenges her to an arrow-shooting competition. She proves the better shot, firing her arrow through a wedding ring, something Dunai cannot do. Dunai cannot suffer being outshot by his wife and decides to kill her. She apologies for foolishly outperforming her husband and begs for her life, saying that she is carrying Dunai's child, a magical baby. She warns Dunai not to act too impulsively:

> А й теперь-то ты Дунаюшко хмѣльнешенекъ,
> А й теперь Дунаюшко пьянешенекъ,
> А убьешь ты меня ту молоду жену,
> А й ты сдѣлашь двѣ головки безповинныихъ,
> У меня съ тобой во чревѣ есть чадо посѣяно,
> По колѣнкамъ у него есть ножки въ серебри,
> По локоточкамъ у него есть ручки въ красномъ золоти,
> А назади у него пекетъ свѣтелъ мѣсяцъ,
> От ясныхъ очей какъ будто лучъ пекетъ.

> Because now you, Dunaiushka, are tipsy,
> Because now, Dunaiushka, you are drunk,
> And if you kill your young wife
> Then you will take two innocent lives
> In my bosom you and I have an offspring sired,
> And up to his knees his legs are silver,
> And up to his elbows his arms are of gold,
> And at his back a bright moon glows.
> From his clear eyes it is as if a ray is burning.

(Gil'ferding 1896:2:100–114)

Dunai slays Nastasiia regardless and cuts open her womb, revealing a fetus just like the one the slain woman had described. He then takes his own life by falling on his sword. Here the song becomes an etiological narrative, saying that the flowing blood became the source of the Dunai (Danube) River.

Bogatyri and their *kniaz* are vain and easily offended. Bragging leads to trouble time after time so that *byliny* feature a regular formula, typically found in the introductory section or *zachin*, which says that a wise man boasts of his parents, while a foolish man boasts of his wealth or his young wife.

У стольняго города у Кіева,
У ласкова князя у Владиміра
Заводилось пированье, почестенъ пиръ
На всихъ на князей, на бояровъ,
На русскихъ могучихъ богатырей,
На всихъ поляницъ на удалыихъ.
Красно солнце на вечери,
Почестенъ пиръ у нихъ на весели.
Вси на пиру пьяны веселы,
Вси на пиру наѣдалися,
Вси на пиру напивалися,
Вси на пиру поросхвастались:
Умный похвасталъ отцемъ матерю,
А безумный похвасталъ молодой женой.

In the capital city of Kyiv,
At the home of the kind *kniaz* Vladimir,
Feasting started, a feast of honor,
For all of the princes and the boyars,
For the mighty Russian *bogatyrs*,
For all of the *polianytsy*, the women of valor.
The bright sun approaches evening,
And the feast of honor is in full swing;
All at the feast are drunk and joyous,
All at the feast have eaten their fill,
All at the feast have drunk their full measure,
All at the feast begin to boast:
The wise man boasted of his father and mother,
The foolish man boasted of his young wife.

(Gil'ferding 1896:2:405–411)

Stavr Godinovich is just such as foolish man. At a banquet in Kyiv, he lists his wonderful possessions but then says that none can compare to his young wife who can outwit all of the assembled princes and boyars. Vladimir, insulted, responds by throwing Stavr in prison. A servant informs Vasilisa Nikulichna, Stavr's wife, of her husband's predicament. She disguises herself as a man and goes to rescue her foolish spouse by claiming to be a suitor courting Vladimir's daughter. Everyone falls for Vasilisa's disguise except the daughter, who demands tests of gender. Vasilisa passes all the tests—playing chess, shooting arrows, and engaging in a wrestling match—and no one, except Vladimir's daughter, suspects that she is a woman. She tries to reveal her true identity to her husband and even he does not realize that she is anyone other than the *bogatyr* she is pretending to be. Vasilisa sheds her disguise in the end and saves her foolish husband. In other texts, Vladimir himself is not above insulting his *bogatyri* by not honoring them properly. When he does so, their anger leads to serious consequences. Thus, when the *kniaz* fails to invite Ilia Muromets to a feast, the *bogatyr* goes around Kyiv shooting down gilded church roofs and offering the gold to beggars so that they can buy drink.

Heroes can resort to cheating on each other and trying to steal other men's wives. When Dobrynia Nikitych goes on a quest, Alesha Popovich courts his wife Nastasiia. His false accounts of seeing Dobrynia's dead body finally get her to accept his proposal, and a wedding celebration for the two of them begins. In this Russian version of the widespread return story pattern, Dobrynia appears at the marriage banquet disguised as a *skomorokh* and drops his wedding ring into his wife's goblet. She, of course, recognizes the ring and is reunited with her spouse. *Bogatyri* are not always selfless defenders of the homeland. In a widely recorded song, Kalin Tsar and his troops threaten Kyiv. Ilia Muromets calls upon the other *bogatyri* to help him defend the homeland. They refuse, saying that Vladimir does not feed them, so why should they work for him? Only when Ilia takes on the burden of fighting the enemy single-handedly and shows signs of success do they join the fight.

While *byliny* sing of powerful knights in the service of the prince or of fabulously wealthy merchants, they often valorize those of lowly origin. Mikula Selianinovich, a mythological *bylina* hero, plows the earth and is portrayed as an archetypical peasant. Ilia Muromets is also a peasant, not a nobleman. Furthermore, in this particular version of his acquisition of his great strength, he is a cripple who cannot walk and is forced to sit on the stove. Since the stove (*pech*) is a large structure built into the wall of the home with a shelf for the elderly and the infirm, Ilia's incapacity is underscored. Three *kaliki* arrive and magically cure him, either with their words or by giving him an elixir to drink. Ilia is not only cured but gains superhuman strength—and an obligation to follow the course of justice imposed on him by his debt to the mendicants.

While peasants like Ilia can join the ranks of noble warriors, noblemen, and even *Kniaz* Vladimir, can be foolhardy. In the *bylina* about Ilia Muromets and Solovei Razboinik, the Nightingale Robber, Ilia brings the brigand to Kyiv as a gift to his *kniaz*. Vladimir insists on hearing the renowned and fearsome whistle of the captured Solovei. Ilia warns against this, but Vladimir persists, and Ilia loosens Solovei's bonds, gives him the drink of green wine that he requests, and orders him not to whistle with full force. The brigand does as ordered and causes death and destruction even at half volume—at which point Ilia is forced to kill his captive.

> Засвисталъ какъ Соловей тутъ по соловьему,
> Закричалъ разбойник по звѣриному,
> Маковки на теремахъ покривились
> А околенки во теремахъ розвыпались
> Отъ него отъ полсвисту соловьяго,
> А что есть-то людюшокъ, такъ вси мертвы лежатъ,
> А Владимíръ князь-от стольне-кіевской
> Куньей шубонькой онъ укрывается.

> And here Solovei whistled as nightingales do,
> And here he yelled like an animal,

> And the tops of towers began to bend,
> And the windows in the towers shattered,
> Just from his whistling at half volume,
> And as for the people, they are all lying there dead,
> And as for Vladimir, the *kniaz* of Kyiv,
> He is hiding under a sable cloak.
>
> (Gil'ferding 1896:2:11–19)

Women play an important and active role in *byliny*, a fact that few non-folklorists know. *Bylina* women have size, power, and agency. The *polianitsa* is a woman warrior, as large as, if not larger than, her male counterparts and a formidable combatant. A formula used in several songs has *Kniaz* Vladimir addressing both the *bogatyri* and the *polianitsy* in his service, treating the two as equals. In the *bylina* "Ilia Muromets and His Daughter," the daughter is a *polianitsa* who approaches Kyiv, demanding a worthy opponent. Alesha Popovich rides out to confront her but is so frightened that he withdraws to the city. Dobrynia Nikitych follows and also demurs. The task of fighting the *polianitsa* and protecting Kyiv falls to Ilia Muromets. He fights the powerful warrior-woman on horseback but cannot subdue her. The two then engage in hand-to-hand combat. They trade insults and Ilia calls the *polianitsa*'s mother a whore, not realizing that his own liaison with this woman produced his opponent. The *polianitsa* initially overcomes Ilia but cannot kill him because it is not his fate to die in battle. When they fight again, Ilia gets the better of his adversary but stays his hand: some instinct stops him from delivering the fatal blow. The combatants part ways. The *polianitsa* is grateful to have her life spared, but she cannot forget that Ilia insulted her mother and returns to fight him once more. This battle again goes to Ilia and, sadly, he kills his daughter. While the *polianitsa* does die, she is shown to be her father's equal and powerful enough to intimidate both Alesha and Dobrynia. There is another *bylina*, usually referred to as "Ilia and His Son." It is similar in content to the song about Ilia Muromets and his daughter, and the son, Ilia's near-equal in combat, is also killed. This pair of songs presents women and men as equivalent.

Women are not demure; they are aggressive and initiate sex. *Byliny* tell of a youth who seeks employment in the service of the king of Lithuania or Poland. His first job is as a lowly stable hand. He works his way up to chamberlain. In this position, he serves the king's daughter. The nature of his service expands to pleasuring her in bed, in some versions at her request. Everything is fine until the youth gets drunk and brags of his conquests in a public tavern, at which point he is immediately hauled off for execution. The youth gets word to the princess who either takes him back or, finding out that he has family, sends him home to his wife and children with a substantial monetary gift. While the liberated woman here is a foreigner, some Russian women are also presented as sexually aggressive, such as in the *bylina*, mentioned earlier, where Apraksiia, *Kniaz* Vladimir's wife, tries to seduce the leader of the *kaliki*. In some versions of the song about Alesha and Tugarin, it is implied that Apraksiia grants Tugarin favors until Alesha Popovich rids the land of the boastful invader and sets things right in court. Sviatogor's wife is sexually forward. Sviatogor keeps her in a crystal coffin like a priceless jewel, releasing her while he sleeps. Ilia Muromets comes upon the sleeping Sviatogor and marvels at his size. At this point the wife emerges and seduces Ilia. When Sviatogor awakens and becomes aware of what has happened, he kills his wife and becomes blood brothers with Ilia.

Although women are pictured as having strength, wit, and sexual desire, *byliny* do not present a society where women are treated equally. While Apraksiia and the Lithuanian/Polish princess are not punished, other women who act on their sexual desires are, such as Sviatogor's wife, just mentioned. Women who outperform their husbands, like Dunai's Nastasiia, are also killed. Some women are executed through torture. Ivan Godinovich courts a woman who is promised to another. When her father refuses to break the engagement for the sake of the Russian *bogatyr*, he takes her by force. The original suitor, often given a name that implies Turkic or otherworldly origin, sets out in pursuit. As the two heroes fight, the original fiancé tempts his betrothed with offers of queenship, and she not only helps him capture Ivan but allows him to "enjoy himself" with her. When Ivan finally breaks free, he appears willing to take back the woman whom he had so ardently pursued. But then he executes her in a most cruel manner, cutting off first her legs, then her arms, and finally her lips. Women, it seems, should know that Russian men are always to be preferred.

> Тутъ молодой Иванушко Годиновичъ
> Становилъ Настасью супротивъ соби,
> Во свои во бѣлы онъ во ручушки
> А онъ бралъ свою да саблю вострую,
> Й онъ смахнулъ своей да саблю вострую,
> Да срубилъ ей ножки по колѣночкамъ.
> Говорилъ да Иванушко енъ таковы слова:
> —А почто-то эти ноженки-ты рѣзвыи?
> —Оплетали-то татарина поганого,
> —А й того Федора Иванова.—
> И смахнулъ своей онъ саблей вострою,
> Отрубилъ ей ручки по локоточкамъ,
> Говорилъ да Иванъ да таковы слова:
> —А й почто-то эти ручки бѣлыи?
> —Обнимали-то татарина поганого,
> —А й того Федора Иванова.—
> Онъ смахнулъ еще да саблей вострою,
> Отрубилъ-то ей уста сахарнiи,
> Говорилъ да Иванушко да таковы слова:
> —А й почто эти уста сахарнiи?
> —Цѣловали-то татарина поганого,
> —А й того Федора Иванова.—
> А ще тутъ Настасьюшкѣ славу поютъ,
> Ей славу поютъ да вѣки по вѣку.

> And there young Ivanushka Godinovich,
> He stood Nastas'ia opposite him,
> And in his white hands,
> He took a sharp sword,
> And he brandished the sharp sword
> And he chopped off her legs at the knee,
> And Ivan Godinovich spoke these words:
> "Why do I need these frisky legs?
> They encircled a pagan Tatar.
> That one, that Fedor Ivanov."
> And he brandished his sharp sword,
> He chopped off her arms at the elbow,
> Ivan spoke the following words,
> "Why do I need these white arms?
> They embraced a pagan Tatar.
> That one, that Fedor Ivanov."
> He brandished his sharp sword again,
> He chopped off her lips like sugar,
> And Ivan Godinovich spoke these words:
> "Why do I need these lips like sugar
> They kissed a pagan Tatar.
> That one, that Fedor Ivanov."
> And there they sing Nastasiushka's glory,
> They sing her glory from one epoch to the next.
>
> (Gil'ferding 1896:2:116–122)

The oral tradition was multifaceted and complex. *Byliny* could be sung at night to help pass the time after a hard day's work. They could be performed while working to help ease a repetitive task. They could be entertainment at an evening event such as the *posidelki*, which were held to help young people meet and marry. Although most of the performers were men, collectors such as Gil'ferding recorded texts from women. While one might have expected women to favor songs that featured *polianitsy* and underscored the power of women, this was not the case, at least if one goes by Gil'ferding's collection. There, powerful and sexually aggressive women appear in texts performed by men, while women singers favor more romantic subject matter: songs that end with the union of lovers.

Bylina Heroes in the Fine Arts and Popular Culture

Bylina heroes appeared in the fine art of the late nineteenth century. Ilia Muromets, Dobrynia Nikitych, and Alesha Popovich on horseback were immortalized in Viktor Vasnetsov's 1881 painting known to all Russians (see Fig. 20.2). It was part of his folklore and mythology series. Less well-known are Vasnetsov's painting of Ilia Muromets alone and Nikolai Roerich's 1910 painting also of Ilia. Nikolai Rimskii-Korsakov composed an opera based on Sadko, first staged in 1898. These works of fine art were roughly contemporaneous to the period when *byliny* were still alive as an oral tradition and being collected and published.

The living tradition started to die out with the beginning of the twentieth century. Better communication with the Russian north, the growing availability of print and media, and the Soviet push for modernization reduced the demand for oral performance. Soviet policy affected the *bylina* tradition more directly as well. Because *byliny* were heroic, they fit Soviet ideals, encouraging officials to claim them as part of the Soviet ethos, the people's view of history. The location of the action in Ukraine supported Soviet goals because it seemed to say that Ukraine was part of Russia, not the separate nation that Ukrainians wanted it to be. *Byliny* were also attractive because Soviets wanted to portray Soviet-era struggles as part of the grand scheme of history, a direct evolution of the heroic era. To accomplish their goals, they had professional folklorists "help" the singers compose new epics on Soviet topics. These were called *noviny*, from the word "new" (*novyi*), as opposed to *byliny/stariny*, songs of bygone times. As Miller describes in his book, *Folklore for Stalin*, performers were coached in singing about Lenin. They were taken to the openings of new subway stations and told to sing about the glories of Soviet technical accomplishments. Kriukova, for example, originally a traditional singer, became well known in the Soviet era and produced texts about Soviet accomplishments such as this ode to icebreakers.

> Сказать-то нам не про старинушку,
> А сказать-то нам про новинушку,
> Про жизнь про новую, про теперешнюю,
> Про удалых добрых молодцев-папанинцев,
> Про богатырей-то славна советских,
> Про их-то славное хожденьице окиянское.
> Не на пароходах-то ходили они паровых,
> Не на черненых больших караблях,
> Не на парусных-то легких лодочках,
> Они носились-плавали на лединочке;

> We will tell not about the olden times,
> We will tell about what is new,
> About new life, about (the life) of today,
> About daring goodly heroes, the Papanitsy (a Russian geographical society)
> About glorious Soviet heroes,
> About their glorious ocean voyage,
> They did not venture forth on steam ships,
> And not on big black vessels,
> And not on light sailing vessels,
> They went and sailed forth on icebreakers.

(Sokolov 1939:30)

FIG. 20.7. Marfa Kriukova—a composer of *noviny*.
(*Source*: Unknown author. Photograph of Marfa Kriukova 1940.)

There were also odes to tractors and the mechanization of farming. Forced folklore cannot live, and epic singing died out: both the *noviny* and the traditional *byliny* (Fig. 20.7).

While the Soviets were not successful in starting a new oral tradition glorifying Soviet accomplishments, they did begin the transition of *bylina* heroes into the sphere of popular culture. The 1956 film *Ilia Muromets* (English: *The Sword and the Dragon*) told the story of Ilia by conflating episodes from several oral epics into one cinematic text. More importantly, it promoted Soviet ideals such as struggle on behalf of the motherland. It presented a squeaky-clean version of Ilia's adventures, with no sexual exploits, no heroic hubris, and no questioning of loyalty to the ruler. Ilia does father a son he knows nothing about, and the boy is raised by the Turkic enemy to be a warrior against Russia. When the father and son struggle, however, the younger combatant immediately recognizes the justice of his father's cause and switches his allegiance to Russia. A film about Sadko with numerous folk tale and pop culture elements was produced in 1953 (Fig. 20.8). The idea that *bylina* heroes represent the best of Russia/the Soviet Union was further underscored by naming a powerful aircraft after Ilia Muromets and a submarine after Sadko.

FIG. 20.8. Sadko from the 1953 film.

(*Source: Sadko*. 1953. Directed by Aleksandr Ptushko, Mosfilm.)

Even more influential in the popular imagination was Irina Karnaukhova's book *Russkie bogatyri* retold for children and first published in 1949 then reissued in 1963 and subsequently. Like the film described above, it presented "clean" versions of *bylina* heroes, men with no psychological struggles, no sex, and no doubts about their mission to serve Russia. Female combatants were absent—there were no more *polianitsi*. Generation after generation grew up with this book, and when the Soviet Union collapsed and newly independent and commercially oriented film studios such as Melnitsa started looking for material that would be truly Russian and yet competitive with the animated features produced in the West, they remembered Karnaukhova. The result was *Alesha Popovich i Tugarin Zmei* (*Alesha Popovich and Tugarin the Dragon*), produced in 2004, followed by *Dobrynia Nikitych i Zmei Gorynych* (*Dobrynia Nikitych and the Dragon Gorynych*) in 2006 and *Ilia Muromets i Solovei Razboinik* (*Ilia Muromets and Solovei the Brigand*) in 2007. Once it had introduced these three heroes to the public, the Melnitsa Studio went on to produce a series of *Tri Bogatyria* (*Three Bogatyrs*) films, one almost annually, and to do so with good commercial success. While these do draw on *byliny*, though very loosely, they also use folk tale elements; literary works, namely Pushkin's poem "Shamakhanskaia Tsaritsa" ("The Queen of Shamakhan"); and,

FIG. 20.9. Screen capture from the Tri Bogatyri animated series parodying the Vasnetsov painting. *Tri Bogatyri i Shamakhanskaia Tsaritsa*, 2010.

(*Source*: *Tri Bogatyri i Shamakhanskaia Tsaritsa*. 2010. Directed by Sergei Glezin, Melnitsa Studio, St. Petersburg.)

of course, characters drawn from popular Western cinema such as the talking horse Iulii, presumably based on the donkey in the Shrek films produced by Dreamworks (Kononenko 2014) (Fig. 20.9).

Conclusion

Byliny as an oral traditional genre flourished in the Russian north into the first part of the twentieth century. The oral epics were complex and dealt with the real issues of the people who sang them and their audiences. They acknowledged fierce pride, especially the overconfidence of the young, while reminding all that pride must be tamed for successful communal life. Men and women were both shown as wanting power, status, and recognition of their abilities, while acknowledging that their desires need to be held in check for the communal good. The epics, as performed by ordinary people, both women and men, transposed the action onto a time long ago, a place far away, and a social class that the singers knew only from song. This allowed *byliny* to speak of pressing frustrations and concerns. Perhaps saying that even those with money and power had to temper their desires made it easier for the ordinary fishermen and villagers of the far north to do the same.

There have been some attempts by lovers of antiquity to recapture the traditions of the ancient past. Performers sing to the accompaniment of *gusli* and dress in medieval garb, with flowing robes or colorful, heavily embroidered costumes. These reconstructions are very attractive. The performers have clear, conservatory-trained voices and play beautifully polished *gusli*. While appealing, the reconstructions are nothing like the performances by peasants, fishermen, and widows from whom Rybnikov, Gil'ferding, and other folklorists working in the Russian north recorded their *bylina* texts. These are reconstructions for the stage and a modern audience. The oral tradition is gone, but what lives on are the heroes who have migrated to popular culture: Ilia Muromets, Dobrynia Nikitych, Alesha Popovich, and to a lesser extent Sadko, especially as they are portrayed in Melnitsa films and their spinoffs such as video games.

Notes

1. See the *zachin* to the song about Stavr Godinovich quoted below, under "*Bylina* Content."
2. For an example of a *kontsovka*, see the end of the scene between Nastasia and Ivan Godinovich below, under "*Bylina* Content," where the singer speaks of Nastasia's glory. This *kontsovka* does not address the audience because it is the end of an episode, not the end of the *bylina* as a whole.

Works Cited

Astakhova, A. M. 1938–1951. *Byliny severa*. Moscow: Akademiia Nauk.

Astakhova, A. M. 1948. *Byliny Ivan Gerasimovicha Riabinina-Andreeva*. Petrozavodsk: Goslitdat.

Bailey, James, and T. G. Ivanova. 1998. *An Anthology of Russian Folk Epics*. Armonk, NY: M. E. Sharpe.

Bezsonov, P. (Petr Aleeksevich). 1861–1864. *Kaleki perekhozhie: Sbornik stikhov i izsledovaniia P. Bezsonova*. 3 vols. Moscow: Tipografiia A. Semena.

Danilov, Kirsha. 1977. *Drevniia rossiiskiia stikhotvoreniia sobranyia Kirsheiu Danilovym*, eds. A. P. Evgen'eva and B. N. Putilov. Vtoroe dopolnennoe izdanie. Moscow: Nauka.

Gil'ferding, A. F. (Aleksandr Fedorovich). 1894, 1896, 1900. *Onezhskie byliny zapisannye Aleksandrom Fedorovichem Gil'ferdingom letom 1871 goda*. Vols. 1–3. St. Petersburg: Tipografiia imperatorskoi akademii nauk.

Grigorev, A. D. 1910–1939. *Arkhangel'skiia byliny i istoricheskie pesni, s napevami zapisannymi posredstvom fonografa*. 3 vols. Moscow: Akademiia nauk.

Karnaukhova, I. V. 1963. *Russkie bogatyri: Byliny v perekaze dlia detei*. Leningrad: Gosudarstvennoe izdatel'stvo detskoi literatury.

Kireevskii, P. V. 1971. *Sobranie narodnykh pesen P. V. Kireevskogo; Zapisi v Simbirskoi i Orenburgskoi guberniakh*, eds. A. D. Soimonov and N. M. Iazykov. Leningrad: Nauka.

Kolpakova, N. P. 1957. *Novye zapisi bylin na Pechore*. Moscow: Akademiia Nauk SSSR.

Kononenko, Natalie. 1998. "Clothes Unmake the Social Bandit: Sten'ka Razin and the Golyt'ba." In *Playing Robin Hood: The Legend as Performance in Five Centuries*, ed. Lois Potter, 111–135. Newark, NJ–London: Delaware University Press.

Kononenko, Natalie. 2014. "Post-Soviet Parody: Can Family Films about Russian Heroes Be Funny?" In *Family Films in Global Cinema: The World Beyond Disney*, eds. Noel Brown and Bruce Babington, 171–185. New York–London: I. B Tauris.

Kononenko, Natalie. 2019a. "Maksim Volkov, Vitalii Mukhametzianov: *Sadko* (2017)." *Kinokultura*, 63/January. http://www.kinokultura.com/2019/issue63.shtml.
Kononenko, Natalie. 2019b. *Ukrainian Epic and Historical Song: Folklore in Context*. Toronto: University of Toronto Press.
Likhachev, Dmitrii S. 1985. *Slovo o Polku Igoreve i kul'tura ego vremeni*. Leningrad: Khudozhestvennia literatura.
Likhachev, Dmitrii S. 1986. *Slovo o Polku Igoreve*. Leningrad: Nauka.
Mann, Robert. 1989. *Lances Sing: A Study of the Igor Tale*. Columbus, OH: Slavica Publishers.
Mann, Robert. 2005. *The Igor Tales and Their Folkloric Background*. Jupiter, FL: Birchbark Press.
Markov, Aleksei. 1901. *Belomorskiia byliny*. Moscow: A. A. Levenson.
Miller, Frank J. 1990. *Folklore for Stalin: Folklore and Pseudofolklore in the Stalin Era*. Armonk, NY: M. E. Sharpe.
Miller, V. F. 1908. *Byliny: Novoi i nedavnei zapisi, iz raznykh mestnostei Rossii*, eds. Elena Nikolavena Elionskaia and A. Markov. Moscow: Sindolnaia tipografiia.
Oinas, Felix J. 1971. "The Problem of the Aristocratic Origin of Byliny." *Slavic Review*, 30/3:513–522.
Oinas, Felix J. 1978. "Russian Byliny." In *Heroic Epic and Saga: An Introduction to the World's Great Folk Epics*, ed. Felix J. Oinas, 236–256. Bloomington, IN: Indiana University Press.
Onchukov, N. E. 1904. *Pechorskiia byliny*. St. Petersburg: Tipografiia N. Sokolova i V. Pastora.
Rybnikov, Pavel. 1990. *Pesni: Sobrannye P. N. Rybnikovym; v trekh tomakh*, ed. Boris N. Putilov. Petrozavodsk: Kareliia.
Sokolov, B. M., and Iu Sokolov. 2007. *Neizdannye materialy ekspeditsii B. M. i Iu. M. Sokolovykh, 1926–1928, po sledam Rybnikova i Gil'ferdinga*, eds. V. M. Gatsak and V. A. Bakhtina. Moscow: Nauka.
Sokolov, Iu. 1939. *Byliny M. S. Kriukovoi: zapisali i kommentirovali E. Borodina i R. Lipets*. Moscow.
Zguta, Russell. 1978. *Russian Minstrels: A History of the Skomorokhi*. Philadelphia: University of Pennsylvania Press.

CHAPTER 21

DUMY
Ukrainian Folk Epic

NATALIE KONONENKO

EPIC poetry is extremely important to Ukrainians because they see it as the genre that legitimizes Ukrainian claims to statehood. Especially in those periods when the territory that would become Ukraine was under foreign rule, epic was proof that there was a unique Ukrainian essence that justified the call for an independent state. Ukrainian epic songs, *dumy* (singular *duma*), came from the folk and were a distinctive form of expression, implying that the people themselves were different from their political masters. Indeed, Ukrainian *dumy* are distinctive in form and content. What makes Ukrainian *dumy* unique in form is their irregular line length and the presence of rhyme. The *duma* lines run from three to sixteen syllables. Rhyme occurs in tirades, end-rhyming groups that are not regular, like stanzas, but have varying numbers of lines coinciding with a particular topic. For example, all lines describing one topic such as a storm at sea typically have the same end rhyme, and when the topic changes to human reaction to the storm, the rhyme switches as well. The texts are relatively short, focusing on the most dramatic part of an event, such as the death of a hero and his bravery in confronting his demise. In terms of content, *dumy* are distinctly Ukrainian in the sense that when the action occurs in places that are named, these can be located on or near the territory of present-day Ukraine. While some actors are nameless Kozaks (Cossacks), those figures who are named can often be linked to historical personages. Similarly, some of the events described can be connected to Ukrainian history—if not to specific battles, then to known historical circumstances.

Because having an epic poetry was a claim to potential statehood, Ukrainian epics began to be collected early in the nineteenth century. This was the beginning of romantic nationalism, and the recording of *dumy* began not long after the collection of German tales published by Wilhelm and Jacob Grimm, folktale collectors whose goal was to find common artistic expression among the folk and unite Germans into one nation. What Ukrainian collectors found was that Ukrainian *dumy*, like other epic poetries, are tales of war, often describing not the battle itself but its results. Many Ukrainian epic heroes die, and it is their courage in the face of death that makes them heroic. Khvedir the Man without Kin is mortally wounded but clings to life long enough to ensure that his page can replace him in battle. The Kozak dying in the Kodyma Valley defiantly shoots at the birds of prey gathering to feast on his remains. Marusia Bohuslavka frees Ukrainians who had been captured in battle by her master, putting her life in jeopardy by doing so. In this sense, Ukrainian epic heroes are like the heroes of other epic poetries. They are like Roland of French epic who bravely fights the Saracens, refuses to call for help, and dies along with his men. They are like Beowulf of English epic who goes to defend his people from a fierce dragon even though he is old and knows that this battle will cost him his life.

Scholars group *dumy* into four cycles, covering the period from the fourteenth through the seventeenth centuries. In chronological order they are, first, songs about Turko-Tatar slavery, which describe the period when the Tatars and the Nogais, a Turkic ethnic group living in the northern Caucasus, raided Ukrainian settlements to capture slaves and sell them to the Ottomans. Next are songs about Kozak battles on land and sea. They reflect the period when Ukrainians went from being individual settlers to forming a community, and Kozaks became an organized military power. *Dumy* about the Kozak uprising (1648–1654) led by Hetman Bohdan Khmelnytskyi come next. Last is a group of songs about everyday life and the struggles that people endured not on the battlefield but at home. It corresponds to The Ruin (1657–1687), when the Hetmanate, a Ukrainian state negotiated by Khmelnytskyi, collapsed and Kozak factions struggled for leadership while disputing where to look for support: Russia, Poland, or the Ottoman Empire. The chaos that characterized The Ruin was as hard on people as any war.

Performers and Performance

Dumy are oral compositions, created during the course of singing. To be able to put together a song rapidly, an epic singer learns a vocabulary of word clusters during his apprenticeship which he expands during his professional life. When performing, the singer follows a traditional plot, building the actual text using word clusters, what Albert Lord called formulas and formulaic expressions, units that fit the metrics and subject matter of *dumy* (1960; Kononenko 1998:111–114).

Dumy likely arose at a time close to the events that they describe. We have no information about the people who started singing these songs, but since Kozaks appear in all *dumy*, including texts connected to the earliest period, it is likely that the composers and first singers were either Kozaks themselves or a special artistic cadre that accompanied Kozak forces. It is they who would have lauded their comrades, especially those fallen in battle (Kononenko 2019:45–48).[1] If this is the case, then the original singers were likely sighted, a situation that was no longer true by the time that *dumy* were written down by literate collectors. When collecting began in the nineteenth century, performing *dumy* was the exclusive right of blind mendicant minstrels called *kobzari* or *lirnyky*.

Kobzari played the *kobza*, a lute that later evolved into the multi-stringed, asymmetrical bandura. *Lirnyky* played the *lira*, a hurdy-gurdy with three strings, a crank connected to a wheel that rubbed the strings, and keys that depressed the strings, producing a melody (Figs. 21.1–21.3).

Kobzari and *lirnyky* were professional musicians. They belonged to guilds which admitted members after a period of apprenticeship that culminated in an initiation rite. The guilds were affiliated with churches and were welfare institutions because only the disabled could become guild members. Ukrainian minstrels traveled the countryside begging at people's homes and at church-related events such as *vidpusty*, special days of atonement.

When begging at a home, *kobzari* and *lirnyky* would perform for a predominantly female audience. Minstrels traveled to earn money during the summer months when the able-bodied men of a household were working in the fields. In the home, mendicants encountered women, children, and the elderly. When arriving at a home, a minstrel sang an introductory begging song. Few of these have been recorded since collectors were interested in epics and little else. The begging songs that we do have appeal to a female audience. They address the eldest woman of the house and compare her to Mary Mother of God, especially Mary of the Protection, the patron saint of Kozaks, typically pictured holding a cloth over the humans she protects. After making the comparison, the singer would ask his audience to pity him and give him alms. Begging songs also reminded listeners that giving alms to blind minstrels is an effective way to ensure that deceased family members, especially those killed in accidents, would attain the kingdom of heaven (Kononenko 1998:211–219).[2] If the family asked the performer to come into the home, he would sing a combination of religious songs called *psalmy*, historical verses, and *dumy*. While *dumy* were the genre of interest to elite collectors, many of whom had nationalist leanings, neither minstrels nor their audiences preferred *dumy* to other songs. Minstrels sang what appealed to the public, and pious, charitable folk often preferred religious verses. Unfortunately, scholars, with their preference for epics, followed closely by historical songs, seldom recorded *psalmy* until P. Demutskyi published his collection in 1903. As for epics, by the time they became the artistic property of mendicants, their subject matter frequently appealed to women and the elderly. Many *dumy* sing of the conflict between a mother who wants to keep her son at home and the son who insists on going to battle to gain fame. In epics, dying Kozaks blame their death not on the enemy but on their own arrogance and their mistreatment of family as they headed to war, subject matter that would appeal to those with unruly sons. When he was done, a *kobzar* or *lirnyk* would sing a song of gratitude similar to the begging song, thus framing the performance.

Kobzari and *lirnyky* played dramatically different instruments but belonged to the same guilds, and these had a highly developed structure likely based on the craftsmen's guilds that supported the churches with which minstrels were affiliated. Minstrel guilds controlled not only membership but also territory so that members of a particular guild were limited to a specific geographical area. Any person who was not a guild member, or a member of a guild other than the one to which a particular territory had

FIG. 21.1. *Kozak Mamai*, a popular folk painting. Mamai plays the symmetrical kobza. Unknown artist. Nineteenth century.

(Courtesy of Rodovid Press.)

FIG. 21.2. Mykhailo Koval, a contemporary sighted singer plays a handmade asymmetrical bandura.

(Photo by author)

been assigned, was punished if he trespassed. Guilds collected dues and held reserve funds, donating to their church and supporting any members who experienced a catastrophe such as a house fire. The officers of a guild were elected at its annual meeting (Kononenko 1998:66–85).

Entry into a guild was through apprenticeship and open to all blind children, male and female. The parents of a blind child negotiated an agreement with an established master, either a *kobzar* or a *lirnyk*. He would take the child on for a predetermined period, usually three years. The first thing taught was coping with blindness, a process that at least one master compared to "seeing with a third eye."[3] This was followed by the rudiments of a performance: the opening begging song and the closing song of gratitude described above. Apprentices lived with their master, and to pay for their training and their upkeep, they would be sent out to beg as soon as they had learned these basics, bringing their earnings back to their master. After the rudiments of begging, apprentices learned religious songs, the *psalmy*. These are apocryphal songs on religious themes such as the life of Saint Varvara (Barbara), Lazarus, the prodigal son, and the need to prepare for unexpected death.[4]

The training of women stopped at this point because performers who knew more songs earned more money, and guilds felt that women were under less pressure to

FIG. 21.3. Playing a lira.

(Photo by author)

produce income. Learning *psalmy* was also the end of training for those men who were less musically inclined or did not want to continue their education. Any person with this much training was allowed to beg on their own. The more adept students proceeded to learning how to play an instrument and singing epics and historical songs. All apprentices had to learn a special language called *lebiiska mova*. Knowing this language was necessary when the minstrel traveled. It was a secret language, known only to guild members. Thus, when a minstrel addressed a stranger in *lebiiska mova* and the latter responded in kind, the minstrel knew that he was talking to a fellow, guild-affiliated mendicant. *Lebiiska mova* also allowed minstrels to discuss topics they did not want revealed to the general public. Because *lebiiska mova* was a secret language, no scholar was able to write down more than snippets until Oleksii Horbach produced a dictionary in 1957. When an apprentice knew a number of songs plus the *lebiiska mova* and the master judged him ready, he would arrange an initiation rite, a ceremony where the initiate appeared before the entire guild, requested permission to join, and paid the members for that privilege with food and drink (Kononenko 1998:86–111).

Most nineteenth-century *kobzari* and *lirnyki* were peasants, usually with a sighted wife and children. A minstrel contributed to his family by singing and begging and possibly by practicing crafts that did not require sight, such as plaiting ropes (Kononenko 1998:58–63). He would beg when weather permitted, meaning in the summer months; and he would follow the circuit assigned by his guild. To travel, the minstrel hired a sighted guide, usually a boy, though sometimes a girl. The child came from a poor family that needed the extra income. As the *kobzar* or *lirnyk* matured and grew in status, he could take on apprentices of his own, earning additional income. Some guilds required a minstrel to have at least ten years of experience and undergo an additional initiation before acquiring the designation of "master" (*pan-maister*) and permission to train others (Kononenko 1998:10–11, 79).

Begging was not the sole source of minstrel music-based income, and *kobzari* and *lirnyky* could be hired for jobs such as playing at weddings and other events. Epics were not performed at dances, and the fact that minstrels knew a variety of songs, including bouncy dance melodies, was ignored by scholars because of their focus on *dumy* alone. In gatherings where only *kobzari* and *lirnyky* were present, such as annual guild meetings, minstrels performed songs that parodied their normal solemn and pious repertory, thus allowing themselves a bit of play and a break from their public stance as pious mendicants (Kononenko 1998:273–283).

Duma Content

Dumy were the most technically complex songs performed by minstrels and popular with audiences as high art. And they were attractive because they were stories of adventure with descriptions of exotic places and exciting, fearsome conflicts. As songs of courage, even in the face of death, they emboldened their listeners. With their descriptions of suffering, they allowed their audiences to have a good cry. Ostap Veresai, a well-known nineteenth-century *kobzar*, specifically stated that bringing the audience to tears was a good way to stimulate their generosity (Kononenko 1998:150).

While the audiences of *kobzari* and *lirnyky* were interested in *dumy* as stories well told, nineteenth- and early twentieth-century collectors who wrote down epic songs valued them as historical documents. With the emphasis on establishing Ukrainian claims to nationhood, scholars with nationalist leanings sought to find Ukrainian historical validity in folklore and considered *dumy* to be the best source of folk historical information. As will be discussed in the section on collecting and scholarship, academics writing as late as the middle of the twentieth century exerted a great deal of effort on matching *duma* content with known historical personages and events, the kind of history recorded in history books. It is my contention that *dumy* do indeed contain historical information, just as earlier scholars had supposed, but that this is information of a different type. Scholars and other members of the elite assumed that the folk who sang and listened to *dumy* were concerned with historical fact and that they understood history in the same way as their educated, urban countrymen. Both assumptions are invalid. *Dumy* were composed by the folk and performed for a folk audience. What they describe is the experiences of ordinary people, not military or political leaders; and recent scholarship that looks at the lives of common folk shows remarkable parallels between *duma* content and studies of everything from the lives of Ottoman slaves to the experiences of rank-and-file Kozaks. Ukrainian epic preserved a historical record not of prominent figures and important battles but of the details of ordinary life (Kononenko 2019:40–43).

What is particularly remarkable about *dumy* is that they maintained an accurate record of fourteenth- to seventeenth-century details which minstrels could not possibly have known. Examples include the types of boats used in Kozak military maneuvers and the minutia of galley slavery. These details were not retained for the sake of minstrel audiences as they were not relevant to their lives. They are there because sung genres retain fossilized information, facts outside the experiences of performers and listeners. Performance studies emphasize the emergence of a text as it is presented to an audience, stressing its adaptation in response to audience reaction (Bauman 1975). The role of the audience is extremely important, as I have discussed in my book on Ukrainian minstrels (1998). In songs, however, certain textual elements can be retained even if their meaning is not known to either the performer or his listeners. With my graduate students, I ran a crowdsourcing experiment that showed that diaspora Ukrainians, even those with a limited knowledge of the language, are able to recognize and translate words in traditional songs, words that refer to objects with which they are not familiar. This is something that they cannot do for prose texts such as folktales and legends because prose texts are not remembered in the same way as songs. Songs can retain information about situations and objects that no longer exist, and recognizing this fact takes us beyond performance studies and to the acknowledgment that folk songs need to be examined not only in the context of performance but also in terms of the historical situations that prompted their composition (Kononenko 2013).

Sample *Duma* Texts

The songs about the period when Tatars and Nogais raided what would later become Ukraine, taking captives to sell to the Ottomans, texts that belong to the first cycle of *dumy*, describe the life of slaves with remarkable accuracy. The "Duma about Marusia Bohuslavka" is considered by some to be a folk version of the life of Roxolana, a

FIG. 21.4. Women slaves in the folk imagination. Tapestry by an unknown artist, *The Harem*, early twentieth century.

(Courtesy of Rodovid Press.)

Ukrainian captive who became the wife of Suleyman the Magnificent (1494–1566), the first sultan to marry instead of using concubines to produce his heirs (see Yermolenko 2010). The *duma* tells of a woman who becomes the wife or consort of a Turkish lord. Marusia is not her master's only slave. He also holds seven hundred Kozaks captive and keeps them imprisoned in a dungeon. Easter approaches, and Marusia, thinking of her Christian faith and pitying her fellow Ukrainians, takes her master's keys while he is away and frees the Kozaks. The men escape, and as they leave, Marusia tells them to inform her parents that she will not be coming home, that ransoming her is futile because she has become "Turkified" (Kononenko 2019:125–130).[5] Recent scholarship on the lives of slave women in the Ottoman Empire shows that women were used for household tasks and had to be sexually available to their masters (Fig. 21.4). Many women, especially if they bore children in captivity, did indeed choose to stay rather than return home; and some did become their masters' wives (Zilfi 2010:109–115).

The topic of ransom is an important one. Capture did not automatically lead to slavery, and anyone who was captured could be released if relatives paid for their freedom (Davis 2003:70–71). "The Captive's Lament" features a conversation between two men. One expresses his wish that his parents ransom him, while the other says that such wishes are futile because the parents would never be able to find him along the slave trader route:

> Товарише, брате мій рідний!
> Та не треба нам в городи християнські поклон посилати
> Своєму батьку й матці більшого жалю задавати,

Бо хотя наш батько й мати будуть добре дбати,
Ґрунти, великі маєтки збувати,
Скарби збірати,
Та не знатимуть, де, в які тяжкі неволі турецкі синів своїх шукати:
Що сюди ніхто на захожає,
І люд хрещений не заїжжає,
Тільки соколи ясненькі літают,
На темниці сідают,
Жалібненько квилят-проквиляют,
Нас всіх бідних невольників у тяжкі неволі турецкі
Добрим здоровьем навітают . . .

(Hrushevska 1927–1931:1:11–12)

My friend, my dear brother,
We should not be sending respects to the Christian cities,
We should not be compounding our father's and our mother's grief,
Because even if our father and our mother did take great care,
Even if they did sell land and possessions,
And amass a great treasure,
They would never be able to determine in which place of Turkish captivity they should seek their sons.
Because no one comes here,
And baptized people do not travel through these parts,
And only bright falcons fly here,
And they alight on our prison,
And they call mournfully and cry,
And to all of us poor captives in harsh Turkish bondage,
They wish good health.

(Kononenko 2019:140–141)

Captivity itself could range from the horrors of galley slavery, a virtual death sentence, to opportunities for slaves to earn money and even to rise to positions within the Ottoman hierarchy (Erdem 1996:16). In the epic "The Escape of Three Brothers from Azov," now a town in Russia located on the Don River, the older two siblings are on horseback, while the youngest is on foot. He begs his brothers to give him a lift, but they refuse because, to accommodate him, they would have to discard the rich garments and other fine goods they carry:

«Браттє миле, браттє любе!
Хоть одинъ ви милосерде майте,
Опрани кульбаки, добичъ изъ коней скидайте,
Мене, брата піхотинця, міждо коні беріте,
Хочъ милю, верстъ увезіте.
Нехай я буду знати,
Куди за вами въ городи Християнські зъ тяжкої неволі втікати.»

То старший братъ згорда словами промовляє:
«Чи подобенство, мій брате,
Щобъ я свое добро Турецьке на шляху покидавъ,
Тебе, трупъ, на коня бравъ?
Одначе ми сами не втечемо,
Ні тебе не довеземо.»

(Hrushevska 1927–1931:1:104–107)

"Oh, my dear brothers, my beloved brothers,
Do me at least one kindness,
Take that fine clothing, take your booty and throw it off your horses,
And take me, your foot soldier brother, upon your horses instead,
Carry me for at least a verst (3500 feet), at least a mile,
So that I may know,
How to follow you, how to escape harsh captivity and flee to the Christian
   cities." Then the oldest brother speaks, saying proudly,
"Would it be proper, my brother,
For me to cast aside Turkish goods and leave them by the road,
And take you on my horse instead?
If I do that, then we ourselves would not escape,
And we won't be able to save you either."

(Kononenko 2019:115–120)

The horseback riders go on ahead while the song describes the sufferings of the youngest. As his strength fails, he climbs a kurgan and succumbs to thirst, hunger, and fatigue. The older two brothers approach home and debate what they will tell their parents. The eldest brother, the one most concerned about his booty, suggests that they lie and say the youngest did not leave with them but stayed behind to earn a bit more before trying to escape. Accumulating wealth in captivity was common enough to be used as a credible excuse, and this is precisely why the older two brothers have precious goods. There are many versions of this popular text, and in all of them, the older two brothers are punished for their callous treatment of their sibling. In many texts, they are attacked and killed by a party sent in pursuit, which takes the goods that they had valued so highly. In some versions they return home, but the parents discover the truth and banish the pair so that their hopes of splitting the estate two ways instead of three come to naught.

Male slaves could not only make money while in captivity but also rise to high positions, as Vezir Ibrahim Pasha (1495–1536) did in real life. In the song "Ivan Bohuslavets," the hero of the title is a Kozak hetman who, along with his men, is held captive by Alkan Pasha. When Alkan Pasha dies, his widow decides that she wants Ivan as her spouse. He agrees on the condition that she not insult his Christian faith. All goes well until Ivan's new wife gets drunk, something a Muslim would not do, and breaks her promise. Ivan Bohuslavets reacts in what seems an extreme manner: he kills his wife, frees all of the men who were his fellow captives, and leads them back to Christian lands

(Kononenko 2019:107–110). Ivan Bohuslavets is probably a fictional character, but a number of Ottoman officials were Christians with high-ranking Muslim wives.

Manumission was a regular practice in the Ottoman Empire. Slaves were routinely given their freedom after seven years, and routes to earlier release were available. Slaves who knew a skilled trade or craft could sell their work and use that money to purchase their freedom. Captives could secure their freedom and rise to high positions through conversion to Islam. The song about Samiilo Kishka is a story about a sixteenth-century hetman and recounts how he frees his men from slavery by taking advantage of Liakh Buturlak, a convert to Islam who serves the Porte as a galley slave overseer. The Christian slaves row the galley of Alkan Pasha, a young man sailing to Kozlov (present-day Yevpatoria) to court the maiden Sandzhakivna. While the Pasha and his men are in town, Liakh Buturlak and Samiilo drink and talk, with Buturlak urging Samiilo to become a Muslim and assume a position of leadership, as he himself has done:

> Ой Кишко Самойлу, Гетьмане Запорожскій,
> Батьку Козацькій! Добро ты вчини:
> Вѣру Христьянську, подъ нозѣ подтопти,
> Хрестъ на собѣ поломи.
> Аще будешъ вѣру Христіянску подъ нозѣ топтати,
> Будешъ у нашего пана молодого,
> За родного брата пробувати.
>
> (Hrushevska 1927–1931:1:44–49)

> Oh, Kishka, Samiilo, Zaporozhian Hetman,
> Father of the Kozaks, do a good deed,
> Trample the Christian faith beneath your feet,
> Break the cross that you are wearing.
> If you trample the Christian faith beneath your feet,
> Then our young master (would accept you as if you were his kin),
> As if you were his own blood brother.
>
> (Kononenko 2019:96–105)

During this discussion, Samiilo gets Buturlak drunk, steals his keys, and walks among his men, freeing them but telling them to pretend to be still chained. Alkan Pasha and his men come back, and the Kozaks attack, killing the Turks, taking the galley, and making their escape. When Liakh Burturlak awakens from his alcohol-induced stupor, he sides with the Kozaks and uses his knowledge of multiple languages to help the Kozaks get past guard posts. This epic has a happy ending, with Samiilo Kishka and his men reaching home safely.

Galley slavery, the fate of the Kozaks in the Samiilo Kishka *duma*, was the most horrible possible result of capture, with men forced to row until they collapsed and died. As described in the Samiilo Kishka song, men were chained to each other and to their oars day and night, making sleep impossible, one of the great horrors of being a galley slave. Galley slavery is the topic of a number of epic songs. The "Lament of the Captives," a shorter text, is a description of beatings, painful exposure to the sun, and the agony of separation from loved ones and one's homeland, ending with an ardent wish for return. The cruelty of the master of the galley is expressed in the following lines:

> Ой кажу, кажу я вам, Турки яниченьки, гей!
> А добре ви дбайте,
> Барзе гадайте,
> По три пучки тернини,
> По чотири червоної таволги
> В руку набірайте,
> З ряду до ряду заходжайте,
> По тричі в однім місті бідного невольника затинайте!
>
> (Hrushevska 1927–1931:1:7–8)

> Oh, I say, I say unto you, Turks, janissaries, hey,
> That you should behave properly,
> That you should guess my meaning well,
> That you should take three bunches of thorns,
> And four bunches of red meadowsweet,
> That you should take them in your hands,
> And walk from row to row,
> Strike each of the poor captives three times in the same spot.
>
> (Kononenko 2019:138–139)

The *dumy* that are typically assigned to the second cycle picture Kozaks as warriors, successful combatants on sea as well as on land. The reason for Kozak success in waterborne assault was the *chaika*, a supremely maneuverable boat, small enough to sneak up on and attack galleys and enemy cities. The small size of the *chaika* had disadvantages, and these are the subject of a number of *dumy*. The epic called "Storm on the Black Sea" tells of a *chaika* overwhelmed by waves. Two brothers are swept into the water and are about to drown when they begin to confess their sins to each other. They speak of their arrogance when they left for war, reciting a catalogue of misdeeds, variants of which appear in a number of texts:

> Се-ж то, нас, браття, не сильна морська хвиля затопляє;
> Се то отцева молитва і материна
> Нас видмо карає;
> Що як ми в охотне війско виряжалися,
> То од отця од матки прощення не приймали,
> Да стару матусю ми од себе, а й стременами одпихали;
> То то-же ми собі превелику гордость мали:
> Старшого брата у себе за брата не мали,
> Сестру середульшу марне зневажали,
> Близькому сусіді хліба і солі ізбавляли,

> То-же ми собі превелику гордость мали:
> Проти Божих церков їджали,
> Шличків із голов не здиймали,
> На своє лице хреста не клали,
> Милосердного Творця на поміч не призивали,
> Да по улицях кіньми вигравали;
> Да проти себе нікого не стрічали,
> Діток малих кіньми розбивали,
> Кров християньску на сиру землю проливали!
>
> (Hrushevska 1927–1931:1:83–84)

> Oh, brothers, it is not the powerful sea wave that is killing us,
> It is our father's prayer, and our mother's
> Which is punishing us,
> Because when we set out for the volunteer army,
> And we did not ask our father and our mother for their blessing,
> And we pushed our elderly mother away from us with our stirrups,
> And we were overcome by arrogance,
> And we did not recognize our elder brother as our kin,
> And our middle sister—we treated her with disrespect.
> And we deprived our neighbor of his bread and salt,
> And we were so arrogant
> That, as we rode past God's churches,
> We did not take our caps off of our heads,
> And we did not cross ourselves,
> And we did not call upon our merciful Creator for help,
> And as we were riding our horses through the streets,
> We did not greet anyone that we met,
> And we let our horses trample small children,
> We spilled Christian blood upon the damp earth!
>
> (Kononenko 2019:200–202)

After confessing their sins, the brothers ask for forgiveness. Their prayers are answered, and they are carried safely to shore. "Oleksii Popovich" is a more colorful text on a similar topic. A storm threatens the fleet on which Oleksii serves as scribe and reader of Holy Scripture. The Kozak leader calls on all men to confess their sins to quell the storm. It turns out that the gravest sinner is the most unexpected: Oleksii. He offers to sacrifice himself to the sea, and in some versions, his little finger is cut off and tossed into the waters. Whether by the letting of blood or the simple act of confession, the sea is calmed, and all reach safety (Kononenko 2019:194–200).

Land battle epics are numerous and often describe the death of the hero. A Kozak seeks booty in the Kodyma Valley, located in south-central Ukraine; but every time he does so, he loses something precious: first his horse, then his friend, and finally his own life (Kononenko 2019:159–163). The *duma* "Kozak Holota" tells of a successful raid. Holota, whose name is a collective noun for indigent masses, looks as bedraggled and impoverished as his name implies. But looks can be deceiving, and when a rich Tatar confronts him, it is the Tatar who dies. The Kozak then acquires his horse and fine clothing (Kononenko 2019:172–175). "The Three Brothers by the River Samarka," near present-day Pavlohrad, die as the result of a fierce battle. The epic describes them lying mortally wounded and calling out, asking each other to fetch water. This is futile since all are completely incapacitated. The older two then ask the youngest to play his trumpet but abandon the idea because it might draw Turkish combatants rather than Christian brothers (Kononenko 2019:69–72). The *duma* entitled "Khvedir, the Man without Kin" also begins after a fierce conflict (Fig. 21.5). A young page is looking for Khvedir, his master, and finds him mortally wounded:

> По потребі, по потребі барзе то по царській,
> То много війська понажено,
> Посічено, на рани смертенні порубано.
> То между тим трупом ніхто живий не пробуває,
> Тілько Хведір бездільний,
> Та безрідний, та безплеменний
> На рани смертенні постріляний
> Та порубаний
> Тілько чуть живий дух в себе має.
>
> (Hrushevska 1927–1931:2:118–120)

> At the behest, at the behest of the tsar,
> Many troops were destroyed,
> They were cut and they were smitten with mortal wounds.
> Among the corpses there is not a soul alive,
> Only Khvedir the man of ill fate,
> The one without kin and without a clan,
> Injured with fatal gunshot wounds,
> Wounded with deep cuts,
> Only he has a bit of life left in him.
>
> (Kononenko 2019:182–185)

Seeing his page, Khvedir passes his armor, clothing, and horse to the youngster, making sure that he can use them properly. Khvedir dies but is assured that another will take his place. Because so many epics focus on the death of their hero, I have posited that these songs might be seen as a kind of male battle lament, expressing grief over the death of their protagonist and serving to guide his soul into the afterlife, as laments sung over those who die natural deaths are supposed to do (Kononenko 1998:171–195). The close relationship between *dumy* and laments is also suggested by the introduction of lament imagery into newer *dumy*, those in the everyday life cycle of songs, a topic discussed below.

Some epics about land battles speak of human failings: inability to recognize the true nature of things. In the *duma* "Matiash the Elder," the old Kozak leads young men on a

FIG. 21.5. A dying Kozak and his horse. P. Shtorm, *A Fire Burns on the Hill*. Mid-twentieth century.

(Courtesy of Rodovid Press.)

foray. When they camp for the night, the youths are carefree and careless, while Matiash is cautious and keeps his horse and armaments by his side. Sure enough, Turks attack. Matiash leads the counterattack, and the youths under his command praise his foresight and apologize for calling him foolish (Kononenko 2019:164–166) (Fig. 21.6). The *duma*

FIG. 21.6. A Mamai-themed painting showing a Kozak encampment with men cooking and drinking and an enemy combatant being tortured by being hung upside down. Unknown artist. Nineteenth century.

(Courtesy of Rodovid Press.)

"Khvesko Handzha Andyber" takes place in a tavern, not in the field. It begins with a description of Andyber, a Kozak who looks bedraggled like Holota. Because of his appearance, he is ignored by the tavern maid and rich patrons. When he becomes a little drunk, he dons his hetman's clothing, and everyone begins to fawn all over him. He accepts the drinks they offer and pours them on his garments, saying that it is they who are being honored and not he (Kononenko 2019:186–192).

The songs from the cycle about the uprising led by Bohdan Khmelnytskyi are different from other *dumy*. Instead of focusing on individuals and their reactions to threatening events, they paint a panoramic picture. Action is seen from a distance, the way history books, rather than those who had witnessed a battle, might describe it. When Kozaks address Khmelnytskyi, they speak as a group; we do not hear the individual voices present in other *dumy*. Actors are often real historical figures, and battles are ones that did occur during the Khmelnytskyi Uprising. Because these *dumy* share many traits with written history, there is reason to believe that they were originally composed by literate seminarians, men with a bookish, rather than a folk, view of events. How seminarian influence on *kobzari* and *lirnyky* might have occurred is easy to explain. In the early stages of the tradition, minstrels lived on church grounds alongside seminarians. Supported by lay brotherhoods of tradespeople, large church complexes provided social services, including schooling for children; housing for the indigent, like the blind, minstrels among them; and food for pilgrims. Pupils, seminarians included, were housed in hospices alongside blind minstrels. Literate seminarians may well have written compositions in honor of Khmelnytskyi because he was considered a patron of the Orthodox

FIG. 21.7. The statue of Bohdan Khmelnytskyi in Kyiv.

(Photo by author)

Church, and *kobzari* and *lirnyky*, living in close proximity, might have picked up these compositions and adapted them to their repertory (Kohut 2011; Kononenko 2019:207–209) (Fig. 21.7).

When collectors encountered Khmelnytskyi *dumy*, they were enthralled by them because they named real places, people, and events. The folk did not share this attitude. Khmelnytskyi *dumy* were not popular, and nineteenth-century *kobzari* and *lirnyky* seldom knew these songs. Collector zeal has preserved some of these texts. The one most like *dumy* about earlier conflicts is the story of Khmelnytskyi and Barabash, the keeper of Kozak registers.[6] It tells that, when Khmelnytskyi got Barabash drunk and learned that Kozaks were being cheated of their rightful pay, he became enraged and rebelled against the *Rzeczpospolita*, the Polish–Lithuanian Commonwealth, which made a practice of hiring Kozak forces with promises of payment and then reneging on those promises (Kononenko 2019:215–220). Even this *duma* lists historical personages:

> Оттогди-то Хмелныцькый як сіи слова зачував,
> Так на кума свого Барабаша велыке пересердые мав,
> Сам на доброго коня сидав,
> Слугу свого повіреного з собою забырав.
> Оттоди-то прыпало йому з правои рукы
> Чотыры полковныкы:
> Первый полковныче Максыме Олшанськый,
> А другый полковныче Мартыне Полтавськый,
> Трейтій полковныче Ивана Богуне,
> А четвертый Матвій Бороховычу.
>
> (Hrushevska 1927–1931:2:157–159)

> Well, when Khmelnytskyi heard these words,
> He became greatly enraged with his sworn kin Barabash,
> He himself mounted a fine steed,
> And he took his trusted servant with him.
> And then he was joined on the right hand,
> By four colonels,
> The first colonel was Maksym Olshanskyi,
> And the second colonel was Martyn Poltavskyi,
> And the third colonel was Ivan Bohun,
> And the fourth—Matvii Borukhovych.
>
> (Kononenko 2019:215–220)

The other songs in the Khmelnytskyi cycle describe the battle of Korsun, which occurred on May 26, 1648, a major victory in the Khmelnytskyti Uprising; the 1653 expedition into Moldova where Khmelnytskyi's older son Tymish was killed (Kononenko 2019:232–236); and the treaty at Bila Tserkva, signed September 28, 1651, after the defeat at Berestechko on June 28–30, 1651 (Kononenko 2019:239–242). Much of the anger expressed in this *duma* cycle is aimed at Jews who leased land from Polish nobles. Their direct contact with Ukrainians as administrators forced them to bear the brunt of the anger of the oppressed. In the *duma* "The Leaseholders," Jews control hunting and fishing rights, forcing Ukrainians to pay for the privilege of obtaining food for their families. They even control the churches:

Ще-жъ-то жиды рандари въ томъ не пересталы:
На славнуй Украйни вси козацьки церкви зарондовалы.
Которому бъ то давъ Богъ козаку альбы мужику,
Дытыну появыты:
То нейды до попа благословитьця,
А пойды до жида рандана, да положъ шостакъ,
Щобъ позволивъ церковъ одчиныты,
Тую дытыну окрестыты.

(Hrushevska 1927–1931:2:173–174)

And the Jews, the lease-holders, did not stop there,
In glorious Ukraine they took control of all the churches,
So that if God gave a Kozak or a peasant,
Gave him a child,
Instead of going to the priest to have his child blessed,
He had to go to the leaseholder-Jew and give him a sixpence,
So that he would open up the church,
So that the man could have his child baptised.

(Kononenko 2019:225–230)

The cycle ends with a song about Bohdan Khmelnytskyi's death which occurred on August 6, 1657, his younger son Iurii's misbehavior, and the struggle for succession to the position of hetman (Kononenko 2019:243–247).

The *dumy* in the final cycle, the one that corresponds to The Ruin (1657–1687), are often referred to as songs of everyday life. The Ruin was a period when the population of Ukraine suffered from squabbling among Kozak leaders, and the songs that reflect this period are not stories of war but complaints about human misery. "Kozak Life" tells of a woman whose husband leaves to join the Kozaks. Unable to tend the farmstead on her own, she takes to drink. When her husband returns, he beats her instead of sympathizing with her plight (Kononenko 2019:256–260). "The Step-Father" tells of tensions between a young man and the man who took his dead father's place. In this and other songs, poverty, not search for military glory, forces men to leave home and seek wage labor or earn money as a soldier. Some consider marrying for money to alleviate the family's plight (Kononenko 2019:266–268). Many texts tell of a sister as she cries for her departing brother and asks him when he will come home (Kononenko 2019:263–266). The brother responds by listing impossible situations, thus informing his sibling that he will never return:

«Сестро,» каже, «мила,
Родина сердешна!
Ой сподівайся мене тоді в гості,
Якъ будуть о Петрі бистрі ріки-озера замерзати,
Объ Різдві калина в лузі процвітати,
Пойди ти, сестро, до тихого Дунаю,

Возьми ти сестро, піску у білу руку,
Посій ти, сестро, на коміню:
Коли той буде пісокъ на біломъ камені зіхожати,
Синімъ цвітомъ процвітати,
Хрещатимъ барвінкомъ біленький камінь устилати,
Разними красними цвитами украшати,
Тоді, сестро, буду до тебе въ гості прибувати,
Твого життя при бідности доглядати.»

(Hrushevska 1927–1931:2:281–282)

"Sister," he said, "my dear one,
My own beloved kin,
You can expect me to come visit you,
When on the feast of Saints Peter (and Paul) the rivers and the lakes freeze over,
When a rowan tree blooms in the field at Christmas.
Go, sister, go down to the quiet Danube River,
Take, sister, take sand in your white hands,
And sow that sand, sister, upon a white rock.
When the sand starts to sprout on that white rock
When it blooms with blue flowers,
When it covers the stone with cross-shaped periwinkle,
When it adorns it with colorful flowers,
That is when, sister, I will come and be your guest,
That is when I will take care of you in your poverty.

"The Widow and Her Three Sons," one of the most popular of *dumy* and attested in several versions, is part of this cycle. It tells of a woman who refuses to send her sons away as hirelings and takes on wage labor herself. She succeeds in raising the boys to maturity, ruining her own health. The family prospers, and as the sons start to entertain friends, they become embarrassed by their mother's sickly and shabby appearance. They decide to kick her out of the home she had so struggled to create. A compassionate neighbor takes the woman in. At this point the household of the ungrateful sons falls into ruin. Realizing that the cause of misfortune is their treatment of their mother, they ask her to return. She agrees in some versions but not in others, and in those cases where she does return, she brings her sons renewed prosperity (Kononenko 2019:84–87, 282–287).

The everyday-life *dumy* are an interesting mix of the military subject matter typical of epic with other genres. Like laments, these *dumy* poetically describe the fact that the departing Kozak will not return and use language that greatly resembles that found in laments (Fig. 21.8). The images in the text quoted above are almost identical to lament imagery (see also Kononenko 2019:275–278). Everyday-life *dumy*, like ballads, sing of conflicts between young wives and their mothers-in-law, and in some versions of "The Widow and Her Three Sons" it is this conflict that prompts the ejection of the widow from her home. Songs like "The Dream" may be adaptations of *dumy* about slavery. In

FIG. 21.8. Saying goodbye. Unknown artist, mid-twentieth century.

(Courtesy of Rodovid Press.)

this *duma,* a young man is urged to marry an orphan girl rather than a rich widow because the orphan will have no family other than her in-laws, allowing them to shape her as they please (Kononenko 2019:271–274). This is reminiscent of young slave girls raised and molded by rich Ottoman families to become spouses for their sons (Zilfi 2010:167). Songs like "The Dream" show that Ukrainian epic was a living art form that continued to evolve.

Duma Collecting and Scholarship

Dumy were first published in 1819 by Mykola Tsertelev (1790–1869). He belonged to a group of gentlemen influenced by the Romantic movement who met to discuss literature and culture. When Kirsha Danilov's collection of Russian epics appeared in print (first in 1804 and then again in 1818; see chapter 17, this volume) and created a sensation, this group searched for epics on Ukrainian territory, and Tsertelev produced *An Experiment in Collecting Little Russian (Ukrainian) Songs* (*Opyt sobraniia malorossiiskikh pesnei*). Tsertelev's work made such an impression that many collectors wrote down and published *dumy*. Mykhailo Maksymovych published one work in 1827, another in 1834, and a third in 1849. Izmail Sreznevskyi put together three volumes which appeared between 1833 and 1838. Panteleimon Kulish was an important collector who also discussed the nature of Ukrainian epic and his interaction with singers. *Zapiski o Iuznoi Rusi* (1856) and *Istoriia vozsoeedinenia Rusi* (1874) are among his many publications.

A dramatic shift in how collecting was approached came in the middle of the nineteenth century. Early publications gave texts only. Texts were viewed as important. The performers of *dumy*, because they were blind mendicants, were seen as mere vessels that carried heroic songs created long ago; they were deemed unworthy of attention. With the growing interest in village life, the attitude toward *kobzari* and *lirnyky* changed. A seminal case study by Hryhoryi Bazylevych (1853) focused on villagers and included a description of the minstrel Andrii Shut. After the publication of Bazylevych's article, collectors began to include information on performers along with texts.

Knowledge about *kobzari* and *lirnyky* grew. The writer and collector of folklore Panteleimon Kulish interviewed Shut and other performers. The artist Lev Zhemchuzhnikov painted them and also brought the *kobzar* Ostap Veresai to public attention. Veresai appeared at scholarly gatherings, and the Frenchman Alfred Rambaud wrote about him, making him and the Ukrainian epic tradition known in the West. Porfirii Martynovych recorded minstrel biographies. Other important collectors included Mikhail Speranskyi, Mykola Sumtsov, Oleksandr Malynka, Valerian Borzhkivskyi, and Vasyl Horlenko. Mykola Lysenko transcribed the music of minstrel performance. *Dumy* were increasingly seen as a complex performance genre. Scholars, specifically Opanas Slastion and Hnat Khotkevych, learned how to sing *dumy* themselves.

Even as scholars realized that Ukrainian *dumy* were a living tradition, they continued to see them as a record of the historical past and sought to connect them to famous personages and battles. Platon Lukashevych's *Little Russian and Red Russian Folk Epics and Songs* (1856) arranged its texts by historical figures. Kulish "reminded" minstrels of historical facts. Volodymyr Antonovych and Mykhailo Drahomanov (1874–1875) published a multivolume work in which they sought to include all known *duma* texts, plus historical songs, arranged chronologically. Kateryna Hrushevs'ka (1927–1931) produced the definitive work of this period, two volumes with all known *duma* texts, extensive annotation connecting texts to historical fact, plus available information about the performer of each variant.

Volume one of Hrushevs'ka's work came out in 1927 and volume two appeared in 1931. By this time Soviet power was firmly established, and epic songs came under suspicion precisely as expressions of Ukrainian nationalism. Almost all copies of Hrushevs'ka's volume two were destroyed, and efforts were made to confiscate volume one. Hrushevs'ka was exiled and died in 1948. Scholars in western Ukraine were able to do some folklore work, and Filaret Kolessa, helped by poet Lesia Ukrainka and her gift of a wax-cylinder recorder, published *dumy* with musical annotation (Kolessa 1910–1913, 1920). But working with *dumy* was perilous. A widespread legend that may be based in fact states that Josef Stalin was so afraid that Ukrainian epic would foment nationalism that he had *kobzari* and *lirnyky* invited to a sham conference and then executed.[7] The importance that *dumy* had acquired made it impossible to destroy them altogether, and their publication continued during the Soviet period, only now incorporated into the Soviet fold. *Dumy* were still presented as a historical record, and this record led into the Soviet period, with folklorists given the task of helping minstrels compose *dumy* about Lenin, Stalin, the construction of tractor factories, and other Soviet themes (Pavlii et al. 1955; Miller 1990). In the text called "About Lenin and Stalin," the two leaders speak to the working masses and call them to action:

> Гей, з заводів трударі,
> З підземелля шахтарі
> І ви, селяни-бідняки
> Та знедоволені батраки!
> Добре ви дбайте,
> Зброю вірную до рук забирайте,
> Разом з нами в бій вирушайте,
> Ворога лютого та ненависного проганяйте!
> А годі вже перед ним на коліна упадати,
> Вже ж бо час настав кайдани розірвати,
> Волю здобувати!
>
> (Pavlii et al. 1955:337–339)

> Oh you factory workers,
> And you miners who work underground,
> And you, villagers, you poor folk,
> And you discontented laborers!
> Listen well and take heed,
> Collect your armaments and take them in your hands,
> Set out to battle along with us,
> Expel the fierce and despised enemy!
> You have fallen on your knees before him long enough,
> The hour has come to break apart your shackles,
> And to gain your freedom.

Some scholars were able to do more classical work, and Borys Kirdan worked on the artistry of minstrels and their modification of texts.

With the collapse of the Soviet Union and the independence of Ukraine, old texts that had been virtually inaccessible were republished. The Harvard Ukrainian Research Institute and the Rylsky Institute of Folk Art, Folklore, and Ethnography in Kyiv both tried to be the first to assemble and publish all extant *duma* texts. Their competition ended with the Rylsky Institute's producing a facsimile edition of Hrushevs'ka in 2004 and, in 2007, a large volume of *duma* melodies with corresponding texts compiled by Sofiia Hrytsa.[8]

In the early days of Ukrainian independence, Ukrainian *dumy*, as the genre that would lead Ukrainians to statehood, carried a great deal of prestige. Pavlo Suprun (1937–2019), a blind *kobzar*, received a great deal of attention and composed a *duma* about Chornobyl. His "Duma pro Chornobyl" was not picked up by other minstrels and

FIG. 21.9. Pavlo Suprun, a blind singer (died 2019), plays a factory-made asymmetrical bandura as he begs outside St. Michael's cathedral in Kyiv.

(Photo by author)

did not enter the tradition. Interest in Suprun waned and he was relegated to singing for money outside St. Michael's church in Kyiv (Fig. 21.9).

Most contemporary *kobzari* and *lirnyky* are not blind and are different from the minstrels of the past. Many are highly educated, research their repertories, and perform for elite audiences. Taras Kompanichenko has sought to revive old instruments and to show that *dumy* were performed in the context of many other song types. Jurij Fedynskyi is both a singer and a maker of traditional instruments. He runs a summer retreat where he teaches the handcrafting of instruments, especially the bandura. Mykhailo Khai, a *lirnyk*, holds a doctoral degree and is a published author. Mykhailo Koval is a retired schoolteacher who plays a handmade bandura and researches and seeks to revive traditional crafts such as weaving. For these men minstrelsy is a labor of love and not a way to earn a living. They perform at festivals such as those held at Mamaeva Sloboda, a recreated Kozak village in Kyiv, and at folklore conferences. The Honchar Museum in Kyiv holds an annual minstrel festival where performers gather. Kompanichenko, Fedynskyi, and others travel abroad to perform. There are bandura enthusiasts outside Ukraine, and these include Andrij Hornjatkevyc and Victor Mishalow in Canada and Hryhorii Kytasty in the United States. *Duma* performances today, whether in Ukraine or among the Ukrainian diaspora, are staged events performed in contexts that evoke Ukrainian tradition (Fig. 21.10).

FIG. 21.10. A contemporary Kozak re-enactment at Mamaeva Sloboda in Kyiv.

(Photo by author)

Conclusion

Ukrainian epic has survived for over seven centuries, meeting the needs of performers and audiences. *Dumy* probably originated in the fourteenth century as a way to honor fallen comrades, and I have argued that they shared many features with laments since singing a person into the afterlife was believed necessary for the repose of the soul. In the nineteenth and early twentieth centuries, and perhaps as early as the seventeenth, *dumy*, along with other songs, were a way for blind mendicants to make a living, giving them dignity and purpose. In this period, *dumy* adapted to address the concerns of their civilian audiences such as the suffering caused by poverty and the unhappy results of family strife, even as they retained a number of striking details from the periods when they were first composed. Today *dumy* are performed on stage rather than in the home or the churchyard. They are sung at events dedicated to tradition and civic pride. The texts of *dumy* are no longer being modified to reflect current circumstances, and new *dumy* are not being created. The songs forcibly composed during the Soviet era have been discarded. Since Ukraine is now a nation-state, *dumy* are no longer needed to support claims to independence. They remain very much alive as emblems of Ukrainian courage and national pride.

Notes

1. The Mexican corridos described by McDowell (2000) offer an interesting parallel. They were composed to honor fallen rebels shortly after their demise.
2. Translations of begging and gratitude songs are mine, probably the only translations in English. The source of each text, some archival, is given at the end of each song.
3. Translation from a statement by Kuchuhura-Kucherenko (Kononenko 1998:97).
4. Translations of sample *psalmy*, along with their sources, are given in Kononenko (1998:220–238).
5. This and most subsequent song references are to my translations of sample texts. Translations are accompanied by publication information for the Ukrainian original and a discussion of the historical situation that the text reflects.
6. Ivan Barabash was killed in 1648 in a Kozak uprising (date of birth not known). He supported cooperation with the *Rzeczpospolita* but was probably not the keeper of Kozak registers.
7. Oles Sanin's *Povodyr* (*The Guide*) gives a filmic version of this event. It follows an American boy who becomes the guide to a minstrel and witnesses the execution of *kobzari* and *lirnyky*. The narrator is the boy as an adult, and he admits that there is no record of this incident. While very much alive in the public imagination, there is indeed no documentary evidence for it. Orders to execute individual minstrels have been found but nothing about a mass execution.
8. For a detailed account of Ukrainian epic scholarship with complete bibliographic information, see Kononenko (1998:282–298 plus notes to the bibliographic essay).

Works Cited

Antonovych, Vladimir, and Mikhail Drahomanov. 1874–1875. *Istoricheskie pesni malorusskogo naroda*, 2 vols. Kyiv: Izdatelstvo russkogo imperatorskogo geograficheskogo obshchestva.

Bauman, Richard. 1975. "Verbal Art as Performance." *American Anthropologist*, New Series, 77/2:290–311.

Bazylevych, Hryhorii (Bazilevich Grigorii), sviashchennik. 1853. "Mestechko Aleksandrovka, Chernigovskoi guberni, Sosnitskogo uezda." *Etnograficheskii sbornik*, 1:313–336. Reprinted in *Chernigovskie gubernskie vedomosti*, 1854, nos. 12–14.

Davis, Robert C. 2003. *Christian Slaves, Muslim Masters: White Slavery in the Mediterranean, the Barbary Coast, and Italy, 1500–1800*. Houndmills–New York: Palgrave/MacMillan.

Demutskyi, P. 1903. *Lira i iii motivy; zibrav v Kyiivshchyni P. Demutskyi*. Kyiv: Notopechatnaia i drukarnia I.I. Chokolova.

Erdem, Y. Hakan. 1996. *Slavery in the Ottoman Empire and Its Demise, 1800–1909*. London: MacMillan Press; New York: St. Martin's Press.

Horbach, Oleksa. 1957. *Argo ukraiins'kykh lirnykkiv*. Munich: Naukovy zapysky Ukraiins'koho Vil'noho Universitetu.

Hrushevs'ka, Kateryna. 1927–1931. *Ukrainski narodni dumy*, 2 vols. Kharkiv-Kyiv: Derzhavne Vydavnytstvo Ukrainy.

Hrytsa, Sofiia. 2007. *Ukraiins'ki narodni dumy*. Kyiv: Ukrainian Academy of Sciences.

Kohut, Zenon. 2011. "The Khmelnytsky Uprising, the Image of Jews, and the Shaping of Ukrainian Historical Memory." In *Making Ukraine: Studies on Political Culture, Historical*

Narrative, and Identity, 242-270. Edmonton-Toronto: Canadian Institute of Ukrainian Studies Press.

Kolessa, Filaret. 1910-1913. *Melodii ukraiins'kykh narodnykh dum.* Materialy do ukraiinskoi etnolohii, nos. XIII and XIV. Lviv: Etnohrafichna komisiia naukovoho tovarystva im. Shevchenka.

Kolessa, Filaret. 1920. *Ukraiins'ki narodni dumy.* Lviv: Prosvita.

Kononenko, Natalie. 1998. *Ukrainian Minstrels: And the Blind Shall Sing.* Armonk, NY-London: M. E. Sharpe.

Kononenko, Natalie. 2013. "Groupsourcing Folklore Sound Files: Involving the Community in Research." *Canadian Slavonic Papers/Revue canadienne des slavists*, 55/1-2:131-150.

Kononenko, Natalie. 2019. *Ukrainian Epic and Historical Song: Folklore in Context.* Toronto: University of Toronto Press.

Kulish, Panteleimon. 1856. *Zapiski o iuzhnoi Rusi.* St. Petersburg: Tipografiia A. Iakobsona.

Kulish, Panteleimon. 1874. *Istoriia vozsoedinenia Rusi.* St. Petersburg: Tipografiia Tovarishchestva "Obshchestvenniia Pol'za."

Lord, Albert B. 1960. *The Singer of Tales.* Cambridge, MA-London: Harvard University Press.

Lukashevych, Platon. 1856. *Malorossiiskie i Chervonorusskie narodnye dumy i pesni.* St. Petersburg: Tipografiia Eduarda Pratsa.

Maksymovych, Mikhail. 1827. *Malorossiiskie pesni, izdannye M. Maksimovichem.* Moscow: Tipografiia Avgusta Semena.

Maksymovych, Mikhail. 1834. *Ukrainskie narodnye pesni.* Moscow: Universitetskaia tipografiia.

Maksymovych, Mikhail. 1849. *Sbornik ukrainskikh pesen.* Kyiv: Tipografiia Feofila Gliksberga.

McDowell, John H. 2000. *Poetry and Violence: The Ballad Tradition in Mexico's Costa Chica.* Urbana-Chicago: University of Illinois Press.

Miller, Frank J. 1990. *Folklore for Stalin: Russian Folklore and Pseudofolklore of the Stalin Era.* Armonk, NY-London: M. E. Sharpe.

Pavlii, P. D., M. S. Rodina, and M. P. Stelmakh, eds. 1955. *Ukraiinski narodni dumy ta istorychni pisni.* Kyiv: Vydavnytstvo akademii nauk ukraiinskoii RSR.

Sreznevskyi, Izmail. 1833-1838. *Zaporozhskaia starina.* Parts I-III. Kharkiv: Universitetskaia tipographiia.

Tsertelev, Nikolai. 1819. *Opyt sobraniia starinnykh malorossiiskikh pesnei.* St. Petersburg: tipografiia. K. Kraia.

Yermolenko, Galina I., ed. 2010. *Roxolana in European Literature, History and Culture.* Farnham-Burlington, VT: Ashgate.

Zilfi, Madeline C. 2010. *Women and Slavery in the Late Ottoman Empire: The Design of Difference.* New York: Cambridge University Press.

CHAPTER 22

SOUTH SLAVIC EPIC AND THE PHILOLOGY OF THE BORDER

DAVID F. ELMER

The epic genre, for all that it may seem like a self-evident category, populated by narratives about the heroic exploits of noble individuals and freighted with the weight of collective (since the nineteenth century, often national) aspirations, is notoriously difficult to define.[1] Traditions of heroic poetry have been documented among speakers of all the south Slavic national languages; while the typical songs of some of these traditions have more the character of "ballads" (another muddled generic term), the traditions on which the present essay focuses—those of the central zone of the Dinaric Alps, a territory stretching from Croatia in the northwest through Bosnia-Herzegovina, southern Serbia, and Montenegro—exhibit a broad family resemblance to many other traditions and texts commonly recognized as "epic."[2] The features of this poetry that secure its place within the epic family include lengthy, often complex narratives reported in many hundreds or, not infrequently, thousands of verses; an expansive narrative technique that can, in its most developed forms, exploit digressions, detailed descriptions, flashbacks (analepses), and, very commonly, copious amounts of quoted speech; a focus on the heroic, usually martial exploits of exceptional men (and very occasionally women); and an emphasis on the group affiliations of these individuals, whose identities, in spite of a superficial individualism expressed by a commitment to personal autonomy, are defined in collective terms, that is, with respect to their confessional allegiances as either Muslims or (Orthodox or Catholic) Christians. The tradition (or traditions) of south Slavic heroic poetry can, then, be classed without much controversy as an epic tradition.

The significance within this tradition of confessional affiliation as a line of demarcation expressed not only in the story-worlds of the songs (determining, e.g., who counts as a hero and who counts as a villain) but also in the repertoires and narrative techniques of the tradition-bearers is a reflection of the historical circumstances in which the tradition developed.[3] The core of the region in which epic singing was cultivated lies precisely along the frontiers that for centuries separated the Ottoman Empire, administered by a Muslim ruling class, from its Christian neighbors, the Habsburg Empire and the

Venetian territories on the Adriatic coast. From the mid-sixteenth century to the early twentieth, those who lived along these frontiers—many of them military colonists settled there in order to defend the border—became intimately familiar with the realities of frontier life, including frequent skirmishes, cross-border raids, and migration (indeed, a large proportion of frontier dwellers were themselves migrants or refugees).[4] These lived experiences left deep traces on the tradition, clearly visible, for example, in two of the best-known plot types, referred to by John Miles Foley, after Albert Lord, as the "Return Song" and the "Wedding Song."[5] Both of these hinge on cross-border movement and depredation, the former recounting the return home or rescue of a hero who has been held captive for many years on the other side of the frontier and the latter describing the kidnapping or attempted kidnapping of a bride by a foreign commander. Moreover, the very diffusion of these plot types, versions of which were collected from Muslim as well as Christian singers, attests to the movement of tradition-bearers across the border and the transmission of songs between communities.[6] The south Slavic epic tradition is, fundamentally, a tradition of the border.[7]

The general contours of this tradition have been outlined numerous times.[8] While it is impossible to say with any certainty how far back in time the tradition extends, epic singing among the south Slavs can be traced back at least to the fifteenth century.[9] It is not unreasonable to suppose that the first Slavs to arrive on the Balkan peninsula in the sixth century already brought with them some form of epic song, although the traditions recorded by modern ethnographers need not descend from this hypothetical early tradition (cf. Auty 1980:197). As documented in the large, influential collections by which it is chiefly known,[10] the tradition is characterized by a distinctive, stichic verse form: the *deseterac* (pl. *deseterci*), a ten-syllable line with an obligatory caesura after the fourth syllable.[11] Epic-style songs in *deseterci* are still composed and performed, but as an orally transmitted art form, relying on inherited themes and specialized compositional techniques, the tradition is more or less defunct.[12]

In its traditional form, south Slavic epic poetry has played an important—indeed, central—role in the comparative study of oral poetry and in the development of the so-called oral-formulaic theory, a model developed by Milman Parry and Albert Lord for the oral composition in performance of poetic narratives through the manipulation of traditional verbal formulas and thematic units. In the 1930s, by conducting extensive fieldwork in then-Yugoslavia (Fig. 22.1), Parry obtained an essential "proof of concept" in support of his arguments regarding the traditional and oral character of the Homeric epics; in his own subsequent writing, supported by additional fieldwork, Lord made south Slavic epic the center of a more broadly comparative study.[13] The model articulated by these two scholars is a "theory" only in its application to texts for which no firm data can be obtained regarding the manner and circumstances of their composition (the *Iliad*, *Beowulf*, etc.). It is an empirical fact that the traditional south Slavic singers observed and documented by Parry, Lord, and many others composed their songs in performance by drawing on traditional repertoires of formulas and themes.[14]

Traditionally, songs were typically performed by solo performers providing their own accompaniment with a musical instrument—in northwest Bosnia, the *tambura*, a

FIG. 22.1. Jovan Govedarica (left), Milman Parry (center), and Mićo Savić, Gacko, 1934 or 1935.
(Photographer unknown. Photo courtesy of the Milman Parry Collection of Oral Literature, Harvard University.)

plucked instrument with two strings, but elsewhere, and more commonly, the *gusle*, a bowed, one-stringed instrument (Fig. 22.2).[15] More rarely songs were sung or recited without instrumental accompaniment.

The songs themselves can be categorized according to various schemes. They are commonly classified into various "cycles" defined with reference to the figures or events

FIG. 22.2. Unidentified singer with *gusle*, Gacko, 1934 or 1935.
(Photograph by Milman Parry. Photo courtesy of the Milman Parry Collection of Oral Literature, Harvard University.)

they depict: thus, in addition to various "unhistorical" songs (on religious, legendary, or mythical themes), scholars speak of a "Kosovo cycle" (relating to the 1389 Battle of Kosovo), a "Marko Kraljević cycle" (songs in which the legendary prince of Prilep is the hero), a "*hajduk/uskok* cycle" (describing the exploits of outlaws—*hajduci* and *uskoci*), and so on.[16] Muslim epic is sometimes considered as its own "cycle" alongside many others, but such a classification obscures both the diversity of Muslim epic, which can itself be divided into numerous "cycles," and the fact, alluded to above, that the single most salient dividing line within the broader tradition is the one between Muslim and Christian epic.[17] The difference between these two branches of the tradition—which do indeed share many common formulas, themes, plots, and characters—is registered most immediately by the typical difference in length between Muslim and Christian songs: while the latter usually do not exceed five or six hundred verses in length, the former are typically around a thousand verses long and not uncommonly extend to several thousand.[18] This crude measure, of course, is an indicator of more substantial differences in style and aesthetics, most notably a marked affinity for the accumulation of descriptive detail among Muslim (Bosniak) singers.[19] While it would be reductive to attribute these differences of length and style to any narrow set of causes, the development of a relatively more expansive aesthetic in Muslim milieux was undoubtedly favored by factors specific to those milieux, above all the custom of listening to performances of epic song during the long nights of Ramadan, when singers were permitted and encouraged to elaborate their narratives over many hours, sometimes even continuing their song at the following night's gathering.

To return to the notion of south Slavic epic song as a "tradition of the border," shaped by many centuries of contact and intermingling between groups, it is worth noting that a close relationship can be observed between the Muslim branch of the south Slavic tradition and the neighboring Albanian tradition of epic song as performed in Kosovo and northern Albania. Numerous convergences of musical form and performance style, of plot and character, and of lexicon indicate that the traditions have developed in mutual contact. Performers in both traditions sing in strikingly similar styles, with Albanian *lahutars* accompanying themselves on the *lahuta*, an instrument that is essentially the same as the *gusle* played by south Slavic *guslars* (although the *lahuta* typically has a slightly longer neck). Although the metrical constraints in Albanian epic song are somewhat less rigid than those of the south Slavic *deseterac*, Albanian epic singers exhibit a distinct decasyllabic tendency in the composition of (sung) verses; since octosyllabic patterns are more typical of Albanian versification, this decasyllabism is itself an indication of close contact with the south Slavic tradition (see Skendi 1954:174–179; Scaldaferri 2021:79–82). Numerous heroes appear in both south Slavic and Albanian songs (Đerđelez [Gjergj Elez] Alija, Arnaut Osman [Osman "the Albanian"], and others). In both traditions, songs about the brothers Mujo and Halil enjoyed special popularity, and both traditions preserve (independent) versions of the story of the Battle of Kosovo.[20] Finally, in both traditions one encounters a shared lexicon of Turkish loanwords (Skendi 1954:144–146; Lord 1972:305–307; cf. Friedman 2012:293–294), many of them relating to horses or other heroic accoutrements (SSl. *đogat*, Alb. *gjokat*, "white horse"; SSl. *dorat*, Alb. *dorin*, "reddish-brown horse"; SSl., Alb. *topuz*, "club, mace"), features of domestic space or material culture (SSl. *odžak*, Alb. *oxhak*, "hearth, house"; SSl. *džezva*, Alb. *xheze*, "coffee pot"), and, of course, aspects of the practice of Islam (SSl., Alb. *avdes*, "ablution"; SSl., Alb. *namaz*, "prayer"). One also encounters Bosnian/Serbian loanwords in Albanian songs and Albanian loanwords in Bosnian songs.[21]

All of these convergences speak, of course, to the movement and mingling not just of traditions but also, in the first place, of tradition-bearers—individuals whose engagements with members of other groups were sufficient to enable the cross-fertilization of epic traditions. When he visited Sandžak (i.e., the old Ottoman Sanjak of Novi Pazar, a region that today straddles the border between Serbia and Montenegro and abuts Kosovo and northern Albania) in 1934 and 1935, Milman Parry found several bilingual singers of Albanian descent. One of these, Salih Ugljanin, could sing epic songs in both Albanian and Bosnian and claimed even to be able to translate songs from one language into another (Schmaus 1938a:274–77; Kolsti 1990) (Fig. 22.3). Discussions of the relationship between Slavic and Albanian traditions have often focused on the question of who borrowed what from whom (cf. Schmaus 1938a:277; Skendi 1954:200–202). The potential for such discussions to take on a nationalistic edge is memorably captured in Ismail Kadare's novel *The File on H*, a fiction, inspired by the fieldwork of Parry and Lord, in which two Harvard scholars collecting oral epics in Albania are pursued by Serbian agents because they seek to show that the Albanian tradition is the original one (Kadare 1997).[22] For my present purposes, however, more important than the particular paths and mechanisms of diffusion is the simple fact that the convergences between south Slavic and Albanian epic song attest to patterns of contact and intermingling that justify the designation of both traditions as "traditions of the border."

FIG. 22.3. Salih Ugljanin, Novi Pazar, 1934 or 1935.
(Photograph by Milman Parry. Photo courtesy of the Milman Parry Collection of Oral Literature, Harvard University.)

The Philology of the Border

The present essay aims to extend the notion of a "tradition of the border" by examining "borders" of various kinds that have been traced through the territory of south Slavic epic song. In framing my remarks this way, I am intentionally invoking the rich literature on borderlands as distinctive cultural spaces, including such landmark works as Gloria Anzaldúa's *Borderlands—La frontera* (1987). One of the dominant themes of this literature is that a border is not so much a line of demarcation as a zone of contact and intermingling, where cultural oppositions are not only constructed but also internalized, reflected upon, complicated, and deconstructed.[23] Moreover, music and song have long featured prominently in this literature as examples of the cultural complexity typical of borderlands.[24] The south Slavic epic tradition is no less exemplary in this regard, both as a product of a border region that saw centuries of close contact and intermingling between distinct groups and as itself an expression or manifestation of that intermingling. The "borders" I will focus on in the following pages, however, are not borders in the usual, spatial sense of the word. They are, instead, metaphorical lines of demarcation that have, historically, shaped the ways in which south Slavic epic is approached and understood. I suggest that the tradition itself can be viewed as a kind of borderland, where the tracing of boundaries invites reflection not just on the differences thereby created but also on the extent to which certain features or inhabitants of the territory escape conclusive assignment to one or the other side of the divide.

Since the "map" of this territory (to continue my metaphor) is usually keyed to published collections and written documents, even if the documents themselves derive more or less directly from oral tradition, the approach taken here will also be a text-centered one, which I will call a "philology of the border."[25] Some comment on this coinage is in order. "Philology" is a capacious term. Rooted in scholarly traditions going back to classical antiquity, it embraces a wide variety of critical and interpretive reading practices. Historically, however, it has been closely tied to the practice of textual criticism, that is, to the study of manuscripts and manuscript traditions. Philology is the method by which the readings of those manuscripts are scrutinized and judged to be either authentic (the words of the author) or spurious, the product of corruption and error in the copying of manuscripts.[26] In other words, philology is traditionally a method for making distinctions, for separating true from false readings—we might say, for drawing a border between them. A "philology of the border," on the other hand, is a *recursive* philology: it takes as one object of examination the very act of discrimination itself. It attends simultaneously to the dynamics of both inclusion and exclusion that are instantiated to an extent in every text.[27] And it finds a natural point of focus in texts that in one way or another elude easy classification. In the pages that remain I apply such a recursive "philology of the border" to several problems of classification that have arisen in the history of the scholarship on south Slavic epic song.

Vuk Stefanović Karadžić, *Hasanaginica*, and the Boundaries of the Serbian Nation

Formal efforts to classify south Slavic epic and subject it to serious scholarly study begin with Vuk Stefanović Karadžić (1787–1864). "Vuk," as he is commonly known, was born to a peasant family in the Serbian village of Tršić, then in the Ottoman Empire.[28] He received only a few years of formal education, but after fleeing to Vienna in late 1813 at the end of the First Serbian Uprising, he embarked upon a career as a linguist, ethnographer, folklorist—and above all, philologist—that eventually earned him an international reputation; his monumental collection of epic and lyric songs *Srpske narodne pjesme* (1841–1865) remains a standard point of reference for any discussion of south Slavic folklore. In later years, Vuk credited the friendship, advice, and patronage of Jernej Kopitar (1780–1844), a Slovene working in Vienna as the imperial censor for Slavic and Greek publications, for shaping his career.[29] According to Vuk, it was Kopitar who encouraged him to collect and publish folk songs, offering him Johann Gottfried von Herder's *Stimmen der Völker in Liedern* (1807) as an example (Wilson 1986:90). Vuk's subsequent activity as a collector was part of a larger project, conceived in terms of a Herderian romantic nationalism, aimed at the linguistic and cultural consolidation of a Serbian national identity.

As a first step in this program, in 1814 Vuk published, with Kopitar's encouragement, a collection of one hundred lyric and eight epic songs under the title *Mala prostonarodnja slaveno-serbska pjesnarica* (*A Little Slaveno–Serbian Songbook of the Common People*). The songs were patently selected to provide a picture, even a definition, of Serbian national identity; particularly in the selection of epic songs "the boundaries of [the] nation are determined" (Rihtman-Auguštin 2004:17; cf. Beissinger 2017:140–141).[30] Thus, the first text in the epic section, "The Song of Miloš Obilić," stages a confrontation between representatives of Orthodox Slavdom and of the "Latin" (i.e., Catholic) world. Sent by Prince Lazar to collect tribute from "the Latins," who cite the magnificence of their cathedral as a way of asserting their superiority over Lazar's principality, Miloš (a hero of the Kosovo cycle) responds with a lengthy catalogue of Orthodox monasteries (Karadžić 1814:90)[31]:

> vi ste mudri Gospodo Latinska
> jeste mudri, al' zborite ludo:
> da vi znade naše manastire,
> slavni naši Cara zadušbine
> kakovi su, i koliki li su:
> da vidite Lavru Studeničku,
> ne daleko od Novog-Pazara,
> da vidite Đurđeve Stupove,

> kod Deževe starie dvorova,
> zadušbine Cara Simeona . . .
>
> You are wise, Latin sirs,
> you are wise, but you speak nonsense:
> if only you knew our monasteries,
> foundations of our glorious emperors,
> how great they are and how many:
> if you could see the Lavra of Studenica,
> not far from Novi Pazar,
> if you could see the Pillars of St. George,
> near the ancient halls of Deževa,
> foundations of Emperor Simeon [i.e., Stefan Nemanja] . . .

Miloš's speech, on which the song centers, constitutes a kind of sacred geography of the (Orthodox) Serbian nation.[32] Notably, however, the Serbian nation as defined by Vuk's *Pjesnarica* is not limited to followers of the Orthodox faith but includes also "Serbs of the Mohammedan law," to whom are ascribed the sixth and seventh of the epic songs, "The Marriage of Hajkuna, Sister of Beg Ljubović" and "The Sorrowful Song of the Noble Wife of Hasan Aga."

The second of these songs, commonly known by the title *Hasanaginica* ("The Wife of Hasan Aga"), is something of an exception in Vuk's collection.[33] The song describes a tragic domestic drama: Hasan Aga repudiates his wife when her "modesty" (*stid*) prevents her from visiting him in the field as he recovers from a wound.[34] Against her wishes she is given in marriage to a *kadi*, and, as the wedding procession passes her former home and she stops to greet her children, Hasan Aga enjoins the children to turn away from their mother "with her heart of stone"; overcome with sorrow, the woman dies on the spot. Unlike the other songs in the *Pjesnarica*, which Vuk claimed to have learned in his youth and to have reproduced from memory, *Hasanaginica* was taken (without acknowledgment in the 1814 edition) from a published source.[35] In 1774, the Venetian abbot Alberto Fortis published the text, along with an Italian translation, in his *Viaggio in Dalmazia*, an account of his travels in Venetian Dalmatia. By the time Vuk decided to include Fortis's text—replacing some lexical forms typical of Dalmatian dialects with forms more typical of Vuk's Serbian—the song was already known internationally.[36] A German translation by Friedrich Werthes, included in his partial translation of Fortis's book (Werthes 1775), caught the attention of Goethe, whose own version, based on Werthes's translation, appeared in 1778 in Herder's *Volkslieder* (the first edition of *Stimmen der Völker in Liedern*).[37] Goethe himself was unable to read the song in the original language, but he did make an effort to reproduce the distinctive rhythm of the *deseterac* (including even the obligatory caesura), as one immediately sees in his rendering of the song's famous beginning (Herder 1778:309):

> Was ist weisses dort am grünen Walde?
> Ist es Schnee wohl, oder sind es Schwäne?

> Wär es Schnee da, wäre weggeschmolzen,
> Wären's Schwäne, wären weggeflogen.
> Ist kein Schnee nicht, es sind keine Schwäne.
> 'S ist der Glanz der Zelten Asan Aga;
> Niederliegt er drein an seiner Wunde.

The corresponding lines in Vuk's *Pjesnarica* are as follows (Karadžić 1814:113)[38]:

> Šta se beli u gori zelenoj?
> Il' je snieg, il' su labudovi?
> Da je snieg već bi okopnio;
> Labudovi već bi odletili.
> Nit' je snieg, nit su labudovi,
> Nego šator age Asan-age,
> Gdi on leži od ljutie rana . . .

> What gleams white on the green mountain?
> Is it snow, or are they swans?
> If it were snow, it would already have melted;
> swans would already have flown away.
> Neither is it snow, nor are they swans,
> rather the tent of the aga Hasan Aga,
> where he is lying gravely wounded . . .

Nor were the translations of Werthes and Goethe the only ones to have appeared in the years prior to the publication of the *Pjesnarica*: by 1814, the song had already been translated into French, Hungarian, Latin, and English, in addition to Italian and German.[39] The wide international circulation of the song must inevitably have conditioned Vuk's decision to include it, in spite of the fact that it did not belong to the traditions of Tršić, which he purported to represent in his songbook. The song was among the most internationally recognizable symbols of south Slavic identity in the early nineteenth century. Any anthologizer of south Slavic folk song who had an eye on a wider European readership would have felt enormous pressure to include it.[40]

In his response to the expectations of an international readership and his engagement with an emerging market for "world literature," Vuk can be seen as instantiating what Étienne Balibar has referred to as the "philological model of the border," based on the "paradigm of translation," according to which national identities are defined in part by the ability of national languages to be translated into each other (Balibar 2014:87–88, 94–97). Vuk's publication of a "Serbianized" *Hasanaginica* is an effort to place the "Serbian" language, and thus the "Serbian" nation, in the chain of equivalences by which national identities are partly defined. From the standpoint, however, of the "philology of the border" proposed in this essay, what is most notable about Vuk's *Hasanaginica* is that the effort to make the song a vehicle of a specifically "Serbian" identity overwrites other possible ways of framing the identity represented by the text. Fortis, and Herder following him, presented the song as belonging to the "Morlachs," a period exonym referring to the Slav peasants of the Dalmatian hinterland.[41] How Fortis obtained the text is not entirely clear, but it must have been transcribed in Dalmatia from an informant who might have been either Christian or Muslim.[42] The song clearly reflects the influence of a Muslim milieu at some point in its development, but it could easily have circulated in Christian communities as a representation of the "Turks." The question "To whom does *Hasanaginica* 'belong'?" has accordingly been a source of controversy for well over a century (Wolff 2001:192, citing Lucerna 1905).[43] The controversy is itself an indication of the fact that the identity encoded by the text is difficult to pin down, even fluid, insofar as it depends as much on where and how the text circulates as it does on who the original tradition-bearers might have been.

Hasanaginica and the Boundary between "Women's Songs" and "Men's Songs"

Examined from the point of view of the "philology of the border," *Hasanaginica* slips from the confines of the national category to which Vuk assigned it. National identity, however, is not the only form of classification Vuk imposes on his material. The *Pjesnarica* is divided into two sections, the first of which is labeled *Pesne ljubovne i različne ženske* ("Love Songs and Various Women's Songs") and the second *Pesne muželske, koe se uz gusle pjevaju* ("Men's Songs, Which Are Sung to the *Gusle*"). This binary, gendered opposition has become one of the most fundamental and firmly rooted ways of categorizing south Slavic oral poetry. To the best of my knowledge, it originates with Vuk's 1814 *Pjesnarica*, although Vuk claimed there in a footnote to be reproducing popular terminology.[44]

Vuk provided a fuller discussion of the opposition—subtly reconfigured as an opposition between "women's songs" (*ženske pjesme*) and "heroic songs" (*junačke pjesme*)—in the introduction to the first volume of *Narodne srpske pjesme* (Karadžić 1824:xvii–xx; it is in this reconfigured form that the opposition has become a fixture in the field). There he distinguishes the two categories on several dimensions, including soloist versus ensemble performance, performance before an audience versus group participation, and a focus on the quality of the song text versus a focus on the musical quality of the singing, with the first element in each of these oppositions characterizing "heroic" songs. Essentially, however, the opposition singles out and privileges one specific style of singing—the singing of decasyllabic songs to the accompaniment of the *gusle*—consigning everything else to the category of "women's songs," even as Vuk himself acknowledges that the so-called women's songs are *not* sung exclusively by women.

The gendered line of demarcation drawn by Vuk and sustained by subsequent generations of scholars has served simultaneously to define the genre of epic within the broader tradition of south Slavic folk song and to privilege that genre by presenting it as an ostensibly unitary form in opposition to the diversity of forms included among the "women's songs."[45] On closer inspection, however, it turns out to be not so easy to draw a firm line around the category of epic song and harder still to draw it in terms of gender. Already in his discussion of 1824, Vuk concedes two important points: in the first place, he acknowledges the existence of songs that stand, as he puts it, "on the border between women's songs and heroic songs" and that cannot be comfortably situated in either category.[46] At the same time, he acknowledges that there are, in fact, women who know how to sing (epic) songs to the *gusle*, a fact confirmed by subsequent researchers (Karadžić 1824:xvii).[47] When one keeps in view such observations and the ethnographic data on which they are based, it quickly becomes apparent that Vuk's distinction is not so much a matter of ethnographic description as an ideologically freighted effort to privilege the category of epic. The shift in Vuk's terminology between 1814 and 1824 is indicative of the ideological character of this distinction. By shifting from "women's versus men's songs" to "women's versus heroic songs," Vuk confounded the categories of performer ("women's songs") and song content ("heroic songs"), subtly suggesting an equivalence between heroism and masculinity and assigning to men—the unspoken counterparts to the women who notionally transmit "women's songs"—responsibility for the performance (in every sense of the word) of the heroic ideals of the nascent Serbian state.[48]

Hasanaginica is in fact a perfect example of a song that escapes Vuk's system of classification. In terms of its decasyllabic metrical form, the song could in principle be sung to the *gusle*; formally, it is not really distinguishable from properly "heroic" songs. But its resolute focus on domestic affairs and its focalization from the point of view of Hasanaginica place the song more squarely among the "ballads" that have also been collected in the south Slavic epic zone, often as part of women's repertoires; Dalmatia was particularly rich in such ballads.[49] Vuk lamented the fact that he was never able to find a singer who knew the song.[50] But if he thought of it as a "heroic" ("men's") song, he was probably looking in the wrong place. Though it had been thought by many scholars that the song had disappeared from the tradition, it was "rediscovered" in the 1930s—in the repertoires of Dalmatian women, where it had doubtless been all along.[51] Strictly speaking, then, the song belongs among the "women's songs." But the fact that, even after its "rediscovery" by scholars, the song has continued to be published in anthologies of "epic songs" is an indication of the extent to which Vuk's bipartite, gendered system of classification inscribes a divide in a region of the tradition that exhibits more continuity than difference.

Orality and Literacy, Traditional and "Post-Traditional"

If the scholarly "rediscovery" (though it was never really lost) of *Hasanaginica* in the 1930s destabilized the canons of Vuk's gendered boundary, the fieldwork conducted by

Parry and Lord in the same period established the south Slavic epic tradition as the principal canon by which the boundary between oral and written poetry was, for a time, to be fixed. As noted in the introductory section of this essay, Parry traveled to then-Yugoslavia in order to obtain empirical confirmation of his theory regarding the oral composition of the Homeric poems, guided by the work of Matija Murko (cf. Parry 1971:439). Although Parry's published and unpublished writings reveal a keen interest in the songs he collected, Parry was ultimately interested not in the songs themselves but in what they could teach him about the workings of oral poetry more generally. He sought "evidence on the basis of which could be drawn a series of generalities applicable to all oral poetries; which would allow me, in the case of a poetry for which there was not enough evidence outside the poems themselves of the way in which they were made, to say whether that poetry was oral or was not, and *how* it should be understood if it was oral" (Parry 1971:440).[52] In other words, Parry sought to use the south Slavic epic tradition to establish principles by which any given text could be securely assigned to one side or the other of the divide between orality and literacy.

Parry, who died tragically just three months after concluding his fieldwork, never fully articulated the "generalities" he sought; that task was left to his student and assistant, Albert Lord, whose 1960 book *The Singer of Tales* (2019) offered a definitive formulation of the results of their investigations. The principal criterion put forward there for establishing oral composition is the use of formulas and formulaic expressions, with the formula understood, following Parry, as "a group of words which is regularly employed under the same metrical conditions to express a given essential idea" (Lord 2019:4).[53] The materials collected by Parry and Lord provided ample evidence of the use of such formulas by south Slavic epic singers, as can be readily seen in a chart provided by Lord in his book. The chart, reproduced here with Lord's translation, uses solid and broken underlining to indicate formulas and formulaic expressions, respectively, in an excerpt of "The Song of Baghdad" as sung by Salih Ugljanin on November 22, 1934 (Lord 2019:47–48)[54]:

Jalah reče, / zasede đogata;

Đogatu se / konju zamoljila:

"Davur, đogo, / krilo sokolovo!

Četa ti je / o zanatu bila;

Vazda je Mujo / četom četovao.

Vodi mene / do grada Kajniđe!

Ne znam đadu / ka Kajniđi gradu."

Hajvan beše, / zborit' ne mogaše,

Tek mu svašta / šturak umijaše.
-------- ---------

Ode gljedat' / redom po planini.
------- -----------

Uze đadu / ka Kajniđi gradu,
------ -------------

Pa silježe / planinama redom,
-------- -----------

Pa ga eto / strmom niz planinu,
------- -------------

I kad polju / slježe kajnićkome,
------ -------------

Kome stati / polje pogljedati . . .
---------- ----------

With "By Allah" she mounted her horse;
She implored the white horse:
"Hail, whitey, falcon's wing!
Raiding has been your work;
Ever has Mujo raided.
Lead me to the city of Kajniđa!
I know not the road to the city of Kajniđa."
It was a beast and could not talk,
But the steed knew many things.
He looked over the mountains
And took the road to the city of Kajniđa,
And crossed one range after another,
Until lo he rushed down the mountain,
And when he descended to the plain of Kajniđa,
Were anyone to look out over the plain . . .

Lord observes that "one quarter of the whole lines and one half of the half lines are formulas" and that "there is no line or part of a line that did not fit into some formulaic pattern." This, for Lord, would be incontestable proof that the text was composed orally, even if one did not happen to know that Ugljanin was illiterate.

Lord offered the excerpt above, and by extension the larger body of material he and Parry collected from the singers they encountered in Yugoslavia, as a paradigmatic example of the near total formularity that could, he argued, be expected in a genuinely oral composition. In practice, it often proved difficult, at least in part because of the lack of a suitably large corpus against which a sample could be tested, to demonstrate a similar degree of formulaic density in texts of uncertain provenance (cf. Lord 1968:19–21). Nevertheless, the test of formulaic density was put forward by Lord, and adopted by others, as "the surest proof now known of oral composition" (Lord 2019:54–55; cf. Notopoulos 1964:19). Just as importantly, Lord declared, at least initially, that a text subjected to such a test would have to be judged to have been composed *either* orally *or* by a fundamentally literate technique. The divide that separated the mindset of oral composition from that of the written text was, he insisted, absolute. In response to certain Homerists and medievalists who had characterized poems such as the *Iliad* and *Beowulf* as "transitional texts" that combined elements of oral style with compositional techniques made possible by writing, Lord declared any such straddling of the divide an impossibility; those appealing to the notion of a "transitional text" were, he argued, seeking an impossible reconciliation of their preferred model of (literate) authorship with the elements of oral style present in their texts (Lord 2019:138).

As research progressed, however, and the comparative study of oral poetry grew to encompass a wider range of traditions, it became increasingly clear that the boundary between orality and literacy is both harder to fix and more permeable than Lord had initially supposed. The model of oral composition he elaborated is explicitly a model of composition *in* performance; but, as emphasized by Ruth Finnegan, there are many traditions across the globe that separate composition from performance and consequently exhibit a greater reliance on memorization and a lesser reliance on formulas (in Parry's sense of the term) than Lord's model would envision (Finnegan 1976:131–161).[55] At the same time, formulas—even a preponderance of formulas—can be observed in texts composed in writing (cf. Lord 1968:24). In short, the model of oral composition sought by Parry and elaborated by Lord is simply not as generalizable across traditions as Parry had hoped. Moreover, even within the south Slavic domain, Lord eventually recognized the existence of "transitional texts" that lie, so to speak, on the border between oral and written, noting that, in terms of formulaic density, some of the written decasyllabic poems of the eighteenth-century Dalmatian friar Andrija Kačić-Miošić are indistinguishable from genuinely oral texts (Lord 1995, with discussion of Kačić on pp. 225–233).

To be sure, the materials collected by Parry and Lord, who consciously avoided working with singers influenced by written texts, are undeniably the product of a traditional technique of oral composition in performance. Nevertheless, an attempt has recently been made to impose on these materials a distinction that in many ways mimics the orality–literacy divide, by distinguishing "traditional" from "post-traditional" singers. In a series of writings, including a posthumously published paper, Zlatan Čolaković has argued that Parry's most talented singer, Avdo Međedović (Fig. 22.4), was not in fact a representative of his tradition but an exceptionally creative artist who had broken with the tradition to produce non-traditional songs: a "post-traditional" singer (Čolaković 2004, 2007a, 2007b, 2019). Čolaković extended his arguments about Međedović, whom Lord called "our Yugoslav Homer," to "Homer" himself, who should also be seen, in his view, as a "post-traditional" singer.[56] He thus effectively reversed the force of the analogy developed by Parry and Lord: where they had offered the poetry of Međedović and his peers as an argument in favor of the oral and traditional character of the *Iliad* and *Odyssey*, Čolaković offered Međedović's poetry as an argument in favor of the artistic singularity of the Homeric texts. Like the earlier notion of the "transitional text," his argument has found favor among Homerists attracted by the possibility of accommodating the figure of a uniquely gifted, original "author" within a model of oral composition.[57]

FIG. 22.4. Albert Lord and Avdo Međedović, Bijelo Polje, 1950 or 1951.
(Photographer unknown [Miloš Velimirović?]. Photo courtesy of the Milman Parry Collection of Oral Literature, Harvard University.)

Čolaković is right to observe that Međedović's singing diverged in several ways from that of other singers recorded by Parry and Lord. His songs are notably longer than is typical for his tradition. Luka Marjanović calculated an average length of something less than a thousand verses for songs in the Muslim tradition and found songs exceeding three thousand verses to be exceptional (1898:xi). Of the thirteen songs that Međedović either sang or dictated for Parry, only one was less than a thousand verses in length (and this one was a song that came to Međedović from a Christian tradition)[58]; eight were more than five thousand lines long, and two, the longest south Slavic epics ever recorded, exceeded twelve thousand verses, approximating the length of the *Odyssey* in terms of number of lines.[59] Međedović extended his songs to these extraordinary lengths by employing traditional techniques of *okićenje* ("ornamentation") more liberally than many other singers. As Lord explains, with emphasis on the traditional nature of such techniques, "Catalogues are extended and also amplified by descriptions of men and horses; journeys are described in detail; assemblies abound in speeches" (Lord and Bynum 1974:10).[60] Moreover, Međedović used nonformulaic expressions in his singing more frequently than other singers in his tradition, in which many songs, as we have seen, were virtually entirely formulaic (Lord 2019:140).

The differences that set Međedović apart from many of his peers can be observed in the results of an experiment Parry conducted in August 1935. Wishing to understand how Međedović, as a master of his art, acquired and adapted material from other singers, Parry arranged for him to be present when another *guslar*, Mumin Vlahovljak, sang "The Wedding of Bećiragić Meho," a song that Međedović had never heard. When Vlahovljak had finished, Parry asked Međedović whether he would now be able to sing the song, and Međedović, saying that he thought he could sing it even better, proceeded to perform a version that was nearly three times as long as Vlahovljak's (6,313 verses compared to 2,294).[61] Every section of the song was expanded by the addition of descriptive details, similes, speeches, or "human touches of character" that "imparted a depth of feeling that had been missing in Mumin's version" (Lord 2019:83). Međedović's handling of the song's opening theme, the description of an assembly of warriors presided over by Mustajbeg of the Lika, illustrates his technique. Vlahovljak devotes twenty verses to this theme, Međedović eighty-six; he takes twenty-four verses just to describe Mustajbeg and the hero seated to his right (PN 12471, ll. 52–75):

> londža se je turska pokupila
> u Kanidži na kamenoj londži
> londže turske trijes i šes aga.
> Age sede redom i besede.
> Ko l' je kolu beše u ičelu?
> Beg Mustajbeg, tursko ogledalo,
> kod beglera ostali begleri.
> Bega carska pera zaklupila,
> zlatna pera i to pod fermanom.
> Bega sedam bajraktara dvori,
> na vitke se sablje poduprli,
> baš ki lale cara u divane.
> Do beglera s desne stran' kolena
> A gazija Bosne vojskovođa,
> Hrnja Mujo od cijele vojske.

Mujo begu sedi kraj kolena,
i četir' ga dvore bajraktara.
Na serdara pera Alotmanska.
Na glavi mu kapa okovata.
Na njoj sedam pera carevije,
da je prvi gazalija carski.
Zlatna dela i zlatna još pera,
mrka brka i čela široka,
napuštene veđe više čela.

A Turkish assembly was gathered
in Kanidža, in the stone hall,
a Turkish assembly of thirty-six agas.
The agas sit in order of rank and talk.
Who was at the head of that circle?
Beg Mustajbeg, paragon of the Turks;
beside the Beg sat the other begs.
An imperial plume adorned the Beg,
a golden plume that he wore by imperial decree.
Seven standard-bearers attended the Beg.
They leaned on slender sabers,
just as the Sultan's courtiers attend him in council.
At the Beg's right knee,
a hero, the commander of Bosnia,
Hrnja Mujo with command over all the army.
Mujo sits at the Beg's knee,
and four standard-bearers attend him.
The *serdar* wears the Ottoman plume:
on his head, an ornate cap,
on the cap seven imperial plumes,
since he is the first hero of the empire.
A golden hero, and the plume, too, is golden.[62]
His mustaches were dark and his brow broad,
over his brow his eyebrows extended far.

Međedović employs the same "expansion aesthetic" throughout his performance.[63]

In a conversation with Parry's assistant Nikola Vujnović recorded after Međedović's performance, Vlahovljak—clearly discomfited by having witnessed the performance of a "better" version of his song—criticizes the use of excessive ornamentation, strongly implying, without saying so directly, that Međedović has falsified or corrupted the song (PN 12472, discussed at Elmer [2010:280–286]). For Čolaković, Vlahovljak's remarks provide confirmation of his view that Međedović is a "post-traditional" singer, a performer who has left his tradition behind to pursue his own, original artistic vision (Čolaković 2007b:571, 574; 2019:8, 36–38).[64] And yet, Međedović himself believed that his "ornaments," which were largely derived from what he had learned from other singers, provided a truer picture of the Bosnian heroes than songs that lacked such embellishments; he did not see himself as departing from the tradition but, on the contrary, as fortifying it (PN 12467, discussed at Elmer [2010:286–289]).⁶⁵ Is it fair to characterize his willingness to "improve" Vlahovljak's song as the attitude of a "post-traditional" singer?

In terms of the theoretical apparatus of Parry and Lord, the mere fact that Međedović was able to compose in performance such astonishingly long songs—at an often astonishingly high rate of delivery—is itself a strong argument against "post-traditionality" (cf. Danek 2012:40, n43). Parry stressed that the reliance on traditional expressions and traditional themes was a consequence of the pressures faced by the oral poet composing in performance—that it was, in fact, the only way to meet such pressures.⁶⁶ While it is true that Međedović, in comparison to other singers in his tradition, employed a greater number of formulas not present in that tradition (i.e., formulas of his own invention) and demonstrated a remarkable ability to compose apparently non-formulaic expressions in performance, this is entirely to be expected within the terms of Lord's account of oral tradition. Every singer creates new phrases; some of these become part of the singer's repertoire of formulas, and some of these formulas enter the tradition (Lord 2019:44–46). The songs of a talented singer like Međedović will naturally include a higher proportion of phrases not found in the broader tradition. But such a singer is nevertheless wholly dependent as much on a traditional technique as on the "pool" of traditional phrases and themes: the singer's ability to create is the product of the internalization of traditional verbal and thematic patterns.⁶⁷

The fundamental error of Čolaković's position is that it denies the "traditional" singer any meaningful form of creativity. For him, "traditional" poems are "created and transmitted orally by singers of tales who do not resemble poet-artists, but 'artisans who recreate.' . . . The essential characteristic of tradition is its conservatism" (Čolaković 2019:2). In contrast to the vast majority of folklorists, who emphasize the many ways in which individual creativity and traditional resources interact in the creation of oral poetry and other forms of traditional art, Čolaković seems to uphold a doubly Romantic vision: on the one hand, there is the traditional "artisan," who is devoted simply to the recreation of what has been handed down and whose individual voice is therefore subsumed into a tradition that stretches back into time immemorial (one senses the looming shadow of *das Volk*); on the other hand, there is the creative "artist," who, by virtue of their own originality, breaks free of the tradition and creates something entirely new and unreproducible. No less than Vuk's distinction between "women's songs" and "heroic songs," this dichotomy carries an unmistakably ideological charge, which comes very close to being made explicit in the concluding sentence of Čolaković's last essay: "Studying Homer with all of this in mind gives us an insight into the beginnings and origin of Western, essentially post-traditional and non-traditional, culture" (Čolaković 2019:27). Međedović and Homer, as "post-traditional" singers, become symbols of an alleged break with tradition that supposedly defines "Western culture."

That is not to say that the effort to discern the limit of south Slavic oral epic tradition is necessarily an ideological, rather than empirically grounded, endeavor. Lord, in his essay on the "transitional text," points to the case of Filip Višnjić, a blind singer who himself composed and dictated to Vuk a sequence of songs about the First Serbian Uprising: "when Višnjić tried to recount history, departing from the traditional themes (although his style was certainly authentic), he created a nontraditional song. No other singer could learn it and sing it without memorizing it" (1995:224). Čolaković makes a similar claim about Međedović (and "Homer"): "Their extended songs, as we know them, were unrepeatable and not learnable within the tradition. Singers would not be able to learn them . . . by the traditional mode of listening, but only by memorizing written texts" (2019:9). But there are significant differences between Međedović and Višnjić. While Međedović occasionally uses traditional themes in novel ways, his epics nevertheless employ the same thematic "lexicon" as other songs in the tradition; when Čolaković characterizes his songs as "unrepeatable," he seems to have in mind mainly their prodigious length, achieved by the proliferation of descriptive detail and other forms of ornamentation ("Their *extended* songs . . ."). Presumably, if another singer were given the opportunity to listen to such an extended song in its entirety, they would be able to assimilate and recreate its narrative sequence, built as it is out of traditional themes. In the case of Višnjić's songs about the First Serbian Uprising, by contrast, the narrative sequence is determined not by traditional themes and plot structures but by Višnjić's understanding of recent historical events. Since composition-in-performance relies on the manipulation of traditional themes as well as on the manipulation of traditional formulas, it is the thematic novelty of these songs that makes them difficult to assimilate by traditional means. Like Višnjić's great hero Đorđe Petrović (Karađorđe), who, at the conclusion of "The Beginning of the Revolt against the Dahis," envisions his eventual crossing of the Serbian frontier into Bosnia (Karadžić 1841–1865, vol. 4, no. 24, ll. 624–28), Višnjić himself has in a sense crossed into new territory with these songs.

Nevertheless, it must be emphasized that, while Višnjić may have composed a song on a new, and therefore "untraditional," topic, he was himself a fully traditional singer.[68] If he has stepped into untraditional territory, the boundary, arguably, has not been so much crossed as displaced. The border of tradition is in some sense always a receding horizon, and border-crossers like Višnjić effectively expand the territory of the tradition. The composition of new songs on new topics is not an inherently untraditional phenomenon; to the contrary, it is essential to the growth and vitality of any tradition, just as it provides the notional point of origin of every tradition.[69] Under the right circumstances, the novel songs of a singer like Višnjić might well be taken up by others and so enter the "pool of tradition," although they would undoubtedly be changed in the process.

In Lieu of a Conclusion, a Coda

Limits, boundaries, and definitions are fundamental tools of analysis in the study of any domain of human creativity, the endless variety of which would quickly overwhelm our critical faculties without them. No less important, however, is the critical evaluation of such boundaries and definitions—the "philology of the border"—since the binaries they create are all too readily absorbed by ideological structures of valorization. There is nothing particularly novel or innovative about the approach taken in this essay; the practice of such a "philology" is widespread in the humanities. Nevertheless, it seems worthwhile to stress the importance of the "philology of the border" particularly in the case of oral epic since epic poetry has over and over again been subject to valorization as the embodiment of the values of "the nation," among the south Slavs as elsewhere.

The figure of Avdo Međedović himself provides an instructive case in point. Regardless of whether he has been seen as a "traditional" or a "post-traditional" singer, he has repeatedly been offered as a symbol of Bosniak culture: either of the richness of that culture's traditions or of the creative originality those traditions are capable of fostering. From time to time, however, it has been hinted, or even claimed outright, that Međedović was Albanian.[70] The debate over Međedović's ethnicity has, predictably, taken on a decidedly nationalistic character, with echoes of Kadare's *The File on H*.[71] To judge by the interviews Parry recorded with him, his own conception of his identity was complex: he refers to himself as a "Bosniak" and as a "Turk" (but never as an "Albanian"); at various times he frames his identity in terms of religion, geography, and kinship (but generally not in terms of ethnicity).[72] Moreover, he was highly conscious of the fact that the world in which he encountered Parry was a radically different one from the world of his youth, when, as a soldier in the Ottoman army, he traveled to Albania, Macedonia, Bulgaria, and Greece.[73] In truth, an "Albanian" identity—for which there is no conclusive evidence—is probably the least apt of the many possible identities to which Međedović might have laid claim, in the account of political anthropologist Ivan Čolović (2011:188):

> The materials made up of Avdo's own statements, Parry's and Lord's photo-documentation, testimonies by Avdo's contemporaries and relatives, as well as various interpretations of his songs all indicate that this folk bard was at times a little bit of a Bosniak, Turk, Albanian, Muslim, Montenegrin, a man from Rovci, from Sandžak, Yugoslav, a Balkan man, and a Slav. This identity spectrum was in part a fruit of a strategy Avdo Međedović (circa 1875–1955) used in order to survive in several wars in which he took part, and in several states in which he lived, and in part, it was a fruit of identity strategies of those who wrote about him in different periods. None of his identities is either true or false, and every one of them is a part of the political history of Avdo Međedović and his *gusle*, which, as we can see, hasn't run its course yet.

To make the same point in somewhat different terms, we might say that, more than a "Bosniak" or an "Albanian," more than a "Yugoslav Homer," Avdo Međedović was a man of the border.

Acknowledgments

I am grateful to Ronelle Alexander, Dorian Jurić, Peter McMurray, Gregory Nagy, and Robert Romanchuk for offering valuable feedback on drafts of this essay.

Notes

1. On the difficulty of isolating "epic" as a genre cross-culturally and within any given cultural setting, see Bynum (1976, esp. pp. 41–45) and Martin (2005), who emphasizes the fluidity of generic boundaries.
2. According to Bynum (1979:1; cf. Jurić 2020:14), this region is the only one in which "oral epos as an indigenous tradition in South Slavic has been convincingly documented." Heroic poetry is attested among speakers of Bosnian, Bulgarian, Croatian, Macedonian, Montenegrin, Serbian, and Slovene (and among neighboring speakers of Albanian, Greek, and Romanian).
3. See Jurić (2020:15) for the salience of religion (rather than modern ethnic categories) as the "axis" along which branches of the tradition diverge.
4. On the so-called *triplex confinium* as a frontier zone characterized by more or less constant conflict and frequent migration, see the essays collected in Roksandić and Štefanec (2000); also Bracewell (2006), offering a critical review of the various ways this frontier zone has been represented in historiography. Bracewell (2000:37) and Roksandić (2000:243–244) emphasize the distinctive culture of this frontier zone and the shared customs that united those dwelling on opposite sides of the border.
5. For schematic descriptions of these plot types, see Foley (Return Song 1990:361–363; Wedding Song: 2004:37–38). Both plot types were identified by Lord (2019:128–130), who discusses also the overlap between them.
6. Foley's descriptions of the "Return Song" and the "Wedding Song" (see previous note) are based on the Muslim tradition, but numerous examples of both types have been collected from Christian singers as well. On historical patterns of migration and their influence on the development of the tradition, see Koljević (1980:301–302, with reference to Christian tradition).
7. On the so-called Krajina epic (see below, note 17) as an expression of a distinctive identity associated with life on the frontier, see Kunić (2024). Schmaus (1958) discusses traces of epic traditions tied specifically to *martolos*, border guards stationed along the Ottoman frontier and often recruited from migrants or local Christian populations. Buturović (1991:286–290) includes the *martolos* in her discussion of the ways in which "[c]hanges in the border of the Bosnian pashalik . . . were instrumental in enriching its oral traditional repertoire." The south Slavic epic tradition is hardly unique as a "tradition of the border." One thinks immediately of the Byzantine epic *Digenis Akritis*, the eponymous hero of which bears a name that encodes a construction of the Arab-Byzantine border as a region of contact and hybridity: *Digenis* means "double-born," referring to split Arab/Byzantine parentage, while *Akritis* means "border soldier" (technically, these are epithets; the hero's given name is Basileios). See also Paredes (1958:xii: "Borders and ballads seem to go together"). Robert Romanchuk (personal communication, July 30, 2021) points out to me the example of the Ukrainian "Turkish-Tatar" *dumy*, which "arose among the Zaporozhian Cossacks who guarded the border of the Polish-Lithuanian Commonwealth from the Tatars."
8. Concise overviews are provided by Coote (1978) and Auty (1980). Braun (1961) is more comprehensive but focuses on the Christian tradition; for the Muslim tradition, see Buturović (1992). Lord (2019; originally published 1960) remains the classic description of the tradition from the standpoint of compositional technique.
9. The two *bugarštice* included in Petar Hektorović's *Ribanje i ribarsko prigovaranje* (1568) are generally regarded as the earliest recorded examples of south Slavic oral epic. (For the term

bugarštica, see below, note 11.) The earliest recorded examples of songs in the *deseterac* meter date to the eighteenth century; see below ("Vuk Stefanović Karadžić, *Hasanaginica*, and the Boundaries of the Serbian Nation") for discussion of one of these. Bynum (1986) provides a rich description of the earliest textual evidence for south Slavic oral epic, a song in *bugarštica* meter recorded by Rogeri de Pacienza in *Lo Balzino* (1497); though the song in question is a dance song, it clearly draws on epic tradition. Buturović (1992:296) judges that the remarks of Turkish chronicler Ibn Kemal (1469–1534) about the hero Đerđelez Alija presuppose an epic tradition. On the evidence for the presence of south Slavic singers of heroic songs in the Crown lands of Poland, including Ukraine, in the fifteenth and early sixteenth centuries, see Hrushevsky (2012:485–486). (I thank Robert Romanchuk for this reference.)

10. The major published collections of texts are *Srpske narodne pjesme* (see Karadžić, 1841–1865, published in five volumes with an earlier version published in 1824 under the title *Narodne srpske pjesme* [see Karadžić, 1824]); *Hrvatske narodne pjesme* (in ten volumes, published by Matica Hrvatska, 1896–1942 [see Marjanović, 1898]); *Narodne pjesne Muhamedovaca u Bosni i Hercegovini* (see Hörmann, 1888, two volumes). Bogišić (1878) collects the surviving *bugarštice* (on which see note 11), along with older examples of songs in *deseterci*. The website of the Milman Parry Collection of Oral Literature at Harvard University (http://mpc.chs.harvard.edu) provides access to numerous field recordings and transcriptions made in the 1930s and 1950s by Milman Parry and Albert Lord. The Vienna Phonogrammarchiv has published on compact disc and CD-ROM the collection of field recordings made in 1912–1913 by Matija Murko in Bosnia and Herzegovina (Murko 2017). Bynum (1986:305–306) lists some 160 collectors "whose accumulations are either certainly or probably still accessible to the modern researcher in some form or part."

11. In earlier phases of the tradition, the *deseterac* coexisted with the longer verse of the so-called *bugarštica*. (*Bugarštica* lines vary in length but gravitate toward fifteen syllables.) While it is sometimes supposed that the *bugarštica* is the "older" form of epic, the relationship between *bugarštice*, which seem to have died out some time in the eighteenth century (but cf. Stolz 1969:154), and decasyllabic epics is far from clear; see Bogišić (1878:1–89), Schmaus (1959), and Coote (1978:272–273) for discussion. Roman Jakobson (1966) argued that the *deseterac* derives from an Indo-European prototype. Stolz (1969:155–56) points out that in Bulgaria and Macedonia songs of an epic character were sung in octosyllabic verses (the octosyllable is primarily a lyric and ballad meter in Bosnian/Croatian/Serbian traditions). The 4 + 6 structure of the *deseterac* is often characterized as a rigid constraint, and indeed one rarely encounters departures from it in published collections. In performance, however, singers not uncommonly produced hypo- or hypermetrical verses.

12. On the political manipulation of newly composed (i.e., non-traditional) epic songs during the wars of Yugoslav succession in the 1990s, see Žanić (2007).

13. Parry's published works are collected in Parry (1971). Lord (2019) is the definitive formulation of the model of composition in performance developed by Parry and Lord, centered on south Slavic oral epic but with consideration also of the Homeric poems *Beowulf*, *Digenis Akritis*, and other texts and traditions. Lord (1991) presents further comparative studies. Robert Kanigel (2021) has written an engaging account of Parry's life and work, with scattered snapshots of Lord. For the Milman Parry Collection of Oral Literature, which contains the many thousands of recordings and texts collected by Parry and Lord, see above, note 10.

14. Coote (1978:277) emphasizes the prominence the south Slavic epic tradition has enjoyed as "[u]ntil recently . . . the only model of oral composition that has been thoroughly documented and investigated."

15. In parts of Bulgaria and North Macedonia epics are sung to the accompaniment of the *g'dulka/ćemane*, known as the *lira* in Greece (Lord 1972:301). The word *gusle*, it should be noted, is morphologically plural.
16. Kleut (1994) offers a critical overview of several such classificatory systems, emphasizing the difficulties involved in the assumption, on which they are generally based, that songs can be meaningfully correlated with historical events. As Kleut points out, such systems represent an extension of the organizational principles applied by Vuk Stefanović Karadžić in *Srpske narodne pjesme* (1841–1865). Similar classifications are offered by Coote (1978:260–269) and Auty (1980:198–199).
17. Čubelić (1970), for example, treats Muslim epic as one "cycle" among others. For a classification of Muslim epics based on the collection of Kosta Hörmann, see Buturović (1976:157). The collector Luka Marjanović, guided by the terminology of his informants, divided the materials he collected in northwestern Bosnia into two "cycles" according to the principal scenes of action (1898:xxxiv): "songs of the Lika" (*ličke pjesme*), situated in and near the Lika district, and "Hungarian songs" (*unđurske pjesme*), situated along the Slavonian frontier. This same classification was known and referred to by singers of the following generation (Bynum 1979:5). Schmaus, following Matija Murko, distinguished two broad "types" of Bosnian Muslim epic, tied to geographical regions but distinguished according to formal characteristics (i.e., Schmaus's "types" are not "cycles" distinguished according to content): the "Krajina type," from the frontier region of northwestern Bosnia, and the "Hercegovinian type" or "southern Muslim type" (Schmaus 1953a:300, 1953b:95, 110–12; criticism of Schmaus's classification at Buturović 1992:149–161).
18. These very approximate figures refer to collected *texts*, which are themselves only a proxy for "living" epic song. Traditional singers in all branches of the tradition could expand or contract their songs, and the pace of delivery varied widely. It is also important to note that wide variation in length can be observed in the Muslim tradition (cf. Buturović 1992:586).
19. For the poetics of ornamentation in Bosniak epic, see below, note 60. I use the term "Bosniak" to refer to the Muslim, Slavic-speaking inhabitants of any part of the territory of the former Yugoslavia. "Bosnian" refers to the territory of Bosnia or an inhabitant thereof, also to the language spoken by Bosniaks.
20. For Albanian songs about the Battle of Kosovo, see Schmaus (1938b) and Lord (1984). Robert Elsie's translations of selected Albanian songs are available in Di Lellio (2009). Kadare (2000) reflects, in fiction, on the relation between the south Slavic and Albanian Kosovo traditions.
21. On Slavic loanwords in Albanian songs, see Skendi (1954:146–149). In Bosnian songs from Sandžak, one not infrequently encounters the Albanian word *besa*, "solemn pledge, sworn word," a word (and concept) that carries great weight in Albanian culture. Veis Sejko has devoted an entire monograph to shared elements in south Slavic and Albanian epic traditions (2002).
22. The novel originally appeared in 1981 in the Albanian magazine *Nëntori* under the title *Dosja H*. In *Elegy for Kosovo* (2000; originally published in 1998 as *Tri këngë zie për Kosovën*) Kadare portrays Albanian and Serbian epic traditions about the Battle of Kosovo more as parallel traditions originating in a shared experience.
23. Cf. Madrid (2011:4): "Rather than a separating fence or a dividing river, the border is instead a porous line that has always allowed transnational flows and has prevented the segregating discourses that the idea of the border helps to create from actually being a reality." We can compare Bracewell's (2000:37) description of the Balkan *triplex confinium*:

"the frontier can be seen not just as a line of demarcation between civilizations, polities and identities, but also as a zone of shared interests and values"; Roksandić (2000:243) speaks of a "united borderland region."

24. See, for example, the classic study of Américo Paredes (1958); cf. Corona and Madrid (2008:5): "[M]usic is the perennial undocumented immigrant; it has always moved beyond borders without the required paperwork."

25. I adapt this term from Emily Apter's discussion of the philosophy of Étienne Balibar (Apter 2020:97, 111); note, however, that Balibar's "philological model of the border," discussed briefly in the following section, is somewhat different from the approach I am outlining here.

26. This formulation refers to "Lachmannian" textual criticism, focused on the reconstruction of an archetype for surviving manuscripts. On "new philology," which focuses attention on individual manuscripts as unique and revealing instantiations of a text and treats textual variation as a meaningful phenomenon (and not just as the product of "error"), see Nichols (1990). Aspects of my "philology of the border"—for example, consideration of different contexts of reception of *Hasanaginica* (see the following section)—could be considered examples of "new philology," adapted for oral tradition.

27. Particularly when we are dealing with oral tradition, every text is the product of an act of demarcation since the text has been "collected," textualized in one form or another, and cut off from the discourse and social practice in which it was embedded.

28. Wilson (1986) remains the most complete account of Vuk's life. Hajdarpasic (2015:20–37) offers a valuable account of Vuk's work as language reformer, with particular emphasis on the importance of Bosnia and Herzegovina in Vuk's cultural geography. Tršić, situated approximately 100 km southwest of Belgrade, and about 20 km east of the Serbian–Bosnian border, was destroyed in the early nineteenth century in the course of the Serbian struggle for independence from the Ottoman Empire but has been restored as a museum and "ethno-park."

29. Wilson (1986:86–88) situates Kopitar's interest in Vuk in the context of a Habsburg policy of fostering the national consciousness of Slavs within the Austrian Empire in order to counter Russian influence (cf. pp. 2–3, 81–83).

30. Burke (1978:287–288) lists Vuk's *Pjesnarica* among forty-eight key works marking the "discovery of the people" (i.e., *das Volk*) in eighteenth- and nineteenth-century Europe. On the "discovery" of "the people" (*narod*) among the south Slavs, see Hajdarpasic (2015:18–20 and passim).

31. I quote the text in Vuk's orthography. Miloš's catalogue extends for forty-two verses in total.

32. Vuk does not cite sources for the songs in the *Pjesnarica*; he claimed to have heard them in Tršić and memorized them in his youth (Karadžić 1814:19; but see below for the so-called *Hasanaginica*, which he took from a published source). Especially in the case of this early work, it is legitimate to question whether Vuk has accurately reproduced traditional material or whether he has reshaped it according to his own canons of style, content, etc.

33. In the *Pjesnarica*, as in Vuk's source (see below, this section), the protagonists are referred to as Asan Aga and Asanaginica, and the text is thus sometimes referred to as *Asanaginica*. When Vuk reprinted the song in volume 3 of *Srpske narodne pjesme*, he changed the spelling to Hasan Aga and Hasanaginica, to better comport with his experience of the ikavian dialect used by Dalmatian singers (cf. Pasarić 1908:548; Jurić 2020:9); the title *Hasanaginica* has come to be preferred in the scholarship.

34. No indication is given of how Hasan Aga received his wound; one presumes that he received it in a duel or battle, either of which would be a typical theme in a properly epic song. The text's silence on this point is a kind of generic sign-posting: as a description of the strictly domestic consequence of a martial encounter that is passed over in silence, the song positions itself in opposition to more strictly "heroic" or "epic" narratives. This is already an indication that Vuk's classification of the text among epic songs deserves closer scrutiny (see the next section for further discussion).
35. Vuk does acknowledge his source in volume 3 of *Srpske narodne pjesme* (Karadžić 1841–1865:vol. 3, 527), where he also laments the fact that he was never able to hear the song "among the people" (*u narodu*).
36. For a cursory overview of Vuk's editorial interventions, see Butler (1980:417); Butler provides both Vuk's text and a facsimile of Fortis's original.
37. For Goethe's use of Werthes's translation, see Rölleke (1975:427, n126). Herder did not credit Goethe by name, but he did acknowledge that the translation was not his own—a "subtle homage" according to Rölleke. Goethe published his version, with slight changes, under his own name in the first volume of *Goethe's Werke* (Goethe 1806:111–114).
38. These lines provide a standard example of so-called Slavic antithesis, a rhetorical figure typical of south Slavic folk poetry (essentially, a priamel consisting of rhetorical questions that are answered negatively before the focal topic is named).
39. Isaković (1975:7–8) lists twenty-two translations into eleven languages in a list that extends only until 1841.
40. According to Wolff (2001:191), Vuk sent Goethe a copy of the *Pjesnarica* inscribed with the following dedication: "A Slav sends to the greatest German, alongside the original of the 'Mourning Song of the Noble Wife of the Hero Asan Aga,' also the first publication of Serbian folk songs."
41. On the term *Morlacchi* and its gradual effacement, see Wolff (2000, 2001:173–191). Wolff (2001:190–191) emphasizes that Herder's *Volkslieder* established *Morlackisch* as a national category equivalent to "German," "English," etc.: once again, Balibar's "philological model of the border" at work.
42. Muljačić (1975) speculates that Fortis might have obtained the song from a Christian peasant woman who worked for him as a domestic servant. Fortis's text is, however, evidently connected in some way to a manuscript tied to Giulio Bajamonti, a doctor in Split who was a close associate of Fortis and had a strong interest in south Slavic folk epic; Bajamonti even wrote an essay (heavily influenced by the ideas of Giambattista Vico) comparing south Slavic epics with the Homeric poems, titled "Il Morlacchismo d'Omero" (1797). On Bajamonti, his interest in folk epic, and the "Split manuscript" as the probable source for Fortis's text, see Murko (1935b, esp. 370–377). (Muljačić [1975:39] expresses skepticism about the "Split manuscript.") Murko asserts that the text derives from a Muslim milieu, although it may have been collected from a Christian informant (1935b:355, 366). Elsewhere, Murko (1951:192–193) notes that, in Dalmatia, ballads depicting Muslim settings often entered the repertoires of Christian women who worked in Muslim households, suggesting that *Hasanaginica* is among such songs.
43. The question is further complicated by the fact that a text that may reasonably be considered to be a "multiform" of *Hasanaginica* appears in the "Erlangen manuscript" (Erlangen, Universitätsbibl. 2107), a compilation of songs that appears to have been made in the first decades of the eighteenth century by an Austrian official collecting material from south Slavic soldiers serving in the Habsburg *Militärgrenze*, some distance

from Dalmatia (Gesemann 1925:cii–civ). This song, the sixth in the manuscript, likewise recounts a tragic misunderstanding, leading to divorce, between Asan Aga and his wife, although the song ends more happily for Asanaginica: on her own initiative, she marries the man who provoked Asan Aga's jealous suspicion by praising her beauty (Gesemann 1925:5–8). A song similar to the Erlangen text, collected in Gacko from Hasnija Hrustanović, can be found in the Milman Parry Collection of Oral Literature (PN 2854; for the text, see Vidan 2003:210–212). In contemporary Bosniak culture, *Hasanaginica* is claimed as a symbol of Bosniak identity.

44. "All those songs that are not decasyllabic and cannot be sung to the *gusle* are called in common Serbian [*prosti serblji*] 'women's songs'" (Karadžić 1814:23).

45. Note again the heading in the *Pjesnarica*: *pjesne ljubovne i različne ženske* ("Love Songs and Various/Diverse Women's Songs"). For the diversity of women's song traditions among the south Slavs, see Vidan (2003:12); Vidan's book offers an authoritative account of the traditional ballads sung by Bosniak women.

46. Karadžić (1824:xix–xx): "Some songs are, as it were, on the border [*na međi*] between women's songs and heroic songs, so that a person doesn't know among which he should take them to be [Vuk goes on to cite several songs from his collection] . . . Such songs bear a stronger resemblance to heroic songs than to women's songs, but it would be rarely heard that people would sing them to the *gusle* (even if to women), and, because of their length, neither are they sung like women's songs, but are only recited."

47. Murko (1951:189–205) provides a detailed discussion of female epic singers, noting that such singers are exceptional at the eastern end of the epic zone but more common toward the west, especially in Dalmatia. Antonijević (1960) presents a study of one female singer in particular.

48. Nenić (2012) offers an exemplary discussion of the ideological dimensions of the gendering of epic performance as "men's songs."

49. Dukić (1992:35) refers to *Hasanaginica* as the "paradigm" of the ballad genre. The song's generic ambivalence, however, is indicated by the fact that, while Dukić includes it in his anthology of oral epics from Dalmatia (1992:117–119), the subsequent volume in the same series, devoted to oral *lyric* from Dalmatia, likewise includes the song (Perić-Polonijo 1996:311–313). For a nuanced discussion, informed by south Slavic oral poetry, of the ballad in relation to epic, lyric, and drama, see Perić-Polonijo 1988, who notes that ballads are often considered to be "border-line poems" (p. 41) and characterizes *Hasanaginica* as an "epic ballad" (p. 43, n4). Schmaus (1959:169–170) notes how widespread ballads are in the south Slavic epic zone and how difficult it is to distinguish them from heroic epics purely on the basis of form and style. The rich ballad tradition of Dalmatia and the prominence of ballads in women's repertoires are well illustrated by the collection made by Andro Murat (1996) on the island of Šipan, near Dubrovnik, in the late nineteenth century; Perić-Polonijo, the editor of the collection, offers a useful discussion of the genres represented in it (pp. 13–23). See also (Coote 1978:270) and note 42 above.

50. See above, note 35.

51. In 1932 Milan Ćurčin published a version dictated to him by the sculptor Ivan Meštrović, which Meštrović had learned as a child from his grandmother in Dalmatia. Matija Murko (1935a) subsequently recorded the song from a female singer, Pavle Kuvelić, on the island of Šipan.

52. The most significant of Parry's unpublished "writings" are the series of commentaries he composed—orally, by dictating them to a wax-cylinder "Parlograph" machine—in

late 1934. These were intended to be part of a large study to which Parry gave the title *Ćor Huso* (the title refers to a legendary singer of the generation preceding that of Parry's informants). The quotation is taken from this work, excerpts from which are printed in Parry (1971). The complete transcriptions of Parry's commentaries are conserved in the Milman Parry Collection of Oral Literature.

53. Cf. Lord (2019:139): "Formula analysis, providing, of course, that one has sufficient material for significant results, is, therefore, able to indicate whether any given text is oral or 'literary'"; (pp. 154–155): "This is the surest proof now known of oral composition." At pp. 140–141 Lord also discusses thematic composition and non-periodic enjambment as canons of oral style, but formula analysis remains his principal diagnostic tool.

54. Formulas are determined by their recurrence in a corpus of some twelve thousand verses sung or dictated by Ugljanin. "Formulaic expressions" are phrases that, while not repeated verbatim within that corpus, are constructed according to a repeated pattern.

55. Finnegan (1976) writes, "to speak as if there is a definite break between [oral literature and written literature] is an exaggeration, and a misleading one. The two terms are, I would argue, relative ones, and to assign any given piece unequivocally to either one category or the other—as if they were self-contained and mutually exclusive boxes—can distort the nature of the evidence" (p. 137). Lord's response to her observations, suggesting the possibility of "written composition without writing," follows on pp. 175–176.

56. I enclose the name "Homer" in quotation marks to signal my own view that "Homer" is best understood as a construct of the Homeric tradition (cf. Nagy 1996:20–22).

57. See Fowler (2007) and Danek (2012). Richard Janko, another prominent Homerist, edited Čolaković (2019) for publication.

58. PN 12463, "The Illness of Emperor Dušan in Prizren," 645 lines. Međedović learned this song from a singer named Mihajil Božović (Lord and Bynum 1974:54).

59. The *Odyssey* totals roughly 12,100 lines (the exact number varies according to the edition). Međedović's longest songs are PN 6840, "The Wedding of Meho, Son of Smail," with 12,323 lines, and PN 12389 + 12441, "Osmanbeg Delibegović and Pavičević Luka," with 13,331 lines. The astonishing length of Međedović's longest songs is a consequence of the fact that Parry had asked him to sing or dictate the longest songs in his repertoire and to develop them fully; such lengths were not typical even for Međedović.

60. Lord notes that while Međedović learned many of his *kite* "ornaments" from other singers, he invented some of them himself. On the technique of ornamentation in the Bosniak tradition and in Međedović's own practice, in comparison also with Homeric poetics, see Elmer (2010).

61. For a description of the experiment and comparison of the two versions, see Lord 2019:82–86, 237–249. Parry conducted a similar experiment involving Nikola Vujnović and Salih Ugljanin; while the two singers' versions exhibit a number of differences, they are approximately the same in length (Lord 2019:108–109, with n4).

62. The golden "Ottoman" (*Alotmanska*) plume, glossed, somewhat confusingly, as "seven imperial plumes," is likely a reference to a *çelenk* (*čelenka* in Međedović's Bosnian), a jeweled aigrette like the one awarded to Admiral Nelson by Sultan Selim III (and stolen from the National Maritime Museum in London in 1951); such jewels served as military decorations. Nelson's exceptionally ornate *çelenk* had thirteen rays or "plumes" and a clockwork mechanism that caused the central diamonds to rotate. The young hero of Međedović's "The Wedding of Smailagić Meho" wears no less than six rotating *čelenke* (PN 6840, ll.1659–74; text at Bynum and Lord [1974:102–103], translation at Lord and Bynum [1974:101]).

63. I take the notion of an "expansion aesthetic" from Martin (1989:196, 205–230).
64. Čolaković writes, "traditional singers find Međedović's style intolerable" (2019:9) but provides no evidence for this claim apart from the indirect criticism of a single singer, Vlahovljak, who had been put into an embarrassing position by Parry's experiment; see further Elmer (2010:284).
65. Čolaković, who accuses Lord of deliberately withholding evidence that would counter his notion of Međedović as a traditional singer (2019:8, n40), does not provide the relevant passages from this text or discuss their significance. His paraphrases of Međedović and other singers are frequently tendentious.
66. See Parry (1971:439) and Lord (2019:166). Čolaković (2019:8) denies the link between oral composition in performance and reliance on tradition ("this assertion is completely wrong") but does not engage with Parry's reasoning, endeavor to show where the fault lies, or offer any counterexample apart from his own idiosyncratic presentation of Međedović and "Homer."
67. On the concept of the "pool of tradition," deliberately formulated by Lauri Honko to capture the complexity of the relationship between individual creativity and collective tradition, see Honko (1998:70–71, 2000:18–19).
68. Cf. Koljević (1980:281–282) on the traditional and formulaic character of Višnjić's language, even in his songs about the First Serbian Uprising. Dorian Jurić (personal communication, July 26, 2021) makes a direct comparison between Višnjić and Međedović as traditional singers: "These are traditional singers being given untraditional tasks, which a malleable art is able to accommodate." My remarks in this paragraph owe much to the exchange in which this comment was offered.
69. I write "notional" in order to acknowledge Lord's cautionary remarks about the illogicality of the concept of an "original" in oral tradition (Lord 2019:106–108).
70. See Berisha (1998:295–303) and Neziri (2006:77–81). Three arguments are offered in support of "Albanian" ethnicity: (1) In the photograph featured on the cover of *The Singer of Tales*, Međedović is wearing a white skull cap, which is ordinarily a marker of Albanian identity; (2) he acknowledged kinship with Hajro Ferizović and the Ferizi clan, Ferizi being a common Albanian surname; (3) he used a number of Albanian words in his songs and conversation. Neither individually nor taken together are these arguments decisive. Međedović's lexicon of Albanian words could easily be explained as belonging to the patois of his region of Montenegro, where he regularly mingled with Albanian speakers. His reference to possible kinship with Hajro Ferizović is elliptical (text at Bynum and Lord [1974:15]), and Ferizović himself makes no reference to Albanian ancestry in the interviews he gave for Parry. (In Montenegro there are many fully "Slavicized" families with distant Albanian origins [cf. Jireček 1916:69].) The white skull cap is an oddity—in photos taken by Lord in 1950 or 1951, Međedović wears a dark fez more typical for Montenegrin "Bosniaks" (see Fig. 22.4)—but it is hardly enough to support the claim that Međedović was Albanian.
71. For an example of the kind of rhetoric that has attended this controversy—in which Zlatan Čolaković also participated—see the texts assembled in the appendix to Čolović (2011).
72. See PN 12436, the first of several interviews with Međedović recorded by Parry, translated by David Bynum in Lord and Bynum (1974:37–51; an original-language transcription is printed in Bynum and Lord [1974:1–21]). There Međedović speaks of himself as a member of a company of "Bosniaks" (*Bošnjaci*) in the Ottoman army (Lord and Bynum 1974:45). Later in the same conversation, recalling experiences under German authorities at the end of the First World War, he uses the phrase "we Turks" (*mi Turci*; p. 49).
73. For Međedović's account of his military service, see Lord and Bynum (1974:41–46).

Works Cited

Antonijević, Dragoslav. 1960. *Milena guslarka*. Beograd, Serbia: Naučno delo.
Anzaldúa, Gloria. 1987. *Borderlands/La Frontera: The New Mestiza*. San Francisco, CA: Aunt Lute Books.
Apter, Emily. 2020. "Cosmopolitics." In *Thinking with Balibar: A Lexicon of Conceptual Practice*, eds. Ann Laura Stoler, Stathis Gourgouris, and Jacques Lezra, 94–116. New York: Fordham University Press.
Auty, Robert. 1980. "Serbo-Croat." In *Traditions of Heroic and Epic Poetry*. Vol. 1, *The Traditions*, ed. A. T. Hatto, 196–210. London: Modern Humanities Research Association.
Bajamonti, Giulio. 1797. "Il Morlacchismo d'Omero." *Nuovo Giornale Enciclopedico d'Italia*, March:77–98.
Balibar, Étienne. 2014. "At the Borders of Europe: From Cosmopolitanism to Cosmopolitics." *Translation: A Transdisciplinary Journal*, 4:83–103.
Beissinger, Margaret H. 2017. "History and the Making of South Slavic Epic." In *Archaeology and Homeric Epic*, eds. Susan Sherratt and John Bennet, 135–155. Oxford: Oxbow.
Berisha, Anton Nikë. 1998. *Qasje poetikës së letërsisë gojore shqipe*. Prishtina, Kosovo: Rilindja.
Bogišić, Baltazar. 1878. *Narodne pjesme iz starjih, najviše primorskih zapisa: sa raspravom o "Bugaršticama" i s rječnikom*. Belgrade, Serbia: Državna štamparija.
Bracewell, Wendy. 2000. "Frontier Blood-Brotherhood and the Triplex Confinium." In *Constructing Border Societies on the Triplex Confinium*, eds. Drago Roksandić and Nataša Štefanec, 29–45. Budapest: Central European University.
Bracewell, Wendy. 2006. "The Historiography of the Triplex Confinium: Conflict and Community on a Triple Frontier, 16th–18th Centuries." In *Frontiers and the Writing of History, 1500–1850*, eds. Steven G. Ellis and Raingard Esser, 211–227. Hannover-Laatzen: Wehrhahn.
Braun, Maximilian. 1961. *Das serbokroatische Heldenlied*. Göttingen: Vandenhoeck & Ruprecht.
Burke, Peter. 1978. *Popular Culture in Early Modern Europe*. New York: Harper & Row.
Butler, Thomas. 1980. *Monumenta Serbocroatica: A Bilingual Anthology of Serbian and Croatian Texts from the 12th to the 19th Century*. Ann Arbor: Michigan Slavic Publications.
Buturović, Đenana. 1976. *Studija o Hörmannovoj zbirci muslimanskih narodnih pjesama*. Sarajevo: Svjetlost.
Buturović, Đenana. 1991. "The Geographic Extent and Chronological Coordinates of South Slavic Moslem Oral Epic." *Oral Tradition*, 6/2–3:284–302.
Buturović, Đenana. 1992. *Bosanskomuslimanska usmena epika*. Sarajevo: Svjetlost.
Bynum, David E. 1976. "The Generic Nature of Oral Epic Poetry." In *Folklore Genres*, ed. Dan Ben-Amos, 35–58. Austin: University of Texas Press.
Bynum, David E. 1979. *Bihaćka Krajina: Epics from Bihać, Cazin, and Kulen Vakuf*. Vol. 14, Serbo-Croatian Heroic Songs. Cambridge, MA: Harvard University Press.
Bynum, David E. 1986. "The Collection and Analysis of Oral Epic Tradition in South Slavic: An Instance." *Oral Tradition*, 1/2:302–343.
Bynum, David E., and Albert Bates Lord, eds. 1974. *Ženidba Smailagina sina: kazivao je Avdo Međedović*. Vol. 4, Serbo-Croatian Heroic Songs. Cambridge, MA: Center for the Study of Oral Literature.
Čolaković, Zlatan. 2004. "Homer: Ćor Huso ili Avdo, rapsod ili aed?" *Almanah*, 27–28:47–68.
Čolaković, Zlatan. 2007a. "Post-tradicionalna epika Avda Međedovića i Homera." In *Epika Avda Međedovića: Kritičko izdanje/The Epics of Avdo Međedović: A Critical Edition*, 1:47–89. Podgorica, Montenegro: Almanah.

Čolaković, Zlatan. 2007b. "The Singer above Tales." In *Epika Avda Međedovića: Kritičko izdanje/The Epics of Avdo Međedović: A Critical Edition*, 2:567–597. Podgorica, Montenegro: Almanah.

Čolaković, Zlatan. 2019. "Avdo Međedović's Post-Traditional Epics and Their Relevance to Homeric Studies." *Journal of Hellenic Studies*, 139:1–48.

Čolović, Ivan. 2011. *The Balkans: The Terror of Culture. Essays in Political Anthropology*. Baden-Baden: Nomos.

Coote, Mary P. 1978. "Serbocroatian Heroic Songs." In *Heroic Epic and Saga: An Introduction to the World's Great Folk Epics*, ed. Felix J. Oinas, 257–285. Bloomington: Indiana University Press.

Corona, Ignacio, and Alejandro L. Madrid. 2008. "Introduction: The Postnational Turn in Music Scholarship and Music Marketing." In *Postnational Musical Identities: Cultural Production, Distribution, and Consumption in a Globalized Scenario*, eds. Ignacio Corona and Alejandro L. Madrid, 3–22. Lanham, MD: Lexington Books.

Čubelić, Tvrtko. 1970. *Epske narodne pjesme: izbor tekstova s komentarima i objašnjenjima i rasprava o epskim narodnim pjesmama*. Zagreb, Croatia.

Ćurčin, Milan. 1932. "Hasanaginica u Narodu (Meštrovićeva Verzija)." *Nova Evropa*, 25/3–4:119–130.

Danek, Georg. 2012. "Homer und Avdo Međedović als 'Post-Traditional Singers'?" In *Homer, gedeutet durch ein großes Lexikon: Akten des Hamburger Kolloquiums vom 6.–8. Oktober 2010 zum Abschluss des Lexikons des frühgriechischen Epos*, ed. Michael Meier-Brügger, 27–44. Berlin: de Gruyter.

Di Lellio, Anna, ed. 2009. *The Battle of Kosovo 1389: An Albanian Epic*. London–New York: I. B. Tauris.

Dukić, Davor. 1992. *Zmaj, junak, vila: antologija usmene epike iz Dalmacije*. Split, Croatia: Književni krug.

Elmer, David F. 2010. "Kita and Kosmos: The Poetics of Ornamentation in Bosniak and Homeric Epic." *Journal of American Folklore*, 123/489:276–303.

Finnegan, Ruth. 1976. "What Is Oral Literature Anyway? Comments in the Light of Some African and Other Comparative Material." In *Oral Literature and the Formula*, eds. Benjamin A. Stolz and Richard Stoll Shannon, 127–166. Ann Arbor: Center for the Coördination of Ancient and Modern Studies, University of Michigan.

Foley, John Miles. 1990. *Traditional Oral Epic: The Odyssey, Beowulf, and the Serbo-Croatian Return Song*. Berkeley: University of California Press.

Foley, John Miles. 2004. *The Wedding of Mustajbey's Son Bećirbey as Performed by Halil Bajgorić*. FF Communications No. 283. Helsinki: Suomalainen Tiedeakatemia.

Fowler, Robert. 2007. "Introduction." In *Epika Avda Međedovića: Kritičko izdanje/The Epics of Avdo Međedović: A Critical Edition*, ed. Zlatan Čolaković, 2:539–544. Podgorica, Montenegro: Almanah.

Friedman, Victor A. 2012. "Balkan Epic Cyclicity: A View from the Languages." In *Balkan Epic: Song, History, Modernity*, eds. Philip V. Bohlman and Nada Petković-Djordjević, 293–300. Lanham, MD: Scarecrow Press.

Gesemann, Gerhard. 1925. *Erlangenski rukopis starih srpskohrvatskih narodnih pesama*. Sr. Karlovci, Serbia: Srpska kraljevska akademija.

Goethe, Johann Wolfgang von. 1806. *Goethe's Werke*, Vol. 1. Tübingen: J. G. Cotta.

Hajdarpasic, Edin. 2015. *Whose Bosnia?: Nationalism and Political Imagination in the Balkans, 1840–1914*. Ithaca, NY: Cornell University Press.

Herder, Johann Gottfried. 1778. *Volkslieder*, Vol. 1. Leipzig: Weygand.
Honko, Lauri. 1998. *Textualising the Siri Epic*. FF Communications No. 264. Helsinki: Suomalainen Tiedeakatemia, Academia Scientiarum Fennica.
Honko, Lauri. 2000. "Text as Process and Practice: The Textualization of Oral Epics." In *Textualization of Oral Epics*, ed. Lauri Honko, 3–54. Berlin–New York: Mouton de Gruyter.
Hörmann, Kosta. 1888. *Narodne pjesne Muhamedovaca u Bosni i Hercegovini*, 2 vols. Sarajevo: Zemaljska štamparija.
Hrushevsky, Mykhailo. 2012. *History of Ukraine-Rus'*. Vol. 6, *Economic, Cultural, and National Life in the Fourteenth to Seventeenth Centuries*, trans. Leonid Heretz. Edmonton–Toronto: Canadian Institute of Ukrainian Studies.
Isaković, Alija, ed. 1975. *Hasanaginica: 1774–1974: prepjevi, varijante, studije, bibliografija*. Sarajevo: Svjetlost.
Jakobson, Roman. 1966. "Slavic Epic Verse: Studies in Comparative Metrics." In *Selected Writings*, 4:414–463. The Hague: Mouton & Co.
Jireček, Konstantin. 1916. "Albanien in der Vergangenheit." In *Illyrisch-albanische Forschungen*, ed. Ludwig von Thallóczy, 1:63–93. Munich–Leipzig: Duncker & Humblot.
Jurić, Dorian. 2020. "Back in the Foundation: Chauvinistic Scholarship and the Building Sacrifice Story-Pattern." *Oral Tradition*, 34:3–44.
Kadare, Ismail. 1997. *The File on H*. London: Harvill Press.
Kadare, Ismail. 2000. *Elegy for Kosovo: Stories*. New York: Arcade.
Kanigel, Robert. 2021. *Hearing Homer's Song: The Brief Life and Big Idea of Milman Parry*. New York: Knopf.
Karadžić, Vuk Stefanović. 1814. *Mala prostonarodnja slaveno-serbska pesnarica*. Vienna: G. Ioanna Šnirer.
Karadžić, Vuk Stefanović. 1824. *Narodne srpske pjesme*, Vol. 1. Leipzig: Breitkopf & Härtel.
Karadžić, Vuk Stefanović. 1841–1865. *Srpske narodne pjesme*, 5 vols. Vienna: Jermenski manastir.
Kleut, Marija. 1994. "The Classification of Serbo-Croat Oral Epic Songs into Cycles: Reasons and Consequences." In *The Uses of Tradition: A Comparative Enquiry into the Nature, Uses and Functions of Oral Poetry in the Balkans, the Baltic, and Africa*, eds. Michael Branch and Celia Hawkesworth, 75–81. London: School of Slavonic and East European Studies.
Koljević, Svetozar. 1980. *The Epic in the Making*. Oxford: Clarendon Press.
Kolsti, John. 1990. *The Bilingual Singer: A Study in Albanian and Serbo-Croatian Oral Epic Traditions*. New York: Garland.
Kunić, Mirsad. 2024. "The Many Deaths of Mustaj Beg of Lika." In *Singers and Tales in the Twenty-First Century*, eds. David F. Elmer and Peter McMurray, 231–61. Cambridge, MA–London: Milman Parry Collection of Oral Literature.
Lord, Albert B. 1968. "Homer as Oral Poet." *Harvard Studies in Classical Philology*, 72:1–46.
Lord, Albert B. 1972. "The Effect of the Turkish Conquest on Balkan Epic Tradition." In *Aspects of the Balkans: Continuity and Change. Contributions to the International Balkan Conference Held at UCLA, October 23–28, 1969*, eds. Henrik Birnbaum and Speros Vryonis, 298–318. The Hague: Mouton.
Lord, Albert B. 1984. "The Battle of Kosovo in Albanian and Serbocroatian Tradition." In *Studies on Kosova*, eds. Arshi Pipa and Sami Repishti, 65–83. Boulder–New York: East European Monographs, distributed by Columbia University Press.
Lord, Albert B. 1991. *Epic Singers and Oral Tradition*. Ithaca, NY: Cornell University Press.
Lord, Albert B. 1995. "The Transitional Text." In *The Singer Resumes the Tale*, ed. Mary Louise Lord, 212–237. Ithaca, NY: Cornell University Press.

Lord, Albert B. 2019. *The Singer of Tales*, 3rd ed. Cambridge, MA–Washington, DC: Milman Parry Collection of Oral Literature and Center for Hellenic Studies. (Originally published 1960.)

Lord, Albert Bates, and David E. Bynum, eds. 1974. *The Wedding of Smailagić Meho, by Avdo Međedović*. Vol. 3, Serbo-Croatian Heroic Songs. Cambridge, MA: Harvard University Press.

Lucerna, Camilla. 1905. *Die südslavische Ballade von Asan Agas Gattin und ihre Nachbildung durch Goethe*. Berlin: A. Duncker.

Madrid, Alejandro L. 2011. "Transnational Encounters at the U.S.–Mexico Border: An Introduction." In *Transnational Encounters: Music and Performance at the U.S.–Mexico Border*, ed. Alejandro L. Madrid, 1–16. Oxford: Oxford University Press.

Marjanović, Luka. 1898. *Hrvatske narodne pjesme, knjiga treća: junačke pjesme (Muhamedovske)*. Zagreb, Croatia: Matica hrvatska.

Martin, Richard P. 1989. *The Language of Heroes: Speech and Performance in the* Iliad. Ithaca, NY: Cornell University Press.

Martin, Richard P. 2005. "Epic as Genre." In *A Companion to Ancient Epic*, ed. John Miles Foley, 9–19. Malden, MA: Blackwell.

Muljačić, Žarko. 1975. "Od koga je A. Fortis mogao dobiti tekst 'Hasanaginice'?" In *Hasanaginica: 1774–1974: prepjevi, varijante, studije, bibliografija*, ed. Alija Isaković, 39–49. Sarajevo: Svjetlost.

Murat, Andro. 1996. *Narodne pjesme iz Luke na Šipanu*, ed. Tanja Perić-Polonijo. Zagreb, Croatia: Matica hrvatska.

Murko, Matija. 1935a. "Asanaginica sa Šipana." *Nova Evropa*, 28/4–5:112–119.

Murko, Matthias. 1935b. "Das Original von Goethes 'Klaggesang von der edlen Frauen des Asan Aga' (Asanaginica) in der Literatur und im Volksmunde durch 150 Jahre, part 1." *Germanoslavica*, 3:354–377.

Murko, Matija. 1951. *Tragom srpsko-hrvatske narodne epike: putovanja u godinama 1930–1932*, 2 vols. Zagreb, Croatia: Jugoslavenska akademija znanosti i umjetnosti.

Murko, Matija, collector. 2017. *Epic Folk Songs from Bosnia and Herzegovina: The Collections of Matija Murko (1912, 1913)*. Sound Documents from the Phonogrammarchiv of the Austrian Academy of Sciences: The Complete Historical Collections 1899–1950, Series 16, OEAW PHA CD 40.

Nagy, Gregory. 1996. *Homeric Questions*. Austin: University of Texas Press.

Nenić, Iva. 2012. "(Un)Disciplining Gender, Rewriting the Epic: Female Gusle Players." In *Musical Practices in the Balkans: Ethnomusicological Perspectives. Proceedings of the International Conferences Held from November 23 to 25, 2011*, eds. Dejan Despić, Jelena Jovanović, and Danka Lajić-Mihaljović, 1–14. Belgrade, Serbia: Belgrade Institute of Musicology of SASA.

Neziri, Zymer Ujkan. 2006. *Studime për folklorin*, Vol. 1. Prishtina, Kosovo: Instituti Albanologjik i Prishtinës.

Nichols, Stephen G. 1990. "Introduction: Philology in a Manuscript Culture." *Speculum*, 65/1:1–10.

Notopoulos, James A. 1964. "Studies in Early Greek Oral Poetry." *Harvard Studies in Classical Philology*, 68:1–77.

Paredes, Américo. 1958. *"With His Pistol in His Hand": A Border Ballad and Its Hero*. Austin: University of Texas Press.

Parry, Milman. 1971. *The Making of Homeric Verse: The Collected Papers of Milman Parry*. Oxford: Clarendon Press.

Pasarić, Josip. 1908. "I opet Andrićevo 'Iznenadjenje.'" *Savremenik*, 3/9:545–557.
Perić-Polonijo, Tanja. 1988. "The Ballad and the Lyric Poem." In *Balladen und andere Gattungen/Ballads and Other Genres*, 41–51. Zagreb, Croatia: Zavod za istraživanje folklora.
Perić-Polonijo, Tanja. 1996. *Tanahna galija: antologija usmene lirike iz Dalmacije*. Split, Croatia: Književni krug.
Rihtman-Auguštin, Dunja. 2004. "Vuk Karadžić: Past and Present; or, On the History of Folk Culture." In *Ethnology, Myth and Politics: Anthropologizing Croatian Ethnology*, ed. Jasna Čapo Žmegač, 13–21. Aldershot: Ashgate.
Roksandić, Drago. 2000. "Stojan Janković in the Morean War, or, of Uskoks, Slaves and Subjects." In *Constructing Border Societies on the Triplex Confinium*, eds. Drago Roksandić and Nataša Štefanec, 239–288. Budapest: Central European University.
Roksandić, Drago, and Nataša Štefanec, eds. 2000. *Constructing Border Societies on the Triplex Confinium*. Budapest: Central European University.
Rölleke, Heinz, ed. 1975. *"Stimmen der Völker in Liedern": Volkslieder*, by Johann Gottfried Herder. Stuttgart: Reclam.
Scaldaferri, Nicola. 2021. "Text, Music, Performance." In *Wild Songs, Sweet Songs: The Albanian Epic in the Collections of Milman Parry and Albert B. Lord*, ed. Nicola Scaldaferri, 69–84. Cambridge, MA: Milman Parry Collection of Oral Literature and Center for Hellenic Studies.
Schmaus, Alois. 1938a. "Beleške iz Sandžaka (I)." *Prilozi proučavanju narodne poezije*, 5:274–280.
Schmaus, Alois. 1938b. "Kosovo u narodnoj pesmi Muslimana (srpska i arnautska muslimanska pesma o Kosovu)." *Prilozi proučavanju narodne poezije*, 5:102–121.
Schmaus, Alois. 1953a. "Episierungsprozesse im Bereich der slavischen Volksdichtung." In *Münchener Beiträge zur Slavenkunde: Festgabe für Paul Diels*, eds. Erwin Koschmieder and Alois Schmaus, 294–320. München: Isar Verlag.
Schmaus, Alois. 1953b. *Studije o Krajinskoj epici*. Zagreb, Croatia: Jugoslavenska Akademija znanosti i umjetnosti.
Schmaus, Alois. 1958. "Die Frage einer 'Martolosen'-Epik." *Die Welt der Slaven*, 3:31–41.
Schmaus, Alois. 1959. "Gattung und Stil in der Volksdichtung." In *Rad Kongresa folklorista Jugoslavije u Varaždinu 1957*, ed. Vinko Žganec, 169–173. Zagreb, Croatia: Udruženje folklorista Jugoslavije.
Sejko, Veis. 2002. *Mbi elementet e përbashkëta në epikën shqiptaro-arbëreshe dhe serbokroate*. Tirana, Albania: Bargjini.
Skendi, Stavro. 1954. *Albanian and South Slavic Oral Epic Poetry*. Philadelphia, PA: American Folklore Society.
Stolz, Benjamin A. 1969. "On Two Serbo-Croatian Oral Epic Verses: The *Bugarštica* and the *Deseterac*." *The Bulletin of the Midwest Modern Language Association*, 2/1:153–164.
Vidan, Aida. 2003. *Embroidered with Gold, Strung with Pearls: The Traditional Ballads of Bosnian Women*. Cambridge, MA: Milman Parry Collection of Oral Literature.
Werthes, Friedrich, trans. 1775. *Die Sitten der Morlacken aus dem Italiänischen übersetzt*. Bern: Typographische Gesellschaft.
Wilson, Duncan. 1986. *The Life and Times of Vuk Stefanović Karadžić, 1787–1864: Literacy, Literature, and National Independence in Serbia*. Ann Arbor: Michigan Slavic Publications.
Wolff, Larry. 2000. "Disciplinary Administration and Anthropological Perspective in Venetian Dalmatia: Official Reflections on the Morlacchi from the Peace of Passarowitz to

the Grimani Reform." In *Constructing Border Societies on the Triplex Confinium*, eds. Drago Roksandić and Nataša Štefanec, 47–56. Budapest: Central European University.

Wolff, Larry. 2001. *Venice and the Slavs: The Discovery of Dalmatia in the Age of Enlightenment.* Stanford, CA: Stanford University Press.

Žanić, Ivo. 2007. *Flag on the Mountain: A Political Anthropology of War in Croatia and Bosnia-Herzegovina, 1990–1995.* London: Saqi.

CHAPTER 23

SOUTH SLAVIC WOMEN'S BALLADS

AIDA VIDAN

For centuries women's ballads have permeated the cultural landscape of the South Slavic lands.

The post–World War II period of intense industrialization, urbanization, and the rise of literacy, combined with migrations due to the violent disintegration of Yugoslavia in the 1990s, effectively brought an end to this tradition. However, its footprint in both world archives and cultural memory continues to generate a discourse which casts light not only on the societies in which it thrived but also on creative processes, dissemination, and layers of signification pertinent to other traditions.

Even though mostly attributed to female performers, the gender delineation is relative since there are examples of male singers performing ballads, as well as men and women composing hybrid songs that exhibit features of both epic and ballad styles. What is thus important to stress from the outset is the shared nature of the decasyllabic meter most typically used in South Slavic ballads and epics, as well as the compositional structure that allows for the formulas and themes to permeate songs irrespective of their length and the performer's gender and cultural background. In other words, despite their stylistic, thematic, and performative idiosyncrasies, the South Slavic ballads are deeply embedded in oral traditional poetics. They draw from the wealth of its building blocks common to all verse genres and relying on the listener's general knowledge of the tradition, the two elements essential for opening up the creative space in which the singer can compose in performance.[1]

South Slavic Ballad: The Form, the Theme, the Performer

Before addressing diachronic aspects of collecting South Slavic ballads, it is necessary to provide at least a provisional definition of the genre, in particular given differing perspectives on the length, tragic nature, musicality, and performative character.

Considering the Balkans' cultural diversity, there is potentially a broad swing of the pendulum when it comes to various elements contained in any definition. For practical reasons necessitated by the current analysis, the South Slavic ballad is defined as a formulaic deca- or octosyllabic narrative song characterized by dramatic complexity and a relative economy of thematic units with a focus on a personal conflict and its emotional and psychological implications.

Below is an example of several decasyllabic verses from a song by Zehra Šaković (Parry no. 2903) describing how the main character, Zlata, resolves to dress up and depart her parents' home, protesting her father's rejection of her captive beloved and his plans to marry her off to a more appropriate suitor. The girl's traditional attire and her ritualistic performative femininity reveal, however, a deep rift in the established practices punctuating her agency and ultimate rejection of patriarchy as she secretly runs away to execute her own will. What is more, this segment is counterpointed later in the song with another instance of re/dressing when Zlata visits her beloved's mother, discards her feminine outfit, and puts on male attire. She borrows her beloved's horse from his mother and travels to a warrior contest disguised as a man to win it and to seek the release of her captive beloved as a reward.

Although in this multiform the reasons for her beloved's captivity are never revealed, it is implied that her mission has both a love motivation as well as a note of political intervention.[2] Parallel to her being kept captive to patriarchy, her beloved, a Muslim, is imprisoned due to the clashes with the neighboring Christian forces (he is said to be held in the "Lenđer grad," typically perceived as a Christian coastal city in the local lore). In the first instance of dressing and leaving home in protest without a male guardian, Zlata overturns the Muslim patriarchal code, while in the second example her masculine attire and command of a horse and weapons signify refusal of the male political checkerboard in quest of a dignified life irrespective of political/religious designations. Thus, her acts of re/dressing mark restructuring of the traditional behavioral practices and serve as an ultimate condemnation of a patriarchal/military world order (Fig. 23.1).

Furthermore, in terms of their prosodic qualities, the decasyllabic verses below, even though formulaic in nature and thus encountered in multiple songs, exhibit a marvelous wealth of poetic features such as the usual caesura after the fourth syllable, the internal rhyme, multiple instances of assonance and alliteration, and examples of anaphora contributing to the cumulative effect of the character's action. Even this brief example, which uncovers only a part of the multilayered meanings and resonances, thus indicates the powerful expressive economy of the balladic decasyllable:

> Sve mislila, na jednu smislila,
> pa se povi po svilenu pasu,
> pa izvadi svileno odjelo,
> pa oblači Zlatija devojka.
> Pripe peču, prigrnu feredžu,
> pa izlazi odaji na vrata.

> She was thinking and suddenly decided,
> and she wrapped her silken waist,

and she took out her silken attire,
and the maiden Zlata put it on herself.
She put on her veil and threw on her cloak,
and stepped through the door outside the room.

While, for instance, the song length among female Muslim performers in Herzegovina in the 1930s oscillated from several tens to several hundred lines,[3] a female Catholic singer from the island of Šipan (Croatia) in the late nineteenth century provided multiple ballads of over a thousand lines which in their thematic scope gravitate to the balladic spectrum while bearing epic qualities in terms of their digressive nature.[4] Relying only on the statistical determinant of length thus does not necessarily point to the inherent qualities of balladic genre. A more productive criterion appears to be the combination of thematic focus dealing with the character's internal struggle and a dramatic charge which typically structures the plot in a series of swift and succinct turns of events.

The element of the tragic outcome as one of the defining components of this genre in older periods can be eliminated especially in the context of the comparative multiform approach demonstrating that a gifted singer is capable of rendering any segment of the song, including its end, in any number of modalities. While traditionally some songs are more likely to conclude in a certain way, there undoubtedly always exist multiforms (recorded or unrecorded) which provide an alternate outcome. Similarly, depending on the culture and performative circumstances, some songs were sung only vocally,

FIG. 23.1. Milman Parry Collection, Image 299: "Woman on a horse, Gacko," Lord, 1933–1935.

while for others a *tepsija* (round pan) was used to reverberate and enhance the singer's voice. Women singing with a *gusle*, a one-string traditional instrument used in men's performances of epics, is rare (Murko 1951:190, 193; Vidan 2003:19). Still, irrespective of the accompaniment, the performative circumstances for South Slavic female singers have traditionally been entirely different from those customary for male singers. While epic singers commonly sang with the *gusle* in a public setting and often during a religious occasion such as Ramadan in Muslim communities or various social and religious gatherings in the Christian areas, female singers did not enjoy such exposure in traditional environments. On the contrary, their singing would not typically be characterized as a "performative event" since they usually sang while taking care of household chores or children (Murko 1951:190; Vidan 2003:17). In this sense the singer and her audience, consisting of family members or friends, functioned in a domestic atmosphere of their household conducive to intimate narratives. Similarly, the focal point was not the mastery of the performer (even though this aspect is necessary and implied). An intrusion of foreign elements, including scholarly activity (described in greater detail in section Milman Parry and Albert Lord: New Collecting Practices and Women Singers), disturbed this fine balance and resulted in materials of poorer quality than those collected by the members of the singer's immediate circle.

Earliest Collecting Efforts and Dynamics between the Oral and the Printed

Despite being somewhat overshadowed by the role the local epics played in explaining the structure of Homer's *Iliad* and *Odyssey*, women's ballads represent a critical body of material contributing to our deeper understanding of the process of composition in performance, diachronic and synchronic transmission of oral materials, as well as the connections oral traditional poetry has to the mythological strata. During their trips to the Balkans in the 1930s, Milman Parry and Albert Lord, with their field-altering research methodology, initially focused on recording the epics by male singers in both written and audio forms. However, they also recognized the importance of the shorter genres, including ballads, and committed considerable resources and time to collecting as many songs as possible.[5] It is owing to their phenomenal efforts that we inherited not only one of the richest repositories of oral traditional poetry in the world, housed in Harvard's Widener Library, but along with it also a wealth of ethnographic data allowing us to map geographic, cultural, linguistic, performative, and personal details in an attempt to understand how various circumstances affected the creative process.

The collecting of South Slavic ballads had a long history that preceded Parry's and Lord's undertaking. Looking at the Renaissance period with the oldest extant texts entails a reformulation of both the notion of collecting practice and genre due to a highly permeable boundary between the oral and the written in the earlier eras (Lord 1987; Vidan 2024). This boundary has been recently problematized with regard to other genres as well (Nagy 2020; Amodio 2020; Ziolkowski 2010). Coming on the wings of a flourishing literary culture especially in the southern Croatian province of Dalmatia, the local writers had a developed awareness of the traditional lore which informed both their language and thematic interests. In particular, the prosperous urban environments of Dubrovnik, Split, and Hvar emerged as literary centers, which in the liminal zone of Italian influences established a highly original literary output. It is worth noting the example of Petar Hektorović's piscatorial eclogue *Ribanje i ribarsko prigovaranje* (*Fishing and Fishermen's Conversation*, 1556, published 1568; see Hektorović 1997), an account of his three-day-long journey between the islands of Hvar and Šolta with two fishermen who share their philosophical outlook on life. The epistolary poem consists of 1,684 verses which also include two *bugarštice* (fifteen-syllable verse songs) sung, as one of the fishermen says, "[a]fter the Serbian fashion" (*sarbskim načinom*; Hektorović 1997:66) and which Maja Bošković-Stulli convincingly argued belong to the balladic corpus (Bošković-Stulli [1988] 1991; Lord 1987:340). This early text incorporates evidence of not only a complex interaction between written and oral expression but also dissemination of oral traditional materials across ethnic and cultural boundaries. Even though examples from the Renaissance are sparse, later periods provide a greater number of works, in particular epics, showing mutual influences.[6]

Approximately forty balladic texts are preserved also in the Erlangen manuscript dated ca. 1716-1733 and discovered in 1913 in the Erlangen University Library (Erlangenski rukopis, 2022). It was written in the church version of the Cyrillic script, and its orthography reveals that it was likely collected by a German native speaker. Its adorned 530 leaves contain 217 songs and include, among others, a ballad about a magical fish which has mythological roots (no. 34 in Medenica and Aranitović 1987). Already this example points to subcutaneous connections of South Slavic balladic materials with mythological motifs of Indo-European origin, in this case a dragon cycle (Vidan, 2025), while the manuscript itself serves as a bridge between the older and newer strata of the tradition. The mix of all three regional dialects (štokavian, čajkavian, and kajkavian) indicates that the collector gathered the materials indiscriminately and included them in no particular order. The manuscript was first published in 1925 by Gerhard Gesemann as *Erlangenski rukopis starih srpskohrvatskih narodnih pesama*.

Another early example of one of the most famous South Slavic ballads, "Hasanaginica" (in Croatian with English translation provided in the Appendix), was published in 1774 by the Italian abbot Alberto Fortis in his *Viaggio in Dalmazia*, which made it accessible (in Italian and Croatian) to Western readers, including Johann Wolfgang von Goethe (Goethe, 1987:313–316) and Johann Gottfried Herder (Herder, 1990:213–216), the former offering his own iteration based on F. Werthes' German translation. The widely disseminated song appearing subsequently in a cohort of multiforms (including Parry no. 2676 by Hasnija Hrustanović) in multiple collections from the Bosnian/Croatian/Montenegrin/Serbian language continuum tells a story of the bashful wife of Hasanaga who, for a mysterious reason, fails to visit her wounded husband. Consequently, she is punished by being sent away to remarry but dies of sorrow for her children. The character of Hasanaginica remains an epitome of tragic fate due to the rigid patriarchal customs, while the song, with its memorable opening containing a prime example of the Slavic antithesis, is considered one of the most dramatically charged and enigmatic texts. Thus, already in the eighteenth century the South Slavic ballads captured the romantic imagination of Western literary circles, a testimony to this genre's remarkable aesthetic qualities. What is more, the Western interest in European liminal spaces rested in part on the region's status of a non-conforming rebel in the zone where foreign rule imposed by the Venetians, Ottomans, Hungarians, and Habsburgs effectively prevented the early formation of nation states and linguistic determination. The praise for the autochthonous tradition and insurgent spirit thus stands in stark opposition to the region's political subjugation.

The Legacies of Vuk Stefanović Karadžić and Nikola Andrić

The strong ties between the processes of language standardization and oral traditional literature, including ballads, are particularly evident in the work of the Serbian ethnographer and linguist Vuk Stefanović Karadžić (1787–1864) who, encouraged and assisted by the Viennese linguistic circles (in particular Jernej Kopitar, himself of Slovenian background), engaged in a broad spectrum of collecting and publishing activities. In many ways, Karadžić's ethnographic efforts mark a new stage in ballad collecting practices. Even though his ethnic misnomers in publication titles did not accurately reflect the sources of ballads and epics which came not only from Serbian Orthodox but also Croatian Catholic, Montenegrin Orthodox, and Bosnian Muslim singers, his contribution to preserving the South Slavic oral heritage and anchoring language modernization processes in it is undeniable. Starting with *Mala prostonarodnja slaveno-serbska pjesnarica* (1814, Vienna) and *Narodna srbska pjesnarica* (1815, Vienna) to a more ambitious four-volume series *Srpske narodne pjesme* (vols. 1–3 came out in 1823 and 1824 in Leipzig, vol. 4 in 1833 in Vienna; see Karadžić 1969), in a cohort of nineteenth-century collectors, Karadžić was the most efficient in making South Slavic ballads and epics available to both domestic and foreign reading audiences.[7] The input from Western folklorists such as Jakob Grimm shortly after the publication of the first two Leipzig volumes in 1824 included both congratulatory notes and commentaries on linguistic and subject matter. In fact, with Kopitar's assistance, Grimm and Karadžić established contact as early as 1814 during Grimm's stay in Vienna, and Karadžić visited him repeatedly in Berlin through 1857 (Kropej 2013:222–223). Grimm's own interest in Slavic philology and conviction that common people's oral expression should be a foundation for language standardization encouraged Karadžić to carry on with his work. Of particular interest in Grimm's exchanges with Karadžić were several ballads with strong mythological links and broad Indo-European diffusion such as the ballad of the immured wife (Dundes 1989, 1995; Jurić 2020) and the one of the serpent-groom (Vidan, 2025).

In the heat of nationalist debates of the 1990s as Yugoslavia was disintegrating, it was precisely ballads and epics with deeper historical layers that prompted various ethnic groups to claim ownership over them. Already in 1908, the ballad of the immured wife known as "Zidanje Skadra" ("The Building of Skadar"), widespread throughout the Balkans and beyond, whose multiform Karadžić collected during 1820–1821, became contested ground when Nikola Andrić, the editor of the Croatian series *Hrvatske narodne pjesme* (*Croatian Folk Songs*), posthumously accused Karadžić of plagiarism. While selecting materials for the Croatian book series, Andrić discovered a text nearly identical to Karadžić's taken down around the same time by a local collector in southern Croatia (Jurić 2020). Given a lack of expected variance Andrić concluded that Karadžić somehow appropriated it from the Croatian collector. An extended and tumultuous series of accusations between the Serbian and Croatian scholars ensued throughout the twentieth century but failed to elucidate the cause of the improbable overlap. Emphasizing the artificiality of ethnic boundaries in traditional singing and singers' general obliviousness to larger ethnic claims in earlier periods, Dorian Jurić (2020) maps out the contentious history of this song up to the most recent nationalistically tainted scholarship. Relying on the earlier research by Alan Dundes (1989, 1995), he elaborates the non-linear diffusion model of this song and makes a claim that its concurrent existence in oral and written sources in the first half of the nineteenth century affected its stability and opened up a possibility for some singers to learn it from printed editions, including Karadžić's own (Jurić 2020:12, 21).

Thus, from their very appearance Karadžić's editions with ethnically charged titles initiated reactions ranging from contestations to laudations both at home and in the West. The balladic corpus they made widely accessible coupled with the linguistic impact they generated created an interest that has not waned even two hundred years after their first publication. At the time Karadžić was active, the tradition had already existed in the Balkan area for centuries, all along absorbing various influences and modifying them to reflect the local mores. Karadžić himself gave primacy to ballads and lyric songs over epics in 1824, in volume 1 of the Leipzig edition of his *Srpske narodne pjesme*: "Concerning the age of our songs, I would say that we have women's songs that are older than heroic songs because we have few heroic songs that are older than Kosovo and there is not a single one that comes from before the Nemanjići period, while among women's songs some may be even a thousand years old" (Karadžić 1969:vol. 1, 539).[8] Even though his statement is speculative, it reflects an awareness of both the longevity and complexity of the oral tradition in the region.

As evident from previous examples, proprietary ethnic arguments which obfuscate diffusion patterns in favor of politically motivated goals disregard the basic functional mechanisms guiding the creation of oral poetry and propose the existence of an urtext belonging to a specific ethnic entity. This teleological approach conveniently overlooks the polyphonic nature of oral creation possible by reliance on the building blocks contributed by a multitude of antecedent singers belonging to adjacent language continuums. What is more, it erases a multicultural facet of orality, thus precluding investigation of motifs and stories disseminated across multiple ethnic groups and languages, a phenomenon well documented already by Antti Aarne in 1910 and subsequently elaborated by Stith Thompson and Hans-Jörg Uther (Uther et al. 2004). In doing so, it effectively also undermines understanding of mythological schemes which predate more recent religious, historical, and political developments. Finally, a similarly outdated discourse arguing for exclusivity or either oral or written literary format has neglected a dynamic and productive exchange between the two, as discussed above. Interaction between living oral tradition and printed *pjesmarice* (songbooks) was even more pronounced in the later periods with the rise of publishing enterprises. Already Matija Murko noted this in the course of his research in 1931–1932 (1951:67, 69–70), while Parry and Lord during their trip to the region in 1934–1935 collected hundreds of popular booklets printed in the period from the late nineteenth century onward and discussed at length the mutual influences between orality and institutionalized printed materials (Lord 1968:10–15, esp. n35).

The second large output of South Slavic ballads collected was by the Croatian publishing house Matica hrvatska in a series *Hrvatske narodne pjesme* (*Croatian Folk Songs*), in particular volumes 5, 6, 7 and 10 (Andrić 1909; Andrić 1914; Andrić 1929; Andrić 1942) which, although published in the early part of the twentieth century, were written down in the second half of the nineteenth century by a group of collectors. The aforementioned Andrić was the driving force behind this important edition. While Karadžić focused on the songs at the expense of the singer, whose identity was most often neglected, the Matica hrvatska collaborators were instructed to note down the name of the singer and the locality (Murko 1951:189); and many ended up gathering multiple versions of songs, some of which were subsequently included in the published edition. One of the greatest contributors was Andro Murat, who wrote down 149 songs from several Šipan singers, including his mother, the prolific and talented Kate Murat née Palunko.[9] Many of the songs from this manuscript were included in the Matica hrvatska ten-volume series, while the entire corpus consisting of numerous ballad–epic hybrid song forms was published more recently in *Narodne pjesme iz Luke na Šipanu* (Murat 1996). Baldo Melkov Glavić, another outstanding collector from the Dubrovnik area working around the same time, gathered songs in mixed genre (1889) and contributed numerous texts to the Matica hrvatska series. In many regards the collections of these two researchers are comparable, largely because they both worked around the same time, focused on the same region, and showed a great deal of interest in songs performed by women. Both Murat and Glavić were known for their accuracy and left relatively detailed records of their collecting practices.

Matija Murko and the Ethnography of South Slavic Oral Tradition

The principal contribution of Matija Murko, a Slovenian scholar who taught in Prague and undertook multiple trips in the Balkans from 1909 through 1932, is not necessarily in recordings of ballads but rather in ethnographic data pertaining to female singers. Even though he originally planned to focus on epic singers in his *Tragom srpskohrvatske narodne epike. Putovanja u godinama 1930–1932* (*Tracing the Serbian-Croatian folk epic. Travels in the years 1930–1932*) published only in 1951, once he encountered vibrant communities of female performers, he decided to include his findings in a chapter devoted to them. His volume presents a wealth of data with lists of individual singers, their biographical details, family origin, notes on education and literacy, as well as information about their repertories, sources of learning songs, descriptions of performances, and reputation. Based on his observations, he concluded that in the 1930s the epics (we can assume also some hybrid forms in this category) were better preserved among women than men on the Dalmatian islands; however, he did not encounter female *guslari* anywhere. From his field notes it is clear that, due to regional cultural variations, Catholic singers living on the coast had a greater exposure to epic songs which they not only internalized but also performed in the less constricting societal circumstances when compared to their Muslim counterparts living inland (Vidan 2003:17). Even though they did not use the *gusle* and did not have the same public exposure or recognition as male singers, female singers in Dalmatia interacted with the epic segment of the tradition (Murko 1951:190–193) and, I would argue, adopted it to reflect their own perspectives and preoccupations, as evident from the example of Kate Murat.

Murko was the first to attempt recording of traditional songs in the Balkans, but his imperfect equipment allowed him to capture only approximately thirty verses at the time (Murko 1951:24; Murko [1929] 1990:14–16). Still, even these brief clips, which he compared with texts taken down from dictation, were sufficient to observe on a smaller scale what Parry and Lord were eventually able to demonstrate on a much larger corpus and with greater precision: in different iterations of the same song, "entire verses appeared in a wholly new form or simply disappeared" (Murko [1929] 1990:16). In fact, Murko became aware of this phenomenon as early as 1913 when a fieldwork protocol set by the Vienna Phonogrammarchiv forced him to first write down the opening of the song he was to record (Tate 2011:344). Surprised with variations he discovered, he continued to investigate it during his subsequent trips. Even though Murko did not use or define the term "formula" as later developed by Parry and Lord, he identified some of the essential constitutive elements of traditional songs: "The singers retain their songs as long as they do thanks to the well-known epic repetitions, utilized for example for messages, and to the various clichés reserved to celebrate aspects of feminine beauty, heroes, costumes, horses, arms, duels, and so on" (Murko [1929] 1990:17). What is more, he underscored the fact that these songs are not memorized: "Can one picture for himself what it is to sing long poems, without error in subject matter, in irreproachable poetic verses, with the greatest of speed? This is not possible except among singers who do not learn the poems by heart, or word for word, but who re-create them anew each time in brilliant improvisation, thanks to their 'science' of language and of poetry" (Murko [1929] 1990:19). Murko was clearly aware of the special nature of language employed in traditional verses irrespective of the singer's gender or the song genre, as well as of the singer's ability to recreate the song anew during each performance. He eventually became critical of the cult of epic singers, making him initially overlook the rich tradition of female singing to which he dedicated most of his 1932 trip. He noted that he "arrived in the last moment because the excellent female singers were very old (around 85) or had passed away" (Murko 1951:190). Murko's stress on ethnographic data and performance context in addition to his sensitivity to the impact of his own research process on singers (for example, he used battery-powered equipment that he could bring to villages with no electricity to record in singers' own settings) place him well ahead of his time. Some of the questions he initiated were tackled by Parry and Lord but also by later scholars such as Richard Bauman and Charles Briggs, who pointed out the need for researchers "to deconstruct this notion of natural context by confronting their own influence on what their local sources offered them" (1990:71).

Murko's lasting impact is most visible in his influence on Milman Parry whom he met in Paris in 1928 (Parry 1971:439). Parry likely became familiar with Murko's Sorbonne lectures published in 1929 before undertaking his own expeditions to the Balkans in 1933 and 1934–1935 (Tate 2011:332), the latter with his assistant Albert Lord. Since Murko was yet to learn about the still living practice of women singing in his 1931–1932 trip, it is unlikely that in 1928 he could have shared much about this portion of the tradition with Parry. In other words, between 1931 and 1935 both Murko and Parry independently of one another discovered female performers in the southern regions of what was then Yugoslavia, with the former focusing on ethnographic data and the latter on collecting the songs in addition to interviewing a group of singers (Fig. 23.2).

Milman Parry and Albert Lord: New Collecting Practices and Women Singers

Although Parry was primarily interested in recording longer songs by male singers in order to explain the composition of the Homeric epics, once he encountered gifted female singers, he decided to include shorter genres as a part of his project as well. Together with Lord and a local singer and guide, Nikola Vujnović, he looked to expand their network in the field. Toward this goal they recruited and trained two educated native speakers who had access to the local communities in the hinterland of Dubrovnik and could thus collect songs from the otherwise unreachable mostly Muslim women

FIG. 23.2. Milman Parry Collection, Image 818: "On market day Serb and Albanian, Moslem and Christian mingle," Parry, 1933–1935.

groups. These two young men, Ibrahim Hrustanović and Hamdija Šaković, wrote down nearly two thousand songs, primarily from their mothers, close relatives, and family friends. Based on my research of family relations and manuscripts, they were joined by Halid Dizdarević, a son of one of the principal singers, who also contributed to this core corpus. Unlike with the first two collectors, unfortunately there are no interviews with him about his fieldwork. Once the word spread in the area about Parry's and Lord's research, other individuals (some incentivized by small monetary awards) started sending notebooks with songs to the scholars. Among these there were children of illiterate singers who wrote down their mothers' or relatives' songs, but some clearly copied texts from popular songbooks or even from one another (Bartók and Lord 1951:249). As only scant data about both the singers and these other scribes exist, the reliable nucleus of the collection constitutes the songs written down by Ibrahim, Hamdija, and Halid in addition to some 250 songs Parry and Lord recorded by phonograph.

The Parry Collection of Oral Literature contains a total of 11,396 ballads and lyric songs by 309 singers, of whom 257 are female and 52 are male. From this corpus 466 are by Hasnija Hrustanović, 330 by Emina Šaković, and 338 by Đula Dizdarević, the three most gifted singers whose songs were written down by their sons, Parry's and Lord's close associates. Emina and Đula were sisters and, having grown up together and lived in close proximity, represent a unique case for studying how the stability of a song may be affected through singers' multiple exposures to the same narrative pattern. Both Halid and Hamdija (most likely first cousins) collected songs from both women. All three singers were illiterate and, except for Emina who was fifty-four at the time, unsure of their birth year. At one point in the interview Hamdija mentions that his aunt Đula was about sixty-seven years old, while Ibrahim Hrustanović guessed that his mother Hasnija was about the same age. Of the three, Hasnija was most prolific and produced about 10,000 verses, but Emina's and Đula's statistics are not far behind (Fig. 23.3).

FIG. 23.3. Milman Parry Collection, Image 584: "Đula Dizdarević," Lord, 1933–1935.

Ibrahim Hrustanović, Hamdija Šaković, and Halid Dizdarević not only were reliable collectors instructed not to alter or improve songs but also belonged to the Gacko Muslim community of southern Bosnia and Herzegovina, where they grew up and were thus well received. This opened the door of many traditional homes for them, but even they reported challenges when collecting in the remote villages where they were less known. Parry and Lord met with Ibrahim's family, which was critical for befriending other members of the community, including the local muezzin Salih Zvizdić. It was Zvizdić who made arrangements for a recording session in his house, where it was allowed for women to visit and perform for the foreign researchers (Fig. 23.4). Approximately 250 songs recorded on phonograph disks during these sessions constitute the corpus for the ethnomusicological study *Serbo-Croatian Folk Songs* authored by Bartók and Lord in 1951. In addition, Parry and Lord, assisted by Nikola Vujnović, conducted and recorded interviews with a group of female singers as well as with Ibrahim and Hamdija, capturing invaluable data about their lives and singing, the process of collecting, as well as the social environment in general. Still, when compared to the conversations with the male singers, these interviews were not as comprehensive and probed less into what James Porter calls "singer's epistemics," a reference not only "to the social functions that the singer perceives a particular song to have in the context of performance and use but also, just as crucially, to the complex of meanings that the singer brings to the song in the context of undifferentiated daily life" (1985:190). The singers' own interpretation of the meaning they generate is critical when it comes to our analytical and classifying processes as well as for understanding the contextual frameworks. As Flemming Andersen puts it, "[w]e need to complement our textual studies with observations made by the singers themselves" since "singers themselves distinguish among different types of songs in their repertoires" and, furthermore, "they can provide invaluable information on the meanings and functions of the ballads they sing" (1991:26).

The protocol of recording the materials in two modes, on phonograph disks by foreign scholars and in writing by family members, yielded important insights about the effect of the researcher on the collection process. While the recorded sessions resulted in data pertaining to music, pitch, voice coloration, hesitations, and other metalinguistic details, at the same time it became apparent how the performative act suffered in terms of the length and complexity of the song. At times the women complained that they forgot the song or became confused due to the presence of unfamiliar individuals and strange equipment (Vidan 2003:88). By contrast, the singers felt at ease singing for their kin in the privacy of their homes, which resulted in far fewer truncated performances and songs of overall greater quality but with no audio recordings.[10] In addition, multiple singing sessions (Ibrahim, Hamdija, and Halid gathered songs over a period of several months) produced numerous multiforms, thus allowing for comparative analysis of various performances of the same song by the same singer but also comparisons of multiforms by the singers related through

FIG. 23.4. Milman Parry Collection, Image 720: "Left to right—Hanifa Hrustanović, Mulja Zvizdić, Ziba Zvizdić," Lord, 1933–1935.

family or close contacts in the community. Furthermore, it is possible to trace these songs in the larger corpus of South Slavic materials published by Karadžić, the Matica hrvatska series, as well as materials gathered by later collectors such as Olinko Delorko in the 1950s and 1960s.[11]

Oral Composition and Ballads

The sheer scope of verbal art coming from this one relatively small geographic region makes it possible to recreate a canvas of various patterns including formulas, themes,[12] narrative trajectories, functions, character typologies, mythological elements, and so on. Ultimately, such density of sources enables us to gain a deeper insight into "traditional referentiality," which John M. Foley saw as critical for understanding oral traditional songs. According to him, it "entails the invoking of a context that is enormously larger and more echoic than the text or work itself, that brings the lifeblood of generations of poems and performances to the individual performance or text. Each element in the phraseology or narrative thematics stands not simply for that singular instance but for the plurality and multiformity that are beyond the reach of textualization" (Foley 1991:7). Foley's important contributions, as with many other scholars, were in the area of epic; but his theory is equally valid and applicable to the ballads and, if anything, more readily tested given the number of multiforms, in particular in Herzegovina and southern Dalmatia. As Foley emphasized, members of traditional society almost never had a singular experience of listening to any given song. On the contrary, they were immersed in the environment of traditional singing and internalized a range of patterns with their vast semantic potential. The collective thus generated the meaning on which individual performances rested but also served as a repository of referentiality. For this reason, its members could anticipate certain configurations and follow without trouble even when the singer omitted or mixed up information, conflated or bifurcated narrative units, or produced entirely new narrative combinations. In Foley's words, the meaning of structures is derived "from the natural and inherent associations encoded in them and accessible to the informed audience" (Foley 1991:39). The concepts of multiformity and traditional referentiality are thus correlated in the sense that the latter is constituted through the plurality of the former in the most immediate terms and ultimately through the entire tradition as such. In this sense songs from the Gacko community serve as a unique laboratory which is linked not only to the other balladic but also epic corpora and provides an excellent testing ground for further development of these theories.

In his last book, published posthumously, Lord devoted a chapter to textual stability, variation, and memorization in the ballad (Lord 1995:167–186), in which he differentiates between "remembering" and "memorizing" based on the examples from Francis James Child's collection and Bosnian text 12a and its multiforms (Parry No. 6391a) from his and Bartók's volume (Bartók and Lord 1951). He positions ballads in the middle ground between lyric songs with their pronounced textual stability and epic songs where variance is more evident. By examining a cohort of multiforms he concludes that ballads are characterized by a sense of textuality as the singers are aware of recognizable texts, but songs nonetheless exhibit modulations on the levels of both the verse and thematic units, a sufficient proof that songs are not memorized. Lord thus deduces that ballad singers remembered the songs rather than memorized them (1995:177), but in the unfinished chapter he left us, he did not have a chance to correlate the notions of remembering and creativity. When a larger sample is examined in conjunction with ethnographic data, the evidence emerges that (a) textual stability in ballad oscillates in the manner similar to epics and (b) awareness of extratextual elements is critical in understanding processes of innovation in the ballad. Taking Lord's analysis a step further, I looked into the question of stability of the same theme across genres in two ballads and two epic multiforms to demonstrate how the same thematic unit can be deployed creatively in otherwise dissimilar narratives. The two ballad plots under investigation differed from one another as well as from the epic. Similar to epic singers, stability (not fixity!) of certain themes in ballads becomes more pronounced if frequently employed in songs popular in the repertoire of the same singer (Vidan 2003:22–30). As expected, the same theme is more succinct in its balladic iterations than in its epic versions.

Below are two examples of the same opening theme employed in two entirely different narratives. Hasnija Hrustanović's song (Parry no. 12220) tells a story of a girl who is promised in marriage by her brother to a man she does not love and therefore makes secret arrangements to be stolen by another young man whom she does love. By contrast, the song by Emina Šaković (Parry no. 2460) deals with a wife's infertility, which is eventually overcome but nearly brings the marriage to the brink of collapse.

> U čardaku na visokoj kuli
> svilu tkala materina Duda,
> na čardaku među jastucima
> gledajući naspram pendžerima,
> gledajući kad će dragi doći.
> Tad na vrata sluga Huseine,
> pa đevojci 'vako govorijo:
> "Hanumice, Dudo materina!
> Daj muštuluk da ti nešto kažem."
> "Kaži, Huso, šta je tebi drago,
> ako bude za muštuluk, Huso,
> dobro ću te danas darivati."
>
> (Hasnija Hrustanović, Gacko, 1935)

> In the upper room in the lofty tower
> mother's child Duda wove silk,
> in the upper room amidst pillows,
> and kept glancing toward the windows,
> glancing to see if her beloved was coming.
> Then the servant Husein appeared at the door,
> and thus spoke to the maiden:
> "Little lady Duda, mother's child!
> Give me a reward, I will tell you something."
> "Say, Husein, whatever you wish.
> If it merits a reward, Husein,
> I will give you a lavish gift today."
>
> (Parry no. 12220)

> Vezak vezla u Mostaru Zlata
> na čardaku, na visokoj kuli,
> na čardaku, kraj džamli pendžera.
> Vezak vezla, pjesmu ispjevala
> gdje Alibeg vjernu ljubu kara,
> on je kara što nema evlada.
> To je ljubi vrlo mučno bilo,
> pa izlazi uz bijelu kulu
> i eto je u gornje čardake.
> Ona roni suze od očiju
> i proklinje svoju milu majku:
> "Moja majko, dugo jadna bila!
> Što me dade begu Alibegu
> da me kori i dnevi i noći
> što ja nemam od srca evlada."
>
> (Emina Šaković, Gacko, 1935)

> Zlata sat embroidering in Mostar
> in the upper room, in the lofty tower,
> in the upper room, by the glass window.
> She sat embroidering and sang a song
> about Alibeg scolding her, his faithful wife,
> for she had no child of her own.
> This caused her much grief,
> and she stepped upstairs in the white tower,
> and then she went to the upper rooms.
> She was shedding tears from her eyes
> and cursing her dear mother:
> "My mother, may misfortune befall you!
> Why did you give me to Alibeg
> to scold me every day and night
> because I have no child of my own."
>
> (Parry no. 2460)

Narrative Patterns and Mythological Elements

In addition to smaller units of meaning—formulas, blocks of lines, and thematic units—being shared by all traditional verse genres, instances of the subject matter overlapping in longer narrative songs are not a rarity either. Despite societal divisions in the performative spaces of men and women and different thematic preoccupations overall, some stories reflected universal appeal and, as such, were adopted and adapted by both groups. However, the singers opted to emphasize different aspects of the same basic plot, render it in different amounts of detail, and present a different point of view, ultimately expressing their own fe/male perception of the world. Examples of such songs include the "rescue and wedding" and the "return" categories among the most prominent ones. The former group tells of a hero coming to his imprisoned friend's rescue with the help of the captor's daughter. Among many, the epic performed by a male singer entitled "Hasan of Ribnik Rescues Mustajbey" published in *Serbocroatian Heroic Songs* (Parry and Lord 1953–1954) is a good example. Among female performers from Gacko Stoja Bjeloglav's "Marko Kraljević in the Azap Prison" (Parry no. 2485) stands out, as does Kate Murat's song "The Wedding of Banović Stjepan" (text no. 46 in Murat 1996) recorded on the island of Šipan. Many more examples abound (Vidan 2003:20–22). Stoja's song is 49 decasyllabic verses, Kate Murat's is longer at 403 lines, while the recorded epic multiforms by men oscillate between 700 and 1300 lines. What is important to stress is that in a number of songs by female performers it is the maiden who frees the captive man and marries him afterward, reflecting a moment of agency that the societies in which the singers lived so often denied them.

The plot of the "return song," which in its most basic pattern replicates many elements found in the *Odyssey* (Lord 1962; Lord 1980), consists of the following sequence: absence of the hero, devastation of his home by his competitors, return of the hero, his retribution, and rejoicing. Albeit less frequently encountered than in epics and focusing on the most emotionally charged segments, the story appears also in the ballad corpus of the Milman Parry Collection and is sung by Hasnija Hrustanović (Parry no. 2897; Vidan 2003:222–224). These narratives woven from the collective memory resonate with and reveal mythological schemes which are often entwined with elements not exclusive to the given cultural group, as the previous example clearly demonstrates. "The story in oral tradition is always and by necessity permeated by the myth," emphasized Lord (1959:4), echoing research of earlier scholars such as Natko Nodilo and Vatroslav Jagić and anticipating contributions by Roman Jakobson, Vyacheslav Ivanov, Vladimir Toporov, Vitomir Belaj, Radoslav Katičić, and others, many of whom grounded their theories on the examples from the South Slavic balladic corpus. Of course, not every ballad has a mythological aspect, but sometimes even songs which on the surface deal with human affairs—such as the widespread narrative about incest between a brother and a sister at harvest—reveal more complex relations. In this case the mythological subtext is signaled through a formulaic distich, with the metaphor of lightning indicating the wrath of the principal thunder deity at a moral transgression. Đula Dizdarević and Emina Šaković both performed this song on multiple occasions (Parry nos. 11754, 11724, 1318, 1036), as did several other singers, totaling fifty-three multiforms in the Parry Collection alone (Vidan 2003:65–72, 188–191). It is thus justified to say that, like in epics, in ballads too myth can serve as a unifying principle linking South Slavic ballad to Indo-European tradition.

Organizing a wide range of ballads into neat thematic categories is bound to generate all kinds of problems, in part because even though some songs are characterized by relative textual stability, others do not conform to these patterns and attest to the singers' creative abilities. For instance, songs opening with what looks like the same or a relatable plot, can diverge when the singer introduces new elements or recombines the existing ones into new narrative trajectories. Thus, the plot dealing with "kidnapping of the bride" can be developed in any number of ways and includes segments that deal with the liberation of the bride, wedding of the bride, demise of the bride, and so on. Given how interwoven some of the plotlines are, any classification calls for an open-ended system. Organizing South Slavic ballads along chronological lines that reflect different points in a traditional woman's life provides some insight into the thematic preoccupations of the singers. In the most general terms, several periods are discernible: pre-married life, married life, parenting, and death (anticipation of own death or experiencing that of a family member). The category of pre-married life can further be divided into songs dealing with an unwanted marriage, obstacles to marriage, assault of a maiden, and sibling or parent relationships. Songs focusing on married life unsurprisingly deal with a good or evil husband and a good or evil wife, in/fertility and offspring, various family member interventions, and an evil mother-in-law. The parenting group of songs can typically be divided into songs on good versus evil parents, while songs on death divide along the lines of announcement of demise to different characters. Each category in each principal group has further subdivisions, reflecting an extremely productive thematic paradigm.

Conclusion

In conclusion, developments of the last several decades point to a greater orientation toward examining performative circumstances (drawing on ethnopoetics and an ethnography of speaking) and application of information technology in the study of traditional verbal art. As Foley underscored, the structuralist approach which is at the core of oral formulaic theory had to be balanced with the so-called performance-oriented approach (Bauman and Briggs 1990; Foley 1995). Even though earlier researchers, including Murko, Parry, and Lord, were aware of the relevance of the ethnographic perspective, in the 1970s and early 1980s the emphasis started shifting more radically from textual analysis of oral heritage toward a more inclusive approach that takes into consideration various metalinguistic, cultural, social, historical, and anthropological elements. This change occurred, however, at a time when the majority of oral traditional genres, including the ballad, were in the process of disappearing or had already ceased to exist. For many performances from this part of the world the only record that remains is that of the text. Moreover, uneven collecting and editing practices have rendered some of the texts unusable for certain types of analysis. In other situations where texts have not been edited, the paralinguistic components that accompanied the performances are lost. In yet other scenarios, when materials are recorded, interference from the research protocol is noted. And yet, despite these concerns, due to the vast quantity and quality of the material, the South Slavic ballads that have reached us continually offer new avenues of exploration. Dynamism and multivocality inherent to a living oral tradition are silenced by turning a performance into a single printed text. Foley proposed to further expand the textual analysis by creating electronic editions of epic songs equipped with various layers of information including the singer's biographical data, interviews, recordings and transcripts of the song, and English translations, in addition to performance-based commentaries and explanations of concepts rooted in the culture of traditional singing (Foley 2005:239, 245). While some of these tasks have been accomplished for the epics, projects of this scope pertaining to South Slavic ballads, including searchable databases, are only now entering their final stages.

While some information is irretrievably lost, digital projects will make South Slavic ballads available not only to the researchers but also to the communities from which they originated. Moreover, the existing wealth of material in its modernized iteration has the potential to provide the frameworks for both immersion into the polyphonic landscape of oral song and access to its realms of referentiality through the accompanying scholarly apparatus. This, of course, can never substitute for the experience of listening to the singer composing the ballad in performance in the intimate atmosphere of her home, but it can allow us to hear voices and stories that resonate beyond the world in which they once existed.

Notes

1. I use Albert Lord's notion of "composition in performance," which is essential for understanding the creative aspect of both epic and ballad songs in the South Slavic region. While improvisation implies an impromptu performance whose signification does not draw from the wealth of traditional formulaic patterns and themes, composition in performance suggests that the singer is capable of producing varied iterations of a given song in the moment of performance precisely because their utterance and overall creativity are facilitated by the antecedent tradition. See, in particular, Lord's "Poetics of Oral Creation" (1959:1).
2. The concept of multiform is Lord's. Rather than employing the term "variant," which implies a hierarchical relationship among related songs and existence of the Urform, multiformity signifies their equal status and the fact that the same idea may appear in different iterations. Lord first introduced this concept in his Singer of Tales (1960:120) and elaborated it further in his multiple articles, most notably in The Singer Resumes the Tale, ed. Mary Louise Lord (1995:23).
3. Based on the holdings from the Milman Parry Collection of Oral Literature, Harvard University.
4. The singer in question is Kate Murat née Palunko from the island of Šipan near Dubrovnik, and some of her songs could be considered hybrid cases. What makes this singer particularly interesting is that songs were collected from her by two family members in three different periods: the first batches of approximately two thousand verses were written down by her brother, Vice Palunko, in 1860–1862 and 1869–1871 (Matica hrvatska ms. 139). The third collecting was done by her son Andro Murat in 1884–1885, at which time almost sixteen

thousand lines were written down and eventually published in Murat, *Narodne pjesme iz Luke na Šipanu* (1996). Both collectors left detailed notes about their editorial polices. The example of Kate Murat provided an exceptional opportunity for a comparative study of the output of a nineteenth-century female singer, in particular with regard to the development of her singing abilities and the question of multiforms by the same performer.

5. Parry's principal works were published posthumously in *The Making of Homeric Verse: The Collected Papers of Milman Parry* in 1971, while Lord's seminal *Singer of Tales* came out in 1960. Neither, however, addresses the question of ballads in depth. Lord's later book *The Singer Resumes the Tale* (1995) devotes a chapter to oral traditional lyric poetry in which he provides a comparative analysis of South Slavic lyric songs and Latvian *dainas* and includes an unfinished chapter on textual stability in the ballad. His 1951 volume co-authored with Béla Bartók is an ethnomusicological study of South Slavic shorter genres (Bartók and Lord 1951).

6. To mention only the pinnacle epic works of the Baroque, the Enlightenment, and the nineteenth-century National Revival period which directly draw from oral traditional poetics and focus on historical developments, especially the centuries-long Ottoman advancements in the region, Ivan Gundulić's octosyllabic *Osman* (ca. 1626, oldest extant copy ca. 1651), Andrija Kačić Miošić's decasyllabic historical account *Razgovor ugodni naroda slovinskog* (*Pleasant Conversation of Slavic People*, 1756), Ivan Mažuranić's *Smrt Smail-age Čengića* (*The Death of Smail-aga Čengić*, 1846), and Petar Petrović Njegoš's *Gorski vijenac* (*The Mountain Wreath*, 1847).

7. In the 1891–1898 edition the volumes containing ballads are nos. 1 and 5. In the 1969 series edited by Vladan Nedić ballads are mostly included in vol. 1.

8. The Kosovo battle was in 1389; the Serbian dynasty of Nemanjići ruled from the mid-twelfth century to the second half of the fourteenth. Andrić similarly speculates that women's songs may be older and considers a possibility that "our heroic men's songs evolved from women's songs" (1996:623).

9. Šipan is an island in the vicinity of Dubrovnik. For more details on Kate Murat, see note 4.

10. This further confirms Bauman's and Briggs's theory mentioned above about researchers' interference with their sources.

11. Delorko's principal publications are *Hrvatske narodne balade i romance* (*Croatian Folk Ballads and Romances*, 1951) and *Ljuba Ivanova. Hrvatske starinske narodne pjesme sakupljene u naše dane po Dalmaciji* (*Ljuba Ivanova. Croatian Old-time Folk Songs Collected in Our Times in Dalmatia*, 1969), but his eighteen manuscripts contain 2,365 songs (held in the Institut za etnologiju i folkloristiku in Zagreb/Institute of Ethnology and Folklore). His fieldnotes, biographical data on singers, song summaries, observations on influences, popularity, and concordances of songs with other sources are of great interest.

12. I rely on Lord's definition of "theme" as "groups of ideas regularly used in telling a tale in the formulaic style of traditional song" (Lord 1960:68).

13. A lengthy scholarly debate concerns the terms *nozve* and *bešice*, as well as translation choices for a number of other lexical items. These include not only the usual problems of versification, rhythmic patterns, semantic realm, figures of speech, register, cultural connotations, and various subcutaneous resonances, but also issues stemming from Fortis's imperfect orthography which captured only approximately the singer's pronunciation and resulted in various ambiguities. Although some scholars argue for interpretation of *nozve* as "knives," I lean here to understanding it as "slippers" (from *nazuti*), in particular since -ž in *noževi* ("knives") is not marked with -x, the letter Fortis

systematically employs for this phoneme. On the other hand, *uboske*, later transliterated as *uboške*, is likely an error standing for *u bošči* (from Turkish *bohça*, "bundle"), rather than *ubog* ("poor") and resulting in "pauper/orphan clothes." The mother gives caring gifts of fine clothes/footwear to all her children, including the youngest, and in my view, similarly does not make a gendered choice giving knives to the older boys and clothes to the girls. Finally, for the epithet *rđavskoga*, referring to mother's heart in the final segment Fortis originally had *argiaskoga* from Turkish *agr* ("powerful," "haughty," "arrogant"), which is translated here figuratively. For a detailed treatment of translation issues in *Asanaginica*, see Arnautović (2021).

14. I am grateful to Ellen Elias Bursać for her comments and suggestions. The disparity in the name of the principal character H/Asanaginica (the wife of H/Asan aga) is due to a variance in regional spelling and pronunciation. Fortis's first rendition is entitled "Xalostna pjesanza plemenite Asan-aghinize," wherein he partly employs Italian orthography for the local language.

Works Cited

Amodio, Mark C. 2020. "Introduction: The Pathway(s) from Oral-formulaic Theory to Contemporary Oral Theory." In *John Miles Foley's World of Oralities. Text, Tradition, and Contemporary Oral Theory*, ed. Mark C. Amodio, 1–12. Leeds: Arc Humanities Press.

Andersen, Flemming G. 1991. "Technique, Text, and Context: Formulaic Narrative Mode and the Question of Genre." In *The Ballad and Oral Literature*, ed. Joseph Harris, 18–39. Cambridge, MA: Harvard University Press.

Andrić, Nikola, ed. 1909. *Hrvatske narodne pjesme*. Vol. 5, Ženske pjesme. Romance i balade. Zagreb: Matica hrvatska.

Andrić, Nikola, ed. 1914. *Hrvatske narodne pjesme*. Vol. 6, Ženske pjesme. Pričalice i lakrdije. Zagreb: Matica hrvatska.

Andrić, Nikola, ed. 1929. *Hrvatske narodne pjesme*. Vol. 7, Ženske pjesme. Ljubavne pjesme. Zagreb: Matica hrvatska.

Andrić, Nikola, ed. 1942. *Hrvatske narodne pjesme*. Vol. 10, Haremske pričalice i bunjevačke groktalice. Zagreb: Matica hrvatska.

Andrić, Nikola. 1996. "Andro Murat. Prilog člancima 'Sabirači matičinih hrvatskih narodnih pjesama.'" In *Narodne pjesme iz Luke na Šipanu*, coll. Andro Murat, ed. Tanja Perić-Polonijo, 623–632. Zagreb: Matica hrvatska.

Arnautović, Armina. 2021. "Through Linguo-stylistic Analysis to a New Retranslation of the Ballad 'Hasanaginica.'" *ExELL (Explorations in English Language and Linguistics)*, 9/2:143–183.

Bartók, Béla, and Albert B. Lord. 1951. *Serbo-Croatian Folk Songs*. New York: Columbia University Press.

Bauman, Richard, and Charles L. Briggs. 1990. "Poetics and Performance as Critical Perspectives on Language and Social Life." *Annual Review of Anthropology*, 19:59–88.

Bošković-Stulli, Maja. 1991. "Balladic Forms of the Bugarštica and Epic Songs." *Oral Tradition*, 6/2–3:225–238. First published 1988 in Croatian in *Forum*, 5–6:501–511.

Delorko, Olinko. 1951. *Hrvatske narodne balade i romance*. Zagreb: Zora.

Delorko, Olinko. 1969. *Ljuba Ivanova. Hrvatske starinske narodne pjesme sakupljene u naše dane po Dalmaciji*. Split: Matica hrvatska.

Dundes, Alan. 1989. "The Building of Skadar: The Measure of Meaning of a Ballad of the Balkans." In his *Folklore Matters*, 151–168. Knoxville, TN: University of Tennessee Press.

Dundes, Alan. 1995. "How Indic Parallels to the Ballad of the "Walled-up Wife" Reveal the Pitfalls of Parochial Nationalistic Folkloristics." *The Journal of American Folklore*, 108/427:38–53.

Erlangenski rukopis. 2022. *Hrvatska enciklopedija*. Mrežno izdanje. Leksikografski zavod Miroslav Krleža, 2021. http://www.enciklopedija.hr/Natuknica.aspx?ID=18295. Accessed July 16, 2022.

Foley, John Miles. 1991. *Immanent Art. From Structure to Meaning in Traditional Oral Epic*. Bloomington, IN: Indiana University Press.

Foley, John Miles. 1995. *The Singer of Tales in Performance*. Bloomington, IN: Indiana University Press.

Foley, John Miles. 2005. "From Oral Performance to Paper—Text to Cyber-Edition." *Oral Tradition* 20/2:233–263.

Fortis, Alberto. 2004. *Put po Dalmaciji*. Split: Marjan tisak.

Gesemann, Gerhard. 1925. *Erlangenski rukopis starih srpskohrvatskih narodnih pesama*, Vol. XII, Zbornik za istoriju, jezik i književnost srpskog Naroda. Sr. Karlovci: Srpska kraljevska akademija.

Glavić, Baldo Melkov, coll. and ed. 1889. *Narodne pjesme, iz usta i rukopisa*. Dubrovnik: D. Pretner.

Goethe, Johann Wolfgang. 1987. *Sämtliche Werke*. Vol. 1: *Gedichte 1756–1799*, ed. Karl Eibl. Frankfurt am Main: Deutscher Klassiker Verlag.

Hektorović, Petar. 1997. *Ribanje i ribarsko prigovaranje/Fishing and Fishermen's Conversation*, trans. Edward D. Goy. Stari Grad: Centar za kulturu.

Herder, Johann Gottfried. 1990. *Werke in zehn Bänden*. Vol. 3: *Volkslieder. Übertragungen. Dichtungen*, ed. Ulrich Gaier. Frankfurt am Main: Deutscher Klassiker Verlag.

Jurić, Dorian. 2020. "Back in the Foundation. Chauvinistic Scholarship and the Building Sacrifice Story-Pattern." *Oral Tradition*, 34:3–44.

Karadžić, Vuk S., coll. and ed. 1969. *Srpske narodne pjesme*, Vols. 1–4, ed. Vladan Nedić. Belgrade: Prosveta.

Kropej, Monika. 2013. "The Cooperation of Grimm Brothers, Jernej Kopitar and Vuk Karadžić." *Studia Mythologica Slavica*, 16:215–231.

Lord, Albert B. 1959. "The Poetics of Oral Creation." In *Comparative Literature. Proceedings of the Second Congress of the International Comparative Literature Association*, Vol. 1, ed. Werner P. Friederich, 1–6. Chapel Hill, NC: University of North Carolina Press.

Lord, Albert B. 1960. *The Singer of Tales*. Cambridge, MA: Harvard University Press.

Lord, Albert B. 1962. "Homeric Echoes in Bihać." *Zbornik za narodni život i običaje južnih Slavena*, 40:313–320.

Lord, Albert B. 1968. "Homer as Oral Poet." *Harvard Studies in Classical Philology*, 72:1–46.

Lord, Albert B. 1980. "The Mythic Component in Oral Traditional Epic: Its Origins and Significance." In *Classical Mythology in Twentieth-Century Thought and Literature*, eds. Wendell M. Aycock and Theodore M. Klein, 145–161. Lubbock, TX: Texas Tech Press.

Lord, Albert B. 1987. "The Nature of Oral Poetry." In *Comparative Research on Oral Traditions: A Memorial for Milman Parry*, ed. John Miles Foley, 313–349. Columbus, OH: Slavica.

Lord, Albert B. 1995. *The Singer Resumes the Tale*, ed. Mary Louise Lord. Ithaca, NY: Cornell University Press.

Medenica, Radoslav, and Dobrilo Aranitović, eds. 1987. *Erlangenski rukopis. Zbornik starih srpskohrvatskih narodnih pesama*. Nikšić: Univerzitetska riječ.

Murat, Andro, coll. 1996. *Narodne pjesme iz Luke na Šipanu*, ed. Tanja Perić-Polonijo. Zagreb: Matica hrvatska.

Murko, Matija. 1951. *Tragom srpsko-hrvatske narodne epike. Putovanja u godinama 1930–1932*. Zagreb: Jugoslavenska akademija znanosti i umjetnosti.

Murko, Matija. 1990. "The Singers and Their Epic Songs." In *Oral Formulaic Theory. A Folklore Casebook*, trans. and ed. John M. Foley, 3–30. New York: Garland. First published 1929 as *La Poésie populaire épique en Yougoslavie au début du XXe siècle*. Paris: L'Institut d'études slaves.

Nagy, Gregory. 2020. "Orality and Literacy Revisited." In *John Miles Foley's World of Oralities. Text, Tradition, and Contemporary Oral Theory*, ed. Mark C. Amodio, 17–22. Leeds: Arc Humanities Press.

Parry, Milman, coll., and Albert B. Lord, ed. 1953–1954. *Serbocroatian Heroic Songs*, Vol. 1: Novi Pazar: English Translations; Vol. 2: Novi Pazar: Serbo-Croatian Text. Belgrade: Srpska akademija nauka; Cambridge, MA: Harvard University Press.

Parry, Milman. 1971. "Ćor Huso: A Study of Southslavic Song." In his *The Making of Homeric Verse: The Collected Papers of Milman Parry*, ed. Adam Parry, 437–464. Oxford: Clarendon Press.

Porter, James. 1985. "Problems of Ballad Terminology: Scholars' Explanations and Singers' Epistemics." In *Ballad Research. The Stranger in Ballad Narrative and Other Topics*, ed. Hugh Shields, 185–194. Dublin: Folk Music Society of Ireland.

Tate, Aaron Phillip. 2011. "Matija Murko, Wilhelm Radloff, and Oral Epic Studies." *Oral Tradition*, 26/2:329–352.

Uther, Hans-Jörg, Antti Aarne, and Stith Thompson. 2004. *The Types of International Folktales. A Classification and Bibliography: Based on the System of Antti Aarne and Stith Thompson. Part I: Animal Tales, Tales of Magic, Religious Tales, and Realistic Tales, with an Introduction*. FF Communications 284. Helsinki: Suomalainen Tiedeakatemia, Academia Scientiarum Fennica.

Vidan, Aida. 2003. *Embroidered with Gold, Strung with Pearls: The Traditional Ballads of Bosnian Women*. Cambridge, MA: The Milman Parry Collection of Oral Literature and Harvard University Press.

Vidan, Aida. 2024. "Držić's Magician and Lucić's Captive Maiden: Oral Sources and the Croatian Renaissance Drama." In *Singers and Tales in the 21st Century*, eds. David F. Elmer and Peter McMurray, 307–325. Cambridge, MA: The Milman Parry Collection of Oral Literature and Harvard University Press.

Vidan, Aida. 2025. "The South-Slavic Serpent-Groom Ballad: A Myth of Rebirth." In *Dragons Ancient, Medieval, and Modern*, ed. Joseph F. Nagy, in press. Chicago: Brepols; Los Angeles: UCLA Center for Medieval and Renaissance Studies.

Ziolkowski, Jan M. 2010. "Straparola and the Fairy Tale: Between Literary and Oral Traditions." *The Journal of American Folklore*, 123/490:377–397.

APPENDIX

Asanaginica

Što se b'jeli u gorje zelenoj?	What glistens white in the green highlands?
Al' su sn'jezi, al' su labutove?	Is it traces of snow or is it flocks of swans?
Da su sn'jezi, već bi okopnuli,	If snow, it would have long since melted
labutove već bi poletjeli:	swans would have long since flown away:
Ni su sn'jezi, ni su labutove,	It is neither snow nor is it swans,
nego šator age Asan-age.	but it is the tent of agha Asan-agha.
On boluje u ranami ljutimi,	He lies suffering of fierce wounds,
oblazi ga mati i sestrica,	his mother came to see him, his sister too
a ljubovca od stida ne mogla.	but his beloved could not for the shame.
Kad li mu je ranam' bolje bilo,	When his wounds were partly healed
ter poruča vjernoj ljubi svojoj:	he sent word to his faithful beloved:
"Ne čekaj me u dvoru b'jelomu,	"Wait not for me in my white manor,
ni u dvoru, ni u rodu momu."	neither in my manor, nor among my kin."
Kad kaduna r'ječi razumjela,	When the lady understood the words
još je jadna u toj misli stala,	misery halted her in her thoughts,
jeka stade konja oko dvora;	there sounded horses by the manor
i pobježe Asanaginica	and in haste Asanaginica took flight,
da vrat lomi kule niz pendžere.	in neck-break haste, her turret's windows past.
Za njom trču dve ćere djevojke:	Her two girl daughters came running after
"Vrati nam se, mila majko naša!	"Come back to us, our beloved mother!
Nije ovo babo Asan-ago,	Here's not our father Asan-agha,
već daidža, Pintorović beže!"	rather Pintorović bey, our uncle!"
I vrati se Asanaginica,	And thus returned Asanaginica,
ter se vješa bratu oko vrata.	she hurled herself around her brother's neck.
"Da, moj brate, velike sramote,	"Oh, my brother, what a grievous dishonor,
gdi me šalje od petero dice!"	for him to banish me from my five children!"
Beže muči, ne govori ništa,	The bey stood silent, uttered not a word,
već se maša u džepe svione,	but he reached in his silken pockets
i vadi joj knjigu oprošćenja,	and took out the letter of annulment
da uzimlje potpuno vjenčanje,	asking her to collect her dower,
da gre s njime majci u zatrage.	and with it return to her mother.
Kad kaduna knjigu proučila,	When the lady looked over the letter
dva je sina u čelo ljubila,	she kissed her two sons on their brows
a dve ćere u rumena lica,	and her two daughters on their rosy cheeks,
a s malahnim u bešice sinkom,	yet from her tiny son in the cradle
od'jeliti nikako ne mogla,	part she could not by any means,
već je bratac za ruke uzeo,	but her brother took her by her hands
i jedva je (s) sinkom rastavio,	hardly able to tear her from the little one,

ter je meće k sebi na konjica,	and mounted her beside him on his horse,
s njome grede u dvoru b'jelomu.	with her to the white manor he set off.
U rodu je malo vr'jeme stala,	She stayed for a short time among her kin,
Malo vr'jeme, ne nedjelju dana,	a short time, not even a week,
dobra kado i od roda dobra	a good lady from a good family,
dobru kadu prose sa svi strana,	a good lady sought after from all sides,
da najveće Imoski kadija.	most ardently by the Imotski judge.
Kaduna se bratu svomu moli:	The lady begged her dear brother:
"Aj, tako te ne želila, braco,	"Oh brother, let me not long for you,
nemoj mene davat' za nikoga,	do not marry me off to anyone
da ne puca jadno srce moje,	lest my poor heart burst
gledajući sirotice svoje!"	at the sight of my little orphans!"
Ali beže ne hajaše ništa,	But the bey paid no heed
već nju daje Imoskomu kadiji.	and he gave her to the Imotski judge.
Još kaduna bratu se moljaše,	Yet again the lady begged her brother
da njoj piše listak, b'jele knjige,	for a white letter to write in her stead
da je šalje Imoskom kadiji:	and to send it to the Imotski judge:
"Djevojka te l'jepo pozdravljaše,	"The maiden sends you her kind greetings
a u knjizi l'jepo te moljaše:	and in her letter she kindly begs you:
kad pokupiš gospodu svatove,	once you gather the noble guests together,
dug podkljuvac nosi na djevojku;	that you bring a long veil for the maiden,
kada bude agi mimo dvora,	when she passes by the agha's manor
nek ne vidi sirotice svoje!"	that she see not her little orphans!"
Kad kadiji b'jela knjiga dođe,	When the judge received the white letter
gospodu je svate pokupio,	he gathered the noble guests together,
svate kupi, grede po djevojku.	gathered the guests, went for the maiden.
Dobro svati došli do djevojke	The guests merrily reached the maiden's
i zdravo se povratili s njome.	and in a good spirit set off back with her.
A kad bili agi mimo dvora,	But as they passed by the agha's manor
dve je ćerce s pendžera gledahu,	the two daughters watched her from the window
a dva sina prid nju izhođahu	and the two sons ran out to meet her
tere svojoj majci govorjahu:	and thus they spoke to their mother:
"Vrati nam se, mila majko naša,	"Come back to us, beloved mother,
da mi tebe užinati damo!"	let us make for you a light supper!"
Kad to čula Asanaginica,	When Asanaginica heard these words
starišini svatov govorila:	she said to the wedding party elder:
"Bogom brate, svatov starišina,	"By God, brother, wedding party elder,
ustavi mi konje uza dvora,	have my horses stop by the manor
da darujem sirotice moje!"	so I can give gifts to my little orphans!"
Ustaviše konje uza dvora,	They had the horses stop by the manor,
Svoju dicu l'jepo darovala:	she gave fine gifts to her children:
svakom sinku nozve pozlaćene,	to each son gold-embroidered slippers,

svakoj ćeri čohu do poljane
a malomu u bešice sinku,[13]
njemu šalje uboške haljine.
A to gleda junak Asan-ago
ter dozivlje do dva sina svoja:
"Hod'te amo, sirotice moje,
kad se neće milovati na vas,
majka vaša srca rđavskoga!"
Kad to čula Asanaginica,
b'jelim licem u zemlju udarila,
uput se je s dušom rastavila,
od žalosti, gledajuć sirote!

to each daughter broadcloth to the ground
and for the tiny son in the cradle,
for him she sent clothes in a bundle.
All along hero Asan-agha watched this
then he called out to his two sons:
"Come on here, my little orphans,
since no pity there is for you,
in your mother's heart of stone!"
Upon hearing this Asanaginica
with her white face struck the ground,
in a flash she parted with her soul
out of sorrow, gazing upon her orphans.

(Unknown singer; Fortis 2004:65–69; translated by Aida Vidan[14])

Prose: Folktale and Legend

CHAPTER 24

FOLK TALES IN GREECE

MARIA KALIAMBOU

THE modern Greek term for folk tale, παραμύθι (*paramýthi*), has a history as long as the genre itself. In ancient Greek the word *paramýthi* derives from the verb παραμυθέομαι (*paramythéomai*), observed first in Homer and later in Herodotus and Plato, meaning to give advice or offer consolation and comfort. Plato uses the terms τιτθών μύθοι (*titthon mythoi*, stories by nursing women) and γραών ύθλοι (*graon ythloi*, stories by old women), commonly referred to in English as "old wives' tales," which pejoratively evaluates stories narrated by old women such as grandmothers, mothers, or nurses as unreliable. The meaning of *paramýthi* has changed over time and reflects various theoretical and methodological debates. It began to mean "fantastic story" in medieval times and became interchangeable with the word "myth" (a narrative in the sacred realm that is believed in). The etymology of the term demonstrates the blending of two major genres of oral literature: myths and folk tales (*para* + *myth*[*i*], meaning next to the myth). The term itself implies an intergeneric dialogue between tales and myths and, thus, complicates the definition of the genre folk tale. Today the term *paramýthi* is associated with folk tales and mostly stories for children. In colloquial speech, it means an untrue story—such as in "Don't tell me tales!" In other words, the Greek term for folk tales alludes to fundamental issues that occupy folk tale scholarship: the function of the tales (consolation), the narrators (old women), the quality of the narratives (untrustworthy, fantastic stories), and their generic characteristics (close relationship to myths). All of these topics will be addressed to greater or lesser degrees in this chapter. In the final analysis, however, naming a genre in oral tradition creates controversy for scholars, whereas for narrators the terminology is insignificant.

COLLECTORS AND SCHOLARS

Foreign Fascination

As in the other southeast European cultural traditions, western European scholars and travelers were the first who collected, translated, and published folklore genres in Greece. In the late eighteenth century, European travelers, fascinated by Greece and its perceived exoticism, were the first to attempt a collection of folk material. The French traveler and writer Pierre Augustin Guys was "one of the first fieldworkers" (Papachristophorou 2016:427) who documented Greek folk culture in 1783 in his correspondence, including among his records some stories told by women.[1] In 1843 Jean Alexandre Buchon, another French traveler, published three folk tales in his travelogue (pp. 261–280).[2] The same year, a Greek of the diaspora, Georgios Eulampios, issued, in Saint Petersburg, a collection of Greek folksongs and the magic tale "Water of Life" (ATU 551[3]) in Greek and Russian along with some information regarding its performance (Eulampios 1843; Hatzitaki-Kapsomenou 2002:97–98).

Scholarship about Greek folk tales began later in the second half of the nineteenth century with Johann Georg von Hahn, the Austrian consul in Greece, who published in 1864 a collection of Greek and Albanian folk tales in Leipzig (Grimm 1990). Because Hahn did not know Greek and therefore could not speak to the original sources, he asked students from local schools to collect material which he later translated into German without paying special attention to the linguistic aspects of the original stories. He aimed to establish a categorization system to organize and catalogue the material. Indeed, his collection comprises "the first attempt" (Thompson 1946:414)[4] in folk tale scholarship to create an international tale-type catalogue, a predecessor of the ATU. Hahn's collection, which due to its German translation had little influence in Greece itself, nonetheless began the tradition of folk tale scholarship concerning Greece.

In 1879, the Danish classicist Jean Pio published a collection of Greek tales, based on the manuscripts of Hahn and his own material, in Copenhagen. In the preface (written in French) Pio emphasizes his passion for the Greek language and his strong desire to save the "rich treasure" of the folk tales. Pio was a linguist who was deeply interested in the idiomatic aspects of the folk material; thus, in contrast with Hahn, he tried to preserve the character of the language. Pio's collection is a wonderful example of an interlinguistic play: a Danish scholar writes a preface in French, but the main volume is in dialectal Greek. In his preface he explains that for part of his material he "made undergo real examinations" two locals who told him the stories to make sure his spoken dialect was correct (iii–xi, here x).

Other foreign scholars in the nineteenth and early twentieth centuries wanted to prove the continuity of literature from ancient until modern times and study the linguistic purity of oral material. Classicist Bernard Schmidt wished to find ancient mythological themes in modern Greek narratives (Meraklis 1993:74), whereas linguists Carl Dieterich and Paul Kretschmer and literature scholars Émile Legrand and Louis Roussel investigated the linguistic "treasures" hidden in folk tales.

It was not until the beginning of the twentieth century that the British scholar Richard McGillivray Dawkins (1871–1955) established folk tale scholarship about Greece (Hatzitaki-Kapsomenou 2002:140). His major contribution was to move away from the ideological trap of continuity. Dawkins critiqued previous scholars who had searched for ancient remnants in modern Greek stories by arguing that their endeavors were methodologically difficult to prove and distracted from the independent value of modern Greek narratives. He instead lays out a comparative approach in his four significant collections of folk tales, where he compares Greek versions with stories from other cultural traditions (1916, 1950, 1953, 1955). He provides an extensive list of the variants of each folk tale and then translates the one most interesting to him. Dawkins aimed to show the concrete local characteristics of the folk tales and to embed them in their historical circumstances. Moreover, he was interested in the narrators themselves as well as the performative aspects of the stories. Dawkins's contribution to Greek folk tale and folklore is unsurpassed. Rightly, Robert Georges named Dawkins "one of the giants of the century in the field of folktale scholarship" (1965:212).

Greek Scholarship

Folk tales became an object of academic inquiry to Greek scholars when folklore as a discipline emerged in Greece at the end of the nineteenth and beginning of the twentieth centuries. Influenced by the historical, political, social, and theoretical movements in central and western Europe, Greek scholarship echoed the romantic zeitgeist of the time in searching for "authentic" national traits in oral literature. Nikolaos G. Politis (1852–1921), known as the father of Greek folklore, was the first to systematically collect, categorize, and analyze oral literature. Politis was a charismatic and informed scholar (Puchner 2002) whose work remains important for many disciplines (folklore, anthropology, literature, linguistics, history).[5] In dialogue with his European colleagues, especially those of German romanticism and English evolutionism, Politis paid attention to the relics of folk culture in order to prove Greece's connection with its ancient past. He had been interested in folk tales from an early age—he published his first article at the age of fifteen, wrote several commentaries on collections of Greek folk tales, translated foreign tales (one by Hans Christian Andersen) into Greek, and initiated national competitions to collect oral material. In 1909, Politis baptized all genres of oral literature μνημεία του λόγου (monuments of speech) and placed folk tales first in his canon.[6] Influenced by the Grimm brothers' collection with annotations by Johannes Bolte and Jiří Polívka,[7] Politis compiled a catalogue of folk tales (still an unpublished manuscript to this day) accompanied by substantive comparative materials from many cultural traditions around the world (Kaliambou 2012). His attempt to systematize these materials would pave the way for his successors.

Georgios Megas (1893–1976), student of Politis and later professor at the University of Athens, followed the steps of his mentor, contributing to folk tale scholarship by initiating collections and publishing folk tales in journals. In his capacity as professor, between the years 1957 and 1963 he tasked his students with collecting folk tales from their places of origin. Through them he collected more than four thousand folk tales. The collection, which resides at the University of Athens and the Folklore Society of Greece, continues to be enriched with published and unpublished material, exceeding 23,000 texts as of 2012 (Megas 1978:ix; Megas et al. 2012:13). Additionally, Megas understood the necessity of creating a folk tale catalogue; therefore, working from the international catalogue by Aarne-Thompson (the AT Tale-Type Index that preceded the ATU), he compiled the first volume of animal tales—published in 1978, two years after his death.

A group of scholars spearheaded by Anna Angelopoulou (together with Aigli Brouskou, Marianthi Kaplanoglou, and Emmamouela Katrinaki) continued Megas's work on cataloguing Greek folk tales and between 1994 and 2007 published five volumes of magic tales (Angelopoulou and Brouskou 1994, 1999; Angelopoulou et al. 2004, 2007). In 2012, Folklore Fellows Communications by the Finnish Academy published a one-volume catalogue of Greek magic tales in English, an honor and important step to the internationalization of the Greek folk tale. The editors followed the method of the French cataloguers Paul Delarue and Marie Louise Tenèze, which includes "number, title, synthesis of versions, number of versions per geographical region, and the translated versions and commentary" (Megas et al. 2012:17).

Along with the projects of cataloguing and archiving, Greek folk tale scholarship was pursued with renewed interest and efforts in the late twentieth and early twenty-first centuries. Professor of folkloristics Michalis Meraklis (b. 1932) carried out research on folk tales by bringing "the biology of the tale" into discussion, namely the embeddedness of the stories in their social and historical environments, which often reveals the stories' local idiosyncracies (Avdikos 1994:135). Teaching folk tales and folklore at the university level and producing new doctoral dissertations and research projects are crucial for continued interest in folk tales. Although autonomous folklore departments do not exist in Greece, courses on folk tales are taught in departments of literature and language, history and archaeology, and ethnology. Also, departments of education for preschool and elementary students teach folk tales with an emphasis on the applied aspect of the material for educational purposes.

Fruitful avenues for future scholarship on Greek folk tale include interdisciplinary dialogue with a broad spectrum of discourses including comparative literature, gender studies, diaspora studies, disabilities studies, film studies, creative writing, music, visual culture, and more. Modern Greek folk tale scholarship would be further enriched by considering the expanding universe of stories through translations as well as the possibilities in digital humanities for folk tale analysis (Haase 2016).

History of the Greek Folk Tale

The history of the Greek folk tale runs parallel to the history of Greek literature. The Greek folk tale has evolved over centuries, built on two pillars: a long oral and written autochthonous literary tradition coupled with influences from continuous cultural exchanges with neighboring peoples. The central question in folk tale research, about the beginning of the genre, carries special weight given the long Greek history. The Greek folk tale is inevitably linked with antiquity. Three entire tales have survived from antiquity through ancient literary texts: the tale of Meleager (ATU 1187: Meleager, catalogued as a "tale of the stupid ogre"), the tale of Cupid and Psyche (ATU 425B: The Search for the Lost Husband), and the tale of Polyidus (ATU 612: The Three Snake Leaves), the latter two of which are magic tales. Additionally, several isolated motifs and episodes can be traced back to ancient literature, such as in the Homeric epics (ATU 410: Sleeping Beauty, ATU 753: Christ and the Smith, ATU 974: The Homecoming Husband, ATU 1137: Blinded Ogre, Polyphemus), Herodotus's *History* (ATU 736A: Polykrates's Ring, ATU 950: Rhampsinitus, ATU 985: Brother Rescued), drama, Hesiod's *Theogony*, Aesop's fables, Apuleius's *Metamorphoses* (ATU 425: The Search for the Lost Husband), and Apollodorus's *Library* (Papachristophorou 2016:426; Kakridis 1978:55–66).

Recent scholarship has highlighted some new findings: the motif of the friendship between two men, with one dying for the other (ATU 516: Faithful John, ATU 516C: Amicus and Amelius, two variants of a magic tale) passed from antiquity through the Middle Ages and then into modern literature (Classen 2006). Additionally, two ancient Greek narratives of miraculous healings ascribed to Asclepius, the god of medicine, are related to the "religious" folk tale ATU 753A: Unsuccessful Repetition (Bernao Fariñas 2015). A fable tradition was also known in antiquity. In particular Aristophanes, as a connoisseur fabulist, included fables in his comedies in the Aesopic style of speaking animals (such as the entire play *Birds*). In his comedy *Peace* Aristophanes uses "an extended version of an Aesopic fable with Trygaios flight to heaven on the dung beetle" (Pertsinidis 2009:209). Aesop's fables have enriched the modern Greek oral tradition, and some are included in the catalogue of animal tales (ATU 64: Torn-off Tails, ATU 279*: Snake Trying to Surround Crab Refuses to Straighten Himself, ATU 122C: The Sheep Persuades the Wolf to Sing).

Information about folk tales and their narration in the Byzantine period remains a research desideratum. Politis (1911–1912) believed that oral genres (proverbs, myths, and legends) circulated in Byzantium, and he traces folk tale motifs in Byzantine texts. The story of the personified dragon who holds the water from the village, abducts girls, and forces the princess to marry him (ATU 300: The Dragon Slayer) is mentioned in Byzantine sources (Meraklis 1979). The oldest known version of the type ATU 1525E (Thieves Steal from One Another), catalogued in "anecdotes and jokes," is found in two Greek texts of the fifteenth and sixteenth centuries before it developed in variants from other Balkan cultural traditions and the Caucasus, specifically Georgia, demonstrating, therefore, the Byzantine cultural heritage of these areas (Braccini 2021). The medieval novel Καλλίμαχος και Χρυσορρόη (*Kallimachos and Chrysorroi*), saved in an anonymous manuscript of the first half of the fifteenth century, abounds with folk tale motifs (such as a golden castle, magic objects, an apple causing magical sleep, resurrection after removal of the poisonous apple, abduction by a beast, and many more) and episodes where the magic abilities of the heroes belong to folk tales (Polemis 2021:39–50).

Greece's connections with oriental cultures are known from antiquity: tales and motifs from Egyptian and Hebrew cultures were documented by Herodotus and Homer. Also, versions of the Arabic *Pañcatantra* are translated into the Byzantine text Στεφανίτης και Ιχνηλάτης (*Stephanites and Ichnelates*) translated at the end of the eleventh century by Symeon Seth, who intentionally shortened the text to adjust it to the Byzantine reader's preference and infused it with Byzantine cultural references and moralizing messages which reflect the didactic tone of the original (Hölzlhammer 2020).

During the almost four hundred-year stretch of Ottoman occupation (1453–1821), Ottoman cultural elements were likewise introduced into the Greek repertoire of traditional narrative. Oral exchanges with Turkish material were influential to the development of the folk tale genre in Greece. For instance, "specific folktale characters, such as the bey, the kadi, the terrifying Arab, and even the Hodjas" testify to the oral exchanges between the two cultures (Papachristophorou 2016:427). Other genres of oral literature, such as the shadow theater of Karagöz, were also imported by the Ottoman Turks and widely disseminated in Greece (Chatzipantazis 2021). The *Arabian Nights* was introduced to Greek audiences through oral transmission before the Greek translation in the eighteenth century by way of western European chain translations or frame tales (Papachristophorou 2004:311).

Western European influences in Greek oral and written tradition have been visible since medieval times, during the Crusades and the Frankish and Venetian occupations of Greek territories. After the catalytic intervention of western Europeans in the Greek Revolution of 1821—which enabled the establishment of the Greek state in 1830—European magic tales entered the Greek tradition through translations. They circulated either as expensive publications for the affluent or in the form of cheap booklets widely disseminated among audiences of children (Kaliambou 2006). Moreover, since the middle of the nineteenth century children's magazines[8] and schoolbooks have included translated stories from European traditions. All the above media offered tales by the best-known compilers, collectors, editors, and authors of European tales, both oral and literary: Charles Perrault, the Brothers Grimm, and Hans Christian Andersen, among others (Fig. 24.1).

CHARACTERISTICS: STYLE AND CONTENT

The Greek folk tale tradition includes all of the tale types classified in the international ATU catalogue: animal, magic, religious, and realistic tales; tales of the stupid ogre; anecdotes and jokes (jocular tales); and formula (or chain) tales. Indeed, Greek folk tales possess stylistic and aesthetic elements of the European folk tale as described by Max Lüthi (1982), such as one-dimensionality, depthlessness, abstract style, isolation and universal interconnection, sublimation and all-inclusiveness. At the same time, some stories are Greek oikotypes, meaning local forms distinctive to a specific cultural tradition. Folk tales are "like the chameleon, which remaining always the same animal is said to vary its colour according to its background" (Dawkins 1948:52). With these words Dawkins emphasizes how the environment plays an important role in the character of the stories. Stories may be similar across nations but reflect individual traditions to fit each particular background—thus, they may display "well marked national characteristics" (Dawkins 1948:52). In a similar vein, Meraklis claims that although folk tales serve

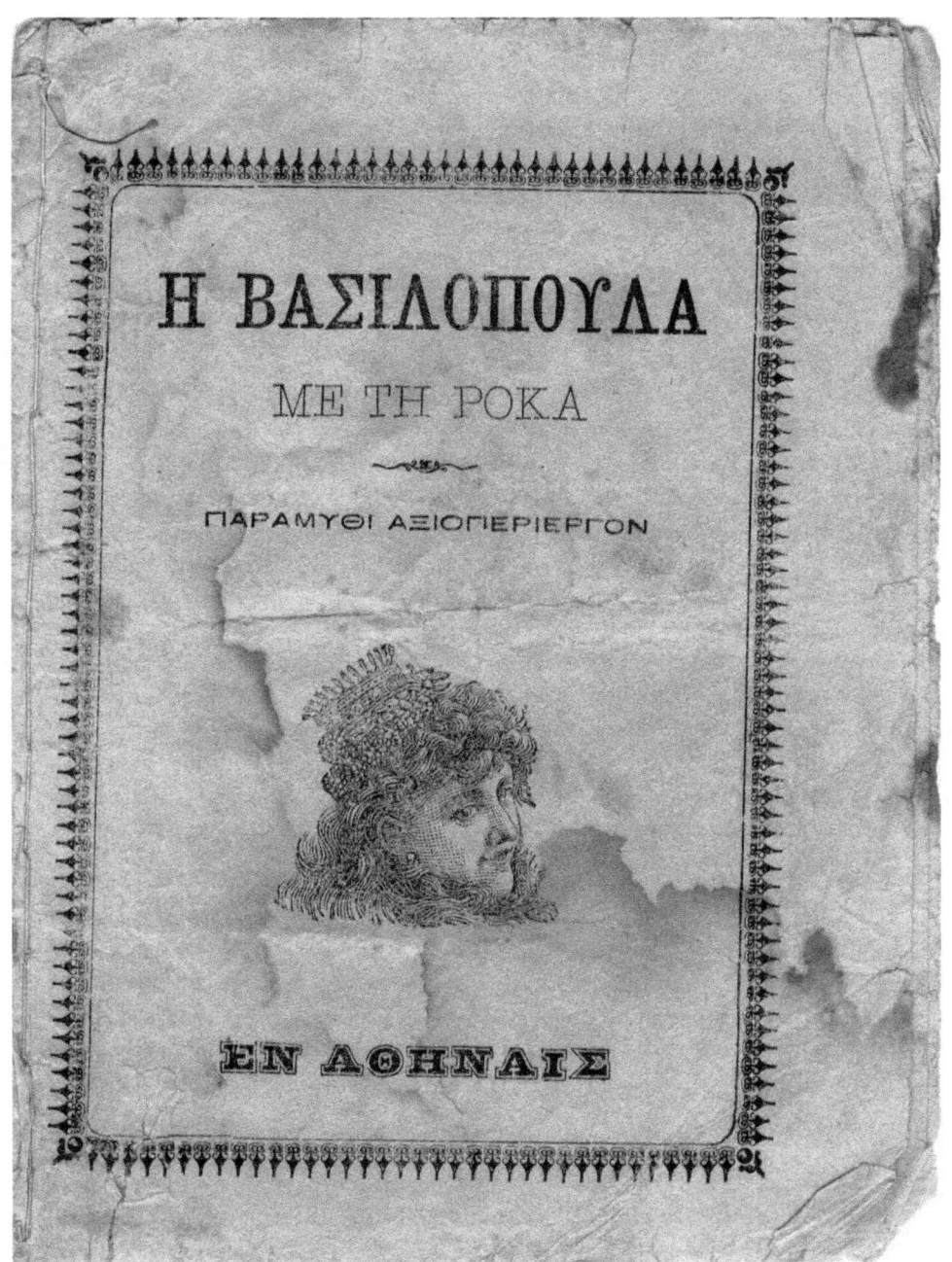

FIG. 24.1. Η βασιλοπούλα με τη ρόκα. Παραμύθι αξιοπερίεργον. Εν Αθήναις ("The Princess with the Spindle. A Curious Folktale." Athens). The booklet, published anonymously in the 1880s, contains one of the first translations of "Sleeping Beauty" in Greek.

(Courtesy of Ελληνικό Λογοτεχνικό και Ιστορικό Αρχείο; The Hellenic Literary and Historical Archives, Athens, Greece. Library collections).

to unite people since they share similar features across geographical borders, they also reflect specific ethnographic traits of the group which narrates them ([1973] 2001:46). What are the exact characteristics of Greek folk tales, and how are Greek stories different from stories from other cultures? Many scholars of Greek folk tale, from the nineteenth century to the present day, have weighed in on these questions and offered ways to answer them.

Style

In the introduction to his collection of folk prose narratives, Greek folklorist Demetrios Loukatos (1908–2003) outlines the basic characteristics of Greek folk tales. He compares these with other oral prose genres and with tales from other linguistic and cultural traditions. According to him, Greek folk tales follow a simple and uncomplicated narrative structure; narrators propel the plot with simple and spare words. They do not want to weary their audiences: thus, prolonged episodes are generally absent in Greek storytelling (Loukatos 1957:ιε and ιστ). Raconteurs even mention their tendency to be brief with phrases such as για να μην τα πολυλογούμε ("Let's not talk a lot!") (Hatzitaki-Kapsomenou 2002:283).

Consequently, the language in Greek folk tales is simple, direct, and laconic. Narrators use their everyday language and even their dialects, allowing them to compose stories with a vivid local touch. Besides the units of speech, the narration is mostly in the present tense and paratactic form, thus furthering the direct style of storytelling. Additionally, dialogue is integrated in the narrative in a continuous, linear manner as in folk theater and is distinguished by the single verb λέει ("he/she/it says").

> "Τι έχεις μέσα στο σακί;" Λέει: "Κάτι απίδια που μου δώσανε στο χωριό, τα 'ριξα μέσα." Λέει: "Για να δω!" Ανοίγει εκείνος το σακί, βλέπει ο άλλος τα πράματα. Λέει: "Γιατί μου 'πες ψέματα;" Λέει: "Ε, έτσι στο 'πα για να γελάσω."

> "What do you have in the sack?" He says: "Some pears they gave me in the village and threw [them] in." He says: "Let me see." He opens the sack, and the other sees many things. He says: "Why did you lie to me?" He says: "Eh, I told you this to laugh!"
>
> (Loukatos 1957:κ)

Greek folk tales start and conclude with formulaic expressions, mostly rhymes or short songs, which are common devices in other southeast European oral traditions as well. Alfred Messerli, in his extensive study on the formulaic expressions of European folk tales, believes that the beginning and ending of the folk tale are key to an understanding of the entire story. After the pivot of folk tale scholarship toward narrators and the emphasis on their importance not only as text mediators but also as artists, the opening and closing formulas in stories have attracted increased scholarly attention: they define the narrative process (Messerli 2022:88). The beginning and ending of a folk tale demonstrate the narrator's creativity, and with these two framing devices "they win over the public." Some formulas are designed to entertain and draw laughter from the audience. Openings and closings are indispensable since they put the "frame" of the narrative in constant dialogue with the narrative itself, creating a metatextual reflection.

At the beginning of a folk tale, narrators create contrasts between fantasy and reality, whereas at the end they bring their audiences back to reality. For example, the initial words "Now the story begins. Good evening to your worships" (Τώρα ξεκινά η ιστορία. Καλησπέρα της αφεντιάς σας) (Megas 1970:70) inform and prepare the audience for the world of magic. Similarly, the playful shifting between truth and reality, evidenced in the sentence "Once there was, though perhaps there never was, a king" (Είχεν κι αν είχεν έναν βασιλέα) (Dawkins 1953:229), intrigues the audience and encourages them to pay close attention. The most common opening formula in Greek folk tales is a short rhyme which refers to the spinning of a thread, metaphorically alluding to the spinning of the narrative:

> Κότσινη κλωστή κλωσμένη,
> 'Σ την ανέμην τυλιμένη,
> Δος της τσούννον να γυρίση
> Παραμύτθι ν'αρτσινίση.
>
> Red thread twisted well,
> Neatly wound upon the reel;
> Set the reel a turning do,
> And I'll tell a tale to you.
>
> (folk tale from the island Astypalaia, Dawkins 1950:41)

Closing statements such as "There! That's what they call a happy ending!" (Νά! αυτό είναι που λένε καλά υστερνά) (Megas 1970:127) or "All the same I was not there, and you are not to believe the story" (Μήδε γω ήμουνα κει μήτε σεις να το πιστέψετε) (Dawkins 1953:242) demonstrate more playful techniques to provoke doubt in the truthfulness of the story and to help the audience return to real life. The most common closing formula, "And they lived right well, may we live better" (και ζήσαν αυτοί καλά, κι εμείς καλύτερα) (Megas 1970:74), urges us to consider our own lives. The distance between the real and the unreal worlds is minimized: in a consoling tone, the narrator reminds us that we also live well. Fantasy is beautiful, but reality surpasses it.

Besides the above-mentioned opening and/or closing formulas, Greek folk tales may incorporate other oral genres, such as folk songs, proverbs, or riddles. For instance, narrators use rhymes from well-known folk songs to describe the beauty of a young woman:

> Τον άμμο τον αμέτρητο βάνει μαργαριτάρι,
> Τα κοχλιδάκια του γιαλού βάνει δαχτυλιδάκια,
> Και του κοράκου το φτερό βάζει καμαροφρύδι.

> She wears as pearls the countless sand,
> She dons the seashells as rings,
> And paints her eyebrow raven black.
>
> (Hatzitaki-Kapsomenou 2002:152)

Storytellers also embed proverbs in Greek folk tales to reinforce narrative points. Examples of aphorisms in folk tales include "save the anger of the night for the morning after" (τον αποψερνό θυμό φύλαγέ τον το πωρνό) and "What goes around, comes back around" (ό,τι κάμεις, θα βρεις) (Hatzitaki-Kapsomenou 2002:153). Additionally, several of the short animal fables in the modern Greek tradition conclude with a proverbial phrase that delivers the moral of the story. For instance, the phrase "the fox leaves whatever it cannot reach hanging" ("sour grapes"; όσα δε φτάνει η αλεπού τα κάνει κρεμαστάρια) concludes the well-known Aesop fable "The Fox and the Grapes." Loukatos names these short allegorical proverbs, which are positioned at the end of animal stories and briefly include the story itself, "proverb-myths" (παροιμιόμυθοι) and argues that because of their brevity these stories are the most remembered and told by the people ([1972] 1998).

Content

Certain recurring motifs and episodes belong to the *ars narrandi* of any good Greek storyteller (Dawkins 1953:xviii, xix), although many of them are common throughout European and other folk tale traditions. The childless couple who wishes to have a baby but must agree to relinquish it at a certain age is a common introductory episode in folk tales; the motif of the hero entering the underworld through falling into a well is "a convenient piece of padding to lengthen any story"; the episode of the heroine narrating her turmoil in front of everyone, without the listeners in the story being able to leave the room, is likewise a frequent ending; and the motif of the three gifts to the displaced wife or the three dresses of the beautiful heroine (picturing the earth, the sea, and the sky) also adorn the main body of many folk tales. Elaborating on these recurrent motifs, Chryssoula Hatzitaki-Kapsomenou adds more of them to Dawkins's list: the isolation of the hero or heroine in a tower; the keys that open forty rooms, with the last one reserved for the forbidden chamber; the abundance of food when the hero reaches an unknown palace; the difficult tasks or riddles a princess sets for her suitors; the crossing of three roads from which the hero has to choose one to proceed on his journey; the three fountains pouring oil, honey, and wine; and finally the motif of abundant hospitality to any foreigner (2002:145, 146).

The local folk tale world sounds familiar to its listeners. "Everything happens easily and occurs nearby. The king and the princess watch their kingdom from their window, the good Fate meets people on the street and talks to them, poor people and orphan girls enter the palaces effortlessly" (Loukatos 1957:ιστ). Greek folk tales refer to known events, and they are representations of the narrators' and their audiences' expectations.

As Lutz Röhrich argues ([1956] 1991), folk tales depict reality and, as such, reflect the living environment in which they are told. Indeed, the world of traditional Greek folk tales becomes modern and adapts to the current environment: "the room becomes a balcony, the loom a sewing machine, the oil lamp an electric one, the prince becomes heir, the horse a car," etc. (Loukatos 1957:ιζ).

Furthermore, abstract ideas in Greek folk tales are transformed into concrete, material substances. For example, the blessings of the parents come in the form of a horse, or a mother gives her wish to her traveling daughter enclosed in a tobacco box (Meraklis 1990:155, 156). The Greek folk tale directly narrates horrible acts (brutal murders, horrific punishments, etc.) without any reservation or shame. As Loukatos argues, the folk tale has "historical memory"; these things might have happened in earlier times, and the story does not change them (1957:ιζ).

For example, one version of the Greek magic tale "Cinderella" (ATU 510A) from the beginning of the twentieth century reveals the particularity of the story to the cultural and historical environment of the village Nymfaio in rural northern Greece (Loustas 1996:141–144). The story, a classic magic tale, represents, in a local rendition, one of the main social problems of that time: the mass migrations to America, Canada, and Australia. In this Greek "Cinderella," the father leaves his wife and three daughters behind and goes to foreign lands "to find a better job" and build a better life. Additionally, the Greek "Cinderella" distinguishes itself by its strong religious elements: the beautiful poor heroine finds her prince not at a ball but in the church, during the most powerful sermon of the year, the Resurrection liturgy on Easter Sunday. Thus, the story reflects the lived experiences of the locals, where religious practices played an important role in their everyday lives, and migration emptied small villages.

Dawkins also extrapolates some local characteristics that prevail in Greek folk tales. He argues that, compared to other folk tale traditions, the "Greeks prefer a more intellectual, a more practical, and often a slightly mocking tone in their stories" (1948:53). According to Dawkins, the religious tale "The Greater Sinner" (ATU 756C: Two Sinners) has a "peculiarly Greek" form (1953:473–476). The story follows a penitent sinner (the first sinner) who has to fulfill an impossible task in order to be pardoned for his crimes. A traveler (the second sinner) meets and insults him, and the first sinner kills him, which, surprisingly, proves to be his salvation from his previous sins. The explanation is that the second sinner whom he killed has committed greater sins than the first sinner did: namely, the second sinner has either hindered a happy marriage or kept the water supply away from the people. This specific folk tale is also common among southeast Europeans, and the Greek story seems to be closest to the Bulgarian, Serbian, and Romanian versions. For Greeks, interfering with God's will by hindering a happy marriage was unacceptable. Similarly, water was of paramount importance: it was considered an "unlawful deed" to withhold water or poison the wells. These elements, however, are not emphasized in versions from other folk tale traditions.

A variety of characters circulate in modern Greek folk tales. Some remain the same as in the ancient Greek literary tradition, such as the lamia (an evil female vampire who eats horses and drinks the blood of her family members), water nymphs (nereids), and the three female Fates who define the destiny of a newborn baby. The *drakos* (a personified ogre) with mostly evil characteristics appears commonly. Other characters demonstrate influences from the Greek tradition's encounter with its neighboring peoples. One evil male character in Greek folk tales is the beardless man, well known in other southeast European countries (Serbia, Bosnia and Herzegovina, Croatia, Bulgaria) and Turkey, as well as in Arabic and Judaic narratives. A man without a beard has negative connotations in Greek culture. The lack of a moustache (and a beard) symbolizes lack of masculinity (Megas 1977:1285). The beardless man is sly and dangerous and brings bad luck. Greek proverbs demonstrate that the type of the beardless man is well situated in Greek culture. To mention one example, Φυλάξου από άνθρωπο σπανό και μαλλιαρή γυναίκα ("Beware of a beardless man or a hairy woman"). The magic tale "The Servant Who Took the Place of His Master" (ATU 531: The Clever Horse) describes the story of a poor boy who, in search of his prince-godfather, meets a villainous beardless man. The latter forces the boy to change places with him under an oath of silence, and only if the beardless man dies should the boy reveal the misdeed imposed by him. The boy is sent to fetch the golden-hair maiden, who sets two difficult tasks on him, which he achieves with the help of ants and bees. Upon their return, the villainous beardless man kills the boy, but the maiden revives him with the water of life; thus, he is free from his oath and narrates the truth to the prince and the king. At the end, the boy marries the maiden with golden hair (Dawkins 1953:182–189). The beardless man also appears in tales that include the telling of falsehoods or feature the stupid ogre (Meraklis [1973] 2001:56–57).

Besides magic, animal, religious, and other tales, there is a rich repertoire in the Greek tradition of anecdotes and jokes.[9] Some of these stories may mediate vulgar and obscene scenes, using humor and "bad" words which, however, do not shock the audience—since this manner of speaking belongs to their everyday lives. According to the information of some collectors, narrators had profane and "very immoral" stories in their repertoires and sometimes competed with each other for "the foulest story" (Hatzitaki-Kapsomenou 2002:147).

A group of jocular Greek folk tales refers to the topic of death and the dead. One joke satirizes the belief that there is communication between the living and the dead and ridicules the gullibility of people (ATU 1540: The Student from Paradise [Paris]), whereas in another anecdote the living "imitate" dead people in order to avoid returning their debts (ATU 1654: The Robbers in the Death Chamber) or to avoid work (ATU 1951: Is the Wood Split?). In spite of their initial macabre character, these jocular stories through their cheerful mood give rise to satire and social criticism as they mock the weaknesses of human behavior, such as gullibility, laziness, stinginess, theft, etc. (Kaliambou 2017). Parallel to those amusing stories, three magic tales which display jocular elements address the topic of Death[10] and how humans unsuccessfully attempt to deceive him (ATU 330: The Smith and the Devil, ATU 331: The Spirit in the Bottle, and ATU 332: Godfather Death). These folk tales demonstrate humorously how easily humans interact with Death and are not afraid to have close relationships with him, to trick him, or to get rid of him even if temporarily (Kaliambou 2020).

As in folk tales from other cultures, the Greek magic folk tale does not include explicit eroticism; it does not narrate erotic scenes. Love, however, is of paramount importance. Love, even at first sight, is a strong motivation for the heroes and heroines, and marriage remains the culminating event, as Vladimir Propp (1968) identified: the motif of marriage is the last (thirty-first) function in the folk tale structure. Moreover, sexual intercourse between a couple is never explicitly stated, only subtly inferred. In "The Folktale of the Beardless Man" a king who wanted to meet his people visits the house of a young and beautiful woman. "He could not hold back his love for her, and he made a child with her" (Hatzitaki-Kapsomenou 2002:278). In the story "The Brave Father and His Brave Son" the narrator narrates a homosexual harassment scene in which drunken sailors bullied, stalked, and tried to sexually assault the young good-looking hero of the story:

σαν φάγανε και σφίξανε και κάμποσο βίνο . . . και γινήκανε (με συγχώρεση) σαν τα γουρούνια, σηκώνουνται και πάνε να τον πειράζουνε. Τότες αυτός σηκώνεται 'ποκεί και πάει αλλού. Μα κείνοι θέλανε κι άλλα πράματα, γιατί ήτανε κομματάκι νόστιμος, κι όπου πήγαινε τον κυνηγούσαν από πίσω.

After they ate and drank lots of wine . . . and they became (forgive me) like pigs, they stand and go to assault him. He moves from there and goes somewhere else. But they wanted different things, because he was good looking, and wherever he went they hunted him following him from behind.
(Hatzitaki-Kapsomenou 2002:327)

In the same story, when the young man enters the room where the princess waits, the narrator claims "You know what they did afterwards" (Τι κάνανε πλια, σεις τα ξέρετε), and indeed later the story reveals that the young woman was pregnant and delivered a boy (Hatzitaki-Kapsomenou 2002:329).

Performance

The idea of the female narrator is an ancient one, if one takes into account Plato's derogatory phrase "old wives' tales" referring to stories told by old women to entertain children. In modern Greece, the first known female narrator was the elderly Paraskevi (κερά-Παρασκευή), who lived in Ermoupolis, on the island Syros, at the end of the nineteenth century. Lady Paraskevi narrated folk tales to Hahn, the Austrian consul in Greece and systematic collector of Greek tales, and to his Danish collaborator Pio. Hahn created a collection of stories named "The Folktales by Lady Paraskevi" (Τα παραμύθια της κερά Παρασκευής), which marks "the first time in the history of Greek folktales that a folk female narrator exists not anonymously but instead gives her name

FIG. 24.2. Hahn, Johann Georg von. 1864. *Griechische und Albanesische Märchen*. Leipzig: Wilhelm Engelman. The lithograph shows a group of women, a man, and children listening carefully to an old woman storyteller. The group is located in Athens on the slopes of the Acropolis.

to the collection of the tales she narrated" (Kaplanoglou 2021:152). As Pio writes in the preface to his 1879 edition of folk tales, Lady Paraskevi was crucial to both the Austrian and Danish collectors because she helped them to understand the local idioms in the tales (Fig. 24.2).[11]

Ethnographic accounts of modern Greece attest that narrators are not only women but also men who wanted to amuse their friends (Dawkins 1948:65). Kaplanoglou, in her ethnographic research in the 1990s on Greek islands and on communities of Asia Minor descendants, observes that men were talented narrators. For example, Ioannis Goulas (Ιωάννης Γκουλάς) would perform a single story for three consecutive nights! The narrator would interact with his audience, checking to see if children were listening by asking them "Where did we stop?" (πού είχαμε μείνει;), and he would interrupt his story at a critical point so that he could continue from there the next day, creating a cliffhanger (Kaplanoglou 2001:257). Besides adults, children also narrated stories, mostly to their peers (Kaplanoglou 2001:119).

Storytellers are usually amateur narrators from all social strata who learn the stories mostly from their family members. Even today storytellers come from all walks of life, from truck drivers to monks (Pelasgos 2017:495–501). Nowadays there are also professional storytellers educated in Greece or abroad, with a large repertoire from various traditions, who perform to children and adult audiences (Anagnostopoulos 2017:719). They improvise during their narration and use theatrical and musical techniques to adorn their performances. The modern storyteller Stelios Pelasgos (2008:187f.) started seminars for adults and children in the 1990s to revive oral performances in Greece. Since then, festivals have spread throughout Greece with storytellers performing to larger audiences at events similar to theater performances. A recent documentary film captures storytellers who learned the art of storytelling through listening to older narrators (maybe the last ones, according to the director Vassilis Loules) from the Greek countryside (Loules, 2014).

Folk Tales in Popular Culture and Children's Literature

Popular booklets of folk tales were the main medium for the distribution of folktales in Greece at the end of the nineteenth and beginning of the twentieth centuries (Kaliambou 2006).[12] They were small, usually published with twelve, sixteen, or thirty-two pages; had typographical errors; and generally circulated anonymously. Most of the time they had a colorful cover which functioned as a buying incentive. They were affordable, with prices equivalent to a piece of bread. The material in the booklets was diverse in origin and represented mixed traditions. Some were traditional Greek oral stories, but the majority were translated works from the best-known European collections by Perrault, the Brothers Grimm, and Andersen and from foreign traditions from all over the world (Figs. 24.3 and 24.4).

The adaptation of the original texts into Greek popular booklets ranges from free and innovative handling of the material to faithful translations (Kaliambou 2007b). A booklet from 1914, for example, published a unique version of "Little Red Riding Hood" (ATU 333). The heroine is a girl from a minority group, the Aromanian Vlachs, with the entire story located in their village. The story takes place around Christmastime, and the little girl brings her grandmother "Christmas food." In this creative version, epithets strengthen the emotional atmosphere: the little girl is "unfortunate" (άμοιρο) or "a beautiful little angel" (ωραίο αγγελούδι); the bad wolf is "a wild and heartless beast" (το άγριο και άσπλαχνο θηρίο); the forest is "big where at night you could hear only wild wolves' howling" (μεγάλο δάσος που την νύχτα δεν ήκουε κανείς τίποτα παρά να ουρλιάζουν οι αγριόλυκοι). The free adaptation climaxes with the terrifying atmosphere of the ending, resembling popular crime and detective novels: "[the wolf] knew that soon he will give up his spirit on the rough ground and he will pay with his wretched and black guts for the innocent human blood" (ήξερε πως κι αυτός σε λίγο θα ξεψυχήσει επάνω στο άγριο χώμα και θα πληρώσει με τα έρημα και μαύρα σωθικά του τ'αθώο κι ανθρώπινο αίμα).[13]

FIG. 24.3. This is an example of a standardized booklet of folk tales by popular publishers. Τα ωραιότερα παραμύθια. Η ακατάδεχτη αρχοντοπούλα. Εκδόσεις Σ. Δαρεμά, Αθήναι (*The Most Beautiful Fairy Tales. The Strange Princess*, Athens: S. Daremas, n.d. [ca. 1950s]).

(Courtesy of publisher Daremas, Athens.)

Contrary to the free translations, Hans Christian Andersen's tales are an example of faithful popularization into the Greek booklets (Kaliambou 2005). During the years ca. 1930–1970, when Andersen's tales were massively distributed through popular booklets, publishers preferred translations close to the original. The only notable interventions refer to cultural differences such as religious rituals. For example, in Andersen's fairy tale "The Bell" the translator intervenes in the text only in order to explain rituals unknown in Greek culture, such as confirmation in the Catholic Church. Andersen's

FIG. 24.4. Ιστορίες και παραμύθια. Η Σταχτομπούτα. Το Βασιλόπουλο και η Γοργόνα. Η Πολιτεία των Τριτώνων (*Stories and Folktales. Cinderella. The Prince and the Mermaid. The City of Tritons*, Athens: Saliveros, n.d. [ca. 1950s]). As the name of the series, *Stories and Folktales*, indicates, this popular booklet contains a variety of genres.

(Courtesy of Ελληνικό Λογοτεχνικό και Ιστορικό Αρχείο; The Hellenic Literary and Historical Archives, Athens, Greece. Library collections.)

reception changed drastically after the 1970s, with substantial adaptations, reductions of the stories, more visual elements than textual ones, etc.[14]

Folklore continues to inform culture and society. Folk tales have entered all aspects of life and are found everywhere: in advertisements, in songs, in graffiti. Comic books draw inspiration from animal fables or folk tales, as can be seen with the current comic writer Arkas (Katsadoros 2019:143–153). In the twentieth century, educators showed increased interest in the use of folk tales for children's instruction. Aesop's fables belong to the canon of a child's education; they are taught in schools and thus gain even more popularity among the younger generations. Children remember short stories, even more so if they have a didactic verse at the end.

Authors of children's literature employ traditional and modern tales in their texts. Antigone Metaxa-Krontira (1905–1972), well known under the pseudonym "Aunt Lena," contributed significantly to the dissemination of folk tales among children. She authored several books of folk tales and created the first radio programs and the first theater for children in Greece (Kaliambou 2008:623). Today, this theatrical tradition continues with professional performers—storytellers who embellish their performances with folk tales.

Conclusion

Greek folk tales have a long tradition in Greek history and culture. As sources of local history, folk tales represent the regional characteristics of the people narrating them. Yet, Greek folk tales have also been open to dialogue with other cultures through both oral and literary avenues. They have been enriched through influential exchanges with western European traditions. Moreover, Greek folk tales demonstrate the broader cultural tradition that Greece shares with other Mediterranean and southeast European peoples.

Greek folk tales have been narrated by women, men, and even children on various occasions during their leisure activities. They have touched all possible issues of their everyday lives in symbolic ways. Folk tales continue to be a beloved genre in Greek culture. Today, new literary creations and professional performances of narratives continue the long tradition of oral storytelling. They mostly belong to children's entertainment and education. Nevertheless, the new and expanding dimensions of folk tales today as well as the evolving research directions of the genre may well show the dynamism that oral traditional prose narrative has in Greek culture and beyond.

Notes

1. In his four-volume correspondence, Guys described the everyday life of the Greeks (architecture, clothing, religion, customs, marriage and death rituals, oral narratives, dance

1. and music, art, etc.). Notes on storytelling and some tales are in the first volume (Guys 1783:letter XXII, 347–364).
 2. The three folk tales were (1) "Rodia" (Aarne-Thompson-Uther Tale-Type Index [ATU] 709: Snow White), (2) "Le Dracophage" (ATU 304: Dangerous Night-Watch + 552: Girls Who Married Animals), and (3) "Le Petit Rouget Sorcier" (ATU 303: The Twins or Blood Brothers + 555: The Fisherman and His Wife).
 3. The ATU is a catalogue of seven major folk tale categories; each tale type in each category, assigned a number, refers to a traditional, recurrent, independent narrative plot.
 4. For Stith Thompson the greatest weakness of Hahn's catalogue was that his system did not differentiate between tale types and motifs (recurrent elements in tales that persist independently in tradition).
 5. A similar important personality who reformed the Serbian language and was the first to collect oral literature (including folk tales) and other folklore extensively was the Serb Vuk Stefanović Karadžić (1787–1864).
 6. Politis made this distinction in his introductory article on Greek folklore in the newly created journal Λαογραφία (Laografia, Folklore). The phrase μνημεία του λόγου ("monuments of speech"), with its singular archaeological character, was an attempt to connect the newly established nation to ancient predecessors through folklore (see Herzfeld 1982:10).
 7. The German folklorist Johannes Bolte together with the Czech Slavicist Jiří Polívka published in five volumes a standard work in folk tale scholarship, namely a complete new edition of the annotations of the Brothers Grimm tales (Grimm et al. 1913–1932).
 8. The well-known and widely distributed children's journal in the nineteenth century Διάπλασις των Παίδων (Formation of the Children) was one of the main sources for folk tales for children (see Kaplanoglou 1998).
 9. Just to list a few of them, ATU 1533: The Wise Carving of the Fowl, ATU 1535: The Rich and the Poor Farmer, ATU 1626: Dream Bread, ATU 1641: Doctor Know-All, ATU 1696: What Should I Have Said?, ATU 1730: Entrapped Suitors, ATU 1920: Contest in Lying, ATU 1920D*: Climbing to Heaven.
10. Death in Greek culture is a masculine noun and is male.
11. An iconic stereotypical image of a grandmother narrating stories to her grandchildren is the subject of a painting by the Greek painter Nikolaos Gyzis, The Folktale of the Grandmother (Το παραμύθι της γιαγιάς, 1884; http://ebooks.edu.gr/ebooks/v/html/8547/2003/Anthologio_E-ST-Dimotikou_html-empl/index09_00.html).
12. A similar phenomenon occurred also in neighboring Bulgaria (see Roth 1993).
13. Folk tales published in popular booklets share common elements with popular novels. Linguistic elements (such as shifting from standard to everyday language; restricted vocabulary; use of colloquial expressions, adjectives, and adverbs; diminutive and superlative forms; metaphors and comparisons; dialogues and direct speech) as well as aesthetic characteristics (sentimentalization, moralization, dichotomization, and amplifications of the stories) demonstrate the "dialogue" between the two prose genres, novel and folk tale (Kaliambou 2007a).
14. Interestingly enough, Andersen's tales were introduced in the last three decades of the nineteenth century into Greek culture by Greek intellectuals who intervened in subtle and latent ways in the original translations providing further indoctrination and moralization in the stories.

Works Cited

Anagnostopoulos, Vasilis. 2017. "Η παραδοσιακή αφήγηση και οι σύγχρονοι παραμυθάδες. Η περίπτωση της Θεσσαλίας." In Το παραμύθι από τους αδερφούς *Grimm* στην εποχή μας. Διάδοση και μελέτη, eds. Michalis Meraklis, Georgios Papantonakis, Christos Zafeiropoulos, Marianthi Kaplanoglou, and Georgios Katsadoros, 717–724. Athens: Gutenberg.

Angelopoulou, Anna, and Aigli Brouskou. 1994. Επεξεργασία παραμυθιακών τύπων και παραλλαγών ΑΤ *700-749* (Γεωργίου Α. Μέγα, κατάλογος ελληνικών παραμυθιών, αρ. 2). Athens: Historical Archive Hellenic Youth, General Secretary of New Generation.

Angelopoulou, Anna, and Aigli Brouskou. 1999. Επεξεργασία παραμυθιακών τύπων και παραλλαγών ΑΤ *300-499* (Γεωργίου Α. Μέγα, κατάλογος ελληνικών παραμυθιών, αρ. 3). 2 vols. Athens: Historical Archive Hellenic Youth, General Secretary of New Generation.

Angelopoulou, Anna, Marianthi Kaplanoglou, and Emmanouela Katrinaki. 2004. Επεξεργασία παραμυθιακών τύπων και παραλλαγών ΑΤ *500-559* (Γεωργίου Α. Μέγα, κατάλογος ελληνικών παραμυθιών, αρ. 4). Athens: Historical Archive Hellenic Youth, General Secretary of New Generation.

Angelopoulou, Anna, Marianthi Kaplanoglou, and Emmanouela Katrinaki. 2007. Επεξεργασία παραμυθιακών τύπων και παραλλαγών ΑΤ *560-699* (Γεωργίου Α. Μέγα, κατάλογος ελληνικών παραμυθιών, αρ. 5). Athens: Historical Archive Hellenic Youth, General Secretary of New Generation.

Avdikos, Evangelos. 1994. Το λαϊκό παραμύθι. Θεωρητικές προσεγγίσεις. Athens: Odysseas.

Bernao Fariñas, Óscar M. 2015. "The Structural Device of 'Unsuccessful Repetition' in Two Ancient Greek Healing Narratives. Insights into the Composition of the Iamata of Epidaurus." *Fabula*, 56/1–2:1–16.

Braccini, Tommaso. 2021. "Pine-Cones for Moss: A Late Byzantine/Early Modern Greek Version of ATU 1525E, Thieves Steal from One Another." *Fabula*, 63/3–4:353–366.

Buchon, Jean-Alexandre. 1843. *La Grèce continentale et la Morée: Voyage, séjour et études historiques en 1840 et 1841.* Paris: Librairie de Charles Gosselin.

Chatzipantazis, Theodoros. 2021. Το παραδοσιακό δραματολόγιο του Καραγκιόζη. Από τον προφορικό αυτοσχεδιασμό στο παραλογοτεχνικό ανάγνωσμα. Herakleion: Panepistimiakes Ekdoseis Kritis.

Classen, Albrecht. 2006. "Das Motiv des aufopfernden Freundes von der Antike über das Mittelalter bis zur Neuzeit." *Fabula*, 47/1–2:17–32.

Dawkins, Richard M. 1916. *Modern Greek in Asia Minor. A Study of the Dialects of Sílli, Cappadocia and Phárasa, with Grammar, Texts, Translations and Glossary. With a Chapter on Subject-Matter of the Folktales, by W. R. Halliday.* Cambridge: Cambridge University Press.

Dawkins, Richard M. 1948. "Some Remarks on Greek Folktales." *Folklore*, 59/2:49–68.

Dawkins, Richard M. 1950. *Forty-Five Stories from the Dodekanese. Edited and Translated from the Mss. of Jacob Zarraftis.* Cambridge: Cambridge University Press.

Dawkins, Richard M. 1953. *Modern Greek Folktales.* Oxford: Clarendon Press.

Dawkins, Richard M. 1955. *More Greek Folktales.* Oxford: Clarendon Press.

Eulampios, Georgios. 1843. Ο Αμάραντος ήτοι τα ρόδα της αναγεννηθείσης Ελλάδος. Δημοτικά ποιήματα των νεωτέρων Ελλήνων, συλλεχθέντα, ρωσσιστί μεθερμηνευθέντα και δια φιλολογικών και ιστορικών σημειώσεων εξηγηθέντα. Athens: Vivliopoleio Noti Karavia. Photomechanical reprint.

Georges, Robert A. 1965. "Richard M. Dawkins: A Commemorative Essay on the Tenth Anniversary of His Death." *Folklore*, 76/3:202–212.
Grimm, Gerhard. 1990. "Hahn, Johann Georg von." In *Enzyklopädie des Märchens*. eds. Rudolf Wilhelm Brednich, Hermann Bausinger, Wolfgang Brückner, Lutz Röhrich, Rudolf Schenda. Band 6:376–378. Berlin: Walter de Gruyter.
Grimm, Jacob, Wilhelm Grimm, Johannes Bolte, and Jiří Polívka. 1913–1932. *Anmerkungen zu den Kinder- und Hausmärchen der Brüder Grimm*. Neu bearbeitet von Johannes Bolte und Georg Polívka. 5 vols. Leipzig: Dieterich'sche Verlagsbuchhandlung, Theodor Weicher.
Guys, Pierre Augustin. 1783. *Voyage littéraire de la Grece, ou lettres sur les Grecs, anciens et modernes, avec un parallèle de leurs moeurs*, 3rd exp. ed. Paris: Veuve Duchesne.
Haase, Donald. 2016. "Challenges of Folktale and Fairy-Tale Studies in the Twenty-First Century." *Fabula*, 57/1–2:73–85.
Hahn, Johann Georg von. 1864. *Griechische und albanesische märchen*. Leipzig: Wilhelm Engelman.
Hatzitaki-Kapsomenou, Chryssoula. 2002. Το νεοελληνικό λαϊκό παραμύθι. Thessaloniki: Aristotle University of Thessaloniki, Institute of Modern Greek Studies, Manolis Triantafyllidis Foundation.
Herzfeld, Michael. 1982. *Ours Once More: Folklore, Ideology, and the Making of Modern Greece*. Austin: University of Texas Press.
Hölzlhammer, Lilli. 2020. "Altindische Weisheit in Byzanz: Zu den didaktischen Erzählstrategien in Symeon Seths Stephanites und Ichnelates und seinen arabischen Vorgängern." *Fabula*, 63/1–2:96–118.
Kakridis, Ioannis Th. 1978. Οι αρχαίοι Έλληνες στη νεοελληνική λαϊκή παράδοση. Athens: Morfotiko Idryma Ethnikis Trapezis.
Kaliambou, Maria. 2005. "Hans Christians Andersens 'Reise' in Griechenland. Zur Rezeption seiner Märchen seit Ende des 19. Jahrhunderts." *Fabula* 46/1–2:78–88.
Kaliambou, Maria. 2006. *Heimat–Glaube–Familie. Wertevermittlung in griechischen Populärmärchen (1870–1970)*. Münchener Schriften zur Neogräzistik 3. Neuried: Ars Una.
Kaliambou, Maria. 2007a. "Popularmärchen und populärer Roman: Ein 'Dialog' zwischen den Gattungen." *Fabula* 48/1–2:60–72.
Kaliambou, Maria. 2007b. "The Transformation of Folktales and Fairy Tales into Popular Booklets." *Marvels & Tales: Journal of Fairy-Tale Studies* 21/1:50–64.
Kaliambou, Maria. 2008. "Metaxa-Krontira, Antigone." In *The Greenwood Encyclopedia of Folktales and Fairy Tales*, ed. Donald Haase, 2:623. Westport, CT: Greenwood Press.
Kaliambou, Maria. 2012. "Άγνωστο αρχειακό υλικό παραμυθιών του Νικολάου Πολίτη" In *Nikolaos G. Politis and the Research Center of Greek Folklore of the Academy of Athens. Proceedings of the International Research Conference (Athens December 4–7, 2003)*, eds. Aikaterini Polymerou-Kamilaki, Paraskeuas Potiropoulos, and Panagiotis Kamilakis, 23:343–373. Athens: Research Center of Greek Folklore of the Academy of Athens.
Kaliambou, Maria. 2017. "'. . . Έφυγεν εκεί όπου δεν πεθαίνουν.' Αναπαραστάσεις των νεκρών στα ελληνικά παραμύθια." Λαογραφία 43:177–199.
Kaliambou, Maria. 2020. "Παρέα με τον Χάρο. Οι σχέσεις των ανθρώπων με τον θάνατο στα ελληνικά λαϊκά παραμύθια." Εθνογραφικά 15:117–124.
Kaplanoglou, Marianthi. 1998. Ελληνική λαϊκή παράδοση. Τα παραμύθια στα περιοδικά για παιδιά και νέους (1836–1922). Athens: Ellinika Grammata.

Kaplanoglou, Marianthi. 2001. Παραμύθι και αφήγηση στην Ελλάδα. Μια παλιά τέχνη σε μια νέα εποχή. Το παράδειγμα των αφηγητών από τα νησιά του Αιγαίου και από τις προσφυγικές κοινότητες των Μικρασιατών Ελλήνων. Athens: Patakis.

Kaplanoglou, Manrianthi. 2021. Παραμύθια και καθημερινή ζωή. Θεωρητικές και εμπειρικές παράμετροι μιας λαογραφικής έρευνας στη Ρόδο. Athens: Patakis.

Katsadoros, Georgios. 2019. Αισώπειοι μύθοι. Πρόσληψη και μετάπλαση στη λαϊκή και λόγια παράδοση. Athens: Gutenberg.

Loukatos, Demetrios. 1957. Νεοελληνικά λαογραφικά κείμενα. Βασική Βιβλιοθήκη Αετού, 48. Athens: Zacharopoulos.

Loukatos, Demetrios. 1998. Νεοελληνικοί παροιμιόμυθοι. Athens: Hestia, Nea Helleniki Vivliothiki. First published 1972.

Loules, Vassilis, director. 2014. Πέρασα κι εγώ από κει κι είχα παπούτσια από χαρτί. Παραμύθια για πάντα. Documentary film, writer Vassilis Loules a nd Kostas Mahairas. E-Trikala Production, Greece.

Loustas, Nikolaos. 1996. Λαογραφική μελέτη Νιβεάστας, Νέβεσκας, Νυμφαίου Φλωρίνης. Thessaloniki (author's publication).

Lüthi, Max. 1982. *The European Folktale: Form and Nature*, trans. John D. Niles. Bloomington, IN: Indiana University Press.

Megas, Georgios A. 1970. *Folktales of Greece*. Translated by Helen Colaclide. Foreword by Richard M. Dorson. Chicago, IL: University of Chicago Press.

Megas, Georgios A. 1977. "Bartloser." In *Enzyklopädie des Märchens*, eds. Kurt Ranke, Hermann Bausinger, Wolfgang Brückner, Max Lüthi, Lutz Röhrich, Rudolf Schenda. Band 1:1284–1288. Berlin: Walter de Gruyter.

Megas, Georgios A. 1978. Το ελληνικό παραμύθι. Αναλυτικός κατάλογος τύπων και παραλλαγών κατά το σύστημα *Aarne-Thompson (FFC 184)*. Τεύχος πρώτον: Μύθοι ζώων. Athens: Academy of Athens, Research Center of the Greek Folklore.

Megas, Georgios A., Anna Angelopoulos, Aigli Brouskou, Marianthi Kaplanoglou, and Emmanouela Katrinaki, eds. 2012. *Catalogue of Greek Magic Folktales*, coord. Anna Angelopoulos, trans. Deborah Brown Kazazis. Folklore Fellows Communications 303. Helsinki: Suomalainen Tiedeakatemia, Academia Scientarum Fennica.

Meraklis, Michael. 1990. "Griechenland." In *Enzyklopädie des Märchens*, eds. Rudolf Wilhelm Brednich, Hermann Bausinger, Wolfgang Brückner, Lutz Röhrich, Rudolf Schenda. Band 6:143–161. Berlin: Walter de Gruyter.

Meraklis, Michalis. 1993. "Το ελληνικό παραμύθι." In Έντεχνος λαϊκός λόγος, Michalis Meraklis, 73–91. Athens: Kardamitsa.

Meraklis, Michalis. 2001. Τα παραμύθια μας. Athens: Entos. First published 1973.

Meraklis, Michael. 1979. "Byzantinisches Erzählgut" In *Enzyklopädie des Märchens*, eds. Kurt Ranke, Hermann Bausinger, Wolfgang Brückner, Max Lüthi, Lutz Röhrich, Rudolf Schenda. Band 2:1096–1112. Berlin: Walter de Gruyter

Messerli, Alfred. 2022. "'Sie bleiben dort, ich aber kehrte hierher zurück.' Anfang und Ende im europäischen Volksmärchen." *Fabula*, 63/1–2:52–95.

Papachristophorou, Marilena. 2004. "The Arabian Nights in Greece. A Comparative Survey of Greek Oral Tradition." *Fabula*, 45/3–4:311–329.

Papachristophorou, Marilena. 2016. "Greek Tales." In *Folktales and Fairy Tales: Traditions and Texts from around the World*, 2nd ed., eds. Anne E. Duggan and Donald Haase, 2:425–429. Santa Barbara, CA: Greenwood Press.

Pelasgos, Stelios. 2008. Τα μυστικά του παραμυθά. Μαθητεία στην τέχνη της προφορικής λογοτεχνίας και αφήγησης. Athens: Metaixmio.
Pelasgos, Stelios. 2017. "Η ενσάρκωση των παραμυθιών των Grimm. Από τους Έλληνες φορτηγατζήδες στους Έλληνες καλογέρους." In Το παραμύθι από τους αδερφούς *Grimm* στην εποχή μας. Διάδοση και μελέτη, eds. Michalis Meraklis, Georgios Papantonakis, Christos Zafeiropoulos, Marianthi Kaplanoglou, and Georgios Katsadoros, 495–501. Athens: Gutenberg.
Pertsinidis, Sonia. 2009. "The Fabulist Aristophanes." *Fabula*, 50/3–4:208–226.
Pio, Jean. 1879. Νεοελληνικά παραμύθια. *Contes populaires grecs, publiés d'après les manuscrits du Dr. J.-G. de Hahn*. Copenhagen: A. F. Høst.
Polemis, Ioannis, ed. 2021. Καλλίμαχος και Χρυσορρόη. Thessaloniki: Aristotle University of Thessaloniki, Institute of Modern Greek Studies, Manolis Triantafyllidis Foundation.
Politis, Nikolaos G. 1909. "Λαογραφία." Λαογραφία, 1:3–18.
Politis, Nikolaos G. 1911–1912. "Δημώδη Βυζαντινά Άσματα." Λαογραφία, 3:622–652. Reprinted in Nikolaos G. Politis. 1980. Λαογραφικά σύμμεικτα, 4:186–209. Athens: Academy of Athens, Research Center of Greek Folklore.
Propp, Vladimir. 1968. *Morphology of the Folktale*, 2nd ed., trans. Laurence Scott, introduction by Svatava Pirkova-Jakobson, rev. and ed. with a preface by Louis A. Wagner, new introduction by Alan Dundes. Austin: University of Texas Press.
Puchner, Walter. 2002. "Politis, Nikolaos Georgiou." In *Enzyklopädie des Märchens*, eds. Rudolf Wilhelm Brednich, Hermann Bausinger, Wolfgang Brückner, Helge Gerndt, Lutz Röhrich, and Klaus Roth. Band 10:1142–1145. Berlin: Walter de Gruyter.
Röhrich, Lutz. 1991. *Folktales and Reality*, trans. Peter Tokofsky. Bloomington, IN: Indiana University Press. First published 1956.
Roth, Klaus, ed. 1993. *Südosteuropäische Popularliteratur im 19. und 20. Jahrhundert*. Munich: Münchner Vereinigung für Volkskunde, Südosteuropa-Gesellschaft.
Thompson, Stith. 1946. *The Folktale*. New York: Holt, Rinehart and Winston.

CHAPTER 25

SLOVAK TALES AND THE COLLECTIONS OF PAVOL DOBŠINSKÝ

JANA PIROŠČÁKOVÁ

PAVOL Dobšinský (1828–1885) was a Lutheran pastor, folklorist, Romantic poet, translator, literary critic, journalist, key member of the nineteenth-century Slovak national revival movement, and the most significant and best-known Slovak collector of folk tales. His collections of folk tales are among the most frequently published Slovak books and almost certainly the most widely read nineteenth-century Slovak works of literature. At the time of their initial publication (the second half of the nineteenth century), when the number of readers of Slovak literature on the territory of today's Slovakia only slightly exceeded the number of Slovak writers, Dobšinský's collections helped broaden the circles of readers of Slovak books and contributed to the establishment of the newly codified standard Slovak as a literary language (Kraus 1993). Dobšinský extensively censored and edited the collected folk tales before their publication, mainly with the goal of eliminating their erotic elements and earthy humor, which are typical of folk narratives. Thanks to his interventions, the folk tales that were originally aimed at adult audiences became favorite and recommended reading for children (Vojtech 1999:102). They are still perceived as children's literature today, and as such, Dobšinský is also considered a children's literature author.

Dobšinský's collections comprise the foundational and representative works of Slovak folklore studies. Folklore scholars consider them essential for research on the Slovak folk tale tradition (Gašparíková 2004b; Michálek 2008), yet they also emphasize that they "do not capture the earlier phases [in the development of the tradition] authentically" (Gašparíková 2004b:665). This is because the collections are marked by (1) a limited range of genres, with a marked preference for magic or fairy tales[1] that does not correspond to the characteristic repertoire of folk storytellers; (2) a preference for certain themes (the material in these collections does not capture the whole spectrum of folk storytelling as documented in later folklore-collecting projects); and (3) an overall mode of narration, condensed folk tale poetics, and storytelling style, considered characteristic features of Dobšinský's folk tales. The magic tales in his collections show a level of storytelling and stylistic accomplishment that collectors find only among exceptionally talented folk storytellers. These aesthetic qualities place Dobšinský's folk tales at "the pinnacle of European literary folklore" (Leščák 1986:359). Indeed, select folk tales from Dobšinský's collections have been translated into more than twenty languages.[2]

Beginning with the Czech scholar of Slavic and folklore studies Jiří Polívka (1858–1933), who prepared and issued an extensive catalogue of Slovak folk tales recorded and published in the nineteenth century (1923b, 1924, 1927, 1930, 1931), scholars have pointed out that the folk tales from Dobšinský's collections were not authentic examples of folk magic tales (Polívka 1923a; Melicherčík 1959; Brtáň 1969; Gašparíková 1986b; Leščák 1986; Leščák and Sirovátka 1982; Marčok 1986; Šmahelová 1989; Kraus 2000; Michálek 2008). Nevertheless, for over a hundred years, they were systematically used in editorial and educational practices as examples of folk prose, which created the impression that folk tales as a genre resembled the tales from Dobšinský's collections. Over time, readers erroneously came to identify Dobšinský's tales with folk magic tales. In other words, the tales from Dobšinský's collections, which presented folklore in an idealized form, were elevated to the status of models for literary culture.

The objective of this chapter is to answer the following questions regarding Dobšinský's work in the context of the Romantic conception of national art: (1) What is the characteristic style of Dobšinský's tales? (2) How did Dobšinský edit the tales before their publication? and (3) How and why was his preference for certain types of magic tales reflected in his collections? In this chapter, I demonstrate and explain how the characteristic style of tales from Dobšinský's collections was the result of purposeful editing of Slovak folk magic tales under the influence of Romantic ideas about the form and function of folklore. Like other Slovak Romantics as well as folklore collectors in nineteenth-century Europe, Dobšinský considered folklore an integral part of the artistic tradition of his nation. Along with language, folklore constituted an important aspect of national identity that national revivalists could use to demonstrate that Slovak culture was just as valuable as the cultures of other Slavic as well as non-Slavic nations. Slovak Romantics viewed folklore as national art and, as elsewhere in Europe, idealized it.

Dobšinský's Collections and Authentic Folklore

Dobšinský published two extensive collections of folk tales. The first, *Slovak Tales: Book I. Tales of Ancient Legendary Times* (*Slovenské povesti, Kniha I. Povesti prastarých báječných časov*), was compiled between 1858 and 1861 in collaboration with August Horislav Škultéty (1819–1892), an ethnographer, writer, and director of the first Slovak *gymnázium* (secondary school), located in Revúca. It included sixty-four tales in six volumes (Fig. 25.1).

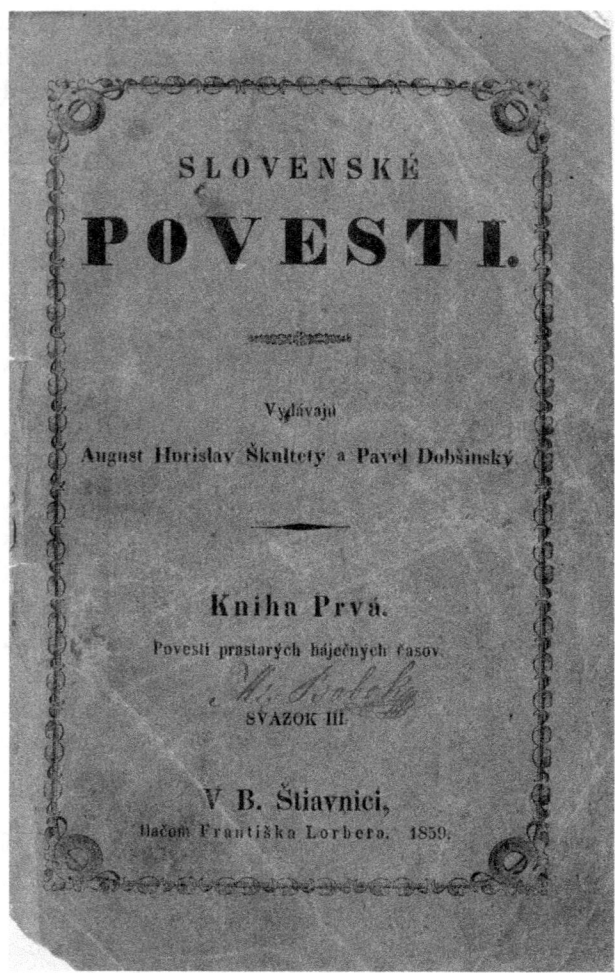

FIG. 25.1. Cover of *Slovenské povesti*, Kniha I. *Povesti prastarých báječných časov*/*Slovak Tales, Book I. Tales of Ancient Legendary Times*, Volume 3, 1859. The Slovak National Library, Martin, Slovakia.

The seventh volume was not published, but Dobšinský later included the tales from it in his next collection, *Simple National Slovak Tales* (*Prostonárodné slovenské povesti*), which included ninety-three tales in eight issues and was published between 1880 and 1883 (Fig. 25.2). Dobšinský presented them as "authentic and original Slovak tales," "relics of the remote past" (Škultéty and Dobšinský 1858:III–IV), which he brought to their readers "completely untouched . . . in the same simplicity and precise narrative structure that the people use to tell them" (Dobšinský 1880a:5). These statements imply that we can find authentic samples of folk tradition in the collections. However, Dobšinský published only a negligible number of tales on the basis of folk storytelling; the majority of the tales were derived from older sources, and they typically were carefully rewritten.

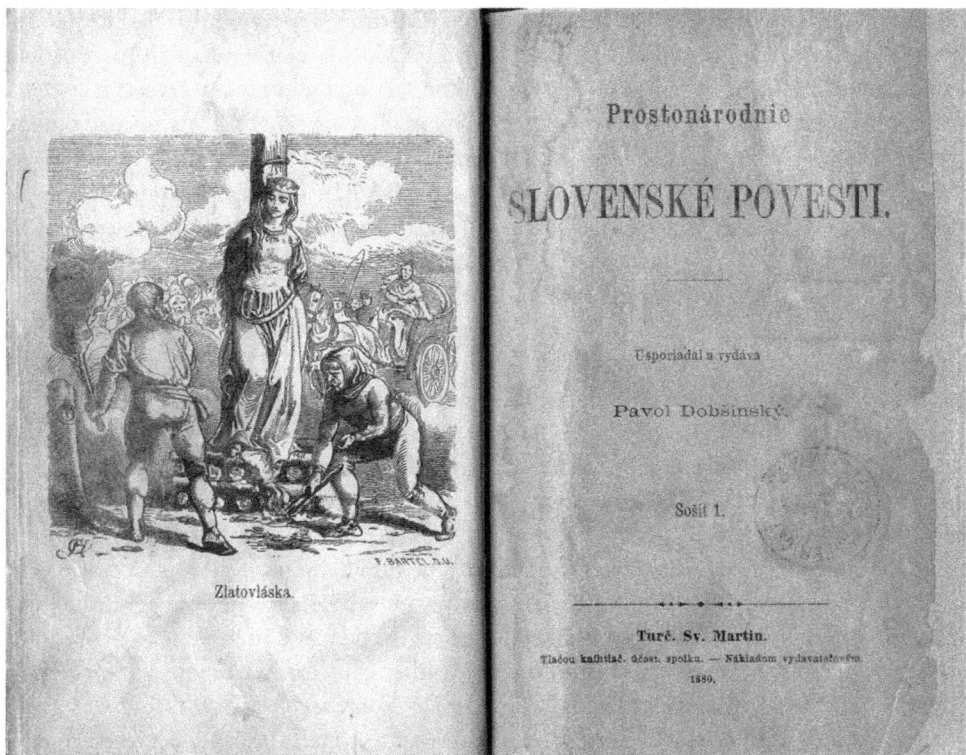

FIG. 25.2. Title page of *Prostonárodné slovenské povesti/Simple National Slovak Tales*, Volume 1, 1880, with an illustration. The Slovak National Library, Martin, Slovakia.

He considered that the authentic forms of folklore, which he experienced in folk storytelling, did not meet the high standards that the Romantics set for folklore and its function as a showpiece of national identity. In other words, the model for the Romantics was not folklore in itself but an idealized form of folklore. In his introduction to *Slovak Tales*, Dobšinský explicitly outlined his selective approach on the basis of qualitative criteria, stating that "not every narrative that circulates in these modern times among the Slovak communities, however, is an authentic and original Slovak tale. There are quite a few told among the people that are not worthy of the name tale" (Škultéty and Dobšinský 1858:V). An "authentic and original Slovak tale" that would be worthy of publication, according to Dobšinský, did not include any type of folk narration but only the type of narrative that met selective criteria for composition, style, language, genre, content, and theme. At the same time, the acceptable narrative also had to demonstrate superior aesthetic qualities and impeccable moral principles. Only tales that met all of these criteria could, in Dobšinský's view, adequately represent its collective author—the Slovak people (Škultéty and Dobšinský 1858).

This historical context explains an additional reason why Dobšinský published literary rather than authentic folk tales in his collections. That reason was practical.

His collections were published at a time when, for the majority of Slovaks, it was not common practice to read literary works written in Slovak. The movement for national emancipation led by Lutheran intellectuals in the second half of the nineteenth century therefore faced a challenging task: to teach Slovaks of all levels of society to read Slovak books. This was the goal that Dobšinský was striving to meet by publishing his tales: "As far as reading is concerned, our nation is still one that has to be fed with milk before it can get accustomed to more nourishing food. Tales are such milk that our Slovaks will find palatable and will teach them to love reading and get accustomed to Slovak books" (letter, May 30, 1858, quoted in Melicherčík 1959:83). *Slovak Tales* and *Simple National Slovak Tales* were arranged in ways that included "an extensive selection of tales edited to meet the needs of contemporary readers" (Melicherčík 1959:94) and thus presented a modified and constructed picture of Slovak folklore.

Although neither comprehensive data on the sales of the individual editions nor analyses of audience response are available, the reception of Dobšinský's tales among the transmitters of folk tradition shows that Dobšinský met or even exceeded his key editorial goal. The collections of folk narratives in the twentieth century demonstrate that the tales from his collections became widely available to the public thanks to frequent editions in inexpensive issues and thus also reached the transmitters of folk tradition. They influenced the form of oral narration even among illiterate storytellers and in regions with predominant populations of ethnic minorities such as Ruthenians (e.g., Žeňuchová 2004, 2006). This occurred to such an extent that folklore scholars today are not certain when to classify certain variants as the result of the reception of Dobšinský's tales (Gašparíková 2004b:663) or whether the striking similarities between the collected folk samples and his published tales resulted from the standardization and stabilization of characteristic features of folk narratives over time. Folklorists tend to conclude that the similarities stemmed "from indisputable reception" and point out that the signs of acceptance of Dobšinský's collections within the folk tales gathered in the field during the interwar period "exceeded those resulting from other possible influences of print models" that can be identified (Gašparíková 2004b:663). In the central European context, this is seemingly a unique instance of the influence of print publication of tales on folk tradition. For example, parallel collections by the Czech folklorist Karel Jaromír Erben (1811–1870), *A Hundred Simple National Tales and Legends in Original Slavic Dialects* (1865) (*Sto prostonárodních pohádek a pověstí slovanských v nářečích původních*) and *Selected National Legends and Tales of Other Slavic Branches* (1869) (*Vybrané báje a pověsti národní jiných větví slovanských*), influenced folk storytellers' narratives only minimally (Gašparíková 1986a:382).

Content Sources and Editing Methodology

Except for ten tales that we can assume Dobšinský collected himself, he drew on material from older manuscript collections for the remaining 147 tales, including over 400 tales gathered by more than fifty collectors.³ According to folklore studies scholars, these collections "represent exceptional source material in the European context" (Urbancová 1983:68). In compiling *Simple National Slovak Tales*, Dobšinský also drew on material from two older editions. These included the first collection of Slovak tales (*Slovak Tales*), ten tales published in 1845 by the Romantic poet, prose writer, journalist, translator, and politician Ján Francisci (1822–1905), under the pen name Janko Rimavský, as well as a collection of sixty-four Slovak tales and legends by the most significant Czech writer and collector of the nineteenth century, Božena Němcová (1820–1862), *Slovak Tales and Legends*, published in Prague in 1857–1858.

Dobšinský's work on these collections involved a variety of editing and creative strategies that went beyond simple adaptation of older manuscript or book texts. We can describe his strategies for preparing the tales for publication because the source materials are available, which allows us to analyze and compare potential sources with the published tales. This analysis is possible thanks to the source information associated with the title of each tale along with the contemporary inventories of tales that were compiled by Dobšinský,⁴ and modern catalogues (Polívka 1923b, 1924, 1927, 1930, 1931; Gašparíková 1993, 2001, 2004a) point to potential models. However, we must take into consideration that the source information is not completely reliable for several key reasons. Not all variants that the source information points to can be viewed as models for the published tales (e.g., Polívka 1923b:75, 77; 1927:61, 127, 194, 429; 1930:188, 286, 196), and there are specific discrepancies and inconsistencies (e.g., Polívka 1924:95–98, 366–373). Moreover, Dobšinský had a specific agenda in publishing his sources. For tales that were adopted from older manuscript collections, he consistently recorded accessible versions and direct models. However, for tales that he adapted and edited on the basis of older manuscript collections, he did not always clearly reference print models.

For tales adapted from the volume by Francisci, Dobšinský did not acknowledge his source, but he attributed authorship to storytellers who contributed to their composition. For example, he attributes the source for the tale "Good Day, Little Bridge" ("Pamodaj šťastia, lavička"; ATU 480D*) to a Lutheran pastor, Ľudovít Reuss (1822–1905). The version of the tale by Reuss was recorded in the early 1840s under the didactic title "A Good Heart Finds Its Reward" ("Dobré srdce nájde odmenu") in the *Codex of Revúca A* (a manuscript collection of Slovak folk tales). Francisci significantly reworked the tale for the purposes of his edition. When we compare Dobšinský's version with the assumed model and with Francisci's adaptation of Reuss's tale, it is evident that the direct model for the tale in *Simple National Slovak Tales* was Francisci's version. This was the case for all the tales that Dobšinský adopted from Franscisci's collection (Pácalová 2010:300–313).

Dobšinský was more transparent in the case of tales adopted from Němcová. He acknowledged her as a source for eleven tales, for example "The Journey toward the Sun and the Moon" ("Cesta k slncu a mesiacu"; ATU 460A) as "told by B. Němcová's Janko and Miko Sochorík, Juro Šulek, and Štefan Márton from Trenčianska" (1882b:26). In fact, Dobšinský published other tales from Němcová's collection without citing the Czech writer but only her sources—the same treatment that he gave to tales adopted from Francisci's collection. For example, "Peračina"⁵—which contains the superstition that if one finds the bloom of the fern on the night of the feast of St. John the Baptist, the earth will open and reveal a hidden treasure—is a translation of Němcová's text. However, instead of acknowledging her as the source, Dobšinský credits the Romantic poet and collector Samo Chalupka (1812–1883) from whom Němcová heard about the superstition. Dobšinský also realized that Němcová collected a lot of material that the Slovak Romantics did not record on their home territory, and this was precisely the type of material that he adopted from her collections. The omission of Němcová in editorial notes for some of the tales can be interpreted as Dobšinský's intending to return them to the Slovak tradition (or the Slovak cultural context).

In order to examine the relationships between acknowledged models and published tales in Dobšinský's collections, it would be necessary to analyze each text individually. When Polívka attempted to explore the relationships between the tales published in the collection *Slovak Tales* and their acknowledged models, he came up with three principal approaches: (1) the tale was prepared for publication by the author of the model, (2) the tale was prepared for publication by the author on the basis of the record by another collector, or (3) the tale was prepared for publication on the basis of several older versions (1923a:76–83). On the basis of comparative analyses of acknowledged models alongside the published texts, Polívka came to the conclusion that

> we cannot analyze all of the tales in this collection [to] demonstrate how each of them was reworked. The selected examples sufficiently demonstrate that the collection does not offer reliable and authentic samples of Slovak folk storytelling but only shows the type of material that was circulating among the Slovak people and the approximate forms that were used to narrate it.
>
> (1923a:83)

In *Simple National Slovak Tales*, the most common form of source reference is to one older variant that was the most immediate model for the given tale. The references contain the name of the collector who recorded the tale and sometimes information on its local origin and dialect. For example, "Cinderfella–Foul Face" ("Popolvár-hnusná tvár"; ATU 530) was "narrated in the country dialect of the Muráň Valley by S. Ormis" (Dobšinský 1882b:31). A writer and teacher, Samo Ormis (1824–1875) recorded the same tale in the *Codex of Revúca* in approximately 1843–1844, and Dobšinský published it in the seventh issue of *Simple National Slovak Tales* with minimal changes (Fig. 25.3). The published text is almost a word-for-word transcription of the model. He applied the same method to more than a third of the tales that were based on materials from manuscript collections in this edition. Another group of texts in this edition consists of tales that are based on a single direct source. Dobšinský reworked the models before publication. This is the case for another tale by Ormis recorded in 1843 in the *Codex of Revúca C*, "The Wise Boy" ("Múdry chlapec"; ATU 327A; published in the fifth issue in 1881), as well as all the tales that were taken from the collections of Francisci and Němcová. Indeed, as Dobšinský prepared tales from Němcová's collection for

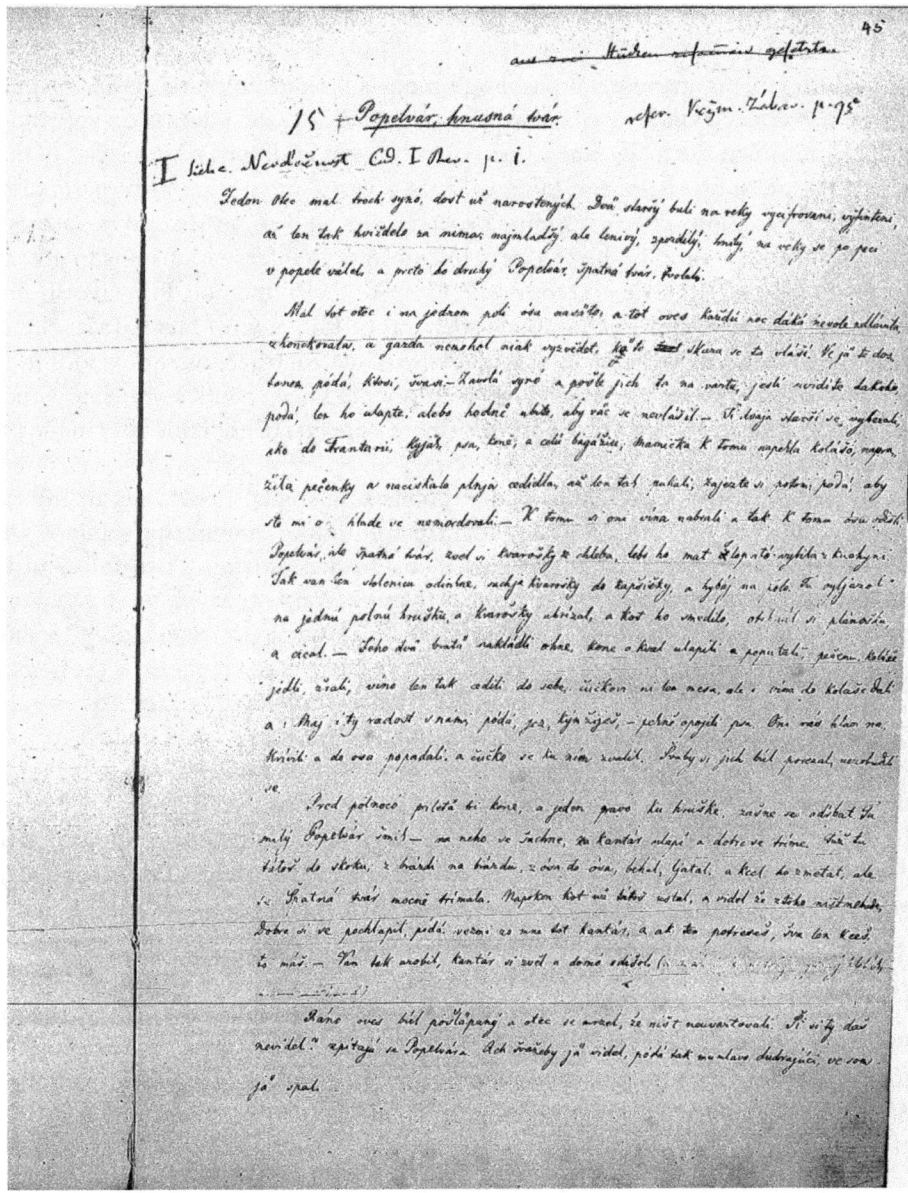

FIG. 25.3. Manuscript of the magic tale "Popolvár–hnusná tvár"/"Cinderfella–Foul Face" (ATU 530) recorded by Samo Ormis in *Codex of Revúca* in approximately 1843–1844. Pavol Dobšinský published this magic tale in volume 7 of *Prostonárodné slovenské povesti*/*Simple National Slovak Tales* in 1882. Manuscript is held in the Literary Archive of the Slovak National Library, Martin, Slovakia, signature B465.

publication in *Simple National Slovak Tales*, he translated them from Czech to Slovak (Pácalová 2010:314–318).

The editing of the manuscript and book models includes different levels of intervention in the vocabulary, syntax, word order, additions of idiomatic expressions, modifications of contextual sequencing, corrections or additions to the levels of content and theme, abbreviations of long passages, stylistic modifications of parts of the original, modifications of the storyline or characters, and so on (Pácalová 2010:250–252, 303–318; 2014a, 2014b). The objective of Dobšinský's interventions was to give the published tales unified style and form and to make them resemble folk tales in their original authentic versions as he knew them from folk environments (Melicherčík 1959:174). For this reason, he included eight tales in dialect (there were only four in the previous edition) and eight that he most likely adopted from a folk storyteller without any consideration of earlier written models (there were two tales of this kind in the previous edition).

In *Slovak Tales*, the source information points to a single model only in the case of about a third of the tales. All tales adapted from older manuscript versions were published only after Dobšinský reworked them. In the remaining two-thirds of the tales, the source information points to more than one variant, which is why the notes on source information have a different structure. The first part refers only to those collectors who recorded the first variants of the respective tales, followed by the name of the storyteller who prepared the text for publication or edited its language. For example, "Longbeard" (*Laktibrada*; ATU 431) was "recorded by Jonatan Čipka Hradovský[6] from Malý Hont and Ondrej Návoj and narrated by Pavol Dobšinský from Gemer" (Škultéty and Dobšinský 1858:13).

In this collection, the references to the collectors reflect different relationships between potential models and the published versions of the tales, including (1) one of the listed variants is the direct model; (2) the published tale was composed on the basis of several variants, one of which tends to be dominant (e.g., as in the tale "Longbeard"); or (3) in rare cases, the published version of the tale material is autonomous, and the only function of the source notes is to record accessible variants. The comparison between the published tales and their potential models therefore points to more complex methods of preparing tales for publication in *Slovak Tales* than editorial corrections or retellings (reworkings) of a single model like in *Simple National Slovak Tales*.

The "Ideal" Form of the Slovak Tale in *Slovak Tales*

Almost half of the tales in *Slovak Tales* (and the tales in *Simple National Slovak Tales* that were originally intended for publication in the seventh issue of *Slovak Tales*) were written by Dobšinský, Škultéty, and their collaborators[7] on the basis of several variants. The tale "Longbeard" was written by Dobšinský on the basis of an older record in *Simple*

National Journal IV ("*Prostonárodný zábavník IV*") published in 1845 (Polívka 1927:327) and in some respects inspired by the version of the tale recorded by Jonatan Dobroslav Čipka (1819–1861), "Two Sisters" ("Dve sestry") from the *Codex of Tisov* from 1843 (Pácalová 2014a:4–5) (Fig. 25.4). This approach to preparing the tales for publication was characteristic of the collection *Slovak Tales*. Folklore scholars in Slovakia identify this approach as the compilation-stylization method. It is considered a unique and original method of reworking tales in the broader European context (Leščák 1986:359).

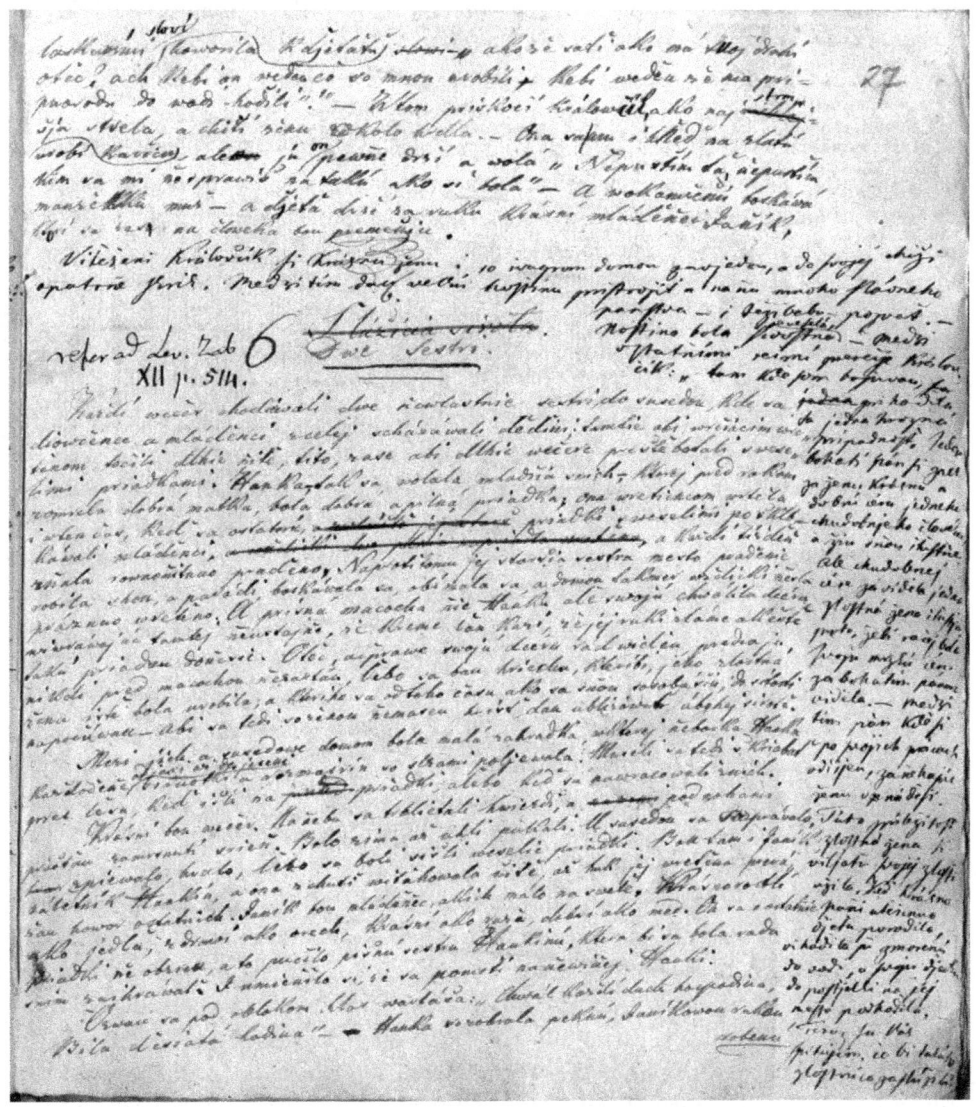

FIG. 25.4. Manuscript of the magic tale "Dve sestry"/"Two Sisters" (ATU 431) by Jonatan Dobroslav Čipka from *Codex of Tisov* from 1843. Manuscript is held in the Literary Archive of the Slovak National Library, Martin, Slovakia, signature B466.

The compilation-stylization method entails excerpting material and motifs from models and incorporating them into the new text, often preceded by reduction and stylistic reworking. In practice, this approach requires thorough knowledge of the source material. Collections of both tales as well as primary materials show that Dobšinský mastered his source materials. His manuscripts *The Inventory* and *A Selection of Individual Original Slovak Tales* (1858–1859) contain a database of variants from manuscript collections, technical notes on the generic classifications for certain tales as well as on the quality of the texts, and notes on how to proceed with further processing of the recorded texts. For example, in *A Selection of Individual Original Slovak Tales*, for the tale "Mataj" (ATU 756B), he added the following note: "The origin: from Daxner, storylines in Dx and Ormis need to be compared, the endings good in Orm. From Jančo, how the angel shows him the way out of hell" (quoted in Polívka 1923a:94). "Mataj" was prepared for the seventh volume of *Slovak Tales* by Škultéty, and it was published in the second issue of *Simple National Slovak Tales*. According to the information in the source note, it was "narrated by Štefan Marko Daxner from Malohont, Samo Ormis from Gemer, and Jozef Jančo from Šariš; prepared by A. H. Škultéty" (Dobšinský 1880b:12). A comparison of the models with the printed text shows that Škultéty proceeded methodically according to Dobšinský's instructions. The tale is based on Daxner's variant and adopts selected motifs from the other recorded variants (Polívka 1930:85–86).

Škultéty's text, which was published in *Simple National Slovak Tales*, was the fourth variant that followed three older reworkings of the material "Robber Madej" by Daxner, Ormis, and Jančo. In relation to its models, it presented a type of ideal variant. Folklore as well as Slovak studies scholars give it different names. An overview of the scholarly terminology that describes it suggests its essence; it is called "an objective form of the Slovak tale" (Melicherčík 1959:93), "the nationally representative variant" (Leščák and Marčok 1977:32–37), "the ideal original form of the tale" (Horálek 1979:23–25), "optimal resonance" (Leščák and Sirovátka 1982:94), "a prototype" (Kraus 1999:134), "a model variant" (Kraus 2000:28, 31), and "a literary construct—palimpsest" (Pácalová 2016c:16).

The fact that the basis for the preparation of tales for publication in *Slovak Tales* consisted of compiling older records was pointed out earlier by Polívka (1923a:79) as well as more recently (Brtáň 1969; Leščák and Marčok 1977; Marčok 1986; Kraus 2000; and others). However, this process cannot really be categorized as compilation because its organizing principle is a stylizing and creative approach that exceeds editorial competencies. The published tales are not merely edited models but products of individualized creativity that correspond to the Romantic concept of authorship (Pácalová 2016c:20), in which the author is believed to be present in the literary work. David L. Cooper (2012) and other Anglo-American literary scholars consider this type of "creativity" in the realm of literary forgery.[8] Moreover, the source material itself is not produced by folklore collecting in the modern sense. It is composed of qualitatively heterogenous records that range from simple narrative structures that resemble oral folk storytelling, which Dobšinský preferred in *Simple National Slovak Tales*, to markedly literary and stylized narrative forms.

Most of the source material that Dobšinský used for his collections was recorded in the first half of the nineteenth century, a period when Slovak collectors did not have a domestic model to draw on in recording tales and preparing them for publication. They proceeded more or less intuitively. The first collections of tales published by Francisci in 1845 did not reach a wider public and did not influence the manner in which tales were later recorded and edited. The second important aspect of the period context is the fact that the recording of tales by the generation of Slovak Romantics overlapped with the quest for form in Romantic prose. Among the writers who were also collectors, this tendency was manifested in markedly stylized literary writing, which was influenced by the Romantic imagination to such an extent that we can describe it as Romantic (Pácalová 2010:93–120, 2015c:37–47). Čipka can serve as a characteristic Romantic author. Let us consider a brief example from his tale "Two Sisters," which was one of the source variants for Dobšinský's tale "Longbeard":

> Idú, dlho idú, až prídu do velikej pustej hori. Po stromoch bolo počuť krkanie havranou, a po dolinách vitie vlkou. Blížilo sa k večeru, a žjadná náďeja, že bi prišli do ďedini ľebo do mesta. I zatňe oťec ostrou sekerou do visokej jedli, zatňe do druhej, do treťej, a z narúbaních stromou vistaví malí domček praviac, že tej noci tu prenocujú.[9]

> On and on they went until they reached a tall deserted mountain. They could hear the croaking of the ravens in the trees and the howling of wolves in the valleys. The evening was approaching, and there was no hope of reaching a village or a town. So the father swung his axe and cut down a tall fir, and then cut down a second one, and then a third one, and with the trees he cut down he built a little house and said that they would spend the night there.
> (quoted in Polívka 1927:330–331)

By contrast, Dobšinský's version of the passage is: "Otec vzal sekeru na pleče, pobral sa aj s dcérou preč a zaviedol ju do hory. Tu zoťal stromy a vystavil jej jeden domček" ("The father put an axe over his shoulder, took his daughter, and led her into the forest. There he cut down trees and built a little house for her") (Škultéty and Dobšinský 1858:15).

Dobšinský reworked the passage from Čipka's tale because he considered it to be excessively literary; it did not correspond to his idea of an "original, authentic Slovak tale" and thus was not fit for publication. He made a telling comment about another tale by Čipka in *Selected Original Slovak Tales* when he referred to Čipka's "poetic narration of a novel kind that is foreign to the tales" (Dobšinský [1923] quoted in Polívka 1923a:96) (Fig. 25.5). In his editions Dobšinský "removed such corruptions of individual narrative styles" from the tales (Marčok 1986:401) and revised them into forms that better corresponded to his ideal of the folk tale, or—to paraphrase the remark made by Dobšinský cited above—to the narrative mode typical of folk tales. Dobšinský used this revision process to unify earlier manuscript versions of tales that were recorded in the 1840s.

Dobšinský also reworked recorded versions that he considered simple and aesthetically ineffective or, in some respects, erroneous by refining their language, style, and

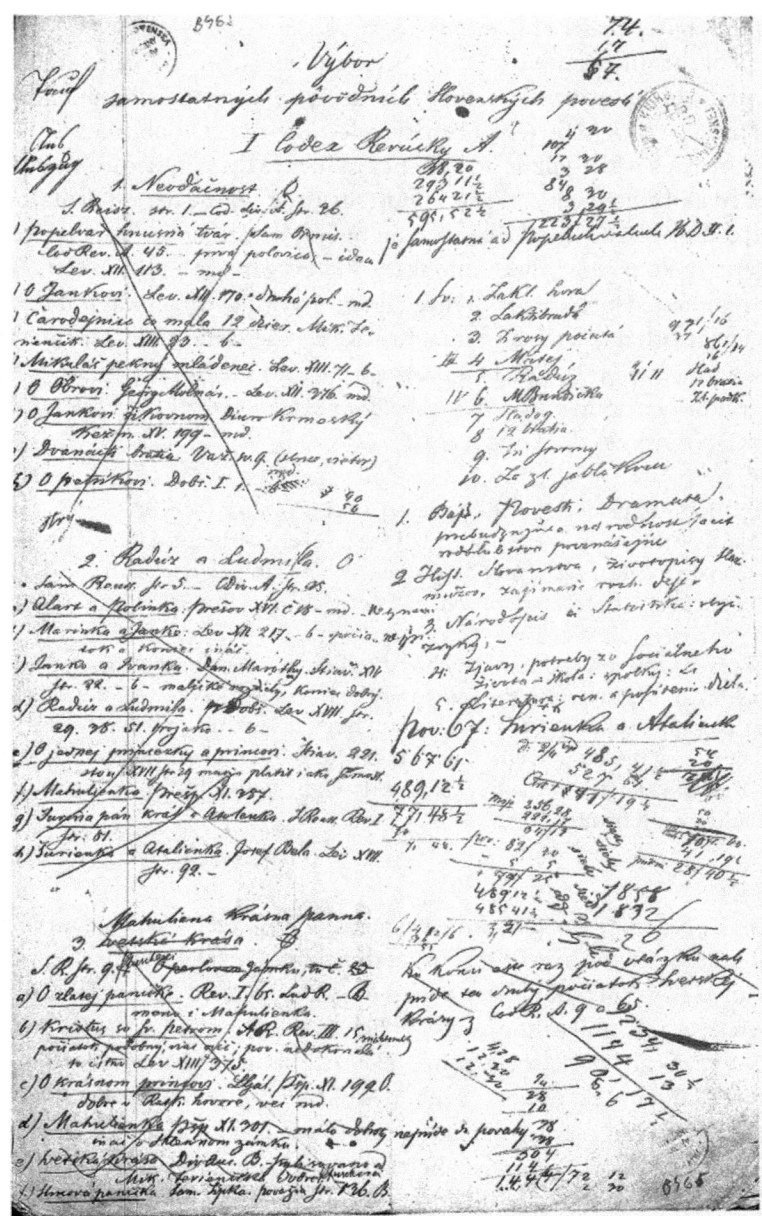

FIG. 25.5. Manuscript sample of *Výber samostatných pôvodných slovenských povestí/Selected Original Slovak Tales* from 1858 by Pavol Dobšinský. Manuscript is inserted into *Codex of Revúca*. Manuscript is held in the Literary Archive of the Slovak National Library, Martin, Slovakia, signature B465.

narrative structure (e.g., Leščák 1986:361–362; Kraus 2000:29–30). In the process of reworking them, he applied a wide range of interventions (discussed earlier in connection with the editing of models for *Simple National Slovak Tales*). It was, however, characteristically in *Slovak Tales* where he strove to include the features of tale poetics from the older recorded versions and use the models of poetics inspired by this process to rework tales recorded earlier as well as write new variants. In this process he focused on stabilizing the constitutive elements of tale poetics, especially of their structural elements (Gašparíková 1986b:40), as well as on preserving the distinctive characteristics of narrative style (Marčok 1986:400). Typical interventions therefore included an increased use of commonplaces—that are less frequent in the manuscript versions than in the published texts—and a consistent inclusion of introductory and concluding formulas (Gašparíková 1986b:46). This conventional sign of folk tale poetics is not necessarily always present in folk prose. While all of the tales published by Dobšinský are framed by introductory and concluding formulas,[10] such formulas appear in only about a third of the 585 tales published in the collection *Simple National Slovak Tales I–III* (Gašparíková and Filová 1993, 2001, 2004). The reasons why Dobšinský intentionally foregrounded such signs of folk expression were not merely aesthetically motivated. He also used these signs to give his readers a signal about the genre: "Attention, you are reading a folk tale!" The poetic elements of the tales in *Slovak Tales* are based on fixed structures of language and the illusion of "authentic" folk storytelling, which Dobšinský achieved through the implementation of elements of folk prose associated with orality (mnemonic and ritual features). In this way he created a specific style of Slovak storytelling that came to be received as traditional (Gašparíková 1986b:41). In other words, Dobšinský's contemporaries perceived his published folk tales, which were a result of purposeful reworking, as characteristic of the genre. Thanks to their purported normativity, the tales from Dobšinský's collections eventually became viewed as canonical texts representative of Slovak folk tales (Kraus 2000:28, 31; 1999:134) and guided future storytellers (Gašparíková 1986b:41).

Dobšinský's Collections and the Romantic Interpretation of Tales

The theoretical principles of the compilation-stylization method were established in editorial practices by Škultéty in his older, unpublished project from the turn of the forties and fifties of the 19th century, on which he collaborated with Reuss and Čipka (Pácalová 2015b; Melicherčík 1959:90–93). In the introduction to their work-in-progress collection, Škultéty, Reuss, and Čipka explain that almost every tale was "received from different corners of Hungary."[11] They became convinced that individual records "varied in their modes of narration but rarely in their central idea and substance"; therefore, they decided to "choose one of them and fill it in as necessary" (quoted in Polívka 1923a:51).

They proceeded in this manner because they realized that variability was a characteristic feature of tales. They clearly explained the basis for the compilation method, which leads to the creation of a model variant: "Different traditions were compared, and each united into one whole, so it was hardly possible to add or leave out anything" (letter to Jozef Podhradský, quoted in Polívka 1923a:49). Škultéty, Reuss, and Čipka were inspired by the work of Samuel Reuss (1783–1852), a Lutheran pastor and ethnographer who considered the collection of tales an accumulation of material for scholarly analysis according to the principles of the mythological school (which recognized fundamental relationships between language and mythology that, proponents of it maintained, were mirrored in folk tales) in the 1840s (Piroščáková 2019a:71–75; Hammel 2018). As such, they sought to approximate the original language of the narratives because they were convinced that the tales reflected the lives of their creators and transmitters (Fig. 25.6).

Dobšinský and Škultéty followed different objectives when they created the model variants for *Slovak Tales*. In these narratives they recognized signs of the "the period 'culture building'" (Cooper 2012:33) and considered them proof of the linguistic and cultural maturity of the nation that "created" and transmitted them. Therefore, the tales they published were intended to evoke the most authentic form of each tale, one that represented the "ideal" linguistic, aesthetic, and moral qualities of the Slovak nation.

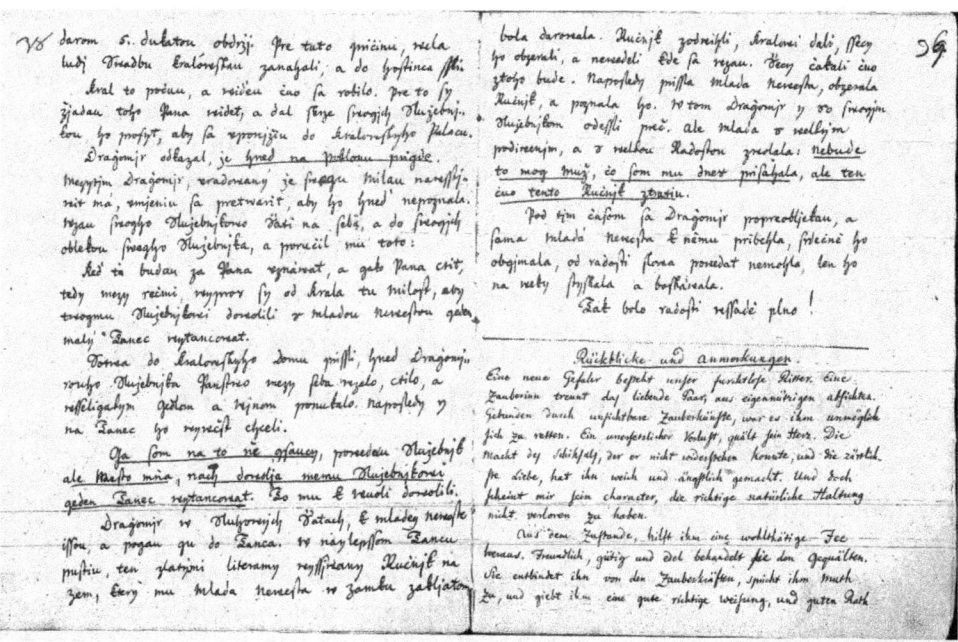

FIG. 25.6. The end of the magic tale "1te sage"/"1st Tale" (ATU 326) and comments to the tale in German (*Rückblicke und anmerkungen*) by Samuel Reuss in the *Codex of Revúca* in approximately 1840. Manuscript is held in the Literary Archive of the Slovak National Library, Martin, Slovakia, signature B465.

Such tales could then fully represent the nation in competition with other small nations that aspired to autonomy and independence in the Habsburg Empire.

However, the concept of a mythological school was not alien to Dobšinský, and a decade after *Slovak Tales* was issued, he developed it in an extensive treatise titled *Reflections on Slovak Tales* (Úvahy o slovenských povestiach) (1872) (Bužeková and Krekovičová 2008; Kováčik 2002; Melicherčík 1959:148–168). In this essay, he reconstructed the views of ancient Slovaks on divinity, communal life, and the concept of humanity on the basis of Slovak magic tales.[12] The material platform for this work consisted of collections published up to that point, including *Slovak Tales and Legends* by Němcová and older manuscripts in which magic tales were particularly well represented. Francisci published only magic tales in his collection. Dobšinský's and Škultéty's *Slovak Tales* included sixty magic tales and, as a curiosity, two "Animal Tales,"[13] one "Tale of the Stupid Ogre," and one "Anecdote." In *Simple National Slovak Tales*, Dobšinský also included several "Religious Tales" and "Realistic Tales," but magic tales comprised a two-thirds majority of the tales in this collection. This proportion roughly corresponds to the generic representation in the collection by Němcová and in manuscript collections.[14]

The preference for the magic tales in the Slovak context corresponds to the preferences of collectors in the broader European context, in which collectors purposely sought them out and recorded them because they "perceived them as 'real' tales" or tales sui generis (Otčenášek 2012:54) and considered them "a type that reflected a high level of artistic development" (Gašparíková 2004b:594). For European collectors, magic tale material represented "an important source of evidence for the belief systems of their ancestors" (Uther 2011:I:9). The reworking and editing of tales undertaken by collectors at the end of the eighteenth and in the nineteenth century were motivated by the objective of recovering connections between folklore and mythology (the mythological school). For example, Erben, mentioned earlier, reworked the material of "Three Hairs from the Devil's Beard" (ATU 461) in the Czech magic tale "Three Golden Hairs of the Wise Old Man" ("Tri zlaté vlasy deda Vševeda") in a way that transformed the devil into the sun. Erben justified this adaptation with reference to the ancient worship of the sun associated with solar mythology (Otčenášek 2012:69).

Dobšinský also had other purposes in his imitation of the folk tradition. He published tales in order to showcase the high-level cultural development on the part of the Slovaks while also providing appropriate reading material for the nation. Dobšinský's approach to editing the tales was not influenced only by the Romantic conception of national art as context for explaining the characteristic structure of his tales. He also closely followed the Romantic approach for interpreting the tales that developed during the first half of the 1840s. This mode of interpretation significantly influenced the understanding of tales among the generation of collectors that included Dobšinský and directly shaped the form of the early manuscript collections, which later served as the key source of material for him. The fact that magic tales were predominantly represented in his collections is not exceptional and corresponds to the generic preferences for the source material in the European context. There is another phenomenon characteristic of the

Slovak environment which is reflected in the manuscript collections from the 1840s as well as in the book editions of tales by Dobšinský: the preference for content influenced by the Romantic interpretation in the selection of the themes, motifs, and characters.

In the first half of the 1840s, the Romantic interpretation of tales was significantly influenced by the leading figure of the Slovak Romantic and national revival movements, the politician, codifier of standard Slovak, poet, translator, and literary critic Ľudovít Štúr (1815–1856). Štúr's review of Francisci's *Slovak Tales* (1845) and his chapter devoted to tales in the monograph *On the National Tales and Songs of Slavic Tribes* (*O národných povestiach a piesňach plemien slovanských*) (1853) belong to the foundational texts on the theory of folk tales. Štúr's lectures dedicated to the tales, however, had the most significant influence on the form of the manuscript collections of the 1840s. They were delivered during the spring of 1844 as part of his set of lectures on the art of the Slavs and circulated among his contemporaries in numerous copies.[15]

Štúr viewed folk tales as a set of magic tales. He presented them as an artistically mature type of narrative and the oldest forms of linguistic expression that preserved the early worldview of the Slavs in "its pure and uncorrupted" state (he rejected the possibility of using them, however, to reconstruct historical events). The original and conceptually foundational element of his interpretation was the motif of the spell as a constitutive element of magic tales. He explained the spell as a form of metamorphosis in which the will of the subject under the spell is not decisive, yet the subject is the cause of the spell, which is a punishment for sins, such as in "The Three Raven Brothers" ("Traja zhavranení bratia"; ATU 451), in which the angry mother curses her sons and thus turns them into ravens. Štúr differentiated between spells and types of metamorphoses, which in his view reflected a voluntary and intentional union between humans and nature. He pointed out the example of "Radúz and Ľudmila" (ATU 313), in which the female protagonist transforms herself and her fiancé into various things and people. On the basis of the magic tales he examined, Štúr classified the characteristic types of spells, their length, and methods of removing spells. He determined that the gravest types of spells were those that could be removed only through maintaining silence, such as in "The Maiden Who Seeks Her Brothers" (Štúr 1987:84–86).

Romantic collectors broadened this concept. Under the category of spells they also included the transformation of humans into animals, objects, or rocks as well as limitations on the protagonist's movement, speech, or other life functions. These spells thus reflected unsatisfactory life situations experienced by the protagonist. In magic tales, such a broadly conceived concept of the spell is expressed through a set phrase which, for example, stolen princesses use to welcome heroes: "Och, ako dlho som tu už zakliata!" ("Oh, how long I have been under a spell!"). Among magic tale motifs, the Romantics were particularly drawn to the kidnapping and imprisonment of a victim—typically by a dragon or a soulless monster—whom they considered symbols of the greatest physical or psychological force that the creators of the tales could imagine (Reuss ca. 1840–1843:71–72 [manuscript note below Reuss's text]). The protagonist who overcame such a powerful enemy had to be equally and exceptionally powerful. Therefore, the dragon-slayer is at the pinnacle of the hierarchy of (male) heroes in Slovak magic tales.

This motif recurs in Dobšinský's collections as well as in his manuscript sources in "The Dragon-Slayer" (ATU 300)[16] and "The Ogre's (Devil's) Heart in the Egg" (ATU 302)[17] as well as in material classified as "The Clever Horse" (ATU 531)[18] and "The Princess on the Glass Mountain" (ATU 530).[19] The typical companion of the hero in this type of material is the clever magical horse, which is special because it can foretell the future and flies with extraordinary speed. When carried on the horse's back, the hero can cover the same distance in one day that his brothers traverse in a whole year. This magical helper is described as *tátoš* (steed), and the term still evokes a magic-tale horse to Slovak speakers.

The greatest authority from the previous generation of national revivalists, the poet, collector of folk songs, aesthetician, and linguist Ján Kollár (1793–1852), placed the steed in the highest position in the pantheon of demonic creatures associated with evil in folk superstition in his *National Songs* (*Národné spievanky*) (1834). By contrast, the younger Romantic generation re-evaluated and transformed the figure of the steed, turning it into the most important helper of the hero. In this role the steed passed into the poetic inventory of motifs in Slovak Romantic poetry (Pácalová 2016b; Piroščáková 2019b) in which it symbolized the strength and courage to fight associated with the ideal national hero of the Slovak Romantics: one who struggles for the sake of the social good. This context is evident in the lines of Dobšinský's poem "The Warrior" ("Bojovník"), which he wrote during the revolutionary year of 1848:

> Sadnem si ja na koníka,
> na vraného tátošíka,
> nech svet vidí bojovníka,
> svetov nízkych protivníka.
>
> I will straddle my horse,
> my wild steed,
> may the world see the warrior
> the conqueror of the nether worlds.
>
> (Dobšinský [1848] 1966b)

The recorded material shows that the motif of the spell was attractive for the Romantics, especially in material in which the setting (a castle or a forest) is enchanted along with a character (most commonly a princess). The spell is typically lifted from her as well as from her community and country. Dobšinský's collections also included tales that can be categorized under ATU 330A, "The Fight on the Bridge"[20]; ATU 301, "The Three Stolen Princesses"[21]; ATU 303, "The Twins or Blood-Brothers"[22]; ATU 304, "The Dangerous Night-Watch"[23]; ATU 326, "The Youth Who Wanted to Learn What Fear Is"[24]; and ATU 402, "The Animal Bride."[25] For the Slovak Romantics (atypically in the context of Romanticism), subjectivity (or individuality) was not the most important feature of the tales. Instead, they attached more importance to the hero's actions for the good of the community. In this value system, the lifting of the spell from the princess was significant because the whole country and society were saved along with her. Therefore, tales of this type were considered more valuable than tales in which the objective of the hero's quest was more individualistic—for example, in tales categorized as ATU 400, "The Man on a Quest for His Lost Wife"[26]; ATU 408, "The Three Oranges"[27]; or ATU 516, "Faithful John."[28]

The magic tale motif in which the lifting of the spell from the princess benefits the whole community calls for a suitable groom for the king's daughter, one who will prove to be a wise and promising future ruler, a guarantor of the independence, safety, and stability of the entire country. This requirement was very timely in the context of the ongoing national and emancipatory movements of the nineteenth century. This is the reason why the Slovak Romantics used the tales as sources of accessible metaphors that pointed to developments outside of literature. Such metaphors were particularly important for strengthening the movement for national emancipation that situated Slovaks in the context of broader historical developments and in relation to other Slavic and non-Slavic nations (Piroščáková 2019b). The historical perspective that these writers modeled corresponds to the Romantic prototype of the superhuman "who does not escape into idyllic versions of the past but creates a new future suited to his own philosophy of history" (Horyna 2005:103).

This prototype of a superhuman was, according to the Slovak Romantics, ideally represented in the hero of "Cinderfella the Greatest" (Rimauskí [Rimavský] 1845; Dobšinský 1882a) (Fig. 25.7). This magic tale represented a convergence of the most compelling material: "The Dragon-Slayer," "The Three Stolen Princesses," and "The Ogre's (Devil's) Heart in the Egg." The name of the hero was also significant. In the introduction to the tale it is a derogatory nickname derived from his family and social situation (the youngest of three royal sons, who is mocked and put down by everyone, not respected or trusted by anyone, and whom neither his parents nor his brothers love) and typical activities (lounging on top of the hearth and playing with ashes). In the Slovak Romantic imagination, Cinderfella was promoted to a Romantic literary hero and a prototype of a national hero (Čepan 2002). The Romantics were particularly interested in this figure especially because of his key character trait, which they attributed to the Slovak nation in their interpretations of the tale. They were also intrigued by the metaphorical potential of the hero's name derived from the word "cinder" (*popol*) and by the central theme of the tale, in which "the youngest son defies the world's destiny" (Rimauskí [Rimavský] 1845:X). Cinderfella—or the man of the hearth—kills the witch as well as her three invincible dragon sons, who keep princesses, and a soulless monster imprisoned underground. He absorbs the witch's magical powers and becomes the most powerful man in the world. The story of Cinderfella echoes the myth of the phoenix as well as Christ-like imagery. First, he symbolically burns (dies) only to rise from the ashes (to be resurrected) and then grows stronger through this regeneration (in "Cinderfella the Greatest," the monster without a soul first kills Cinderfella; then the princess, whom Cinderfella, the hero, has come to liberate, resurrects him). At the highest level of abstraction, Cinderfella represented a symbol of national destiny (Čepan 2002). Although

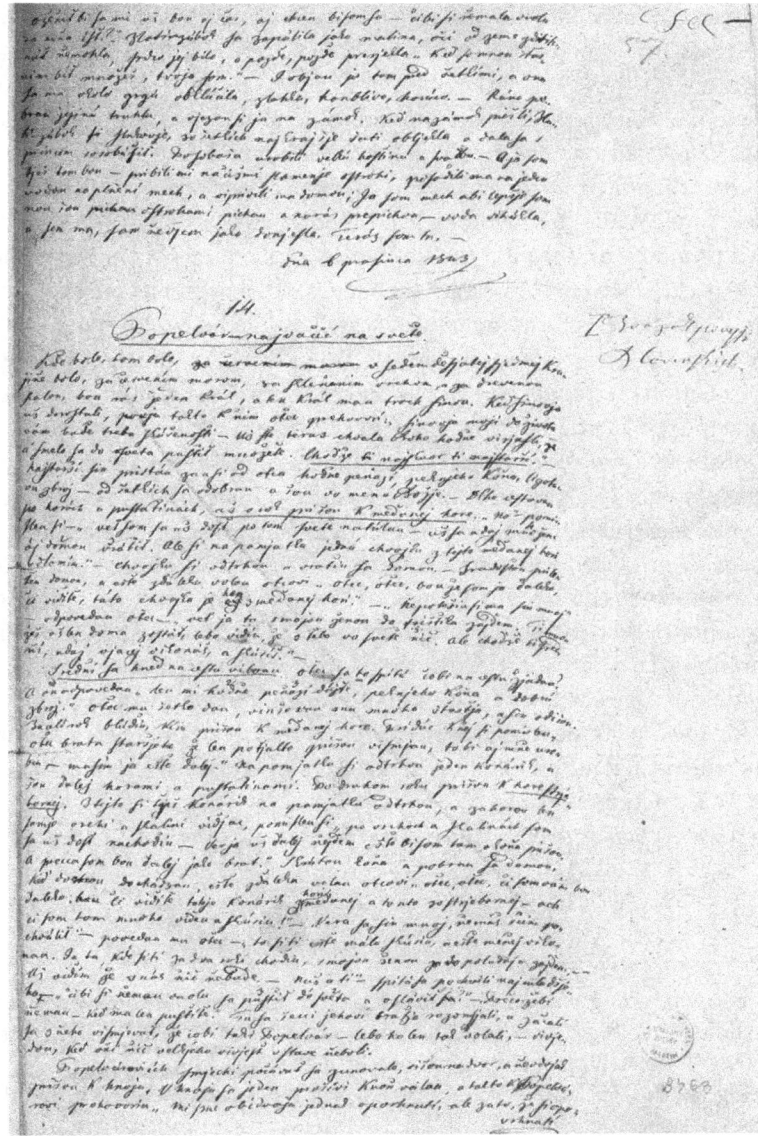

FIG. 25.7. Manuscript of the magic tale "Popolvár najväčší na svete"/"Cinderfella the Greatest" by Ján Francisci in *Codex diversorum auctorum A* from 1843 that Francisci published in *Slovenské povesti/Slovak Tales* in 1845 and later published by Pavol Dobšinský in his edition *Prostonárodné slovenské povesti/Simple National Slovak Tales* in 1882. Manuscript is held in the Literary Archive of the Slovak National Library, Martin, Slovakia, signature B463.

the Slovak nation was equally passive as Cinderfella in the opening of the tale, a time would come when it would "rise from the ashes" like Cinderfella (Dobšinský [1846] 1966a).

Magic tales that feature the broader motif of generational succession and the specific character of Cinderfella were compelling for the Romantics because they provided artistic expression for their optimism about historical development, which was necessary in their time. While the mythological school viewed folk tales as narratives that commented primarily on the past, the Romantics of the mid-1840s (before the revolution of 1848–1849) looked to the narratives as sources of hope for a better future position of the Slovaks in the Habsburg monarchy as well as for their achievement of national rights. They perceived folk tales as optimistic forecasts of the future: "In these tales the future of our nation is strongly and clearly reflected, and only a blind man does not see this future in the tale 'Cinderfella the Greatest'" (Rimauskí [Rimavský] 1845:X).

Pavol Dobšinský's project of collecting and meticulously preparing and editing the many folk tales in his well-known publications proved to be influential and indeed critical for the nineteenth-century architects of Slovak literature, culture, and nationhood. The folk tales he produced were demonstrably not published directly as performed by storytellers, nor—in his preference for magic tales—were they entirely representative of the larger tradition. Yet they served another purpose in the broader picture of Slovak national aspirations. They formed what the Romantics of the time viewed as valuable, even "ideal," models of folk narrative furnishing powerful metaphors of hope and brighter prospects for the Slovak people. Dobšinský and others like him believed that Slovak magic tales represented the eschatological record of a better destiny for the nation and a promise of future national existence.

Translated from the Slovak by Katarina Gephardt

Notes

1. These are what are termed "Tales of Magic" in the Aarne-Thompson-Uther (ATU) International Tale-Type Index, ATU numbers 300–749 (Uther 2011); see also https://sites.ualberta.ca/~urban/Projects/English/Content/ATU_Tales.htm.
2. The first English translations were of two Slovak folk tales published in London (1889) and Boston (1890) by Albert Henry Wratislaw (1822–1892) in his *Sixty Folk-Tales from Exclusively Slavonic Sources*. They were "The Gold Spinner" ("Zlatá priadka"; ATU 500) and "Are You Angry?" ("Hneváte sa?"; ATU 1000 + 1008 + 1010 + 1012). The folk tales in Slovak publications of Dobšinský's collections are not classified in the ATU Tale-Type Index, although some of them are included by the Slovak folklore scholar Viera Gašparíková in an issue of *Slowakische Volksmärchen* from the series *Die Märchen der Weltliteratur* (2000). For the purposes of this chapter, however, all of the folk tales and material referenced have been classified using the ATU Tale-Type Index. For additional English translations of Dobšinský's folk tales, see Cooper (2001).
3. The basic description of these manuscript collections was completed by Polívka (1923a:4–33); a more detailed description is in Pácalová (2010:9–120), and for selected collections,

see Pácalová (2015a, 2015c, 2018). They are housed in the Literary Archive of the Slovak National Library in Martin, Slovakia.
4. These are the *The Inventory* and *A Selection of Individual Original Slovak Tales*. They contain a chronological inventory of all manuscript collections that Dobšinský had at his disposal up to 1858. The originals are in the manuscript collection *Codex of Revúca A, B, C*, transcribed and published by Polívka (1923a:86–110).
5. This tale cannot be classfied in the ATU Tale-Type Index.
6. Jonatan Čipka Hradovský was the pseudonym of Jonatan Dobroslav Čipka.
7. In addition to Dobšinský and Škultéty, the source information refers to another fifteen contributors, the most productive of whom, with a contribution of eight tales, was one of the most important Slovak Romantic poets, Ján Botto (1829–1881). See Pácalová (2014a:12; 2010:236–237) for more detailed discussions of these contributors.
8. See also Cooper (2012) for references to further reading on this topic.
9. The orthography reflects Slovak usage before the first language codification of 1846.
10. Typical introductory formulas: "Bol raz jeden kráľ" ("Once upon a time there was a king"); "Kde bolo, tam bolo" ("Where it was, there it was"). Typical concluding formulas: "Žili šťastne, kým nepomreli" ("They lived happily ever after"); "Žijú až podnes, ak nepomreli" ("They are still alive today if they have not died").
11. The authors refer to Upper Hungary, or the northern part of multiethnic Hungary inhabited predominantly by Slovaks. Hungary was a part of the Habsburg monarchy.
12. In the preface to *Simple National Slovak Tales*, Dobšinský summarized the contents of his monograph: "I have also attempted to write *Reflections on Slovak Tales* in which, in addition to the clarification of the content, significance, and antiquity of Slovak tales, I explain the views and concepts of our Slav ancestors related to the world and nature, on divinity, the soul and immortality, and humanity as well as to the moral and legal customs and relations, both familial and civic" (1880a:4).
13. This and the subsequent generic categories are the classifications utilized in the ATU Tale-Type Index; see Uther (2011) and https://sites.ualberta.ca/~urban/Projects/English/Content/ATU_Tales.htm.
14. While the ATU Tale-Type Index is employed in the classification of folk tale plot lines, as Gašparíková aptly points out, the method of editing a tale can modify the tale type (2004b:595–597). Several examples illustrate this. In *Slovak Tales*, "About the Little Tom Cat" ("O kocúrikovi"; ATU 545B) adapts the magic tale material of "Puss in Boots" in a way that creates a humorous effect. This is how Dobšinský probably understood the tale because he did not translate it into standard Slovak but published it in dialect, which he primarily used for anecdotes and jokes. He was convinced that the folk language underscored the comic effect of the tales (Doruľa 1982, 1987, 1990; Gašparíková 1980).

In the same collection, Dobšinský also used dialect for the publication of "Are You Angry?" ("Hneváte sa?"), which, according to the ATU classification, belongs to Tales of the Stupid Ogre (Giant, Devil). In the version published by him, there are no supernatural characters, but it is a humorous tale in which a farmhand and his master compete to make each other angry. Another tale published in dialect is "We Three Brothers" ("My traja bratia"). The ATU Tale-Type Index includes material on three brothers who pledge themselves, in exchange for a large amount of money, always to say the same words. Among Tales of Magic, it is classified as ATU 360, while among Anecdotes and Jokes, it is ATU 1697. In Dobšinský's tale, the three brothers come to an agreement with the devil. However, the magic tale is narrated in language that creates a humorous effect.

The opposite process, in which the material from folk tales without supernatural elements is adapted to include elements of the magic tale, is evident in *Simple National Slovak Tales* in "Klinko and King Kompit" ("Klinko a Kompit kráľ"). It connects several motifs from Religious Tales as well as Anecdotes and Jokes (ATU 1525A + 804B + 1072 + 1071 + 1084), but its basic narrative structure follows the pattern of the magic tale. This is evident in the composition as well as the ending of the tale in which, thanks to his exploits, a clever man wins the hand of the princess and half of the kingdom. This tale was also published under the title "Clever" by Němcová, but she edited it in such a way as to make it correspond to a humorous tale type.

15. The manuscript of the lectures was not preserved, so all that remains are written records by audience members. A complete edition of the lectures based on these records was published by Pavol Vongrej (Štúr 1987). Before this publication, a magazine edition from 1875, edited by the lesser Romantic writer Andrej Truchlý-Sytniansky (1841–1916), was considered the canonical version of Štúr's lectures. Sytniansky published an incomplete and censored text (Vongrej 1981, 1987) in which he omitted the passages dedicated to the folk tale because, in his view, they did not correspond to the image of Štúr that his contemporaries constructed following his tragic death (Pácalová 2016a).
16. See "The Enchanted Mountain" ("Zakliata hora"); "Kuchta the Winner" ("Víťaz Kuchta"); "Three Whistles" ("Tri píšťalky"); "The Son of Poor Parents" ("Chudobných rodičov syn"); "Dalai Lama" ("Dalajláma"); "The Knight Who Ruled the World" ("Svetovládny rytier"); "The Little King, the Little Cook, Cinderman" ("Kráľčík, kucharčík, popeľčík"); "Cinderfella the Greatest" ("Popolvár najväčší na svete"); "Baláž"; "The Good Marksman" ("Dobrý strelec"); and "The Enchanted Sister" ("O zakliatej sestre").
17. See "Cinderfella the Greatest," "The Father's Grave" ("Otcov hrob"), "Vintalko," "The Sun Horse" ("Slncový kôň"), and "The Enchanted Sister."
18. See "The Golden Horseshoe, the Golden Feather, the Golden Hair" ("Zlatá podkova, zlaté pero, zlatý vlas"); "Vintalko"; "The Bad Brother" ("Zlý brat"); and "The Black-Haired Prince" ("Čiernovlasý princ").
19. See "Cinderfella–Foul Face," "Kuchta the Winner," and "The Father's Grave."
20. See "Vintalko," "The Sun Horse," and "Baláž."
21. See "Cinderfella the Greatest" and "Splitwood" ("Lomidrevo") or "Toppleoak" ("Valibuk").
22. See "The Enchanted Mountain."
23. See "The Good Marksman."
24. See "Nebojsa."
25. See "Mrs. Pussy Cat" ("Pani mačička") and "The Enchanted Castle" ("Zakliaty zámok").
26. See "Berona."
27. See "The Three Lemons" ("Tri citróny").
28. See "Worldly Beauty" ("Svetská krása") and "Mahuliena, the Golden Maiden" ("Mahuliena, krásna panna").

Works Cited

Brtáň, Rudo. 1969. "August Horislav Škultéty (1819–1892)." In *Literárne postavy Gemera* I., ed. Július Bolfík, 84–120. Bratislava, Slovakia: Obzor.

Bužeková, Tatiana, and Eva Krekovičová. 2008. "Dobšinského 'Úvahy o slovenských povestiach' vo svetle súčasných folkloristických a slavistických výskumov." *Slovenský národopis* 56/1:18–27.

Čepan, Oskar. 2002. "Bottov asketický hrdina." *Slovenská literatúra* 49/2:89–106.
Cooper, David L. 2001. *Traditional Slovak Folktales Collected by Pavol Dobšinský*, ed. and trans. David L. Cooper. Armonk, NY: M. E. Sharpe.
Cooper, David L. 2012. "Padělky jako romantická forma autorství. Rukopisy královédvorský a Zelenohorský ze srovnávací perspektivy." *Česká literatura* 60/1:26–44.
Dobšinský, Pavol. 1923. "Výbor samostatných pôvodných slovenských povestí." In *Súpis slovenských rozprávok* 1, ed. Jiří Polívka, 86–110. Turčiansky Sv. Martin, Slovakia: Matica slovenská. Manuscript written 1858.
Dobšinský, Pavol. 1880a. *Prostonárodnie slovenské povesti*, Vol. 1. Turčiansky Sv. Martin, Slovakia: tlačou Kníhtlačiarskeho účastinárskeho spolku–nákladom vydavateľovým.
Dobšinský, Pavol. 1880b. *Prostonárodnie slovenské povesti*, Vol. 2. Turčiansky Sv. Martin, Slovakia: tlačou Kníhtlačiarskeho účastinárskeho spolku–nákladom vydavateľovým.
Dobšinský, Pavol. 1882a. *Prostonárodnie slovenské povesti*, Vol. 6. Turčiansky Sv. Martin, Slovakia: tlačou Kníhtlačiarskeho účastinárskeho spolku–nákladom vydavateľovým.
Dobšinský, Pavol. 1882b. *Prostonárodnie slovenské povesti*, Vol. 7. Turčiansky Sv. Martin, Slovakia: tlačou Kníhtlačiarskeho účastinárskeho spolku–nákladom vydavateľovým.
Dobšinský, Pavol. 1966a. "Časy." In *Keby si počul všetky tie výchrice . . . Výber neznámej slovenskej poézie z polovice 19. storočia*, ed. Pavol Vongrej, 148. Bratislava, Slovakia: Tatran. Manuscript written 1846.
Dobšinský, Pavol. 1966b. "Bojovník." In *Keby si počul všetky tie výchrice . . . Výber neznámej slovenskej poézie z polovice 19. storočia*, ed. Pavol Vongrej, 170. Bratislava, Slovakia: Tatran. Manuscript written 1848.
Doruľa, Ján. 1982. "Význam Slovenských povestí pre výskum slovenskej lexiky." *Slovenský národopis* 30/2:90–97.
Doruľa, Ján. 1987. "O jazyku rozprávok zo zbierky Pavla Dobšinského." In *Literárnomúzejný letopis* 21, ed. Imrich Sedlák, 71–89. Martin, Slovakia: Matica slovenská.
Doruľa, Ján. 1990. "O jazyku slovenských ľudových rozprávok." *Slovenská reč* 55/3:129–146.
Erben, Karel Jaromír. 1865. *Sto prostonárodních pohádek a pověstí slovanských v nářečích původních*. Prague: I. L. Kober.
Erben, Karel Jaromír. 1869. *Vybrané báje a pověsti národní jiných větví slovanských*. Prague: Spolek pro vydávání laciných knih českých.
Gašparíková, Viera. 1980. "Slovenské humoristické podania v diele Boženy Němcovej a Pavla Dobšinského." *Slovenský národopis* 28/3:423–432.
Gašparíková, Viera. 1986a. "Rozprávky Pavla Dobšinského v dobovom kontexte a ich živý odkaz." *Slovenský národopis* 34/3:381–389.
Gašparíková, Viera. 1986b. *Slovenská ľudová próza a jej súčasné vývinové tendencie*. Bratislava, Slovakia: Národopisný ústav SAV.
Gašparíková, Viera. 1993. "Porovnávacie komentáre k jednotlivým rozprávkovým textom." In *Slovenské ľudové rozprávky*, Vol. 1, eds. Viera Gašparíková and Božena Filová, 619–748. Bratislava, Slovakia: VEDA.
Gašparíková, Viera. 2000. "Slowakische volksmärchen." In *Die Märchen der Weltliteratur*. Munich: Hugendubel.
Gašparíková, Viera. 2001. "Porovnávacie komentáre k jednotlivým rozprávkovým textom." In *Slovenské ľudové rozprávky*, Vol. 2, eds. Viera Gašparíková and Božena Filová, 905–1053. Bratislava, Slovakia: VEDA.
Gašparíková, Viera. 2004a. "Porovnávacie komentáre k jednotlivým rozprávkovým textom." In *Slovenské ľudové rozprávky*, Vol. 3, eds. Viera Gašparíková and Božena Filová, 511–574. Bratislava, Slovakia: VEDA.

Gašparíková, Viera. 2004b. "Slovenská rozprávka v ľudovom podaní." In *Slovenské ľudové rozprávky*, Vol. 3, eds. Viera Gašparíková and Božena Filová, 591–675. Bratislava, Slovakia: VEDA.

Gašparíková, Viera, and Božena Filová. 1993. *Slovenské ľudové rozprávky*, Vol. 1. Bratislava, Slovakia: VEDA.

Gašparíková, Viera, and Božena Filová. 2001. *Slovenské ľudové rozprávky*, Vol. 2. Bratislava, Slovakia: VEDA.

Gašparíková, Viera, and Božena Filová. 2004. *Slovenské ľudové rozprávky*, Vol. 3. Bratislava, Slovakia: VEDA.

Hammel, Robert. 2018. "Samuel Reuss ako encyklopedista." *Slovenská literatúra* 65/4:264–277.

Horálek, Karel. 1979. *Folklór a světová literatura*. Prague: Academia.

Horyna, Břetislav. 2005. *Dějiny rané romantiky. Fichte–Schlegel–Novalis*. Prague: Vyšehrad.

Kollár, Ján. 1834. *Národnié zpiewanky čili pjsně swětské Slowáků w Uhrách gak pospolitého lidu tak i wyššjch stawů, sebrané od mnohých, w porádek uwedené, wyswětlenjmi opatřené a wydané od Jana Kollára. Djl perwý.* Budin, Hungary: král. Universická tiskáreň.

Kováčik, Ľubomír. 2002. "Dobšinského mytologická teória slovenskej ľudovej rozprávky." In *Mytologizmus v slovenskom literárnom romantizme*, 14–19. Banská Bystrica, Slovakia: Univerzita Mateja Bela.

Kraus, Cyril. 1993. "Účasť literatúry na kodifikácii spisovnej slovenčiny." *Slovenské pohľady* 109/7:32–36.

Kraus, Cyril. 1999. *Slovenský literárny romantizmus. Vývin a tvar*. Martin, Slovakia: Matica slovenská.

Kraus, Cyril. 2000. "Poznámky na tému Dobšinského rozprávky." *Slovenské pohľady* 116/12:28–33.

Leščák, Milan. 1986. "Kultúrnohistorický význam diela Pavla Dobšinského." *Slovenský národopis* 34/3:359–367.

Leščák, Milan, and Viliam Marčok. 1977. "Dobšinský dnes." *Romboid* 11/11:32–37.

Leščák, Milan, and Oldřich Sirovátka. 1982. *Folklór a folkloristika*. Bratislava, Slovakia: Smena.

Marčok, Viliam. 1986. "Literárna hodnota Dobšinského rozprávok." *Slovenský národopis* 34/3:399–405.

Melicherčík, Andrej. 1959. *Pavol Dobšinský. Portrét života a diela*. Bratislava, Slovakia: Slovenské vydavateľstvo krásnej literatúry.

Michálek, Ján. 2008. "Pavol Dobšinský a jeho miesto v slovenskej kultúre." In *Pohľady do vývinu slovenského jazyka a ľudovej kultúry*, ed. Ján Doruľa, 270–275. Bratislava, Slovakia: Slavistický ústav Jána Stanislava SAV.

Němcová, Božena. 1857–1858. *Slovenské pohádky a pověsti*. Prague: Nákladem kněhkupectví Josefa Šálka.

Otčenášek, Jaroslav. 2012. *Antropologie narativity. Problematika české pohádky*. Prague: Etnologický ústav Akademie věd České republiky.

Pácalová, Jana. 2010. *Metamorfózy rozprávky (od Jána Kollára po Pavla Dobšinského)*. Bratislava, Slovakia: Ars Poetica–Ústav slovenskej literatúry SAV.

Pácalová, Jana. 2014a. "Rozprávky-palimpsesty (K podobám autorstva a subjektivity v rozprávkach slovenských romantikov) I." *Slovenská literatúra* 61/1:1–12.

Pácalová, Jana. 2014b. "Rozprávky-palimpsesty (K podobám autorstva a subjektivity v rozprávkach slovenských romantikov) II." *Slovenská literatúra* 61/2:89–106.

Pácalová, Jana. 2015a. *Codexy tisovské. K prameňom slovenských rozprávok*. Bratislava, Slovakia: Slavistický ústav Jána Stanislava Slovenskej akadémie vied–Ústav slovenskej literatúry Slovenskej akadémie vied.

Pácalová, Jana. 2015b. "Kniha, ktorá nevyšla." *Studia bibliographica Posoniensia* 10/1:168–180.
Pácalová, Jana. 2015c. "Romantický rozprávkar Janko Rimavský." In *Rozprávkar Janko Rimavský*, 7–52. Bratislava, Slovakia: Slavistický ústav Jána Stanislava Slovenskej akadémie vied–Ústav slovenskej literatúry Slovenskej akadémie vied.
Pácalová, Jana. 2016a. "Nádeje a sklamanie (prednášky o poézii slovanskej v redakcii Andreja Trúchleho-Sytnianskeho)." In *Štúr, štúrovci, romantici, obrodenci*, ed. Peter Zajac, 283–298. Bratislava, Slovakia: Ústav slovenskej literatúry SAV.
Pácalová, Jana. 2016b. "Romantický subjekt a ideál žertvy (paradigma popolvárovského hrdinu)." In *Autor a subjekt*, ed. Ľubica Schmarcová, 34–51. Bratislava, Slovakia: Literárne informačné centrum.
Pácalová, Jana. 2016c. "Simulovanie kolektívneho autorstva ako súčasť romantickej koncepcie autora (na príklade Slovenských povestí Augusta Horislava Škultétyho a Pavla Dobšinského)." In *Autor a subjekt*, ed. Ľubica Schmarcová, 13–33. Bratislava, Slovakia: Literárne informačné centrum.
Pácalová, Jana. 2018. "Oprašovanie pokladov: K možnostiam textologického spracovania rukopisných rozprávkových zbierok–Codexy revúcke." *Etnologické rozpravy* 25/1:25–44.
Piroščáková, Jana. 2019a. "Ad Fontes (Codexy revúcke)." *Slovenský národopis* 67/1:63–85.
Piroščáková, Jana. 2019b. "Sonda do podhubia. Motív zakliatej krajiny v slovenskom romantizme." In *Slovenský romantizmus: Synopticko-pulzačný model kultúrneho javu*, eds. Peter Zajac and Ľubica Schmarcová, 121–146. Brno, Czech Republic: Host.
Polívka, Jiří. 1923a. "O sberateľoch a sbierkach slovenských rozprávok." In *Súpis slovenských rozprávok*, Vol. 1, 1–158. Turčiansky Sv. Martin, Slovakia: Matica slovenská.
Polívka, Jiří. 1923b. *Súpis slovenských rozprávok*, Vol. 1. Turčiansky Sv. Martin, Slovakia: Matica slovenská.
Polívka, Jiří. 1924. *Súpis slovenských rozprávok*, Vol. 2. Turčiansky Sv. Martin, Slovakia: Matica slovenská.
Polívka, Jiří. 1927. *Súpis slovenských rozprávok*, Vol. 3. Turčiansky Sv. Martin, Slovakia: Matica slovenská.
Polívka, Jiří. 1930. *Súpis slovenských rozprávok*, Vol. 4. Turčiansky Sv. Martin, Slovakia: Matica slovenská.
Polívka, Jiří. 1931. *Súpis slovenských rozprávok*, Vol. 5. Turčiansky Sv. Martin, Slovakia: Matica slovenská.
Reuss, Samuel. ca. 1840–1843. "Zweyte sage." In *Codex revúcky B* [manuscript]. Literárny archív Slovenskej národnej knižnice v Martine, Starý fond, signatúra B465.
Rimauskí (Rimavský), Janko. 1845. *Slovenskje povesťi*. Levoča, Slovakia: Werthmüller a sin.
Škultéty, August Horislav, and Pavel Dobšinský. 1858. *Slovenské povesti. Kniha I. Povesti prastarých báječných časov*, Vol. I. Rožňava, Slovakia: Ladislav Krek.
Šmahelová, Hana. 1989. *Návraty a proměny. Literární adaptace lidových pohádek*. Prague: Albatros.
Štúr, Ľudovít. 1853. *O národních písních a pověstech plemen slovanských*. Prague: František Řivnáč.
Štúr, Ľudovít. 1987. *O poézii slovanskej*. Martin, Slovakia: Matica slovenská.
Urbancová, Viera. 1983. "Koncepcia dejín slovenskej etnografie." *Slovenský národopis* 31/1:57–76.
Uther, Hans-Jörg. 2011. *The Types of International Folktales. A Classification and Bibliography Based on the System of Antti Aarne and Stith Thompson*, Vols. I–III. Helsinki: Suomalainen Tiedeakatemia, Academia Scientiarum Fennica. Second printing. See also *Aarne-Thompson-Uther Classification of Folk Tales*: https://sites.ualberta.ca/~urban/Projects/English/Content/ATU_Tales.htm.

Vojtech, Miloslav. 1999. "Dobšinský Pavol." In *Slovník slovenských spisovateľov*, ed. Valér Mikula, 101–102. Prague: Libri.
Vongrej, Pavol. 1981. "Neznámy text Štúrových prednášok." *Slovenské pohľady* 97/2:95–101.
Vongrej, Pavol. 1987. "Poznámky a komentáre." In *O poézii slovanskej*, 101–125. Martin, Slovakia: Matica slovenská.
Wratislav, Henry Albert. 1889. *Sixty Folk-Tales from Exclusively Slavonic Sources*. London: E. Stock.
Žeňuchová, Katarína. 2004. "Ľudová próza zo zbierok Sama Cambla a Volodymyra Hnaťuka – prameň etnickej, jazykovej a religióznej identifikácie Slovákov." *Slavica slovaca* 39/2:115–123.
Žeňuchová, Katarína. 2006. "Pôsobenie Samuela Cambla medzi dialektológiou a folkloristikou." *Slavica slovaca* 41/1:3–16.

CHAPTER 26

VLADIMIR PROPP AND RUSSIAN WONDERTALES

SIBELAN FORRESTER

In the anglophone world (as in German-speaking nations and many others), folk tales and especially wondertales—the latter known as "fairy tales" in English by non-specialists—are one of the primary genres that come to mind when we think about folklore. The brothers Jakob and Wilhelm Grimm compiled and edited their famous nineteenth-century collection of fairy tales in German with the idea that these tales contained the essence of an *ethnos* and were ideal material for educating children in that national spirit. In the late nineteenth and early twentieth centuries, Andrew and Nora Lang edited some two dozen "fairy books" with a more international reach, bringing together tales in English and in translation; these were purchased by parents and libraries and were available to children well into the twentieth century; many of them are still in print today. The wondertales comprise an important area of historical folklore research, from the index of tale types compiled by Antti Aarne and later updated by Stith Thompson and then Hans-Jörg Uther (now known as the ATU Tale-Type Index) to folklore dissertations that assemble all known variants of a particular tale. The wondertales have inspired psychologists, filmmakers, and visual and plastic artists as well as authors and scholars of literature. In Russian, the term for wondertales is волшебные сказки ("magical [folk] tales"), and the folklorist and scholar most closely associated with them is Vladimir Yakovlevich Propp (1895–1970) (Fig. 26.1). Propp published several works on Russian folk tales, including what is probably the best-known study of folk tales in the world, *Morphology of the Folktale* (Морфология сказки, 1928). He taught for decades at Leningrad State University, including a long-standing special course on folk tales, and he left a great impact on generations of folklorists and others who still remember him fondly.

This chapter will present a brief biography of Propp, followed by a more detailed discussion of his three books on Russian folk tales, and will conclude with some information about the Russian wondertales Propp worked with in today's cultural and popular discourse.

Vladimir Propp

FIG. 26.1. Vladimir Propp later in life.

Vladimir Propp: Life and Work

Propp was born into a well-off Russified German family in St. Petersburg on April 29 (April 17 Old Style), 1895, and christened Hermann Waldemar.[1] His father worked in a business that supplied flour to all the German bakeries in St. Petersburg, which was then the imperial capital of Russia but had a thriving German and Russified-German community. The family could afford a governess for the children, and Propp grew up essentially trilingual in French, German, and Russian—quite useful for a scholar. He entered St. Petersburg University in 1913, specializing in *Germanistik*; in his third year (with the university's name already changed to fit the city's change to the less Germanic-sounding Petrograd), he switched to Russian and Slavic philology. As a university student he was not called up into the Russian army when the First World War began, but he took a six-week first-aid course and in 1915 started working in an infirmary, eventually qualifying as a nurse. Propp later wrote that this new contact with the uneducated Russian folk (народ) inspired in him a spiritual as well as intellectual connection to Russian culture. This was also when he first developed a strong interest in Russian orthodoxy, something he had to keep quiet for many Soviet years but described in his late diaries and memoirs, published only after his death.

In 1918 Propp graduated from Petrograd University with a degree in Slavic and German philology (literature and literary history)—notably, his degree was not in folklore, although German philology offered a good entrée into that topic given the prominence of the Grimms and other collectors in nineteenth-century German verbal culture. For several years after graduation Propp taught German language and other subjects at various institutions in and around the city, designing instructional materials for Russian-speaking students of German. In 1932 he accepted an invitation to teach at his alma mater, now called Leningrad State University, and he taught there for the rest of his life.

While he was studying at university Propp worked as a tutor, and he described the experience of reading Aleksandr Afanas'ev's collection of Russian folk tales (on which more below) and suddenly perceiving patterns in the events and plots of the tales—that is, specifically, in the wondertales:

> У меня проклятый дар: во всем сразу же, с первого взгляда, видеть форму. Помню, как в Павловске, на даче, репетитором в еврейской семье, я взял Афанасьева. Открыл № 50 и стал читать этот номер и следующие. И сразу открылось: композиция всех сюжетов одна и та же.
>
> I have a cursed gift: to see the form in everything at once, from the first glance. I remember how in Pavlovsk, at a summer house, working as a tutor in a Jewish family, I picked up Afanas'ev. I opened to [tale] number 50 and started reading it and the ones following. And it hit me at once: all the plots have the same composition
>
> (entry from January 27, 1969, Пропп 2002:10).[2]

This insight sparked Propp's work on the tales' morphology, a monumental project of reading and research that took ten years until it was published as a relatively brief book in 1928, under the editorship of the linguist and literary historian Viktor Zhirmunsky. The book initially received warm reviews, though interest then dropped off for a time.

Many of Propp's early scholarly friends and supporters were, like Zhirmunsky, the Petrograd developers and practitioners of the "formal method," which reacted against the previous fashion for biographically and historically based literary scholarship. We now refer to it as "formalism" or the "formal school." By the time his first book appeared (actually, it was his first scholarly publication), it was already becoming dangerous for a Soviet scholar or writer to be accused of formalism: the term was used in contrast with the stress on "correct" ideological content that was soon to be fixed in literature as socialist realism. But it was in another connection that Propp was arrested in 1930: he was accused of belonging to some kind of illegal German nationalist movement. He spent several months in prison, and this left a lasting mark on his attitude toward life in the Soviet state. Of course, "Propp" is a markedly non-Russian name, yet (unlike many twentieth-century political and literary figures) he never changed it or adopted a pseudonym in hopes of passing as an ethnic Russian. It is sadly ironic that a man so enchanted and inspired by Russian culture would be treated as an enemy alien, and unfortunately this was not the only case of such treatment during his lifetime.

Propp was not himself a collector or fieldworker, and he was largely self-educated as a specialist in folklore. He read encyclopedically for every project or course he undertook and became familiar with archives and collections and with the work of many of Russia's outstanding folklore collectors and editors (who eventually included some of his own students). His approach to folk narratives was informed by sensitive and knowledgeable references to literature. After the *Morphology* was published, he began presenting his work on folklore and folkloristics. In 1932 he was invited to teach in the Department of Romance and Germanic Philology at Leningrad State University; in 1937 he moved to the new Department of Folklore, which eventually merged with the Department of Russian Literature, all comprising part of the university's new Филологический факультет ("Philological Faculty"). Propp continued to read, ponder, and write about literature until the end of his life, even when his teaching was mostly about folklore. His 1939 doctoral thesis was later published, in revised and expanded form, as *Historical Roots of the Wondertale* (*Исторические корни волшебной сказки*), the second of his three major publications on folk tales.

Propp and his family were evacuated from Leningrad along with the university during the devastating siege of the city in March 1942, and he continued teaching in evacuation in Saratov. (His mother and older sister, who remained in the city, both died of starvation.) As the university's students and personnel were to return to Leningrad in 1944, Propp had trouble as a German getting permission to travel back with them, and his passport was taken away. Apparently, it was only support from the rector of the university that brought him back from evacuation and perhaps spared him (yet another) arrest as an enemy alien.

Historical Roots of the Wondertale (*Исторические корни волшебной сказки*) started its life as a final chapter of the *Morphology*. Propp considered it essentially that study's second part: *Morphology* explains how the wondertale is organized; *Historical Roots* attempts to explain why. Adapted from his dissertation, it was published in 1946 and almost at once harshly attacked. A long and threateningly negative review published in *Советская этнография* (*Soviet Ethnography*), for example, accused the book of infiltrating Soviet scholarship with "bourgeois traditions," anti-Marxism, idealism, religious ideas, "sycophancy" (due to the many foreign works cited in the book's extensive bibliography), and of course formalism. After the terrible suffering but also the relative cultural freedom of the war years, 1946 saw a bad moment of high Stalinist reconsolidation of scholarly and cultural control; besides scholars, it struck creative writers such as Anna Akhmatova and Mikhail Zoshchenko, and it quickly developed into the "anti-cosmopolitan" campaign, aimed mainly at Jews but not fond of Germans either. After a meeting at the university where Propp was scolded and encouraged to perform self-criticism, and where he did so, he suffered a heart attack. For several years after this he was unable to publish any significant work, although he did not lose his job at the university.

Only after Stalin's death in 1953 did Propp's situation improve. In 1955 the first Leningrad edition of his book on the Russian heroic epos appeared (*Русский герои‚ческий эпос*; a second, corrected edition was published in Moscow in 1958). Anatoly Liberman's introduction to a selection of translated excerpts from texts by Propp points out that Propp had learned his lesson from the previous harassment and did not cite a single non-Russian scholar in his book (Propp 1984b:xvi). Here, Propp distinguished the

Russian epic songs, былины (*byliny*), from other long narrative forms, including folk tales (though a few Russian folk tales do recycle or parody былина plots), and he traced their development in relation to the history of Russia while of course attending to their patterns. The epic songs were considered to have historical relevance—unlike the tales, which the folk (aside from small children) clearly recognized as entertaining fantasy— and the similarity of the Homeric epics to *byliny* granted Russian epic a higher generic status than many other kinds of folklore. This time Propp was criticized, though much more mildly, for using *only* Russian and Soviet sources in his notes and bibliography.

In 1963 Propp published his fourth monograph, *Русские аграрные праздники* (*Russian Agricultural Feastdays*). As he had done with the wondertales, here he approached the traditional seasonal festivals as a group so that the similarities and variations within a shared body of ritual actions became evident. At the same time, translations of *Morphology* into various Western European languages were finally bringing him international renown; he had a chance to respond to criticism by the French structuralist Claude Lévi-Strauss and declared, among other things, that he was not a structuralist but a semiotician. In 1969, in response to the growing interest abroad, Propp's *Morphology* was reissued in a second Soviet edition. Toward the end of his life the scholar was widely known and respected at home; his seventieth birthday in 1965 was celebrated at the university with scholarly presentations and festive toasts.

Two more books written by Propp were published posthumously. *Проблемы комизма и смеха* (*Problems of Comedy and Laughter*, published as *On the Comic and Laughter* in the 2009 English translation by Debbeche and Perron) was assembled and completed by his widow, Elizaveta Antipova, and appeared in 1976; it treats literary works more than folk and ethnographic material. *The Russian Folktale* (*Русская сказка*), based on lecture notes for his specialized course at Leningrad State University and the notes of some of his students, appeared in 1984; it will be discussed below. Later in life Propp had begun serious study of Russian church architecture and icons, collecting icons and pictures and applying the same approach to their patterned elements that characterized his previous scholarship. Several articles and material from folklore collections he edited have been translated into English, for instance, the article and selection of texts in *Down along the Mother Volga: An Anthology of Russian Folk Lyrics* (Reeder 1975). Personal notes and memoirs published long after his death reveal that as a young man he was inspired by Russian orthodoxy, even enrolling briefly in seminary in 1921, a year during the Russian Civil War when seminary experience would have offered no possible professional advancement or benefit. This aspect of Propp's spiritual and intellectual life was inspired, he wrote, by works of religious philosophers Vladimir Solov'ev and Pavel Florensky. Perhaps working with Russian folklore, especially as the genres he most often studied (wondertales, epic songs) slipped into the past, helped him keep a connection to that principle even in the darker hours of his life in the Soviet Union. Various other published volumes have collected Propp's articles and other writings or listed his complete bibliography.

Propp married twice: first to Serafima Pavlovna Sokolova (with whom he had daughters Maria and Elena) and then to Elizaveta Yakovlevna Antipova, with whom he had a son, Mikhail, born in 1937. Late in life Propp and his wife were run off their feet caring for a grandson, but even after turning seventy he continued to teach his special folk tale course rather than retiring completely. In the 1960s, finally freed from the earlier pressures, he worked on his memoirs and a fictionalized autobiography. In one section of the latter, he expresses pity for the boy Fedya, who is clearly based on himself: "Бедный мальчик! Он с мамой говорит по-немецки, а с другими—по-русски и иногда путает языки. Да, несчастный . . . . Может ли быть скучнее судьба, чем родиться немцем, евреем или поляком в великодержавной России?" ("The poor boy! He speaks German with his mother but Russian with others and sometimes mixes up languages. Yes, he's unfortunate . . . . Can there be a fate more tedious than to be born a German, a Jew, or a Pole in the great state of Russia?") (Пропп 2002:26). Propp died on August 22, 1970, in Leningrad—the same city where he had been born, just with a different name.

It is important to know something about Propp's life, including the periods when he faced repression (1930, 1944, 1947–1953), because that determined the conditions in which he worked—not only the material conditions, as he might have called them, that provoked a heart attack or fainting in front of his students during class but also the intellectual barriers that kept him (as he himself recognized and regretted) from accessing and engaging with more recent scholars and scholarship from elsewhere in the world, plus the psychological pressures that compelled him, or perhaps his editors, to insert Soviet cant into many of his publications. (The worst of that has largely been removed unannounced in later editions; we may also speculate about the reasons for this editing, and it is not always clear whether editors of newer publications had access to original manuscripts.) Liberman's lengthy introduction to Propp's career (see Propp 1984b) describes many concrete instances of hostile criticism of and outright attacks on Propp; he cites the scholar and philologist Olga Freidenberg, who wrote to her cousin Boris Pasternak that Propp, "who had been mercilessly harassed because he was German, began to lose his sense of dignity, which he had preserved for so long" (Pasternak 1982:268). Liberman bitterly derides the Marxist bent of some of Propp's works (though he praises the worthwhile insights in every work), asserting that Propp was sincere in the Marxism he adopted after 1928. We might ask in return: what was Propp supposed to do? Unlike Liberman, who emigrated from the USSR in 1975 (five years or so after Propp's death in 1970), Propp was, or at least felt that he was, stuck in place. Besides perhaps fearing for his family, he may well have found the laws of historical development that Marxism and thence dialectical materialism imposed on culture congenial to his insights in *Historical Roots* and other works. The Marxist ideas were in harmony with other scientific and scholarly theories of the late nineteenth century, and the idea of evolving and predictable "stages" (стадии) specified allowed him to push his analysis back into the past, much as historical linguistics had done, to posit the wondertale's sources and explain the formations he found in the materials.

Propp's Folk Tale Scholarship

Three books by Propp especially address the folk tale, and even today these three (especially *Morphology* and *The Russian Folktale*) provide an excellent introduction to the topic for specialists as well as students of folklore and folk culture in Russia. Propp originally gave his first book the title Морфология волшебной сказки (*Morphology of the Wondertale*), but the editor simplified it for a more general appeal to readers, who would be familiar with the word сказка ("folk tale") tout court. Recent Russian editions of the book have begun restoring the original title. Although the 1928 title refers to any folk tale, the book clearly concentrates on wondertales, proceeding from Propp's original insight into the patterns that structure them but do not apply to other kinds of folk tales. Just as the word "morphology" can refer to the study of form in various branches of biology or other natural sciences, the book argues for a structure or grammar of the tales. Propp identifies seven essential types of characters, characterized by their role in the tale rather than by other features: these are the dispatcher, the donor, the false hero, the helper, the hero, the princess, and the villain. The donor, for example, gives the hero some needed thing but may at the same time be a character of many positive or negative kinds. Propp isolates thirty-one *functions* of the wondertales, labeled with letters of the alphabet to underline that the functions come in predictable order and then adorned with numbers to distinguish subtypes. Some functions appear together: thus, a kidnapping (function A1) must be followed by a rescue (various flavors of R). Propp deduced the functions from detailed comparative analysis of various Russian wondertales—not for nothing did it take him ten years to complete the book. One function is the same even if it is performed by different characters or by different means. The approach in *Morphology* organized, and in a way professionalized, study of this important folk genre. In longer and more complex wondertales, multiple *moves* add suspense or prolong pleasure by lengthening the narrative, returning to an earlier point in the sequence of functions and deferring the ending—Propp took his term "move" (ход) from chess and similar games. The classic ending is marriage and coronation of the hero—which might well be read as a single thing since in the Russian Orthodox marriage ceremony crowns are held over the bride and groom and "crowning" (венчание) is a synonym for "wedding."

In many cases the precision of Propp's system will break down if applied to individual tales, but it is nevertheless a profound contribution to the study of wondertales. Even a folklorist who finds Propp's method unhelpful must take it into account in outlining the plan for any study of folk tales. In literary or film adaptations of wondertales, Propp's system makes it easy to see where authorial fantasy departs from folk tradition while perhaps offering steps for a creator to follow. It is significant that he based his system on Russian (and occasionally other Slavic) materials, rather than the west European tales on which most European folk tale scholarship had previously relied. The work has had a huge impact on literary theory and subsequently on the study or teaching of any kind of formulaic literature, sharpening perception of patterns in other forms of discourse.

The *Morphology* burst into world prominence when it was translated into English in 1958, thanks largely to Roman Jakobson (originally a youthful member of the formal school, by 1958 a famous linguist teaching at Harvard University). The book was reviewed in 1960 by Claude Lévi-Strauss, which brought it to the attention of prominent literary theorists in France, and then picked up and applied to new folk material by Alan Dundes, who was to become a renowned and influential scholar of folklore in the anglophone world. Propp's work was simultaneously a formative influence on structuralist literary theory and its heirs and a new and influential tool for practical study of folk material—and it was soon applied to all kinds of genres and phenomena, much as Propp directed his sense for pattern at a variety of topics of his own. For folklorists, his approach offered a productive alternative or supplement to the tale types listed by Antti Aarne (updated later by Stith Thompson and then Hans-Jörg Uther [Uther 2004, 2011]) and to motif indices. The book has been critiqued and its approach adapted many times and from various directions, but it remains a fundamental, even classical work in the history of folklore studies and of intellectual discourse. The revised translation into English published in 1968 has been in print ever since.

Once when revising the syllabus for a course on Russian folklore, I had left my copy of *Morphology* at home. A quick trip to the library revealed that one of their copies was on reserve for an advanced seminar in English literature, while the other copy was on reserve for a seminar in French. Any approach to discourse can find Propp's famous book useful and consider it a necessary precondition for a scholarly study. When it was rediscovered in the 1950s, Western scholars were stunned that these insights had been published so many years before.

It is also true that the book is awkwardly written, and one might well question some of the functions that Propp so labored to discover and systematize: they become so general, in his effort to keep the system shapely, that some divisions begin to blur. One might raise objections about the gender of the prescribed characters: a fair number of well-known Russian wondertales feature heroines rather than heroes ("Finist, the Bright Falcon," "Father Frost," "Vasilisa the Beautiful" and various other tales of Baba Yaga), whereas the princess is generally a kidnapped victim, a tester, or a reward (Figs. 26.2–26.4). For this and other reasons many scholars have adapted elements of Propp's system to use in their own work. Folklore scholar and Germanist Jack Zipes (1988:10) has reduced it to eight steps, while Alan Dundes discerned two sequences "in what people think of as 'story': assignment of task to accomplishment of task, and lack to lack liquidated" (2007:123). All the same, specialists in cultural studies and literary theory, even if they do not read the book or apply its approaches, must be aware of its importance in the development of theory. Knowledge of the functions and their order may help in distinguishing the real thing from "fakelore"—though perhaps it also works as a manual for composing fakelore. Besides Propp's engagement with Claude Lévi-Strauss (much of whose work on factors structuring human society and their interpretation was done before Propp's work was widely available in the West), he has been compared to Joseph Campbell, whose *Hero with a Thousand Faces* (1949) also appeared before Propp

FIG. 26.2. Ivan Bilibin's illustration of Baba Yaga flying in her mortar, emphasizing the red-capped mushrooms, fly agaric, on the forest floor.

(Ivan Bilibin, 1900, watercolour and ink on paper, Association Goznak, Moscow)

became widely known in the West. Campbell draws more on myth than on folk tales—and his book is easier reading than the *Morphology*.

As mentioned above, Propp's second monograph, *Historical Roots of the Wondertale* (*Исторические корни волшебной сказки*), strives to find the *Why?* to Morphology's *How?* Why are there such similarities among wondertales from very different and very distant cultures, and can elements of initiation rituals be reconstructed by back-forming

FIG. 26.3. Ivan Bilibin, Vasilisa the Beautiful leaving Baba Yaga's hut with a skull full of fire.
(Ivan Bilibin, 1899, watercolour and ink on paper, Association Goznak, Moscow)

from a wide international sweep of folk and ethnographic material? Propp assumed that analogous conditions of production in hunter–gatherer societies would produce similar ritual elements, meaning that material from very distant places and from more recently recorded "primitive" cultures could supplement information drawn from Russian wondertales and ethnographic material, where the past was buried more deeply. The book draws on an enormous trove of folk and ethnographic material, though lack of access to more recent scholarship from outside the USSR gives the work an old-fashioned feeling even in its updated, post-Stalin-era form: it reflects the assumptions, sometimes

FIG. 26.4. Ivan Bilibin, Vasilisa the Beautiful encounters the White Knight, the spirit of dawn before sunrise.

(Ivan Bilibin, 1900, watercolour and ink on paper, Association Goznak, Moscow)

imperialist and even racist, of scholars of comparative religion from the late nineteenth and early twentieth centuries.

In fact, in Propp's presentation the assumptions of late nineteenth-century anthropology and ethnography seem to fit well with Marxist ideas about the ways different societies develop, meaning that "primitive" societies can stand in for earlier stages of more "advanced" societies such as that of the Soviet Union, or at least its European parts. The book is tremendously erudite, incorporating material from folk tales, comparative religion, anthropology, and ethnography, as recorded all over the world. Propp argues that wondertales are based in actual initiation rituals from pre-agricultural stages of human civilization. The Russian wondertales preserve narratives from adolescent rites of passage in animist forest hunting cultures: tales evolved into narratives to be told for entertainment once those rituals were no longer practiced as (in the case of Russia) forest culture was largely replaced by agriculture, a different set of practices more based on practical understanding of how to manipulate the earth to grow food. Propp asserts that the classical wondertale rescue from danger was added once actual sacrifice (such as to a dragon, associated with rain and thus with fertility) was no longer performed: if a hero had come to intervene in the era when the sacrifice was part of religion, not yet distanced into mythology, it would have been blasphemous. The link to adolescent rites of passage explains why so many wondertales end with marriage, the step that brought an adolescent in traditional society into the adult world.

This seems to mesh well with the stages of historical development posited by Marxism, which Propp eagerly credits in his work, plentifully citing Friedrich Engels in particular. His book appeared just as the anti-cosmopolitanism campaign was gaining steam, though, and so was subjected to violent attacks by professional academic thugs who saw much better than the well-intentioned scholar which way the cultural wind was blowing. We cannot say what kind of pressure was applied to Propp, though his humiliating self-criticism in 1948 and comments from observers like Freidenberg, mentioned above, show that it had a devastating moral and physical effect on him. The texts and publication history of *Historical Roots* and subsequent books by Propp might offer material for studying how political and social pressures impact the ideas a scholar can pursue. Everything Propp wrote offers intriguing ideas and (often) analysis, but his transformation under Stalin may feel similar to Dostoevsky's repudiation of his own youthful left-wing opinions after arrest, mock execution, imprisonment, hard labor, and exile. Although Propp left behind the Russified-German community he had been born into, his experience of prison in 1930 showed him what the system could do to someone who did not conform. Academic freedom continues to be an issue around the world today, and we might ask how much continuing life as a scholar and researcher is worth, compared to the price of refusing to compromise.

There are several distinct editions of *Historical Roots*: the original from 1946, inevitably shaped by the need to cite Stalin (along with Lenin, Marx, and Engels) and surely by other concessions necessary to get it into print; one from 1986, with the worst of those rhetorical elements removed; one from 1996, published by St. Petersburg State University and already a post-Soviet version; reprints from various years by Labirint Publishers (2002, 2004, 2009, 2011, 2014); and multiple editions from 2020 and 2021, though these last may be simple reprints of earlier editions. The increasing number of publications now available suggests that the book intrigues readers and/or has become required reading in some academic programs. The 1946 and 1986 editions, of course, are now bibliographic rarities.

A new English translation of *Historical Roots* is in progress, but as of this writing the book is available only in fragments in English, mainly in the 1984 collection of excerpts from Propp's works edited by Anatoly Liberman, *Theory and History of Folklore* (Propp 1984b). Liberman notes in his brief initial "Editor's Note" that "[e]veryone interested in oral literature, in the history of literature, in comparative literature, in Russian folklore, in structuralism, in the impact of Marxist ideas on the humanities, and in the state of the art in the Soviet Union" should find Propp (and this anthology of his writings in particular) of interest (Propp 1984b:viii). Liberman's detailed and punctilious seventy-two-page (!) introduction offers an unparalleled survey of information on Propp's scholarly and critical reception, along with copious information and opinion about linguistics and an extended discussion of Lévi-Strauss, compared and contrasted to Propp. Liberman criticizes Propp's subordination to Marxist theory in his writings after 1928, and especially to Soviet requirements for scholarly citation, accusing Propp of being "all right with Big Brother" (p. lii). Propp's compromises seem to exemplify what Vladislav Zubok calls a Faustian bargain between senior scholars and the Soviet state (2009:124). On the one hand, ideological demands were enforced in published attacks or at department meetings, if not by arrest and worse, while, on the other hand, compliant scholars were rewarded with summer houses, scholarly prestige, membership in research institutes or the Academy of Sciences, and the like. Presentations of Propp's work and biography by scholars in Russia are, understandably, much more sympathetic, perhaps criticizing his compromises implicitly, gently hinting at the pressures he faced (arrest and imprisonment in 1930; the 1944 ban from returning to Leningrad, where his whole life was located; the harassment that led to a heart attack), and implying, though never stating outright, that he was not wrong to act as he did.

Propp's posthumous book *The Russian Folktale* (*Русская сказка*, Propp 1984a) actually does treat folk tales of every kind, not merely wondertales. The book is based on Propp's own lecture notes from his special course on folk tales at Leningrad State University, which he had begun to expand into written form, supplemented by notes of his students. While the book concentrates on the study of folk tales that were told in Russian by ethnic Russians, it offers a great deal of other information: an overview of the history of folk tale collection, especially but not only in Russia and the USSR; attention to folklore as a source of secular literature in Western Europe (starting with Basile, Boccaccio, Chaucer, and various French authors of literary fairytales); and then the history of folk tale studies, including west European exemplars but highlighting Russian collectors and scholars. Propp emphasizes the different varieties of folk tale collections, from the often haphazard mass of manuscripts in the archives of the Russian Geographical Society that Afanas'ev was asked to edit to Ivan Khudiakov's, collected by the editor himself and usually providing some information about where a tale was recorded and who the teller was. Some collectors would work to assemble the whole repertoire of one talented or famous teller, while others would invite different inhabitants of one village to tell tales, even if some of them overlapped. Propp continues his survey of collectors into the twentieth century and the Soviet period, mentioning the collections of workers' folklore that have received less attention from scholars abroad.

The Russian Folktale provides a separate chapter for each of the four main kinds of tales: wondertales or "magic tales" (волшебные сказки), "novellistic tales" (whose name, derived from "novella" rather than "novel," intends to locate these tales as a transitional form between folk oral genres and literary stories), cumulative tales (as when one character after another forms a chain to pull out a stubborn turnip), and animal tales. The length of these chapters decreases tellingly from the first through the last one: Propp has the most to say about wondertales, second most about the novellistic tales, and so on. In any case, the Russian corpora of cumulative and animal tales is smaller than the others. The presentation of ideas from *Morphology* in the chapter on wondertales is clearer and easier to assimilate than in *Morphology* itself since Propp has worked out over time how to present the information in a lecture. If *Morphology* is often dry and mechanical in style, *The Russian Folktale* shows its origins in lectures: Propp often slows down discernably to emphasize the importance of what he is about to say, essentially telling his students to pick up their pencils and prepare to take notes. Occasionally the book includes skeletal sections that stand in for the elaborated versions Propp must have given from memory in his lectures. *The Russian Folktale* was translated into other languages (such as Italian) years before the translation into English was published in 2012, with a foreword by Jack Zipes (Propp 2012) (Fig. 26.5).

Folk tales seem not to have been compromised as "fakelore," as were the Soviet *noviny* (narratives about revolutionary and political figures composed along the lines of traditional epic songs, *byliny*), since epic songs had higher status and were expected to respond to historical events; nevertheless, by the 1960s the oral genre was already dying out, if not dead, even in distant villages. Tellers were aware that Soviet culture frowned on all the kings and princes, and with the quick spread of literacy in the 1920s and 1930s teachers and then parents were more likely to read a printed version to children but even more likely to choose Soviet "folk tales" for children, like Arkadii Gaidar's "Сказка о военной тайне" ("Tale of the Military Secret," 1933). The Soviet state and its cultural apparatus cunningly used popular culture to confine folklore in safe compartments: updated narratives arrived via newspapers, books, theater (including local amateur performances), then movies, and eventually television.

Propp continues to be widely cited in scholarly literature, sometimes to signal that a folklore scholar has checked all the boxes or to signal application of the *Morphology*'s insights to new kinds of formulaic discourse, such as detective stories or romance literature. Recent citations in English include articles or books on Icelandic sagas, internet mythology, Thai animation, and young adult fantasy series. One recent work in digital humanities engages thoroughly with Propp's *Morphology*, moving toward the possibility of Proppian-style machine analysis of tales, which that author recognizes is a time-consuming, laborious task that requires both close attention and very good knowledge of the culture concerned: "blind reproduction or validation of a morphological analysis is a prohibitively difficult endeavor, requiring a scholar with the necessary skills to retrace the years-long paths of reading, analysis, and synthesis required to generate a morphology by hand" (Finlayson 2016:56).

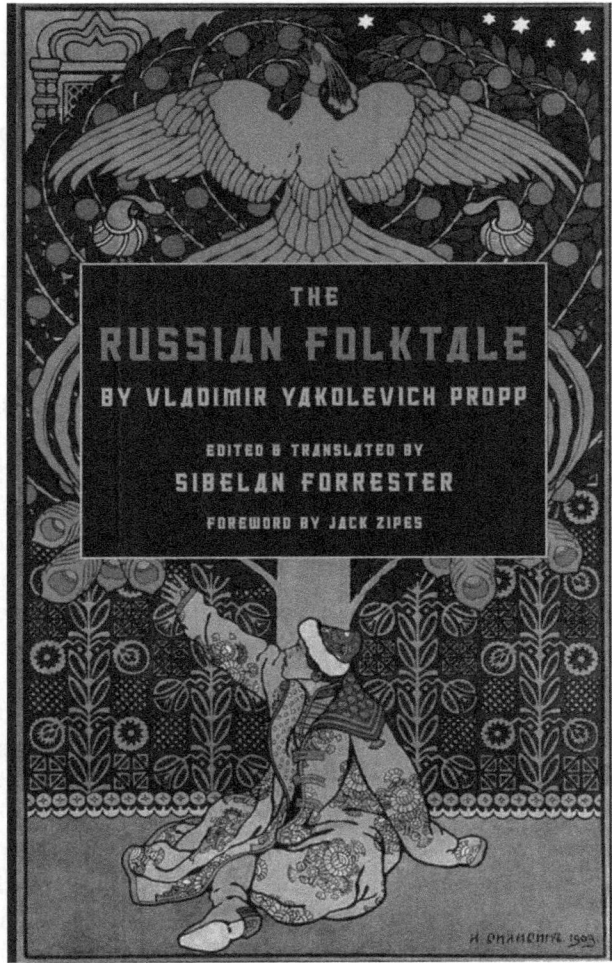

FIG. 26.5. The cover of the 2012 translation of Propp's study *The Russian Folktale*, featuring Ivan Bilibin's illustration of "The Firebird."

(Wayne State UP, 2012)

Nonetheless, it truly is tempting to approach wondertales via Propp's analysis with artificial intelligence: his analytic work strives to identify a system, synthesizing its insights into tables of data that could be manipulated for all kinds of purposes. In practice, however, even for the hundred tales from Afanas'ev that are distilled in the *Morphology*, Propp's work is more illuminating than exhaustive. He tends, like Campbell, to want to include everything in a master narrative, though he uses the wondertale as opposed to myth. This may help explain why his analysis is so male-centric; looking at both male and female heroes might require different approaches and thus could potentially complicate the model.

Afanas'ev Past and Present

The foundational collection of Russian folk tales is the one edited and published by Aleksandr Afanas'ev (1826–1871), who was invited to work with the quite motley archives of the Russian Geographical Society. The initial five volumes appeared between 1855 and 1863 and contain nearly six hundred tales, making the collection one of the largest in the world. It is very much worth noting that the texts (as opposed to the order of tales, commentary, and other apparatus) in this foundational collection were barely revised after initial publication, unlike the tales in the Grimms' collections, which were revised several times in new editions (see Haase 1993). Afanas'ev himself approached the texts of the tales as ethnographic material rather than as primers in "being Russian," and his death in 1871 left future publication in the hands of other editors. Individual tales from the Народные русские сказки (*Folk Russian Tales*) have been edited and adapted for all kinds of Russian editions and projects, but the fundamental collection has changed only slightly over time (aside from adjustment to the new Russian orthography and re-arrangement of its elements). Afanas'ev's mythological school commentaries (à la Max Müller) on certain tales are no longer provided alongside the tales concerned, but they are still included at the end of the edition, as appendices. Propp notes in *The Russian Folktale* that Afanas'ev already perceived the four main types of Russian folk tales correctly and that he was planning to organize them differently in the next edition, which appeared after his death. The posthumous editions, of which the most complete and scholarly versions became standard in three volumes, reflect this understanding; the wondertales, in particular, are all given together in series. Afanas'ev provides variants of tales, useful to scholars if not as interesting for readers; this also conveys recognition that versions of folk tales depend on individual tellers as well as particular instances of performance. Those tales that are clearly in Belarusian and Ukrainian, or in adjacent dialects from southern and western Russia, are included among the Russian tales but not edited or translated into standard Russian. The complete three volumes of Afanas'ev's tales, along with notes and commentary, have been translated into English by Jack Haney (Afanas'ev 2014, 2015, 2021); many individual tales or briefer selections have been translated into English since the early twentieth century, including Norbert Guterman's translation of over 175 tales (Afanas'ev 1976), with an afterward by Roman Jakobson (Fig. 26.6).

Afanas'ev's collection has had multiple afterlives in addition to the star turn in Propp's *Morphology*. Briefer selections of tales, without apparatus but still identified as tales from Afanas'ev, have been published for children—or for general readers, like the tales beautifully illustrated in fin-de-siècle "folk" style by artist Ivan Bilibin. Afanas'ev's collection solidified into a three-volume set that has been re-edited multiple times, always under the editorial guidance of whoever is the leading folklorist of the day in Russia, then the Soviet Union, and then Russia again. For the 1955 edition, that was Propp himself (Афанасьев 1955–1957). One should also mention the *Заветные сказки* (sometimes translated as *Forbidden Tales*) that Afanas'ev had assembled, which treated

FIG. 26.6. The cover of the Pantheon edition of Norbert Guterman's translation of a selection of tales from Afanas'ev.

political, religious, and sexual themes that Russian imperial censorship would not have passed; these were first published abroad by subscription in the nineteenth century. Since tales that mocked Orthodox priests often included sexual elements, only a few of those "obscene" tales made it through the puritanical Soviet censorship into published collections of that era. A collection of the *Forbidden Tales* was published right after the end of the USSR, with naughty lubok-style illustrations and an archaic font. Aside from questions of censorship, that sub-collection of Afanas'ev's is a reminder that authentic folk tales (which, in this case, almost entirely lack any elements of the wondertale) were told for and to adults as much as for children.

Nevertheless, the folk tale as a living oral genre, which Jakobson and his folklorist co-author Petr Bogatyrev asserted was alive and widespread in the Moscow region in the 1920s (Jakobson and Bogatyrev [1928] 1982:33), died away with the spread of literacy and other forms of popular entertainment (radio, cinema, television). The exceptions are professional tellers who perform at libraries or in living museums, often in folk costume—but they tend to have memorized the texts they recite. The versions published by Afanas'ev and others continue to be read for pleasure and for artistic inspiration. These include Bilibin's beautiful stylized illustrations; Nadezhda Teffi's humorous story "Нянькина сказка про кобылью голову" ("A Nanny's Tale about a Mare's Head," 1910), in which upper-class parents hire a tale-telling peasant nanny for their children and swoon over the dreadful tale she tells; Marina Tsvetaeva's folkloric long poems, especially "Царь-Девица" ("The Tsar-Maiden," 1922), which combines elements of both versions of that tale from Afanas'ev; Vasilii Shukshin's humorous "До третьих петухов" ("Before the Cock Crows Thrice," 1976), which mixes folk tale characters—starting with the hero, Ivan the Fool—together with literary heroes who share shelves in the library and typical Soviet behaviors among folk characters like Baba Yaga or Zmei Gorynych, whom Ivan encounters "in the wild." Folk tale characters are used for humor: one anecdote has a mother threatening that if her child does not finish her breakfast kasha Baba Yaga will come, to which the child responds: "So will she really finish eating my kasha?" Scholars continue to discover and interpret the ways tales (still most often taken from Afanas'ev) enter material and popular culture, film, television, theater, and literature.

Wondertales today are strongly associated with children (not adolescents); folk characters show up in decorations for day care centers and kindergartens, in cartoons and feature films (the wretched pastiche of folk tale elements in the humorous live-action Soviet Baba Yaga movies is nonetheless enjoyed by viewers; more recent animated treatments span a variety of approaches). Folk tale elements may be discerned in many of the best-loved children's cartoons, such as *Ёжик в тумане* (*Hedgehog in the Mist*, 1975). Since adults are familiar with wondertale plots from their own childhoods, references in artistic works of any kind will be meaningful to them. A quick survey of recent literary publications shows a body of original works with the generic title or subtitle "сказка."

As long as Russian folk tales, and especially Russian wondertales, occupy such a large part in the culture, Propp's insights will continue to be sought out. Although his *Russian Folktale* touches on many important collectors and editors of Russian folk tales, his work on wondertales helps to keep Afanas'ev in the center of the perception and study of Russian folk tales. Propp's writings offer profound insights into Russian folk culture, its structures and its roots; his *Morphology of the Folktale* in particular has proved to be useful and even obligatory for scholars who work in fields quite far from its origins.

Notes

1. Both the Russian Empire and the Soviet Union imposed Russian patronymics on their citizens, so Propp's legal name in both states includes the patronymic formed from his father's name, Jakob, translated into Russian Yakov.
2. Here and elsewhere all translations are mine unless otherwise noted.

Works Cited

Афанасьев, Александр. 1955–1957. *Народные русские сказки в 3 тт.* Подгот. текста, предисловие и примечания В.Я. Проппа. Москва: Гослитиздат.

Afanas'ev, Aleksandr. 1976. *Russian Fairy Tales*, trans. Norbert Guterman. Afterword by Roman Jakobson. New York: Pantheon.

Afanas'ev, Aleksandr. 2014, 2015, 2021. *The Complete Folktales of A. N. Afanas'ev*, trans. and ed. Jack V. Haney. 3 vols. Jackson: University Press of Mississippi.

Campbell, Joseph. 1949. *Hero with a Thousand Faces*. Princeton: Princeton University Press.

Dundes, Alan. 2007. "Structuralism and Folklore: Introduction." In *The Meaning of Folklore: The Analytical Essays of Alan Dundes*, ed. and introduction Simon J. Bronner, 123–144. Louisville: University Press of Colorado; Logan: Utah State University Press.

Finlayson, Mark Alan. 2016. "Inferring Propp's Functions from Semantically Annotated Text." *The Journal of American Folklore*, 129/511:55–77.

Haase, Donald, ed. 1993. *The Reception of Grimms' Fairy Tales. Responses, Reactions, Revisions*. Detroit: Wayne State University Press.

Jakobson, Roman, and Petr Bogatyrev. 1982. "Folklore as a Special Form of Creativity." In *The Prague School: Selected Writings, 1929–1946*, ed. Peter Steiner, trans. Manfred Jacobson, 32–46. Austin: University of Texas Press. First published 1928.

Pasternak, Boris. 1982. *Correspondence with Olga Freidenberg*, ed. with commentary by Elliott Mossman. New York and London: Harcourt Brace Jovanovich. Cited from Liberman, "Introduction," in Propp 1984b, p. xv.

Пропп, Владимир. 1928. *Морфология сказки*. Ленинград: Государственный институт истории искусств.

Пропп, Владимир. 1955. *Русский героический эпос*. Ленинград: Ленинградский Государственный Университет.

Propp, Vladimir. 1958. *Morphology of the Folktale*, trans. Laurence Scott, introduction by Svatava Pirková-Jakobson. Bloomington: Indiana University Research Center in Anthropology, Folklore and Linguistics.

Пропп, Владимир. 1963. *Русские аграрные праздники*. Ленинград: Ленинградский Государственный Университет.

Propp, Vladimir. 1968. *Morphology of the Folktale*, 2nd ed., trans. Laurence Scott, ed. Louis A. Wagner, introduction by Alan Dundes. Austin: University of Texas Press.

Пропп, Владимир. 1976. *Проблемы комизма и смеха*. Москва: Искусство.

Пропп, Владимир. 1984a. *Русская сказка*. Ленинград: Издательство Ленинградского Государственного Университета.

Propp, Vladimir. 1984b. *Theory and History of Folklore*, trans. Adriana Y. Martin and Richard P. Martin, ed. with introduction and notes by Anatoly Liberman. Minneapolis: University of Minnesota Press.

Пропп, Владимир. 2002. *Неизвестный В.Я. Пропп. Древо жизни. Дневник старости. Переписка*. Предисловие, сост. Антонины Н. Мартыновой. Санкт-Петербург: Издательство «Aleteia».

Propp, Vladimir. 2009. *On the Comic and Laughter*, trans. Jean-Patrick Debbeche and Paul J. Perron. Toronto: University of Toronto Press.

Propp, Vladimir. 2012. *The Russian Folktale*, ed. and trans. Sibelan Forrester, foreword by Jack Zipes. Detroit, MI: Wayne State University Press.

Reeder, Roberta, ed. and trans. 1975. *Down along the Mother Volga: An Anthology of Russian Folk Lyrics*, introduction by V. Ja. Propp. Philadelphia: University of Pennsylvania Press.

Uther, Hans-Jörg. 2004, 2011. *The Types of International Folktales. A Classification and Bibliography. Based on the System of Antti Aarne and Stith Thompson*. 3 vols. Helsinki: Suomalainen Tiedeakatemia, Academia Scientiarum Fennica.

Zipes, Jack. 1988. "The Changing Functions of the Fairytale." *The Lion and the Unicorn*, 12/2:7–31.

Zubok, Vladislav. 2009. *Zhivago's Children: The Last Russian Intelligentsia*. Cambridge, MA–London: Belknap Press of Harvard University Press.

CHAPTER 27

SUPERNATURAL LEGENDS IN THE WESTERN BALKANS

DORIAN JURIĆ

WHILE the Slavic Balkans have largely been associated with oral epic singing in international folklorist circles, the region boasts a dynamic and fertile tradition of oral narrative genres. In this chapter I provide a brief overview of Slavic Western Balkan supernatural legends, focused most particularly on those of the Bosnians, Croats, Montenegrins, and Serbs. I make some observations in dialogue with the work of other scholars, outline some avenues for future research, and argue that novel theoretical practices and renewed collection projects in the region must be accompanied by a return to the production of "survey studies"—comprehensive overviews of singular supernatural beings based on large-scale systematization of extant oral traditional materials combined with synchronic and diachronic mapping. Data in this chapter are drawn from various published sources, as well as from my own historical research with unpublished manuscripts in the archive in the Department of Ethnology at the Croatian Academy of Sciences and Arts and contemporary ethnographic research, predominantly conducted in Croatia and Bosnia-Herzegovina.[1]

ORAL NARRATIVE IN THE WESTERN BALKANS

Oral prose narratives (Bosnian, Croatian, Montenegrin, and Serbian [hereafter BCMS]; *pripovijetke/pripovetke*, Macedonian [Mac.] *prikazna*, Slovenian [Slov.] *pripoved*) in the Slavic Western Balkans follow the most common folkloristic division (Bascom 1965)[2] of myth (*Mit*), folktale (BCMS and Mac. *bajka* [also BCMS *skaska*, Mac. *skazna*], Slov. *pravljica*), and legend (Croatian and Bosnian *predaja*, Serbian and Mac. *predanje*, Slov. *povedka*, *pripovedka*), although a smaller subset of hagiographic stories, miracles tales, and other legends which lack a strong localized character are often separated out under the recognizable title *legenda* (Botica 2013:435–449).[3] Finer analytical genres taken from German, English, Russian, and Finnish folkloristics are used by specialists; however, tellers and folklorists generally convene on these categories. This is with good reason: the categories largely derive from native terminology (e.g., *predaja*, best glossed as "tradition," from the verb *predati*, to convey, surrender, or pass on) often have broad applications in common usage and carry extended morphological configurations that produce a useful vernacular lexicon (e.g., *pripovedati*, to tell a story, as the verb form of *pripovetke*). Of course, as elsewhere, this nomenclature is often foregone in lieu of simple terms like "story"/"tale" (BCMS *priča*, Slov. *zgodba*). In the BCMS languages it is also common to discuss these stories by nature of their transmission with the stock phrasing that the story was *prenošena s koljena/kolena na koljeno/koleno*, literally, passed on/transferred from knee to knee, that is, from one generation to the next.

Traditionally, oral narratives, like songs and other folklore, were performed domestically during family gatherings, feasts, weddings, holidays, work (shucking corn, drying tobacco, washing clothing, etc.), and travel. The arts were particularly cultivated after harvest and during winter when field work and other duties were suspended. At these times families and friends would gather *na selo/sijelo/silo* (BCMS lit. at a session/for a sit) to eat, drink, and converse. Oral traditions were an integral part of these gatherings as entertainment and as critical modes of transmission for traditional knowledge and cultural memory (Bošković-Stulli 1967:311–312; Murko 1951:343–335). Legends as a genre, though, are generally unique in not requiring and often completely lacking a formal storytelling occasion, even if their deployment may be reserved for a suitable, etic audience (Šešo 2010a:103–104). Heavily tethered to locations and events, discourses on belief, etiological reasoning, and prescriptive and proscriptive behavior, legends are most often shared spontaneously and are not "set apart from the flow of conversation through the use of distancing formulas" (Tangherlini 1994:8). It is thus a prompted and functional genre rather than a performative one, or at least one not rendered wholly as performance.

Like most other regions of Europe, early published examples of this lore largely appeared in highly adapted form in medieval and renaissance missals, prayer books, and treatises which served didactic functions in Christian (and Muslim) discourse (Botica 2013:441; Mencej 2017:153–155; Milošević-Đorđević 1991:317–318; Valk 2015:143–150). At that time, tales often passed fluidly between both oral and written texts which were not so heavily divided in their essential features—they took on variant forms, were often anonymous, and were redacted and altered with abandon (Bošković-Stulli 1963:7). Finally approached as a worthy topic of scientific enquiry in the romantic nationalist movements of the nineteenth century, oral prose narratives took on a new life by serving as nascent national literature in the scholarly zeitgeist. In this frame, the texts were treated with reverence as a window into national pasts and the mentality of the folk; their forms, however, were still deemed unsightly and primitive compositions, demanding heavy emendation to make them suitable for public consumption (Valk 2015:150–158). This perception shifted over the following decades as folkloristic approaches to oral traditions were refined. However, the category of legends, and particularly supernatural legends (most commonly *demonološke/a predaje/predanja* in BCMS), was often one of the last to be accurately and consistently presented "as narrated" in published scholarly collections.

SUPERNATURAL LEGENDS

What have been variously titled "supernatural," "belief," "mythic," or "demonological" legends are common narratives that focus on encounters between humans and supernatural beings. These tales describing the nexus between the human and the daemonic realms were so often viewed in early scholarship as lacking narrative forms—as unstructured, reported speech—that in anthropological, ethnological, and folkloristic texts they were regularly subjected to two forms of butchery. The more narratively polished subset, the fabulates (more on these subcategories anon), were heavily reworked by collectors and editors to fit belletristic literary norms, while their rough-hewn counterparts, the memorates, most often had their contents stripped from their cultural, social, and performative contexts and were then briefly summarized and collated under headings like "superstitions" or "pagan beliefs" (Dégh 1996:36; Dégh and Vázsonyi 1974:233–234). True empirical studies of these materials only began to be conducted in the middle of the twentieth century when widespread collection, ethnographic research among tale tellers, and comparative analyses began to reveal the artistry, purpose, diffusion, and structural properties of legends.

What the genre lacked in historical representation, however, it made up for in abundance, vigor, and adaptability. As numerous scholars later noted, many ancient legends are alive and well into the present day, and new legends are regularly added to their ranks. The legend is the genre that best made the jump from rural to urban environments following the industrial revolution and subsequent urban expansions, and traditions thought extinct have a propensity for resurfacing in unlikely ways, places, and forms. Many factors have contributed to legends proving such a resilient form of oral narrative, including the mutable nature of the genre, its connection with phenomena that run the spectrum of verisimilitude among tellers, the ease with which it assimilates novel subject matter, and its common linkage to physical space, moral precepts, and didactic functions.

Legend has also been recognized as a genre sensitive to ideology and dependent on social structures and worldview. Indeed, scholars have argued that the functional purpose of legends is to extol communal value systems and norms in traditional societies (Holbek 1991:188–189, cited in Asplund Ingemark 2006:2). Thus, aspects of belief in legends are recognized as a foundational element of the genre. Early scholars connected legendry directly with concepts of belief, contending that the primary function of legends is to provide evidence that keeps traditional worldview alive (Christiansen [1958] 1977:4); any hesitation by narrators to admit personal experience with the supernatural was read as an erosion of traditional values (Dégh 1996:39), while statements of disbelief were seen as the incursion of modern analytical thinking and omitted from publication (Roper 2018). More recent scholarship has stressed veracity and belief in legends as a process: the performance event is often couched in wider discourses where the reliability of traditional beliefs is presented, discussed, and debated (Dégh 1996). Legends act as a vocabulary for discussing problems or as a process of "veracity negotiation" (Dégh 2001:16). The factual depiction of events in the narrative and the fusion of personal experience with belief are integral stylistic features that authenticate the story by providing temporal, spatial, and personal data (Dégh 1996:39, 41); locating the narrative in well-known surroundings; and imbuing the structure of the story with a truth value or a "rhetoric of truth" (Oring 2012:151–152). This is true even when lived faith in the subject matter has been lost (Bošković-Stulli 1963:11) or the narrator prefaces the telling with statements of suspicion or disbelief.

Starting with the writings of the Grimm brothers (1816:v), legends have generally been defined in contrast to folktales. The Grimms focused largely on the real or presumed historicity of legends, but later scholars, particularly Max Lüthi, have fleshed out and extended the comparison (see particularly Lüthi 1961; Lüthi [1966] 1976; Lüthi [1982] 1986). Lüthi described legends as artistically simpler than folk tales but more emotionally engaging. While elements of the miraculous and supernatural are an organic and integrated component of folk tales, the world of humans and the world of the fantastic coexist in a manner mundane and prosaic to the characters. Legends, on the other hand, focus on the jarring and generally frightening points at which the heterogeneous human and supernatural realms collide (Dégh 1996:41). While supernatural beings in folk tales are, in Lüthi's words, only "figures," in legends they are real creatures ([1982] 1986).

Supernatural Legends in the Western Balkans

Lüthi's framing of legends accurately describes those of the Western Balkans where the supranormal realm lies adjacent to the human, and encounters are inevitable. The cast of characters in that realm is quite colorful and consists of common and lesser-known figures. The major roster in the tales are vampires/werewolves[4] (*vampir, vukodlak/ volkodlak, kudlak, tenac*), fairies/nymphs (*vila* [pl. *vile*], *samovila, samodiva, juda, rusalka*), witches (*veštica/vištica/vještica, coprnica*) and warlocks (*vrač, coprnik*, Slov. *vidovin*), succubi/nightmares (*mora*), devils (BCMS *vrag, đavao, belaj*, Slov. *hudič, krut*), and ghosts of various kinds. The minor cast is much larger but lesser known and employed, including such figures as dog-headed beings (*psoglav/pasjeglavec*), fates (*rojenice, suđenice, usud*), shamanic village protectors (*kresnik/krsnik, zduhač, vjedogonja*), fairy/nymph healers or paramours (*vilenjak, vilenica*), supernatural donkeys (*orko*), and a number of wild people, plague figures, small dwarves and imps, and various other beings (on all of these and more, see Đorđević 1952; Đorđević 1953; Jurić 2019; Jurić 2023; Kropej 2012; Lovrenčević 1970; Lozica 1995; Marjanić 1999; Marks 2007; Mencej 2017; Šešo 2003; Zečević 1981).

These stories teach and enforce the idea that the human realm is relegated to the village and the diurnal world of noise and bustle, while the world of the supernatural is the "other realm"—deep nature, graveyards, and other places designated unfit for humans to tread for long or at all. This other realm belongs to the quiet and the nocturnal and may turn even familiar, habited locations into dangerous sites. Liminal zones just outside the village such as crossroads, meadows, fields, and mills are shared in shift-work, belonging to the dark forces until cock's crow when they revert to human ownership (Bratić 2013:esp. 193–213; Jurić 2024:203).

> Кад је било око пола ноћи, отвори вампир воденична врата, виде да нема никог, уђе у воденицу, скине покров са себе и метну га на воденични кош, па седе крај ватре и почне кувати качамак. Док је он кувао качамак, вампирче свуче полако покров са коша и тури га себи у недра. Кад је дошло време, почеше петли да кукуречу; вампир скочи и поче тражити покров, али га не могаше наћи, и онда седне крај ватре и почне плакати.
>
> (Čajkanović 1927:409–410)

> When it was around midnight, the vampire opened the watermill's door, saw that there was no one [inside], entered the mill, took his shroud off and placed it on the mill's hopper, and then sat beside the fire and started to cook polenta. While he was cooking polenta, the *vampirče*[5] carefully took the shroud down from the hopper and stuffed it in his shirt's breast. When the time came, roosters began to crow; the vampire leapt up and began to seek the shroud but he couldn't find it. Then he sat beside the fire and began to cry.

Unfortunately, the balance of those realms is not kept reciprocally; while foolhardy humans may seek wealth or knowledge by intruding into the supernatural realm, most recognize the power imbalance and stay away, only falling into danger through happenstance. Supernatural beings, on the other hand, often intrude into the human realm with intentions that range from benign to malignant. The strongest and most upstanding humans may gain some great power from interacting with the supernatural but often at the cost of retaining their relationship to their human collective—for example, some folk healers are taught their arcane knowledge by *vile* but become marginal figures in human society—or else are put in the uncomfortable position of having to keep their supernatural benefits secret from their peers, a task that generally proves futile (Bratić 2013:202–207; Jurić 2019:278–280, 292–293, 314–315). Most commonly, though, interaction with the supernatural realm leaves a metaphysical stain of illness and exhaustion, inevitably leading to the wasting away and death of even those who successfully escape direct contact (Bratić 2013:194–196). And this only accounts for benign or mercurial supernatural forces, let alone the predatory ones like vampires and witches who intentionally prey on humans.

In supernatural legends, the dichotomy of the real, known world and the unknowable other world is mapped onto physical space through the work of imagination and the symbolic action of narrative. This causes social and environmental "other" places—both impenetrable and deep nature, as well as neighboring villages—to become localized zones for the supernatural and makes social others more prone to being depicted as, in fact, supernatural others (Tarkka 2015:17). Thus, *vile* are nature spirits living in deep, impenetrable, or dangerous natural areas but are also sometimes said to dress like Turks or be imported from India (Bošković-Stulli 1975:94; Jurić 2019:81–82, 84). Accusations of witchcraft or designation as a vampire was often cast upon Albanians, Roma, Turks, and various "others" who lived in neighboring villages or moved into Slavic settlements. Vampire narratives are rife with subtle and overt descriptions of the monster as an ethnic other:

> Okopavaj oni, okopavaj. Dignu ploču, a moj vukozlak sidi u grebu i podvija noge po turski i govori: "Sad ubi ti mene, kad nisan umija ja tebe!"
>
> (Banović 1918:187)
>
> They dig, dig it out. They lift the lid, and my vampire is sitting in the grave, his legs crossed in the Turkish [manner] and he says, "Now you kill me, since I didn't know [how to kill] you!"

That is to say that the narrative linkage between the supernatural and location means that the physical distance of otherworldly places and times is subservient to their normative distance (Koski 2008:340–342). Though cultural norms depicted in narrative and in reality often differ (cf. Honko [1981] 2013:180), they generally coalesce on zones of danger. The places of the supernatural are those where humans should not be or where they may be but not at those times—encounters happen during the dark of night (*gluho/gluvo doba*, lit. the deaf time) or at an inauspicious/inopportune/evil time/moment (*u zao čas*). The entrance of the human into normatively distant places and times violates taboos, and the deed invokes the intrusion of the supernatural (Koski 2008:342). Camilla Asplund Ingemark (2006:9–10) has recently connected this sharing of local geography to Bakhtin's idea of the "chronotope," or time–space, suggesting that humans enter a chronotope of enchantment when their well-known landscapes become alien territory in supernatural encounter. This model works well for northern European lore but generally does not fit the southeastern model where, in supernatural encounters, locations do become multispacial (perhaps better bispacial) but are never multitemporal or synchronic (Asplund Ingemark 2006:12–13). In general, supernatural time in the Western Balkans is the same as mundane human time (Jurić 2024:200), making encounter events between the numinous and humans less chronotopic and perhaps more akin to Foucault's ([1984] 1998) concept of heterotopias, worlds within worlds that mirror but also upset what is outside of them.

Locality, Localization, Migration, and Mapping

This heterotopic nature is particularly apt for natural sites which, by their dynamic nature and *milieu dominance* (Eskeröd 1947:82–83), exert a particular *valence*, a quality of possessing a minimal set of features that accrue specific narratives of a similar ilk (Laime 2018:80). *Vile*, for instance, often reside in various cavities in the earth, on lofty mountains, or in high cliffs in oral narratives (Jurić 2023). The presence of such karstic speluncae in a communal milieu will exert an influence on tradition-bearers to invent novel lore about them, to experience certain encounter events in a traditionally conditioned manner—for instance, a numen (Honko 1964:17) met at the cave will likely be experienced or later interpreted as a *vila*, rather than any other being (Bahna 2015; Honko 1964:18; Laime 2018:81)—and to *localize* or *familiarize* (Honko [1981] 2013:174) imported migratory legends or widely known tale types to that site.

Questions of locality, localization, and migration in contemporary legend-telling contexts can be greatly improved with attention to modern ethnographic practices and confident mapping of frequency and movement. Luka Šešo, a leading contemporary expert on Croatian supernatural legends and their performative contexts, has suggested that the "sincerest" belief in supernatural beings is found among those who remain in a single rural area over the course of their life (2010a:109). My own passive folklore collection in the Bilogora and Podravina regions of Croatia over the last ten years has suggested to the contrary that belief may migrate with people if the migration is between rural sites; the stories, however, tend to remain rooted to their original soil. I have had the opportunity of collecting legends and other related lore in the Bilogora region (specifically around the city of Daruvar) not only from families who trace their lineages back generations in situ but also from a sizeable diaspora of Bosnian Croats who migrated to the region predominantly from the Pougarje district of Bosnia-Herzegovina (just east of Jajce) in the 1980s. This research has revealed a sharp divide, with local lore unfailingly neglected by the Bosnian incomers who have retained the stories they learned in childhood.

In 2021, in a village 15 km removed from the city of Daruvar, one discussant, Šimo (Šimun) Bliznac (b. 1955 in Pougarje) related a legend (here the *legenda* variety) to me about *vile* that he had learned as a child from his mother:

> Čovjek, koji je bio . . . je l'? . . . glavni u to vrijeme. Postojala je magla i postojale su vile. E sad, Bog je pitao toga čovjeka, šta 'oće da . . . ukine Bog. Il' da ostanu vile, il' da ostane magla. Veli, "ako ukinem maglu, nećete imat' kiše, neće vam ništa moći rod't' bez kiše, a ako vam ostavim vile, onda imat ćete problema sa vilama." Onda je rek'o da se ukinu vile.

> A man, who was . . . you know? . . . important in that time.[6] Fog existed and *vile* existed. Well now, God asked that man what he would like to . . . [what he would like]

that God do away with. Either for *vile* to remain, or for fog to remain. He [God] said, "if I abolish fog, you will have no rain, nothing will grow for you without rain, and if I leave you *vile*, then you will have problems with *vile*." Then he [the important person] said that he would [have God] abolish *vile*.

Šimo followed this story with a detailed general description of *vile*, before declaring that he knows no other narratives. As often happens in such situations, the legend prompted discussion about his home region with his sister-in-law (present at the telling) who grew up in a neighboring village. She reminded him of some of Pougarje's topography which elicited recall, prompting Šimo to deliver a string of lore specific to his home region.

The legend about the abolishment of *vile* prompted a "belief statement," or dite (von Sydow 1977b) about two approximately forty- or fifty-foot-deep sinkholes/caverns (*smetvine*) in the region. In the spring, these fill up with rainwater and, purportedly, with unseen but audible underground currents. *Vile* were said to live within them (Fig. 27.1). Talk of *vila* chasms prompted a legend about an odd impression in a nearby meadow called *Prosinovo okno* (likely "millet's shaft," i.e., pit in the millet field) where locals mowing the field are said to have watched the earth devour their picnic lunch in a sinkhole. This, in turn, elicited a string of related tales regarding fatal mishaps provoked by various actors breaking prohibitions on working on Annunciation (*Blagovijest*, March

FIG. 27.1. The chasms (*smetvine*) in Pougarje in which *vile* are said to reside.

(Credit: Dorian Jurić.)

25), as well as stories about Pougarje's infrastructure built during Ottoman rule (roughly 1500–1878). After this litany of folklore, I asked about a supernatural being local to the Bilogora region, the *Imbrica* or *Mâli* (a dangerous, diminutive horseman), who is known, at least in name, to most residents;[7] but Šimo could relate no tales, descriptions, or proscriptions.

This example speaks to the integral role that childhood plays in the retention of oral traditions[8] but also to the way that legends migrate. "Narratives connected to the local, familiar sphere are more likely to match the contextual knowledge of the listeners and therefore to be relevant to them" (Koski 2008:339), but a nostalgic once-local sphere may exert a greater influence than contemporary surroundings. This calls attention to the need for careful ethnographic interviewing in tandem with collecting projects. Such data reveal much about how legends move, as well as when and how they are or are not localized. Competent contemporary mapping of such migrations provides the ability to draw conclusions that can speak back to materials collected over the last century as well as processes of successful migration, retention, and localization.

Migration itself can also be an impetus for narrative creation, particularly under fraught circumstances when movement is forced. For a region where, as the Bosnian author Meša Selimović once said, the waves of history ceaselessly break upon the people like a reef, studies on the fertile topic of war-related legendry have remained surprisingly tethered to medieval and early modern strife. The numinous can manifest in the heat of battle—the Serbian folk hero Marko Kraljević materializing before his co-nationals in a skirmish in World War I (Petrovich 1914:64n1) bears strong resemblance to the miracle of angelic (likely *šehiti* [martyrs]) horsemen helping Bosniak and mujahideen forces in the 1990s (Li 2019:80–81)—but supernatural legends most commonly occur after turmoil has ended. After the wars of secession in the 1990s, as former refugees, soldiers, and other displaced people resettled into their homes and communities and tried/try to rebuild their former lives, legends often became both a product of and a tool for making sense of trauma. In these cases, localization manifests in displacement and return, with supernatural beings produced as a by-product of the transformation of homes (through bloodshed) from familiar into foreign realms. Mirjam Mencej (2021) has recently explored the role that ghost legends play in returning a modicum of social power and sense of justice to the Bosniak survivors of the Srebrenica massacre, while Šešo has given examples of supernatural encounters conditioned by tradition but manifesting as a product of war trauma (2016:223–230):

> I meni se, kad je ovaj rat bio, počelo pričinjavati da na mene, dok spavam, skače ona crna mačka mora od koje nisam mogao maknuti. Nisam znao je li san ili java. Znao sam da to ne može biti, ali opet se nisam mogao oteti tom dojmu da jest. (225)

> When this war was going on, it seemed to me too that, while I was sleeping, a black cat, a *mora*, was jumping on me and I couldn't escape from under it. I didn't know if it was a dream or real. I knew that it couldn't be [real] but, nevertheless, I couldn't shake that feeling that it was.

Careful exploration of the link between supernatural legends and recent political unrest could bring to light a range of novel legends serving important societal and psychological roles while telling an even more complex story about the relationship between monsters and movement.

Mapping Monsters

In 2019, I produced a doctoral thesis meant to serve as an updated reference work on the Western Balkan *vila*. For this revised survey study, I gathered a wide range of primary and reliable secondary folklore data collected between the years 1814 and 1914 from forty-five published texts and 133 unpublished or partially published manuscripts. Using a modern, performance-focused theoretical approach and comparative methodology based on contemporary understandings of tradition diffusion, materials were systematized to elicit emic story patterns and motifs and generic variation in depiction, then plotted geographically to distinguish core traditions from the regional or idiosyncratic. Already, this systematic approach has illuminated the historical diffusion of various story patterns (Jurić 2019; Jurić 2020b), clarified a number of basic features of the *vila* in aggregate (Jurić 2023), elucidated genre-specific depictions (Jurić 2019:356–361), and helped to refine comparative data in a wider Eurasian context (Jurić 2019; Jurić 2024). Such a scheme only becomes more refined as new material is added and reflects an ongoing research project to which I continue to add both historical and contemporary data.

This thorough, regionally focused, being-centered model is perhaps a prime example of the merits of meso-, rather than macro- or micro-, level analytical frames. It avoids the many problems of large-scale comparative projects like the Aarne–Thompson–Uther (ATU) tale-type index or, in a regional context, the Krstić index (Krstić 1984) or the *Ethnographic Atlas of Yugoslavia* (Šešo 2010b:117–119), which must by nature of their scope remain superficial. At the same time, being-centered surveys also remain above the myopic level of intensive studies of singular motifs or works on supernatural beings which limit their purview to national boundaries or individual tropes. Herbert Halpert (1971:49–50) has noted that a comprehensive legend index would need to be action- rather than character-focused because of the tendency for motifs to latch on to diverse beings in migration—a tendency very common for the *vila* which is a *tradition dominant* (Eskeröd 1947:81)[9] in the South Slavic context (Jurić 2023).[10] Despite this, a narrow regional scope (here linguistic) sets an arbitrary but practicable boundary which elicits a largely stable depiction apposite for strong delineation of motifs and traits useful for comparative research. Building catalogues and mapping traditions allows for a more expansive view on systems of oral traditional practices, the tracing of trends synchronically and diachronically, and the delineation of core content from the regional or idiosyncratic. This provides a matrix to which many questions can be posed and subsequently answered, including modern problems and critical questions from past research—for example, the forms that supernatural legends take.

MEMORATES, FABULATES, AND LEGENDS

In his cited 1934 essay "Kategorien der prosa-volkdichtung," Carl Wilhelm von Sydow (1977a) presented a novel categorical system of prose folk narrative genres. The most lasting and versatile of these are the memorate and fabulate, though von Sydow's lack of concrete utilization of his system in case studies[11] meant that their exact use has shifted over time under the aegis of various scholars. While many folklorists treat the memorate as a category of legend, von Sydow was clear in defining it as a related but independent genre (Pentikäinen [1968] 1973:220; von Sydow 1977a:73). The term was formulated to encompass "the narratives people tell about their own purely personal experiences" that "show neither poetic character nor tradition" (73), which is to say, that lack collective and traditional elements, and thus folkloristic traits. While von Sydow did not explicitly state that memorates require a supernatural element, that reading was implied given that his wider categorical system involved a similar secular category, the chronicate (Pentikäinen [1968] 1973:221); this conception was later cemented in the writings of Lauri Honko (Bahna 2015:17). Von Sydow defined fabulates as "short, single-episodic narratives in the background of which stand some sort of experiences and observations . . . [that were] shaped by the storytelling art of the folk" (1977a:74) His definition centers on the communal processes that produce the fabulate, its fixed pattern or motif, and its use as proof for a traditional article of faith. He further introduced two critical considerations that endure in scholarship devoted to these sub-genres: the fundamental opposition between fabulate and memorate and the conception that fabulates are akin to folk tales (74). Beyond this, though, he left the definition of fabulate so broad and vague as to make it nearly synonymous with legend, engendering much later confusion surrounding the term (Pentikäinen [1968] 1973:221). Subsequent scholars highlighting various aspects of his definition came to very different conclusions. Pentikäinen outlines four conventional uses of the fabulate after von Sydow: "1) as the main concept of prose tradition; 2) as a synonym for legend; 3) in the distinction memorate–fabulate, in which legend is the cover concept; 4) for an invented story without the background of tradition" ([1968] 1973:233). Most of this writing also cemented the concept of fabulate as synonymous with another common term, "migratory legend" (Christiansen [1958] 1977:5; Dégh 1971:61).

In their famous reassessment of the memorate genre, Linda Dégh and Andrew Vázsonyi (1974) trace the early scholarship following from von Sydow. As later folklorists employed his system, it quickly became apparent that tales about personal and unique encounters with the supernatural retained their first-hand character in second- and third-hand retellings, prompting a softening of his original definitions and the deployment of increasingly convoluted terminology to account for hybrid statuses and subcategories (Dégh and Vázsonyi 1974:226). Dégh and Vázsonyi systematically dissect von Sydow's definition of the memorate, showing that it can in no way be said to exist independently of the legend genre, if it can be said to exist at all.

Personal encounters with the supernatural inevitably draw on traditional knowledge and prior accounts to give them structure, content, and meaning; first-hand accounts can be passed on in toto to other tellers, particularly in family environments (Gwyndaf 1984); tellers often have a tendency to shift third-person narratives to first person, either for stylistic effect or to enhance claims of veracity (Bošković-Stulli 1991:190; Dégh and Vázsonyi 1974:228–229); and folklore collection projects can never capture all examples and variants of tales that do or have existed in a region. Based on these facts, Dégh and Vázsonyi convincingly argue that a tale can never be definitively proven to be a memorate. And yet, stories must begin somewhere, and people are known to have experienced personal encounters with the supernatural. These inevitabilities prompt the authors to propose novel terminology, the "proto-memorate," to account for the a priori understanding that memorates must exist as a starting point for supernatural legends. Contemporary scholars have largely abstained from this nomenclature, which explains well a theoretical surety but is redundant in practice. What was required was a shift in paradigm about the nature of memorates rather than more jargon.

Those, including this author, looking to simplify the latticework of complex terminology woven by legend scholars over the twentieth century often treat memorates and fabulates as the primary subdivisions of legends (Pentikäinen's third definition above)—the poles of a continuum between unique and individual experiences, on the one hand, and generic and collective, ones on the other. As Lutz Röhrich ([1958] 1969:223) has suggested, memorates are the "prelude to the legend," legends in nascency, and hardly an independent genre. The memorate must be seen as an uncertain genre, but it is important to remember that folklorists have long been honest about how all genres are porous categories. They act as tools, helping to clarify material just enough to allow for analytical assessment and conclusions to be rendered (Georges 1971:3). Robert A. Georges (1971) has even shown how the simplest definitions of the broadest category "legend" cannot contain all examples and breaks down under scrutiny. The memorate is a category with intrinsic ambiguity, but the realization that true memorate status must always be conjectured demands a renewed call to exhaustive collection projects and frequency mapping. As David Bynum once noted, the structure of repetitive complementarity in oral traditions means that, generally, patterns and motifs are never entirely represented in a single telling of a fable. Rather, their complete meaning only becomes clear over multiple tellings as the multiforms take their place on a spectrum of nominal change (1978:70, 103–104). An extensive and comparative catalogue of oral traditions is the only means to approximate a system for verifying the status of memorates.

Given the structural freedom involved in legend-telling, comparison must rest predominantly on content and smaller integers of stylistic patterns. In *vila* legends, many motifs—children, men, or horses taken and returned by *vile* (Jurić 2019:286–289, 303–304); villagers encountering *vile* dancing roundels at night (275–277); etc.—follow a very limited range of traditional story patterns and variants. They contain a conservative number of stock elements regardless of whether they were/are told as having occurred to unnamed individuals, named but vague characters, fellow villagers, family members, or the tellers themselves. Simpler supernatural beings with a limited catalogue of motifs related to them display such conformity to a higher degree. A large majority of *Orko* legends (cf. Lozica 1995; Vuletić-Vukasović 1934), for instance, follow the same common pattern:

Лука Гуда с Мајкова с Рожетића, у дубровачкому запутио се у глухо доба ноћи пјеше пут града. Кад је дошао између Брсечина и Трстенога у Смоковачу, нашао испод рогача товара (магарца) без улара гђе пасе. Нико га не чува, готово у пустињи, па ти он узјаше на њ, па хајд пут Трстенога. . . . Кад је Лука дошао до Михајла (цркве), товар се успрегне, неће напријед, него све расте, а Лука зове у помоћ, али га нико не чује, као да му дигло глас. Једва се дочепао звоника на Михајлу и ту се прихитио, а товара нестало низ баштине. Лука је остао у кампањелу (звонику) све до зоре, а онда му је Кусија донио скалу (љеству) и сашао, али није отишао пут града. Страшиво је у Смоковачи.— Други су напртили мијех вина, те је оживио.

(Vuletić-Vukasović 1934:173–174)

Luka Guda from Majkovi, Rožetići region, in the Dubrovnik [area] set off toward the city on foot in the witching hour of the night. When he came between Brsečine and Trsteno in Smokovača, he found an ass without a halter grazing under a carob tree. No one was watching over it, in a completely barren area, so he mounted it and off to Trsteno . . . . When Luka got to Mihajl (church), the ass stops, it won't go forward, instead it begins to grow. Luka calls out for help but no one hears him, as though his voice rose up too. He barely caught hold of the bell tower on Mihajl and held tight while the ass vanished from the field. Luka remained in the campanella (bell tower) until dawn and then Kusija brought him a ladder and he descended, but he didn't take the path to the city. It's spooky in Smokovača—some others were packing a wineskin and then he [Luka] came to.

Dégh and Vázsonyi have outlined the process by which fabulates are recycled into memorates (1974). Given limited structural forms, it can never be confirmed whether collected memorates represent fabulates reworked as memorates or true (proto) memorates where experience itself has been shaped by tradition. The distinction, however, is largely unimportant. The materials themselves even seem to hint at this secret reality too. We often sense the teller's wink and nod in historical texts where a common and migratory fabulate is reworked as an event that occurred to a fellow villager who is named vaguely, like Mare the Vlach (Banović 1918:195), or given an alliterative, humorous-sounding name like Mar Đon Đuraš or Prenk Pilju (Dučić 1931:272, 273). This is not only a problem of historical data but even occurs in modern materials (see examples in Dragić 2017; Šešo 2016). The point is hardly novel, but charting, comparing, and analyzing these materials systematically is the only method for recognizing stock and collective traditions that are stylistically presented otherwise and for isolating those legendary equivalents of hapax legomena that can be tentatively assumed to be true memorates, though which are rarely able to be definitively categorized.

Novelty, Surprise, and the Subversion of Expectations

A useful and underexplored tool for identifying idiosyncratic lore is the ability to recognize subversion of traditional expectation. Just like informant disbelief (Roper 2018), humorous, novel, surprising, and subversive turns in the performance of oral traditions were for decades treated as a sign of degradation and corruption of lore that was regularly idealized and romanticized as a once sacred inheritance from ancient cultural roots. If oral traditions were, in the Herderian sense, the patrimony of the nation, handed down from time immemorial, then it was assumed that they should be treated with sanctity and respect. It was unimaginable that peasant tradition-bearers would not do their best to convey that information logically and credibly (Jurić 2020b:23), that they would inject fantasy and humor into genres that were generally treated seriously (Perić-Polonijo 1996:13–19), or that they would intentionally subvert expectations to add novelty to familiar stories in order to shock or surprise listeners. This is in fact a common practice found in even the earliest materials and which continues today.

Of the two most common definitional foci of the term "fabulate"—communal legends that travel easily versus legends that border on folk tales and include heightened levels of the fantastic—I think it is important to embrace the former and reject the latter. The communal definition positions legends on a useful sliding scale between individual (memorates) and communal (fabulates) while allowing for a clearer contextualization of the fantastic in legend-telling. Kaarina Koski (2008:337–339) has argued that increased use of fantastic elements in legend-telling is less a reflection of the narrator's use of shifting or hybrid genres and more the teller's individual decision in each tale (or each performance) to diminish elements of veracity in favor of compelling storytelling and audience engagement. Subversion of traditional expectation when handled poorly often draws oral traditional material into the territory of irony or satire—the bane of verisimilitude—but, when handled competently, can in fact lend heavy tones of believability, suggesting to listeners "this is not the tired old story you are used to hearing but, in fact, something that really happened!"

A tale collected in 2008 near the Dalmatian city of Drniš (Dragić 2017:224–225) employs the very common motif of a human who comes upon a *vila* with her hair tangled in a bush or bramble. In these legends, which are found throughout the Western Balkans (Jurić 2019:306–307), the *vila* pleads with the human to untangle her hair, warning or threatening that if the helper breaks a single hair, the *vila* will die, sometimes with ill consequences for the aide as well. The resolution in these tales is always the same:

the human succeeds in untangling the hair and is blessed with some sort of gift, ability, or power from the *vila*. It comes as a shock then for listeners in this milieu to hear the version Manda Sučić heard from her mother:

> Jednom . . . dok su tako išle po selim, jednoj vili zapela kosa za draču. Zvala ona cilu noć, mol'l'a da joj neko pomože, al' niko od stra nije smijo iz kuće. Kažu da je jednom starom didu bilo je ža' slušat', pa un jadan oša joj pomoć.
> Rekla njemu vila da ako joj pomože otpetljat kosu da će se opet vrat't' u mladost i dugo živ't, al' da joj nesmi ostat' nijedna dlaka. Tijo stari opet da bude mlad, jer žena mu već davno umrla, a dice nisu imali pa joj tako otpetljava kosu skoro cilu noć, a kad ju je oslobodjo, jadan, umra. Privar'la ga vila. Da joj nije otpetlja kosu una b' umrla kad bi svan'lo, a ovako umra un nisritan.
>
> (Dragić 2017:224)

> Once . . . when they [*vile*] went about the villages like that, the hair of one *vila* got caught in a bramble. She called out the whole night, begged someone to help her, but none dared leave his house out of fear. They say that one old man couldn't bear to hear her suffering, so that poor fellow went out to help.
> The *vila* told him that if he helped her untangle her hair she would [repay him and] return his youth and he would live long, but that he mustn't leave even a single hair [in the bramble]. That old man wanted to be young again, for his wife had died long before and they didn't have any children. Well, he spends almost the whole night untangling her hair but, when he had freed her, the poor fellow died. The *vila* tricked him. If he hadn't untangled her hair, she would have died at sunrise but, in this way, that poor man died [instead].

Here we find the untraditional claim that *vile* offer de-aging to humans, an idea that has been lifted from the pages of Marin Držić's 1550 play *Novela od Stanca* (*The Novela of Stanac*) and injected into a traditional plot (see my treatment of this very trope in Jurić 2023:53). Moreover, the generally beneficent and fair-dealing *vila* in this motif has been turned on her head to make a statement about the dangerous nature of these mercurial supernatural beings. For Sučić, the *vile* can never be trusted. The subversion of a traditional element not only adds a measure of surprise to the narrative but also makes the telling even more frightening, suggesting that "even the good things you have heard about *vile* are untrue!" It also leads to a denouement in which the guileful and deceptive nature of the *vile* leads to their special demise and, through detection via the stock motif of braiding horses' manes (Jurić 2019:303-304), another common motif is explained, that is, why the *vile* are no longer among humans (297-298):

> Kad su ujtra ga našli drugi seljani nisu znali šta mu ju' bilo. Al' kad su posli' ošli u štalu vid'li su da su svim konjima ispletene pleten'ce. Unda su vid'li da su to bile vile pa im više niko nikad nije tijo pomoć. Tako su ti kroz neko vrime sve one pomrle.
>
> (Dragić 2017:224-225)

When the other villagers found him in the morning, they didn't know what had happened to him. But later, when they went into the stables and saw that all the horses had braids, then they saw that it had been *vile* and no one wanted to help them anymore. That's why, after some time, they all died out.

Filling in the Gaps

Zeal for ethnographic folklore collection in the Western Balkans seems to come in cycles. The most extensive collection projects occurred between the 1880s and the 1930s as the fields of ethnology and folkloristics became formalized and, in the face of rapid industrialization, rural exodus, and the proliferation of state-sponsored education programs, a fear was prompted that rural peasant culture would be lost forever. Extensive folklife and folklore collection projects carried out by academics and lay scholars were generally encouraged by and published in academic journals such as the *Glasnik zemaljskog muzeja* (*Herald of the National Museum*), the *Srpski etnografski zbornik* (*Serbian Ethnographic Review*), and the *Zbornik za narodni život i običaje* (*Review on Folk Life and Customs*). Such journals accepted a wide range of materials, sometimes publishing full monographs but also mining submitted manuscripts for passages or sections that could be published in groupings based on topic or region (see Jurić 2020a). This wave of research and publishing was upended in the political turmoil of the early twentieth century. The masterworks of many great scholars (e.g., Veselin Čajkanović, Tihomir R. Đorđević, Matthias Murko) that were researched and written in the interwar period often did not see publication until the 1950s or later, and journals that continued to publish through these difficult times (often with haphazard continuity due to various political and economic disruptions) generally published archived material from older collection projects. Following the Second World War, socialist Yugoslavia brought with it an ethos that simultaneously celebrated peasant culture but also denigrated old belief systems, both formal and informal, as superstitious and backward. While the farmers' old customs could be celebrated, they were expected to be relegated to an unenlightened past now overcome. Agriculturalists were respected in the socialist ethos, but the real hero was the factory worker who left the village behind. The 1940s and 1950s thus continued a period largely dedicated to collation and passive analysis of earlier collected materials. From the mid-1950s to the 1980s a renewed passion for collection swept across the region's scholarly circles, prompted by the performative turn in international folkloristics. Leading scholars like Maja Bošković-Stulli in Croatia and Serbia's Nada Milošević-Đorđević returned to rural regions of their nations to see what remained of past oral prose traditions and to study the tales not only for content but also for stylistic features of performance and interconnections between the tales and the tellers' social contexts. Growing nationalist tensions in the 1980s and the brutal wars of secession in the 1990s caused another break in research stability, but a renewed wave of collection work, growing since the late 1990s, is producing a wealth of data. This is allowing scholars to once again "check in on the folk" to see what is still being told, where, and what role these traditions are playing in contemporary contexts.

A new, younger cadre of local scholars have answered a call in modern folkloristics to use ethnography and participant observation to understand the role served by legends in the lives of contemporary tellers. Luka Šešo has spent the last two decades seeking out remnants of supernatural legendry, predominantly in the Dalmatian hinterland. Taking a largely functionalist approach, he has pursued many lines of questioning regarding the social roles that supernatural legends serve in modern society (2016:165–247), as well as developing a simple system for categorizing informants based on their expressions about and relationships to the veridical character of tales about the supernatural (2010a; 2016:148–164). He breaks these down into (1) interlocutors unfamiliar with supernatural beings or traditional beliefs, generally residents of urban and tourist centers; (2) potential interlocutors restrained by skepticism; (3) those who express themselves with strong self-censorship and rationalization arising from ethnopolitical problems; (4) the greatest number of interlocutors (he calls them "traditionalists") who are well versed in legends, even detailing them as occurring to friends or family but inevitably adding mild auto-censure or rationalizations to the telling, such as "but that all happened long ago" or "other people believe these things but I do not"; and (5) those who express a strong belief in supernatural beings as a reflection of their immobility and traditional professions. Šešo's research has revealed a number of contemporary examples of story patterns long thought extinct, highlighting robust continuities between past and present oral traditions in certain localities. Some of his explications of the utility of such lore are heretofore unknown and offer to tell us as much about the past as the present, the exemplar of this being a contemporary account of a man abducted by *vile* as a child. Despite the mystery surrounding the case, his neighbors reveal that he was fleeing an abusive father, returned home when hunger overcame him, and used the story of abduction to avoid immediate and future punishment (2016:238–243).

Slovenian folklorist Mirjam Mencej (2017:59–75) has similarly brought attention to the four discourses that are used to discuss practices and behavior related to witchcraft in Styria. Those are witchcraft (read "traditional folk"), Christian (cf. Valk 2015:143–150), rational, and New-Age discourses (cf. Radulović and Đorđević-Belić 2021:17). This systematization is highly productive, mirrors discourses on a range of supernatural beings beyond witches and in the wider Balkan sphere, and, aside from the New-Age category, is apposite for discussion of historical archival materials as well. These and a number of other theoretical considerations recently proposed or refined (see, e.g., Mencej 2017:75–90 on repertoire; Radulović and Đorđević-Belić 2021 on the utile concepts of disenchantment and re-enchantment expanded from the work of Max Weber) will become useful tools in the field researches of contemporary scholars who continue to comb largely rural regions for thriving or moribund traditions.

The amount of contemporary data recently collected and published has not only revealed that legends remain resilient in a range of locations but also disproven Christiansen's contention ([1958] 1977:4) that legends must die out when kindred experience of the beliefs dies out. Modern tellers might couch their narratives in rationalist discourse that attempts to rhetorically distance them from feared perceptions of backwardness or gullibility (Šešo 2016:159–160; Radulović and Đorđević-Belić 2021:17) or feel compelled to explain the traditions' generic conventions for a modern audience (Milošević-Đorđević 1991:319–321); however, the traditions prevail, sometimes grow, and regularly adapt to modern society. Informants remain links in the chain of custom that connects them to their forebears, even if particular regions have been more prone to being cut off by various global and national flows, demographic gutting through mass economic emigration, or heightened levels of urbanization.

Though we know of a number of oral traditional genres that have gone extinct in the Western Balkans over the span of the last century (folk tale and oral epic song in traditional models, among others), as well as a range of modern foreign and native traditions that have grown to threaten the value of older models or to turn them into ossified practices aimed at tourists, legend continues to prove a robust genre. I am not inclined to join the many older generations who have prematurely rung its death knell. Instead, a more pressing concern, particularly in a postwar context where tensions and trauma remain, has been a tendency to trace national lines over traditions that have never been beholden to them. Postwar political and ideological concerns remain myopic frames for the study of oral traditions, even if there has been considerable easing starting in the 2010s. No one in this region, or in the wider international sphere, is interested in resurrecting a failed (and often equally misrepresentative) Yugoslav model; but studies focused on exclusively national depictions ignore the immense overlap across Balkan national and linguistic boundaries (see Jurić 2020b: particularly 19).

The histories of particular names of beings and the movements of motifs and story patterns follow complicated and elaborate trajectories. Only detailed systematization, mapping, and comparison can begin to reveal when, where, and how a *vukodlak* is like or unlike a *vampir*, a *kudlak*, or a *tenac* or when, where, and how a Bosnian *vila* is like or unlike a Croatian, Montenegrin, or Serbian *vila*, a Bulgarian *samovila*, a Macedonian *juda*, a Greek Nereid, or Romanian *iele* (Jurić 2019:5–12; Jurić 2023). Renewed and comprehensive synchronic and diachronic mapping, analysis, and other forms of comparative work must be the next step to contextualize a new wave of ethnographic material being added to our store of knowledge. Only this will provide the ability to fully trace the trajectories of various traditions and the innovations, alterations, diminishments, and extinctions that affect them. The answer to pernicious and lasting questions regarding the origins and spread of supernatural beings and their oral traditions will only be found in such efforts.

Notes

1. The folklore collection, ethnography, archival research, and participant observation that inform this chapter have been conducted throughout all the nations of the former Yugoslavia (2013); in Zagreb, Croatia (2013, 2014, 2015–2016, 2019, 2022); rural regions immediately west of the city of Virovitica (2008, 2013, 2014, 2015, 2022); around the city

of Daruvar (2015–2016, 2022); as well as in the Bosnian cities of Tuzla (2016) and Bihać (2022). All translations in this chapter are my own.

2. William Bascom's (1965) codification of English-language folklore nomenclature is likely the most commonly used today, though there are other practices. While the term "folk tale" can be used to describe a range of lore, Bascom formalized the term "folktale" as a single word to gloss the German *Märchen*. I follow this nomenclature however, here, the words are separated to conform with other chapters in the handbook. His other two glosses—*Sagen* as legend and *Mythen* as myth—are straightforward and nearly universal. I prefer the blanket term "oral narrative" to encompass these three categories rather than Bascom's "prose narrative."

3. This is common to folkloristics in Slavic nations and not unheard of in English-language scholarship. See, for instance, Scullion (1984).

4. There are both pure and blended depictions of these two figures in local traditions. The name *vukodlak* (lit. wolf-hair) has shifted meaning over history, starting as a celestial phenomenon before assuming vampire characteristics (Đorđević 1952:4; Perkowski [1989] 2006:351–363). Today, due to Western influence, the two are largely treated exclusively and highly influenced by depictions in Western media.

5. A baby born of a vampire and a human woman, generally his wife to whom he returns after death and reanimation. A *vampirče* has the ability to recognize and kill vampires (Đorđević 1952:204–205).

6. The name of the political figure or leader used in this legend seems to have been lost in the course of time. I probed Šimo for who this figure might be or at least what social station he might have held. He only replied that he did not know but that it was "someone important. A king, a ban [viceroy] or something . . . who knows?"

7. Once a well-known figure in this region (Lovrenčević 1970:81–84), today this diminutive horseman, dressed in brown with a red hat, is mostly known as a vague spirit who "fairy leads" people, particularly in one forest where locals harvest *kotrč* mushrooms (lumpy bracket [*Polyporus umbellatus*]). In a fashion known throughout Europe, his influence is obviated by turning one's pockets inside-out.

8. My own father, born in 1954 in the Podravina region of Croatia but who moved to Canada as a child, still retains vivid memories of the bridge over a small creek in his home village under which the local children told him a great black hand waits to snatch unsuspecting children as they cross.

9. That is, popular supernatural beings who subsume the motifs, behavior, and lore of others over time. See particularly Lauri Honko's ([1981] 2013:176–179) treatment of Eskeröd's concepts of milieu and tradition dominance.

10. This was one of the many impediments to creating the Aarne-style legend-type indexes that were begun and abandoned several times in the twentieth century (Dégh 1996:41; Hand 1971). It also remains a problem in Thompson's motif index (Jurić 2019:18n22), where useful delineation of narrative tropes (e.g., F365.6 Fairies steal cattle) coexists with vague description (e.g., F231.2 Fairy's feet) and all packaged in Anglocentric language that leads with comparative assumptions. A being-centered map of the kind I propose here, of course, cannot boast the broad applicability of indexes like the ATU. Rather, it helps to contextualize the grounded, emic patterning of those tropes to specific beings while lending a heightened level of refinement to cross-cultural comparative work.

11. Juha Pentikäinen's ([1968] 1973) critical adumbration of von Sydow's systems and terms remains the most competent overview of this work.

Works Cited

Asplund Ingemark, Camilla. 2006. "The Chronotope of Enchantment." *Journal of Folklore Research*, 43/1:1-30.
Bahna, Vladimir. 2015. "Memorates and Memory: A Re-Evaluation of Lauri Honko's Theory." *Temenos*, 51/1:7-23.
Banović, Stjepan. 1918. "Vjerovaña. (Zaostrog u Dalmaciji)." *Zbornik za narodni život i običaje južnih Slavena*, 23:185-214.
Bascom, William. 1965. "The Forms of Folklore: Prose Narratives." *Journal of American Folklore*, 78/307:3-20.
Bošković-Stulli, Maja. 1963. *Narodne pripovijetke*. Zagreb: Zora and Matica hrvatska.
Bošković-Stulli, Maja. 1967. "Narodne pripovijetke i predaje Sinjske krajine." *Narodna umjetnost*, 5/6:303-432.
Bošković-Stulli, Maja. 1975. "Usmene pripovijetke i predaje s otoka Brača." *Narodna umjetnost*, 11/12:5-159.
Bošković-Stulli, Maja. 1991. "Fantastika u usmenoj prozi (kazivanja Srba iz Hrvatske)." In *Pjesme, priče, fantastika*, 160-197. Zagreb: Matica hrvatska.
Botica, Stipe. 2013. *Povijest hrvatske usmene književnost*. Zagreb: Školska knjiga.
Bratić, Dobrila. 2013. *Gluvo doba. Predstave o noći u narodnoj religiji Srba*. 2nd ed. Belgrade: Biblioteka XX vek.
Bynum, David E. 1978. *The Dæmon in the Woods: A Study of Oral Narrative Patterns*. Cambridge, MA: Harvard University Press.
Čajkanović, Veselin, ed. 1927. *Srpske narodne pripovetke*, Vol. I. Beograd and Zemun: Grafički zavod "Makarije."
Christiansen, Reidar Thoralf. 1977. *The Migratory Legends*. New York: Arno Press. First published 1958.
Dégh, Linda. 1971. "The 'Belief Legend' in Modern Society: Form, Function, and Relationship to Other Genres." In *American Folk Legend: A Symposium*, ed. Wayland D. Hand, 55-68. Berkeley, CA: University of California Press.
Dégh, Linda. 1996. "What Is a Belief Legend?" *Folklore*, 107:33-46.
Dégh, Linda. 2001. *Legend and Belief. Dialectics of a Folklore Genre*. Bloomington, IN: Indiana University Press.
Dégh, Linda, and Andrew Vázsonyi. 1974. "The Memorate and the Proto-Memorate." *Journal of American Folklore*, 87/34:225-239.
Đorđević, Tihomir R. 1952. *Vampir i druga bića u našem narodnom verovanju i predanju*. Beograd: SAN.
Đorđević, Tihomir R. 1953. *Veštica i vila u našem narodnom verovanju i predanju*. Srpski etnografski zbornik knj. 66. Beograd: SAN.
Dragić, Marko. 2017. "Vile u tradicijskim pričama šibenskoga i splitskoga zaleđa." *Godišnjak Titius*, 10/10:219-240.
Dučić, Stevan. 1931. *Život i običaji plemena Kuča*. Belgrade: Srpska Kraljevska Akademija.
Eskeröd, Albert. 1947. *Årets äring*. Stockholm: Nordisk Museet.
Foucault, Michel. 1998. "Of Other Spaces (1967), Heterotopias." Trans. Jay Miskowiec. https://foucault.info/documents/heterotopia/foucault.heteroTopia.en/. Accessed July 11, 2022. First published in French 1984.
Georges, Robert A. 1971. "The General Concept of Legend: Some Assumptions to Be Reexamined and Reassessed." In *American Folk Legend: A Symposium*, ed. Wayland D. Hand, 1-20. Berkeley, CA: University of California Press.

Grimm, Jacob, and Wilhelm Grimm. 1816. *Deutsche sagen*. Berlin: Nicolaischen Buchhandlung.
Gwyndaf, Robin. 1984. "Memorates, Chronicates and Anecdotes in Action: Some Remarks towards a Definition of the Personal Narrative in Context." In *The 8th Congress for the International Society for Folk Narrative Research: Bergen, June 12th–17th, 1984*, eds. Reimund Kvideland and Torunn Selberg, 217–224. Bergen: Forlaget Folkekultur.
Halpert, Herbert. 1971. "Definitions and Variation in Folk Legend." In *American Folk Legend: A Symposium*, ed. Wayland D. Hand, 47–54. Berkeley, CA: University of California Press.
Hand, Wayland D., ed. 1971. *American Folk Legend: A Symposium*. Berkeley, CA: University of California Press.
Holbek, Bengt. 1991. "On the Borderline between Legend and Tale." *Arv, Nordic Yearbook of Folklore*, 47:179–191.
Honko, Lauri. 1964. "Memorates and the Study of Folk Belief." *Journal of the Folklore Institute*, 1/1–2:5–19.
Honko, Lauri. 2013. "Four Forms of Adaptation of Tradition." In *Theoretical Milestones: Selected Writings of Lauri Honko*, eds. Pekka Hakamies and Anneli Honko, 173–188. Helsinki: Academia Scientiarum Fennica. First published 1981.
Jurić, Dorian. 2019. "Singing the Vila: Supernatural Beings in the Context of Their Traditions." PhD dissertation, McMaster University, Hamilton, Ontario, Canada.
Jurić, Dorian. 2020a. "'Josip Tomec Collector': Class and Folklore Collection in Nineteenth-Century Croatia." *Journal of American Folklore*, 133/527:27–52.
Jurić, Dorian. 2020b. "Back in the Foundation: Chauvinistic Scholarship and the Building Sacrifice Story-Pattern." *Oral Tradition*, 34:3–44.
Jurić, Dorian. 2023. "Where Does the *Vila* Live? Returning to a Simple Question." *Folklore*, 134/1:48–72.
Jurić, Dorian. 2024. "Western Balkans: 'A *Vila* like a *Vila*.'" In *The Exeter Companion to Fairies, Nereids, Trolls and Other Social Supernatural Beings: European Traditions*, eds. Simon Young and Davide Ermacora, 196–216. Exeter: University of Exeter Press.
Koski, Kaarina. 2008. "Narrative Time-Space in Belief Legends." In *Space and Time in Europe: East and West, Past and Present*, ed. Mirjam Mencej, 337–353. Ljubljana: Oddelek za etnologijo in kulturno antropologijo, Filozofska fakulteta.
Kropej, Monika. 2012. *Supernatural Beings from Slovenian Myth and Folktales*. Studia Mythologica Slavica Supplementum 6. Ljubljana: Collegium Graphicum.
Krstić, Branislav. 1984. *Indeks motiva narodnih pesama Balkanskih Slovena*. Belgrade: Srpska akademija nauka i umetnosti.
Laime, Sandis. 2018. "The Place Valence Approach in Folk Narrative Research: The 'Church Sinks Underground' Motif in Latvian Folklore." In *Storied and Supernatural Places: Studies in Spatial and Social Dimensions of Folklore and Sagas*, eds. Ülo Valk and Daniel Sävborg, 80–92. Helsinki: Finnish Literature Society and Studia Fennica Folkloristica.
Li, Darryl. 2019. *The Universal Enemy: Jihad, Empire, and the Challenge of Solidarity*. Stanford, CA: Stanford University Press.
Lovrenčević, Zvonko. 1970. "Mitološke predaje bilo-gore." *Narodna umjetnost*, 7/1:71–100.
Lozica, Ivan. 1995. "Dva demona: Orko i macić." *Narodna umjetnost*, 32/2:11–63.
Lüthi, Max. 1961. *Volksmärchen und volkssage. Zwei grundformen erzählender dichtung*. Bern: Franke Verlag.
Lüthi, Max. 1976. "Aspects of the *Märchen* and the Legend." In *Folklore Genres*, ed. Dan Ben-Amos, 17–33. Austin: University of Texas Press. First published in German 1966.
Lüthi, Max. 1986. *The European Folktale. Form and Nature*, trans. John D. Niles. Bloomington, Indianapolis: Indiana University Press. First published in German 1982.

Marjanić, Suzana. 1999. "Zaštitna sredstva protiv more kao žensko-niktomorfnog demona." *Treća: Časopis Centra za ženske studije*, 2/1:55–71.

Marks, Ljiljana. 2007. "'Ni o drvo, ni o kamen ...': Magične formule u hrvatskim predajama o vješticama." *Narodna umjetnost*, 44/2:27–42.

Mencej, Mirjam. 2017. *Styrian Witches in European Perspective: Ethnographic Fieldwork*. London: Palgrave Macmillan.

Mencej, Mirjam. 2021. "The Dead, the War, and Ethnic Identity: Ghost Narratives in Post-War Srebrenica." *Folklore*, 132/4:412–433.

Milošević-Đorđević, Nada. 1991. "Continuity and Change in Folk Prose Narrative." *Oral Tradition*, 6/2–3:316–324.

Murko, Matthias (Matija). 1951. *Tragom srpsko-hrvatske narodne epike. Putovanja u godinama 1930–1932*. Zagreb: Jugoslavenska akademija znanosti i umjetnosti.

Oring, Elliott. 2012. "Legendry and the Rhetoric of Truth." In *Just Folklore: Analysis, Interpretation, Critique*, 104–152. Los Angeles, CA: Cantilever Press.

Pentikäinen, Juha. 1973. "Belief, Memorate, and Legend." *Folklore Forum*, 6/4:217–241. First published 1968.

Perić-Polonijo, Tanja. 1996. "Predgovor." In *Narodne pjesme iz Luke na Šipanu*, by Andro Murat, ed. Tanja Perić-Polonijo, 7–36. Zagreb: Matica Hrvatska.

Perkowski, Jan Louis. 2006. "The Darkling: A Treatise on Slavic Vampirism." In *Vampire Lore: From the Writings of Jan Louis Perkowski*, 317–488. Bloomington, IN: Slavica Publishers. First published 1989.

Petrovich, Woislav M. 1914. *Hero Tales and Legends of the Serbians*. London: George G. Harrap & Company.

Radulović, Nemanja, and Smiljana Đorđević Belić. 2021. "Disenchantment, Re-Enchantment and Folklore Genres: Introduction." In *Disenchantment, Re-enchantment and Folklore Genres*, eds. Nemanja Radulović and Smiljana Đorđević Belić, 7–26. Belgrade: Institute for Literature and Arts.

Röhrich, Lutz. 1969. "Die deutsche volkssage. Ein methodischer abriß." In *Vergleichende sagenforschung*, 217–286. Darmstadt: Wissenschaftliche Buchgesellschaft. First published 1958.

Roper, Jonathan. 2018. "Folk Disbelief." In *Storied and Supernatural Places: Studies in Spatial and Social Dimensions of Folklore and Sagas*, eds. Ülo Valk and Daniel Sävborg, 223–236. Helsinki: Finnish Literature Society and Studia Fennica Folkloristica.

Scullion, John J. 1984. "Marchen, Sage, Legende: Towards a Clarification of Some Literary Terms Used by Old Testament Scholars." *Vetus Testamentum*, 34/3:321–336.

Šešo, Luka. 2003. "O krsniku: Od tradicijske pojave u predajama do stvarnog iscjelitelja." *Studia ethnologica Croatica*, 15:23–53.

Šešo, Luka. 2010a. "'Ja o tome znam, ali ne želim pričati': Tradicijska vjerovanja u nadnaravna bića u unutrašnjosti Dalmacije." *Narodna umjetnost*, 47/2:97–111.

Šešo, Luka. 2010b. "Problem istraživanja nadnaravnih bića u hrvatskoj etnologiji i folkloristici." In *Mitski zbornik*, eds. Suzana Marjanić and Ines Prica, 115–125. Zagreb: Institut za etnologiju i folkloristiku, Hrvatsko etnološko društvo, and Scarabeus-naklada.

Šešo, Luka. 2016. *Živjeti s nadnaravnim bićima: Vukodlaci, vile i vještice hrvatskih tradicijskih vjerovanja*. Zagreb: Jesenski i Turk.

Tangherlini, Timothy. 1994. *Interpreting Legend: Danish Storytellers and Their Repertoires*. New York: Garland.

Tarkka, Lotte. 2015. "Picturing the Otherworld: Imagination in the Study of Oral Poetry." In *Between Text and Practice: Mythology, Religion and Research*, Special issue of *RMN Newsletter*, eds. Frog and Karina Lukin, 10:17–32.

Valk, Ülo. 2015. "Discursive Shifts in Legends from Demonization to Fictionalization." *Narrative Culture*, 2/1:141–165.

von Sydow, Carl Wilhelm. 1977a. "Kategorien der prosa-volksdichtung." In *Selected Papers on Folklore*, ed. Richard M. Dorson, 60–88. New York: Arno Press.

von Sydow, Carl Wilhelm. 1977b. "Popular Dite Tradition: A Terminological Outline." In *Selected Papers on Folklore*, ed. Richard M. Dorson, 106–126. New York: Arno Press.

Vuletić-Vukasović, Vid. 1934. "Prizrijevanje." *Srpski etnografski sbornik* 50/4:155–195.

Zečević, Slobodan. 1981. *Mitska bića srpskih predanja*. Belgrade: Vuk Karadžić and Etnografski muzej.

CHAPTER 28

POLISH URBAN LEGENDS AS A FOLKLORE GENRE

MARTA WÓJCICKA

From the very beginning, Polish studies on urban legends (*legendy miejskie*, sing. *legenda miejska*) have emphasized that stories of this sort belong to folklore. This was based on the following criteria: the popularity of the story within a specific social group, the collective nature of story creation (and the resulting variants), spontaneity, the casual nature of such storytelling, and its oral character (Simonides and Hajduk-Nijakowska 1989:411). In other words, urban legends comprise a contemporary folk genre involving

> a set of conventions that govern storytelling [which] includes ways of creating stories, their semiotic organization, the intentional attitude of the speaker towards the listener, and typical applications. These folk-genre-related conventions [both] determine how the world is described and what its ontological status is as well as define the positions of the speaker and the listener, the communicative intent they share, and the means of expression that are used.
>
> (Bartmiński 1990:15)

What makes folk genres distinctive is their naturalness, meaning that they function within syncretic (verbal/somatic/situational) communication (Bartmiński and Niebrzegowska-Bartmińska 2009:140). This examination of urban legends, as a contemporary folk genre, includes considerations of research on the genre in Poland, form, diction or choice of words, the narrator, the audience, communication context (circumstances, time, and place), the subject matter and function of the narrative, its purpose and performance, and the ontology of the depicted world or reality that is represented (cf. Bartmiński and Niebrzegowska-Bartmińska 2009; Niebrzegowska-Bartmińska 2012). This chapter provides a descriptive and analytical discussion of these considerations in the study of urban legends as a prose narrative folk genre. It argues that the genre expresses relevant, meaningful stories of an apocryphal nature that address issues of truth and fiction as well as right and wrong. They reflect social, political, and economic conditions in contemporary Poland.

Urban Legends in Poland: State of the Art

Urban legends have been the subject of international research since the 1940s. The 1980s were a breakthrough period in the study of these texts. It was then that the first collections of the genre appeared (Dale 1978; Dale 1984; Brunvand 1981; Brunvand 1984; Brunvand 1986; Brunvand 1989; Smith 1983, 1986). Polish folklorists and anthropologists have been interested in urban legends since the late 1960s. The first Poles to study them were Dorota Simonides (1969) and Dionizjusz Czubała (1985, 1993, 2005, 2014). Initially, urban legends were treated as a type of memoir story (Czubała 1985). Later, their genealogical distinctiveness was recognized and emphasized. Such narratives were defined as "short, single-thread stories in prose, about some unusual present-day events that are likely to spread rapidly and over large areas" (Czubala 1985:83) or as "stories that are current, spontaneous, and emotional for both the teller and the listener" (Czubala 2014:7). Urban legends, which tend to be short-lived, are most likely to emerge during periods of social unrest (Czubala 1985:85).

Studies of urban legends focus, on the one hand, on what makes them different from other folk prose genres and, on the other, on what makes them similar especially to folk tales (oral traditional, fictional stories without specified time or place told for entertainment) including common elements that they share with them. In the 1970s, urban legends were likened to folk tales. Both genres were viewed as embracing similar storytelling conventions that relied on making the narrative seem authentic and realistic (Simonides and Hajduk-Nijakowska 1989:410). Later analyses helped identify differences between these genres in their distinct initial and final formulae, intentions, and ways of describing the world (Wójcicka 2013). In folk tales, some narrators use framework testimony formulae (statements at the beginning and/or end of tales) and at times refer to collective sources, whether unspecified ("people say") or family members. For urban legends, by contrast, sources are typically family, friends, or the media. Differences in the ways testimony formulae are used in folk tales and urban legends (extra-generational vs. intra-generational relations, respectively) demonstrate different types of interactions between people today and in the past. Even though both genres describe unusual things or events, "folktales look for explanations of some unknown or disturbing phenomena almost exclusively in the supernatural world, while urban legends do so by referring to the human psyche" (Wójcicka 2013:56). Both genres seek to allay fears caused, for example, by some ostensibly supernatural phenomena, while urban legends find "explanations" in other causes such as disease. Urban legends are also intended to ridicule human vices, make people laugh, and educate them, among other things.

Polish studies on urban legends have focused especially on the topics commonly addressed by the genre. Indeed, the subject matter usually constitutes the basis for identifying different types of urban legends, including automotive, political, medical, erotic, economic, religious, parapsychological, and morbid, as well as those related to assaults, robberies, monsters, extraterrestrials, oddities, or anomalies (Czubala 1993:138). Urban legends can be comical or disturbing; they recount disgusting things or events, animal attacks, winning (money or prizes), children left unattended, murders, gang violence, new technology, and strange accidents (Przybyła-Dumin 2013). What is also typical of this genre is the setting (usually highly urbanized areas), time (present day) (Rydzewska 2004:118), and links with the media, which not only popularize urban legends but also generate them (Hajduk-Nijakowska 2005:148).

What has become evident in the study of urban legends is that the only constant distinguishing feature of this genre is its function—to express social anxieties (Rydzewska 2004; Hajduk-Nijakowska 2005). As argued by Klaus Thiele-Dohrmann, urban legends offer "a way for people to give vent to their fears and aggression," and telling them is a means to "help relieve stress and make the world around us predictable again" (Hajduk-Nijakowska 2005:145). But urban legends serve not only expressive but also ludic, educational, social, and, especially, communicative functions. Moreover, they provide commentary on current social situations (Rydzewska 2004:120) and project public sentiments and the need to find someone to blame for tragedy (Hajduk-Nijakowska 2005:153). Urban legends make social gatherings more fun and enjoyable because "story-sharing helps create bonds" (Napiórkowski 2013:22), and retelling, itself, is a cultural practice (Napiórkowski 2013:22) and, for some, therapeutic. As stories that sometimes resemble myths (narratives that furnish accounts of significant, even sacred, phenomena), urban legends "serve to make reality more accessible, explaining the unknown by referring to what is known" (Napiórkowski 2013:25).

This interest by Polish folklorists has resulted in the publication of urban legend compilations. Many stories that were in circulation in Poland at different points in time can be found in Dionizjusz Czubala's 1993 publication, and a large number of stories are included in a 2013 study by Agnieszka Przybyła-Dumin. In 2014, Czubala published a collection of urban legends based solely on orally transmitted texts. But there has also been another tide of Polish interest in urban legends that is associated with the internet. Enthusiasts of such narratives have created a website to collect urban legends shared online.[1]

FORM

Urban legends are (originally) oral or written (secondarily oral) stories, either collected by folklorists and published or circulated online. They generally have a two-part structure. This includes sections external to the story (extratextual) and those internal to the story (intratextual). Extratextual sections are about the pragmatic aspects of the urban legend (describing when and how the speaker found out about it), or they constitute a summary of it—either modal ("It's true" or "I don't know if it's true") or moralistic ("It's human nature"). And intratextual sections are related to the events described in the story. Extratextual sections (in italics, for the most part, in the urban legends excerpted here) often provide a frame for the narrative, as in the example below. The initial statement specifies the time and place of the event, while the final passage is a testimony formula (in which the performer refers to the source from which they obtained the message but declines to take a position, suspending judgment):[2]

> *A few years ago, there was this accident in Tarnowskie Góry.*[3] A mother left her baby outside [a store] in a stroller and went inside. She heard her baby crying but didn't want to stop her shopping. When she finished, she went out of the store, but her baby started screaming even louder. She couldn't calm it down, and she discovered that there was a rat [in the stroller]. When she was buying milk in the store, a rat had come out of the sewer. And it had gone under the baby's blanket and bitten the baby badly. I don't know whether the baby survived. *I heard this story a few years ago from some friends of mine. And now when I'm traveling somewhere with my baby, I often have this incident in the back of my mind.*
>
> (Czubala 2014:236)

Extratextual content at the end of an urban legend can include formulae that serve to provide evidence that supports the authenticity of the story (e.g., where it was heard—in the example below, at the hospital). Intratextual content often has a two-part structure. Part one describes the situation with a surprising—funny or tragic—ending (using either short or compound/complex sentences). Part two explains why it ended the way it did (employing multiple complex sentences). The first part is dominated by additivity, which is typical of orality ("A woman got pregnant, and she gave birth to a Black baby. And her husband got mad"), while the latter is likely to focus on causality ("And only then did they discover that it was the husband who transmitted the sperm of the Black man, and that's why his wife gave birth to a Black baby"):

> A woman got pregnant, and she gave birth to a Black baby. And her husband got mad. But she swore she hadn't had sex with any Black man or any other man. She went to a doctor, and she swore blind that she was telling the truth. So the doctor examined her husband. And it turned out that he had had sex with his neighbor upstairs. So the doctor examined the neighbor. And he found that she had slept with a Black man. And only then did they discover that it was the husband who transmitted the sperm of the Black man, and that's why his wife gave birth to a Black baby. *I heard this story from other patients in the hospital I was at in January.*
>
> (Czubala 2014:198)

A similar two-part structure can be seen in the example below. The story contains two sequences, preceded by a concise, existential, formulaic expression with the numerical concept ("two") that introduces it.[4] The main characters are two roommates, and what happens to them seems to be a matter of chance, which is emphasized by the last sentence of the story:

> *A story about two girlfriends/roommates from one of Warsaw's dorms.* One evening, the girls went to a student party. After some time, one of them became tired and returned to her room. But the girls only had one key to their room, so she didn't close the door so that her roommate could get inside when she came back. After a while, the other girl came to the room for a second to get something, and when she saw her roommate sleeping, she didn't turn the lights on. She only took the thing she came to get and went back to the party. When she returned to the room early in the morning, she discovered her roommate was dead, the room was full of blood, and on the wall someone had written "Had you switched the lights on, you'd be lying next to her."
>
> (I: Ernest Ziemiński, born in 1980; C: Marta Ziarno, recorded on June 8, 2011, in Lublin)[5]

There are also urban legends that have a tripartite structure, such as in the story below. Here, the attempt to put a light bulb inside one's mouth is made first by a student, second by a taxi driver, and finally by the student's friend. While the first student was motivated by the bet he had made, the taxi driver and second student were driven by curiosity and skepticism:

> *This story allegedly happened in one of the dormitories in Łódź.* During some booze-up, a guy made a bet with his friends that he would put the wider part of a light bulb inside his mouth. And he managed to win the bet, but when he wanted to pull the light bulb out, it turned out to be difficult, and he couldn't do it. After a few attempts, his friends decided to take him to the hospital to have the bulb removed. They ordered a taxi and took their friend to the hospital. The taxi driver couldn't hold back an ironic smile because he had never seen anything like that before. When the doctor saw the student with a light bulb in his mouth, he also made some scathing comments about it. But he helped the student, and after a minor surgical procedure, the bulb was out. The students went back to the party only to find another friend with a light bulb in his mouth. It turned out that he hadn't seen the first attempt and couldn't believe it, so he decided to try this himself. The students then knew what to do and took the other friend to the hospital as well. And by chance, they ended up with the same doctor. When he saw the second student, the doctor couldn't help but laugh out loud. And he showed the students why—when he drew the curtain in his office, they saw the taxi driver from the first cab sitting there with a light bulb in his mouth as well.
>
> (I: Ernest Ziemiński, born in 1980; C: Marta Ziarno, recorded on June 8, 2011, in Lublin)

The urban legends cited above provide grotesque ways to expose what contemporary people dread and fear and how they perceive themselves: losing a child due to inattention, infidelity and being caught, random murders, and foolish acts of bravura.

Although brief and informal, each narrative is structured and constructed in stock and formulaic ways, including extratextual and intratextual content. Extratextual passages attest to the source and "veracity" of the tales: whom the storyteller heard them from as well as where and when the actions took place. All are localized and/or provide temporal frameworks. Intratextual content comprises the core of the story, the message.

DICTION

While rooted in oral tradition, urban legends employ their own distinctive diction or choice of words. They use rhetorical devices typical of folklore such as formulae, epithets, and, at times, euphemisms instead of metaphors. A formula is a primary rhetorical device used in both traditional and contemporary folklore. It is not only a structural component of urban legends or part of their frame, however. As "the offspring of tradition, collectivity, and orality" (Bartmiński 1975:6), formulae also help the narrator create and reproduce stories and aid the audience in recognizing and understanding them. In urban legends, both initial and final formulae are most frequently testimony formulae, which show the narrator's attitude to what they are talking about. The most popular testimony delimiters in urban legends are perception verbs (e.g., *słyszeć*, "to hear"), used either alone or with additional information about the place and/or time of the event described in the story, such as in "We heard it not that long ago because it happened in Pińczów" (Czubala 1996:113). The frame of an urban legend also includes authenticity formulae, or formulae of truth, either of alethic (assertive) modality, as in "Let me tell you a true story" (Czubala 1996:27), or epistemic modality, for example, "They say there is this illegal company operating in Poland that buys little girls and sends them to the West" (Czubala 1996:37).

Epithets, such as "a huge rat" (Czubala 1996:80, 81), "giant rats" (Czubala 1996:81), "greedy dogs" (Czubala 1996:18), "a greedy pointing dog" (Czubala 1996:18), "an unfortunate plumber" (Czubala 1996:14), or "false teeth" (Czubala 1996:17), are intended to emphasize the terror of the situation described in the story. Adjectives such as "huge," "giant," and "greedy" are used to portray animals that can injure or even kill the characters. Such epithets show that urban legend is a genre which presents a certain part of reality in an expressive way to describe some risk. Epithets are also compositional devices: firmly embedded in the storyteller's lexicon, they organize the text, introducing the protagonist and/or objects of the story.

Another rhetorical device that is frequently used to describe the world in this genre is euphemism, found primarily in urban legends about sexual exploits. Traditional folk texts, such as folk songs, express eroticism using metaphors. In urban legends that revolve around the topic of sex, however, narrators use euphemistic descriptions of intercourse itself ("coitus," "doing it," "providing services to millionaires only," "receiving men," "going inside [a woman] for erotic purposes," "making love," "[the lady was] having an interaction with a dog") or of male or female reproductive organs ("grabbed his ...," "his thing was burned").

Moreover, the style used in urban legends about cultural taboos such as sex or death is like that of a report. It is additive, relying on simple or compound sentences, themselves composed of simple clauses, joined by conjunctions. This serves to create a distance from the narrated events. Such stories typically contain many verbs:

> This one family got a parcel from America, and there was a can inside. And they thought it was a soup mix, so they ate it. But it turned out that the can contained the ashes of their aunt who had gone to America some time back. And she died, and it was her will to be buried in Poland. [Before she died] she had asked someone to send her ashes to Poland.
> (I: Urszula Morąg, born in 1967 in Skaryszew, living in Dąbrówka Nagórna; C: Dagmara Morąg, Radom, 2011)

As an orally performed narrative genre, words, word groups, and sentences are the building blocks of urban legends. Narrators turn to an arsenal of such devices in order to tell stories effectively.

The Narrator and the Audience

With urban legends, there is a dual narrator. Its two realizations are the speaker and the actual, or internal, narrator. Speakers, who are external (Wójcicka 2013), convey the story in its current variant and build the variant, usually on the basis of the tale they have heard themselves. Actual, or internal (Wójcicka 2013), narrators (of which there may be several) are mentioned by the storyteller as the "author(s)" from whom the narrative was originally heard. In the urban legend cited below, the (external) speaker is a man who makes reference to the original (internal) narrator of the story. By using a testimony formula (*My grandmother told me, and she herself had heard from a friend of hers*), he mentions the actual (internal) narrator, a friend of his grandmother's, whose "liaison" between the internal and external narrators is his grandmother. This allows the speaker (or external narrator) to "not take a stand and keep his personal opinion to himself" on whether certain events took place, although he does not shun value judgments (*They managed to live this lie for a few months*) (Bartmiński 1989:52):

> *My grandmother told me, and she herself had heard from a friend of hers*, that some family that lived in Chełm with their grandmother had been hiding her dead body (when she died) in order to continue to receive her generous old-age pension. *They managed to live this lie for a few months*. The truth came out when the postman who delivered pensions in that area was replaced, and the new guy categorically demanded that the old lady receive the money herself. At that point the family had

no choice but to admit that she was dead. The old lady was finally buried in a cemetery, and the family went to prison.

(I: Grzegorz Adamczuk, living in Chełm, a student; C: Bożena Skolimowska, May 18, 2010, Chełm, Lubelskie Province)

Urban legends are generally examples of "stories having a specific [internal] narrator, thus revealing a kind of a double consciousness" (Bartmiński 1989:52).

The actual (internal) narrator described by the speaker not only is the original source of the story but also makes it sound more (or less) credible. This is because retelling someone else's story is a way to relate to it and lend credence to it or, on the contrary, to distance oneself from it. In order to authenticate the message of the source used, people known by their first and last names, loved ones, family members, or friends are typically cited by the narrator. By contrast, to dissociate themselves from the story, speakers refer to some unspecified group, the media, the community, or people in general. An internal narrator is described by the speaker in the next example as she starts the story. The people whom the speaker mentions (an old lady and a doctor known by his last name) are believed by the speaker to make the narrative seem more authentic:

People in our community used to say that there were some worms in bananas imported from Africa or South America. And there was this old lady who would say that her sister's son, or grandson, had eaten those bananas with the worms. And they didn't know what was wrong with him. And they tried to do some magic to make him feel better, so, you know. . . . And then there was this doctor, Pojasek, who said that those bananas must have been eaten unwashed. And the old lady said that no, they were washed, but she saw some worms squirming inside, and the boy died because of those worms.

(I: Genowewfa Januszewska, born in 1940, Biłgoraj; C: Paulina Januszewska)

Evident from the above example, there can be a number of internal narrators. They create what is known as a narration within a narration; Jan Brunvand calls this a "friend of a friend," which represents the way an urban legend circulates among people. Each previous narrator mentioned by the speaker is intended to make the legend seem more authentic, but in fact the multi-level structure of the narration often makes the story less plausible.

In an urban legend, the internal narrator (implied by the story) serves as an intermediary, an interpreter, or, less frequently, an observer of the tale. Intermediaries connect the community in which the story is circulating with the audience. They are the depositary of the narrative from some more or less remote past, which they change and update. The intermediary retells the information. This fact is demonstrated by multiple testimony formulae, such as the following:

A friend of mine told me about this accident. She had come at five in the morning to attend her lectures and saw something terrible at the station in Katowice. This was a year ago, after some concert at the "Spodek,"[6] I think. She saw a large group of people at the ticket office. A few skinheads were beating some boy; they were spitting on him, kicking him, and cutting him with razor blades. There were a lot of bystanders, but no one did anything about it. Only after the police came was this stopped.

(Czubala 2014:285)

The interpreter or external speaker, on the other hand, not only retells the story but also adds some explicit comments (in italics below), which are intended as generalizations or serve to confer a moralistic tone, such as in the following:

AIDS is a venereal disease, after all. And I ask myself sometimes whether this isn't God's punishment for what is happening in the world right now. In Germany, this has escalated into perversion. I'm no saint myself, and I used to play around like this myself, but recently a friend of mine came back from Germany. He told me there are restaurants there where waitresses are naked, wearing only aprons. And when they walk by, men grab them by their butts. And they only smile at them and say "Zwei [two] Mark." And when someone grabs them by the pubic hair, they say "Drei [three] Mark." And they immediately add the amount to their bill. *And how can they not be infected if it's like this?* By the way, have you heard about the big shots in Arłamów? *Those communist pigs* had a luxury holiday resort in the Bieszczady Mountains. They used to go hunting there. And they would have naked whores pander to their whims. There were dozens of naked Negro women there, and those guys took them whenever they wanted. *And they were from Africa, for God's sake! And how could they not be infected?*

(Czubala 2014:214)

Finally, the speaker can also serve as the observer of the events, although this happens much less frequently. In such cases, this is emphasized by the verb *widziec* ("to see") used in the first-person singular, for example:

This happened in Warsaw. I saw it with my own eyes . There were drug addicts sitting in front of this huge store. Sitting and begging for money. A policeman came and wanted to chase them away. But they had those long pins, and they stabbed him to death in front of other people. And he died there. No one helped him. Because people there are callous.

(Czubala 2014:208)

The audience, as portrayed in the urban legend, is someone living during the same time as the internal narrator, someone who might have heard about the well-known events described in the story. Often already at the beginning of the narration the storyteller mentions this common knowledge, entering into a dialogue with the audience by asking the question "By the way, have you heard about Jantar[7]—you know, the singer? I've heard she's alive" (Czubala 1996:38). In many urban legends with elaborate openings, the speakers designate themselves as the audience of the tale that they are about to retell. Thus the story itself describes a communication context surrounding the spreading of the story.

The Communication Context

An important part of many urban legends is the description of the situation in which speakers heard the story that they are now retelling. That description—the communication context—is embedded in the narrative and covers the circumstances, time, and/or place it was told and heard. The story is typically about events described by a relative (such as a grandmother or uncle) or a friend. In the following, the communication context (in italics) includes the circumstances and time when, as the speaker recalls, she was the audience of a story "retold by older people":

> *When I was a child, I once heard a legend that had been popular for a few years back then. I heard it being retold by older people.* They'd say that some people were riding around the city in a black car and kidnapping children from the streets. And that organs were harvested from those children for transplants. So mothers were afraid to let children go to school alone or play outside on their own in the evenings.
> (I: Jadwiga Ozimek, 1953, Tuszyn, living in Radom; T[8]: Marta Ozimek, 2011)

People know urban legends from the media as well. Here, the circumstances ("information" in a newspaper) and place (a Polish town) comprise the speaker's communication context:

> *I think I might have read it in* Polityka.[9] There was this information about some criminal being arrested. The police had put him in a cop car and had taken him to the police station. And then he told them he had AIDS and threw himself at them and started biting them. So the policemen fled in panic, and he walked away casually. They'd rather let him escape than have themselves and all the other inmates infected. *It happened in Otwock, I think.*
> (Czubala 2014:212)

The exact time of the event in the narrative is usually not specified in urban legends. The time at which the story was told indirectly points to when the speaker heard it. Many people come and go to places where a listener-cum-speaker may hear a tale (a train, village, or sanatorium). This contributes to the dissemination of unbelievable stories since the constant movement of people makes it impossible to confirm them. For example, in one urban legend, the speaker's communication context includes "Those are street rumors, or even bus rumors. And they are fairly popular, especially among people who interact with others in buses or queues. People say that it happened in the Old Town" (Czubala 1996:66). Specific information about the time and place at which a story was heard can be provided if it is intended to make it seem more authentic or to distance the speaker from it (this is often the case with tales from the media). Normally, however, narrators cannot recall the exact time or place they have heard a story unless this can be connected to some important event in their life and/or specific individual memories (such as a trip their parents took to Greece).

Subject Matter and the Function of Urban Legends

The most important characteristic of urban legends is that they reflect social sentiments, problems, risks, and concerns. Urban legends are the "product of urban civilisation" (Czubala 2014:16) and expose fundamental anxieties of contemporary society. Moreover, they are, above all, tales about the storytellers themselves and their value systems and worldviews. Telling a story is a pretext for contemplating, evaluating, and drawing conclusions about the world around us. The inspiration for an urban legend is usually some true but astonishing event such as an unusual rash, the disappearance of a student, or some other strange or sensational event, coupled with the lack of information or understanding about how or why such events actually happened or indeed happen at all.

The topics explored in urban legends change as fast as the world around us. If we were to examine the ways this genre and its themes in Poland have evolved over time, we would see what social, cultural, and economic problems have been on the minds of Polish citizens more or less since the 1960s. But analysis of this is not an easy task. In other words, there is no systematic study of when people first become interested in specific urban legend topics nor when they lose interest in them. However, there are some general trends.

In the 1960s, the topics that were popular in urban legends in Poland were about vampires, newborn babies on railway tracks, catalepsy, winning a Mercedes, and winning the lottery. In the 1970s, there were stories about members of a family drinking a powder that turned out to be their aunt's ashes, a hippie who killed his own mother, men in black cars abducting children to use their blood to cure rich people in western Europe, the kidnapping of Anna Jantar (a Polish singer who died in a plane crash in 1980) into a harem, finding severed hands, being blinded by razor blades, castrated rapists, selling human flesh, sexual eccentricities, and gifts donated abroad that were stolen. In the 1980s, some urban legends were political stories associated with the lifting of martial law and the Solidarity movement. Some were about Polish goods exported to the Soviet Union for next to nothing (meat hidden under lumps of coal, ham under grains of wheat), Polish natural resources secretly mined by Soviet companies, former big shots such as Leonid Brezhnev treated with blood from Polish newborns, vast fortunes illegally accumulated by government officials (e.g., the cars owned by Piotr Jaroszewicz,[10] golden handles on the doors at the home of Edward Gierek[11]), and dignitaries' wives shopping abroad (e.g., Gierek's wife traveling to Paris for a haircut). During that time, there were also urban legends about the assassination attempt by the KGB on (the Polish pope) John Paul II, Russians bugging the telephone exchange in Warsaw, and Red Army soldiers raping Polish women. The decades-long economic crisis in communist Poland, when stores had insufficient supplies of almost everything, was known as "queue folklore" (when urban legends about goods hidden on purpose in warehouses to make the nation economically deprived were rampant).

In post-communist Poland of the 1990s, the topics were much the same (members of the government living dissolutely, scandals, etc.) but were about different people (e.g., the son of Lech Wałęsa[12] cruising around town in expensive cars). Some anticlerical legends started to appear[13] (e.g., about priests burning sex shops or women being blackmailed during confession because of admitting to having used birth control). With the rise of capitalism and Polish society's improved standard of living, there were more stories demonstrating fear of thieves and criminals (e.g., about a woman being robbed and blinded with a razor blade, a thief tearing someone's ear off to grab an earring, and a crook cutting off someone's finger to steal a ring). This was the time of what Czubala describes as "market legends"—stories about cutlets made of dog meat, roast rat, and selling clothes taken off of dead bodies (as well as cadaveric poison in a wedding dress, yucca with venomous spiders, and infected bananas). In the 1990s, the tales that were particularly numerous were those about HIV (intentional infecting by drug addicts but also accidental infections at the hairdresser's, the dentist's, or a hospital or from a prostitute). Other recorded stories included one about "a hitchhiker who disappeared" and one about "a death car."

In the first decade of the 2000s, common topics included exploding toilets, lost winnings, child rape, sex with a dog, poison from a corpse, a surgical tool left in someone's belly, a tampon in someone else's abdomen, surgical errors, dangerous plants, water veins, human flesh, dog and cat meat, mice in bottles, rats eating children, and spiders in food. The year 2010 marked the era of the Smoleńsk urban legends, which circulated and were popular mainly online, about a catastrophic airplane crash that killed Poland's president and numerous government, military, and church officials.[14] This national disaster became a widely discussed topic of Polish public debate and was subject to various conspiracy theories, none of which has ever been verified.

The above overview of topics addressed by urban legends shows what Poles have feared over the past few decades and how stories that circulate in public furnish scapegoats to explain the unknown as well as ways to connect socially with others. Indeed, urban legends are like a mirror that reflects the times in which they are popular. They are influenced by the historical, economic, and political realities of the people who tell them, revealing social contexts and popular sentiments. Urban legends of the 1960s developed from folk tales (vampires, catalepsy) and were related to death and the underworld. In the 1970s and 1980s, urban legends were told to explain the realities of that time, such as the lack of goods in stores. They sought reasons for that in the actions of the Polish United Workers' Party and the communist political system in Poland at the time. The next decades, from the collapse of communism in 1989 on, would see politicians as the main culprits who were to blame for shortages and threats. Wealth became a bone of contention among different social groups. Those who were better off became objects of suspicion (they "must have stolen something," e.g., gifts donated by the West). The social (and economic) stratification that would gain momentum in the years after 1989 would contribute to the development of stories about illegal accumulation of wealth, stealing, and fraud by those who were more successful in life. Urban legends became a vehicle for expressing frustration, especially when Poland was undergoing a dramatic rise of capitalism (often called "wild capitalism").

Poles feared HIV in the 1990s, possibly more than anything else; hence, there were many sexual, lifestyle, and sexual-orientation topics in urban legends. Later, stories came to reflect a decrease in trust placed by the public in professions that had enjoyed it up until then (e.g., priests and doctors). That trend was, perhaps, connected with the development of the media industry in Poland, which focused on sensational and lurid news. Journalism described as tabloid or "fast food journalism" (Allan 2006:212) not only provided topics for urban legends but also influenced the way people perceived the world. In the first decade of the 2000s, urban legends reflected the fear of foreigners (e.g., dog meat sold by the Arabs or Chinese). In such tales, "foreigners create an anti-world and anti-culture, which is, by definition, perceived as a threat to culture" per se (Napiórkowski 2013:122).

By documenting social contexts and public sentiments, urban legends serve several important functions, among them defensive, cognitive, and evaluative. Defensive functions are warnings against hazards and risks posed, for instance, by the mythologized West, new lifestyles, nature, or technological advancements. At the same time, by exaggerating those dangers, urban legends reinforce public anxieties and provide protection against a vision of the world that would force the carriers of culture to reconsider their outlooks. They are the vehicles for and the creators of social stereotypes. Cognitive and etiological functions explain the unknown and the disturbing by identifying scapegoats: someone to blame (politicians, priests, western Europe, hippies, drug addicts, Arabs, etc.). Evaluative and integrative functions perform a number of roles in uniting people around the worldviews that they communicate and appraise, their refusal to accept disinformation and manipulation by the media, and the very pleasure of listening to unusual stories in social gatherings.

Purpose and the Performance of Urban Legends

Urban legends have specific purposes, which differ from the functions they serve. While the function of the narrative affects or resides in the audience or recipient of the "message," the purpose or intention is communicated by the storyteller in performance and is conveyed in the text, through words. Purpose is expressed by acts of speech and is revealed in the storyteller's use of various discursive techniques that serve to scare, warn, entertain, and/or amuse the audience in performance.

Verbs explicitly describe the intention of the narrator. The verb "to scare" (*straszyć*) and a synonym, "to frighten" (*przestraszyć*), figure in the following:

> There was once this common belief that some people drove around Lublin in a black car and kidnapped children. This was to *scare* children into not approaching any black cars, probably due to the fact that during the time of the Polish People's Republic,[15] similar cars were used by the Security Service. In any case, this story was used to *frighten* children so that they stayed near their parents or their homes, or else someone from a big black car would kidnap them. *I heard this from a friend of mine, or actually a friend of my mom's, and my mother also told me that there were such rumors being spread in Lublin.*
> (I: Magdalena Gnyp, 1984, Lublin; T: Magdalena Wójtowicz, 2009)

The verb "to warn" (*ostrzegać*) reflects the storyteller's purpose in this cautionary urban legend:

> In Katowice there is this incredibly rich lady. She has a university education and can speak several languages. She receives men very rarely because she carries herself with dignity. She's like an elite prostitute and provides her services to millionaires only. She charges more for a single night than other women can earn in a month. Regulars at the local cafe know her, and the staff bow low to her whenever they see her. She used to be an extremely attractive woman, but recently, having gotten HIV, she has become emaciated and ugly. *Those who know this, warn others*, but she still infects foreigners. She must have many prominent people on her conscience.
> (Czubala 1993:64)

The above examples reveal explicit reasons for which each speaker tells an urban legend. The stories are related specifically to make listeners aware of something or to scare them in order to warn them against some menace. Such storytelling is intended to explain unclear, uncertain, mysterious, or dangerous situations (such as child abduction or AIDS infection) and to make them seem, as a result, less threatening. Therefore, the primary goal is not to entertain but to explain various realities and allay fears or concerns. In other words, storytelling purposes, such as providing entertainment and didactic intent (e.g., warning against sex with random partners), are secondary to the narrator's main objective (Wójcicka 2013).

Explicitly expressed purposes are rare, however, in urban legends. More often the purpose is implicit or inferred; for instance, the intention of the speaker may be to instill fear, often of an irrational nature (as occurs at times in certain traditional folk tales, such as fables). For example,

> When I was in secondary school, I used to go to the countryside during summer holidays to visit a friend of mine. And I remember her grandmother telling us this story about a girl who was preparing for a party, and she wanted her hair to look nice, but she didn't have hair spray, so she used sugar with water. And so she backcombed her

hair to make it look nice, and she went out. But it was in the summertime, and she was passing some fruit trees along the way. And bees attacked her. And she was bitten so badly that she actually died next to those trees. They didn't manage to save her. *And there is this legend that she appears there every year, and no one walks anywhere near that place during that time of the year because strange things happen.*

(I: Anna Ozimek, 1979, Pionki, living in Radom; T: Marta Ozimek, 2011)

Another inherent purpose of urban legends may be to warn people against violating some not expressly stated, yet obvious, common-sense "rules" of behavior, for example, related to being a mother and raising children or to having limited trust in strangers:

A few months back my flatmate told me that she had heard this story when she was in Kraków. And this was apparently for real. A woman comes shopping to one of Kraków's shopping malls. She wants to buy some magazines. So she goes to a newsstand. And she leaves her stroller in front of the newsstand for a moment. You know, this is a small place, so she couldn't get in there with the stroller. It takes her no more than five minutes to buy the magazine. And when she turns around she sees that there is no child, no stroller, no child. Wait, no, I mean, the stroller was there but the child was not in the stroller. So she reports it to the security—that her child is missing. The security blocks the doors, and everyone starts to look for that kid. After about fifteen minutes, they find her, because this was a baby girl, you know, but she has her hair cut, and she is dressed in boys' clothes. It turns out that someone tried to abduct her. *So that's the story. But I don't know if it's true or not, but . . . it's scary.*

(I: A. N., 1986; T: Magdalena Kiewel, Warsaw, 2009)

Urban legends are meant to intrigue, spark interest, and/or surprise the audience, so they are often told for entertainment purposes. This entertainment is also due to their subject matter, which often breaks some cultural, for example, sexual, taboos:

Some couple went to a cinema in Katowice. There aren't many filmgoers in cinemas nowadays, so they were interrupted by no one. But suddenly someone moved, and the girl got scared, and her muscles contracted. The movie ended. The lights went on. And the girl was moaning with pain. They had to call in a doctor. I heard about this about six months ago.

(Czubala 1996:48)

Another common purpose of urban legends is to make the audience laugh, such as when the speaker relates a surprising or even ridiculous incident. Often the storyteller makes fun of social vices (greed or hypocrisy) or a social group (e.g., stereotypically portraying the police), for instance:

Friends of a friend of my friend, or someone like that, decided to experiment with some illegal substances, and then they felt like driving a car in the middle of the night. One of them came up with this brilliant idea to go to a roundabout and drive around it in reverse. So they are going around and around, and suddenly they hit a car driving in the right direction. The police show up immediately, and those guys start to panic and are afraid to get out of the car. After a moment a policeman approaches them, and when they roll their windows down, they hear him saying "No worries, gentlemen. That guy has a BAC of 0.20 percent and he's trying to convince me that you've been driving around the roundabout in reverse!"

(I: Katarzyna Rodzik, born in 1986; C: Marta Ziarno, May 15, 2011, Warsaw)

If the function of urban legends is, overall, to articulate social anxieties in a myriad of different ways, the purpose of the genre may be said to scare and/or warn, that is, to remind its audiences of certain realities and truths, and/or to shock, amuse, and entertain. And it is expressly through performance that these purposes are communicated.

THE ONTOLOGY OF THE DEPICTED WORLD

The world, as depicted by urban legends, is real from the storyteller's point of view. Something that goes beyond our imagination yet does not come from another realm (as is the case with folk tales) enters our everyday life, which we all know so well. This quotidian reality means shopping for groceries, eating bananas, buying a (yucca) tree, going to the cinema, riding a bus, partying, and so on. Indeed, situations portrayed in urban legends are typical or ordinary—as are the people described in them; each is an "everyman"—not known by name. For example,

> *There's this story. My aunt once told me that* a friend of hers had bought a tree, or a flower, named yucca. And she brought it home with her husband. And one time, when she was watering it, the flower started to shiver. So she contacted some people she had found online who specialised in such things. They came, examined the tree, and found a scorpion's egg near its roots and said it was to hatch soon.
>
> (I: Estera, 1991, Łęczna; R: recording; and T: Marta Kalinowska, 2011)

In this and other such stories, characters relate to events and things that everyone is afraid of (even though the frame of the narrative might also suggest that the speaker is distancing themselves from them). What is recounted are experiences that anyone could have. Portraying characters in this way is akin to how characters are typically represented in folk tales. They have no individual, distinctive, or unique features; they are relatable to all and are universal.

A hidden, but perhaps the most important, character in an urban legend, however, is the narrator. Observations by narrators, as well as their conclusions and versions of events often seem more significant than the events themselves. Who are the narrators of such stories? They are people who are confused by the flood of events and often contradictory information surrounding them, including media coverage. They are people who seek to explain things around them that might be dangerous for their own health, survival, or worldview. But they do not refer to the supernatural (ghosts, apparitions, lamiae, and otherworldly figures) for these explanations as do storytellers of traditional folk tales. Instead, they look for answers in the behaviors and attitudes of the people in their midst: AIDS victims who inject the virus into people who travel with them by bus; a gang that abducts a girl or woman, takes her abroad, and sells her to a brothel; someone who cheats other people; someone else who deliberately infects others with some disease or does something for fun that puts others at peril. They look to human nature, which manifests itself in trickery and a lack of moral standards, where the risk is the result or consequence of a joke, such as a Pole in Libya selling his wife, by accident, to an Arab. The narrators of urban legends seem to show that it is often the most common elements of the world around us that threaten us: plants, pets (a cat attacking its sleeping owner and choking them to death), or everyday items that are intended to help but become lethal instead (HIV in dressings produced by HIV carriers, a washing powder stored under the bed that eventually causes a grandmother to become ill). Even a house, a space which is seemingly safe and familiar, is not free from harm that can invade it (indeed, at home, people can also hide things that they do that are not commonly accepted by society, even bestiality). Alternatively, danger might come from the outside. Many stories take place at the cinema, supermarket (kidnapping), city pool (razor blades at the slide), disco (date-rape drugs), workplace, or on the road (abduction, murder). Traveling (and diseases associated with being away from home) is also particularly perilous. Furthermore, many events take place at night or in the dark, which creates the feeling of unease but can also symbolize the dark side of human nature.

The following urban legend—about the "impossible" happening on the outskirts of society—in a forest and lake far from the city borders—reflects the very notion that the narrator and his own questions about and obsession with the events recounted are more telling than the narrative itself. The italicized words represent the "external" voice of the narrator: the framing portions of the story and his "thinking out loud":

> *I have heard that* [Marek W., the student from Lublin who has gone missing] *was found in a forest, with his body cut up and his internal organs taken out. I know this sounds ridiculous, but this is what my own mother told me. But . . . nah, this is impossible, because it takes too much testing to match organs from two different people. No, this can't be true. But, you know, this is what my mother told me, that* he was found in the forest, cut in half, and all his major organs were missing . . . in some forest near Lublin. *But I've also heard a different version from a friend of mine. He told me that* the body had been found in the artificial lake, and the body looked the same, but this time he had his eyes sewed up . . . *I'm telling you,* his eyes were stitched up, and there was a gaping hole in his chest and stomach with no organs inside. *Yup, in the artificial lake. But this thing with his eyes, it got me thinking. Why stitch up his eyes? Why would anyone want to do this? This makes no sense. I came back a couple of weeks ago . . . a week ago, or two maybe? And, you know, my mum . . . I'm almost thirty, and she started panicking that she'd come pick me up, because* they had found that boy without his organs. *Oh! I've also heard that his . . . from someone else, that* he'd been set up by his uncle, who's in debt, and that uncle had taken him to a party, and

after the party some people in a van came and took him somewhere. *So, that's about it. No joke, three people, three different stories. People need the excitement, yes....* But the truth is that the prosecutor's office has not found any evidence of any third party's involvement. *But if you've been watching CSI: New York or Miami, then you know that they either tell the truth or feed you some false information to get to the information they are really interested in. And in this case, you need to ... how did he find himself, you know,* a drunk guy who walks out of a club and suddenly finds himself eight kilometers away from Lublin, drowned in a lake, where water is only some fifty centimeters deep. *You know ... well ... but what's important is that people have something to talk about ... and it becomes front-page news for two weeks, and everyone's talking only about this.*

(Wójcicka 2014:159)

The ontology—the nature of being, what exists, and what is real—of the depicted world is both implicitly and explicitly addressed in this urban legend. The italicized sections represent the parts of the story that put reality, as understood by the narrator, into question. The storyteller struggles with what is truth and what is not as he introduces his "unbelievable" tale and then proceeds to reveal that two other versions of it also exist. What is real in this narrative? And what is not? It is precisely these questions that illustrate why urban legends are so powerful: they intersect with, yet never entirely resolve, what is truth and what is fiction.

In other words, urban legends straddle the boundary between reality and fantasy—but in our own world and on our own terms. They hover between what we believe and what we find hard to believe. And in this juncture between real and unreal, in this "depicted world," we find meaning. Our worst fears are elicited: we are warned, we are shocked, we are amused. It is the apocryphal nature of this "depicted reality" that draws us to urban legends. They stir us precisely because they mediate between certainty and impossibility.

Narrators of urban legends look for reasonable explanations of events by referring not to the make-believe or to scientific knowledge but to common knowledge and their own observations (Wójcicka 2013). Traditional folk stories (magic tales and other folk tales) show distinct models of people and the world based on fantasy. In these stories, an order is grounded on the dichotomy between good and evil, punishing what is wrong, rewarding what is right, portraying home as a sacred space and the world as animistic. By contrast, while urban legends are also narrative folklore genres, they use anti-models. Perpetually veering between fact and fiction and good and bad behavior, they represent a world that is ambiguous, in which it is difficult—almost impossible—to distinguish between what is true and what is false, what is right and what is wrong.

Notes

1. See https://mitologiawspolczesna.pl (accessed August 31, 2023).
2. The urban legends discussed here are presented only in English translation but can be accessed in Polish in the sources indicated. All translations of them are mine.

3. Tarnowskie Góry and other places cited in the texts are names of various cities and towns in Poland.
4. Compare the term "contracted sentence," introduced by Vilem Mathesius (1947); see also Wójcicka (2010:118–123).
5. "I" refers to the informant, "C" to the collector of the urban legend.
6. The Spodek, located in Katowice, is a sports and entertainment hall and venue for cultural events that opened in 1971.
7. Anna Jantar was a Polish pop singer who died at the height of her career in a plane crash in 1980 at age twenty-nine.
8. "T" refers to the person who transcribed the urban legend.
9. *Polityka* is a Polish opinion-forming social and political weekly of a liberal-leftist character, published from 1957 on in Warsaw.
10. Piotr Jaroszewicz was a Polish politician and communist activist who served as deputy prime minister (1952–1970) and prime minister (1970–1980).
11. Edward Gierek was a communist politician and first secretary of the Central Committee of the Polish United Workers' Party in 1970–1980.
12. Polish politician, trade union activist, and dissident Lech Wałęsa was leader and hero of the democratic opposition in the Polish People's Republic, co-founder and first chair of "Solidarity," and president of the Republic of Poland from 1990 to 1995.
13. These were in response to the involvement of the Catholic Church in Poland, which supported right-wing politicians in elections as well as strict anti-abortion laws adopted by the government and the introduction of compulsory religious education in schools (cf. Czubala 2014:55).
14. These urban legends were generated by the crash of a Polish aircraft in the Russian city of Smoleńsk in April 2010 in which ninety-six people died. The passengers were all members of the Polish delegation to the celebrations for the seventieth anniversary of the Katyn massacre (which occurred in World War II).
15. The Polish People's Republic was the official name of Poland from 1952 to 1989.

Works Cited

Allan, Stuart. 2006. *Kultura newsów*. Krakow: Wydawnictwo Uniwersytetu Jagiellońskiego.
Bartmiński, Jerzy. 1975. "Wokół Lordowskiej koncepcji formuły." *Literatura Ludowa*, 6:3–11.
Bartmiński, Jerzy. 1989. "Językowe sposoby porządkowania świata. Uwagi na marginesie biłgorajskich relacji o kosmosie." In *Etnolingwistyka*, Vol. 2, ed. Jerzy Bartmiński, 49–58. Lublin: Wydawnictwo Uniwersytetu Marii Curie-Skłodowskiej.
Bartmiński, Jerzy. 1990. *Folklor–język–poetyka*. Lublin: Zakład Narodowy im. Ossolińskich.
Bartmiński, Jerzy, and Stanisława Niebrzegowska-Bartmińska. 2009. *Tekstologia*. Warsaw: Wydawnictwo Naukowe PWN.
Brunvand, Jan Harold. 1981. *The Vanishing Hitchhiker, American Urban Legends and Their Meanings*. New York–London: Norton.
Brunvand, Jan Harold. 1984. *The Choking Doberman and Other "New" Urban Legends*. New York–London: Norton.
Brunvand, Jan Harold. 1986. *The Mexican Pet: More "New" Urban Legends and Some Old Favorites*. New York–London: Norton.

Brunvand, Jan Harold. 1989. *Curses! Broiled Again. The Hottest Urban Legends Going*. New York–London: Norton.
Czubala, Dionizjusz. 1985. *Opowieści z życia. Z badań nad folklorem współczesnym*. Katowice: Wydawnictwo Uniwersytetu Śląskiego.
Czubala, Dionizjusz. 1993. *Współczesne legendy miejskie*. Katowice: Wydawnictwo Uniwersytetu Śląskiego.
Czubala, Dionizjusz. 1996. *Nasze mity współczesne*. Katowice: Fundacja dla Wspierania Śląskiej Humanistyki.
Czubala, Dionizjusz. 2005. *Wokół legendy miejskiej*. Bielsko-Biała: Wydawnictwo ATH.
Czubala, Dionizjusz. 2014. *Polskie legendy miejskie. Studium i materiały*. Katowice: Thesaurus.
Dale, Rodney M. 1978. *The Tumour in the Whale*. London: Duckworth.
Dale, Rodney M. 1984. *It's True. It Happened to a Friend: A Collection of Urban Legends*. London: Duckworth.
Hajduk-Nijakowska, Janina. 2005. *Żywioł i kultura. Folklorystyczne mechanizmy oswajania Traumy*. Opole: Wydawnictwo Uniwersytetu Opolskiego.
Mathesius, Vilem. 1947. "O tak zwanym aktualnym rozczłonkowaniu zdania," trans. M. R. Mayenowa. In *O spójności tekstu*, ed. M. R. Mayenowa, 7–12. Wrocław: Ossolineum.
Napiórkowski, Marcin. 2013. *Mitologia współczesna*. Warsaw: Wydawnictwo Naukowe PWN.
Niebrzegowska-Bartmińska, Stanisława. 2012. "Miejsce wartości w opisie gatunków mowy." In *Język a kultura. Akty i gatunki mowy w perspektywie kulturowej*, ed. Anna Burzyńska-Kamieniecka, 23:33–41. Wrocław: Wydawnictwo Uniwersytetu Wrocławskiego.
Przybyła-Dumin, Agnieszka. 2013. *Proza folklorystyczna u progu XXI wieku na podstawie badań terenowyc*. Chorzów–Katowice: Wydawnictwo Naukowe "Śląsk."
Rydzewska, Joanna. 2004. "Folklor albo cień oficjalnej cywilizacji." *Kultura Popularna*, 3/9:111–123.
Simonides, Dorota. 1969. *Współczesna śląska proza ludowa*. Opole: Powiatowy Instytut Śląski.
Simonides, Dorota, and Janina Hajduk-Nijakowska. 1989. "Opowiadania ludowe." In *Folklor górnego śląska*, ed. Dorota Simonides, 393–454. Katowice: Wydawnictwo "Śląsk."
Smith, Paul. 1983. *The Book of Nasty Legends*. London: Routledge and Kegan Paul.
Smith, Paul. 1986. *The Book of Nastier Legends*. London: Routledge and Kegan Paul.
Wójcicka, Marta. 2010. *Dawno to temu, już bardzo dawno . . . Formuły ramowe w tekstach polskiej prozy ludowej*. Lublin: Wydawnictwo Uniwersytetu Marii Curie-Skłodowskiej.
Wójcicka, Marta. 2013. "Urban Legends in Poland." In *Estonia and Poland: Creativity and Tradition in Cultural Communication. Vol. 2: Perspectives on National and Regional Identity*, eds. Liisi Laineste, Dorota Brzozowska, and Władysław Chłopicki, 43–58. Tartu: ELM Scholarly Press.
Wójcicka, Marta. 2014. *Pamięć zbiorowa a tekst ustny*. Lublin: Wydawnictwo Uniwersytetu Marii Curie-Skłodowskiej.

PART IV

MUSIC, SONG, IDENTITY, AND PERFORMANCE

Ethnoreligious Identity: Music and Song

CHAPTER 29

THE *SEVDALINKA* AS TRADITIONAL BOSNIAN LOVE SONG

NIRHA EFENDIĆ

THERE is extensive literature on the Bosnian folk love song, which has been called the *sevdalinka* (pl. *sevdalinke*) since the end of the nineteenth century. The nature of publications about this type of song is diverse and interdisciplinary. Literary historians, theorists, and critics have written about it, then melographers, musicologists, and ethnomusicologists but also sociologists, psychologists, cultural historians, and publicists of various profiles. The root of the word itself contains the Arabic word *sawda'*, meaning "black color," which is why it is often described as a song with a melancholic feeling. But orientalist Abdulah Škaljić translates this root and the word that came from it (*sawdah*, adopted and transformed in the Bosnian language as *sevdah*) as "love longing" (1979:561). Although this type of song would get its first lexicographic treatments only in the 1970s, the first literary-theoretical definition of the term *sevdalinka* appeared in the early twentieth century—precisely in 1909. Indeed, it was the definition of literary historian Pavle Popović, in his 1909 overview of lyric poetry in the monograph *Pregled srpske književnosti* (*Review of Serbian Literature*[1]), that initiated the literary-theoretical discussions that followed throughout the twentieth century. Popović underlined the following: "Among these songs, the so called 'sevdali songs' stand out, and they are Bosnian love songs with many Mohammedan [Muslim] elements [and] with much passion and longing" (1909:82–83).

A few years later, in his study about Serbo-Croatian literature in Bosnia and in the chapter "Die bosnischen Sevdalinke" ("The Bosnian *Sevdalinke*"), the Croatian literary historian Dragutin Prohaska apostrophized its urban origin (1911:170–171), which affected later study of the *sevdalinka* as a typical urban song. Bosnian authors Hamza Humo and Jovan Kršić wrote about the *sevdalinka* in the 1920s and 1930s.[2]

Their observations are mostly reduced to the joint conclusion that it is a kind of song that had been listened to by upper-class urban society. In his doctoral dissertation defended in Vienna in 1936, *Volkmusik Bosniens und der Herzegovina* ("Folk Music of Bosnia and Herzegovina"), Fr. Branimir Marijić (2022) described the *sevdalinka* as a song that arose in Bosnian cities that were inhabited by a Muslim population. The novelist Ahmed Muradbegović named this kind of song as *Pesma feudalne gospode*— "the song of feudal lords" (1940). The first translations of *sevdalinke* into German, French, and Czech were published in the same period. Among the foreign researchers in Bosnia, the work of the Czech melographer and collector of folk traditions Ludvík Kuba, German Slavists Leopold Karl Goetz and Gerhard Gesemann, as well as French publicist René Pelletier had a significant impact on European knowledge of Bosnian lyric oral poetry.

A stronger interest in the *sevdalinka* among local publicists emerged in the 1940s, and they issued articles in magazines and daily newspapers, which resulted in broadcasts of the *sevdalinka* on the radio. By the beginning of World War II, Sait Orahovac, Hasan Kadragić, Ivan K. Ostojić, and Dušan Umičević produced several shorter pieces about the *sevdalinka* (Maglajlić 2011). An entire series of publications focusing on literary and theoretical definitions of the genre was created in the period after World War II. A significant contribution to this work was made by cultural historian Alija Bejtić (1953), who searched for the historical identities of characters mentioned in some of the *sevdalinka* songs. Literary historian Muhsin Rizvić defined *sevdalinke* as "lyrical memoirs" (1963). In 1969, German Slavic studies researcher Wolfgang Eschker defended his PhD dissertation on the function of figures of speech in the oral transmission of the *sevdalinka*, and he later published it as a monograph (1971). Literary historian Hatidža Krnjević also dealt with the literary-theoretical definition of the *sevdalinka* in her essay "O poetskoj prirodi sevdalinke" ("About the Poetic Nature of the *Sevdalinka*," 1976).

Following World War II, in the period of the standardization of Bosnian national literature, Popović's acknowledgment of "Bosnian … songs with many Mohammedan elements" doubtless influenced further definitions of the *sevdalinka* as a Muslim urban song created in the territory of Bosnia and Herzegovina. For example, in the *Encyclopedia of the Lexicographic Institute*, "Bosnian–Herzegovinian *sevdalinke*" are identified as "Muslim urban folk songs; their origin should be sought in our folk songs and Islamic–Oriental music" (Kostrenčić and Protega 1962:695–696). Finally, in the lexicographic "round-up" on the issue of understanding the *sevdalinka*, literary historian Munib Maglajlić proposed the following definition: "The *sevdalinka* is a *Bosnian* love song, whereby the term Bosnian includes and covers song elements from Herzegovina and Sandžak[3] as well" (2011:152). From all of the above interpretations, it can be concluded that the *sevdalinka* is an oral lyric song of the urban cultural area of Bosniaks and that it reaches beyond the borders of modern Bosnia and Herzegovina. More precisely, it extends to the wider area of the Balkans, wherever Bosniaks have lived.

Anthologies: The Cultural-Historical Development of the *Sevdalinka*

Different collections of the *sevdalinka*, which have been issued continuously for more than 130 years, have contributed to the theoretical definition of the song genre in literature but also to the focus by researchers on the *sevdalinka* as love song, a genre that has long intrigued the wider public. The oldest collection of *sevdalinke*, titled *Hercegovke i Bosanke. Sto najradije pjevanih ženskih pjesama* (*Herzegovinians and Bosnians. One Hundred of the Most Popular Women's Songs*), was published in Sarajevo in 1888 by teacher and folklorist Ivan Zovko who compiled this collection. The most recent and so far youngest anthology was prepared by Semir Vranić and Zanin Berbić in Sarajevo in 2021, *Zaboravljeno blago. Stotinu bosanskih narodnih pjesama sa notnim zapisima* (*Forgotten Treasure. One Hundred Bosnian Folk Songs with Melodies*). The second part of this anthology, with the same title, is now in the process of being published.

The major anthologies that specifically cite the *sevdalinka* or *sevdah* include the following editions, listed here chronologically: *Sevdalinke. Narodne biser-pesme za pevanje* (*Sevdalinka songs. Folk Gems for Singing*), by Janko Veselinović (1895); *Bosanske sevdalinke za klavir, za jedno i dva grla* (*Bosnian Sevdalinka Songs for Piano, for One or Two Voices*), by Bogoslav Kečerovský (1907); *Sevdalinke. Izbor iz bosansko-hercegovačke narodne lirike* (*Sevdalinka Songs. Selection of Bosnian–Herzegovinian Lyric Folk Songs*), by Hamid Dizdar (1944); *Sevdalinke, balade i romanse Bosne i Hercegovine* (*Sevdalinka Songs, Ballads, and Romances of Bosnia and Herzegovina*), by Sait Orahovac (1968); *101 sevdalinka* (*101 Sevdalinka Songs*), by Munib Maglajlić (1978); *Sevdah Bošnjaka* (*Sevdah of the Bosniaks*), by Muhamed Žero (1995); *Sevdah nadahnut životom* (*Sevdah Inspired by Life*), by Omer Pobrić (1996); *Sevdalinke 1 i 2* (*Sevdalinka Songs 1 and 2*), by Vehid Gunić (2003); *Za gradom jabuka. 200 naljepših sevdalinki* (*Apple Tree behind the City. The 200 Most Beautiful Sevdalinka Songs*), by Ivan Lovrenović (2004); *Sevdalinka, alhemija duše* (*Sevdalinka, Alchemy of the Soul*), by Esad Bajtal (2012); *1001 sevdalinka* (*1001 Sevdalinka Songs*), by Šahbaz Jusufović (2016); and *Sevdalinke* (*Sevdalinka Songs*), by Muhamed Žero (2021).

The *sevdalinka* is a song genre that has delighted the world beyond its place of origin, in both a literary and musical sense. One of its most important distinguishing characteristics compared to other genres is reflected in its openness and potential for adaptation to different types of influences throughout its centuries-long existence and development. The circumstances under which the *sevdalinka* was created and developed were a result of the penetration of "Eastern" or "Oriental" culture in Balkan society along with its Islamic characteristics due to the Ottoman Empire. Moreover, its durability was made possible by the members of the Balkan population who embraced Islam. In other words, "From Ludvik Kuba to Cvjetko Rihtman and Vlado Milošević, and we can include Béla Bartók there as well, musicologists, without any exception, consider [the *sevdalinka*] to be a Bosniak song, an urban song, a type of love song" (Buturović 2011:31).

Starting with the first significant appearance of the *sevdalinka* in the sixteenth century, the surrounding Eastern (Ottoman) culture preserved its domination in the Balkans until the very end of the nineteenth century. Still, as historian and culturologist Smail Balić observes, in terms of its music, the *sevdalinka* also preserved its Slavic character: "Despite the influence of the Arab–Turkish musical tradition through Turkish songs in the Balkans and through Islamic devotional songs, the main elements of Bosnian music remained independent. Therefore, they cannot be attributed an Oriental origin" (1994:60). Literary historian and folklorist Đenana Buturović makes a similar assumption about this type of love song. Pointing out the specific character of the first account of a *sevdalinka* as an "adaptation" of an old Slavic love song, Buturović concludes at the end of her detailed analysis of the origin and creation of the *sevdalinka* that it is "a literary subgenre of lyric love song, and the melody in this area is subject to change at any given moment, depending on the performer and the taste of the audience" (2011:45).

The most complete answer to the question about the origin and development of the *sevdalinka* song type was offered by Maglajlić (1997) in his chapter "Sredina i vrijeme nastanka i trajanja sevdalinke" ("The Environment and Period of the Creation and Duration of the *Sevdalinka*"), in which he describes the origin of the genre in the following words:

> The *sevdalinka* was likely created when the Eastern lifestyle was more fully accepted in the part of Bosnia's population that adopted Islam, when specific urban environments emerged with all the essential institutions, when city districts, or mahalas, were formed in which houses possessed all the necessary spaces in accordance with each owner's wealth: a fenced courtyard with a small gate (*kapidžik*), a courting window (*ašik-pendžer*) and more—in other words, when life began to take place in the environment that formed the well-known background of events in the *sevdalinka*. (1997:215)

This passage shows us that the backbone of the origin of the *sevdalinka* in most examples is courting, although there are numerous *sevdalinke* that describe and commemorate certain cities or better-known parts of cities. According to the American Slavist Masha Belyavski-Frank (2018), *sevdalinke* are urban songs which reflect the middle and upper classes and the lifestyle of these milieux, starting from the concept of the *mahala* (i.e., neighborhood) (Fig. 29.1). Belyavski-Frank also describes some important facts related to the *sevdalinka* and courting:

> An essential component of the cultural background of the *sevdalinka* is the process of courting or *ašikovanje*, which comes from the Arabic word *ašik* (to love). . . . In some ways *ašikovanje* was like the courtly love of medieval France. The man had an

ideal woman, whom he did not touch, and whom he admired and loved from afar. (2018:26–27)

Literary historian Sead Šemsović (2021) claims that the *sevdalinka* appears only in locations and communities in which such courting was a socially acceptable and widespread practice.

FIG. 29.1. *Mahala*—neighborhood as a space of realizing the *sevdalinka* (1900).
(Folklore Archives of the National Museum of Bosnia and Herzegovina.)

The *Sevdalinka* as Love Song

The First Account of a Sevdalinka

The first indication of the existence of the *sevdalinka* takes us back to the distant Middle Ages. According to the latest research of Maglajlić (2016), the earliest data on the existence of an oral love song go back to 1574, to an incident that took place in the market in the city of Split, on the Dalmatian coast. This comes down to us through the chronicles of the duke of Split, who sent his reports about the events in his city to the Senate in Venice. In the middle of the nineteenth century, the Croatian writer Luka Botić researched these reports and translated the fascinating content, which also contained the story of the unhappy love between a Catholic woman from Split, Marija Vornić, and a young Muslim man, Adil, from Klis (also in Dalmatia). That relationship was not permissible due to their cultural and religious differences. However, Adil sang a song to his beloved Marija, and the duke of Split included this event in his reports in Italian. After the unexpected events which shook the Vornić family, the love story ended in tragedy. Obeying the wishes of her wealthy parents, Marija was sent to a convent, where she was accompanied by her sister Ivanica. "Poor Mara," as she was described back in the day by philosopher from Split Franjo Bokutlija, died of grief and exhaustion in the convent. Her sister remained with the nuns forever. This is how the unfortunate story of the first account of the life of the *sevdalinka* in this region ended.

In his adaptation of the "old Slavic love song," Botić used the thirteen-syllable verse form of South Slavic lyric poetry, exemplified in the first two verses below, adding a chorus in the widespread epic decasyllable such as in the third and fourth lines. Buturović notes that the verses of this song are "Bosniak-Muslim" as well as "Croat-Christian" (2011:42):

> U Turčina đulvodica slatko miriše,
> Al' je ljepša djevojčica, ljepša od ruže;
> A ja Turčin ginem za djevojkom,
> Za djevojkom, krotkom golubicom!
>
> The Turk's rosewater smells sweetly,
> But the girl is prettier, prettier than a rose;
> And I the Turk am dying for the girl,
> For the girl, a gentle dove![4]

The Life of the Sevdalinka

After this early reference, there followed a longer period in which we have no testimonies of the existence and development of the type of song that was named *sevdalinka* only in the late nineteenth century. The silence was to be interrupted by transcriptions of several *sevdalinke* that can be found in the *Erlangen Manuscript*,[5] which was collected in the first half of the eighteenth century. After that, several *sevdalinke* were recorded in Vuk Karadžić's[6] *Pjesnarica* (*Songbook*) published in Vienna in 1814. The late nineteenth and early twentieth centuries would be marked by more intense collecting of Bosnian folk songs, including the *sevdalinka*.

In order to gain insight into the social framework in which the *sevdalinka* existed in the second half of the nineteenth century, the testimony of the Bosnian poet Safvet-bey Bašagić[7] provided in his 1912 *Bošnjaci i Hercegovci u islamskoj književnosti* (*Bosniaks and Herzegovinians in Islamic Literature*) is of particular importance. Referring to poet Arif-bey Rizvanbegović Stočević (who wrote in Turkish under the pseudonym Hikmet), Bašagić recalled an anecdote that his father (Ibrahim-bey) heard once while visiting Rizvanbegović's (Hikmet's) home. This early information not only is significant for a glimpse into the milieu in which lyric song was listened to but also mentions a specific song, recognizable today as a *sevdalinka*, which cheered up those present in the halls of Fehim effendi Đumišić, who hosted a dinner that night. Here is Bašagić's narration:

> My father told me that, when the Turkish Parliament convened for the first time, Fehim effendi Đumišić invited all the Bosnian and Herzegovinian delegates for dinner. Fehim effendi heard from someone that at that time there was a Sarajevan woman in Constantinople who was known as a good singer. Sparing neither cost nor effort to prepare a real Bosnian dinner for the guests, he brought the singer to his palace to sing a few songs for them. Among the guests was Hikmet at his own table, because there was no joy for him without alcohol. Everybody knew about this weakness of his, and nobody held it against him. My late father said that he was observing Hikmet and his mood the whole time while the fiddler and singer were performing. [Hikmet] sat still, which was rare for him; he looked seriously and listened to everything with a kind of deep reverence and childlike fascination. Among others, the Sarajevan lady sang the *sevdalinka* with the following verses:
>
> > Kun' ga, majko, i ja ću ga kleti,
> > Samo, stani, ja ću započeti:
> > Tamnica mu moja njedra bila, [i td.]
> >
> > Curse him, mother, I will curse him too,
> > But wait, I shall begin:
> > May my bosom be his dungeon, [etc.]
>
> Upon hearing this, Hikmet jumped to his feet and shouted in great excitement: "My people is the greatest poet!", and then he began to explain to the guests the beauty of the folk song based on Arabic poetry. Everyone gasped in amazement: What marvels Hikmet found in that song.
>
> (Bašagić 1912:162–163)

Motifs

The range of motifs present in the *sevdalinka* is surprisingly wide and diverse. Many songs whisper about the pain of love, the joy of meeting the beloved, the trouble of parting, the sunset that brings the possible arrival of the beloved. On the other hand, numerous verses preserve the memory of the pain of parting, the unrequited love, the betrayal or pain caused by jealousy. Although the focus is placed on the description of feelings, sometimes a song provides a detailed description of the lover, such as the one expressed in these verses:

> Bijeli zubi, dva niza bisera,
> Biser usta, kutija šećera,
> Perčin mu je tura ibrišima,
> Dvije oči, dvije trnjinice,
> Obrvice s mora pijavice.

> White teeth, two strings of pearls,
> Pearly mouth, sugar box,
> His braid is a strand of silk thread,
> Two eyes, two blackthorns,
> The eyebrows like whirlpools from the sea.[8]

In these songs, we often see a girl longing for her beloved boy who is far away, and because of her inability to meet with him, she develops and elaborates a detailed plan in her imagination in order to find out more about him. In one song, a curious maiden plants a pine tree and begs it to grow tall quickly so that she can climb it and observe the wider environment from its high branches and thus find out where her beloved is and what he is doing:

> Je l' moj dragi u bilomu dvoru,
> Boluje li ili ašikuje,
> Volila bih čuti da boluje,
> Neg za drugom da on ašikuje . . .

> Is my beloved in his white palace,
> Does he suffer in pain or is he in love,
> I would prefer to hear that he is in pain,
> Rather than in love with another . . .[9]

Thus, she prefers the possibility of her lover being ill to the possibility of his having given his heart away to another girl.

The girl sometimes calls on water in the songs to carry her greetings to the loved one, and sometimes her imagination takes her to dreams in which she finds herself in the role of water that flows close to her beloved. In one particularly beautiful song, the girl wishes to be the water that springs up near the shop in which her beloved spends most of his days so that she may ease the torment of his thirst on a hot day, but also her thirst for him, which she skillfully weaves into the following verses:

> Ne bi l' Ahmi žeđa dodijala,
> ne bi li se vodice napio,
> ne bi l' mene s vodicom popio!
>
> Hopefully Ahmo will be tired of thirst,
> And he will drink the water,
> So he may drink me up with water![10]

Exaggerations of the extent to which the hearts of lovers are affected, and the commotion they can cause in general, are the subjects of numerous love songs. One particularly frequent motif in this regard is the overemphasized power of "dark eyes." Numerous examples confirm that the power of "magic eyes" has become almost a myth. In a famous *sevdalinka*, a girl from Travnik sets the city on fire "with her dark eyes through a glass-paneled window,"[11] a girl from Derventa seduces the entire neighborhood with the eyes of a hawk,[12] a girl from Mostar is beloved by her entire town because of her dark eyes "and mostly by the lord Alaj-bey,"[13] while in another example, a dark-eyed girl is even reprimanded because her agency has caused an uproar, which is why she is criticized:

> Sve si momke do jednoga,
> Svojim licem primamila,
> A divojke rasrdila,
> Crnim okom i pogledom!
>
> You lured all the boys,
> With your face,
> And you enraged all the girls,
> With your dark eyes and your gaze![14]

Another extremely common motif in the *sevdalinka* is that of a girl's curse, which can be real and apparent or feigned. The very content and meaning of the curse differ from case to case. In the primary meaning, the girl invokes a real curse on the boy who rejected her, while in the secondary meaning the formula of the curse is based on the principle of contradiction. It is used to emphasize the desired outcome as effectively as possible: may the beloved be imprisoned in a dungeon, not a dark and damp one but in the dungeon of his lover's bosom; may he be chained, not by iron chains but by his lover's hands; may he be shackled, not in heavy iron shackles but in bracelets; may he be bitten, not by the poisonous teeth of a snake but by his lover's white teeth; may he be carried away by water, not to a faraway and dark place but to the palace of his beloved;

may he be hanged, not on an evil tree but on his beloved's neck; may he be hit by a gun, not with a lead bullet but with his beloved's gold coin (Efendić 2015).

In the unfulfilled dreams, in the longing behind the latticed window, only a real encounter with the loved one can heal the wounds caused by the longing for a meeting. So in the verses of a song, a sad girl asks herself:

> Što moj dragi za sunca ne dođe,
> Što ne dođe, da mi kahar prođe?
>
> Why hasn't my beloved come during the daylight,
> Why hasn't he come to take my sorrow away?[15]

There are numerous motifs in the *sevdalinka* songs, and we have mentioned only a few. The fundamental sentiment in these songs is the love between beloveds; less frequently it is jealousy or love between spouses, and the emotions vary from longing, subtle trembling, and amorous glances to very openly sensual and passionate feelings.

Performers, Guardians, and Transmitters of Tradition

The available literature on *sevdalinke* focuses mainly on the recording and development of the genre as oral literary lyric poetry, the motifs, and, in general, the worldview and spiritual culture that emerge from the *sevdalinke*, considered the crown jewels of South Slavic traditional lyric song. Very little attention, however, has been paid to the fact that it has been the performers who have kept *sevdalinke* alive until the present day, that the singers have played the most important role as their guardians. This tradition accordingly remembers many singers and performers.

The situations in which *sevdalinke* were traditionally performed were typically gendered. They included very intimate female gatherings, where girls sang while they embroidered or listened to *sevdalinke* while a metal tray (*tepsija*) was spun. When the *tepsija* was used, two skilled girls would be engaged. One of them would spin the tray on a table, producing a continuous, characteristic sound to accompany the other girl, who would hover over the tray and sing a song into it, which would amplify the overall sonic effect in a distinctive manner (Fig. 29.2). In male settings, boys performed the songs accompanied by a *saz* (a long-necked stringed musical instrument of the lute family originating in the Ottoman Empire) (Fig. 29.3). While girls and women sang in private, boys' or men's performances were freer because male musicians could go out into public spaces, into the coffeehouses.

The performance of songs in the coffeehouses enabled the initial commercial recordings, which are, as a rule, older than the scientific field recordings (Karača Beljak 2019). There are also certain differences between scientific field and commercial

FIG. 29.2. Spinning the tray (*tepsija*) (1954).
(Folklore Archives of the National Museum of Bosnia and Herzegovina.)

recordings, especially when it comes to the choice of repertoire and musicians. Indeed, the earliest recordings of *sevdalinka* singing were commercial, dating as far back as 1906. For example, "the Mustafa Sudžuka Trio was recorded in Sarajevo performing the song 'Kad ja pođoh na Bentbašu' (*When I went to Bentbaša*)" (Karača Beljak 2019:79). The German Franz Hampe from Berlin recorded Salih Kahrimanović singing the still very popular *sevdalinka* "Snijeg pade na behar na voće" ("Snow Fell on Blossoms, on Fruit") and playing the *saz* in Sarajevo for British Gramophone Records in 1907. This was a time when such public performances were popular and frequent in Sarajevo. On the other hand, Kuba, who had recorded songs and tunes only a decade earlier, did not have any recording instruments at his disposal; and he relied on his knowledge of notation and his own skill to transcribe tunes he heard with a pencil. The first recordings—made with cumbersome but for long-ago 1907 extremely advanced technology—were a way to achieve a more direct contact with the singer. This helped to permanently preserve the memory of significant *sevdalinka* performers from this period. We must not forget that local poets of the early twentieth century were very deeply inspired by romantic verse as much as by oral traditional songs, and thus they created poems which were a result of the fusion of the two. There is also the unquestionable influence of the *starogradska* (literally "old city") music, urban traditional folk music which was formed by translations of the Russian and Hungarian romance song genre from the late nineteenth and early twentieth centuries.

The poems of local literary authors were also gradually given the "clothing of a melody," following the model of traditional poetic creation. The *sevdalinka*, as well as the newer songs called *novokomponovana narodna muzika* (newly composed folk

FIG. 29.3. A member of a feudal family with *saz* (1898).
(Folklore Archives of the National Museum of Bosnia and Herzegovina.)

music) which stood shoulder to shoulder with the *sevdalinka*, became an equal part of the important singing repertoires. There are songs by numerous poets, such as Safvet-beg Bašagić, Aleksa Šantić, Musa Ćazim Ćatić, Osman Đikić, and later Jozo Penava, Ismet Alajbegović Šerbo, Jovica Petković, Rade Jovanović, as well as other particularly prominent vocalists, who both sang and composed, such as Zaim Imamović. All of them were building a new world, a world in which the *sevdalinka* received a confirmation of its centuries-old value but also a new appearance with which it would continue to delight the world outside of Bosnia and Herzegovina throughout the twentieth century and beyond.

Bora Janjić and Sofka Nikolić were among the most popular singers from the 1920s who sang the *sevdalinka* and whose performances were recorded. The emergence of the first gramophones also contributed to the acclaim of songs preserved by these performers in their repertoires. However, what caused the popularity of the songs among the broader public was, without any doubt, the appearance of singers in the program of Radio Sarajevo (immediately after the Second World War). In the beginning, the *sevdalinka* was broadcast live on the radio, performed by pairs of singers and accordion players—the most significant of which were the duets of Alajbegović and Petković (Karača Beljak 2019). Performances by this duo are preserved in the archive records from the 1960s. The first auditions[16] for singers were held around the same time. The singers who performed for the program of Radio Sarajevo during those years carried the aura of *sevdalinka* masters, such as Zaim Imamović and Nada Mamula, later Safet Isović, Zehra Deović, and Himzo Polovina (see A-V Link 1), as well as Zumra Mulalić, Beba Selimović, Nedžad Salković, Zora Dubljević, and for a while Zekerijah Đezić and Ljubica Berak. Isović started his musical career as a vocal soloist of Radio Sarajevo. As Isma Kamberović points out,

> His delightful voice won over composer Jozo Penava and accordion player Ismet Alajbegović Šerbo. Their fruitful collaboration started at that time. He became one of the best *sevdalinka* performers. Isović brought the *sevdalinka* closer to the wider masses, and he became their favorite singer (he started in the late 1950s). (2018:99)

A little while later, listeners of the Radio Sarajevo program would be thoroughly delighted by the voice of Hanka Paldum. Tamara Karača Beljak notes that

> The work of trained musicians became visible in the 1960s. Their production work, their way of performing the *sevdalinka* created a new dimension and a new direction . . . they prepared recording material, wrote down lyrics and arranged music, first for the Tamburica Orchestra, and as of 1970, also for the Folk Orchestra. The work of Beluš Jungić, Ljubinko Miljković, Zvonko Nevžala, and Jozo Penava especially stands out. (2019:82)

With the exception of notable performances in specialized "ethno" music shows (televised music programs with both older and newly composed *sevdalinke*) broadcast by TV Sarajevo in the 1980s, there was a renewed interest in singing accompanied by the *saz* during the aggression against Bosnia and Herzegovina (1992–1995). A significant number of performances of *saz* player Avdo Lemeš and singer Emina Zečaj accompanied by Mehmed Gribajčević were recorded. Adding this to the valuable material recorded for the TV Sarajevo shows whose archive tapes contain audio recordings of *saz* players Selim Salihović, Muhamed Mešanović, Ćamil Metiljević, Hašim Muharemović, Himzo Tulić, Avdo Vrabac, and Behka and Igbal Ljuca, it is no exaggeration to say that the Radio–Television of Bosnia and Herzegovina houses notably precious archives representing a reliable basis for studying the traditional performance of the *sevdalinka*.

A musician worthy of mention from the period before the 1992–1995 war was the *sevdalinka* performer Hamdija Šahinpašić (born in 1914 in Pljevlje, Sandžak, North Montenegro). Šahinpašić appeared several times on the TV show *Meraklije*,[17] which had a cult status and was edited and presented by renowned journalist, publicist, and *sevdalinka* collector Vehid Gunić. Šahinpašić boasted a repertoire of three hundred *sevdalinke*, which Montenegrin ethnomusicologist Miodrag Vasiljević titled "Yugoslav Folk Songs from Sandžak as Sung by Hamdija Šahinpašić from Pljevlje"; it was published in Moscow in 1967. This collection of songs represents an extremely important archive of the Sandžak heritage, as well as certain linguistic and performance characteristics related to the *sevdalinka* in that region. It was not until 2002 that Šahinpašić's collection was published in Sarajevo as *Po Taslidži pala magla* (*Fog Fell on Taslidža*). Hamdija Šahinpašić died in Sarajevo in 2003.

The first two decades of the twenty-first century are notable for the releases by Damir Imamović, grandson of *sevdalinka* master Zaim Imamović and son of Nedžad Imamović. Damir, third in a line of exceptional *sevdalinka* performers, covered new ground researching the *sevdalinka* sound and experimenting with different genres (see Imamović 2017). His important work earned him the Best of Europe Award for an album produced in 2020. The album is named *The Singer of Tales*, as in the book by Albert B. Lord (1960), which is dedicated to an understanding of oral composition by the great Balkan singers of traditional epic poetry. Apart from Imamović, more recent notable *sevdalinka* performers include Amira Medunjanin, Vanja Muhović, and Božo Vrećo. The latest musically trained generation of *sevdalinka* performers brings us new, fresh names such as singer Selma Droce, the excellent accordion player Damir Galijašević, as well as *saz* player and vocalist Zanin Berbić (see A-V Link 2) and performer Lejla Čaušević.

Concluding Remarks

As this story of the *sevdalinka* is brought to a close, a final tribute to the many performers who have unstintingly kept the genre alive includes two videos that illustrate distinctive examples of the sound and performance of the *sevdalinka*. One represents a traditional twentieth-century rendition and the other, a twenty-first-century performance that is both traditional and innovative. Both performers are, without a doubt, iconic. The first features the voice of Himzo Polovina (1927–1986), an old-style *sevdalinka* interpreter singing "Dunjaluče, golem ti si" ("Oh World, You Are Vast") from the 1970s–1980s against historic footage of Sarajevo filmed in 1915 (A-V Link 1). The second features Zanin Berbić (b. 1996), a representative of the new, contemporary generation of

FIG. 29.4. Zanin Berbić, a contemporary young performer and singer of the *sevdalinka* with *saz* (2021).

(Photo from private collection of N. Efendić.)

sevdalinka musicians. He sings "Čador penje beže Ljuboviću" ("Ljubović Bey Is Pitching His Tent") in a video from 2020 (A-V Link 2) and is also shown in Fig. 29.4 playing the *saz*.

Efendić-A-V Link 1
A-V Link 1: Himzo Polovina, "Dunjaluče, golem ti si" (video, 2012 ▶).
Efendić A-V Link 2
A-V Link 2: Zanin Berbić, "Čador penje beže Ljuboviću" (video, 2020 ▶).

All of the abovementioned artists—Polovina, Berbić, and the larger community of *sevdalinka* performers of the past and present—have devotedly and diligently perpetuated the performance and memory of the *sevdalinka*, which represents a tradition of some of the most beautiful love songs in the Balkans. Not only that but these notable performers have made the *sevdalinka* accessible and comprehensible to the broader public, bringing their own emotions to the songs as they have performed them. In this way, they spread their understanding of the layered and sometimes intricate, often allegorical content of the *sevdalinka*. The new generations of young musicians, whose singing repertoire nurtures the genre, emphatically put their own seal on the contemporary performance of the *sevdalinka*; but they also pass on its story, persistently pushing the boundaries of its fame.

Notes

1. This and all subsequent translations are mine.
2. See for example Kršić (1938) and Humo (1934).
3. Sandžak is a geographic area mostly inhabited by a Bosniak population living in the neighboring countries of Bosnia and Herzegovina, and it includes the southern part of Serbia and northern part of Montenegro.
4. See Maglajlić (2016:12). The reports of the duke of Split were published by Vincenzo Solitro (1844). The annex in which Botić published the translation of some sections of the reports of the duke of Split is titled "Izvori za 'Bijednu Maru'" ("Sources for 'Poor Mara'"; 1949:239–241). Referencing based on a secondary source is found in Maglajlić (2016). See "Bijedna Mara" ("Poor Mara"; Botić 1949). A musical drama in three acts based on Botić's work was staged for the first time in 1932 by Niko Bartulović. More recently, composer Josip Hatze composed the opera Adel i Mara (Adel and Mara), and the Croatian National Theater premiered it in 2017, directed by Ozren Prohić and based on a libretto by Branko Radica.
5. The *Erlangen Manuscript* is a collection of oral poems compiled by an unnamed collector in today's Western Balkans around the 1720s. This collection was found in Erlangen, Germany and is considered one of the oldest inscribed collections of Serbian oral poems.
6. Vuk Stefanović Karadžić (1787–1864) was a Serbian linguist and anthropologist, known as one of the most important reformers of the Serbian language. He also collected oral poetry, including materials originating in Bosnia.
7. Safvet Beg Bašagić (1870–1934) was a Bosnian writer and one of the most renowned poets of Bosnia and Herzegovina at the beginning of the twentieth century.
8. "Komšinice, boli me srdašce" ("Neighbor, My Heart Aches") (Zovko 1893). Vol. III, Song No. 173.
9. "Bor sadila Vakufka divojka" ("A Girl from Vakuf Planted a Pine Tree") (Kurtagić 1937).
10. "Što sam mlada, da sam voda hladna" ("I Wish I Were Cold Water") (Kasumović 2000).
11. "Što se ono Travnik zapalio?" ("Why Is Travnik Ablaze?") (Kukić 1954).
12. "U divojke oči sokolove" ("A Girl Has the Eyes of a Hawk") (Bradarić 2018).
13. "Što s' na Mostar sinja magla svila?" ("Why Is There Dark Fog upon Mostar?") (Zovko 1893).Vol. II, Song No. 38.
14. "O djevojko karakašli" (O dark-eyed girl), Zovko (1893), Vol. II, Song No. 25.
15. "Kamen gori, a biser govori" ("The Stone Burns and the Pearl Speaks") (Zovko 1893).
16. Auditions took place in order to select vocalists qualified to sing on live radio.
17. *Meraklija* can be translated as "hedonist," "pleasure-seeker," or someone who enjoys everything (plural *Meraklije*). The TV music show *Meraklije* in Bosnia was transmitted every weekend, containing mainly *sevdalinke* and hosting different interpreters of the *sevdalinka*.

Works Cited

Bajtal, Esad. 2012. *Sevdalinka, alhemija duše*. Sarajevo: Rabic.
Balić, Smail. 1994. *Kultura Bošnjaka, muslimanska komponenta*, 2nd ed. Zagreb: R&R.
Bašagić, Safvet-beg. 1912. *Bošnjaci i Hercegovci u islamskoj književnosti. Prilog kulturnoj historiji Bosne i Hercegovine*. Sarajevo.

Bejtić, Alija. 1953. "Prilozi proučavanju naših narodnih pjesama." *Bilten instituta za proučavanje folklora Sarajevo*, 2:387–405; 3:105–124.

Belyavski-Frank, Masha. 2018. *Miris dunja. Odabrane sevdalinke iz Bosne i Hercegovine/ The Scent of Quinces. Selected Traditional Love Songs from Bosnia-Herzegovina*. Sarajevo: Univerzitet u Sarajevu, Institut za jezik i Zemaljski muzej BiH.

Botić, Luka. 1949. "Pripovijest iz narodnog života u Dalmaciji, u drugoj polovici šesnaestog vijeka." In *Izabrana djela*, 89–171. Zagreb: Jugoslovenska Akademija Znanosti i Umjetnosti.

Bradarić, Smajl O. 2018. *Narodne umotvorine (iz Dervente i okolice većinom)*. Sarajevo: Slavistički komitet i Zemaljski muzej BiH.

Buturović, Đenana. 2011. "Sevdalinka. Naučni esej." *Znakovi vremena*, 14/54:28–45.

Dizdar, Hamid. 1944. *Sevdalinke. Izbor iz bosanskoherceogvačke narodne lirike*. Sarajevo: Izdanje državne krugovalne postaje.

Efendić, Nirha. 2015. *Bošnjačka usmena lirika—Kulturnohistorijski okviri geneze i poetička obilježja*. Sarajevo: Zemaljski muzej BiH i Slavistički komitet.

Eschker, Wolfgang. 1971. *Untersuchungen zur improvisation und tradierung der sevdalinka an hand der sprachlichen*. Munich: Verlag Otto Sagner.

Gunić, Vehid. 2003. *Sevdalinke 1 i 2*. Tešanj: Planjax.

Humo, Hamza. 1934. "Sevdalinka na rubu dvaju društvenih sistema." *Pravda* (January 6–9), 30:10483–10485.

Imamović, Damir. 2017. *Sevdah*. Zenica: Vrijeme.

Jusufović, Šahbaz. 2016. *1001 sevdalinka*. Tuzla: BKC Tuzla.

Kamberović, Isma. 2018. *Bošnjački nekrolog (2005–2017)*. Gradačac: BZK Preporod.

Karača Beljak, Tamara. 2019. *Uvod u etnomuzikologiju. Etnomuzikološka čitanka Bosne i Hercegovine za studente muzičke teorije i pedagogije*. Sarajevo: Muzička akademija UNSA i Institut za muzikologiju.

Karadžić, Vuk Stefanović. 1814. *Mala prostonarodna slaveno-serbska pjesnarica*. Vienna: K. S. V.

Kasumović, Ahmet. 2000. *Bošnjačke narodne pjesme Srebrenika i okoline*. Gračanica: Grin Gračanica.

Kečerovský, Bogoslav. 1907. *Bosanske sevdalinke za klavir, za jedno i dva grla*. Sarajevo: J. Studničke i dr.

Kostrenčić, Marko, and Miljenko Protega, eds. 1962. *Enciklopedija leksikografskog zavoda*, Volume 6. Zagreb: Jugoslovenski Leksikografski Zavod.

Krnjević, Hatidža. 1976. "O poetskoj prirodi sevdalinke." In *Uporedna istraživanja instituta za književnost i umetnost*, 73–87. Belgrade: Institut za književnost i umetnost.

Kršić, Jovan. 1938. "Bosanska sevdalinka." *Žena danas*, 1/24:4–5.

Kukić, Stevo K. 1954. *Narodne pjesme iz Bosne*. Manuscript Collection of Ethnology Department, National Museum of Bosnia and Herzegovina, Manuscript 102, Song No. 40.

Kurtagić, Muharem. 1937. *Muslimanske narodne pjesme, ženske*. Manuscript collection, Matica hrvatska, V/31:197.

Lord, Albert B. 1960. *The Singer of Tales*. Cambridge, MA: Harvard University Press.

Lovrenović, Ivan. 2004. *Za gradom jabuka. 200 naljepših sevdalinki*. Sarajevo: Dani.

Maglajić, Munib. 1978. *101 sevdalinka*. Mostar: Prva književna komuna.

Maglajlić, Munib. 1997. "Sredina i vrijeme nastanka i trajanja sevdalinke." In *Bošnjačka književnost u književnoj kritici, knjiga II*, eds. Đenana Buturović and Munib Maglajlić, 210–215. Sarajevo: Alef.

Maglajlić, Munib. 2011. "Leksikografsko određenje sevdalinke." *Novi izraz*, 53–54:146–153.

Maglajlić, Munib. 2016. "O pjesnicima i pjevačima sevdalinke." In *101 sevdalinka*, 3rd ed., 5–20. Dubrovnik: Preporod.

Marijić, Branimir. 2022. *Volkmusik Bosniens und der Herzegovina/Narodna glazba Bosne i Hercegovine*, eds. Jasmina Talam and Fr. Ante Marić. Mostar–Sarajevo: Hercegovačka franjevačka provincija Uznesenja BDM, Franjevačka knjižnica, Muzička akademija UNSA, Informativni centar Mir.

Muradbegović, Ahmed. 1940. "Sevdalinka, pesma feudalne gospode." *Politika*, December 5.

Orahovac, Sait. 1968. *Sevdalinke, balade i romanse Bosne i Hercegovine*. Sarajevo: Svjetlost.

Pobrić, Omer. 1996. *Sevdah nadahnut životom*. Visoko: Muzički atelje "Omega."

Popović, Pavle. 1909. *Pregled srpske književnosti*. Belgrade: Štamparija "Davidović."

Prohaska, Dragutin. 1911. *Das Kroatisc-Serbische schriftum in Bosnien und der Herzegovina/ Croatia-Serbian Literature in Bosnia and Herzegovina*. Zagreb: Dionička tiskara u Zagrebu.

Rizvić, Muhsin. 1963. "Ogled o sevdalinci." *Izraz*, 13/11:454–466.

Šahinpašić, Hamdija. 2002. *Pa Taslidži pala magla: Narodne pjesme iz Sandžaka po pjevanju Hamdije Šahinpašića iz Pljevalja*. Sarajevo: Šahinpašić.

Šemsović, Sead. 2021. *Usmena poezija Bošnjaka*. Sarajevo: Slovo bosansko.

Škaljić, Abdulah. 1979. *Turcizmi u srpskohrvatskom jeziku*, 4th ed. Sarajevo: Svjetlost.

Solitro, Vincenzo. 1844. *Documenti storici sull'Istria e la Dalmazia*. Venezia: Coi tipi della ved. di G. Gattei.

Vasiljević, Miodrag A. 1967. *Jugoslovenske narodne pesme iz Sandžaka. Po pevanju Hamdije Šahinpašića iz Pljevalja*. Moscow: Muzljik.

Veselinović, Janko M. 1895. "Sevdalinke." In *Sevdalinke. Narodne biser-pesme za pevanje*, 5–6. Belgrade.

Vranić, Semir, and Zanin Berbić. 2021. *Zaboravljeno blago. Stotinu bosanskih narodnih pjesama sa notnim zapisima*. Sarajevo: Baybook.

Žero, Muhamed. 1995. *Sevdah Bošnjak*. Sarajevo: NIPP Ljiljan.

Žero, Muhamed. 2021. *Sevdalinke 505 pjesama sa notnim zapisima*. Sarajevo: Dobra knjiga.

Zovko, Ivan. 1888. *Hercegovke i Bosanke. Sto najradije pjevanih ženskih pjesama*. Sarajevo: Tisak i naklada tiskare Spindler i Löschner.

Zovko, Ivan. 1893. *Tisuću narodnih ženskih pjesama*. Manuscript collection, Matica hrvatska. Vol. III, Song No. 173; Vol. II, Song No. 25, 38, and 202.

CHAPTER 30

THE TRADITIONAL YIDDISH FOLK SONG

MICHAEL LUKIN

THE very notion of a "Yiddish traditional song" might be viewed as an oxymoron. Traditional poetry and music, it is largely understood, developed in close connection with agricultural cycles (Ling 1997:1), in living conditions that did not permit rapid changes or significant influence from passing fashions, often as a result of a cultural preference for orality over literacy. But eastern Yiddish speakers, for the most part, comprised an urban and relatively mobile population: the majority were never directly engaged in agricultural work and lived in shtetls (i.e., small market towns situated within the territories of the Polish–Lithuanian Commonwealth);[1] their occupations and the lack of long-standing ties to land and estate meant frequent migrations across fairly distant regions where Jews were permitted to reside (Hundert 2007). Moreover, during the time of settlement in the Slavic countries (from approximately the fifteenth century onward), most of eastern Ashkenazi Jewry was literate and thus much exposed to various written texts (Stampfer 2010:190–210).

Nonetheless, speakers of eastern Yiddish (or eastern Ashkenazim), a population that numbered approximately 10 million on the eve of the Holocaust, developed a traditional repertoire; its phenomenology is explored in this chapter.[2] Traditional Yiddish songs have been documented from the second half of the nineteenth century until the decades that followed the Holocaust, when their last performers were still alive.

My interpretation of the term "traditional folk songs" follows Galit Hasan-Rokem's definition of the dimension of "tradition" in Jewish folklore (2002:957): "the group's concept that their cultural heritage contains traditional values and modes of expression that are transmitted from generation to generation ... one of the means by which the historical-chronological identity of the group is strengthened and its continuity sustained." Despite the fact that the eastern Yiddish community had none of the hallmarks of a society that would produce traditional songs, a repertoire that matches Hasan-Rokem's definition did emerge in the shtetl, far from the rural, oral societies and their way of life. Although most Yiddish songs lacked a fixed social function, many did display conservatism and an orientation toward aesthetic ideals, formal norms, and patterns; they were recognized by the performers as conventions transmitted orally from generation to generation, tested over an extended period of time, and reflecting contextual, musical, and poetic traditional values. These norms and patterns touch on prosody, poetic motifs, musical modality, forms, rhythms, and ways of singing. All of these songs maintained complex interrelations with parallels in their non-Jewish surroundings, both rural and urban, differing from them in various details while at the same time adopting and adapting some of their features.

In addition to referring to specific norms and patterns, the label "traditional" emphasizes three further dimensions of such songs: first, their distinctness from non-Jewish songs circulating in the Yiddish-speaking realm; second, their remoteness from Yiddish songs of literary origin; and third, their ties with other Jewish traditional repertoires, especially klezmer music (i.e., music played by traditional Jewish semi-professional instrumentalists).

We begin with a brief examination of the affinities to these significant components of the eastern Yiddish speakers' soundscapes, which can advance our understanding of the traditional songs' repertoire. Then, following a discussion of the cultural conservatism displayed in eastern Yiddish folk songs, we survey three different genres within the corpus: lullabies, lyric songs, and ballads. Spanning roughly four centuries, this rich body of traditional songs is worthy of study.

Non-Ritual Songs of Eastern Ashkenazi Soundscapes

Evidence suggests that eastern European Jews enjoyed their neighbors' songs, performing them either in their respective Slavic languages or in Yiddish translation, adapted for Jewish contexts (Rubin 1966). Rabbi Moshe Haim Ephraim (1748, Medzhybizh–1800, Sudylkiv), grandson of the founder of the Hasidic movement (Israel ben Eliezer, ca. 1700, Okopy Gory Świętej Trójcy–1760, Medzhybizh, known as the Baal Shem Tov) recalls in his book of sermons (2011:142): "As I heard from my grandfather . . . the nations of the world sing 'lidir' [songs]—in all of them is concealed an aspect of awe and love, spreading from the higher to the lower spheres" (the original Hebrew text uses the Yiddish word *lidir* and not its Hebrew equivalent, likely intending to emphasize the folkish nature of the songs). The passage refers to a mystical search for so-called divine sparks—but nonetheless provides a glimpse into a significant ethnomusicological phenomenon: in addressing the collective experience of the Jewish audience, it also makes clear that the beauty of the surrounding nations' *lidir* was recognized.

However, the impact of the co-territorial traditions on the formation of the inner Yiddish traditional repertoire was not particularly strong. In this sense, the Yiddish speakers' entire corpus of folk songs resembled that of the klezmer: as

Walter Feldman has demonstrated (2016:209–211), the latter comprised distinct repertoires, allowing for the coexistence of co-territorial melodies along with the "core" repertoire. The geographical scope of Yiddish singing constitutes another general parallel to klezmer music: both overlapped with the geographical distribution of eastern Ashkenazi liturgical tunes. Accordingly, numerous traditional Yiddish songs were only peripherally shaped by the surrounding non-Jewish languages and melodies. Close variants were documented in Bessarabia and Poland, Ukraine, and Lithuania—regions whose languages, musical styles, and repertoires differed significantly from one another.

This transnational dimension, the similarity of singing traditions throughout a variety of countries, was unique to the songs of the eastern Ashkenazim; it was not evident in the western Ashkenazi communities (Feldman 2022). The latter were more embedded in the local cultural contexts in general, and in local soundscapes in particular; residing in French, Italic, and Germanic lands, western Yiddish speakers often recognized local songs as their own (Matut 2011). And yet, after migrating to central/eastern Europe, Jews' attitude to their surroundings—at least concerning music, songs, proverbs, and folk tales—shifted.[3] Instead of absorbing local folklore, these newcomers developed their own repertoire, corresponding to old western European and Slavic traditions. This process marked the beginning of the emergence of traditional Yiddish singing and dictated its aesthetics and cultural meanings.

From early modernity and until the Holocaust's aftermath, various popular songs, distributed primarily via cheap Yiddish booklets, became an additional significant component in the Jewish shtetl's soundscape. These were attached to fixed tunes fashionable at the time—"historical songs," laments, songs about ethics and proper conduct—as well as couplets composed by preachers, jesters, and bards, and, in the late nineteenth century, songs of social movements and theater.[4] Yiddish popular songs of literary origin were always oriented toward innovation and current affairs, displaying awareness of their authors' personalities and copyrights; aimed at commercial success; and, to some extent, subject to elite control. Limiting creative freedom in each performance and thus preventing the diversity of different versions, these orientations dictated poetic, musical, and performance choices that were different from those inherent to the traditional songs.

The rapid disappearance of the traditional repertoire and the domination of songs of literary origin were noted at the beginning of the twentieth century.[5] As my own fieldwork in Israel (1998–2010) has demonstrated, most contemporary informants primarily recalled the stagey songs of the late nineteenth and early twentieth centuries, while the traditional songs—old songs about unrequited love, old ballads, lullabies that were not of literary origin, and paraliturgical multilingual songs—were remembered fragmentarily and only by individual folk singers.[6] Fedchenko and Gidon (2008) reached similar conclusions based on their fieldwork in Podolia (a region located in southwestern Ukraine, at the left bank of the Dniester River) in 2005–2007. Today, traditional songs are available as archival audio recordings, transcriptions, and published collections (Feldman and Lukin 2017).

The temporal boundaries of the evolution of the eastern Yiddish traditional songs' repertoire span from the language's emergence (approximately fifteenth century) to the upheavals of the twentieth century. Urbanization, modernization, emigration, lingual assimilation, vigorous antagonism to Yiddish in mandatory Palestine, and most noticeably the fatal blow that the Jewish shtetl suffered during the First World War, followed by its complete annihilation in the Holocaust—all led to the total disappearance of the traditional Yiddish repertoire.

In the absence of living witnesses who learned the traditional songs in their natural habitat within the lively Yiddish-speaking communities of eastern Europe, only two routes can allow us to deduce the social contexts and performance dimensions: a comparative analysis of the Yiddish and non-Jewish songs' lyrics and melodies and an examination of literary testimonies and cultural-historical scholarship.

Cultural Conservatism and Eastern Yiddish Folk Repertoires

The methodology noted above (that is, an interdisciplinary approach that merges comparative analysis, testimonial examination, and historical research) reveals five factors that defined the emergence and persistence of the Yiddish traditional folk song in its heyday: (1) eastern Yiddish speakers' general conservatism; (2) a creative rearrangement of poetic and musical patterns that originated in the western European realm, primarily in Germanic lands, which were perceived as time-tested and thus representative of the ideals of what is proper and beautiful; (3) an exposure to pan-European traditional song genres that stimulated the emergence of Yiddish ecotypes (ethnic variants), notwithstanding the conservatism; (4) a distinct musical orientation toward the "core repertoire" of klezmer music, a traditional institution that has gained widespread social recognition; (5) folk intertextuality, or the awareness of poetic and musical interconnections between different genres.

While four of the five factors (nos. 2–5) touch upon music, the general conservatism embraced numerous aspects of life—primarily those related to religious customs but also those including non-liturgical music and verbal folklore. This conservatism was not due to obedience to rabbinical control; it was a behavioral norm. Linguist Zelda Kahan Newman (2000) has compellingly demonstrated that some colloquial Yiddish intonation patterns, as well as Talmud-study chanting tunes, have been preserved since the early Middle Ages. One of the most salient explanations for this preservation, she asserts, is reverence for the practices of former generations as a cultural value.

Nonetheless, the community's conservatism did not mean a total lack of cultural dialogue with its surroundings, nor did it signify limited innovation. Historian Moshe Rosman (2002) coined the term "innovative tradition" to explain the peculiar combination characteristic of Polish–Lithuanian Jews: conservative medieval norms of daily conduct coupled with an openness to the modern spirit, including perceptions and behaviors shared with non-Jewish neighbors. This concept accords with the formation and spread of traditional Yiddish folk songs, which also aligned with the four additional cultural dynamics.

Overall, the five factors are interrelated: general conservatism (1) led to an orientation toward inner sources of musical inspiration (4, 5) and to adherence to the preservation of old Germanic traditions brought to eastern Europe as early as the migrations from the west (2); nonetheless, this form of preservation of German songs and song elements displayed significant freedom to alter and adjust local Slavic traditions (3). Finally, Yiddish folk intertextuality (5) implied that melodies could be considered independent texts, allowing an interplay between textual semantics and the associations rising from different musical genres (4). This intertextuality aligns with a society that considered literacy the uppermost value, granted text a central role in culture, and broadly recognized the practice of contrafact—adapting new song texts to familiar tunes—as a central foundation in disseminating handwritten and printed songs beginning in premodern times (Feldman 2016:47; Matut 2012:324–327; Turniansky 1989). With these cultural dynamics in mind, the phenomenon of innovative singing tradition is examined below. To this end, we survey functional, lyric, and narrative repertoires, exploring the genres of lullabies, lyric songs, and ballads, respectively, and tracing their place in Jewish and local cultures.[7]

Traditional Lullabies

Our exploration of traditional lullabies is divided into two: first, we will relate to the lullabies' verbal aspects; then we will analyze the musical elements. The traditional Yiddish lullaby, we will find, fulfilled three dominant functions: soothing, safeguarding, and inauguration.[8]

The lyrics of traditional Yiddish lullabies display an apparent affinity to the German lullaby tradition (Sadan 1961; Lukin 2020b). This is particularly noticeable given the absence of the Yiddish repertoire's key motif in Slavic lullabies: raisins and almonds brought to the baby by a little white or golden goat. Our discussion will focus on those Yiddish lullabies that contain this imagery; they are documented around eastern Europe, with the earliest evidence relating to the 1840s (Wiener 1898a:5–6; Wengeroff 1908:27). These lullabies are the most representative of the older layers of the Yiddish folk song repertoire. The motif refers to a traditional Ashkenazi treat for children (Wengeroff 1908:83), and its wide distribution in Yiddish lullabies should be examined in light of its no less impressive distribution in German ones, which is evident over a wide geographic area beginning in premodern times.

According to Emily Gerstner-Hirzel (1973:924), this typical formulation—"Zucker, Rosine un Mandelkern/ißt das kleine Kindchen gern" (Sweets, raisins, and almonds/ the little child eats them happily[9])—has an extensive history in German song. It appears in a thirteenth-century rhymed romance in upper-middle German, "Mai und Beaflor," in the form of a rhyme identical to that in the lullaby—*mandelkern-gern*: "weize, rîs, mandelkern/wehset in dem lande gern" (wheat, rice, almonds/grow beautifully in the soil). Although it is not known when the change from *rîs* (rice) to *rosine* (raisin) took place, it is clear that in an orally transmitted song, the sound shapes and advances the text's development no less than the content; for our purposes, it is significant that the poetic motif has long been present in the German cultural realm (Tahir Ul-Haq 1978:96).

Dov Sadan (1961) has observed the German roots of another image as well: the little goat, white or golden, granting this gift to the baby. Its etymology displays an inclination toward creative rearrangement of German poetic heritage among eastern Yiddish speakers: in German songs, the gift-givers are only parents or birds; there is no mention of a goat. According to Sadan, the motif emerged as a result of a new interpretation of the German rhyme "Wiegeli-Ziegeli" (*Ziegel/Dachziegel* = bricks/roof tiles):

> Nunni, bulli, Wiegeli,
> Ufem Dach es Ziegeli,
> Vögeli het Naestli gemacht,
> Meiteli, schlaf die ganzi, ganzi Nacht.

> Nunni, bulli [lulling syllables], a little cradle,
> On the roof a little brick,
> The little bird made a little nest,
> Girl, sleep all through the night, all through the night.

Sadan makes note of the antithetic parallelism—"above is the shingle/brick (*Ziegel/Dachziegel*)/below is the cradle (*Wiegele*)"—and explains that while roofs in Jewish eastern Europe were generally covered with straw rather than shingles, and because a goat was often close to the cradle, the word *Ziegeli* received a new meaning based on the German/Yiddish homonym *Ziegel/tsigl*: kid, instead of the original meaning, shingle.[10]

Three facts demonstrate that this lullaby was not integrated into the Jewish repertoire in the decades preceding its mid-nineteenth-century documentation[11] but rather brought to eastern Europe during the Ashkenazi migrations in the early modern period: first, the transition from shingle to kid must have taken place over the course of a number of generations; second, the motif was widespread throughout eastern Europe in numerous versions and was not a local phenomenon—this process of distribution and multiplication of versions also took time; and finally, the tunes to which lullabies with this motif were sung differed from the parallel songs in German.

The last intensive contact between German and eastern Yiddish speakers occurred in the seventeenth century. From then on, the gap between the two folk traditions widened (in musical aspects, Idelsohn 1932:vol. 9, viii–ix; as concerning language, Kerler 1999:34–40; in terms of everyday conduct, Rosman 2002). Thus, we can assume that German lullabies that included the expressions *tsigele* and *rozhinkes mit mandlen* were brought to eastern Europe before the eighteenth century and spread among Jews from then on.

What were the motivations for the preservation of German motifs and their creative adaptation to new surroundings?

First, they reflect caution and conservatism in all aspects of protecting babies: verbal formulas tested over time, and perceived as transferring the wisdom of older generations to newborns, should not be changed; the lullaby thus fulfills the traditional function of safeguarding.

Second, the "golden/white goat" motif might have taken hold thanks to a known charm for putting a baby to sleep: placing a goat's horn next to the baby's head. It is mentioned by Zekharia Simaner (d. 1715) from the Lithuanian town of Plungė in the *Book of Memory* (1708:33) and by Eliyahu ben Yehuda (1520–1590) of the Polish town Chełm (ca. 1725:23b, 173). If the motif related to the charm, it was a mimetic device. However, without comprehensive fieldwork, it is impossible to know how widespread these charms were and to what extent they influenced the world of folklore imagery, especially considering the plethora of charms for calming babies referred to in the same books.

The third reason for the affinity to German lullabies is that the two images, the goat and its gifts, belonged to the Ashkenazi "Golden Age," symbolizing the idyll of days gone by. Their inclusion in the lullaby's lyrics may have been dictated by one of its traditional functions, namely, inauguration—presenting the baby with the cultural values of the society into which it is born. Adherence to community traditions rather than coterritorial ones when welcoming a new member emphasized its fundamental values: general conservatism and lingual and social hesitancy with regard to Slavic village culture.

Alongside the apparent affinity to German heritage of this and many other Yiddish lullabies, the stock of their poetic motifs is not particularly exceptional within the Slavic landscape. Valentin Golovin counted twenty-one typical motifs found in the Russian repertoire (2000:21–41). Table 30.1 illustrates that twelve are present in the Jewish repertoire as well (nos. 2, 3, 5, 7, 14, 15, 19–21 in Golovin's classification do not appear in the extant documentation of traditional Yiddish lullabies). This proximity stems from the cross-cultural nature of the motifs themselves; nevertheless, the comparison illustrates that the Jewish lullaby was not a foreign implant in the eastern European landscape, despite the lack of complete correspondence between the Jewish and Slavic stocks of motifs:[12]

One of the most common motifs in Yiddish lullabies is learning Torah, an Ashkenazi cultural ideal from medieval times and until the modern era.[14] The earliest Ashkenazi evidence of wishing the acquisition of literacy and advances in learning upon newborns is found in the eleventh-century prayer book *Machzor Vitry* (Baumgarten 2004:93):

> It is a custom that at a convenient time, shortly after the circumcision ceremony, ten [men] gather. And they take a Pentateuch. And the little one is in the cradle dressed like on the day of his circumcision ceremony in grandeur. And they place *a book on him* and say "let this one [the boy] keep what is written in this [the Pentateuch]." ... *And they put a quill and ink in his hand so that he will be a scribe*, adept in the Torah of God.
>
> (Italics mine)

The motif "Yankele will learn Torah" resonates with this testimony and appears, in various modifications, in numerous Yiddish lullabies. Although the motif of learning is absent in the traditional Slavic repertoire, it should be noted that it corresponds to motifs 9 and 10 in Table 30.1 (wishes of sleep/growth, future well-being and success), reflecting, again, a selective and partial adaptation of the co-territorial cultural norms to

Table 30.1. Shared Yiddish/Russian Motifs (According to Golovin's Classification)

Category identified by Golovin	Yiddish parallel	Source	Origin in the source cited
1. Expelling the harmful influence	The mother will come home and expel the *kozele* (female mature goat).	Mlotek and Slobin (2007:67)	Poland
4. Threat and/or warning	The girl who cries and is not willing to calm down is taken away and thrown into the bag.	Ginzburg and Marek (1901:60, 65)	Kaunas region, south-central Lithuania
6. Feeding or refreshment	Kasha in a little pot, bread to smear with butter.	Wiener (1898b:48)	Białystok, northeastern Poland
8. Giving gifts	The daddy will buy little shoes.	Ginzburg and Marek (1901:61)	Vitebsk, Belarus
9. Sleep as growth	Wake up again, with healthy body parts.	Cahan (1957:#340)	Siedlce, eastern Poland
10. Well-being and success in the future	Yankele will study Torah, he will write little scrolls, and an honest Jew will he always remain.[13]	Wiener (1898b:48)	Bessarabia
11. Expressing an attitude about the baby	Sleep well, my greatness! Close your beautiful eyes.	Ginzburg and Marek (1901:68)	Kaunas region
12. Calming and deepening the sleep	Sleep, sleep, sleep, the daddy will travel to the village.	Cahan (1957:#336)	Novogrudok, western Belarus
13. Marking the baby or its location	Sleep, my daughter, beautiful and nice, in your cradle; I will sit close to you.	Ginzburg and Marek (1901:65)	Tukums, southern Latvia
16. Rocking	Sleep, my child, I will rock you.	Kisselgof (1912:39)	No location mentioned
17. Reference to family members	Lyulinke lyuli, the daddy is not here.	Nadel (1905)	Kolomyia, Galicia (western Ukraine)
18. Worries of the soother (mother)	You are squeaking and crying, and not willing to sleep, and make your mother unhappy with this.	Ginzburg and Marek (1901:60, 65)	Kaunas region

the Jewish way of life. Moreover, several Yiddish lullabies comprise a refrain "lyulinke-lyu-lyu," shared by eastern Slavs. The inclusion of the motif of learning and the Slavic component again fulfills the function of inauguration, presenting the baby with the world into which it is born.

Thus, the poetics of the traditional Yiddish lullaby display two features: German roots, relating to three traditional lullaby functions, and an adaptation of the verbal patterns to the norms of the eastern European shtetl. The image of a golden or white goat bringing raisins and almonds, combining German heritage with a creative reflection of the Slavic surroundings, exemplifies both.

The music of the traditional Yiddish lullaby reveals other essential features. It displays a distinct musical orientation toward klezmer music in its *intonatsia* and in rhythmic, formal, and melodic diversity and modes.[15] Most have a musical form that consists of two or three asymmetrical parts; rhythms that generally combine three to six different patterns; and melodic contours that involve embellishments, leaps, and a certain degree of asymmetry. The rhythmic asymmetry is sometimes dictated by the tonic prosody of the lyrics, shared by all traditional Yiddish folk songs—a relatively stable number of stressed syllables and a variable number of unstressed ones. Yet, the asymmetry also appears when the versification does not require it, representing a consistent aesthetic ideal, as in the example shown in Fig. 30.1.

Here, the melodic segment "r" appears six times in three different renditions, of which two end on the third degree of the scale (B) and four others on the tonic (G). Moreover, the segment represents a variety of word–sound relations: three sounds are attached to three syllables three times (3/3), three sounds per two syllables appear once (3/2), five sounds per two syllables appear once (5/2), and five sounds attached to three syllables appear once (5/3). Thus, no verbal–musical element repeats; when such a repetition almost takes place (in the second measure of the first line and the second measure of the third line), the last note differs in length (by a quarter and a dotted eighth, respectively).

FIG. 30.1. "Under Yankele's Cradle" (Mlotek and Slobin 2007:78).
"Under Yankele's cradle there stands a pure-white little kid. The little kid went off to trade in raisins and almonds. Raisins and almonds are very sweet, my baby will be healthy and spry."

(Translated from Yiddish by Mlotek and Slobin.)

FIG. 30.2. "Clap Hands" (Mlotek 1972:7).
"Clap hands, clap hands! Daddy will buy you shoes, and you will run to 'kheyder.'"

(Translated from Yiddish by Mlotek.)

FIG. 30.3. "Grandfathers and Grandmothers" (Slobin 2000:388).
"The grandpas and grandmas are standing outside, with broad bags, with long ends, a girl who weeps, and won't be quiet, they take and throw into the bag."

(Translated from Yiddish by Slobin.)

This rhythmic behavior reveals the extent to which the change was a key aesthetic principle.

Rhythmic and melodic diversification also stand out in the example shown in Fig. 30.2. Part A contains two almost identical phrases, ending on a long note, whereas part B comprises two different phrases, each with a long note in the middle, rather than at the end; furthermore, the melodic contour of both phrases in part A is balanced, moving upward, then downward, and then back to the initial sound, whereas both phrases of part B emphasize the melodic movement upward.

Leaps in the melodic contour, resembling instrumental music, are quite frequent, as in the example shown in Fig. 30.3, which is also marked by asymmetry and diversification

FIG. 30.4. "A White Goat Comes Along" (Mlotek and Slobin 2007:67).
"A little white goat comes along, and wants to bite my Khanele. Mother comes home, and chases the little goat away. Sleep, my little girl, sleep. You will marry a man, a rabbi, you will marry a man, a scholar, your father and mother will be happy."

(Translated by Mlotek and Slobin.)

The melody shown in Fig. 30.4 represents a relatively developed musical form, found in other types of Yiddish songs as well—especially in serial songs (cumulative and non-cumulative), in paraliturgical folk paraphrases of canonical Hebrew chants, and in ballads. This use of the tripartite form in a lullaby melody illustrates the aforementioned folk intertextuality: the melody is represented before the baby as a ready-made product. The typological characteristics of this musical form, shared by lullabies, ballads, serial cumulative and non-cumulative songs, and folk paraphrases of liturgical poems, are instructive: the opening section (O) is based on motives of Talmud "study tunes" (Idelsohn 1932:vol. 8, 70–71), that is, emphasizing the natural minor pentatonic scale's degrees—1, 3, 4, 5;[16] the middle section (M) repeats the formula of counting and is usually marked by modal and rhythmical neutrality, ensuring a lack of tension and enabling multiple repetitions of the same motive;[17] and the concluding section (C) brings rhythmic and modal change, resembling klezmer *intonatsia* and reinforcing the sense of tonic. "Study tunes" were always sung by individuals to themselves or study-mates; klezmer music, in contrast, was always played in the public sphere. Hence, the musical semiotics of this form display a juxtaposition of the learned individual and the common collective, echoing two paramount wishes to the babies—successful learning and happy marriage.

The relative complexity of musical forms in most lullabies and their frequent correspondence with instrumental music and other song genres emphasize the central place that music takes in the poetic–musical composition of the traditional Yiddish lullaby: both components, lyrics and tunes, are considered equally important in the genre. This perception distinguishes the Jewish repertoire from the eastern Slavic landscape:

according to several studies, the music in most Slavic traditions serves as a framework for chanting magical verbal formulas and is of secondary importance; the words are considered the lullaby's critical component. For example, Izaly Zemtsovsky describes the formulaic eastern Slavic lullabies' tunes thus (1976:888):

> In the lullaby tunes, trochaic motives are prevalent. The melodies are generally based on a trichord of a minor third [three notes whose range comprises a tone and a half], sometimes enriched with a sub-fourth [a sound distanced from the lowest note of the main three notes by three and a half tones] or neighboring tones. The lullabies are meant not only for rocking the child but also as a magical protection against evil forces and a spell against death.

The affinity of such formulaic tunes to the genre of magic spells, ritual songs such as lamentations, or calendrical songs performed at the end of the year (*Koliadki*), noted by Zemtsovsky, has also been underscored by Laurel Osborn (1995:35–37), Valentin Golovin (2000:90–103), and Sheryl Allison Spitz (1979). The dominance of lyrics over tunes is expressed in the prosody of the traditional Ukrainian and Belarusian lullabies' lyrics: the number of syllables is generally fixed or varies only slightly, and the musical rhythm does not change throughout the lullaby. Mazuryna characterizes the typical tunes of Belarusian lullabies as "round," soft, and wave-like (2016:93).

The magic-transformational function observed in Slavic lullabies is rare in Yiddish ones. Most of the Yiddish verbal formulas, although featuring conservatism and emphasizing the functions of safeguarding and inauguration, are neither magical nor obligatory and hence do not dominate the music. This indifference to the role of lyrics within the poetic–musical composition is reflected in the following instruction by Zekharia Simaner in the *Book of Memory* (1708:32–33): "The nursing mother should make the baby happy with a song that causes it to sleep." The inclusion of this recommendation, self-evident and therefore superfluous to the modern reader, among healing and magical charms and instructions for writing amulets, demonstrates a belief in the specific power of music. According to it, the baby's happiness, which causes it to fall asleep, stems primarily from singing, whatever the song, and it appears that the words have no particular importance; content is secondary to practice.

This charm was copied from Sephardic[18] sources, and scholarship on Sephardic lullabies acknowledges a similar attitude toward texts. The most widespread texts performed at the cradle in Sephardic families were "romances"—medieval ballads whose dramatic narratives often told of murders, love affairs, kings, and warriors (Weich-Shahak 2015:22). These songs suited the function of soothing thanks mainly to their length and repetitive melodies; they, too, reflected indifference to lyrics' impact on babies. The wide distribution in eastern Europe of the *Book of Memory*, which was reprinted more than twenty times between its first printing in 1708 and the end of the nineteenth century, indicates that the charms it contained and the worldviews they reflected were shared by eastern Ashkenazi Jews as well.

In music, much like as in poetics, these distinct features of the Yiddish lullabies did not necessarily separate them completely from surrounding musical contexts. The melodic patterns Zemtsovsky identified in Slavic lullabies are common in Jewish melodies as well; however, in the Yiddish lullaby, the monotonous character of the trochaic chains is often veiled by dotted or asymmetrical rhythms, as in Fig. 30.1. Moreover, Yiddish lullabies' tunes correspond to the Slavic repertoire in their preference for ascending opening sounds and in their modality—most contain motivic chains shared by Jews and Slavs, including many motives based on a third, anchored in natural minor, or Nikriz and Hijaz modes.[19]

This Jewish–Slavic musical dialogue within the repertoire of lullabies was examined by Moisei Beregovski (1892–1961), a prominent Ukrainian-Jewish scholar of Yiddish speakers' folk music, in 1935 (Slobin 2000:522–525). He compared another version of the lullaby "Under Yankele's Cradle" to the Ukrainian lullaby "Oi, nu liuli liuli, naletili guli" (Oi, nu, liuli liuli, birds flew down). Identifying three musical motives shared by both lullabies and exploring sociomusical ties between the two ethnic groups, he emphasized that each developed the same motives in its own manner.

Lullabies belong to the "functional" repertoire, that is, songs whose performance contexts, poetics, and music are dictated by consistent functions rather than by a narrative or the dominance of emotions. Consequently, the five factors noted above interact in this repertoire with soothing, safeguarding, and inauguration functions. In other words, the approach to the lullaby's poetic and musical patterns—as proven by generations and therefore significant for inauguration functions and efficient for soothing and safeguarding—was shaped by cultural conservatism. The traditional perception of a lullaby as primary music led to klezmer's influence and correspondence with other song genres; these inspirations infused lyrics and music with equal importance, facilitating the soothing and inauguration functions. Finally, the shared eastern European cultural experience in lulling babies to sleep led to the integration of co-territorial musical modes, motives, and several poetic motifs in the Yiddish lullaby.

Traditional Lyric Songs

The traditional Yiddish lyric repertoire reveals vague yet discernable memories of once-relished lyric German folk songs: their traces—poetic images, single verses, or stanzas—became the building blocks of the Yiddish reincarnations. The reason for this is, most likely, that the lyric songs did not follow a straightforward narrative, focusing instead on the realm of emotion—despair, longing, nostalgia, dreams, and hopes (Winick 2014:469). Improvisatory composition in the performance of such songs made it possible to incorporate one or two such elements in a Yiddish lyric song and fostered further unstructured development.

This affinity to old German elements, documented all over Jewish eastern Europe, requires explanation. I suggest that it resonates with an unspoken perception that reflects the cultural conservatism of eastern Ashkenazim: time-tested formal devices and imagery are beautiful and can reveal genuine emotion. This conservatism is especially striking in the absence of any ritual or functional control over the choices of words and tunes; it therefore represents an accurate "folk idea" (Dundes 1971). Indeed, in eastern Europe, lyric songs were primarily sung solo among members of Jewish society's lower stratum, such as apprentices and female servants; public performances outside of the workplace were avoided. The lack of refrains in most songs reflects typical characteristics of their traditional performance—the absence of an audience and instrumental accompaniment. The examination of the poetics and music that emerged within these contexts demonstrates that, as in the case of lullabies, the lyric repertoire's evolution reveals the cultural traits outlined above.

Various versions of the following lyric song were documented in the early twentieth century in the Kaunas region, the Pinsk and Minsk regions (Belorussia), Kostopil (Rivne region, western Ukraine), Bessarabia, and the Warsaw region.

> Volt ikh geven a feygele,
> Volt ikh tsu dir gefleygn,
> Az du zolst visn mayn troyer harts
> Mit mayne farveynte eygn.
>
> Volt ikh geven a fishele,
> Volt ikh tsu dir geshvumen,
> Az du volst visn mayn farbitern harts,
> Volstu tsu mir gekumen.
>
> Oy, volt ikh gehat ferd un vogn,
> Volt ikh tsu dir geforn,
> Az du volst visn mayn farbitert harts
> Mit mayne opgeshnitene yorn.
>
> Volt ikh gehat tint un feder,
> Volt ikh tsu dir brivelekh geshribn,
> Az du volst geleyent mayne farbiterte briv,
> Volstu in khaloshes geblibn.
>
> If I were a little bird,
> I would fly to you,
> So that you should know my sad heart
> And my bleary eyes.
>
> If I were a little fish,
> I would swim to you,
> So that you should know my bitter heart
> And would come to me.

Oh, if I had horses and coach,
I would drive to you,
So that you should know my bitter heart
And my lonely being.

If I had ink and pen,
I would write to you little letters,
So that having read my bitter letter,
You would faint.

Its broad proliferation during the eighteenth century in Jewish eastern Europe is confirmed by a contrafact ascribed to one of the most powerful Hasidic Belarusian leaders of the time—Rabbi Menachem-Mendel of Vitebsk (1730–1788). In his paraliturgical chant, the love theme is transferred into the realm of religious longing for God (Zalmanoff 1948:19):

Volt ikh hobn gilderne fliglen,
Volt ikh tsu dir fliyen.

Volt ikh hobn gilderne reder,
Volt ikh tsu dir forn.

Volt ikh hobn ferd un zatl
Volt ikh tsu dir geritn.

Volt ikh hobn tint un feder,
Volt ikh tsu dir geshribn.

Volt ikh hobn a golden ring,
Volt ikh tsu dir gegebn.

If I had wings of gold,
I would fly to You.

If I had wheels of gold,
I would travel to You.

If I had a horse and saddle,
I would ride to You.

If I had ink and pen,
I would write to You.

If I had a ring of gold,
I would give it to You.

The ascription likely reflected reality: the song was most probably created in the eighteenth century, when the parallel between the longing for God and lovers' longing became a widespread metaphor;[20] moreover, no later religious contrafacts of Yiddish love songs are known. Juda-Leib Cahan (1957:484) has noted that various German songs containing a parallel wish to be a bird were included in Johann Gottfried Herder's *Stimmen der Völker* (1778) and subsequent classical collections of German folk songs, whereas the most similar version mentioning the bird, the horse, and the saddle ("Wohlauf ihr Narren, zieht all mit mir," "Farewell You Fools, All Go with Me") was documented in 1547 and ceased to exist in oral tradition at the end of the eighteenth century.[21] The possibility of a later borrowing from German-speaking communities is slim: this Yiddish song apparently preserved an old German model that survived in oral tradition in remote areas of eastern Europe from early modernity until the years following the Holocaust.

The perception of the old as beautiful finds support in an examination of the typical prosody and characteristic compositional tools and imagery of Yiddish lyric songs—all display a high level of uniformity and reveal the five cultural factors discussed above.

Prosodic features include a preference for tonic verse, usually of three or four stresses in one line of a quatrain stanza, and a partial alternate rhyme of the second and fourth lines (abcb). Thus, the prosodic schema of the last stanza above is as follows (stressed syllables are in bold; rhymes are underlined; numbers at the end of each line mark the proportion between the stressed and unstressed syllables; since the position of stresses in eastern Yiddish is flexible, in the actual performance of a song, the musical–poetic complex defines it):

> **Volt** ikh **gehat tint** un **feder**, (4/8)
> Volt **ikh** tsu dir **brivelekh geshribn**, (3/10)
> Az **du** volst geleyent mayne farbiterte **briv**, (4/13)
> **Vol**stu in khaloshes geblibn. (3/9)

As in traditional lullabies, the rhythmic asymmetry stands out and is a typological characteristic of the traditional lyric repertoire.[22]

The principles of composition involve anaphoric structures (each stanza is anchored in the same pattern: "If I were/had ... so that you should") and associative chaining ("bitter heart" corresponds with "bitter letter"). Other versions of this song also include two more characteristic features—spontaneous changing of the narrative time between stanzas (e.g., the first stanza in the present, the second in the past, the third in the future) and a mixture of first-, second-, and third-person speech. Yiddish lyric songs share all these features with numerous other eastern European traditions.

In terms of imagery, the traditional vocabulary of Yiddish lyric songs, like that of lullabies and ballads, adheres to an assortment of diminutives; a scarcity in descriptions of nature, persons, or objects; and an emphasis on actions. Many lyric songs comprise antithetical parallelisms, juxtaposing a description of neutral scenery to inner emotion, for example (Orshansky 1867:31, Yiddish song published in Russian translation):

> A little fire is burning in the little stove,
> And smoke flows from the fireplace.
> When I remember my dear friend,
> My soul strives to leave my body.

The first half of this stanza describes the setting of a house in indifferent fashion; it is only the second half that reveals that the image should be understood as a metaphor: the "fire" of longing burning in the heart is not seen outside, just as the fire burning in the stove is only hinted at by smoke.

Alongside inspiration from the old German lyric repertoire, some metaphors were inspired by ballads. In the example above, the image of smoke as suggesting a "burning" emotion echoes a famous Yiddish riddle-ballad song, whose erotic subtext hints at the wedding night (Krauss 1896:69, Galicia): "Vus iz hekher fin dem hoyz in vus iz geshtinker vi der moyz? In vus far a hoyz iz nit du kin tish? In vus far a takh iz nit du kin fish?" "What is taller than a house and who is faster than a mouse? Which house does not have a table, and which water does not have fish? [smoke, cat, bathhouse, *mikve* (ritual bath)]." While the two latter images openly refer to the preparations for the wedding, the first two refer to it only covertly, likely interpreting chimney smoke as hinting at burning emotion or as a phallic symbol and a cat catching a mouse as the loss of virginity. Whether inspired by old German songs or old Yiddish ballads, the imagery of Yiddish lyric songs, as of lullabies, corresponds with the surrounding eastern European landscape, especially in its emphasis on love and loneliness.[23]

Balladic inspiration is also discernable in the melodies of the traditional lyric songs in eastern Yiddish. The most prominent musical form of their tunes is the four-phrase structure ABCD, typical of English and Spanish ballads as well.[24] Beregovski provides three examples of possible German prototypes of Yiddish lyric songs, all three in four-phrase form, which he emphasizes graphically (1948:74–75) (Fig. 30.5).

FIG. 30.5. (a) "Frau von Luxemburg," 1540 (Erk and Böhme 1893:368, as represented by Beregovski). (b) "Der Herr von Braunschweig," fifteenth century (Erk and Böhme 1893:224, as represented by Beregovski). (c) "Zwei gespielen," 1540 (Erk and Böhme 1893:248, as represented by Beregovski).

The formal resemblance of these early modern exemplars to the melody of two versions of the song "If I Were a Little Bird" is apparent (Fig. 30.6).

Along with the formal similarity to ballads' tunes, the modality, development of melodic contours, typical cadenzas, and melismas are shared with the music of the eastern Slavic surroundings. At the same time, the modality of Yiddish lyric songs is often inspired by the klezmer core repertoire; the two most prominent modes—the natural minor and the altered Phrygian mode, represented in the example above—are also the most recognized in the latter.

Traditional lyric songs in eastern Yiddish, we have seen, drew inspiration from old German lyric songs, premodern ballads, neighboring Slavic lyric traditions, and the klezmer repertoire. The sum of these parts reveals the traditional folk perception of beauty and sincerity within the eastern Ashkenazi realm, attained using the right proportion of the above elements. Although no one today can be interviewed to verify these suggestions, comparative analysis of tunes and texts of the lyric repertoire demonstrates

FIG. 30.6. Beregovski (2013, vol. 2:1, upper stave, and 2:2, lower stave).

that its most widespread exemplars usually integrated multiple affinities to different cultural contexts, with no preference given to any one of them.

Traditional Ballads

Of the inspirations for the traditional lyric songs listed above, the ballads' impact on their musical forms and traditional imagery invites further examination. The wealth of the Yiddish balladic repertoire and discernable traces of old ballads in various other genres point to its wide distribution in the earliest stages of Jewish settlement in Polish–Lithuanian towns (Mlotek 1965). The Yiddish ballad does indeed demonstrate the eastern Ashkenazi Jews' full participation in the European song tradition: its ecotypes include such international ballad types as "Riddles and Impossible Tasks," "Choice of Profession/of a Groom according to Profession," "Request for an Overnight," and "The Homecoming Husband," to mention just a few (Lukin 2022). Following Mlotek (1965), I suggest that the dissemination of the Yiddish ballad preceded the flourishing of the lyric Yiddish repertoire, whose development was inspired by the dominance of lyric folk songs in the eastern Slavic regions. The emergence of the Yiddish balladic ecotype included changes in narratives, a shift to klezmer-like tunes, and the adaptation of the traditional four-phrase forms to the lyric texts.

Several underpinnings of the international balladic genre were best suited to the Jewish community's cultural realm in the shtetl. In performance contexts, these were the lack of a fixed social function and solo performance. Like lyric songs, Yiddish ballads were usually performed inside homes, and during work, with the exception of particular ballads sung for a bride (Lukin 2022). In terms of imagery, the ballad's typical disinterest in a specific natural landscape resonated with the preferences of urban society, as did the focus on the relations between genders and between family members. Finally, the migratory nature of balladic plots fueled their propagation in all regions of Jewish settlement. On the formal level, incremental repetitions and an abundance of dialogue and everyday speech quotations are especially significant. The structural principle of repetition characterizes numerous traditional Hebrew texts, among them prayers and paraliturgical chants, familiar to all. This proximity of indigenous repertoires to ballads might have stimulated a quick appropriation of the latter. As for the various modes of direct speech and dialogues, the researchers assumed their significance in the cultural realm of the shtetl. To emphasize it, a scholar of Yiddish literature and culture, David Roskies, coined the terms "shtetlspeak" and "sthtetlfolk" (2022). He explains (p. 47), with reference to Walter J. Ong:

> The shtetlfolk, which is to say, the people of Kasrilevke and Shklov, are both literate and highly talkative; literacy feeds orality and vice versa, because the study of

canonical texts is always done out loud, either in unison or in constant dialogue, and Ong's essential list of oral attributes—a load of epithets and other formulary baggage, an additive rather than an analytic style, redundancy, a conservative or traditionalist mindset, personal engagement, and complete lack of distancing—permeate all ages and social strata.[25]

Numerous features of family-ballad aesthetics resonate indeed with this "shtetlspeak." Historian Tamar Salmon-Mack, relying on rabbinical sources, describes the effect of the typical Jewish home's congestion—with living quarters shared with neighbors and diminishing personal living space in the Polish–Lithuanian shtetl—on a distinct culture of gossip (2012:259–276). She also notes long periods of absence of husbands and significant age disparities between spouses in frequent second marriages; these social conditions might well resonate with the ballads' imagery—particularly their focus on the community's assessment of the actualities of life—and their language, often recalling gossip.

In addition to these generic features, the ballad's popularity and significant impact on other genres might have stemmed from the lack of traditional epic singing in Yiddish-speaking society. Thanks to overall literacy, Yiddish epic poetry was transmitted via books and therefore did not influence folk singing. Thus, the ballad was the only narrative genre available for spontaneous oral musical creativity.

Processes of the cultural adaptation of German, Slavic, and central European ballads into the Yiddish ecotype are described in my previous study on klezmer's influence on older Yiddish ballads (Lukin 2022). For the current discussion, it is significant to ask why old Yiddish ecotypes did not preserve the typical western European four-phrase ballad musical form. The answer appears to be twofold. First, klezmer music was suited to one essential feature of the balladic genre: a narration about dramatic events, meant to evoke a strong emotional response among the listeners yet told from the perspective of an objective bystander, emotionally removed from the affairs described. This artistic effect was successfully achieved not only by klezmer-like short tunes but also by the adherence to the tripartite form, containing the opening, middle, and concluding sections, outlined above. Another explanation for the dissociation of the older Yiddish ballads from the typical ballad tunes might be the latter's appropriation by the lyric songs and the rise of the lyric genre. The four-phrase form became associated with songs of longing, despair, and love and might thus have been perceived as less suitable for the telegraphic style of the old ballad.

The proximity to klezmer tunes shared by ballads and lullabies created specific musical links between these two repertoires. In the next pair of examples (Figs. 30.7 and 30.8), the first melody belongs to a lullaby, and the second is a Yiddish ecotype of the German ballad "Großmutter Schlangenköchin" (a dialogue between mother and daughter, who complains about life in her in-laws' home; it ends with the daughter's death). The similarity between these two melodies is apparent, as is the distance between the message of the lyrics of the second song (the ballad) and the emotions its melody is meant to evoke.

FIG. 30.7. "Aylelule, Sleep My Dear Child," lullaby (Brounoff 1911:8).
"Aylelule [lulling meaningless syllables], sleep, my dear child, shut your eyes swiftly. Close them, then open them, you should sleep well and maintain good health."

FIG. 30.8. "Where Have You Been, My Little Daughter?," ballad (Cahan 1938:#134).
"Where have you been, my little daughter? By my in-laws, the warriors, my beloved mother."

These links between the different genres stimulated the crystallization of a musical style less tied to specific poetic features. They produced tunes that resembled the klezmer *intonatsia* but which, unlike real instrumental music, were suitable for the limited human voice and allowed for rhythmical flexibility dictated by the traditional tonic versification. Numerous Yiddish songs, displaying equal affinity to more than one genre, were sung to such tunes.

No less prominent in the traditional Yiddish repertoire is the tripartite musical form. Figures 30.9 and 30.10 show two examples of its use in ballads. As in the lullabies, the tripartite tunes incorporate the *intonatsia* of individual learning in their beginnings, juxtaposed to dance-like motives at their endings; the two are separated by enumeration-like motives. All three types of motives emphasize the referential function of the balladic texts and strengthen the emotional remoteness of the speaker-performer.

The affinities to various inner Jewish musical contexts encouraged the circulation of this tripartite form in multiple genres listed above, though within each genre its musical semiotics were interpreted differently. Especially prominent in two types of functional songs—serial songs and folk paraphrases—it provides another example of interconnections between different song types and of melodic patterns characteristic of the whole traditional Yiddish repertoire.

FIG. 30.9. Tripartite form in ballad melodies (Cahan 1957:55).
"Once occurred an event as follows: a man left his young wife. He is gone away from her, and delayed his coming back for many many years, ocean of years, in a foreign country. The lovely Khane found herself bound in a religious marriage [unable to dissolve the union]."

FIG. 30.10. Tripartite form in ballad melodies (Cahan 1957:90).
"Just listen to me, you, pretty girl! Just listen to me, you, lovely girl! What will you do on such a long journey?—I will traverse every street, exclaiming, 'Who requires laundry services?'—all for the sake of being with you!"

Conclusion

Numerous inner links between song genres attest to the high degree of consistency in the traditional layer of songs by eastern Yiddish speakers, whose processes of emergence began, most likely, in the sixteenth century. This layer is marked by specific poetic and musical characteristics that distinguish traditional Yiddish songs from songs of literary origin and songs of neighboring ethnic groups: poetic tonic prosody, an aesthetic ideal of asymmetry shared by lyrics and tunes, specific musical forms, and idiosyncratic imagery. All display the preservation of old western European patterns, inspiration from the klezmer tradition, and a dialogue with Slavic surroundings.

Each of the three major genres—functional, lyric, and narrative—interpreted these choices in its own way. Preserved Germanic poetic motifs in lullabies fulfilled the functions of safeguarding and inauguration; the latter was also emphasized in musical and lyrical markers of the Slavic surroundings. Eastern Slavic influence stands out in the traditional lyric repertoire, and the incorporation of old German elements in it, particularly of the four-phrase form, was perceived as adding to its beauty. Finally, in ballads, preserving old narrative types meant singing about truth and sharing narratives about moral values tested over generations.

All three genres highlight the traditional prestige of klezmer music, although none implies performance with instrumental accompaniment. The affinity to klezmer music differs between the genres: in lullabies, rhythmic klezmer-like *intonatsias* represented the power of music and hinted at weddings, serving for soothing and inauguration; in lyric songs, the klezmer-like modes and motives assured an intimate feeling of home, of belonging to an insiders' discourse; and in ballads, the rhythmic happy tunes emphasized distancing from the dramatic events described.

The eastern Yiddish speakers' cultural conservatism and remoteness from a rural way of life dictated these aesthetic choices. However, the traditional Yiddish repertoire cannot be interpreted broadly as German texts adapted to klezmer melodies. Just as the image of a little white goat bringing raisins and almonds appeared in the eastern Ashkenazi cultural realm and not in German or Slavic traditional lullabies, so, too, the aesthetics and semiotics of other genres emerged through constant dialogue with multiple cultural contexts. As my fieldwork has demonstrated, scant information can be gleaned from interviews with living descendants of eastern European communities. Therefore, a comparative analysis of written, printed, and audio-recorded texts and tunes, as well as voice qualities and performance styles represented on archival audio recordings, enriched by an examination of literary testimonies and historical research, was selected as the only available methodology. It revealed folk intertextuality—an awareness of the differences between the inherited German, local Slavic, and inner eastern Ashkenazi contexts—in all probability an outcome of the Yiddish speakers' high literacy rate and frequent migrations across Europe. This methodology also underlined the traditional perception of a multiplicity of affinities as an aesthetical ideal. As the analysis has demonstrated, these cultural dynamics contributed to the development of a traditional eastern Yiddish folk repertoire.

Acknowledgments

I would like to thank Abigail Wood, Galit Hasan-Rokem, and Margaret Beissinger for their assistance. This research was supported through The Israeli National Authority for Yiddish Culture.

Notes

1. Between the approximate fifteenth century and the Holocaust, the eastern Yiddish speakers resided in the regions encompassing present-day Lithuania, Belarus, Poland, and western Ukraine.
2. For eastern Yiddish, see Beider (2018); for the state of tradition in the aftermath of the Holocaust, see Slobin (1983:11; 1995:19); for the collections and history of study, see Feldman and Lukin 2017.
3. On the historical background of Ashkenazi migrations to eastern Europe, see Stampfer (2012).
4. On the stylistic differences between folk and early modern printed songs, see Lukin (2022:109–110); similar differences between late modern Yiddish songs are discussed by Slobin (1983:7).
5. Bar-Itzhak (2010:77–112), Loeffler (2010:75–79), Safran (2010:186–195, 222–224).
6. My field recordings are held by the Sound Archives of the National Library of Israel.
7. On the taxonomy of folk songs based on the predominance of the lyric, narrative, or functional dimension, see Hasan-Rokem (2002:957).
8. A different Hebrew version of parts of this section was published in Lukin (2020b).
9. Translations are mine unless otherwise indicated.
10. Indirect evidence of the goat's presence in Jewish homes and the folkloric identification of the goat as a "Jewish" animal is brought by Belova (1999:524): in Ukrainian, Belarusian, and Polish villages, the goat was sometimes called "the Jews' cow," "the Jews' animal." Belova also brings a folk superstition documented in Podolia, according to which "Petronia" birds were created from the goat excrement the Jews hid in their feather pillows. That is, as this Slavic superstition indicates, the goat was found not only in every Jewish household but also next to the bed.
11. In addition to Wengeroff's testimony, it was mentioned by Moisei Berlin (1861:78–79) and quoted by the Yiddish writer Mendele Moykher Sforim (Werses 1983:287).
12. Several categories are exemplified in multiple lullabies, and nearly every traditional lullaby is documented in numerous versions. Rather than give all bibliographical details of this vast documentation, only one reference for each category and each song is provided.
13. Wiener (1898a:5–6) dwells on the differences between the wishes for a baby boy (learning Torah) and a baby girl (a successful arranged marriage), as the published folk lullabies reflect them. However, without a focused ethnographic study, it is not clear how much these differences were seen as significant in practice.

14. Tahir-Ul-Hak (1978:139) surveyed many collections of lullabies in a variety of traditions in eastern Europe, including archival recordings preserved in the Freiburg Archive, and concluded that although the motif of learning itself appears in a Finnish lullaby, only in Yiddish lullabies is scholarship frequently presented as a prominent cultural ideal.
15. The term *intonatsia* was introduced by the prominent Russian musicologist Boris Assafiev as a designation of a musical motive (motive—a short sequence of sounds representing a distinct musical idea) belonging to a certain group of motives sharing both musical and semantic characteristics. See Zemtsovsky (1997:189–192).
16. The term "pentatonic scale" designates here a sequence of five notes derived from the seven pitches of the minor scale, excluding any semitones.
17. The term "the formula of counting" pertains to concise musical patterns found in counting rhymes, commonly shared among children's repertoires. Musical constructs characterized by "modal and rhythmical neutrality" embody a balance where no specific note takes rhythmic or melodic dominance over others.
18. Sephardim are descendants of Jews expelled from Spain in 1492 and residing in the Ottoman Empire, the Italic lands, and the Netherlands. Since most books created by them were in Hebrew, they became available to all other diasporas, including the Ashkenazi communities. The charm appeared previously in the books *Paths of Faith*, Venice, ca. 1545, and *Provisions for the Way*, Sabbioneta, 1567.
19. On the modality of Yiddish folk songs, see Beregovski's description (Slobin 2000:294–296). Nikriz, or "Dorian-Ukrainian," scale is a minor natural scale with raised fourth and sixth degrees (g-a-b♭-c#'-d'-e'-f'-g'); Hijaz or "Altered Phrygian," scale is a major scale with lowered second, sixth, and seventh degrees (g-a♭-b-c'-d'-e♭'-f'-g').
20. Biale (1997:144): "The love song between God and Israel had now become a poem of sexual relations between the Hasid and the divine."
21. "Wollt Gott, ich wär ein kleins Vögelein, Waldvöglein klein, Zur Lieben wollt ich mich schwingen . . . /Wollt Gott, ich wär ein klein Pferdelein, Artig Zeltelein, Gar sanfte wollt ich ihr traben" ("Would that I were a little bird, little forest bird, I would swing myself to the beloved . . . /Would that I were a little horse, [with] a good saddle, I wanted to trot her very gently"). For information about this German song, see Arnim and Brentano (1987:537).
22. The formal features of Yiddish lyric songs' versification are discussed by Harshav. For a prosodic analysis that combines Harshav's insights with those of Weinreich and Moser, and for references to these studies, see Lukin (2022:133, note 38).
23. Analyzing Polish folk music, Czekanowska (1990:91, 135) sees this atmosphere as a particular influence of the eastern Slavic traditions.
24. On the scholarship of this form in Yiddish lyric songs, see Lukin (2020a:95–102).
25. Roskies (2022) alludes to the fictitious shtetl called "Kasrilevke," which was created by the renowned Yiddish writer Sholem Aleichem, and the Belarusian shtetl Shklov as depicted in the three volumes of stories by another prominent Yiddish writer, Zalman Shneour.

Works Cited

Arnim, Ludwig Achim, and Clemens Brentano. 1987. *Des Knaben Wunderhorn: Alte Deutsche Lieder*, ed. Heinz Rölleke. Vol. 1. Stuttgart: Reclam.

Bar-Itzhak, Haya. 2010. *Pioneers of Jewish Ethnography and Folkloristics in Eastern Europe*, trans. Lenn J. Schramm. Ljubljana: Scientific Research Centre of the Slovenian Academy of Sciences and Art.

Baumgarten, Elisheva. 2004. *Mothers and Children: Jewish Family Life in Medieval Europe*. Princeton, NJ: Princeton University Press.

Beider, Alexander. 2018. "Yiddish in Eastern Europe." In *Languages in Jewish Communities, Past and Present*, eds. Benjamin Hary and Sarah Bunin Benor, 276–312. Berlin–Boston, MA: De Gruyter Mouton.

Belova, Olga. 1999. "Koza." In *Slavjanskie drevnosti: Etnolingvisticheskij slovar'*, ed. Nikita Ilyich Tolstoy, Vol. 2, 522–524. Moscow: Institut slavjanovedenija Rossijskoj Akademii Nauk; Mezhdunarodnye otnoshenija.

Ben Yehuda, Eliyahu. 1725. *Mif'alot elokim*. Zholkva: Tasha"m.

Beregovski, Moisei. 1948. "Di muzikalishe oysdruk-mitlen fun der yidisher folkslid," Typescript. Russian Institute for the History of the Arts, F. 45. Op. 1. ed. khr. 38. 99 leafs, St. Petersburg.

Beregovski, Moisei. 2013. *Evreiskii muzykal'nyi folklor; v 5 tomach na 5 diskach*. Kiev: Dukh i Litera.

Berlin, Moisei. 1861. "Ocherk etnografii evrejskogo narodonaselenija v Rossii." *Zapiski Imperatorskogo Russkogo geograficheskogo obshhestva: Issledovanija i materialy*, 1:1–94.

Biale, David. 1997. *Eros and the Jews: From Biblical Israel to Contemporary America*. Berkeley, CA: University of California Press.

Brounoff, Platon. 1911. *Jewish Folk Songs*. New York: Harris.

Cahan, Juda-Leib. 1938. *Yidisher folklor*. Vilnius: YIVO.

Cahan, Juda-Leib. 1957. *Yiddish Folksongs with Melodies*. New York: YIVO.

Czekanowska, Anna. 1990. *Polish Folk Music: Slavonic Heritage, Polish Tradition, Contemporary Trends*. Cambridge–New York: Cambridge University Press.

Dundes, Alan. 1971. "Folk Ideas as Units of Worldview." *The Journal of American Folklore*, 84/331:93–103.

Erk, Ludwig, and Franz Magnus Böhme, eds. 1893. *Deutscher Liederhort: Auswahl dervorzüglicheren Deutschen Volkslieder, nach Wort und Weise aus der Vorzeit und Gegenwart*, Vol. 1. Leipzig: Breitkopf und Härtel.

Fedchenko, Valentina, and Dina Gidon. 2008. "Pesni na idishe." In *Shtetl, XXI vek*, eds. Valery Dymshits, Alexander Lvov, and Alla Sokolova, 261–276. St. Petersburg: Evropeiskii Universitet.

Feldman, Walter Zev. 2016. *Klezmer: Music, History and Memory*. New York: Oxford University Press.

Feldman, Walter Zev. 2022. "Ethnogenesis and the Interrelationship of Musical Repertoires Among the Jews of Eastern Europe," *Shofar: An Interdisciplinary Journal of Jewish Studies* 40 (2): 1–12.

Feldman, Walter Zev, and Michael Lukin. 2017. "East European Jewish Folk Music." Oxford Bibliographies. Jewish Studies. New York: Oxford University Press.

Gerstner-Hirzel, Emily. 1973. "Das Kinderlied." In *Handbuch des Volksliedes*, eds. Rolf Wilhelm Brednich, Lutz Röhrich, and Wolfgang Suppan, Vol. 1, 923–967. München: W. Fink.

Ginzburg, Saul, and Piotr Marek, eds. 1901. *Evrejskie narodnye pesni v Rossii*. St. Petersburg: Voskhod.

Golovin, Valentin. 2000. *Russkaja kolybel'naja pesnja v fol'klore i literature*. Åbo: Akademis Förlag.

Hasan-Rokem, Galit. 2002. "Jewish Folklore and Ethnography." In *The Oxford Handbook of Jewish Studies*, ed. M. Goodman, 956–974. Oxford: Oxford University Press.

Hundert, Gershon D. 2007. "The Importance of Demography and Patterns of Settlement for an Understanding of the Jewish Experience in East-Central Europe." In *The Shtetl: New Evaluations*, ed. Stephen Katz, 29–38. New York–London: New York University Press.

Idelsohn, Abraham Zebi. 1932. *Thesaurus of Oriental Hebrew Melodies*. Leipzig: Hofmeister.

Kerler, Dov-Ber. 1999. *The Origins of Modern Literary Yiddish*. New York: Clarendon Press.

Kisselgof, Zusman. 1912. *Lider-zamelbukh: Far der yidisher shul un familye*. St. Petersburg: Juwal.

Krauss, Salomo. 1896. *Am Ur-Quell: Monatschrift für Volkskunde*, Vol. 6. Hamburg: G. Kramer.

Ling, Jan. 1997. *A History of European Folk Music*, trans. Linda Schenck and Robert Schenck. Rochester, NY: University of Rochester Press.

Loeffler, James. 2010. *The Most Musical Nation: Jews and Culture in the Late Russian Empire*. New Haven, CT: Yale University Press.

Lukin, Michael. 2020a. "Servant Romances: Eighteenth-Century Yiddish Lyric and Narrative Folk Songs." In *Jews and Music-Making in the Polish Lands*, eds. François Guesnet, Benjamin Matis, and Antony Polonsky, 83–107. Polin: Studies in Polish Jewry 32. London: Littman Library of Jewish Civilization.

Lukin, Michael. 2020b. "Shir ha-eres ha-mesorati be-yidish ke-yetsira mizrach ashkenazit." *Jerusalem Studies in Jewish Folklore*, 33:133–188.

Lukin, Michael. 2022. "At the Crossroads: The Early Modern Yiddish Folk Ballad." *Shofar: An Interdisciplinary Journal of Jewish Studies*, 40/2:105–142.

Matut, Diana. 2011. *Dichtung und Musik im frühneuzeitlichen Aschkenas*, 2 vols. Leiden–Boston, MA: Brill.

Matut, Diana. 2012. "What Happened in Hamburg: A Yiddish Document about Polish Jews in Germany during the Early Modern Period." In *Leket: Yiddish Studies Today*, eds. Marion Aptroot, Efrat Gal-Ed, Roland Gruschka, and Simon Neuberg, 321–356. Düsseldorf: Düsseldorf University Press.

Mazuryna, Natalja. 2016. "Prajavy invaryjantnasci i varyjantnasci w belaruskih narodnyh kalyhankah suchasnaga zapisu." *Vesci BDPU*, 1/87:91–95.

Mlotek, Eleanor. 1965. "Traces of Ballad Motifs in Yiddish Folk Song." In *The Field of Yiddish: Studies in Language, Folklore, and Literature*, ed. Uriel Weinreich, 2nd collection, 232–253. The Hague: Mouton.

Mlotek, Eleanor. 1972. *Favorite Yiddish Songs of Our Generation*. New York: Workmen's Circle Education Department.

Mlotek, Eleanor G., and Mark Slobin, eds. 2007. *Yiddish Folksongs from the Ruth Rubin Archive*. Detroit, MI: Wayne State University Press.

Moshe Hayim Ephraim. 2011. *Degel machaneh efrayim*. Jerusalem: Makhon Daat Yosef.

Nadel, Arno. 1905. "Jüdisches Wiegenlied: Volksmelodie." *Ost und West: Illustrierte Monatsschrift für modernes Judentum*, 5:701–702.

Newman, Zelda Kahan. 2000. "The Jewish Sound of Speech: Talmudic Chant, Yiddish Intonation and the Origins of Early Ashkenaz." *The Jewish Quarterly Review*, 90/3–4:293–336.

Orshansky, Ilya. 1867. "Prostonarodnye pesni russkih evreev." *Gakarmel*, 20:31–32.

Osborn, Laurel. 1995. "Lullabies of Ukraine in the Context of Ukrainian Folksong Tradition: A Textual and Musical Analysis of the Repertory from the Zinoviy Lys'ko Published Collection, Ukrainian Folk Melodies, 1967–." PhD dissertation, University of Saskatchewan.

Roskies, David G. 2022. "Shtetlspeak: The Triumph of the Dialogical in Zalman Shneour's Shklov." *Shofar: An Interdisciplinary Journal of Jewish Studies*, 40/1:38–62.

Rosman, Moshe. 2002. "Innovative Tradition. Jewish Culture in the Polish–Lithuanian Commonwealth." In *Cultures of the Jews: A New History*, ed. David Biale, 519–570. New York: Schocken Books.
Rubin, Ruth. 1966. "Slavic Influences in Yiddish Folk Songs." In *Folklore and Society: Essays in Honor of Benjamin A. Botkin*, ed. Bruce Jackson, 131–152. Hatboro, PA: Folklore Associates.
Sadan, Dov. 1961. "Tsimukim ushkedim." *Machanayim*, 53:124–130.
Safran, Gabriella. 2010. *Wandering Soul: The Dybbuk's Creator, S. An-Sky*. Cambridge, MA: Belknap Press of Harvard University Press.
Salmon-Mack, Tamar. 2012. *Tan du: Al nisuyin umashbereyhem be-yahadut polin-lita, 1650–1800*. Tel Aviv: Ha-kibbutz Ha-meuhad.
Simaner, Zecharia. 1708. *Sefer zekhira*. Hamburg: Tahamish Rahz.
Slobin, Mark. 1983. "Studying the Yiddish Folksong." *Journal of Jewish Music and Liturgy*, 6:7–11.
Slobin, Mark. 1995. "Ten Paradoxes and Four Dilemmas of Studying Jewish Music." *The World of Music*, 37/1:18–23.
Slobin, Mark, ed. 2000. *Old Jewish Folk Music: The Collections and Writings of Moshe Beregovski*. Syracuse, NY: Syracuse University Press.
Spitz, Sheryl A. 1979. "Social and Psychological Themes in East Slavic Folk Lullabies." *Slavic and East European Journal*, 23/1:14–24.
Stampfer, Shaul. 2010. *Families, Rabbis and Education: Traditional Jewish Society in Nineteenth-Century Eastern Europe*. Oxford: Littman Library of Jewish Civilization.
Stampfer, Shaul. 2012. "Violence and the Migration of Ashkenazic Jews to Eastern Europe." In *Jews in the East European Borderlands: Essays in Honor of John D. Klier*, eds. Eugene M. Avrutin and Harriet Murav, 127–146. Boston, MA: Academic Studies Press.
Tahir-Ul-Haq, Ilona. 1978. *Das Lied der Juden im osteuropäischen Raum: Seine Funktionen im Prozess der Erhaltung und Veränderung des sozialen und kulturellen Normensystems und in der Bewältigung aktueller Lebenssituationen*. Frankfurt am Main: P. Lang.
Turniansky, Chava. 1989. "Yiddish 'Historical' Songs as Sources for the History of the Jews in Pre-Partition Poland." In *Poles and Jews: Perceptions and Misperceptions*, ed. Władysław T. Bartoszewski, 42–52. London: Littman Library of Jewish Civilization.
Weich-Shahak, Susana. 2015. "Musico-Poetic Genres in the Sephardic Oral Tradition. An Interdisciplinary Approach to the Romancero, Coplas and Cancionero." *European Journal of Jewish Studies*, 9/1:13–37.
Wengeroff, Pauline. 1908. *Memoiren einer Grossmutter: Bilder aus der Kulturgeschichte der Juden Russlands im 19. Jahrhundert*. Berlin: M. Poppelauer.
Werses, Shmuel. 1983. "Shirey am bitsirat Mendele." In *Studies in Aggadah and Jewish Folklore*, eds. Issachar Ben-Ami and Joseph Dan, 285–300. Jerusalem: Magnes.
Wiener, Leo. 1898a. "Popular Poetry of the Russian Jews." *America Germanica*, 2/2:1–27, 33–59.
Wiener, Leo. 1898b. "Aus der russisch-jüdischen Kinderstube." *Mitteilungen der Gesellschaft für jüdische Volkskunde*, 2:40–49.
Winick, Stephen D. 2014. "Folklore and/in Music." In *A Companion to Folklore*, eds. Regina Bendix and Galit Hasan-Rokem, 464–482. Malden, MA: Wiley-Blackwell.
Zalmanoff, Shmuel. 1948. *Book of Chasidic Songs*. Brooklyn, NY: Hevrat Nihoah.
Zemtsovsky, Izaly. 1976. "Narodnaia muzyka." In *Musykal'naia enciklopedia*, ed. Iuri Keldysh, Vol. 3, 887–904. Moscow: Sovetskii kompozitor.
Zemtsovsky, Izaly. 1997. "An Attempt at a Synthetic Paradigm." *Ethnomusicology*, 41/2:185–205.

CHAPTER 31

KLEZMER MUSIC IN EASTERN EUROPE AND AMERICA

WALTER ZEV FELDMAN

WITHIN the two decades from 1980 to 2000 the word "klezmer" became perhaps the newest Yiddishism in the English language. Today it is rather well known—at least in Jewish circles—that the Yiddish word "klezmer" was derived from two Hebrew words, *klei* (vessel, instrument) and *zemer* (song). As ancient Hebrew had no generic term for "music," *zemer* was one of a number of words within the semantic range of what we would call "music." So a *klei-zemer* was a musical instrument. Metaphorically, *klei-zemer* could become a musician who was a "vessel of song." But this new meaning occurred only in Bohemia and then in all the rest of northeastern Europe, approximately five centuries ago. It was unknown to speakers of other Jewish languages elsewhere in the world.

Originally having three syllables (*klei-zemer*), in the Yiddish language it became shortened to the two-syllable *klezmer*, with the irregular plural *klezmorim*. By the end of the 1990s a semantic shift was occurring, and this is reflected in the *American Heritage Dictionary* entry of 2000. Now the first meaning of klezmer was "an itinerant Jewish folk musician" and secondarily "the music played by such a folk musician" (Feldman 2016:61). Throughout its history, the klezmer musicians' guild in Europe was exclusively instrumental. A member of such a guild was never "itinerant" but was based in a city or in a predominantly Jewish town. Within the following decade—in English and other Western languages, but not in Yiddish or in modern Hebrew—the second meaning has overtaken the first. To most of the world "klezmer" is now a kind of music, analogous to jazz or flamenco. So a "klezmer" must be a musician who plays "klezmer." Linguistically this is, of course, a bit sloppy—in the English language flamenco is not performed by "flamencos," nor is jazz played by "jazzes."

Contrary to recent popular "folklore" in America, there were no klezmorim in medieval Europe. Klezmer was a new term for a member of the Jewish musicians' guild, first appearing in Renaissance-era Prague and then spreading to the Polish-Lithuanian Commonwealth (mentioned in a Jewish communal source in Kraków in 1595 and a guild document in Lwów in 1629). The word appears on seventeenth-century tombstones in the Old Jewish Cemetery of Prague (Zaagsma 2000). It also was found in earlier Jewish texts written in Bavaria, but this state soon expelled the Jews, so the term never acquired much currency in the German Empire (or its successor states), until the second half of the eighteenth century. Christian sources from Bohemia and Moravia, from the seventeenth and eighteenth centuries, describe the prominent role of the Jewish musicians (i.e., klezmorim) both in Jewish weddings and playing for dances of Christian patrons. Their rather close interactions with professional Christian musicians in the cities seem to have been distinctive to these Czech lands (Sehnal 1997). But these sources do not describe unique features of the klezmer performance within the Jewish community, particularly in the synagogue just prior to the Sabbath, which are suggested in the Jewish sources. These professional patterns of the klezmorim in the Czech lands seem to have come to an end within a generation following the Habsburg Emancipation of the Jews toward the end of the eighteenth century. Elsewhere, throughout eastern Europe, the klezmer guild continued to be exclusively urban, flourishing in cities such as Vilna, Berdichev, and Iași, as well as in innumerable private towns (*shtetl*). Klezmorim rarely lived in villages (*dorf*).

Uniquely among any known Jewish cultures worldwide, the klezmorim created a single system of musical genres, both for listening and for dancing, throughout a very wide geographical territory, stretching from the Baltic to the Black Sea. Like the Yiddish language, it was diffused eastward and northward from Bohemia and the Danubian regions in the course of the later sixteenth century. By the end of that century and the beginning of the next, the klezmer guild was established throughout the broad Polish-Lithuanian Commonwealth, which was now the home to the vast majority of the Jewish population of Europe.

The new Yiddish linguistic usage reflected the upward mobility of Jewish instrumentalists, who were at last permitted to form their own guild, as can be seen from the Lwów charter of 1629. This Jewish musicians' guild had a monopoly (Yid. *khazuke*) on performance at Jewish weddings. The guild retained the same name—klezmer—and most of the same privileges for almost four centuries throughout Jewish eastern Europe, which soon became largely—although not completely—hereditary. The klezmorim also developed a distinctive jargon of Yiddish—at times called *labushaynski*—so that they could speak to one another at weddings without being understood. Although following the Russian annexation of much of the Polish-Lithuanian Commonwealth (1793–1795) the tsarist imperial government did not recognize Jewish communal organizations, the klezmorim still had de facto control over Jewish wedding music. This situation continued until the Russian Revolution (1917).

For over three centuries the instrumentation of the klezmer ensemble was highly fixed, as first specified in the Czech sources. The klezmer *kapelye* was led by a violin and accompanied by a second violin (*sekund*), a portable cimbalom (*tsimbl*), and a bowed bass. At times a baroque wooden flute also appeared in the ensemble. Rarely a flautist or even a cimbalist might be a band leader. The clarinet became accepted in the klezmer ensemble in certain regions by the first half of the nineteenth century. By the last third of the century—starting in the Russian Empire—the clarinet was integrated into a larger ensemble of up to a dozen men (an *orkestra* or *kompania*), including also brass and percussion. Still, the first violin often remained the leader. Due to the dates of the appearance of sound recording, this larger ensemble is much better documented than the older groups with the violin and cimbalom or the flute and cimbalom. In the pre–World War I era an intermediary small ensemble with both clarinet and violin was recorded repeatedly in Russian Ukraine and Poland.[1]

THE KLEZMER REPERTOIRE

As some notated evidence for klezmer music appears by the end of the eighteenth and the first half of the nineteenth centuries, we can observe a stylistic distinction between the Jewish "North" (Lithuania, Belarus, Northern Poland) and the Jewish "South" (Ukraine, Galicia, Moldova). In most cases this difference had little to do with local Gentile musical styles. As the preeminent Yiddish linguist Max Weinreich wrote, "Not only Jewish history but 'Jewish geography' too is a separate topic, which occasionally agrees with general geography, but more frequently does not" (1973, 1:47). In general, the repertoire that the klezmorim created for their Jewish public shows a deep interaction of predominantly four musical repertoires, which I describe as "stocks" (Feldman 2016:11–20). These were the elements of the synagogue liturgy (*nusakh*), central and western European dance music from the Renaissance and then from the Baroque eras, and Ottoman music of various social categories. During the nineteenth century a fifth stock emerged from Ottoman and formerly Ottoman Moldova. I have termed this latter the "transitional" klezmer repertoire.

Particularly in the seventeenth and especially in the early eighteenth centuries, as Ashkenazic Jews settled in Ottoman Moldova, a kind of Ottoman musical koine was created in northeastern Europe. While some of this repertoire was restricted to the internal use of the Ashkenazic Jewish communities, other examples evidently were performed for the local aristocracies. It is not unlikely that the creation of the "Sarmatian theory" among the Polish aristocracy encouraged the klezmorim to create "orientalized" musical genres. This well-known pseudo-history of the sixteenth to eighteenth centuries had claimed that the Polish aristocracy had been descended from invading Alanic/ Iranian Sarmatians from the Central Asian steppes. Only the Polish peasantry were descended from native Slavs! This supposed "Oriental" origin for the Polish aristocracy led to their adoption of various customs and sartorial habits both from Ottoman Turks and from the Crimean Tatars.

A rare example from a Polish aristocratic wedding in Warsaw from 1674 reveals dancing groups of Turks, Jews, Gypsies (Roma), and Karaites at the same event (Geshuri 1959). Another example of this phenomenon was the appearance of Jewish musicians from the Prague ghetto to perform "Turkish music" for the Habsburg emperor Leopold II in 1791 (Nettl 1923). An Ottomanized klezmer violin repertoire is recorded in the later eighteenth century in Berlin in the Aaron Beer MS (Idelsohn 1932:144). Within the following generation the noted cantor and violinist Hirsch Weintraub of Dubno in Volhynia created a manuscript (ca. 1830) of his own klezmer melodies. Many of these display a fusion with Baroque, Ashkenazic prayer *nusakh* and Ottoman *makam* elements but a stylistic configuration noticeably distinct from the klezmer repertoires of the end of the nineteenth century (Feldman 2016:238–242).

The wedding orator (*badkhn*) guided the klezmorim through several moods, expressed both musically and through his improvised verses. Some of these moods might be quite introspective and even mournful. Nevertheless, the wedding feast itself featured a great deal of dancing, both of a quasi-ritualistic and of a social nature. Jewish dance was largely a unified system, combining two major elements: one deriving from popular and aristocratic dance of the Baroque era—especially the contradance *sher*—and the other based on improvised movements, indigenous to the Jews themselves. The vocabulary of east European Jewish dance music featured elements attributable to the five "stocks" which created the klezmer repertoire. It is noticeable that no co-territorial dance culture contributed significantly to this fund of dances. The one striking exception is the Moldovan culture, for highly specific historical reasons.

Already by the early eighteenth century Ottoman Moldova had become the scene of lively interaction between Jewish and non-Jewish professional musicians (Feldman 2020, 2022). The surviving notated sources for the popular urban music of both Iași and Bucharest display a confluence of Greco–Ottoman and Western musical practices. In Iași there is a strong suggestion of a Jewish klezmer influence in this mixture as well (Feldman 2022). The "native" music of Romanian-speaking peasants and shepherds plays a very small role in this musical combination.

There is documentary evidence for the joint appearances of klezmer and Moldovan *lăutar* (professional Romani, pl. *lăutari*) musicians in Istanbul from the end of the eighteenth and into the earlier twentieth centuries (Feldman 2020:9). There is no doubt that this musical back and forth must have produced somewhat different effects on the Ashkenazic communities prior to the Ottoman withdrawal from the Danubian Principalities (as seen in the Weintraub manuscript from Dubno ca. 1830) and then afterward. The Ottoman/Phanariot withdrawal was a prolonged affair, stretching from the Russo–Turkish war of 1828, through the Unification of the Principalities in 1859, and then the official independence of the new Kingdom of Romania in 1881. During this entire period, the "native" Romanian musical element gradually became more prestigious and hence more acceptable to urban dwellers, both Christian and Jewish.

From the Ottoman eighteenth century and even through the succession of Russian and then Romanian rule in the various territories of historical Moldova, klezmorim and *lăutari* came to form a single professional class. Yiddish became the professional language of the *lăutari*, and there was also some intermarriage between Jewish klezmorim and Romani/Gypsy (*țigan*) *lăutari*. In some towns the leader of a "Jewish" band was a Gypsy and in others the leader of a Gypsy band was a Jew.

At the same time some Greco-Turkish musical elements began to penetrate into Jewish music together with their urban Moldovan adaptations as well as more purely Moldovan folkloric elements. Hence, they entered the klezmer repertoire together with genre names in the Romanian language and with their Moldovan choreographic patterns. And it was this Moldovanized musical style that formed the basis for the "transitional repertoire" of the klezmorim. Thus, on the one hand, they should be regarded as a separate repertoire; but, on the other, to the Ashkenazic Jews in much of eastern Europe they would have appeared as a newer continuation of the Greco-Turkish musical components that had already won acceptance within Jewish musical culture for centuries. Very likely it was this combination of both continuity and novelty that led to the continued vitality of the transitional repertoire in eastern Europe.

East European Jewish dance fused mainly west European dance figures with a distinctive body posture and system of Jewish gestures and other upper-body movements. Where the ethnic Moldovan group dances were adopted, the Jews danced them with typical Jewish body posture and at much slower tempos than their Moldovan versions. Even the originally German contradance *sher* featured sections of free improvisation of each male and female dancer (Feldman 2016:261–268; Netsky 2015). Jewish dance culture also developed a distinction between the dancing of the community and more virtuosic dancing of a soloist, known as a *tentser*. A few such *tentsers* actually became professionals and performed with the klezmer ensembles. Some *badkhonim* were also solo *tentsers*. Each community also contained non-professional men and women who received high regard for their dancing, both as leaders and as soloists. The best known of these latter solo dances were termed *khosidl* and *skotshne*. Despite the name, *khosidl* was not a dance of Hasidic Jews per se but represented a degree of Hasidic influence on the non-Hasidic majority (Feldman 2016:318–321). The klezmer music for these dances usually represented specific compositional techniques, with modulations and rhythmic shifts. The *skotshne* could also be a complex, dance-like melody performed for listening. These were the compositions of well-known klezmorim, and they often commanded a higher price from the dancers.

Scholarship

The notated and sound collections, some contextual materials, and biographies on the music of the klezmorim are mainly the product of the late tsarist and early Soviet periods. This situation is due to the unique role of Jewish musicians in the creation of the Russian conservatory system (Loeffler 2010). The earliest article on the subject was "Evreiskie Orkestry" ("The Jewish Orchestras") published in Petersburg in 1904 by the non-Jewish musician Ivan Lipaev. Relevant literature is mainly written in Russian and some in Yiddish. The major collectors and scholars were Zusman Kiselgof (Belarus, 1878–1939), Joel Engel (Moscow, 1868–1927), Moyshe (Moisie) Beregovski (Kyiv, 1892–1961), and Sofia Magid (Petersburg, 1892–1954). The first two participated in the famous folkloric Anski (Ansky) Expeditions just prior to World War I. Beregovski worked as part of a Jewish institute in Kyiv in the 1920s and early 1930s and was able to conduct many field expeditions. In the mid-1930s he supervised the Jewish Music Ensemble of the Ukrainian Soviet Socialist Republic in Kyiv, led by the klezmer violinist I. Rabinovitch (see Wollock 2000). Beregovski wrote the first dissertation with the topic of klezmer music at the Moscow Conservatory in 1944. The major collections of recorded sound and manuscripts are still housed in Kyiv and in Petersburg. Outside of the Soviet Union, significant historical research into professional Jewish performance was conducted by E. Lifschutz (1930), based in Vilna.

Stalin's repression and then the Holocaust put an end to both the Soviet and the Polish-Lithuanian branches of this research. In 1960 the Polish-Jewish folklorist Isaac Rivkind published a major Hebrew-language historical study on the klezmorim from his position at the Jewish Theological Seminary in New York. This was a lengthy critique of the famous musician Joachim Stutschewsky's Hebrew *Ha-Klezmerim* (1959). After 1960 there was a general dearth of publication until the post-revival scholarship, led by Mark Slobin, Hankus Netsky, Joel Rubin, and myself. Slobin, Netsky, and Rubin also focus on klezmer music as one of their areas of expertise in their academic positions. Starting in the 1980s Slobin has been both publishing on the klezmer revitalization and translating many of the major writings of Beregovski. Outside of the United States, Vasile Chiseliță, in his capacity as researcher in the Moldovan Academy of Sciences in Chișinău, has treated some klezmer topics in the course of his work on Moldovan instrumental music (2008, 2012). He shows that the north Moldovan peasants have created versions of different Jewish dances both for actual dancing and as ceremonial music at the wedding feast. I treat this phenomenon as well in my recent article (Feldman 2020).

The Wedding (*Khasene*)

Almost as a corollary of the new dominance of the entirely male klezmer ensemble and the male wedding orator was the absence of the voices of women. Virtually alone among all other Jewish communities, the eastern Ashkenazim did not allow women to sing either love or wedding songs during the wedding. As Beregovski stated, "It should be noted that no ritual wedding songs existed in the Yiddish language" ([1962] 1982:292). Some of the much earlier Jewish wedding songs from Renaissance Germany were still known even in nineteenth-century eastern Europe. They were sung in the week prior to the ceremony and only by young servant boys and girls—never by members of "respectable" households (Sholokhova 2022). Unlike many other cultures of eastern Europe, among the Jews instrumental music and the singing of songs were never connected. Rather, many Yiddish folk singers created new songs based on klezmer dance melodies. This situation arose—certainly by the beginning of the nineteenth century—as the Yiddish song became increasingly female and hence private.

In order to reimagine the Jewish wedding in eastern Europe, we must understand something of the role of the other professional wedding character, the *badkhn* or wedding orator (see Lifschutz 1930/1952). Unlike the klezmer, the *badkhn* would not necessarily be part of a hereditary lineage, although at times he might marry into a klezmer family. Only an individual with both literary talent and broad humor could become a *badkhn*. Since he had been a yeshivah student, he was in a sense a "spoiled rabbi," much as the Irish speak of a "spoiled priest," who was never ordained.

The significant moments in the wedding were accompanied by multipart compositions utilizing rhythms not usual for Jewish dancing, especially varieties of three-quarter time. The wedding was announced in the early morning by the *dobriden* ("good morning"), and it closed with the melodies leading the relatives homeward through the streets (*gas nign*, *zay gezunt*, and *gezegenish marsh*). The klezmorim greeted important guests with a composed *mazltov* melody. Other melodies were used in various moments of the wedding (Feldman 2016:137–162). Our main source for all of these is the notations collected by Beregovski as these customs quickly died out in America. The best klezmorim serenaded the in-laws and other honored guests at their table with melodies of their own composition, including versions of the *tish nign*, the *zogekhts*, and especially the *gedanken* ("meditations"). This latter combined rubato playing with references to both dance and non-dance melodies. Some of these klezmer composers performed nothing else at the wedding, leaving all other music to more junior band members.

While studying the music and wedding customs of the east European Jews, one is struck by the prominence of introverted, even tragic musical expressions for much of the wedding—especially its earlier sections, prior to the legal marriage ceremony under the wedding canopy, the *khupe*. While the anthropological scheme of separation, transition, incorporation will fit most wedding customs in the world (including Jewish ones), the eastern Ashkenazim stressed the "separation" phase to an extreme that was foreign to other Jewish communities. The locus classicus of this tragic mood was the *kaleh baveynen* ceremony—"causing the bride to weep," or the "bride's lament." Connected to, but not an essential part of, the "veiling of the bride" ritual (*kaleh-badekn*), the bride's lament was conducted by the *badkhn*, who improvised the poetic texts, and not by a rabbi.

Scholarship on the wedding customs of Christian peasants of northeastern Europe points to the predominance of a melancholy mood through much of the period leading up to the wedding day (Slobin 1992). Recent research in the Republic of Moldova documents the analogous "song of the bride" ritual (*cântecul miresei*) in all regions of the republic, including those southern regions that never had a high concentration of Jewish inhabitants (Badrajan 2002:118). How much significance should we attribute to these co-territorial non-Jewish wedding customs?

Since the *kaleh baveynen* ceremony is without any reliable Jewish *halakhic* (legal) precedent, does not require the presence of a rabbi, and is absent among all other Jewish communities worldwide—whether Sephardic, Ashkenazic, or other—we can safely conclude that it is based upon non-Jewish, probably pagan customs of a very broad region of eastern Europe. It would seem that this mood of prenuptial sorrow for the bride tied in well with the penitential mood of much early modern rabbinic thinking about the significance of the wedding ceremony. This confluence of mood may have rendered it relatively easy for Ashkenazic Jews to adopt these originally non-Jewish wedding customs, especially if there had already been an earlier, Knaanic (Slavic-speaking) Jewish precedent.[2]

Apart from the dances mentioned earlier, the wedding also featured a few ritual dances that were performed prior to the general dancing. The most important of these were the *makhetonim tants*, in which the elderly parents of the bride danced facing one another. The music to this dance was often identical to the *khosidl* genre. Another kind of melody was employed for the mimetic ritual known as the *broygez tants*, or "dance of anger." This was a unique moment for parody in the wedding, in which the mothers of the bride and of the groom executed an improvised dance based on mimetic gestures. The underlying theme of this pantomime was the competition and mutual dislike of the two mothers-in-law. This would be followed by a resolving *sholem-tants*, or "dance of reconciliation." This latter was one of the only places where the community was allowed to sing along, and it led into the general round dance known as *freylekhs* in the south and *redl* or *karakhod* in the north.

Apart from the wedding, some leading klezmorim attached themselves at times to the courts of nineteenth-century Hasidic *rebbes* (leaders). In such cases they might collaborate with the court cantor (*khazn*) to create listening melodies for the *tish*, the ritual table of the *rebbe*. Beregovski's research confirms such patterns, and in his introduction to his long unpublished 1946 collection of Hasidic wordless melodies (*niggunim*), he emphasized the partly instrumental character of these vocal melodies (Beregovski: 1999 [1946]).[3]

In addition, as professional musicians, the klezmorim played both popular cosmopolitan west European genres for the aristocracy—and for some wealthier Jews—and local dances for the peasantry.

Patterns of Klezmer Music and Jewish Dance in America

Following the mass immigration after the Russian pogroms of April 1881, usually junior members of klezmer lineages from the Russian and Austrian Empires settled in New York, Philadelphia, and some other American cities. Rarely, a senior and illustrious klezmer—such as the Molodovan violinist Milu Lemisch (1847–1918)—emigrated to the United States and founded a musical dynasty. The immigration of klezmer families to both North and South America is an important factor in the study of klezmer music in the twentieth century and beyond. This immigration led to the creation of abundant commercial sound documentation and some published and unpublished notations (mainly in New York and Philadelphia), beginning early in the twentieth century, and the presence of practicing hereditary klezmorim. These factors helped to produce the klezmer revitalization of the later 1970s, which then spread worldwide.

Immigrant klezmorim came from both the Jewish north and the south, but following World War I the immigrants' musical taste shifted emphatically to the Jewish south (see Feldman 2016, chapter XII). Within this southern group, dance music focused increasingly on the "transitional" repertoire created by Bessarabian klezmorim or their students. The immigrant klezmorim quickly made contact with one major Balkan group—the Christian Greeks. Their contacts ultimately went back to both Moldova and Istanbul and were avidly perpetuated by Greek musicians in New York and Philadelphia. By the 1920s in America several Greek recordings of klezmer melodies were made for a mainly Greek audience. Istanbul-born Greek musician/entrepreneur, Theodotos (Tetos) Dimitriades (1897–1971), became a producer for the music of Dave Tarras (Tarrasiuk; 1897–1989), the most prominent of all the immigrant klezmorim (more about Tarras in the section "The Klezmer Revitalization").

Even before 1900 the proletarianized Jewish immigrants could not maintain the more elaborate Jewish wedding customs and their music (Loeffler 2000). Klezmer music in America became restricted to dance music. Whereas in the first immigration period klezmer listening music from the Jewish wedding could still be published in New York City—or even performed in concert—after World War I, the published or commercially recorded klezmer repertoire was almost exclusively in the dance genres (Shapiro 1902).

A large proportion of the immigrant members of klezmer lineages branched out into mainstream American music of several types. Later the American-born generation often bypassed the klezmer repertoire altogether in favor of orchestral or popular musical work (Logan 1949). *Landsmanshaft* immigrant organizations usually insisted on hiring known local klezmorim, but after World War II these organizations were less active (see Weisser 1985). The shrinking traditional klezmer dance repertoire in use in America could be played either by klezmorim or by *musikers* (non-klezmer Jewish musicians) (Netsky 2002). By then the repertoire was usually simply described as "playing Jewish" or "the bulgars." The Yiddish-speaking *landsmanshaften* were predominantly "traditionalist," petit-bourgeois, and moderately religious. They usually stood in opposition to the bundist and other socialist groups who were avowedly Yiddishist. Yiddish song of various types held some status in the latter groups but rarely among the *landsmanshaften*, where it was considered a private, female repertoire. Conversely, klezmer music was too much bound up with the traditional Jewish life-cycle events to appeal to most of the bundists, socialists, and communists.

Already by the 1940s east European Jewish dance was changing in significant ways in America. Even among native Yiddish speakers, the gestural emphasis in the upper-body movements of Jewish dance began to appear overly "exotic" or "oriental" in America (Feldman 2016:171–175). Music for the solo dances *khosidl* and *skotshne*, which were entirely based on improvised steps and hand gestures, ceased to be composed and almost ceased to be danced at Jewish weddings in America. The old contradance *sher* maintained its vitality, using a variety of older and newer melodies (Netsky 2015), and the general circle *freylekhs* (or Belarussian *redl*) maintained its function in weddings.

The dominant choreographic trend consisted of Jewish variants of the Bessarabian line dances *bulgar*, *zhok*, *hora*, and *honga* (*hangu*). The leading klezmorim—especially Naftule Brandwein (1884–1963) and Dave Tarras—continued to compose new melodies for these dances. But the generation of Jews born after World War II rarely learned to dance them, much less the traditional style of performance.

The career of the dancer and modern choreographer Nathan Vizonsky (1898–1968) exemplifies a rare public stage treatment of Jewish dance. Born in Łódź to a Hasidic family, he studied both dance and acting in Europe. Upon coming to America in the 1920s he settled in Chicago and established a Yiddish dance troupe, which performed widely in the Midwest. He choreographed a major Yiddish dance pageant at the Chicago World's Fair in 1933, which, alas, was not filmed. His publication on Jewish dance from 1942 is a small but important document.

By the mid-twentieth century (and even somewhat earlier) the clarinet had replaced the violin as the leading klezmer instrument in America. Secondarily the trumpet and trombone became the vehicles for klezmer performance. Since both the leading immigrant klezmorim (Shloymke Beckerman, Brandwein, Tarras, et alia) and the American-born generation (the Epsteins, the Musiker brothers, and Sid Beckerman) were all clarinetists, the living transmission of musical articulation was mainly suited to the clarinet. In addition, almost the entire surviving klezmer dance repertoire was adjusted to the rhythms, tempos, modalities, and modulations of the dance known as *bulgar* or *bolgar*, creating what I earlier termed the "bulgar/freylekhs hybrid" (Feldman 1994).

A minority of the members of the klezmer lineages who had been born in America did choose to continue to perform and to create new versions of the klezmer repertoire. Notable were the clarinetists Max Epstein (1912–2000), Sid Beckerman (1919–2007)—the son of the illustrious Shloymke Beckerman (d. 1974)—as well as his cousin the accordionist Sam Beckerman, Dave Tarras's accompanist. The two brothers Sam (1916–1964) and Ray Musiker (b. 1927) constitute almost a class by themselves. Sam was a respected jazz saxophonist, who became the son-in-law of Tarras and integrated him into his innovative production "Tanz" in 1955. His brother Ray is a major clarinet stylist and a composer of new klezmer melodies (Byom 2017).

Another reality of the klezmer performance of the mid-twentieth century was the inclusion of Yiddish song. Traditionally the klezmorim had never performed songs or worked together with singers, other than the wedding *badkhn*. Once the Yiddish theater developed, it was by definition within the public sphere, however. Klezmer music had been one source for songs of the Yiddish theater in Europe, but this became rather less the case in America. While Tarras himself became a favorite accompanist for Yiddish theatrical singers, most Yiddish theater musicians were not klezmorim. But as the role of the klezmorim and their repertoire declined within Jewish life-cycle events, some of the American-born musicians teamed up with female singers. A classic case was the clarinetist Marty Levitt (1931–2008) and his wife, singer Harriet Kane, in New York.

We can view klezmer music as one of the celebratory and dance musics of immigrants in America but—following the Holocaust—one that was largely cut off from any possible re-enforcement from the "old country." As a professional music of a hereditary caste, it could make only limited inroads to the wider American Jewish public. Nevertheless, within these narrower confines (mainly within the southern transitional dance repertoire) it made significant stylistic gains, mainly under the brilliant guidance of the clarinetist Tarras.

The Klezmer Revitalization

There is still no authoritative history of the process known as the "klezmer revival" or "klezmer revitalization." In general, we might divide it into three eras:

1. The early revitalization: 1975–1990
2. The second period: 1990–2001
3. The third period: 2001–present

The Early Revitalization: 1975–1990

In general, the first period was a movement among American "baby boomers," somewhat under the influence of both the introduction of south Balkan music and dance and the Irish music revival. A movement toward Bulgarian, Macedonian, and Serbian dance and song had begun in several American and Canadian cities by the 1960s. While this Balkan music and dance movement was never entirely Jewish, Ashkenazic Jews were prominent in much of the east and the west coast.

The American Jewish involvement in Balkan music can be seen, for example, in the women's choral group The Pennywhistlers, created by New York singer Ethel Raim in 1962. While Raim grew up in a Yiddish-speaking home, the group's repertoire featured very little Yiddish but was primarily Bulgarian, Russian, and Macedonian. The first group to adopt the name "Klezmorim," was formed in Berkeley in 1975 and was a spin-off of this south Balkan dance movement.

The next significant stage in this movement was accomplished by the present writer, in conjunction with Raim, for whose group he was previously an accompanist, together with the mandolinist/clarinetist Andy Statman. Like Raim, Feldman came from a Yiddish-speaking immigrant home in the Bronx. Yiddish dance was part of his familial background, especially as Feldman senior had grown up in the north Bessarabian town Edinets—a major center of klezmer music and dance. The preeminent klezmer Dave Tarras had fled his native Ukraine and studied in Edinets prior to emigrating to New York. Together with Statman, Feldman explored the only Balkan musical community with any presence in New York City—the Greeks. Several of their Greek (and Armenian) musical mentors were already performing Jewish klezmer music for their own audiences long before the revitalization. Originally learning from Greek teachers—who employed the identical tuning—Feldman took the step of reviving the klezmer cimbalom (*tsimbl*), which had apparently been abandoned everywhere after the World War II era.

Together, Feldman and Raim—through the Balkan Arts Center, co-directed by Martin Koenig—obtained a grant from the National Endowment for the Arts to study with and present Tarras and his accompanists. The resulting concert in November 1978, "Jewish Klezmer Music: A Tribute to Dave Tarras," marked the first public appearance of this term in English. It was also a crucial inspiration both to aspiring klezmer musicians and to Yiddish singers and songwriters. After 1985, Statman soon gravitated toward Hasidism, and he pursued his own idiosyncratic blend of klezmer, Hasidic music, jazz, and bluegrass.

Following the impetus of the Tarras concert in 1978, two groups billed as "klezmer" appeared in the next two years. In 1979 Henry Sapoznik, Yiddish singer Michael Alpert, and songwriter Joshua Waletzky combined to form Kapelye (Yiddish for "the klezmer band"). In 1980 Hankus Netsky—a scion of a klezmer family from Philadelphia—put some of his students at the New England Conservatory into his Klezmer Conservatory Band (KCB). But in both cases Yiddish song held a central position. Thus, in a very short time "klezmer" became a kind of promotional term for a mix of the same Yiddish popular and theatrical song that had been part of American Jews' listening before there was any kind of "revitalization," along with some actual Yiddish folksongs, in Kapelye. Both the klezmer listening and wedding ritual repertoire and the Jewish dance to which instrumental music had been the accompaniment were still in a near-moribund state.

Adrienne Cooper's and Henry Sapoznik's initiative of 1985 in creating KlezKamp as a teaching festival and Alpert's research on the remaining Yiddish singers, dancers, and at least one European-born amateur fiddler (Leon Schwartz, 1901–1989) with a major klezmer repertoire enriched the resources of the revitalization movement. A handful of authentic hereditary klezmorim, willing to offer technical guidance, linked the revival movement to aspects both of American klezmer practice—mainly on the clarinet—and occasionally of east European practice.

In Chicago, clarinetist Kurt Bjorling started his own group in 1984, called the Chicago Klezmer Ensemble. In time the group came to include Joshua Huppert and later Deborah Strauss on violin, Eve Monzingo on piano and cimbalom, and Al Ehrlich on bass. They began recording in 1987 and 1988. For some years Strauss played in Netsky's KCB. Later she formed a klezmer and Yiddish vocal duo with mandolinist/singer Jeffery Warschauer. Over time Strauss also became a noted Ashkenazic dance teacher.

During the 1980s the leading Yiddish dance researcher was Lee Ellen Friedland of New York, who had studied folklore at the University of Pennsylvania. But after publishing a couple of significant articles, she dropped out of the field. In California and in New York City in the same period Alpert conducted major dance research with recent immigrants from the Soviet Union, especially with Polish klezmer dancer Ben Bazyler and with the Ukrainian-born singer and dancer Bronya Sakina. Among the latter's student was the Californian dancer and dance ethnographer Sue Ellen Foy, who shortly afterward moved to Hungary.

The Second Period: 1990–2001

The second phase of the revitalization was symbolized by the fall of communism (1989) and the reunification of Germany. These events rapidly led into what historian Diana Pinto had termed the "Decade of the Jews" (i.e., the 1990s). European countries, led by Germany, began to reckon more openly with the legacy of the Holocaust. The main significance for Jewish music of these world-shaking events was the opening up of a large and wealthy market for klezmer music in Germany. This new audience helped to focus several American Jewish musicians and groups on the older, European aspects of the klezmer repertoire and style. Foremost of these at that time was the New York–based Klezmatics, which had been founded by trumpeter Frank London and violinist Alicia Svigals in 1986. They soon added Lorin Sklamberg as their Yiddish singer, as the group sought to create a balance between vocal and instrumental music. By the mid-1990s the Klezmatics were able to avail themselves of senior clarinetist Ray Musiker (b. 1927), who showed interest in guiding the younger group. By this time Svigals also began to compose successfully in the European klezmer dance style, releasing her solo album *Fidl* in 1996. Chicago-based Kurt Bjorling was soon replaced on clarinet by New Yorker David Krakauer, who came to klezmer music through jazz and has continued to create a new musical synthesis since the early 1990s. Kraukauer is widely seen as a key innovator in modern klezmer and is well regarded in classical music. After Svigals left the Klezmatics in 2001, the group continued with the violin of Lisa Gutkin.

Aspiring non-Jewish klezmer musicians in Europe were very much aided by American Jewish musicians who expatriated themselves to Germany, Austria, and Hungary. Among the foremost of these were pianist/accordionist Alan Bern and clarinetist Joel Rubin, who initially led the virtuosic klezmer and Yiddish group in the late 1980s Brave Old World. By the early 1990s they were led by Bern, with Yiddish singer Michael Alpert, clarinetist Kurt Bjorling, and California bassist Stuart Brotman. Their 1992 CD *Beyond the Pale* represented another landmark in integrating klezmer and Yiddish song performance.

Rubin collaborated with Austrian-based expat accordionist and cimbalist Joshua Horowitz to record a brilliant CD of Beregovski's wedding and dance transcriptions in 1992, under the title *Bessarabian Symphony*. Earlier Rubin had studied and worked with the Epstein brothers, perhaps the foremost surviving American klezmer clan. By this time German clarinetist Christian Dawid formed his own duo with his Dutch accordionist wife Sanne Moricke. He later would play occasionally with Brave Old World. While also doing fieldwork with non-Jewish Ukrainian performers of klezmer music in Podolia, Dawid remains perhaps the most influential performer of traditionally based klezmer music in Germany.

Horowitz combined with the Cleveland-based accordionist Walt Mahovlich (a performer of non-Jewish east European musics) and violinist Steven Greenman to form the ensemble Budowitz, which performed often in central Europe. At the end of the 1990s Bjorling collaborated with the leading Gypsy/Romani cimbalist of Europe (the

Hungarian Kálmán Balogh) to perform perhaps the most creative European klezmer-based performances of the decade, through their 1999 concert tour of Holland and Belgium. In Budapest two American expat musicians, the fiddler Bob Cohen and the accordionist Christina Crowder, formed Di Naye Kapelye in 1989. The post-Soviet immigration to Brooklyn of the north Moldovan clarinetist German Guildenstern (1934–2006) led to a renewed interest in the Bessarabian roots of Dave Tarras's music, notably in the playing of his student the Russian-born mathematician Alex Kontorovich, also supported by Sapoznik through his Living Traditions organization.

Parts of this phase of the revitalization were documented in the 2000 Canadian film by David Kaufman *The New Klezmorim: Voices Inside the Revival of Klezmer and Yiddish Music*, based on performances at the new KlezKanada festival, held north of Montreal.

At the same time the faddish quality of this "Decade of the Jews," highlighted by such Jewish music festivals as Kraków and even Ancona, Italy (locations with almost no local Jews), encouraged the emergence of non-Jewish musical groups with little or no contact with European Jewish musical performance. These groups created various hybrids of wind- and horn-based American klezmer dance music with south Balkan and Romanian Gypsy styles (i.e., *muzica lăutărească*) or (in Poland) folkloric peasant repertoires (Waligorska 2013). While attracting audiences in Germany, Poland, or Italy, they had little effect on the movements within klezmer music as performed by Jewish musicians or their non-Jewish students and followers in Europe.

In 1998 the present author conducted extensive interviews with the last European-born klezmer ensemble leader, the Galician violinist, poet, and journalist Yermye Hescheles (1910–2010), long based in New York. Collaborating with Greenman, Alpert, and Brotman, he founded an ensemble using the traditional klezmer instrumentation of first violin, second violin, cimbalom, and bass. Their 1999 recording *Khevrisa: European Klezmer Music* (with Svigals as a guest artist) was issued by Smithsonian Folkways (DC) in 2000 and led to extensive tours in Europe in the early 2000s. This was followed soon by a period of new klezmer composition on the part of Greenman, continuing until today. Greenman remains one of the few successful new composers in the non-dance European genres of klezmer music. Also in the early 2000s Feldman returned to Yiddish dance and began teaching workshops at the major Canadian and European festivals. Among his students was Helene (Khayele) Domergue (Zilberberg) from Paris, who had taught Yiddish dance in France and at various European festivals.

Despite the conservatory background of several of the musicians active in this "second period" of the revitalization, there was very little attempt to "classicize" the klezmer repertoire in a manner comparable to what the students of Rimsky-Korsakov had accomplished in the late tsarist empire (see Loeffler 2010). The two high-profile figures in this period were the Argentine/Israeli clarinetist Giora Feidman and the renowned Israeli (Polish) violinist Itzhak Perlman. Feidman (the son of a Bessarabian klezmer) created classicizing arrangements, with some influence from the clarinet of Dave Tarras. After appearing in the play *Ghetto* in 1984, Feidman has retained his popularity in Germany as a voice for reconciliation between Germans and Jews (Rubin 2015). His influence upon the klezmer revitalization in North America has been minimal, however. Perlman performed a mixture of Yiddish songs and American klezmer dance music. Numerous commercial recordings document their performances of Yiddish and klezmer material.

The Third Period: 2001–Present

After 2001, the landscape altered once again. In Europe the philosemitism of the previous decade began to dissolve. As Rubin notes, "German interest in all things Jewish—including klezmer music—declined in the early 2000s" (2015:207). This was also symbolized by the closing in 2006 of the Berlin Heckesches Hoftheater, which had hosted regular performances of klezmer and Yiddish music since 1993 (Rubin 2014:34). Nevertheless, thanks to festivals such as Yiddish Summer Weimar (organized by Alan Bern since 1999); the Kraków Festival of Jewish Culture; London Klezfest; klezmer festivals in Petersburg, Kyiv, and Kharkiv; as well as the Canadian KlezKanada Festival, European and Russian klezmer students are interacting with American teachers continuously. It is no longer possible to divide the klezmer world neatly into a North American zone and a European zone. Yiddish Summer Weimar in particular has also allowed klezmer scenes of some quality to develop among non-Jewish musicians in locales as mutually distant as Czechia and Japan.

By this period the primary function of klezmer music was not the wedding, although of course some klezmorim play them too from time to time. And traditional Ashkenazic dance largely died out everywhere by the 1960s. The lack of knowledge about Jewish dance among Jewish wedding guests below age eighty limits the viability of the klezmer dance repertoire. After the pioneering dance research of Lee Ellen Friedland and Michael Alpert in the 1980s, a few knowledgeable dancers still teach it, as far afield as Russia and Japan. These include Avia Moore in Canada and the United States and Helene Domergue in France. Steven Weintraub had studied with the noted Yiddish modern dancer Felix Fibich (1917–2014) from Poland. Fibich had been the husband and dance partner of Judith Berg (1912–1992), the choreographer for the 1937 Yiddish film *Der Dybbuk*. Feldman had studied with Tarras—a first-rate dancer as well as the leading klezmer—and he teaches dance in the United States, Canada, Germany, Israel, Russia, and many other countries; but Ashkenazic dance still leads a fragile and sporadic existence. Since 2019 Feldman's student Natalia Holava is actively teaching Ashkenazic dance in Belarus and elsewhere, frequently working with the klezmer violinist Aleksei Rozov from Moscow.

By the middle of the first decade of the 2000s, conservatory-trained Jewish musicians and singers from Russia, Ukraine, and Latvia (and to a lesser extent Moldova and Belarus) were confident enough with the style and repertoire to perform and teach Jewish and non-Jewish musicians at home and abroad. In many cases this also involved a relearning of the Yiddish language, often from grandparents as well as through courses. Lacking any living exponents of the klezmer violin, it would seem that younger conservatory-trained violinists utilized the almost century-old ethnographic recordings of Anski, Engel, Kiselgof, and Magid to reconstruct the Jewish violin style of articulation.

After several of these musicians emigrated to Germany, they became a factor there, in Holland, and in Denmark. Violinists Aleksei Rozov and Boris Itzkovitch remain in Moscow and Mitia Khramtsov in Petersburg. Stas Rayko from Kharkiv and his student Mark Kovnatsky from Moscow now reside in Germany. Rayko in turn taught the Jewish klezmer ensemble Shtetl Band Amsterdam, then (2006) led by bassist Gregor Schaefer, with violinist Bert Vas and violist Iefke Wang. Later, both Schaefer and Wang composed in the European klezmer idiom. Shtetl Band Amsterdam also recorded with clarinetist Christian Dawid. The Israeli-born violinist Amit Weisberger settled in France in 2007 and established an influential klezmer ensemble. The Paris-born clarinetist Marine Goldwasser leads a klezmer ensemble there and works with Yiddish singers.

The Moldovan Lemisch klezmer clan had branches as far afield as Athens, Istanbul, and Beirut. In Montreal a scion of the Lemisches—trombonist Rachel Lemisch—combined with her husband Jason Rosenblatt in the innovative ensemble Shtreiml, featuring combinations of klezmer with Turkish popular music. They have recently relocated to Jerusalem, where Jason's brother Elie has long been performing klezmer violin.

The potential for creative interaction of Arab or other Muslim and klezmer musicians has developed in several places, far more than in Israel/Palestine (where it had existed in the nineteenth century). A landmark of this possibility is the *Three Klezmer Dances* from 2008 by the Boston-based Syrian composer Kareem Roustom, scored for string orchestra and tambourine and based on the recordings of Naftule Brandwein and the transcriptions by Beregovski and Kiselgof.

The possibilities for classical/klezmer cooperation were also explored in 2007–2009 by the collaboration of the present writer and Christina Crowder with clarinet virtuoso Alexander Fiterstein (born in Minsk and now a professor of clarinet at Johns Hopkins University in Maryland). The American violinist Noah Bendix-Balgley—son of Yiddish dance teacher Brian Bendix—composed his *Fidl-Fantazye: A Klezmer Concerto* for the Pittsburgh Symphony (2011–2014) and now works as concertmaster of the Berlin Philharmonic. In Italy, the Kyiv-born violist/violinist Igor Polesitsky from the Maggio Musicale Fiorentino also leads the Klezmerata Fiorentina, with a repertoire largely based on Beregovski's field collection in Ukraine. Polesitsky had been the student of Kyiv concertmaster Abram Shtern (1918–2014), who had been the last student of Leopold Auer (1845–1930), and had a klezmer musical background as well.

A generation of aspiring klezmer violinists in the United States are often accompanied by Pete Rushefsky, a leading cimbalist, who has composed several klezmer suites in a European-influenced style. He also directs the Center for Traditional Music and Dance in New York City. In Montreal, in the younger generation, Daniel Kunda Thagard is bringing a traditional style on the cimbal to a high level. The klezmer violin now has a critical mass of younger performers not only in America but also worldwide, including Abigale Reisman, Zoe and Annie Aqua and Jake Shulman-Ment in the United States, Ilana Cravitz in the United Kingdom, and Daniel Hoffman and Gershon Leyzerson in Israel. Within America the line of clarinetists going from Tarras to Statman has its leading contemporary exponent in New Yorker Michael Winograd. His CDs *Bessarabian Hop* (2013) and *Storm Game* (2015) are original developments of this trend.

In all of these movements there is generally a balance between the use of recorded models and prolonged contact with Jewish klezmer musicians, whether in the United States, Canada, Europe, Turkey, or Japan. The younger Russian, Ukrainian, Moravian, Dutch, German, French, British, American, and Israeli violinists and clarinetists form a committed group of musicians who seem likely to carry aspects of both the European and the American klezmer styles into the next millennium.

Notes

1. This was the so-called Belf orchestra, researched by J. Wollock (1997).
2. After the fall of the Khazarian Empire, Jews became speakers of the East Slavic Rus language for the next four to five centuries. Even earlier, Jews in Moravia and Bohemia had adopted the Czech language. The rabbis referred to both the West Slavic and the East Slavic languages spoken by Jews as the language of "Knaan." The Germanic/Slavic/Hebrew fusion language—later known as "Yiddish"—seems to have arisen first in the Czech lands. Judeo-Rus would be replaced by Yiddish in Galicia, Ukraine, and Lithuania proper by the mid-sixteenth century and in eastern Belarus only in the mid-seventeenth century.
3. On the Yiddish song and melody terminology, see Feldman (2016:43–47) and my "Introduction to the Study of the Yiddish Folk Song" on the online site Inside the Yiddish Folksong (www.yiddishfolksong.com).

Works Cited

Badrajan, Svetlana. 2002. *Cântecul Miresei: Muzica în ceremonialul nupțial din Basarabia.* Chișinău, Moldova: Editura Epigraf.

Beregovski, Moyshe. 1982. "Jewish Folk Songs." In *Old Jewish Folk Music: The Collections and Writings of Moshe Beregovski*, ed. and trans. Mark Slobin, 285–302. Philadelphia: University of Pennsylvania Press. First published 1962.

Beregovski, Moyshe. 1999. *Evreiskie napevy bez slov.* Moscow: Kompozitor. Written 1946.

Byom, Clara. 2017. "Mixing in Too Much Jewish: American Klezmorim in New York City from 1950–1970." MA thesis, The University of New Mexico Albuquerque, New Mexico.

Chiseliță, Vasile. 2008. "Interferențe culturale evreiești în muzica tradițională de dans din Basarabia și Bucovina." *Anuarul Institutului de Etnografie și Folclor "Constantin Brăiloiu,"* 19:201–222.

Chiseliță, Vasile. 2012. "Rezonanțe işene și basarabene în biografia muzicienilor Lemisch: Surse, dileme, controverse." *Anuarul Muzeului Literaturii Române Iași*, 5:47–64.

Feldman, Walter Zev. 1994. "Bulgărească, Bulgarish, Bulgar: The Transformation of a Klezmer Dance Genre." *Ethnomusicology*, 38/1:1–35. Revised version in *American Klezmer: Its Roots and Offshoots*, ed. Mark Slobin, 84–124. Berkeley: University of California Press, 2002.

Feldman, Walter Zev. 2016. *Klezmer: Music, History and Memory.* New York: Oxford University Press.

Feldman, Walter Zev. 2020. "Klezmer Tunes for the Christian Bride: The Interface of Jewish and Romanian Expressive Cultures in the Wedding Table Repertoire from Northern Bessarabia." *Revista de Etnografie și Folclor, New Series*, 1–2:5–35.

Feldman, Walter Zev. 2022. "Francois Rouschitzki's 'Musique Orientale' (1834) as a Source for the Creation of Urban Music in Moldova." *Revista de Etnografie și Folclor*, 1–2:146–160.

Geshuri, M. S. 1959. "Klezmorim Yehudim." In *Encyclopedia of the Jewish Diasporas*, Vol. II, ed. I. Gruenbaum, 473–478. Warsaw–Jerusalem–Tel-Aviv: Encyclopedia of the Jewish Diasporas Co.

Idelsohn, Abraham Zevi. 1932. *The Synagogue Song of the German Jews in the 18th Century*, Vol. 6, Thesaurus of Hebrew-Oriental Melodies. Leipzig: Friederich Hofmeister.

Lifschutz, E. 1930. "Badkhonim un Leytsonim bay Yidn." In *Arkhiv far der Geshikhte fun Yidishen Teatr un Drame*, ed. Jacob Shatzki, 38–74. YIVO: Vilna–New York; English translation: "Merrymakers and Jesters among Jews," *YIVO Annual of Jewish Social Sciences*, 7(1952):43–69.

Lipaev, Ivan. 1904. "Evreiskie orkestry." *Russkaia Muzykal'naia Gazeta*, 4:101–103; 5:133–136; 6:169–172; 8:205–207.

Loeffler, James Benjamin. 2000. "In Search of 'A Respectable Wedding': Jewish Weddings on the Lower East Side, 1881–1914." MA thesis, New York: Columbia Universit.

Loeffler, James Benjamin. 2010. *The Most Musical Nation: Jews and Culture in the Late Russian Empire*. New Haven, CT–London: Yale University Press.

Logan, Andy. 1949. "Profiles: Five Generations." *The New Yorker* (29 October): 32–51.

Netsky, Hankus. 2002. "The Klezmer in Jewish Philadelphia, 1915–70." In *American Klezmer: Roots and Offshoots*, ed. Mark Slobin, 52–72. Berkeley: University of California Press.

Netsky, Hankus. 2015. *Klezmer: Music and Community in Twentieth-Century Jewish Philadelphia*. Philadelphia, PA: Temple University Press.

Nettl, Paul. 1923. *Alte jüdische Spielleute und Musiker*. Prague: J. Fleisch.

Rivkind, Isaac. 1960. *Klezmerim: Pereq be-toldot ha-amanut ha-'amamit*. New York: Futuro Press.

Rubin, Joel E. 2014. "With an Open Mind and with Respect: Klezmer as a Site of the Jewish Fringe in Germany in the Early Twenty-First Century." In *Dislocated Memories: Jews, Music, and Postwar German Culture*, eds. Tina Frühauf and Lily Hirsch, 31–56. New York: Oxford University Press.

Rubin, Joel. 2015. "Music without Borders in the New Germany: Giora Feidman and the Klezmer-İnfluenced New Old Europe Sound." *Ethnomusicology Forum*, 24/2:204–229.

Sehnal, Jiří. 1997. "Jewish Dance Bands in Moravia." *Hudebni Věda*, 34/3:292–302.

Shapiro, Herman S. 1902. *The European Jewish Wedding*. New York: Hebrew Publishing Company.

Sholokhova, Lyudmila. 2022. "The Yiddish Wedding Folk Songs of East European Jews: Function, Ethnography, Sociology, Texts and Music." In Special issue of *The Shofar: An Interdisciplinary Journal of Jewish Studies* (in press).

Slobin, Mark. 1992. "Europe/Peasant Music Cultures of Eastern Europe: Ritual Music of the Wedding." In *Worlds of Music*, ed. Jeff Todd Titon, 171–182. New York: Schirmer Books.

Stutschewsky, Joachim. 1959. *Ha-klezmerim. Toldotehem, orah-hayehem ve yetsirotehem*. Jerusalem: Mosad Bialik.

Waligorska, Magdalene. 2013. *Klezmer's Afterlife: An Ethnography of the Jewish Music Revival in Poland and Germany*. New York: Oxford University Press.

Weinreich, Max. 1973. *The History of the Yiddish Language*, ed. Paul Glaser, trans. Shlomo Noble and Joshua Fishman. New Haven, CT: Yale University Press. (Translation of *Geshikhte fun der Yidisher Sprakh*, YIVO, 1973).

Weisser, Michael. 1985. *A Brotherhood of Memory: Jewish Landsmanshaftn in the New World*. New York: Basic Books.

Wollock, Jeffrey. 1997. "European Recordings of Jewish Instrumental Folk Music, 1911–1914." *Association for Recorded Sound Collections Journal*, 28/1:36–55.

Wollock, Jeffrey. 2000. "The Soviet Klezmer Orchestra." *East European Jewish Affairs*, 30/2:1–36.

Zaagsma, Gerben. 2000. "The Klezmorim of Prague: About a Jewish Musicians' Guild." *East European Meetings in Ethnomusicology*, 7:41–47.

Further Reading

Beregovski, Moyshe. 2015. *Jewish Instrumental Folk Music: The Collections and Writings of Moshe Beregovski*, 2nd ed., rev. Kurt Bjorling. Evanston, IL: Kurt Bjorling; revision of Beregovski 2001, ed. Mark Slobin. Syracuse: Syracuse University Press.

Beregovski, Moyshe. 1987. *Evreiskaia narodnaia instrumental'naia muzyka*, ed. Max Goldin. Moscow: Sovetskii Kompozitor.

Feldman, Walter Zev. 2003. "Remembrance of Things Past: Klezmer Musicians of Galicia, 1870-1940." *Polin*, 16:29–57.

Feldman, Walter Zev, and Michael Lukin. 2017. *Oxford Bibliography of East European Jewish Folk Music*. Oxford: Oxford University Press.

Kiselgof, Zusman, E. Khazdan, and L. Guralnik, eds. 2000. *Evreiskie narodnyie melodii, zapisanue Z.A. Kiselgofom*. St. Petersburg: Tsentr evreiskoi muzyki.

Kostakowsky, Wolff. 2001. *The Ultimate Klezmer*, arranged and ed. Joshua Horowitz. Owings Mill, MD: Tara Publications.

Lausevic, Mirjana. 2007. *Balkan Fascination: Creating an Alternative Music Culture in America*. Oxford: Oxford University Press.

Levitt, David. 2019. *The Levitt Legacy Klezmer Folio*, Vol. 1, ed. Christina Crowder. New York: Klezmer Institute.

Nettl, Paul. 1927. "Die Prager Judenspielleutezunft." In *Beiträge zur böhmischen und mährischen Musikgeschichte*, 70–91. Brno: R. M. Rohrer.

Rubin, Joel. 2017. "'Ich habe zwei Heimaten': An International Klezmer Community Coalesces in Berlin." *GVS/SMPS (Gesellschaft für die Volksmusik in der Schweiz)*, 18:52–59.

Rubin, Joel. 2020. *New York Klezmer in the Early Twentieth Century: The Music of Naftule Brandwein and Dave Tarras*. Rochester, NY: Rochester State University Press.

Sapoznik, Henry. 1999. *Klezmer! Jewish Music from Old World to Our World*. New York: Schirmer.

Slobin, Mark. 1984. "Klezmer Music: An American Ethnic Genre." *Yearbook for Traditional Music*, 16:34–41.

Slobin, Mark. 1986. "A Fresh Look at Beregovski's Folk Music Research." *Ethnomusicology*, 30:253–260.

Slobin, Mark. 2000. *Fiddler on the Move: Exploring the Klezmer World*. New York: Oxford University Press.

Balkan Romani Music Traditions

CHAPTER 32

ROMANI (GYPSY) MUSIC IN BULGARIA AND MACEDONIA

LOZANKA PEYCHEVA

THE focus of this study is on Romani (Gypsy) music[1] in Bulgaria and North (Vardar) Macedonia[2] and how it has changed over time. While the early Ottoman period is briefly considered, the main historical frame here spans the first decades of the nineteenth century to the present day—a period of nearly two centuries in which Romani music has undergone significant transformations. Macedonia and Bulgaria are home to numerous European Romani communities, and many of the most prominent Romani musicians known locally and abroad are from this region (Silverman 2012:6–7). The evolution of Romani music in these two neighboring countries has been a process of constant formation, transformation, permanent reproduction (each time in a new way), and accumulation of cultural codes that represent values, perceptions, and meanings relating to particular time periods. The resources that I have employed for analyzing the evolution of Romani music are earlier studies, publications, archival documents, and interviews that convey the ethos of different historical periods, supplemented by years of my own empirical field research from 1988 to 2008 in dozens of settlements in different regions of Bulgaria as well as several cities in Macedonia.

Romani musicianship is the offspring of the traditional craft of music-making, a craft that has developed for centuries in the Balkans within ever-changing socioeconomic conditions and cultural traditions. Balkan Romani musicians[3] have been professionals for hundreds of years, marketing their products and adapting their performances to Romani as well as non-Romani patrons (Vukanović 1962:42, 60; Peycheva and Dimov 2004; Peycheva 2011; Silverman 2012:4). In the course of this development, they became professionally involved in the performance of ritual, festive, and everyday events of local communities. They constantly created and re-created musical codes and idioms through the dynamics of their occupation. Romani music in Bulgaria and Macedonia proverbially consists of a constitutive duality: it is simultaneously old and new, traditional and popular, authentic and commercial, real and imagined, concrete and abstract, amateur and professional. It combines traditional and modern, folk and popular, and ethnic and global elements; it is an amalgam of many musics, styles, and repertoires.

The music that traditional Romani musicians produce is distinguished by how they master sound and acquire repertoire. Most of them are autodidacts and musically non-literate, learning and making the music they perform by ear. They are active players who constantly discover and rediscover music styles and repertoires of songs and dances that they are free to interpret and enhance with new content. Romani musicians have earned a reputation for being outstanding instrumentalists and singers; they are well known to improvise while playing, constantly transforming traditional local (rural) folk and popular music (in some of its most essential features), embellishing individual details to their own taste, and adding ornaments that "appear" delicate and beautiful; indeed, according to some researchers (and many musicians themselves), Roma play music spontaneously "from the soul" (Vukanović 1962:59; Peycheva 1999:183, 222). Practically speaking, however, Romani music involves continuous interaction between individual musical talent and economic need as musicians reproduce and mix the codes of various cultures—changing patterns and transitioning from old to new musical styles and from one historical period to the next. To be sure, the Romani music that has evolved over the centuries in Bulgaria and Macedonia is profoundly informed by history itself.

My research here focuses on Romani music from Bulgaria and Macedonia in a broad historical context and examines its chronological development in four consecutive periods. The first section presents the music profession as one of the artisan *esnafi* (guilds, sg. *esnaf*) in the medieval Ottoman Empire, in which itinerant Gypsies or *tsigani* (sg. *tsiganin*) participated as a stratum. The second covers the early modern period between the liberation of Bulgaria (1878) and the establishment of socialist rule in Bulgaria and Yugoslavia (1944). It outlines widespread practices and developmental changes related to the distinctive characteristics of Gypsy musical creativity in everyday life, rituals, festive entertainment, and the burgeoning recording industries. The third traces the reproduction of the policy of "re-educating the masses" through the institutionalization of Gypsy music and the stages of its development during the socialist period (1944–1989 in Bulgaria and 1944–1991 in Macedonia). The fourth considers the transition from socialism to capitalism in the 1990s. It treats the opening of new capitalist markets as well as the transformation of Romani music into an asset of the media, including music and festival industries which commercialize and promote Gypsy music in new expressive arenas. This study provides a story of Romani music, tracing its development in Bulgaria and Macedonia from a product of traditional craft to produced sound which has combined different music idioms with Western technologies and is associated with various cultural industries, markets, and mass culture. As such, it has broad social significance.

Itinerant Professional Gypsy Musicians in the Ottoman Empire

In the nineteenth century, the territories of present-day Bulgaria and North Macedonia were provinces of the Ottoman Empire. At that time, no linguistic, religious, or ethnic boundaries were drawn between Bulgarians and Macedonians (Roudometof 2002:88–92).

Gypsy musicians had a specific place in the Ottoman Empire, which ruled the Balkans for over five hundred years, starting in the fourteenth century. During this period music as a craft was associated with the Gypsy population mainly in Balkan cities (Ziroevich 1981:233, 235). As Elena Marushiakova and Veselin Popov point out, "In the tax register from 1522–1523, Gypsies were most often recorded as musicians (*sazende*)"; according to the list of *esnafi* in Istanbul prepared in the seventeenth century on the orders of Murad IV, the musicians' *esnaf* included three hundred people, most of whom were Gypsies (2000:48–52). Tatomir Vukanović writes that "Gypsy bear guides and their songs accompanied by a tambourine" were mentioned as historically common in the sixteenth century (1962:43). In the centuries-old structure of the Ottoman guilds, professional Gypsy musicians were associated with *mehteri* (musicians), *mehter-millets* (musician-communities), *davuldzhii* (drummers), *chalgadzhii* (small music bands), *svirdzhii* (whistlers), and *zurnadzhii* (*zurna* musicians), all of them professional designations (Peycheva 2011:211).

Today's practitioners of the *zurna* (double-reed, traditional woodwind instrument; pl. *zurni*), often termed *zurla* in the past (Gerov [1897] 1976:166) and *surla* (Macedonian word for *zurna*) (Rice 1982; Silverman 1996:246), and clarinet in Bulgaria and Macedonia are the descendants of musical families who practiced their craft in the Ottoman Empire (Peycheva 2011:211) (Fig. 32.1). In various sources during the Ottoman period (travelogues, archival materials, studies), the *zurna* is mentioned as one of the musical instruments associated with the Ottoman military music of the Janissary Corps. The military orchestras in the Ottoman Empire were reported to be composed exclusively of Romani musicians (Peycheva and Dimov 2002:27).

With the formation and development of a strong and self-reliant urban craft and commercial class of artisans as well as small shopkeepers and traders who flourished in the first half of the nineteenth century in some of the Ottoman cities (Daskalov 2004:56), a new type of urban music culture whose pioneers in the vast majority of cases were professional musicians, often of Gypsy origin, was born in the territories of the present-day states of Bulgaria and Macedonia. Urban music in some parts of the Ottoman Balkans was *chalgiya*. As Borivoje Džimrevski notes, the term *chalgiya* (pl. *chalgii*) meant a small orchestra with an indefinite number of musicians and instruments that developed an Oriental musical style[4] (1985). Typical instruments for *chalgii* were violin (one or two), clarinet, lauta, saz, tambura, santur, and tambourine. Džimrevski suggests that the *chalgiya* tradition dates

FIG. 32.1. Family *zurna* musicians from Petrich, Bulgaria, descendants of the famous *zurna* master Ismail Kurtov (in framed photo).

(Photo by Lozanka Peycheva, 2002.)

back to the late eighteenth century. According to him, the *chalgiya* bands were the result of the urban music and folklore tradition, which creatively flourished in the nineteenth and twentieth centuries (1985:8, 12). The music performed by *chalgiya* orchestras differed from local rural folk music in terms of instruments (most of the local instruments typically used by villagers were not used in *chalgiya* bands, and *chalgiya* ensemble instrumentation was not known to the rural population), style (*chalgiya* musicians performed in many, often unrelated, styles and elaborate new ways of looking at older styles, as well as creating their own specific style idiom in which stylistic boundaries remained open), repertoire (*chalgiya* orchestras performed diverse musics for variable audiences and musical tastes), and cultural contexts (*chalgiya* orchestras performed their music in mostly non-rural contexts, offering distinctive forms of sociability specific to people who lived in semi-urban and urban environments). The musicians of the *chalgiya* groups, usually traveling professional Gypsy performers, were without specific localization and played to different audiences in different situations: from private family gatherings to public community holidays, from *sabori* (local church holidays) to regional annual *panairi* (fairs)—markets where traveling traders traded freely in the Ottoman Empire (Buchanan 2006:99–100).

Raina Katsarova gives an account of music performed by traveling professional Gypsy musicians in the nineteenth century in her study of the musical life of the Bulgarian town of Koprivshtitsa. At that time traveling was a form of sociality, a way of living together for professional Gypsy musicians. Peripatetic Gypsy musicians performed at various occasions and used the venues of the vast imperial markets (city pubs and inns, fairs, etc.) to offer their customers music for entertainment and enjoyment. Katsarova's research on the state of urban musical life in Koprivshtitsa is a story about the main types of music that met the musical requirements of the town's population at that time (from the 1830s to the end of the 1870s). During their constant journeys in the nineteenth century, Koprivshtitsa's men working abroad, traveling merchant-drovers, and traveling Gypsies—professional musicians—had the opportunity to hear and learn many new songs, and they were not only Bulgarian but also Turkish, Greek, Serbian, and Bosnian songs; Gypsy violinists who toured Macedonia, Thrace, and northern Bulgaria also picked up new songs and instrumental motives, extended phrases, and melodies (Katsarova 1938:388).

According to archival materials, nineteenth-century professional Gypsy musicians sang and played various musical instruments: *zurna*, *gŭdulka* (rebeck), violin (called *kemane*, *ibrishovska tsigulka*), lauta, santur, mandolin, saz, drum, tambourine, etc. Only Gypsies were included in instrumental formations composed of *zurni* and *tŭpan* (double-headed drum, pl. *tŭpani*). The archival sources show that various instrumental formations called *chalgii*, *chalgadzhii*, etc. were similar in cultural functions in urban musical life. The two main musical formations associated with Gypsy musicians in the nineteenth century—the *zurna-tŭpan* and the *chalgiya* orchestras—have their historical sequels, transformations, and developments to this day (Peycheva 1999:29–31).

As Ventsislav Dimov summarizes, the new *chalgiya* music in the Ottoman cities during the *Vŭzrazhdane* (Bulgarian revival, ca. 1762–1878) was more urban than rural, more modern than traditional. He describes *chalgiya* as an original synthesis, a "hybrid hodge-podge" between Oriental and European. *Chalgiya* was modern urban music in the Balkans, a local ethnic variant of Balkan urban music in the nineteenth century (Dimov 2020:23–24).

THE COMMERCIALIZATION OF ROMANI MUSIC IN POST-OTTOMAN SPACES (1878–1945)

In the post-Ottoman era the evolution of music-making among Gypsies can be seen as the result of major political, economic, social, and cultural transformations involving an awakening of Balkan nationalisms. These transformations coincided with the early modernization of music practices in southeastern Europe. Vukanović terms this modernization "Balkan Europeanization," pointing out that it contrasted with the Ottoman past identified with Oriental musical culture, widespread in southeast European cities: "When the South Slav countries were liberated from Turkish dominion, the towns rapidly adopted the Middle European way of life, and Turkish music began to disappear not only in Serbia but also in . . . Macedonia [,] . . . Bulgaria [,]" and other Balkan countries (1962:47). During this period, Gypsy musicians continued to make music professionally. They employed both older, traditional as well as newer, modern performance practices in diverse social and cultural contexts, developing different themes and styles and often attracting completely different audiences. As before, they played at weddings and festivals as well as family and calendar events for clients from different local, ethnic, confessional, and social groups. Moreover, they performed, often all day long, at regional fairs (*panairi*) or coffeehouses and pubs where men drank together (Peycheva 1999:237–238).

Carol Silverman emphasizes that Romani music of the Balkans was a commodity to be sold and "has been a particularly important element in the traffic of popular and commercially mediated musics at least since World War II and possibly earlier" (1996:236). Indeed, by the early decades of the twentieth century (1930s–1940s), some Romani musicians had begun to have commercial success as recording artists (Ramadan Lolov, Ahmed Babakov, Karlo Aliev, etc.). They became popular in Bulgaria with the help of the market distribution of music during this early period of the gramophone and radio industry. Distinctive music styles for Romani musicians at this time were associated with several types of instrumental formations emblematic of their musical craft: the *zurna-tŭpan* and the *chalgiya* orchestras established in the Ottoman Empire, newly created *duhovi muziki* (wind bands), and urban *salonni orkestri* (salon orchestras) (Fig. 32.2). These formations were in some ways case-specific. For instance, *zurna-tŭpan* groups were affiliated with local family and calendar festivities in village and urban life, while *salonni orkestri* started to supply musical entertainment in restaurants, taverns, and cinemas (Buchanan 2006:117). By the turn of the century Rom-dominated *chalgiya*-related urban professional ensembles "existed all over the Balkans," performing in nightclubs, taverns, and coffeehouses (Buchanan 2006:116).

Bulgaria

Zurna-tŭpan instrumental ensembles were gradually being replaced by other small music groups composed of Romani musicians (Peycheva 1999:79). In other words, traveling Romani musicians formed or participated in small ensembles (the number of musicians varied between four and about ten) called *svirdzhii, kemendzhii, chalgadzhii*, as well as *bandi* (bands) and *muziki* (bands). The musical instruments used in these small ensembles (violin, clarinet, double bass, accordion, santur, tambourine, drum, etc.) were of differing origins (Turkish, local, and west European) and were grouped in various combinations. Such chamber music ensembles, composed mainly of Romani musicians, existed under different names throughout the Balkans; in Macedonia they

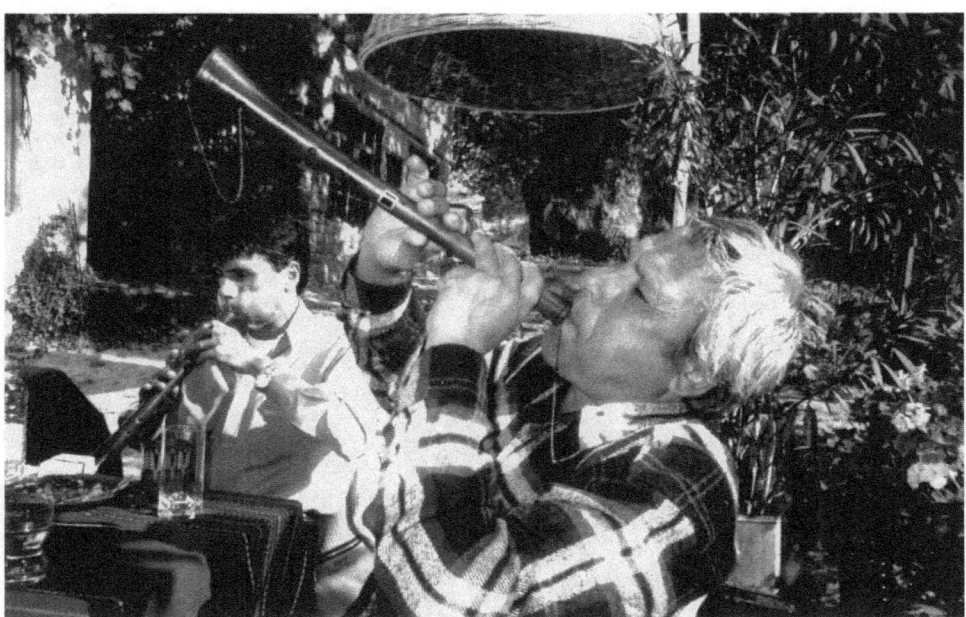

FIG. 32.2. *Zurna* musicians Demko (father) and Samir (son) Kurtovi from Kavrakirovo village, Petrich region, Bulgaria.

(Photo by Ventsislav Dimov, 2001.)

were called *chalgii*. They performed a diverse repertoire, including local folk songs and instrumental tunes, urban songs, tunes and dances of ethnic minorities, music of neighboring Balkan peoples, and modern west European dance tunes (waltzes, mazurkas) (Peycheva 1999; Vŭlchinova-Chendova 2000; Buchanan 2006:114–116).

Small village wind bands (*duhovi muziki*) of Romani musicians (the number of musicians varied between five and fifteen) were formed mostly in northern Bulgaria and usually included instruments with diverse musical functions: melodic (clarinet, trumpet, flugelhorn), harmonic (baritone, bass), and rhythmic (big and small drums, cymbals). Many of these Romani musicians received musical training and received musical literacy in military orchestras where they worked as professional musicians. Wind bands played at weddings, funerals, and other family and calendar events. Their repertoire was diverse, dominated by local folk music, popular tunes, hits, and modern European dance music (Peycheva 1999:80, 82, 83, 95, 203–205, 235) (Fig. 32.3).

In Bulgaria, urban salon orchestras and pub bands were created with the participation of Romani musicians. The musicians added their imprint to the interpretation of the wide range of styles and genres performed by them for various communities living together, including popular songs, boulevard songs (a genre matrix for the invention of sweet-sentimental songs for mass audiences, with hints of "pornographic content" (Balareva 1967:114), characteristics of subcultural productions, and reflections of the urban life of boulevards), arrangements of celebrated orchestral

FIG. 32.3. XIVth International Festival Romfest in Stara Zagora, Bulgaria. In the hotel after the competition program, the informal festival continues with the Romani brass band *Belite lebedi* (White Swans) from Sliven, Bulgaria.

(Photo by Lozanka Peycheva, 2006.)

pieces, Bulgarian *hora* (dances), *kitki* (folk song medleys), folk songs, patriotic songs, and many American dances popular in Europe (Balareva 1967; Buchanan 2006:117).

The first half of the twentieth century was a formative period in the growth of factories in the private sector and, accordingly, in the commercialization of "Gypsy music" in the Bulgarian music industry. Dimov describes in detail the production of "Gypsy music" of the several private record companies that were developing the growing record industry in Bulgaria (2007). As he points out, one of the earliest recordings featuring Gypsy musicians dates back to 1911—the Sofia Gypsy Gaydari band playing the song "Yana boli belo gŭrlo" ("Yana's Fair Throat Hurt"). As professionals at the time, Romani musicians performed "all kinds of music—from Bulgarian folk through popular urban music to world artistic (music)" (Dimov 2007:186–187, 189). Hence, the growing popularity of Romani musicians, rising stars of the gramophone industry, who emerged as the most successful performers of Bulgarian folk music: Ramadan Lolov (clarinet), Gosho Lolov (clarinet), Ahmed Babakov (clarinet), Ahmed Saliev (bagpipe), and Carlo Iliev (flugelhorn). Some of them became decisive figures in the development of Bulgarian folk music. Records of popular (Bulgarian, Balkan, west European) and art (European) music included Romani musicians: Peyo Budakov (violin), Mustafa Kurdoolu (cimbalom), Atanas Sotirov—the "Golden Gypsy" (violin)—etc.

In the second half of the 1930s, when radio emerged as a distribution path, some Romani musicians became popular artists through broadcasting. During these years independent record companies and radio networks merged, and radio as a national cultural institution gave wide publicity to the Romani instrumentalists who performed and developed Bulgarian local folk music. They were an integral part of radio programs (Peycheva 2008:274–277). Improvised and creative Gypsy music-making as well as *chalgiya*-like idioms, such as popular local music in the then popular music style— sentimental Balkan urban songs (included in the repertoire of salon orchestras and other instrumental groups)—were not well received because they were not recognized as official expressions of the Bulgarian nation and therefore had limited access to national radio. They were stigmatized in public discourse and critically attacked on two accounts: on the one hand, as "meaningless and low-brow" and, on the other, as "non-Bulgarian" and alien to local folk traditions (Dimov 2001:115–116).

Macedonia

For various historical reasons depending on the conflicts involving Greece, Serbia, and Bulgaria, between the Congress of Berlin (1878) and the end of World War II, the borders of Macedonia were repeatedly redefined. Macedonia was the last part of Europe to be liberated from the Ottoman Empire, at which time (1912) its territory was divided into three zones, each governed by a nation-state wishing to consolidate control of the newly conquered region (Rice 1982:122; Roudometof 2002:99). One of them, Vardar Macedonia, comparable to the territory of present-day North Macedonia, was assigned to the administration of Serbia. After World War I, Serbia effectively took control of the territory of former Ottoman Macedonia (Roudometof 2002:95).

Zurna-tŭpan instrumental ensembles flourished mainly in Macedonia (Rice 1982:122–123). Kosta Manojlović published his observations from 1924 on wedding customs in the village of Galichnik, located in western Serbia. He mentions the involvement of the *zurna-tŭpan* formations at some points in the ritual scenario of the traditional local wedding. Before the wedding, the musicians play in the evening by the lighted fire:

> the sound of the bells and the muffling thud of the drum are carried out in the dark night, and they echo far across the mountains; early in the morning on the wedding day, the bridegroom and his relatives, accompanied by drums and *zurnas*, go to their mother's or father's grave—if they have died—to beg their forgiveness for marrying.
>
> (Manojlović 1926:86–87)

The lack of political independence in Macedonia before 1912 slowed down the processes of economic modernization, including in the field of music. This delayed the transformation of Gypsy music into a commodity for the music industry. Romani musicians continued to be active and developed the "old-city" *chalgiya* style and legacy practices of previous generations of *chalgiya* musicians at weddings, celebrations of traditional big calendar and religious holidays, name-day celebrations, parties for *esnaf* patrons, fairs, cafés, etc. As Džimrevski remarks, *chalgiya* was a typical representative of old-town instrumental Oriental music culture in Macedonia. He examines the practice of *chalgiya* groups in different cities there and notes that *chalgiya*, as a musical tradition, was deeply rooted in the everyday life of the urban population and particularly prevalent and established in the *chalgiya* centers, especially Veles, Ohrid, Bitola, and Skopje. Romani musicians predominated in these ensembles in Macedonia; about 65% of the *chalgiya* musicians were Roma: "Along with the *zurna* and drum, the *chalgiya* for musically gifted Roma was a spiritual music-style identity" (Džimrevski 1985:12, 16–17). As Alexandra Kuzman notes, the right to play in cafés in Skopje was given to those musicians who were members of the *chalgadzhi esnaf* and held membership cards with its seal (2019:89).

In the interwar years (1918–1941), the practice of playing "café" or *kafana* (tavern or pub, pl. *kafane*) music developed in what was then the Kingdom of Yugoslavia. *Kafane* were the central sites for male entertainment: "the *kafana* has been a place where people can drink alcoholic beverages, eat, listen to the music, dance and have a good time in the company of friends" (Hofman 2010:143). Live music has long been one of the most important features of *kafane*. Romani *kafana* musicians performed for diverse audiences: in orchestras that played "light" or "serene" salon music, in unstandardized ensembles (with an unspecified number of musicians and instruments; labeled as *ciganski ansambli* [Gypsy ensembles]) performing folk music in urban pubs, and in restaurants and hotels (Dumnić-Vilotijević 2019:143, 154–155). Moreover, as Ana Hofman observes, until World War II, the women who performed in public as *kafana* singers "were mainly Roma who usually danced or sang in urban environments" (2010:145).

During the 1930s, in some Macedonian cities (such as Prilep), the local *chalgiya* ensembles gradually disappeared, giving way to ensembles that performed new musical styles (Kuzman 2019:104). These changes were necessitated and promoted by the advent of new technologies—the recording industry and radio—which institutionalized and popularized folk music. The virtual lack of information, however, on the institutionalization of Gypsy music from southern Serbia (Vardar Macedonia) in the interwar years, when radio represented a new form of music distribution, reveals that Romani musicians (and their specific aesthetics of music-making) had limited access to the programs of representative Yugoslav media. Maria Dumnić-Vilotijević analyzes the ideological component that defined the politics of Radio Belgrade (which began broadcasting in 1929) concerning the airing of music performed by Roma. The main intention of radio editors was to create a concept or construct of national music and regulate a specific national repertoire along with ensembles and acceptable ways of performing folk music. This ideology, tied to the romantic ideal of "authentic national folklore," served as a basis for criteria and procedures aimed not only at rejecting Gypsy-Oriental or urban folk improvised music that distorted "authentic national" expression but also at limiting the number of Gypsy performers of Serbian folk music. Negative attitudes on the part of the music editorial staff toward Romani music were evident (Dumnić-Vilotijević 2019:142–143, 148–149). The restrictions imposed ignored Gypsy musicians in the public music mainstream and left them out of distribution networks through local broadcast media. It is not surprising, then, that in these conditions Gypsy musicians from southern Serbia (Vardar Macedonia) did not become star performers and could not reach the same levels of popularity as Romani musicians on Bulgarian radio at the time.

The Institutionalization of Music-Making: Roma during Socialism (1944–1989/1991)

Socialist regimes and government communist ideology were established in Bulgaria and Macedonia in 1944. As Silverman rightly points out, "Post–World War II communist regimes in Eastern Europe officially downplayed ethnicity but nevertheless defined Roma as a social problem" (2012:10). Socialism as official state ideology determined the ways in which Romani music was resituated in both Macedonia and Bulgaria. The ruling governments institutionalized various Romani social and cultural forms. Macedonian Romani organizations—such as music and dance ensembles—proliferated in Skopje (Silverman 1996:234). Gospodin Kolev describes similar processes in Bulgaria: the creation of neighborhood Romani community centers as local organizations in which the music community was constantly represented through amateur choirs, small orchestras, and other music and dance ensembles; this occurred in Sofia, Pleven, Vidin, Yambol, and Sliven (2010:58–61). Institutionalization of this sort provided various avenues of entry and access to publicity and covered the diverse socialist-sponsored music contexts at the local level (both urban and rural) in which Roma were able to participate: concerts, folk festivals, and competitions. A few Romani orchestras and singers who performed frequently were broadcast on the radio in Sofia and Skopje. Romani musicians continued to be employed in Bulgarian and Macedonian popular and folk music and in cultural industries—media, music, and film.

Bulgaria

A closer look at the development of Gypsy music during the socialist period shows that the specialized formative policy of the ruling Communist Party toward the Gypsies in Bulgaria was aimed at integrating them into Bulgarian society and was relatively tolerant from the late 1940s to the mid-1970s. In the beginning of the socialist period in Bulgaria a policy was adopted for establishing Gypsies as an equal and distinct ethnic community within the Bulgarian nation; they were actively involved in the "construction of a new life" (Marushiakova and Popov 1993:88). In the first decades, the Bulgarian state took care of the "education of the Gypsies," and newspapers intended for them were published, such as *Romano essi* ("Romani Voice"), *Neve Roma* ("New Roma"), and *Nov pŭt* ("New Road") (Kolev 2010:70). The first Gypsy theaters and ensembles were organized in various Bulgarian cities: in 1947 the theater "Roma" was established in Sofia (Marushiakova and Popov 1993:88). Romani musicians who were interviewed claimed that a Gypsy music ensemble performing popular music (*estrada*) was formed in Stara Zagora in 1944–1945; a Gypsy music theater was founded in Ruse in 1947, which traveled and performed "all over Bulgaria"; and in 1954 a Gypsy music-theater formation was established in Vidin (Peycheva 1999:239–240). In the late 1940s, a government-controlled movement for "cultural emancipation of Romani music" began in Bulgaria: "Romani Theatres and ensembles were created, old Gypsy songs were sought, new songs were composed in the Romani language, part of which are recorded on gramophone records and broadcasted on national radio" (Dimov 2007:190). There were a variety of ways in which official socialist cultural policy institutionalized Romani music and its performers as social actors. Kolev (a representative of the Romani political elite and expert on the state policy toward Roma during the Bulgarian communist regime) writes that in the early years of socialism in Bulgaria, conditions were created, promoted by the Bulgarian government, "for developing the artistic and musical talent of the Gypsy population" (2010:60). The performance and composition of Gypsy music and songs were encouraged; the movement for amateur creativity, artistic amateurism (called *hudogestvena samodeinost*, or artistic self-activity) was rapidly growing, involving various forms of activity among the Gypsy population (Kolev 2010:95). Starting in the autumn of 1944 and in subsequent years there were "neighborhood Gypsy *chitalishta*" (community centers)—cultural institutions with educational functions, the mission of which was to establish places for the creative expression of local communities— intended "exclusively for the local people, for the Roma" (Kolev 2010:58). All urban community centers had amateur groups (composed of non-professionals) to perform music and dance: mixed choirs, dance ensembles for performing Bulgarian and Gypsy dances, instrumental groups with local traditional folk instruments in villages, and orchestras composed of modern instruments (violin, accordion, guitar). For members of these local cultural institutions, being a singer, musician, or dancer was a hobby, not an occupation.

The socialist politics of creating an ideologized mass culture through "civilizing" entertainment was visible when professional Romani performers appeared in the official arena to develop their careers as public personas. Some of them (such as Peyo Budakov and Angelo Malikov) remained performers mainly of entertainment music (named *estradna*, *leka*, *zabavna*, or *ganrova muzika*), while others (such as Boris Karlov, Ibro Lolov, Traycho Sinapov) became famous performers of Bulgarian folk music (termed *narodna muzika*). For instance, Budakov, celebrated as a violinist, singer, and director of a salon and folk music orchestra, broadcast a live entertainment music concert twice a week on Radio Sofia (1944–1945). As Dimov notes, "the Gypsy minority was the first in Bulgaria to organize and broadcast its rich musical program in order to express its cultural identity, present its traditions, and thus declare itself to its community and the national audience," which took place on January 14, 1946, in a half-hour evening radio broadcast on the Occasion of the Holiday of the Gypsy Minority in Bulgaria (2019:230).

Another one of the mechanisms by which the institutionalization of Romani music in socialist Bulgaria was realized was the work of Romani songwriters for the monopoly state gramophone record company Balkanton.[5] The most successful creators of Gypsy music during the socialist period, identified as "distinctive Gypsy composers" who authored "new, really fun songs and music," included Yashar Malikov, Hasan Chinchiri,[6] and Angelo Malikov[7] (Kolev 2010:60, 95, 76, 96–102). Some of their songs were very popular among local audiences at that time (Peycheva 1999:215–216; Dimov 2007:190–193). According to Yashar Malikov, September 9, 1944 (when the forcible imposition of communist rule in Bulgaria took place) was a watershed moment for Gypsy music in Bulgaria: after the political turnaround in Bulgarian history, new, humorous, fast Gypsy songs were born. These songs are called *nevo gilya* (newly composed Gypsy songs with old-time roots). The *nevo gilya* songs were sung in Romani, the names of their authors were known, and the songs were popularized through the media (Peycheva 1999:57; Dimov 2007:194).

The attitude of the authorities toward Gypsy music began to change during the late 1970s and early 1980s, when a new policy toward Gypsies in Bulgaria was established. This policy was connected with attempts at Romani ethnocultural depersonalization and, in the long run, their complete assimilation into the "Bulgarian socialist nation." In pursuit of this policy, formal recognition of Gypsies was restricted in order to adopt the official position that "Gypsies do not exist in Bulgaria at all" (Marushiakova and Popov 1993:89–92). An illustrative example of repressive actions by the authorities includes the closure of the Romani dance group and dramatic theatrical company at the Vasil Drumev Community Center in Sofia's Philipovtsi neighborhood in 1980 (Marushiakova and Popov 1993:91).

Because of media censorship directed against Gypsies, Gypsy music disappeared from Bulgarian radio in the 1980s. Sharing her field experience from that time, Silverman writes that working with Roma in socialist Bulgaria was challenging because, by 1984, they did not officially "exist" (2012:16). The repressive measures failed, however, to stifle entirely either Romani musicians or their creativity, reflected—in the 1980s—in their participation in the genre dubbed wedding music (*svatbarska muzika*) performed in "wedding orchestras" (*svatbarski orkestri*) (Silverman 2012:131–133). Wedding orchestras were comprised of a combination of clarinets, saxophones, trumpets, violins, accordions, electric guitars and basses, synthesizers, drum kits, and above all sound systems; in some isolated cases local traditional instruments such as the *kaval* (wooden flute) and/or the *gajda* (rural bagpipe) were played (Rice 1996:183; Peycheva 1999:88). As Silverman notes, wedding music "was a viable niche in the second economy, especially for Roma" (1996:239). Romani musicians in wedding orchestras worked outside of official music institutions. Some observations regarding the *svatbarski orkestri* and analysis of the nature of this practice indicate that wedding music, as a hybridization of Bulgarian traditional music with other Balkan or popular idioms, was a fusion genre, characterized by various local, "Western," and "Eastern" influences; it was a powerful, meaningful, grassroots alternative to the music of professional, state-sponsored folk ensembles (Rice 1996:192; Buchanan 1996:203, 225; Silverman 2012:16).

Macedonia

After the end of World War II, Macedonia became a republic in the Yugoslav Federation, where socialism sought a formula for the integration of its constituent ethnic groups. Yugoslavia after World War II was an extremely diverse country in ethnic, religious, and cultural terms. In the context of Yugoslav multiculturalism, a policy was pursued to integrate the various ethnicities; but the existing official hierarchy—*narodi* (nations), *narodnosti* (nationalities), and *etničeski grupi* (ethnic groups)—in which Roma were included showed other attitudes and understandings of the ethnic structure of the population. However, as it turned out, culture, especially music, was an area in which groups could display their distinctiveness; and the state supported the cultural activities of diverse communities that took place in both old and new specifically cultural contexts (Silverman, 2012:10).

The *zurla-tŭpan* instrumental ensemble as a Romani cultural phenomenon in Macedonia remained a common alternative to the progressively more widespread modern ensembles consisting of clarinet, trumpet, accordion, and drum (Rice 1982:135). The structuring of media publicity in the Yugoslav Republic of Macedonia was organized in order to promote Romani musicians who performed Macedonian music. Silverman remarks: "During the socialist period, Radio Skopje rarely broadcast music identified as Romani, but the Radio did regularly broadcast Macedonian music performed by Roma" (Silverman 1996:246). This suggests that repertoire selection was the principle that determined the admission of Romani musicians to the official public sphere. Prominent *zurla* and *tŭpan* musicians in Macedonia were regularly hired by state-funded radio and folklore ensembles, which gave widespread media, festival, and concert visibility to the music of this distinctively Romani instrumental combination (Silverman 2012:128).

Another notable example in this regard was the Chalgiya Orchestra, formed after World War II by Radio Skopje, which played live on the radio until the mid-1950s and revitalized nineteenth-century *chalgiya* music. The Skopje Radio Chalgiya Orchestra recorded a large number of Macedonian *chalgiya* songs and local dances and created, in studio conditions, a new *chalgiya* sound which had specific features: characteristic rhythmic and intonational precision, frequent modulations in improvisation sections, and the avoidance of glissandos (typical of Veles, Ohrid, and Bitola *chalgiya* music); some songs included an accordion, which led to a significant change in the sound of the *chalgiya* (Kuzman 2019). Kuzman draws a dividing line between the spontaneous, "non-standard" tavern and wedding *chalgiya* style appreciated in live performance and the recorded "standard" style created on radio, emphasizing that the warmth of sound characteristic of "true" *chalgiya* masters was missing to some extent in the Skopje radio station *chalgiya* (2019:171, 173, 217). As Sonia Seeman remarks, "most Macedonians were aware that *chalgiya* musicians during this period were Romani" (2012:12–13). She emphasizes the fluidity of *chalgiya* tradition and claims that "with the establishment of [the Socialist Federal Republic of] Yugoslavia, state managers consciously exploited the mutability of *chalgiya* and codified stylistic practices in order to represent a more singular Macedonian—and less Ottoman Turkish—ethno national identity" (2012:7).

As Hofman (2010) points out, as the early 1960s unfolded, the organized institutionalization of *kafana* music and its performers started, and in the mid-1960s *zabavna muzika* (entertainment music), also called *estrada*, was the most frequently broadcast genre on all of the republic radio stations in socialist Yugoslavia. Hofman uses "estradization" to describe the ways in which the state created order and organized the institutionalizing of *kafana* music and its performers. The main goal of estradization, she argues, was to establish ordered, rational state control in a domain which operated in an unofficial and illegal manner in this period and furnish the performers with a stable, legally framed, and officially recognized position: "Institutionalization would enable *estrada* workers to gain the dignity enjoyed by other artists, as well as legalization of the music vocation and control of the professional activities, by providing the *estrada* workers regular employment, pensions and health insurance" (Hofman 2010:151–152).

An example of the "cultivation" of *kafana* musicians through organized presentation and controlled production as well as the estradization of Romani music in Macedonia was the artistic career of the celebrated Romani singer Esma Redzhepova. Redzhepova (born in 1943 in Skopje) emerged in the 1960s as an important public persona. Proclaimed the "queen of Gypsy music," she was "perhaps the most famous Romani singer in the world" (Silverman 2012:201). Silverman aptly notes that Esma's renown and success were due in no small part to her mentor and husband Stevo Teodosievski, a Macedonian accordionist who managed her career from the outset and whose astute and varied endeavors to create a specifically Romani niche for Esma in the commercial world proved highly successful (2012:207). To all this can be added that Esma developed a distinctive vocal style and musical idiom which became a strong personal brand. Her emotional voice and notably specific singing style were irreducible to the style of other Romani vocalists from Shuto Orizari (a large, iconic Romani neighborhood in Skopje) due to the fact that her constructed approach was innovative, unusual, and incomparably more complex than that of the local Romani song tradition.[8] It is important to emphasize that Esma, who began as an anonymous singer and became a world-renowned, popular star and Romani singer in the public domain, raised the Romani singing tradition to an unprecedented aesthetic level and changed the global reception of Romani singing.

Silverman points out that as part of the multicultural agenda of Josip Broz Tito[9] during the Yugoslav socialist period, Romani music was made publicly available through recordings as well as radio and television programs in Macedonia; yet the state music industry and institutions were, at the same time, discriminatory to Roma (2012:32). For instance, representatives of the Romani community, including musicians (some of whom were widely popular), were often featured in the media; but Radio Skopje rarely broadcast music identified as Romani. Media representations of Romani music performances become more visible in the late 1980s when, as Silverman notes: "Weekly Romany music and news programs were introduced ... and in 1990 a weekly Romany television show with news and music was introduced" (Silverman 1996:246).

Romani/Gypsy Music in Post-Socialist Bulgaria and North Macedonia

The fall of the Berlin Wall in 1989 unlocked a new phase related to Roma and their music in the transition from socialism to capitalism in Bulgaria and Macedonia. With the change of political systems at the end of 1989 and the cultural transformations that have occurred over the past several decades, Romani musicians are expanding their contacts and travels beyond Bulgaria and Macedonia, bringing Balkan "exoticism" and "authenticity" to the global market—a market mediated by record companies, managers, festivals, and clubs.[10] The cooperation between various Romani musicians and collaborations between Romani and non-Romani musicians have increased and are more diverse in nature since the 1990s. Romani music continues to be performed in a wide variety of traditional settings but has also reached new cultural contexts and naturally serves as a means to express ethnic identity. Moreover, in today's globalized and consumer-oriented society, some Romani musicians turn out to be commercially successful: "[s]ome performers (Kristali, Ćita, Amza) are very well paid; some are not" (Silverman 2012:293) (Fig. 32.4).

Bulgaria

In Bulgaria of the 1990s, Romani musicians actively and creatively responded to new historical circumstances and opportunities to rethink their music and seek pluralistic forms of musical expression. Wedding orchestras were still important players in the music life of the first decade of post-communism. Musicians inherently gravitated toward Gypsy song and dance and composed new songs as well as *kyučetsi*, a solo dance form deeply embedded in the social and musical life of Balkan Romani communities (Peycheva 1995; Silverman 1996:244; Silverman 2012:107).

Likewise in the 1990s, new small instrumental groups (orchestras, bands) were formed, developing diverse musical styles and entering the media and commercial recording industry as active representatives of the Romani community. The structures and mechanisms of cassette culture (Manuel 1993) were established on the Bulgarian market at that time (Peycheva and Dimov 1994a). This was a decade when the record industry in Bulgaria impulsively produced dozens of Gypsy music albums that were eclectic, multilingual, expressive, and provocative, highlighting the varied sensibilities of creating and perceiving Romani music (Peycheva 1995).

FIG. 32.4. XVth International Festival Romfest in Stara Zagora, Bulgaria. Lozanka Peycheva interviews Amza Tairov (keyboard) from North Macedonia.

(Photo by Ventsislav Dimov, 2007.)

In the early 1990s a new commercial phenomenon emerged, called *pop folk*, *chalga*, or *ethnopop*, interpreted as a fusion of pan-Balkan styles with popular Gypsy, Turkish, and wedding music. *Chalga* is clearly among the many musical styles and genres that Roma have contributed to in Bulgaria (Silverman 2012:274). Seeman observes that the *chalga* genre is one of local appropriations of Ottoman sound features (2012:27). And according to Silverman, "The Orient is evoked in *chalga* via symbolic Eastern instrumental styles" (2012:189). There is no fixed instrumentation in Romani *chalga* ensembles. They combine instruments such as clarinets, saxophones, trumpets, electric guitars and basses, synthesizers, drum kits, tarabukas, and sound systems. Indeed, *chalga* performers provide accompaniment to individual singers' repertoires. Some top-selling Romani *chalga* singers seeking collaboration with musicians have used a variety of ensembles to record a commercially produced *chalga* song repertoire. The *chalga* musical idiom has been widely distributed through commercial cassettes, CDs, radio, and television programs (Dimov 2001; Statelova 2003; Silverman 2012:77). Over the years, some Romani vocalists have switched to mainstream *chalga* environments and have acquired star status on the *chalga* stage (such as Sophie Marinova and Azis). At the same time, *chalga* became the focus of heated debate. It should not be surprising that attitudes toward the genre polarized Bulgarian society (Silverman 2012:194). In certain social circles, *chalga* encountered fierce resistance because it was assumed that it was aesthetically banal, tart, kitsch; it disturbed the imaginary "purity" of Bulgarian music and was purportedly a conduit of decline, cynicism, viciousness, pornography, and debauchery (Dimov 2001).

Over time, the music performed by Romani musicians was becoming more varied and very layered. There were different groups of Roma who performed and listened to diverse music that interested them—Romani, Bulgarian folk, Turkish, etc. New developments in the arrangements and composition of Romani music were visible, with an emphasis on blending innovative techniques and diverse styles. Featured in their projects were experimental ensembles and performers who deconstructed the boundaries between styles and, in novel ways, affirmed musical hybridity in new pop and fusion forms: Gypsy rap (Gypsy Aver and Kitka orchestras), Gypsy folk (Gypsy folk orchestra), Gypsy jazz (RomaNeno Project—Gypsy passion and jazz improvisation).

As a part of these developments was Romfest—the National Romani Music and Dance Festival with international participation (1993–2009), held in the town of Stara Zagora (Peycheva and Dimov 1994b; Peycheva 2003; Peycheva and Dimov 2005; Silverman 2012:163–167). This festival has been taken up as policy by festival organizers and Romani activists in Bulgaria, but Romani musicians participating in the festival are generally not politically active. Romfest sought to give visibility to Romani musicians in official public space and was also an arena in which participants experienced exchanges of emotions and enthusiastic excitement in addition to enjoying various ways in which Romani music could be conceived (Figs. 32.5 and 32.6).

Music created by Romani musicians forms part of the sociocultural and political complexity of the post-socialist decades. Compared to the previous period, when the communist regime supported the production of the song genre *nevo gilya*, Romani music is now more hybrid and carries different layers of meaning that go beyond the specific conditions and local contexts from which it emanates (Peycheva 1999:216). It intersects, for example, with elements of different ethnomusics, among which the Balkan and Oriental ones predominate. Furthermore, songwriters are not always Roma; and many of the songs are performed in Bulgarian. Not surprisingly, Romani composer and musician Angelo Malikov criticizes the lack of an authentic Romani song form: "Unfortunately today, the true Romani song is forgotten. . . . No one sings those old Romani songs that touched the sensitive Romani soul" (2005:70). Romani musicians whom I have interviewed over the years have shared that authentic, old Romani music is "slow and sad" (Hasan Chinchiri) and that something "spiritual and true" is embedded in the erstwhile genres (Philip Simeonov-Fekata) (Peycheva 1999:215, 220).

North Macedonia

As a result of the collapse of the Yugoslav project, the former Federal Republic of Macedonia began to construct the apparatus of an independent modern state in 1991.

FIG. 32.5. XIVth International Festival Romfest in Stara Zagora, Bulgaria; young dancers on stage.

(Photo by Lozanka Peycheva, 2006.)

As a newly autonomous state recently renamed North Macedonia, it seeks to strengthen national identity and improve overall conditions for its citizens.

How does Romani music fit into this transformation? In Macedonia today an independent, viable, but somewhat unstable commercial recording industry regularly produces a variety of Romani performers, although fewer than in Bulgaria (Silverman 2012). Various institutionalized events are also organized, such as calendar holidays (e.g., St. George's Day) and contests (e.g., the Roma Vasilitsa Singing Competition), which provide a stage for performances by Romani musicians. The first Macedonian Romani music festival Šutkafest took place in Skopje in 1993 and had great cultural and political importance (Silverman 2012:33, 169–170, 210). Important efforts made to provide media coverage of Romani culture and music and promote their public prestige included, in the 1990s, two private Romani television channels and several Romani radio stations that operated in Macedonia as well as two half-hour specialized weekly broadcasts aired on national television, which apparently made an impression on the public (Silverman 2012:33, 221). The *zurla-tŭpan* tradition in Macedonia remains important for the Romani community because these musical instruments are deemed necessary for particular ritual events: the henna ceremony for the bride, processions in the

FIG. 32.6. XIVth International Festival Romfest in Stara Zagora, Bulgaria; the audience in the summer theater.

(Photo by Lozanka Peycheva, 2006.)

wedding, circumcision ceremonies, etc. (Silverman 1996:247). *Zurla-tŭpan* bands also perform on a variety of different stages in Macedonia. Through their relationship with various cultural industries (record, concert, festival), individual musicians or bands appear in public music venues (Angelov 2020:323–328). Festivals, such as the Golden Zurla—a Romani *zurna* and *tŭpan* festival that took place in Tetovo in 2018—are organized in Macedonia to present the *zurna* music tradition.[11] In addition, Gorancho Angelov provides examples of several newly composed Macedonian songs in which the *zurna* is featured as a leading instrument (2016:219).

In general, in post-communist Macedonia, Romani music-making is active, strong, and lively. Romani musicians in North Macedonia still perform important roles, providing music for the events of everyday life as well as weddings and other in-group festivities of various communities. Moreover, demonstrating their innovative strategies to adapt to recent historical and cultural circumstances, they continue to perform a variety of diverse styles: local forms of *chalgiya*, Romani-style brass band performances, local traditional folk music, and other popular styles of the day. The creative enthusiasm, permanent activities, and flexibility of Romani performers to adapt to new challenges have made these developments possible. In short, there are vibrant old and new genres of Romani music created through combinations of various musical codes, repertoires, styles, and preferred performative techniques that are conditioned by community tastes, sensibilities, and ways that individuals interact in various socio-musical contexts.

Conclusion

The functioning and development of the professional Romani music communities in Bulgaria and Macedonia depend on specific historical forms of political and social relations that have been turning points or starting points for the evolution of various musical styles and genres. Although they are not usually favored by the authorities, Romani musicians manage to adapt to changing conditions, and the music they perform fits in with the spirit of the times in whatever style and genre forms may appear at a particular historical moment.

In Bulgaria and Macedonia, a number of small formations are perpetually associated with Romani music: the *zurna-tŭpan* instrumental ensembles, *chalgiya* groups, *duhovi muziki*, salon orchestras, wedding orchestras, studio groups, and ad hoc bands assembled for the purpose of a specific sound or video recording. Each of these small instrumental or vocal–instrumental ensembles makes music in a broad range of styles and creatively develops many different approaches to performing diverse musical repertoires that respond to various audiences. Although their repertoires are sometimes very wide-ranging, in most cases musicians fulfill what audiences require of them and what they expect will suit their tastes (Vukanović 1962:59).

As interpreters and improvisers, Romani musicians deal creatively with the tension between their own and other ethnic musics. Folk music from Bulgaria and Macedonia remains a powerful generator for Romani music and professional Romani musicians. At the same time, Romani musicians have a specific contribution to the functioning, interpretation, and stylistic transformations in the development of this music, which they model and change in quite uninhibited ways with an emphasis on artistic subjectivity, unique self-expression, and their own individual imprint.

Music-making provides one of the few public arenas for the affirmative articulation of Romani identity. Musicianship has been a viable Romani profession for hundreds of years, and "Gypsy music" is often perceived as a positive romantic stereotype associated with Roma (Silverman 2012:249). Part of the explanation for this is probably related to the mystique of the proverbial "Gypsy music idiom," coupled with the warmth and mastery with which Romani musicians charge their performances. Their intuitive ability to evaluate their clients' emotional moods, filter them through musical language, and respond appropriately with performance is legendary. This creates, for many, energetic moments of intense and spontaneous oneness and togetherness in which the music played by Roma "from their souls" resonates deeply with the experiences of their audiences. Although in most cases Romani musicians—like all Roma—remain marginalized in everyday life, they achieve influence and recognition outside their

FIG. 32.7. Third Symposium of the International Council for Traditional Music Study Group on Music and Dance in Southeastern Europe, 17–23 April 2012, Berovo, Macedonia. Romani musicians play; researchers of Roma and Balkan music and dance. "Bachiyata" area near Berovo.

(Photo by Ventsislav Dimov, 2012.)

own ethnic boundaries through music. They are perceived and appreciated by their fans, both in- and out-group, as mediators who, through the Romani/Gypsy music that they perform, bring a depth of meaning and understanding to the lives of their listeners (Fig. 32.7).

Notes

1. The exonym "Gypsy" is widely known and has circulated for centuries during various historical periods. In recent years the politically correct endonym "Roma," perhaps as a response to post-communist sociopolitical and cultural changes in Bulgaria and Macedonia, became central to public consciousness and is used by authorities, Romani activists, scholars, media, the entertainment industry, and other public producers and consumers of culture. In this chapter, I use "Gypsy" in some cases and in others "Roma" (noun plural) and "Romani" (adjective). This chapter focuses on various historical moments and how Roma (Gypsies) and Romani (Gypsy) music-making have played important roles within the changing contexts of Bulgarian/Macedonian cultures over time. I use "Gypsy" mostly in the early historical sections of the chapter and "Roma/Romani" in the subsequent

sections, especially as usage historically has changed among Bulgarian/Macedonian speakers. Moreover, when I write about Roma more generally, I use "Roma/Romani." And when I translate passages into English, if the author uses "Gypsy" (*tsiganin*, etc.) in another language, I translate it as "Gypsy."
2. North Macedonia has been the name of Vardar Macedonia since 2019; I call it "Macedonia" when I refer to it generally and "North Macedonia" when I refer to it from 2019 on.
3. Most professional Romani musicians are men. But there are also female professionals, especially singers and dancers.
4. Derek Scott writes that orientalist signs are contextual and that there is not *one* orientalist style. Musical orientalism, associated with exoticisms and exotic-sounding music played by Gypsy bands, employs elements such as augmented seconds, ornamented lines, elaborate "ah!" melismas for voice, sliding or sinuous chromaticisms, rapid scale passages, ad libitum sections, irregular rhythms, and other orientalist stereotypes as markers of cultural difference. Scott emphasizes that "The augmented second was increasingly used to connote 'Gypsy'" ([1998] 2016:140).
5. Songs by Hasan Chinchiri, produced by the state record company Balkanton, include "Cherniyat muzikant" ("The Black Musician"; https://www.youtube.com/watch?v=ryuApoRxEFI), "Sviri, Sali" ("Bashal, Sali" ["Play, Sali"]; https://www.youtube.com/watch?v=yPzSDLHTaMI), and "Tsvetentse" ("Flower"; https://www.youtube.com/watch?v=LWToLT20ZvA).
6. The first part of this video features Hasan Chinchiri conducting his orchestra; in the second part, Chinchiri plays the violin: https://www.youtube.com/watch?v=boUb3jzQ6Fo.
7. This video features Angelo Malikov on the cimbalom: https://www.youtube.com/watch?v=ITyWDq2Pjj8.
8. Esma Redzhepova's best-known song was "Chaje Shukarije" ("Beautiful Girl"): https://www.youtube.com/watch?v=UcEJzOHH1mw. See also "Romano Horo": https://www.youtube.com/watch?v=fP9FYpp6p6s.
9. Tito was the leader of the Socialist Federal Republic of Yugoslavia from 1944 to his death in 1980.
10. Yet, as Silverman observes, in this process these institutions and sites are controlled by non-Roma (2012:244–252, 293).
11. See https://www.youtube.com/watch?v=7hfBThA19g8.

Works Cited

Angelov, Goranco. 2016. "Traditional Musical Instruments Used in Strengthening the National Identity of the Macedonian People since 1989." In *Music and Dance in Southeastern Europe: Myth, Ritual, Post-1989, Audiovisual Ethnographies*. Fifth Symposium of the International Council for Traditional Music Study Group on Music and Dance in Southeastern Europe 2016, eds. Ivanka Vlaeva, Lozanka Peycheva, and Ventsislav Dimov, 215–221. Blagoevgrad: University Publishing House "Neofit Rilski."

Angelov, Gorancho. 2020. "Zurladzhiskata traditsiya vo Republika Makedoniya." PhD dissertation, Institute of Ethnology and Folklore Studies with Ethnographic Museum, Bulgarian Academy of Sciences, Sofia.

Balareva, Agapiya. 1967. "Salonni orkestri." In *Entsiklopediya na Bŭlgarskata muzikalna kultura*, eds. Venelin Krŭstev, et al., 114–115. Sofia: BAN.

Buchanan, Donna A. 1996. "Wedding Musicians, Political Transition, and National Consciousness in Bulgaria." In *Retuning Culture: Musical Changes in Central and Eastern Europe*, ed. Mark Slobin, 200–230. Durham, NC: Duke University Press.

Buchanan, Donna. 2006. *Performing Democracy: Bulgarian Music and Musicians in Transition*. Chicago: University of Chicago Press.

Daskalov, Roumen. 2004. *The Making of a Nation in the Balkans: Historiography of the Bulgarian Revival*. Budapest: Central European University Press.

Dimov, Ventsislav. 2001. *Etnopopbumŭt*. Sofia: Zvezdan.

Dimov, Ventsislav. 2007. "Tsigani/Romi v Bŭlgarskata muzikalna industriya." In *Integraciyata na romite v bŭlgarskoto obshtestvo*, eds. Velina Topalova and Alexey Pamporov, 183–201. Sofia: Institut po sociologiya pri BAN.

Dimov, Ventsislav. 2019. *Muzikata za naroda na mediyniya front: Mekata vlast na narodnata i populyarna muzika v socialisticheska Bŭlgaria*. Sofia: Universitetsko izdatelstvo "Sv. Kliment Ohridski."

Dimov, Ventsislav. 2020. "Etnopop muzika i vlast na Balkanite (kak edna hibridna muzika stava meka sila v kulturnite voyni: mediyno-antropologichni prochiti)." In *Mekata vlast na populyarnata muzika v mediite (po primeri ot Bŭlgariya i Balkanite)*, ed. Lozanka Peycheva, 12–63. Sofia: Universitetsko izdatelstvo "Sv. Kliment Ohridski."

Dumnić-Vilotijević, Maria. 2019. *Zvuci nostalgije: Istorija starogradske muzike u Srbiji*. Belgrade: Chigoja shtampa.

Džimrevski, Borivoje. 1985. *Čalgiskata tradicija vo Makedonija*. Skopje: Makedonska Kniga.

Gerov, Nayden. 1976. *Rechnik na Bŭlgarskiya ezik*. Fototipno izdanie. Chast vtora E–K. Sofia: Bŭlgarski pisatel. First published 1897.

Hofman, Ana. 2010. "Kafana Singers: Popular Music, Gender and Subjectivity in the Cultural Space of Socialist Yugoslavia." *Narodna umjetnost*, 47/1:141–161. https://www.academia.edu/246139/KAFANA_SINGERS_POPULAR_MUSIC_GENDER_AND_SUBJECTIVITY_IN_THE_CULTURAL_SPACE_OF_SOCIALIST_YUGOSLAVIA. Accessed September 7, 2021.

Katsarova, Raina. 1938. "Chŭrtici ot muzikalniya givot na Koprivstitsa predi Osvobogdenieto." In *Yubileen sbornik Koprivshtitsa*, Tom 2, 378–423. Sofia: Pechatnitsa "Hudognik."

Kolev, Gospodin. 2010. *Bŭlgarskata komunisticheska partiya i ciganite prez perioda 1944–1989*. Sofia: Centŭr za publichni politiki.

Kuzman, Alexandra. 2019. "*Čalgiskata* muzika kako izraz na makedonskata graganska kultura i identitet." PhD dissertation, Universitet "Sv. Kiril i Metodij," Institut za makedonska literatura, Skopje.

Malikov, Angelo. 2005. "Romskata muzika i pesen—Sredstvo za samoidentifikaciya i edinenie na etnosa." In *Muzika, Romi, Medii*, eds. Lozanka Peycheva and Ventsislav Dimov, 69–71. Sofia: Zvezdan.

Manojlović, Kosta P. 1926. "Svadbeni obichaji u Galichniku." *Glasnik Etnografskog muzeja u Beogradu*, 1:84–93.

Manuel, Peter. 1993. *Cassette Culture: Popular Music and Technology in North India*. Chicago: University of Chicago Press.

Marushiakova, Elena, and Vesselin Popov. 1993. *Ciganite v Bŭlgaria*. Sofia: Club '90.

Marushiakova, Elena, and Vesselin Popov. 2000. *Ciganite v Osmanskata imperiya*. Sofia: Izdatelska kŭshta "Litavra."

Peycheva, Lozanka. 1995. "Muzikalniyat polilingvizŭm na tsiganite v Bŭlgaria (nablyudeniya vŭrhu 84 audiokaseti)." *Bŭlgarski Folklor*, 21/6:58–72.

Peycheva, Lozanka. 1999. *Dushata plache, pesen izliza*. Sofia: TerArt.

Peycheva, Lozanka. 2003. "Romfest—konstruirane na identichnost chrez muzika (vŭrhu Romski gledni tochki kŭm edin romski muzikalen festival)." *Bŭlgarsko Muzikoznanie*, 27/4:161–173.

Peycheva, Lozanka. 2008. *Mezhdu seloto i vselenata: starata folklorna muzika ot Bŭlgaria v novite vremena*. Sofia: Akademichno Izdatelstvo "Prof. Marin Drinov."

Peycheva, Lozanka. 2011. "Romska muzikalna kultura na Balkanite: Muzika i muzikanti, instrumenti i formacii, lica i obrazi." *Naselenie*, 29/3–4:209–235.

Peycheva, Lozanka, and Ventsislav Dimov. 1994a. "Demokasetite: za edin neizsledvan fact ot Sofiyskiya muzikalen pazar." *Bŭlgarski Folklor*, 20/4:25–34.

Peycheva, Lozanka, and Ventsislav Dimov. 1994b. "Vtori festival na romskata muzika i pesen." *Bŭlgarski Folklor*, 20/5:125–127.

Peycheva, Lozanka, and Ventsislav Dimov. 2002. *Zurnadzhiiskata Traditsiya v Yugozapadna Bŭlgaria/The Zurna Tradition in Southwestern Bulgaria*. Sofia: Bŭlgarsko Muzikoznanie Izsledvaniya.

Peycheva, Lozanka, and Ventsislav Dimov. 2004. "The Gypsy Music and Musicians' Market in Bulgaria." In: *Mitteilungen des SFB "Differenz und integration" 6: Segmentation und komplementaritat*, 14:189–206. Halle/Saale: Orientwissenschaftliches Zentrum.

Peycheva, Lozanka, and Ventsislav Dimov. 2005. *Muzika, Romi, Medii*. Sofia: Zvezdan.

Rice, Timothy. 1982. "The Surla and Tapan Tradition in Yugoslav Macedonia." *Galpin Society Journal* 35:122–137.

Rice, Timothy. 1996. "The Dialectic of Economics and Aesthetics in Bulgarian Music." In *Retuning Culture: Musical Changes in Central and Eastern Europe*, ed. Mark Slobin, 176–253. Durham, NC: Duke University Press.

Roudometof, Victor. 2002. *Collective Memory, National Identity, and Ethnic Conflict: Greece, Bulgaria, and the Macedonian Question*. Westport, CT: Praeger.

Scott, Derek B. 2016. "Orientalism and Musical Style." Chapter 8. In *Musical Style and Social Meaning: Selected Essays*, 137–163. London–New York: Routledge. https://www.researchgate.net/publication/292514680_Orientalism_and_musical_style. Accessed March 10, 2022. First published 1998.

Seeman, Sonia Tamar. 2012. "Macedonian Čalgija: A Musical Refashioning of National Identity." *Ethnomusicology Forum*, 21/3:1–32. https://www.researchgate.net/publication/260098314_Macedonian_Calgija_A_Musical_Refashioning_of_National_Identity. Accessed March 10, 2022.

Silverman, Carol. 1996. "Music and Marginality: Roma (Gypsies) of Bulgaria and Macedonia." In *Retuning Culture: Musical Changes in Central and Eastern Europe*, ed. Mark Slobin, 231–253. Durham, NC: Duke University Press.

Silverman, Carol. 2012. *Romani Routes: Cultural Politics & Balkan Music in Diaspora*. New York: Oxford University Press.

Statelova, Rosemary. 2003. *Sedemte gryaha na chalgata: Kŭm edna antropologiya na etnopop muzikata*. Sofia: Prosveta.

Vukanović, Tatomir. 1962. "Musical Culture among the Gypsies of Yugoslavia." *Journal of the Gypsy Lore Society*, Series 3, 41:41–61.

Vŭlchinova-Chendova, Elisaveta. 2000. *Gradskata tradicionna instrumentalna praktika i orkestrovata kultura v Bŭlgaria (sredata na XIX–kraya na XX vek)*. Sofia: Poni.

Ziroevich, Olga. 1981. "Romi na podrucju danashne Yugoslavie u vreme turske vladavine." *Glasnik Etnografskog muzeja u Beogradu*, 45:225–245. https://books.google.bg/books?id=yuF4BgAAQBAJ&pg=PA235&lpg=PA235&dq=%D0%BC%D0%B5%D1%85%D1%82%D0%B5%D1%80%D0%B8&source=bl&ots=VtKovuOzJ5&sig=ACfU3UobSk4g-g31shdC3gjDCdGp_5Ayeg&hl=bg&sa=X&ved=2ahUKEwiK2faFlY72AhUrR_EDHQMmCPUQ6AF6BAgKEAM#v=onepage&q=%D0%BC%D0%B5%D1%85%D1%82%D0%B5%D1%80%D0%B8&f=false. Accessed February 20, 2022.

CHAPTER 33

THE MUSIC OF URBAN *LĂUTARI* IN SOUTHERN ROMANIA

SPERANȚA RĂDULESCU AND
MARGARET HIEBERT BEISSINGER

ROMANI musicians in the historic Romanian Principalities, the southern and northeastern regions of what is now Romania, have long played a central role in traditional music-making for both Romanian and Romani communities. Known as *lăutari* (sg. *lăutar*), male Romani traditional professional musicians—both rural and urban—have been part of the Romanian cultural and social landscape for centuries. *Lăutari* learn and transmit their art through the male kin line within the family. Starting at an early age, boys acquire their skills "by ear" from *lăutar* fathers and other older male relatives in an oral traditional process that most *lăutari*, to this day, perpetuate. For generations *lăutari* in southern Romania have virtually monopolized traditional music-making at life-cycle and other family and festive gatherings for both out-group and in-group events.

As part of their unique history in Romania, *lăutari*, along with most other local Roma, were enslaved for centuries by the Romanian princes and ruling elite as well as the boyars and clergy (Achim 1998).[1] The bondage endured by Roma, which began soon after they migrated into the Balkans and settled in the Romanian Principalities during the fourteenth century, was extensive, lasting until the mid-nineteenth century (Parvulescu and Boatcă 2022:70). Romani slaves provided the labor for elite Romanian society, from working in the fields to making music in the courts, estates, and monasteries. Based in large part on the service roles that Roma assumed during the many years of slavery, they have traditionally been classified into subgroups (*neamuri*) that were rooted in long-established occupational identities. These included bear trainers, coppersmiths, goldsmiths, tinkers, and spoonmakers, among many others; musicians were called *lăutari*. Up until the mid-nineteenth century, the boyars whose households included court ensembles typically used the slave *lăutari* whom they owned, but they sometimes also engaged others, such as the "prince's slaves" from the city or, at times, musicians of other ethnicities. Even before their official release from bondage, some *lăutari* could ply their trade freely, provided they paid taxes to the ruler. In fact, some of them were organized as early as the eighteenth century in guilds led by a *staroste* (Bobulescu 1922:141–147).

During the first half of the nineteenth century, urban *lăutari* performed a variety of instrumental and vocal-instrumental music genres for their "masters" and attending families and guests. These included "worldly" or "blue heart songs" in Romanian or Neo-Greek (Moisil 2020; Gheorghiță 2020a), Romanian village and city dance music, and fashionable salon pieces such as mazurkas, cracoviennes, polonaises, ecossaises, marches, romances, and serenades that young boyars composed and then hired musicians to perform on their behalf under the windows of the women whom they wooed.[2] Melodic formulas and "oriental" melisma—perpetuated since at least the time of Phanariot rule (1711–1821)[3] and perhaps even in previous centuries—adorned most of their songs (Garfias 1981; Filimon [1863] 2017).

Urban *lăutari* also performed light classical music in versions that they picked up by ear from the small ensembles of "German music"[4] that had long been subsidized by the ruling elite and boyars (Moisil 2020). Starting around 1830, they sometimes would hear military bands as well that performed dance music, popular songs, marches, waltzes, overtures, and opera passages for city dwellers (Gheorghiță 2020b). Thus, *lăutari* became acquainted with Western-style tonality and tonal harmonization, which they later adopted in the music of their own repertoires.[5] When ordinary people hired *lăutari* to entertain at inns, fairs, or family celebrations, the musicians performed Romanian folk songs and dances, ballads, epic songs, and/or various genres of other ethnic groups.

The abolition of slavery in the Romanian Principalities (Moldova in the northeast and Wallachia in the south) took place in 1855 and 1856, respectively; full emancipation was finalized in 1864 (Crowe 2007:xii). In the aftermath of emancipation during the second half of the nineteenth century, many *lăutari* still resided near monasteries and boyar courts where they had been enslaved—in villages as well as cities (Achim 1998:79). Their livelihood became, at that time, providing "musical services" to the villagers and townspeople at weddings, baptism parties, and other family events (Rădulescu 2017a:510).

In the meantime, urban *lăutari* in the second half of the nineteenth century represented a strong, growing community. They maintained ties with one another, cemented by kinship and neighborhood as well as by professional collaboration. Moreover, due to the importance of Romani musicians earning their income through performances for local non-Roma, the social contacts between them and urban dwellers (Romanians and other ethnicities) were substantial and evidently cordial. Of all the Romani subgroups in Romania, *lăutari*, especially in the cities, were among the most "assimilated." Many lost much or most of their proficiency in the Romani language over the course of the nineteenth century.

The story that unfolds in the pages ahead begins in the eventful second half of the nineteenth century when Romania was comprised of the principalities of Wallachia and Moldova along with part of the historic region of Dobrogea. In 1859 the union of

Wallachia and Moldova took place. The united principalities were renamed Romania in 1866. Romanian independence from Ottoman rule was recognized in 1878, and in 1881 the Kingdom of Romania was established (Michelson 2000). By the end of the century, the entire population included almost 6 million inhabitants. According to the census of December 1899, 92.2 percent of them were Romanians, 4.3 percent were Jews, and 3.5 percent were "others," including various small ethnic groups.[6] Roma were not censused at that time (and clearly not recognized as a distinct racial group) but were officially considered Romanian. Nonetheless, it is likely that they accounted then for between 7 and 7.5 percent of the total population of the country (Achim 1998:83).[7]

This chapter focuses on two urban Romani genres, *arii naționale* (national arias) and *muzica lăutărească* (*lăutar* music). Both were, for the most part, created and perpetuated by male *lăutari* during the late nineteenth and early-to-mid-twentieth centuries, respectively, and performed in the cities of Wallachia (such as Bucharest and Craiova) and, to a certain degree, Moldova (such as Iași). Furthermore, each of the genres resonated in distinctive settings. *Arii naționale* gained renown not only in the urban centers of the Romanian Principalities but eventually also in late nineteenth-century western Europe. By contrast, *muzica lăutărească* was (and still is for many) a beloved genre heard primarily in more intimate urban surroundings, especially among Roma and later among Romanians as well. These two distinctly different genres, both produced and performed by urban Romani musicians, virtually all men, reflect the adaptability of *lăutari* as musicians and the range of their performance expertise. *Lăutari* proverbially pride themselves on their exquisite talent and skills as well as being innately able to read their audiences, determining which music they wish to hear and performing virtually "any" music requested.

Nineteenth-Century Urban Music in Romania

Music provided rich and diverse forms of popular culture in the nineteenth-century cities of the Phanariot-ruled Romanian Principalities. It was promoted to a great extent by Romani musicians. A number of prominent cultural figures documented it. The earliest account was furnished by the musician (church singer) and writer Anton Pann (1790–1854), an Ottoman subject who published *Spitalul amorului sau Cîntătorul dorului* (*The Hospital of Love or the Singer of Longing*) in 1830. It was an informative miscellanea of pieces from the nineteenth-century cities of Wallachia and included some rural folk songs and many urban songs that appear to be early *manele*,[8] as well as other Phanariot "worldly songs," romances, and unclassifiable songs with verses not in the traditional Romanian octosyllabic meter. All of them are written in Pann's church musical notation (Pann [1830] 2009). Another was by the well-known politician-scholar Mihail Kogălniceanu (1817–1891), who wrote "Esquisse sur l'histoire, les moeurs et la langue des

Cigains connus en France sous le nom de Bohémiens" ("Sketch of the History, Mores, and Language of the Cigains [Gypsies], known in France as Bohemians") (published in Berlin in 1837).[9] The author Nicolae Filimon (1819–1865) also wrote about Romani musicians and was the first to devote an article worthy of attention to them ([1863] 2017). In it he observes and comments on the "orientalization" of the music performed by *lăutari*, which, in his opinion, had begun in the eighteenth century during the Phanariot period. He maintained that the music was "collected from the musicians of the Greek rulers and from the excursions they incessantly made around the big cities of the Orient" (Filimon [1863] 2017).

The "orientalized" music survived long after the end of the Phanariot period and the restoration of local rulers (which took place in 1822). As Walter Zev Feldman remarks, it may even be that the landscape of folk music in the nineteenth-century Romanian cities, towns, and villages was dominated by Greek Phanariot and post-Phanariot music.[10] He notes that "[b]y post-Phanariot music, I understand a Balkan fusion music with a Greek–Turkish dominant feature, which existed in the Romanian Principalities of Wallachia and Moldavia especially in the cities, during the Phanariot rule" (Feldman 2016:27)—in other words, "the augmented second between the third and fourth degrees of the minor mode" (Rădulescu 2017b:182n1), evident throughout nineteenth-century melodies published by numerous musicians such as Anton Pann and Dimitrie Vulpian (1848–1922). As Rădulescu points out, "[t]his second must have been very common in the urban and rural pieces of the time" (2017b:182n1). Vulpian, whose music publications bore the ubiquitous and distinctive "augmented second," issued two important (and hefty) volumes of *Horele noastre* (*Our Horas*[11]) that he had "collected and arranged for piano"; each contained five hundred melodies (Vulpian 1908). In the meantime, many other musicians were beginning to publish notations of folk songs (usually dance tunes) on broadsheets. They were minimally harmonized and labeled "national," a tag that was beginning to be applied to almost every institution and product, including *arii naționale*, which we turn to now.

ARII NAȚIONALE: A NEW URBAN MUSIC FOR ROMANIA

The term *arie națională* (pl. *arii naționale*) refers to a popular instrumental genre that arose in the second half of the nineteenth century (Rădulescu 2017b:182). It was performed by urban *lăutari* in a *taraf* (pl. *tarafuri*), a small ensemble composed of traditional instruments.[12] *Arii naționale* were either dance melodies or songs without words—newly created or re-created by *lăutari* in performance and based on traditional urban or rural music. Sometimes embellished with passages of concert virtuosity, *arii naționale* were characterized by tonal harmonies and "European-style" orchestrations. They broke, in a sense, from the Balkan character of the post-Phanariot music of the day and provided a means for *lăutari* and the nineteenth-century urban world to connect with west European trends.

Arii naționale appeared at the height of the nationalist era in central and southeastern Europe, spanning several decades from the second half of the nineteenth century to the first decades of the twentieth. It was a time when the peoples of eastern Europe—Poles, Czechs, Slovaks, Romanians, Croats, Serbs, and so on—were increasingly determined to construct nations in which they were no longer second-class citizens of one or another of the empires that subjugated them: Russian, Austro-Hungarian, or Ottoman. The nationalist ideology and political project derived from this were elaborated and put into circulation by the bourgeoisie and intelligentsia educated in Western universities. In Romania, this ideology was embraced over several decades even by ordinary people living in cities as well as in some villages. Among the educated, it stimulated intellectual discourse. Among many others, however, it encouraged and generated a desire to express their aspirations in cultural terms for the construction of a national state: a Romanian nation. In other words, Romanians sought "specific, unifying sound symbols accessible to all: boyars, bourgeois and intellectuals educated in the West, as well as ordinary citizens" (Radulescu 2017b:182).

As a new music performed by *lăutari* that emerged spontaneously in the urban centers, *arii naționale* served to build an accessible popular culture and instill solidarity. They targeted the burgeoning middle class and the common people in the cities of the Romanian Principalities, soon to be christened Romania, and eventually in the villages. Adopted in the repertoires of both urban and rural *lăutari*, this music contributed to the fortification of the nation through distinct Romanian, but also European, cultural emblems that resonated powerfully in the Romanian political context of the 1860s through the 1930s. Having gained its independence from centuries-long Ottoman suzerainty and almost immediately becoming a kingdom, nationalist aspirations were fervently embraced, and *arii naționale* became meaningful expressions of them.[13]

By 1900 *arii naționale* had become popular in most regions of Romania. "România, România" ("Romania, Romania") "Hora mărțișorului" ("The Mărțișor[14] Hora"), "Hora națională" ("The National Hora"), "Am un leu și vreau să-l beau" ("I've Got a Penny, and I Want to Drink It Up"), "Ceasornicul" ("The Clock") "Sârba lui Pompieru" ("Pompieru's Sârbă"[15]), and "Căruța poștei" ("The Post Wagon") were representative of the genre. "Hora Staccato," an *arie națională* that became a famous, perennial recital piece, was composed in 1906 by Grigoraș Dinicu (1889–1949), a celebrated, virtuosic urban *lăutar* violinist from a long family of Bucharest Romani musicians (Fig. 33.1; see Cosma 1996a:185–228).[16]

Arii naționale acquired their European character primarily through their firm absorption of tonality and tonal harmonization but also through their equal and symmetrical melodic phrases, grouped into distinct sections in moderate contrast.[17] Most of the *arii naționale* were accompanied by a traditional dance rhythm, that of the hora (in 2/4 meter) or sârbă (2/4 in compound time: 3/8 + 3/8), produced by the *lăutar* instruments *cobză* (kobza—a stringed, lute-like instrument) or *țambal* (cimbalom). However, the

FIG. 33.1. Grigoraș Dinicu, *lăutar* violinist
(credit: https://en.wikipedia.org/wiki/Grigora%C8%99_Dinicu#/media/File:Grigoras_Dinicu_02.jpg; accessed March 12, 2024).

pace of each dance varied considerably since both, especially the hora, in principle allow for either slower or more dynamic tempos.

Arii Naționale Showcased in Europe

Following Romania's new political status (independence from the Ottoman Empire in 1878 and, three years later, its elevated standing as a kingdom), its diplomatic contacts with western Europe and beyond multiplied. Due to this the authorities within the monarchy sensed the need, on a cultural level, to represent Romania music-wise not only through local genres but also through a more European-sounding music, especially in official political contexts. As in the past, various diplomatic events continued to take place with music produced by urban Romani musicians—*lăutari*.[18] Yet Romanians recognized the necessity for music that also reflected somewhat of a more "Western" sound, particularly for public occasions. Indeed, the World's Fairs held in Paris in 1889 and 1900, at which Romania took part, represented precisely such an imperative. And, as it turned out, the best-known *lăutari* of Bucharest were the musicians who were solicited for this international stage, and it was they who famously delivered.

The general delegates to the two World's Fairs in Paris, local politicians and elite intellectuals, chose the most famous urban *lăutari* to journey across Europe to represent Romania at its own pavilion (see Parvulescu and Boatcă 2022:69). But as they prepared for the 1889 World's Fair in Paris, the Romanian delegates soon realized that they would be confronted there with an unusual clientele: foreign, unfamiliar audiences. Moreover, it is unclear whether anyone was occupied with which repertoire the *lăutari* should perform at the Romanian pavilion. In the end, it was most likely the Romani musicians themselves who proposed or made a first selection of the music that would represent Romania. It was they who had to find a solution that would satisfy the international public yet also simultaneously express themselves. And, in fact, they did: they promoted *arii naţionale*, a distinctive new genre that was unlike European music but at the same time compatible with it. For this occasion, the *lăutari* composed pieces such as "Sârba expoziţiei" ("Exhibition [World's Fair] Sârbă"), "Marşul naţional" ("National March"), "Hora de concert" ("Concert Hora"), and "Ciocârlia" ("The Skylark") (Cosma 1996a:103–105).

The *lăutari* and their music turned out to be a sensation at the World's Fairs in Paris. At the 1889 exposition, the *lăutar taraf* headed by violinist Ionică Dinicu (1854–1929)[19] performed to great acclaim at the Romanian Pavilion (Fig. 33.2). Due to both their "Gypsy" identity and the novelty of their repertoire, they became a curiosity there and were warmly received by the French and international public. Indeed, the success of the *lăutari* and their music, abundantly reflected in the press of the time, boosted their personal careers (see Bibesco 1890).

"Gypsy" musicians from Hungary also performed at the 1889 World's Fair. But, as Annegret Fauser notes, the acclaim derived by the Hungarian Romani musicians there was "tempered by the even more exotic and more 'authentic' gypsy music from Romania" (2005:257).[20] At the same time, although the performances on the part of the *lăutari* delighted countless spectators at the World's Fairs in Paris, some disgruntled Romanian intellectuals apparently were not particularly thrilled that their country was exhibited—and celebrated—through an exotic and orientalist lens (Minea 2021). There was likely some amount of racism on their part as well given the choice of *lăutari* as opposed to Romanian peasants to represent the country in Paris.

Once back in Romania after the World's Fair, the *lăutar* "stars" performed the new *arii naţionale* for their fellow city dwellers. As a result, their less-traveled local *lăutar* confrères easily picked up the music by ear and proceeded to play it in cities, towns, and even some villages, promoting the genre throughout Romania. Appearing at both the 1889 and 1900 World's Fairs, the Bucharest *lăutar* violinist Sava Pădureanu (1848–1918) became an international celebrity and subsequently performed widely—such as in Britain, Russia, and Monte Carlo (Fig. 33.3). In 1908 he was invited with his *taraf* to take part in a concert alongside Eugène Ysaÿe at the Palais des Beaux Arts in Paris (see Cosma 1996a:103–116). Around the same time, fellow Romani musicians were likewise hired to entertain visitors at summer spa resorts across Europe (Cosma 1996a).

FIG. 33.2. *Lăutar taraf* (ensemble) of Ionică Dinicu, *lăutar* violinist and leader of the *taraf*; Romanian Pavilion at the 1889 Paris World's Fair
(credit: https://ro.wikipedia.org/wiki/Anghelu%C8%99_Dinicu#/media/Fi%C8%99ier:P._Nadar_-_Exposition_universelle_de_Paris._Section_roumaine_-_Bande_de_Dinicu.jpg; accessed March 12, 2024).

The lasting success of *arii naționale* was also due in part to the inclusion of some of them in George Enescu's best-known compositions, his two "Romanian Rhapsodies" (Op. 11) for orchestra. Performed for the first time in 1903, the "Romanian Rhapsodies" were extremely popular and widely disseminated, especially after the establishment in 1920 of the first radio station in Romania. Moreover, the middle class, eager for national affirmation, adored *arii naționale*. At the Romanian Athenaeum (Romania's "temple" of art music and most iconic concert hall, located in Bucharest), the audiences of the interwar period often requested encores, crying *Naționale, naționale!* ("National arias, national arias!") (Pârvulescu 2003).

Arii naționale continued to be performed throughout the first decades of the twentieth century and, to some extent, after the Second World War. And although their popular base was within the perimeters of the "Old Kingdom" (the historic principalities of Wallachia and Moldova), the genre also made its way into certain city restaurants in Transylvania and Banat, two regions that formed part of the Austro-Hungarian Empire until 1918. It may be that the inhabitants of these areas were more familiar with central

FIG. 33.3. Sava Pădureanu, *lăutar* violinist
(credit: https://ro.wikipedia.org/wiki/Fi%C8%99ier:Sava_Padureanu.jpg; accessed March 12, 2024).

European music, whose imprint was evident in the music performed by local musicians there, including *lăutari*.

Moreover, while most of the *lăutari* in Romania have been Roma, *klezmorim* (Jewish musicians) and *lăutari* at times intersected and cooperated in music-making, especially before the Second World War in Moldova. The *klezmorim* performed *arii naționale* at parties for Romanians but also at their own gatherings. At the time of their massive emigration to Israel in the 1950s through the 1970s, many Jews left Romania with the sounds of this music in their ears and fingers. Indeed, for a long time, *arii naționale* remained a well-liked genre of the *klezmorim* repertoire, as attested by peasants and villagers from Botoșani County in northeastern Moldova.[21] Even in the early 2000s, in the cities of the far northeast of Romania, there were *lăutari* who asserted that their elderly customers still requested *arii naționale* at parties. Indeed, in relatively recent interviews, a few *lăutari* from this region claimed that *arii naționale* represented music not only for Romanians but for "everyone."

Although no longer occupying a central role in local popular music, *arii naționale* from the end of the nineteenth and the beginning of the twentieth centuries continue to circulate in Romania. They appeal to a somewhat limited public but are still performed in a number of select venues. These include restaurants frequented by tourists (there is no *lăutar* violinist, nor even "folk" fiddler, who does not have in his repertoire "Ciocârlia," which he may bring out especially when facing a "cultured" foreign audience). *Arii naționale* are also heard at receptions as well as upscale clubs and other dining establishments, where they are performed as café-concert music that blends into a discreet, "refined" sonic background. As a genre that was established and performed by urban *lăutari*, *arii naționale* remain a part of the diverse repertoire that Romani musicians have shared over the years with "all of Romania": Roma, Romanians, Hungarians, Jews, and various other communities that have been delighted and entertained by the genre.

Muzica Lăutărească as Urban Song and Dance for Roma

Muzica lăutărească (*lăutar* music), a distinctive style and form of song and dance music performed by urban *lăutari* originally for other *lăutari* and their families, started to emerge in urban environments in the south (and, to some extent, the east) of Romania during the first several decades of the twentieth century, possibly even earlier. However, there is little clear evidence in this regard—of either written or audio records—to attest to the early history of the music. The scholars at that time, Romanian folklorists, were instead concerned exclusively with rural music, which they considered relevant for the cultural identity of the majority population—ethnic Romanians.[22]

Muzica lăutărească was initially created and performed as vocal–instrumental or purely instrumental music for urban Romani in-group consumption (Costache 2021:29–30; Beissinger 2024a:52). Although it evolved over time and eventually was embraced by many Romanians as well, it was originally urban music performed within *lăutar* circles at their own parties and social gatherings in the cities of Wallachia and, to a lesser extent, Moldova (Rădulescu 2017a:510). *Muzica lăutărească* did not aim to appeal to an out-group audience as did *arii naționale*, which became a type of "national" genre that "represented" individuals and groups throughout and even beyond Romania.

Nor did *muzica lăutărească* resemble the communist-era mass-produced "folk" music, *muzica populară*, overseen by the political elite in Romania who sought through socialist dogma to artificially "homogenize" the multiethnic inhabitants of Romania into a single harmonious "nation." Instead, *muzica lăutărească* responded at the outset to the small ethnic and socially marginalized subgroup of Romani musicians. It was—at least at the beginning—a party and "table" music (*Tafelmusik*) produced by professional Romani musicians for connoisseurs—themselves and their families. During the wedding banquets of the sons and daughters of *lăutari*, it was and still is, to some extent, customary for some of the guests (themselves musicians) to perform as soloists alongside the *taraf* hired by the groom's father, who traditionally hosts the event. *Muzica lăutărească* includes two genres: lyric songs and dance music.

Lyric Songs

The lyric songs of *muzica lăutărească* are often called *cântece de ascultare* (songs to listen to). They are performed as a vocal genre accompanied by a small instrumental ensemble or *taraf*. The songs make up a somewhat heterogeneous category, which includes pieces from various sources and different historical periods. Regardless of their derivations, however, the songs of *muzica lăutărească* are marked by a distinctively comparable performance style. While on rare occasions the lyrics are performed in Romani or a mixture of Romani and Romanian, they are by far most frequently sung in Romanian. *Lăutari*, who have traditionally performed much of their vocal repertoire in Romanian to Romanian-speaking patrons or customers, manipulate the poetic register of the language with great savvy, imagination, and feeling. In other words, *lăutari* have long been native speakers of Romanian singing to other native speakers—both Romanians and Roma.

Muzica lăutareasca songs were and are typically sung by men. A small number of iconic female singers, however, also represent the tradition, the best-known of whom include Romica Puceanu (1927–1996) and Gabi Luncă (1938–2021).[23] The songs are performed at banquets or gatherings at *cârciumi* (taverns or pubs, sg. *cârciumă*) or restaurants—among a circle of customers or friends and/or family seated close to the musicians or for all of the guests. The *taraf* is normally limited in size: in early ensembles simply a violin and small cimbalom, while later ensembles became somewhat larger, comprised of combinations of violin, small or large cimbalom, accordion, and/or bass viol. The singer, who is sometimes one of the instrumentalists, adopts one of the vocal timbres specific to the genre: a dramatic chest voice, head voice (falsetto), or (more rarely) a conventional operetta voice. What is important to musicians and audiences alike is not so much the native quality of the voice but its expressiveness. The songs are more or less ornate and include varying degrees of melisma, interspersed or sustained throughout with vibrato, in a relatively free rhythm and in a fairly moderate tempo.

No matter how "oriental" the ornaments and melismata or how "Balkan" the scale systems underlying the songs (Garfias 1981),[24] the accompaniments by the musicians are conceived in terms of tonality. The steps of one mode or another are reinterpreted from the perspective of the Western tonal functions determined by the musicians. When the first violinist (*primaș*) wishes to indicate to his accompanists the beginning of a song or a change of harmony, he plays before his bandmates two or three bichords or utters the name of a note: the tonic of the key in which his fellow instrumentalists should begin the accompaniment or the one to which they should modulate. Until about the mid-twentieth century, the *primaș* would indicate the tonalities or "tones" (*tonurile*, sg. *ton*) using A, C, D, G, etc. In the "classical" period of *muzica lăutărească* (the 1950s through the 1980s), the harmonic discourses of the accompaniment were economic on both the vertical and horizontal planes. Their texture was homogeneous and realized by the continuous reiteration of a single formula of harmonic figuration, called a *țiitură* (pl. *țiituri*). There are several such *țiituri* from which the *primaș* chooses, and he imposes on the other musicians the one he considers appropriate for the piece but also for the tempo of his projected execution. These include the figuration *de of* (of woe) in 10/16 (3 + 2 + 3 + 2), the regular "hora" figuration (2/4 with sixteenth-note subdivisions and accents on the second half of each quarter note), and the "rushed *țiitură*" (*țiitura gonită*)—a figuration in binary meter with subdivisions of triplets performed at an accelerated tempo in which the accompanists deliberately avoid accents.[25] Sometimes "incidents" occur in the succession of the tonic, dominant, and subdominant chords: the most frequent consists of attacking a diminished seventh chord with which, through different enharmonic transformations, the *lăutari* modulate to a more distant tonality.

The accompaniment has a relatively autonomous trajectory. Its pulsations are often inconsistent with the unequal pulsations of the melodies. In other words, its rigorously measured and predictable rhythm is superimposed on the rubato of the melodies, a type of "flowing rhythm," as Judit Frigyesi terms it (1993). Robert Garfias remarks on the relation between melody and accompaniment, from which it follows that melodic phrases are not only relatively rhythmically free but also elastic as they swell or shrink at the will of the solo performer and determine the expansion or constriction of the corresponding accompaniment:

> the accompanying ensemble supports the free, lyrical melody with the fixed and regular quadruple pattern of the Rom style hora. Over this the vocal melody seems to float, yet so clear and firm is the rhythmic accompaniment that it is only by listening carefully that one notices that the total number of measures in any phrase is likely to be irregular and that . . . at each return of the melody in any performance, the number of measures required for each phrase may vary greatly. The number of measures during which the accompaniment continues to sustain any particular harmony is determined by how long the singer decides to hold the particular pitch which is being harmonized. (1996:11)

Furthermore, in music performed by *lăutari*, the dynamic register exploited by the musicians is typically wider than in other types of traditional music, such as that performed by Romanian peasants. It can range from a delicate pianissimo to a vigorous fortissimo.

The song lyrics overall speak of deep emotions: pain, love, betrayal, the misery of poverty, harsh imprisonments that involve separation from family and children, and, perhaps most of all, confrontation with the presumed enemy, the proverbial *duşman* (pl. *duşmani*). The enemy, an amorphous, recurrent theme, is a person or perhaps plight that, while undefined, is deeply and powerfully embedded in the verses. It may well be that the "enemy" is a subconscious personification of the discrimination that Roma have been subjected to throughout the ages and up to this day, an affliction that persists. Two immaculate figures in the songs of *muzica lăutărească* are unambiguously articulated however: the mother—a holy icon, whose old age, loneliness, or death is felt with melodramatic acuteness—and one's precious children.

As oral traditional compositions that "belong" to all and are a part of *lăutar* folklore, the songs of *muzica lăutărească* are rendered in countless versions by different, as well as the same, singers. No song is ever sung exactly the same. The poetry of *muzica lăutărească* is loosely stanzaic and sung in a generally trochaic octosyllabic meter,[26] the predominant form of oral traditional Romanian lyric (and narrative) song. It likewise is distinguished by mono-rhyme (two or more verses that are marked by end rhyme or assonance). Introductory formulas, found throughout Romanian oral poetry, customarily signal the beginning of songs or passages within them. They too form part of the lyrics of *muzica lăutărească*. They typically begin with *Foaie verde* ("Green leaf"), followed, in the second half of the line, by plant imagery; and these verses rhyme with the subsequent verse(s) (see the examples below).

In one version of "Mahala şi ţigănie" ("City Slum and Gypsy Ghetto"), a much-loved accordionist and male vocalist from the "golden age" of *muzica lăutărească*, the *lăutar* Florică Roşioru, sings of pain: the struggles and anguish of living in the fabled *mahala* (a slum-like neighborhood on the outskirts of a city or town), just making it through each day:

> Foaie verde iasomie,
> Mahala şi ţigănie,
> Mahala şi ţigănie;
> de când am intrat în tine,
> N-a rămas carne pe mine,
> n-a rămas carne pe mine.
> Puţinică ce-a rămas, *of, of,*
> tot s-a fript şi tot s-a ars.
>
> Dacă stau s-o cântăresc,
> nici o litră nu găsesc;
> Nici o litră, nici un gram,
> că-i mâncată de duşmani.
> Rău ma dor picioarele
> Bătând mahalalele
> Pe la toate mândrele,
> Pe la toate mândrele.

Green leaf of the jasmine,
City slum and Gypsy ghetto,
City slum and Gypsy ghetto,
Ever since I entered you,
There is no meat left on my bones,
There is no meat left on my bones.
The little bit that has remained, *oh, oh*,
Has all been roasted and all been burnt.

If I stop and try to weigh it,
I can't find even a little bit [a quarter of a kilo],
Not a quarter of a kilo, nor even a gram
'Cause it's been eaten up by my enemies.
My feet hurt so badly
As I make the rounds all over the city slums,
To all of my sweethearts,
To all of my sweethearts.

The interjections *of, of* (in italics) in the second-to-last line of the first stanza do not form part of the metrically complete verse itself but are extra-syllabic and index Romani-coded exclamations "of woe." The fourth verse of the second stanza references "enemies" (*duşmani*), the nebulous presence who or which has "eaten up" the strength and will of the singer. His feet that "hurt so badly" vividly express the overall aching and helplessness that he feels.

Another quintessential example of a lyric *muzica lăutărească* song, here rendered by the earliest legendary female singer of the genre, Romica Puceanu, conveys emotions of unhappy love, "De când te iubesc pe tine" ("Ever Since I've Loved You") (Fig. 33.4). The exclamations addressed to the beloved (in italics) are sung at the beginning and/or end of metrically complete verses, spontaneously and expressively underscoring the overall sense of the singer's discontent:

Foaie verde mărgărit,
Fir-ai, neică, afurisit!
Atunci când te-am cunoscuti,
Nu ştiu ce rău ţi-am făcut,
Dragă, Nu ştiu ce rău ţi-am făcut, *nene*.
De când te iubesc pe tine,
Dragă, eu nu mai am zile bune.
Dacă nu te cunoşteam,
Mai fericită eram,
Mai fericită eram, *dragă*.

Foaie verde trei migdale,
Neică, cine mi te-a scos în cale?
Puică, nu mai blestema,
Că nu este vina mea,
Dragă, că nu este vina mea, *dragă*!
De vină-i norocul tău,

Că te-a scos în drumul meu,
Dragă, că te-a scos în drumul meu, dragă.

Green leaf of the lily of the valley,
May you be cursed, beloved!
Back when I first met you,
I don't know how I wronged you,
My dear, I don't know how I wronged you, *beloved*.
Ever since I've loved you,
My dear, I haven't had good days.
If I had never met you,
I'd be happier now,
I'd be happier now, *my dear*.

Green leaf of three almond trees,
Beloved, Who made you cross my path?
Sweetheart, don't curse me anymore,
'Cause it's not my fault,
My dear, 'cause it's not my fault, *my dear*!
It's your luck that's to blame,
'Cause it made you cross my path,
My dear, 'cause it made you cross my path, *my dear*.

FIG. 33.4. Romica Puceanu, Romani vocalist (https://ro.wikipedia.org/wiki/Romica_Puceanu#/media/Fi%C8%99ier:Romica_Puceanu1.jpg; accessed March 12, 2024).

The lyrics of the songs of *muzica lăutărească* offer virtually anyone overwhelmed by troubles, anxiety, or pain, regardless of race, ethnicity, or gender, a reason to identify with them. The songs often elicit unabashedly deep emotional responses, including tears, by listeners and singers alike.

Dance Music

Muzica lăutărească for dancing is dominated by *hore lăutărești* (*lăutar* horas). These are in many ways comparable to the Romanian rural horas of southern Wallachia. But they differ primarily in their specific scale structures, moderate tempo, and style of dance. With regard to scales, there are two main variants: either a major scale with an augmented second between steps II and III or a minor scale with an augmented second between steps III and IV. They correspond to the *hijaz* and *nikriz makams* (melody types of Turkish music), respectively (Garfias 1981:100). The "augmented seconds" that lend the songs a certain "oriental" color also exist, in certain proportions, in other ethnic Romanian traditional rural and urban music. The scales typical of *muzica lăutărească* melodies for dancing are further distinguished by an abundance of micro-intervals almost imperceptible to the ear, which finely color the melodic discourse (micro-intervals that are rarer, but not absent, in the other oral traditional music of ethnic Romanians).

The dances of *muzica lăutărească* also differ through their moderate-tempo hora accompaniment in which the musicians markedly stress the subdivisional beat, that is, the offbeat rhythmic formulas which, in turn, inform and support the Romani dancers in the dynamic virtuosic figures that they perform with their feet and palms. While Romanians typically dance the *hora mare* (large hora) in a circle formation with hands held at shoulder height, Roma traditionally dance the *hora lăutărească* individually, as a solo dance, thus enabling them to execute the distinctive rhythmic foot-stamping, as well as arm and hand movements including clapping and finger-snapping (Beissinger 2005:43). A young *lăutar* violinist from the village of Dobrotești in Teleorman County (southwest of Bucharest) distinguished between the Romanian and "Gypsy"[27] hora in 1998, pointing out that "There's no difference in terms of the instruments; it's a difference of musical style.... For a Romanian hora you play a hundred trills, but for a Gypsy hora you play three hundred! Romanians dance with one stomp [on the floor] per beat, while Gypsies stomp three times per beat!" (Rădulescu 2004:71).

Muzica Lăutărească *as an Emblem of Romani Identity*

As the twentieth century proceeded, *muzica lăutărească* became a type of sonic emblem of Romani identity, a powerful "voice to those silenced by racism and prejudice" (Radano and Bohlman 2000:xiii). It also embraced a cultural symbol that, while gradually becoming more public (that is, appealing to ethnic Romanians), was also profoundly private, a means for Romani musicians from southern Romania to express "their own" racial (or ethnic) and occupational niche (see Beissinger 2001). *Muzica lăutărească* was and is not performed throughout Romania but rather primarily in the southern cities of the country, especially in Wallachia.[28] Indeed, it is such a "niche" form that traditional Romani musicians in Transylvania do not perform it. It is not part of the tradition there, and their customers (Romanians, Hungarians, and other Roma) do not request it at restaurants and parties. In Transylvania, a part of Romania that is culturally quite distinct from the southern, more "Balkan" zone, such as reflected in the music and other ways, Roma perform their "own" ensemble music.

Furthermore, most rural Romani musicians, even in the south, have not mastered *muzica lăutărească* either since they specialize in traditional Romanian music for their rural customers. As a result, they are not usually hired to perform *muzica lăutărească*, although they have immense admiration for it. Thus, when Romani musicians in southern Romanian villages organize a celebratory event (such as a wedding), they typically hire urban *lăutari*, who superbly produce *muzica lăutărească*, so that they can celebrate and dance with style as the festivities take place.

Most Romani musicians in southern Romania consider *muzica lăutărească* the epitome of Romani music and music-making and by far their favorite musical form (Voiculescu 2005:277; Beissinger 2016:130, 138n150): the "most beautiful music in the world!" as Victor Gore (1931–2008), an early performer of the genre who both sang and played the accordion, relayed in an interview (Fig. 33.5).[29] *Muzica lăutărească* is viewed

FIG. 33.5. Victor Gore, *lăutar* accordionist and vocalist

(credit: https://ro.wikipedia.org/wiki/Victor_Gore; accessed March 12, 2024).

as a complex and difficult genre to perform but, above all, a genre that "only *lăutari*" can "genuinely" render. This opinion has repeatedly been expressed by *lăutari* over decades of field experience: Roma are unquestionably "superior musicians," and Romanians "simply cannot perform Romani music" properly, least of all *muzica lăutărească*. *Lăutari* typically maintain that, try as they may, Romanians are not "endowed" with "the gift of music" as are Roma (see Beissinger 2001; Rădulescu 2004).

Muzica Lăutărească: Song and Dance for City Dwellers in Southern Romania

Muzica lăutărească eventually transcended the in-group circles of the *lăutar* communities, which happened surely after World War II, if not earlier. As it spread, it was performed not only for Roma but also progressively for Romanians, especially the common people and middle class, in neighborhood *cârciumi* throughout Bucharest and other southern cities such as Craiova, Slatina, Balş, Piteşti, Târgovişte, Buzău, Giurgiu, Brăila, and Constanţa. It may be that, by the end of the interwar period, *muzica lăutărească*—which at that time had not reached its peak but was about to culminate as a musical form (with distinct characteristics)—might have been adopted as repertoire even in the elite restaurants in the center of Bucharest, along with *arii naţionale*. In short, *muzica lăutărească* became a favorite music of many ethnic Romanians, especially those from the poor city neighborhoods with whom the style and messages of the songs resonated.

In the communist era, *muzica lăutărească* was withdrawn from the central urban restaurants, in all probability because it was not "authentic Romanian folklore." It was still performed, however, here and there in small taverns on the outskirts of cities: this was perhaps one of the reasons it acquired and gradually consolidated its alternative name, *muzica de mahala* ("slum music")[30] (Garfias 1996). From the mid-twentieth century through the 1970s its popularity reached unprecedented heights. This was the "classic" age of its great interpreters, such as the brothers Aurel (Fig. 33.6) (1928–1989) and Victor Gore, Florea Cioacă, Dona Dumitru Siminică, Fărâmiţă Lambru (Fig. 33.7) (1927–1974), Marcel Budală, Ion Onoriu, Vasile Năsturică, and Florică Roşioru, along with the female vocalists Romica Puceanu and Gabi Luncă (see Beissinger 2024b).

Well-known masterpieces of *muzica lăutărească* of that era include songs such as "Pe drumul mănăstiresc" ("On the Monastery Road"), "Mahala şi ţigănie" ("City Slum and Gypsy Ghetto"), "Stinge, Doamne, stelele" ("Snuff Out the Stars, Lord"), "Blestemat să fii de stele" ("May the Stars Curse You"), "Doi tovarăşi am la drum" ("I'm on My Way with Two Comrades"), "Nici nu ninge, nici nu plouă" ("Neither Snow nor Rain"), "Inimă Supărăcioasă" ("Peevish Heart"), "Inel, inel de aur" ("A Ring of Gold"), "La şalul cel

FIG. 33.6. Aurel Gore, *lăutar* violinist
(credit: https://ro.wikipedia.org/wiki/Aurel_Gore; accessed March 12, 2024).

negru" ("The Black Shawl"), "La ciolpan cu frunza lată" ("Old Tree with Broad Leaves"), "De când te iubesc pe tine" ("Ever Since I've Loved You"), and "De ești supărată" ("If You're Angry") (see Vasilescu 2015). Yet only a few recordings produced by Electrecord (the sole record company label during the communist period) and some footage made by Romanian television (broadcast exclusively on New Year's Eve in 1973 and 1975 when the communist government made a few ideological concessions) have been preserved. Otherwise, *muzica lăutărească* was excluded from radio broadcasting. In the 1980s, however, Electrecord obtained the rights to produce a few *muzica lăutărească* records every year (in addition to the more than one hundred annually issued "authentic folklore" records). Apparently, this exception was only made to enable the record company to survive financially. *Muzica lăutărească* records sold far better than "authentic folklore" albums, despite the fact that "folklore music" was intensely promoted by the national-communist state. These were the "classic" years of *muzica lăutărească*, when it was still one of the most popular urban song genres in the cities (see Vasilescu 2015).

Since the 1980s, *muzica lăutărească* has undergone significant changes. The orchestral apparatus expanded and diversified, adding the large cimbalom. As a consequence, the harmonic density and the number of distinct chords used in the accompaniment increased. Moreover, the medium and low registers began to exceed the high ones in intensity. Thus, the sound center of gravity of the music descended, and the sonic discourse became ponderous. The melodies were kept more or less in the same stylistic register but lost some of their expressiveness. Even the distinctive vocal timbres, including falsetto, gradually faded away, becoming a characteristic of the past.

FIG. 33.7. Fărâmiță Lambru, *lăutar* accordionist and vocalist
(credit: https://ro.wikipedia.org/wiki/F%C4%83r%C3%A2mi%C8%9B%C4%83_Lambru; accessed March 12, 2024).

Muzica Lăutărească after 1989

Popular culture in Romania was greatly affected by the revolution and collapse of communism in December 1989. Not surprisingly, the 1990s and early 2000s brought new innovations to Romani music-making. Perhaps the most significant development involved the wholesale adoption in public celebratory music-making at both Romani and Romanian festive family events of *manele* (sg. *manea*), Romania's local version of the Balkan ethno-pop song-dance genre (see Beissinger 2007; Beissinger et al. 2016). Emblematic of new freedoms after decades of repressive communist rule, *manele* became the rage in the 1990s and well into the twenty-first century and was unquestionably the most popular dance music at weddings, baptism parties, and other celebrations at which *lăutari* performed during those years. *Manele* were (and continue to be) performed primarily by young male Romani musicians, the vocalists of whom are often called *maneliști*. Due in part to a multitude of new liberties throughout society, the genre generated an unprecedented celebrity culture that included stars such as Adrian (Copilul) Minune, Vali Vijelie, Florin Salam, and many others (see Beissinger et al. 2016).

Muzica lăutărească persisted in this new post-communist environment, but it also evolved. The dance-form *hora lăutărească* had long been a requisite part of in-group Romani weddings and other celebrations and gatherings. After 1989 it also increasingly became an integral part of Romanian life-cycle festivities at which *lăutari* were hired. Changes in *muzica lăutărească* in the momentous 1990s and beyond included, in particular, new and altered instrumentation and the development of an overall more elaborate and virtuosic style of performance. These shifts paralleled the quality of sonic experience that *manele* simultaneously offered. Ensembles began to include the synthesizer (*orgă*), capable of incorporating the timbres of absent instruments (such as the cimbalom, accordion, and second violin). Acoustic instruments, especially the violin and eventually the accordion, were replaced with electric violins and accordions and became the norm. Moreover, thanks to the adoption of electrified "tools" and sophisticated amplification devices, the levels of volume in performance steadily increased, sometimes resulting in ear-splitting reverberations. Virtuosity and technical mastery became priorities, including dense melodic ornamentation and the adoption of "mainstream" harmonies foreign to the classic *lăutar* style. These shifts affected many *lăutari*, particularly those who were still relatively young when the revolution took place.

After 1989, both *muzica lăutărească* and *manele*, clearly urban Romani genres, penetrated rural environments as well. At ethnic Romanian village nuptial and other family celebrations, wedding guests, often in traditional courtyard settings, would dance to *manele* and the *hora lăutărească* for hours. While *manele* and *muzica lăutărească* had already provided in-group Romani dance music for decades, a post-1989 fascination with these forms seized both urban and rural Romanians, coinciding with the advent in the 1990s of new cultural, social, political, and economic freedoms. Repeatedly observed in fieldwork at weddings and other festivities in the late 1990s and the early twenty-first century in both cities and villages of southern Romania, Romanian guests often preferred the *hora lăutărească* over the traditional Romanian *hora mare* (see Beissinger 2005).

Overall, in post-1989 Romania, the transformations in musical terms of *muzica lăutărească* have proceeded in several distinct directions. One of them concerns a type of standardization, in other words, a "remodeling" of songs that are naturally characterized by fluid structures into songs with "ordinary," predictable rhythmic-melodic structures that are equal and symmetrical. This is achieved through procedures similar to those by which traditional rural musical forms are converted into conventional "official" folklore presented in the media. They entail the normalization not only of melodic phrases (and their subordination to Western rhythms) but also of the harmony or accompaniment, coupled with a suppression of oral compositional initiatives, often impromptu, on the part of the performers. These are overseen by conductors of folk orchestras who undertake to "standardize" (and even "improve") traditional music for performance purposes. Thus, the *tarafuri* that perform Romani music and advertise on the internet populate YouTube with audio and video recordings made in the studio that often adhere to these practices of normalization;

as a result, they usually lack spontaneity. Furthermore, they undermine the underlying principles of folklore (both musical and verbal) as oral composition in performance within given contexts and frameworks.

Another transformation affecting *muzica lăutărească*, due in large part to the collapse in 1989 of erstwhile cultural, social, and political "borders," concerns the invention of "pan-Gypsy" music, a syncretic undertaking in which musical sounds and phrases—clichés from various international Romani music traditions—are combined in performance. It is based on the fusion of conventional elements from Balkan, Russian, Hungarian, French, and Spanish Romani music traditions, among others, which are familiar from recordings, radio broadcasts, television shows, the internet, and iconic films such as Emir Kusturica's *Time of the Gypsies* and *Black Cat, White Cat* (with "Gypsy" music arranged by Goran Bregović) or Tony Gatlif's "Gypsy" Trilogy (*The Princes, Latcho Drom*, and *Gadjo Dilo*) featuring Romani musicians. "Pan-Gypsy" music was promoted by the internationally known Romani virtuoso cimbalom player Marius Mihalache (from Bucharest) and his *taraf* around 2010, which served to articulate his direct link to "Gypsy" music writ large and put his name on the map, especially in Europe and North America, where "Gypsies" are often seen as exotic, and their role as musicians provides identifiable stereotypes.

Yet another development within contemporary *muzica lăutărească* is the hybridization of *lăutar* music with various forms and genres of non-Romani European music. Most of the "crossbreeding" is done randomly by borrowing and adopting instruments and melodic, harmonic, and rhythmic structures from virtually any source, often discovered by the musicians' browsing the internet. Potpourris typically display an amalgamation of different styles: café-concert, well-known popular songs, rural "folk" music, and jazz, to name a few. There is also a relatively new hybrid form as of the first decade of the 2000s: mixing *muzica lăutărească* with well-known "hits" of the fine-art or "classical" music repertoire. For example, typical *lăutar* melodies are replaced with themes borrowed from familiar works by Bach, Mozart, Schubert, Chopin, Rachmaninov, Khachaturian, and others, possibly embellished with *lăutar*-style ornaments. This was launched and made popular by one of the most influential performers of early twenty-first-century *muzica lăutărească*, the virtuosic accordionist Ionică Minune (b. 1959). He has been innovative in terms of crossbreeding *lăutar* music with the fine-art music canon as well as setting new standards for technical mastery of the accordion and is a type of guru for young Romani musicians, especially those who have studied or are studying in music high schools or universities. Many of them learned to play traditional instruments via oral traditional channels in their families but have chosen also to pursue more formal music training in order to augment their occupational credentials. They include accordionists, who typically study piano, as well as violinists and clarinetists. A good number of them, especially accordionists, have become epigones of Ionică Minune, whose style they emulate and whose contact with him, even for a handful of private lessons, will, they hope, raise their *lăutar* skills and thus their professional status.

Conclusion

Arii naționale were the earliest "original" Romanian music with both a national and European relevance. As a genre composed and performed by *lăutari*, it underscores the unique role that Romani musicians have played and continue to play in the rich cultural fabric of Romania. *Arii naționale* were central to the cultural representation of Romania in Europe as displayed at the two World's Fairs in Paris in 1889 and 1900. Comparable "national" urban folk music rendered by Romani musicians has perhaps emerged in other countries of eastern Europe as well. For example, the urban Hungarian popular song genre *nóta* can be viewed as a possible "national music"—performed by Romani musicians in cafes and restaurants in Hungary and elsewhere in central Europe (see Sárosi 1978:151–196). But the parallels and connections between Romani or "Gypsy" music as a "national" tradition with broad relevance need not be limited to eastern Europe. Flamenco in southern Spain, too, is a music and dance tradition with roots in Andalusian Gitano (Calé) artistic expression that has long been synonymous with Spanish "national" culture.

"Classical" Romani *muzica lăutărească* might have shared the fate of Brazilian samba, Portuguese fado, or even Greek *rebetiko*; in other words, it could have become a kind of sonic blazon of its country of origin, Romania. But it fell victim to a few mischances that were beyond the control of the artists who perpetuated it. For one, *muzica lăutărească* missed the optimal moment: when it was in full swing, on a high artistic level, and admired by a great many inhabitants of southern Romania (especially in the 1950s–1980s), it was strangled by the communist political regime, which did not recognize its existence and drastically squelched or, at best, limited its media coverage. Moreover, due to distinctly different musical traditions and tastes in Transylvania, northern Moldova, and part of Banat (territories that together account for more than a third of the country), people there looked at *muzica lăutărească* rather with indifference. Then, by the time the popularity of "classical" *muzica lăutărească* had grown among intellectuals who could give it impetus, the incentive of the musicians had begun, in subtle ways, to wane, and the "golden age" of the genre was passing. The top-down controls of communism were exhausting, even debilitating. By the rocky and difficult 1990s, as people everywhere in eastern Europe were coping with post-communism, the "transition," and attempts to find a place in the new order of things, some *lăutari* were beginning to lose hope in the future of their profession, putting a damper on protecting and perpetuating the cultural heritage that many or most of them had traditionally passed from generation to generation.[31]

The brilliant and original road on which *muzica lăutărească* set off in the first half of the twentieth century is not closed, however. *Lăutari* have always been able to "turn old into new," to recover and recycle, after several decades, forgotten or outmoded pieces and styles.[32] Moreover, they have always approached *muzica lăutărească* with resilience and creativity, as an emblem of their racial identity and occupation. This same strength and inspiration will most likely pave the way for the future of *muzica lăutărească*. What will come out of it will probably be a new and different music, generated, in part, by the *muzica lăutărească* of the past, but one that will resemble tomorrow's present.

Notes

1. The first written evidence of Romani slavery in the Romanian Principalities derives from 1385 (Achim 1998:21).
2. "Some young men and ladies from different classes of society find a noble amusement in the composition of horas and other national cantilenas, which they give to the *lăutari* to perform" (Filimon [1863] 2017).
3. "Phanariot rule" refers to the period from 1711 to 1821, when those who governed Wallachia were appointed by the Sublime Porte from among the Greek nobles of the Fanar district of Constantinople.
4. "German music" at that time meant any music from the West (Moisil 2020:131).
5. However, we have no evidence to clearly indicate that the small urban ensembles practiced tonal-harmonic accompaniment before the end of the nineteenth century. William Beatty-Kingston writes in 1888, quite ambiguously, "the music of Dacia [the ancient region in parts of what is now Romania] is essentially, almost exclusively, melodic. Harmony does not enter into its being; it has never created a vocal duet, trio or part-song; its horas (*derivatur* chorus) are sung in unison" (114).
6. See https://en.wikipedia.org/wiki/Demographic_history_of_Romania (accessed January 22, 2024).
7. This estimate puts the total Romani populace at that time between 420,000 and 450,000 residents.
8. The *manea* (pl. *manele*) performed at that time was a genre "associated with Turkish musics" possibly in existence in the Romanian Principalities as early as the mid-seventeenth century (Moisil 2016:45, 58n4).
9. Kogălniceanu also produced a Romani–Romanian dictionary in 1857.
10. Personal communication between Rădulescu and Feldman.
11. A hora is a traditional Romanian circle dance in duple meter.
12. A *taraf* is a small (vocal-) instrumental ensemble comprised of two to seven or so traditional musicians (during the nineteenth century, even up to twelve—when their employer could afford to pay them) (Moisil 2020). The musicians were by and large professionals (they supported themselves and their families by making music): chiefly *lăutari* but also, at times, *muzicanți* (sg. *muzicant*), musicians who could read music.
13. And at the end of World War I (1918), "Greater Romania," with the incorporation of Transylvania, Bukovina, Bessarabia, and parts of Banat, Crișana, and Maramureș, was formed.
14. *Mărțișor* is the celebration of the beginning of spring, on March 1, when special trinkets with red-and-white tassels are gifted especially to girls and women.
15. Costache Pompieru was the name of a well-known *lăutar* at the time, while the fast-paced *sârbă* is a traditional Romanian dance in 2/4 compound time: 3/8 + 3/8.
16. Dinicu studied at the Bucharest Conservatory and became a well-known violinist nationally as well as internationally. While concertizing in Vienna in 1932, Jascha Heifetz played "Hora Staccato" in a recital and explained to a Romanian journalist there how several years

earlier while in Bucharest he had heard Dinicu play it (in *lăutar* fashion, without music). Heifetz had been so enamored of the piece that he had asked Dinicu "to give [him] permission to transcribe 'Hora' and add it to [his] concert repertoire," which Dinicu granted him (Cosma 1996a:206).

17. They were accompanied with predictable tonic, dominant, and subdominant chords, possibly of the sixth degree chord, presented through harmonic figurations. These figurations may have started to form at that time around the kobza (*cobză*) or small (portable) cimbalom (*țambal*).

18. Typical was the musical entertainment of *lăutari* such as Angheluș Dinicu (1838–1905), a celebrated pan-pipe (*nai*) player who performed at the gala receptions at the Royal Palace in Bucharest and at the Palace at Poiana Stânei (in Prahova) for the state visit of Emperor Franz Joseph of Austria-Hungary in September 1896 (Cosma 1996b:235).

19. Ionică Dinicu was the father of the famous *lăutar* violinist Grigoraș Dinicu.

20. As Fauser points out, regarding the 1889 World's Fair, "the Romanian gypsies were perceived as more 'authentic' musicians [than the Hungarian Roma] because they were unspoiled by the urban music business—a widespread approach towards Hungarian gypsies that endured well into the twentieth century with the writings of Béla Bartók, who himself favored the music of Romanian gypsies over those of Hungary" (2005:257).

21. This detail was provided and reconfirmed in 2006–2007 by various elderly Romanians, who in turn had heard it from Jews who returned in the summers to the small towns of Moldova in order to visit their native land and reconnect with inhabitants there whom they knew from their youth. In Botoșani County in 1930, there were 315,780 Jews from a total of 451,892 Jews in Romania. See https://kehilalinks.jewishgen.org/botosani/botosani.html (accessed March 2, 2024).

22. Romanian ethnomusicologists have long ignored *muzica lăutărească* for two main reasons. The first is that the nationalist-communist regime did not allow scholars to research the music that they found worthy but rather limited research to what was recommended to them. And what was imperatively recommended was the traditional rural music of ethnic Romanians. The cultural apparatchiks of the communist regime also considered that there was no Romani music since the Roma "did not exist"; that is, they were not considered or recognized as a minority ethnic group (and, in fact, were not censused as such). The second reason is that, under constant ideological pressure, ethnomusicologists had learned to practice a sort of self-censorship: they stayed away from problematic subjects in order to avoid career obstacles. Moreover, a great many had come to believe that the most important subject of research was indeed—since there could be no other—"the folklore of Romanian peasants." The consequence of this was that the long-avoided music performed by Roma in Romania ceased to attract the attention of many scholars or even to exist for them.

23. See Beissinger 2024b for a discussion of their repertoires.

24. Robert Garfias identifies the Turkish *makams* that underlie the *lăutar* melodies, of which the most frequently encountered are *hijaz*, *nikriz*, and *segah* (1981:100). It appears that these *makams* were inserted into the music of the *lăutari* not necessarily directly, from Turkish music but through the filter of the music brought to the Principalities by the Greek rulers from the Fanar quarter of Istanbul (1711–1821), together with a large number of ethnic Greeks. Turkish court music belonged to earlier times and never enjoyed the great popularity of Greek music in the Romanian cities of the eighteenth and nineteenth centuries (Gheorghiță 2020a).

25. This is executed in order to obtain a compact textural effect and to suggest the free unfolding of the melodic lines over it.
26. Romanian octosyllabic meter (with feminine verse endings) implicitly also includes lines of seven syllables (the masculine verse form).
27. "Gypsy" here reflects the usage of the *lăutar* (*hora țigănească*, from *țigan*, pl. *țigani*).
28. It is also performed, but less commonly, in Iași and a few other cities in Moldova.
29. Victor Gore, interview with Beissinger (Bucharest, June 25, 1998).
30. The term *muzica de mahala* was already in circulation in the nineteenth century (Gheorghiță 2020a), although there are no tangible data that link it to *muzica lăutărească* of the mid-twentieth century.
31. In the 1990s, very poor years for most of Romania's citizens, some of the sons of *lăutari* rejected the job of their fathers who were perennially short of money and in search of customers (and who, in some cases, also discouraged them from perpetuating it). The crisis of the *lăutar* occupation lasted about a decade.
32. After all, *manele* represent, in some ways, an outgrowth of *muzica lăutărească*.

Works Cited

Achim, Viorel. 1998. *Țiganii în istoria României*. Bucharest: Editura enciclopedică.
Beatty-Kingston, William. 1888. *Music and Manners. Personal Reminiscences and Sketches of Character*. Vol. I: *Music*. New York: Harper & Brothers.
Beissinger, Margaret H. 2001. "Occupation and Ethnicity: Constructing Identity among Professional Romani (Gypsy) Musicians in Romania." *Slavic Review*, 60/1:24–49.
Beissinger, Margaret H. 2005. "Romani (Gypsy) Music-Making at Weddings in Post-Communist Romania: Political Transitions and Cultural Adaptations." *Folklorica: Journal of the Slavic and East European Folklore Association*, 10/1:39–51.
Beissinger, Margaret H. 2007. "*Muzica Orientală*: Identity and Popular Culture in Postcommunist Romania." In *Balkan Popular Culture and the Ottoman Ecumene: Music, Image, and Regional Political Discourse*," ed. Donna A. Buchanan, 95–141. Lanham, MD: The Scarecrow Press.
Beissinger, Margaret. 2016. "Romanian *Manele* and Regional Parallels: 'Oriental' Ethnopop in the Balkans." In *Manele in Romania: Cultural Expression and Social Meaning in Balkan Popular Music*, eds. Margaret Beissinger, Speranța Rădulescu, and Anca Giurchescu, 95–138. Lanham, MD: Rowman & Littlefield.
Beissinger, Margaret H. 2024a. "Lăutari, Music-Making, and Social Practices of Live Performance in Southern Romania." In *The Routledge Handbook of Popular Music and Politics of the Balkans*, ed. Catherine Baker, 49–60. London: Routledge.
Beissinger, Margaret H. 2024b. "'Songs of Pain': Muzica Lăutărească and the Voices of Romica Puceanu and Gabi Luncă." *Music & Minorities*, 3:1–26.
Beissinger, Margaret, Speranța Rădulescu, and Anca Giurchescu, eds. 2016. *Manele in Romania: Cultural Expression and Social Meaning in Balkan Popular Music*. Lanham, MD: Rowman & Littlefield.
Bibesco, Georges. 1890. *Exposition Universalle: La Roumanie*. Paris: Imprimerie Typographique J. Kugelmann.
Bobulescu, Constantin. 1922. *Lăutarii noștri. Din trecutul lor*. Bucharest: Tip. Națională.
Cosma, Viorel. 1996a. *Lăutarii de ieri și de azi*, 2nd ed., rev. exp. Bucharest: Editura du Style.

Cosma, Viorel. 1996b. *Interpreți din România. Lexicon: Dirijori—Cântăreți—Instrumentiști—Regizori.* Vol. I: *A–F.* Bucharest: Editura GALAXIA.
Costache, Ioanida. 2021. "Sounding Romani Sonic-Subjectivity: Counter History, Identity Formation, and Affect in Romanian–Roma Music." PhD dissertation, Stanford University.
Crowe, David M. 2007. "Introduction." In *A History of the Gypsies of Eastern Europe and Russia*, xi–xvi. New York: Palgrave Macmillan.
Fauser, Annegret. 2005. *Musical Encounters at the 1889 Paris World's Fair.* Rochester, NY: University of Rochester Press.
Feldman, Walter Zev. 2016. *Klezmer: Music, History and Memory.* Oxford: Oxford University Press.
Filimon, Nicolae. 2017. "Lăutarii și compozițiunile lor." https://lecturadigitala.ro/ro/articole/alte-scrieri/151-lăutarii-si-compozitiunile-lor-nicolae-filimon. Accessed January 22, 2024. First published 1863.
Frigyesi, Judit. 1993. "Preliminary Thoughts toward the Study of Music without Clear Beat. The Example of 'Flowing Rhythm' in Jewish Nusah." *Asian Music*, 24/2:59–88.
Garfias, Robert. 1981. "Survivals of Turkish Characteristics in Romanian Musica Lăutărească." *Yearbook for Traditional Music*, 13:97–107.
Garfias, Robert. 1996. "The Development of the Romanian Urban Gypsy Song from Its Probable Origins in the Folk Doina." The Romanian Doina. Unpublished manuscript. https://www.academia.edu/33194266/The_Romanian_Doina. Accessed February 24, 2024.
Gheorghiță, Nicolae. 2020a. "Practici muzicale laice la curțile domnești și boierești din Valahia și Moldova în epoca fanariotă (1711–1821)." In *Noi istorii ale muzicilor românești*, I, ed. Valentina Sandu-Dediu and Nicolae Gheorghiță, 35–78. Bucharest: Editura Muzicală.
Gheorghiță, Nicolae. 2020b. "Muzicile militare moderne în Țara Românească și Moldova în secolul al XIX-lea." In *Noi istorii ale muzicilor românești*, I, ed. Valentina Sandu-Dediu and Nicolae Gheorghiță, 263–290. Bucharest: Editura Muzicală.
Kogălniceanu, Mihail. 1837. *Esquisse sur l'histoire, les moeurs et la langue des Cigains connus en France sous le nom de Bohémiens.* Berlin: Librairie de B. Behr.
Michelson, Paul E. 2000. "Romania (History)." In *Encyclopedia of Eastern Europe From the Congress of Vienna to the Fall of Communism*, ed. Richard Frucht, 667–691. New York: Garland Publishing, Inc.
Minea, Cosmin. 2021. "Roma Musicians, Folk Art and Traditional Food from Romania at the Paris World Fairs of 1889 and 1900." In *World Fairs and the Global Moulding of National Identities: International Exhibitions as Cultural Platforms, 1851–1958*, eds. Joep Leerssen and Eric Storm, 144–169. Leiden, the Netherlands: Brill.
Moisil, Costin. 2016. "A History of the *Manea*: The Nineteenth to the Mid-Twentieth Century." In *Manele in Romania: Cultural Expression and Social Meaning in Balkan Popular Music*, eds. Margaret Beissinger, Speranța Rădulescu, and Anca Giurchescu, 45–61. Lanham, MD: Rowman & Littlefield.
Moisil, Costin. 2020. "Muzica în Principatele Române de-a lungul secolului al XIX-lea." In *Noi istorii ale muzicilor românești*, I, ed. Valentina Sandu-Dediu and Nicolae Gheorghiță, 131–163. Bucharest: Editura Muzicală.
Pann, Anton. 2009. *Spitalul amorului sau Cîntătorul dorului*, with a preface by Nicolae Gheorghiță. Bucharest: Compania. First published 1830.
Parvulescu, Anca, and Manuela Boatcă. 2022. *Creolizing the Modern: Transylvania across Empires.* Ithaca, NY: Cornell University Press.
Pârvulescu, Ioana. 2003. *Întoarcere în Bucureștiul interbelic.* Bucharest: Humanitas.

Radano, Ronald, and Philip V. Bohlman. 2000. "Preface." In *Music and the Racial Imagination*, xiii–xv. Chicago: University of Chicago Press.
Rădulescu, Speranța. 2004. *Taifasuri despre muzica țigănească/Chats about Gypsy Music*. Bucharest: Paideia.
Rădulescu, Speranța. 2017a. "Muzica Lăutărească." In *Bloomsbury Encyclopedia of Popular Music of the World: Genres: Europe*, eds. Paolo Prato and David Horn, 510–511. London: Bloomsbury Academic.
Rădulescu, Speranța. 2017b. "National Ideology, Music and Discourses about Music in Romania in the Twentieth Century." *Musicology Today: Journal of the National University of Music Bucharest*, 31:181–195.
Sárosi, Bálint. 1978. *Gypsy Music*. Budapest: Corvina Press.
Vasilescu, Costel. 2015. *Anii de glorie ai muzicii lăutărești*. Bucharest: Editura EIKON.
Voiculescu, Cerasela. 2005. "Production and Consumption of Folk-Pop Music in Post-Socialist Romania: Discourse and Practice." *Ethnologia Balkanica*, 9:261–283.
Vulpian, Dimitrie. 1908. *Horele noastre culese ș-arangiate pentru piano de D. Vulpian*. Bucharest: Librăria Soce et Cie.

CHAPTER 34

ROMANI MUSICAL LABOR AND CULTURAL POLITICS IN SOUTHEASTERN SERBIA

ALEXANDER MARKOVIĆ

DOOM-TA-DOOM-TA-KA ... *DOOM-rakka-DOOM-ta-ka*. It's a summer evening in 2010 in Vranje, a town in far southeastern Serbia. I hear the distinctive drum pattern of a tune in 9/8 meter drift through my apartment window as I work on the day's field notes. The sounds float out of a courtyard overhung with leafy grapevines on this summer night, announcing an intimate gathering at a Serb neighbor's home. The hosts have hired a few Romani musicians to entertain their guests. Quickly, the percussive pops and taps of hands striking the small, hourglass-shaped *tarabuka* drum are joined by the strains of clarinet and accordion. As the music picks up, I recognize the tune: "Sobinka," a melody named after the Sobina neighborhood.[1] I hear various guests burst out in appreciative whistles, exclaim "op," and begin to clap to the beat. Many in Vranje associate "Sobinka" with older, and thus "authentic," local music. The tune's additive 9/8 meter (2+2+2+3) places it within the *Vranjski čoček* ("čoček of Vranje") genre, reinforcing associations with regional folklore and tradition.[2] As I lean on the windowsill to listen, my landlady emerges from her apartment next door to stand on her porch and take in the music. She winks at me, a soft smile spreading across her face as she hums the familiar melody.

In Vranje, Romani musicians are specialized artisans, professionals who learn, cultivate, and elaborate myriad musical repertoires that are central to family celebrations, local folklore, and regional pride. Even as non-Roma have long disparaged Roma as "lowly Gypsies," Romani professional entertainers—musicians whose primary livelihood comes from performing music for pay—are integral to the cultural and historical fabric of Vranje society.[3] Romani musical services also build relationships between Serbs and Roma through shared cultural space in the context of important rituals, of emotional exuberance, of economic exchange, of historical legacies, and of cultural innovation.[4] These phenomena support discourse about Vranje's "unique" culture within Serbia, within the former Yugoslavia, and even internationally. Because they perform—and thus embody—coveted music and dance practices, in other words, Roma are the linchpin in locals' efforts to tap into Vranje's broader cultural cachet. Taking Vranje as an illustrative case study, this chapter examines the seminal role that Roma play in regional folklore, community relations, and identity narratives for locals—for *Vranjanci*, "people of Vranje," including Serbs and Roma alike.[5]

Dynamic Traditions: Regional Cultural History and Romani Musical Labor

In Vranje, music, dance, folklore, and celebratory culture connect Serbs and Roma much more intensely than do other spheres of local life. Here, as throughout the Balkans, Roma have long dominated professional musical performance (Seeman 1990; Brandl 1996; Beissinger 2001; Keil and Vellou-Keil 2002; Pettan 2002; Seeman 2012; Silverman 2012; Seeman 2019). Romani musical labor effectively builds relations across ethnic lines that are otherwise policed through entrenched segregation and inequality. Serbs and Roma alike laud Romani musicians' impressive performance chops and profound command of repertoire. *Vranjanci* often assert that Roma are irreplaceable when it comes to producing the right celebratory atmosphere for nurturing "authentic" expressive culture and folkloric traditions in the region. Romani skills evolved through centuries of musical work and cultural innovation, and Romani professional entertainers remain key players in local identity politics, cultural heritage, and community life in the present.[6]

An Ottoman document from the reign of Ottoman sultan Selim II (r. 1566–1574) provides the earliest record of Romani musicians in Vranje, describing a *džemat* (official grouping) of Muslim Roma who performed for the town's military garrison in return for tax exemptions (Vukanović 1978; Vukanović 1987).[7] Romani musicians in the region also performed for the civilian populace at entertainment venues and for family celebrations. Two ensemble types predominated in nineteenth-century Vranje: *čalgija* orchestras (derived from Ottoman urban musical ensembles) and the *surla* (double-reed shawm) and *goč* (large double-headed drum) ensembles that would later give way to brass bands.

Romani *čalgija* musicians performed in a predominantly urban musical style, much like those in other nearby Balkan Ottoman towns.[8] These ensembles featured clarinet (*grneta*), violin (*ćemane*), and frame drums with zils (*dajre*);[9] they probably also included the *ut* or *lavta* (short-necked fretless lutes), much like ensembles in Kosovo and Macedonia. *Čalgija* musicians performed in taverns (*kafane*, literally "coffeehouses") and at family life-cycle celebrations for all of Vranje's ethnic communities—Turks, Albanians, Serbs, Jews, Tsintsars (Aromanians), and Roma. While instrumentalists were traditionally men, historically Romani women also performed as *dajre* frame drum players, singers, and dancers. Malika Eminović (popularly known as Koštana), a famous Romani entertainer in late nineteenth-century Vranje, performed with an ensemble comprised of her male relatives and was purportedly trained to play the tambourine, sing, and dance by her mother (Stanković [1902] 2005).

When Serbia annexed Vranje from the Ottomans in 1878, however, rapid political and cultural changes altered the conditions of Romani musical labor. Most local Muslims moved south into remaining Ottoman territories. Christian urbanites who remained were joined by an influx of Serbian Orthodox peasants from the surrounding area, as well as civil servants from northern Serbia. Officials and educators sought to integrate the local populace into a "modernizing" Serbia, and many Ottoman-era practices were derided as foreign or primitive. Central Serbian musical styles became increasingly influential, including the *starogradska muzika* ("old urban music") promoted by Belgrade-based national radio programs in the period between the two world wars (see Dumnić 2013).

Vranje's urban ensemble retained its basic form, but from the early to mid-twentieth century more "modern" instruments gradually supplanted older, Ottoman-style instrumentation. Acoustic guitars eventually replaced the *ut*, and musicians increasingly used the upright bass (*bas* or *kontrabas* in Serbian) instead of the *dajre* drum for rhythmic accompaniment. Gradually orchestras also incorporated accordion and later saxophone. After World War II, these urban ensembles were increasingly called *kafanski orkestri* ("kafana restaurant orchestras"). They remained popular among both Serbs and Roma, providing entertainment at local taverns, hotels, and family parties. *Kafana* orchestras were quite versatile in terms of repertoire, instrumentation, and performance contexts, playing everything from regional folk music (such as *ćoček* dance tunes and late Ottoman-era urban ballads) to commercialized forms of folk and pop (such as Yugoslav-era "newly composed folk music" and European "schlager" songs); some even incorporated numbers from international styles like jazz. Romani professionals who performed in *kafana* bands considered the ensemble and its repertoires to be more prestigious than other local styles because they were "more cosmopolitan" and more lucrative. Older musicians note that the best *kafana* bands were hired to perform for the summer at hotels on the Adriatic coast, far from Vranje, and in front of Yugoslav audiences with diverse musical tastes. They claim that *kafana* performers thus enjoyed higher status than musicians in genres that catered primarily to local clientele and celebrations such as weddings.[10]

Yet this regional repertoire is critically important to community life and identity in the Vranje area. Even as the urban *kafana* ensemble has lost popularity since the 1990s, the iconic brass band music remains in high demand for community celebrations. Romani musicians' opportunistic experimentation with novel instruments drove the early twentieth-century emergence of brass bands. Brass eventually replaced older ensembles comprised of two oboe-like, double-reed shawms called *surle* (sg., *surla*) and one or two large double-headed drums, locally known as *gočevi* (sg., *goč*).[11] Throughout the southern Balkans, Roma have long monopolized the *surla/zurla/zurna* genre, and the instruments were often considered to be exclusively "Gypsy" (Rice 1982; Keil and Vellou-Keil 2002; Silverman 2012; Seeman 2019). The *surla* and *goč* were used in Ottoman military *mehter* bands, and Romani *mehter* musicians adapted these instruments to civilian celebratory culture and regional folk music (Silverman 2012; Seeman 2019). The loud, piercing sound of the *surla* and deep bass of large *goč* drums were perfect for big outdoor events before the advent of amplification. Romani *surla-goč* music became closely associated with the ritual tunes and dance music central to celebrations like weddings and religious feast days.

Changing demographics and cultural politics eventually affected demand for *surla-goč* ensembles. A few precious photographs from festive gatherings show Romani *surla-goč* ensembles entertaining Serbian patrons into the 1920s; other accounts indicate that some bands remained active until World War II.[12] However, demand for this music steadily declined as cultural holdovers of Ottoman rule were fast disappearing.[13] Serbs increasingly equated *surla* and *goč* music with Muslim Turkish culture, rejecting it as a vestige of a bygone era.[14]

The simultaneous rise of brass bands in the area hastened the decline of *surla-goč* ensembles. Brass bands are similarly loud and highly mobile, making them equally suited for outdoor events. At the same time, the relative novelty of brass instruments made them attractive. Already in the 1830s, Serbia's first post-Ottoman ruler, Milan Obrenović, invited an Austrian bandmaster to put together a Central European–style band at his court—effectively importing the initial concept, instrumentation, and repertoire from the very "West" to which newly independent Serbia's elites looked for models of modern nationhood (Golemović 1997; Golemović 2002; Zakić and Lajić-Mihajlović 2012).

Oral histories indicate that Vranje musicians first encountered brass instruments in the military during the two Balkan wars (1912 and 1913) and World War I (Milovanović and Babić 2003:103–104). Local musicians tell how their fathers and grandfathers learned to manage large ensembles and adapt musical arrangements to brass while serving in army bands (see also Milovanović and Babić 2003:101–104; Golemović 2002). On returning home, enterprising Romani musicians experimented with these instruments, transferring ritual music, songs, and instrumental dance tunes from *surla* and *goč* to the brass medium. Romani family histories show that many former *surla* players took up trumpets in response to growing local demand, effecting a gradual turnover from one musical form to the other (Milovanović and Babić 2003).

Because of this tie to *surla-goč* traditions, Romani musicians also monopolized the emergent brass genres; to date, locals see Romani musicians and brass bands as essentially synonymous, and very few non-Roma perform in brass ensembles. Key elements of regional brass band styling illustrate the *surla-goč* legacy as musicians creatively balanced continued demand for older aesthetics and repertoires with popular interest in new sounds. When Vranje brass ensembles perform older local dance tunes, the mid-brass instruments generally drone while the leading trumpet and clarinet players perform melody and improvise—much like the respective roles of leading (first) and droning (second) *surla* musicians (see Rice 1982; Keil and Vellou-Keil 2002; Silverman 2012). Well into the 1970s and 1980s, many brass ensembles preferred a shorter clarinet (similar to an E-flat clarinet) whose higher pitch evokes the sound of a *surla*. Early commercial recordings of the famous Bakija Bakić ensemble show these sonic echoes of *surla-goč* aesthetics, particularly on tracks featuring older dance tunes like "Vranjanka" ("the Vranje dance/tune," an iconic local form in 7/8 meter) and "Preševka" ("the tune/dance from Preševo," a town near the North Macedonian border).[15]

Despite some continuity with older forms, however, brass band culture in the early twentieth century also involved intense experimentation as Roma developed this emergent genre. As baritone horns and tubas entered the local scene, musicians interrogated the musical capacities of these mid-brass instruments, using them to amplify the drone underneath a melody, to boost percussive dynamics, or to heighten select dimensions of the melody. Gradually, these innovations produced a more dynamic, textured, and "fuller" sound in brass ensembles than was true of the older *surla-goč* genre. By the mid-twentieth century, brass bands more or less consistently featured the instrumental lineup seen today: one clarinet (*grnata*) or (later) saxophone, two to four rotary valve flugelhorns (*trube*), two to four baritone horns (*mali basovi*), one tuba (*veliki bas*), a snare drum (*doboš*), and the large double-headed *goč* drum with a cymbal (*sahan* or *činela*) mounted on top.

From World War II onward, brass bands became the preeminent musical ensemble at Vranje community celebrations such as weddings, baptisms, send-off parties for compulsory military service, and religious feast days. Regular exposure to military bands familiarized locals with the sound and aesthetics of brass (Golemović 1997; Timotijević 2005:154–156). Close associations between brass and the national military also lent significant cultural cachet to these ensembles as elites intensively cultivated Serbian national identity among the populace. Some also came to see brass as more modern and "European-sounding" than the *surla-goč* music of the region's past. Popular demand for brass bands surged; people claim that there were more than thirty standing brass bands in the Vranje area by the 1950s and 1960s. A local brass band competition was established at the "Karanfil Devojče" cultural festival in Vranjska Banja, predating the national brass competition at Guča, which began in 1961.

The burgeoning popularity of the Guča Brass Band Festival in western Serbia has increased the importance of Romani brass ensembles in Vranje. Regional Romani ensembles often win the most coveted awards at Guča, and resulting public acclaim boosts their national visibility through recording deals, television appearances, and high-end performances. Other media platforms—like the soundtracks of internationally popular Emir Kusturica films dating from the 1990s—exposed wider audiences to south Serbian Romani brass.[16] Throughout the former Yugoslavia, and later on the international "world music" scene, the music's dynamism and versatility drew an ever-larger fan base. These developments have amplified local pride in Vranje's brass musicians as *Vranjanci* revel in the growing cachet associated with Balkan brass music abroad.

Vranje's Romani musicians thus capitalized on a novel instrumental ensemble to accommodate the reactionary cultural politics of a post-Ottoman Serbia, crafting a new performance medium to expand their professional opportunities as entertainers. Working musicians at the time were still primarily oriented toward local contexts, however, meaning that their experimentation with brass focused on enhancing interpretation of regional folk repertoires. Musicians carefully husbanded aspects of antecedent genres to engage with important affective and symbolic dimensions of local celebratory culture, preserving the ethos of Vranje folk music within the emergent brass idiom. Early Romani brass musicians engaged with popular trends in selective and judicious ways, in other words, conservatively tailoring performance practices to foster broad-based demand for their services—accompanying rituals and celebratory dancing at weddings, for example, as the veritable bread and butter of their existence as working musicians. This dynamic continues in present-day brass band work and how elders train new generations of Romani musicians.

The development of Vranje brass band culture illustrates how deeply Romani musical labor has shaped regional cultural history. Despite widespread derision of Roma in general, Serbs nevertheless rely on Romani professionals as preeminent carriers of valued folklore and traditions. Romani skills anchor community life and actively embody the performative culture around which regional identity narratives cohere, creating spaces for Vranje Serbs and Roma to elaborate relations in dynamic ways.

Deeply Affected: Romani Brass, Sentiment, and Community Life

Romani performance practices elicit strong emotions in Vranje. Musicians catalyze intense experiences for participants, where ritual and celebratory affect allow people to more deeply embody notions of self, of family, and of collective identities through a sense of shared traditions. Roma cultivate specialized knowledge of the ritual and dance repertoires specific to life-cycle and community celebrations—important folklore deeply embedded in symbolic life and identity politics. Elder *Vranjanci* in particular argue that such events absolutely require brass band accompaniment, scoffing at the notion that any other genre might substitute. Because music, ritual, and social ties in Vranje are in many ways mutually constitutive, people value Romani practitioners for their ability to produce the affective states that participants need to "really feel" key social and symbolic dimensions of community life.

Vranje's celebratory culture revolves around *ćef*—a state of heightened excitement and pleasure.[17] People can attain it by enjoying food, drink, and good company; but engaging with music and dancing are perhaps the strongest ways to generate *ćef*. Locals most often experience *ćef* at events like baptisms, religious feast days, and weddings, where brass music is the preeminent genre for key ritual and dance music at life-cycle celebrations. *Ćef* manifests through conventionalized, collective forms of self-expression and interaction. In response to dynamic drumming, a stirring solo, or the strains of one's favorite tune, people whistle, clap, snap fingers, throw back their heads while closing their eyes, spread their arms high, or shout out in pleasure; they may also embrace fellow celebrants, clink glasses with neighbors, or link arms at the elbow with a close friend to quaff swigs of alcohol (Fig. 34.1). This excitement also moves people to participate more actively in dancing or engage with musicians. They crowd closer to performers, draw instruments toward their ear or face so that they are in the "blast zone" of sound, and tip musicians (sometimes lavishly) in return for solicitous attention. As much as *ćef* is about individual pleasure, then, it is also a form of collective feeling that intensifies social interactions and is witnessed by fellow celebrants.

While there are many different celebratory contexts in Vranje, Roma and Serbs alike are particularly excited by—and articulate about—weddings. The importance of family and community concerns that underpin wedding celebrations make them especially joyful, but also symbolically weighty, events. *Vranjanci* enthusiastically expound on the

FIG. 34.1. Romani woman moved by music at a celebration in 2010, demonstrating *ćef*.
(Photograph by the author.)

"ideal" or "traditional" wedding complex. The primary focus are rituals that refashion the status of the bride and groom, signal changing roles of family members, and constitute new relationships between two families. Especially significant are those practices that confirm the elder status of the couple's parents (particularly the groom's parents), and the bride's transferal from her birth family to her marital family (i.e., the groom's household).

All of the major celebratory and ritual practices revolve around specific musical repertoires and dancing supported primarily by Romani brass musicians. Only Romani brass bands in Vranje perform the tune "Turski Mekam" ("Turkish Mekam"), for example, which traditionally signals the start of weddings and which musicians often play to welcome successive groups of arriving guests.[18] Ritual figures like the *starejko* (groom's maternal uncle) have special status and roles too, and they often have Romani musicians play for them while they engage in playful celebratory destruction out of sheer joy (i.e., hurling roof tiles into the courtyard to watch them shatter) or to provide an "honor escort" when they depart wedding celebrations.

One event in particular illustrates well the strong connection between Romani musical practice, affect, and community life—the ritual dance event known as *Svekrvino Kolo*, "the groom's mother's dance." In Vranje, the first portion of the wedding was traditionally called the *zasevka*, implying the "sowing" of a field for ritual actions performed by the groom's mother, or *svekrva* (in Serbian). She leads *Svekrvino Kolo* during this opening event at weddings, reveling in a ritual that gives her special pride of place at the celebration. Both Roma and Serbs perform the *Svekrvino Kolo* ritual, and locals explain that many women "live for" the opportunity to marry off a son in order to dance with motherly pride in front of assembled wedding guests.[19] Perhaps no other moment of the wedding is so viscerally exciting. Even onlookers who do not participate look forward to witnessing when the groom's mother "begins to dance" (*zaigruje* in local Serbian dialect) (Fig. 34.2).

Patriarchal gender norms imbue this ritual-dance with intense power. In Vranje, a bride's status depends heavily on her ability to contribute to her new family—not only in terms of labor but also by reproducing it through the children she bears (Sugarman 1997; Zlatanović 2003; Silverman 2012). Male children are particularly important as they are the ones who will perpetuate her in-laws' family lineage and name (Sugarman 1997; Zlatanović 2003). After she bears a male child, then, there is no greater event for a married woman than the marriage of that son. As Zlatanović (2003)[20] argues in her analysis of Serb weddings, the groom's mother confirms her status in her marital family by successfully raising a son and increases her standing by becoming an elder who now supervises "her" own new bride.

Women palpably radiate joy and pride during this ritual dance, feelings considerably heightened through their bodily experiences of dancing *Svekrvino* to brass band music. *Vranjanci* have very visceral reactions to *Svekrvino*. Hearing (and feeling) the throbbing beats of the drum, swaying one's body to the rhythm while dancing, spontaneously lifting one's arms during evocative musical improvisations—all galvanize an

FIG. 34.2. Jovica Ajdarević brass band follows the groom's mother as she leads *Svekrvino Kolo* at a Serb wedding in Preševo in 2011.

(Photograph by the author.)

"intensity" of experience that in turn underlines the ritual's symbolic import. Romani brass musicians thus provide the musical soundscape and performative engagement that boosts the affective punch of *Svekrvino*.[21]

Svekrvino Kolo carries great emotional weight because of its semantic connections to patriarchal notions of marriage, gender roles, and community relations. As she dances, the *svekrva* periodically throws out handfuls of ritual contents—wheat, candies, coins, sugar cubes, etc.—from a decorated sieve to bless the couple and bring fertility to their union (Zlatanović 2003:66–67). The groom's mother figuratively "sows" these blessings by tossing the sieve's contents just as a farmer sows his field with seeds (hence *zasevka*). Through *Svekrvino* the groom's mother symbolically transfers her own established fertility to her daughter-in-law and son through contagious ritual actions rooted in metaphors of agricultural and "natural" productivity (Zlatanović 2003; Silverman 2012). *Svekrvino Kolo* is also a very public event, performatively constituting the family's wider social circle. Large numbers of assembled kin and invited guests accompany the groom's mother during the dance, arranged in the line next to her in order of seniority and importance. They dance along with her to show their support and approval during this milestone in the family's life (Fig. 34.3).

FIG. 34.3. Extended family and friends dance with the mother of the groom during *Svekrvino Kolo* at a Romani wedding in 2010.

(Photograph by the author.)

Locals dance *Svekrvino Kolo* to a suite of melodies in a slow 7/8 meter (3+2+2).[22] Musicians always open with the specific *Svekrvino Kolo* melody, then perform other melodies in the same meter to create variety and extend the duration of the ritual while periodically returning to the *Svekrvino* tune.[23] *Svekrvino* customarily begins with the *goč* drum performing solo for a time, as if to emphasize the exciting pull of the percussive motif. Indeed, the drummer often performs directly in front of the *svekrva* throughout. *Vranjanci* say, "Without the *goč*, there is nothing!" Many women enthusiastically comment that the "heavy" beating of the *goč* drum (referring to the slow tempo of the dance) automatically makes them feel butterflies in their stomach and sparks the desire to dance.

Musicians interact closely with the *svekrva* as she dances, using improvisation to heighten her emotional state. In addition to the slow, syncopated beating of the *goč* drum, the leading trumpet, saxophone, or clarinet uses periodic solos to raise the level of excitement. Celebrants especially respond to microtonal melodic improvisations, much beloved in local musical culture for the pleasure they induce. Performers launch into wailing solos that draw out specific pitches, add complex ornamentation, or else deploy exaggerated slow pitch slides, all executed over the almost trance-inducing percussive background of the mid-brass instruments and drum. Corporeal engagements by, and with, the musicians also produce affective intensity. The groom's parents and relatives often request specific "modes of attention" from the musicians in order to frame the ritual moment (Csordas 1993). During solos by the melodic instruments, for example, musicians may approach the *svekrva* while she dances, bending (or kneeling) to play toward her feet, pointing the bells of their instruments toward her face, or playing next to her ear to direct the musical energy at her in a very physical way.

The complex interaction of dance movements, melodic improvisation, rhythmic support, and public performance pushes *Svekrvino Kolo*'s sentimental significance for celebrants (especially the *svekrva*) into a state of affective "high." The embodied experience of *Svekrvino* with its iconic musical accompaniment draws together diverse threads of symbolic meaning, cultural continuity, family dynamics, and collective feeling for participants. Affect produced through musical sounds and bodily practices (by musicians and celebrants alike) really drives the power of the *Svekrvino* ritual, in other words; and these dynamics constantly reaffirm Romani importance for reproducing social life and cultural connections in Vranje.

Romani brass bands thus mediate the interconnection between collective feeling, identity, and folklore. Romani entertainers are seminal culture-bearers in this context because they husband older repertoires and customary practices, even as they also constantly elaborate these "living traditions." The affective power that Roma create at community events by means of expert skills and knowledge also lubricates the social relations that form the bedrock of local people's lives. Romani performers' ability to foster intense emotion and social connection through performance, therefore, galvanizes important cultural processes that define family, marriage, gender, and sociality in Vranje.

Exotic by Proxy: Ottoman Legacies, Identity Politics, and Romani Expressive Culture

Aside from their outsized impact on local musical heritage and their skill at producing celebratory affect, Vranje Roma are essential figures in regional identity politics. The importance of music and dance in Romani community life positions them as "middlemen" whose practices link *Vranjanci* to a distinctive cultural heritage within Serbia more broadly. More specifically, locals admire how Roma (still) cultivate musical and dance aesthetics shaped by centuries of Ottoman rule. These "Eastern" forms are seen as "unique" to Vranje, allowing locals to garner prestige and other forms of renown beyond their hometown.

Local narratives of regional pride often center on the area's Ottoman legacies. Tropes of Ottoman Vranje carry considerable cultural cachet by legitimating local claims to urban cosmopolitanism and historical continuity. Moreover, stereotypes that depict Vranje as Serbia's most exotic, "Eastern" place support local claims of cultural distinctiveness within the nation (Zlatanović 2008). These narratives generate cultural capital by engaging with the positive valences of orientalist tropes, including claims that heightened sensuality and good musical taste are inherent to local character (Zlatanović 2008:155). At times, these tropes effectively counter widespread narratives that lament the history of "oppressive" Ottoman rule in Serbia.

Romanticization of Ottoman Vranje traces back to the early twentieth-century literary works of Borisav (Bora) Stanković (Zlatanović 2008). Born in Vranje shortly before the end of Ottoman rule, Bora—as *Vranjanci* generally refer to him—penned several works whose storylines were set in town around the end of the Ottoman period.[24] His literary opus quickly became popular and has since entered the canon of classical Serbian literature. Bora's sentimental treatment of the Ottoman look and feel of turn-of-the-century Vranje strongly influenced characterizations of the town's "local color" in Serbia and Yugoslavia more broadly (Zlatanović 2008). Popular narratives evoke an exotic space still deeply marked by the Turks—narrow streets, enclosed gardens, melismatic song, the crooning of the clarinet, the rustling of women's silken *šalvar* pants, and above all the purportedly passionate temperament of the locals.[25]

People from Vranje liberally traffic in such romantic images because of their national popularity (Zlatanović 2008:148–150, 154). They often use the phrase *Borino Vranje* ("Bora's Vranje") interchangeably with *Staro Vranje* ("Old Vranje") in nostalgic talk about the beauties of the old town and its culture (Zlatanović 2008). A Facebook group dedicated to "Old Vranje" sees members posting old photos of the town, many from the late nineteenth and early twentieth centuries. Users' responses vacillate between enthusiastic praise for the way the town once was and bitter laments about the disappearance of "authentic" landmarks and the old ambience. *Vranjanci* obtain symbolic capital by claiming intrinsic cultural value and deep history via Ottoman legacies—rejecting, by contrast, notions that Vranje is merely an impoverished peripheral backwater in contemporary Serbia (see Zlatanović 2008:157–158).

Thus, *Vranjanci* are keen to emphasize links to the Ottoman period through cultural forms that carry positive connotations. They point to cuisine, language, traditional attire, and architecture as proof of genuine cultural continuity with Ottoman times. Music and dance practices provide an especially powerful link to this past because they also generate strong feelings and nostalgic associations with community celebrations. People affectionately describe older songs, music, and dances as "old Turkish things" (*stare turske stvari*, in Serbian). Sometimes these repertoires are simply glossed as *pusto tursko*, literally meaning "cursed Turkish" but in effect implying intense, bittersweet emotion about something of value.[26] Stage presentations and film adaptations of Bora Stanković's works feature copious amounts of Vranje folk music, popularizing these repertoires throughout the former Yugoslavia (Zlatanović 2008:150–152). Well-known Yugoslav-era folk singers, such as Staniša Stošić, also promoted Vranje's musical heritage on the national stage through recordings and performances for radio and television. While most commercial recordings stylized Vranje music in ways that altered important aspects of local practice—to make them more "palatable" for nonlocal audiences unfamiliar with Ottoman-derived aesthetics—popular acclaim for this music nevertheless boosts its symbolic value for locals seeking cultural capital (Zlatanović 2008:150–152).

Vranjanci point to specific ensembles, particular repertoires, and a distinctive musical style to demonstrate Ottoman cultural influence. Key aspects of musical form and aesthetics draw from late Ottoman practices. Additive meters such as 7/8 (3+2+2), 9/8 (2+2+2+3), and 12/8 (3+2+2+3+2 or 3+2+2+2+3) are common, and locals prize rhythmic syncopation for creating the distinctive groove of local music. *Vranjanci* contrast these features with "monotonous" even meters (primarily 2/4) associated with central Serbia, the nation's proverbial heartland. Extensive microtonality (i.e., the use of smaller intervals than is typical in Western classical music) also marks the distinctive sound and improvisational potential of Vranje folk music. Romani musicians argue that these *polutonovi* (literally "half-tones" but in practice meaning semitones) are among the most aesthetically pleasing facets of local music, and many stress that this microtonality makes local musical palates (and especially Romani musical tastes) "like those of Turks." Ottoman musical echoes even influence conventions for soloing and improvisation. Romani musicians refer to instrumental solos as *gazeli* (*gazel*, sg.), a term that generally meant a vocal improvisational solo in late Ottoman parlance. Local people prize evocative *gazeli*, with particularly superb improvisations instantly drawing intense bodily and exclamatory responses from audiences.

Regional dance repertoires also illustrate Ottoman cultural influence. Dance tunes like *Pembe* (from the Turkish for "pink"), *Serez* (the Turkish name for a district in today's northern Greece), and *Djošino Tursko Kolo* ("Djoša's Turkish dance") suggest origins in the Ottoman period. Serbs in particular sometimes associate drawn-out leg lifts (with the knee bent up to a 90-degree angle) in slower dances like *Pembe* and *Preševka* with Muslim/Albanian/Turkish dance aesthetics (Fig. 34.4).

Perhaps the strongest association with Ottoman culture coheres around *čoček* music and dance, however. The term comes from the Ottoman Turkish *köçek*, a type of professional male dancer who performed in a solo fashion at court celebrations and public entertainment venues until the mid-1800s (see Seeman 2019). In the Balkans at large, the term *čoček* (or *qyqek, kyuchek*) may indicate dance forms, metric patterns, or repertoires of tunes depending on the specific region and ethnic group in question (see also Silverman 2012). In Vranje, *čoček* encompasses a large repertoire of tunes in highly syncopated 2/4, 4/4, or 9/8 meters. *Čoček* also refers to two-line dance forms (for tunes in 4/4 and 2/4 vs. in 9/8), as well as improvisational solo dancing featuring subtle movements of the hands, arms, shoulders, and pelvis.

Local discourses explicitly connect *čoček* with the urban culture of Old Vranje. While *čoček* is especially important to Roma, Serbs also embrace *čoček* as part of their

FIG. 34.4. Romani men execute higher leg lifts while dancing *Pembe*, an older "heavy" dance form, in 2010.

(Photograph by the author.)

traditional music and dance culture. *Čoček* in 9/8 is known as *Vranjski čoček* ("Vranje čoček"), explicitly highlighting connections to the area's past. Throughout the Balkans various groups connect the 9/8 meter with Turks and Turkish legacies, especially in Turkish Thrace, Bulgaria, and parts of Macedonia (Silverman 2012; Seeman 2019). Ethnographic accounts from Vranje in the 1930s indicate that *Vranjanci* still called it *čoček avası* at the time, using a localized form of the Turkish word for "tune" (*havası*) (Janković and Janković 1951b:146, 152–153). Both Serbs and Roma dance *Vranjski čoček*, but Serbs consider it to be the most "authentic" (essentially, the oldest) *čoček* style in their community; it is also the only dance form that Serbs refer to as *čoček*.[27] Serbs also generally imbue *čoček* with orientalist notions of Ottoman Turkish influence, highlighting "sensual" dimensions of the solo form of the dance. *Vranjanci* often claim that "every woman in Vranje knows to dance with her hips and belly." Even as they assert an inherent ability to dance solo-type *čoček*, Serbs also posit an exotic continuity between *čoček* and "belly dance" to strengthen the connection to an "Eastern," Ottoman heritage.

Čoček in 9/8 also conjures Old Vranje's Ottoman holdovers further abroad. Choreographed suites of "dances from Vranje" performed by nearly every dance ensemble in Serbia and the diaspora feature stylized interpretations of *Vranjski čoček* as a grand finale. Women performers dressed in the brightly colored *šalvar* pantaloons, short vests, and silk blouses of Ottoman-era attire dance *ćoček* in 9/8 while tapping elbows, knees, and hips with a tambourine (*dajre*). Officially, this segment of the choreography depicts Ottoman-era *čengije* or *ćoček(inj)e*—predominantly Romani women who sang, played the *dajre*, and danced for pay in taverns and at celebrations (Sugarman 2003; see also Seeman 1990; Silverman 2012; Seeman 2019). The ubiquity and popularity of this choreography illustrate how connections between *ćoček*, Romani entertainers, and romantic stereotypes underpin notions of Vranje's distinctive expressive culture.

In essence, Serbs often need Roma in order to access Old Vranje cachet because it is specifically Romani musical labor and expressive culture that maintain iconic Ottoman-derived forms. Extant Romani music and dance practices bridge the temporal and cultural gap between the Ottoman era and the present day. For one thing, Roma liberally pepper the pages of Bora Stanković's classic works, generally appearing as musicians and singers who entertain townspeople with masterful skill. The plot of Stanković's play *Koštana* revolves around a Romani heroine who sings and dances professionally as a *čengija*, beguiling the town's elite Serbian youth with her talent and exceptional beauty. Stanković consistently ties the emotional depth and passion of his characters to their appreciation, even need, for music provided by Romani artists. Because popular Vranje stereotypes often draw from Stanković's works, they also reinforce close connections between Roma, music, and Ottoman Old Vranje. Moreover, *Vranjanci* can actively cultivate (and perform) the archetypal lust for life described in Stanković's opus by engaging with Romani musicians.

In practice, too, Serbs see Roma as culture-bearers who continue older Ottoman legacies. *Vranjanci* argue that Roma retain traditional practices to a much greater extent than Serbs, pointing out, for example, that most Roma still hold extended three-day weddings with the full gamut of rituals and customs. Romani women in Vranje attend weddings in attire derived from Ottoman-era urban clothing: silk blouses with wide sleeves, short vests, and most importantly *šalvare* (Fig. 34.5). Throughout Serbia, this sartorial ensemble evokes (Ottoman) Vranje, familiar to all who have seen folk dance performances or theater productions of Stanković's plays.

Romani-style *ćoček* dance makes for yet another valued link to the Ottoman past. *Ćoček* comprises the vast majority of the dance repertoire at Romani events. *Romski ćoček* is the most common form. It may be danced as a line dance or in the solo style derived from late Ottoman practices. Romani professional *čengije* or *ćočekinje* performed similar solo *ćoček* in taverns and at celebratory gatherings during the Ottoman period (see Seeman 1990; Sugarman 2003; Silverman 2012; Seeman 2019). Solo Romani *ćoček* connotes a deep, ongoing cultural link to the Ottoman past by conjuring images of these *čengije* entertainers (Fig. 34.6).

Furthermore, Vranje's Roma are the de facto tradition-bearers as musical professionals who preserve the older repertoires associated with the Ottoman period. Ottoman society considered musical performance for pay to be a low-class profession, shameful because performers use bodily skills to produce pleasurable states for paying patrons (Sugarman 2003; Shay 2014). This was despite high demand for professional

FIG. 34.5. Groom's mother and the bride lead the dance line at a Romani wedding in the 1980s, dressed in traditional attire marked by *šalvare*.

(Photograph by the author.)

musicians' and dancers' expert services to support important life-cycle rituals and create pleasurable experiences. Because of the stigma against performing for pay, such work often fell to Romani communities whose marginalization meant that this was one of the most lucrative of the limited economic options available to them (Sugarman 2003; Silverman 2012; Seeman 2019). Vranje Romani professional knowledge—honed over generations of musical labor—means that they not only maintain key repertoires but also guide clientele through essential rituals at celebrations, practices whose cultural scripts can be traced back to the late Ottoman period.

Serbs can also use Roma as proxies to tap into a cosmopolitan urban identity with deep historical roots. Ottoman urban lifestyles historically connoted higher socioeconomic status and conferred greater cultural capital by virtue of their connection to imperial centers of power (Seeman 2012; Seeman 2019). Throughout the Ottoman-controlled Balkans, town-dwellers emphasized their privileged status by contrasting urban lifestyles with rural peasant practices. By the nineteenth century, growing numbers of non-Muslims residing in towns and cities readily adopted the hallmarks of Ottoman urban culture to confirm their place as cosmopolitan residents—many spoke Turkish in addition to their mother tongue, cultivated distinctively Ottoman urban forms of dress (such as *šalvare* among women), and so on (Hadži Vasiljević 1932; Pettan 2002; Seeman 2019).

FIG. 34.6. Young Romani woman dances solo *čoček* at a wedding in 2007.

(Photograph by the author.)

Music and dance practices were no exception. Urban *čalgija* musical ensembles were considered more prestigious in part because of their connections to Ottoman court and high-art music, as opposed to *zurla-tapan* (*surla-goč*) bands and other forms of music associated with rural communities (or the "raucous" outdoor celebrations of commoners) (Pettan 2002; Seeman 2012:300; Seeman 2019). *Čalgija* music continued to connote prestige and cosmopolitanism for patrons in neighboring Macedonia and Kosovo well into the twentieth century (Pettan 2002; Seeman 2012:299–301). Similarly, Romani musical services even today allow Vranje Serbs to perform (often in visceral, embodied ways) cultural prestige rooted in valued Ottoman urban legacies.

In sum, music and dance mean that Roma can act as cultural bridges to prized aspects of the town's Ottoman past. Serbs are often anxious that decades of nation-building and modernization projects have weakened iconic practices that continue to "live" in Romani communities. When Roma sing, play, and dance, they offer Serbs opportunities to tangibly (re)connect with exoticized cultural differences that invoke an alluring past. Vranje Serbs can harness pro-Ottoman "Oriental" tropes, in fact, subtly complicating black-and-white narratives of Ottoman-derived backwardness without overtly threatening their belonging to a "European" Serbian national identity. Elements of self-exoticization in these narratives also portray locals as deeply emotional and possessed of an inherent zest for life, a positive but also purportedly Eastern subjectivity that Romani entertainers help bring out during musical events (Zlatanović 2008:155–157; see also van de Port 1998:177–206). Romani performers allow local Serbs to safely access Ottoman cultural forms through living folklore, claiming regional "authenticity," prestigious urbanity, and an exotic otherness that brings valuable cachet in spite of popular derision for "Turkish times" in Serbian national discourse.

Conclusion: Recognizing Romani Rootedness

All across Europe, critics have long argued that Roma do not really belong in the societies where they live. Tropes of "Gypsy" nomadism, backwardness, and depravity figure prominently in racist narratives that promote Romani exclusion or even cleansing from national spaces (Hancock 1987; Stewart 2013; McGarry 2017). Aside from deriding Romani bodies and lifestyles, anti-"Gypsy" diatribes also often claim that Roma have no "real" (or "good") folklore and culture of their own, instead using and corrupting cultural forms of those around them. Music and dance are frequent targets in these narratives. In the Balkans people contrast ostensibly "Gypsy" instruments like the violin, clarinet, and *zurla/surla*—associated with paid performers—with "pure" folk instruments performed by amateur (generally rural) non-Romani musicians. Even musical scholarship has often sought to differentiate Romani musical practices from those of national majorities, claiming that Roma perform purely out of economic self-interest, do not possess their "own" music but rather perform that of others, have little knowledge of musical theory, and even "corrupt" the national musical traditions of others through hybrid practices and out of a desire to please the masses (Bartók 1947; Djordjević [1933] 1984:36–39; cf. Silverman 2012). Nationalist detractors cynically criticize the value of Romani music-making by exploiting essentialisms that link Romani musical practices with inherent "Gypsy" inferiority.

Yet on the ground in places like Vranje, we see that in reality Roma have long been dynamic partners in cultural production and "tradition." Far from merely "taking" the expressive forms of others to regurgitate them in performance contexts, Romani professionals constantly elaborate expressive culture through careful innovation. Moreover, they may be "pillars" of folkloric heritage, serving as a kind of living memory of community cultural histories by maintaining valued practices. Roma cultivate profound insights into the cultural worlds of their neighbors, mastering intricate details of ritual, social, and aesthetic life in order to secure their livelihoods.

These performance skills and expertise embed Roma firmly within local communities, in the end; and Romani performers drive practices that shape cultural reproduction, social life, and identity politics with far-ranging impacts. Romani musicians act as a kind of interstitial glue within communities, providing services that create intense spaces for people to strengthen (or renegotiate) family bonds and social relations. Their musical labor channels collective affect, where intense feeling in extraordinary situations heightens celebrants' reflexive engagement with issues of gender, family, sociality, and identity, among others. Whether as *tamburica* players, violinists, accordionists, or brass musicians, Romani musicians throughout Serbia are integral to the sociocultural fabric of life—in spite of the intense marginalization and ubiquitous racism that often disavow Romani worth and belonging in the nation.

Notes

1. See https://www.youtube.com/watch?v=J5txVVdgXNo for a 1960s recording of "Sobinka," performed by locally renowned Romani clarinetist Kurta Ajredinović.
2. *Čoček* denotes a broad genre of music, as well as dance forms, associated with Ottoman cultural legacies throughout the Balkans and often with Romani communities in particular. There are myriad *čoček* melodies, generally in highly syncopated 2/4, 7/8, or 9/8 meter; and Romani musicians constantly improvise new tunes. In Vranje, people distinguish between two "subcategories": tunes in 9/8 with one specific dance form known as *Vranjski čoček* versus all other music in 2/4 (or 4/4 or even 8/8) that accompanies a different dance form.
3. I use the word "Gypsy" in quotation marks when discussing how non-Roma stereotype Roma; primarily non-Romani peoples assigned names like "Gypsy," *Ciganin, Zigeuner*, etc., to Romani groups; and these often have pejorative connotations. In all other circumstances I use Roma (adj., Romani) out of respect for the way that most Romani communities refer to themselves.
4. Serbs and Roma constitute the two main ethnic groups in Vranje and in the villages surrounding the town. According to the 2011 census, Serbs comprise roughly 92 percent of the urban population, while Roma make up nearly 6 percent of the town's residents. Significant Romani communities, including musicians, also exist in nearby Vranjska Banja and the village of Pavlovac, alongside Serbs. Census data on Roma are often problematic, however, as some Roma may prefer to affiliate with other ethnic groups to avoid social stigma (there are Roma who are primarily Serbian-speaking Orthodox Christians and refute Romani origins, for example, although other Roma and Serbs reject this claim). Moreover, many Roma have emigrated to northern and western Europe since the European Union dropped restrictive visa requirements for Serbian citizens as of January 1, 2010; consistent emigration has lowered numbers of full-time Romani residents in the region, but the extended diaspora maintains strong ties with the home region, returning

5. I conducted seventeen months of fieldwork focused on Romani musical labor and ethnic relations in Vranje, spread over various stays between 2006 and 2011, with a year-long consecutive residency from 2009 to 2010. I worked with Serbs and Roma alike, inquiring about musical practices, folk tradition and cultural innovation, and performative dynamics at celebrations; I also investigated how ethnic relations and music were informed by politics, economics, and social concerns. In addition to participant observation, including documenting musical events such as weddings in both Romani and Serb communities, I interviewed Romani musicians, Romani community members, and Serbs across a broad spectrum of generation, socioeconomic class, and gender to obtain a cross section of local perspectives on music and dance, regional folk culture, and ethnic identity in the area.
6. Romani professional musicians make their living primarily by tendering musical services for pay at community celebrations among both Roma and Serbs. Romani musicians preserve specialized knowledge of local musical aesthetics, diverse repertoires, and key elements of ritual and celebratory folk culture; musicians are generally trained within families, where elders pass down knowledge through traditional methods (including learning by ear), and many ensembles are formed around extended family groups.
7. Most likely as part of *mehter* ensembles associated with Ottoman military and government. Such ensembles accompanied soldiers, including the janissary corps, into battle but also performed for court ceremonies (and those of provincial officials). *Mehter* bands comprised a variety of wind and percussion instruments, several of which—such as the double-reed *zurla* (*surla*) shawm and the large double-headed drum known as *davul* (but also *tapan* or *goč* in the Balkans)—also became popular in local folk music, likely as a result of Romani musicians' transferring these instruments to community circles. See Seeman (2019) for a more in-depth discussion of *mehter* music and its connection to Romani musicians historically.
8. See Seeman (1990 and 2012) for a more in-depth discussion of the instrumentation, musical style, and historical development of comparable urban *čalgija* music in Macedonia. Historically, ensembles in Vranje were likely similar to the group in this video of *čalgija* musicians from Veles, Macedonia, performing on clarinet, violin, *džumbuš* (*cümbüş* in Turkish), and *dajre* (tambourine-like frame drum): https://www.youtube.com/watch?v=Gz5yJCgQSos.
9. The root *čalgi-* in the name for the musicians/ensemble type derives from the Turkish verb "çalmak," meaning to strike or to play, pointing to a clear connection with Ottoman urban culture (Seeman 1990; Seeman 2012; Seeman 2019).
10. See Seeman (2012:300) for a similar distinction between less prestigious outdoor ensembles, known as *kaba čalgi*, that played for weddings and more highly regarded ensembles that played indoors at urban events (known as *indži čalgi*, or fine/refined ensembles) in Macedonia.
11. This ensemble type is widespread throughout the southern Balkans; see Keil and Vellou-Keil (2002). Vranje ensembles were much like this one at a Romani wedding in Skopje, Macedonia: https://www.youtube.com/watch?v=CZAd7C5QTzc (accessed January 19, 2016).
12. See Vukanović (1987) for one such photograph.
13. Similar transformations of Ottoman-influenced musical practices took place several decades prior in central Serbia after independence from Ottoman rule during the mid-nineteenth century (see Djordjević [1933] 1984:30).

14. See Pettan (2002) for the situation in Kosovo in the late twentieth century, where *surla* and *goč* bands were associated with Muslims and not sought out by Serbs in the midst of rising political tensions with Albanians. Compare this with accounts by Serbian dance researchers Ljubica Janković and Danica (1951a) whose fieldwork in eastern Kosovo during the 1930s demonstrates that local Serbs still regularly hired Romani *surla* and *goč* musicians. According to Robert Leibman, older Serbs in this region still preferred such ensembles as late as 1972, asking him to bring out such musicians when he sought to film the community's dance repertoire (personal communication).
15. See this recording of the tune "Vranjanka," for example: https://www.youtube.com/watch?v=ieC6JcAZsJM (accessed August 1, 2018).
16. Kusturica's most famous films, such as *Underground* and *Black Cat, White Cat*, centered plot lines and characters around tragicomic approaches and absurdist fantasy, often as commentary on sociopolitical disintegration amidst calamities like war. Romani characters (and actors) figured in several of his films, often to heighten absurd or chaotic elements; and Romani brass music provided a raucous soundtrack to support such scenes.
17. *Ćef* comes from the Ottoman Turkish *keyif*, and this concept (and name) are common in many other Balkan regions once under Ottoman rule (e.g., Albanian *qejf*, Greek *kefi*).
18. In Ottoman and Turkish musical practice, *mekam* refers to general rules for composing and improvising (similar to modes); *mekams* are named and vary in terms of range and typical melodic contours. In Vranje, however, *mekam* has come to refer to solo, usually unmetered improvisation, without reference to the musical theory behind the Ottoman-derived *mekam* system; some, like the one discussed here, have even become fairly standardized in terms of melody and improvisational turns.
19. When a daughter marries, her mother does not perform this dance ritual; instead, it is the privilege of the young woman's mother-in-law because the ritual symbolism focuses on male children and perpetuation of the groom's family lineage.
20. For a detailed analysis of wedding rituals in the Serbian community in Vranje, comparing pre–World War II weddings with those of the 1990s, see Zlatanović (2003).
21. See *Svekrvino* at this 2010 Romani wedding in Vranje: https://www.youtube.com/watch?v=rlQGPeQ1I3Y.
22. Indeed, many ritual tunes and dances in Vranje are set to a slow 7/8 meter, so locals closely associate it with the most intense moments (and feelings) of celebrations. Slow tunes in 7/8 meter are also associated with important ritual dancing in other Balkan communities, such as among Serbs in eastern Kosovo and in many Romani communities in Kosovo and Macedonia (see Seeman 1990:23; Silverman 2012:28).
23. Here is the standard *Svekrvino Kolo* melody, performed by the Dejan Avdić brass band from Vranjska Banja: https://www.youtube.com/watch?v=-17-s1OGyFM.
24. Although the exact date is unknown, Bora was likely born in 1876. The expanding Serbian state conquered Vranje and officially ended Ottoman rule in 1878.
25. *Šalvare* (from Turkish, also locally known as *dimije*) are a type of wide, baggy pants drawn in and secured at the waist by a drawstring. In the late Ottoman period, they were typical elements of urban women's attire, particularly among wealthier classes, across religious and ethnic lines. They were generally seen as a marker of town culture via Ottoman urban practices, in contrast to the woolen skirts worn by peasant women (generally Christians) in villages surrounding towns. While most Christian urban women abandoned *šalvare* in favor of newer, central Serbian urban styles after the Ottoman period, Romani women in

Vranje have continued to wear them (albeit only on festive occasions in recent decades), and people see them as distinctively Romani folk attire.

26. *Pusto* in Serbian literally means "deserted" or "abandoned," but in a colloquial sense the word can be translated as "cursed." For English speakers the translation may seem anything but affectionate, but it is regularly used in a laudatory way. For example, older Vranje residents often talk about *pusta mladost*, or "cursed youth," to reflect on the beauty of younger days, gone too quickly and missed very much. Because intense feeling is highly valued, when Serbs apply the term *pusto* to old "Turkish-era" repertoires they do so to emphasize how deeply they enjoy them.

27. Serbs also dance to tunes in 4/4 or 2/4, but many call the dance *Sa*. Roma, on the other hand, always refer to these tunes as *čoček*, sometimes qualifying them as *Romski* (Romani) *čoček* to differentiate them from *Vranjski Čoček* in 9/8. As such, they also claim the former style of *čoček* as distinctively Romani.

Works Cited

Bartók, Béla. 1947. "Gypsy Music or Hungarian Music?" *The Musical Quarterly*, 33/2:240–257.

Beissinger, Margaret. 2001. "Occupation and Ethnicity: Constructing Identity among Professional Romani (Gypsy) Musicians in Romania." *Slavic Review*, 60/1:24–49.

Brandl, Rudolf M. 1996. "The 'Yiftoi' and the Music of Greece: Role and Function." *The World of Music*, 38/1:7–32.

Csordas, Thomas J. 1993. "Somatic Modes of Attention." *Cultural Anthropology*, 8/2:135–156.

Djordjević, Tihomir. 1984. "Cigani i muzika u Srbiji." In *Naš narodni život*, Vol. 3. Belgrade: Prosveta. First published 1933.

Dumnić, Marija. 2013. "The Creation of Folk Music Program on Radio Belgrade before World War Two: Editorial Policies and Performing Ensembles." *Muzikologija*, 14:9–29.

Golemović, Dimitrije. 1997. "Mesto i uloga limenih duvačkih orkestara u narodnoj muzičkoj praksi Srbije." In *Etnomuzikološki ogledi*, 211–226. Belgrade: Biblioteka XX vek.

Golemović, Dimitrije. 2002. "Šta i kako." In *Dragačevski trubač*, 12–13.

Hadži Vasiljević, Jovan. 1932. "Vranjska gradska nošnja ranijih godina." *Glasnik etnografskog muzeja u Beogradu*, 7:6–31.

Hancock, Ian. 1987. *The Pariah Syndrome: An Account of Gypsy Slavery and Persecution*. Ann Arbor, MI: Karoma Publishers.

Janković, Ljubica, and Danica Janković. 1951a. "Gnjilanci i gnjilanske narodne igre: Opšti pregled na narodnu kulturu, stanovnike, istoriske prilike i narodni život u gnjilanskoj oblasti." In *Narodne Igre*, br. 6, 47–142. Belgrade: Prosveta.

Janković, Ljubica, and Danica Janković. 1951b. "Vranjanci i vranjanske narodne igre." In *Narodne Igre*, br. 6, 143–228. Belgrade: Prosveta.

Keil, Charles, and Angeliki Vellou-Keil. 2002. *Bright Balkan Morning: Romani Lives and the Power of Music in Greek Macedonia*. Middletown, CT: Wesleyan University Press.

McGarry, Aidan. 2017. *Romaphobia: The Last Acceptable Form of Racism*. London: Zed Books.

Milovanović, Krsto, and Dragan Babić. 2003. *Srpska truba*. Belgrade: Narodno Delo.

Pettan, Svanibor. 2002. *Rom Musicians in Kosovo: Interaction and Creativity*. Budapest: Institute for Musicology of the Hungarian Academy for Sciences.

Rice, Timothy. 1982. "The Surla and Tapan Tradition in Yugoslav Macedonia." *The Galpin Society Journal*, 35:122–137.

Seeman, Sonia Tamar. 1990. "Music in the Service of Prestation: The Case of the Rom of Skopje, Macedonia." In Continuity and Transformation in the Macedonian Genre of Chalgija." MA Thesis, University of Washington.

Seeman, Sonia Tamar. 2012. "Macedonian *Čalgija*: A Musical Refashioning of National Identity." *Ethnomusicology Forum*, 21/3:295–326.

Seeman, Sonia Tamar. 2019. *Sounding Roman: Representation and Performing Identity in Western Turkey*. New York: Oxford University Press.

Shay, Anthony. 2014. *The Dangerous Lives of Public Performers: Dancing, Sex, and Entertainment in the Islamic World*. New York: Palgrave Macmillan.

Silverman, Carol. 2012. *Romani Routes: Cultural Politics and Romani Music in Diaspora*. New York: Oxford University Press.

Stanković, Borisav. 2005. *Koštana: Komad iz vranjskog života s pesmama*. Belgrade: JRJ. First published 1902.

Stewart, Michael. 2013. "Populism, Roma, and the European Politics of Cultural Difference." In *The Gypsy "Menace": Populism and the New Anti-Gypsy Politics*, ed. Michael Stewart, 3–24. New York: Columbia University Press.

Sugarman, Jane C. 1997. *Engendering Song: Singing and Subjectivity at Prespa Albanian Weddings*. Chicago: University of Chicago Press.

Sugarman, Jane C. 2003. "Those 'Other Women': Dance and Femininity among Prespa Albanians." In *Music and Gender: Perspectives from the Mediterranean*, ed. Tallia Magrini, 87–118. Chicago: University of Chicago Press.

Timotijević, Miloš. 2005. *Karneval u guči: Sabor trubača 1961–2004*. Čačak: Legenda.

van de Port, Mattijs. 1998. *Gypsies, Wars, and Other Instances of the Wild: Civilization and Its Discontents in a Serbian Town*. Amsterdam: Amsterdam University Press.

Vukanović, Tatomir. 1978. *Etnička istorija i kulturna baština Vranjskog gravitacionog područja u doba oslobodjenja od Turaka 1878*. Vranje: Radnički Univerzitet.

Vukanović, Tatomir. 1987. *Muzička kultura u starom vranju*. Vranje: Nova Jugoslavija.

Zakić, Mirjana, and Danka Lajić-Mihajlović. 2012. "(Re)Creating the (Folk Music) Tradition: The National Competition of Brass Orchestras at the Dragačevo Trumpet Festival." *New Sound*, 39/1:58–79.

Zlatanović, Sanja. 2003. *Svadba—Priča o identitetu: Vranje i okolina*. Special Editions 47. Belgrade: Institute of Ethnography SASA.

Zlatanović, Sanja. 2008. "The Literary Opus of Bora Stanković and the Construction of a Local Identity." *Ethnologia Balkanica*, 12:147–166.

*Folk and Popular Music in
Post-communist Eastern Europe*

CHAPTER 35

BLUEGRASS AS *FOLK* MUSIC IN THE CZECH REPUBLIC

LEE BIDGOOD

When Czechs perform bluegrass music today, they use instruments and techniques developed in the United States: the five-string banjo and F-style mandolin, the flat-top dreadnought guitar, a fiddle used for breakdowns and harmonic layering, and a double bass for bottom-end rhythm (Video 1 ▶). Singers take on a country-like crooner role or join together in close-harmony hymns, choruses, and laments—often using the Czech language (Video 2 ▶) but sometimes in English (Video 3 ▶).[1]
  Video 1 https://youtu.be/t_k39NqCry8
  Video 2 https://youtu.be/ePU3yfTHiMw
  Video 3 https://youtu.be/C4Vx5iKwVOU
While it might seem unlikely for central Europeans to devote themselves to the performance of this form of Americana, there is significant context for this Czech bluegrass. Since the early 1900s Czechs have undertaken "Americanist" projects based on ideas and materials from the United States. Czech *bluegrassáci*[2] ("bluegrassers," an insider term both in Czech and US bluegrass circles) are people involved as musicians, luthiers, parents, spouses, audience members, customers—music makers, per Small (1998). Czech bluegrassers engage in Americanism alongside individuals who maintain US military vehicles, recreate battles from the US Civil War, and dress up as Native Americans, cowboys, and gold prospectors. Calling participants in these scenes "Americanists" (Bidgood 2017:129–130), I consider their activities as negotiations between Czechness and Americanness: they exist in a persistent liminal/liminoid state (Turner 1974) with transformative power that depends on connections to both Czech and American realities (Boyce-Tillman 2009). Attention to Czech bluegrass music making provides new perspectives on the connections between "folk" and "folklore" in central European contexts.
  As an acoustic form of country music that emphasizes its vernacular elements, bluegrass is sometimes considered a commercial popular form and sometimes as traditional music. Bluegrass fits with Jason Toynbee's criteria for popular music: it developed in

and through mass media and serves a mixed constituency that includes middle- and working-class as well as diasporic communities. It also plays out the paradox that Toynbee identifies among popular musics that both "identify and represent particular social groups" and seek to "sing for *all* the people" (Toynbee 2000:xix). There is a professional industry and a market for bluegrass; at the same time bluegrassers worldwide create the music in non-commercial contexts where the social/cultural capital of authenticity and the pathways of transmission are as important as economic capital (DeWitt 2009). In the United States and elsewhere, bluegrass has become a means for mediating tensions and paradoxes that arise between ideas of folk, traditional, and popular music. This chapter explores cases (including some from my ethnographic fieldwork), highlighting ways that Czechs have integrated and distinguished *folk*, folkloric, and bluegrass within local and global contexts.

Video 1. Czech–Slovak–Dutch band G-Runs and Roses performs the classic bluegrass song "Molly and Tenbrooks" at *Balbínova poetická hospůdka* (Balbín's Poetic Little Pub) in downtown Prague, February 4, 2019. (Credit: Lee Bidgood.)

Video 2. At an informal jam in an apartment building basement in Prague a group of amateur Czech musicians performs "Karolína," a popular retexting of Michael Martin Murphey's song "Carolina in the Pines," March 14, 2019. (Credit: Lee Bidgood.)

Video 3. Goodwill (from the Czech city of Ostrava) perform their original song "Glad to Be Dead" with a contemporary edge at the *Muzikantský kemp na Kosodrevine* (Kosodrevina Musicians' Camp) in the Slovakian Lower Tatra mountains, January 11, 2019. (Credit: Lee Bidgood.)

Clarification of Terms

Czech bluegrassers have explained to me that what they sing and play is neither *folklor/folklorní* (folklore/folkloric) nor *lidový* (folk, meaning "of the people"); they do not ordinarily play the styles and repertories that have been designated as regional or local cultural heritage (e.g., vocal songs from a certain village or a dance done by members of a specific group). Nor do they perform repertory that was created by the singer-songwriters who have created a vibrant Czech *folk* scene since the 1960s. The term *tradiční* (traditional) is used by Czech bluegrassers to describe bluegrass projects that draw on early versions of the style or are otherwise antiquated.

Discussing this range of terms, usages, and sounds, I also draw on linguist Tom Dickins's concept of a spectrum in the field of Czech *folk*-related music. The spectrum concept allows Dickins to use categories derived from American and other global sources: *folk* (inflected by the work of singer-songwriters like Bob Dylan and Joni Mitchell), *country* (derived from American country music), and *tramp* music (a form rooted in Czech romanticization of America in the early 1900s) within the range of vernacular forms that provide Czechs a sense of rootedness and community and a means for negotiating ideas of authenticity (Dickins 2017).

Bluegrass in a Global Context

The history of bluegrass is informed by the hillbilly music industry that emerged in the United States during the early 1900s when records of rural string band musicians were marketed to the wider US public. Hillbilly records and barn dance radio shows gained audiences nationwide (Peterson 1997; Wolfe 1999; Berry 2008) and even reached audiences as far afield as South Africa and Australia (Bidgood and Přibylová 2022).

Bill Monroe (1911–1996) was a mandolinist, singer, and bandleader (after 1939 his group was known as Bill Monroe and His Blue Grass Boys) whose changing cast of sidemen (contracted supporting musicians, some of whom were female) would shape their namesake style for more than half a century. Seeking to decenter Monroe in the 1950s, fans and music makers adopted the term "bluegrass" to refer to acoustic, string band–accompanied country music (Rosenberg 2005:102). Bluegrass in this decade was flexible; it allowed musicians and fans to react against the polished "Nashville sound" of country music and the clamor of rock and roll but also to embrace the financial possibilities pop-crossover could provide. During this time, bluegrass was in the mainstream of American popular music, and recordings and broadcasts reached audiences abroad thanks to US military media of occupation forces in Japan and Germany (Bidgood and Přibylová 2022).

During this period urban, middle-class revivalists around the world found in bluegrass an alternative to commercial country and pop, one whose standardized format for participatory music making provided clear roles for participants (Rosenberg 1993). Festivals allowed fans and musicians (some of whom found they could make their living through bluegrass) to share in music making. The first American bluegrass festivals were in Virginia in the first half of the 1960s; the first outside the United States was likely in New Zealand in 1967; the Banjo Jamboree bluegrass festival first held in Kopidlno, Czechoslovakia, in 1973 is the longest-running European festival (Video 4 ▶ and Fig. 35.1).

Video 4 https://youtu.be/yGRLYdIOGIA

Bluegrass is more marginal in the Czech Republic than in the United States, where there is an industry group (the International Bluegrass Music Association, established 1985) and a Recording Academy award category (or "Grammy"), established in 1989; still, films like *Bonnie and Clyde*, *Deliverance*, and *O Brother, Where Art Thou* give the music a globally recognized presence. Bluegrass affords its diverse range of participants ways to revise received narratives (e.g., highlighting the contributions of Black Americans to string band music; see Barbour-Payne 2016) as well as nostalgic rearticulations of community such as the aggressive neotraditional precision of "mash" (an approach that emphasizes coordination instead of polyphony in the ensemble; see Cassell 2021).

Czech bluegrass activity includes many of these approaches, such as the nostalgic traditionalism of bands like Sunny Side and BG Cwrkot who emulate the sound and dramaturgy of 1950s bluegrassers. In contrast, Druhá Tráva ("Second" or "Other" Grass)

FIG. 35.1. A fan, Ondřej Kozák, and Ralph Schut at the Banjo Jamboree festival in Čáslav, a yearly event of the *Bluegrassová Asociace České Republiky* (Bluegrass Association of the Czech Republic), June 22, 2019.

(Credit: Lee Bidgood.)

perform original songs by Robert Křešťan written in a literary mode that does not reference a rural past. Bands like G-Runs and Roses and Milkeaters perform a mix of older material, tongue-in-cheek pop covers, as well as original compositions, mostly within the "mash" framework that rearticulates bluegrass's driving rhythm.

While there is an actual bluegrass industry in the United States, only a handful of Czech bluegrassers and bands make their living entirely from the music. Participants in the Czech scene usually have day jobs, even if they are paid for performing at festivals, country saloon bars, and other venues where bluegrass is a part of the living tradition of Czech Americanism. Pub jams have long been a key part of bluegrass activity for players of all levels, a weekly social and musical meeting where the sharing of beer and song around a table fosters strong community connections. For example, in 2019 I tracked down some musicians in Prague who I used to jam with during visits in 2002–2008 and found that the core members of the same group were still meeting (Fig. 35.2).

Despite its rootsy trappings, grassroots community, and being the "best-documented genre of country music," bluegrass was not initially recognized as "folklore" (Malone and Laird 2018:659; Rosenberg 2018:133). Robert Cantwell has called the style "an original characterization . . . a 'representation,' of traditional Appalachian music," perhaps implying distance from an authorized "tradition" (1984:xi). Neil Rosenberg writes in

FIG. 35.2. Guitarist and singer Zdeněk, along with his bass-playing wife Věra (not pictured), supported the Czech-language bluegrass jam at the *U Supa* pub in southwest Prague I first visited in 2002. This session on April 11, 2019, took place at a new jam location, the *Krok Zpět* restaurant in southern Prague.

(Credit: Lee Bidgood.)

the 1980s that, "Today bluegrass is in many ways more of a traditional art that it was when the folk revivalists discovered it" as practitioners at the community level share it in "traditional" ways (2005:366). While commentators on string band revivals have foregrounded ambivalence about the ability of newcomers and "outsiders" to inhabit and express the music, Rosenberg (1993) discusses the possibility of a shift from being a "revivalist" to being a "specialist" in bluegrass. This possibility for transformation is key to the global popularity of bluegrass.

Video 4. At the 2019 Banjo Jamboree festival in Čáslav, banjoists join in playing "Foggy Mountain Breakdown" (a tune made famous by US banjoist Earl Scruggs), an annual tradition at the event. (Credit: Lee Bidgood.)

BOHEMIAN FOLKLORE IN CONTEXT

My ethnographic fieldwork with Czechs has focused on bluegrass, consisting of participant observation, interviews, as well as documentary projects like the film *Banjo Romantika* (Lange 2015).[3] Since I first started traveling to the Czech Republic in 2000, though, I have also become aware of how folkloric music has been produced, examined, and celebrated in Bohemia and Moravia, two historically significant regions which, along with Silesia, make up the current territory of the country—and which show differing approaches to Americanism.

The mid-nineteenth-century Czech national revival accompanied awareness of *das Volk* growing throughout Europe. The "Gubernatorial Collecting" carried out by Austrian authorities in 1819 gathered and transcribed "folk songs, but also ballads and various kinds of very unsophisticated tunes" (Pilková 1988:35). Later collectors/composers such as Antonin Dvořák and Leoš Janáček supported nation-building with their presentation of folkloric material. The eastern region of Moravia, distant from metropolitan and industrial centers, was a key collecting field and still fascinates composers, collectors, and ethnologists searching for cultural rarities in bucolic rural locales.

In contrast, the more westerly Bohemia was designated by Austrian rulers as an industrial zone that by the end of the eighteenth century led the Czech-speaking lands in terms of manufacturing (Myška 1996:200). By 1919 Bohemia contained approximately 20 percent of the Austro-Hungarian Empire's population and 70 percent of its industrial capacity (Reidinger 2007:23). Rural migration to industrial centers such as Prague and Pilsen likely reduced Bohemians' ties to home territories and folklores.

Ethnic differences were exploited through the first half of the 1900s as Czechs expelled Germans from territory in north Bohemia newly established as part of the interwar Czechoslovak Republic (1918–1938), a move that was countered after the German takeover of the Sudetenland in 1938 (when Czechs were expelled) and then repeated after the Second World War with another expulsion of Germans. Musical life was affected by ethnicity politics: Bohemian Germans comprised a significant portion of the workforce in the west Bohemian town that in German was known as Schönbach. Tomáš Dvořák and Marek Rejhon (2019) explain how displacement of ethnically German workers from this center of stringed instrument manufacturing meant that the best makers of American-style jazz guitars moved across to Germany as the town was renamed Luby u Chebu.

In a 2019 interview, Czech old-time musician Martín Žák recalled the ethnically diverse landscape of northern Bohemia and how it homogenized through the first half of the 1900s. He recalls meeting with a Bohemian German woman spared the post–World War II expulsion and allowed by a Czech authority to choose one of hundreds of confiscated zithers, musical markers of German ethnicity (Žák personal interview, 2019). Žák's interest in this instrument in his region has an Americanist slant: he plays the Americanized version of the instrument known as the autoharp (Žák 2010).

Postwar changes to Czechoslovakia included the ascendancy of the Communist Party in 1948, new official interest in folklore (especially through spectacular displays of folklore as propaganda), and popular disillusion with local Bohemian and Moravian vernacular forms as a result. Musicologist Michael Beckerman argues that while after 1948 there was ambivalence about "official" folklore, informal use of folkloric material remained a way to offset "the deleterious influence of large Russian army ensembles" and to undertake and express a quest for ideals, even for "purity" (1996:47–48).

The separation of the Czech Republic and Slovakia in 1993 after the fall of communism in 1989 saw continued interest in folklore and continuity in practices of scholarship. The practice of *národopis* (ethnology) still holds a strong place in Czech academic circles; theory and practices from recent Western discourse on ethnography, anthropology, and folkloristics are slowly being adopted (Balaš 2018) accompanied by studies that critique past practices of Czech(oslovak) ethnology (Kratochvíl 2015). Histories such as Tyllner's *Tradiční hudba: Hledání kořenů* (*Traditional Music: Searching for Roots*, 2010) and Houda's studies of folk festivals during the normalization period (2013, 2019) represent evolving scholarly approaches. While ethnomusicologists like Zuzana Jurková (2014) have focused on urban folklore, Czech Americanism seems seldom worthy of scholarly attention. Exceptions include Jan Pohunek (2018) and the circle of scholars of the *Od folkloru k world music* (*From Folklore to World Music*) colloquium led by Irena Přibylová and Lucie Uhliková.[4] As the next section indicates, there are further examples of vernacular music forms which have not fit historically strict definitions for Czech *folklór* but have permeated Czech culture for centuries.

HISTORICAL CASE: ALTERNATIVE VERNACULARS

The history of Czech music practices provides a background for Czech *folk* culture. An early Czech vernacular urban song form, *kramářské písně* (vendors' or hawkers' songs), accompanied commercial transactions in urban market locations and spread through non-commercial person-to-person transmission through the nineteenth century (Thořová 2010). Other forms of urban vernacular songs such as the *Staropražské písničky* (Old Prague Songs) composed by Karel Hašler (1879–1941) were published and performed in cabarets in the 1910s and spread through oral circulation.[5] These vernacular folk-spectrum forms, especially early twentieth-century tramp music, are the foundation for Czechs' engagement with bluegrass.

Tramping music (*trampská hudba*) is the most direct predecessor to Czech bluegrass, notable for its pervasive and paradigm-setting Americanism. The informal Czech tramping movement established ca. 1900 patterns of Americanist recreation that continue today.[6] Early tramps pursued outdoor recreation in reaction to industrialization and urbanization, creating songs to provide a soundtrack for imaginative play around campfires in the Czechoslovak woods. Tramp songs (*trampské písně*) became commercial commodities as artists like the Melody Boys and the *Ztracenkáři* (a group linked to the tramp camp *Ztracená naděje*, or Lost Hope) made recordings of songs like *Cariboo* ("Caribou," by Jaroslav Mottl, ca. 1926) and *Vlajka* ("Flag," by Jan Korda, ca. 1928) that were featured on records and in films such as *Dobrý tramp Bernášek* (*The Good Tramp Bernášek*, dir. Karel Lamač, 1933) (Video 5 ▶).

Video 5 https://youtu.be/_KLZaQqfaAI

The verses of *Cariboo* narrate a first-person account of a caribou hunt at dawn, presumably in the animal's North American territory. The free phrasing and minor tonality of the melody, along with lines like *V plamenech posvátných hruď tvá se pálí—hlas předků vznešených volá už z dáli* ("In sacred flames your chest is burning—the voice of noble ancestors calls from afar") in the third verse indicate how Czechs have imagined and valued Native American spirituality. *Vlajka* is more clearly about the nostalgia intrinsic to the tramp experience, particularly the way that it allows one to reflect on past pleasure, as in the words of the second verse: *Po letech sám až zabloudíš v ten kraj a staneš tam, kde býval kdys tvůj ráj* ("Years later when you wander alone back to that place and find yourself where your paradise once was").

Tramp songs showed international connections, especially to global dance fads of the early 1900s, through their labeling as foxtrot, tango, waltz, or blues (Kotek 1998:106–118). As in other areas of tramp cultural production (architecture, literature, sport, etc.), these songs used exotic themes like maritime life and the American West—and included international string band instrumentation featuring the Spanish or Viennese guitar, the Italian/Iberian mandolin, and various forms of the Black Atlantic banjo. The recording of *Hvezdička* ("Little Star") by the *Setleři* ("Settlers"; Supraphon, 1931) features slide steel guitar sounds indicating that tramp musicians were (like American hillbilly musicians of the period) part of the contemporary global fascination with Hawaiian music.

Through the period of Communist Party primacy (1948–1989), tramping and tramp singing became naturalized as a part of Czech recreation and musical life, often facilitating self-realization through nostalgia for "golden eras" of the pre-communist and interwar periods (Jehlička and Kurtz 2013:326). Jiří Wabi Ryvola (1935–1995) connected the exotic "elsewhere" to romantic corners of Czech landscapes, as in his 1976 song *Zvláštní znamení woodcraft* ("The Special Sign of Woodcraft"); Ryvola's text evokes the *siluety hor a stromů, starejch opuštěnejch lomů* ("silhouettes of mountains and trees, of old abandoned quarries") including mention of the *maskovaný kombinézy po všech armádách* ("camouflage uniforms from all sorts of armies") that had become one of the canonic forms of Czech tramp dress after the Second World War (Pohunek 2018:73–74; Symonds and Vařeka 2014:172). In the 1984 song *Ročnik 47*, ("Class/Year of 47") Stanislav Wabi Daněk (1947–2017) describes older tramps squeezing into the camouflage outfits of their youth (in Czech, *svý tělo . . . napasovat do maskáčů z mládí*), walking *zas jdeme známým údolím, tak jako v čase naší zašlý slávy, a slova městem neředěná snášejí se do vyrezlý trávy* ("again through the familiar valley, as in the time of our bygone glory, and the words undiluted by the city drift into the carved grass"). Tramp songs keep alive a "glowing coal" (*žhavej uhlík*) that recalls times in the woods camping and singing with friends.

Continuing a history of music making at the border of folklore and *folk*, Czech tramps created new forms of Czech Americanist culture. The arrival of bluegrass brought new ways to continue connecting people and places with story and sound and to shape self and community.

Video 5. Students in the Charles University Faculty of Humanities Global String Band perform the tramp song *Cariboo* (Jaroslav Mottl) at the *Kampus Hybernská* in Prague, May 22, 2019. (Credit: Lee Bidgood.)

HISTORICAL CASE: THE BANJO AS A *FOLK* INSTRUMENT

Czechs first encountered bluegrass via radio during the 1950s when the Munich US Armed Forces Network (AFN) station included country music shows in its programming (Craig 1988). Bluegrass became a key part of Czech folk-spectrum music making during the normalization period (1968–1989), offering opportunities for instrumental virtuosity and grounding of musical activity in real and imagined territories. The history of the banjo in the Czech lands can illustrate how Czechs learned about and re-created bluegrass and how they created new kinds of *folk* expressions.

A product of the transit and terror of the Black Atlantic (Gilroy 1993; Winans 2018), the banjo is a defining part of bluegrass for many participants. Marko Čermák, banjoist for the pathbreaking groups Greenhorns and White Stars, first heard the banjo played in a bluegrass context thanks to AFN broadcasts. In a 1998 memoir he recalls listening to the radio at a friend's home:

> From Pavel's radio resounded that strange English and then in the next moment the banjo—fantastic, devilish, interpolated with the whinnying of horses. I probably stopped breathing and my heart must have stopped. Then there were songs about cowboys, they played mandolins, violin, harmonica, guitars—all instruments that I knew well from cabins, from pubs, from the campfire. But this was music, it grooved, and that fantastic banjo.
>
> (Čermák 1998:9)

Working on his own, Čermák could not reproduce the sounds he heard on the radio (Bidgood 2017:32–33). Pete Seeger's 1964 visit to Czechoslovakia brought Czech bluegrassers important information about the banjo and shaped the ways this instrument became part of Czech *folk* music making.

Seeger's performances were announced in Czech as *folklorní, lidový, populární*, and related to the labor movement (Přibylová 2018:241–243, 246). With his leftward leanings, Seeger could connect for Czechs the vernacular nature of bluegrass-related music and Communist Party ideology—not without issues, however. When Seeger sang a song of protest against the war in Vietnam, audience members whistled (an expression of distaste), perceiving his stance as a repetition of Czechoslovak government propaganda (Deitch 2001:5).

Recollections of a March 28, 1964, Prague symposium held as part of Seeger's visit show concerns about "folkness" on all sides. In his memoir *The Incompleat Folksinger* Seeger recalls audience questions: "'What is the relationship of American folk music to Big Beat rock-and-roll?' 'What is bluegrass music?' 'Are the blues considered folk music?' I was on the spot, knowing that I wasn't an authority, but trying my best to answer" (1992:512–513). Jiří Tichota, musicologist and member of the *folk* group Spirituál kvintet (Spiritual Quintet), reports that Seeger was surprised to learn that Czechs did not consult street singers (*pouliční zpěváci*) in seeking folk music. Tichota explained to Seeger that in Czech contexts urban folklore did not exist anymore and that folkloric music was drawn from the distant past (Přibylová 2018:255).

Reflecting on his conversations at the 1964 symposium, Seeger commented on this collective "forgetting" of folk music:

> experience has shown in Britain and elsewhere that folk music can survive even its revivalists. And I'm willing to bet that a few years from now young Czechs will realize that they have a helluva lot of fine tunes and rhythms and poetry that they can use to make their lives more musical, to understand where they came from and where they want to go, and to use as a basis for their own imagination and creativity. (1992:512–513)

Irena Přibylová observes that developments following Seeger's visit would validate his prediction: the emergence of songwriters (*písničkářů*) and a musical phenomenon that would be called *folk* (2018:255).

Along with songwriting, the banjo added a new and exciting sound to *folk* music making. In the 1970s a younger generation followed Čermák's model in making their own instruments since access to Western instruments and parts was still difficult. Along with fellow enthusiasts Ladislav Ptáček and Pavel Krištůfek, Jaroslav Průcha set out to create the metal parts needed to build a banjo. Drawing on a strong tradition of manufacturing in a market that can support niche enterprises, these makers learned how to cast, shape, plate, and polish metal banjo parts. They now create and sell banjos domestically and abroad; Průcha parts are used in the bluegrass community not only in Europe but by major bluegrass retailers in the United States (Fig. 35.3). The iconic Gibson Company used Czech parts in its instruments (Bidgood 2017:59–60).

Taking a ride on an intercity bus or entering a blue-collar workplace in the country today, one often gets an earful of Prague-based Country Radio, which since the early 1990s has broadcast a mix of foreign and domestic music—as of 2020 the percentages were 70 percent domestic and 30 percent foreign.[7] In addition to country and bluegrass music, the station broadcasts *folk* and tramp musics—all of which feature the banjo, a ringing note of Americanism that is also a celebration of Czechness (Fig. 35.4).

FIG. 35.3. Luthier Jaroslav Průcha at his workshop in Buš, a village south of Prague, playing a banjo that he built as a teenager in the early 1970s. May 25, 2016.

(Credit: Lee Bidgood.)

FIG. 35.4. This advertisement for Country Radio states that the station supplies *klidné rádio do neklidné doby* ("calm radio for un-calm times"), a slogan that I have seen used since 2002. Image captured December 5, 2018, in southeast Prague near the station's studios.

(Credit: Lee Bidgood.)

Old Time and *Folklor*

In August of 2009 I met with members of the band Rakovnickej Potok (Rakovník Creek), named for the town where they live, about 50 kilometers north of Prague. I had learned of this group from YouTube videos posted in 2006 by user "elzamando" in which the group's four members play driving, shuffle-bowed fiddle, bass and guitar rhythm, and "old-time" down-picking on an open-back banjo. I was eager to speak with them during this short fieldwork trip: they were some of the first Czech string band players I had found with interests centered on this bluegrass-adjacent string band revival approach.

It is difficult to articulate concisely the ways that bluegrass and old-time players distinguish themselves from each other. Many contemporary definitions of old-time music hinge on a "pre-bluegrass" status; this claim of priority makes sense in the context of popular music in the early 1900s, when "people distinguished between the old-time music of the last century and the more modern music of ragtime, jazz, and Tin Pan Alley. Old-time was identified with sentimental parlor songs, minstrel songs, minstrel music, fiddlers, fiddle contests, and square dances, and with the rural areas of the nation" (Titon 2001:xiv). As noted above, revivalists of old-time music have sought recordings and musicians whose musical modes were "weirder" (more metrically irregular, with more extensive microtonal variation, with rarer lyrical content, etc.), marking their activities as "old time" to distinguish them from bluegrass and more commercially successful (and less faithful) re-creations of folk music, such as those by the Kingston Trio (Allen 2010). Many old-time musicians continue this reactive identification, drawing their repertory and style from commercially released hillbilly records from the 1920s–1940s and from field recordings made by elderly players (Jones-Bamman 2017:48–52) (Video 6 ▶).

Video 6 https://youtu.be/Ey7N729EPFA

When I met with Rakovnickej Potok, we sat on the lawn outside the home of banjoist Jindřich "Jindra" Matuška, where he builds banjos as a hobby. Jindra spoke in our interview about the ways that old time affords him experiences he prefers over those that bluegrass provides: the homophonic texture and less spectacular instrumental playing that often characterize old-time playing are more approachable and more about community coherence. Bluegrass, they explained, features individuals and flashy instrumental solos, in an atmosphere of competition.

Potok's members described how they have learned their band repertory from songbooks, tablatures, and social media sites. They perform this material in their town and region, where audiences do not speak much English. Moreover, singing in English is difficult for the singers in the group, as Jindra added: "Many texts of traditional American pieces I find complicated, like the phonetics. Sometimes to sing the long 'A' gets me . . . some words, making them sound nice is complicated" (Rakonickej Potok personal interview, 2009). To avoid these issues, the group has retexted common old-time songs with Czech lyrics, sometimes following the original idea.[8] Potok guitarist

Libor Štěpánek's version of "Cluck Old Hen" (*Stará slepice*) hews closely to the original, centering its text on a chicken that has not laid an egg since last spring. Štěpánek's version (italic) with my translation in parentheses is here, followed by the corresponding excerpted verses as sung in the United States.

Ta stará slepice/snensla loni vajec nejvíce
Pro chlapy z nádraží/co na stavbu trati vyráží

(That old hen/laid the most eggs last year
For guys from the station/working out on the track)
My old hen's a good old hen/She lays eggs for the railroad men
Sometimes one, sometimes two/Sometimes enough for the whole dang crew

Slepice jsem stará/nesnesla jsem nic už od jara

(I'm an old hen/I haven't laid anything since spring)[9]
Cluck old hen, cackle and sing/You ain't laid an egg since way last spring

In addition to these retextings, which are common in Czech folk-spectrum music, the group takes a further step in grounding their Americanism in local culture: "So we try to, with old time music, for example, insert Czech folk songs" (Rakonickej Potok personal interview, 2009). Czech folkloric songs that the group performs include *Široký, hluboký* ("Wide, Deep"), *Holka modrooká* ("Blue-Eyed Girl"), and *Na rozloučení* ("Farewell").[10]

Jindra commented that "When we sing Czech folk songs here in the Czech lands and play the banjo on them, it's weird, because there has always been a violin, clarinet or bass, yes [in folkloric music], but we still try to maintain the Czech tradition in a way . . . the common songs are also earthy [*zemitý*]" (Rakovnickej Potok personal interview, 2009). Adjectives that members of the group used to contrast old time and bluegrass included *zemitý*—derived from the Czech noun *země*, meaning land or earth. When I asked about the word, Honza provided a technical definition, "coming from the earth," while Jindra explained that it is "kind of natural or normal" (Rakonickej Potok interview, 2009). As members of the group elaborated on these definitions, they opened a discussion of the group's philosophy of revival. Honza ventured that "it feels to us a little like a return to somewhere, a return to some kind of simplicity, some kind of roots, to originality, to simplicity" (Rakovnickej Potok interview, 2009).

Video 7 https://youtu.be/6bLgmPkHc7E

The group performs a juxtaposition of "Cumberland Mountain Deer Race" with the Czech folkloric song *Holka modrooka* ("Blue-Eyed Girl"). The two songs share the same melody, and Pete Seeger played them together during his 1964 concerts. Potok's text (by Olda Bauer) concerns a deer hunt on the banks of the Cumberland River (the title is literally that: *Lov jelenů na břehu řeky Cumberland*). On a past version of their website, the group claims "while the Americans present the song as originally an American folk tune, we know our own [song when we hear it]!"[11] With other songs a parenthetical subtitle lists an American song as the original used for the Czech-texted copy, here instead of citing Uncle Dave Macon (whose version of the "Cumberland Mountain Bear Chase" originally inspired Seeger's version of the song), the group lists the Czech song Holka Modrooka as the source, arguing that (this little part of) bluegrass-related music is always already Czech (Video 7 ▶).

Video 6. Czech band Trativod ("Dry Well") blends bluegrass and old-time elements (particularly the open-back banjo and downstroke style), performing the traditional American song "June Apple" at the Bluegrass Party festival in the central Bohemian town of Mlékojedy, June 1, 2019. (Credit: Lee Bidgood.)

Video 7. Members of the band Rakovnickej Potok perform *Lov jelenů na břehu řeky Cumberland* ("Deer Hunt on the Banks of the Cumberland River") in the town of Rakovník, August 12, 2009. (Credit: Lee Bidgood.)

HISTORICAL CASE: WESTERN AND EASTERN IN *BALADA PRO BANDITU*

Dramatic adaptations of Ivan Olbracht's 1933 novel *Nikola Šuhaj loupežník* (*Nikola Šuhaj the Robber*) have juxtaposed tramping's vocabulary of Wild West motifs and bluegrass-forward folk-spectrum music with more folkloric vernacular elements. A key part of the story's appeal is its exotic setting, a territory that at the time of Olbracht's writing was administered by Czechoslovakia and referred to as "Subcarpathian Rus" (*Podkarpatská Rus*). An interstitial mountain region between Czechoslovakia, Hungary, and Ukraine, the Rus was a far-off place where Czechs could safely imagine bandits, wild landscapes, and adventures.

Adapted as *Balada pro banditu* (*Ballad for a Bandit*) the story was first dramatized for theater in the Moravian city of Brno in 1975 and then produced for film in 1978 (dir. Vladimír Sís). In both cases the story was presented as a *trampský muzikal* (tramp musical) that puts together dramatic elements of the western film genre with a presentation of a folk tale from a rural area. The film was accompanied by the Greenhorns—at this point in their career forced to use the Czech form of their name *Zelenáči* due to restrictions on the use of the English language following the 1968 Soviet invasion and subsequent atmosphere of "normalization."

Sís's film cuts between two settings: the mountains of Olbracht's story and a Czechoslovak tramping gathering where an audience engages with a live production of the drama. The former setting has the "feel" of a filmed drama, with folkloric clothes, dwellings, and action accompanied by nondiegetic music. The latter setting is more informal and experimental, with a Western-like production of the story (with cowboy bravado, galloping about, and gunfights) in an outdoor amphitheater at a gathering resembling a large *potlach* (tramp reunion) or one of the popular *Porta* festivals (founded 1967) that featured folk-spectrum music, complete with campfire, guitars, military backpacks, and cowboy hats (Kneller 2014).

The songs by Miloš Štědroň (music) and Milan Uhde (lyrics) reference at times central European folklore, tramp themes, and country musics, foregrounding the folk-spectrum mix that was formed in the 1970s. The soundtrack is dominated instrumentally by the Greenhorns' bluegrass-type instrumentation, including banjoist Marko Čermák, who appears with the band in the film (Mládková 2017). The opening number, *Zabili, zabili* ("They Killed, They Killed"), represents Americanist elements. In the film production harmonica and slide resophonic guitar (from Greenhorns Tomáš Linka and Josef Dobeš) provide subdued harmonic gestures during the verses sung by the female lamenting the death and hasty burial of the male lead; Marko Čermák's banjo adds energy to the faster-paced instrumental pre-chorus section.

The ballad *Ani tak nehoří* ("It Doesn't Burn") hews more toward folklore, with fingerpicked guitar and flute more prominent. The images in the somewhat cryptic text (the verses describe pale legs, a priest's candle, apples, brandy, and a small garden that can hurt more than a wound to the heart) are elliptical enough to suggest they are the remnant of some obscure folksong tradition. In a 1983 recording cast member Miroslav Donutil and the Czech Television titles list Miloš Štědroň as composer but, instead of crediting Milan Uhde, state that the song has a folkloric text (*lidový text*), indicating how *folk* productions often fulfill the role of folklore.[12]

Iva Bittová, who played the female lead in the film, has fused *folk* and folkloric music with jazz, experimental, and other forms of art music in the decades since. In an analysis of some of Bittová's most folklore-adjacent recordings, Julie Brown (2020) describes a "post-revival" space in which "personal folk music" can oppose a mainstream, finding that Bittová's intersectional performances and improvisation create an idiosyncratic and potentially productive mode of folklorism. Americanist folk-spectrum music helps facilitate these sorts of negotiations, especially at the borders where *folk* and folklore meet.

Western and Eastern Folklores: Jiří Plocek

The lived experience of an individual can help shed some light on the ways that musical experience bridges divides that might arise from concerns about authenticity and identity—concerns that tend to separate *folk* and folklore in the Czech context. Jiří Plocek is a mandolinist, musical organizer/entrepreneur, and writer/commentator with significant work histories both in radio work and in chemistry. At some points his careers blended: through a chemistry post-doc in the United States at Indiana University Bloomington in 1993–1994, Plocek focused his interests in bluegrass. Plocek has also documented current and historical folkloric music in the Moravian region and taken part in some of the most in-depth experiments to fuse bluegrass with folkloric musics.

In an interview I conducted with Plocek in 2019, he related his history with bluegrass—the music that first captured his attention as a young person. It is a story similar to those told by many of his generation: in the early 1970s, as a teenager, he attended a concert by the band Zelenáči and was inspired to take up the banjo. Plocek became interested in exploratory, progressive music from American musicians like Tony Trischka (a banjoist with Czech heritage) as well as mandolinists Sam Bush and Andy Statman. After switching to the mandolin in the 1980s, Plocek experimented in open forms of bluegrass with bands based in the Moravian city of Brno: Classic Newgrass Quartet and Blue Mill Water Band. As he put it, "I wanted to find my new music. Grass, but new" (Plocek interview 2019). Eventually he was invited to support singer-songwriter Robert Křešťan in Poutníci (Pilgrims), a forerunner to Druha Tráva (Fig. 35.5).

Plocek became interested in local folkloric music when his early search for a mandolin led him to a local tamburitza group (*tamburářský soubor*); the organizer gifted him an instrument made by the Cremona company of Luby u Chebu, a flat-topped mandolin with f-holes that did not fit in with the tamburitza (an instrument family with roots in Bulgaria, Croatia, and Macedonia). He gained more than just an instrument from the experience: "I found out that there was a great mandolin tradition here, from the time of the First Republic. And it came from . . . a time when nations were emancipated, and nation-states were formed after the First World War, so there was a great cultural connection with the Slavic nations in the Balkans" (Plocek interview 2019).

After this brush with regional folkloric music, Plocek was plunged into it, thanks to Petr Surý (1957–2022), bassist for Poutníci. While Plocek had no experience playing folkloric music, "he [Surý] loved it and could play it, he had a huge [collection] of Romanian, Hungarian, Slovak, and Balkan recordings, especially Romanian, he had a lot, we listened to it and said, 'Jesus and Mary, as if I could ever play that!'" (Plocek interview 2019). In 1985 Surý brought Plocek to play some of this material with the *Brněnský rozhlasový orchestr lidových nástrojů* (Brno Radio Orchestra of Folk Instruments):

> I was invited there to record some Romanian folklore they played, they had it in the score, they needed an instrument called a *cobză*, an instrument of the lute type . . . played with a quill, a feather . . . goose or hen, I don't know. But no one had the instrument here, and no one knew how to play it. And my friend [Surý] tells the conductor, "Well, I have a friend who plays the mandolin, it's a plucked instrument, so it could imitate the *cobză* part." So they invited me and I went there to record.
>
> (Plocek interview 2019)

Plocek was also inspired by the genre boundary–crossing recordings of US mandolinist Andy Statman. "I tried to come up with instrumentals there sometime in '84, '85, that would take these national or cultural roots into account. I was inspired by Andy Statman, because when I heard him use Jewish terms or just Eastern European terms in bluegrass, for example, I thought, 'That's the way!'" (Plocek interview 2019). Along with

FIG. 35.5. Mandolinist Jiří Plocek (second from left) with the Classic Newgrass Quartet at the 1983 Banjo Jamboree festival, when that event took place near Kopidlno (Hradec Králové region).
(Credit: Jiří Plocek.)

Poutníci banjoist Luboš Malina, Plocek founded Teagrass (a bluegrass band) in 1990, the year after the Velvet Revolution in which the Communist Party ceded its control of Czechoslovakia. The group's core became Plocek, Surý, and Mišo Vavro on guitar, with guests added for recordings to convey the lineup of a bluegrass band or a folklore band with the hammered dulcimer–like *cimbál* (cimbalom) and clarinet of Moravian music, as well as the *tarogáto*, panpipes, and flutes of other regional styles. The group's 1995 recording *Cestou na východ* (*Eastbound*) includes musical material from the Moravian region, Slovakia, Romania, Hungary, Serbia, Croatia, and Ukraine.

Their goal was to journey to these locales through music but through a bluegrass lens; as the liner notes put it, the project is "the synthesis of seemingly quite diverse musical styles and opinions—in essence, we set out from Moravia headed further east (or rather southeast) to discover local musical treasures, while keeping on our Western glasses to a large extent" (Plocek 1995; author's translation). In an interview for the film *Banjo Romantika* banjoist Luboš Malina, Plocek's Poutníci bandmate and occasional contributor to Teagrass, has indicated that his song "Remembering" is an overt attempt to play something that sounds like Czech folkloric music on a quintessentially American instrument (Lange 2015) (Video 8 ▶).

Video 8 https://youtu.be/wIfupTrtEmk

In our interview, Plocek reflected on some of the reasons why folklore has had a troubled role in recent Czech history: "here the culture was influenced by a lot of things. Life under Austria–Hungary, [the] interwar [period], both of those terrible wars, then the communists, yeah. All this distorted the perception of our roots, because those people were not free" (Plocek interview 2019). Starting with musical Americanism and its gestures toward the wide-open spaces of the Wild West and then creating Teagrass during what might be seen as freedom after 1989, Plocek's explorations have helped join folklore and folk-spectrum musics: "on that journey I met American music and on that journey I also deeply met our traditional music . . . and actually through the return to our traditional music . . . I actually have returned to my roots and to my way. Maybe with that trip to bluegrass and improvised music of an individual character, I contributed something to our tradition" (Plocek interview 2019; Plocek 2014).

Video 8. Banjost Luboš Malina performs elements of his composition "Remembering" at his home in rural north Bohemia, July 11, 2011. (Credit: Shara Lange and Lee Bidgood.)

REFLECTION: *FOLK* AND POLITICS

Plocek's connecting of *folklór* and folk-spectrum sounds subtly challenges the idea that *folk* music is politically engaged and that folklore exists in a realm far from politics. Joseph Grim Feinberg (2018) confronts this notion head-on in his analysis of the pursuit of authenticity by Slovak folkloric dance groups and his consideration of the term "folklorism." He argues that post-1989 efforts to remove nationalism (redressing the legacy of propagandistic, Soviet-style folkloric projects) did not propose a politics to replace those of the Communist Party, and thus participants became focused on experience and affect. This process of depoliticization is one that political scientist Justin Acome (2013) has noticed in bluegrass in the United States and comprises an important area of research for scholars of vernacular music: what are the politics advanced by the agendas of "depoliticized" folk/folkloric musics? This question points to the future of folk-spectrum music–related cultural projects—and research that might document and analyze them.

As to methodology, the ethnographic engagement of scholars such as Feinberg and Acome sheds light on the grassroots-level participation in these musical areas. At the same time, larger-scale survey or other interpretive work could establish links between music and politics and distinguish the characteristics of cohorts of genre and generation. It seems useful to consider not only folk-spectrum musics within Czech contexts but also the ways that this range of musical approaches might prove a useful frame of analysis elsewhere.

Feinberg's account highlights tactics used by participants to "work through" the tensions in Slovak folkloric music and dance and create a pragmatic and self-limiting approach to authenticity: "Caught between the inauthenticity of public life and the inaccessibility of authentic folklore, but having renounced political transformation as a means of overcoming this tension, the authentic folklore movement seeks tentative resolution to the tension in the non-publicly public, intimately collective, fleeting yet enduring experience of shared joy" (2018:161–162). In discussing the social utility of the experience of joy through folkloric music and dance, Feinberg discusses changes to the political utility of these practices in the atmosphere of nationalist sentiment that arose in the Czech Republic (and other parts of Europe) after 2014 in response to the growing stream of immigrants from Africa and the Middle East.

During a 2018–2019 fieldwork/teaching stint in Prague—as I was learning about the political climate, with right-wing populist politicians taking anti-immigrant stances—I also noticed new uses of the "folk" term. The Czech participants in the Balfolk movement organize events during which participants learn folkloric dances from a variety of European locales, all accompanied by live music.[13] *Folklorni mejdlo* (Folklore Soap) is another recent movement that celebrates folkloric music and dance, focusing on the Moravian *cimbál* ensemble, created by and directed at younger participants (Hrbáčková 2018).[14]

The blend of participatory and presentational valences of these experiences affords participants a variety of means for the realization of self and community—some of the same affordances offered by the various forms of Czech Americanism. Surges in popularity of these physically participatory pursuits might be due to the skepticism among Czech youth about the value of media (especially social media) as a means for creating and sustaining social relations. Furthermore these neo-folkloric practices provide opportunities for immediate, low-barrier-to-entry participation—in contrast to bluegrass and *folk* music, which stress instrumental virtuosity and refined lyricism, respectively.

Another aspect that might disincline Czech youth participation in folk-spectrum music is the conservative/nationalist attitude of some participants, a politics sometimes made evident in the display of the Confederate flag. While this iconic symbol of hate and prejudice has been under attack in the United States recently, it has maintained a semiotically active profile elsewhere in the world, including the Czech Republic. Musicians display images of the flag, fly it at their *chaty* (vacation cottages), and even use it to name businesses, such as *U Starého Rebela* (The Old Rebel Pub), an eating, drinking, and bluegrass performance venue run by a bluegrasser in the East Bohemian town of Sloupnice for many years (Fig. 35.6). Mandolinist Honza Skovajsa, a longtime bluegrasser and child of a couple who has played Czech tramping, country, and bluegrass music since the 1970s, told me in a 2016 conversation that now that he is in his thirties, he is disenchanted with bluegrass and has been directing his energies toward klezmer music since it feels more like a natural or comfortable thing for him to do. He also mentioned a frustration with (largely older) bluegrassers who express conservative and nationalistic views, especially on social media.

FIG. 35.6. The stage at *U Starýho Rebela* (the Old Rebel Pub) in Sloupnice (Pardubice region), May 17, 2008. The Confederate flag flanks photographs of bluegrass icons Lester Flatt, Bill Monroe, and Earl Scruggs.

(Credit: Lee Bidgood.)

Conclusion

The "Americanist generation" of Czechs hooked by the banjo and bluegrass in the 1970s will not live forever. A deejay at Prague's Country Radio once shared with me his confidential concern that the station's currently very large listenership will diminish as members of this age cohort die. Perhaps the pan-European and/or local folkloric dance and music scene will complement, compete with, or replace Czech Americanism.

In recent years I have kept up with fieldwork contacts in the Czech Republic via Facebook since I have been unable to visit in person. I have observed conversations about nationalism, arguments for and against vaccination, etc. that echo the discourse I observe in the United States. I wonder how world-changing events like COVID-19 (a pandemic that erupted during the writing of this text) might affect the ways that folk-spectrum music works in Czech contexts and elsewhere. Responses to this pandemic have created fuel for the fires of "culture wars" and have limited musical community-building and commerce.

Amidst the substantial hardships, however, there are possibilities for artistry, collaboration, and connection. Czechs cultivated folk-spectrum music making through the hardship and horrors of a long twentieth century—through world wars, a period of totalitarian rule, and the for-profit privatization by opportunistic oligarchs that followed. Work by artists, organizers, and scholars (in creating, presenting, and interpreting expressive culture) continues to blur divides between folk, folkloric, and popular music, a process that could be an important part of sustainable and resilient society now and in the future.

Notes

1. For a representative survey of Czech bluegrass-related media, see Bidgood (2017:153–160).
2. I use italics to indicate Czech usage, even if the origin of a phrase is English—for example, in band names, festival titles, etc. All translations are mine.
3. More information, media, and photos from my fieldwork, as well as links to other writings, are accessible via my website: https://www.leebidgood.net.
4. The annual colloquium is held in collaboration with the festival *Folkové Prázdniny* (Folk Holiday) in the town of Náměšť nad Oslavou. Proceedings of the meetings are published each year and are accessible online (https://www.folkoveprazdniny.cz/kolokvium-uvod, accessed November 10, 2021).
5. For Bronislava Volková, Hašler "personified the essence of Czech popular culture. . . . A certain celebratory nationalism comprising a folk character found a permanent place in his songs about Czech identity, which still have an enduring effect on the Czechs" (2015:124). Volková states that these songs "eventually became so ingrained in the nation that many people are still not sure today whether they are simply folk songs or songs written by a composer-poet" (p. 125).
6. *Tramping in Bohemia* (Buff 2011) provides a glimpse of tramping in contemporary and historical contexts (https://vimeo.com/258509063, accessed November 20, 2021).
7. http://www.countryradio.cz/o-radiu/ (accessed August 10, 2020).
8. There are historical cases of transatlantic borrowing: the melody for the popular song known in the United States as "Roll out the Barrel" was written by Czech composer Jaromir Vejvoda in 1927. Models for Czech Americanist retexting were provided by groups like the Greenhorns (Bidgood 2018).
9. English verses from the Traditional Tune Archive online repository, the kind of source that Rokovnickej Potok members consult when retexting songs (https://tunearch.org/wiki/Annotation:Cluck_Old_Hen_(1), accessed November 20, 2021). Many of Rakovnickej Potok's retextings are on that website, in PDF form, with chords. The A4 format indicates printing and placement in a clear plastic page protector in a binder, for use as a memory aid at pub jams and performances, a phenomenon I have often observed among Czech Americanist musicians (http://www.rakovnickej-potok.cz/SONGY/03-Stara_slepice(zp).pdf, accessed November 21, 2021).
10. *Široký, hluboký*, collected in the Kouřím district by Karel Jaromír Erben in 1864 (http://folksong.eu/cs/melody/21958, accessed November 11, 2021); *Holka Modrooká* is a common song; my son learned it in his Czech preschool in 2018–2019. *Na rozloučení* is associated with Bohemian regions, not Moravian ones, indicating how this group emphasizes folklore that is more local to them.
11. https://web.archive.org/web/20090620014225/http://www.rakovnickej-potok.cz/Pisne.php#15 (accessed October 28, 2022).

12. https://www.youtube.com/watch?v=GCL0ZIb21V0 (accessed May 25, 2020).
13. *Bal folk* is a francophone term, the condensed form "balfolk" is used in the Czech Republic (http://festival.balfolk.cz/, accessed August 1, 2020) and in the United States (Wharton 2019) to refer to the recent cosmopolitan movement that emphasizes accessibility, rootedness, and live music.
14. http://folklornimejdlo.cz/ (accessed August 1, 2020).

Works Cited

Acome, Justin. 2013. "Bluegrass Nonsense Politics." PhD dissertation, The Ohio State University.

Allen, Ray. 2010. *Gone to the Country: The New Lost City Ramblers and the Folk Music Revival.* Urbana, IL: University of Illinois Press.

Balaš, Nikola. 2018. "Academia without Contention? The Legacy of Czechoslovak Ethnography and Folklore Studies in Czech Anthropology." *Sociologický Časopis/Czech Sociological Review*, 91/3:343–370. https://www.ceeol.com/search/article-detail?id=692550.

Barbour-Payne, Yunina. 2016. "Carolina Chocolate Drops: Performative Expressions and Reception of Affrilachian Identity." In *Appalachia Revisited: New Perspectives on Place, Tradition, and Progress*, eds. William Schumann and Rebecca Adkins Fletcher, 43–58. Lexington, KY: The University Press of Kentucky.

Beckerman, Michael. 1996. "Kundera's Musical Joke and 'Folk' Music in Czechoslovakia, 1948–?" In *Retuning Culture: Musical Changes in Central and Eastern Europe*, ed. Mark Slobin, 37–53. Durham, NC: Duke University Press. https://doi.org/10.1215/9780822397885-003.

Berry, Chad. 2008. *The Hayloft Gang: The Story of the National Barn Dance.* Urbana, IL: University of Illinois Press.

Bidgood, Lee. 2017. *Czech Bluegrass: Notes from the Heart of Europe.* Urbana, IL: University of Illinois Press.

Bidgood, Lee. 2018. "The Americanist Imagination and Real Imaginary Place in Czech Bluegrass Songs." *Popular Music and Society*, 41/4:390–407.

Bidgood, Lee, and Irena Přibylová. 2022. "Bluegrass: Popular Folk Music Globalized from the Bottom Up." In *The Oxford Handbook of Global Popular Music*, ed. Simone Krüger Bridge, 699–713. Oxford: Oxford University Press. https://doi.org/10.1093/oxfordhb/9780190081379.013.14.

Boyce-Tillman, June. 2009. "The Transformative Qualities of a Liminal Space Created by Musicking." *Philosophy of Music Education Review*, 17/2:184–202. https://www.jstor.org/stable/40495499.

Brown, Julie. 2020. "Duetting with Bartók and Others Bittová's Post-Revival 'Personal Folk Music.'" In *Remixing Music Studies: Essays in Honour of Nicholas Cook*, eds. Ananay Aguilar, Ross Cole, Matthew Pritchard, and Eric Clarke, 148–163. New York: Routledge.

Buff, Margot, director. 2011. *Tramping in Bohemia.* 30 minutes. https://vimeo.com/258509063.

Cantwell, Robert. 1984. *Bluegrass Breakdown: The Making of the Old Southern Sound.* Urbana, IL: University of Illinois Press.

Cassell, Thomas. 2021. "In Seeking a Definition of Mash: Attitude in Musical Style." MA thesis, East Tennessee State University.

Čermák, Marko. 1998. *Banjo z mlžných lesů: Trail stezkou času; Greenhorns, White Stars, Paběrky; škola hry na pětistrunné banjo; tabulatury; zpěvník.* Naděje, CZ: Country Home.

Craig, R. Stephen. 1988. "American Forces Network in the Cold War: Military Broadcasting in Postwar Germany." *Journal of Broadcasting & Electronic Media*, 32/3:307–321. https://doi.org/10.1080/08838158809386704.

Deitch, Gene. 2001. Liner notes for *Pete Seeger in Prague 1964*. Flyright Records, CD.

DeWitt, Mark. 2009. "Louisiana Creole Bals de Maison in California and the Accumulation of Social Capital." *The World of Music*, 51/1: 17–34. https://www.academia.edu/12805959/Louisiana_Creole_Bals_de_maison_in_California_and_the_Accumulation_of_Social_Capital.

Dickins, Tom. 2017. "Folk-Spectrum Music as an Expression of Alterity in 'Normalization' Czechoslovakia (1969–89): Context, Constraints and Characteristics." *The Slavonic and East European Review*, 95/4:648–690. https://doi.org/10.5699/slaveasteurorev2.95.4.0648.

Dvořák, Tomáš, and Marek Rejhon. 2019. *Bohemian Jazz Guitars Tribute: Neznámý příběh československých jazzových kytar/The Unknown Story of Czechoslovak Jazz Guitars*. Kladno, CZ: Halda.

Feinberg, Joseph Grim. 2018. *The Paradox of Authenticity: Folklore Performance in Post-Communist Slovakia*. Madison, WI: University of Wisconsin Press.

Gilroy, Paul. 1993. *The Black Atlantic: Modernity and Double Consciousness*. New York: Verso.

Houda, Přemysl. 2013. *Intelektuální protest, nebo masová zábava?: Folk jako společenský fenomén v době tzv. normalizace*. Prague: Academia.

Houda, Přemysl. 2019. *Normalizační festival: Socialistické paradoxy a postsocialistické korekce*. Prague: Karolinum Press.

Hrbáčková, Anežka. 2018. "Folklorní mejdlo: Prague 'Folklorists' as a Cultural Cohort." *Národopisná Revue*, 28/2:119–129. http://cejsh.icm.edu.pl/cejsh/element/bwmeta1.element.desklight-91af3976-0afc-4fb6-928f-12b6edeafad4.

Jehlička, Petr, and Matthew Kurtz. 2013. "Everyday Resistance in the Czech Landscape: The Woodcraft Culture from the Hapsburg Empire to the Communist Regime." *East European Politics and Societies*, 27/2:308–332.

Jones-Bamman, Richard. 2017. *Building New Banjos for an Old-Time World*. Urbana, IL: University of Illinois Press.

Jurková, Zuzana, Peter Balog, Hana Černáková, Jakub Jonáš, Pavla Jónssonová, Veronika Seidlová, et al. 2014. *Prague Soundscapes*. Prague: Karolinum Press.

Kneller, Rosavera. 2014. *The Porta Festival, 1967–1969: Tramping and the Forging of a Czechoslovak Wilderness*. MA thesis, University of North Carolina at Chapel Hill.

Kotek, Josef. 1998. *Dějiny české populární hudby a zpěvu (1918–1968)*. Prague: Academia.

Kratochvíl, Matej. 2015. "'Our Song!' Nationalism in Folk Music Research and Revival in Socialist Czechoslovakia." *Studia Musicologica*, 56:397–405. https://doi.org/10.1556/6.2015.56.4.7.

Lange, Shara, director. 2015. *Banjo Romantika: American Bluegrass Music and the Czech Imagination*. 56 minutes. Light Projects.

Malone, Bill C., and Tracey Laird. 2018. *Country Music USA: 50th Anniversary Edition*. Austin, TX: University of Texas Press.

Mládková, Nela. 2017. "Dramatizace Olbrachtova Nikoly Šuhaje loupežníka." Thesis, Charles University Pedagogical Faculty. https://dspace.cuni.cz/handle/20.500.11956/2121.

Myška, Milan. 1996. "Proto-Industrialization in Bohemia, Moravia." In *European Proto-Industrialization: An Introductory Handbook*, eds. Sheilagh Ogilvie and Markus Cerman, 188–207. Cambridge: Cambridge University Press.

Peterson, Richard. 1997. *Creating Country Music: Fabricating Authenticity*. Chicago: University of Chicago Press.

Pilková, Zdeňka. 1988. "Eighteenth Century Folk Music in the Czech Lands: Comments on the State of Research." In *Janáček and Czech Music*, eds. Michael Beckerman and Glen Bauer, 34–37. Stuyvesant, NY: Pendragon Press.

Plocek, Jiří. 1995. Liner notes for *Cestou na východ/Eastbound*. Teagrass. G-Music, CD.

Plocek, Jiří. 2014. "Moje Muzikantská Cesta Do Ameriky a Zpět." In *Od folkloru k world music: Svět v nás, my ve světě*, eds. Irena Přibylová and Lucie Uhlíková, 116–125. Náměšť nad Oslavou, CZ: Městské kulturní středisko.

Pohunek, Jan. 2018. *Století trampingu/A Century of Tramping*. Prague: Národní Muzeum.

Přibylová, Irena. 2018. "Pete Seeger v Československu v roce 1964: Pamětníci, legendy a odkaz." In *Od folkloru k world music: O paměti*, eds. Irena Přibylová and Lucie Uhlíková, 239–262. Náměšť nad Oslavou, CZ: Městské kulturní středisko.

Reidinger, Melinda. 2007. "Islands of Bourgeois Self-Realization in a Sea of Changes: A Century of Czech Cottaging." PhD dissertation, University of Virginia.

Rosenberg, Neil V. 1993. "Starvation, Serendipity, and the Ambivalence of Bluegrass Revivalism." In *Transforming Tradition: Folk Music Revivals Examined*, ed. Neil Rosenberg, 194–202. Urbana, IL: University of Illinois Press.

Rosenberg, Neil V. 2005. *Bluegrass: A History*, 20th anniv. ed. Urbana, IL: University of Illinois Press.

Rosenberg, Neil V. 2018. *Bluegrass Generation: A Memoir*. Urbana, IL: University of Illinois Press.

Seeger, Pete. 1992. *The Incompleat Folksinger*. Lincoln, NE: University of Nebraska Press.

Sís, Vladimír, director. 1978. *Balada Pro Banditu*. 89 minutes.

Small, Christopher. 1998. *Musicking: The Meanings of Performing and Listening*. Lebanon, NH: University Press of New England.

Symonds, James, and Pavel Vařeka. 2014. "Cowboys and Bohemians." *Journal of Contemporary Archaeology*, 1/1:165–193.

Thořová, Věra. 2010. "Kramářská píseň jako inspirační zdroj české písně lidové." *Český Lid*, 97/1:51–74. https://www.jstor.org/stable/42640291.

Titon, Jeff Todd. 2001. *Old-Time Kentucky Fiddle Tunes*. Lexington, KY: University Press of Kentucky.

Toynbee, Jason. 2000. *Making Popular Music: Musicians, Creativity, and Institutions*. Oxford: Oxford University Press.

Turner, Victor. 1974. "Liminal to Liminoid, in Play, Flow, and Ritual: An Essay in Comparative Symbology." *Rice Institute Pamphlet–Rice University Studies*, 60/3:53–92. https://scholarship.rice.edu/handle/1911/63159.

Tyllner, Lubomír. 2010. *Tradiční hudba: Hledání kořenů*. Prague: Etnologický ústav Akademie věd České republiky.

Volková, Bronislava. 2015. "The Greats of Czech Popular Culture (1900–2000): Roots, Character, and Genres." *Russian Literature*, 77:123–134. http://dx.doi.org/10.1016/j.ruslit.2015.01.009.

Wharton, Anne. 2019. *Entering the Bal: Strategies of Adoption in a North American Elective Folk-Dance Community*. MA thesis, Texas Tech University.

Winans, Robert B., ed. 2018. *Banjo Roots and Branches*. Urbana, IL: University of Illinois Press.

Wolfe, Charles K. 1999. *A Good-Natured Riot: The Birth of the Grand Ole Opry*. Nashville, TN: Country Music Foundation Press/Vanderbilt University Press.

Žák, Martin. 2010. *Zápisky osamělého poutníka s autoharfou*. Naděje, CZ: Country Home.

CHAPTER 36

FOLKTRON

Folklore Influences in Contemporary Bulgarian Popular Music

ASYA DRAGANOVA

SITUATED at the geographical and symbolic crossroads between the perceived cultural constructs of "East" and "West," on the border between Europe and Asia, Bulgaria and the Balkan Peninsula as a whole constitute an organic melting pot of musical influences. Bulgarian popular music, across all genre categories, frequently draws upon the richness of diverse musical traditions to attain distinctiveness (Draganova 2019; Stankova 2019). Taking an ethnographic approach to research, this chapter focuses specifically on the commercially established genre of pop-folk, in juxtaposition to the more niche, folklore-inspired emerging sounds associated with artists such as the members of band Oratnitza and artist Nikola Gruev known as Kottarashky. Pop-folk involves references to multiple Balkan folk traditions, such as Turkish and Gypsy, in combination with elements of globally recognized genres such as pop, disco, and dance music. However, while pop-folk has attained a profit-oriented style that achieves widespread appeal through accessible and sexualized politics of representation, the genre does not fully embrace the ways in which folklore heritage is explored within other genres of contemporary Bulgarian popular music. This chapter treats folklore as a source of artistic continuity, legitimacy, and inspiration, rather than as a museumized and fixed culture (Peycheva 2020; Nettl 1992:382) inherently associated with the past.

With an "aura" of authenticity and uniqueness (Benjamin [1936] 1999; Lomax 1968), folklore of the Balkan crossroads is celebrated as a valuable source of creative identity, inspiration, and pride. It is a pathway to alternativity (Holland and Spracklen 2018): an opportunity to move away from a formulaic approach to popular music. Within Bourdieusian terms, folklore(s) acts as a resource for attaining distinction within the fields of cultural production, defined by struggle and competition (Bourdieu 1993). Music is able to build imaginary connections with ethnic, national, and regional identities through the markers of recognition employed in the interaction between artists and audiences, even when they are separated in space and time or divided by technologies of sound reproduction (Draganova et al. 2021; Gilroy 1991:186). The imagined connections with individual and shared identities, however, bring significant cultural responsibilities, as well as dividends to be derived from pursuing a connection with the "local" by exploring elements of music traditions.

In the context of a globalized field dominated by the English language, the lingua franca of popular music, in this chapter I also interpret the use of the Bulgarian language in popular music as another "folklore" resource of distinction and a marker of identity (Draganova 2019:140–161; Hill 2007:3). For American ethnomusicologist Alan Lomax (1956:50) and Bulgarian–French philosopher Julia Kristeva (1995:43), language can be transmitted in the emotion of vocal patterns and in the patterns of musical thought. Both language and music are defined by rhythm, sound, musicality, and structures that communicate individual and collective meanings. This chapter seeks to establish a context for the development of pop-folk as a commercial genre within popular music and address the alternative means through which Bulgarian and Balkan folklore heritage has been explored within a range of more niche styles with elements of experimentation that have resisted the development of a clearly constructed genre category. Here, I interrogate the perceived cultural benefits and tensions emerging from the use of folklore references in contemporary popular music.

The title of this chapter is borrowed from the name of Oratnitza's 2015 album *Folktron* (Fusion Embassy). The album title plays with the name of the Japanese–American TV series *Voltron*. In the famous animation, Voltron is the name of the "Defender of the Universe," who is a robot that consists of five lion robots, each of them representing a different kind of force. This sense of fragmentation, of elements complementing each other, captures some of the key concepts within the chapter: the interaction between influences and the symbolic dialogue between "local" and "global" embodied in popular music. *Folktron*, in essence, is about mixing the unmixable, about exploring territories: it is a crossroad where (re)invention can "succeed" or "fail."

The notion of a "Folktron"—a whole within which distinct elements interact together—captures well the crossroad-like location of the Balkans between the cultural constructs of Europe and Asia, "West" and "East." The dynamic transitions which define the histories and present situations of the region suggest diversity, richness, and incredible potential. Yet, those characteristics have also become the basis for the creation of a Balkan stereotype of instability, marginality, and inferiority (Todorova [1997] 2009). *Folktron* as an overarching theme in the chapter represents an attempt to conceptualize the challenges in referencing tradition in pursuit of contemporary artistic achievement and originality. The word "folktron" itself is, of course, made up and successfully articulates the mixing of the "unmixable" into something new, yet familiar.

"Balkanism": A Cultural Context

The crossroad location of the Balkans, together with the dynamic transitions which define their histories, suggests diversity, cultural richness, and opportunities. At the same time, it has become the basis for the creation of Balkan stereotypes of instability, marginality, and inferiority (Goldsworthy [1998] 2013; Todorova [1997] 2009). These stereotypes, referred to as "Balkanism," have become profoundly internalized. This, I argue, suggests inherent complexities associated with conceptualization and performance of contemporary local identities, drawing upon folklore influences through popular music.

Akin to Edward Said's orientalism (1978), the Balkan stereotype is a distinctive phenomenon of its own (Bjelić 2011; Todorova [1997] 2009), which can be summarized as the chaotic "other" within Europe itself. The Balkans can, therefore, be described as a "nest" of orientalism (Bakić-Hayden and Hayden 1992) as eastern Europe and particularly the Balkans have been framed in psychoanalytic terms as a pathology, as a failure of the subject (Kristeva 2000; Žižek 1999). The process of constructing "Balkanism"—in association with poverty, violence, backwardness—has been established over a prolonged period of time and can be linked with the Balkans' disadvantaged position within the Ottoman Empire. For example, Bulgaria was under Ottoman control between 1396 and 1878. More recent historical developments have contributed to the continued construction of negative stereotypes: the association of part of the region, including Bulgaria, with the restrictive communist regimes in the Eastern Bloc and the complex post-communist transitions, defined by corruption and the rise of mafia structures (Nikolova 2018:2–3; Glenny 2008, 2012). If the unconscious is structured as a language (Lacan [1977] 1997), then for Slavoj Žižek "Balkan" embodies, in Western fantasy, inherent transgression and the European Unconscious (1999). Kristeva, a prominent contemporary philosopher from Bulgaria who has lived and worked in France for most of her life, suggests that Bulgaria and the Balkans embody violence and the European "abject"—"the crisis of the European subject" (2000:70–71). These arguments suggest that Bulgaria and the Balkans take on a peripheral position symbolically, and not only geographically, within the center–periphery model of Europe dominated by the perceived "West." The internalization of negative stereotypes, alongside the ongoing social and economic challenges rooted in post-communist transition, creates a lack of "European confidence" (Sotirova 2021; Roberts 2009, 2010).

The decade worth of continual fieldwork which informs this chapter suggests that those who are involved in making popular music frame it as a potential participant in the construction, consolidation, and celebration of more "confident" contemporary Bulgarian identities that symbolically participate in the global cultural dialogue. At the same time, popular music can embody and enhance negative stereotypes (Stankova 2019; Kourtova 2012). This chapter seeks to contribute to normalizing the Balkans (Bjelić 2011) where, according to Todorova ([1997] 2009), negative stereotypes have become self-designations accepted as legitimate facts. By focusing on contemporary popular music, I seek to contextualize contemporary practices within popular music culture and express how they connect with the past to construct visions of the present and future.[1] The findings presented here are derived from thirty-six open-ended ethnographic interviews with music artists and industry figures as well as observations at live music events in Bulgaria (predominantly Sofia and Burgas regions) and the United Kingdom (London, Canterbury, Birmingham). This continuously updated fieldwork began in 2012. As a Bulgarian and an amateur musician living and working in the United Kingdom, I provide a critical insider perspective which allows for both insight into and distance from the studied field (Blackman and Kempson 2016:1–16; Savin-Baden and Major 2012:68–70). The methodological approach also incorporates textual and discourse analyses: engaging with musical output—in terms of its musical, lyrical, and visual content—as well as the broader industry, social, and political contexts within which it emerges. This chapter is informed by and contributes to popular music studies, media and cultural studies, and cultural sociology.

Angels and Demons of Pop-folk: Designating Value in Bulgarian Popular Music

Pop-folk has been a prominent subject for public and academic discussion in contemporary Bulgarian popular music in the context of post-communism. Defining the musical content of this ethno-pop stylistic is not straightforward; importantly, it involves rhythms, figures, and ornamental styles of vocal delivery identified as Romani and Turkish, with elements and instruments used in pop, disco, and dance music (Dimov 2010). For ethnomusicologist Timothy Rice, "pop-folk is an outgrowth of Bulgarian Rom music and the music of Bulgaria's Balkan neighbours" (2004:91). While in everyday language pop-folk is often referred to as *chalga*, I avoid this usage because *chalga*, which translates as "to play" and "to entertain" from Turkish, is also associated with *svatbarska muzika* (wedding music)—the music of wedding orchestras (Levy 2009; Buchanan 1995). In terms of instrumentation, style, and repertoire, *svatbarska muzika* and pop-folk are, in some regards, similar; yet, while related, they should not be considered synonymous, especially as pop-folk grew into a commercial phenomenon (Draganova 2019:122–135; Statelova 2008). *Svatbarska muzika*, on the other hand, is associated with more "indigenous" acoustic instruments and live performance, with a focus on improvisation rather than strictly structured songs.

Pop-folk as a style developing in the 1990s overthrew all the limitations imposed by the communist regime (1944–1989) and radically challenged the "standards" of the pre-1989 communist state–approved and –supported popular culture (Dimova 2019; Buchanan 2007a, 2007b). During the forty-five-year communist period, music recording and publishing were reliant on the state-controlled label Balkanton and the facilities of the Bulgarian National (at the time People's) Radio and Television. Bulgarian pop, referred to as "Estrada," under communism, was carefully composed by professionally trained musicians, with complex harmonies and poetic lyrics riddled with sophisticated metaphors (Draganova 2019:25–27). Love, for example, the most common of topics in popular music, was idealized and intellectualized and detached from the direct expression of sexual desires. For example,

> Не посрещай зората без обич за мен
> Не посрещай светът е за двама
> Пак ще грее в очите ти приказен ден
> Даже мен да ме няма
>
> Don't welcome the dawn without love for me
> The world's made for two
> So the light of a beautiful day will glow again in your eyes
> Even if I, even if I am not there
>
> From "Светът е за двама" ("Svetŭt e za dvama,"
> "The World Is for Two"; single, Goranov 1982)
> Lyrics by Dimitar Tochev; performed by Orlin Goranov
> Translation by Asya Draganova[2]

Or

> А душата виновно, виновно мълчи
> само сянката мина през нея.
> Само вятърът, вятърът вейна едва,
> пиле някакво изписука.
> Ах каква, ах каква синева сме забравили
> някога тука.
> Синева, синева.
>
> As the soul remains in guilty silence
> Crossed by a single lonely shadow
> Only the wind, only the wind moves slightly—
> The cry of an unknown bird—
> Ah, the azure, the azure we'd forgotten
> Once upon a time somewhere around here
> Azure, azure.
>
> —From "Синева" ("Sineva," "Azure"; Diana Express 1976)
> Lyrics by Pavel Matev, performed by Vasil Naydenov

The post-communist period opened unprecedented opportunities for challenging the dominant—until then—cultural norms and created a new range of available themes and expressions. Pop-folk, in contrast to the lyrical aesthetic demonstrated above, puts raw sexual expressions at the forefront alongside largely trivialized versions of love, passion, and jealousy. Furthermore, if pre-1989 music and cultural expressions of materialistic pursuit were unthinkable, in the style of pop-folk the demonstration of wealth and ambitions of richness are prominent themes. Sashka Vaseva's "classic" pop-folk song lyrics demonstrate that:

> Левовете в марки сменям аз,
> вино за да пия в този час.
> Доларите стават, левовете не.
> Аз ще се напия в долари поне.
>
> Нямаш мили, нямаш мили, нямаш ти пари.
> Нямаш мили, нямаш мили, марки–долари.
> Стана страшно, стана мрачно нямаш ли пари,
> а да пия и да пия цял ден не върви.
>
> Levs in Deutsche Marks I exchange
> To drink wine at this time
> Dollars are alright, but levs are not ok
> Let me get drunk in dollars at least.
>
> You have no money, my dear man
> You have no real money, no Deutsche Marks, no dollars
> This is so scary, dark
> That alcohol won't save me here.
>
> Sashka Vaseva, "Левовете в марки" ("Levovete v marki,"
> "Levs into Deutsche Marks"; Vaseva 1996)

Visually and lyrically, the materialist obsession of pop-folk persists into its contemporary outputs. For example, this hit by singer Anelia with over 11 million YouTube views presents largely nonsensical lyrics where the identifiable themes are carelessness and material success:

> Пука ми, пука ми, пука ми на,
> дреме ми, дреме ми, дреме ми на . . .
> Голяма си гъзарка, цяла хилядарка,
> Анелия, Анелия,
> голяма си гъзарка, лепиш ги като марка,
> Анелия, Анелия.
>
> I don't give a . . .
> I don't give a . . . I'm so posh, a thousand means nothing:
> Anelia, Anelia
> I'm so posh, wasting money like it's stamps,

Anelia, Anelia
—From "Гъзарка" ("Gŭzarka," "Posh Girl"; single, Anelia 2020)
Lyrics by Petya Radeva, performed by Anelia

Exhibiting some similarities with early gangster rap, early pop-folk's iconography revolves—and continues to revolve—around expensive cars, lavish jewelry, luxury locations, hyperfeminine and hypermasculine sexualized bodies (Baker 2020; Dimova 2019; Statelova 2005). Pop-folk very much reacted to the challenges of the post-communist period by building an escapist world of the nouveau riche, materialist dreams, and primal sexual fantasies. The lyrics largely responded to and embodied the lawless environment of the early 1990s, riddled by mafia violence and a mass urge to take advantage of the transitional moment to utilize new opportunities to create wealth, especially as private initiative had been suppressed for more than four decades under the communist regime. Pop-folk captured the opportunistic spirit of the moment—songs were quickly and cheaply produced, and even plagiarism was a widely accepted practice.

The radical opposition between pop-folk and pre-1989 popular music is not confined to lyrical themes and linguistic style. Pop-folk draws upon Romani music and a range of other folkloristic influences, often classified and perceived as "oriental," in combination with recognizable pop-song structures and electronic instruments. This contradicts directly the mono-ethnic nature of communist popular culture, which aimed at purity of Bulgarian-ness and encouraged a separation from any Ottoman influences and other ethnic references in music (Levy 2004:50; Peycheva 1999). Pop-folk is, to an extent, a derivative of "Gypsy" wedding orchestra music (*svatbarska muzika*)—a distinct underground phenomenon from pre-1989, a musical activity that happened under the radar of the "official" stage performances approved and encouraged by the state. Folklore influences, in the communist context, were carefully reworked into beautifully crafted, complex musical works that bridged the "gap" between the classical and folklore (Peycheva 1996, 2020). This was achieved through the reinvention of folklore via complex and intricate new arrangements of familiar songs. Examples of that are the folklore choirs such as the National Radio and Television and Philip Koutev ensembles. Folklore was "cleansed" of "dirty" topics, for example, sexual or humorous content; and the out-of-this-world sound of women's voices articulated a desexualized bodilessness (Buchanan 2007b:255; Silverman 2004:231), one that sonically elevated the music from the human to the cosmic realm. For example, one of the most internationally recognizable, signature Bulgarian musical outputs was *Le Mystère des Voix Bulgares* (*The Mystery of Bulgarian Voices*), the first album of which was compiled by Marcel Cellier, released in 1987, and nominated for a Grammy (Bulgarian State Television Female Choir 1987). *Obrabotena muzika* (processed music), reworked folklore music defined by transformation, polishing, processing, and cultivation (Peycheva 2020:1), as a format was a successful attempt to "translate" the richness of Bulgarian folklore to the language of the global musical imagination, which is in harmony with the notion of "world music" (Stankova 2019; Buchanan 1995, 2007a; Rice 1994, 2004).

And while the communist state was busy establishing a "purified," "high-art" version of Bulgarian musical identity (Levy 2004), wedding orchestras and their *chalga*—or "play"—which later informed the commercial style of pop-folk, became a pan-Balkan phenomenon with its reiterations in Serbia and other ex-Yugoslav countries (*turbo-folk*), Romania (*manele*), and Greece (*laika*). Pop-folk, however, remains a divisive subject in contemporary Bulgarian culture, and radically opposed value judgments are ascribed to the style. "Defenders" of its style suggest that it is a cosmopolitan genre, which captures local specificity and global formats to deliver a dialogue and synthesis of globalized cultural influences (Kourtova 2012; Levy 2004). In contrast to a range of other styles within Bulgarian popular music which are distinctly mono-ethnic, pop-folk is associated with openness toward the participation of minority groups in the construction of the style, especially Roma: a group that experiences significant issues of segregation and discrimination. From these perspectives, pop-folk can be interpreted as a socially progressive phenomenon in popular culture. Its popularity, the accessibility of the well-known song format, the familiarity of the rhythms, and the heuristic thematic content of the genre expressing relatable sentiments of love and jealousy suggest that this can be "music of the people" and that criticisms of it come from a classist, high-brow position of elitism. Yet, contemporary pop-folk, removed from its rougher 1990s beginnings, "sells" to its audiences images of material abundancy and luxury, "perfect" lifestyles, and "expensive" bodies dressed in designer clothes and professional makeup. The songs from the genre, in terms of their visual and lyrical content, do not express social experiences of poverty, marginalization, and class struggle (Dimova 2019:101).

The accessibility of pop-folk, along with its evident popularity, has resulted in the formation of a sizeable sector within local music industries, most notably represented by Payner—the largest music label in the country—and the related media channels under the umbrella brand Planeta. The total capital of Payner assets is 2,142,000 levs, equivalent to 1,071,000 euros (Bulgarian Registry Agency 2021). This might not sound particularly impressive from the perspective of "major" global music companies, but it is worth pointing out for context that Bulgaria is the poorest country in the European Union, with average annual earnings of only 6,000 euros (Eurostat 2019). Furthermore, for comparison, other key local labels such as Virgin Records and Monte Music, have only declared 5,000 levs capital (Bulgarian Registry Agency 2021).

For the local context, Payner resembles a "major" music label, existing in symbolic opposition to all other labels which can be interpreted as "independent." This dominance over the commercial music field, in combination with the distinctly formulaic content promoted by pop-folk—in terms of song structure, the perceived superficiality of the thematic content, and stereotyped sexualities—results in a "mainstream," sell-out image of the style, one that alludes to manufactured success and inauthenticity, markers of a "lower" artistic value of the genre. Within the pop-folk field itself, commercial success is interpreted as a key goal and strategic focus. According to Rumen Apotolev from Payner, whom I interviewed in 2014:

People listen to music on our TV channel with their eyes. This means that there will always be people who will like us; we will have a target whatever happens. . . . [This is] an industry that brings in lots of money, and people cannot look at us like we're some common *chalga*-singers. We have become part of the country's business, which has caused incredible amounts of agitation, excitement, and interest.

(quoted in Draganova 2019:130–133)

Indeed, pop-folk's popularity has been the subject of undying public criticism. Borrowing tropes and language from pop-folk itself, the style has been described as "sinful" (Statelova 2005) and as an "apple of discord" (Draganova 2019:122), particularly in relation to some of the dangerous stereotyped sexual identities associated with the style. Female singers such as Galena, Emanuela, Desi Slava, Preslava, and Andrea are the most prominent artist representatives of the genre, formulating its own star system. This may sound empowering; yet, the focus on large breasts and lips, excessive markers of femininity, and Barbie doll–like near-caricature constructions of heteronormative sexual appeal create a limiting space for women in the field and are problematic in the context of twenty-first-century feminism (Baker 2020). The "roles" that women perform are those of lovers, betrayed sexual partners, and temptresses, supported by songs and videos like "You're not Around" (Bilyanish 2021), "He" (Danna 2020), and "With You" (Maria 2020), where women's fulfillment and happiness are portrayed as entirely dependent on romantic and sexual relationships with men. "Female pop-folk celebrities, whatever their own ethnic background, provide sensual and entrepreneurial fantasies and embody mastery of the codes of consumer culture," argues Catherine Baker (2020:353). This complements the ways in which Apotolev of Payner describes female singers (or "girls," as frequently referred to in my interview of him in 2014) as moldable identity products that translate well across a range of sectors:

Most of them have personal image makers, who develop a specific approach towards the singer's image, a different stage persona for in front of the audience and within society. If one of our singers is ready to get naked, then another [singer] will never do that. . . . It is not just image interests we have; it is also business and trading interests, which are dictated by our relationships with many other sectors. The advertising sector has to be aware of how each singer looks and presents herself so that she can be sold as a marketing image to relevant companies.

(quoted in Draganova 2019:130–133)

While male performers are not as prominent in pop-folk, their images conform to similar heteronormative gendered stereotypes. Male artists such as Galin, Fiki, and Antonio are, by and large, muscular and loaded with markers of material wealth as a key element of desirable masculinity. Over the two to three years since 2019, duets that involve male and female singers have become very popular in pop-folk. While somewhat expanding the genre repertoire of formats, duets like "Unique" (Hoang and Ilian 2019), "Just Sex" (Galin ft. Diona 2020), and "In Everybody's Mouth" (Emilia ft. Fiki

2020) affirm a hypersexualized hetero norm. There is, of course, the important exception of pop-folk Romani homosexual singer Azis, famous for provocative performances which combine markers of masculinity (muscular, beard) with markers of hyperbolized femininity expressed in dress, choreography, and singing techniques. While his presence in a homophobic media environment is important, his commercialized, "shock" interpretations of queerness affirm an exotic stereotype rather than normalization (Karakashyan 2020:50–53; Draganova 2019:133; Kimmel 2007:258–259). Overall, the image of the field is determined by a "sex sells" soft porn–like aesthetic and defined by a singer-based "star system" where demonstrating wider musical skills, such as instrumental, are outside the discourse.

Pop-folk is a significant music industry phenomenon locally. According to my observations, most new video releases score around 500,000 views on YouTube in their first week on average, which is significant considering that the language of the song lyrics is Bulgarian, which is only spoken in Bulgaria, and the country's population is just over 6,500,000 (National Statistical Institute 2021). Yet, due to its divisive character, the genre remains relatively isolated from non-specialized platforms, except in televised celebrity and talent formats such as *Like Two Drops of Water* (*Kato dve kapki voda*, NOVA TV, 2013–to date). A notable exception to this "rule" is musician and showman Slavi Trifonov and his Ku-Ku band who have been a quintessential element in national television prime time. Their repertoire consists of authored songs that accommodate some of the wedding band *chalga* roots of the pop-folk genre as well as its "classic" post-communist themes of lawlessness, financial success, and lust. These are complemented by reinventions of highly recognizable Bulgarian/Macedonian region folk songs such as "Jovano, Jovanke" ("Dear Jovana, Sweet Jovanka") and "Nazad, nazad, mome Kalino" ("Go Back, Go Back, Maiden Kalina"). These reinventions include new, contemporary instrumental arrangements contributing to the accessibility of the songs and highlighting their singalong qualities. With this combination of contemporary sound and the "patriotic" sentiment contained in performing folk music, Trifonov has successfully appealed to a mainstream audience and mainstream nationalism (Kourtova 2012), managed to fill up entire football stadiums' and major arenas' worth of audiences for his performances with his band, and entered mainstream politics in 2020 with his own populist party, There is Such a People. The party won the second round of pre-term general elections in 2021 yet failed to form a government.

The connection with folklore music is tendentiously pursued by the wider pop-folk business. For example, Payner has a dedicated TV channel (Planeta Folk) for folk music and multiple artists signed to its "folk" subcategory. At the same time pop-folk's connection with folk music remains complex as the genre involves, with a mix of folklore traditions, an interplay between the perceived "European" and "Eastern" creating visual and lyrical thematic connections with the imagined *orient*: a symbolic space of highly exoticized passion, mystery, sexual energy, and dynamism.

Pop-folk actively plays with folklore influences from the Balkan region and farther East, and its suggested connectivity with folklore and locality participates in the branding and marketing of the genre. While this is a cosmopolitan, dialogic approach to music—where "global" and pan-Balkan "local" interact—the dependency of the genre on materialism and sexualization, alongside the repetitive formulaic musical and thematic content, trivializes and exploits the musical traditions that are employed by the genre. These themes of mostly "primal" nature coincide and re-affirm some of the Balkan stereotypes and symbolically oppose perceived European, or "Western," cultural conventions. It is impressive that a genre performed mostly in Bulgarian—and therefore associated with a small market—can reach a sizeable industry status and popularity in the wider region including Greece and Turkey. Yet, the limited vocabulary of pop-folk and the tropes which some may identify as vulgar question the aesthetic and cultural value of the style which dominates the market.

In my fieldwork, music figures critical to pop-folk have suggested that the traditions that the genre plays with require being explored tastefully and with "respect." Throughout interviews, musicians and producers such as Boyko Petkov and Vasko the Patch observed that the eclectic nature of pop-folk creates a mockery of the richness of Romani, Bulgarian, and other local folk influences. As music journalist Ivaylo Kitsov summarized in a research interview with me in 2014,

> Our only salvation is folklore. This is our mega power which more and more people are starting to realise, but they don't know what to do with it. You may have power, and this power might be incredibly destructive. Some musicians are great and know how to "touch" folklore with clean hands. . . . And there are no politics involved here, the world takes whoever is skilful and whoever is good, whoever is interesting.

Within Bulgarian popular music, pop-folk with its appeal to the "primal" represents a form of "nesting orientalism" (Bakić-Hayden 1995) that embodies and reinforces stereotypical perceptions opposed to an idealized European-ness. Within the "social imaginary" (Appadurai 1996), the genre has played a divisive role (Kourtova 2012:147–150). While the popularity and commercial success of the genre frame it as a normalized form of entertainment, the celebrations of absurd hypersexualization and luxury construct a contemporary form of Balkanism.

Alternative Sounds: Folklore-Inspired Aesthetics in Contemporary Popular Music

Guitarist and composer Miroslav Ivanov, whose most recent album Little Alien (2019) explores folkloristic and futuristic themes, observed in an interview I took in 2021 that

> Every good musician knows that Bulgarian folklore is unique and can become a signature style. For me, artistry has to do with quality, not whether something is Bulgarian

or not Bulgarian. Bulgarian folklore is aesthetic, and Bulgarian musicians, especially composers, love using it as an expressive language, like blues or jazz. Bulgarian folklore is clearly not inferior to these or any other key global influences in popular music.

While pop-folk may be the *vanguard* in contemporary Bulgarian popular music, Bulgarian and wider Balkan folklore influences are explored across a range of styles including pop, rock, jazz, and experimental music: this is a holistic rather than an isolated ongoing trend. Folklore here is not the static subject of collection, preservation, and performance in "original" form (Sharp 1965) but a continuum and, indeed, an "expressive language," as formulated by Ivanov. Instead, ideas of "hybridization, fusion, remix, cover, remake, intertextuality, transtextuality, or acculturation" are central here (Peycheva 2020:2). This is a living and evolving aesthetic influence that participates in the construction of contemporary music and cultural identities. Musician and promoter Kottarashky, who plays with field recordings of folklore motifs from around Bulgaria as well as electronica, has had successful outputs such as the soundtrack to *Blind Vaysha*, Theodore Ushev's Oscar-nominated animation (2016). Kottarashky, in one of my interviews with him in 2014, says,

> In most cases music inevitably bears some local influences, if you listen carefully. For example, [in] genres like new wave and punk, like the band Review, which are pretty well-developed here, even though they are global genres, you can still grasp some specificity of Bulgarian sound in them. Especially the lyrics!

For some musicians, Bulgarian folklore borrowings—the iconic asymmetric meters, distinctive rhythms, traditional instruments, vocal patterns, and themes—are purposefully pursued as a source of distinction. For others, folklore is an unconscious, tacit influence that structures musical thought, particularly through the lyrics and their own rhythm and musicality. Artists who perform in Bulgarian can establish a more intimate connection with their local audiences—to enable a cultural process—as they employ a range of linguistic references, humor, and collectively recognized cultural references (Hall 1997:19–40). Yet, the specificity of the native language bleeds into the music even if it is performed in another language as it dictates how lyrical ideas are structured (Kristeva 1995); language is in the nuances of vocal sound present in the pronunciation or accent (Stankova 2019:21–25). Using Bulgarian language and folklore can be a designated and consciously pursued aspect of artist identity or be present as subtle, tacit influences. Musician Stefan Valdobrev, who composes for theater and film as well as having a remarkably successful career in pop-rock with the band Usual Suspects, describes folklore as a frame of mind, a way of thinking in songwriting. In *Book about Songs* (2020), he writes,

> I love Bulgarian folklore, but my aim is not to re-work it but to delicately incorporate it into my author music, to embrace it within my own style and not to necessarily be on its designated territory. (p. 69)

> I value contemporary, smart takes in the use and interpretation of folklore. As Bulgarians are so proud of their folklore, we often feel we need to show the world our music's complexity. But embellishment is to be found in simplicity. (p. 93)

The use of folklore influences is not a current "trend" on the surface; it is a theme interwoven into the make of Bulgarian popular music, a persistent practice approached within all genre categories in a variety of ways and not necessarily as an intended signature or selling point of artists. Folklore references are part of the musical imagination and repertoire. Alongside the "high-art," professionalized incarnations of folklore present in works such as the complex choir compositions and performances associated with *Le Mystère des Voix Bulgares*, folklore heritage is interpreted by musicians as an accessible resource open to interpretation. Like Charles Wright-Mills's "sociological imagination" (1959), the "folklore imagination"—as I would frame it—is an aesthetic and expressive space of self and collective identity-exploration. It is drawn upon in a variety of styles such as heavy metal by bands like Smallman, Voyvoda, and Vrani Volosa; rock and indie music with artists such as Revu, Mental Architects, and Meridua; electronic music with artists such as Kink and Balkansky; and jazz artists including Teodosii Spassov, Ivo Papazov, and Yıldız İbrahimova.

Despite the complexities and richness of folklore heritage, it belongs to "the people": it adapts and changes and is not to be an isolated "pocket" of culture (Nettl 1992). This is not about the invention of tradition or *fakesongs* (Harker 1985; Hobsbawm and Ranger 2012) but rather organic continuations through experimentation. My experience of attending music performances by popular artists such as Valdobrev, cited above, includes audiences' finding opportunities for active participation, particularly in folklore-inspired elements in songs, such as the transition of pop songs "Tya" (1998) and "Eto taka" (2018) ("She" 1998 and "Like That" 2018) into the folklore song "Ripni Kalinke" ("Get Up, Dear Kalina"). This seamless transition from Valdobrev's song, reinvented in a new version 20 years after the original was recorded, into the folklore song "Ripni Kalinke" highlights the similarities that the music carries, the inspiration drawn from folklore, if not in terms of lyrical themes,[3] then in terms of harmonic progressions and rhythm. Usually, during the final part of the live performances of this song, as it moves from its original format to a folklore rendition, the instrumental accompaniment stops and the audience takes over the sonic environment by singing and creating rhythm with clapping or stomping. Guitarist Ivanov, who performs with the Usual Suspects among many other bands, as well as solo, stated in an interview in 2021,

> I draw inspiration from folklore, but I am not a folklore musician as my background is in rock, jazz, and blues. . . . I have found ways of incorporating it into my music in the three solo albums I have had so far. The folklore influences in my music are a form of fantasy, a form of an imagination because after all, I am not a folklore specialist, so my take is rock- and jazz-informed. In "Wind" from my first album, my guitar solo seeks to mimic the traditional sound of bagpipes, and in my latest album "Thracian

beetle" has a folklore theme, as well as "Orpheus," which has folklore nuances, especially thanks to the participation of kaval player Zhivko Vasilev.

For much-celebrated Bulgarian musicologist Stoyan Djoudjeff, folklore itself is like a native language—it shapes musical expressions sometimes subconsciously and without being strategically pursued (Djoudjeff 1935, 1936, 1939 in Naydenova 2013:36–42). This is confirmed by folk revivalist Lomax, who suggests that folklore is unconsciously transmitted in everyday life, in the emotion of communication, and in vocal patterns, even though those processes are often difficult to rationalize (Lomax 1956:48–50). But while for some artists folklore is an element of their wider approach to music, for others it is a central focus, even if they are creating contemporary re-inventions and original authored music rather than pursuing "true to the original" preservationist goals. These artists contribute to the ongoing process of creating a body of work on the principle of *avtorski pesni v naroden duh*, or authored songs in folk spirit (Peycheva 2020). For example, the band Oratnitza, whose members are not professionally trained folklore musicians, employs indigenous acoustic instruments to perform music which can be broadly described as Bulgarian folklore-based. Yet, those instruments are not necessarily associated with the region: the kaval, *tŭpan* (drum), and *gaĭda* (bagpipe), which make regular appearances in their work, are traditionally associated with Bulgaria and the Balkans; yet, the cajón which dominates the rhythm section of the band, and the didgeridoo, originate from Peru and Australia, respectively. Not only does the band expand the instrumental repertoire associated with performing Bulgarian folklore; but using common elements such as irregular music meters, they also draw parallels and connect Bulgarian folklore with trap, dub step, and drum and bass. In an interview, they suggested that while this has attracted younger audiences, it has also attracted some negative reactions from folklore "puritans" whose take on folklore is defined by preserving the perceived "original" or the *obrabotena muzika* (processed, or reworked, music) model consolidated during the communist regime, where interpretations were highly professionalized and complex. Referring to internationally recognized award-winning kaval player Spassov, Oratnitza's Hristiyan Georgiev said in an interview in 2014,

> People like Teodosii Spassov offered a ground-breaking approach that challenged a model which was . . . made of concrete. He showed that change can happen and many musicians afterwards started to interpret folklore music their own way: they demonstrated how one folklore song can be played on the guitar, on the bass; it can be interpreted in all sorts of styles—in jazz, in rock, in. . . . This is change, the birth of diversity; this is how it is done. Once this was all taboo: to sing a folklore song in one of the styles I just listed.

Models such as *obrabotena muzika* explore socially "acceptable" topics through the expressive language that uses contemporary interpretations of folklore. Topics include the beauty and fertility of nature as a metaphor for love (e.g., "Chereshchitsa rod rodila"/"A Cherry Tree Gives Fruit," Ensemble Philip Koutev 1983), the performance of Bulgarian rituals (e.g., "Lazarski Boueneck"/"The Lazarus Girls Dance the Boueneck," Bulgarian State Television Female Choir 1994), and the significance of labor (Dimova 2019), for example, in popular tunes such as "Dilmano Dilbero" dedicated to the unlikely topic of sowing and reaping peppers (performed and recorded by multiple choirs including Ensemble Philip Koutev 1989). Oratnitza, in contrast, performs songs dedicated to themes like hangover in "Гано, Гано" ("Gano, Gano" [Gano = woman's name, vocative case] from Folktron, 2015):

> Гано, Гано бела Гано, мари,
> що не станеш сутрин рано, мари
> да пометеш равни двори.
>
> Gano, oh, fair-skinned Gano, dear,
> why don't you get up early, dear,
> to sweep up in your garden?

And laziness in the song "Леле Свашке" ("Lele Svashke," "Oh Mother-in-law"; from Oratnitza 2012), a song addressed by the mother of a son to his new mother-in-law:

> Леле свашке, пуста свашке, църна лисицо
> откога' се теб сродихме къща запустихме.
> Откогато твойта щерка снаха ми стана,
> от тогава, леле свашке, болест ме захвана . . .
> Леле свашке, пуста свашке, 'айде да си траемо,
> кусурите що' ги имат сал' двете да знаемо.
>
> Oh mother-in-law: you sneaky black fox, may you be forsaken.
> Since becoming relatives with you, the house has tumbled down in dust,
> Since your daughter has become my daughter, too,
> Since then, oh mother-in-law, I've caught a strange disease . . .
> Oh mother-in-law: may you be forsaken, but let's just both keep quiet about the faults of our children that each of us now knows.

Oratnitza also explores the connectedness between the indigenous music from geographically distant locations; for example, the Australian didgeridoo is part of the band's sonic signature. Furthermore, songs like "Ethiopia" (*Alter Ethno* 2018) takes inspiration from both Bulgarian and Ethiopian rhythms and instrumentation to explore the parallels between the musical traditions within a jazz format. Oratnitza's music and lyrics demonstrate that the use of folklore's expressive tools can be flexible, rather than static, and used to explore a wide range of topics, some of them associated with humor and everyday life, without moving to trivialization and formulaic content as argued in relation to pop-folk.

Contemporary "non-professional" folklore-oriented artists within Bulgarian popular music also challenge mono-ethnic and nationalistic perceptions of folklore. For example, bands such as Eriney, Kayno Yesno Slontse, Irfan, and Isihiya perform music inspired by folklores from Europe, the Balkans, and the Arab region. In a context where Bulgarian identities are historically built in symbolic opposition to the Ottoman control which dominated the past and lasted for five hundred years, references to Turkish as well as Arabic influences identified as "oriental" can challenge critics and audiences. As Plamena Kourtova notes,

> For some, the internalized self-perception of Bulgarians as Balkan reinforces their rejection of the Oriental as a stereotype for their crudeness, barbarity and lack of sophistication. For others, the eclecticism of the music stands as a symbol of regional pride and national belonging. Both, however, exist within the same social totality and therefore stand as conflicting but interdependent aspects of its underlying principles. (2012:162)

Multi-instrumentalist Evgeni Chakalov addressed a peculiar kind of "political correctness" which suggests that the similarities between Bulgarian and Turkish folklores are purposefully excluded from the discourses of Bulgarian folklore, despite the fact that five hundred years of mingling cannot be left without a legacy. Similarly, when experimenting with instruments, Chakalov encounters a particular form of resistance. In an interview in 2013, he said,

> At some performances, Arabic-inspired compositions were not as welcome as the Bulgarian. In Bulgaria there has always been this political correctness issue. When I get a Gallic bagpipe I get asked "why not a Bulgarian bagpipe? What sort of Bulgarian are you?" Playing the Gallic bagpipe and not the Bulgarian is some sort of crime. I just like the sound of the Gallic bagpipe more: Bulgarian folklore is beautiful but cannot be everyone's favourite music. . . . I played for a folklore ensemble; the lute player ran away somewhere, and I replaced him with electric guitar which resulted in some nice experiments. Among the people I played with, none would go home and listen to "authentic" folklore anyway.

Music that explores folklore references carries metaphors for inter-ethnic relationships, which poses challenges to experimentation. As a result of that, these symbolic interactions in music cannot be simplified to an artistic dialogue or a play on eclecticism: they can be political and contested.

A perceived category that successfully surpasses these challenges is so-called Balkan music, which employs the aesthetic of wedding orchestras to capture the authentic energy and charm of the crossroad location of the Balkan Peninsula as a melting pot of ethnic groups and influences. This field is attuned to the notion of world music, which enables global audiences to "imagine" places by picking up on their "exotic" quirks and is represented by Bosnian (identifying as Yugoslav) artist and film score composer Goran Bregović and his Wedding and Funeral Orchestra, Romani brass band Fanfare Ciocârlia, American-based "immigrant Gypsy punks" Gogol Bordello and Kultur Shock, and electronic band Balkan Beat Box. The ways in which these artists avoid the potential cultural clashes and conflicts embodied in their music derived from mixed influences is through humorous self-awareness taken as far as satire. This is a form of branding based upon a positive, or at least "fun," interpretation of Balkan and wider east European stereotypes. Examples of that are Kultur Shock's 2006 album *We've Come Here to Take Your Jobs Away* and Gogol Bordello's exaggerated east European accents. Overall, the image of Bulgaria and the Balkans within the global musical imaginary is defined by the distinctiveness of folklore. For example, Bulgarian folklore has been incorporated in the work of artists including Peter Gabriel, Kate Bush, Leftfield, Steve Vai, and U2 (Draganova 2019:151). The international recognition and cultural translation (Draganova 2021; Maitland 2017) are largely to be accredited to the unprecedented success of *Le Mystère des Voix Bulgares*, which was acclaimed by artists such as George Harrison, Frank Zappa, and David Bowie and inspired the emergence of Bulgarian choirs all over the world (Stankova 2019).

In a research conversation, musician Robert Wyatt, associated with the psychedelic, progressive Canterbury Sound and jazz styles within popular music, told me that whenever he felt he was experimenting in music and trying out something new, it was only to find out that it already existed in Bulgarian folklore. Wyatt, a songwriter, singer, and instrumentalist emblematic of British progressive and experimental music, is associated with acts such as the Wilde Flowers, Soft Machine, and Matching Mole, as well as being known for his extensive solo career (Draganova et al. 2021; O'Dair 2014). He is another "Western" internationalist musician whose imagination is fascinated by Bulgarian folklore. In conversation, Wyatt and his wife—artist and Wyatt's manager Alfreda Benge—spoke to me about Bulgarian folklore as something "magical" and "inspirational," complex and unique: their favorite European folklore. In e-mail correspondence with me in 2017, Wyatt wrote,

> It'd be sad if your unique culture were totally swamped by our ubiquitous musical Big Mac factories! ... A Bulgarian habit we often used, unusual here at that time in popular music: uneven, irregular time-signatures. I wish I'd heard Bulgarian folk music when I was a teenager—it would have helped me understand those rhythms, how to adapt them for my phrasing on drums!

Wyatt is associated with the Canterbury Sound—a signature style within popular music linked to progressive rock, psychedelic music, and jazz—and the time that he refers to in our conversation is the 1960s, when he began to play with bands. The legacy of this perceived scene is represented by experimentation and artistic freedom (Draganova et al. 2021). The parallels with Bulgarian music that Wyatt draws are, therefore, a confirmation of the flexibility and universality of folklore as a source of inspiration.

The goals of reaching for this artistic resource are not necessarily commercial and do not need to lead to trivialization or standardization. Rather, the diversity of the musical examples presented in this section articulates that the use of folklore is a pathway to alternativity—moving away from mainstream banality into a field of experimental potential (BCMCR 2020/2021; Holland and Spracklen 2018; Scott 2012). Experimentation is tied to freedom and confidence—elements which strongly counteract the negative stereotypes under the umbrella of Balkanism.

Conclusion

Music's relationship with place is not only geographical. Music is a metaphor for place, too, and we imagine, romanticize, and live place through it (Draganova and Blackman 2018). The use of folklore resources within Bulgarian popular music offers attractive opportunities for artistic distinction and attaining signature style in popular music. Incorporating folklore into recognizable formats—mixing them with genres, styles, instruments, and expressive tools familiar to international audiences promotes a dialogic, cosmopolitan approach to popular music. This "conversation" through popular music enables a symbolic interaction—participation in a globalized and diverse cultural fabric. Isolating "tradition" into static, museumized forms might aim to preserve; but to live, music needs to breathe, to evolve, and to change together with the wider social and cultural contexts. The "folklore imagination" presents artists with an aesthetic spectrum, a flexible language of artistic expression. Opportunities to experiment suggest freedom and confidence, progressive politics of identity that can challenge existing negative Balkan stereotypes of backwardness. At the same time, a commodified approach to folklore traditions from the region can result in trivializing heritage. The notably successful genre of pop-folk builds problematic bridges between folk and celebrations of mafia, materialism, and hypersexual heteronormativity. Pop-folk has produced a sizable sector of cultural production and can be framed as "just" an entertainment industry; at the same time, the genre is a metaphor for postcommunist turmoil which reproduces new forms of Balkanism or nests of orientalism. Yet, the "Folktron" of Bulgarian popular music—the urge to explore and experiment with different folklore elements to invent new, yet relatable sound—goes beyond this commercial genre and into more niche areas of musical creativity. Like the animated robot hero Voltron, "Folktron" is a figure of the imagination: a cultural crossroad turned into a superpower; and it is through the diversity of the music that we imagine Bulgaria as well, as a dynamic place of curiosity, authentic energy, and contradiction.

Notes

1. This is a continuation of research that began with my doctoral study finalized in 2016, dedicated to popular music in contemporary Bulgaria. My PhD dissertation became the basis for the monograph *Popular Music in Contemporary Bulgaria: At the Crossroads* (2019) and was the beginning of continually updated fieldwork data collection.
2. This and all subsequent translations from Bulgarian to English are mine. This and all subsequent song-text excerpts in this chapter can be heard in performance on YouTube by searching for the artist's or group's name and the title of the song.

3. Valdobrev's song is about youth, love, and discovery, while "Ripni, Kalinke" is about performing Bulgarian traditional dance as a form of resistance against the oppressors of Bulgarian identity and tradition.

Works Cited

Appadurai, Arjun. 1996. *Modernity at Large: Cultural Dimensions of Globalization*. London: University of Minnesota Press.

Baker, Catherine. 2020. "What Female Pop-folk Celebrity in South-east Europe Tells Postsocialist Feminist Media Studies about Global Formations of Race." *Feminist Media Studies*, 20/30:341–360.

Bakić-Hayden, Milica. 1995. "Nesting Orientalisms: The Case of Former Yugoslavia." *Slavic Review*, 54/4:917–931.

Bakić-Hayden, Milica, and Robert Hayden. 1992. "Orientalist Variations on the Theme "Balkans": Symbolic Geography in Recent Yugoslav Cultural Politics." *Slavic Review*, 51/1:1–15.

BCMCR (Birmingham Centre for Media and Cultural Research). 2020/2021. *Research Theme 2020/2021: Alternativity*: https://bcmcr.org/research/category/alternativity/. Accessed January 31, 2021.

Benjamin, Walter. 1999. "The Work of Art in the Age of Mechanical Reproduction." In *Illuminations*, ed. Hannah Arendt, 152–196. London: Pimlico. First published 1936.

Bjelić, Dusan. 2011. *Normalising the Balkans: Geopolitics of Psychoanalysis and Psychiatry*. Aldershot: Ashgate.

Blackman, Shane, and Michelle Kempson, eds. 2016. *The Subcultural Imagination: Theory, Research and Reflexivity in Contemporary Youth Cultures*. London: Routledge.

Bourdieu, Pierre. 1993. *The Field of Cultural Production: Essays on Art and Literature*. Cambridge: Polity Press.

Buchanan, Donna A. 1995. "Metaphors of Power, Metaphors of Truth: The Politics of Music Professionalism in Bulgarian Folk Orchestras." *Ethnomusicology*, 39/3:381–416. http://www.jstor.org/stable/924628. Accessed January 31, 2021.

Buchanan, Donna A. 2007a. "'Oh, Those Turks!' Music, Politics, and Interculturality in the Balkans and Beyond." In *Balkan Popular Culture and the Ottoman Ecumene*, ed. Donna Buchanan, 3–54. Lanham, MD: Scarecrow Press.

Buchanan, Donna A. 2007b. "Bulgarian Ethnopop along the Old *Via Militaris*: Ottomanism, Orientalism, or Balkan Cosmopolitanism." In *Balkan Popular Culture and the Ottoman Ecumene*, ed. Donna Buchanan, 225–268. Plymouth: Scarecrow Press.

Bulgarian Registry Agency. 2021. *Inquiries*: https://portal.registryagency.bg/. Accessed January 31, 2021.

Dimov, Vencislav. 2010. "Music as Media in the Field of Ethnomusicology." *Bulgarian Musicology*, 2/3:23–40. [Димов, Венцислав. 2010. "Музиката като медия в сферата на етномузикологията." *Българска музикология*, 2/3:23–40.]

Dimova, Zlatina. 2019. "Chalga as a Factor for Deformation of Cultural Identity in Post-communist Bulgaria." In *Language, Literature and Other Cultural Phenomena Communicational and Comparative Perspective*, eds. E. Parpală and C. Popescu, 98–109. Craiova: Editura Universitaria Craiova.

Djoudjeff, S. 1935. "On Style in Music and the Bulgarian Style." *A. S. O.*, 1/2:83–84. [Джуджев, С. 1935. "За стила в музиката и българсия стил." *А. С. О.*, 1/2:83–84.]
Djoudjeff, Stoyan. 1936. "Bulgarian Folklore Dance." *Zlatorog*, 17/8:369–372. [Джуджев, Стоян. 1936. "Българският народен танц." *Златорог*, 17/8:369–372.
Djoudjeff, Stoyan. 1939. "Sound and Rhythm in Bulgarian Speech." *Golden Horn*, 20/9:441–445. [Джуджев, Стоян. 1939. "Звук и ритъм в българското слово." *Златорог*, 20/9:441–445.]
Draganova, Asya. 2019. *Popular Music in Contemporary Bulgaria: At the Crossroads*. Bingley: Emerald.
Draganova, Asya. 2021. "The 'New Flowers' of Bulgarian Punk: Cultural Translation, Local Subcultural Scenes, and Heritage." In *Oxford Handbook of Punk Rock*, eds. George McKay and Gina Arnold. New York: Oxford University Press. https://academic.oup.com/edited-volume/38573.
Draganova, Asya, and Shane Blackman. 2018. "No Blue Plaques 'In the Land of Grey and Pink': Popular Music Alternativity in the Lived and Imagined City of Canterbury." In *Alternativity and Marginalisation*, eds. Samantha Holland and Karl Spracklen, 219–237. Bingley: Emerald Publishing.
Draganova, Asya, Shane Blackman, and Andy Bennett, eds. 2021. *The Canterbury Sound in Popular Music: Scene, Identity and Myth*. Bingley: Emerald.
Eurostat. 2019. *Wages and Labour Costs*: https://ec.europa.eu/eurostat/statistics-explained/index.php/Wages_and_labour_costs. Accessed January 31, 2021.
Gilroy, Paul. 1991. "Sounds Authentic: Black Music, Ethnicity, and the Challenge of the 'Changing' Same." *Black Music Research Journal*, 11/2:111–136.
Glenny, Misha. 2008. *McMafia: A Journey through the Global Criminal Underworld*. New York: Vintage.
Glenny, Misha. 2012. *The Balkans: 1804–2012: Nationalism, War and the Great Powers*. London: Penguin Books.
Goldsworthy, Vesna. 2013. *Inventing Ruritania: The Imperialism of the Imagination*. London: Yale University Press. First published 1998.
Hall, Stuart. 1997. "The Local and Global." In *Culture, Globalization and the World-System*, ed. Anthony King, 19–40. London: Macmillan.
Harker, David. 1985. *Fakesong: The Manufacture of British 'Folksong' 1700 to the Present Day*. Milton Keynes: Open University Press.
Hill, Sarah. 2007. *"Blerwytirhwng?" The Place of Welsh Pop Music*. Aldershot: Ashgate.
Hobsbawm, Eric, and Terence Ranger, eds. 2012. *The Invention of Tradition*. Cambridge: Cambridge University Press. Originally published 1983.
Holland, Samantha, and Karl Spracklen, eds. 2018. *Alternativity and Marginalisation*. Bingley: Emerald Publishing.
Karakashyan, Kosta. 2020. "Positive Media Representation of the Bulgarian LGBTQ+ Community and Shifting National Attitudes towards Homosexuality." MA thesis, United Nations Educational, Scientific and Cultural Organization.
Kimmel, Michael S., ed. 2007. *The Sexual Self: The Construction of Sexual Scripts*. Nashville, TN: Vanderbilt University Press.
Kourtova, Plamena. 2012. "Slavi Trifonov and the Commodification of Nationalism: Popular Culture, Popular Music, and the Politics of Identity in Postsocialist Bulgaria, 1990–2005." PhD dissertation, Florida State University.
Kristeva, Julia. 1995. "Bulgarie, ma souffrance." *L'Infini* 51/Autumn:42–52.
Kristeva, Julia. 2000. *Crisis of the European Subject*, trans. S. Fairfield. New York: Other Press.

Lacan, Jacques. 1997. "The Agency of the Letter in the Unconscious, or Reason since Freud." *Écrits: A Selection*, trans. A. Sheridan, 146–178. London: Tavistock. First published 1977.

Levy, Claire. 2004. "Who Is the 'Other' in the Balkans? Local Ethnic Music as a Different Source of Identities in Bulgaria." In *Music, Space and Place: Popular Music and Cultural Identity*, eds. Sheila Whiteley, Andy Bennett, and Stan Hawkins, 42–57. Aldershot: Ashgate.

Levy, Claire. 2009. "Folk in Opposition? Wedding Bands and the New Developments in Bulgarian Popular Music." *Music and Politics*, 3/1:1–12.

Lomax, Alan. 1956. "Folk Song Style: Notes on a Systematic Approach to the Study of Folk Song." *Journal of International Folk Music Council*, 8/1956:48–50.

Lomax, Alan. 1968. *Folk Song Style and Culture*. Washington, DC: American Association of Advanced Science.

Maitland, Sarah. 2017. *What Is Cultural Translation?* London: Bloomsbury.

Naydenova, Gorica. 2013. *From Philosophy to Folklore: The Unknown Stoyan Djuzhev*. Sofia: Mars 09. [Найденова, Горица. 2013. *От философия до фолклористика: Непознатият Стоян Джуджев*. София: Марс 09.]

National Statistical Institute. 2021. *2021 Population Census and Housing Census in the Republic of Bulgaria Act*: https://www.nsi.bg/en/content/17050/basic-page/2021-population-census-and-housing-census-republic-bulgaria-act. Accessed April 6, 2022.

Nettl, Bruno. 1992. *The Study of Ethnomusicology: Thirty-one Issues and Concepts*. Champaign: University of Illinois Press.

Nikolova, Ivelina. 2018. "Modern Morality That Gives Life to Vices: Glimpses of the Image of Moral Decay in Bulgaria." *HTS Teologiese Studies/Theological Studies*, 74/1:a4633. https://doi.org/10.4102/hts.v74i1.4633.

O'Dair, Marcus. 2014. *Different Every Time: The Authorised Biography of Robert Wyatt*. London: Serpent's Tail.

Peycheva, Liliana. 1999. "The Enchanted Music: Chalga According to Romani Musicians." *Bulgarian Musicology*, 1:58–65. [Пейчева, Лиляна. 1999. "Изкушената музика: Чалгата според ромските музиканти." *Българска музикология*, 1:58–65.]

Peycheva, Liliana. 1996. "The Media: Death-Life of Bulgarian Folk Music." *Bulgarian Folklore*, 5:29–34. [Пейчева, Лиляна. 1996. "Медиите: Смърт–живот на българската фолклорна музика." *Български фолклор*, 5:29–34.]

Peycheva, Lilyana. 2020. "Traditions in the Discussions about the *Obrabotvane* of Folklore in the *Avtorski Pesni v Naroden Duh* from Bulgaria." *Arts*, 9/3:89.

Rice, Timothy. 1994. *May It Fill Your Soul: Experiencing Bulgarian Music*. Chicago: University of Chicago Press.

Rice, Timothy. 2004. *Music in Bulgaria: Experiencing Music, Expressing Culture*. New York: Oxford University Press.

Roberts, Ken. 2009. *Youth in Transition: Eastern Europe and the Rest*. Basingstoke: Palgrave Macmillan.

Roberts, Ken. 2010. "1989: So Hard to Remember and so Easy to Forget." In *1989: Young People and Social Change after the Fall of the Berlin Wall*, eds. Carmen Leccardi, Charles Feixa, Sijka Kovahceva, Herwig Reiter, and Tatjana Sekulic, 15–29. Strasbourg: Council of Europe.

Said, Edward. 1978. *Orientalism*. New York: Vintage Books.

Savin-Baden, Maggi, and Claire Howell Major. 2012. "Personal Stance, Positionality and Reflexivity." In *Qualitative Research: The Essential Guide to Theory and Practice*, 69–79. London: Routledge.

Scott, Michael. 2012. "Cultural Entrepreneurs, Cultural Entrepreneurship: Music Producers Mobilising and Converting Bourdieu's Alternative Capitals." *Poetics*, 40/3:237–255.

Sharp, Cecil James. 1965. *English Folk Song: Some Conclusions*. London: Mercury.

Silverman, Claire. 2004. "'Move over Madonna': Gender, Representation, and the 'Mystery' of Bulgarian Voices." In *Over the Wall/after the Fall: Post-communist Cultures through an East-West Gaze*, eds. Sibelan Forrester, Magdalena J. Zaborowska, and Elena Gapova, 212–237. Bloomington: Indiana University Press.

Sotirova, Nadezhda. 2021. "'Good Job, but Bulgarian': Identifying "Bulgarian-ness" through Cultural Discourse Analysis." *Journal of International and Intercultural Communication*, 14/2:128–145. https://doi.org/10.1080/17513057.2020.1760919.

Stankova, Maria Vassileva. 2019. "Globalization, Nationalism and Cultural Translation in Bulgarian Folk Singing." PhD dissertation, New York University.

Statelova, Rosemary. 2005. *The Seven Sins of Chalga*. Sofia: Institute for Arts Research. [Стателова, Розмари. 2005. *Седемте гряха на чалгата*. София: Институт за изследване на изкуствата.]

Statelova, Rosemary. 2008. "Chalga Girls and Chalga Boys: Weak Music and Luscious Physique." *Through the Years: Rosemary Statelova On*, 70/2011:124–134. [Стателова, Розмари. 2008. "Чалга момичета и чалга момчета: Слаба музика и пищна физика." В *През годините: Розмари Стателова на*, 70/2011:124–134.]

Todorova, Maria. 2009. *Imagining the Balkans*, updated ed. Oxford: Oxford University Press. First published 1997.

Valdobrev, Stefan. 2020. *Book of Songs*. Sofia: Bookmania. [Вълдобрев, Стефан. 2020. *Книга за песните*. София: Книгомания.]

Wright Mills, C. 1959. *The Sociological Imagination*. Oxford: Oxford University Press.

Žižek, Slavoj. 1999. "The Spectre of Balkan." *Journal of the International Institute*, 6/2. http://quod.lib.umich.edu/j/jii/4750978.0006.202/--spectre-of-balkan?rgn=main;view=fulltext. Accessed January 31, 2021.

Songs/Albums

Anelia. 2019. "Posh Girl," single. Dimitrovgrad: Payner [Гъзарка].

Bilyanish. 2021. "You're not Around," single. Dimitrovgrad: Payner [Няма те, няма].

Bulgarian State Television Female Choir. 1994. "Lazarus Girls Dance the Boueneck." *Le Mystère des Voix Bulgares*. Ritual, New York: Nonesuch/Elektra [Лазарски буенек].

Bulgarian State Television Female Choir. 1987. *Le Mystère des Voix Bulgares* (album), compiled by Marcel Cellier. Stockholm: Disques Cellier.

Danna. 2020. "He," single. Dimitrovgrad: Payner [Той].

Diana Express. 1976. "Azure." *Diana Express*. Sofia: Balkanton [Синева].

Emilia ft. Fiki. 2020. "In Everybody's Mouth." *Shark*. Dimitrovgrad: Payner [На всикките в устата].

Ensemble Philip Koutev. 1983. "A Cherry Tree Gives Fruit." *Ensemble Philip Koutev*. Sofia: Balkanton [Черешчица род родила].

Ensemble Philip Koutev. 1989. "Dilmano Dilbero." *Bulgarian Poliphony 1*. Sofia: Balkanton [Дилмано Дилберо].

Galin ft. Diona. 2020. "Just Sex," single. Dimitrovgrad: Payner [Просто секс].

Goranov, Orlin. 1982. "The World Is for Two," single. Sofia: Balkantone [Светът е за двама].

Hoang, Ani, and Ilian. 2019. "Unique," single. Dimitrovgrad: Payner [Уникат].

Ivanov, Miroslav. 2019. *Little Alien*, independent release. Sofia.

Kottarashky. 2016. *Blind Vaysha Soundtrack*. Berlin: Asphalt Tango.

Maria. 2020. "With You," single. Dimitrovgrad: Payner [С теб].

Oratnitza. 2012. *Oratnitza*. Sofia: Fusion Embassy.

Oratnitza. 2015. *Folktron*. Sofia: Fusion Embassy.

Oratnitza. 2018. *Alter Ethno*. Sofia: Fusion Embassy.

Shock, Kultur. 2006. *We Came to Take Your Jobs Away*. San Francisco: Koolarrow Records.

Valdobrev, Stefan, and the Usual Suspects. 1998. "Tya," *Towards*. Sofia: City Studio [Тя].

Valdobrev, Stefan, and the Usual Suspects. 2018. "Eto taka," *20 Years of Towards*. Sofia: Orpheus Music.

Vaseva, Sashka. 1996. "Levs in Deutsche Marks." *Inflation and Love*. Dimitrovgrad: Payner [Инфлация и любов].

CHAPTER 37

ALBANIAN-LANGUAGE *ETNOPOP* AND THE EMERGENCE OF A "BALKAN" REGIONAL MUSIC SPHERE

JANE C. SUGARMAN

IN the summer of 2005, a pop music arranger in Kosova named Florent Boshnjaku finished an arrangement that he hoped would become a hit song (Fig. 37.1). All that it needed was lyrics. He first e-mailed an mp3 of the arrangement to a lyricist who was then studying in London. When the lyricist e-mailed back a text, it wasn't quite what Boshnjaku felt the song needed. So he turned to Bekim Latifi, known as MC Beka, and e-mailed him the mp3 file just as Latifi was departing for Switzerland, as he did each weekend, to deejay at a dance club in Zurich. Latifi wrote some verses on the airplane and then, once in Switzerland, e-mailed them back to Kosova. Knowing that Boshnjaku rarely reads his e-mail, he sent a text message to his cellphone, telling him that the lyrics had been sent. At 3 p.m. the next day, Boshnjaku read the text message and found the lyrics in his e-mail. Two hours later, singer Vullnet Sefaja, for whom the song was destined, arrived at the studio to review them; and by 7 p.m. the recorded song, "Ah sa keq" ("Oh How Terrible"), was complete.[1]

As this anecdote suggests, the period since the late 1980s has seen a revolution in the production and distribution of recorded music within and beyond southeastern Europe. With the collapse of socialist governments throughout the region, music personnel in virtually all countries began to found private music studios and production houses. These new firms largely replaced state radio–television stations and recording companies, which had in the socialist period been the centers of music production. Whether or not state broadcasting outlets continued to function, private radio stations and television channels were also established and became, at least initially, the primary

FIG. 37.1. Arranger Florent Boshnjaku in his studio in Prishtina, Kosova, July 2006.
(Photograph by the author.)

outlets for airing new productions. Gradually, each national group came to have its own monolingual music industry, composed of a combination of public and private enterprises.

Within music studios themselves, the composition and arrangement of songs were likewise transformed by the adoption of synthesizer- and computer-based methods of production. By the 2000s, the rise of social media and the availability of new digital technologies transformed music distribution still further. All these processes occurred in a period when both producers and consumers of recorded music were experiencing greater personal mobility, whether through periodic short-term travel, as in this chapter's opening anecdote, or through long-term labor outmigration. For those national groups with a large migrant population, the new national industries were, in fact, diasporic and transnational.

During the first decade of the 2000s, virtually all industries in the region promoted similar musical genres that alluded in some way to the region's folklore, or to "ethnic" sounds more generally. These included *turbo-folk*, whose production was centered in Serbia but whose audience extended to other Slavic speakers in and from the former Yugoslavia; *chalga* in Bulgaria; *manele* in Romania; *laïkó* in Greece; *Türk pop* in Turkey; and what was most often called *etnopop* in Albanian-speaking areas.[2] Initially, no single forum emerged to bring these compatible genres into regular contact with each other.

Rather, each national industry presented itself to its audience as the primary source of music for that national group. As this chapter details, however, behind the scenes music personnel in the various countries began to interact with increasing intensity.

This study traces the development of the Albanian-language genre of *etnopop* beginning in the first decade of the 2000s, primarily in Kosova and North Macedonia, and examines the use in its production of new digital technologies. As I will argue, at the heart of *etnopop* production lay a paradox. On the one hand, new communication and production technologies enabled Albanian speakers both to maintain close contact transnationally as a self-identified national group and to create an extensive music industry whose products were often a focal point of transnational social interaction. On the other hand, these same technologies enabled, and often encouraged, personnel within the industry to engage with non-Albanian producers and performers in neighboring countries. The result was a situation in which the Albanian industry maintained a facade of autonomous existence for much of its audience while in fact fostering intricate transnational interconnections. Ultimately, such interactions contributed to what has emerged as a complexly organized southeast European regional music sphere.

Summoning the Albanian "Transnation"

A new private, transnational Albanian-language music industry began to coalesce in the waning days of socialism. In 1988, the government of the Yugoslav Republic of Serbia, led by Slobodan Milošević, began to rescind the autonomy of the Albanian-majority province of Kosova.[3] Following months of protests by Kosovar Albanians, Serbian police entered the headquarters of Radio-Television Prishtina on July 5, 1990, and forcibly removed all Albanian employees. Up to that time, the station had produced the great majority of recordings and video performances of Albanian music of all types for the whole of Yugoslavia. Over the next two years, as Yugoslavia began to break apart, the socialist system in neighboring Albania collapsed, to be replaced by a parliamentary democracy with a capitalist economy.[4] In the aftermath of these developments, personnel in Albania joined with Albanians in the former Yugoslavia—in Kosova, what is now North Macedonia, Montenegro, and Serbia—as well as with Albanians in the diaspora, to cobble together a network of music studios, production companies, and broadcast media so as to be able to record and disseminate various types of Albanian music. Soon a division of labor emerged, with production and distribution concentrated in the former Yugoslavia and its diaspora and broadcast media centered in Albania.

Albanian-language music production could not have developed as it did were it not for the availability of relatively inexpensive music technologies that were just coming to market beginning in the late 1980s. In the very early 1990s, Albanian arrangers in Kosova and North Macedonia began to prepare songs on synthesizer-based digital audio workstations (DAWs) such as the Korg M1 and Roland JV-1000. Already by the mid-1990s, they had transferred their skills to computer-based programs such as Cubase and Logic. The albums they produced, as well as a very few produced by artists in Albania, were then distributed to homeland and diaspora sites by new production companies located both in the former Yugoslavia and in guestworker sites in Germany and Switzerland (see Sugarman 2004). Within Albania, the state radio–television continued to dominate the recording and broadcast of domestic artists well into the 1990s. In order to address the lack of Albanian-controlled broadcast media in Kosova, however, it also launched a satellite television program in 1993 that broadcast news and cultural programming both to the former Yugoslavia and to diaspora sites in western Europe.[5] By the early 2000s, a media non-governmental organization in Switzerland reported that Kosova had one of the highest concentrations of satellite dishes in the world (Brunner 2002).

In subsequent years the Albanian industry became further integrated as artists from Albania sought to release recordings on labels in the former Yugoslavia and its diaspora, while those in Kosova and North Macedonia sought to appear on television in Albania. All sought to capitalize on the ever-growing audience in the diaspora, which emerged as the most lucrative market for all Albanian musical products. Not all Albanians in all sites came to consume the same types of music, but the new industry did bring together artists and musical styles that, before 1990, had been known primarily to audiences within each region or state, making them available to much larger audiences grouped into class-, gender-, or generation-based "taste cultures." As performers, arrangers, and distributors collaborated increasingly across state borders, productions could no longer be identified exclusively with any one of the region's nation states.

Following the Kosova War (1998–1999), Kosova became a protectorate of the United Nations. By the early 2000s, both Albania and Kosova were home to multiple radio and television channels, as well as myriad new recording studios, video production companies, and distribution firms. Despite different political histories as well as historic differences in folkloric forms and styles of state-sponsored music, a popular music mainstream emerged in which performers, arrangers, lyricists, distributors, and media outlets all participated. Recordings of artists from all homeland areas, as well as ones living in the diaspora, recorded in a variety of sites, continually entered this industry and circulated throughout it, at a level of integration exceeding that of the 1990s.

The Emergence of *Etnopop*

Beginning with the first decade of the 2000s, one of the most prominent genres that circulated through the Albanian industry came to be known as *etnopop*. The song with which this chapter begins, "Ah sa keq," very much exemplified the genre. At its core was a computer-based Western-style dance track with verses and a chorus, each based on a repeating ostinato. Other than language, the features that rendered the track audibly "Albanian" were produced through digital means: a melody wafting through the instrumental lines, recorded originally on a rural end-blown flute (*fyell*), and then cut up and reassembled so as to fit the song's structure; a synthesized timbre in the accompaniment that evoked the sound of the two-stringed plucked lute *çifteli*; and a synthesized frame drum (*daire*) pattern that came to the fore in the interlude between the song's two verses. In arrangements such as this, Albanian folklore achieved a sort of afterlife. The historic associations of each of these sounds—the *fyell* with shepherds' melodies, the *çifteli* with men's celebratory gatherings, and the *daire* with women's singing at weddings or on calendrical holidays—were stripped away in the service of a track in which allusions to folklore lived on as decorative devices that nevertheless resonated with Albanian listeners as markers of their sense of collective identity.

In one respect, "Ah sa keq" was somewhat unusual for *etnopop* in that its singer was male. In the early 2000s Albanian *etnopop* was dominated by young female singers, generally of urban background and often quite highly educated. As a result, even when their lyrics were written by men, their songs frequently addressed the state of youthful gender relations from an assertively female, and at times overtly feminist, perspective. Despite its male lead, "Ah sa keq" too had a feminist theme. After verses that described a husband's panic when he awoke to find his wife gone from their home, the chorus provided a playful punchline:[6]

> Ah sa keq pa ty kur shkon
> Asgjë ktu në shpi nuk bon
> Pse më ik e shkon në punë
> Ah kjo mendjen krejt ma lun.
>
> Oh it's terrible without you when you've gone
> Nothing here in the house is right.
> How could you run away and go to work?
> It's driving me out of my mind.

A-V Link 1: Vullnet [Sefaja] Marigona, "Ah sa keq" (audio, 2006 ▶).

In an interview in 2004, Shkumbin Kryeziu, head of the Labia music production company in Prishtina, described to me *etnopop*'s overall sound as "pop music with folkloric, Oriental, and Balkan elements."[7] These elements could be ones associated with Albanian rural folklore, such as specific melodic or rhythmic structures, or instruments such as the *çifteli* or the *fyell*. Or they could allude to older urban instruments such as the clarinet, the short-necked lute (*ud*), or the goblet drum (*tarabuka*) or to the use of Ottoman *makam*-s (melodic modes). Beyond Albanian territories, allusions to Turkish folk instruments or to Egyptian-style *raqs sharqi* dance drumming became popular, as did sounds with a "Mediterranean" flavor, most frequently flamenco-style Spanish guitar.[8] Despite using a variety of "ethnic" rhythmic patterns, the great majority of songs were in a brisk duple meter, and the singers' vocal production was unequivocally Western, reinforced by the frequent use of backup singers in emulation of Anglophone pop productions.

Why *etnopop* at this particular historical junction? In the years immediately following the war (1998–1999), as industry personnel confirmed for me, productions of "folk music" fell out of favor among listeners, especially in Kosova. On the one hand, the commercial folk music that had been a top-selling genre in the 1990s, which included many Romani and Turkish elements, was avoided by some media outlets because it offended the tastes of many cultural officials (see Sugarman 2007). Eventually it became associated primarily with the live occasions at which it originated, such as weddings, other family celebrations, and middle school graduation parties. On the other hand, patriotic productions in a "folkloric" style reminded many people of the war period, when such recordings dominated musical production (Sugarman 2010). Several interviewees emphasized to me that listeners wanted to hear music that was "upbeat" and "optimistic"; as producer Fatos Kadiu explained, something *ma happy* (more "happy").[9] After all, *Kosovarë* (Kosovar Albanians) had survived a war and the Milošević era and were eager to build a new future for their society.

In the very early 2000s, many Albanian pop music productions closely emulated Western models, and particularly those from the United States. While many male performers took up hip-hop, female performers were inspired by a host of US singers in a "neo-soul" or R&B style: from Aaliyah and Erykah Badu to Destiny's Child and Alicia Keys to Mariah Carey and Christina Aguilera. Although the hip-hop recordings soon became top sellers, the R&B recordings, while often admired for their artistry, did not.[10] Now the pendulum of public opinion began to swing the other way: there began to be criticisms that "all productions sounded the same" and that there was nothing that distinguished these recordings as "Albanian."

The solution was to create a style of music with a Western basis, often deliberately emulating US compositional procedures, that still alluded to something "local": what arranger Florent Boshnjaku referred to me as *diçka e jona*: "something of ours." That "something" did not have to come from Albanian folklore but could be any combination of features that expressed Albanians' historic relationship to neighboring areas around the Mediterranean, while avoiding elements that were too specifically "Slavic." Through this process, folkloric sounds began to be heard as belonging to a larger, regional category of *etno*. As producer Shkumbin Kryeziu explained, listeners didn't need to hear music that was exactly like that from the United States or Great Britain because they could hear such music on MTV or in fact on many local radio and television stations. And it was important that there be songs in the Albanian language, with "good" texts.

Mostly it was young people of marriageable age who were buying cassettes and CDs in this period, so the new songs were overwhelmingly intended to be performed or aired at dance events that attracted them in large numbers. In Kosova and North Macedonia, these were held at a host of new clubs or, in the summer, at large outdoor parties. In the diaspora, they could be held at periodic "youth evenings" (*mbrëmje rinore*) or at clubs such as the one at which MC Beka deejayed (Fig. 37.2). The songs thus needed to be in meters and tempos that could be danced to: whether for club dancing (*vallëzim*), solo or couple *çoçek* dancing, or line dancing (*valle*).[11] While some songs drew rhythmic

FIG. 37.2. Poster advertising a live appearance in 2008 by Kosovar singers Edona Llalloshi and Sinan Vllasaliu at the Albanian dance club Rinora 4 in Rümlang, Switzerland.

inspiration from Western pop or Eurodance, others were based on duple-meter Turkish or Arabic rhythmic cycles, which were more suited to local types of dance.

Etnopop was not a uniquely Albanian phenomenon, however. By the late 1990s and early 2000s, arrangements sharing some of these same features were being produced in Turkey, Greece, Romania, Bulgaria, Serbia, and North Macedonia, sometimes with clearly local referents but often with similar vocabularies of "ethnic" timbres and textures. Although in Turkey arrangements frequently featured live studio musicians, those from other areas were largely computer-based. Singers elsewhere in the region drew on techniques meant to reference their national group's folklore, whether it be the slow vibrato used by Serbian *turbo-folk* singers, the focused sound of Bulgarian *chalga* singers that many of them learned at folk music school (Livni 2014:73), or specific regional ornaments. In contrast, one can hear the deliberately Western vocal style used by Albanian *etnopop* singers as a sonic signaling of the strong orientation that *Kosovarë* in particular adopted in this period toward North Atlantic political entities, and especially toward the United States.

The *etno* trend was also not merely a regional one. Initially it was inspired, at least in part, by the 1990s fashion in western European dance clubs for "ethnically" flavored tracks such as Algerian singer Cheb Khaled's "Didi" ("Take," 1992); Egyptian singer Amr Diab's "Ya nour al-ayn" ("Light of My Eyes," 1996), which had helped to popularize flamenco guitar; and Turkish singer Tarkan's "Şımarık" ("Spoiled," known in English as "Kiss Kiss," 1997). By 1999 productions in the Anglophone industry had begun to engage with various Middle Eastern sounds, including Jay-Z's "Big Pimpin'," co-produced with Timbaland, which sampled an Egyptian instrumental piece, and "Desert Rose," Sting's collaboration with Algerian singer Cheb Mami. The trend broadened in the early 2000s to include Timbaland and Missy Elliott's bhangra-infused hit "Get Ur Freak On" (2001) and Jay-Z's collaboration with bhangra performer Punjabi MC ("Beware of the Boys," 2002), as well as Scott Storch's Arab-flavored arrangements for Beyoncé ("Baby Boy," "Naughty Girl," 2003) and 50 Cent ("Candy Shop," 2005). Shakira's 2002 album *Laundry Service* introduced elements of Andean and Arab music into Anglophone pop, as well as—through video performances—her penchant for dancing Arab *raqs sharqi* during instrumental interludes. Throughout southeastern Europe, music personnel as well as audiences were well aware of these productions: they could access them through music programming on local broadcast media or transnational cable or satellite outlets. Albanian *etnopop*, which took ideas from many of them, can thus be seen as representing a claim made by singers and composer-arrangers in Albanian territories to be participating in locally inflected ways in what was emerging as a broad transnational musical trend.

THE BEGINNING OF REGIONAL INTERACTIONS

Early in the 2000s, Albanian *etnopop* musicians began to interact with productions from neighboring states, initially through the practice of "covering." By "covering" I mean the pairing of new lyrics in one's own language with the melody, and perhaps the entire arrangement, of a song originally sung in another language. Covering of this sort has a long history in southeastern Europe, documented back at least to the nineteenth century.[12] In the 1990s, performers of Albanian commercial folk music routinely covered songs from Greece and Turkey: significantly, the two countries in the region that had long had private music industries (Sugarman 2006; Sugarman 2007). By the 2000s, however, musicians throughout southeastern Europe were covering each other's productions to an unprecedented degree, in ways that sometimes traversed forbidden political boundaries. Source recordings also came from outside the region: from India as well as Egypt and Tunisia. Perhaps the prime example in the Albanian industry was an album from 2003 on which two songs covered recent Bulgarian hits while a third was a cover of an Indian film song that had also been covered in Serbia.

In a context in which virtually all arrangements were computer-generated, the practice of covering helped to detach them from their texts. This situation was reinforced by a change in the way that studio personnel prepared them. In an older form of composition, a song would begin with lyrics that were then set to a melody with accompaniment, whether by the lyricist or by a separate composer. The composer might prepare the arranged version themselves or prepare a "demo" version that was then assigned to an arranger.[13] One Kosovar *etnopop* singer who followed this format in many of her songs was Edona Llalloshi, as illustrated by her 2004 hit, "S'dua hiç" ("I Don't Wish at All"):[14]

> S'dua hiç të jemi miq
> Se nga fjalët që u thanë
> U bë gremi që po na ndanë
> S'dua hiç të jemi miq
> Më duhet dashuria
> Nuk më mjafton veç miqësia.
>
> I don't wish at all to be friends
> For because of the words that were spoken
> An abyss now separates us.
> I don't wish at all to be friends
> I must have love:
> Friendship just isn't enough.

A-V Link 2: Edona Llalloshi, "S'dua hiç" (video, 2004 ▶).

In this case, Llalloshi commissioned a song from prom- inent songwriter Ilir Berani, who composed both lyrics and music. His demo recording then went to arranger Xhevdet Gashi for the final production, which combined a Spanish-style dance rhythm with *tarabuka* embellishments and *çifteli*-like accompanying timbres.

In this period, however, many arrangers had begun to adopt a new approach to composition, pioneered by R&B and hip-hop arrangers in the United States, in which tracks originate with a rhythmic "groove." This procedure was demonstrated to me during a 2004 visit to the studio of arranger Nexhat Mujovi, known as Wirusi ("The Virus"), in Tetovo, North Macedonia (Fig. 37.3).[15] There Mujovi talked me through his creation of

FIG. 37.3. Arranger Nexhat Mujovi-"Wirusi" in his studio in Tetovo, North Macedonia, December 2004.

(Photograph by the author.)

a song called "Taxi," sung by Kosovar singer Nora Istrefi, that was about to be released for New Year's 2005. Mujovi had first prepared a *gruv* composed of a very sparse bass line and multiple percussion tracks that highlighted a repeating *tarabuka* pattern. Over this he had layered various short melodic and chordal motives, drawing on pitches of the Ottoman *makam Hicaz*, with some repeating at regular intervals and others appearing only at certain points. Among these motives were short violin interjections reminiscent of Turkish or Egyptian music that complemented the *tarabuka* pattern. Over these basic "instrumental" parts Mujovi had added a synthesized vocal melody that the singer would perform once lyrics were prepared. The completed track had then been assigned to a lyricist, in this case Aida Baraku, a rare woman in the Albanian industry. Challenged with a particularly prickly vocal line, she had created a narrative about a woman waiting in the rain for a taxi after a breakup with her partner:[16]

> A ka një taxi për autostradë
> Vetëm e femër ani çka
> A ka një taxi le t'jetë paradë
> rrugës e sonte ani çka . . .

> Is there a taxi going to the main road?
> Just a woman
> Is there a taxi? Let there be a parade
> Along the road this evening.

A-V Link 3: Nora Istrefi, "Taxi" (audio, 2004 ▶).

Mujovi played the finished recording for me, with solo and backup vocals added as well as sounds of cars passing on the road, and asked me what I thought of it. *Beyoncé shkon në Orient*, I replied ("Beyoncé goes to the Orient"). He was delighted. Istrefi had commissioned from him a dance-club song with a bit of an "Oriental" flavor and had said that she particularly liked Beyoncé and Destiny's Child. In the middle of the song he had inserted a long *tarabuka* solo so that she could perform a "belly dance" in live performances. When I returned to Prishtina and spent a few days typing up field notes at an internet café, Beyoncé's song "Naughty Girl" played regularly through the sound system, and I realized that she had already gone to the Orient: the song features several elements of Middle Eastern musical performance, including the scale of *makam Hicaz* and frequent Arab-style violin interjections. In his homage to Beyoncé, Mujovi's song had brought her sound back to a world area where *makam*-based melodies and *tarabuka* solos were right at home.

The new type of compositional procedure that Mujovi described paved the way for several new types of interaction between figures in the Albanian industry and members of other national groups. Once arrangements were self-contained computer files, they could be disseminated via hard drive or e-mail far from the arranger's studio. And since they existed separate from a text, there was no reason why the arranger had to be Albanian. As a result, beginning in 2001, several prominent pop singers in Kosova began to commission songs from non-Albanian arrangers in neighboring North Macedonia. Among the first was a song entitled "Mos ma ndal" ("Don't Stop Me"), commissioned by star singer Adelina Ismaili from arranger Marion Filipovski, known as "Maki" (Fig. 37.4). The lyrics, created by Ismaili, told the story of a young woman who became annoyed when her boyfriend went out to clubs every night and left her at home. In response, she decided to do the same:[17]

> Shoki jem dola dhe unë
> Me pi edhe me vallzu
> Ndoshta edhe unë knaqna
> Djemt e tjer duke i shiku
> S'po ma nin hiç me kon je
> Veç vazhdo me çika rri
> Por të lutem mos ma ndal
> U knaq edhe unë si ti.

> My friend, I too have gone out
> To drink and to dance,
> And perhaps I too will enjoy myself

Looking at the other young men.
It doesn't bother me where you've been
So continue to sit with the girls,
But I ask you not to stop me
From enjoying myself as you do.

A-V Link 4: Adelina Ismaili, "Mos ma ndal" (video performance for New Year's 2002 ⓘ). Received by young women as a feminist anthem, the song was rapidly propelled to megahit status. Ismaili made "belly dance" moves a highlight of her video performances, perhaps serving as an inspiration for Istrefi's subsequent appearances.

As Maki told me in a 2004 interview, he had long been drawn to synthesizer-based pop music.[18] For Ismaili's song, he utilized available timbres that evoked the sound of the *çifteli*, as well as a vocal texture in which Ismaili's melody was paired with a moving drone. This type of melody-and-drone singing is characteristic of Albanian rural singers in parts of western North Macedonia and in the 1990s had become popular among commercial folk singers in Kosova as well (see Sugarman 2007). It is also characteristic, however, of much south Slavic rural singing, including that of Macedonians

FIG. 37.4. Arranger Marion Filipovski-"Maki" in his studio in Skopje, North Macedonia, December 2004.

(Photograph by the author.)

and Bulgarians. Maki explained to me that his familiarity with this style came not from Albanian practices but from years of listening to folk music programming on Macedonian Radio-Television, as well as from recordings of the Bulgarian vocal group Trio Balkana. Albanian audiences, however, greeted the arrangement very much as their own. The result was a song that was not in a strict sense "Albanian," in that its composer-arranger was Macedonian; but it was also not Macedonian, not only because it was sung in the Albanian language but also because Maki had never prepared any such arrangement for a Macedonian singer. Soon the great majority of Kosovar pop singers were commissioning songs from Maki and other arrangers in North Macedonia, motivated in part by a relative scarcity of Albanian arrangers and in part by the sheer novelty that the Macedonian styles were injecting into the industry.

If an arrangement did not have to be created by a person of the same national background as the singer, there was no reason why only one singer should benefit from a good arrangement. Some arrangers thus began licensing their productions to singers of different national groups. The earliest notable example was initiated in 2003, when Kosovar arranger Enis Presheva, Jr., was contacted by a young Turkish speaker from North Macedonia, Hakan "Kaan" Mazhar, who was living in Turkey (Fig. 37.5). Mazhar asked Presheva to orchestrate a computer-based demo arrangement that he had prepared and to record it with studio musicians in Istanbul. Presheva's setting, which

FIG. 37.5. Arranger Enis Presheva, Jr., in his and Xhevdet Gashi's studio in Prishtina, Kosova, July 2002.

(Photograph by the author.)

featured flamenco-style guitar, prominent *tarabuka*, *arabesk*-style violin interjections, and an interlude of jazzy scat singing, can be heard as the apotheosis of the eclecticism of *etnopop*. Presheva was so pleased with it that he licensed it for Kosovar singer Leonora Jakupi and commissioned an Albanian-language text, entitled "Ti nuk ekziston" ("You Do Not Exist"), from Kosovar rapper and lyricist Memli Krasniqi:[19]

> Larg nga sytë e mi dua të jesh ti
> Se s'kupton
> Mos u bo fëmijë se koha po të shkon
> Larg nga sytë e tu do t'jem edhe unë
> Për gjithmonë
> Unë të kam tregu asgjë nuk më mungon
> Se ti për mua nuk ekziston.
>
> Far from my gaze you must remain
> Because you don't understand
> Don't be childish because your time has passed.
> Far from your gaze I will be
> Forever
> I've told you that I lack for nothing
> Because for me you do not exist.

Notably, the videospot for Jakupi's version was produced by the Macedonian firm Tomato Productions.

A-V Link 5: Leonora Jakupi, "Ti nuk ekziston" (video, 2003 ▶).

Presheva assumed that the only other version of the arrangement that would eventually be recorded would be one by Mazhar in Turkish. Unbeknown to him and Jakupi, however, Mazhar had already licensed the demo version to Serbian singer Daniel Djokić, whose song "Ne mogu od nje" ("I Can't Because of Her") debuted on Serbian radio stations just before the appearance of the Albanian-language version. It was not until 2014 that Mazhar released his own performance, entitled "Yolumu bulurum" ("I'll Find My Way"), this time with a new setting by Macedonian arranger Darko Dimitrov.

Taking Stock of *Etnopop*

By the middle of the first decade of the 2000s, North Macedonia was emerging as a major node in networks of covering, arranging, and licensing. There are several reasons for this. First is the complicated makeup of the country's population, which consists of Macedonians, who speak a Slavic language; Albanians; Turks, who frequently know themselves to be of Albanian descent (Ellis 2003); Roma; and other smaller groups. North Macedonia is thus the preeminent site in the region where Slavic, Albanian, Turkish, and Romani speakers come into extended contact. Second, in the 1950s, through an agreement between Yugoslavia and Turkey, large numbers of Muslims in North Macedonia and Kosova emigrated to Turkey, initiating what has been a steady flow back and forth of family members as well as cultural products. The Albanian cultural sphere thus extends considerably eastward to include individuals living in Turkey such as Mazhar. Third, Macedonians listen avidly to a broad spectrum of Slavic-language pop music. In the period of socialist Yugoslavia, many developed a taste for Yugoslav rock as well as newly composed folk music (*novokomponovana narodna muzika*), and that has continued to the present. Beginning in 2003, however, Bulgarian producers began to enter the Slavophone music market aggressively when they inaugurated FEN TV, a music video channel screening Bulgarian *chalga* productions virtually around the clock. FEN was immediately licensed to cable operators in North Macedonia as well as Albania, although not in Kosova.[20] With such a rich menu of Slavophone genres available through the local media, Macedonians developed only a very small popular music industry of their own: one major reason that arrangers there were seeking out Albanian clients. Those same media made Serbian and Bulgarian, as well as Macedonian, productions accessible to Albanian arrangers in North Macedonia to emulate or directly copy.

Initially, all of the phenomena that I have noted—covers, multiple licensing, and use of non-Albanian arrangers—operated in a context where Albanian industry personnel assumed that their audiences were not aware of the music produced in neighboring countries. Fairly quickly, however, listeners brought each of these strategies to public attention: through internet discussion forums, newspaper and magazine articles, and even exposés on Kosovar state television. Covers, identified as "borrowed songs" (*këngë të huazuara*) or "stolen songs" (*këngë të vjedhura*), met with the most extensive and negative reaction. On the one hand, they were seen as a dishonest practice that betrayed, as one journalist wrote, "a fatal lack of creative imagination" on the part of industry personnel.[21] On the other, they were seen as threatening the purity of Albanian culture and hence national identity itself: as one particularly fraught online posting put it in 2005, "As if you were to put poison in your own blood."[22] Before multiple licensing was understood, Albanian songs that resulted from that process were also taken to be covers and met with the same disapproval. Fearing a similar reaction to the use of non-Albanian arrangers, production houses initially camouflaged their names on album cover art, using Filipovski's nickname "Maki," rendering Darko Dimitrov as "D. D.," and Albanianizing Robert Bilbilov's name as "Robert Bilbili." This subterfuge was quickly dropped, however, once it became common knowledge that arrangements were being prepared by non-Albanians. By the middle of the first decade of the 2000s, it was clear that, despite criticism of all these practices, industry personnel continued to engage in them, and audiences continued to consume the productions in large quantities.

A second set of issues, for both producers and audiences, was how to characterize the new genre. In 2004, Baki Jashari, who was then head of programming at Radio Kosova, described to me a recording that began with solo *çifteli*, suggesting a rural "folk" song (*këngë popullore*), then incorporated elements of an urban song (*këngë qytetare*), and then turned into a "popular" song (*këngë argëtuese*). Should such recordings be programmed as folk or as popular music?[23] Arranger Xhevdet Gashi similarly remarked to me that many productions fell somewhere between folk and pop, although he added that he would classify them all as popular music. But he struggled with labels. When was a song *etnopop*? When should it be called *pop-folk* or *folk-pop*?[24] Some more elite urbanites chose to refer to the genre as *turbofolk*—in this case, a derogatory term that aligned it both with Serbian production and with the superficiality and commercialism that were often associated with it.[25] Gashi was one of several industry personnel who pointed out to me the growing similarity among regional styles of music, asserting that "songs no longer have a national identity but rather a Balkan identity." His studio partner, arranger Enis Presheva, Jr., told me of playing for Gashi an arrangement that he had recorded in Turkey with Turkish studio musicians. Did it sound Albanian enough? Would audiences think it sounded too Turkish? "It doesn't sound like it is from anywhere," was Gashi's response.[26]

A Regional Sphere Coalesces

One of the reasons that arrangers became involved in multiple music industries was economy of scale: working in relatively small industries that offered only limited possibilities for CD sales, arrangers actively sought out opportunities to bring in extra income by traversing ethnonational and state borders. A second motivation was the possibility of greater professional recognition and of collaborating with a greater range of regional artists. In the early 2010s, a young arranger in Albania named Flori Mumajesi achieved such recognition when he introduced a new type of *etnopop* arrangement into the Albanian industry. In the 2011 televised music competition *Top Fest*, he performed his song "Tallava," named for a vocal genre often performed by individuals identifying as Romani or Egyptian (*egjiptian*). Verses of the song were sung by Mumajesi himself, over an arrangement filled with bubbly synthesized sounds. The "hook" and interlude for the arrangement, however, were provided by an uncredited Albanian Romani vocalist, singing an ornamented melody in a recognizably Romani style and backed by additional Romani voices. In the chorus, Mumajesi's voice and those of the Romani singers intertwined.[27] Such a combination would not have been imaginable in an arrangement from Kosova at that time, where references to Romani music would have aligned the production in people's minds with commercial folk music. In the years to follow, however, multiple arrangers produced similar songs with "hooks" sung by Romani vocalists.

A-V Link 6: Flori Mumajesi, "Tallava" (audio, 2011 ▶).

Mumajesi was one of a number of younger arrangers who benefited from a new media outlet called "Balkanika Music Television," which was introduced in 2005 by the same Bulgarian company that produces FEN TV. Balkanika rotated blocks of music videos from southeast European countries under the rubric "One television—One world—The musical world of the Balkans."[28] For the countries that participated in its programming, Balkanika TV dramatically changed the perceived audience for music productions:

rather than aiming them at members of a single national group, singers and arrangers could now aim at a broader, "Balkan" audience. Kosova was initially conspicuously absent from Balkanika TV: not only because the station was not available there but also because Kosova was not recognized by the channel as a country. In neighboring Albania, however, where both FEN TV and Balkanika were available since their inception, singers and arrangers were gradually able to develop a regional profile.

Having had a major success on Balkanika TV with another song featuring a Romani soloist, Mumajesi began to license some of his Albanian-language songs to Bulgarian *chalga* singers. Soon after "Tallava" debuted on Albanian television, he not only licensed the song's arrangement to Bulgarian singer Stefani for a song titled "Ne se pravi" ("Do Not Pretend") but also sang (in Bulgarian) on the recording and appeared in the song's video.[29] This strategy was an extension of the multiple licensing of the early 2000s. Rather than doing it surreptitiously, however, Mumajesi carried out the practice overtly, even posting press releases to Albanian newspapers and websites announcing his collaborations. Thereafter credits for musical productions frequently named the composer of the licensed arrangement.

A-V Link 7: Stefani and Flori, "Ne se pravi" (video, 2011 ▶).

"E di": The Regional Wanderings of an *Etnopop* Song

In recent years, the practices described here have become less common as musicians in each national industry have pursued distinctive artistic directions in their productions. Nevertheless, two clusters of releases illustrate both the extent to which these practices continue and recent attitudinal shifts toward them. In October 2016, a video of Serbian *turbo-folk* singer Viki Miljković's song "Rođendan" ("Birthday") was posted on YouTube, which has become perhaps the most widely accessed outlet distributing southeast European commercial musics.[30] Visually the video, shot in Greece, very much fit what I have come to think of, from Albanian productions, as a "summer hit" trope: a singer in flowing summer clothing vacationing at a seaside resort, with some combination of clear Mediterranean waters, boats, balconies, pastel houses with blue trim, and bougainvillea figuring prominently (Fig. 37.6).[31] To an upbeat melody, accompanied by clarinet and violin riffs, Miljković sang of making the best of a bad relationship:

> I live my life as if
> Every day is my birthday
> And so I celebrate!
> I live my life, but I'm running out of time
> Now every night
> Is as if it is my last.

FIG. 37.6. Screenshot of Viki Miljković, "Rođendan." (https://www.youtube.com/watch?v=NIGyRttyU6o).

(Serbia, 2017.)

A-V Link 8: Viki Miljković, "Rođendan" (video, 2017 ▶).

Under the video, listeners from the Bosnian–Croatian–Serbian-speaking realm posted praises of the production. Further down, however, more far-flung listeners registered some skepticism. Bulgarians pointed out *chalga* singer Galena's hit "Pak li" ("What, Again?") from 2012, while Macedonians referred to Suzana Gavazova's song "Opasen" ("Dangerous"), which was released shortly after Galena's. Another poster identified Romanian singer Mădălina's "Nici tu nici eu" ("Neither You nor I"), first posted on YouTube in 2015. Then there were the Albanian listeners, insisting—often in vain—that the "original" was Kosovar singer Nora Istrefi's song "E di" ("I Know"), released in 2006.

Istrefi's version was indeed the first. Consistent with her vocal style, the video of her song situated her in a particularly "Western" milieu, showing her walking through a luxury hotel in a series of designer outfits, and singing—as did Miljković—about a no-good guy (Fig. 37.7):[32]

> E di, e di
> Njoh mashkuj si ti
> E ti loqk s'je si ta
> Je veç më i zi.
>
> I know, I know
> I know men like you
> And you, sweetheart, are not like the others:
> You are even worse!

FIG. 37.7. Screenshot of Nora Istrefi, "E di." (https://www.youtube.com/watch?v=ZAumSOqTdes).
(Kosova, 2006.)

The song's novel arrangement, by Artan Kastrati, juxtaposed Istrefi's R&B-inflected vocals with sampled *surle* (loud double-reed pipes) and a dense mix of rhythmic lines evocative of frame and goblet drums.

A-V Link 9: Nora Istrefi, "E di" (video, 2006 ▶).

Several years after the Albanian-language release, it would appear that Kastrati licensed the melodic content of the song to a Bulgarian team that transposed Galena's version, and its accompanying video, considerably eastward. Filmed in a cistern beneath Istanbul, the video played up the "Oriental" flavor characteristic of many *chalga* performances by combining Galena's undulating movements, and those of a sea of female dancers, with whirling Mevlevi dervishes and images of poisonous snakes and insects (Fig. 37.8). While the basic melody and harmonic setting of the song remained the same, the decorative features of the new arrangement exchanged one set of *etno* elements for another. The brash *surle* riffs of Istrefi's version were exchanged for clarinet and violin motifs with a pronounced Romani flavor, and the syncopated bass line was transformed into a Turkish *düyek* rhythmic cycle. The theme of male duplicitousness remained:

> Again, again?
> You need me for an hour?
> Only when you're alone do you feel as if I exist.
> Again, again?
> Did I go crazy over you?
> As always I couldn't tell you no.

This new arrangement then became the basis for all subsequent versions: those by Gavazova, Mădălina, Miljković, as well as a few other Serbian, Romanian, and Romani singers. It is unclear from YouTube postings whether anyone besides Galena's team contacted Kastrati regarding the song, or Galena's arranger Kalin Dimitrov, or whether the remaining versions are uncredited (and uncompensated) covers.[33]

FIG. 37.8. Screenshot of Galena, "Pak li." (https://www.youtube.com/watch?v=Ez_OBbMWE6w). (Bulgaria, 2012.)

A-V Link 10: Galena, "Pak li" (video, 2012 ▶).

At the time that Miljković's version was released, the complicated travels of Istrefi's song throughout the region confirmed that both covering and licensing continued to be ways that musical materials circulated within and among Balkan states. Judging from YouTube comments below the accompanying videos, some listeners appeared to be loyal overwhelmingly to their particular national industry and seemed taken aback when confronted with information that a song was a cover. Others were clearly consuming productions from throughout the region—whether on YouTube; on Balkanika Music Television, its website, or its YouTube channel; or through other avenues—and readily pointed out the multiple versions. Despite this awareness, there was a competitiveness among the postings as to which version was the original or the best, as well as a general disparagement of the ubiquity of covering (often referred to as "stealing") within the various music industries.

A-V Link 11: Tea Tairović, "Hajde" (video, 2021 ▶).

A more recent instance of pan-Balkan covering has unfolded quite differently. In 2021, Serbian singer Tea Tairović released a music video of a song entitled "Hajde" ("C'mon"), whose first line, "Nek noćas gori Balkan" or "May the Balkans be lit tonight," alluded to its regional resonances (Fig. 37.9).[34] The song first appeared in 2004 as the Albanian-language song "Qyqeku," created and recorded by Kosovar singers Kastriot Grajqevci and Gazmend Rexhepi of the rock band Kozanostra and seemingly inspired by the many songs for the dance çoçek that were released by the Albanian industry in the 1990s (*qyqek* is a Kosova spelling of *çoçek*; see Sugarman 2007). Gradually, the song became a staple of Kosovar wedding bands and New Year's television programming and, as "Hajde

FIG. 37.9. Screenshot of Tea Tairović, "Hajde." (https://www.youtube.com/watch?v=boroNuv9oGY). (Serbia, 2021.)

luj qyqek" ("C'mon, Dance Çoçek"), was rerecorded by a series of performers, mostly of commercial folk music rather than *etnopop*, including the Pro Band (2012), Remzie Osmani (ca. 2014), and Yllka Kuqi and Ylli Demaj (2017) (Fig. 37.10). In 2018, it traveled both to Bulgaria, recorded by *chalga* singers Desi Slava and Fiki as "Da vdignem mnogo shum" ("Let's Make a Lot of Noise"), and to Romania, recorded by *manele* singers Vali Vijelie and Liviu Puștiu as "E mare petrecere" ("It's a Big Party"). All the versions paid tribute to the continuing popularity of *çoçek* dancing throughout the region. Tairović's 2021 recording in fact appealed to multiple audiences by including shout-outs in the Romanian language between verses.

A-V Link 12: Kozanostra, "Qyqeku" (video, 2004 ▶)

Within days of its posting, Albanian websites had identified the original of Tairović's song and were reporting that Grajqevci was preparing to file suit for violation of copyright against the various singers who had recorded covers (see, e.g., Syri.net 2021). Soon after, Tairović broke with years of industry practice by openly identifying the original song's Albanian title in a posting on YouTube:

> Thanks to those who love my song "Hajde," my heart is full! Much respect to the original version "Hajde luj qyqek" and to the author who gave me the exclusive rights to record my version of the song in Serbian and Romanian language! May a united Balkans burn most brightly!

A-V Link 13: Yllka Kuqi and Ylli Demaj, "Potpuri 2018" (video performance, 2018); "Hajde luj qyqek" begins at 1:48 ▶.

FIG. 37.10. Screenshot of Yllka Kuqi and Ylli Demaj performing "Hajde luj qyqek" for New Year's 2018 programming on the YouTube channel *n'Kosovë*. (https://www.youtube.com/watch?v=uhnA8Z5ohaI).

Authorship credits on the original posting were not, however, altered, nor was the song identified as being from Kosova. With her posting Tairović brought the issue of region-wide covering, and thus of commonalities in musical taste that "unite the Balkans," to broad public attention. Since its appearance, YouTube comments beneath various versions of the song have begun to strike a less contestatory tone, with listeners from throughout the region complimenting the various artists on their renditions.[35]

It can be helpful to think of such patterns of circulation as another "afterlife" of folklore. Beginning in the 1990s, with the fall of socialism and the founding of private music industries throughout the Balkan region, a period of uncertainty ensued in some states because new intellectual property laws had not yet been codified to replace whatever existed in the socialist period. Within the transnational Albanian industry, and particularly in the case of commercial folk music, newly created songs like "Hajde luj qyqek" circulated much like older folk songs. Singers learned them from a recording, performed them at weddings and other occasions, and rerecorded them—all without attention to copyright claims. In the broader region, songs in one language were covered and circulated among other linguistic groups in a similar "folkloric" spirit. There are now new laws throughout the region; but they are honored only to varying degrees, and it has been hard to curb entrenched practices. At least in the Albanian industry, many artists have not registered their work and thus stand no chance of profiting as their songs are rerecorded. "Hajde luj qyqek" seems to have been caught in this set of circumstances. Created in the early 2000s, it circulated for years among Kosovar singers without notice. But when the composer became aware of Tairović's Serbian-language version, and the profits that were accruing to it, he approached her team. According to one person in the music industry with whom I consulted, singers now often credit a song's origins openly, as Tairović did, and thus admit that the song is a cover, without necessarily compensating the composer monetarily. That may well be the case in this instance.

One Planet under a Groove

In 1996, a team of media specialists in Australia proposed that the development of new cable and satellite television technologies together with neoliberal economic transformations that included media privatization in many world regions were contributing to the rise of several prominent regional media spheres that challenged the primacy of productions from the United States and western Europe (Sinclair et al. 1996). These spheres were usually an outgrowth of what the authors termed "geolinguistic regions": world areas in which countries were united by language and by a legacy of shared social practices. Similarly, US media specialist Michael Curtain (2003) drew attention to the importance of "media capitals": cities that, rather like Sassen's "global cities," had become regional centers of media production in which infrastructure and personnel were heavily concentrated. In musical terms, such regions began to consolidate in the early twentieth century, through both radio transmissions and the development of recording and film industries. Today prominent musical "geolinguistic regions" include Spanish-speaking Latin America, with Miami as one prominent "media capital"; Chinese-speaking East Asia, in which Hong Kong has dominated; and the Arab-speaking Middle East, in which Beirut and then Dubai has assumed the position once occupied by Cairo. In contrast, the countries of southeastern Europe, while united by the shared legacies of the Austro-Hungarian and Ottoman Empires and, for many, of socialist cultural policies, have been slow to develop a regional media-sphere in any explicit form. This is true not only because of the multiplicity of languages spoken within the region but also because of political antagonisms that are often of long standing and that in many cases are still festering. Similarly, while music production within each state is often concentrated in a single city, none has emerged as a regional center of production in which music personnel from multiple states are concentrated.

Addressing the ethnic conflict that characterized southeastern Europe in the 1990s, Rogers Brubaker (2002) promoted the notion of relative "groupness": the idea that populations go through periods of placing greater or lesser emphasis on a particular group identity. Seen in this light, the 1990s marked a period of intense "groupness" in the region. Citizens of formerly socialist states were restructuring their societies to be free-market democracies. In addition, those living in the Yugoslav successor states were engaged in intensive nation-building efforts that often involved the promotion of highly nationalistic ideologies. More so than other national groups, Albanians found themselves reconstituting their identity on a transnational basis: both because they live in large numbers in several different homeland states and because massive emigration from all areas has produced an extensive Albanian diaspora.

The music industries that developed throughout the region during this period played a considerable role in this nation-building process, promoting images of discrete national cultures, however similar those cultures might be. This was particularly the case in the former Yugoslavia, where highly nationalist productions fueled the wars of the 1990s. By the early 2000s, however, national industries began to serve simultaneously as sites of diligent boundary maintenance and of the tentative exploration of regional affinities: hence, on the one hand, the policing among Albanians of practices such as "covering" and use of "foreign" arrangers and, on the other, a reaching-out to neighboring groups through various types of collaboration. Practices such as covering, multiple licensing, and use of foreign arrangers thrived precisely because of the lack of a single regional media-sphere: they were ways for musicians to benefit from stylistic and technical innovations originating among neighboring groups, and to increase their audience, without having to challenge their state's or nation's image of national unity. By cobbling together a transnational industry, Albanian musicians and producers were able to offer their consumers songs with meaningful lyrics crafted in their own language, as well as to draw in profits offered to them by their large diaspora.

By the middle of the first decade of the 2000s, within the context of a more stable political landscape, outlets such as Balkanika Music Television and YouTube precipitated more overt cross-border collaboration as well as musical consumption. What emerged was a different kind of regional sphere, one in which no single language or language family was hegemonic. Rather than production being concentrated in a single "media capital," the southeast European music sphere developed as a relatively egalitarian marketplace in which each national industry offered its wares for regional consumption.

This emergent regional sphere was in turn embedded in larger circuits of production and circulation. In 2006 I purchased a pirate CD in Albania entitled *Balkan Hits 2005*. The title referred not to a specifically "Balkan" playlist but to the range of musics that were being listened and danced to in the region at that time. In addition to expected songs from the "greater Balkans"—Italy, Slovenia, Romania, Bulgaria, Greece, Turkey, and Algeria—the CD included tracks from Sweden, Puerto Rico, Jamaica, and Colombia. Among them were a Greek cover of a Turkish song and a Romanian cover of an Arab song. Two of the artists were themselves "diasporic": Arash, an Iranian singer living in Sweden who has actually arranged songs for Albanian performers, and Lola Ponces, an Argentine singer living in Italy, whose English-language song quoted Cheb Khaled's "Didi." The range of musical styles represented, and particularly the inclusion of various Latin and Caribbean artists, signaled future directions for Albanian musicians who, in the 2010s, began to produce tracks heavily inflected with elements of reggaeton, dancehall, and Latin trap in addition to regional *etno* features.

Today, singers and arrangers in southeastern Europe, with radio and television transmissions as well as YouTube, social media, and various streaming services at their disposal, follow intensively innovations and trends emerging on a global scale. In particular, the "groove"- and "loop"-based compositional procedure that arrangers adopted in the early 2000s, together with a common corpus of "ethnic" samples and globally circulating rhythmic patterns available via computer, today link a range of dance-based musical styles spread geographically from South Asia through the Middle East and Europe to Afro-diasporic genres in North America and the Caribbean. On radio and television programs, on streaming sites, and in dance clubs across southeastern Europe and its diaspora, young people consume hit recordings spanning that entire sphere and hear their own industry's productions fitting seamlessly into the flow of styles: "one planet under a groove," as it were.

In such a context, what does it mean to speak today of "Albanian music"? Within the complex, multiethnic, and trans-state environment that is the Albanian music industry, it is at times only the language, the persona of the singer, or perhaps the addition of a sampled folk instrument that marks a pop production as "Albanian." Contemporary Albanian music is not so much a range of historically informed genres as it is a label and a marketing category: its Albanian-ness resides in the community it gathers around itself, regardless of its sound, and even the nationality of its producers and audience. On the one hand, it may speak less and less to listeners who seek in it a confirmation of the distinctiveness of their national culture through the foregrounding of folkloric elements. But, on the other, it is helping to define "Albanian-ness" in new, fresh, and unexpected ways.

Acknowledgments

This chapter includes some substantially revised, expanded, and updated parts of an earlier article by the author (Sugarman 2006). Field research for this study was conducted in Kosova and North Macedonia between 2002 and 2011, supported by faculty research grants from Stony Brook University and the Graduate Center of the City University of New York. My deepest thanks to the many individuals who set aside time to speak with me on this topic. Many thanks also to Alma Bejtullahu for introductions to some music personnel in Prishtina in 2002 and to the Bejtullahu family for use of their apartment in my first visits.

Notes

1. Throughout this chapter I use the shorthand designation "arranger" (Alb. *aranzher*) to indicate individuals who also compose original songs. I was told this anecdote by Boshnjaku in an interview in Prishtina on July 6, 2006.
2. Contributions to Buchanan (2007a) offer overviews of several of these genres. In addition, see, for Serbian *turbo-folk* (also referred to as *neofolk*), Gordy (1999), Kronja (2004), Baker (2008), Grujić (2009), Cvoro (2014), and Simić (2019); for *chalga* (also known as *etnopop* or *popfolk*), Kurkela (1993), Dimov (2001), Rice (2002), Statelova (2005), Apostolov (2008), Silverman (2012:177–197), and Livni (2014); for *manele* (also known as *muzică orientală*), Beissinger et al. (2016); for *türk pop*, Karahasanoğlu and Skoog (2009); and for *laïkó*, Dawe (2003). Kurkela (1997) and Archer (2012) consider subsets of these genres in a broader regional context.

3. At the time, the province was known in Serbian as "Kosovo" and since 1990 by the older designation of "Kosovo i Metohija." I use the form "Kosova" here since that is the name used by the Albanian majority; for the same reason, I use the form "Prishtina" for the capital city. For information on Kosova in the late 1980s and 1990s, see Reineck (2000), Maliqi (1998), Clark (2000), Pula (2004), and Judah (2008:64–74).
4. For accounts of Albania during this period, see Biberaj (1998), Vickers and Pettifer (2000), and Abrahams (2015).
5. This broadcast was financed by the Kosova Albanian government-in-exile, headquartered in Germany (Pula 2004:825).
6. Vullnet (Sefaja) Marigona, "Ah sa keq." Text Beka, music Florent Boshnjaku, *fyell*, Shaqir Hoti. Selection #1 on the album *Boll mo*. Vizioni-Libonia, 2006.
7. Interview with Shkumbin Kryeziu, November 16, 2004.
8. *Raqs sharqi* is a type of Arab solo dance most often called "belly dancing" in English.
9. Interview with Fatos Kadiu, October 18, 2004.
10. Among the singers who recorded in an R&B style in this period were Arta Bajrami, Eliza Hoxha, and Alma Bektashi.
11. Çoçek (Alb. *çoçek* or *çyçek*; Serb. and Mac. *čoček*; Bulg., *kyuchek*; cf. Turk. *çiftetelli*; Gk. *tsifteteli*) is a style of solo dance, descended from Ottoman forms, in which the dancer emphasizes movements of the head, arms and hands, and torso. Among Albanians, it is often danced by couples facing each other. The name derives from the Ottoman word *köçek*, which referred to a type of professional dancer, usually a young male. For Albanian *çoçek* dancing, see Sugarman (2003, 2007).
12. For early instances of covering, see Katsarova (1973), Peeva (2003), Koço (2004:187), Sugarman (2006), and Buchanan (2007b).
13. Gender is important here: the great majority of Albanian music industry personnel have been male.
14. Edona Llalloshi, "S'dua hiç." Text and music Ilir Berani, arranged by Xhevdet Gashi. Selection #1 on the album *S'dua hiç*. Vizioni-Libonia, 2004. I interviewed Llalloshi on November 4, 2004.
15. Interview with Nexhat Mujovi in Tetovo, December 23, 2004.
16. Nora Istrefi, "Taxi." Text Aida Baraku, music Nexhat Mujovi-Wirusi. Selection #5 on the album *Ëngjëll*. Arboni, 2005. On the same album, the song "Negativ," arranged by Florent Boshnjaku, was created through a similar commission.
17. Adelina Ismaili, "Mos ma ndal." Text Adelina Ismaili, music Marion Filipovski-Maki. Selection #1 on the CD compilation *16 mega hite—Vetëm për shpirtin tuaj*. Labia, 2002.
18. Interview with Marion Filipovski in Skopje, North Macedonia, December 22, 2004. See Bicevski (1986) and Kaufman (1968) for melody-and-drone singing in North Macedonia and Bulgaria, respectively.
19. Leonora Jakupi, "Ti nuk ekziston." Text Memli Krasniqi, music Kaan, arranged by Enis Presheva, Jr. Selection #1 on the album *Krejt ndryshe*. Zëri i Drenicës, 2003. I discussed the song's production in 2004 with Krasniqi on September 19, producer Agim Rama on October 21, and Presheva on December 18.
20. See FEN's website: http://www.fentv.bg. As of 2023, the station categorizes the music it plays as "popfolk" (*chalga*), "pop," "folklore," and "Balkan" (including Serbian *turbo-folk*, Romanian *manele*, and Greek *laïkó*).
21. See Uka (2003). Her criticism extended beyond the music: "Our singers steal not only foreign songs and music but they also steal the style of foreign singers, their manner

of dancing, their dramatic movements, their dress . . . in a word, even their image!" Although her article singled out covers of Serbian songs, those were a rarity.

22. Anonymous posting on the website of Kosovar television station TV21 on April 20, 2005.
23. Interview with Baki Jashari and Selvete Krasniqi-Ismaili at Radio Kosova, November 11, 2004.
24. Interview with Xhevdet Gashi, December 7, 2004.
25. In his 2012 article on what he refers to as "Balkan pop-folk styles," Archer discusses the Albanian commercial folk music of the 1990s (see Sugarman 2007) together with Serbian *turbo-folk* and Bulgarian *chalga*. But Albanian *etnopop* is a much closer parallel to those genres, hence its being dismissed by more elite Albanians as *turbofolk*. They dismiss the commercial folk music also but refer to it as *tallava*, alluding to a Romani vocal genre that many commercial folk singers perform.
26. Interview with Enis Presheva, Jr., on December 18, 2004.
27. See "Flori Mumajesi—Tallava," posted on YouTube April 15, 2011, https://www.youtube.com/watch?v=5-WS0FMZ5zI. I believe that these artists identify as "Roma." However, in Albanian-populated regions there are also individuals often identified by scholars as Roma who speak Albanian as their first language. In North Macedonia and western Kosova, and increasingly in Albania, a number now identify as "Egyptians" *(egjiptianë)*, and trace their origins to that country, since many of the words used to identify them in local languages derive from that word (as does the English "Gypsy"). For Albania, see particularly Ohueri (2016).
28. This was the channel's initial slogan when I first saw it in 2006; by the 2010s it had become "Bridge of the Balkans!" (http://www.balkanika.tv/en/about-us.html; accessed October 12, 2016). Ana Hofman (2014:54–55) notes that, at least in its early years, the station favored productions in a "global pop style" and marginalized genres such as *turbo-folk*, *chalga*, and *manele*. This in fact gave an edge to Albanian productions, in which folkloric elements were subordinated to more Western features.
29. Stefani and Flori, "Ne se pravi," with lyrics by Yordan Botev, was released by Ara Music in late 2011. Mumajesi's earlier hit, "Origijinale," sung by Aurela Gaçe ft. Dr. Flori and Marsel (Selita), was released in Albania in 2010 and won Balkanika's "Balkan Music Awards" in 2011.
30. Viki Miljković, "Rođendan," released on YouTube on October 28, 2016, by Wave Music.
31. A prime Albanian example of this trope is the video for the song "Vespa," sung by Xhensila (Myrtezaj) ft. Endri Prifti, released in 2014; see also Greek singer Malu's video for the song "Tous eipes pos," released in 2015.
32. Nora Istrefi, "E di." Selection #6 on the album *Opium*. Text by Beka, music by Artan Kastrati. Arboni, 2006.
33. Galena, "Pak li." Text Marieta Angelova, music Artan Krasniqi, arranged by Kalin Dimitrov. Payner, 2012. First posted on YouTube on April 22, 2013. Other versions posted on YouTube include Sekil, "Loli sharpa," and Džefrina and Južni Ritam Show, "Shala nane avri taro udar" (all Romani musicians from North Macedonia, 2013); Suzana Gavazova, "Opasen" (North Macedonia, 2013; music video posted 2014); Mădălina, "Nici tu nici eu" (Romania, 2015); Sandra Repac, "Šaj laj" (Serbian-language version of Gavazova's "Opasen," 2016); and Elis Armeanca, "La maxim vreau să-mi trăiesc viața" (Romania, 2017).

34. Tea Tairović, "Hajde." Text Sanja Vučić and Tea Tairović, arranged by Vojan Bašić. Video by xVisual. T Music, 2021. First posted on YouTube on May 21, 2021.
35. I am indebted to blogger Emily Gray (2022) for drawing my attention to "Hajde"; her article provides a perceptive analysis of cross-border covering. See also the video posted by "Balkan Mashup" at https://www.youtube.com/watch?v=7aLZ5aqaBF8, which juxtaposes the Serbian-, Bulgarian-, and Albanian-language recordings (although it implies that the song is from Albania). Kosovarë who might have taken Tairović's gesture as a welcome one, in an era when political tensions between Serbia and Kosova have often been intense, were disappointed when a more recent video production, for the song "Balkanija," featured the flags of all the states of the region with the pointed exception of Kosova (https://www.youtube.com/watch?v=fHyTXVUa5ok). The success of "Hajde" recalls an earlier instance of covering, when Kosovar singer Vera Oruçaj's çoçek song "Lujmi" (1994) was covered by Serbian singer Jovana Tipsin as "Ruža puna trnja" (1997).

Works Cited

Abrahams, Fred C. 2015. *Modern Albania: From Dictatorship to Democracy in Europe*. New York: New York University Press.

Apostolov, Apostol. 2008. "The Highs and Lows of Ethno-Cultural Diversity: Young People's Experiences of *Chalga* Culture in Bulgaria." *Anthropology of East Europe Review*, 26/1:85–97.

Archer, Rory. 2012. "Assessing Turbofolk Controversies: Popular Music between the Nation and the Balkans." *Southeastern Europe*, 36:178–207.

Baker, Catherine. 2008. "When Save Met Bregović: Folklore, Turbofolk and the Boundaries of Croatian National Identity." *Nationalities Papers*, 36/4:741–764.

Beissinger, Margaret, Speranța Rădulescu, and Anca Giurchescu, eds. 2016. *Manele in Romania: Cultural Expression and Social Meaning in Balkan Popular Music*. Lanham, MD: Rowman and Littlefield.

Biberaj, Elez. 1998. *Albania in Transition: The Rocky Road to Democracy*. Boulder, CO: Westview Press.

Bicevski, Trpko. 1986. *Dvoglasjeto vo SR Makedonija*. Skopje: Institut za Folklor "Marko Cepenkov."

Brubaker, Rogers. 2002. "Ethnicity without Groups." *European Journal of Sociology*, 43/2:163–189.

Brunner, Roland. 2002. "Experience and Lessons Learned? Case Studies. d) Kosovo." Part 3 of the report, *How to Build Public Broadcast in Post-Socialist Countries*. Zürich, Switzerland: Medienhilfe. http://archiv2.medienhilfe.ch/topics/PBS/bs-kos.pdf. Accessed October 28, 2002 (no longer active).

Buchanan, Donna A. 2007a. *Balkan Popular Culture and the Ottoman Ecumene: Music, Image, and Regional Political Discourse*. Lanham, MD: Scarecrow Press.

Buchanan, Donna A. 2007b. "'Oh, Those Turks! Music, Politics, and Interculturality in the Balkans and Beyond." In *Balkan Popular Culture and the Ottoman Ecumene: Music, Image, and Regional Political Discourse*, ed. Donna A. Buchanan, 3–54. Lanham, MD: Scarecrow Press.

Clark, Howard. 2000. *Civil Resistance in Kosovo*. London: Pluto Press.
Curtain, Michael. 2003. "Media Capital: Towards the Study of Spatial Flows." *International Journal of Cultural Studies*, 6/2:202–228.
Cvoro, Uroš. 2014. *Turbo-Folk Music and Cultural Representations of National Identity in Former Yugoslavia*. Abingdon–New York: Ashgate.
Dawe, Kevin. 2003. "Between East and West: Contemporary Grooves in Greek Popular Music (c. 1990–2000)." In *Mediterranean Mosaic: Popular Music and Global Sounds*, ed. Goffredo Plastino, 221–240. New York: Routledge.
Dimov, Ventsislav. 2001. *Etnopopbumât*. Sofia: Bâlgarsko Muzikoznanie.
Ellis, Burcu Akan. 2003. *Shadow Genealogies: Memory and Identity among Urban Muslims in Macedonia*. New York: Columbia University Press.
Gordy, Eric D. 1999. "The Destruction of Musical Alternatives." In *The Culture of Power in Serbia: Nationalism and the Destruction of Alternatives*, 103–164. University Park: Pennsylvania State University Press.
Gray, Emily. 2022. "'Let's Light up the Balkans': How an Albanian Wedding Tune Became the Serbian Song of the Summer." *Kosovo 2.0*. https://kosovotwopointzero.com/en/lets-light-up-the-balkans/. Accessed September 13, 2022.
Grujić, Marija. 2009. "Community and the Popular: Women, Nation and Turbo-Folk in Post-Yugoslav Serbia." PhD dissertation, Central European University, Budapest.
Hofman, Ana. 2014. "Balkan Music Awards: Popular Music Industries in the Balkans between Already-Europe and Europe-to-Be." In *Mirroring Europe: Ideas of Europe and Europeanization in Balkan Societies*, ed. Tanya Petrović, 41–63. Leiden, the Netherlands: Brill.
Judah, Tim. 2008. *Kosovo: What Everyone Needs to Know*. Oxford–New York: Oxford University Press.
Karahasanoğlu, Songül, and Gabriel Skoog. 2009. "Synthesizing Identity: Gestures of Filiation and Affiliation in Turkish Popular Music." *Asian Music*, 40/2:52–71.
Katsarova, Raina. 1973. "Balkanski varianti na dve turski pesni." *Izvestiya na Instituta za Muzikoznanie*, 16:115–133.
Kaufman, Nikolay. 1968. *Bâlgarskata mnogoglasna narodna pesen*. Sofia: Nauka i Izkustvo.
Koço, Eno. 2004. *Albanian Urban Lyric Song in the 1930s*. Lanham, MD: Scarecrow Press.
Kronja, Ivana. 2004. "Turbo Folk Music and Dance Music in 1990s Serbia: Media, Ideology and the Production of Spectacle." *Anthropology of East Europe Review*, 22/1:103–114.
Kurkela, Vesa. 1993. "Deregulation of Popular Music in the European Post-Communist Countries: Business, Identity and Cultural Collage." *World of Music*, 35/3:80–106.
Kurkela, Vesa. 1997. "Music Media in the Eastern Balkans: Privatised, Deregulated, and Neo-traditional." *International Journal of Cultural Policy*, 3/2:177–205.
Livni, Eran. 2014. "*Chalga* to the Max! Musical Speech and Speech about Music on the Road between Bulgaria and Modern Europe." PhD dissertation, Indiana University, Bloomington.
Maliqi, Shkëlzen. 1998. *Kosova: Separate Worlds—Reflections and Analyses 1989-1998*. Prishtina–Peja: MM Society and Dukagjini Publishing House.
Ohueri, Chelsi West. 2016. "Mapping Race and Belonging in the Margins of Europe: Albanian, Romani, and Egyptian Sentiments." PhD dissertation, University of Texas at Austin, Texas.
Peeva, Adela, director. 2003. *Chiya e tazi pesen?/Whose Song Is This?* Documentary film, produced by Slobodan Milovanovich and Paul Pauwels. VHS and DVD formats, 70 minutes.
Pula, Besnik. 2004. "The Emergence of the Kosovo 'Parallel State,' 1988–1992." *Nationalities Papers*, 32/4:797–826.

Reineck, Janet. 2000. "Poised for War: Kosova's Quiet Siege." In *Neighbors at War: Anthropological Perspectives on Yugoslav Ethnicity, Culture, and History*, eds. Joel M. Halpern and David A. Kideckel, 354–378. University Park: Pennsylvania State University Press.

Rice, Timothy. 2002. "Bulgaria or Chalgaria: The Attenuation of Bulgarian Nationalism in a Mass-Mediated Popular Music." *Yearbook for Traditional Music*, 34:25–46.

Silverman, Carol. 2012. *Romani Routes: Cultural Politics and Balkan Music in Diaspora*. New York: Oxford University Press.

Simić, Marina. 2019. "Music of the Others: Locating the (Turbo-) Folk Critique." *Contemporary Southeastern Europe*, 6/2:22–37.

Sinclair, John, Elizabeth Jacka, and Stuart Cunningham, eds. 1996. *New Patterns in Global Television: Peripheral Vision*. Oxford: Oxford University Press.

Statelova, Rosemary. 2005. *The Seven Sins of Chalga: Toward an Anthropology of Ethnopop Music*. Sofia: Prosveta.

Sugarman, Jane C. 2003. "Those 'Other Women': Dance and Femininity among Prespa Albanians." In *Music and Gender: Perspectives from the Mediterranean*, ed. Tullia Magrini, 87–118. Chicago: University of Chicago Press.

Sugarman, Jane C. 2004. "Diasporic Dialogues: Mediated Musics and the Albanian Transnation." In *Identity and the Arts in Diaspora Communities*, eds. Thomas Turino and James Lea, 21–38. Warren, MI: Harmonie Park Press.

Sugarman, Jane C. 2006. "Inter-Ethnic Borrowing and Musical Modernity in 'Balkan' Popular Musics Past and Present." In *Urban Music in the Balkans: Drop-Out Ethnic Identities or a Historical Case of Tolerance and Global Thinking?*, ed. Sokol Shupo, 64–75. Tirana, Albania: Documentation and Communication Center for Regional Music.

Sugarman, Jane C. 2007. "'The Criminals of Albanian Music': Albanian Commercial Folk Music and Issues of Identity since 1990." In *Balkan Popular Culture and the Ottoman Ecumene: Music, Image, and Regional Political Discourse*, ed. Donna A. Buchanan, 269–307. Lanham, MD: Scarecrow Press.

Sugarman, Jane C. 2010. "Kosova Calls for Peace: Song, Myth and War in an Age of Global Media." In *Music and Conflict*, eds. John O'Connell and Salwa el-Shawan Castelo-Branco, 17–45. Urbana, IL: University of Illinois Press.

Syri.net. 2021. "Flet këngëtari që e krijoi këngën 'Hajde luj qyqek', paralajmëron padi për të drejta autoriale." Syri.net. https://www.syri.net/syri_kosova/jeteosestil/254712/flet-kengetari-qe-e-krijoi-kengen-hajde-luj-qyqek-paralajmeron-padi-per-te-autoriale/. Accessed June 3, 2023.

Uka, Antigona. 2003. "Folku i vjedhur serb: Hit në Kosovë?" *Eurozëri*, 25:10–11.

Vickers, Miranda, and James Pettifer. 2000. *Albania: From Anarchy to a Balkan Identity*, updated ed. New York: New York University Press.

PART V
THE FOLKLORE OF EVERYDAY LIFE

Folk Wit, Wisdom, and the Spoken Word

CHAPTER 38

CHASTUSHKI

LAURA J. OLSON AND SVETLANA ADONYEVA

In the Russian tradition, *chastushki* are short rhymed folk songs that may be sung by a single singer, by several singers taking turns, or by a group in unison. They are often declaimed or sung on a simple melody to the accompaniment of accordion or balalaika. The word *chastushka* has the Russian root *chasto* ("often"), which in this case may refer to the frequent beat of this song genre: singers often declaim or sing *chastushki* quickly. However, *chastushki* can also be sung slowly and legato (as in the variant from the Russian Volga and central region called *stradaniia*); these slower variants usually involve some homophonic group singing. In Russia, *chastushki* are called by many names depending upon the region or type: *korotushki*, *prigudki*, *pripevki*, *perepevki*, *pribaski*, *stradaniia*, *sbirushki*, *matani*, and *zavlekashi*. A *chastushka* is one stanza long, can consist of two or four lines (occasionally six or other multiples of two), often has the meter of trochaic trimeter or tetrameter, and usually rhymes in a pattern such as AA, AABB, ABAB, ABBB, or ABCB.

In the Ukrainian tradition, *chastushki* are called *chastivki*, *tryndy*, *vytrybėnki*, *drybushachki*, *rėdzin'kiia*, *karotsen'kiia*, and *kolomyiki*; and in Belarus they are most often called either *prypeŭki* or *chastushki*. Local folk names for this type of song in Belarus include *prypevy*, *papeŭki*, *padpīavalki*, *padskoki*, *taradaĭki*, *braniushki*, *taptushki*, *zabaŭki*, *skakukhi*, *plīasukhi*, *krutsīolki*, *vytushki*, and *vydrahantsy* (Tsishchanka 1971:141–144). As Ivan Tsishchanka points out, collectors often did not record the local names for the genre but combined all short ditties into one category, losing some of the specificity of each type. Scholars began to use the Russian term *chastushka* for all of these types starting in the 1930s (Tsishchanka 1971:144–145). In the twentieth century and later, Ukrainian and Belarusian *chastushki* do not differ significantly from the Russian in their basic form, style, or subject matter; however, the manner of playing and singing developed under the influence of preexisting local musical styles, and their content reflects life in these countries (Novak 1999; Ivanyts'kyi 2004; Fiodaraŭ 1989:247).

History

Observers of Russian culture began to comment upon the *chastushka* as a new type of song during the second half of the nineteenth century. Russian scholars have discussed many different theories about how *chastushki* began their existence. Several scholars saw likenesses between *chastushki* and Russian lyric songs with a mix of contemporary folkloric and literary content which became popular in the nineteenth century (V. S. Bakhtin 1966:14; Lazutin 1960:48). Sergei Lazutin demonstrated that short sections of lyric songs began to be sung as separate songs and eventually as four-line *chastushki* in the second half of the nineteenth century; prior to that, those were not generally recognized as songs in and of themselves (1960:48–49). Several scholars likened *chastushki* to short songs with stereotyped content that were sung by a soloist to introduce or end a round-dance or a folk dance with playacting. Such songs seemed to be among the forerunners of the *chastushka*, although Vladimir Bakhtin cautions that *chastushki* never were accompanied by playacting (1966:14). Z. Vlasova (1971) found that *chastushki* were adapted from almost every kind of lyric folk song, such as songs about family life, love songs, cruel romances, urban folk songs, folk songs adapted from poems, dance songs with playacting, historical songs, and recruits' songs. *Chastushka* composers took the parts of the songs that were most aphoristic and laconic; sometimes they adapted the first four lines of the song (Vlasova 1971:108). According to Vlasova, the *chastushka* was not a sign of the death of the lyric folk song, as D. Zelenin (1903:78), A. Gorelov and Z. I. Vlasova (1965:18), and others had argued; rather, the lyric folk song and *chastushka* each continued to exist and mutually influence each other. Besides direct borrowing, both drew from the same source: the language of folklore (Vlasova 1971:110).

Stephen Frank has argued that *chastushki* had great social significance in the late nineteenth century because their entrance into Russian village culture helped to change the way young people expressed themselves. These short, satirical songs could be critical of serfdom, agricultural work, government authorities, or parental authority; could mock the local priest or deacon; or could make uncritical reference to drunkenness and brawls (Frank 1992:723–724). Whereas previously the folklore genres of mummery and folk theater allowed for public satire through physical comedy, the *chastushka* gave greater access to a verbal satirical, critical, or rebellious voice.

Native Ukrainian and Belarusian short songs similar to *chastushki* appear to have predated the appearance of *chastushki* in Russia. Some Soviet Russian commentators erroneously remarked that in Ukraine and Belarus *chastushki* appeared only under Russian influence, after the First World War (Sokolov 1941:401). However, sources allow us to date the collection of Belarusian *chastushki* to the late nineteenth century (Tsishchanka 1971:13, 15). Belarusian nativity plays (*batleika*)—a genre which dates back to the sixteenth century—contained short, witty, improvised ditties on contemporary themes that twentieth-century scholars called *chastushki* (Tsishchanka 1971:130–131). Ukrainian folk dances, such as the *kolomyika, shumka, kozachka, chabarashka, talalaika, gopak*, *vprisiadka*, and *drobushechki*, accompanied by instrumental folk music and short rhymed sung couplets, may have been among the sources that influenced or gave rise to the Russian *chastushka*; Vladimir Bakhtin points out that they considerably predate it as collections of these dance songs date to the early nineteenth century (Alexander 1976; V. S. Bakhtin 1966:21–22, 257). These folk dance genres are related to the Belarusian *skakukha*, *pliasushka*, and *podskok* and the Polish *krakoviak*, *mazurka*, *kuiaviak*, etc. To take the case of one specific dance song type, the Ukrainian *kolomyika* originated in eastern Galicia among the Hutsul people, and the earliest collections were in the 1860s; it remains popular in western Ukraine and, like the *chastushka*, has come to be sung outside of dance contexts as well as within folk dances (Polferov 1931; Zachyniaev 1907; Ivanyts'kyi 2004). The features linking the Ukrainian, Belarusian, and Polish dance song genres with the Russian *chastushki* include their size (all are monostrophic) and the literary poetics of all of these texts (i.e., their rhyme and metrical schemes) (V. S. Bakhtin 1966:22).

Content and Collection

From the very beginning of *chastushka* collecting, Russian scholars have made numerous attempts to categorize *chastushki* by content; later, Soviet scholars divided *chastushki* by historical time period based upon content (Meshkova 2001). Most classifications based upon content are simply lists of themes. They are not particularly helpful since all rely on a scholar's determination of the most important aspects of the content of any given *chastushka*—and many *chastushki* contain subject matter from more than one category (such as love and nature). Still, in our view a broad division into four groups based upon generalizations about content can be useful: (1) *chastushki* having to do with everyday life, love, and relationships; (2) *chastushki* about sex, many of which use the Russian cursing language *mat*; (3) *chastushki* that participate in public discourse of politics, including those expressing official ideology or anti-official protest; and (4) humorous *chastushki* based upon a principle of nonsense, illogicality, or parody.

The largest group is *chastushki* about everyday life. This is the content for which the genre is known, and the category includes *chastushki* about love or lost love; interpersonal relationships between friends, villagers, or family members; aspects of everyday life, such as nature, weather, furniture, clothing, or food; and simple events or observations of the lyrical "I." Very typical is content containing some emotional reflection and elements from nature or everyday life:

> Я косила осенью,
> Любовалась озимью:
> —Эта озимь, эта рожь—
> До чего милой хорош.

> I scythed in the fall
> I loved to look at the winter crop
> —That winter crop, that rye—
> Oh, how good looking is my dear one.
>
> (Eleonskaia 1914:No. 206)

Erotic *chastushki* mention or hint at acts of sex and/or feature names for male or female genitalia. They are often raucously funny; they are not necessarily meant to excite the audience sexually, but this could be one of their functions. As Boris Uspenskii (1994) points out, each Russian village had its master of telling erotic folk texts; these were told to young men in order to positively influence their sexual development. Similarly, we can imagine that exposure to erotic *chastushki* would have been considered not only appropriate but salutary for young men. We emphasize their transgressive function in the section on pragmatics below. They were used in certain parts of Russia and Belarus during weddings; for example, in Ulyanovsk oblast they were sung by elder women on the second and third days of the wedding (Matlin 2019; see below under "Pragmatics").

Like erotic *chastushki*, political *chastushki* also have a primarily transgressive function. These include *chastushki* that satirize elements of everyday life so as to imply systematic problems with the government or authority figures, satirical *chastushki* that directly mention institutions or authority figures, *chastushki* that convey political propaganda (i.e., composed under the guidance of government organs to support and spread the point of view of the authorities), and *chastushki* that are not composed specifically to support the government's point of view but nonetheless do so (such as patriotic *chastushki*).

We place illogical humorous *chastushki* in a separate category because although they use images from everyday life, they are not "about" everyday life (they are not "about" anything). Their intent is simply to entertain. This category includes *neskladukhi* and *nebylitsy*.

POETICS

This section will first describe the poetic features of Russian *chastushki* of everyday life, as well as erotic and political *chastushki*, and then describe nonsense *chastushki* and those from Belarus and Ukraine.

The most significant differences between Russian *chastushki* and traditional lyric folk songs lie in the set size of the *chastushka* stanza (four lines), the predominant use of the syllabo-tonic metric system (a verse structure based on word stress and the number of syllables), and the rhyme scheme. Russian folk songs do not have a set stanza size and use tonic (accentual) verse. Further, *chastushki*, like literary poetry, often have an ABAB rhyme scheme that seems to emphasize the "finished" nature of the piece, whereas traditional Russian lyric folk songs lack rhyme or have accidental or internal rhyme (Lazutin 1981; Alexander 1976).

Russian *chastushki* and their Ukrainian and Belarusian cousins are easy to remember and to repeat; therefore, similar content, themes, or phrases often appear in many variations. In fact, referring specifically to the four-line *chastushka*, it is easy for a singer to create a new text by taking the first line of a *chastushka* and adding three different lines or taking the first two lines and adding two different lines. In fact, we may divide four-line *chastushki* into one-part and two-part texts; the two-part texts predominate and are exactly the type of *chastushki* that can easily give birth to new *chastushki*. In the one-part texts, the first two lines and the second two lines are united by syntax and together comprise a single sentence. In two-part *chastushki*, the first two lines and the second two lines can each stand alone syntactically. There is often parallelism, in which the second half imitates the syntax of the first half (Lazutin 1981). In *chastushki* with such parallel structure, the last line often serves as a kind of "punchline," delivering potentially surprising, humorous, or especially significant content.

Chastushki may also be divided into monologues and dialogues; the majority of *chastushki* are monologues, although since *chastushki* are meant for public singing, they presuppose a dialogue (i.e., another *chastushka* sung in response). Monologue *chastushki* may be divided into those that tell a narrative and those that are primarily descriptive. The narratives are usually not highly involved but report a single event from everyday life. Additionally, some monologues are couched in the form of a direct or rhetorical address to a person or thing (Lazutin 1981).

The following is an example of a monologue *chastushka* with a narrative, in one part, with rhyme scheme ABCB:

> На беседу я пришел,
> Кругом поклонился,
> Увидал: милашки нет—
> Назад воротился.

> I came to the party (*beseda*)
> And bowed to everyone
> I saw that my girl wasn't there
> And I went back home.

(Simakov 1913:No. 228)

And the following is a two-part monologue with rhetorical address, also with ABCB rhyme scheme:

> Не ходите, девки, замуж;
> Замужем худая жись:
> На вечерку не пускают,
> Говорят, что спать ложись.

> Don't get married, girls;
> Being married is an awful life
> They don't let you go to parties (*vechorki*),
> They tell you to go to bed.
>
> (Eleonskaia 1914:No. 261)

Chastushki are improvised by ordinary people and make use of the language of folklore that people are steeped in; therefore, they are rich in phrases and epithets borrowed from traditional songs, folk tales, proverbs, and popular culture of the time (Vlasova 1971:117, 121). For example, one *chastushka* paraphrases the proverb "He fixes his neighbor's roof, but his own drips" (Чужую крышу кроет, а своя каплет) to make a point about the thrill of the chase:

> Мы чужие крыши кроем
> А свои раскрытые,
> Мы чужих девчонок любим
> А свои забытые.
>
> We fix our neighbor's roofs,
> But our own are open
> We love other people's girls
> And forget our own.
>
> (Eleonskaia 1914:No. 1131)

The previous *chastushka* provides an example of moralizing *chastushki*; more often, however, *chastushki* personalize rather than generalize. Vlasova writes that, in highly economical form, *chastushki* "individualize the passing shades of moods and feelings of the lyric hero," while the lyric song uses a series of images to convey the most common feelings and characteristics (1971:118). The following is a good example of a highly personal expression of the speaker's feeling of rejection, conveyed with a single, highly idiosyncratic image (i.e., the *kvass* from the green mug).

> Зачем было переливать
> Из зеленой кружки квас
> Зачем было подходить
> Когда не стоила я вас.
>
> Why did [you] pour
> The kvass from the green mug?
> Why did [you] come up to me
> If you thought I wasn't worth your time?

(Collected by Ulyanovsk NOTs* 1988 from Elena Shandalova, b. 1927, Iazykovo, Karsun region, Ulyanovsk obl.)[1]

Chastushki use a poetic language that emphasizes realism based in details of ordinary life, rather than symbolism involving abstract concepts. The roles of metaphor, metonymy, logical parallelism (repetition and comparison), and ellipsis dominate; and if abstract concepts are invoked, they are usually "lowered" by comparison with objects or events of everyday life. For example, this two-part *chastushka* with rhyme scheme AABB from a 1913 collection revolves around a single metaphor of burning love but also depicts the loved one in a single detail (gray-eyed boy) and, using metonymy of proximity, compares the immediate feeling of the lyric hero to a burning stick used to light interiors prior to electrification:

> Сероглазый паренек
> Мое сердечко зажег.
> Без лучины, без огня
> Горит сердечко у меня.

> A gray-eyed boy
> Burned my heart.
> Without a lighting-stick, without flame
> My heart is burning.

(Simakov 1913:No. 555)

The following two-part *chastushka* uses repetition for emphasis and presents a metonymy (synecdoche) in which the brown eyes stand for the loved one:

> Кари глазки, кари глазки
> Карие кариночки!
> Они понравились мне
> На первой вечериночке!

> Brown eyes, brown eyes
> Brown, little brown ones!
> I liked them
> At the first party (*vecherinka*)!

(Vlasova 1971:119)

The prior *chastushka* has been reformulated many times:

> Кари глазки, кари глазки,
> Карие кариночки.
> Завлекли они меня
> На прошлой вечериночке.

> Brown eyes, brown eyes
> Brown, little brown ones!

> They attracted me
> At the last party (*vecherinka*).
>
> ("Korobeiniki" 2003)

The following popular *chastushka* makes use of repetition (anaphora, repetition of a word or phrase to start successive clauses) and parallelism to show a comparison between swimming in a river and loving boys; swimming and rivers often figure as metaphors for love or sex in Russian folklore (Plutser-Sarno 2000):

> Хорошо у речки жить,
> Хорошо купаться,
> Хорошо ребят любить,
> Трудно расставаться.
>
> It's nice to live by the river
> It's nice to go for a swim
> It's nice to love guys
> But it's hard to say goodbye.
>
> (Eleonskaia 2014:No. 103)

The following makes use of negative comparison, one of the tropes of Russian folk poetic language; this *chastushka* is also an example of tonic verse, rather than syllabo-tonic, and thus represents an older poetic principle of composition:

> Не туман ложится на землю,
> Не серая роса;
> Со печали помутились
> Мои серые глаза.
>
> It's not fog lying over the earth,
> It's not gray dew;
> It's that my gray eyes
> Became dim from sadness.
>
> (Simakov 1913:No. 1920)

Some *chastushki* create juxtapositions that lack an obvious meaning. In this case they function as reporters or observers of life in all its randomness. They might also be seen as either elevating ordinary life by placing it in poetic form or lowering "high" sentiments, such as in the following two-part monologue with a rhetorical address:

> На столе стоит
> Каша гречнева
> Ой любовь, любовь
> Любовь сердечная.

On the table lies
A bowl of buckwheat kasha
Oh, love, love,
Heart-felt love!

(Collected 1987 by Ulyanovsk NOTs* from Vera I. Podagina, Karsun, Ulyanovsk oblast)

The situation of the person singing the *chastushka* can change the meaning of the lyric. A woman who has recently broken up with her lover might sing the latter *chastushka* wistfully, while another might sing it as if laughing at love: the juxtaposition of such an ordinary detail as porridge with love might seem to undermine the seriousness of the purported love. In this case, the singer followed it with another *chastushka* seeming to give an interpretation to the previous one. The singer warns her girlfriends that real love will be obvious (presumably to the lovers themselves, but she could possibly be hinting that such love is also obvious to others and therefore might give rise to competition):

Любовь сердечная
В глаза бросается
Поверьте девушки,
Для вас касается.

Heart-felt love
Is obvious right away
Believe me, girls,
This applies to you!

(Collected by Ulyanovsk NOTs* in 1987 from Vera I. Podagina, Karsun, Ulyanovsk oblast)

Political and erotic *chastushki* do not differ in their poetics from *chastushki* about everyday life; the primary differences in these categories lie in their content, vocabulary, thematics, and pragmatics. However, our fourth category, nonsense *chastushki*, has its own poetic particularities. V. S. Bakhtin uses the term *neskladukha* for *chastushki* which do not make sense and do not rhyme, while using the term *nebylitsa* for those which do not make sense but generally follow a rhyme scheme. However, the people who compose these genres do not follow a strict division between them, as the following rhyming (ABCB) *neskladukha* demonstrates:

Вы послушайте, ребята
Нескладушу буду петь
На дубу свинья пасется
В бане парится медведь.

Listen, boys,
I'm going to sing a *neskladukha*
A pig was grazing on an oak

> And a bear was steaming himself in the bathhouse!
>
> (V. S. Bakhtin 1966:252)

The following is an example of a non-rhyming nonsense *neskladukha*, in which the lack of expected rhyme contributes to the nonsensical nature of the text:

> Сидит заяц на березе
> При калошах, при часах.
> Я спросила:—Сколько время?
> —Не женатый, холостой.
>
> A rabbit sits on a birch tree
> With rubber boots and a watch.
> I asked him:—What's the time?
> —Not married, a bachelor.
>
> (V. S. Bakhtin 1966:251)

Starting in the Soviet period and to the present day, Ukrainian and Belorussian *chastushki* have been similar in poetics to those from Russia. However, the Ukrainian genre of the *kolomyika*, which accompanies the folk dance of the same name, has a form that differs somewhat from the *chastushka*. The *kolomyika* is syllabic verse, not syllabotonic or accentual, as the Russian *chastushka*: it consists of two (or four) lines of fourteen syllables each (with possible variations on the number of syllables from twelve to sixteen), with a caesura after eight syllables. The two lines rhyme AA, and there may be internal rhymes. The *kolomyika* was originally closely related to the rhythm and movements of the dance which it accompanies (Polferov 1931); later it developed as a genre which may be sung outside of dance contexts.

The following examples demonstrate the closeness of this genre to the folk dance context, as dance emerges as one of the main themes:

> Ой весела коломийка, весела та жвава,
> А від тієї коломийки та й земля дрожала!
>
> Oh the kolomyika is cheerful, cheerful and lively
> And from the kolomyika even the earth trembled!
>
> (Health and Beauty 2013)

> Коломийку заспівати, коломийку грати,
> Або тоту коломийку легко танцювати.
>
> Let's sing the kolomyika, let's dance the kolomyika,
> For that *kolomyika* is easy to dance.
>
> (Shumada 1998)

The other categories of the *kolomyika* content are quite similar to those of the *chastushka*: everyday life and love, humorous satires on politics and sex, being recruited to the army (Ivanyts'kyi 2004:217). The genre itself is named after the geographical region around Kolomyia, a city which was on an important trade route starting in the thirteenth century, currently located in the Ivano-Frankivsk oblast of Ukraine. Several other names were also used locally for the *kolomyika*: *starovits'ka*, *gutsulka*, *sokolivs'ka*, etc. (Zachyniaev 1907:321).

As V. S. Bakhtin has shown, some of the Russian two-line *chastushki* clearly are similar to and were composed under the influence of the Ukrainian two-line dance couplets, such as the following:

Ты играй, играй, двурядочка
Играй повеселей!

Play, play, button-accordion!
Play [more] cheerfully!

(V. S. Bakhtin 1966:257)

Music

The accordion, balalaika, bandura, and similar folk instruments serve as the most common accompaniments to *chastushka*-singing. A single instrument can serve as accompaniment, or several instruments of the same or different types can be played together. In the mid-twentieth century and earlier, groups of singers also sometimes imitated the accordion sound, especially when instruments were not present; these polyphonic melodies with onomatopoeic syllables were called *pod iazyk* ("under the tongue"). Several named instrumental folk melodies (Russian *naigrysh*) are used. The folk melodies may be divided into those to which vocalists dance with quick footwork (Russian *pliasovaia*) and those where dance either is not present at all or is performed only during part of the song or only at a medium-to-slow tempo. The fast-dancing types include *barynia*, *semenovna*, *tsyganochka*, *matania*, *eletskogo*, and *bazar*; the lyric or non-dancing types include *stradaniia*, *dosada*, *kanareika*, and *sharlotskogo* (Semianinov 2016:33, 68–69) (Fig. 38.1).

Historically, prior to the 1920s, musicologists dismissed the musical possibilities of this genre. S. M. Liapunov pointed out that the Russian accordion called *garmon'* (a simple accordion with one, two, or three rows of buttons for playing melody with the right hand and chords or bass notes with the left) seemed as if made especially for simple songs like *chastushki* as it was capable only of playing alternating tonic and dominant major chords and a simple melody (Liapunov and Istomin 1979:233; Semianinov 2016:37) (Fig. 38.2). Starting in the 1920s, Soviet musicologists reversed

FIG. 38.1. Men dance to *chastushki* at holiday in village of Moseevo, Vashkinskii region, Vologda oblast, Russia, July 27, 2001.

(Photo by Svetlana Adonyeva.)

this predominant view and praised the inventiveness of the instrumentalists, especially as they created a driving rhythm with syncopation and varied accents and engaged in interplay between leading and supporting voices within the homophonic chordal structure and polyphonic interplay between the vocal and instrumental parts. This view has come to dominate musicological studies of *chastushki* (Asaf'ev 1987:177–178; Gippius 2000; Semianinov 2016).

For four-line dance *chastushki*, the rhythm is usually duple or, less often, triple meter, with time signatures of 2/4, 4/4, 3/4, or 6/8. The singing part for dance *chastushki* may be declamatory (recitative, with pitch alternation within a second or third), recitative with melodic elements, or melodic; in any case, the ambitus is not larger than a fifth. The melodic structure consists of two almost identical musical sentences (Fiodaraŭ 1989).

The performance manner of the four-line dance *chastushka* generally adheres to the following pattern of dialogue between instrument and singer: after a solo instrumental introduction, the instrumentalist plays an instrumental melody to which a *chastushka* is sung. After a singer sings the *chastushka*, the instrumentalist repeats the same melody with grace notes, ornaments, and other variations while the singer stops singing (and may dance solo, or all participants may dance) for an equal number of lines. Then another singer, or the same singer, sings another *chastushka*, and so on. While accompanying the singing, the instrumental part is often played more softly or with chords only so that the singer can be better heard or featured.

FIG. 38.2. An accordionist examines his *garmon'*. Village ensemble of Ermolovo, Kasimovskii region, Riazan' oblast, Russia, August 1, 1996.

(Photo by Laura J. Olson.)

The pattern for the two-line lyric *stradaniia* type is different and varies considerably from region to region. Here, the singers usually alternate two lines of solo and two lines of group singing in harmony, often followed by the equivalent number of instrumental bars. In some styles, the solo lines are sung quickly, recitative-style, as in a *chastushka*, while the group part is sung slower and follows a particular melody. The two lines sung as a group may be the same text each time or may form an already-agreed-upon sequence. Often the several two-line texts of *stradaniia* cluster around a theme, such as the one the name suggests: *stradaniia* means "suffering."

It should be noted that the number of different melodies and ways of singing and playing within the *chastushka* genre is practically limitless. The foregoing description should be taken as basic and not as exhaustive.

In Ukraine and Belarus, *chastushki* are played similarly to how they are played in Russia, and the various melodies exist with the same names (Fedun 2005:160; Fiodaraŭ 1989). However, *kolomyiki* are distinct. According to Oleksandr Ivanyts'kyi, *kolomyiki* may be divided into two types. Those sung "to dance" are most often sung by men and in a recitative-declamatory fashion; those performed "to sing" (i.e., without dancing) are more often done by women and in a more lyric, melodic fashion (2004:216). The *kolomyika* is traditionally accompanied by a small band consisting of violin, stand-up bass, drum, and cymbals (Ivanyts'kyi 2004:215); other instruments, such as *tsimbalom*, can be included, depending upon location. The dance is played fast, in duple meter; and people dance it in a circle holding hands. A singer/dancer will spontaneously shout out lyrics; often the singers/dancers join in a refrain. Today, the music is usually provided by a band that includes instrumentalists and singers, and the *kolomyiki* texts are known/agreed-upon beforehand; thus, all of the verses can be sung in two-part harmony. Contemporary participant-dancers at an event such as a wedding with *kolomyiki* will typically not participate in the music-making.

Pragmatics

Pragmatics studies the contexts of speech acts and the intentions of the speakers: when and for what purpose do people perform these speech acts? The following remarks are largely based upon the authors' fieldwork (interviews and observations) in Russian villages during the late twentieth and early twenty-first centuries,[2] but similar contexts have been observed for *chastushki* and their musical cousins in Ukraine and Belarus as well (Ivanyts'kyi 2004:207–208; Tsishchanka 1971). We will focus upon the following contexts and purposes: (1) entertainment; (2) courtship; (3) competition (agonism); (4) humor and satire (humorous, transgressive self-expression on the subject of politics or sex); (5) propaganda; (6) ritual functions, such as memorializing of the dead, sending young men off to the army, or as a part of the wedding; and (7) memory.

Entertainment

Chastushki can be used to entertain in any context in which entertainment is warranted. This is a timeless characteristic of *chastushki*, but we can name specific contexts in which the entertainment function of *chastushki* has become its primary raison d'être. In contemporary Russia, Ukraine, and Belarus, *chastushki* and similar genres, like *kolomyiki*, are often performed by professional, semi-professional, or amateur musicians at festivals, at weddings, at contests, on television, etc. Such a public function of *chastushki*—as a folk music genre performed by "musicians" for entertainment to a passive audience, on stage or in a stage-like setting—has been in effect since at least the 1920s, when *chastushki* began to be performed at Soviet state-organized performances. Throughout the Soviet period there have been several famous solo singers, duos, and trios who made their fame by performing *chastushki* (Levin 2004:437). Today, stage performance is the main context in which Russian citizens (majority urban dwellers) are familiar with the *chastushka* genre.

Chastushki performed on stage by a collective or solo musician are not spontaneous; their order is planned out in advance, and their arrangement will often follow a theme. In this way these performances differ significantly from the traditional folk use of *chastushki*, which was spontaneous and emphasized individual self-presentation. When *chastushki* were sung for entertainment by a collective, often the text would underline the collective nature of the performance and the passivity of the audience by addressing the audience using the first-person plural in introductory or closing *chastushki* (V. S. Bakhtin 1966:49):

> А мы частушки сочиняли
> И ногами топали
> А теперь мы вас попросим
> Чтобы вы похлопали!

> We have composed our *chastushki*
> And stomped our feet
> Now we're going to ask you
> To clap your hands!
>
> (Performance by singers in village of Ermolovo,
> Riazan oblast, August 1, 1996, L. J. O. personal archive)

Prior to the point when *chastushki* began to be performed on stage in festivals and competitions organized by the state, *chastushki* were primarily associated with gatherings organized by individuals and groups of young people in villages: here, they were indeed meant to entertain but, more importantly, to facilitate social bonding and courtship and to enable individuals to make their reputations within village society. Today, village dwellers continue to use *chastushka* in spontaneous, family, and social contexts.

Courtship

In Russian villages prior to World War II, courtship occurred at parties of two primary types: young people's indoor parties, known as *besedy, vechorki, posidelki,* and *posidki,* held on evenings during the cold weather seasons, and *gulianiia* (strollings), young people's outdoor parties held during warm weather. Young people themselves would organize such parties, and socializing and courtship were the goals. Often, especially during the winter, girls (*devushki*) would organize the parties by providing the refreshments and arranging the location—often the home of an older couple who were compensated with firewood or food for this service. Here, the girls would do handiwork while also entertaining themselves with songs and games. Boys (*parni*) would arrive sometime during the party, and then the event really got going as flirtation was one of the purposes of such get-togethers. Summer parties during holidays, when the whole village was outside, tended to be an occasion for girls to show off their clothing and personal style, during singing and dancing, to potential grooms and mothers-in-law.

Chastushki were an important accompaniment for both types of parties during the late nineteenth century and throughout the first half to three-quarters of the twentieth century: see, for example, the first two *chastushki* under the section "Poetics," above, which mention the party types *beseda* and *vechorka*. During the outdoor parties, young people would walk through the village in groups. Boys would stroll at the front of a group, placing the accordionist in the center of this row; in the second row would walk the girls, declaiming *chastushki*. The group would stop, and the members would stand in a circle and start dancing in place. While people were dancing, a participant would physically signal their wish to sing a *chastushka* by momentarily stopping dancing; in this way, singers would rarely interrupt each other.

At such parties, young people had an opportunity for self-presentation and for projecting a certain image that contributed to their reputations. In this sense, how they sang *chastushki*, how they danced to *chastushka* music, the words they used in their *chastushki*—all of these actions permitted them to express themselves, enabling them to tighten social bonds and match successfully with a beloved partner (i.e., to become engaged and then married).

Competition

Rivalry, our third function of *chastushki*, was an important component of these *chastushka* exchanges during courtship parties. There was a hard-and-fast rule: if a *chastushka* was insulting to one of the dancers, no one would interrupt it. Anyone who wished to respond would "answer" it with another *chastushka*, an action which they called *otpet'* (i.e., to win a singing competition by having the last word or answering a challenge wittily). Until at least the end of the 1950s, and sometimes later, village communities highly valued the ability to skillfully "otpet'" by declaiming a *chastushka* in response to a *chastushka* that was meant to offend (Fig. 38.3). Boys and girls learned this skill while engaging in informal *chastushka* competitions, in which each stood to gain a desired reputation in the process of courtship: if they sang a pointed remark, a boy could be known as brave and a girl as bold or sassy. During the Soviet period, brave boys and bold girls were viewed as choice partners; skillful accordionists, too, were particularly in demand as romantic partners.

Competition is a principle of social behavior in many cultures: it was described using the term "agon" or agonism in ancient Greece and refers to semi-ritualized competition through which an individual or group gains prestige or reputation. Referring to a type of speech, agon is speech in which a competitor attempts to get the upper hand by breaking rules or conventions of behavior. Such speech makes explicit that which normally is concealed, such as feelings of aggression, desire, etc., and uses the language of invective or carnival language (i.e., the grotesque image of the lower regions of the body, as well as parody and sarcasm) (M. Bakhtin 1984).

FIG. 38.3. After a concert, a male resident and a female seasonal resident exchange *chastushki*. Village of Ivanov Bor, Kirillovskii region, Vologda oblast, Russia, July 17, 2000.

(Photo by Svetlana Adonyeva.)

In Russia agon as a type of speech had its clearest expression in the *chastushki* of village youth. Using the poetic form of the *chastushka*, young men and women would make public remarks about subjects that were generally taboo for a person of their age or gender status to discuss publicly. These would include topics relating to love—who was pairing up with whom, who had broken up, and who was laying a claim for whom—and relating to feelings and desires (including those which were not considered favorable, such as anger, jealousy, and sexual desire). Thus, transgressive speech was one of the basic underlying principles of the chastushka genre. Johann Huizinga has described this playing function of poetic speech as universal for young people's matrimonial games (1971).

Here is an example of the type of challenge which might be used in a competitive *chastushka* exchange:

> Супостатка, тише, тише,
> Погляди, какая тишь,
> Не заглядывай на милого—
> В канаву улетишь

>Be quiet, my opponent,
>Look how quiet it is
>Don't look at my dear one,
>You'll fly into the ditch!

(Adon'eva 2006:161)

As part of this competitive use of the *chastushka* genre, we include a type used by young men to begin and accompany a ritual brawl during outdoor summer holidays. Such *chastushki* were called *pod draku* (i.e., "for a fight"). Groups of young men from different villages would meet during a village holiday and provoke each other to a fight by singing *chastushki* such as the following:

>Ты, товарищ, не ударишь,
>А ударишь–не убьёшь,
>Если я тебя ударю,
>Через пять минут помрешь

>You, my friend, won't even hit me,
>But if you do, you sure won't kill me,
>But if I hit you just one time,
>You'll be dead in five minutes' time.

(Adon'eva 2006:17)

The competitive type of *chastushka*-singing remained one of the most productive and popular genres of folklore for village youth to the end of the 1960s and even, in some locations, into the 1970s. In general, people born in the mid-1960s and 1970s know *chastushki* from their grandmothers and grandfathers and can sing them but did not use *chastushki* in the agonistic fashion we describe here, as did their mothers and fathers. Thus, the *chastushka* as a speech form expressing agon or competition, first mentioned by folklorists at the end of the nineteenth century, had mostly died out by the end of the twentieth century. At the beginning of the twenty-first century, folklorists saw this function expressed only among elders and mostly in the context of performing on stage or remembering their youth (Fig. 38.4). The fact that the *chastushka* gives legitimacy to transgression and allows young people to make or break their reputation for speaking out makes this genre a special type of speech act specifically aimed at this transgressive and competitive function.

Humor and Satire

As young people aged, starting in the 1930s and to at least the end of the twentieth century, the *chastushka* acquired one more function. It allowed men and women to speak out about the taboo topics of politics, war, and sex. It was an important vehicle

FIG. 38.4. A woman declaims *chastushka* for fellow residents and guests after a concert, village of Moseevo, Vashkinskii region, Vologda oblast, Russia, July 27, 2001.

(Photo by Svetlana Adonyeva.)

for self-expression for those who were disempowered. Such taboo *chastushki* could be sung during dancing but often were simply quoted in everyday speech with trusted interlocutors, in which case they were pronounced in a recitative fashion or simply spoken, like a joke:

> Напоили меня пьяною,
> Очнулася в реке:
> Юбки нету, жопа голая
> И трешница в руке.

> They got me drunk
> And I woke up in a river
> Without my skirt, with a bare ass
> And a three-ruble bill in my hand.

> Спасибо Сталину и Ленину
> За помощь старику,
> Всем старухам дали пенсию—
> Лежите на боку.

> Thanks to Stalin and Lenin
> For helping retirees,

> They gave all old women a pension:
> [Now you can] lie on your side [i.e., you don't have to work].
>
> (Singer's commentary:
> Такая пенсия–12 рублей–улежишь тут»
>
> With such a [small] pension of 12 rubles how would you lie and do nothing!)
>
> (Adon'eva 2006:207–208). (Collector's explanation: Prior to 1964, agricultural workers did not receive a pension)

Examples in Ukraine include nationalistic, anti-Soviet *chastivki* arguing for full national liberation from Moscow, such as the following, collected during the period of 1917–1921:

> Я на бочці сиджу
> Під бочкою каша,
> Не думайте москалі
> Що Вкраіна ваша!
>
> I'm sitting on a barrel
> Under the barrel is kasha
> Don't think, Muscovites,
> That Ukraine is yours!
>
> (Sen'ko 1953:4–6)

Later examples include *chastushki* using gallows humor to characterize the Chernobyl disaster (Fialkova 2001, 188).

According to village ethics, there would be no punishment for any *chastushka* utterance because, as the proverb goes, "You can't throw the words out of a song." In other words, *chastushki* were viewed as anonymous, unauthored speech, and no individual bore responsibility for their content. However, the Soviet authorities did put people in prison for singing *chastushki* that were considered ideologically incorrect, especially in the 1930s and 1940s. For example, in 1936 a twenty-one-year-old male tractor driver from Saratov was sentenced to a year and a half in prison for singing the following *chastushka* at a village gathering:

> Вставай Ленин,
> Вставай дедка,
> Нас убила
> Пятилетка.
>
> Get up, Lenin,
> Get up, grandad,
> The five year plan
> Has killed us.
>
> (Davies 1998:156)

The punishment of counterrevolutionary *chastushki* was not just a phenomenon of the height of the purges; it continued after the war. A female *kolkhoz* (collective farm) worker was tried in 1953 for sending anonymous letters containing *chastushki* about party and government leaders and *kolkhoz* life to two local Moscow newspapers and for singing these *chastushki* in her village (Edelman 1999:29). People used *chastushki* as public expressions of discontent, aimed at the purveyors of repressive policies: a sort of answer in a dialogue between the authorities and the "people" (for the metaphor of the dialogue, see Arkhipova and Nekliudov 2010).

As described by A. D. Volkov (b. 1923), who collected political and erotic *chastushki* unofficially, as a hobby, people composed political *chastushki* despite the danger of being arrested; and those that they considered most successful, they would write down and keep (Volkov 1999:290). However, they did not sing them publicly, at least not in the cities. Volkov first heard political *chastushki* during World War II while he was in the hospital and the patients would go on outings in the countryside. Within the hospital itself people spoke them in a whisper rather than singing them (Volkov 1999:492). In the cities, the recitation of political *chastushki* was limited to private contexts, in which people had confidence in each other and could be reasonably certain not to be overheard or observed. But with the advent of Gorbachev's policy of *glasnost* (openness) in 1986, the situation changed dramatically. Volkov wrote, "людей как прорвало!" ("it was as if it burst out of people"). Now it was possible to hear things that earlier people would have been afraid to whisper to each other (Volkov 1999:494).

From the individual's point of view, the use of the *chastushka* form effectively put what one sang in quotes so that individual responsibility was shared with the group. The public village forum functioned as a liminal space in which the sense of being surrounded by "one's own" (*svoi*) held out the promise of one's safety. As Margaret Paxson has argued, politically irreverent *chastushki* performed the function of coalescing villagers' feeling of being a tightly knit group in opposition to the center of power (2005:305–306) (Fig. 38.5).

Today, *chastushki* expressing political satire or erotic jokes make their appearance on the internet in the form of videos or collections of texts. In village contexts such *chastushki* continue to serve as jokes or pranks, such as when recited during a party or when a grandparent teaches a risqué *chastushka* to a grandchild who is too young to understand the joke.

Propaganda

Throughout the Soviet period, officials in charge of the ideological re-education of the population recognized the value of *chastushki* as propaganda. Starting in the 1920s party leaders called for the use of lively, understandable, and relevant means to conduct anti-religious propaganda targeted specifically at rural women, who continued to practice orthodoxy and to believe in the supernatural. In a time of budgetary scarcity, ethnographers were given funds to study folklore, including *chastushki*, with the condition that they "introduce alterations and additions" in publications for mass

FIG. 38.5. A man dances while declaiming *chastushki* with fellow residents and guests after a concert, village of Moseevo, Vashkinskii region, Vologda oblast, Russia, July 27, 2001.

(Photo by Svetlana Adonyeva.)

consumption in order to help with anti-religious propaganda (Andreev 1931:3; Husband 2004:97–98). In other words, *chastushki* were manipulated politically for propaganda: instead of recording spontaneously created *chastushki* directly from the people, Soviet folklorists would compose their own (Gorelov and Vlasova, 1965:12; Tsishchanka 1971:71). Other authors of such texts included Komsomol (Communist Youth League) members and members of so-called agit-brigades, composed of professional and amateur producers of theatrical and musical propaganda in regional houses of culture, factory clubs, and, more rarely, village clubs. The groups based in regional centers often traveled to villages to present their material. Here, they would collect and adapt for new use local *chastushki* and present newly composed texts (Tirado 1993:51–52; Bialosinskaia

1966). Newspapers would print newly composed *chastushki*, and even well-established authors, like Vladimir Mayakovsky, contributed (V. S. Bakhtin 1966:48).

The mode used in the propagandistic texts was a specific type of satire: as one critic described it, "the healthy humor . . . of an optimist" (Gnedin 1935:5; Norris 2009). Such humor remains within the limits of mimesis, leaving intact the principal reference points of good and evil, state and its structures (Ostromoukhova 2009). For example, one set of propaganda *chastushki* criticized the leadership of the *kolkhoz* agronomist in the sowing of millet:

> Агроном Колесников
> По полю гуляет
> Просо поверху лежит
> Он не замечает.
> Припев:
> Хорошо ли сеяли?
> Невнимательно.
> Куры просо поклюют?
> Объязательно.
>
> Agronomist Kolesnikov
> Walks around the field
> The millet is lying on the top
> And he doesn't notice.
> Refrain:
> Did they sow it well?
> Not attentively.
> Will the chickens eat the millet?
> Absolutely.
>
> (Bialosinskaia 1966:229)

Such texts ended up being used only for a short time: they were "disposable" and became folklorized only with significant changes or not at all. One can see the difference between this text criticizing the agronomist's direction of the millet-sowing and the genuinely folkloric texts. The spontaneously created folklore makes use of hyperbole ("The five year plan/has killed us"), irony ("Thanks to Stalin and Lenin/for helping retirees"), and black humor ("Get up, Lenin!"). These *chastushki* are carnivalesque in their evocation of death and rebirth and their reversals of established hierarchies (e.g., calling for Lenin to take on Stalin) (M. Bakhtin 1984:80–81). By contrast, the composed texts use mild expressions with simple negation of the desired behavior ("he doesn't notice"; "not attentively"), without disturbing existing values and hierarchies. As Arkhipova and Nekliudov (2010) point out, such implanted texts would have to correspond to the worldview of the recipients in order to be accepted and transmitted further; in the Soviet Union, they largely did not.

Ritual

The ritual function of *chastushki* arose as a replacement for older ritual genres. During the second half of the twentieth century, the *chastushka* took the place of laments during memorial rituals (Kuleva 2008). People would sing *chastushki* such as the following at cemeteries, when they would go there for the anniversary of a loved one's death. The manner of singing, of course, would differ from ordinary *chastushka*-singing, which tended to be loud and strident; here, the voice might have a softer timbre and volume, and the singing would be without instrumental accompaniment:

> Ой, ни кукушечка кукуют,
> Не соловьюшко поет.
> А не родимая ли мамынька
> Мне голос подает?
>
> Oi, it's not a cuckoo cuckooing,
> It's not a nightingale singing,
> Isn't it my dear mother that bore me,
> Who is calling to me?

(Kuleva 2008:18)

Boys heading to the army or to war also sang particular *chastushki* for the occasion. After they received their call, they would *guliat'* (party)—their families would hold parties for them, and they would visit the parties of other recruits, ride horses around the village, and visit neighbors, family, and friends. During such parties, they would sing *chastushki* in which the speaker, addressee, or subject is a new recruit:

> Некрута вы, некрута,
> Да вам дорожка в никуда!
> Вам дорожка бережком
>
> Да до Череповца пешком.
> Некрутам дается волюшка
>
> Вино и пиво пить,
> А еще дается воля
>
> По гулянкам походить.
> Запрягай-ка батька лошадь
>
> На пристяжку воронка
> Отведи-ка в Красну Армию
> Последнего сынка.
>
> Recruit, hey, recruit,
> You're not going anywhere!

You'll be walking along the riverbank
All the way to Cherepovets.
Recruits are given the freedom
To drink wine and beer,
And they are given the freedom

To go to parties (*gulianiia*).
Dad, harness up the horse

Hitch up our black horse
Lead to the Red Army
Your last son.

(Folklore Archive of Propp Center, St. Petersburg University, Bel 8–4)

Girls and women, meanwhile, would sing *chastushki* about loved ones going off to war, saying goodbye, and being an orphan (Tsentr russkogo fol'klora 2015). Here, too, the *chastushka* took the place of the ritual of lamenting, which formerly had been performed by the female relatives of the men leaving for the army. On the day of conscription, the whole village would gather in a procession to the place where the conscripts were to meet. *Chastushki* would be sung along the way.

In Soviet Russian villages people celebrated this ritual of seeing off the recruits, en masse, with *chastushki*, roughly up until the end of the 1980s. Since conscription was mandatory, and as long as a significant quantity of young people were living in the village, the large quantity of recruits made this a collective ritual in which the whole village participated.

In Russian weddings, *chastushki* began to take the place of laments and ritual songs starting in the 1920s; they also became an important part of the merrymaking of the wedding (Karpukhin 1998:23). Ivan Karpukhin has distinguished two types of *chastushki* associated with the wedding: "1) *chastushki* genetically and thematically connected with the wedding, which are performed during the wedding along with wedding laments and songs; 2) *chastushki* which arose independently of the wedding. They are sung during the wedding party," underlining the wedding's transformation from a highly structured rite of passage "into a cheerful celebration of the creation of a new family" (Karpukhin 2011:174). The latter type of *chastushki* would tend to have the following themes: romance, humor, and making fun of the members of the wedding party, similar to the *koril'nye pesni* ("roasting" songs) that were formerly part of the wedding ritual.

Уж как нордовски ребята
Храбрецы так храбрецы:
Три килОметра бежали,
Испугалися овцы

The guys from Nordovka
Are the bravest of the brave.

> They ran three kilometers
> They were frightened by a sheep
>
> (Karpukhin 2011:175)

Such songs served to describe the current goings-on at the wedding, to bring the appropriate mood to the participants, to allow those attending the wedding to participate actively, and to poeticize the wedding; but they did not form an integral part of the wedding ritual (Karpukhin 2011). They could be sung at other times, outside of the wedding context, and would not seem out of place.

The first type, *chastushki* that were an integral part of the wedding, included *chastushki* that were used during the *devishnik* (bridesmaids' party) and at other moments before the actual wedding ceremony, to provoke the bride to lament. The following example was recorded among Russians in the Republic of Bashkortostan:

> Не ходите, девки, замуж,
> Замужем печаль, печаль.
> Муж на улицу не пустит.
> Скажет: Зыбочку качай.
>
> Don't get married, girls,
> Marriage is sadness, sadness.
> Your husband won't let you out on the street.
> He'll say: rock the cradle!
>
> (Karpukhin 2006:No. 4577)

Girls and women would often sing a whole series of *chastushki* with this same first line, "Don't get married, girls!" (Ne khodite, devki, zamuzh), at the *devishnik*. Starting in the 1970s, when brides no longer were expected to lament, the *devishnik* was converted into a party where the participants sat at a table laden with food, the Russian *zastol'e*. At such a party, similar *chastushki* continued to be sung by the bride's friends (Burmistrov 2008:153).

The Russian traditional wedding had particular laments for a bride who was an orphan (i.e., had lost either mother or father or both); the bride would visit the grave of the absent parent before her wedding and rhetorically address them, imploring them to come to the wedding. *Chastushki* such as the following took over this function.

> По тебя, родима мама,
> На могилушку пришла.
> Ты проснись, родная мама,
> Во замужыце пошла
>
> To see you, my dear mama,
> I have come to your grave
> Wake up, my dear mama,
> I'm getting married!
>
> (Karpukhin 2011:177)

Using similar language and images, both laments and *chastushki* described the bride's emotions in moving to a new family, where she feared she would be asked to work hard or be mistreated. These were sung a cappella, and the mood was not celebratory but thoughtful and intimate.

Erotic *chastushki* were sung—to accordion accompaniment—by wedding participants on the second and third days of the wedding, after the bride and groom had spent their first nuptial night. At this moment in the wedding, erotic songs were seen as a necessary part of the wedding as they would both celebrate and encourage (in quasi-magical fashion) the sexual goings-on of the newly married couple. The erotic *chastushki* were similar in content to the erotic wedding songs they replaced (Karpukhin 2011:177). Often, the *svat* and *svakha*, the parents of the bride or groom (in-laws to each other), were the first to begin such songs:

> Ай сват, ты мой сват,
> Не бери меня за зад!
> Бери меня за перед—
>
> Лучше горе не берет.
> Ай, сваха моя, сваха,
>
> Бело-розовая рубаха,
> Во субботу мыла пол,
> Не поддернула подол.
>
> Oh, [male] in-law, you my in-law,
> Don't take me from behind!
> Take me from the front
>
> You won't be sorry.
> Oh, my [female] in-law, my in-law,
>
> In the light pink shirt,
> On Saturday when you washed the floor
> You didn't tuck up your skirt.
>
> (Morozov 1999:206)

The erotic *chastushki* sung at weddings could have special content referring specifically to the event occurring:

> Как у Тани под подолом
> Птичка гнездышкио свила.
> А другая прилетела,
> Два яичка принесла
>
> Under Tanya's skirt
> A bird wove a nest

>   Another one flew in
>   And laid two eggs!
>
>   (Morozov 1999:208–209)

In general, during the Soviet period, in Russia, Ukraine, and Belarus, as weddings began to emphasize the *zastol'e* ritual on the day of the registration of the marriage as the main part of the wedding, *chastushki* provided a welcome break for wedding guests. Guests would sit at table making toasts and eating and then would take a break for dancing to accordion music and singing (Burmistrov 2008). Indeed, the same pattern held sway at anniversary parties and milestone birthdays, in villages and small towns as well as in cities.

Memory

Chastushki can serve as an instrument of memory and autobiographical retelling. To this day, village-dwelling men and women of the elder generations often remember series of *chastushki* as a connected text that tell a story of their lives. Each *chastushka* is linked in their memory with an event or several events that happened in the past or with emotions they associate with their past. They may keep their *chastushki* in a notebook or perform them, but usually privately, not for an audience. For example, one informant recounted,

> Nowadays I tell them to myself, I sing chastushki by myself. Oh, [I remember] when I was singing chastushki, and Valya [daughter and her family] came over. I was sitting by the window, singing chastushki. They came over. I said, "Oh, if you'd only come earlier, there would have been such a concert!" And they said, "Who was giving a concert?" "I gave a concert, I was singing chastushki!"
>
>   (Folklore Archive of Propp Center, St. Petersburg University, Vash 8–20)

CONCLUSION

The *chastushka* and similar genres in Russian and East Slavic culture are remarkably versatile: they can equally well express joy, laughter, and celebration but also fear, anger, resentment, and grief. With their short form that can easily be adapted through the manner of performance and by changing words or lines, *chastushki* help people express and channel big and small emotions, whatever those emotions might be. For people who grew up with them, they were an indispensable part of weddings and parties; and every aspect of the event was captured in *chastushki*: tears, fears, raucous laughter, and the feeling of all present being bonded together and equalized.

Chastushki are unique in that they provide a platform for expression not only of individual emotions, situations, and processes but of community values, in particular those of openness and equality. These witty, one-stanza couplets allow for the community to move out of static structure and hierarchy into a situation of flexible equality, carnival, or spectacle. A peasant can choose to express their approval of the president or laugh at the government, a girl can criticize her mother, workers can criticize their bosses, a young man can express his fear of leaving home, an old widow can publicly admit her lack of a sexual partner. The community laughs and accepts the sentiments. Whether or not the point of view is challenged, each singer still has a chance to express their point of view and therefore to exercise power through this speech act.

Notes

1. "*Ulyanovsk NOTs" refers to the Scientific-Educational Center "Traditional Culture and Folklore of the Ulyanovsk Volga Region" [Nauchno-obrazovatel'nyi tsentr Traditsionnaia kul'tura i fol'klor Ul'ianovskogo Povolzh'ia], at Ulyanovsk State Pedagogical University, Ulyanovsk, Russia.
2. Olson's fieldwork took place in Riazan', Vologda, Ulianovsk, Saratov, Voronezh, and Kaluga oblasts during trips in 1995, 1996, 1998–1999, 2004–2005, and 2020; collected materials are in her private archive. Adonyeva's fieldwork took place in Vologda and Arkhangel'sk oblasts yearly between 1983 and 2019. These materials are housed at the Folklore Archive of the Propp Center of St. Petersburg University. The corpus of material includes more than two thousand interviews with men and women born between 1899 and the 1980s.

Works Cited

Adon'eva, Svetlana. 2006. *Derevenskaia chastushka XX veka*. St. Petersburg: St. Petersburg State University.
Alexander, Alex. 1976. "The Russian Chastushka Abroad." *The Journal of American Folklore*, 89/353:335–341.
Andreev, N. P. 1931. "Fol'klor i antireligioznaia rabota." *Voinstvuiushchii ateizm*, 1931/12:3.
Arkhipova, A. S., and S. Iu. Nekliudov. 2010. "Fol'klor i vlast'' v zakrytom obshchestve." *Novoe Literaturnoe Obozrenie*, 101. http://magazines.russ.ru/nlo/2010/101/ar6.html.
Asaf'ev, B. V. 1987. *O narodnoi muzyke*, eds. I. I. Zemtsovskii and A. B. Kunanbaeva. Leningrad: Muzyka.
Bakhtin, Mikhail. 1984. *Rabelais and His World*, trans. Helene Iswolsky. Bloomington: Indiana University Press.
Bakhtin, V. S. 1966. *Chastushka*, 2nd ed. Biblioteka poeta, bol'shaia seria. Moscow-Leningrad: Sovetskii pisatel'.
Bialosinskaia, N. S. 1966. "Fol'klor i agitbrigada." In *Sovremennyi russkii fol'klor*, ed. E. V. Pomerantseva, 225–246. Moscow: Nauka.
Burmistrov, N. S. 2008. "Chastushka v svadeb'nom zastol'e." In *Traditsionnoe russkoe zastol'e. Sbornik statei*, eds. A. V. Kostina and L. F. Mironikhina, 148–172. Moscow: Gosudarstvennyi respublikanskii tsentr russkogo fol'klora.

Davies, Sarah. 1998. "The Crime of 'Anti-Soviet Agitation' in the Soviet Union in the 1930's." *Cahiers du Monde Russe: Russie, Empire Russe, Union Soviétique, États Indépendants*, 39/1–2:149–167.

Edelman, O. V., ed. 1999. "Nadzornye proizvodstva prokuratury 58.10." In *Nadzornye proizvodstva prokuratury SSSR po delam ob antisovetskoi agitatsii i propaganda. Mart 1953–1991*: Annotirovannyi catalog. Moscow.

Eleonskaia, E. N. 1914. *Sbornik velikorusskikh chastushek*. Moscow: Komissia po narodnoi slovesnosti pri etnograficheskom otdelenii.

Fedun, Iryna. 2005. "The Folkdances of the Western Polissia Region of Ukraine: Traditions and Innovations." *Traditiones*, 34/1:155–164. https://ojs.zrc-sazu.si/traditiones/article/view/1207.

Fialkova, Larisa. 2001. "Chernobyl's Folklore: Vernacular Commentary on Nuclear Disaster." *Journal of Folklore Research*, 38/3:181–204.

Fiodaraŭ, L. M. 1989. "Muzychnaia chastka." In *Prypeŭki*, ed. Ivan Tsishchanka, 246–249. Minsk: Navuka i tėkhnika.

Frank, Stephen. 1992. "'Simple Folk, Savage Customs?' Youth, Sociability, and the Dynamics of Culture in Rural Russia, 1856–1914." *Journal of Social History*, 25/4:711–736.

Gippius, E. V. 2000. "Intonatsionnye elementy russkoi chastushki." In *Garmonika: Istoriia, teoriia, praktika*, ed. A. N. Sokolova, 27–76. Maikop: AGU.

Gnedin, E. 1935. "Boris Efimov." In *Boris Efimov, Politicheskie karikatury, 1924–1934*. Moscow: Sovetskii pisatel'.

Gorelov, A. A., and Z. I. Vlasova. 1965. *Chastushki v zapisiakh sovetskogo vremeni*. Moscow: Nauka.

Health and Beauty. 2013. "Entsiklopediia tantsa: Kolomyika." http://hnb.com.ua/articles/s-sport-entsiklopediya_tantsa_kolomiyka-2637.

Huizinga, Johan. 1971. *Homo Ludens: A Study of the Play-Element in Culture*. Boston: Beacon Press.

Husband, William B. 2004. "Mythical Communities and the New Soviet Woman: Bolshevik Antireligious Chastushki, 1917–32." *Russian Review*, 63/1:89–106.

Ivanyts'kyi, A. 2004. *Ukraïns'kyĭ muzychnyĭ fol'klor: Pidruchnyk dlia VNZ*. Vinnytsia: Nova Kniga.

Karpukhin, Ivan E. 1998. "Svad'ba russkikh Bashkortostana kak fol'klorno-igrovoi kompleks (Voprosy poetiki i mezhetnicheskikh vzaimootnoshenii)." PhD dissertation, Moskovskii gosudarstvennyi otkrytyi pedagogicheskii universitet, Moscow.

Karpukhin, Ivan E. 2006. *Chastushka (ustami russkikh)*. Ufa: Kitap.

Karpukhin, Ivan E. 2011. "Chastushka na russkoi svad'be i svad'ba v chastushkakh." In *Ot kongressa k kongressu. Materialy Vtorogo Vserossiiskogo kongressa fol'kloristov*, eds. V. E. Dobrovol'skaia, A. B. Ippolitova, and A. S. Kargin, 2:172–186. Moscow: Gosudarstvennyi respublikanskii tsentr russkogo fol'klora.

Chastushki. 2003. "Korobeiniki." http://cqham.qrz.ru/jumor/jumor25.shtml.

Kuleva, Sofiia. 2008. "Chastushki v kul'turnykh traditsiiakh Belozer'ia. Opyt kompleksnogo issledovaniia." PhD dissertation, St. Petersburg State Conservatory, St. Petersburg.

Lazutin, Sergei. 1960. *Russkaia chastushka. Voprosy proizkhozhdeniia i formirovaniia zhanra*. Voronezh: Izdatel'stvo Voronezhskogo universiteta.

Lazutin, Sergei. 1981. *Poetika russkogo fol'klora: Uchebnoe posobie dlia filologicheskikh fakultetov universitetov*. Moscow: Vysshaia shkola.

Levin, L. I. 2004. "Narodnye pesni na estrade." In *Estrada Rossii, XX vek: Entsiklopediia*, ed. Elizaveta D. Uvarova, 432–439. Moscow: Olma-Press.

Liapunov, S. M., and F. M. Istomin. 1979. "Otchet ob ekspeditsii dlia sobiraniia russkikh narodnykh pesen s napevami v 1893 godu." In *Russkaia mysl' o muzykal'nom fol'klore. Materialy i dokumenty*, ed. P. A. Vul'fius, 230–233. Moscow: Muzyka.

Matlin, Mikhail. 2019. *Smekh v russkoi narodnoi svad'be XIX-nachala XXI vv.: Tipologicheskii i funktsional'nyi aspekty.* Doctoral dissertation, Ulyanovskii gosudarstvennyi pedagogicheskii universitet, Ulyanovsk.

Meshkova, O. V. 2001. "O klassifikatsii chastushek." *Vestnik Cheliabinskogo gosudarstvennogo universiteta*, 2/1:102–110. https://cyberleninka.ru/article/n/o-klassifikatsii-chastushek.

Morozov, Igor' A. 1999. "Svadebnyi obriad." In *Fol'klor Sudogodskogo kraiia*, 183–209. Moscow: Gosudarstvennyi respublikanskii tsentr russkogo fol'klora.

Norris, Stephen. 2009, 15–17 May. "'Laughter Is a Sharp Weapon and a Powerful Medicine': Boris Efimov and Soviet Visual Humor." Presented at the Totalitarian Laughter Conference, Princeton University, Princeton, NJ, USA.

Novak, V. S. 1999. *Paleskiia chastushki.* Mazyr: Bely viecier.

Ostromoukhova, Bella. 2009, 15–17 May. "Production of Comic Theater by Soviet Students, 1953–1970." Presented at the Totalitarian Laughter Conference, Princeton University, Princeton, NJ, USA.

Paxson, Margaret. 2005. *Solovyovo: The Story of Memory in a Russian Village.* Bloomington: Indiana University Press.

Plutser-Sarno, Aleksei. 2000. "Review of 'Iz sobraniia A. D. Volkova. v 2 T. T. 1: Eroticheskie chastushki; T. 2: Politicheskie chastushki. M: Ladomir, 1999.'" *Novaia russkaia kniga*, no. 5. http://old.guelman.ru/slava/nrk/nrk5/2.html.

Polferov, Ia. I. 1931. "Kolomyiki." In *Literaturnaia entsiklopediia: V 11 tomakh*, 5:386–387. Moscow.

Semianinov, Iaroslav V. 2016. *Tambovskie chastushki: Istoriia, kommunikativnye formy, zhanrovo-stilevaia klassifikatsiia.* PhD dissertation, Saratovskaia gosudarstvennaia konservatoriia imeni L. V. Sobinova, Saratov.

Sen'ko, H. 1953. *Narodni pripovidky-chastivky pro natsional'no-vizvol'nu borot'bu.* Buenos Aires: Peremoga.

Shumada, Nataliia. 1998. *Zakuvala zozulen'ka. Antolohiia ukraïns'koï narodnoï poetychnoï tvorchosti.* Kiev: Veselka.

Simakov, V. I. 1913. *Sbornik derevenskikh chastushek Arkhangel'skoi, Vologodskoi, Viatskoi, Olonetskoi, Permskoi, Kostromskoi, Iaroslavskoi, Tverskoi, Pskovskoi, Novgorodskoi, Peterburgskoi gubernii.* Yaroslavl': Tip. Nekrasova.

Sokolov, Iu. M. 1941. *Russkii fol'klor.* Moscow: Gosudarstvennoe uchebno pedagogicheskoe izdatel'stvo.

Tirado, Isabel A. 1993. "The Village Voice: Women's Views of Themselves and Their World in Russian Chastushki of the 1920's." *The Carl Beck Papers in Russian and East European Studies*, 1008:1–70.

Tsentr russkogo fol'klora. 2015. "Traditsii. Prichitaniia. Rekrutskii obriad v traditsii Srednei Sukhony (Vologodskaia oblast)." *Culture.ru*. https://www.culture.ru/objects/2108/rekruts kii-obryad-v-tradicii-srednei-sukhony-vologodskaya-oblast.

Tsishchanka, Ivan. 1971. *Belaruskaia chastushka: Pytanni henezisu zhanru.* Minsk: Vydavienctva nabuka i technika.

Uspenskii, Boris. 1994. "'Zavetnye skazki' A. N. Afanas'eva." In *Izbrannye trudy*, eds. E. Babaeva and O. Makhovaia, 2:129–150. Moscow: Gnosis. http://www.philology.ru/literature2/uspen sky-94.htm.

Vlasova, Z. I. 1971. "Chastushka i pesnia: (K voprosu o skhodstve i razlichii)." In *Russkii fol'klor [materialy i issledovaniia]*, 12 (*Iz istorii russkoi narodnoi poezii*):102–122. Leningrad.

Volkov, A. D. 1999. *Politicheskie chastushki*, ed A. V. Kulagina. Moscow: Ladomir (Zavetnye chastushki iz sobraniia A. D. Volkova).

Zachyniaev, A. 1907. *K voprosu o kolomyĭkakh. Spravochnyk kollektsyonera*. St. Petersburg: Tipografiia Imperaterskoi Akademii nauk.

Zelenin, D. K. 1903. *Pesni derevenskoi molodezhi*. Viatka: Izdatel'stvo Viatskogo gubernskogo statisticheskogo komiteta.

CHAPTER 39

WISE AND HUMOROUS WORDS

Hungarian Proverbs, Riddles, and Jokes

ANNA T. LITOVKINA, KATALIN VARGHA,
PÉTER BARTA, AND HRISZTALINA
HRISZTOVA-GOTTHARDT

THE three genres discussed in this chapter have certain features in common. They all are short traditional verbal forms used in everyday communication and belong to oral tradition. Moreover, to varying degrees depending on each genre, literacy and/or urban culture as well as historical period and territory also have had a decisive influence on their evolution and use. As to their origins, they were spoken: they were initially coined by an individual and then gradually spread among the speech community to become anonymous texts, both oral and written, not associated with a particular "author." These short and concise texts contain bits of folk wisdom and may be meant to be humorous and entertaining (jokes, riddles, and anti-proverbs) or not (proverbs).

Proverbs, riddles, and jokes exhibit, however, specific genre characteristics and must therefore be discussed in more depth individually. Accordingly, this chapter is organized into three sections. The first treats Hungarian proverbs. It addresses questions about the nature and origin of proverbs and presents a short review of selected dictionaries of proverbs and proverbial sayings. Then it discusses the main research findings regarding Hungarian proverbs. Lastly, the nature, structural features, and special use of proverb alterations, so-called anti-proverbs, are briefly outlined. The second section discusses Hungarian riddles. After providing an overview of the collection and study of riddles, it treats the subgenres and poetic features of riddles as well as the function and use of the genre in traditional and contemporary Hungarian culture. The third section considers jokes and joking in Hungarian folklore, including joke research, urban and rural layers of jokes, the phenomenon called "the Budapest joke," and joke tales and folk humor. Lastly, contemporary forms of jokes and joking on the internet are overviewed.

Proverbs (*Közmondások*)

Defining what a proverb is proves to be a very difficult task. Archer Taylor, the author of the classic study *The Proverb* (1931), claimed that an all-inclusive, final definition of the genre is an impossibility. Regardless of Taylor's statement, there are literally hundreds of attempts at defining proverbs of various lengths.[1] One of the most precise and comprehensive proverb definitions is provided by Wolfgang Mieder, who states that,

> Proverbs [are] concise traditional statements of apparent truth with currency among the folk. More elaborately stated, proverbs are short, generally known sentences of the folk that contain wisdom, truths, morals, and traditional views in a metaphorical, fixed, and memorizable form and that are handed down from generation to generation. (2004:4)

The Origin of Hungarian Proverbs

If one were to compile a list of genuinely Hungarian proverbs, one would be facing a daunting challenge. Let us look at the following proverbs:

A nép szava Isten szava.
The voice of the people (is) the voice of God.

Nem mind arany, ami fénylik.
All that glitters is not gold.

Aki másnak vermet ás, maga esik bele.
He who digs a pit for others falls into it himself.[2]

The above proverbs are, in fact, very frequently used in Hungary but are not of Hungarian origin. Indeed, similar to Russian, English, French, German, and many other European proverbs, quite a large number of Hungarian proverbs are of foreign origin. But through the centuries or—in the case of very new proverbs—mere decades, they have become part of the Hungarian heritage, and more often than not, an average speaker of Hungarian might not be able to distinguish proverbs of Hungarian origin from those of non-Hungarian origin.

Proverbs coined outside of Hungary can be grouped into the following categories:

1. from Greek–Latin antiquity, as well as from medieval Latin
2. from the Bible
3. calques from other languages (e.g., English, French, German, Russian)
4. other miscellaneous sources

As Mieder points out, "[a] large number of proverbs from various ancient languages and cultures entered the Latin language and eventually reached many of the vernacular languages when medieval Latin proverbs were being translated" (1993:12). Erasmus of Rotterdam, among others, contributed significantly to spreading this classical wisdom throughout Europe. His *Adagia* (1500, 1508, 1536), containing thousands of explanatory notes and essays on classical proverbs and proverbial expressions, was widely read and translated into various European languages (see Mieder 2004:10–11). In Hungary, the first separate Latin–Greek–Hungarian collection was published in 1598, consciously following the Erasmusian tradition (Baranyai Decsi Csimor 1598, see also Barna, Stemler, and Voigt 2004) (Fig. 39.1). A layer of Hungarian proverbs coincides with proverbs from Greek–Latin antiquity, as well as from medieval Latin (Paczolay 2023). Two examples of Hungarian proverbs with their Latin sources and English equivalents include *Nem mind arany, ami fénylik* (Lat., *Non omne quod nitet, aurum est*; Eng., All that glitters is not gold), for which Gyula Paczolay has found equivalents in forty-seven European

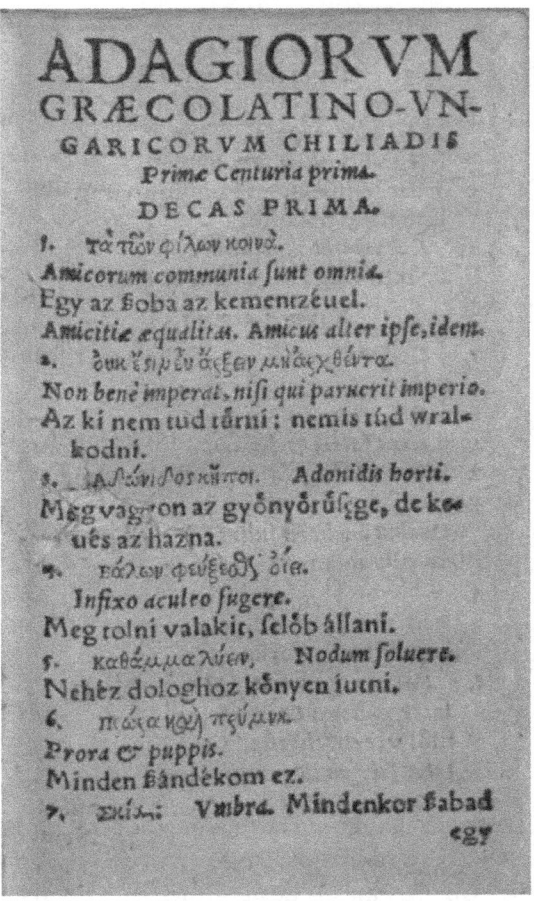

FIG. 39.1. First page of Latin–Greek–Hungarian proverb collection *Adagiorum Graeco–Latino–Ungaricorum Chiliades Quinque*, by János Baranyai Decsi, 1598.

(© National Széchényi Library, Budapest.)

languages (1997:125-129). *Kéz kezet mos* is also of Latin origin (Lat., *Manus manum lavat*; Eng., One hand washes the other) and is found in forty-six other European languages (Paczolay 1997:174-178). A few more Hungarian proverbs of Latin origin include the following:[3]

A baj nem jár egyedül. (Lat., *Nulla calamitas sola.*)
Misfortunes never come alone.

A cél szentesíti az eszközt. (Lat., *Cum finis est licitus, etiam media sunt licita*)
The end justifies the means.

A pénznek nincs szaga. (Lat., *Pecunia non olet*)
Money has no smell.

The Bible, more than any other source, has contributed to the treasury of Hungarian proverbs and sayings, for example:[4]

Nemcsak kenyérrel él az ember.
Man does not live by bread alone (Deuteronomy 8:3; Matthew 4:1-4; Luke 4:4).

Senki sem lehet próféta a saját hazájában.
A prophet is without honor in his own country (Luke 4:24; Matthew 13:57; Mark 6:4; John 4:44).

Szeresd felebarátodat, mint magadat.
Love your neighbor as yourself (Leviticus 19:18; Matthew 19:19; Mark 12:31; Romans 13:9; Galatians 5:14; James 2:8).

The corpus of Hungarian proverbs has also been enriched by English—and, during the last decades, American—proverbs:[5]

A házasságok az égben köttetnek.
Marriages are made in heaven.

A kutya az ember legjobb barátja.
A dog is a man's best friend.

A puding próbája az evés.
The proof of the pudding is in the eating.

Like many other languages, Hungarian has also developed its own proverbs. The richness of this particular proverb stock is demonstrated by a few examples. *Meghalt Mátyás király, oda az igazság* (King Mathias is dead; justice is dead) refers to King Matthias (1443-1490), who is remembered as the most just Hungarian king, emphasizing that with the death of Matthias, justice also died. Literary quotations can also become proverbs (T. Litovkina and Mieder 2005:19-20). For example, the well-known proverb

Aki a virágot szereti, rossz ember nem lehet (He who loves flowers can't be a bad man) originated with the poem "Az árva lyány" ("The Orphan Girl") by Sándor Petőfi (1823–1849), a key figure of the Hungarian Revolution of 1848 and Hungary's national poet:

> Szeresd a virágot
> És ne féltsd szívedet,
> Mert, ki ezt szereti,
> Rossz ember nem lehet.
>
> Love flowers,
> And fear not your heart,
> For he who loves them (flowers)
> Can't be a bad man

This proverb, however, is no longer associated by most Hungarians with Petőfi and his poem.

Dictionaries of Hungarian Proverbs

Proverbs and proverbial sayings from different cultures and languages have been collected for centuries. In fact, there exists an entire field of study called "paremiography" that relates to the listing of proverbs and proverbial sayings in collections and dictionaries. Collecting and publishing dictionaries of proverbs began in Hungary more than four hundred years ago. The first "swallow to make the summer" of Hungarian paremiography was a book authored by János Baranyai Decsi Csimor, entitled *Adagiorum Graeco-Latino-Ungaricorum Chiliades Quinque* (1598), which included about five thousand Latin, Greek, and Hungarian proverbs and proverbial sayings. Since the end of the sixteenth century numerous dictionaries of proverbs and sayings have been published in Hungary.[6] Proverbs have often been included in nineteenth- and twentieth-century collections of Hungarian folk poetry, including a number of notable anthologies and local monographs.[7] For instance, Károly Lábadi (1986) collected proverbs and their variants in Hungarian villages in the area between the Drava and Danube Rivers in present-day Croatia (former Yugoslavia). In his proverb dictionary, Zoltán Ujváry (2001) listed about three thousand proverbial items that he collected in a region called Gömör, located on both sides of today's Slovak–Hungarian border. The collections compiled by Gabriella Vöő (1989, 1999) contain Hungarian proverbs registered in the Folklore Archives of the Romanian Academy in Cluj-Napoca (Romania). Two collections of special interest focus on the paremic knowledge and competence of one informant each, the first being a small landholder from Gömör County (Ujváry 1996) and the second a "common Székely peasant" from Transylvania (Tánczos 2008:251–350).

Other influential Hungarian proverb scholars include Gyula Paczolay, who deals primarily with comparative paremiography. In his collection from 1997 he lists 106 of the "most common European proverbs" which can be found also in the Hungarian language. For many of these proverbs, Paczolay cites equivalents in fifty-five different languages. Some of these common European proverbs are, for example:

Amelyik kutya ugat, nem harap.
A barking dog never bites.

Ajándék lónak ne nézd a fogát.
Don't look a gift horse in the mouth.

Jobb későn, mint soha.
Better late than never.

In 2003, two extensive dictionaries of Hungarian proverbs, proverbial sayings, and idioms were published, both of which mark a novelty in the field of Hungarian paremiography. Vilmos Bárdosi's dictionary (2003) is the first collection of Hungarian idioms, clichés, and proverbs containing an index of thematic categories. Tamás Forgács's volume (2003), on the other hand, is the first collection of Hungarian idioms, sayings, and proverbs based on examples drawn primarily from modern newspapers and magazines, thus providing authentic contexts in order to illustrate the use of each entry.

In 2005, another major paremiographic work followed. In her dictionary of Hungarian proverbs, Anna T. Litovkina includes the meaning and stylistic register of the entries and adds examples of their use in contemporary press and literature. Synonymous and antonymous texts, as well as modifications of traditional proverbs (so-called anti-proverbs) are also listed. The most recent dictionary of Hungarian sayings and proverbs was published by folklorist Ágnes Szemerkényi in 2009 and presents the stock of "classical Hungarian proverbs" from the sixteenth until the twentieth century.

Researching Hungarian Proverbs

The study of proverbs in all their multifaceted aspects such as their origin, structure, meaning, style, pragmatic function, familiarity, frequency of use, etc. is called "paremiology." Hungarian proverbs have been a subject of extensive paremiological research in the past decades. A few of the most significant of these findings include[8] research conducted by Vilmos Voigt and Ágnes Szemerkényi who, in the 1970s, concentrated on folkloristic and semiotic approaches to proverbs and their variants (Voigt 1971; Szemerkényi and Voigt 1972). Szemerkényi went on to treat the everyday use of Hungarian proverbs and sayings, along with their role in social interaction. Besides the primary use of proverbs (i.e., in folklore), she explored their use and function in Hungarian fiction, press, advertisements, etc. (see Szemerkényi 1994).

In 1991–1993, T. Litovkina conducted a paremiological experiment in the form of a sociolinguistic survey and established the "paremiological minimum" of Hungarian (Tóthné Litovkina 1996; T. Litovkina and Mieder 2005:23–29). Based on the answers from the survey, she completed a list of 158 Hungarian proverbs familiar to at least 90 percent of the participants. The single proverb familiar to each participant of the survey was *Aki másnak vermet ás, maga esik bele* (He who digs a pit for others falls into it himself.) Further Hungarian proverbs that have proven to be very well known include the following:

Addig jár a korsó a kútra, míg el nem törik.
The pitcher will keep going to the well until it breaks.

Addig nyújtózkodj, ameddig a takaród ér.
Stretch yourself as far as your blanket reaches.

Ahány ház, annyi szokás.
So many houses, so many customs.

As Mieder states, "proverbs continue to be effective verbal devices and culturally literate persons, both native and foreign, must have a certain paremiological minimum at their disposal in order to participate in meaningful oral and written communication" (1993:53). Establishing a Hungarian paremiological minimum is, therefore, an important achievement in the field of Hungarian paremiology, folkloristics, and linguistics. The results have been used successfully in further ethnolinguistic and sociolinguistic research aimed at exploring popular views of proverbs and anti-proverbs in contemporary Hungarian society and learning how age, gender, and educational background as well as different mechanisms of proverb alteration influence the appreciation of humor in anti-proverbs (Vargha and T. Litovkina 2007; T. Litovkina, Vargha, and Boronkai 2012), discussed next.

Anti-Proverbs

Proverbs have never been considered sacrosanct. On the contrary, they have frequently been twisted and/or used as satirical, ironic, or humorous comments on a given situation. Mieder coined the term *Antisprichwort* ("anti-proverb") for such deliberate proverb innovations, also known as alterations, mutations, parodies, transformations, variations, wisecracks, or fractured proverbs (Röhrich and Mieder 1977; Mieder 1982). His term has been widely accepted by proverb scholars all over the world as a general label for such innovative alterations of and reactions to traditional proverbs. Some anti-proverbs question the truth of a proverb through employing antonyms, transforming the proverb into its opposite, or posing a naive question, for example, *Éhezés közben is megjön az étvágy* (Appetite comes even with starving) as a modification of the traditional text {*Evés közben jön meg az étvágy* (Appetite comes with eating)}.[9] The vast majority of anti-proverbs, however, place the proverbial wisdom only partially into question, primarily by relating it to a particular context or thought in which the traditional wording does not fit, for example, *Madarat tolláról, embert hitelkártyájáról* (A bird is recognized by its feather, a man by his credit card) as an alteration of the traditional Hungarian proverb {*Madarat tolláról, embert barátjáról* (A bird is recognized by its feather, a man by his friend; ~A man is known by the company he keeps)}.[10]

The anti-proverb is not a new genre. Proverb alterations flourished in classical times and in all subsequent eras. Nowadays, however, the genre of transformed proverb is becoming more and more popular, especially due to mass media and the internet. Newspaper and magazine headlines, advertising slogans, cartoons, and caricatures, etc., are some of the major sources for anti-proverbs. In addition, there are numerous lists of playful (often humorous) modifications of traditional proverbs from different languages circulating on the internet and, thus, helping to distribute these new creations to a broad audience. In response to this development, in 2005, the first two collections of Hungarian anti-proverbs were published (T. Litovkina and Vargha 2005a, 2005b). The two volumes contain about 1,500 and over 1,700 proverb parodies, respectively.

Based on T. Litovkina and Vargha's corpus of over seven thousand Hungarian anti-proverbs including examples from oral, written, and internet sources, the most frequently transformed Hungarian proverb is *Addig jár a korsó a kútra, (a)míg el nem törik* (The pitcher will keep going to the well until it breaks; ~The pitcher will go to the well once too often) with all together 178 modifications located, for example,

> *Addig jár a korsó a kútra, (a)míg meg nem telik.*
> The pitcher will keep going to the well until it fills up.
>
> *Addig jár a korsó a kútra, (a)míg szomjas.*
> The pitcher will keep going to the well until it is thirsty.
>
> *Addig jár a korsó a kútra, (a)míg be nem vezetik a vizet.*
> The pitcher will keep going to the well until water is brought into the house.

Among the different types of transformation and humor devices in Hungarian anti-proverbs, one of the most popular is punning (see Vargha and T. Litovkina 2013), for example, puns playing upon personal names. For instance, a number of modifications of the proverb *Nem mind arany, ami fénylik* (All that glitters is not gold) play upon the words *arany* ("gold") and *János Arany* (famous Hungarian poet, 1817–1882, whose surname can be translated into English as "Gold"):

> *Nem mind arany, aki János.*
> All that is János is not gold.
>
> *Nem mind arany, aki költő.*
> All that is a poet is not gold.

There are a number of other techniques of variation and humor in anti-proverbs (which are by no means mutually exclusive):[11]

1. The meaning of a metaphorical proverb is narrowed by putting it in a context in which it is to be interpreted literally: *A falnak is füle van, csak ritkán mossa* (The walls have ears, but they seldom wash them), interpreting literally the traditional proverb *A falnak is füle van* (The walls have ears).

2. The mixing of two (or more) proverbs: *Ki korán kel, ne nézd a fogát* (Don't look in the mouth of one who gets up early) as a contamination of the original proverbs *Ki korán kel, aranyat lel* (He who gets up early finds gold; ~The early bird catches the worm) and *Ajándék lónak ne nézd a fogát* (Don't look a gift horse in the mouth).
3. Applying so-called proverb formulas, that is, particular syntactic structures which are characteristic for proverbs, for example, *Aki birka, marha* (He who is a sheep is an ox/ass), an anti-proverb deploying the proverb formula *Aki X, az Y* (He who X Y).

With the evolution of information technologies and the enormous development of computer-mediated communication we are observing the rapid emergence of the significance of digital visual humor within the domain of anti-proverbs as well. As the findings of research conducted by Hrisztova-Gotthardt et al. (2020) show, traditional proverbs and proverb alterations are often accompanied by images. In the case of anti-proverbs the humorous effect is, indeed, the result of the interplay between the image and the text. The visual element actually helps the (entertaining) message to reach its target population more effectively. The meme shown in Fig. 39.2 is only one of numerous

FIG. 39.2. Internet meme based on the combination of the anti-proverb *Aki másnak vermet ás, az dögöljön meg!* ("He who digs a pit for others should drop dead!") and the globally known meme template of the Grumpy Cat character.

examples of digital visual humor employing proverbs. It is based on the combination of the anti-proverb *Aki másnak vermet ás, az dögöljön meg!* (He who digs a pit for others should drop dead!) and the globally known meme template of the Grumpy Cat character.[12]

Riddles (*Találósok*)

A riddle is a text composed of two parts: a question (or image) and an answer connected by a cognitive link, based on a metaphor, lexical or grammatical ambiguity, or some other "block element." Riddling is a part of the oral and/or literary traditions of all cultures and can be traced back to the ancient civilizations of India and Greece.

Collection and Study of Riddles

The earliest Hungarian records of riddles can be found in two codices and an arithmetic book published in the early sixteenth century. The first riddle book in Hungarian, the *Mesés könyvecske*[13] (*A Small Book of Riddles*, 1629) included three hundred riddles in thirteen conceptual groups, translated from the 1505 edition of the German *Strassburger Rätselbuch* (Voigt 2010:498) (Fig. 39.3).

Throughout the next centuries, riddles could be found in various handwritten and printed sources. Handwritten collections of riddles recorded by students and the clergy are known from the end of the seventeenth century. From the late eighteenth century, riddles were frequently printed on the last pages of chapbooks and almanacs to entertain and educate as well as to fill in the blank spaces. At the same time, following western European examples, periodicals with literary or miscellaneous content, for example, *Mindenes Gyűjtemény* (1789–1792), *Hasznos Mulatságok* (1817–1842), *Regélő* (1838–1842), and *Hölgyfutár* (1850–1862), also published a vast number of riddle texts, mostly sent in by the readers themselves. These sources deserve attention because popular literature and especially "cheap print could have played a role in transmitting themes and motifs between orality and literacy, as well as between different social groups" (Csörsz and Mikos 2019:278).

The scholarly collection of folk riddles in Hungary started in the mid-nineteenth century, motivated by linguistic as well as folkloristic interest, as folklore texts; and especially short forms of folklore, it was thought, preserved the true essence of the Hungarian language. Thus, a considerable number of Hungarian folk riddles were first published in linguistic journals, such as *Magyar Nyelvészet* and *Magyar Nyelvőr*, throughout the second half of the nineteenth century. Riddles were also published in collections of Hungarian folk poetry. The first sizable local corpus, 578 texts from Nagyszalonta,[14] accompanied by comparative notes, was published by Zsigmond Szendrey (1924:133–163, 322–334). He was also the first scholar to attempt to develop a classification of

FIG. 39.3. Cover of *Mesés könyvecske* (*A Small Book of Riddles*), 1629, the first collection of riddles published in Hungarian.

(© Library and Information Centre of the Hungarian Academy of Sciences, Budapest.)

Hungarian riddles, distinguishing two main categories: *találós mesék* (riddling tales) and *találós kérdések* (riddling questions).

After sporadic publications, the collection and analysis of Hungarian riddles gained momentum in the 1970s. Voigt (1993) attempted to record the complete set of riddles known in Mezőcsát, a small town in northwestern Hungary. Separate scholarly volumes of Hungarian riddles were published from different parts of the Hungarian-language area, mostly outside the current borders (Lábadi 1982; Ráduly 1990). János Ráduly (1990:45–58) also studied the sociological aspects of riddling during his fieldwork in Kibéd.[15] The first comprehensive anthology of Hungarian riddles was published in 2010, including all folklore texts that appeared in print in scholarly publications between 1856 and 1924 (Vargha 2010), a total of 3,100 texts. A more complete corpus of Hungarian riddles is underway, and a database that currently contains approximately 10,000 texts is due to be launched in 2026.

Subgenres of Hungarian Folk Riddles

The broad category of riddles and puzzles (Hung. *rejtvény*) consists of miscellaneous texts of both literary and folk riddles. Riddles in a narrower sense (Hung. *találós*) mean only texts from oral tradition, but this category is by no means homogenous. Within this frame, texts share the common features of a question-and-answer format and the exploitation of conceptual or linguistic ambiguity, but several groups of texts can be distinguished based on differences in form and content. This overview follows the basic categories commonly used in international riddle scholarship. Riddles in the strict sense, often referred to as *true riddles* (cf. Petsch 1899; Taylor 1943), form the core of the riddle tradition. These are descriptive, often metaphorical texts that "compare an object to an entirely different object" (Taylor 1943:129) and include both revealing and misleading elements. Objects, characters, and topics are drawn from an environment familiar to both the riddler and the riddlee. But next to the traditional rural lifestyle, new cultural elements introduced to folk practice also appear in riddle texts in short order (e.g., *Uton megy nincs lába, tűz ég a gyomrába? Gőzös.* [1857] [It follows a road, it has no legs, a fire is burning in its stomach? Steam engine.]).

Various linguistic and structural features ensure that a text is distinguished from ordinary questions and recognized as a riddle. First, specific introductory and/or concluding frame elements can be used "in which the respondent is urged to solve the image presented before him" (Kaivola-Bregenhøj 1977:65). The common introductory elements are quite similar in different languages, for example, *Riddle me, riddle me, ree*; *Devine, devine, devinaille* (French); *Adivina, adivina, adivinanza* (Spanish) (Taylor 1943:130; cf. Petsch 1899:49–65). Comparable opening formulas are known in Hungarian riddle tradition but are not commonly used. *Mese mese (mi az?)* (Riddle riddle [what is it?]) occurs regularly in printed sources of riddles before 1850, while the form *Csümő csümő (mi az)?*[16] can be found in archaic texts. In twentieth-century texts, more often than not simply the question *Mi az?* (What is it?) is added to the end or occasionally the beginning of the riddle (e.g., *Nappal tele, éjjel üres. Mi az?* [Full during the day, empty at night. What is it?]). Closing formulas which usually refer to a reward for those who can guess the correct answer or a complete frame with both an opening and a closing element appear only in texts with a literary origin.

Traditional riddles are also often recognizable as fixed-phrase expressions involving formulaic or archaic language. In some languages this involves using a special meter (such as the Kalevala meter in Finnish and Estonian riddles). Hungarian riddles do not use a special meter, but certain poetic features distinguish them from everyday speech. Simple alliteration, for instance, is frequently used in riddles as well as in proverbs and other short forms (Voigt 2011:192), for example, *Hasa hajó, lába lapát, torka trombita.*

Lud. (Its belly is a boat, its foot is a shovel, its throat is a trumpet. Goose.). Other forms of repetition, including parallelism, are also used, often combined with alliteration (*Mihelyt meglesz, mindjárt megmar, Mihelyt megmar, mindjárt meghal. Tűzszikra.* [As soon as it is born, it bites you; As soon as it bites you, it breathes its last. Spark]). The use of onomatopoeic expressions is also common (*Kertben kátyó, házon mátyó, szegen szittyom? Káposzta, macska, szita.* ["Cabbiration" in the garden, "catiration" on the house, "sietion" on the nail? Cabbage, cat, sieve.]). End-rhyme, however, is not typical in Hungarian folk riddles (as opposed to literary ones).

Certain riddling forms are considered incomplete, for they do not provide sufficient information for the riddle to be solved. Many of these are from written sources and have made their way to folk tradition through popular literature (chapbooks, small printed documents, and readers). The largest group among them are *joking questions*, which are direct "wh" questions that shift the frame of reference by punning. The following example is built on the polysemy of the word 'fél' (half/afraid): *Mikor fél a nyúl? Mikor kettőbe vágják* (Ambiguous: 1/When is the rabbit only a half? 2/When is the rabbit afraid? When it is cut in two.). *Wisdom questions* require special knowledge. In Hungarian, they pertain mostly to biblical lore. Some of these are simple questions (*Ki született anya nélkül? Ádám.* [Who was born without a mother? Adam.]), but most depend on a twisted, unexpected wording (*A temető rengett, a koporsó sétált, a halott sírdogált. Jónás a cethalban.* [The cemetery rocked, the coffin walked, the dead man wept. Jonah in the fish.]). *Parody riddles* use and frustrate conventional riddle patterns, with the intention to confuse the riddlee. The most typical examples are texts that have to be understood literally instead of the expected enigmatic interpretation (e.g., *Szarka repül a Tiszán, szalonna csüng az állán, hordó bor az oldalán, ajtó forog a sarkán, kis kutya ül a farkán. Mi az? Ki van mondva.* [A magpie flies over the Tisza (River), bacon dangles from its chin, a barrel of wine on its side, a door swivels around its corners, a little dog is sitting on its tail. What is it? It has been said.]). *Neck-riddles* and *riddle tales* are classified sometimes as tales, sometimes as riddles, depending on the level of the formulation. In texts conveyed as riddles, the puzzle to be solved is presented as a brief story, often in verse; and the solution is its interpretation.

Function and Use of Hungarian Riddles

In Hungarian folk tradition, riddles were told mostly as a form of entertainment and pastime, especially connected to social gatherings and collective activities (e.g., spinning, defeathering, corn husking, and goose grazing). They also played an important part in rites of passage such as courtship, weddings, and wakes (Ráduly 1990:38–45). In the second half of the twentieth century, the disintegration of the traditional rural lifestyle brought significant changes to the riddle genre. Traditional riddles have reached the state of static folklore or have become children's lore. Joking questions and parodistic forms are still popular, especially among the youth. At the same time, their function has changed as they are dialogic only in form. They are not expected to be solved but are presented as a part of humorous discourse mostly in the generic frame of jokes, with the answer functioning as the punchline (Vargha 2013).

Jokes (*Viccek*)

The joke (Hung. *vicc*) "denotes a usually short narrative ending in a humorous punch line" (Attardo 2014:417). A category of jokes is plotless: a pun achieves a humorous effect by using language humor. More generally jokes can also be understood as "an instance of humor" (Attardo 2014:417).

Joke Research in Hungarian Folkloristics

In Hungary, research on jokes focuses on joke as a verbal genre, taking into account the impact of historical, social, and technological changes. Imre Katona, who focused on political jokes, was the scholar most thoroughly involved in collecting and analyzing jokes. He published about 1,500 texts that he collected between 1945 and 1994, broken down into years (Katona 1994) and reflecting the impact of contemporaneous political events on people's everyday lives. Each of the examples below relates to a specific period in twentieth-century Hungarian history. The first references the Hungarian–Soviet borders that were established in 1945:

> János bácsi még az országgyarapodás után, a II. világháború vége előtt új tanyát épített, mely véletlenül épp az 1945-ben megvont magyar-szovjet határra esik. Nem akarják lebontatni, megkérdik az öregtől:
> - Hová akar tartozni?
> - Magyarországhoz.
> - Gondolja csak meg: a Szovjetunió a világ legnagyobb országa, legerősebb a hadserege, legbölcsebb a vezére, és ők már rég a szocializmust építik, mi pedig csak most kezdjük!
> - Hát igen, igen . . . de azok az orosz telek! (Katona 1994:8 [1945])

> Before the end of the Second World War, after Hungary's borders were pushed back, Uncle János built a new farm which happened to be on the Hungarian-Soviet border that was defined in 1945. They don't want to demolish it, so they ask the old man:
> - Where do you want to belong?
> - To Hungary.
> - Just think about it: the Soviet Union is the biggest country in the world, has the strongest army, the wisest leader, and they have been building socialism for a long time, and we are just starting!
> - Well, yes, yes . . . but those Russian winters!

The following example refers to the mass defections following the anti-communist 1956 revolution: *Hogy beszél az okos magyar a buta magyarral?—Telefonon Bécsből.* (Katona 1994:97 [1956]) ("How does the clever Hungarian talk to the stupid Hungarian?"—"On the phone, from Vienna"). The last example, from 1989, the year of the Hungarian regime change, refers to the imminent fall of the socialist system:

> Gorbacsov így szól népéhez:
> —Amikor hatalomra jutottam, a gazdaság a szakadék szélén állt! Büszkén mondhatom, hogy azóta előbbre léptünk. (Katona 1994:224 [1989])

> Gorbachev addresses his people:
> —When I came to power, the economy was on the brink of collapse! I am proud to say that we have moved forward since then.

In addition to analyzing formal and thematic characteristics of political jokes, Katona conducted folkloristic–sociological studies, examining, among other things, the propagation speed of jokes and the fluctuation of their number on an annual, monthly, and even daily basis (1980). Transylvanian researcher Győző Zsigmond has been collecting political jokes among the Hungarian minority in Romania since the 1970s and published a volume (1997) and a small compilation (2003) of them. Political jokes have had a special significance in the socialist and post-socialist countries of Eastern Europe for a long time (see Krikmann and Laineste 2009), and Hungarian texts fit well into the international joke material. At the same time, they also reflect national characteristics, such as Hungarian-language jokes in Romania arising from Hungarian minority status, like the appearance of the cunning Székely (a member of the Hungarian subgroup living in Romania) as the hero of many jokes. For example,

> Elmegy a székely bácsi Pestre. Mikor visszajön, nézik a csomagját, nincs benne semmi se.
> Kérdi a vámos:
> –Bácsi, nem visz semmit az unokáinak?
> –Ezt a követ elvinném, s letenném oda Brassón túl . . .
> (Mármint a határkövet, az országhatárt jelölőt.) (Zsigmond 1997:69)

> A Székely man goes to Budapest. When he goes back to Romania, his luggage is checked, but there is nothing in it.
> The customs officer asks:
> –Aren't you taking anything for your grandchildren?
> –I would take this stone (that marks the border) and put it there, beyond Brașov (city in Romania) . . . .

In other words, the Székely man would like to see Hungary's territory expand significantly, at the expense of Romania's. In addition to political jokes, ethnic (especially Jewish[17]) jokes are a popular research topic, including their role in Jewish communities in Hungary (Papp 2009).

Much of the contemporary research on jokes approaches the genre from a linguistic point of view (pragmatics, sociolinguistics, and cognitive linguistics) as well as by examining them in historical context.[18] Some research explicitly shows the social and cultural embeddedness of certain international themes, for example, "dumb blonde" jokes (Géró 2012) or jokes about marital infidelity (Barta 2012). Jokes often do not coincide with reality. For example, in jokes about adultery, almost twice as many wives as husbands cheat; the husband is the butt of the jokes much more often than the wife. The discrepancy can be explained by the nature of the genre: unexpected outcomes furnish much of the humor. Moreover, as a short genre, jokes simplify and oversimplify (e.g., physicians and secretaries are presumably overrepresented among lovers), and they dramatize.

Urban and Rural Layers of Hungarian Jokes

Since the middle of the twentieth century, the joke has been one of the most vibrant oral genres, spreading until recently mainly by word of mouth, although its written manifestations have long been known. It is popular in all strata of society, but the role of the urban middle class and intellectuals in the development of the joke from a rural to an urban genre is particularly noteworthy. The joke reached its heyday in the big cities at the end of the nineteenth century.

The Budapest Joke

The prototype of Hungarian jokes, the "Budapest joke" (Hung. *pesti vicc*; see Erőss 1982; Buzinkay 1994; Géró and Barta 2016:15–16), originated in the 1860s, at the time of the formation of the Hungarian capital, in an "ethnically, culturally, linguistically, and socially heterogeneous and permanently changing environment" (Géró and Barta 2016:18). In fact, at the end of the nineteenth century, the ever-growing city of Budapest was a melting pot in full effervescence, hence the diversity of the Budapest joke. Written culture played an important part along with the rich oral culture inherited from the rural milieu. Jokes appeared in numerous comic weeklies mostly connected to the political opposition, for example, *Üstökös* (1858–1919), *Ludas Matyi* (1867–1873), and *Borsszem Jankó* (1868–1936) (Buzinkay 1994:229). Jokes were constantly moving between the written and oral modes, and their spread was promoted by social gatherings in a multitude of cafés (a real way of life for their regulars) and cabarets and, in the twentieth century, by an increasing number of published joke collections. "The Budapest joke had its own special qualities," as Géza Buzinkay notes: "It often combined various international motifs, played with words, emphasized puns, and preferred political subjects, conveying the unique outlook of petit bourgeois wisdom" (1994:225). For example,

> Két férfi beszélget a kávéházban.
> –Maga melyik pártba lépett?
> –A radikális pártba.

–Miért éppen oda?
–Szeretem a magányt. (Erőss 1982:88)

Two men are talking in a café.
–Which party did you join?
–The radical party.
–Why that one?
–I like solitude.

Folk Humor and Joke Tales

Although the joke crystallized in the big cities as a genre, it also incorporated many humorous stories of rural folklore. Folk humor appeared in several genres, and these genres went through transformations over time (e.g., Schwank, anecdote, joke tale, etc.) (Landgraf 2013:116–121; cf. Laineste 2016). In this process, a shortening of the texts can be observed from the eighteenth century to the present day: they were polished by use. An increasingly strong typification can also be noted: the concrete figures in the anecdotes gradually become representatives of types. The diverse texts were summarized by Hungarian folklorists in five volumes as part of the Hungarian folk tale catalog (Kovács 1982–1990, Vols. 6, 7A, 7B, 7C, 8; cf. Uther 2004(II):72–510), where humorous stories are arranged primarily on the basis of plots (e.g., stories about fools, married couples, clergymen, etc.).

In the second half of the twentieth century, the similarities between urban jokes and joke tales or funny folk narratives can still be observed, the latter being concise comic stories with a punchline and an entertaining yet normative, behavior-regulating function for the community (Vöő 1981:7). They are longer than jokes, the formulation of the texts is more epic, and they are more old-fashioned in terms of characters and locations. However, a number of similarities can be observed in terms of both the peculiarities of the ridiculed characters (e.g., stupidity, laziness) and the types of conflicts (e.g., marital infidelity, clash between the little man and his superior). In parallel with the disintegration of the traditional way of life, funny short narratives and jokes came to the fore as opposed to more traditional, longer epic forms such as magic tales or historical legends.

Contemporary Forms of Jokes and Joking on the Internet

From the late 1990s, in addition to being transmitted orally, jokes (and other short humorous folklore forms) have spread increasingly through the channels of so-called secondary orality (Ong 1982), in electronic form—first via SMS, then e-mail, social media, etc. The fact that the internet has become an everyday communication arena has had a considerable impact on the humor conveyed. It also accounts for the increasing number of jokes and their rapid spread. As humor scholar Christie Davies states, "The use of e-mail and web sites has a snowball effect, since the existence of an accessible core of jokes stimulates further jokes through imitation, modification, inspiration, emulation, and legitimation" (2003:30). Not only has the mode of transmission changed, but the concept of "joke" has also expanded in meaning: today's joke conveyed by the internet is, widely, no longer a "short narrative ending in a humorous punch line" (as defined at the beginning of this section) but often takes other characteristic forms—first humorous lists, joke cycles, and then verbal–visual jokes (memes, image macros) created as a combination of image and text.

In addition to increased visuality, other specific traits have emerged (e.g., the quick updating of jokes). Fast processing of current topics and news has become typical. Thanks to news broadcast globally in the mass media, people and jokes can also react to events that are distant in space. This was the case, for example, following the terrorist attack on the World Trade Center in New York on September 11, 2001, when the number of jokes transmitted on the internet exploded for the first time (Ellis 2002). In addition to the texts translated from English, the jokes that combined the topic of "9/11" with specific Hungarian characters and topics soon appeared on the Hungarian-language internet. According to Lajos Császi (2003:180) the most frequently heard "WTC" joke in Hungary was the following: *Hallotta, hogy a terroristák fogadást kötöttek Besenyei Péter magyar műrepülő világbajnokkal, hogy át tudnak repülni a WTC két tornya között? Vesztettek.* (Did you hear that the terrorists made a bet with Hungarian aerobatics world champion Péter Besenyi that they could fly between the two towers of the World Trade Center? They lost.) Other popular Hungarian jokes were based on language-specific wordplay: *–Hogy mutatkozik be a német terrorista? –Ich bin Laden* (–How does the German terrorist introduce himself? –Ich bin Laden) or *–Hogy kártyázik a székely az arabbal? –Osszá má, bin Laden!* (–How does the Szekler play cards with the Arab? –Deal, will you, bin Laden!) (homophone with "Osama bin Laden") (Zsigmond 2003:12–13).

Politicians and public figures, as well as actors and celebrities, appear in jokes: they can be heroes or made fun of. The formation of joke cycles around a particularly popular topic or person is also characteristic. One example is the extensive Hungarian joke cycle linked to American actor Chuck Norris, including jokes with special Hungarian references (e.g., the Szent László Hospital in Budapest as well as allusions to the worldwide COVID-19 pandemic): *A koronavírus Chuck Norrist is megtámadta. A vírus azóta a Szent László kórházban lábadozik* (The coronavirus has also attacked Chuck Norris. Since then, the virus is in convalescence at Szent László Hospital).

Jokes based on puns, which do not consist of narrative content and a punchline, are also popular. People often just refer to a joke, quoting part of it (primarily the punchline) (Laineste 2016:18). At the same time, an increasingly important role is played by visuality, in other words, the so-called internet memes. In a general sense, these are "units of popular culture that are circulated, imitated, and transformed by individual Internet users, creating a shared cultural experience in the process" (Shifman 2013:367). Among the various forms of internet memes (which are usually meant to be humorous), some types can be interpreted as verbal–visual jokes. These forms (e.g., image macros and demotivators) combine verbal and visual components and follow the working mechanisms of verbal jokes that consist of a setup and punchline (Dynel 2016:668–684). Humorous memes are also popular in Hungarian-language internet communication, and folkloristic research on them has begun focusing mainly on patterns and variation (Domokos 2014; Vargha 2018).

A specifically Hungarian meme type is the so-called hungaromeme (Balázs 2018:59). Its special feature is the textual part imitating a dialect and the drawing of a "Hungarian" mustache on the face of the person(s) in the picture. The example shown in Fig. 39.4 created in 2013 was the first of this type; the caption—using a faux dialect—is the Hungarian translation of film title *The Amazing Spider-Man*.[19]

The internet has profound implications for the circulation of jokes, and at the same time it opens up new perspectives for joke research: jokes can be captured already in their developmental phase, and the internet helps our work as a kind of time machine, preserving complete conversations on mailing lists or message boards. During 2020–2021, the crisis resulting from the COVID-19 pandemic provided useful opportunities to examine the evolution of jokes. Restrictions to help manage the crisis have radically changed people's lifestyles around the world, and getting over it is greatly aided by humor, which reacts to many of the components of change (e.g., curfew restrictions, home office, distance learning, feeling locked up, and temporary shortages). In addition to the jokes and memes that circulated internationally (e.g., *Sisyphus works from home*), specifically local jokes also appeared. These could refer to officials directly involved in the management of the epidemic or the current political situation, but more often they were about the general poor state and perception of the Hungarian healthcare system (e.g., waiting months for an intervention or the lack of cleanliness in Hungarian

FIG. 39.4. The first example of *hungaromemes*, a meme type combining a faux Hungarian dialect in the textual part and a typical "Hungarian" mustache as an added visual element.

hospitals): *Miért nem regisztráltak még Magyarországon koronavírusos fertőzöttet? –Mert augusztusra kaptak időpontot* (Why hasn't any coronavirus-infected person been registered in Hungary yet? –Because they have an appointment for August); *Két Koronavírus betér egy magyar kórházba. Az egyik megszólal: –Menjünk innen a francba, még elkapunk valamit* (Two coronaviruses enter a Hungarian hospital. One says: –Let's get the hell out of here, we're going to catch something).

Several examples have become specifically Hungarian because of puns based on the Hungarian language, for example, *Hogy kerülje el a koronavírust? –H1N1 almát minden reggel.* (How to avoid the coronavirus? –H1N1 apple every morning) (H1N1 in Hungarian is ambiguous: 1/eat and 2/influenza A virus subtype). Other examples were created—as in every era—by updating earlier jokes:

Kijárási tilalom idején újra aktuális régi történet:
–Mikor fekszik le a jó kislány?
–Hatkor, mert nyolcra otthon kell lennie.

An old story revisited during a curfew:
–When does the good girl go to bed?
–At six, because she has to be home by eight.

Conclusion

The general remarks presented in this chapter have demonstrated how short, traditional verbal genres (proverbs, anti-proverbs, riddles, and jokes) have long provided rich sources of wisdom and humor for Hungarian-speaking communities in eastern Europe. The chapter has surveyed how Hungarian paremiologists, paremiographers, folklorists, and humor researchers, starting already in the sixteenth century but especially since the twentieth, have painstakingly collected, catalogued, and studied these clever, ingenious, entertaining word (and image) patterns. The discussions have also examined how proverbs, anti-proverbs, riddles, and jokes are composed and expressed (orally, in writing, and through images) and the depth of meanings that they convey to their audiences. The authors of this chapter have no doubt that the coming decades will continue to be as productive as the last decades have been and see the birth both of many new texts (in all of these genres, their contents and forms adjusting to changing times) and of new studies, monographs, and dictionaries in the field.

Notes

1. For more on proverb definitions, see Mieder (2004:2–4).
2. These and all subsequent translations from Hungarian are by the authors.
3. For more on Hungarian proverbs of Latin origin, see T. Litovkina and Mieder (2005:65–71).

4. For more on Hungarian proverbs originating from the Bible, see T. Litovkina and Mieder (2005:61–65) and T. Litovkina (2017).
5. For more on English/American proverbs borrowed by the Hungarian proverb stock, see T. Litovkina and Mieder (2005:71–76).
6. For more on dictionaries, see T. Litovkina and Mieder (2005:11–20), T. Litovkina (2013), and Voigt (2013).
7. Further important collections of Hungarian proverbs include Erdélyi (1851), Margalits (1897), and Szemerkényi (2009). For more on proverb collections in Hungarian folkloristics, see Voigt (2013:359–363) and T. Litovkina (2013).
8. For more on this topic, see T. Litovkina and Mieder (2005:9–20), T. Litovkina (2013), and Voigt (2013).
9. All anti-proverbs are followed by their original forms, given in braces.
10. Proverbs are followed by their translations into English and their English-language equivalents (introduced by the sign ~).
11. For more on techniques of variation of traditional proverbs, see Hrisztova-Gotthardt et al. (2018) and T. Litovkina et al. (2021).
12. Source: https://memegenerator.net/instance/32896434/grumpy-cat-aki-msnak-vermets-az-dgljn-meg. Accessed July 23, 2022.
13. From the earliest sources until the middle of the nineteenth century, literary and folk riddles were both generally referred to as *mese*, a term that denotes folk tales and children's stories in contemporary Hungarian. For a discussion of the changing meanings of *mese* with special regard to riddles, see Voigt (1980) and Vargha (2011).
14. Salonta, town in northwestern Romania near the Hungarian border.
15. Chibed, village in Romania, in which the majority of the inhabitants are Hungarian-speaking.
16. Both of these introductory formulae can be translated as "Riddle, riddle, what is it?" *Csümő* is a Romanian loan word meaning "riddle" or "tale" in the dialect spoken by the Hungarian minority in western Moldavia (see Péntek 2016:160).
17. The Jewish community in Hungary used to be one of the largest in Europe, numbering about 800,000 before World War II, with over 120,000 at present.
18. See the following English-language volume on Hungarian humor: T. Litovkina et al. (2012).
19. Source: https://knowyourmeme.com/memes/hungaromem-hungarizalt-memek?_=1614816000000&page=11685. Accessed July 23, 2022.

Works Cited

Attardo, Salvatore. 2014. "Jokes." In *Encyclopedia of Humor Studies*, ed. Salvatore Attardo, Vol. 1, 417–418. Los Angele: Sage Publications.
Balázs, Géza. 2018. "A nyelvi humor antropológiája." *Századvég*, 87/1:57–72.
Baranyai Decsi Csimor, János. 1598. *Adagiorum Graeco-Latino-Ungaricorum Chiliades Quinque*. Bartphae: Iacobus Klöß.
Bárdosi, Vilmos, ed. 2003. *Magyar szólástár. Szólások, helyzetmondatok, közmondások értelmező és fogalomköri szótára*. Budapest: Tinta Könyvkiadó.
Barna, Gábor, Ágnes Stemler, and Vilmos Voigt, eds. 2004. *"Igniculi Sapientiae." János-Baranyai-Decsi-Festchrift*. Budapest: Országos Széchenyi Könyvtár–Osiris.

Barta, Péter. 2012. "Love on the Other Side of the Fence: Hungarian Jokes on Marital Infidelity." In *Hungarian Humour*, eds. Anna T. Litovkina, Judith Sollosy, Péter Medgyes, and Dorota Brzozowska, 185–204. Krakow: Tertium.

Buzinkay, Géza. 1994. "The Budapest Joke and Comic Weeklies as Mirrors of Cultural Assimilation." In *Budapest and New York: Studies in Metropolitan Transformation, 1870–1930*, eds. Thomas Bender and E. Carle, 224–247. New York: Russell Sage Foundation.

Császi, Lajos. 2003. "World Trade Center Jokes and Their Hungarian Reception." *Journal of Folklore Research*, 40/2:175–210.

Csörsz, Rumen István, and Éva Mikos. 2019. "Cheap Print in Eighteenth- and Nineteenth-Century Hungary." In *Cheap Print and the People: European Perspectives on Popular Literature*, eds. David Atkinson and Steve Roud, 274–306. Newscastle upon Tyne: Cambridge Scholars Publishing.

Davies, Christie. 2003. "Jokes That Follow Mass-Mediated Disasters in a Global Electronic Age." In *Of Corpse: Death and Humor in Folklore and Popular Culture*, ed. Peter Narváez, 15–34. Logan: Utah State University Press.

Domokos, Mariann. 2014. "Towards Methodological Issues in Electronic Folklore." *Slovensky Národopis*, 62/2:283–295.

Dynel, Marta. 2016. "'I Has Seen Image Macros!' Advice Animal Memes as Visual–Verbal Jokes." *International Journal of Communication*, 10:660–688. https://ijoc.org/index.php/ijoc/article/view/4101. Accessed July 23, 2022.

Ellis, Bill. 2002. "Making a Big Apple Crumble: The Role of Humor in Constructing a Global Response to Disaster." *New Directions in Folklore*, 6:1–106. https://scholarworks.iu.edu/journals/index.php/ndif/article/view/19883/25953. Accessed July 23, 2022.

Erdélyi, János. 1851. *Magyar közmondások könyve*. Pest: Kozma Vazul.

Erőss, László. 1982. *A pesti vicc*. Budapest: Gondolat.

Forgács, Tamás. 2003. *Magyar szólások és közmondások szótára. Mai nyelvünk állandósult szókapcsolatai példákkal szemléltetve*. Budapest: Tinta Könyvkiadó.

Géró, Györgyi. 2012. "The 'Dumb Blonde' in a Hungarian Context." In *Hungarian Humour*, eds. Anna T. Litovkina, Judith Sollosy, Péter Medgyes, and Dorota Brzozowska, 167–184. Krakow: Tertium.

Géró, Györgyi, and Péter Barta. 2016. "The Hungarian Joke and Its Environs." *European Journal of Humour Research*, 4/1:14–33. https://doi.org/10.7592/EJHR2016.4.1.gero. Accessed July 23, 2022.

Hrisztova-Gotthardt, Hrisztalina, Anna T. Litovkina, Péter Barta, and Katalin Vargha. 2018. *A közmondásferdítések ma: Öt nyelv antiproverbiumainak nyelvészeti vizsgálata*. Budapest: Tinta Könyvkiadó.

Hrisztova-Gotthardt, Hrisztalina, Melita Aleksa Varga, Anna T. Litovkina, and Katalin Vargha. 2020. "The Visual Representations of a Biblical Proverb and Its Modifications in the Internet Space." *European Journal of Humour Research*, 8/2:87–112. https://doi.org/10.7592/EJHR2020.8.2.Hrisztova-Gotthardt. Accessed July 23, 2022.

Kaivola-Bregenhøj, Annikki. 1977. "Means of Riddle Expression." In *Arvoitukset. Finnish Riddles*, eds. Leea Virtanen, Annikki Kaivola-Bregenhøj, and Aarre Nyman, 58–76. Helsinki: SKS.

Katona, Imre. 1980. *Mi a különbség? Közéleti vicceinkről*. Budapest: Magvető Kiadó.

Katona, Imre. 1994. *A helyzet reménytelen, de nem komoly. Politikai vicceink 1945-től máig*. Budapest: Móra.

Kovács, Ágnes, ed. 1982–1990. *Magyar népmesekatalógus 1–9*. Budapest: MTA Néprajzi Kutató Csoport.
Krikmann, Arvo, and Liisi Laineste. 2009. *Permitted Laughter: Socialist, Post-Socialist and Never-Socialist Humor*. Tartu: ELM Scholarly Press.
Lábadi, Károly. 1982. *Hold letette, nap felkapta. Drávaszögi magyar találósok*. Eszék: Magyar Képes Újság.
Lábadi, Károly. 1986. *Ahogy rakod tüzed. Drávaszögi magyar proverbiumok*. Eszék: Horvátországi Magyarok Szövetsége.
Laineste, Liisi. 2016. "From Joke Tales to Demotivators: A Diachronic Look at Humorous Discourse in Folklore." *Traditiones*, 45/3:7–25. https://doi.org/10.3986/Traditio2016450302. Accessed July 23, 2022.
Landgraf, Ildikó. 2013. "Örök körforgásban. Az anekdota műfaja a magyar folklórban." *Ethno-Lore*, 30:114–137.
Litovkina, Anna T. 2005. *Magyar közmondástár. Közmondások értelmező szótára példákkal szemléltetve*. Budapest: Tinta Könyvkiadó.
Litovkina, Anna T. 2013. "New Approaches to Paremiology and Paremiography in Hungary." In *"Вода» в славянской фразеологии и паремиологии." A víz a szláv frazeológiában és paremiológiában/Water in Slavonic Phraseology and Paremiology*, eds. András Zoltán, Oleg Fedoszov and Szabolcs Janurik, 67–101. Budapest: Tinta Könyvkiadó.
Litovkina, Anna T. 2017. *Aki keres, az talál. Bibliai közmondások szótára*. Budapest: Tinta Könyvkiadó.
Litovkina, Anna T., Hrisztalina Hrisztova-Gotthardt, Péter Barta, Katalin Vargha, and Wolfgang Mieder. 2021. *Anti-Proverbs in Five Languages: Structural Features and Verbal Humor Devices*. Cham: Palgrave Macmillan.
Litovkina, Anna T., and Wolfgang Mieder. 2005. *"A közmondást nem hiába mondják" Vizsgálatok a proverbiumok természetéről és használatáról*. Budapest: Tinta Könyvkiadó.
Litovkina, Anna T., Judith Sollosy, Péter Medgyes, and Dorota Brzozowska, eds. 2012. *Hungarian Humour*. Krakow: Tertium.
Litovkina, Anna T., and Katalin Vargha. 2005a. *"Éhes diák pakkal álmodik." Egyetemisták közmondás-elváltoztatásai*. Budapest: privately published.
Litovkina, Anna T., and Katalin Vargha. 2005b. *"Viccében él a nemzet." Magyar közmondás-paródiák*. Budapest: privately published.
Litovkina, Anna T., Katalin Vargha, and Dóra Boronkai. 2012. "On Two Recent Sociolinguistic Surveys Conducted in Hungary on Anti-Proverbs." In *Hungarian Humour*, eds. Anna T. Litovkina, Judith Sollosy, Péter Medgyes, and Dorota Brzozowska, 317–340. Krakow: Tertium.
Margalits, Ede. 1897. *Magyar közmondások és közmondásszerű szólások*. Budapest: Kókai Lajos.
Mieder, Wolfgang. 1982. *Antisprichwörter*, Band I. Wiesbaden: Verlag für deutsche Sprache.
Mieder, Wolfgang. 1993. *Proverbs Are Never Out of Season: Popular Wisdom in the Modern Age*. New York: Oxford University Press.
Mieder, Wolfgang. 2004. *Proverbs. A Handbook*. Westport, CT: Greenwood Press.
Ong, Walter J. 1982. *Orality and Literacy. The Technologizing of the Word*. London: Methuen.
Paczolay, Gyula. 1997. *European Proverbs in 55 Languages with Equivalents in Arabic, Persian, Sanskrit, Chinese and Japanese*. Veszprém: Veszprémi Nyomda Rt.
Paczolay, Gyula, ed. 2023. *Baranyai Decsi János: Adagiorum graecolatinoungaricorum Chiliades quinque – ötezer görög-latin-magyar szólás gyűjteménye (1598)*. Budapest: Akadémiai Kiadó. https://mersz.hu/dokumentum/m1004bdj__1/. Accessed November 14, 2024.

Papp, Richárd. 2009. *Miért kell Kohn bácsinak négy hűtőszekrény*. Budapest: Nyitott Könyvműhely.
Péntek, János, ed. 2016. *A moldvai magyar tájnyelv szótára*. 1. *Moldvai magyar—közmagyar rész. A-K*. Kolozsvár: Erdélyi Múzeum-Egyesület.
Petsch, Robert. 1899. *Neue beiträge zur kenntnis des volksrätsels*. Berlin: Mayer & Müller.
Ráduly, János. 1990. *Hold elejti, nap felkapja. Kibédi találós kérdések*. Bucharest: Kriterion.
Röhrich, Lutz, and Wolfgang Mieder. 1977. *Sprichwort*. Stuttgart: Metzler.
Shifman, Limor. 2013. "Memes in a Digital World: Reconciling with a Conceptual Troublemaker." *Journal of Computer-Mediated Communication*, 18:362–377. https://doi.org/10.1111/jcc4.12013. Accessed July 23, 2022.
Szemerkényi, Ágnes. 1994. *"Közmondás nem hazug szólás." A proverbiumok használatának lehetőségei*. Budapest: Akadémiai Kiadó.
Szemerkényi, Ágnes. 2009. *Szólások és közmondások*. Budapest: Osiris.
Szemerkényi, Ágnes, and Vilmos Voigt. 1972. "The Connection of Theme and Language in Proverb Transformations." *Acta Ethnographica Hungarica* 21:95–108.
Szendrey, Zsigmond. 1924. *Nagyszalontai gyűjtés*. Magyar Népköltési Gyűjtemény XIV. Budapest: Athenaeum.
Tánczos, Vilmos. 2008. *Elejtett szavak. Egy csíki székely ember nyelve és világképe*. Csíkszereda: BOOKART.
Taylor, Archer. 1931. *The Proverb*. Cambridge, MA: Harvard University Press.
Taylor, Archer. 1943. "The Riddle." *Western Folklore*, 2:129–147.
Tóthné Litovkina, Anna. 1996. "Conducting a Paremiological Experiment in Hungary." *Proverbium: Yearbook of International Proverb Scholarship*, 13:161–183.
Ujváry, Zoltán. 1996. *Egy földműves szólásai és közmondásai*. Debrecen: Kossuth Lajos Tudományegyetem Néprajzi Tanszéke.
Ujváry, Zoltán. 2001. *Szólásgyűjtemény*. Budapest: Osiris Kiadó.
Uther, Hans-Jörg. 2004. *The Types of International Folktales: A Classification and Bibliography, Based on the System of Antti Aarne and Stith Thompson*. Helsinki: Suomalainen Tiedeakatemia.
Vargha, Katalin. 2010. *Magyar találós kérdések. 19. századi szövegek antológiája*. Budapest: Tinta Könyvkiadó.
Vargha, Katalin. 2011. "A mesétől a találós kérdésig. Adalékok a magyar szóbeli rejtvények terminológiájához (1789–1935)." *Etnoszkóp*, I/1:96–106.
Vargha, Katalin. 2013. "Rejtvény és vicc határterülete a Magyar Népköltészeti Lexikonban." *Ethno-Lore*, 30:261–291.
Vargha, Katalin. 2018. "Creativity and Humor in the Online Folklore of the 2014 Elections in Hungary." *Folklore: Electronic Journal of Folklore*, 74:7–24. https://doi.org/10.7592/FEJF2018.74.vargha. Accessed July 23, 2022.
Vargha, Katalin, and Anna T. Litovkina. 2007. "Proverb Is as Proverb Does: A Preliminary Analysis of a Survey on the Use of Hungarian Proverbs and Anti-Proverbs." *Acta Ethnographica Hungarica*, 52/1:135–156.
Vargha, Katalin, and Anna T. Litovkina. 2013. "Punning in Hungarian Anti-Proverbs." *European Journal of Humour Research*, 1/3:15–25.
Voigt, Vilmos. 1971. "A szólások változatainak szintjei." *Magyar Nyelvőr*, 95:29–34.
Voigt, Vilmos. 1980. "Hungarian mese: 'riddle' > 'tale.'" In *Folklore on Two Continents: Essays in Honor of Linda Dégh*, eds. Nikolai Burlakoff and Carl Lindahl, 175–179. Bloomington, IN: Trickster Press.

Voigt, Vilmos. 1993. "Egy közösség találós kérdései." In *Csillagok, csillagok, szépen ragyogjatok
. . .* " *Tanulmányok a 65 éves Ág Tibor köszöntésére*, ed. József Liszka, 138–180. Komárom–
Dunaszerdahely: Szlovákiai Magyar Néprajzi Társaság.

Voigt, Vilmos. 2010. "Mesés könyvecske (Märchenbüchlein, 1629). Eine ungarische Fassung des Strassburger Rätselbuchs (1505)." In *Fortunatus, Melusine, Genovefa. Internationale erzählstoffe in der deutsche und ungarische literatur der frühen neuzeit*, eds. Dieter Breuer and Gábor Tüskés, 495–505. Bern: Peter Lang.

Voigt, Vilmos. 2011. "Around Analysis and Hypothesis of Hungarian Alliteration." In *Alliteration in Culture*, ed. Jonathan Roper, 180–194. London: Palgrave Macmillan.

Voigt, Vilmos. 2013. "Précis of Hungarian Paremiography and Paremiology." *Proverbium: Yearbook of International Proverb Scholarship*, 30:347–376.

Vöő, Gabriella. 1981. *Tréfás népi elbeszélések*. Bucharest: Kriterion Könyvkiadó.

Vöő, Gabriella. 1989. *Igaz ember igazat szól. Közmondások a romániai magyar folklórból*. Bukarest: Kriterion.

Vöő, Gabriella. 1999. *Szaván fogjuk. Erdélyi magyar szólások*. Székelyudvarhely: Erdélyi Gondolat Könyvkiadó.

Zsigmond, Győző. 1997. *Három kismacska, kettő közülük kommunista. Erdélyi politikai viccek 1977–1997*. Budapest: Pont Kiadó.

Zsigmond, Győző. 2003. "Hungarian Political Jokes from Romania and Hungary on the Tragic Events of September 11 and Their Consequences." *Semiotische Berichte*, 27/1–4:317–334.

Material Culture

CHAPTER 40

TRADITION AND ADAPTATION IN RUSSIAN FOLK ART

ALISON HILTON

DECORATED household items such as serving dishes displayed on open shelves and embroidered towels draped around icons and windows held special significance during seasonal holidays and rituals marking stages of life such as births, marriages, and funerals. Their designs are closely connected with a sense of heritage and community. The Russian term for folk art is *narodnoe iskusstvo*. *Narod* means the people or folk and connotes nationality and national identity, as do comparable terms in other Slavic languages. In the mid-nineteenth century, art and literature connected with pan-Slavic movements tended to idealize peasant villages as embodying communal values inherited from the original Slav inhabitants. In reality, peasants everywhere, especially serfs in the agricultural zones, suffered demeaning privations. Some became brilliant artists, but others fashioned baskets, pots, and toys during the winter just to make ends meet. After the abolition of serfdom in 1861 fragmented rural social structures, folk arts fell into decline. Regional authorities and a few professional artists made efforts to preserve traditional forms and skills, and a new stage in the evolution of folk art began. The applied arts industries, known as *kustar'*, or small-scale production of crafts for sale, continued through the Soviet era and thrive today.

FOLK ART AND MATERIAL CULTURE: DWELLINGS AND FURNISHINGS

The most conspicuous element of material culture is architecture: the layout of villages and the structure and embellishment of dwellings. A village (*selo, derevnia*) consisted of a row of wooden houses lining a river bank or a dirt road, usually with a church, a bathhouse, windmills, storage sheds, and a blacksmith's shop. A typical farmstead included the dwelling, *izba*, close to the street; a barn; a hayshed; and other buildings encircling a yard with a kitchen garden, usually fenced and set off by a carved gate.

The word *izba* meant a house heated with a clay or tile oven. Variations had to do with local climate and economy, size, the number of walls, and the arrangement of living and storage spaces. The main room, the *izba* itself, defined by the large oven, was the only heated part of the house. In the north (Archangel'sk, Olonets, Vologda, and Novgorod Provinces), large dwellings housed ten to twenty people; the living rooms were raised above the ground over a cellar (*podklet'*) that held livestock and provided heat from animals' bodies during the severe winters. In more temperate central Russia (between the Volga River and Smolensk), houses were more compact, with attached or separate outbuildings; in the south (Kaluga, Orël, Kursk, Voronezh, and Tambov), the rich "black earth" region, houses lacked basements but usually had storage sheds and enclosed yards for stock. Other building types occurred in the Urals, Siberia, the Don River basin, Ukraine, and adjacent regions of eastern Poland. Even after the Bolshevik Revolution and the formation of collective farms, many peasant villages retained the traditional layout and the basic *izba* structure while incorporating new materials such as pressed board for walls, cement blocks for foundations, and sometimes kitchen ranges and piped water.

The *izba* embodied the principles of ornamentation in Russian folk art: clear articulation of ornament in relation to structure and integration of the various components of border ornament, open surfaces, and figurative motifs. Carvings of plant and animal forms or of mythical creatures accentuated the structural functions of the ridgepole of the roof, the gable ends, the horizontal board that separated the triangular pediment from the rectangular base of the house, the uprights at each corner, and the framing of the windows and doors.

Distinctive exterior decoration appeared in north Russia and near Nizhnii Novgorod at the confluence of the Volga and Oka Rivers. The large northern houses provided additional fields for decoration on roofed stairways and passages from one space to another. Carved bands of openwork tracery set off the eaves, the window frames, and the balcony extending across the facade (Fig. 40.1). The most striking feature was the *okhlupen'*, a large figure carved from the root end of the tree used as the ridge-pole, placed so that it protruded over the facade of the house. Shaped as a horse, duck, or deer, the *okhlupen'*, also called *konek* (from *kon'*, meaning "horse"), may have preserved an ancient Slavic or Scandinavian image of a nature deity or protective spirit. Even after the original meaning was forgotten, the *konek* persisted as an essential part of a house.

Along the Volga, houses had broad facades facing the street; decoration emphasized the contrast of the rough horizontal logs and the complex patterns of their notching at the corners. In the Nizhnii Novgorod region, carved boards set off the main architectural features. Vertical boards called "wings" (*krylia*), covering the ends of the roof beams and extending down at the sides, were often carved in openwork patterns like those on the embroidered towels draped around the windows and sometimes described

FIG. 40.1. Oshevnev house, Lake Onega region, 1876. Kizhi Museum-Preserve.

as "carved lace." The frontal board (*lobnaia doska*, from *lob*, "forehead"), also called *krasnaia doska* ("beautiful or "red board"), separated the pediment from the lower part of the facade. Window frames (*nalichniki*), especially the largest (*krasnoe*, "beautiful") window, received elaborate carving in deep relief. During the nineteenth century, carving grew ever more elaborate on all but the most humble houses. The frame of the upper window took the form of an arch supported by columns. Carpenters replaced the single frontal board with two or three parallel boards, stepped back to increase depth and often elaborately carved. The friezes might be extended onto the sides of the house, and would also be richly carved if the house was on a corner and the side visible from the road. By the 1840s through the 1880s, carvers devised complex compositions, mingling purely decorative patterns with figures, and projecting the *lobnaia doska* outward to suggest the mezzanine or balcony of a city house. Many pediments are carved with dates and initials or names of the owners or master carvers.

Along with geometrical patterns and swags of foliage and fruits, decoration included animated birds, animals and mythical beings, the protective spirit (*beregina*), water sprite (*vodianoi*), woman with a fish tail (*rusalka*), paradise bird (*sirin*), and the semi-mythical lion. These magical and protective creatures held pride of place over entryways, which held ritual significance: the gateway leading to the enclosed yard or the doorframe of the house. The style and quality of the carving reflected local traditions, the wishes of the householder, and the skill of the master carver. Practices of architectural decoration developed over long periods in tandem with other aspects of peasant art, particularly those related to the interior arrangement and furnishings of the *izba*, and to the tasks and activities carried out in this setting.

The large clay oven (*pech'*) in one corner to the left or right of the door dominated the interior of the *izba* as its most important feature (Fig. 40.2). The adjacent area (*chulan*), the women's side of the house, contained the water barrel, a table for preparing food, and storage cupboards. Built-in furnishing included raised sleeping platforms (*polaty*) near the oven and low benches (*lavki*) along the other walls used for seating, for sleeping, or to support freestanding cupboards. A loom usually stood in the center of the room. The spiritual focus of the home was the icon corner, located diagonally opposite the oven. Called the *krasnyi ugol'* ("beautiful corner" or "red corner"),[1] it had at least one icon, sometimes an icon case, *bozhnitsa* or *kiot*, and a small table holding candles and family mementoes. The icon corner was the locus of rituals: hospitality, matchmaking, parts of the marriage rites, and preparation for burials.

Interior walls in prosperous houses were at least partly finished, with important features set off by carving or painting. Panels around the oven (*pripechnye doski*), usually painted red or ochre to stand out from the whitewashed clay surfaces, were typical along the Volga. In the northern Karelia, Arkhangel'sk, and Vologda Provinces and east to the

FIG. 40.2. Oshevnev house, interior showing *chulan* (women's side) with *pech'* (oven).

Urals, a long tradition of painting interiors continued in the nineteenth century. Styles ranged from geometrical accenting of structural parts to freehand renderings of plants, animals, and scenes of daily life; rippled patterns imitating the woodwork and marble of city dwellings; or rectangular panels framed like pictures and painted freehand with flowering branches, berries, and birds. Doors of cupboards bore similar motifs: contrasting checkerboard designs or dramatic images like roaring lions (Zhegalova 1983:6). The entire room was treated as an ensemble, with a striking sense of decorative unity, drawn together by a border of red or a contrasting color around each panel, across the walls, and around the frames of windows and doors.

Carved and Painted Utensils

The animals, birds, and hybrid creatures carved on the facades and gates occupied the interior on serving dishes, implements such as distaffs, and embroidered towels. Objects important for hospitality, such as breadboards, saltcellars, and vessels for beverages, were obviously cherished so that some decorations have survived from the early eighteenth century. The *kovsh*, a large boat-shaped bowl for serving mead, beer, or kvass, and small dippers, *nalevki*, for serving or drinking, translated traditional forms of gold and silver liturgical and courtly vessels into wood. They were often shaped as a horse like those on ridgepoles or as a swimming bird, painted with fluid lines to suggest wings, water plants, and rippling waves. Saltcellars took the form of a chair, with a hinged lid, or a bird, whose wings slid open to hold the salt. A museum curator told a story about an expedition to northern Russia to acquire objects for the collection. She especially admired a duck-shaped saltcellar in one peasant's house, but the owner refused to sell it because "without her the house would be impoverished" (Rabotnova 1973:28–29; Hilton 1995:34).

As early as the seventeenth century, craft workers in the market town Khokhloma in the Nizhnii Novgorod district made wooden bowls of all sizes, platters, and canisters shaped and decorated to imitate expensive metalware, using techniques derived from church decoration (Fig. 40.3). Made of linden or aspen wood turned on a lathe, the pieces were primed with clay and polished with powdered silver, tin, or aluminum; painted with cinnabar or heat-resistant oil paints in designs of stylized branches and berries; then covered with linseed oil and varnish; and finally cured in special kilns to create an effect like translucent gold. Velikii Ustiug on the Northern Dvina River in Vologda Province, known for its enamelware and metalware with translucent glass inserts, also produced birchbark canisters (*buraki*) decorated with open-work ornament cut from thin layers of bark and sometimes accentuated with colored tinfoil or mica inserts (Fig. 40.4). Larger objects like breadboards and storage chests with plenty of space for decoration feature scenes of people engaged in activities such as hunting, berry-picking, carriage rides, weaving and spinning, and drinking tea; some probably show artists' families and friends. Inscriptions on many items point to a high level of

FIG. 40.3. Khokhloma tableware, early and mid-twentieth century.

FIG. 40.4. Viazova and unknown artist, birchbark canisters, Velikii Ustiug, Vologda Province, 1982.

literacy, especially in parts of northern Vologda Province settled by merchants and craftspeople, many of them Old Believers exiled from Moscow and Novgorod in the sixteenth and seventeenth centuries.[2] The same artists who provided icons and furnishings for their churches also decorated houses and household implements. Names, dates, and brief texts on containers and distaffs indicate that such pieces were made to order by artists who were recognized for their special skills (Hilton 1995:76–78).

A group of villages on the Northern Dvina River, Navolok, Borok, and Permogore, formed a center for painting on wood. Thanks to signed pieces, we know the names of several artists and families whose members practiced their crafts for generations. One of them, Iakov Iarygin, painted the first known self-portrait of a peasant artist in 1811, showing himself in his workshop, surrounded by his paints and tools. In the 1950s, Pelageia Amosova, daughter of an Old Believer who painted icons and manuscripts as well as utensils and tools, gave researchers valuable information about her training, methods of painting distaffs, and even the local market economy. Trained in the family's traditional icon-painting techniques, using a primer made of glue and honey over the prepared wood, fine lines, and small patches of gold leaf, she and her six brothers set up workshops in three or four villages around the area. Like other peasant artists, they painted only in the fall and winter and usually finished about fifty distaffs each year. "Our work was praised far and wide," Amosova said, adding that customers came more than a day's journey to buy their distaffs (Zhegalova 1983:37–41; Hilton 1995:78–80). Arkhip Ershov, a maker of distaffs decorated with paint and wood inlay in a village near Nizhnii Novgorod, gave a thoughtful response to a scholar's question about the nature of folk art and *narodnost'* ("folk-ness"). He worked in the way his father and his grandfather worked, and "that thread, the thread of tradition, stretched and stretched down to us." But, he added, tradition allowed change: "We each have something of our own, but we still hold on to that thread" (Saltykov 1968:52–53; Zhegalova 1975:6; Hilton 1995:3–4). Far from being an anonymous expression of an innate, Russian love of color and ornament, as romantic theorists claimed, folk art maintained a delicate, shifting balance of local decorative traditions and individual creativity, cumulative originality.

Woodworking and textile arts reached impressive levels of quality in the hands of masters, but every peasant household possessed skill in carpentry and spinning, weaving, and sewing. Among the most varied and well-made domestic objects are those connected with the making and care of fabrics. Tools used for spinning, weaving, and embroidery took up a good deal of space and attention in peasant houses. The massive loom (*tkatskii stan*) constituted an interior architectural feature that received decoration like the beams of houses, often with horse motifs probably related to ancient ornaments found in women's graves (Kruglova 1974:19). Because spinning was a social ritual during long winter evenings, distaffs (*prialki*) enjoyed the most elaborate and varied decoration, and more than forty distinct regional styles are known. *Posidelki* or *besedy*, gatherings of women spinning while they talked and sang, sometimes joined by men, were favorite motifs on distaffs and small storage boxes (Fig. 40.5). Lightweight and portable, distaffs were simple to use. The spinner sat on the horizontal base (*dontse*) to hold the work steady, placed a hank of rough linen on the projecting comb at the top of the distaff blade

FIG. 40.5. Spinning and sewing, detail of painted wood box, Arkhangel'sk, 1980s.

(*lopastka*), and pulled the thread out in a rhythmic motion, to wind it on a spindle. Used among neighbors, distaffs were status symbols, so the decoration was most lavish on the side facing the room. The back of the upright blade might have a space for a small mirror or included names and dates, especially on engagement or wedding gifts. Besides *posidelki*, social scenes such as tea parties and sleigh rides, events important for courtship, were popular embellishments and could include fairly detailed portraits of couples dressed in their best. Accompanying auspicious motifs, such as the *sirin*, the tree of life, and garlands resemble those embroidered on kerchiefs, wedding towels, and garments made by young women for their dowries.

Other tools used for textile arts received hard use, and few are so well preserved as distaffs: the scutcher (*trepalo*) a wooden blade for breaking up the tough flax fibers before spinning, the battledore (*val'ka*) for beating woven linen against stones in the river to soften it, and the rocker (*rubel'*) for smoothing the linen as it dried. The battledore was often decorated with a *rusalka*, perhaps to invoke the water spirit's aid in the task. The rocker, a long, curved board with ridges for smoothing, usually had a handle shaped like a horse, as if the suggestion that it gallops over the cloth might lighten the work. The horse was also a favorite motif on looms and sewing stands (*shveiki*), usually built like distaffs, with a base and a tower ending in a pincushion or a decorative clamp to hold the cloth attached so that the sewer could use both hands for her work. The ancient association of horses or horse-shaped ornaments with women may not have been consciously applied by the makers of these tools, but they remained part of the expected ornamentation. The implements used to make textiles and clothing also had strong visual affinities with the textiles themselves, especially in the case of carved geometrical patterns and the repeated, stylized shapes in weaving and embroidery.

Textile Arts

The *rubakha*, a long, linen shift or shirt, usually with embroidery at the neck, shoulders, and hem, was the basic garment for both women and men. Over it, women usually wore a garment like a wrap-around skirt or a sleeveless jumper. In south Russia and Ukraine, a *poneva*, a broad length of woven cloth was wrapped around the waist and tied with a sash woven with patterns denoting kinship. A full-length embroidered apron and sleeveless jacket completed the costume. The main garment in central and northern Russia, was the *sarafan*, cut on the bias to hang straight from the shoulders, and decorated with embroidery, braided trim, and buttons. Metallic threads and finely worked lace distinguished garments for festive occasions. Headdresses, called *kokoshniki*, designated kinship ties and marital status; their forms varied from region to region, but all were elaborately decorated with gold embroidery, sequins, and river pearls. Paintings and photographs show garments that were actually worn at the time, not for heavy farm work, but for greeting guests and for seasonal ceremonies such as the first day of spring plowing, haymaking, or harvesting (Fig. 40.6). Colorful trim and embroidery articulated the expanse of fabric and highlighted the most important parts of the body, the hem, neckline, and shoulders, akin to the "carved lace" that emphasized the important structural elements of a house.

Embroidery, like architectural carving, incorporated both all-over pattern and symbolic motifs: stylized human figures and mythical creatures. Made for the same occasions as serving bowls and other utensils, towels with broad embroidered borders, tablecloths, and bed valences had ceremonial functions connected with religious or life-stage rituals. In some of the earliest surviving embroideries, large single figures, a tree, bird, horse, or standing woman, dominated the space, with small, stylized designs filling in surrounding areas, while later pieces employed bands of fairly evenly spaced figures or rhythmic, abstract designs (Kalmykova 1981:31–32). Stylized tail feathers of a peacock

FIG. 40.6. Sergei Prokudin-Gorsky, peasant girls in a village near Kirillov on the Sheksna River, 1909 (Library of Congress).

might be conflated with extending branches of trees. The abstract patterns of stitchery inspired invention. Forms such as lozenges or rhomboids, sometimes combined with spirals, swastikas, rays, crosses, or rosettes, could be incorporated into the bodies of figures and animals as well as into geometrical borders.

All women used the skills of spinning, weaving, and embroidery. They also found another type of decoration, printed cloth (*naboika*), appealing with its bright colors, lively patterns, and time-saving production. The basic method employed wood or metal printing blocks covered with oil-based paint and pressed against a wet piece of linen. For a more colorful effect, the boards were covered with a mixture of clay, acid, and glue and pressed onto the fabric, leaving a residue; then the cloth was put into a vat filled with indigo dye and turned a deep blue, while the reserved designs remained white; small stenciled patterns or dots of saffron or red were added later. This could be done on a small scale at home, but master printers and dyers traveled from village to village bringing samples so that each woman could choose a pattern and get the desired length of cloth a few months later.

Specialized Crafts and Regional Markets

Other forms of folk art required materials and tools not available in every household. Workshops for textiles, carving, and metalwork flourished in many regions, along with thriving markets. Factories, defined as workshops with a certain number of craftspeople employed, became famous for production of ceramic and metal utensils. The famous symbol of Russian hospitality, the *samovar* ("self-boiler"), was essentially an urn with a central chimney for burning charcoal surrounded by a vessel for the boiling water, with drafts and valves to regulate temperature and a spout. Ingeniously varied with shapes known as barrel, sphere, pear, and others, they offered scope for virtuosity in the handling of details. Samovars were essential features of every household, from *izbas* and rural estate houses to urban mansions and tenements.

Ivory carving developed in the far north, in the town of Kholmogory near the White Sea, where artists had endless supplies of walrus tusk, whalebone, and even mammoth bone. They made pieces for sale and sent them down the Northern Dvina River to Velikii Ustiug and other trading centers. Ivory and bone carvings inspired artists in the region who worked in humbler materials, using sharp knives to incise pliable layers of birchbark to decorate canisters and small boxes. Besides the foliage and reindeer motifs, the bone and birchbark ornaments included figures such as little cupids that probably came from engravings or illustrated books, sources for carved and gilded decoration of churches as well as secular objects.

Books had been printed in Russia since the sixteenth century, beginning with gospels. Illustrated broadsheets, *lubki*, probably originated as a means of making religious images and other kinds of information available cheaply to everyone. Favorite subjects included animal fables, proverbs, seasonal festivities, natural wonders, and scenes of daily life such as spinning and tea-drinking, often with accompanying printed texts or songs. *Lubki* were made in towns and transported to villages for sale to peasants, a counterpart to objects made by peasants for sale to richer, urban buyers.

The interaction between these levels of commerce became fairly fluid in the late nineteenth century, with the development of *kustar'* art industries. The distinction between folk art and other kinds of applied art is more subtle than simply considering how, by whom, and for whom objects were produced. Objects made by peasants for local use or trade, objects manufactured in towns for sale to peasants or pieces made by peasant artisans for wealthy buyers all had their roles in the development of folk art. People of all regions and classes wanted the objects in their homes to be beautiful as well as useful. Despite different styles, techniques, and costs, there is an underlying connection between a porcelain vase depicting an idealized rural scene made for an aristocrat's palace and a majolica pitcher made in a small factory founded by peasants in villages around Gzhel', south of Moscow, to supply tavernware. Gzhel' pottery often featured little clay figures or animals in uninhibited, playful scenes. Similarly, clay figures and whistles

FIG. 40.7. (Left) Shevelev, clay figures, Kargopol, Arkhangel'sk Province, 1982. (Right) Popuvanov, clay figures, Viatka, Kirov district, 1980s.

made as toys in northern Kargopol and in Viatka in the Ural Mountains showed fantasy and humor in depictions of centaurs and other hybrid creatures. They also showed a keen eye for European fashions, observed among exiles from Poland and other parts of the Russian empire in the mid-nineteenth century (Fig. 40.7).

Toys made up a special category of folk art, one that went beyond the range of any single medium, region, or time period. "The Russians have a peculiar talent for making figures and toys out of the most worthless materials in the world: straw, shavings, ice, dough, they turn all to account," an American visitor wrote in the 1850s (Sears 1855:557). They made *leshi* ("wood sprites") out of pinecones and moss, a horse and sleigh out of scraps of firewood. Two towns were especially famed for toys, Gorodets near Khokhloma on the Volga and Sergeievo, next to the Trinity-Sergei Monastery near Moscow. At Sergeievo, carvers created ingenious moveable toys, some based on folk tales or animal fables, others showing figures in various activities: peasants, soldiers, and the popular hussar and lady promenading in their European fashions (Fig. 40.8). The famous nesting dolls, *matrioshki*, were invented in the 1890s by Sergei Maliutin, a professional artist, working in collaboration with one of the Sergeievo toymakers. More than architectural decoration or the prized tableware and distaffs, toys informally reflected their makers' awareness of the changing world in which they lived.

FIG. 40.8. Carved and painted toys, Bogorodskoe, 1993, 1994.

Designs and Symbolic Meanings

Certain designs and images appeared over a wide range of media, regions, and time periods; and scholars investigating their historical origins have related these animals, mythical creatures, and stylized patterns to images and designs found in ancient burials and carvings on early Christian churches (Vasilenko 1977; Voronov 1924; Kruglova 1987). Carved stone lions flanked the doorways of twelfth-century churches in Vladimir and Suzdal and might have inspired wooden carvings on nineteenth-century houses. The lion and unicorn, a combination derived from western heraldry, appeared over doors and on distaffs, protecting the roof of a house and the tasks of its inhabitants. Animal forms on objects all over the house reinforced the protection and the perhaps subconscious remnants of ancient Slavic beliefs about the forces of nature: the sun, rain, and wind. Like many other ancient cultures, the Slavs believed that the sun rode across the sky on a horse and swam under the world at night on a duck's back; the carved and painted horses and water birds would support the sun's journey. Ancient metal and bone ornaments were highly stylized, and some of the conventional shapes, such as a diamond or rhomboid to symbolize the sun, continued to be carved and embroidered. Even after Grand Prince Vladimir of Kiev adopted Christianity and destroyed the idols of Perun and other Slavic nature gods in the tenth century, belief in the powers of nature persisted among the peasants, a phenomenon known as *dvoeverie*, or dual faith. It is important not to oversimplify this concept; though first used in sermons denouncing the persistence of pagan practices, the term *dvoeverie* later carried a more positive meaning as a balance of parallel presences in Russian Christianity. Familiarity with Slavic divinities—such as the sky gods Perun and Khors; the goddesses Mokosh, symbol of the earth and fertility, and Paraskeva, identified with textile work, women's rituals, and markets; and Iarilo and Kupalo, gods connected with male youth, mid-summer festivals, the sun, and fire—probably made the Christian God and saints relatively easy to recognize and accept (Hilton 1991:59–62). Cut off from Byzantine sources during the long Mongol occupation from about 1237 until the end of the fourteenth century, Russian church decoration and icons evolved in accordance with local practices and beliefs. Artists who worked on the decoration of churches and contributed to the Russian innovation of the carved and gilded iconostasis were also the makers of decorated household articles. Icons of Saints Nicholas and George, venerated as protectors against a variety of dangers, and Elijah with his fiery chariot, conflated with the sun god Iarilo, displayed lively features of folk carving and painting. While peasants prayed to St. George as slayer of the dragon and protector of the land and agriculture and to St. Nicholas, bringer of gifts and rescuer in times of trouble, they never lost the need for the comfort given by the saints' Slavic predecessors (Hilton 1991:67–69).

Carved and painted decoration on dwellings and household articles displayed special heraldic groupings of symbolic or protective power. The composition with two horses and riders flanking a tree with a bird perched or hovering above it had many variations, often with lavish foliage and flowers. The bird, sometimes a peacock or a cockerel, appeared in all media, carvings, ceramics, and painted dishes, sometimes juxtaposed with a rosette symbolizing the sun. The *sirin*, a bird with a woman's face, decorated distaffs, lighting fixtures, cupboard doors, and dowry chests. The *sirin* and her counterpart, *alkonost*, the heavenly bird of joy and sorrow, perched in a tree laden with flowers and fruit, were among the favorite images, depicted on twelfth-century ceramics and enamels from Kiev, embroidered textiles and tiles from the fifteenth century, manuscripts, and *lubki*. Related to the *sirin* and the flowering tree are compositions with central female figures with upraised hands, flanked by birds or horses and riders, with some reference to a tree or branches. These forms visually echo a Christian icon of the Mother of God of the Sign. The image can also be traced to an ancient female nature divinity, in Russia known as Mokosh, Mother Moist-Earth, and found in many cultures, sometimes holding branches or water-weeds, accompanied by fish and birds.

While heraldic motifs from the distant past remained essential in folk art, they also acquired new meanings, and artists altered traditional compositions to accommodate their observations of real life. The process of accretion and adaptation shows why folk art continued to be a living phenomenon. The combination of horses with riders, flowering trees, birds, and other animals with female figures still evoked nature divinities. The figure of a woman with a parasol and rainbow could be a symbol of Mother Moist-Earth or Paraskeva the linen-weaver. Equally, it could represent a fashionably dressed lady with her suitors.

Scenes related to courtship offer good examples of how hierarchical compositions gradually combined with more flexible observations of social interactions. An early distaff from Borok on the Northern Dvina River shows a young man on horseback approaching an imposing house to visit a young woman waiting behind one of the decorated windows. On the back of the blade, a sequel shows the festive sleigh-ride with the betrothed couple surrounded by lavish flowers that promise spring and fertility. Similar

FIG. 40.9. Ol'ga Nikolaeva, *sirin* and sleigh ride, detail from a decorative panel in the style of Borok distaff painting, 1992.

scenes include fluttering birds or a *sirin*, some emphasize the elaborate decoration of the facade, suggesting folk tales featuring a tsar's palace, and others concentrate on the journey (Fig. 40.9). By the mid-nineteenth century, the suitor is treated to a family tea party, and the room's furnishings, including a samovar and a clock, are depicted with all the care a proud householder could wish.

Adaptations

Artists observed and responded to their own surroundings, from the early nineteenth-century painter Iarygin's household scenes to depictions of bazaars and social activities in the early twentieth century. While respecting regional traditions, artists could also express their own interests, as did painter Varlam Riabkov when he modernized the interior of a house in the Urals by adding a puffing railway train (Hilton 1995:51). Scenes of daily life, rare in traditional folk art, grew more frequent as contact between peasants and town dwellers increased. The evolution of folk art depended on the interactions among villages, markets, and towns. The special relationships between gentry landowners and the peasants or serfs who belonged to their estates affected both folk culture and that of the elite. Novels by Lev Tolstoy and others featured scenes in which young nobles visited peasant villages and enjoyed the beauty of singing and dancing during festivities on the first day of haymaking. Such scenes appeared on *lubki* made for peasants and on luxury goods such as porcelain vases and lacquerware. Furniture made by serf artists in Western styles required by the landowners depended upon traditional skills of carving, painting, and inlay work.

On another level, Russian historians and philosophers who pondered questions of national identity believed that what defined Russian culture and distinguished it from that of the West was its Slavic heritage and that peasant life preserved true Slavic traditions that had been lost in the cities. Accordingly, some held that peasants should be protected from exposure to Western influence, but such limitations gradually relaxed. Early in the nineteenth century several serf artists were allowed to study with professional artists and became successful professionals themselves, among them the portraitist Vasilii Tropinin and Alexander Denisov, Nikifor Krylov, and Grigorii Soroka, who painted portraits, scenes of daily life, and landscapes. The latter three were students of Aleksei Venetsianov, an academy-trained painter who retired to his small country estate, freed his serfs, and started an art school for young peasants in which he encouraged observation of nature and daily life but emphasized principles of classical harmony. Most of their works expressed a feeling of calm unity between the land and its people. Very few works known to be by serfs reveal the hardships familiar to the artists (Hilton 1983:249–252).

Ironically, it was Tsar Alexander II's emancipation of serfs in 1861 that disrupted this ideal. Artists began to expose the real conditions of peasant life: the grinding privation and the insecurity in the face of disasters such as fire, storms, hunger, and disease. With the rise of realism in mid-century, artists who depicted peasants with their authentic clothing, wooden utensils, and other crafted objects did so to make a point about crudeness, superstition, and loss of purpose as landless peasants wandered into the cities and the estates decayed.

Folk Art Revival

In contrast to these efforts to expose harsh conditions, other artists and socially conscious patrons studied folk art and encouraged peasants to practice traditional crafts and skills. The first center of activity was Abramtsevo, an estate about forty kilometers northeast of Moscow near the famous Trinity-Sergei monastery. Beginning in the early 1870s, Elizaveta Mamontova and Elena Polenova bought examples of genuine architectural details, utensils, and embroidered towels from villages around the area and built up a study collection to provide models for use in their carpentry and embroidery workshops. They had two important goals: to teach peasants skills that would let them earn livelihoods and to preserve traditional art forms that were gradually being replaced by machine-made goods. A broader, more subjective goal was to "capture the still living creative spirit of the people, and give it the opportunity to develop," in Polenova's words (Sakharova 1964:362–363). Folk songs and tales were part of this "creative spirit," and while searching out decorated objects, Polenova also reread the collection of Russian fairy tales published by Aleksandr Afanas'ev in 1883 and visited local singers and master storytellers to learn and compare their versions. She and Viktor Vasnetsov introduced a genuine folk aesthetic to stage design and book illustration. Authentic sources, objects collected in villages, inspired Vasnetsov's sets and costumes for the opera *Snegurochka* (Snow Maiden). Fairy tales illustrated by Polenova and later by Ivan Bilibin emphasized a colorful, fanciful element. The same fantasy imbued the "Russian-style" architecture of the Abramtsevo studio and of the art colony Talashkino near Smolensk established by Princess Maria Tenisheva a few years later. Folk tales, very rarely the subjects of traditional folk art, became favorite material in all the arts around the turn of the century, notably in Sergei Diaghilev's ballet and opera productions. The folk coloration that permeated Abramtsevo typified the Slavic revival and greatly stimulated the imaginations of artists of the next generation, the early twentieth-century avant-garde.

Among this group, Wassily Kandinsky, Natalia Goncharova, Mikhail Larionov, and Kazimir Malevich all credited Russian icons and folk arts for their own discoveries of new expressive languages of art. Kandinsky took part in ethnographic expeditions beyond the Northern Dvina River, where he felt that he had encountered a new world. "I can remember vividly stepping over the thresh-hold of this amazing spectacle," he wrote, "it was like a fairytale—everything painted with bold and multicolored ornaments" (Kandinskii 1918). Kandinsky painted shimmering fairy-tale subjects and from these works went on to develop insights into the powers of pure color and abstract form. Goncharova, who grew up in linen-producing Vladimir Province, declared that the formal discoveries of cubism had already been exploited by the carvers of painted wooden toys sold at fairs. Larionov chose subjects from popular culture and emphasized the angular graphic styles of folk painting and *lubki*. He emulated the hierarchical compositions of traditional distaffs and embroidered towels in a monumental cycle of paintings personifying the four seasons as large female figures with upraised arms accompanied by smaller paired figures, trees, and birds. Malevich depicted rural life in the simplified styles of *lubki* and, in more ambitious paintings, combined the geometrical properties of folk art and icons. From these sources he derived principles of pure geometrical abstraction.

Paradoxically, efforts to preserve peasant culture around the turn of the century involved not only professional artists but also members of the intelligentsia and aristocracy. Government officials who directed the *zemstvo* system, the district administrations established after the emancipation, supervised and documented the activity of local *kustar'* workshops. The All-Russian Exhibition held in Nizhnii Novgorod in 1896 boasted an entire pavilion devoted to the products of the Russian north, with a substantial representation of folk arts and *kustar'* adaptations. At the Paris World's Fair of 1900, a Russian village built by peasant carpenters housed displays of authentic folk art and Russian-style objects made by both peasants and professional artists. Three museums established under Tsar Alexander III—the Historical Museum in Moscow and the Imperial Russian Museum and the Ethnographical Museum in St. Petersburg—built substantial collections of folk arts through expeditions and research. Promotion of folk arts was not unique to Russia, and government-sponsored exhibitions at trade fairs played an important role in defining national identities, especially in eastern European countries under the rule of the Austro-Hungarian Empire, Prussia, and Russia (Hilton 2019:240–251). Comparable efforts in folk music and dance began around the same time, leading to the formation of ensembles that perform all around the world today. These adaptations of folk culture were not necessarily authentic folk art or duplicates of existing pieces but, as Polenova explained, were meant to validate the evolution of folk art in a natural way.

Bilibin agreed with Polenova's conception of folk art and its role. After lengthy expeditions to Arkhangel'sk, Vologda, Tver', and Olonets Provinces to collect samples of folk art and to photograph the wooden architecture, he published articles on "Remnants of Art in the Russian Village" and "Folk Art of the Russian North" in the journal *Mir iskusstva* (World of Art) (Bilibin 1904) (Fig. 40.10). Authentic folk art was dying out, he feared, and he urged that its last remnants be preserved and allowed to develop naturally. Collecting specimens for museums was not enough; the goal should be teaching young artists traditional skills that could enable them to adapt to changing conditions. Bilibin's reports inspired efforts made throughout the late imperial and Soviet eras to invigorate national artistic traditions. Scholars and artists realized that forms from the past could provide aesthetic fulfillment for modern communities and individuals. Though their original meanings had been lost, familiar forms could help to make even radically new political messages understood. Folk art proved vital to Soviet culture in ways that earlier generations of artists never imagined.

Immediately after the Revolution, Soviet artists and state officials recognized the value of folk styles for communicating with a still resistant rural population. Propaganda posters and paintings on the agit-prop (or agitational-propaganda) trains and steamboats, designed to carry a positive image of the new regime throughout the countryside, often exploited familiar designs from embroidery, wood carving, and *lubki* to advocate literacy and economic progress. Clothing and textile designs of the 1920s and 1930s utilized traditional embroidery and indigo-printed textiles. Professional artists, trained in the new state art institutes, packaged new subject matter in traditional media and folk-like motifs, in embroidered panels, and in decorated breadboards, trays, and boxes. Scenes of collective farmers harvesting and Red Army soldiers marching characterized the new works of "popular art," also termed *narodnoe iskusstvo*. The most striking success came with the lacquer boxes painted by artists in Palekh and neighboring villages in Vladimir Province. Former icon painters, they applied their highly refined skills to a new medium and a variety of subjects ranging from the adventures of

FIG. 40.10. Ivan Bilibin, "Folk Art of the Russian North," title page for *Mir Iskusstva*, 1904.

fairy-tale heroes and princesses to the equally fantastic achievements of Communism, such as rural electrification, celebrated in *The Lamp of Lenin* (1969). The *izba* interior, with a glowing lamp next to a portrait of Lenin, and peasants exclaiming in wonder, combines folk and icon-painting traditions (Hilton 1995:257–267). In contrast to the ways in which large-scale paintings by official socialist realist artists acclaimed peasant prosperity, some Soviet folk art preserved a surprisingly true folk aesthetic.

The late nineteenth-century trend toward centralizing regional craft production continued. Lenin issued a decree, "On Measures to Assist the *Kustar'* Industries," in 1919; and other decrees and allocations of funds followed. Professional artists worked hand in hand with peasants in eight regional schools and workshops, and their products were displayed and sold in the Soviet pavilions at the World's Fairs between 1925 and 1939.

Museums sponsored expeditions to every part of the country and compiled oral and photographic records of artists still working in traditional ways. Vasilii Voronov, a champion of *kustar'* art as integral to the development of national art, made expeditions to the north and the Urals, collected more than six hundred objects, published an influential book on Russian folk art, and later taught at the Institute of Artistic Industry, working chiefly with peasant masters of traditional crafts. (Voronov 1924; Hilton 1995:272–274, 332). An official decree in 1974 required scholars to study theoretical and practical problems of preserving folk art as part of living culture (Nekrasova 1983). Young artists traveled to remote districts to serve as apprentices and learn from the masters of regional crafts. Recognized masters were excused from military service, and outstanding folk artists, musicians, and dancers were honored as national treasures and awarded the designations "People's Artist" and "Laureate of the Lenin Prize," just as composers and academicians were. Every five years, all-union exhibitions and conferences presented and evaluated progress (Nekrasova 1991; Hilton 1995:264–266).

The adaptability of folk art has proven equally important in the late Soviet and post-Soviet eras. The breakdown of authority, the absence of a chain of responsibility, and environmental degradations hurt the folk arts of many regions. As an extreme example, the accident at the Chernobyl nuclear power plant in 1986 made the fields radioactive, and Belorussian artists could no longer get the straw used for their traditional woven straw ornaments. In spite of the excesses of Russian capitalism, however, new markets and competition encouraged ingenuity and quality more than touristic kitsch. Partly thanks to the expanding domestic and foreign tourist market, particularly tours of the ancient Russian towns around Moscow known as the Golden Ring and to Kizhi Island and other architectural preserves in the Russian north, contemporary folk artists have gained new opportunities to practice their art, sell their work, and exhibit at art fairs abroad.

The local resonance of folk arts is even more significant, as the number and variety of exhibitions and publications in the past decades demonstrate. The State Historical Museum in Moscow undertook a major renovation between 1986 and 1997, updated the departments housing folk arts, and held exhibitions such as "The Russian North" in 2019 and "Festive Folk Costume" in 2020. The Russian Museum in St. Petersburg reinstalled its permanent exhibition of folk arts; published a comprehensive, lavishly illustrated guidebook in 2007; and organized several temporary exhibitions and scholarly conferences focusing on the arts of specific regions. Other museums with important folk art collections have modernized their facilities, published new catalogues, organized conferences, developed educational programs, and created engaging web sites. The interaction of scholars and contemporary folk artists at conferences in regional centers, a key component of Soviet arts policy, has not diminished despite cutbacks in state support. These efforts are similar to the work of the St. Petersburg and Moscow music conservatories, which sponsor regular fieldwork by researchers who collect folk music and other materials related to daily life in various regions.

Open-air museums, similar to ethnographic parks in eastern Europe, embody the parallel goals of preservation and education. Mainly from the 1960s through the 1990s, the state placed the surviving examples of wooden architecture under its protection and created museum-preserves at Novgorod, Kostroma, Kizhi on Lake Onega, Malye Korely overlooking the Northern Dvina near Arkhangel'sk, and other sites. Programs for non-specialists, particularly children, often stress conservation of the natural environment along with study of vernacular architecture, domestic crafts, and community festivities (see Titova 2015:18–19). Not only museums but amateur and commercial sites on the internet provide information and demonstrations, for instance, how to decorate clothing with traditional embroidery designs or make Khokhloma-style tableware. Some caution is needed since regional distinctions, so important during most of the past two centuries, are in danger of being lost or muddled. On the other hand, a healthy interest in folk arts as part of Slavic identity offers an alternative to narrow nationalism.

The question remains whether people still make, buy, and use items such as decorated bowls, birchbark containers, embroidered towels or garments, and traditional toys. Recognized centers of craft production are still active, supporting local family businesses as well as the dedicated amateur practice of craft. Among the most notable are the Paraskeva Workshop in Nizhnii Novgorod and the Paraskeva Handweaving Club in St. Petersburg, both named for the ancient Slavic patroness of textile work and women's rituals. It seems that just as the rise of *kustar'* industries, the folk art revival, and early Soviet reworkings of folk art motifs encouraged ingenuity, the new markets and educational resources are stimulating authentic creativity, what we might consider cumulative originality. As Bilibin warned over a century ago, folk art should not stagnate in isolation or survive only in archives and museums. Thanks to its innate adaptability, that seems unlikely to happen.

Acknowledgments

Besides published sources, this study benefited from many informal discussions with Russian scholars. I wish to thank Viktor Vasilenko, Ol'ga Kruglova, Serafina Zhegalova, Svetlana Zhizhina, Maria Nekrasova, and the curators at national and regional museums: the State Historical Museum in Moscow; the Russian Museum and the Ethnographic Museum in St. Petersburg; the Sergiev-Posad Museum-Preserve; the Abramtsevo Estate Museum-Preserve; the museums of local studies in Smolensk, Vologda, Iaroslavl', and Nizhnii Novgorod; and the wooden architecture museum-reserves in Novgorod, Kostroma, Suzdal', and Kizhi.

Notes

1. The proto-Slavic *krasny* meant "beautiful" in a broad sense. In early Russian, it came to mean the color red, associated with divine power in northern icons and with secular power, as in Red Square next to the Moscow Kremlin. Red is ubiquitous in Russian folk arts, painted decoration of houses and utensils and especially costume, and in the nineteenth and twentieth centuries with revolutionary movements that claimed popular support.
2. Old Believers or Old Ritualists were Orthodox Christians who maintained practices developed during Russia's long isolation during and after the Mongol occupation; they rejected

the reforms imposed by Patriarch Nikon of Moscow in the mid-seventeenth century, which were intended to bring Russian liturgy into conformity with Greek Orthodoxy. Severely repressed during the reigns of Tsar Alexei and Peter I, many Old Believer communities fled to the far north or to lands beyond the Volga. There are still active groups in Russia, the United States, and other countries.

Works Cited

Bilibin, Ivan. 1904. "Narodnoe tvorchestvo russkago severa." *Mir iskusstva*, 2/6:265–318.

Hilton, Alison. 1983. "Russian Folk Art and 'High' Art in the Early Nineteenth Century." In *Art and Culture in Nineteenth-Century Russia*, ed. Theofanis G. Stavrou, 237–254. Bloomington, IN: Indiana University Press.

Hilton, Alison. 1991. "Piety and Pragmatism: Orthodox Saints and Slavic Nature Gods in Russian Folk Art." In *Christianity and the Arts in Russia*, eds. William C. Brumfield and Miloš M. Velimirović, 55–72. Cambridge: Cambridge University Press.

Hilton, Alison. 1995. *Russian Folk Art*. Bloomington, IN: Indiana University Press.

Hilton, Alison. 2019. "From Abramtsevo to Zakopane: Folk Art and National Ideals in Russia and Eastern Europe." In Special issue of *Russian History*, eds. Ludmila Piters-Hofmann and Isabel Wünsche, 46/1:240–261.

Kalmykova, Ludmila. 1981. *Narodnaia vyshivka tverskoi zemli*. Leningrad: Khudozhnik RSFSR.

Kandinskii, Vassili. 1918. *Tekst khudozhnika*. Moscow: IZO. Reprinted in John E. Bowlt and Rose-Carol Washton Long. 1980. *The Life of Vasilii Kandinsky in Russian Art*. Newtonville, MA: Oriental Research Partners, 2.

Kruglova, Ol'ga. 1974. *Russkaia narodnaia rez'ba I rospis' po derevu*. Moscow: Izobrazitel'noe iskusstvo.

Kruglova, Ol'ga. 1987. *Narodnaia rospis' severnoi Dviny*. Moscow: Izobrazitel'noe iskusstvo.

Nekrasova, Maria. 1983. *Narodnoe iskusstvo kak chast' kul'tury: Teoriia i praktika*. Moscow: Izobrazitel'noe iskusstvo.

Nekrasova, Maria. 1991. *Narodnoe iskusstvo i sovermennaia kul'tura*. Moscow: Akademiia Khudozhestv SSSR.

Rabotnova, I. 1973. "'Mnogoznachnost' soderzhaniia: Voprosy izuchenniia narodnogo iskusstva." *Dekorativnoe iskusstvo SSSR*, no. 11: 28–29.

Sakharova, Ekaterina. 1964. "Letter to Praskov'ia Antipova, 1885." In *Vasilii Dmitrievich Polenov, Elena Dmitrievna Polenova. Khronika sem'I khudozhnikov*, 362–363. Moscow: Iskusstvo.

Saltykov, Aleksandr B. 1968. *Samoe blizkoe iskusstvo*. Moscow: Prosveshchennie.

Sears, Robert. 1855. *An Illustrated Description of the Russian Empire*. New York: R. Sears.

Titova, Ol'ga. 2015. "Out of the Wood: Interactions between the Kizhi Museum and Its Local Community." In Special issue of *ICOM News, International Council of Museums Magazine*, 68/3-4:18–19.

Vasilenko, Viktor. 1977. *Russkoe prikladnoe iskustvo. Istoki i stanovlenie*. Moscow: Iskusstvo.

Voronov, Vasilii. 1924. *Krest'ianskoe iskusstvo*. Moscow: Gosudarstvennoe izdatel'stvo. Reprinted in *O krest'ianskom iskusstve: izbrannye trudi*, eds. Tatiana Razina and L. I. Sviontkovskaia-Voronova, 28–128. Moscow: Sovetskii khudozhnik, 1972.

Zhegalova, Serafina. 1975. *Russkaia narodnaia zhivopis'*. Moscow: Prosveshchenie.

Zhegalova, Serafina. 1983. "Istoriia odnoi ekspeditsii." In *Prianik, Prialka i Ptitsa Sirin*, eds. Serafina Zhegalova, Svetlana Zhizhina, and Zoia Popova, 14–45. Moscow: Prosveshchenie.

FURTHER READING

Afanasiev, Alekandr, and Ivan Bilibin. 1996. *Russkie Narodnye Skazki/Russian Fairy Tales*, eds. and trans. D. Martin and L. Lisitskaia. Moscow: Terra.

Boguslavskaia, Irina. 2006. *Russian Folk Toys in the Collection of the Russian Museum*. St. Petersburg: Palace Editions.

Dain, Galina. 1981. *Russkaia narodnaia igrushka*. Moscow: Legkaia i pishchevaia promyshlennost'.

Hubbs, Joanna. 1988. *Mother Russia: The Feminine Basis of Russian Culture*. Bloomington, IN: Indiana University Press.

Kononenko, Natalie. 2007. *Slavic Folklore. A Handbook*. Westport, CT–London: Greenwood Press.

Kopanski, Karlheinz. 1998. *Hampelmann & Matrjoschka. Holzspielzeug aus Deutschland und Russland*. Kassel: Wintershall AG.

Opolovnikov, A. V., E. A. Opolovnikova. 1989. *The Wooden Architecture of Russia: Houses, Fortifications, Churches*. New York: Abrams.

Petrova, Evgeniia, ed. 2001. *Fairy Tales in Russia*. St. Petersburg: Palace Editions. Exhibition Catalogue, State Russian Museum.

Ricker, Michael. 2013. *To Spin a Yarn. Distaffs: Folk Art and Material Culture*. Nacogdoches, TX: Stephen F. Austin State University Press.

Vasilenko, Viktor. 1974. *Narodnoe iskusstvo*. Moscow: Sovetskii khudozhnik.

World of Russian Folk Art/Mir russkogo iskusstva: http://www.rusfolkart.org.

CHAPTER 41

FOLK ART REASSESSED
Entangled Material Culture in Rural Romania

ALEXANDRA URDEA AND MAGDALENA BUCHCZYK

To speak about "folk" objects is to assume a boundary between different categories such as *modernity* and *pre-modernity* or *rural* and *urban*, where folklore is ascribed to the pre-modern, the rural. As we know from scholars such as Eric Hobsbawm (1990) and Ernest Gellner (1991), "folklore" is a term imbued with a long political history, which has served different kinds of national projects throughout the nineteenth and twentieth centuries. This literature suggests that folk objects were removed from their initial purposes in the village and began to stand in for, to represent, something else: local or national identity, traditions or rurality (Bendix 2002; I. Popescu 2002; Hedeșan and Mihăilescu 2006). The meaning of the term "folklore" is not the same everywhere, and this is not only because, as the lasting traditions of folk festivals and the United Nations Educational, Scientific and Cultural Organization (UNESCO) tell us, different peoples have different "folk traditions." It is because in diverse settings, the term "folklore" has had other histories, specific political "traditions of invention" (Drace-Francis 2013), and evokes various images in the minds of readers or audiences. The long history of folk artifacts as objects of representation, both in national museums and *in situ*, raises questions about the actors that shape the narratives surrounding these objects. It also prompts reflection on the processes through which certain artifacts are imbued with folk value, power and an aura of authenticity, while others are excluded.

This chapter looks at case studies from Romania to explore how objects are understood and used by people in the countryside, particularly in the settings identified as sources for folk objects. The case studies discussed in this chapter derive from our own archival and ethnographic study, undertaken between 2010 and 2015. This research followed Romanian "folk artifacts" from the 1954 Horniman Museum collection (London) to the places of acquisition and, in some cases, the original owners and makers (Buchczyk 2018; Urdea 2018). Focusing on dress items, pottery, and domestic textiles, our study combines collection history with multi-sited anthropological research. Here, we use the insights from this ethnographic project to reanimate the study of "folk objects" in Romania by revealing the importance of the different narratives around, uses of, experiences with, and perspectives on vernacular objects by diverse social actors. Such a reorientation can enable novel explorations of the social practices and material relations in which "folk objects" are enmeshed, shedding new light on the social, historical, and political entanglements of this material culture.

Collecting Everyday Objects as Folk Art

What sort of things enter the category of Romanian folk objects? For the purpose of this chapter, we refer to all the things one can find in a folklore museum or folk-art exhibition—and in most rural settings: household objects like pottery; textiles that used to embellish house interiors (towels for wall hanging, blankets, bed throws, etc.), indeed the house itself, its architecture and woodcraft; and tools, including musical instruments. We choose to start from these forms of material culture because, in European scholarship and museum practice, this inventory of "folklore" as a category comes with a particular institutional and disciplinary history of selection and valuation (Bendix 1997; Macdonald 2013). This history, rooted in the nineteenth century, entails fixed requirements of authenticity and value, clear geographical boundaries between nation-states and regions, and a presumed close relationship between national or regional identities and objects (Kaneff 2004; Douglas 2011).

Only certain objects from the countryside, representing particular aesthetic qualities or perceived iconic, local features, had the potential to become "folklore" of "folk art" (Kirshenblatt-Gimblett 1998). "Folk" objects were created in rural environments and began to be collected in the nineteenth century by foreign travelers, local intellectuals and aristocrats, and later by museums. Things in people's houses—chairs, wall hangings, beds, pots—were considered collectable when they were imbued with meanings beyond the remit of the household or village: they were transformed into "folk art" and then "national" objects which would be displayed in grand exhibitions around the turn of the twentieth century (I. Popescu 2002; Kallestrup 2006). This history, which we sketch below (see "Folk Objects, the Nation"), is part and parcel of how people understand and use folk objects in today's Romania.

To what extent can collected "folk-art" objects be considered "everyday"? Some of them are objects that have, or seemed to have at one point, a purpose in the home—a chair, a rug, or a pot—while others, such as costumes, were reserved for exceptional situations rather than immersed in everyday experience. Many artifacts, like the textiles used for trousseaus or the special Sunday dress worn to church, were tied in with the performance of gender roles and displayed the social age, the marital status of the wearer, or the wealth of the household. Today, they continue to be displayed on special occasions and used in the performance of belonging, history, and traditions. These objects have enchanted urban collectors with their aesthetics and captivating craft technique. However, the acquisitions of rural dress and material culture in folk-art collections represent rural life in an almost exclusively ceremonial manner, as if every day of the week was Sunday (Hildebrandt 1992). This way, the large part of the folk-art collections mark a perpetual celebration of sorts, underrepresenting the harsh material reality and day-to-day existence in the countryside. The less decorative, mundane objects marking everyday life and labor were often deemed not worthy of folk-art collectors' attention because they contradicted the "authenticity" and the stylistic uniqueness of places. If the relationship between "folk objects" and the everyday is, at best, complicated, how can we understand such material as part of social experience?

A Material Culture Perspective

The disciplines studying material deemed "folklore" or "vernacular" have had different trajectories in eastern and western Europe. Consequently, these terms designated diverse types of objects in these two spaces (Barth et al. 2010). While anthropology emerged in the colonial context and developed around the figure of the timeless "primitive," ethnology and folklore studies in eastern Europe became centered on an internal, also timeless, figure of the "peasant" embodying an ambiguous blend of identity and alterity (Hedeșan and Mihăilescu 2006). Although forms of knowledge and concepts have interacted and traveled between eastern and western Europe, the different academic and political contexts have led to divergent notions of folklore (Kallestrup 2006; Macdonald 2016). This in turn has had a bearing on the place that folklore occupies within popular culture and how people today interact with items identified as "folkloric." For instance, the study of British folklore was embedded in nineteenth-century antiquarianism and cultural survivalism, as well as William Morris's Arts and Crafts movement, which still inspires people today to bring vernacular art and design into everyday life in specific ways (Myrone 2009). Meanwhile in Romania, folklore was incorporated into different statecraft projects, such as the interwar creation of Greater Romania or the legitimation of nationalist communism in dictator Nicolae Ceaușescu's Romania of the 1970s and 1980s (Verdery 1991).

Early on, anthropology's exploration of "other cultures" was deeply interconnected with the study of objects. With the development of functionalism and, later on, structuralism, interest in materiality faded as anthropologists focused on the structures that held societies together or on symbols, which were seen as non-material. From the 1980s onward, influential authors such as Igor Kopytoff (1986), Nicholas Thomas (2009), and Daniel Miller (2005) drew renewed attention to the importance of materiality for understanding culture. Furthermore, a material culture perspective became crucial for understanding different social phenomena, from religion to the power of ideologies, or the relationship between humans and non-humans. Contrary to the distinctions made by UNESCO between tangible and intangible heritage, a material culture perspective assumes that in most cases it is impossible to clearly distinguish between the two (Kirshenblatt-Gimblett 2004; Joy 2013). The material and the immaterial coexist through practice—for example, any dance is expressed through gesture and performance and animated through a range of objects such as instruments, items of clothing, and ornaments. As material culture is linked to embodied action, we need to consider how agency, practice, and things are enmeshed in the dynamic construction of personhood (Buchczyk 2014; Gell 1998; Tesăr 2018; Weiner 1992).

Material culture perspectives offer a range of tools for uncovering the processual and practice-oriented perspectives on "folk art" or "folkloric" objects. Object biographies (Appadurai 1988; Hoskins 2013) allow for the exploration of the historical and social dimensions of the nationalist projects that folk objects were made part of in Romania. National museums, particularly in the socialist period (1947–1989), interpreted "folk objects" as timeless, as an embodiment of identity (Kaneff 2004; Nicolescu 2016). Yet even a simple inventory of all the names used for "folk objects" gives a sense of the wide array of social relations that such items are part of, including *artă populară* (folk art), *artă națională* (national art), and *artizanat*, often used to describe mass-produced or socialism-era folk art. The makers of folk objects were at times addressed as *creatori populari* (folk artists) or *meșteri populari* (folk craftspeople) (Constantin 2009), while the song and dance performances were called *folclor* (folklore), *muzică populară* (popular music), *dansuri populare* (folk dances), or *folclor nou* (new folklore) in the socialist period (see Nicolescu 2016; Urdea 2015). These distinctions matter. For example, by focusing on the lived distinctions between *creatori populari* (folk artists) or *meșteri populari* (folk craftspeople), we can explore the social and political process through which certain objects (and people) are considered valuable, while others are cast aside as "inauthentic" makers and practitioners (Buchczyk 2015, 2021).

In what follows, we highlight some of the ways in which the different types of folk objects are cared for, put on display in local museums, and subject to tensions between pressures of authenticity, commoditization, and social change. By demonstrating the local narratives and practices, we seek to show how folklore is used for a variety of personal or local identity projects. We argue that it provides a form of capital, a cultural currency that allows people from different localities to take part and gain visibility in national and international settings. And it allows for different ways to narrate history, social change, and personal relations through various engagements with the "folk object." In order to understand these situated contexts and actions, we need to examine the emergence of folk material culture as an object of knowledge in Romania.

Folk Objects, the Nation

Since the nineteenth century, folklore and folk art have been interlinked with various politically charged ideas about "the people" and used to forge a national identity (Davison 2005; Herzfeld 2004). In Romania, early scholarship in folklore and folk art was connected to political romanticism and the intellectual genealogy of *Volkskunde*. These studies focused on local and national practices, intersecting with questions about what makes Romanians a "people" (Hedeșan and Mihăilescu 2006). In this academic tradition, rural populations (or peasantry) and their material culture were seen as bearers of an authentic, national character and symbols of the nation (Verdery 1991). Rural objects were acquired mostly by the elites, including members of the Romanian royal family, for example, Queen Marie (consort to King Ferdinand I from 1914 to 1927), and renowned metropolitan collectors (such as Carmen Sylva and Barbu Slătineanu). They were valued for their aesthetic qualities but also came to be seen as linked to particular moral economies, skills, and livelihoods (Urdea 2018). Romanian folk objects were markers of the relationship between the monarchy and "the people," and were used to shape the public perception of the royal household (Kallestrup 2018). In the interwar Romania of the 1920s and 1930s, rural artifacts became collectibles as part of the approach of the new school of sociology initiated by Dimitrie Gusti. For the Gusti school, collecting artifacts became part of integrated data-gathering campaigns that aimed not only at preserving rural material culture but also at shaping rural transformation and national modernization (Mușat 2015). These acquisitions were presented as specimens used in the construction of a new "science of the nation."

The tandem of modernity and preservation of tradition, reforming and collecting, is critical to understanding rural material culture in Romania. It was not only Gusti sociologists who saw folk objects as part of the modernization agenda but also curators and makers of exhibitions. The overlapping ideas of "rural civilization" and "modern living" were exemplified by museum-making practices and exported on a global stage through the Romanian pavilions during world fairs (Demetrescu 2010:162). For example, traditional architecture featured in the Romanian Pavilion of the International Exhibition in Rome (1911), and so-called folkloric architecture was likewise pivotal to the designs of the pavilions exhibited in the world fairs of Barcelona (1929) and New York (1939) (Popescu 2010). Carmen Popescu has demonstrated that Romania's drive for modernization was closely aligned with national traditionalism and notions of "the Romanian soul" (2010:12).

After the Second World War, the country's traditional–modern project was pushed in a socialist direction, accelerating in a Stalinist spirit. In the 1950s, "folklore" was used as "visual propaganda" in exhibitions for export. These shows aimed to spread the word about the benefits of state communism and educate the Western public. The exhibition images of modernization, such as the electrification of the countryside and the construction of new factories and cultural centers, alongside glass cases showing traditional dress and carved "folkloric" architecture (Buchczyk 2018). For example, the 1952 *Rumanian Exhibition: Achievements of the Rumanian People's Republic* in London juxtaposed the communist struggle for the future with the folkloric past. The display combined information panels on the projected statistics of the state Five-Year Plans and sketches of industrial construction with the embroidered blouses and sheepskin jackets worn by rural workers (Buchczyk 2018:163). In the interplay between traditional and modern materiality, folklore was embedded in constructing a new socialist culture. It was mobilized to articulate a new class identity of the peasant-workers, a "symbolic family of people" (Kligman 1988).

Similar to other European contexts, folk objects became part of attempts through which formulations of national heritage or state-sponsored notions of national identity were established and communicated (Herzfeld 1986; Kaneff 2004). Narratives around the past and traditions were framed as part of a "heritage–memory–identity formation" (Macdonald 2013:137), often by linking people, places, and objects. As folklore was used to legitimize national communism, the state invested a great deal in the creation of infrastructure devoted to its production such as heritage organizations, folklore festivals, fairs, and spaces for performance and craft-making. Throughout the country and in almost every rural community, village halls were built and served simultaneously to educate the locals on matters of ideology, modern rural economy, and culture (Urdea 2018). They also provided a space where local folk practices could be turned into folk-art performances and integrated into the national repertoire in sanitized forms. In practice, this meant that villagers performed on local, regional, as well as national stages; and outside their villages they were recognized as representatives of their local "folk culture".

In the mid-1970s, folklore began to play a particularly important role in the official public sphere as Romania entered a period of national communism under Ceaușescu (Verdery 1991). The political isolation from both Western countries and the Soviet Union under Ceaușescu corresponded to a new cultural, inward orientation. Nationalism permeated all folklore and amateur arts, and the annual folklore contest–festival regularly staged between 1976 and 1989, *Cântarea României* ("Song to Romania"), incorporated all the activities carried out through the local houses of culture, from poetry to painting and, of course, performances. Not only were folk dance and song central to the festival, but other artistic productions were often infused with folk themes. And among the presentations selected as winners, nationalist and folklore themes were prime (Urdea 2018). The "Song to Romania" involved the population from every corner of the country, from villages to industrial towns and the capitals of regions. This heavy investment in folklore decreased with the collapse of national communism in 1989. Cultural production in the country was no longer centralized, which meant that the uses and meanings attached to "folklore" during Ceaușescu's period began to be reassessed, as we explore in the section below.

FOLK-ART VALUES—*ARTIZANAT* AND ITS DISCONTENTS

One of the key developments in the production of "folkloric" material culture in postwar Romania was the creation of *artizanat*: an industrialized form of craft production managed through the state-run National Union of Craft Cooperatives (UCECOM) (Constantin 2009). Under socialism, UCECOM generated 11% of the Romanian gross domestic product, with a vast workforce of which 75 percent were women (Anghelache 2018:272). The *artizanat* objects occupied an ambiguous space between rural production and large-scale industrialization, between the peasantry and the "newly urbanized people employed in factories" (Nicolescu 2018:288). This widespread system aspired to produce folk objects that could be seen as both a form of traditional craft and of modern decorative art (Horşia and Petrescu 1972). To achieve this balance, UCECOM engaged museum experts to oversee the design process (Nicolescu 2018:285). They guided and controlled the process both to maintain the "genuine character" of the *artizanat* object and enrich it with new design features (Horşia and Petrescu 1972:74).

Artizanat was situated at the intersection of the planned economy and representational practices of the Socialist Republic of Romania (1947–1989). Across the country, factory-like facilities supported by a network of home-based contractors made folk objects to supply the vast network of state-run folklore gift shops and export Romanian folklore abroad. As in any socialist workplace, the folklore-producing workers were required to meet daily output targets and used modern machinery. Next to factory-style cooperatives, state-run *artizanat* objects were also made by outworkers. Many women wove, embroidered, and sewed *artizanat* textiles in their living rooms, often working through the night, after coming home from a day's work at the collective farm. These objects were based on pattern guidelines and materials provided by UCECOM.

One such folklore-producing outworker was a weaver in a southern Transylvanian village whom Magdalena Buchczyk encountered during her ethnographic fieldwork (2011–2012), in which she traced a collection of Romanian artifacts from the Horniman Museum. At the time of the fieldwork, the octogenarian, known to most people in the village Mrs. Live, had already stopped working in the state-run craft sector and had packed away her loom. During socialism, she had been weaving pieces of fabric with traditional patterns, from wall hangings to large bed throws. Many of these textiles were now carefully folded in a cabinet in her living room. Reflecting on the textiles made for UCECOM, she explained that she had valued the *artizanat* labor as a source of extra income. The engagement with UCECOM was a strategic choice as Mrs. Live could avoid working on the state farm and still reach the full state pension. She also strategically economized with provided materials, enabling her to weave additional pieces for her own use or sale in the village.

Although Mrs. Live understood the value of her labor for the cooperative, the products of her own private work were worth much more. The UCECOM pieces belonged to a separate category of objects, predominantly "red" and "easy to make." In contrast to the red *artizanat* things, the woven objects made from saved material were pieces of high value and required more skill and technical complexity. Displaying smaller wall hangings with more ornate rose patterns, Mrs. Live proudly explained that the objects were made from leftover material from UCECOM commissions according to her own taste and design ideas. These pieces gave her a sense of fulfillment and personal gratification. With the excess yarn, she could express her creativity beyond the confines of the UCECOM design. Her own textiles, seen as unique pieces, were regarded as more valuable by local customers. They were given as gifts or bought by other women in the village who worked in the local factories and had their own disposable income but too little time for crafts. In this way, the red *artizanat* objects and their leftover byproducts circulated in different ways in the local and national markets. While the "red things" from UCECOM commissions were more widespread and could be found in many folk-art shops across Romania and abroad, the little leftover pieces held more personal value and circulated locally, sold exclusively in her home or by word of mouth. The *artizanat* and Mrs. Live's own objects were relational and embedded in multiple symbolic economies in the local and national context.

After 1989, UCECOM production was significantly affected by the post-socialist transformation. In the following decades, production facilities were closed down, and union membership dwindled (Petrescu 2011). A large number of craftspeople and outworkers, previously employed by the cooperative system, were left without work and had to find alternative income streams. As former *artizanat* producers tried to make a living in the precarious post-socialist environment, many left the profession to pursue new careers in the local service economy or administration, or they migrated. In some locations with tourist and heritage profiles, makers were able to establish their own home-based workshops or worked as laborers for other craftspeople (Buchczyk 2021). The *artizanat* products, once essential parts of the Romanian economy and self-representation abroad, came to be seen as inauthentic and kitschy (Nicolescu 2016), no longer considered part of material culture that was worth collecting or presenting in exhibitions.

Artizanat products, with their folkloric patterns and decorative aesthetics, need to be understood as part of a broader constellation of value and hierarchy of objects. In other words, under socialism, some classes of objects (*artizanat*) circulated through the complex system of state folklore shops, while others remained part of the local economy. Although both were part of an interconnected and changing landscape of craft production, they held different power on the local, national, and international stages. Craft makers such as Mrs. Live constructed their own narratives about different sorts of "folk" objects and assigned their meanings and values to material culture. The *artizanat* production example thus demonstrates that "folk objects" occupy a variety of categories and trigger a range of meanings depending on the historical context of their social and political uses and value on the market.

Local Museums and Configurations of Value

During socialist Romania, diverse state-run regional folk and crafts museums were established throughout the country. Meanwhile, post-socialist Romania saw the emergence of local museums. Some of these were rooted in local displays established during the socialist period, while others were established from scratch in the 2000s. Their presence shows that villages are also places of representation and not only spaces where objects live in situ. Through local displays, people try to make sense of objects deemed "folk," often by using them to convey personal histories and how they relate to wider historical narratives. Such memory-based narratives are not entirely severed from the efforts of national folklore museums to reinterpret folk objects in post-socialism. Often, there are tensions at the local level as to how objects should be interpreted, displayed, and cared for.

Overall, villagers and community officials consider local museums the most productive way to put folk items to use, and they often mention that without these displays, such objects are simply left unused and thrown away. In villages people often deplore the "forgetting" of folklore, saying that "no one cares" anymore about the things people made, wore, or used in the past. In most cases this narrative mirrors the realities of depopulation and international migration among the young. Some village women keep dress items and textiles in their wardrobes for special moments, usually when outsiders visit (Urdea 2018). Such items are kept for an indefinite moment when younger family members might claim them, or they are intended to be sold to interested outsiders.

Local museums started opening throughout the Romanian countryside in the 1960s, when collections of folk objects for national, regional, and local exhibitions began in full sway (Nicolescu 2014). Interviews with those who set up such museums show that the museums' rationale was preserving folk culture as a national patrimony, seen as endangered by the modernization of the countryside. Museum professionals from national folklore museums would come to the countryside and help to make the displays of local objects, using their expertise, yet often without further ethnographic fieldwork (Nicolescu 2014). In the region of Vrancea (east-central Romania) in the 1980s, eleven village clusters had established ethnographic collections, two of which were full-fledged "house museums." One of them, the museum of Paltin, was the most developed: it had a "scientifically reorganized" collection, the "conservation of its patrimony was assured," and it numbered 634 pieces. Recent interviews with villagers from around Paltin reveal that people considered the museum to be of great value.

This concerted centralized effort to open local museums stopped in the 1990s when state-sponsored folklore performances, and the state's investment in "folklore," came to a halt after the demise of the socialist state. In the words of the former director of the regional Museum of Vrancea during an interview with Alexandra Urdea, "folklore was liberated from state control" in the 1990s. This historical turning point saw a rise in interest in folklore both from the grassroots and from the ethnologists' and museum professionals' points of view, mirroring not just attempts to redefine identity but the joy of engaging with objects in a new way. But without financial support from the center, all folklore projects struggled afterward.

This is the context in which an unusual number of local museums and collections emerged in villages from the 2000s onward. Some of these became part of a network of local museums throughout the country and benefited from the support of the Romanian Peasant Museum in Bucharest, although, to all intents and purposes, this has generated a hegemonic discourse around folk items already since the 1990s. For example, a publication of the Romanian Peasant Museum describes these local museums as idiosyncratic and labels them "author" museums, code for provincial. In other words, as opposed to regional or national museums which claim to represent wide cultural areas, local "author museums" represent the perspective of one "author," whose interpretations of the objects are imbibed with personal memories.

Urdea's fieldwork in Vrancea included research on two such "author museums" (Fig. 41.1). One of them, called "The Roots of Vrancea," was set up in a little hut that the "author" built for this purpose. The other is set up in a large house, part of which is a holiday residence for an urban family with a great love of all things folkloric. Both comprise objects that likely would not otherwise enter the space of a national museum: they are displayed for their "memory" value and are accompanied by personal narratives. Contrasting with the museums set up by external experts during the socialist period, in the case of the "author museums," local villagers generally do not agree with the curatorial choices of objects. Many locals feel that these museums should strive to represent the village more fully, and they feel excluded from the attention that the "authors" get. In the "The Roots of Vrancea" museum, some of the villagers say that items they donated to the museum are not being displayed or adequately looked after (Urdea 2018).

Museums such as these use objects as retainers of memory, but only some of the "memories" are articulated. Those that sit at odds with current dominant narratives of the nation's modern history are often forgotten. One example is the place of the

FIG. 41.1. The "Grandparents' Museum" in Vrancea, a local ("author") museum set up independently.
(Photograph by A. Urdea, 2012.)

"Song to Romania" festival in such museums. While many villagers remember the festival in a positive light, and the majority of the "authors" had some involvement in it in their youth, this is not reflected in their displays. This is because the use of folklore in the socialist period is generally condemned by state museums, particularly by the Romanian Peasant Museum; therefore, the "authors" of the local museums have trouble making sense of these personal histories in their displays.

Another example is that of craftspeople identified in the past as *creatori populari*, whose objects are now perceived as being less valuable. Before 1989 *creatori* were the people who made folk or folk-inspired objects: textiles, woodcraft, masks, and others. They learned their skills in the village, usually in the family, and took the opportunity to become *creatori* within the framework of state-run folklore productions. In the 1980s their works would be represented in the "Song to Romania" festival, where they were encouraged to make crafts in the vein of old folk items but with their own creative imprint. These new creations were also exhibited in museums as examples of "present-day folk art," in a museological discourse that collapsed social and historical differences and stressed national continuity through folk art. Their work was not so much UCECOM-style *artizanat* but was seen as artistic and unique.

These products were intended to demonstrate that the creativity of the collective folk had not been altered during the socialist period and that socialism helped it flourish. The objects were meant to bridge the contradictions of national communism and merge "folklore" with "present-day transformations"; they often included propaganda symbols (white doves, industrial furnaces, or the hammer and sickle), although in the 1980s many of these symbols signaled nationalism rather than communism. *Creatori* performed their role as transmitters of tradition and national spirituality in a modern communist state. After 1989 regional institutions in charge of folklore performances and crafts helped refashion *creatori* into *meșteri*: craftspeople who made objects with use value and artistic input that had no relation to state ideology. The value of their craft was defined instead by their traditional skills and materials. Yet *meșteri* had had a flourishing pre-1989 career, and their presence and objects often reminded museologists and folklore specialists of the close connection between folklore and national communism.

In the Vrancea region, one local museum was set up by a *creator popular* named Mr. Manu, for whom objects are valuable as art and evidence of the collective creativity of the folk. Unlike other 1980s *creatori*, he did not pursue craftsmanship by reconverting into a *meșter*, so he was no longer invited to display or sell his objects. As we rummaged through the things he had on display in his workshop, he pointed to his heart-shaped embroidered pieces of leather, wood hand-carved into the shapes of snakes or dragons, and other curious objects with names inscribed upon them. However, none of these items allowed him to participate in the fairs held regularly at folk museums across the country, mainly because his objects fall short of authenticity demands, ideological or market value at such fairs. But while Mr. Manu is not especially interested in making authentic crafts, his persona is an embodiment of the imagined "folk" peasant: he wears his felt trousers and embroidered shirt on every occasion and knows precisely how to pose for a good picture (Fig. 41.2). He showed Urdea some of the warm and appreciative

FIG. 41.2. Mr. Manu in his peasant attire, Vrancea.

(Photograph by A. Urdea, 2012.)

comments left in his guest book by various TV producers who have come to film him over the years, whenever an image of "authentic Vranceans" was needed.

Like Mr. Manu's museum, some of the displays encountered in villages are more like collages or idiosyncratic agglomerations, while others have been arranged to tell a coherent narrative through "folklore." To some extent, they have all absorbed the ideas about evaluating and interpreting folklore perpetuated by state museums and other such institutions during the socialist and post-socialist periods, framing folk objects

FIG. 41.3. A room in a traditional house in Vrancea set up as a display of memorabilia and folk crafts. In this example, the room is not for public display but contains artefacts which the owner values as retainers of memory.

(Photograph by A. Urdea, 2012.)

as craft, art, or memorabilia. Alignment to such interpretations from the center was a strategy for the authors of these displays to gain legitimacy. This is not done cynically or with the intention of material gain but rather as a struggle for social confirmation and to a large extent, as for any artistic activity, as part of a search for truth and value. Such negotiations and practices of self-museumification through performance are part of the texture of everyday life (Fig. 41.3). The objects in local museums and exhibitions are performed and used as markers of identity and indices of distinction that represent and reproduce particular normative ideas around production and the use of "folk objects."

Folk Objects in the Home

Objects belonging to rural households have a long history in folklore and museum practice. Since the establishment of the early twentieth-century museums in Romania, rural vernacular architecture and domestic objects have been critical devices for staging the village house and its "folk" material culture in cities. In 1907, the Bucharest-based Museum of National Art displayed a reconstruction of the house of Antonie Mogoș, a rural craftsman from Ceauru village, Gorj County (southeastern Romania). Inspired by the Skansen Open-Air Museum,[1] it served as a blueprint for museum and exhibition practice. In 1911, a replica of the Mogoș house was shown in the Romanian Pavilion of the International Exhibition in Rome. Similar displays of rural, "folkloric" houses were presented in the national pavilions exhibited in Barcelona (1929) and New York (1939) (C. Popescu 2010). The rural material culture was used to represent the country internationally.

In Romania, village houses aimed to showcase a complete picture of the Romanian nation. In 1936, peasant houses were taken to the newly founded Village Museum in Bucharest to be reassembled for public view (C. Popescu 2010:39). During the socialist period, open-air museums displaying houses and their objects were established in some Romanian towns, creating an artificial rural landscape for urban consumption. These museums played a significant part in building a national communist mass culture, disseminating particular representations of rurality through displays, public events, and TV shows (Iosif 2008). The Romanian Village Museum established a philosophy of thinking about "folk objects" as an order of classificatory units, ethnographic zones with geographical boundaries connoting distinct entities with their inhabitants, and material cultures. Every zone had a set of specific dress conventions and categories of objects, materials, tools, and craft production (Formagiu 1974; Istrătescu-Târgoviște 2003; Maier 2009).

These practices of regional classification persisted over time. Educated by the foundational texts of interwar village monographs and informed by iconic displays (such as the Village Museum in Bucharest), consecutive generations of ethnologists and folklore specialists visited the emblematic areas (such as the Maramureș or Vrancea ethnographic zone) to study various local customs and material folklore. One of the most symbolic houses and domestic displays in the Bucharest Village Museum came from the village of Drăguș, central Romania, the site of an extensive monographic study of Gusti's interwar sociological school (Rostas 2000). The Drăguș household aimed to represent a typical house of the Făgăraș ethnographic area, located in southern Transylvania (central Romania). Since then, the style of the Făgăraș district has become vital to the intellectual tradition of Romanian sociology, ethnography, and museum practice. Domestic spaces of Făgăraș and other rural interiors are often represented as noble, harmonious, idealized spaces evoking sentiments of a rustic peasant past and bucolic charm. In museum writing, Romanian peasant households often connote a sense of national aesthetic capacity and taste for beauty, seen as a Romanian feature (Stoica 1984:47). As the cozy home stands for a symbolic family, this national sense of taste is frequently interlinked with ideas of comfort and patriotic affects (Kligman 1988:258).

Museum ethnographers have explored the peasant house, its interiors and practices of storage, collecting, and display of vernacular material culture, as entangled with social relations. For example, scholars have focused on rural domestic displays and "good rooms"[2] to explore their links to ritual rhythms embedded in household networks, practices of embodiment, and kinship (Posey 2005). Ethnographic research on the transformations and revivals of domestic arrangements has also highlighted the social lives and specific dynamics of reinventing domestic displays (Iuga 2010). These approaches provide valuable insights into the performative and affective social practices and personal meanings of objects through time.

In the Făgăraș area, the material culture of these rural domestic spaces requires paying attention to both the objects and spaces with "folk" objects as well as the processes of rejection and change. In a mountain valley village near Drăguș, Buchczyk encountered several abandoned traditional houses similar to the ones found in the museums. In contrast to the curatorial representations of charming pastoral spaces, for people like Mrs. Tave, a villager who had lived in such spaces for decades, their interiors and objects evoked stories of both relatedness and bittersweet sentiments. For Mrs. Tave, the house contained a wealth of biographical narratives, family histories, memories of livelihoods, and critical events. She talked about ambiguous traces of migration, from the photographs of family members living across the ocean to the refrigerator she received as a present from her son in Austria. The house also triggered recollections about the hardships of life in the countryside and the local experiences of collectivization (see Kideckel 1993; Kligman and Verdery 2011). Instead of discussing rustic, traditional domesticity, she took great pride in her new home, located down the road from her previous one. The modern interior and facilities, Mrs. Tave explained, enabled her to live a different, more comfortable life. In contrast to a romanticized curatorial perspective on these spaces, she and other former residents of such homes were not nostalgic for their pastoral past or the aesthetics of a tasteful cottage.

Mrs. Tave's new house did not contain a "good room" wrapped in textiles or "dressed" (*îmbrăcată*) with traditional objects. In this space, the "folk" material culture category was rejected and undesirable, seen as old (*bătrânească*), connoting a past life of poverty and hard labor. Rebuilding and decluttering "folk" objects from the domestic space was considered an escape from drudgery in the direction of modernity and comfort. For people like Mrs. Tave, the old interior was not a nostalgic cottage but a site of memories of hardship, a marker of ruptured relations, and social transformations in the area. The former house had a spectral presence and tended to be kept locked away. The "folk" objects left behind were embedded in powerful stories of change and strong personal feelings about undesirable pasts and aspirational futures. Rather than indices of ahistorical "ethnographic zones," these objects were also part of other narratives and practices. This material culture cannot be understood without exploring the ambivalent experiences and meanings, as well as the related practices of care, rearrangement, rejection, decluttering, and disposal. Objects from a rural house are not only imbued with an aura of rustic locality, but also with ambiguity and affective historical significance.

Beyond Folklore

The "folk-art" aesthetic has entered global consumption: many items in an Ikea showroom are similar to those seen in a folk-art museum. "Tradition never goes out of style," Ikea tells its buyers. Turning everyday objects into art—and, conversely, bringing the category of art into the realm of the everyday—was one of the ambitions of the arts and crafts movements at the turn of the twentieth century in Britain. Its proponent,

William Morris, argued for an aesthetic rooted in the pre-modern world, where each person was the artisan of their own living space, as a way to counter the sense of alienation provoked by industrialization. Then the folklore aesthetic was absorbed by capitalism as folk objects began to be produced and bought as commodities, although craft-making continues to exist alongside factory-produced "folk" objects in Romania as elsewhere.

The wealth of museological and folklore scholarship in Romania devoted to "folk" objects has aimed to generate elaborate classifications of the objects. They have been characterized by particular morphological qualities and assigned to "ethnographic zones," constituting a topography of distinct rural material cultures. Yet, as we have shown, much of the folk rural material culture escapes such classifications when we analyze the object as embedded in a set of complex personal, social, and power relations, and when we consider reinterpretations of folklore in a post-socialist context. Stepping away from the ahistorical zoning perspective allows explorations of the social entanglements in which the objects are situated. Digging into the classificatory logic and the social world of *artizanat* or *artă populară*, and other labels attached to making and remaking "folk" objects opens up new possibilities for investigating changing notions of heritage, social status, and modes of production in a shifting context.

As the examples of the leftover weaving, local museum, and abandoned house demonstrate, the power of folk objects lies in how they evoke memories and are deployed by different actors in various performative and representational projects. A material culture perspective provides a gateway into exploring the complexity of interwoven material, historical, and social domains. Such an approach recognizes that the various nominations of objects (e.g., as *artă populară* or *artizanat*) are part of broader social and historical developments and discourses with very tangible effects. Research exploring daily interactions with these objects points to alterations, re-enactments, and performances, instances of abandoning "folk" objects and constructing new identities and norms. Approaches that focus on object biographies tell us that folk objects occupy multiple roles in various social settings, changing their power and social currency. Ethnographies of material culture build a picture of objects as markers of entangled, ever-shifting social uses, experiences, and meanings. They also tell us more about why some things came to matter or not matter at specific historical moments.

While many state museums in Romania and elsewhere continue to select and display objects following rigid standards of authenticity and belonging to a specific "ethnographic zone," a wealth of other objects deemed "folkloric" are constantly produced, displayed, purchased, kept safe in wardrobes, or mobilized to narrate life histories and perspectives on the past. This capacity of the objects to be representative must not be considered in opposition to their authentic life in situ or seen to diminish their value. While the empirical research of "folk art" or "folkloric" material culture is still considered a specialist field, such things can provide new insights into the social, political, and economic worlds in which they are situated. If "folk" material culture eludes definition, it may be the reorientation from knowledge generated in the city or heritage institution to a range of situated understandings, uses, and values of objects. This reorientation allows us to explore and reassess "folk art" and "folklore" objects in novel ways, shedding light on their social and historical complexities.

Notes

1. The Skansen, established in 1891 in Stockholm, was the first open-air museum and showcased rural and pre-industrial life in Sweden. It served as a prototype for museums of folklore across Europe.
2. Good rooms are representational spaces in domestic space, frequently decorated or dressed with compositions of icons, pieces of pottery, and different types of fabrics covering the surfaces, from walls to beds and tables.

Works Cited

Anghelache, Constantin. 2018. Rolul cooperației meșteșugărești în evoluția și creșterea economică a României. *Romanian Statistical Review: Supplement*, 5:262–279.

Appadurai, Arjun, ed. 1988. *The Social Life of Things: Commodities in Cultural Perspective.* Cambridge: Cambridge University Press.

Barth, Fredrik, Andre Gingrich, Robert Parkin, and Sydel Silverman. 2010. *One Discipline, Four Ways: British, German, French, and American Anthropology.* Chicago: University of Chicago Press.

Bendix, Regina. 1997. *In Search of Authenticity: The Formation of Folklore Studies.* Madison: University of Wisconsin Press.

Bendix, Regina. 2002. "The Uses of Disciplinary History." *Radical History Review*, 84/1:110–114.

Buchczyk, Magdalena. 2014. "To Weave or Not to Weave: Vernacular Textiles and Historical Change in Romania." *Textile: Journal of Cloth and Culture*, 12/3:328–345.

Buchczyk, Magdalena. 2015. "Heterogeneous Craft Communities: Reflections on Folk Pottery in Romania." *Journal of Museum Ethnography*, no. 28:28–49.

Buchczyk, Magdalena. 2018. "Ethnographic Objects on the Cold War Front: The Tangled History of a London Museum Collection." *Museum Anthropology*, 41/2:159–172.

Buchczyk, Magdalena. 2021. "Becoming Heritage Smart: Negotiating the Dilemma of Craft Practice in a Ceramic Center." In *Craft and Heritage: Intersections in Critical Studies and Practice*, eds. Susan Surette and Elaine Paterson, 157–171. London: Bloomsbury Academic.

Constantin, Marin. 2009. "Artizanatul țărănesc în economia de piață din România și Europa Centrală și de Est." *Sociologie Românească*, 7/2:114–129.

Davison, Patricia. 2005. "Museums and the Re-shaping of Memory." In *Heritage, Museums and Galleries: An Introductory Reader*, ed. Gerard Corsane, 202–215. Abingdon: Routledge.

Demetrescu, Ruxandra. 2010. "Modernity, Tradition and the Avant-Garde. Reference Points in Romanian Art Literature, 1908–1946." In *(Dis)Continuities: Fragments of Romanian Modernity in the First Half of the 20th Century*, ed. Carmen Popescu, 143–228. Bucharest: Simetria.

Douglas, Oliver. 2011. "Folklore, Survivals, and the Neo-archaic." *Museum History Journal*, 4/2:223–244.

Drace-Francis, Alex. 2013. *The Traditions of Invention: Romanian Ethnic and Social Stereotypes in Historical Context.* Leiden, the Netherlands: Brill.

Formagiu, Hedvig-Maria. 1974. *Portul popular din România: Catalog tipologic*. Bucharest: Muzeul de artă populară al Republicii Socialiste România.
Gell, Alfred. 1998. *Art and Agency: An Anthropological Theory*. Oxford: Clarendon Press.
Gellner, Ernest. 1991. "Nationalism and Politics in Eastern Europe." *New Left Review*, 189/5:127–134.
Hedeşan, Otilia, and Vintilă Mihăilescu. 2006. "The Making of the Peasant in Romanian Ethnology." *MARTOR: Revista de Anthropologie Muzeului Țăranului*, no. 11:187–201.
Herzfeld, Michael. 1986. *Ours Once More: Folklore, Ideology, and the Making of Modern Greece*. New York: Pella Publishing Company.
Herzfeld, Michael. 2004. *The Body Impolitic: Artisans and Artifice in the Global Hierarchy of Value*. Chicago: University of Chicago Press.
Hildebrandt, Franziska. 1992. *Sieben tage Sonntag? Trachtenpräsentationen im museum am beispiel Hessen*. Frankfurt am Main, Bern, and Paris: P. Lang.
Hobsbawm, Eric. 1990. *Nations and Nationalism since 1780: Programme, Myth*, Reality. Cambridge: Cambridge University Press.
Horşia, Olga, and Paul Petrescu. 1972. *Artistic Handicrafts in Romania*. Bucharest: National Union of Handicraft Cooperatives.
Hoskins, Janet. 2013. *Biographical Objects: How Things Tell the Stories of People's Lives*. Abingdon: Routledge.
Iosif, Corina. 2008. "The Politics of Tradition: Practices of Ethnological Museology under Communism." In *Studying Peoples in the People's Democracies: Socialist Era Anthropology in South-east Europe*, eds. Vintilă Mihăilescu, Ilia Iliev, and Slobodan Naumović, 81–112. Münster: LIT Verlag.
Istrătescu-Târgovişte, Cristian. 2003. *Simbolistică, ornament, ritual în spațiul carpatic românesc: Sau cunoaște-te pe tine însuți*. Timişoara: Brumar.
Iuga, Anamaria. 2010. "The Peasant Room and the Revival of Tradition." *MARTOR: Revista de Anthropologie Muzeului Țăranului*, no. 15:195–204.
Joy, Charlotte. 2013. *The Politics of Heritage Management in Mali: From UNESCO to Djenné*. Abingdon: Routledge.
Kallestrup, Shona. 2006. *Art and Design in Romania 1866-1927*. Boulder, NY: Columbia University Press.
Kallestrup, Shona. 2018. "'Royalty Is No Longer Quite Royal': Word and Image in the Children's Tales of Queen Marie of Romania." *Image & Narrative*, 19/1:23–45.
Kaneff, Deema. 2004. *Who Owns the Past? The Politics of Time in a "Model" Bulgarian Village*. Oxford: Berghahn.
Kideckel, David. 1993. *The Solitude of Collectivism: Romanian Villagers to the Revolution and Beyond*. Ithaca, NY: Cornell University Press.
Kirshenblatt-Gimblett, Barbara. 1998. *Destination Culture: Tourism, Museums, and Heritage*. Oakland: University of California Press.
Kirshenblatt-Gimblett, Barbara. 2004. "Intangible Heritage as Metacultural Production." *Museum International*, 56/1–2:52–65.
Kligman, Gail. 1988. *The Wedding of the Dead: Ritual, Poetics, and Popular Culture in Transylvania*. Berkeley: University of California Press.
Kligman, Gail, and Katherine Verdery. 2011. *Peasants under Siege: The Collectivization of Romanian Agriculture, 1949–1962*. Princeton, NJ: Princeton University Press.
Kopytoff, Igor. 1986. "The Cultural Biography of Things: Commoditization as Process." In *The Social Life of Things: Commodities in Cultural Perspective*, ed. Arjun Appadurai, 64–91. Cambridge: Cambridge University Press.

Macdonald, Sharon. 2013. *Memorylands: Heritage and Identity in Europe Today*. Abingdon: Routledge.
Macdonald, Sharon. 2016. "New Constellations of Difference in Europe's 21st-Century Museumscape." *Museum Anthropology*, 39/1:4–19.
Maier, Radu Octavian. 2009. *Meșteșuguri țărănești. Prelucrarea fibrelor vegetale și animale în spațiul românesc*. Bucharest: Editura Etnologică.
Miller, Daniel. 2005. "Materiality: An Introduction." In *Materiality*, 1–50. Durham, NC: Duke University Press.
Mușat, Raluca. 2015. "Prototypes for Modern Living: Planning, Sociology and the Model Village in Inter-war Romania." *Social History*, 40/2:157–184.
Myrone, M. 2009. "Instituting English Folk Art." *Visual Culture in Britain*, 10/1:27–52.
Nicolescu, G. 2014. "Displaying Historical Materialism in Socialist Romania: The Ventures of Commanding Temporalities." In *TENSES. New Graduate Writing*, eds. Aimee Joyce, Katy Aston and William Tantam, 35–55. London: Goldsmiths, University of London.
Nicolescu, Gabriela. 2016. "The Museum's Lexis: Driving Objects into Ideas." *Journal of Material Culture*, 21/4:465–489.
Nicolescu, Gabriela. 2018. "From Border Fetishism to Tactical Socialism." *East Central Europe*, 45/2–3:279–299.
Petrescu, Claudia. 2011. "Cooperația în România—Actor al economiei sociale." *Calitatea vieții*, 22/4:409–430.
Popescu, Carmen. 2010. "Modernity in Context." In *(Dis)Continuities: Fragments of Romanian Modernity in the First Half of the 20th Century*, ed. Carmen Popescu, 11–101. Bucharest: Simetria.
Popescu, Irina. 2002. *Foloasele Privirii*. Bucharest: Paideia.
Posey, Sarah. 2005. "Masquerade and the Meaning of Work in Rural Romania." PhD dissertation, University College London.
Rostas, Zoltan. 2000. "The Bucharest School of Sociology." *East Central Europe*, 27/2:1–17.
Stoica, Georgeta. 1984. *Romanian Peasant Houses and Households*. Bucharest: Meridiane Publishing House.
Tesăr, Cătălina. 2018. "Marriages, Wealth, and Generations among Romanian Cortorari Roma: Notes on a Future-Oriented Kinship." *Ethnologie française*, no. 4:613–622.
Thomas, Nicholas. 2009. *Entangled Objects: Exchange, Material Culture, and Colonialism in the Pacific*. Cambridge, MA: Harvard University Press.
Urdea, Alexandra. 2015. "A Stitch in Time: Searching for Authenticity through Shifting Regimes of Value in Romania." PhD dissertation, Goldsmiths, University of London.
Urdea, Alexandra. 2018. *From Storeroom to Stage: Romanian Attire and the Politics of Folklore*, Vol. 10. Oxford–New York: Berghahn Books.
Verdery, Katherine. 1991. *National Ideology under Socialism: Identity and Cultural Politics in Ceaușescu's Romania*, Vol. 7. Oakland: University of California Press.
Weiner, Annette. 1992. *Inalienable Possessions: The Paradox of Keeping while Giving*. Oakland: University of California Press.

CHAPTER 42

FOODWAYS IN MOLDOVA

JENNIFER R. CASH

This chapter treats the foodways of the Republic of Moldova, which gained independence from the Soviet Union in 1991. Moldova lies in a historical borderland. Its current borders only appear to separate it from the Romanian lands to its west, with which it is historically and ethnically tied. The republic is largely congruent with the region known from the early nineteenth century until World War II as "Bessarabia," but some of that older territory's land is now within Ukraine, while other land east of the Dniester River is (at least officially) within the country. In addition to Ukrainian "influences" from the north, east, and south, which Soviet nationalities policies emphasized and encouraged, the foodways of the people who live here have been influenced directly by Russian and Soviet rule, as well as by Bulgarians and Gagauz fleeing Ottoman rule and by nineteenth-century colonists invited from various parts of continental Europe. Over several centuries, changing trade routes have introduced new products and spurred the production and exportation of others.

I begin with a theoretical and conceptual orientation to foodways. This is followed by an introduction to Moldova and then a descriptive account of Moldova's foodways organized roughly along the three main trajectories of a contemporary American folkloristic approach to foodways in terms of products, practices, and performance. I have drawn on my fieldwork experience in urban and rural parts of Moldova during the years 1999–2010 but have focused on the elements that seem most continuous with the past and likely future despite changes brought by rural–urban migration, labor migration cycles, and globalization.

Food, Foodways, Folklore

Food has been studied by folklorists since the 1800s in at least two guises—as "folk foods" and as "folklore about food" (the beliefs and customs surrounding food) (Long 2015:1). At its inauguration in 1888, the American Folklore Society included a commitment to documenting food in its mission statement. However, neither in the United States nor in other countries did food become a central concern for folklorists until after the 1960s. A handful of leading anthropologists, some of whom were conversant with folklore studies, did place food (and nutrition) at the center of their work as early as the 1930s (e.g., Claude Lévi-Strauss, Margaret Mead, Audrey Richards). In general, it was European ethnology that led the most developed programs of research into food and foodways through the 1970s, and Don Yoder looked to this research in the 1950s when he began to encourage students in American folkloristics to look beyond "oral traditions" and study "foodways" among many other topics that were "customary" and "material."

European ethnology, as it first reinvigorated folklore's interest in food, still maintained a distinct concern for historically oriented research and emphasized surveying and mapping the distribution of particular ingredients, dishes, terms for food, etc. (e.g., Bringeus 1971; Bringeus and Wiegelmann 1971). By the 1970s, several other leading American folklorists, including Michael Owen Jones, Robert Georges, and Alan Dundes, took up the study of food. Still, major influences in a reorientation to treat food as folklore, full of implicit meanings and integrally tied to local knowledge systems, came slowly. In the 1990s, the *Journal of American Folklore* (*JAF*) published reviews of fewer than six books focused on food—all of them concerning the United States. (More than a dozen books about other topics from the east European region were reviewed during the same decade.) Clearly, interest in food was building in academic circles, however, as articles on food began to appear in the *JAF* as soon as the decade turned over.

The 1997 publication of *Food and Culture* by Carole Counihan and Penny van Esterik can be seen as a watershed for all food studies, although it is most closely associated with developments in the *anthropology* of food. By the 2000s, most American folklorists could be said to differ little from anthropologists; however, folklorists have also articulated distinctions in their approach to the study of food. Specifically, folklore's traditional concern for the systematization of material culture and knowledge systems has resulted in the development of a comprehensive methodological outline for observing, recording, and interpreting research on foodways.

"Foodways" can be defined as a total system of practices and concepts surrounding food and eating (Long 2015:14). Defined this way, its study can be approached from a concern with products, with practices and processes, or with performance. From the angle of the product, the researcher concentrates on food itself: ingredients, recipes, dishes, meals, food culture, and cuisine. From the perspective of practices and processes, one is more interested in oral narratives, instructions, and vocabulary; in customary techniques and styles; and in the material forms that are important in food production and consumption. The practices or processes which are of interest include production, procurement, preservation, preparation, presentation, consumption, cleanup, and disposal (or reuse). The third angle of performance from which a folklorist might approach foodways is the closest to the anthropological approach. Here, the folklorist concentrates on the performance of food contexts and meal systems (physical spaces, occasions, and types of events for specific aspects of foodways including expected meal routines) and on the "performance" of food in terms of how the functions and symbolism of food are revealed and the conceptualizations of food through associated beliefs, evaluation systems, aesthetics, and attitudes.

Food and Foodways in Eastern Europe

Interest in the social and cultural dimensions of food across eastern Europe (southeast Europe included) has been increasing among anthropologists since the 1990s (Harper and West 2003). Signature work has addressed fears of food contamination in post-Chernobyl Ukraine (Phillips 2002), soup kitchens and the problems of charity in Russia (Caldwell 2004), vodka as an alternative currency (Hivon 1998; Rogers 2005), cultural meanings of the potato (Ries 2009), the taste of sausages in Lithuania and the impact of changing EU regulations on local food systems (Klumbyte 2010), and nutrition and household production in Slovakia (Acheson 1997)—to name just a few. That many of these works (and others) remain PhD dissertations or singular articles, however, testifies to the ongoing difficulty in raising a sustained ethnographic discussion about regional foodways in Anglo-American anthropology.

Moreover, few of these works have engaged directly with the relevant local and national traditions of food scholarship, meaning that the possibilities for a new synthesis between folklore, ethnology, and anthropology in the region remain unexplored. European ethnologists have been more successful in this regard (e.g., Mesnil 1992; Mesnil and Popova 2002). American folkloristics can also be said to have generally kept up with the work of east European colleagues better than anthropology did during the latter decades of the Cold War, but—perhaps because it is a smaller field with severely limited intake of new scholars—few folklorists have contributed directly to the development of east European food studies.

Despite growing attention to food across the humanities and social sciences in parallel to the studies of consumption and globalization at the beginning of the twenty-first century, southeast Europe has remained relatively untreated by Western scholarship at the level of either synthesis or full-length study. Rich ethnographic archives exist concerning representative elements of perceived national food cultures for some countries. However, local scholars have still rarely valorized food as an important ethnological subject; Klaus Roth counted only fourteen articles concerning food published in *Bŭlgarska Etnografiia* between 1975 and 1995 (2010:27 note 1). He maintains that food in southeast European ethnological traditions was at best disregarded as a marginal question of history and traditional taste and at worst as politically problematic.

The sustained study of traditional foods would have indeed brought up unpleasant issues for socialist nation-states: Ottoman legacies, status and trade relations expressed through consumption, and the lack of ethnonational distinctiveness in the recent past (Blaszczyk and Rohdewald 2018). The contemporary ethnographic study of food would have been clearly problematic as it would have revealed weaknesses in the new regimes' systems of food production, distribution, and consumption. However, such studies might have also demonstrated how political relations brought new foods, like tinned foods from Vietnam, to the region (see Roth 2010:32).

Moldova: Overview of People and Place

Moldova is a small country, situated in the northeast Balkans and in the Black Sea basin. Its total landmass is 13,067 square miles (33,843.5 square kilometers), comparable in size to the state of Maryland in the United States or about the size of Belgium. At independence, Moldova's population was approximately 4 million. By 2016, it had dropped to about 3 million. Much of the decline is due to outmigration. In addition to the capital of Chișinău, the country counts four other much smaller cities (Bălți, Tiraspol, Orhei, and Cahul). More than half the population continues to live in villages, with a decidedly agricultural profile.

Both culturally and politically, the country is normally divided into four cultural-geographic regions: north, center, south, and east (Transnistria). The central area is the site of the Codru (forest), which was dense deciduous forest prior to the nineteenth century. Most of the country is marked by green and gentle hills; in the south these flatten out into drier steppe-lands. About 75 percent of the country's soils are "black" (chernozem) and particularly good for agriculture. Deposits of sedimentary rocks and related minerals (limestone, chalk, gypsum, sand, etc.) give a distinct quality to some wine varieties. Though the soil is good, adequate water has been a problem for Moldova's agriculture, and the region historically suffered from regular periods of drought.

The most recent census (2014)[1] reported an ethnic profile that could be described as predominantly Moldovan (over 75 percent). Other important ethnic groups, defined primarily by language, were Ukrainian (6.5 percent), Russian (4 percent), Gagauz (4.5 percent), Romanian (7 percent), Bulgarian (1.8 percent), and Roma (0.3 percent). The Romanian category should not be seen as culturally distinct from the Moldovans so much as politically distinct in matters related to education, cultural heritage, language, and geopolitics. Among the 93 percent of the population who declared a religion (including atheism and agnosticism), the 2014 census recorded an overwhelming majority of Moldova's citizens as Christian Orthodox (96.8 percent), with other Christian groups accounting for another 2.5 percent. Muslims (primarily foreigners and their local converted spouses and children) have been among the most discriminated religious groups in the early 2000s, but there is no census category for them—just as there is none for Jews (see below).

Moldova's historical profile in ethnic and religious terms is more complex than suggested by the census. More than three hundred years of Ottoman vassalage produced no substantial conversion to Islam among the local population. However, Bessarabia's border location was marked by complex histories of religious protest and conversion, crisscrossed with experiences of exile and of various privileges and tax exemptions among its minority populations. Some of the Bulgarians and Gagauz who fled the Ottoman Empire in the 1800s were already Christian, while others converted upon settlement. Bessarabia served as a place of refuge for many of Russia's religious minorities (e.g., Old Believers), and Catholic and Protestant settlers were invited by the Russian state from Germany and other west European countries. All of these groups brought some elements of food culture with them, although only a few of their contributions are remembered: the Germans, for example, had a notable influence in the development of the early wine industry.

Bessarabia lost some of its ethnic and religious diversity following the Second World War. In particular, the substantial Jewish population (about 12 percent overall and half of Chişinău) was decimated, both numerically and socially. More than 65,000 Jews remained in 1989 (King 2000:174, see also 24–26), but emigration continued in the early post-Soviet years. Estimates of the Jewish population in 2020 vary between 3,500 and 20,000, making Jews still at least twice as prevalent in the country as Catholics, Old Believers, or Lutherans. Although the 1990s and early 2000s witnessed a Jewish cultural revival in which a handful of Jewish restaurants appeared (King 2000:174), there is little recognition of Jewish food among the general population, even among urban dwellers who suddenly develop a craving for *matzoh* sometime every spring.

Overall, the contribution of ethnic and religious minorities to food culture is generally downplayed. The exception appears with a handful of dishes associated with other Soviet nationalities. For example, barbecued meat skewers are referred to most often as *shashlik* and as a Georgian food and only rarely as the Romanian *frigăruie*. Commonality in foodways, as with other aspects of culture and tradition, is more emphasized than local diversity. Along with shared rural lifestyles dependent on local ecology, shared Christianity is seen as influencing both eating habits (e.g., there are no widespread prohibitions on pork) and the deep symbolism of some products (e.g., bread, wine, salt, water), which are commonly incorporated into political, social, calendrical, and life-cycle rituals (Fig. 42.1).

Legacies of Past Foodways

Moldova's geographical position in a historic borderland means that its foodways can be connected variously to western Europe, the Mediterranean, and the Balkan worlds, as well as to the east Slavic and Russian worlds. In recent food politics, the population's preference for round wheat loaves, as well as the words applied to bread, provide evidence of cultural connections to the West (Buzilă 1999). Local scholars emphasize that the Romanian word for bread (*pâine*) is Latinate and neither Greek-derived nor Slavic. Nevertheless, certain breads used in church liturgical rituals, like *prescură* (small palm-sized, usually round loaves stamped with a religious motif by a wooden *pistornic*), point to enduring connections across Orthodox communities, including Russia (e.g., Arutjunov 2004). The most commonly used word for any ritual bread (*pâine de ritual*),

FIG. 42.1. Ethnic Armenians offering fruit at the annual Festival of Ethnic Groups.

(Chișinău, 2009.)

in or outside the church, is *colac*; but there are many forms beyond that of a circular ring (Buzilă 1999:12–13).

More work has been done on food within the Ottoman Empire than in Moldova or its regional neighbors (see review by Blaszczyk and Rohdewald 2018:1–2). The weightiest social history of food has focused on the issue of charitable food distribution. Charitable kitchens operated across the Ottoman Empire, including in the Balkans, where patronage contributed not only to the authority of the sultan but also to the local lords (Ergin et al. 2007:29–30). It is not known whether charitable kitchens reached Moldova, but there were other aspects of Ottoman foodways that did. As in western Europe, Ottoman elites hungered for meat to such an extent that economic policies in the empire's European peripheries directed the production, sale, and price of steady and increasing amounts of mutton; conflicts focused on Poland–Lithuania's activities in Moldova and the Black Sea coast during the late sixteenth century included concerns over the sheep market (Blaszczyk and Rohdewald 2018:3–4). In at least some regions of Ottoman Europe—and it is not clear whether this was true for Moldova—locals were forbidden to slaughter sheep (for their own consumption) and ordered to eat only goat and beef. Yet the Ottoman market for mutton did encourage pastoralism and transhumance in Moldova, which resulted in both positive and negative images of national culture and identity well into the twentieth century. Soviet ethnography and nationalities policies seized on transhumance as a characteristic that distinguished Moldovans (negatively) from the more sedentary and agricultural Ukrainians.

The direction of trade has fostered development and change in local foodways as well. Aslan (2018) documents, for example, several reorientations of the Ottoman spice trade during the sixteenth to nineteenth centuries. The dominant effect was a successive rerouting more to the east and west so that less spice transited through the Romanian lands and the price of what did make it through was exceedingly high for local markets. With the exception of pepper, which could be grown in the Romanian lands, few of the spices characteristic of Ottoman imperial cooking were incorporated into Romanian (including Moldovan) food. Peppers, on the other hand, still appear widely in everyday food preparation.

In what is now the Republic of Moldova, as throughout the Romanian lands and the Balkans generally, the food habits of elites changed relatively quickly in response to new political and economic orientations (Blaszczyk and Rohdewald 2018). In the Romanian lands, foodways began to diverge in the three major provinces (Transylvania, Wallachia, Moldavia) in the 1600s and were distinct by the mid-1800s. Noblemen in Transylvania turned to German cooking styles (and hired German cooks) from the middle of the seventeenth century (Aslan 2018). Meanwhile, Ottoman-influenced cuisine peaked and then faded in Wallachia and Moldavia from the 1830s as the Phanariots lost their ruling power (Aslan 2018:35). Russian influence on the foodways of Bessarabia (and today's Republic of Moldova) followed the retraction of the Ottoman influence during the nineteenth century and continued during the Soviet period. As described below, twenty-first-century food in the Republic of Moldova therefore unites Russian boiled sausages, pancakes, and boiled dumplings; tinned, pickled, and dried Baltic fishes; peppers, eggplants, spicy *adjika*, and salty sheep's cheese.

In recent memory as in the distant past, new foods and preparations are learned and invented, while others are abandoned and forgotten. Elderly people remember curing ham at home with German techniques before the Second World War and as late as the 1960s; homemade "butter cheese" remains a popular substitute for store-bought varieties. In the first decade of the 2000s, the consumption of pizza, baked potatoes, quiche, pineapple, bananas, and green tea pointed to Moldova's participation in once again expanded networks of trade and migration. The reappearance of store-bought and homemade halvah in the early 2000s signaled more complex relations because halvah is a local food (made with ground sunflower seeds), but the taste for it is often forgotten and then reinvigorated by travel and memory.

Meals (Daily Fare): The Products

Moldova's cuisine makes heavy use of tomatoes, eggplants, onions, cabbage, and sheep's cheese, as well as fresh curds from cow milk, eggs, sour cream, and potatoes. White beans are eaten especially during periods of religious fasting, while chickpeas are stewed together with meaty bones for festive meals in some parts of the country. Green vegetables are uncommon, though lettuces are available in urban areas and a few other greens, like arugula, have been introduced by migrants returning from work in Italy since about 2010.

Meat forms a small portion of most people's daily diet, largely because of its cost and—for rural families—the work of keeping and slaughtering the animals. In the early twentieth century, rural households often kept one or a few pigs for slaughter; today, it is more common to keep several chickens and some ducks. Since independence, and the accompanying economic decline, many rural households keep a milking cow, largely from necessity rather than choice. Milking is considered a woman's task, however, so households without an adult female rarely keep cows. Sheep are more common to the southern reaches of the country. Lamb and veal are eaten, but rarely, with lamb being an ideal (if rarely realized) meal at Easter-time. Freshwater fish are eaten regularly, and various kinds of dry- and wet-smoked fish (whether imported or homemade) are popular on festive tables and during drinking sessions.

White bread (from wheat flour), whether home-baked or store-bought is present at all meals. Rye breads are available commercially. Special breads are baked for major holidays and important rituals. The most common of these is the *colac* (a braided round, pl. *colaci*), which is a critical component in the ritually offered gifts at weddings, baptisms, funerals, and commemorations of the dead (they are subsequently eaten by the recipients). The *pască* is baked for Easter from sweet dough; small cross-shaped breads are baked at Christmas; small *colaci* should be given to caroling children.

Meals are eaten three times daily, with some social snacking. There is not very much differentiation between the content of the meals, and they all run toward the savory end. In theory, lunch is the largest meal of the day and should consist of at least one salad, a soup, and some meat, along with as much bread as is necessary to fill the stomach. Soup is eaten frequently (and is an important source of liquids because water is rarely drunk as such, partly because of water quality). Of these, the most common are *zeamă de pui* (chicken soup) and *borș* (a slightly soured vegetable soup; it is not necessarily a beet soup, as in the Russian version, nor does it necessarily contain *borș acru*, a sour liquid of slightly fermented bran, as in the Romanian version). *Soleankă*, a sour soup of cured meats in a light tomato broth, is much liked but prepared more rarely. Salads of tomatoes and cucumbers are the most common. The meat is most likely to be chicken that has been cooked in the soup broth or a *sos* (gravy) of meat drippings, flour, and broth with small pieces of meat; fried eggs or fried potatoes often stand in for meat, and it is also common to have a meal with just several salads and bread.

Mămăligă (polenta) is considered a "national" dish, as in Romania, but is eaten by all ethnic groups with various accompaniments: scrambled eggs, sheep's cheese, sour cream, and fried pork chunks or fish. *Plăcintă* is a flakey buttery pastry, much like filo, filled with cheese (with and without fresh dill), potatoes, pumpkin, cabbage, sour cherries, apples, or prunes. Most of the country is well suited for growing grapes, and wine (especially red) is the most prominent drink on most household tables and a point of supraethnic national pride (Fig. 42.2). In the northern reaches of the country, distilled

FIG. 42.2. A university student helps harvest wine grapes from his family's hillside allotment.
(Răscăieți, 2009.)

fruit brandies are more common than wine; and throughout the country the distillation of *rachiu* is a popular way of using up excess fruit or wine left in household barrels at the end of the season. Apples, herbs, walnuts, and some other fruits and berries are collected from the old orchards of former collective farms, grazing fields, and roadsides to round out a family's larder and for homemade teas, tinctures, and other remedies. Most families, even in urban areas, preserve some jams, vegetables, and compotes.

Individual preferences for coffee or tea are strongly stated. In general, tea is more commonly consumed—a legacy of Moldova's greater connections to the Russian Empire than to the Ottoman from the nineteenth century (see Blaszczyk and Rohdewald 2018:10). Coffee is consumed in a variety of preparations (boiled in a near-Turkish style, filter-drip, instant, or in an espresso machine, with or without milk). Coffee carries with it some connotations of Ottoman rule but more immediately signals urban, cosmopolitan lifestyles. Sometimes it is associated with Romania (with a wry reference to boiled coffee as Turkish coffee, *cafea turcească*) and more recently, by post-migrants and their families, with Italy. Coffee is also expensive. It is therefore a relatively rare drink in rural areas, where it remains common to prepare teas from self-collected leaves and herbs (including cherry leaves, chamomile, mint, linden, rose hips, and thyme). Urban families tend to drink black teas. Coffee is preferred by women (more than men), professionals, "intellectuals" (including schoolteachers), and people working in the cultural sphere.

The gendered dimension of the preference for coffee or tea seems to correlate with the expectation that women are more "cultured" and refined than men, while men are more traditional and "simple" in their tastes. Coffee and tea, whether part of a meal or consumed outside of mealtimes, are accompanied by cookies, cake, crackers, other pastries, preserves by the spoonful, and sometimes fruit. Fruit is also eaten as a snack on its own outside of mealtimes.

The use of spices is quite restricted. Salt, oil, garlic, onions, dried bay leaf, fresh dill, and parsley constitute the basic spices of everyday and festive cooking. Basil is grown but used only for church and ritual purposes—most often, a long branch of basil is dipped into holy water and then splashed onto people and things in blessing—but small sprigs of basil can be tucked or pinned into a kerchief or shirt collar or placed in a vase on a window sill or table; in these uses it may bring luck and ward off various forms of malevolence and ill-will. Cinnamon is sometimes used in baking. In the south, small green and red chili peppers are used to flavor soups. They may also be nibbled alongside a meal to make it spicier.

Unlike most European countries, Moldova has few products (e.g., cheeses or meats) that have specific names or designated geographic origins. Similarly, because Moldova has not been the direct subject of Europeanization, EU regulations on the manufacture and labeling of foods have raised little public interest or debate—unlike in other east European countries including Romania, Lithuania, Poland, and Hungary, where such regulations have challenged local identities and political solidarities. In rural areas, pigs (as well as all fowl) are slaughtered at home. Wine has proven the one exception to Moldovan products entering European food politics. There are a handful of wineries that produce wines with the status of Protected Geographic Indication, including Purcari, which is seeking the Protected Designation of Origin for its wine. As of 2011, there was only one registered with an *appellation d'origine contrôlée* (Românești red wine), though a few other wineries (Codru, Purcari) were in the process of obtaining such certification (see Ana 2019 and by personal correspondence).

Practices

The above listing was compiled based on my encounters with food in Moldova during fieldwork undertaken across the years 1999–2010. These were years of economic decline and slow recovery as the internal markets of the Soviet Union were broken and not quite replaced. As a Soviet republic, Moldova's primary economic contribution was with the production of food: cereals, fresh and preserved vegetables and fruit, and wine. Even in the Soviet period, the consumption of industrially produced food was relatively low, but in the decade of my most intense fieldwork it was frequently absent from people's daily meals altogether. Daily meals, in rural and urban areas, reflected the prominence of market-crop agriculture, as well as the return of private plots. In rural areas, households strived to produce most of the food they consumed. People in urban areas received gifts of food from relatives in the countryside, sometimes maintained small gardens of their own, and conducted most of their shopping in outdoor markets.

Across the first decades of the 2000s, supermarket shopping increased, but fresh produce and dairy products were still purchased from outdoor markets and sometimes from lone vendors at roadsides. Sometimes people developed favorite vendors; often they complained that vendors did not do enough to attract them as a customer. In lieu of relying on a personal relationship with a friendly and honest vendor, urban shoppers often bought from a vendor who had nominally lower prices or spoke their preferred language. Other aspects of shopping highlighted inconsistencies in product availability and quality too: dairy products had to be tasted (most often with a common spoon) because there were no other ways to distinguish levels of creaminess, fat, sweetness, or saltiness; with dairy vendors rarely in the same market-space twice, consumers had to taste-before-purchasing nearly every time.

In villages, families usually establish close relations with the owner and staff of one or two small shops. Most villages have several small stores selling a wide range of dried goods; fresh bread; commercially produced yogurts, butter, and sour cream; frozen and preserved fish; sausages; and some cheese. Close relations with shop owners and workers are important for sociality, for maintaining an account (i.e., buying on credit), and for receiving accurate advice on which of the commercially prepared meats, fish, and dairy products are fresh and/or delicious. (Irregular and unknown customers, as well as those who do not ask about product quality, may be sold inferior products.)

Most children in Moldova learn to cook basic foods alongside other household chores. In principle, both girls and boys learn all the basic chores inside and outside the house (as part of being adequately "civilized" and having learned all the basic rules of etiquette during their first "seven years at home"). Some boys are praised for demonstrating particular interest in cooking (usually baking), and most adult men help with shopping and participate in some occasional cooking of soups and potatoes as well as periodic food preparation like drying fruits and vegetables, barbecuing, and preparing freshly caught fish. Still, most cooking (like cleaning and childcare) falls with relatively little question or negotiation to women. The willingness of men to undertake some domestic labor contributes to positive stereotypes of ethnic Moldovan men as husbands.

Cooking is learned first by observation and later by doing. From the age of about seven, rural children are likely to be left at home alone for a few hours at a time and may also be expected to care for younger siblings. In such cases, they will be left with instructions for heating up and serving leftover soups, bread, and other food; they are trusted to have mastered the basics of lighting a gas stove, lifting and carrying pots, ladling hot liquids, cutting with sharp knives, and clearing and sweeping. Mothers and grandmothers are likely to involve young children in the preparation of holiday treats, too: stirring doughs or braiding and shaping small breads. First tastes of some foods are offered to children who are milling around the house and kitchen during their preparation. These offerings may pique interest in food and cooking; they certainly transmit a sense that these foods are particularly special and that the children themselves are dear to the cook. These include fresh *brânză* (salty white cheese from sheep's or cow's milk) and *smântână* (sour cream), *plăcintă*, cookies and cakes, newly made jam, sometimes fresh fruit (especially the first of the season), soup with dumplings or homemade noodles, and fruit compotes specially brought up from the cellar and opened for the child. The specialness of the food and child is performed by the cook, who will call the child to table with an air of conspiracy and indulgence. It is a markedly different experience from that of being called to table by a harassed cook who has been cooking hurriedly to meet the needs of a hungry child who must be fed even though the busy cook herself has no time for eating.

Children express interest in cooking at individual levels and rates. Some are interested in baking from middle childhood. By late childhood or early adolescence, most periodically cook for themselves when left alone at home. The common repertoire at this age includes boiled milk, milk rice or macaroni, and fried potatoes. From adolescence, the range expands quickly as children themselves take the initiative to prepare foods that they want to eat: salads and soups are common wishes. Baked goods may appear. *Plăcintă* is attempted relatively late in a cook's progression, as are fried fish and meats with sauces. Bread is among the last foods to be attempted, and many women do not learn to bake it until after marriage or even after childbirth. A young cook's mother (or any other adult female present) will provide critical remarks of all sorts in the cooking endeavor: techniques of cutting; size and shape of ingredients; the adjustment of salt, oil, and other flavorings; arrangement on the serving plate; etc. Although these instructions sound like the transmission of cultural norms, they are more about personal taste and even more about authority. A young cook will receive different instructions for years from the same adult, as well as from different ones. Boys who cook are subjected to much less commentary.

From mid-adolescence, girls are expected to join in some of their family's preparations at major feasts and events. They may spend only an hour or so in the kitchen on the days and evenings before a wedding, funeral, commemorative feast, Christmas, Easter, etc.; but while there they will be set tasks: frying fish or meat patties, peeling and cutting vegetables, stirring the *colivă* (ritual food at funerals), etc. During these preparations, too, girls are subjected to multiple corrections. Boys and men do not cook at major events but set and stoke fires, draw water, fetch and carry ingredients, and sometimes peel onions, potatoes, and garlic or shell walnuts. When a girl succeeds in wrapping *sarmale* (stuffed grape or cabbage leaves) small and tight enough to gain the approval of other women involved in preparations, they will invoke the phrase that the girl is "ready for marriage" (*bună de măritat*). This is not an entirely welcome phrase, and an unmarried girl is likely to disappear from a cooking group around the time that other women start testing it out on her. Because it is not actually difficult to roll small, tight *sarmale*, a girl's exasperated cries that she cannot do it and abandonment of the cooking group probably have more to do with the social relations at play than the mastery of cooking techniques. Cooking alongside other women involves the grueling endurance of ongoing critique over minor and seemingly arbitrary variations in technique and taste (Fig. 42.3).

FIG. 42.3. Two married women showing two unmarried women how to make *sarmale*.
(Căușeni Veche, 2005.)

While most cooking and traditional foods are learned through these informal methods, new dishes are introduced through recipes. Russian and Romanian cookbooks are sold widely in bookstores; recipes are printed in newspapers and women's magazines; and, more recently, women source them from the internet and exchange them through social media. These recipes are essential for providing the "something new" that most women crave at feast time; they tire of reproducing traditional foods at every event and wish for their table to be distinguished from that of their peers. Most recipe-based experimentation happens with salads (e.g., by adding new ingredients like pineapple to a familiar meat and mayonnaise salad), desserts, and presentation (trimming vegetables into flowers, attaching real leaves to fruit-shaped cookies). From middle age, many women will also reveal a personal recipe collection kept in a notebook or on cards. These are compiled discretely and consulted when a woman wants to prepare something particularly special—such as one of the many shaped breads that are holiday-specific. They usually include recipes taken from books, magazines, and foreign sources (including friends from other ethnic backgrounds and trips abroad).

Presumably, these personal collections also include "stolen recipes" learned covertly from other women. Although women teach others by correction during cooking, they rarely provide a verbal explanation of a technique in full. To some degree this would be difficult to do, even if a woman wanted to share her knowledge, because quantities are rarely fixed (only large-scale cooking is habitually planned with reference to quantity, and this is measured out in kilograms). However, it is said that women do not want to share the secrets of their cooking (especially related to bread- and dough-baking) and that when a recipe is shared, the cook will omit an important ingredient or step. Because a recipe will not produce an exact replica, one must "steal" the full recipe by watching the cook in action.

Finally, although much of the traditional model of learning to cook stresses hierarchical relations of authority and control between older and younger women, women also learn cooking as an aspect of friendship. At all ages, girls and women may gather with one or a few friends to learn or perfect certain dishes; as women age, the cooking circles for ritual events are composed increasingly of women who get along with each other; and younger women nearing adult levels of competency in cooking are likely to cook with and for adult female friends—a youngish aunt, older cousin, trusted teacher, or preferred godparent. Cooking with friends allows for a greater range of experimentation and the possibility of "disasters" with food that is burnt, too salty, too sour, etc. but is nevertheless consumed with good nature. Boys rarely have the range of diverse cooking experiences that girls have (Fig. 42.4).

FIG. 42.4. Women preparing *plăcinta miresei* for a *cumetrie* (baptism) party.

(Olăneşti, 2010.)

Food is ideally cooked fresh at every meal, but few women do such frequent cooking past the early years of marriage and motherhood. (Older women caution younger ones against ever starting.) More common is that a woman cooks one major dish per day (e.g., soup, a meat or mushroom "sauce," some baked cakes or savory pies, or boiled or fried potatoes) and augments it with cooked food left from the previous meal or two, along with some freshly cut vegetables ("salads") or a jar of preserved vegetables. In this way, each meal contains several varied dishes, often presented in courses (even breakfast may be served with savory food first and tea/coffee with sweeter foods following). The result is balanced and nutritious meals, but the main aim for most cooks, especially when a "guest" is present, is to create the impression of a feast. Nevertheless, the time spent in the fresh cooking of hot food is restricted to between one and two hours each day.

The overall time spent on food preparation, however, is much greater. Meals also involve shopping (especially for urban households), the heating and replating of leftovers, and cleanup, storage (often by covering serving dishes with plates and refrigerating), and handwashing (there are no dishwashers, and pots are rarely made of stick-free materials). Many women in rural areas bake bread once each week—a process that takes several hours. The additional work of planting, weeding, harvesting, sorting, storing, milling, etc. undertaken by rural households takes several hours or days at key points in the agricultural cycle. There is no strict gender division for these tasks. For example, a group of women may work together during weeding season, but a husband, wife, and older children will periodically sort and re-store their onions and potatoes. Even the limited amount of animal husbandry practiced by most rural households—preparing feed, watering, some cleaning, and letting in/out of chickens and ducks—easily requires up to two hours per day. Households with a milking cow spend more time each day on animal care: men prepare food and water and clean the stall, while women clean and milk the cow and process the milk. They also take a daily turn once every four to eight weeks of pasturing all the cows in the neighborhood or village. Even though animal care is normally considered "men's work," households lacking men often continue to keep animals, even cows; but when women are absent from a household, such animal care usually drops off.

Mealtimes are often staggered as the members of a household often eat separately—especially the mid-day and evening meals—according to their return home. The staggered eating is more pronounced in urban households. Guests are often served upon arrival and not made to wait until the next meal. This means that a woman may be engaged frequently in heating, serving, and cleaning up. (When no woman is home, family members manage on their own but eat a reduced variety of dishes.) Over the course of a year, rural and urban households also make their own preserved vegetables, fruits, jams, and compotes. (Pressed juice is a commonly purchased industrial product for special occasions.) Most of the work of preserving fruits and vegetables is undertaken by women. Men are more likely to take a main role in drying or smoking food but otherwise are more limited to carrying around large quantities of produce, building cooking fires, fetching empty jars, etc. Sometimes women invite one or a few friends to help make preserves, but more often they work alone.

Performance (Gender, House, Hospitality)

Whether in formal scripted performances of the nation, in the everyday welcome of non-residents into a household, or in the many social, calendric, and life-cycle rituals that make life more than the drudgery of work in house and fields, the performance of hospitality indisputably marks Moldova as a particular place (Cash 2013a). This performance unites all resident ethnic groups and is considered to distinguish them from coethnics in other countries. Moldova's inhabitants see few other countries or peoples as hospitable as themselves; only central Asians, peoples of the Caucasus, and perhaps the Scots and Irish draw the admiring comments that are so often applied to the welcomes received with abundant food, warm-heartedness, entertainment, and good cheer in Moldova's villages, near and far. The performance of hospitality, in all but its most political appearances, foregrounds the self-sufficiency of the Moldovan house and household as it is made possible by traditional and complementary gender roles.

The performance of hospitality is very much about the ability of a household to produce food; in turn, the presentation of food is meant to communicate a wide range of skills, values, and activities. These performances also communicate variations and differences between individuals (usually women), households, and regions, with attention focused on disproportionate displays of "pride" (i.e., attempting to appear that one has more than one does), as well as on the "fineness" of attention to detail, aesthetics, or pleasure. Although it is important for feast tables to look nice, some decorative elements (e.g., tablecloths or glassware) may arouse suspicion. Hospitality should be offered freely, fully, and without pretense; table settings that are especially fine may raise suspicions that hosts are (overly) proud or acquisitive or seeking gain from guests by first impressing them. Food, however unlikely it is that a family could "afford" to offer it, is not scrutinized for social meanings other than those of hospitality.

Performances: Bread, Salt, Wine

There are three foods critical to the performance of hospitality: bread, salt, and wine. In the early 2000s, bread with salt typically appeared in formal welcomes, such as when political leaders visited a village, at the opening of public festivals, and at the beginning of concerts and competitions in culture houses. More typical welcomes, of visitors to a family house or of official visitors and important guests at festive meals offstage, paired bread with wine. As a public and political ritual, the formal greeting resonates deeply

FIG. 42.5. A married couple sits in a classic pose as host (*gospodar*) and hostess (*gospodină*) outside their house, joined by an elderly woman. The table is spread with homemade wine and bread, salt, tomatoes, and *brânză*.

(Dișcova, 2006.)

with local tradition and family-based practice, but it also has a long history of political use (Fig. 42.5).

Bread has deep symbolic meanings in Moldova, as in many European societies, including those taken from Christianity. In contemporary Moldova, bread is also strongly associated with hospitality as a matter of both tradition and political elaboration. Traditional hospitality rituals involving the presentation of bread and salt are particularly common, as throughout eastern Europe (Mesnil 1992:7). During the twentieth century, socialist regimes across the region incorporated this traditional ritual into public and political rituals. In Moldova, numerous proverbs and sayings reflect the possibility that a welcome might be made with bread and salt. Local Romanian expressions, for example, include *Ce, să te întâlnesc cu pâine și sare?* (when an expected guest fails to arrive on time, they may be asked sarcastically, "What, should I meet you with bread and salt?") and *M-a întâlnit cu pâine și sare* (about an extraordinarily good welcome, "I was met with bread and salt"). There is also a traditional wedding toast, *Să vă potriviți ca pâinea cu sarea!*, which expresses a wish for the new couple to "get along with each other like bread and salt."

In Moldova, wine is more commonly paired with bread in welcome and many other traditional rituals. For some observers, the presentation of bread and salt in a formal welcome still resonates with past political messages concerning the friendship of the Soviet peoples. Other Soviet nationalities also had formal welcomes involving the presentation of bread and salt, but in Soviet parades, school performances, and other public presentations, Moldova and ethnic Moldovans were differentiated by their jug of wine that invariably accompanied the bread and salt. During Soviet anti-alcohol campaigns, however, Moldova's close association with wine became problematic, resulting in greater public focus on bread and salt as the key symbols of welcome, in divergence from traditional practice.

Bread and salt are fundamental elements of a Moldovan household because they are basic foodstuffs. When people move into a new house, bread and salt should be the first items carried in, to guarantee that the household will always have food. Salt is a practical and indispensable ingredient in the household, but—aside from the sayings that link it to bread—it seems to have little contemporary symbolic weight of its own. To some degree, the very indispensability of salt is its meaning, as expressed in the folktale "Sarea în bucate" ("The Salt in Your Food"), published by Petre Ispirescu, the well-known nineteenth-century collector of traditional Romanian tales.[2] It would be unthinkable to cook or eat without salt, which gives flavor most simply and ubiquitously of all other ingredients. However, salt was used in a wide range of rituals, especially in those involving divination (Asăndulesei 2015).

In contrast, the wine that appears alongside bread in most welcomes and other rituals carries deep symbolic weight. Some of the symbolic resonances of wine (like bread) are undoubtedly linked to Christianity (e.g., blood of Christ) and specifically to orthodoxy. Priests and other religious specialists, however, acknowledge that the widespread use of bread and wine in local rituals expands biblical references and symbolism into popular practices well beyond those envisioned by official church ritual. Some practices can be rendered as elaborations of Christian associations of bread and wine with physical and spiritual life—such as giving away bread and water at crossroads during a funeral procession (as well as offering drinks of wine and water to anyone met en route to the cemetery),[3] offering bread in commemoration of the dead, placing bread and wine on graves, pouring wine on graves, and greeting a wine spill at the table as evidence that a soul is thirsty. Wine in these acts confers spiritual life to its drinker. All of these, however, also draw on the traditional symbols, meaning, and imagery of what has been called the "cult of the dead" in Romanian ethnic and cultural space. In contemporary Moldova, most people prefer to stress the Christian resonances of these practices, although folklorists and ethnographers periodically remind them of pre-Christian and extra-Christian meanings.

Much of the immediate symbolism of bread also exceeds Christian interpretation and is linked in multiple ways to gender, fertility, and reproduction. Some of these links are pragmatic and somewhat contested. For example, married women in rural areas are expected to bake bread, especially after they have children. During the Soviet period, industrially produced bread became available and is described as one of the norms of Soviet life and a definite improvement in women's lives. A return to home-baking (along with cow ownership and home-milking) was one of the first collective responses to post-Soviet economic hardship. Yet there are still women who prefer not to bake and many who even declare that they cannot and still purchase bread that is trucked in daily to the general stores of even the smallest villages. The expectation that women should bake for their families exceeds the pragmatic, however; and with the exception of the Soviet-industrial solution, there is little interest in making it easier for women to fulfill this expectation. As of 2010, women and men still agreed that it was unthinkable that a village in Moldova would ever support a small local bakery like villages in Italy or France. (Only special breads, like *colaci*, are made for sale by small-scale home bakeries [Fig. 42.6].) They could not even imagine that a collective oven would be welcome, even though home baking requires each house to have a large oven, plus regular supplies of firewood and someone strong enough to load and stoke the fire. When women do bake, they face other social expectations, as well as prohibitions. They should be calm and in a good mood during baking; they should not bake bread while menstruating.

Special breads figure in all major life-cycle and calendrical rituals (Figs. 42.7 and 42.8). These include baptism, marriage, funerals and death commemorations, as well

FIG. 42.6. *Colaci* purchased from a home bakery stacked alongside other gifts to be given by the parents of a new child to their *cumetri* (coparents).

(Olănești, 2010.)

FIG. 42.7. A *crăciun* traditionally given to children or hung in animal stalls at Christmastime. Here hung under an icon as decoration.

(Răscăieți, 2010.)

as Christmas, Easter, and *Paștele blajinilor* (Easter of the Dead/Easter of the Blessed), which is celebrated in cemeteries on the Sunday or Monday following Easter. Since the mid-1800s, ethnographers and folklorists have been particularly attentive to documenting marriage rituals, and bread appears at numerous points in these rituals. Even in the most modern weddings of the post-socialist period, *colaci* are offered to the bride's parents when permission to marry her is sought (nowadays on the way to the state registry ceremony); they are exchanged again between the bride's parents and the groom's parents during the wedding. These exchanges are critical and cannot be omitted from the wedding sequence; guests will notice and insist that the ritual be completed. More exciting, however, is the ripping of a bread by the bride and groom. Guests watch this ritual with anticipation, laughter, and much commentary because the party who

FIG. 42.8. Pallbearers and grave diggers receive *pomană*, always including bread with a candle, at subsequent death commemorations in the name of the deceased.

(Căuşeni Veche, 2005.)

pulls the bigger piece is expected to be the boss in the house. (At all weddings I attended, the bride pulled the larger piece.)

Colaci are the most common breads in contemporary wedding rituals, but *jemne* are often mentioned. *Jemne* almost always appear as clearly doubled forms: two doves, a double spiral, doubled knots, and so on. Two *colaci* may also continue to be named as *jemne* when they appear in wedding rituals (Buzilă 1999:329–334). However, no bread that is eaten at a wedding is called "bread"—it is referred to by naming its ritual form. *Plăcinta miresei* (the bride's pie), so named because its crust is thin like the bride's veil, tends to show up only on wedding and baptismal menus; it also requires several experienced women to shake and stretch the dough without tearing it. Although *plăcinta miresei* and special bread forms could be added to the menus of events other than weddings and baptisms, they rarely are. The rarity of these special breads reinforces the connections between bread, women, fertility, and the house as women themselves devote extra cooking attention to their elaboration, preparation, and display against more common forms of festive food.

To date, there is no trend for local folklorists or ethnographers to approach "foodways" as a distinct theme. Many aspects of traditional practice, knowledge, and meanings attached to bread and wine, and less so of salt and water, are transmitted through public folkloric performances and the training of young folk artists (see Cash 2011:77). Plenty of other data exist in short publications and personal archives: generations of folklorists and ethnographers have recorded, in due course, copious data about bread (its forms, techniques for baking), the construction of ovens, rituals in which bread is given and received, and so on. Similarly, the material technologies for wine production (presses, barrels) have been salvaged and preserved, as have the names of grape varietals and oral knowledge concerning the making, cleaning, and repair of barrels; aging; blending; the addition of natural flavorants and preservatives; carbonation (for "champagne"); and distillation (for wine and fruit brandies). Data collected prior to World War II are typically combined in publications and archives concerning "Romania" (as examples from "Bessarabia"). Some exist also for Transnistria, entangled with data gathered from locations in Ukraine. Few scholars, however, have attempted to sift or synthesize these data into full-length studies. The exception is Varvara Buzilă's 1999 book in Romanian, *Bread as Food and Symbol: The Experience of the Sacred*.

Meanwhile, the development of wine scholarship, including on the historical and cultural dimensions, was left until recently in the hands of enologists. The academician Boris Găină remains the leading authority. Wine, however, has gained the mutual interest of local and foreign anthropologists and ethnographers in the decades following independence (e.g., Ana 2019; Bîrlădeanu 2013; Cash 2015; Ciocanu 2015; Iarovoi 2007), as have rituals of drinking (Buzilă 2006; Cojocari and Bîrlădeanu 2013). Unexpected data on drinking practices have been found in old photographs; "toasts" are being deliberately collected in ethnographic fieldwork, as is information on the size, style, and material of wine jugs and drinking glasses. The potential for longue-durée perspectives on wine is good: archaeological evidence exists for wine production in the region from as early as the eight to sixth centuries BCE, with vines and technology brought by Greek colonists. By the seventeenth century, European travelers remarked on the pleasant landscapes and quality wine of the Moldavian principality (Iarovoi 2007:209). Thus, though German colonists are considered the leaders in developing Moldova's wine industry in the nineteenth century, their contributions were only the latest in a longer history of wine production and consumption. Or, in the view of Iarovoi (2007), it is safe to say that wine in Moldova is part of a wider "culture of the grape," which includes consumption of fresh grapes in large quantities; the techniques and technology for preserving grapes, both wet and dry; the development of varietals (including seedless ones for raisins); and the production of other grape-based products like juice and jams. Indeed, there are a number of traditions (and oral folklore) focused on the grape and connected to the regulation of stages in its growing cycle, harvest, and consumption—aside from those traditions focused on wine production and consumption.

Still, there is no strong terroir discourse in Moldova. Microzones of production are known, but common discussion of the links between soil, place, and wine are purely technical; history and people are not drawn into the story (see Ana 2019:ca. 24, 158–159).

Nevertheless, the quality of a homemade wine is seen as proof of the moral qualities of its maker.

Wine and Performance: Social Relations and Ritual Economies

A closer look at wine in Moldova demonstrates how the "performance" of food can reveal important beliefs, evaluation systems, aesthetics, and attitudes surrounding food. Perhaps the first point to make is that wine is considered something other than a beverage: it is said that one does not "drink" (*a bea*) wine but that through the consumption of wine one "partakes in honoring" (*a cinsti*) someone or something (see also Buzilă 2006:489). Moreover, "drinking" is something characteristic of animals: *caii beau apă* ("horses drink water"). When humans gather to consume, the event is already in the realm of the sacred, with special rules applying: it is best not to speak while eating, and "conversation" is often replaced (especially at more formal occasions) with speech acts.

FIG. 42.9. Neighbors share wine and food over the fence during outdoor garden work. Agricultural work is punctuated by sharing food and wine to show respect to workers and transform work itself.

(Răscăieți, 2010.)

The wine glass is raised to offer toasts on auspicious occasions, such as weddings, and to console and memorialize on more solemn occasions. Wine partaken together signals mutual respect—and it is for this reason that it is very nearly impossible to refuse an invitation to drink (Fig. 42.9). Illness (chronic or temporary), the need to drive, and sometimes pregnancy are the only commonly accepted reasons to refuse a drink. Otherwise, refusal can be taken as a grave insult. Yet, interestingly, total abstinence from alcohol, for any reason, is viewed as proof of high moral quality—presumably because it requires iron discipline to refuse consistently on the grounds of preserving one's own health or moral convictions.

In addition to all their other facets, bread and wine are key elements of different local economies. Homemade bread, for example, only participates in economies based on mutuality. It cannot be sold, not least because it is said to have "no price." (The price of commercial bread is widely known and usually criticized as being "too high" in the post-socialist period.) Bread cannot be denied to anyone who asks for it, and bread is exchanged between households without calculation. A house that lacks bread is not subject to moral critique, but it is considered desperately poor. Still, such deep poverty is felt as shameful because even the poorest villagers (who may ask their neighbors for bread) will not claim—in public—ritual offerings of *pomană* (charity) to which they are entitled (Cash 2013b).

On the other hand, wine brokers extensive relations beyond the house and into the realms of the market. Wine can be given as a gift or a loan. Loans of wine are calculated as debts, to be paid off in cash, in kind, or through labor. There is a standard price for wine debts used within villages, as well as market prices for wine grapes and homemade wine. The price of wine used for wine debts within the village is more closely aligned with the market price for labor than the market price for commercially bottled wine.

Feasts (Performing Abundance)

The annual ritual cycle is a rich one. In addition to family events (like birthdays), an ordinary person is likely to attend several life-cycle rituals (weddings, baptisms, funerals) each year. Since 1990, the number of church-related holidays being widely observed has also increased. Easter and Easter of the Dead are now public holidays, with both dates following the common Orthodox calendar. However, as the Romanian Orthodox Church celebrates Christmas together with Catholic and Protestant churches on December 25, while the Russian Orthodox Church celebrates on January 7, both dates are public holidays in Moldova. Local Saints Day festivals are also recognized as public holidays. Almost all of these rituals are centered on a feast, and in recent decades, many celebrations (like those in the Christmas and Easter seasons) that included non-feasting activities and meanings (e.g., divining, caroling, masking) have dropped out of widespread observation. This means that the feast is now the basic and main element of most rituals.

FIG. 42.10. Plates upon plates at a baptismal party.

(Chișinău, 2009.)

Festive meals usually involve two or three courses. Tables are preset with the first course, which consists of a variety of salads, cold meats and cheeses (smoked sausages, fried cutlets, salty cow or goat's cheese, and homemade butter cheese), fresh vegetables, olives, preserved fish, and savory pastries (Fig. 42.10). Bread is on the table too but in small quantities. Salads are a particular focal point for a cook's creativity. One standby is *vinegret*, which contains boiled beets and potatoes, fresh carrots, and dill pickles, with or without mayonnaise. Other salads usually contain mayonnaise and may be based on meat (such as beef tongue, cooked chicken, or imitation crab sticks) or vegetables (potatoes and cabbage are both common bases). A salad of mashed roasted eggplants (*salată de pătlăgea vânătă*) may be served too. Innovation is achieved through the addition of unusual ingredients such as canned corn, pineapple, or mushrooms. One of the most spectacular salads, which may be served as a meal itself in an intimate setting, is the *peşte sub/în şubă* (fish in a [fur] coat): a baking dish or mold is filled with alternating layers of marinated fish (mackerel), grated boiled potato, grated boiled beet, and sometimes chopped onions and boiled eggs; mayonnaise is often spread between the layers and on top.

The first course may also include appetizers such as fried strips of eggplant rolled with garlic and mayonnaise (and sometimes tomatoes) or pastry cups filled with mushrooms or salads. The second course involves two or three hot dishes, such as *năhut* (stewed chickpeas), *sarmale*, or baked chicken or duck. The hot dishes may be staggered, as at weddings, or brought out at the same time. Also, dessert may be served as a final course, but some sweets (colorfully wrapped chocolates, cookies, sweet *plăcintă*, whole or cut fruit) are often on the table from the outset and may be eaten as part of the first course. In any case, the table is rarely cleared of other dishes before the dessert (e.g., cake) is brought out, so latecomers to a festive event may eat from all courses at once. Similarly, multiple drinks (homemade wine, champagne, cognac, compotes of boiled fruit, and sometimes soda) are placed in the center of a festive table, enabling guests to choose their preferred beverage. Coffee and tea are served variably according to the hosts' or guests' preferences. At village weddings, coffee and tea may not be served at all, though one or both are likely to be served as the very final course (with cake) at an urban wedding. It is taken as traditional, especially in villages, that most holidays are observed for three days; so, when guests do not succeed in attending all of the feasts to which they have been invited (orare expected because of reasons of kinship) on the first day, they have time to pay their respects on the second and third days.

Feast menus may be altered to conform with the dietary restrictions that the Orthodox Church recommends at various fasts. Weddings and other celebrations are rarely held during the strictest fasting periods (e.g., Lent) when meat, fish, dairy products, and alcohol are prohibited. There are, however, numerous minor fasts when meat should not be consumed and the menu is adjusted to include only fish.

Food and eating at funerals and memorials distinguish these from other major rituals. The distinctions, however, are subtle and may be missed or intentionally overlooked by some or all of the guests and hosts. Most noticeably, food is expected to be eaten in silence at these events. Nevertheless, as it is still necessary for toasts to accompany wine drinking, there is the possibility for quite extended talking and discussion if the toastmaker strays from a simple invocation of God's mercy. Sometimes, there is more open conversation at a small memorial feast than at other events precisely because there is no music, dancing, or other entertainment to distract the guests. The most important food at a funeral is *colivă*, which is most traditionally prepared from boiled sweetened wheat, although more often now with rice or a quick-cooking farina; this is poured into a round dish and cools into a stiff pudding to be eaten with a spoon; colorful candies form the shape of a cross on the top of the pudding. Although critical to the observation of a funeral, the cooks may "forget" to prepare *colivă* until almost the very last minute. It is often brought to the table, too, as an almost afterthought; and though most guests recognize an obligation to taste it, they do so quite hurriedly and as partially as possible.

Conclusion: Foodways in a Land of Wealth and Poverty

The cost of any individual feast in Moldova is inevitably difficult to calculate. There are some patterns. An urban wedding at a hotel, for example, costs significantly more than an urban wedding at a "café" (middling-quality restaurant with a lot of space for hosting events). Everyone knows that weddings held in the courtyard of a rural house are the least expensive. Actual costs, however, vary widely depending on the actual menu; "contributions" (of gifted food or beverage); decorations; and "connections" or "agreements" with the musicians, master of ceremonies, godparents, salesclerks, restaurant owners, etc. Restaurants give discounts, for example, if the host supplies all the ingredients; and musician friends play at steep discounts. With enough knowledge of these details, people may feel relatively confident of venturing a final calculation, and the organizers of most big events (like weddings) let a certain figure circulate as more or less public knowledge so that guests will give proportionate money gifts to cover the event's monetary cost and leave a little surplus. Often, the publicly known figure is just the figure of the recommended money gift. Nevertheless, the given figure always occludes numerous gifts, discounts, donations, and corners cut. At mid-range urban weddings around 2001, the expected contribution from an unmarried young person was about $20 (USD), while an older "pair" paid double or slightly more than double. With typical guest lists ranging between one hundred and two hundred people, the cost of the wedding was roughly known. Within a decade, the figure had doubled, though the celebrations were also more lavish with a greater range of decorations.

Feasts, whether for happy or sad occasions, are meant to distract attention away from the mundane concerns of everyday life; and they almost always succeed. Descriptions of "typical" feasts focus on the quantity of food and its presentation. Dishes are staggered on the table; courses are announced with intervals of dancing and other entertainment; formal toasting takes over from idle conversation. The whole performance projects impressions of wealth, plenty, and abundance. Some apparently lavish feasts are composed of very simple and inexpensive foods like baked and fresh apples, walnuts, and bread that are artfully arranged between plates of only slightly more costly fare.

People in Moldova ridicule their tendencies to project such images of abundance. Some apply academic terms like "potlatch"; others invoke expressions like "a wedding is proud but starving" (*nunta e mândră și flămândă*); while still others rely on regional stereotypes (e.g., people from the south are simple and generous, while "people from the north would borrow a tablecloth to put on a better display for guests!"). Everyone bemoans the overelaborate celebrations, ritual excess, and misleading presentations of hospitality; but it seems impossible to celebrate otherwise. The performances are so successful that people can rarely calculate a comprehensive market price even for the celebrations they themselves organize. Guests return home, dazzled for days and even years by their hosts' outlay, unflagging hospitality, and genuine desire to raise their guests' spirits.

The feast itself mediates life in the country's continually shifting political and economic fortunes. With independence, the Republic of Moldova slipped quickly from its position in the Soviet imaginary as a "little piece of heaven," where one lived richly and well from the abundance of the land, favorable climate, and fine wines, to become known internationally as "Europe's poorest country" from which women fled to western Europe, risking all manner of exploitation, to earn cash to support their families. The two images, of wealth and poverty, convey some aspects of the rapid changes in Moldova during the twentieth century, especially at either end of the Soviet period, from the 1940s to the 1990s. Yet neither image directly conveys a full picture of the country's economic condition, nor even of the basic availability of food. The two images are better seen as the alternating poles of reality that are continually expressed and mediated through local foodways—the products, practices, and performances.

Notes

1. 2014 Census of the Population and Inhabitants, https://statistica.gov.md/pageview.php?l=en&idc=479&, accessed December 6, 2021.
2. "Sarea în bucate" (ATU international tale-type #923, "Love Like Salt") was first published by Ispirescu in 1887 (https://ro.wikisource.org/wiki/Sarea_%C3%AEn_bucate) and continues to be cited by folklorists and ethnographers in Moldova.
3. Water appears in many rituals, with both positive and negative valences (see Dorondel 2004), but rarely as something to be consumed.

Works Cited

Acheson, Julianna. 1997. "Traversing Political Economy and the Household: An Ethnographic Analysis of Life after Communism in Kojsov, a Rural Village in Eastern Slovakia." PhD dissertation, University of Arizona.

Ana, Daniela. 2019. "Produced and Bottled in Moldova: Winemaking in Flexible Capitalism." PhD dissertation, University of Halle Wittenburg.

Arutjunov, Sergej A. 2004. *Chleb v narodnoj kul'ture: Ètnografičeskie očerki*. Moscow: Nauka.

Asăndulesei, Mihaela. 2015. "The Symbolism of Salt in Holidays as Expressed in the Pioneering Works of Romanian Ethnographers Simion Florea Marian and Tudor Pamfile." In *Salt*

Effect, eds. Marius Alexianu, Roxana-Gabriela Curcă, and Vasile Cotiugă, 241–250. Oxford: Archaeopress.
Aslan, Margareta. 2018. "The Value of Spices in the Romanian Lands during the Ottoman Suzerainty (Sixteenth–Eighteenth Centuries)." In *From Kebab to Ćevapčići: Foodways in (Post-)Ottoman Europe*, eds. Arkadiusz Blaszczyk and Stefan Rohdewald, 25–38. Wiesbaden: Harrassowitz.
Bîrlădeanu, Virgiliu. 2013. "Wine and Speed: Practices of Identity Engineering in the Republic of Moldova (2005–2009)." *History and Anthropology*, 1:36–55.
Blaszczyk, Arkadiusz, and Stefan Rohdewald. 2018. "Introduction: Foodways from Kebab to Ćevapčići and Their Significance in and Beyond (Post-)Ottoman Europe." In *From Kebab to Ćevapčići: Foodways in (Post-)Ottoman Europe*, eds. Arkadiusz Blaszczyk and Stefan Rohdewald, 1–24. Wiesbaden: Harrassowitz.
Bringeus, Nils-Arvid. 1971. *Man, Food, and Milieu: A Swedish Approach to Food Ethnology*. Edinburgh: Tuckwell Press.
Bringeus, Nils-Arvid, and Gunter Wiegelmann. 1971. "Ethnological Food Research in Europe and the USA." *Ethnologia Europaea*, 4:6–13.
Buzilă, Varvara. 1999. *Pâinea. Aliment și simbol: Experiența sacrului*. Chișinău: Știința.
Buzilă, Varvara. 2006. "Obiceiul cinstirii vinului la Moldoveni." *Tyragetia*, XV:488–498.
Caldwell, Melissa. 2004. *Not by Bread Alone: Social Support in the New Russia*. Berkeley: University of California Press.
Cash, Jennifer R. 2011. *Villages on Stage: Folklore and Nationalism in the Republic of Moldova*. Berlin: Lit Verlag.
Cash, Jennifer R. 2013a. "Performing Hospitality in Moldova: Ambiguous, Alternative and Undeveloped Models of National Identity." *History and Anthropology*, 1:56–77.
Cash, Jennifer R. 2013b. "Charity or Remembrance? Practices of Pomană in Rural Moldova." Working Paper No. 144, Max Planck Institute for Social Anthropology.
Cash, Jennifer R. 2015. "The Problems of Paying in Wine: Work, Hospitality, and Self-Sufficiency as Ritual Economy." In *Economy and Ritual: Studies of Postsocialist Times*, eds. Stephen Gudeman and Chris Hann, 31–51. New York–Oxford: Berghahn.
Ciocanu, M. 2015. "Contribuții etnografice la cunoașterea viticulturii țărănești din Basarabia." *Anuarul Muzeului Etnografic al Moldovei*, 15:247–287.
Cojocari, Ludmila, and Virgiliu Bîrlădeanu. 2013. "Război, alcool, identitate. Al doilea război mondial în memoria socială a Republicii Moldova (2001–2009)." In *Istoria recentă altfel: Perspective culturale*, eds. Andi Mihalache and Adrian Cioflâncă, 877–886. Iași: Editura Universității "Al. I. Cuza."
Counihan, Carole, and Penny van Esterik. 1997. *Food and Culture: A Reader*. London: Psychology Press.
Dorondel, Ștefan. 2004. *Moartea și apa: Ritualuri funerare, simbolism acvatic și structura lumii de dincolo în imaginarul țărănesc*. Bucharest: Editura Paideia.
Ergin, Nina, Christoph Neumann, and Amy Singer. 2007. *Feeding People, Feeding Power: Imarets in the Ottoman Empire*. Istanbul: EREN Press.
Harper, Krista, and Barbara West. 2003. "Editors' Notes: Food and Foodways in Postsocialist Eurasia." *The Anthropology of East Europe Review*, 1:5–7.
Hivon, Myriam. 1998. "'Payer en liquide': L'utilisation de la vodka dans les échanges en Russie rurale." *Ethnologie française*, 4:515–524.

Iarovoi, Valentina. 2007. "Vița-de-vie în cultura Moldovenilor." *Buletin Științific. Revista de Etnografie, Științele Naturii și Muzeologie (New Series)*, 20:208–217.

King, Charles. 2000. *The Moldovans: Romania, Russia, and the Politics of Culture*. Stanford, CA: Hoover Institution Press.

Klumbyte, Neringa. 2010. "The Soviet Sausage Renaissance." *American Anthropologist*, 1:22–37.

Long, Lucy M. 2015. *The Food and Folklore Reader*. London–New York: Bloomsbury.

Mesnil, Marianne. 1992. "Patience et longeur de temps: Les leçons du pain." In *Du grain au pain: Symboles, savoirs, pratiques*, ed. Marianne Mesnil, 7–16. Brussels: l'Institut de Sociologie de l'Université de Bruxelles.

Mesnil, Marianne, and Assia Popova. 2002. "L'offrande céréalière dans les rituels funéraires du sud-est Européen." *Civilisation*, 1–2:103–117.

Phillips, Sarah. 2002. "Half-Lives and Healthy Bodies: Discourses on 'Contaminated' Foods and Healing in Post-Chernobyl Ukraine." *Food and Foodways*, 1–2:27–53.

Ries, Nancy. 2009. "Potato Ontology: Surviving Postsocialism in Russia." *Cultural Anthropology*, 2:181–212.

Rogers, Douglas. 2005. "Moonshine, Money, and the Politics of Liquidity in Rural Russia." *American Ethnologist*, 1:63–81.

Roth, Klaus. 2010. "Nahrung als gegenstand der volkskundlichen erforschung des östlichen Europa." In *Esskultur und kulturelle Identität—Ethnologische nahrungsforschung im östlichen Europa*, eds. Heinke Kalinke, Klaus Roth, and Tobias Weger, 27–38. Oldenburg: Bundesinstitut für Kultur und Geschichte der Deutschen im östlichen Europa.

Index

Note: Figures, tables and notes are indicated by *f*, *t*, or *n* following the page number

Aaliyah, 923
Aarne, Antii, 583, 655, 662. *See also* Aarne-Thompson-Uther Tale-Type Index
Aarne-Thompson-Uther Tale-Type Index, 32, 58n1, 606, 608–610, 645–646, 655, 684, 693n10
abiav, 117, 124–132, 125*f*, 127*f*, 128*f*, 131*f*, 132*f*
"About Lenin and Stalin," 536
Academy of Arts (Novi Sad), 305
accommodation, Greek death rituals and, 206–209, 208*f*, 213n9
Acome, Justin, 888
Adagia (Erasmus of Rotterdam), 987
Adagiorum Graeco-Latino-Ungaricorum Chiliades Quinque (Baranyai Decsi), 987, 987*f*, 989
Adam of Bremen, 275
Adamovičs, Ludvigs, 438
Adon'ieva, Svetlana, 171, 176
Adonyeva, S. B., 263
Adonyeva, Svetlana, 257, 263
Aesop, 609, 614, 622
Afanas'ev, Aleksandr, xxvii, 657, 667, 669–672, 671*f*, 1029
agrarian festivals, 343–344, 349–350, 659
Aguilera, Christina, 923
"Ah sa keq," 918, 921–922
Akhmatova, Anna, 658
Akoyunoglou, Mitsi, 210
Albania. *See also* Albanian death rituals
  animism in, 225–228, 229*f*, 237n11–237n16
  assimilation and, 236n2
  Catholicism in, 217, 236n2
  Islam in, 225, 236n2, 237n9
  marriage/weddings in, 217
  naturist belief in, 225–228, 229*f*, 237n11–237n16
  Orthodox Christianity in, 221, 225, 236n2, 237n9
  Ottoman Empire and, 236n2
  prohibitions against death rites in, 220–221, 237n7
  South Slavic epic songs and, 545–546, 561
  under Soviet Union, 216–221, 218*f*, 236n2, 237n5, 237n6
Albanian death rituals, 216–236. *See also* Albania
  animism and, 225–228, 229*f*, 237n11–237n16
  attire and, 232–234, 233*f*
  butterflies and, 227–228, 237n11
  Catholicism and, 217
  crying and, 217, 226, 230–236, 231*f*, 233*f*, 235*f*, 237n17
  dance and, 217
  drums and, 217, 220, 237n7
  gender and, 217, 221, 232–234, 233*f*
  gjamë and, 217, 226
  history and, 216, 236n2
  lacerating of flesh and, 220
  laments and, 220–221, 230–234, 231*f*, 233*f*, 237n17
  meaning of, 216, 236n1
  medicalization and, 236
  naturist belief and, 225–228, 229*f*, 237n11–237n16
  omens and, 224–225, 237n9
  prohibitions against, 220–221, 237n7
  scholarship on, 217–223, 218*f*, 237n5
  snakes and, 228
  songs and, 217, 230–234, 231*f*, 233*f*, 234–236, 237n17

Albanian death rituals (*cont.*)
   under Soviet Union, 216, 217–221, 218*f*, 236n2, 237n5, 237n6
   spirit and, 224–228, 229*f*, 237n11–237n15
   supernatural beliefs and, 224–228, 229*f*, 237n9, 237n11–237n16
   thinking death and, 223–225, 237n8, 237n9
   village life and, 220, 237n6
Albanian epic, 545–546, 562n2, 564n20–564n22
Albanian-language *etnopop*, 918–942
   Balkanika Music Television and, 933–934, 937, 941
   chalga and, 919
   čoček and, 923, 937–938, 939*f*, 943n11
   cover songs and, 930–932, 934–940
   criticism of, 932
   dance clubs and, 923–925, 924*f*, 928
   defining, 922, 933
   emergence of, 921–925, 924*f*
   FEN TV and, 932–934
   gender and, 922, 926, 943n13
   globalization of, 940–942
   Kosovo and, 920–921
   licensing agreements and, 930–940
   manele and, 919
   modern recording techniques and, 918–921
   regional interactions in, 925–931, 927*f*, 929*f*, 930*f*, 943n13
   Serbia and, 920–921
   social media and, 919
   transnational dimensions in, 920–921
   western influence on, 922
   YouTube and, 934–939, 941
   Yugoslavia and, 920–921, 940–941
Albanian population in Kosovo, 61–64, 80n6–80n7
alchemy, 366
Alekseevskii, M. D., 263
Alesha Popovich i Tugarin Zmei (film), 509
Alesha Popovych (*bylina* hero), 485, 489–491, 503–511, 510*f*
Alesul Oilor, 349
Alexander II (Russian tsar), 1028
Alexander III (Russian tsar), 1030
Alexiou, Margaret, 195, 201
Alkan Pasha (*duma* character), 523–524

alliteration, Estonian runosongs and, 139
All-Russia Exhibition, 1029–1030
All Souls Day, 446–447
Alpert, Michael, 780, 781, 782, 783
al Roma, 109, 133
"alternative form of hope," 465–466
Alunāns, Juris, 437–438
Amazing Spider-Man, The (film), 1003, 1003*f*
American Folklore, Journal of, 1056
American Folklore Society, 1055–1056
American Heritage Dictionary, 769
Americanism, Czech bluegrass and, 871–872, 877–878, 889–890
Amosova, Pelageia, 1019
amulets, 366
"Am un leu și vreau să–l beau," 821
Amžina Ugnis (Vydūnas), 438
Ančić, Mladen, 88–89
Ancient Symbolism in Lithuanian Folk Art (Gimbutas), 451
Andersen, Flemming, 588
Andersen, Hans Christian, 607, 610, 619, 620, 622, 623n14
Andrea, 903
Andrić, Nikola, 581–583
"Anecdote," 643
Anelia, 900
Angelopoulou, 608
Angelov, Gorancho, 810
"Animal Bride, The," 645
"Animal Tales," 643
animism, in Albania, 225–228, 229*f*, 237n11–237n16
Ani tak nehoří, 885
Anski Expeditions, 774, 783
anthems
   arii naționale and, 819–826, 822*f*, 824*f*, 825*f*, 840n12, 840n15, 840n16, 841n18, 841n19
   Croat/Croatian weddings and, 87–88, 94–96
   Serbian weddings (Kosovo) and, 65, 80n7
   United States and, 87–88, 104n4, 104n5
   violence and, 88–89
anthologies. *See* collections
"anti–behavior," 387, 397
Antichrist, 404–405, 409, 414–415, 419–421, 423

anti-ponašanje, 386–387
Antipova, Elizaveta Yakovlena, 660
anti-proverbs, 991–994, 993*f*
anti-semitism, 439, 531–532
Antonio, 903
Antonovych, Volodymyr, 535
Anzaldúa, Gloria, 547
"Apocalypse of the Mother of God," 417
apocalypticism
    Antichrist and, 404–405, 409, 414–415, 419–421, 423
    Bolshevik Revolution and, 403, 405
    chapbooks and, 408–409, 415–416, 422–423
    copybooks and, 415–423, 416*f*, 417*f*
    Culiac brothers and, 403–404, 409–413, 411*f*, 412*f*, 415–416, 419–423, 423n1
    Elijah (prophet) and, 404, 409, 414–415, 419–420, 423, 425n18
    Enoch (prophet) and, 409, 414–415, 419–420, 425n18
    John the Baptist and, 410, 419, 425n18
    Maliovantsy and, 407, 425n12
    Mark, Gospel of and, 413–414
    Michael (Archangel) and, 404, 410, 417–423
    Moldovan folk religion and, 403–423, 424n6, 425n13, 425n18
    multi-temporality and, 411, 413
    Old Believers and, 404, 406–408, 422–423, 424n3
    oral narrative and, 413–415, 425n18
    Revelation, Book of and, 408, 414–415
    Skoptsy and, 407, 425n11
    under Soviet Union, 403–404
    two witnesses and, 414–415, 419, 425n18
Apollodorus, 609
Apotolev, Rumen, 902–903
apparitions
    "alternative form of hope" and, 465–466
    at Bryn, 463–464, 469–470, 473–478, 476*f*
    at Dzhubryk, 464–465
    at Fatima, 465, 471, 473
    Greek death rituals and, 199
    at Lourdes, 465, 471, 473
    at Malyi Hvizdets, 464, 466, 468–470, 473, 475–479, 475*f*
    Slavic supernatural legends and, 678, 683
    Ukrainian Marianism and, 459–460, 462–479, 472*f*, 473*f*, 475*f*, 476*f*
    at Vybli, 462–463, 468
    at Zarvanytsia, 465, 470–479, 472*f*, 473*f*
Apraksiia (*bylina* character), 498–499, 504–505
Apsīte, Milda, 439*f*
Apuleius, 609
Aqua, Annie, 784
Aqua, Zoe, 784
Arabian Nights, 610
Arash, 941
Archangelist movement, 404, 409–410, 414–423, 423n2, 425n19
ardeleana, 345
arii naționale, 819–826, 822*f*, 824*f*, 825*f*, 840n12, 840n15, 840n16, 841n18, 841n19
Aristophanes, 609
Arkas, 622
Arkhangel'skiia byliny i istoricheskie pesni s napevami (Grigorev), 496
Arkhipova, A. S., 974
Armed Forces Network, 879
artels, 498
artizanat, 1041–1043
Asanaginica. *See Hasanaginica*
Asclepius, 609
Ashkenazim, 741–747, 752, 758–759, 763–774, 765n18
    cultural conservatism and, 742, 744–745, 747, 752–754, 760, 763
    dance and, 780, 783
    "Golden Age" of, 747
    klezmer music and, 771–776
    literacy of, 741, 747–748, 748*t*
    migration of, 746
    nusakh and, 772
    transnational dimension in song and, 743
Ash Wednesday, 317–318, 323–324
assimilation
    nationalism and, 236n2
    religion and, 236n2
    under Soviet Union, 236n2
Assumption of Mary, Cortorar Romani weddings and, 118, 134n8
Astakhova, Anna M., 496
Athens, University of, 607

Attali, Jacque, 101
attire
    Albanian death rituals and, 232–234, 233f
    Cortorar Romani weddings and, 110, 111f, 112, 113f, 126–127, 127f
    death rites and, 202
    Greek death rituals and, 202
    inverted ritual behavior and, 394
    material culture and, 1021–1022, 1022f
    Paganism and, 448–449
    of *pokladari*, 313f, 331n1
    Romanian community celebrations and, 351–352
    Russian death rituals and, 240–244, 242f, 243f
    Russian folk art and, 1021–1022, 1022f
    Russian weddings and, 32
    Serbian weddings (Kosovo) and, 64f, 67, 72–75, 73f, 77, 77f, 78f, 80n13, 80n15
    Ukrainian weddings and, 14–15, 17, 24–26
ATU. *See* Aarne-Thompson-Uther (ATU) Tale-Type Index
Auer, Leopold, 784
Auerbach, Susan, 201
Auli, 450f
"Aunt Lena" (Antigone Metaxa-Krontira), 622
auseklis, 451–452, 452f
aušrinė, 452
Austria
    Czechoslovakia and, 876
    klezmer music and, 776, 781
    Romania and, 315, 351
"author" museums, 1045, 1045f
autumnal ancestor veneration, 446–448
"Aylelule, Sleep My Dear Child" (Brounoff), 762f
"Az árva lyány" (Petőfi), 989
Azis, 904

Babakov, Ahmed, 798
Baba Yaga, 662, 663f, 664f, 672
badkhn, 772–773, 775, 778
Badu, Erykah, 923
Baiburin, Albert, 168, 171
Bailey, James, 498
bajalice, 386, 388
Bajtal, Esad, 723

Baker, Catherine, 103, 903
Bakhtin, Vladimir, 952–953
Bakhtin, V. S., 963
Bakija Bakič ensemble, 849
Balada pro banditu, 884–885
Balashov, D., 50
Balibar, Étienne, 550
Balić, Smail, 724
Balkan Arts Center, 780
Balkan Beat Box, 910
Balkan Hits 2005 (pirate CD), 941
Balkanika Music Television, 933–934, 937, 941
Balkanism, 897–898
Balkansky, 907
Balkanton music label, 899
ballads
    on bride/in-law conflicts, 8–9, 16, 23–24
    on chastity, 11
    composition of, 590–592
    decasyllabic, 577–578, 593
    Estonian runosongs and, 148–150
    gusle and, 579, 584
    Islam and, 577–581, 584–589 586f, 587f, 589f
    musicality of, 578–579
    octosyllabic, 577
    oral *vs.* written, 579–581
    on reconciliation, 22–23
    Russian, 492
    "singer's epistemics" and, 588
    South Slavic women's (*see* South Slavic women's ballads)
    tragic nature of, 578
    Ukrainian weddings and, 8–9, 11, 16, 21–24
    Yiddish folk song, 759–762, 761f, 762f
balls/*balo*, 317, 332n11, 342
Baltic region. *See also* Estonia; Latvia; Lithuania
    Catholicism in, 430–432
    Crusades and, 140, 276, 282–283, 286, 431–432, 452–453
    defined, 275–276
    early history of, 281–283, 290n6
    gender and, 289
    Germany and, 140–141, 166n3, 432, 438
    Hanseatic League and, 431–432
    history of, 430–432, 431f
    Indo-European influence and, 275

Indo-European mythology and, 435
modern, 287–289
Paris Peace Conference and, 275
Prussia and, 278, 286, 430, 438, 440–441
religion and, 277–279
Russia and, 278, 289n3
under Soviet Union, 432, 438–439, 441, 443
Balts, The (Gimbutas), 443
Balys, Jonas, 277, 280, 440
bandura, 515, 517f, 537, 537f, 963
banjo, 879–880, 881f
Banjo Jamboree festival, 873–874, 874f, 887f
Banjo Romantika (film), 875, 887
baptism
    benedictions and, 373–374
    in Hungary, 373–374
    inverted ritual behavior and, 392
    Russia and, 175–176, 184n8
    Russian childbirth folklore and, 175–176, 184n8
    summer solstice and, 444
Barabash, Iven, 531, 539n6
Baraku, Aida, 927–928
Baranyai Decsi, János, 987, 987f, 989
Barber, E., 41
Bárdosi, Vilmos, 990
Barons, Krišjānis, 288, 290n4, 435–436
Barsov, E. V., 255–256
Bartók, Béla, xxviii, 588, 590, 724
Bašagić, Safvet-beg, 729, 734, 738n7
Basanavičius, Jonas, 439
Basans'ka, Olha, 11
bathhouses, Russian weddings and, 37
Bauman, Richard, 585
Baumanis, Kārlis, 436
Bazyler, Ben, 780
Bazylevych, Hryhoryi, 535
BCMS (Bosnia-Herzegovina, Croatia, Montenegro, Serbia). *See* Bosnia-Herzegovina; Croatia; Serbia
beardless man, 616
bećarac, 91–94, 102
Beckerman, Michael, 876
Beckerman, Sam, 778
Beckerman, Shloymke, 778
Beckerman, Sid, 778
Bedros, Vlad, 422

Beer, Aaron, 772
"Before the Cock Crows Thrice" (Shukshin), 672
"Beginning of the Revolt against the Dahis, The," 560
Bejkova, Avni, 221
Bejtić, Alija, 722
Belaj, Vitomir, 593
Belarus, xxiii, xxxii, 432, 951–955, 965–966, 980
Belite lebedi, 798f
"Bell, The" (H. C. Andersen), 620
Belomoskiia byliny (Markov), 496
Belousov, A. F., 172
Belousova, Ekaterina, 172, 174, 177
Belyavski-Frank, Masha, 724
Bendix, Brian, 784
Bendix-Balgley, Noah, 784
Benedictines, 371–372
benedictions, 368–378
Benge, Alfreda, 911
Bennett, Gillian, 467–468
Ben Yehudin, Eliyahu, 747
Beowulf, 485, 514, 542, 555, 563
Berak, Ljubica, 735
Berani, Ilir, 926
Berbić, Zanin, 722, 736, 737, 737f
berde, 84, 84f
bereavement. *See* Albanian death rituals; death/death rites; Greek death rituals; Russian death rituals
Beregovski, Moyshe, 773–784
Beresnevičius, Gintaras, 443
Berg, Judith, 783
Bergovski, Moisei, 757, 757f, 758f
Berindei, Cosmina-Maria, 413
Berisha, Anton, 217
Berlin Heckesches Hoftheater, 782
Berlin Philharmonic, 784
Bern, Alan, 781
Bernea, Ernest, 407
Beržanskis, Jonas, 439–440
Bērziņa, Aline, 439f
Bessarabia. *See* Moldova
Bessarabian Hop (Winograd CD), 785
Bessarabian Symphony (Rubin & Horowitz CD), 781

betrothal
- *domovyny* and, 14
- rejection of, 14
- *rushnyk* and, 14
- *starosty* and, 13–14
- *svatannia* and, 13–14
- *svaty* and, 13–14
- Ukrainian weddings and, 13–14
- *zmovyny* and, 14

Beyoncé, 925, 928
Beyond the Pale (Brave Old World CD), 781
BG Cwrkot, 873
Biezais, Haralds, 438, 443
"Big Pimpin'," 925
Bilbilov, Robert, 932
Bilibin, Ivan, 663f–665f, 669f, 670, 672, 1029–1030, 1031f
binding, 240
birth. *See* childbirth; Russian childbirth folklore
bisernica, 84, 84f
Bittová, Iva, 885
Bjorling, Kurt, 780–781
Black Cat, White Cat (Kusturica film), 838
black magic, 366–367
blaga rakija, 67
blessings, 368–378
"Blestemat să fii de stele," 834
blind minstrels, 498–499, 514–515, 517, 529, 535–538, 537f
Blind Vasha (Ushev animated film), 906
Bliznac, Šimo, 681–682
blood feuds, laments and, 205–206
bluegrass. *See also* Czech bluegrass
- festivals, 873, 874f
- in film, 873, 877
- global, 873–875, 874f, 875f
- hillbilly music and, 873
- "old-time," 882–884

bluegrassáci, 871
Blue Mill Water Band, 886
body gestures, 202–203, 385, 394
Bogatyrev, Petr, 671–672
bogatyri, 485–511, 491f, 510f
Bogdani, Ramazan, 217
Bohemian folklore, 875–877
Bohlman, Philip, 87, 89

Böhme, Franz Magnus, 757f
boiary, 16–17, 19, 22, 29n8
Bojtár, Endre, 435
Bokutlija, Franjo, 728
Bolshevik Revolution, 403, 405
Bolte, Johannes, 607
bomb-making, 317–319, 322, 330, 332n12, 332n14
Bonnie and Clyde (film), 873
Book about Songs (Valdobrev), 906–907
Book of Memory (Simaner), 747, 752
border areas
- eschatology and, 406–409, 425n13–425n16
- folk religion and, 406–409, 425n13–425n16
- gender as, 551–552
- Islam and, 541–542, 544–545, 551, 556–557
- philology of, 547–548, 550–551, 560–561, 565–566
- South Slavic epic songs and, 541–542, 545–551, 560–561, 565–566
- "tradition of the border" and, 542, 545, 547, 562

Borderlands – La frontera (Anzaldúa), 547
Borino Vranje, 856
Borozdina, Ekaterina, 174
Borzhkivskyi, Valerian, 535
Bosanske sevdalinke za klavir, za jedno i dva grla (Kečerovský), 722
bošča, 72, 73f, 74, 80n13
Boshnjaku, Florent, 918, 919f, 923
Bošković-Stulli, Maja, 580, 690
Bosnia-Herzegovina, 83, 86, 88, 90–94, 92f–94f, 104n2, 104n7. *See also sevdalinka*; Slavic supernatural legends; South Slavic region
"bosnischen Sevdalinke, Die" (Prohaska), 721
Bošnjaci i Hercegovci u islamskoj književnosti (Bašagić), 729
Botić, Luka, 728
Bourdieu, Pierre, 89
Bowie, David, 911
Brandwein, Naftule, 778, 784
Brastiņš, Ernests, 438, 439f, 440, 450–451
brâul bătrân, 345
"Brave Father and His Brave Son, The," 617
Brave Old World, 781

Bread as Food and Symbol: The Experience of the Sacred (Buzilă), 1076
bread ceremony
   Cortorar Romani weddings and, 127, 130
   foodways (Moldova) and, 1070–1077, 1071f, 1073f–1075f
   in Latvia, 448
   in Lithuania, 448
Bregović, Goran, 910
Brezhnev, Leonid, 5, 10
brides. *See* marriage/weddings
Briggs, Charles, 585
Bringa, Tone, 99
Brotman, Stuart, 781, 782
Brounoff, Platon, 762f
broygez tants, 776
Brubaker, Rogers, 940
Bruņenieks, Mārtiņš, 438
Bryn apparition, 463–464, 469–470, 473–478, 476f
Bucharest Village Museum, 1049
Buchczyk, Magdalena, 1042–1043, 1050
Buchon, Jean Alexandre, 606
Budakov, Peyo, 799
Budală, Marcel, 834
Budapest joke, 1000–1001
Budowitz, 781
bugarštica, 563n11, 580
Bula, Dace, 289
bulgar, 778
Bulgaria, 491. *See also* South Slavic region
   chalga in, 807–808
   commercialization of Romani music and, 796–799, 797f, 798f
   ethnopop in, 807–808
   FEN TV and, 932–934
   identity and, 910
   Ottoman Empire and, 901, 910
   pop folk in, 807–808
   Romani music in, 791–799, 801–804, 806–809, 811
   Serbia and, 795–796, 799–801
   under socialism, 801–804, 897–899, 902
   stereotyping, 897–898
   There is Such a People and, 904
Bulgarian National Radio and Television, 899, 901

Bulgarian popular music, 895–912
   authored songs in the folk spirit and, 908
   Balkanism and, 897–898
   Balkanton music label and, 899
   chalga and, 898, 904
   criticism of, 902–903, 905
   dub step and, 908
   electronica and, 907
   "Estrada" and, 899
   folklore-inspired, 905–912
   folk music/instrumentation and, 908–909
   gangster rap and, 901
   gender and, 903–904
   heavy metal and, 907
   humor/satire in, 901, 906, 909–911
   indie music and, 907
   jazz and, 907, 909
   marketing of, 904–997
   obrabotena muzika and, 901, 908
   Payner music label and, 902–904
   pop-folk and, 898–906
   rock music and, 907
   sex and, 903–904
   svatbarska muzika and, 898, 901
   trap music and, 908
   YouTube and, 904
Bŭlgarska Etnografiia, 1057
"bundle" of death clothes, 241, 242f
burial ceremonies. *See* Albanian death rituals; death/death rites; Greek death rituals; Russian death rituals
Bush, Kate, 911
Bush, Sam, 886
butterflies as symbols of resurrection, 227–228, 237n11
Buturović, Đenana, 724
Buzilă, Varvara, 1076
Buzinkay, Géza, 1000
Bylina Severa (Astakhova), 496
byliny, xxvii, 485–511
   artels and, 498
   bogatyri and, 485–511, 491f, 510f
   collections of, 492–496
   content of, 499–506
   cycles in, 486–492
   dumy and, 498
   "epic retardation" in, 495

byliny (cont.)
  in fine art, 492, 494f, 506–510, 508f–510f
  forgery and, 494
  gender and, 501–506, 509
  gusli and, 492, 497–498, 510–511
  Halych cycle and, 491
  history of, 496–499
  hubris and, 501–503
  hyperbole in, 495
  Indo-European influence and, 497
  kaliki and, 498–499, 503–504
  kobzari and, 498
  Kyivan cycle and, 489–491
  lira and, 498
  media and, 507
  myth and, 486, 501, 503, 507
  noviny and, 507–508, 668
  performance of, 492, 497–500, 500f, 503–504, 506–507, 510
  polianitsa and, 490, 501, 504
  in popular culture, 492, 494f, 506–510, 508f–510f
  posidelki and, 498
  Rus' and, 489, 491
  Russian wondertales and, 658–659
  sex in, 504–506
  skomorokhi and, 497–498, 503
  under Soviet Union, 507–508
  stariny and, 492, 507
  Ukraine and, 491, 496, 498, 507
  zachin and, 495, 501
  zapev and, 495
Byliny: Novoi i nedavnei zapisi (Miller), 496
Bynum, David, 686
Byzantine Empire, Greece and, 194–196, 213n2, 213n3, 609–610
Byzantine Rite Christianity, 460–461, 469

"Čador penje beže Ljuboviću," 737
Cahan, Juda-Leib, 756, 762f
căiuți, 351
čajo, Croat/Croatian weddings and, 89–90, 104n6
Čale Feldman, Lada, 103
calendrical cycle, 275–289
  agrarian festivals and, 343–344, 349–350, 659

  Alesul Oilor and, 349
  Ash Wednesday and, 317–318, 323–324
  căiuți and, 351
  Căluș and, 346–348, 347f, 351, 353f, 356n16, 356n17
  Călușerul Transilvănean and, 351, 353f
  capră and, 351, 352f
  Carnival and, 303
  caroling and, 350
  Catholicism and, 336, 340, 342
  cete and, 350–351
  Children's Day and, 336, 354
  Christmas and, 350–353, 352f, 353f, 356n20
  Croatian ethnology and, 325–327, 332n18–333n20
  cultural-artistic societies and, 301–302, 304, 308n11, 308n12, 308n14
  cultural heritage and, 327–328
  dainas/dainos and, 279, 290n3, 290n4
  dance and, 335–355, 336f, 355n3
  dodole and, 295–298, 302
  Epiphany and, 351–352
  ethnochoreology and, 295–307
  ethnography and, 277, 282, 295–298, 303–304, 314, 326–328
  Fărșang and, 340–342, 342f, 356n8
  Fat Monday and, 318–319, 332n12, 332n13
  Festival of Hearts and, 354
  Festivalul datinilor de iarnă and, 351
  Flower Saturday and, 343
  Focul lui Sumedru and, 350
  gadskārtu ieražas and, 280
  gadskārtu svētki and, 280
  Gregorian, 336, 355n3, 424n7
  harvest festivals and, 349–350
  hinkepe and, 284
  Hora la Prislop and, 349
  house-to-house visits and, 338–340, 343, 347, 350, 355
  International Dance Day, 354, 357n23
  International Day of the Romanian Blouse and, 354
  izvorni folklor and, 302
  Julian, 336, 355n3, 405, 424n7
  koledari and, 295–298, 300, 302
  kraljice and, 295–298, 300, 302–303
  Lastovo Carnival and, 311–331

latviskā gadskārta and, 280
Latvju dainas and, 279, 290n4
lazarice and, 295–298, 300, 302, 307n2, 307n3
Lent and, 247, 266n3, 317–318
Marianism and, 283–284, 286
Maslenitsa and, 288
migrant, 281
minority, 281
modern, 287–289, 305–307
myth and, 288, 297, 303
nedeile and, 348–349
newly composed folk music/ instrumentation and, 301
New Year's and, 350–353, 352f, 353f, 356n20
nunta cornilor and, 341, 341f, 356n8
obredna igra and, 299, 303
Orthodox Christianity and, 295–297, 301, 307, 336, 339–340, 346, 355n3
Paganism and, 281–282, 285–287
participatory presentational forms of dance and, 338, 340, 345, 349, 353–355, 356n6, 356n22
Pentecost and, 346–348, 418
ples and, 299, 306
rahvakalender and, 277, 279–280
in Romanian community celebrations, 335–355, 336f, 355n3
Rusalii and, 346–348
saints' days and, 344–345, 348–352, 356n12, 356n13
Sâmbra Oilor and, 343–344
scholarship on, 276–281, 289n2–290n4
secular celebrations and, 353–354, 356n22
in Serbia, 295–307
Shrove Tuesday and, 319–323, 320f–322f, 332n14, 332n15
songs and, 279, 290n3, 290n4
under Soviet Union, 277–278, 301–302, 308n11, 308n12, 308n14
Strânsul Oilor and, 349
summer solstice and (*see* summer solstice)
supernatural beliefs and, 297–300, 303, 342, 348
Târgul de fete and, 349
Terra Mariana and, 283–284, 286
Union Day and, 354
in urban settings, 281, 283–285
village life and, 295–298, 301–307, 308n11, 308n12, 308n14, 344–348, 346f, 347f, 356n12, 356n13, 356n16, 356n17
Volkskalender and, 279–280
zavetina and, 307
Ćaleta, Joško, 327
čalgija orchestras, 846, 861
Calin Didier, 443
Căluș, 346–348, 347f, 351, 353f, 356n16, 356n17
Călușerul Transilvănean, 351, 352f
Campbell, Joseph, 662–663, 669
Cântarea României, 1041, 1046
cântecul miresei, 127–130
Canterbury Sound, 911
Cantwell, Robert, 874
capră, 351, 352f
"Captive's Lament, The," 521–522
captivity. *See also* slavery
in *dumy*, 520–525
Caraveli, Anna, 201, 223
Caraveli-Chaves, Anna, 201
cârciumi, 827, 834
Carey, Mariah, 923
Cariboo (Ztracenkáři), 877–878
Carnival, 303
Ash Wednesday and, 317–318, 323–324
attire and, 313f, 331n1
balo and, 317, 332n11
bomb-making and, 317–319, 322, 330, 332n12, 332n14
chain sword dance and, 312–318, 322–325, 330–331, 331n4, 331n6, 332n8
COVID-19 pandemic and, 328–330
Croatian ethnology and, 325–327, 332n18–333n20
culjanje and, 319, 322, 325, 330, 332n14
cultural heritage and, 327–328
dance and, 312–315, 317–318, 331n4, 331n6, 332n11
Dubrovnik and, 312, 315
Fat Monday and, 318–319, 332n12, 332n13
gender and, 313–314
grube maškare and, 319, 332n13
historical influences on, 314–316
Kapo sale and, 317–319, 323, 332n11
Korčula and, 312–313, 315–317, 331n4, 332n8

Carnival (*cont.*)
   Lastovo, 311–331
   lijepe maškare and, 312–315, 314*f*, 317–320, 322–325, 322*f*, 329–330, 331n6
   Lupercalian, 312
   lyre and, 317–319, 320*f*, 322*f*, 323–325, 330
   masked balls and, 342
   modern, 316–318, 318*f*, 332n10, 332n11
   pokladari and, 312–314, 313*f*, 316–325, 321*f*, 329–330, 331n1, 331n6, 332n8, 332n13
   Poklad puppet and, 312, 316–319, 318*f*, 322–325, 330, 332n10, 332n12, 332n14
   prlina and, 318–319, 332n10
   "professional informants" and, 325
   saints' days and, 317
   sanatur and, 318
   Saturnalian, 312
   Shrove Tuesday and, 319–323, 320*f*–322*f*, 332n14, 332n15
   siege of Lastovo and, 316–317
   under Soviet Union, 316
   supernatural beliefs and, 311–312
   Yugoslavia and, 316
caroling, 350
"Căruța poștei," 821
catacomb church, 404, 424n5
Catangă, Cornelia, 841n23
Catharine the Great, 494
catharsis, laments and, 210
Catholicism. *See also* Christianity; Crusades; Orthodox Christianity; religion
   in Albania, 217, 236n2
   in Baltic region, 430–432
   Benedictines and, 371–372
   benedictions and, 368–378
   calendrical cycle and, 336, 340, 342
   Carnival and (*see* Carnival)
   Catholic Enlightenment and, 366, 378
   charismatic movement and, 379–380
   Croat/Croatian weddings and, 83, 85, 90
   decrees of Trento and, 366
   in Estonia, 277–279
   exorcism and, 370, 377–380
   Franciscans and, 373–374, 376, 378
   geographic concentrations of, xxiv–xxv, xxxiiin 4
   in Hungary, 363–381
   Jesuits and, 378
   laments and, 207, 265
   Lastovo Carnival and (*see* Lastovo Carnival)
   in Latvia, 277–279, 432
   in Lithuania, 277–279, 432
   in Poland, 709, 716n13
   prohibitions against death rites and, 220–221, 237n7
   responsorium and, 374
   in Romania, 336, 340, 342
   sacramentalia and, 369
   South Slavic epic songs and, 541, 548
   South Slavic women's ballads and, 578, 581, 584
   under Soviet Union, 218*f*, 441
   symbolism of, 103
   in Ukraine, 460, 465, 471–472
   white magic and, 366–367
Ćatić, Musa Ćazim, 734
Čaušević, Lejla, 736
"Ceasornicul," 821
ceată, 339
Ceaușescu, Nicolae, 1038, 1041
ćef, 850–851, 851*f*, 865n17
Cellier, Marcel, 901
Čermák, Marko, 879–880, 885
Cestou na východ, 887
cete, 350–351
chain dance. *See also specific dance, e.g. hora*
   gender and, 313, 331n6
   kumpanija and, 313, 331n4
   sword, 312–318, 322–325, 330–331, 331n4, 331n6, 332n8
Chakalov, Evgeni, 910
chalga, xxix, 807–808, 898, 904, 925
chalga, Albanian *etnopop* and, 919
chalgadzhii, 793
chalgiya, 793–796, 799–800, 804–805, 810–811
Chalgiya Orchestra, 804
chalices, Cortorar Romani weddings and, 110–111, 116–118, 117*f*, 133n3, 134n7
Chalupa, Samo, 634
chanting, at Cortorar Romani weddings, 126
"charisma of place," 460, 466–467, 478–479
charismatic movement, 379–380
charms. *See* verbal charms

Charos (Greek personification of death), 194, 200, 207, 213n6
chastity. *See also* sex
　Cortorar Romani weddings and, 109, 112, 116–117, 132, 132*f*
　courtship and, 10–11
　Estonian runosongs and, 159–160
　green orchard metaphor of, 32–33
　hair as a metaphor for, 37–39
　hil'tse and, 17
　Russian wedding songs on, 31–32, 37–39
　signals of, 24–25
　Ukrainian ballads on, 11
chastushki, 951–981
　in Belarus, 951–955, 965–966, 980
　collections of, 953–954
　competition and, 968–970, 969*f*, 971*f*
　content of, 953–954
　context in, 960
　courtship and, 967–968
　dance and, 952–953, 963–966, 964*f*
　as entertainment, 966–967
　folk music/instrumentation and, 963–966, 964*f*, 965*f*
　humor/satire and, 952, 954, 970–973, 974*f*, 975
　kolomyiki and, 951–953, 962–963, 965–966
　lyric songs and, 952
　marriages/weddings and, 977–980
　memory and, 980
　meter of, 951, 954–964
　poetics of, 954–963
　post-communism and, xxix
　pragmatics and, 966–980
　propaganda and, 973–975
　repetition in, 960
　rhyme of, 954–964
　rites/rituals and, 976–980
　scholarship on, 951–954
　sex and, 953–954
　under Soviet Union, 952–953, 962–977, 980
　in Ukraine, 951–955, 962–966, 972, 980
Chicago Klezmer Ensemble, 780
Chicago World's Fair, 778
Child, Francis James, 590
childbirth. *See also* fertility; Russian childbirth folklore
　challenges of research on, 169–170, 183n1
　Cortorar Romani weddings and, 108–109, 113–114, 116–117, 127
　COVID-19 pandemic and, 176–177
　doulas and, 174
　endurance and, 180
　Estonian runosongs and, 150, 153–155
　ethnography and, 168–170, 174
　fairies and, 397
　gender and, 174–177
　inverted ritual behavior and, 385, 392–394, 397
　medicalization and, 170, 172, 174–182, 179*f*, 180*f*, 184n8
　midwives and (*see* midwives)
　modern Russia and, 170–177, 183n2
　myth and, 140
　post-Soviet Russia and, 170–177, 183n2
　rites/rituals and, 168–177, 183n1–183n5, 184n8
　Roma and, 108–109
　scholarship on, 168–178, 183n2
　secrecy about, 169–170
　South Slavic region and, 385, 392–394, 397
　Soviet Union and, 170, 183n1
　supernatural beliefs and, 174–177, 184n8
　verbal charms and, 170, 175
"Child of Mareta," 148–150
Children's Day, 336, 354
Chinchiri, Hasan, 803
Chiseliță, Vasile, 774
Chistov, K. V., 255
choreography. *See also* ethnochoreology
　performance and, 302
　in Serbia, 301, 304–305
"chosen places," 470
christening. *See* baptism
Christianity. *See also* religion; *specific types*, e.g. Catholicism
　autumnal ancestor veneration and, 446–448
　butterflies as symbols of resurrection and, 227–228, 237n11
　Byzantine Rite, 460–461, 469
　in Estonia, 282
　foodways (Moldova) and, 1059–1060, 1062, 1070–1077, 1071*f*, 1073*f*–1075*f*
　geographic concentrations of, xxiv–xxv, xxxiiin 3–n4

Christianity (*cont.*)
   in Latvia, 282
   Lithuania and, 282
   material culture and, 1016, 1019, 1025–1026
   Ottoman Empire and, 193–194
   Russian folk art and, 1016, 1019, 1025–1026
   South Slavic epic songs and, 541–542, 545, 548–549, 551, 557
   South Slavic women's ballads and, 577, 579, 586*f*
   summer solstice and, 443–444
   symbols and, 451
   white magic and, 366–367
Christiansen, Reidar Thoralf, 691
Chubinskii, Pavlo, 5
churchbells, 200
Churilo Plenkovich (*bylina* character), 491
"Cinderella," 615
"Cinderfella-Foul Face," 634, 629*f*
"Cinderfella the Greatest," 646, 641*f*, 648
činimo žito, 67
Cioacă, Florea, 834
"Ciocârlia," 823, 826
Čipka, Jonatan Dobroslav, 636–637, 637*f*, 639, 641–642
Civilization of the Goddess, The (Gimbutas), 443
"Clap Hands" (Mlotek), 750*f*
Classic Newgrass Quartet, 886, 887*f*
Clay, Eugene, 407
"Clever Horse, The," 645
"Cluck Old Hen," 883
ĉoĉek, 845, 857–859, 861*f*, 863n2, 866n27, 923, 937–938, 939*f*, 943n11
Code of Lek Dukagjini, The (Gjeçovi), 217
Codex diversorum auctorum A, 647*f*
Codex of Revúca, 633–634, 635*f*, 640*f*, 642*f*
Codex of Tisov, 637, 637*f*
coffin decoration, 251, 266n4
Cohen, Anthony, 63
Cohen, Bob, 782
Čolaković, Zlatan, 555, 558–560
colax, 122–124
collections
   bylina, 492–496
   chastushka, 953–954
   duma, 514–515, 530–531, 534–537

folk music/instrumentation, 876
Greek folk tale, 605–607, 612, 617–619
klezmer music, 773–774
oral *vs.* written, 579–580
proverb, 989–990
riddle, 994–996, 995*f*
Romanian folk art, 1037–1038
Romani music, 819–820
Russian Geographical Society and, 667, 669
sevdalinka, 723–727, 727*f*, 729, 736
Slovak folk tale, 628–648, 630*f*, 631*f*, 635*f*, 637*f*, 640*f*, 642*f*, 647*f*
South Slavic epic song, 542, 543*f*, 544*f*, 546–561, 546*f*, 556*f*
South Slavic women's ballad, 576, 578*f*, 579–590, 586*f*, 587*f*, 589*f*, 593–595
collective crying, 217, 226, 230–236, 231*f*, 233*f*, 235*f*, 237n17
comic books, Greek folk tales and, 622
commensality, Cortorar Romani weddings and, 113
communism, 217–219, 262, 658, 660, 665–667. *See also* socialism; Soviet Union
community. *See also* Romanian community celebrations; village life
   betrothal and, 13–14
   courtship and, 10–12
   Estonian runosongs and, 139–141
   evil eye and, 7–8, 15
   family life and, 171–172, 183n5
   jealousy and, 6–8
   klub and, 17, 19*f*, 27
   Serbian weddings (Kosovo) and, 66–67, 74
   skladka and, 11–12
   under Soviet Union, 171–172, 183n5
   supernatural beliefs and, 6–8, 10, 12
   tensions within, 6–10
   theft and, 8
   tsyhanshchyna and, 25–26, 26*f*
   wedding preparations and, 15–17, 29n6–29n8
"comparative links," 470
competition, *chastushki* and, 968–970, 969*f*, 971*f*
composition
   of ballads, 590–592
   formulaic expressions and, xxviii, 514

of oral narrative, 590–592
oral vs. written narrative and, 552–560, 579–581
Contest of Serbian Villages, The, 302, 308n11, 308n12, 308n14
continuity in Greek folklore, 193–195, 213n1–213n3
Cooper, Adrienne, 780
Cooper, David L., 638
Corrsin, Stephen D., 314–315
Cortorar Romani weddings, 108–133. *See also* Roma; Romania
   abiav and, 117, 124–132, 125*f*, 127*f*, 128*f*, 131*f*, 132*f*
   al Roma and, 109, 133
   Assumption of Mary and, 118, 134n8
   attire and, 112, 113*f*, 126–127, 127*f*
   bread ceremony and, 127, 130
   cântecul miresei and, 127–130
   chalices and, 110–111, 116–118, 117*f*, 133n3, 134n7
   chanting and, 126
   chastity and, 109, 112, 116–117, 132, 132*f*
   childbirth and, 108–109, 113–114, 116–117, 127
   Christmas and, 118
   colax and, 122–124
   commensality and, 113
   between cousins, 109
   COVID-19 pandemic and, 108
   devils/demons and, 124
   dissolution of, 108–109, 114–116
   dowry and, 113–117, 115*f*, 134n5, 134n6
   Easter and, 108, 118
   family life and, 109, 110, 112–116
   fertility and, 108–109, 113–114, 116–117, 127
   flag rituals and, 125, 125*f*
   Gadge and, 109, 116, 133n1
   gender disparities and, 110, 112–116, 113*f*, 115*f*
   gogitul miresei and, 125–130, 127*f*, 128*f*
   hair and, 126
   identity and, 109
   înțelegerea and, 118–120, 119*f*, 134n8
   obstacle ritual and, 131, 131*f*
   Orthodox Christianity and, 118, 134n8
   penden pes and, 112
   private nature of, 109, 133n1
   puberty and, 112, 113*f*
   reciprocity in, 114–116
   social order and, 110, 112–116
   songs and, 127–130
   tocmeala and, 114–115, 118, 119*f*, 120–122, 124, 125, 134n9
   trousseau and, 113–114, 115*f*, 134n6
   xanamika and, 112, 121
Cossak. *See* Kozak
Counihan, Carole, 1056
Country Radio (Prague), 880, 881*f*
courting, 10–11, 14, 724–727. *See also* love
courtship
   chastity and, 10–11
   chastushki and, 967–968
   dosvitky and, 10–12, 27
   games and, 10
   hromada and, 10
   Lent and, 11
   road magic and, 12
   skladka and, 11–12
   Ukrainian weddings and, 10–13, 13*f*
   vechornytsi and, 10–12, 27
   vulytsia and, 12, 13*f*, 27
COVID-19 pandemic, xxx
   childbirth and, 176–177
   jokes about, 1002–1003
   Lastovo Carnival and, 328–330
   law enforcement and, 108
   masks and, 329–330
   in Romania, 108
   Russia and, 176–177
   in Serbia, 307
Cravitz, Ilana, 784
"Creating Health Care Consumers" (Temkina & Rivkin-Fish), 174
Creed, Gerald, 304
Croat/Croatian weddings, 83–104. *See also* Croatia
   anthems and, 87–88, 94–96
   attention and, 95–96
   bećarac and, 91–94, 102
   Bosnian Croats and, 90–94, 92*f*–94*f*, 104n7
   čajo and, 89–90, 104n6
   Catholicism and, 83, 85, 90
   devils/demons and, 96, 103
   domoljubne tamburaške pjesme and, 86
   firearms at, 98–99, 104n9

Croat/Croatian weddings (*cont.*)
    flag rituals and, 83–94, 84*f*, 86*f*, 92*f*–94*f*,
        104n4–104n6
    humor/satire and, 85, 92, 99
    identity and, 83–90, 84*f*, 86*f*, 91,
        104n4–104n6
    kapije, od and, 91–92, 92*f*
    law enforcement and, 89–90
    memory and, 101
    motor vehicles and, 92–99, 92*f*, 94*f*, 104n9
    pyrotechnics at, 97–100, 98*f*
    sexual orientation and, 90
    songs and, 86–88, 91–94
    under Soviet Union, 85–86
    supernatural beliefs and, 87, 96, 103, 104n9
    tambura music and, 84–86, 84*f*, 86*f*, 89–103,
        92*f*, 93*f*, 94*f*, 98*f*, 104n7, 104n9
    territoriality and, 100–104, 105n10
    in urban settings, 98–99
    witches/witchcraft and, 103
Croatia. *See also* Croat/Croatian weddings;
    Slavic supernatural legends; South Slavic
    region
    Bosnian refugees in, 83, 86, 104n2
    Carnival and (*see* Lastovo Carnival)
    "Croatian Spring" and, 83
    cultural heritage and, 327–328
    donkeys and, 316–319, 318*f*, 321*f*, 322, 325, 330
    Dubrovnik and, 312, 315
    ethnology and, 325–327, 332n18–333n20
    feminism in, 103
    independence of, 88
    Korčula and, 312–313, 315–317, 331n4, 332n8
    Life Partnership Act and, 90
    media in, 91, 96
    Muslim Bosniak refugees in, 83, 104n2
    Romani refugees in, 83–84, 104n2
    Serbian refugees in, 83–84, 104n2
    siege of Lastovo and, 316–317
    under Soviet Union, 85–86, 316
    supernatural beliefs in, 103
    Yugoslavia and, 83, 85–88, 95–96, 103, 316
Crowder, Christina, 782, 784
crowning day, 30, 39, 43–44, 48–50
Crusades. *See also* Catholicism
    Baltic region and, 140, 276, 282–283, 286,
        431–432, 452–453

    Greece and, 610
    "Livonia" and, 431–432
crying, Albanian death rituals and, 217, 226,
    230–236, 231*f*, 233*f*, 235*f*, 237n17
Császi, Lajos, 1002
Culiac, Alexandru, 403–404, 409–413, 411*f*,
    415–416, 419–423, 423n1
Culiac, Grigore, 403–404, 409–413, 412*f*, 415–
    416, 419–423, 423n1
Culiac, Ion, 409
Čulinović-Konstantinović, Vesna, 102
culjanje, 319, 322, 325, 330, 332n14
cultural-artistic societies, 301–302, 304,
    308n11, 308n12, 308n14
Cultural Heritage, UNESCO Convention for
    Safeguarding of the Intangible, 288
culture. *See also* material culture; popular
    culture
    calendrical cycle and, 327–328
    Carnival and, 327–328
    communism and, xxviii–xxx
    conservatism and, 742, 744–745, 747,
        752–754, 760, 763
    as distinct from national boundaries,
        xxiii–xxv, xxiv*f*
    Estonian runosongs and, 142, 164–165
    Lastovo Carnival and, 327–328
    under Soviet Union, xxviii
Cupid and Psyche, tale of, 609
curses
    community and, 7
    folk religion and, 409, 416, 418–419
    Greek death rituals and, 205, 207
    in Hungary, 363, 368, 370–371, 377–378, 381
"Curses of the Archangel Michael, The," 419
Curtain, Michael, 940
čveger, 385
Cvetkovich, Ann, 86, 96
Czech bluegrass, 871–890. *See also* bluegrass;
    Czech Republic/Czechoslovakia
    Americanism and, 871–872, 877–878,
        889–890
    banjo and, 879–880, 881*f*
    bluegrassáci and, 871
    Bohemian folklore and, 875–877
    festivals and, 873, 874*f*
    folklorní and, 872

lidový and, 872
"old-time," 882–884
as popular music, 871–872
Porta festivals and, 884–885
pub jams and, 874, 875*f*
tramp songs and, 877–878, 884–885
vernacular songs and, 877–879
wild west motifs in, 884–885
Czech Republic/Czechoslovakia. *See also*
   Czech bluegrass
   Austria and, 876
   ethnology and, 877
   Germany and, 876
   history of, 875–877
   kramářské písně and, 877
   politics and, 888–889
   under Soviet Union, 876, 878, 879–880
   vernacular and, 877–879
Czubała, Dionizjusz, 699–700
dainas/dainos, 279, 290n3, 290n4, 432–451,
   433*f*, 437*f*, 439*f*, 440*f*, 442*f*, 446*f*, 450*f*
dance
   Albanian death rituals and, 217
   Albanian *etnopop* and, 923–925, 924*f*, 928
   ardeleana and, 345
   Ashkenazim and, 780, 783
   badkhn and, 772–773, 775, 778
   balo and, 317, 332n11
   brâul bătrân and, 345
   broygez tants and, 776
   bulgar and, 778
   calendrical cycle and, 335–355, 336*f*, 355n3
   Căluș and, 346–348, 347*f*, 351, 353*f*, 356n16,
      356n17
   Carnival and, 303, 312–315, 317–318, 331n4,
      331n6, 332n11
   ceată and, 339
   chain (*see* chain dance)
   chastushki and, 952–953, 963–966, 964*f*
   choreography and, 301, 304
   cultural-artistic societies and, 301–302, 304,
      308n11, 308n12, 308n14
   dodole and, 295–298, 302
   ethnochoreology and, 295–307
   flag rituals and, 63, 64*f*
   freylekhs and, 776–778
   gender and, 297–298, 313, 331n6, 339
   honga and, 778
   hora and (*see hora*)
   house-to-house, 338–340, 343, 347, 350, 355
   karakhod and, 776–777
   khosidl and, 773, 776–777
   klezmer music and, 770–784
   koledari and, 295–298, 300, 302
   kraljice and, 295–298, 300, 302–303
   kumpanija and, 313, 331n4
   Lastovo Carnival and, 312–315, 317–318,
      331n4, 331n6, 332n11
   in Latvia, 436, 437*f*, 443–444
   lăutari and, 832
   lazarice and, 295–298, 300, 302, 307n2,
      307n3
   in Lithuania, 443–444
   makhetonim tants and, 776
   masked balls and, 342
   modern, 305–307
   newly composed folk music/
      instrumentation and, 301
   obredna igra and, 299, 303
   Paganism and, 436, 437*f*, 443–444
   participatory presentational forms of, 338,
      340, 345, 349, 353–355, 356n6, 356n22
   performance and, 302
   pjevanje u kolu and, 92
   ples and, 299, 306
   raqs sharqi, 922, 925
   redl and, 776–777
   Romanian community celebrations and,
      337–352, 341*f*, 346*f*, 347*f*, 352*f*, 354–355, 356n6,
      356n7, 356n13, 356n20, 356n22, 357n23
   Romani music and, 832
   ruga bal and, 345
   ruga foeni and, 346*f*
   sârbă and, 338, 345, 356n7
   in Serbia, 295–307
   sher contradance and, 772–773, 777
   sholem-tants and, 776
   skotshne and, 773, 777
   under Soviet Union, 301–302, 308n11,
      308n12, 308n14
   supernatural beliefs and, 297–300, 303
   svekrvino kolo and, 65, 67–71, 69*f*–71*f*, 73,
      75–76, 80n12, 852–855, 865n23
   sword (*see* sword dance)

dance (*cont.*)
   tentser and, 773
   village life and, 295–298, 301–307, 346–348, 347*f*, 356n16, 356n17
   in Yugoslavia, 295–296, 298, 300–301, 303–304, 307
   zhok and, 778

"dance of life," 209
Daněk, Stanislav Wabi, 878
Danforth, Loring, 197–198, 204
"Dangerous Night-Watch, The," 645
Danilov, Kirsha, 495–496, 534
Danube river, mythologizing of, 43
Daukantas, Simonas, 436
"Da vdignem mnogo shum," 938
Davies, Christie, 1001
Davis-Floyd, Robbie, 172
davuldzhii, 793
Dawid, Christian, 781, 784
Dawkins, Richard McGillivray, 606–607, 610, 614–615
Daxner, Štefan Marko, 638
death/death rites, 169, 183n1, 245*f*, 246*f*. *See also* Albanian death rituals; Greek death rituals; Russian death rituals
   accommodation and, 206–209, 208*f*, 213n9
   animism and, 225–228, 229*f*, 237n11–237n16
   attire and, 202, 240–244, 242*f*, 243*f*
   autumnal ancestor veneration and, 446–448
   binding and, 240
   body gestures and, 202–203
   bread ceremony and, 448
   "bundle" of death clothes and, 241, 242*f*
   church bells and, 200
   coffin decoration and, 251, 266n4
   crying and, 217, 226, 230–236, 231*f*, 233*f*, 235*f*, 237n17
   drums and, 217, 220, 237n7
   Easter and, 247, 266n3
   in Estonia, 287
   Estonian runosongs and, 144–145
   ethnography and, 193–194, 217–223, 230
   feminism and, 201–206, 202*f*, 204*f*
   gender and, 199–209, 202*f*, 204*f*, 208*f*, 213n5, 213n6, 213n9, 217, 221, 232–234, 233*f*, 245, 247, 264–266
   grave goods and, 244, 247–249, 248*f*, 249*f*
   grave-markers and, 243, 243*f*
   in Greek folk tales, 616
   hair and, 202
   hierarchy of, 203
   hora de pomană and, 345–346
   howling deceased back to life and, 254
   immediate aftermath of death and, 199–201, 213n5, 213n6
   inverted ritual behavior and, 392–394
   Kapu svētki and, 447
   korifea and, 205
   lacerating of flesh and, 195, 202, 220
   laments and, 193–213, 202*f*, 204*f*, 220–221, 254–266, 255*f*
   in Latvia, 287
   Lent and, 247, 266n3
   lullabies about, 144–145
   market economy and, 253–254
   Meatfast Saturday and, 247, 266n3
   medicalization and, 236
   modern, 253–254, 262–263
   myth and, 217, 225–226
   naturist belief and, 225–228, 229*f*, 237n11–237n16
   omens and, 224–225, 237n9
   orphans and, 232, 263–265
   Orthodox Christianity and, 193–195, 198–199, 206–208, 213n2, 213n3, 240–250, 266n3
   ossuary and, 198, 198*f*
   pain and, 203–206
   prohibitions against, 220–221, 237n7
   puzuri and, 448
   remembrance and, 247–250, 248*f*, 249*f*
   rites/rituals and, 171, 183n3
   scholarship on, 255–256, 262–263
   "screaming the dead" and, 201–202, 202*f*
   secondary burial and, 198, 198*f*
   šiaudinis soda and, 448
   snakes and, 228
   under Soviet Union, 216, 217–221, 218*f*, 236n2, 237n5, 237n6, 250–253, 252*f*, 256, 266n4
   speaking for the dead and, 201
   spirit and, 224–228, 229*f*, 237n11–237n15
   supernatural beliefs and, 199

thinking death and, 223–225, 237n8, 237n9
Trinity Saturday and, 247, 266n3
Troitsa and, 247, 266n3
Victory Day and, 252, 252f
village life and, 263–265
washing and, 240–244
zaochnoe otpevanie and, 250–251
Death Rituals of Rural Greece (Danforth), 197–198
de Beauplan, Guillaume Levasseur, 5, 19
"De cănd te iubesc pe tine," 835
Dee, John, 365
Deeds That Were Done in the Year 1920, The (A. Culiac), 410, 411f
"De ești supărată," 835
Dégh, Linda, 685–687
Delarue, Paul, 608
Deleuze, Gilles, 88, 100–101, 105n10
Delibašić, Mirko, 98–99
Deliverance (film), 873
Delorko, Olinko, 589
del Rio, Martin, 365
Demaj, Ylli, 938, 939f
Demidov, Prokopii A., 495–496
demons. *See* devils/demons; exorcism
Demutskyi, P., 515
Denisov, Alexander, 1028
Deović, Zehra, 735
Derzhavin, Gavriil, 257
"Desert Rose," 925
deseterac, 542, 545, 549, 563n11
design meanings, 1025–1027, 1027f
desire, Estonian runosongs and, 158–160
Destiny's Child, 923, 928
dever, 68, 76, 392, 396
devils/demons. *See also* exorcism
 Cortorar Romani weddings and, 124
 Croat/Croatian weddings and, 96, 103
 Hungary and, 363, 366, 368, 370–371, 373, 377–380
 Latvian religious folklore and, 449
 Lithuanian religious folklore and, 449
 Moldovan folk religion and, 407, 418, 421, 423, 426n21
 possession by, 379
 Serbia and, 297
 Slavic supernatural legends and, 677–678

Slovak folk tales and, 643, 645–646
South Slavic region and, 388, 391, 395–396
Ukraine and, 461
devishnik, 32
Diab, Amr, 925
Diaghilev, Sergei, 1029
Dickins, Tom, 872
diction
 Estonian runosongs and, 139
 Polish urban legend and, 703–704
 Russian wedding songs and, 31–32
"Didi," 925, 941
"Dievs, Svētī Latviju" (Baumanis), 436
Dievturi/Dievturība, 281–282, 432, 438–442, 440f, 444, 449–451
"Dilmano Dilbero," 909
diminutive forms of address in laments, 257–261
Dimitriades, Theodotos, 777
Dimitrov, Darko, 931–932
Dimitrov, Kalin, 936
Dimov, Ventsislav, 795, 802–803
Di Naye Kepelye, 782
Dinicu, Angheluș, 840n18
Dinicu, Grigoraș, 821, 822f, 840n16
Dinicu, Ionică, 823, 824f, 841n19
dirges, 195. *See also* laments
Diuk Stepanovich (*bylina* character), 491
divination, 10, 366
divorce, dissolution of Cortorar marriage and, 108–109, 114–116
divych vechir, 16–17
"Dixie," 88, 104n5
Dizdar, Hamid, 722
Dizdarević, Đula, 586–587, 587f, 593
Dizdarević, Halid, 586–588
Djokić, Daniel, 931
Djordjević, Tihomir, 299
Djošino Tursko Kolo, 857
Djoudjeff, Stoyan, 908
dobriden, 775
Dobrynia Nikitych (*bylina* hero), 485, 489–491, 491f, 503–511, 510f
Dobrynia Nikitych i Zmei Gorynych (film), 509
Dobrý tramp Bernášek (film), 877
Dobšinský, Pavol, xxvii, 628–648, 630f, 631f. *See also* Slovak folk tales

Dobšinský, Pavol (*cont.*)
   as editor, 628, 632–636, 639, 640*f*, 641–645, 648
   impact of, on oral narrative, 632
   literary forgery and, 638
   Lutheranism and, 628, 632
   magic and, 628–629, 635*f*, 637*f*, 642*f*, 643–646, 647*f*, 648
   romantic nationalism and, 628–629, 631, 634, 639, 641–648
   source attributions by, 633–634, 636
dodole, 295–298, 302
dog-headed beings, 678
"Doi tovarăşi am la drum," 834
Domergue, Helene, 782, 783
domoljubne tamburaške pjesme, 86
domovyny, 14
donkeys, 316–319, 318*f*, 321*f*, 322, 325, 330, 679, 687
"Don't Touch My Plain" (Škoro), 94–96
Donutil, Miroslav, 885
Dostoyevsky, Fyodor, 223, 666
dosvitky, 10–12, 27
doulas, 174
Down along the Mother Volga: An Anthology of Russian Folk Lyrics (Reeder), 659
dowry, Cortorar Romani weddings and, 113–117, 115*f*, 134n5, 134n6
"Dragon-Slayer, The," 645, 646
Drahomanov, Mykhailo, 535
drakos, 616
"Dream, The," 533–534
Droce, Selma, 736
drums, Albanian death rituals and, 217, 220, 237n7
druzhky, 16–17, 19, 21–22, 24, 29n8, 30
Držić, Marin, 689
dual narrator, 704–706
Dubljević, Zora, 735
Du Boulay, Juliet, 201, 207–209, 213n9
Dubrovnik, 312, 315
dub step, 908
"Duma about Marusia Bohuslavka," 514, 520–521
"Duma pro Chornobyl" (Suprun), 536–537
Dumnić-Vilotijević, Maria, 800
dumy, xxvii, 513–539
   anti-semitism in, 531–532
   bandura and, 515, 517*f*, 537, 537*f*, 963
   blind minstrels and, 498–499, 514–515, 517, 529, 535–538, 537*f*
   byliny and, 498
   captivity in, 520–525
   collections of, 514–515, 530–531, 534–537
   content of, 519–534
   cycles, 514, 519–534
   defined, 514
   ethnography and, 542
   on family life, 9, 29n4
   features of, 513–514
   formulaic expressions and, 514
   galley slaves in, 522, 524–525
   gender and, 517–518
   guild system and, 515, 517–519
   heroism in, 513–514
   kobzari and, 498, 514–519, 516*f*, 529–531, 535–539
   Kozak battle cycle in, 514–515, 520–529, 528*f*, 529*f*, 538*f*
   Kozak uprising cycle in, 514, 529–532, 530*f*, 539n6
   laments and, 533–534
   lebiiska mova and, 518–519
   lira and, 498, 514–515, 517, 518*f*, 519, 537
   Marianism and, 515
   orphans and, 534
   performance of, 514–519, 516*f*–518*f*
   poverty in, 531–534
   ransom in, 521–522
   rhyme in, 513
   Ruin cycle in, 514, 532–535
   scholarship on, 514, 519–520, 534–537
   under Soviet Union, 535–536, 539n7
   Turko-Tatar slavery cycle in, 514, 520–525, 521*f*, 533–534
   Ukrainian nationhood and, 513–514, 519, 535–536, 538
   vidpusty and, 515
Dunai (*bylina* character), 501, 505
Dundes, Alan, 582, 662, 1056
Dundulienė, Pranė, 443
"Dunjaluče, golem ti si," 737
dvoeverie, xxvi
Dvořák, Antonin, 876

Dvořák, Tomáš, 876
dwellings, 1013–1017, 1015*f*, 1016*f*, 1048–1050
Dybbuk, Der (film), 783
Dzhubryk apparition, 464–465
Džimrevski, Borivoje, 793–794, 800
Đezić, Zekerijah, 735
Đikić, Osman, 734
Đumišić, Fehim effendi, 729

"E di," 934–936, 928*f*
Efimenkova, B. B., 262–263
Ehrlich, Al, 780
Eisen, Mattias Johann, 141
electronica, 907
Eleusinian Mystery Cult, 195
Elijah (prophet), 404, 409, 414–415, 419–420, 423, 425n18
Elliott, Missy, 925
Emanuela, 903
"E mare petrecere," 938
Eminović, Malika, 846–847
Encyclopedia of the Lexicographic Institute, 722
endurance, childbirth and, 180
Enescu, George, 824
Engel, Joel, 773–784
Engelman, Wilhelm, 618*f*
Engels, Friedrich, 666
Enoch (prophet), 409, 414–415, 419–420, 425n18
Ephraim, Moshe Haim, 742
epic poetry, xxvii. *See also* oral narrative
   Albania and, 545–546, 561
   anti-semitism in, 531–532
   artels and, 498
   bogatyri and, 485–511, 491*f*, 510*f*
   border areas and, 541–542, 545–551, 560–561, 565–566
   bride as epic hero in Russian wedding songs and, 38–39
   bugarštica and, 563n11
   byliny and (*see byliny*)
   Catholicism and, 541, 548
   Christianity and, 541–542, 545, 548–549, 551, 557
   collections of, 492–496, 514–515, 530–531, 534–537
   cycles in, 486–492, 514, 519–534, 543–545
   defining, 541
   deseterac and, 542, 545, 549
   dumy and (*see dumy*)
   "epic retardation" in, 495
   formulaic expressions and, 514
   gender and, 501–506, 509, 551–552
   groom as epic hero in Russian wedding songs and, 42
   gusle/guslars and, 544*f*, 545, 551–552, 561
   Habsburg Empire and, 541
   Halych cycle and, 491
   heroic epic songs, xxvii
   heroism in, 551–552
   hyperbole in, 495
   Islam and, 541–542, 544–545, 551, 556–557
   kaliki and, 498–499, 503–504
   Karadžić and, 548–552, 559–560
   kobzari and, 498, 514–519, 516*f*, 529–531, 535–539
   Kosovo cycle in, 544, 548
   Kozak battle cycle in, 514–515, 520–529, 528*f*, 529*f*, 538*f*
   Kozak uprising cycle in, 514, 529–532, 530*f*, 539n6
   Kyivan cycle and, 489–491
   lahuta/lahutars and, 545
   lira and, 498, 514–515, 517, 518*f*, 519, 537
   loan words and, 545
   Marko Kraljević cycle in, 544
   marriage/weddings and, 542, 549, 557
   novelty in, 560
   noviny and, 507–508
   okićenje and, 557–559
   oral *vs.* written, 552–560
   Orthodox Christianity and, 541, 548–549
   Ottoman Empire and, 541, 548, 561
   performance of, 545, 551–552, 555, 557–560
   philology of border areas and, 547–548, 550–551, 560–561, 565–566
   polianitsa and, 490, 501, 504
   posidelki and, 498
   post-traditionality and, 558–560
   "return song" type of, 542, 593
   Ruin cycle in, 514, 532–535
   Russian folk epics and (*see byliny*)
   sex in, 504–506
   skomorokhi and, 497–498, 503

epic poetry (*cont.*)
  songs and, 32
  South Slavic (*see* South Slavic epic songs)
  stariny and, 492, 507
  Turko-Tatar slavery cycle in, 514, 520–525, 521*f*, 533–534
  Ukraine and, 513–514
  Venetia and, 542, 549
  "Wedding Song" type of, 542
  zachin and, 495, 501
  zapev and, 495
"epic retardation," 495
Epimenides of Crete, 195
Epiphany, 351–352
"Epistle of Our Lord Jesus Christ Which Was Sent by God from Heaven," 417
epithets, 619, 703
Epstein, Max, 778
Epstein Brothers Orchestra, 781
Erasmus of Rotterdam, 987
Erben, Karel Jaromír, 632, 643
Erdeljan, Jelena, 470
Erikson, Thomas Hylland, 62–63
Eriney, 910
Erk, Ludwig, 757*f*
Erlangen Manuscript, 729, 738n5
Erlangenski rukopis starih srpskohrvatskih narodnih pesema (Gesemann), 580
Erlangen University, 580
Ermak (*bylina* character), 492
Ershov, Arkhip, 1019
"Escape of the Three Brothers from Azov, The," 522–523
eschatology
  applied, 408
  border areas and, 406–409, 425n13–425n16
  chapbooks and, 408–409, 415–416, 422–423
  copybooks and, 415–423, 416*f*, 417*f*
  defined, 403
  ethnography and, 405
  in Moldovan folk religion, 403–423
Escher, Wolfgang, 722
esnafi, 792–793, 800
"Esquisse sur l'histoire, les moeurs et la langue des Cigains connus en France sous le nom de Bohémiens" (Kogălniceanu), 819–820

Estonia. *See also* Baltic region
  as Baltic state, 275–276
  calendrical cycle and, 275–289
  Catholicism in, 277–279
  Christianity in, 282
  Crusades and, 140, 276, 431–432
  death rites in, 287
  early history of, 281–283, 290n6
  Hanseatic League and, 431–432
  hinkepe and, 284
  history of Baltic region and, 430–432, 431*f*
  "Livonia" and, 431–432
  Livs/Livonians and, 283–285, 290n6
  Lutheranism and, 277–279
  Marianism and, 283–284, 286
  Maslenitsa and, 288
  modern, 287–289
  mumming and, 288
  Paganism in, 285–287
  Paris Peace Conference and, 275
  Pleiades and, 281
  Protestantism and, 277–279
  rahvakalender and, 279–280
  religious intersectionality and, 285–287
  scholarship on, 276–281, 289n2–290n4
  under Soviet Union, 164
  urban settings and, 283–285
"Estonian Ballads" (Tormis), 150
Estonian Folk Calendar (Lätt & Hiiemäe), 280
Estonian Folklore Archives, 141–142, 164, 279–280
Estonian Folklore Council, 288
Estonian runosongs, 139–165
  alliteration and, 139
  ballads and, 148–150
  Baltic Germans and, 140–141, 166n3
  burdens of motherhood and, 145–147
  chastity and, 159–160
  childbirth and, 150, 153–155
  community and, 139–141
  culture and, 142, 164–165
  death and, 144–145
  desire and, 158–160
  diction and, 139
  evil eye and, 155
  family life and, 140, 145–150

features of, 139
fertility and, 163
Finnic people and, 139–140, 165n1
folk music/instrumentation and, 141
gender and, 147–150
genitalia and, 156–157
human sacrifice and, 148
identity and, 139–141, 166n3, 166n4
illegitimate children and, 148–150
infanticide and, 147–150
lullabies and, 142–145
parallelism and, 139
poetic form of, 139
pregnancy and, 150–155
public domain and, 141–143
recordings of, 141
repetition and, 139
resentment and, 158–160
rhyme and, 139
sex and, 155–164
stanzas and, 139
stichic form in, 139
supernatural beliefs and, 142, 154–155
trochaic meter and, 139
unfixed song texts and, 139
unwanted children and, 147–150
verbal charms and, 140, 154
witches/witchcraft and, 146
"Estrada," 899
Esztergom book of rituals, 377
"Ethiopia," 909
ethnicity/ethnicization
of Kosovo, 61–66, 64f, 65f, 79n5, 80n6–80n10
oral narrative and, 582–583
"placarding," 63
ethnochoreology. *See also* choreography; ethnography
Carnival and, 303
cultural–artistic societies and, 301–302, 304, 308n11, 308n12, 308n14
defined, 295, 307n1
izvorni folklor and, 302
modern, 305–307
narodna igra and, 299, 307n5
newly composed folk music/instrumentation and, 301

obredna igra and, 299, 303
orska igra and, 299, 307n5
ples and, 299, 306
in Serbia, 295–307
under Soviet Union, 301–302, 308n11, 308n12, 308n14
village life and, 295–298, 301–307
in Yugoslavia, 295–296, 298, 300–301, 303–304, 307
zavetina and, 307
Ethnochoreology. Traces (Vasić), 305
Ethnographic Atlas of Yugoslavia, 684
Ethnographic Museum (St. Petersburg), 1030
ethnography. *See also* ethnochoreology
apparitions and, 462–464
calendrical cycle and, 277, 282, 295–298, 303–304, 314, 326–328
childbirth and, 168–170, 174
death rites and, 193–194, 217–223, 230
dumy and, 542
eschatology and, 405
folk religion and, 461–465, 479
Greece and, 618
magic and, 363, 365, 381
marriage/weddings and, 5, 85, 87, 89, 103, 110
oral narrative and, 584–585
Romanian folk art and, 1049
Russian wondertales and, 665–666
Slavic supernatural legends and, 690–692
South Slavic epic songs and, 552
South Slavic women's ballads and, 579, 581, 584–585, 591, 594
ethnology
Croatian, 325–327, 332n18–333n20
Czech Republic and, 877
foodways (Moldova) and, 1056–1058
Ethnology and Folklore, International Society for, 281
Ethnology and Folklore Research, Institute of (Zagreb), 326, 328
"ethno" music shows, 735–736
ethnopop. *See* Albanian-language *etnopop*
etnopop. *See* Albanian-language *etnopop*
"Eto taka," 907
Eulampios, Georgios, 606
euphemism, 703–704

evil eye
- community and, 7–8, 15
- Estonian runosongs and, 155
- inverted ritual behavior and, 392, 395–396
- Russian childbirth folklore and, 175–177, 184n8
- South Slavic region and, 392, 395–396

evil forces/spirits. *See* supernatural beliefs

"Evreiskie Orkestry" (Lipaev), 773

exorcism, 370, 377–380, 407, 411, 416, 418–419. *See also* devils/demons

Experiment in Collecting Little Russian (Ukrainian) Songs, An (Tsertelev), 534

fables, 609
fabulates, 677, 685–688
Faculty of Music (Belgrade), 305
Faculty of Philosophy (Belgrade), 303
fairies/nymphs
- childbirth and, 397
- Greek folk tales and, 615
- Slavic supernatural legends and, 678–682, 682f, 684, 686–692, 693n7, 693n9
- water nymphs and, 615

fairs. *See* festivals
fairy tales. *See* magic tales; Russian wondertales
"Faithful John," 646
fakelore, 662, 668
fakesongs, 907
family life
- ballads on bride/in-law conflicts and, 8–9, 16, 23–24
- betrothal and, 13–14
- burdens of motherhood and, 145–147
- community and, 171–172, 183n5
- Cortorar Romani weddings and, 109, 110, 112–116
- daughter's relationship with in-laws and, 6–10, 7f, 16, 28n2
- *dumy* on, 9, 29n4
- Estonian runosongs and, 140, 145–150
- *neamo* and, 110–111, 134n4
- in Russian wedding songs, 34–35, 45–48, 58n3, 58n5
- Serbian weddings (Kosovo) and, 76–77
- under Soviet Union, 171–172, 183n5
- tensions within, 6–8
- Ukrainian weddings and, 6–10, 7f, 21, 24, 28n2

Fanfare Ciocârlia, 910
Fărşang, 340–342, 342f, 356n8
"fast food journalism," 710
Fates, the, 616
Fatima apparition, 465, 471, 473
Fat Monday, 318–319, 332n12, 332n13
Fedchenko, Valentina, 743
Fedor Alekseevich (Tsar of Russia), 254
Fedorova, P., 43
Fedosova, Irina, 32, 256
Fedynskyi, Jurij, 537
Feidman, Giora, 782
Feinberg, Joseph Grim, 888–889
Feldman, Walter, 743
Feldman, Walter Zev, 820
Feldman, Zev, 779–780, 782–783
female. *See* gender
feminism, 103, 201–206, 202f, 204f
FEN TV, 932–934
fertility. *See also* childbirth; supernatural beliefs
- Cortorar Romani weddings and, 108–109, 113–114, 116–117, 127
- Estonian runosongs, 163
- Russian weddings and, 31–32, 38, 40–41, 50
- Ukrainian weddings and, 15, 17, 29n7

festivals
- bluegrass, 873, 874f
- *duma*, 537, 538f
- of klezmer music, 782–783
- laments and, 203
- *Porta*, 884–885
- Romanian community celebrations and, 348–349
- Romani music, 798f, 807f, 809, 809f, 810f, 849
- Serbian Romani music and, 849

Festivalul datinilor de iarnă, 351
Fibich, Felix, 783
Fidl (Svigals album), 781
Fidl-Fantazye: A Klezmer Concerto (Bendix-Balgley), 784
50 Cent, 925
"Fight on the Bridge, The," 639

Fiki, 903, 938
File on H, The (Kadare), 546, 561
Filimon, Nicolae, 820
Filipovski, Marion (Maki), 928–930, 929*f*, 932
fine art, *byliny* in, 492, 494*f*, 506–510, 508*f*–510*f*
Finland, songs about sex in, 164
Finnegan, Ruth, 555
Finnic people, 139–140, 165n1
Finnish Academy, 608
Finnish lament movement, 210
firearms, at Croat/Croatian weddings, 98–99, 104n9
Fire Burns on the Hill, A (Shtorm) (painting), 528*f*
First Serbian Uprising, 548, 560
"First Tale" (S. Reuss), 642*f*
Fiterstein, Alexander, 784
flag rituals
    Confederate flag and, 88, 104n5
    Cortorar Romani weddings and, 125, 125*f*
    Croat/Croatian weddings and, 83–94, 84*f*, 86*f*, 92*f*–94*f*, 104n4–104n6
    Serbian weddings (Kosovo) and, 63–64, 64*f*, 65*f*, 80n7
    songs and, 87–90, 104n4–104n6
    violence and, 88–90
Florensky, Pavel, 659
Flower Saturday, 343
Foaie verde, 829–831
Focul lui Sumedru, 350
"Foggy Mountain Breakdown," 875
Foley, John Miles, 542, 590
folk art. *See* Romanian folk art; Russian folk art
"Folk Art in the Russian North" (Bilibin), 1030, 1031*f*
Folk Dance Research of Serbia, Centre for, 305, 308n18
folk epic. *See* epic poetry
Folklore Archive, St. Petersburg State University, 240
Folklore Fellowship Communications, 608
Folklore for Stalin (Miller), 507
Folklore Society of Greece, 607
Folklorní mejdlo, 889
folk music/instrumentation. *See also* songs
    bandura and, 515, 517*f*, 537, 537*f*, 963
    banjo and, 879–880, 881*f*
    blind minstrels and, 498–499, 514–515, 517, 529, 535–538, 537*f*
    bluegrass (*see* Czech bluegrass)
    Bulgarian popular music and, 908–909
    chastushki, 963–966, 964*f*, 965*f*
    collections of, 876
    Czech (*see* Czech bluegrass)
    Estonian runosongs and, 141
    gender and, 517–518
    guild system and, 515, 517–519
    gusle and, 544*f*, 545, 551–552, 561
    gusli and, 492, 497–498, 510–511
    kanklės and, 433
    kapelye and, 770
    klei-zemer and, 769
    klezmer (*see* klezmer music)
    kobza and, 498, 514–519, 516*f*, 529–531, 535–539
    kokles and, 433, 440*f*
    lahuta and, 545
    lăutari and, 772
    lira and, 498, 514–515, 517, 518*f*, 519, 537
    lyre and, 317–319, 320*f*, 322*f*, 323–325, 330
    newly composed (*see* newly composed folk music/instrumentation)
    popular culture and, 449–450, 450*f*
    Romani (*see* Romani music)
    rubato and, 775
    sanatur and, 318
    saz and, 732, 733–736, 734*f*, 737*f*
    skomorokhi and, 497–498, 503
    starogradska muzika, 733–734
    tepsija and, 732, 733*f*
folk religion. *See also* Moldovan folk religion
    apocalypticism and, 403–423, 424n6, 425n13, 425n18
    Archangelist movement and, 404, 409–410, 414–423, 423n2, 425n19
    Bolshevik Revolution and, 403, 405
    border areas and, 406–409, 425n13–425n16
    catacomb church and, 404, 424n5
    chapbooks and, 408–409, 415–416, 422–423
    copybooks and, 415–423, 416*f*, 417*f*
    Culiac brothers and, 403–404, 409–413, 411*f*, 412*f*, 415–416, 419–423, 423n1
    curses and, 409, 416, 418–419

folk religion (*cont.*)
   defined, 406
   eschatology in, 403–423
   ethnography and, 461–465, 479
   exorcism and, 407, 411, 416, 418–419
   heavenly letters and, 408–409, 416–417, 425n16, 425n19
   Inochentie of Balta and, 404, 407–410, 419–420, 424n6, 425n13
   Maliovantsy and, 407, 425n12
   modern, 404, 424n4–424n6
   myth and, 404, 433–443, 450–452
   Old Believers and, 404, 406–408, 422–423, 424n3
   oral narrative and, 413–415, 425n18
   in Romania, 424n6
   Sabbath and, 417, 425n19
   seeker culture and, 404, 424n4
   Skoptsy and, 407, 425n11
   under Soviet Union, 403–406, 410, 422, 423n1, 424n5, 424n10
   Tătuniştii and, 410
   in Ukraine, 461–462, 478
   verbal charms and, 408–409, 416, 417f, 418–419, 421–423, 426n22
folk songs. *See* songs
"Folktale of the Beardless Man, The," 617
"Folktales by Lady Paraskevi, The" (Hahn), 617–618
folk tales/fairy tales, xxvii. *See* Greek folk tales; magic tales; myth; Russian wondertales; Slovak folk tales
Folktron (Oratnitza album), 896, 911
Food and Culture (Counihan & van Esterik), 1056
foodways (Moldova), 1055–1082
   anthropology of, 1056
   bread and, 1059–1060, 1062, 1070–1077, 1071f, 1073f–1075f
   Christianity and, 1059–1060, 1062, 1070–1077, 1071f, 1073f–1075f
   defined, 1056–1057
   ethnology and, 1056–1058
   feasts and, 1078–1081, 1079f
   gender and, 1066–1070, 1067f, 1068f
   influences on, 1059–1061, 1060f
   material culture and, 1081–1082

   Ottoman Empire and, 1057–1061, 1063
   performative hospitality and, 1070–1081, 1071f, 1073f–1075f, 1077f, 1079f
   preparation and, 1064–1070, 1067f, 1068f
   products and, 1061–1064, 1063f
   rites/rituals and, 1059–1060, 1062, 1070–1077, 1071f, 1073f–1075f, 1078–1081, 1079f
   scholarship on, 1055–1058
   wine and, 1077–1078, 1077f
Forbidden Tales (Afanas'ev), 670–671
Forgács, Tamás, 990
forgery, 494, 638
formalism, Russian wondertales and, 657
formulaic expression, xxviii, 514, 661
formula of counting, 751, 765n17
Forry, Mark, 99
Fortis, Alberto, 549, 580
"Forty Pilgrims Plus One," 498–499
Foucault, Michel, 680
"Fox and the Grapes, The" (Aesop), 614
Foy, Sue Ellen, 780
Franciscans, 373–374, 376, 378
Francisci, Ján, 633–634, 639, 644, 647f
Frank, Stephen, 952
Frankish Empire, Greece and, 610
Franz, Adolf, 370
Franz Joseph (emperor of Austria-Hungary), 840n18
"Frau von Luxemburg" (Erk & Böhme), 757f
Freidenberg, Olga, 660, 666
freylekhs, 776–778
Friedland, Lee Ellen, 780, 783
funerals. *See* Albanian death rituals; death/death rites; Greek death rituals; Russian death rituals
Funk & Wagnall's Standard Dictionary of Folklore, 440
furnishings, 1013–1017, 1015f, 1016f, 1028
Fyli, Glykeria, 203

Gabor Roma, 116, 122, 133n3, 134n4
Gabriel, Peter, 911
Gadge, 109, 116, 133n1
gadskārtu ieražas, 280
gadskārtu svētki, 280
Gaidar, Arkadii, 668
Găină, Boris, 1076

Galena, 903, 935–937, 937f
Galijašević, Damir, 736
Galin, 903
galley slaves, 522, 524–525
games, 10, 394
gangster rap, 901
"Gano, Gano," 909
Gashi, Xhevdet, 926, 930f, 933
Gatlif, Tony, 838
Gavazova, Suzana, 935–936
Gavazzi, Milovan, 326, 333n19
gedanken, 775
Gediminas (Grand Duke of Lithuania), 439, 441
Gellner, Ernest, 1036
gender. *See also* patriarchy/paternalism
   accommodation and, 206–209, 208f, 213n9
   Albanian death rituals and, 217, 221, 232–234, 233f
   Albanian *etnopop* and, 922, 926, 943n13
   Baltic region and, 289
   as border areas, 551–552
   Bulgarian popular music and, 903–904
   byliny and, 501–506, 509
   Carnival and, 313–314
   chain sword dance and, 313, 331n6
   childbirth and, 174–177
   Cortorar Romani weddings and, 110, 112–116, 113f, 115f
   dance and, 297–298, 313, 331n6, 339
   death rites and, 199–209, 202f, 204f, 208f, 213n5, 213n6, 213n9, 217, 221, 232–234, 233f, 245, 247, 264–266
   dumy and, 517–518
   epic poetry and, 501–506, 509, 551–552
   Estonian runosongs and, 147–150
   female ballad singers and, xxviii
   folk music/instrumentation and, 517–518
   foodways (Moldova) and, 1066–1070, 1067f, 1068f
   girl fairs and, 348–349
   gjamë and, 217, 226
   Greek death rituals and, 195, 199–209, 208f, 213n5, 213n6, 213n9
   Greek folk tales and, 617–618, 618f
   heroism and, 551–552
   Islam and, 221
   klezmer music and, 774
   laments and, 195, 201–206, 202f, 204f, 264–266
   Lastovo Carnival and, 313–314
   lăutari and, 827, 841n23
   in Lithuania, 441, 443
   lyric songs and, 827, 841n23
   medical paternalism and, 174
   oral narrative and, 617–618, 618f
   performance and, 617–618, 618f
   rites/rituals and, 171, 183n4
   Romani music and, 813n3, 846–847
   Russia and, 174–177, 181
   Russian death rituals and, 245, 247, 264–266
   Serbia and, 297–298
   Serbian Romani music and, 846–847
   Serbian weddings (Kosovo) and, 67, 79
   sevdalinke and, 732, 733f
   songs and, 217, 501–506, 509, 774
   South Slavic epic songs and, 551–552
   South Slavic women's ballads and (*see* South Slavic women's ballads)
   sword dance and, 313, 331n6
   Târgul de fete and, 349
   unwanted children and, 147–150
   Yiddish folk songs and, 774
genitalia, Estonian runosongs and, 156–157
Gennady of Novgorod, 390
Georges, Robert, 607, 686, 1056
Georgiev, Hristiyan, 908
Gephardt, Katarina, 648
Germania (Tacitus), 431
Germany
   Baltic region and, 140–141, 432, 438
   cultural influence of, on Yiddish folk songs, 743–749, 753, 756–760, 763
   Czechoslovakia and, 876
   Estonian runosongs and, 140–141, 166n3
   klezmer music and, 781–785
   Latvia and, 432, 438
   Lithuania and, 432, 438
   Nazism and, 288, 438, 452–453
   Volkskalender and, 279–280
Gerstner-Hirzel, Emily, 745
Gesemann, Gerhard, 580, 722
"Get Ur Freak On," 925
Ghetto (play), 782

ghosts. *See* apparitions
Gidon, Dina, 743
Gierek, Edward, 708, 716n11
gifts, midwives and, 175
Gil'ferding, Aleksandr, 489, 492, 495–496, 497*f*, 499, 500*f*, 501–506
Gimbutas, Marija, 438, 443, 451
girl fairs, 348–349
gjamë, Albanian death rituals and, 217, 226
Gjeçovi, Shtjefën Konstandin, 217
Gjidede, Pavlo, 230
Glasnik zemaljskog muzeja (journal), 690
glasnost, 432, 441, 973
Glavić, Baldo Melkov, 583
global bluegrass, 873–875, 874*f*, 875*f*
goats, in lullabies, 745–747, 748*t*, 749, 751, 763, 764n10
"God Bless America," 87
Goethe, Johann Wolfgang von, 549
Goetz, Leopold Karl, 722
Goffman, Erving, 222
gogitul miresei, 125–130, 127*f*, 128*f*
Gogol Bordello, 910–911
golden/white goat motif, 745–747, 748*t*, 749, 751, 763, 764n10
Goldstein, Diane, 178, 180–181
Goldwasser, Marine, 784
Golovin, Valentin, 747, 752
Goncharova, Natalia, 1029
"Good Day, Little Bridge," 633
"Good Heart Finds Its Reward, A" (L. Reuss), 633
Gorbachev, Mikhail, 973
Gore, Aurel, 835*f*
Gore, Victor, 833–834, 833*f*
Gorelov, A., 952
Goulas, Ioannis, 618
Govedarica, Jovan, 543*f*
Grajqevci, Kastriot, 937–938
"Grandfathers and Grandmothers" (Slobin), 750*f*
Grandparents' Museum, 1045
grave goods, 244, 247–249, 248*f*, 249*f*
grave-markers, 243, 243*f*
Grcevich, Jerry, 94–95, 99
"Great Hymn of the Archangel Michael," 421
Great Lent. *See* Lent

"Great Sinner, The," 615
Greece/Greeks. *See also* Greek death rituals; Greek folk tales
Byzantine Empire and, 194–196, 213n2, 213n3, 609–610
continuity in Greek folklore and, 193–195, 213n1–213n3
Crusades and, 610
Eleusinian Mystery Cult and, 195
Epimenides of Crete and, 195
ethnography and, 618
Frankish Empire and, 610
klezmer music and, 772–773, 777, 779
laografia and, 194, 213n1
modern, 193–197, 213n1–213n3
nationalism in, 193–195, 213n1–213n3
Orthodox Christianity in, 193–195, 198–199, 206–208, 213n2, 213n3
Ottoman Empire and, 193–195, 213n1–213n3
Philhellenes and, 193–194
Plutarch and, 195
professional storytellers and, 618–619
Revolution of 1821 in, 610
Thesmophoria Mystery Cult and, 195
Turco–Greek War (1920–1922) and, 213n2
Venetia and, 610
Greek death rituals, 193–213. *See also* Greece
accommodation and, 206–209, 208*f*, 213n9
anger with God and, 202–203, 207
apparitions and, 199
attire and, 202
body gestures and, 202–203
Charos and, 194, 200, 207, 213n6
church bells and, 200
curses and, 205, 207
feminism and, 201–206, 202*f*, 204*f*
gender and, 195, 199–209, 202*f*, 204*f*, 208*f*, 213n5, 213n6, 213n9
hair and, 202
hierarchy of, 203
Homer and, 195, 200
immediate aftermath of death and, 199–201, 213n5, 213n6
inheritance and, 195
korifea and, 205
lacerating of flesh and, 195, 202
laments and, 193–213, 202*f*, 204*f*

modernization and, 196–197
moirologistria and, 200
omens and, 199
Orthodox Christianity and, 193–195, 198–199, 206–208, 213n2, 213n3
religion and, 202–203, 206–208
scholarship on, 183–199, 199f, 213n1–213n3
"screaming the dead" and, 201–202, 202f
secondary burial and, 198, 198f
semiotics of, 197–199, 198f
Solon and, 195
speaking for the dead and, 201
supernatural beliefs and, 199
urban settings and, 196–197
violence and, 195
Greek folk tales, 605–622. *See also* Greece
beardless man and, 616
characteristics of, 610–617, 611f
collections of, 605–607, 612, 617–619
comic books and, 622
content of, 614–617
continuity in, 193–195, 213n1–213n3
death in, 616
drakos and, 616
epithets in, 619
fables and, 609
the Fates and, 616
gender and, 617–618, 618f
history of, 608–610
lamia and, 615
love in, 617
media and, 610
oikotypes and, 610
performance of, 617–619, 618f
in popular culture, 619–622, 620f, 621f, 623n13, 623n14
profanity in, 616
professional storytellers and, 618–619
scholarship on, 606–608
sex in, 617
style of, 612–614
term for, 605
water nymphs and, 615
Greenhorns and White Stars, 879, 884–885, 886
Greenman, Steve, 781, 782
green orchard metaphor, 32–33

Gregorian calendar, 336, 355n3, 424n7
Greimas, Algirdas Julien, 443
Gribajčević, Mehmed, 735
Griechische und Albanesische Märchen (Engelman) (lithograph), 618f
Grigorev, A. D., 496
Grimm, Jakob, xxvii, 513, 581–582, 610, 655, 656, 669, 678
Grimm, Wilhelm, xxvii, 513, 610, 655, 656, 669, 678
grooms. *See* marriage/weddings
"Großmutter Schlangenköchin," 760, 753f
grube maškare, 319, 332n13
Gruev, Nikola, 895
G-Runs and Roses, 874
Guattari, Felix, 88, 100–101, 105n10
Guča Brass Band Festival, 849
Guidelines for Folk Research (Institute for Ethnography, Tirana), 219, 237n5
Guildenstern, German, 782
guilds
lăutari and, 818
National Union of Craft Cooperatives and, 1041–1043, 1046
in Ottoman Empire, 792–793
Romanian folk art and, 1041–1043
Romani music and, 792–793
guild system, 283, 331
dumy and, 515, 517–519
klezmer music and, 769–770
lebiiska mova and, 518–519
Gulag, identity and, 178
Gunić, Vehid, 723, 736
gusle
South Slavic epic and, 544f, 545, 551–552, 561
South Slavic women's ballads and, 579, 584
gusli
byliny and, 492, 497–498, 510–511
"Gusta mi magla padnala na toj mi ramno Kosovo" (folk song), 65
Gusti, Dimitrie, 407, 425n14, 1040
Guterman, Norbert, 670, 671f
Gutkin, Lisa, 781
Gutslaff, Pastor, 148
Guys, Pierre Augustin, 606
Gypsies. *See* Roma

habitus, 89
Habsburg Empire
　klezmer music and, 772
　Slovakia and, 648
　South Slavic epic songs and, 541
Hahn, Johann Georg von, 606, 617, 618*f*
hair
　beardless man and, 616
　Cortorar Romani weddings and, 126
　čveger and, 385
　Greek death rituals and, 202
　as a metaphor for maidenhood, 37–39, 45
　Russian wedding songs and, 37–39, 52–53
　Ukrainian weddings and, 24
"Hajde," 937–940, 930*f*
"Hajde luj qyqek," 937–940, 931*f*
Ha-Klezmerim (Stutschewsky), 774
Håland, Evy Johanne, 201
Halemba, Agnieszka, 465
Halpert, Herbert, 684
Halych cycle, 491
Hampe, Franz, 732
Haney, Jack, 670
Hanseatic League, 431–432
Harapi, Zef, 227
Harrison, George, 911
Hart, Laurie Kain, 206–207, 209
Harvard Ukrainian Research Institute, 536
harvest festivals, 349–350
Hasanaginica, 549–552, 580–581, 596n13, 600
"Hasan of Ribnik Rescues Mustajbey," 593
Hasan-Rokem, Galit, 741
Hasdeu, Bogdan Petriceicu, 407, 413–415, 426n20
Hasidim, 742, 755, 773, 776, 778, 780
Hašler, Karel, 877
Hasznos Mulatságok, 994
Hatzitaki-Kapsomenou, Chryssoula, 606, 612, 614, 616, 617
"He," 903
healing. *See also* medicine/medicalization; shamans
　benedictions and, 372–376
　charismatic movement and, 379–380
　magic and, 366–367
　Slavic supernatural legends and, 678–679
　social media and, 380

Hearts, Festival of, 354
heavenly letters, 408–409, 416–417, 425n16, 425n19
heavy metal, 907
Hedgehog in the Mist (cartoon), 672
Heifetz, Jascha, 840n16
Hektorović, Petar, 580
Helmreich, Stefan, 95
heraldry, 1026–1027, 1027*f*
Hercegovke i Bosanke. Sto najradije pjevanih ženskih pjesama (Zovko), 723
Herder, Johann Gottfried von, xxvi, 141, 166n4, 286, 435, 548–550, 580, 756
Heretz, Leonid, 408
Herodotus, 605, 609
heroism
　bogatyri and, 485–511, 491*f*, 510*f*
　bride as epic hero in Russian wedding songs and, 38–39
　in *dumy*, 513–514
　in epic poetry, 551–552
　gender and, 551–552
　groom as epic hero in Russian wedding songs and, 42
　heroic epic songs and, xxvii
　mother as folk hero in Russian childbirth folklore and, 178–180, 179*f*, 180*f*
　in South Slavic epic songs, 551–552
Hero with a Thousand Faces (Campbell), 662–663
Hertz, Leonard, 406
Hertz, Robert, 198
Herzfeld, Michael, 194, 196–197
Hescheles, Yermye, 782
Hesiod, 609
Hetman Bohdan Khmelnytskyi (*duma* character), 514, 529–532, 530*f*
Hiiemäe, Mall, 280
Hikmet (Arif-bey Rizvanbegović Stočević), 729
hillbilly music, 873
hil'tse, 17
Hinduism, 436–437, 451, 460
hinkepe, 284
Historical Museum (Moscow), 1030
Historical Roots of the Wondertale (Propp), 658, 660, 663–667

History (Herodotus), 609
Hitler, Adolph, 453
Hobsbawm, Eric, 1036
Hoffman, Daniel, 784
Hofman, Ana, 800, 805
Holava, Natalia, 783
Holka modrooká, 883–884
Hölgyfutár, 994
Holocaust, 741, 744, 756, 774
Holst-Warhaft, Gail, 201
Homer, 195, 200, 555, 559–561, 579, 585, 605, 609, 659
Honchar Museum, 537
honga, 778
Hont, Malý, 636
hora
    klezmer music and, 778
    lăutari and, 820–823, 828, 832, 837, 840n11
    Romanian community celebrations and, 338, 340–343, 345–346, 348, 349, 354, 356n7
"Hora de concert," 823
hora de pomană, 345–346
Hora la Prislop, 349
hora lăutărească, 832
hora mare, 832
"Hora mărțișorului," 821
"Hora Națională," 821
"Hora Staccato," 821, 840n16
Horbach, Oleksii, 519
Horele noastre (Vulpian), 820
horilka, 15, 19, 23
Horlenko, Vasyl, 535
Hornjatkevyc, Andrij, 537
Horowitz, Joshua, 781
hospitality, performance of, 1070–1081, 1071f, 1073f–1075f, 1077f, 1079f
Houda, Přemysl, 877
house-to-house dance, 338–340, 343, 347, 350, 355
howling deceased back to life, 254
Hoxha, Enver, 217, 236n2, 237n16
Hradovsky, Jonatan Čipka, 636–637, 637f, 639, 641–642
Hrebeljanović, Lazar, 62, 79n5, 80n9
Hrisztova-Gotthardt, H., 992
Hroch, Miroslav, 63, 78

hromada, 10
Hrushevs'ka, Kateryna, 535–536
Hrustanović, Hanifa, 589f
Hrustanović, Hasnija, 586–587, 591, 593
Hrustanović, Ibrahim, 586–588
Hrvatske narodne pjesme (Andrić), 582–583
Hrytsa, Sofiia, 536
hubris, *byliny* and, 501–503
Hufford, David, 174–175, 177, 466
Huizinga, Johann, 969
human sacrifice, Estonian runosongs and, 148
Humo, Hamza, 721
humor/satire
    in Bulgarian popular music, 901, 906, 909–911
    chastushki and, 952, 954, 970–973, 974f, 975
    Croat/Croatian weddings and, 85, 92, 99
    jokes and (*see* jokes)
    Polish urban legends and, 699, 702, 712–713
    riddles and (*see* riddles)
    Russian weddings and, 50, 54–55
    in Russian wedding songs, 54–55
    tambura music and, 99
    Ukrainian weddings and, 17, 21–23, 25–26, 26f
Hundred Simple National Tales and Legends in Original Slavic Dialects, A (Erben), 632
hungaromeme, 1003, 1003f
Hungary
    alchemy and, 366
    amulets and, 366
    analogy approach to study of, 364
    baptism in, 373–374
    benedictions and, 368–378
    black magic and, 366–367
    Catholic Enlightenment and, 366, 378
    Catholicism in, 363–381
    charismatic movement and, 379–380
    curses in, 363, 368, 370–371, 377–378, 381
    devils/demons and, 363, 366, 368, 370–371, 373, 377–380
    divination and, 366
    exorcism and, 370, 377–380
    healing and, 366–367
    historicity and, 363–365
    icons and, 378

Hungary (*cont.*)
   jokes in (*see* jokes)
   lidérc and, 379
   magic in, 363–381
   medals and, 378
   midwives and, 367
   necromancers and, 367
   Orthodox Christianity in, 379
   Paganism in, 363–365, 367
   Protestantism in, 366–367
   proverbs of (*see* proverbs)
   relics and, 378
   riddles in (*see* riddles)
   romantic nationalism in, 363–364
   scholarship on, 363–365
   shamans and, 364, 367
   songs as spells and, 366
   specialists in magic and, 368–369
   supernatural beliefs in, 363–381
   táltos and, 367
   trances and, 367
   Transylvanian nobility and, 116, 134n7
   verbal charms and, 366–371, 374–375, 381
   white magic and, 366–367
   witches/witchcraft and, 365–368, 378
   words of magic and, 366–367
hunting, in Russian wedding songs, 39–42, 58n4
Hupel, August Wilhelm, 286
Huppert, Joshua, 780
hurdy-gurdy. *See* lira
Hurt, Jakob, 141–142, 278–279
Hvezdička (Setleři), 878
hyperbole, in epic narrative, 495

Iaroslav the Wise, 491
Iarygin, Iakov, 1019
Iazykov, N. M., 497
Ibrahimova, Yildiz, 907
Ibrahim Pasha (vezir), 523
icons
   Hungary and, 378
   krasnyi ugol' and, 1016
   Pohonia Monastery of the Dormition of the Mother of God and, 465, 473, 475
   Ukrainian weddings and, 17, 23
   Zarvanytsia apparition and, 472

identity. *See also* nationalism
   Bulgaria and, 910
   of closeness, 470
   Cortorar Romani weddings and, 109
   Croat/Croatian weddings and, 83–90, 84*f*, 86*f*, 91, 104n4–104n6
   Estonian runosongs and, 139–141, 166n3, 166n4
   Gulag and, 178
   habitus and, 89
   Latvia and, 178, 443
   lăutari and, 832–834, 833*f*
   Lithuania and, 443
   Roma and, 109
   Romania and, 1039–1041
   Romanian folk art and, 1039–1041
   Romani music and, 832–834, 833*f*
   Russian folk art and, 1027–1028
   Serbian weddings (Kosovo) and, 60–61, 64*f*, 67, 72–74, 73*f*, 74–75, 80n13, 80n15
   violence and, 88–90
Idolishche (*bylina* character), 490–491
"If I Were a Little Bird" (Bergovski), 758, 758*f*
igritsy, 50
"Ilia and His Son," 504
Iliad (Homer), 555, 579
Ilia Muromets (*bylina* hero), 485–491, 490*f*, 495, 502–511, 510*f*
Ilia Muromets i Solovei Razboinik (film), 508–509
Iliev, Carlo, 798
illegitimate children, Estonian runosongs and, 148–150
Imamović, Damir, 736
Imamović, Nedžad, 736
Imamović, Zaim, 735, 736
Imbrica, 683, 693n7
immigrants. *See* migration
Imperial Russian Museum, 1030
"Inappropriate" (Mäkelä & Tarkka), 164
Incompleat Folksinger, The (Seeger), 880
incorporation, rites/rituals and, 168
incubus, 379
indie music, 907
Indo-European influence
   Baltic region and, 275
   byliny and, 497

Latvia and, 430, 435–436, 438, 443, 451
Lithuania and, 430, 435–436, 438, 443, 451
South Slavic region and, 397
South Slavic women's ballads and, 580, 582, 593
"Inel, inel de aur," 834
"In Everybody's Mouth," 903
infanticide, Estonian runosongs and, 147–150
Ingemark, Camilla Asplund, 680
Ingold, Timothy, 101, 103
inheritance, Greek death rituals and, 195
"Inimă Supărăcioasă," 834
initiation, 169
in-laws. *See* marriage/weddings
innovative tradition, 744–745
Inochentie of Balta, 404, 407–410, 419–420, 424n6, 425n13
inspiration, Yiddish folk songs and, 744–745
instruments, musical. *See* folk music/instrumentation
înțelegerea, 118–120, 119f, 134n8
International Dance Day, 354, 357n23
International Day of the Romanian Blouse, 354
intersectionality, religion and, 285–287
Inventory, The (Dobšinský), 638
inverted ritual behavior, 385–398. *See also* rites
  "anti-behavior" and, 387, 397
  anti-ponašanje and, 386–387
  attire and, 394
  bajalice and, 386, 388
  baptism and, 392
  body gestures and, 385, 394
  childbirth and, 385, 392–394, 397
  čveger and, 385
  death rites and, 392–394
  dever and, 392, 396
  evil eye and, 392, 395–396
  fairies and, 397
  games and, 394
  marriage/weddings and, 392–394
  naopako ponašanje and, 387, 398n5
  nisam živ and, 386
  Paganism and, 397–398
  provlačenje and, 388, 390
  razbijanje sudova, 390, 392–393
  religion and, 390
  in Russia, 390–391

  spitting and, 385, 394–395
  types of, 388–390, 389f, 395–397
  verbal charms and, 386–391, 389f, 394–397
  violence and, 385, 392–394
  werewolves and, 392
  živ nisam and, 386, 396
Ionian University, 210
Irfan, 910
Isihiya, 910
Islam
  in Albania, 225, 236n2, 237n9
  border areas and, 541–542, 544–545, 551, 556–557
  Bosnian refugees in Croatia and, 83, 104n2
  butterflies as symbols of resurrection and, 227–228, 237n11
  gender and, 221
  geographic concentrations of, xxiii–xxv, xxxiiin 5
  Ottoman Empire and, 193–194
  prohibitions against death rites and, 220–221, 237n7
  sevdalinke and, 721–724, 728–729
  South Slavic epic songs and, 541–542, 544–545, 551, 556–557
  South Slavic women's ballads and, 577–581, 584–589 586f, 587f, 589f
  under Soviet Union, 218f
Ismaili, Adelina, 928–929
Isović, Safet, 735
Istoriia vozsoeedinenia Rusi (Kulish), 535
Istrefi, Nora, 927–928, 934–936, 936f
Itzkovitch, Boris, 784
"Ivan Bohuslavets," 523–524
Ivančan, Ivan, 313, 315, 331n3
Ivan Godinovich (*bylina* character), 491, 505–506, 672
Ivanov, Miroslav, 905–908
Ivanov, Vyascheslav, 397, 593
Ivanova, T. G., 498
Ivanyts'kyi, Oleksandr, 965
izba, 1014, 1016, 1031
izvorni folklor, 302

Jagić, Vatroslav, 593
Jakobson, Roman, 593, 662, 670–672
Jakupi, Leonora, 931

Janáček, Leoš, 876
Jančo, Jozef, 638
Jāņi, 444
Janissary Corps, 793, 864n7
Janjić, Bora, 735
Jankó, Borsszem, 1000
Janović, Danica, 295, 298–300, 303, 305, 307n5, 308n6
Janović, Ljubica, 295, 298–300, 303, 305, 307n5, 308n6
Janta, Anna, 706, 708, 716n7
Jaroszewicz, Piotr, 708, 716n10
Jashari, Baki, 932
Jay-Z, 925
jazz, 907, 909
jealousy, community and, 6–8
Jenkins, Richard, 64
Jesuits, 378
"Jewish Klezmer Music: A tribute to Dave Tarras," 780
Jewish Music Ensemble, 774
Jewish people/Judaism
　anti-semitism and, 439, 531–532
　Ashkenazim (*see* Ashkenazim)
　dance and, 770–784
　folk songs and (*see* Yiddish folk songs)
　geographic concentrations of, xxiii, xxv
　guild system and, 769–770
　Hasidim and, 742, 755, 773, 776, 778, 780
　innovative tradition and, 744–745
　kaleh baveynen ceremony and, 775–776
　klezmer music and (*see* klezmer music)
　Landsmanshaft organizations and, 777
　literacy of, 741, 747–748, 748t
　Lwów charter of 1629 and, 770
　marriage/weddings and, 770–772, 774–778, 780–781, 783
　migration of, 741, 743–746, 764
　nusakh and, 772
　sher contradance and, 772–773, 777
　"shtetlspeak" and, 760
　under Soviet Union, 658
　Talmud and, 744, 751
　Torah and, 747–748, 748t
　transnational dimension in song and, 743
　in Ukraine, 460
Jewish Theological Seminary (NY), 774

John of Kronstadt, 408
John Paul II, 379, 709
John the Baptist, 410, 419, 425n18, 444
jokes, xxvii, 985, 998–1004
　Budapest, 1000–1001
　memes and, 1003, 1003f
　political, 998–999, 1002
　puns and, 1002–1004
　rural folklore and, 1001
　scholarship on, 998–1000
　social media and, 1001–1004, 1003f
　urban settings and, 1000–1001
Jones, Michael Owen, 1056
Joninės, 444
Jordan river, mythologizing of, 43
"Journey of the Mother of God into Hell, The," 418, 421
"Journey toward the Sun and the Moon, The," 633
"Jovano, Jovanke," 904
Jovanović, Rade, 734
Julian calendar, 336, 355n3, 405, 424n7
Jurić, Dorian, 582
Jurková, Zuzana, 877
Juška, Antanas, 436
"Just Sex," 903
Jusufović, Šahbaz, 723

Kabakova, Galina, 171
Kačić-Miošić, Andrija, 555
Kadare, Ismail, 546, 561
Kadiu, Fatos, 923
"Kad ja pođoh na Bentbašu" (Karača Beljak), 732
Kadragić, Hasan, 722
kafana, 800, 805
kafanski orkestri, 847
Kalėdos, 448–449
kaleh baveynen ceremony, 775–776
kaliki, 498–499, 503–504
Kalin Tsar (*bylina* character), 490, 495, 503
Kallas, Oskar, 141
Kallimachos and Chrysorroi, 609
Kaloian (Bulgarian ruler), 490–491
Kaltsouni, Nota, 211f
Kama, Pikne, 148
Kamberović, Isma, 735

Kamsi, Kolë, 223
Kandinsky, Wassily, 1029
Kane, Harriet, 778
kanklės, 433
Kapaló, James, 462
Kapas, Halyna, 17
kapelye, 770, 780
kapije, od, 91–92, 92f
Kaplanoglou, Marianthi, 618
Kapo sale, 317–319, 323, 332n11
Kapu svētki, 447
Karača Beljak, Tamara, 732, 735
Karadžić, Radovan, 79n5
Karadžić, Vuk Stefanović, xxvii, 386, 398n2, 548–552, 559–560, 581–583, 589, 729, 738n6
karakhod, 776–777
"Karanfil Devojče" cultural festival, 849
Karnaukhova, Irina, 509
Karpukhin, Ivan, 977
Kasian Mikhailovich (*bylina* character), 498–499
Kassabian, Anahid, 101
Kassis, Kyriakos, 203
Kastrati, Artan, 936
Katičić, Radoslav, 593
Katona, Imre, 998–999
Katsarova, Raina, 795
Kaufman, David, 782
Kaufman, Dimitrina, 223
Kaufman, Nikolai, 223
Kayno Yesno Slontse, 910
Kečerovský, Bogoslav, 722
Keys, Alicia, 923
Khai, Mykhailo, 537
Khaled, Cheb, 925, 941
Khevrisa: European Klezmer Music (Hescheles CD), 782
Khmelnytskyi, Bohdan, 514, 529–532, 530f
Khmelnytskyi, Iurii, 532
khosidl, 773, 776–777
Khotkevych, Hnat, 535
Khramtsov, Mitia, 784
Khrushchev, Nikita, 250, 252
Khudiakov, Ivan, 667
"Khvedir, the Man without Kin," 527
"Khvesko Handzha Andyber," 529

Kingston Trio, 882
Kink, 907
Kircher, Athanasius, 366
Kirdan, Borys, 536
Kireevskii, Piotr, 496–497
Kiselgof, Zusman, 773–784
Kitsov, Ivaylo, 997
klei-zemer, 769
KlezKamp, 780
KlezKanada, 782, 783
Klezmatics, 781
Klezmer Conservatory Band, 780
klezmer music, 769–785
  Ashkenazim and, 771–776
  Austria and, 776, 781
  badkhn and, 772–773, 775, 778
  broygez tants and, 776
  bulgar and, 778
  collections of, 773–774
  dance and, 770–784
  dobriden and, 775
  festivals of, 782–783
  freylekhs and, 776–778
  gedanken and, 775
  gender and, 774
  German interest in, 781–785
  Greece/Greeks and, 772–773, 777, 779
  guild system and, 769–770
  honga and, 778
  hora and, 778
  intonatsia and, 749, 751, 761, 765n15
  kapelye and, 770
  karakhod and, 776–777
  khosidl and, 773, 776–777
  klei-zemer and, 769
  labushaynski and, 770
  Landsmanshaft organizations and, 777
  lăutari and, 772, 825–826
  Lwów charter of 1629 and, 770
  makam and, 772
  makhetonim tants and, 776
  marriage/weddings and, 770–772, 774–778, 780–781, 783
  mazltov medody and, 775
  migration and, 776–785
  Moldova and, 771–775, 777, 782–784
  Ottoman Empire and, 771–772

klezmer music (*cont.*)
   performance of, 770–779, 781, 783–784
   Poland and, 771, 782–783
   redl and, 776–777
   repertoire and, 771–773
   revitalization of, 779–785
   rubato and, 775
   Russia and, 770–773, 776, 779, 782–783, 785
   scholarship on, 773–774
   sher contradance and, 772–773, 777
   sholem-tants and, 776
   skotshne and, 773, 777
   under Soviet Union, 773–774, 780
   tentser and, 773
   tish nign and, 775–776
   transitional, 771, 777
   Ukraine and, 771, 774, 779–781, 783–785
   in United States, 776–785
   Yiddish folk songs and, 742–744, 749, 751, 753, 758–761, 763
   Yiddish theater and, 778
   zhok and, 778
   zogekhts and, 775
klub, 17, 19*f*, 27
Knowledge Society, 277
kobza/kobzari, 498, 514–519, 516*f*, 529–531, 535–539
Kogălniceanu, Mihail, 819–820
Kõivupuu, Marju, 287
kokles, 433, 440*f*
koledari, 295–298, 300, 302
Kolessa, Filaret, 535
Kolettas, Ioannis, 194, 213n2
Kolev, Gospodin, 801–802
Kollár, Ján, 645
kolo
   pjevanje u kolu and, 92
   Serbian weddings (Kosovo) and, 63, 65, 67–71, 69*f*–71*f*, 73, 75–76, 80n12
   svekrvino, 65, 67–71, 69*f*–71*f*, 73, 75–76, 80n12, 852–855, 865n23
kolomyiki, 951–953, 962–963, 965–966
Kolpakova, Natal'ia P., 496
Kompanichenko, Taras, 537
Komsomol, 974
Kontorovich, Alex, 782
Kopitar, Jernej, 548, 581

Kopytoff, Igor, 1038
Korčula, 312–313, 315–317, 331n4, 332n8
korifea, 205
Kornienko, Halyna, 6*f*
korovai, 14–15, 21, 23, 24*f*, 28
korovainytsi, 14–15, 28
Korsun, battle of, 531
Koshcheishche, Tsar (*bylina* character), 491
Kosovo. *See also* Serbian weddings (Kosovo)
   Albanian-language *etnopop* and, 920–921
   Albanian population in, 61–64, 80n6–80n7
   Battle of (*see* Kosovo, Battle of (1389))
   ethnicization of, 61–66, 64*f*, 65*f*, 79n5, 80n6–80n10
   flag rituals and, 63–64, 64*f*, 65*f*, 80n7
   identity in, 60–61
   religious paraphernalia in, 62
   Romani population in, 61–62
   Serb population in, 61–66, 64*f*, 65*f*, 79n5, 80n6–80n10
   under Soviet Union, 61
   United Nations administration in, 60–62, 72, 79, 921
   Yugoslavia and, 61, 67
Kosovo, Battle of (1389), 66, 79n5, 80n9
Kosovo cycle in South Slavic epic songs, 544, 548
Kosovo Liberation Army, 61–62
Kostsos, Vangelis, 211*f*
Kottarashky, 906
Kourtova, Plamena, 910
Koutev, Philip, 899, 901
Koval, Mykhailo, 13, 517*f*, 537
Kovnatsky, Mark, 784
Kozák, Ondřej, 874*f*
Kozak battle cycle in *dumy*, 514–515, 520–529, 528*f*, 529*f*, 538*f*
"Kozak Holota," 526–527
"Kozak Life," 532
Kozak Mamai (painting), 516
Kozak uprising cycle in *dumy*, 514, 529–532, 530*f*, 539n6
Kozanostra, 937
Krakauer, David, 781
Kraków Festival of Jewish Culture, 783
Kraljević, Marko, 683

kraljice, 295–298, 300, 302–303
kramářské písně, 877
Krasniqi, Memli, 931
krasnyi ugol', 1016
krásota, 33–39
Křešťan, Robert, 874, 886
Kretschmer, Dieterich, 606
Kretschmer, Paul, 606
Krėvė-Mickevičius, Vincas, 438
Kristeva, Julia, 896, 897
Kristić Index, 684
Krištůfek, Pavel, 880
Kriukova, Marfa, 507, 508f
Krnjević, Hatidža, 722
krolevets rushnyk, 15, 29n7
Kršić, Jovan, 721
Kryeziu, Shkumbin, 922–923
Krylov, Nikifor, 1028
Kuba, Ludvik, 722, 723, 733
Kuçi, Yllka, 938, 939f
Kūčios, 448
KUD (cultural-artistic societies), 301–302, 304, 308n11, 308n12, 308n14
Kūka, 448
Kuksa, Tatiana, 174, 176, 181–182
Kūlgrinda, 441, 448
Kulish, Penteleimon, 534–535
Kultur Shock, 910–911
kum, 67–68
Kurdoolu, Mustafa, 799
Kursite, Janina, 443
Kurtov, Ismail, 794f
Kurtovi, Demko, 797f
Kurtovi, Samir, 797f
Kusturica, Emir, 838
Kuzman, Alexandra, 800, 804
Kyivan cycle, 489–491
Kytasty, Hryhorii, 537

Lábadi, Károly, 989
labushaynski, 770
lacerating of flesh, 195, 202, 220
"La ciolpan cu frunza lată," 835
Lāčplēsis (Pumpurs), 437–438
lahuta/lahutars, 545
Laime, Sandis, 285, 286–287, 443
Lambru, Fărâmiță, 834, 836f

laments
  Albanian death rituals and, 220–221, 230–234, 231f, 233f, 237n17
  blood feuds and, 205–206
  of the bride, 31–39
  catharsis and, 210
  Catholicism and, 207, 265
  crying with words and, 230–234, 231f, 233f, 237n17
  death rites and, 193–213, 202f, 204f, 220–221, 254–266, 255f
  diminutive forms of address in, 257–261
  dumy and, 533–534
  features of, 257–261
  feminism and, 201–206, 202f, 204f
  festivals and, 203
  Finnish lament movement and, 210
  gender and, 195, 201–206, 202f, 204f, 264–266
  Greek death rituals and, 193–213, 202f, 204f
  Homer and, 195, 200
  korifea and, 205
  metaphors of, 257–261
  moirologistria and, 200
  of the mother, 34–35, 58n3
  nationalism and, 193–195, 209–210, 213n1–213n3
  nisiotika and, 204–205
  Orthodox Christianity and, 198–199
  performance of, 31–32, 261–262
  post-modern, 209–213, 211f
  professional, 232–234, 233f
  Protestantism and, 207, 265
  revival of, 209–212, 211f
  rhyme and, 260–261
  rhythm in, 260–261
  Russian death rituals and, 254–266, 255f
  Solon and, 195
  under Soviet Union, 256
  speaking for the dead with, 201
  violence and, 195
  weddings and, 203
lamia, 615
Lamp of Lenin, The, 1031
Landsmanshaft organizations, 777
landwirtschaftliche Volkskalender, Der (Yermoloff), 280

Lang, Andrew, 655
Lang, Nora, 655
Language of the Goddess, The (Gimbutas), 451
laografia, 194, 213n1
laografía, defined, xxv–xxvi
Larionov, Mikhail, 1029
"La şalul cel negru," 834–835
Lastovo Carnival, COVID- 19 pandemic and, 328–330
Lastovo Carnival, 311–331. *See also* Carnival
  Ash Wednesday and, 317–318, 323–324
  attire and, 313*f*, 331n1
  balo and, 317, 332n11
  bomb-making and, 317–319, 322, 330, 332n12, 332n14
  chain sword dance and, 312–318, 322–325, 330–331, 331n4, 331n6, 332n8
  Croatian ethnology and, 325–327, 332n18–333n20
  culjanje and, 319, 322, 325, 330, 332n14
  cultural heritage and, 327–328
  dance and, 312–315, 317–318, 331n4, 331n6, 332n11
  Dubrovnik and, 312, 315
  Fat Monday and, 318–319, 332n12, 332n13
  gender and, 313–314
  grube maškare and, 319, 332n13
  historical influences on, 314–316
  Kapo sale and, 317–319, 323, 332n11
  Korčula and, 312–313, 315–317, 331n4, 332n8
  lijepe maškare and, 312–315, 314*f*, 317–320, 322–325, 322*f*, 329–330, 331n6
  lyre and, 317–319, 320*f*, 322*f*, 323–325, 330
  modern, 316–318, 318*f*, 332n10, 332n11
  pokladari and, 312–314, 313*f*, 316–325, 321*f*, 329–330, 331n1, 331n6, 332n8, 332n13
  Poklad puppet and, 312, 316–319, 318*f*, 322–325, 330, 332n10, 332n12, 332n14
  prlina and, 318–319, 332n10
  "professional informants" and, 325
  saints' days and, 317
  sanatur and, 318
  Shrove Tuesday and, 319–323, 320*f*–322*f*, 332n14, 332n15
  siege of Lastovo and, 316–317
  under Soviet Union, 316

  supernatural beliefs and, 311–312
  Yugoslavia and, 316
Latifi, Bekim (MC Beka), 918, 923
Lätt, Selma, 280
Latvia
  as Baltic state, 275–276
  calendrical cycle and, 275–289
  Catholicism in, 277–279, 432
  Christianity in, 282
  Crusades and, 276, 282–283, 286, 431–432, 452–453
  death rites in, 287
  Dievturi/Dievturība, 281–282, 432, 438–442, 440*f*, 444, 449–451
  early history of, 281–283, 290n6
  gadskārtu ieražas and, 280
  gadskārtu svētki and, 280
  Germany and, 432, 438
  Hanseatic League and, 431–432
  identity and, 178, 443
  latviskā gadskārta and, 280
  Lutheranism and, 277–279
  Marianism and, 283–284, 286
  modern, 287–289
  nationalism in, 439, 443, 450–453, 452*f*
  Paganism in, 281–282, 285–287
  Paris Peace Conference and, 275
  Protestantism and, 277–279
  religious intersectionality and, 285–287
  scholarship on, 276–281, 289n2–290n4
  under Soviet Union, 432, 439
  tribes of, 282
  urban settings and, 283–285
  werewolf trials in, 285
  witchcraft trials in, 285
"Latvian Folk Beliefs" (Šmits), 280
Latvian Guards Organization, 451–452, 452*f*
Latvian religious folklore, 430–453. *See also* Baltic region; Latvia
  anti-semitism in, 439
  attire and, 448–449
  auseklis and, 451–452, 452*f*
  autumnal ancestor veneration and, 446–448
  bread ceremony in, 448
  calendrical cycle and, 275–289
  Catholicism in, 277–279, 432

Crusades and, 276, 282–283, 286, 431–432, 452–453
  dainas/dainos and, 432–451, 433f, 437f, 439f, 440f, 442f, 446f, 450f
  dance in, 436, 437f, 443–444
  devils/demons and, 449
  Germany and, 432, 438
  Hanseatic League and, 431–432
  Hinduism and, 436–437, 451
  history of Baltic region and, 430–432, 431f
  identity and, 178, 443
  Indo-European influence and, 430, 435–436, 438, 443, 451
  Jāņi and, 444
  Kapu svētki and, 447
  kokles and, 433, 440f
  Kūķa and, 448
  Līgo and, 444
  "Livonia" and, 431–432
  Livs/Livonians and, 282–285, 290n6
  masking in, 448–449
  mumming in, 448–449
  nationalism in, 439, 443, 450–453, 452f
  "New Age" spirituality and, 453
  orphans and, 434
  Paganism in, 281–282, 285–287, 430–453
  perkonskrusts and, 452
  popular culture in, 449–453, 450f, 452f
  puzuri and, 448
  religion's impact on Paganism and, 438
  religious intersectionality and, 285–287
  Roma and, 449
  Russia and, 432
  Sanskrit and, 436–437
  under Soviet Union, 432, 439
  summer solstice in, 443–445, 445f, 446f
  swastika and, 452–453
  symbols and, 450–453, 452f
  ugunskrusts and, 452
  Veļu laiks and, 447
  winter solstice in, 448–449
  Ziemassvētki and, 448–449
Latviešu ornamentika (Brastiņš), 450–451
latviskā gadskārta, 280
Latvju dainas, 279, 290n4
Laundry Service (Shakira album), 925
Laurinkienė, Nijolė, 443

lăutari, 817–840
  arii naționale and, 819–826, 822f, 824f, 825f, 840n12, 840n15, 840n16, 841n18, 841n19
  cârciumi and, 827, 834
  dance and, 832
  gender and, 827, 841n23
  guilds and, 818
  hora and, 820–823, 828, 832, 837, 840n11
  identity and, 832–834, 833f
  klezmer and, 772
  klezmer music and, 825–826
  lyric songs and, 827–832, 831f, 841n23, 842n25, 842n26
  manele and, 819, 836–837, 840n8
  muzica de mahala and, 834, 842n30
  muzica lăutărească and, 819, 826–827, 832–834, 833f, 841n22
  muzica populară and, 827
  "pan-Gypsy" music and, 838
  performance of, 818–821, 823–828, 832–839, 840n2
  Phanariot rule and, 818–820, 840n3
  sârbă and, 821, 823, 840n15
  staroste and, 818
  taraf and, 820, 827, 837, 840n12
  tonality and, 827–828, 841n25
  trochaic octosyllabic meter and, 829, 842n26
law enforcement, 89–90, 108
Lawson, John, 194
Lay of Igor's Campaign, 492, 494–495
lazarice, 295–298, 300, 302, 307n2, 307n3
Lazutin, Sergei, 952
"Leaseholders, The," 531–532
lebiiska mova, 518–519
Leftfield, 911
Legenda Duminicii, 417
"Legend of the Sunday," 417
legends. See folk tales; Polish urban legends; Slavic supernatural legends
Legrand, Émile, 606
Lemeš, Avdo, 735
Lemisch, Milu, 776, 784
Lemisch, Rachel, 784
Lenin, Vladimir, xxviii, 5, 507, 536, 971–972, 1031–1032

Lent, 11, 247, 266n3. *See also* Carnival; Lastovo Carnival
  Ash Wednesday and, 317–318, 323–324
  Fat Monday and, 318–319, 332n12, 332n13
  Shrove Tuesday and, 319–323, 320*f*–322*f*, 332n14, 332n15
Leopold II (Habsburg emperor), 772
Leutloff-Grandits, Carolin, 61
Lévi-Strauss, Claude, 659, 662, 667
Levițchi, Feodosie, 419, 425n13
Levitt, Marty, 778
Levkievskaya, Elena, 250
Leyzerson, Gershon, 784
Liakh Buturlak (*duma* character), 524
Liapunov, S. M., 963
Liberman, Anatoly, 658, 660, 667
Library (Apollodorus), 609
licensing agreements, 930–940
lidérc, 379
lidir, Yiddish folk songs and, 742
lidový, 872
Liepiņš, Zigmārs, 437
life-cycle. *See* childbirth; death; marriage/weddings
Life Partnership Act (Croatia), 90
Lifschutz, E., 774
Līgo, 444
lijepe maškare, 312–315, 314*f*, 317–320, 322–325, 322*f*, 329–330, 331n6
Like Two Drops of Water (TV series), 904
Lindquist, Galina, 465
Lipaev, Ivan, 773
lira, 498, 514–515, 517, 518*f*, 519, 537
Listova, Tatiana A., 172
Lithuania. *See also* Baltic region; Lithuanian religious folklore
  as Baltic state, 275–276
  calendrical cycle and, 275–289
  Catholicism in, 277–279, 432
  Christianity and, 282
  Crusades and, 276, 282–283, 286, 431–432, 452–453
  dainas/dainos and, 279, 290n3, 290n4
  early history of, 281–283, 290n6
  Mindaugas and, 282–283
  modern, 287–289
  nationalism in, 443, 450–453, 452*f*
  "New Age" spirituality and, 453
  Paganism in, 285–287, 430–453
  Paris Peace Conference and, 275
  Poland and, 283
  religious intersectionality and, 285–287
  Rzeczpospolita and, 531, 539n6
  scholarship on, 276–281, 289n2–290n4
  under Soviet Union, 432, 438–439, 441, 443
  tribes of, 282
  Vytautas the Great and, 283
Lithuanian Folklore Archive, 277
Lithuanian Folk Songs, 280
Lithuanian religious folklore, 430–453. *See also* Lithuania
  All Souls Day and, 446–447
  attire and, 448–449
  aušrinė and, 452
  autumnal ancestor veneration and, 446–448
  bread ceremony in, 448
  Catholicism in, 432
  dainas/dainos and, 279, 290n3, 290n4, 432–451, 433*f*, 437*f*, 439*f*, 440*f*, 442*f*, 446*f*, 450*f*
  dance in, 443–444
  devils/demons and, 449
  gender in, 441, 443
  Germany and, 432, 438
  Grand Duchy of, 432
  Hinduism and, 436–437, 451
  history of Baltic region and, 430–432, 431*f*
  identity and, 443
  Indo-European influence and, 430, 435–436, 438, 443, 451
  Joninės and, 444
  Kalėdos and, 448–449
  kanklės and, 433
  Kūčios and, 448
  Kūlgrinda and, 441, 448
  Latvju dainas and, 279, 290n4
  masking in, 448–449
  mumming in, 448–449
  nationalism in, 443, 450–453, 452*f*
  orphans and, 434
  Paganism and, 430–453
  Poland and, 432
  popular culture in, 449–453, 450*f*, 452*f*
  racism in, 440
  Rasos and, 444

religious intersectionality and, 285–287
Romuva and, 432, 433f, 438, 440–442, 444, 449
Russia and, 432
Sanskrit and, 436–437
šiaudinis soda and, 448
under Soviet Union, 432, 438–439, 441, 443
sulaužtinis kryžiukas and, 452
summer solstice in, 443–445, 445f, 446f
sutartinės and, 441
swastika and, 452–453
symbols and, 450–453, 452f
Vėlinės and, 446–447
Visuomybė and, 440–441
winter solstice in, 448–449
Zoroastrianism and, 440
Litovkina, Anna T., 990–992
Little Alien (Ivanov album), 905
"Little Red Riding Hood," 619
Little Russian and Red Russian Folk Epics and Songs (Lukashevych), 535
"lived religion," 462
Living Traditions, 782
Livonia, 282–285, 290n6
"Livonia," 431–432
Livs/Livonians, 282–285, 290n6
Ljuca, Behka, 735
Ljuca, Igbal, 735
Llalloshi, Edona, 924f, 926
loan words, South Slavic epic songs and, 545
Lolov, Gosho, 798
Lolov, Ramadan, 798
Lomax, Alan, 896, 908
London, Frank, 781
London Klezfest, 783
"Longbeard," 636, 639
Longinović, Tomislav, 304
Lord, Albert B., xxvii–xxviii, 736
 dumy and, 514
 South Slavic epic songs and, 542, 546, 552–560, 556f
 South Slavic women's ballads and, 578f, 579, 583–591, 587f, 589f, 593–594
Loukatos, Demetrios, 612, 614–615
Lourdes apparition, 465, 471, 473
love. *See also* courting
 of God, 755–756

in Greek folk tales, 617
paramours in Slavic supernatural legends and, 679
songs of (*see sevdalinka*)
Lovrenović, Ivan, 723
Lucijanović, Melko, 315, 332n7
Lukashevych, Platon, 535
lullabies
 death and, 144–145
 Estonian runosongs and, 142–145
 formula of counting and, 751, 765n17
 goats in, 745–747, 748t, 749, 751, 763, 764n10
 intonatsia and, 749, 751, 761, 765n15
 modality of, 753
 musical aspects of, 749–753, 749f–751f, 749n15–752n18
 pentatonic scale and, 751, 765n16
 Sephardic sources of, 752, 765n18
 verbal aspects of, 745–749, 748t, 764n10
 Yiddish folk songs and, 745–753, 748t, 749f–751f, 749n15–752n18, 764n10
Luncă, Gabi, 827, 834
Lupercalian Carnival, 312
Lüthi, Max, 610, 678
Lutzkanova-Vassileva, Albena, 96
Lwów charter of 1629, 770
lyre, 317–319, 320f, 322f, 323–325, 330
lyric songs, xxvii
 chastushki and, 952
 gender and, 827, 841n23
 lăutari and, 827–832, 831f, 841n23, 842n25, 842n26
 tonality and, 827–828, 841n25
 trochaic meter and, 829, 842n26
 trochaic octosyllabic meter and, 829, 842n26
 Yiddish folk, 51f, 753–759, 758f
Lysenko, Mykola, 535

Macedonia. *See also* South Slavic region
 commercialization of Romani music and, 799–801
 Romani music in, 791–793, 795–796, 799–801, 804–806, 808–811
 Serbia and, 795–796, 799–801
 under socialism, 804–806
MacPherson, James, 494

Mădălina, 935–936
Maggio Musicale Fiorentino, 784
magic. *See also* magic tales; supernatural beliefs; witches/witchcraft
　Albanian death rituals and, 224–228, 229f, 237n9, 237n11–237n16
　alchemy and, 366
　amulets and, 366
　benedictions and, 368–378
　black, 366–367
　childbirth and, 174–177, 184n8
　Croat/Croatian weddings and, 87, 96, 103, 104n9
　divination and, 366
　Estonian runosongs and, 142, 154–155
　ethnography and, 363, 365, 381
　exorcism and, 370, 377–380
　Greek death rituals and, 199
　healing, 366–367
　in Hungary, 363–381
　inverted ritual behavior and (*see* inverted ritual behavior)
　myth and, 364, 397–398
　necromancers and, 367
　road, 12
　Russian weddings and, 32
　Serbia and, 297–300, 303
　shamans and (*see* shamans)
　songs as spells and, 366
　specialists in, 368–369
　spells and, 366
　táltos and, 367
　trances and, 367
　Ukrainian weddings and, 6–8, 10, 12, 13f, 15–16
　verbal charms and (*see* verbal charms)
　white, 366–367
　words of, 366–367
magic tales, xxvii. *See also* Greek folk tales; magic; myth; Russian wondertales; Slovak folk tales
　Aarne-Thompson-Uther Tale-Type Index of, 32, 58n1
　Russian wedding songs and, 32
Magid, Sofia, 773, 783
Maglajlić, Munib, 722, 723, 724, 728
Magyar Nyelvészet, 994

Magyar Nyelvőr, 994
mahala, 724–727, 727f
"Mahala și țigănie," 829–831, 834
Mahovlich, Walt, 781
maidenhood. *See* chastity
"Maiden Who Seeks Her Brothers, The," 644
"Mai und Beaflor," 746
makam, 772
Mäkelä, Heidi Henriika, 164
makhetonim tants, 776
Maki (Marion Filipovski), 928–930, 929f, 932
Maksymovych, Mykhailo, 534
Mala prostonarodnja slaveno-serbska pjesnarica (Karadžić), 548–551, 581, 729
male. *See* gender
Malevich, Kazimir, 1029
Mâli, 683, 693n7
Malikov, Angelo, 803, 808
Malikov, Yashar, 803
Malina, Luboš, 887–888
Malinowski, Bronislaw, 263
Maliovannyi, Kondrat, 425n12
Maliovantsy, 407, 425n12
Malyi Hvizdets apparition, 464, 466, 468–470, 473, 475–479, 475f
Malynka, Oleksandr, 535
Mamaeva Sloboda festival, 537, 538f
Mami, Cheb, 925
Mamontova, Elizaveta, 1028
Mamula, Nada, 735
Mänd, Anu, 283
manele, 819, 836–837, 840n8, 919
"Man on a Quest for His Lost Wife, The," 646
Manu's Museum, Mr., 1046–1047, 1047f
Marianism, 459–479
　"alternative form of hope" and, 465–466
　apparitions and, 459–460, 462–479, 472f, 473f, 475f, 476f
　benedictions and, 375
　Bryn apparition and, 463–464, 469–470, 473–478, 476f
　cult of, 283–284, 286
　dumy and, 515
　Dzhubryk apparition and, 464–465
　Fatima apparition and, 465, 471, 473
　folk religion and, 417–418, 421
　Lourdes apparition and, 465, 471, 473

Malyi Hvizdets apparition and, 464, 466, 468–470, 473, 475–479, 475f
Paganism and, 438
Pohonia Monastery of the Dormition of the Mother of God and, 465, 473, 475
rituals and, 476–478
"Ukrainian Jerusalem" and, 471, 473f, 474f
Vybli apparition and, 462–463, 468
Zarvanytsia apparition and, 465, 470–479, 472f, 473f
Marie (Romanian queen consort), 1040
Marijić, Branimir, 722
Marjanović, Luka, 556–557
Mark, Gospel of, 413–414
market economy, Russian death rituals and, 253–254
"Marko Kraljević in the Azap Prison," 593
Marko Kraljević cycle in South Slavic epic songs, 544
Markov, A. V., 496
"Marriage of Hajkuna, Sister of Beg Ljubović, The," 549
marriage/weddings, 5–28, 60–79, 83–104, 108–133, 169. *See also* Cortorar Romani weddings; Croat/Croatian weddings; Russian weddings; Russian wedding songs; Serbian weddings (Kosovo); Ukrainian weddings
abiav and, 117, 124–132, 125f, 127f, 128f, 131f, 132f
in Albania, 217
al Roma and, 109, 133
anthems and, 65, 80n7, 87–88, 94–96
Assumption of Mary and, 118, 134n8
attention and, 95–96
attire and, 14–15, 17, 24–26, 32, 64f, 67, 72–75, 73f, 77, 77f, 78f, 80n13, 80n15, 112, 113f, 126–127, 127f
ballads and, 8–9, 11, 16, 21–24
bathhouses and, 37
bećarac and, 91–94, 102
betrothal (*see* betrothal)
blaga rakija and, 67
boiary and, 16–17, 19, 22, 29n8
bošča and, 72, 73f, 74, 80n13
Bosnian Croats and, 90–94, 92f–94f, 104n7
bread ceremony and, 127, 130

Breshnev era and, 5, 10
bride's role in, 76–77, 77f, 78f
čajo and, 89–90, 104n6
cântecul miresei and, 127–130
Catholicism and, 83, 85, 90
ceremony and, 17–25, 18f–20f, 24f
chalices and, 110–111, 116–118, 117f, 133n3, 134n7
changes in custom practices, 67–68
chanting and, 126
chastity and (*see* chastity)
chastushki and, 977–980
childbirth and, 108–109, 113–114, 116–117, 127
Christmas and, 118
činimo žito and, 67
civil, 17
colax and, 122–124
commensality and, 113
community and, 6–14, 66–67, 74
courtship and (*see* courtship)
between cousins, 109
COVID-19 pandemic and, 108
crowning day and, 30, 39, 43–44, 48–50
daughter's relationship with in-laws and, 6–10, 7f, 16, 28n2
dever and, 68
devishnik and, 32
dissolution of, 108–109, 114–116
divination and, 10
divych vechir and, 16–17
domoljubne tamburaške pjesme and, 86
domovyny and, 14
dosvitky and, 10–12, 27
dowry and, 113–117, 115f, 134n5, 134n6
druzhki and, 30
druzhky and, 16–17, 19, 21–22, 24, 29n8
Easter and, 108, 118
epic narrative and, 542, 549, 557
ethnography and, 5, 85, 87, 89, 103, 110
family life and, 6–10, 7f, 21, 24, 28n2, 76–77, 109, 110, 112–116
fertility and, 15, 17, 29n7, 31–32, 38, 40–41, 50, 108–109, 113–114, 116–117, 127
firearms at, 98–99, 104n9
flag rituals and, 63–64, 64f, 65f, 80n7, 83–94, 84f, 86f, 92f–94f, 104n4–104n6, 125, 125f
Gadge and, 109, 116, 133n1

marriage/weddings (cont.)
  games and, 10
  gender disparities and, 110, 112–116, 113f, 115f
  gogitul miresei and, 125–130, 127f, 128f
  hair and, 126
  hair ceremony and, 24
  hil'tse and, 17
  horilka and, 15, 19, 23
  hromada and, 10
  humor/satire and, 17, 21–23, 25–26, 26f, 50, 54–55, 85, 92, 99
  icons and, 17, 23
  identity and, 60–61, 64f, 67, 72–74, 73f, 74–75, 80n13, 80n15, 83–90, 84f, 86f, 91, 104n4–104n6, 109
  igritsy and, 50
  înțelegerea and, 118–120, 119f, 134n8
  inverted ritual behavior and, 392–394
  journey to the groom's house and, 49–50
  kaleh baveynen ceremony and, 775–776
  kapije, od and, 91–92, 92f
  klezmer music and, 770–772, 774–778, 780–781, 783
  klub and, 17, 19f, 27
  kolo and, 63, 65, 67–71, 69f–71f, 73, 75–76, 80n12
  korovai and, 14–15, 21, 23, 24f, 28
  korovainytsi and, 14–15, 28
  krásota and, 34–39
  krolevets rushnyk and, 15, 29n7
  kum and, 67–68
  laments and, 203
  law enforcement and, 89–90
  length of festivities surrounding, 67
  memory and, 101
  modernization and, 27–28, 28f
  mothers-in-law and, 65, 67–71, 69f–71f, 73–76, 77f, 78f, 80n12
  motor vehicles and, 92–99, 92f, 94f, 104n9
  myth and, 43
  obstacle ritual and, 131, 131f
  omens and, 10, 15–16
  Orthodox Christianity and, 74, 76, 118, 134n8
  patriarchal nature of, 67, 79
  penden pes and, 112
  poizd and, 18–21, 20f
  post-wedding events and, 25–26, 26f, 49–50
  preparations for, 14–17, 29n6–29n8
  private nature of, 109, 133n1
  prychet and, 15, 23
  prydane and, 23
  puberty and, 112, 113f
  pyrotechnics at, 97–100, 98f
  reciprocity in, 114–116
  reconciliation and, 22–23
  rushnyk and, 14–15, 23, 24f, 27, 29n7
  Serbian Romani music and, 851–855, 853f, 854f, 860f, 861f, 865n18, 865n19, 865n22
  Serb population in post-war Kosovo and, 61–66, 64f, 65f, 79n5, 80n6–80n10
  sex and, 17, 23
  sexual orientation and, 90
  shyshky and, 14, 16, 23
  skladka and, 11–12
  skrynia and, 15, 28
  social order and, 110, 112–116
  songs and, 65–66, 80n9–80n10, 86–88, 91–94, 127–130 (see also Russian wedding songs)
  South Slavic epic songs and, 542, 549, 557
  stari svat and, 68
  starosty and, 13–14, 18–19, 20f
  supernatural beliefs and, 6–8, 10, 12, 13f, 15–16, 32, 87, 96, 104n9
  svakhi and, 30, 38–39
  svashka and, 18–19, 21
  svatannia and, 13–14
  svaty and, 13–14
  svekrvino kolo and, 65, 67–71, 69f–71f, 73–76, 77f, 78f, 80n12
  svitilka and, 18, 21
  tamada and, 27
  tambura music and, 84–86, 84f, 86f, 89–103, 92f, 93f, 94f, 98f, 104n7, 104n9
  territoriality and, 100–104, 105n10
  tocmeala and, 114–115, 118, 119f, 120–122, 124, 125, 134n9
  trousseau and, 113–114, 115f, 134n6
  tsyhanshchyna and, 25–26, 26f
  tysiatskiĭ and, 30
  ukrains'ke and, 15, 17
  vechornytsi and, 10–12, 27
  violence and, 88–90

voritne and, 19, 21
vulytsia and, 12, 13*f*, 27
women in, 66, 74–75
xanamika and, 112, 121
zaigruvanje and, 65, 67, 71–72, 74, 76
zamesuvanje and, 67–68, 72
zmovyny and, 14

"Marşul naţional," 823
Márton, Štefan, 633
Martynenko, Hanna, 12
Martynovych, Porfirii, 535
Marushiakova, Elena, 793
Marusia Bohuslavka (*duma* character), 514, 520–521
Marxism, 217–219, 262, 658, 660, 665–667
masking
    COVID-19 pandemic and, 329–330
    Fărşang and, 340–342, 342*f*
    grube maškare, 319, 332n13
    Kalėdos and, 448–449
    lijepe maškare, 312–315, 314*f*, 317–320, 322–325, 322*f*, 329–330, 331n6
    masked balls, 342
    Ziemassvētki and, 448–449
Maslenitsa, 288
"Mataj," 638
Matching Mole, 911
material culture, 1038–1039
    attire and, 1021–1022, 1022*f*
    books and, 1023
    Christianity and, 1016, 1019, 1025–1026
    design meanings and, 1025–1027, 1027*f*
    dwellings and, 1013–1017, 1015*f*, 1016*f*
    foodways (Moldova) and, 1081–1082
    furnishings and, 1013–1017, 1015*f*, 1016*f*, 1028
    heraldry and, 1026–1027, 1027*f*
    ivory and, 1023
    izba and, 1014, 1016, 1031
    krasnyi ugol' and, 1016
    okhlupen' and, 1014
    Old Believers and, 1019, 1033n2
    pottery and, 1017–1019, 1018*f*, 1023–1024, 1024*f*
    regional markets and, 1023–1024
    revivals and, 1028–1033
    Roma and, 110
    specialized crafts and, 1023–1024, 1024*f*, 1025*f*
    tableware and, 1017–1021, 1018*f*, 1020*f*
    textiles and, 1019–1022, 1020*f*
    toys and, 1024, 1025*f*
    utensils and, 1017–1021, 1018*f*, 1020*f*
    woodworking and, 1018*f*, 1019
"Matiash the Elder," 527–528
Matthias (Hungarian king), 988
Matuška, Jindřich "Jindra," 882
Matveevna, Mariya, 254
Matyi, Ludas, 1000
Mauss, Marcel, 61
Mayakovsky, Vladimir, 975
Mazhar, Hakan "Kaan," 930–931
mazltov medody, 775
MC Beka, 918, 923
Meatfast Saturday, 247, 266n3
medals, Hungary and, 378
Međedović, Avdo, 555–561, 556*f*
medicine/medicalization. *See also* healing
    Albanian death rituals and, 236
    benedictions and, 372–376
    childbirth and, 170, 172, 174–182, 179*f*, 180*f*, 184n8
    death rites and, 236
    medical paternalism and, 174
    menopause and, 180–181
    Russian childbirth folklore and, 177–182, 179*f*, 180*f*
    supernatural beliefs and, 174–177, 184n8
Medunjanin, Amira, 736
Megas, Georgios, 607–608
Mehmeti, Fadil, 221
mehter, 793, 848, 864n7
mehter-millets, 793
Meleager, tale of, 608–609
Melody Boys, 877
memes, 993–994, 993*f*, 1003, 1003*f*
memorates, 677, 685–688
memory
    chastushki and, 980
    Croat/Croatian weddings and, 101
    "point-system of memory" and, 100, 105n10
    tambura music and, 100–104, 105n10
men. *See* gender
Menachem-Mendel of Vitebsk, 755

Mencej, Mirjam, 683, 691
menopause, Russian childbirth folklore and, 180–181
Menoudakis, Nikos, 211f
Mental Archhitects, 907
Mėnuo Juodaragis festival, 450, 450f
Meraklije (TV program), 736, 738n17
Meraklis, Michalis, 608, 610, 612
Meridua, 907
Mešanović, Muhamed, 735
Mesés könyvecske, 994, 995f
Messerli, Alfred, 612
Metamorphoses (Apuleius), 609
metaphor, 32–33, 37–45, 257–261
Metaxa-Krontira, Antigone ("Aunt Lena"), 622
meter
  chastushki, 951, 954–964
  Estonian runosongs, 139
  lyric songs, 829, 842n26
  octosyllabic, 829, 842n26
  Serbian Romani music, 854, 857–859, 865n22, 866n27
Metiljević, Ćamil, 735
Michael (Archangel), 404, 410, 417–423
midwives
  gifts and, 175
  Russian childbirth folklore and, 174–177
  supernatural beliefs and, 174–177, 184n8, 367
Mieder, Wolfgang, 986–987, 991
migration
  Bohemian, 876
  calendrical cycle and, 281
  of Jewish peoples, 741, 743–746, 764
  klezmer music and, 776–785
  Landsmanshaft organizations and, 777
  nisiotika and, 204–205
  supernatural beliefs and, 681, 683–685, 687, 693n9
Mikula Selianinovich (bylina character), 486, 501, 503
Miljković, Viki, 934–936, 935f
Milkeaters, 874
"Millal maksan memme vaeva," 145–146
Miller, Daniel, 1038
Miller, Frank, 507
Miller, Vsevolod, 496

Milošević, Slobodan, 209, 920, 923
Milošević, Vlado, 723
Milošević-Đordjević, Nada, 690
Mindaugas (Grand Duke of Lithuania), 282–283
Mindenes Gyűjtemény, 994
minority calendrical cycle, 281
minstrels. See folk music/instrumentation; songs
Minune, Adrian, 836
Minune, Ionică, 838
Mir iskustva (journal), 1030, 1031f
Misāne, Agita, 443
Mishalow, Victor, 537
Mladenović, Olivera, 300, 302–304, 308n12, 308n14, 308n16
Mladić, Ratko, 79n5
Mlotek, Eleanor, 749f–751f
Moldova, census data on, 1058–1059
Mogoș, Antonie, 1048
moirologistria, 200
Moldova, 403–406, 424n7–424n10. See also Moldovan folk religion
  Bolshevik Revolution and, 403, 405
  dumy and, 531
  foodways in (see foodways (Moldova))
  Julian calendar and, 405, 424n7
  klezmer music and, 771–775, 777, 782–785
  Orthodox Christianity in, 403–409, 414–415, 419–422, 423n2, 424n3, 424n5–424n7, 425n11, 425n15, 425n18, 425n19
  Ottoman Empire and, 1057–1061, 1063
  religion in, census data on, 1059
  Romania and, 405–406, 424n6, 424n8, 424n9
  Russia and, 404, 408, 410, 422–423, 424n3, 424n5, 424n8, 424n10–425n13, 425n18
  shamans and, 404
  under Soviet Union, 403–406, 410, 422, 423n1, 424n5, 424n10
Moldovan Academy of Sciences, 774
Moldovan folk religion. See also folk religion; Moldova; Orthodox Christianity
  apocalypticism and, 403–423, 424n6, 425n13, 425n18
  Archangelist movement and, 404, 409–410, 414–423, 423n2, 425n19

Bolshevik Revolution and, 403, 405
catacomb church and, 404, 424n5
chapbooks and, 408–409, 415–416, 422–423
copybooks and, 415–423, 416f, 417f
Culiac brothers and, 403–404, 409–413, 411f, 412f, 415–416, 419–423, 423n1
curses and, 409, 416, 418–419
devils/demons and, 407, 418, 421, 423, 426n21
eschatology in, 403–423
exorcism and, 407, 411, 416, 418–419
heavenly letters and, 408–409, 416–417, 425n16, 425n19
Inochentie of Balta and, 404, 407–410, 419–420, 424n6, 425n13
modern, 404, 424n4–424n6
Old Believers and, 404, 406–408, 422–423, 424n3
oral narrative and, 413–415, 425n18
Sabbath and, 417, 425n19
seeker culture and, 404, 424n4
under Soviet Union, 403–406, 410, 422, 423n1, 424n5, 424n10
Tătuniștii and, 410
verbal charms and, 408–409, 416, 417f, 418–419, 421–423, 426n22
Monroe, Bill, 873
Montenegro. *See* Slavic supernatural legend; South Slavic region
Monzingo, Eve, 780
Moore, Avia, 783
Moricke, Sanne, 781
"Morlachs," 550–551
Morphology of the Folktale (Propp), xxvii, 655, 659, 661–663, 668–669, 672
Morris, William, 1038, 1051
Moscow Conservatory, 774
"Mos ma ndal," 928–930
Most Beautiful Fairy Tales, The. The Strange Princess, 620f
Mother of God. *See* Marianism
motor vehicles
    Croat/Croatian weddings and, 92–99, 92f, 94f, 104n9
    tambura music and, 95–96

mourning. *See* Albanian death rituals; death/death rites; Greek death rituals; Russian death rituals
Muharemović, Hašim, 735
Muhović, Vanja, 736
Mujovi, Nexhat (Wirusi), 926–928, 927f
Mulalić, Zumra, 735
Muller, Carol, 87, 89, 104n5
multiformity, South Slavic women's ballads and, 577–578, 580, 582, 588–591, 593
multitemporality, 411, 413
Mumajesi, Flori, 933–934
mumming, 281, 288, 448–449
Muradbegović, Ahmed, 722
Murat, Andro, 583
Murat, Kate, 583–584, 593
Murko, Matija, xxviii, 553, 583–585, 594
Museum of National Art (Bucharest), 1048
musical instruments. *See* folk music/instrumentation
Musiker, Ray, 778, 781
Musiker, Sam, 778
Musin-Pushkin, Aleksei, 492, 494
Muslims. *See* Islam
Mustafa Sudžuka Trio, 732
muzica de mahala, 834, 842n30
muzica lăutărească, 819, 826–827, 832–834, 833f, 841n22
muzica populară, 827
Mystére des Voix Bulgares, Le (Cellier), 901, 907, 911
myth
    byliny and, 486, 501, 503, 507
    calendrical cycle and, 288, 297, 303
    childbirth and, 140
    death rites and, 217, 225–226
    folk religion and, 404, 433–443, 450–452
    Indo-European, 435
    magic and, 364, 397–398
    marriage/weddings and, 43
    oral narrative and, 592–593
    South Slavic epic songs and, 544
    South Slavic women's ballads and, 579–580, 582–583, 590–593

"Nanny's Tale about a Mare's Head, A" (Teffi), 672
naopako ponašanje, 387, 398n5

Narbutas, Teodoras, 436, 437
narodna igra, 299, 307n5
Narodna srbska pjesnarica (Karadžić), 581
Narodne igre (Janković & Janković), 295
Narodne pjesme iz Luke na Šipanu (Murat), 583
Narodne srpske pjesme (Karadžić), 551
Narodni običaji korčulanskih kumpanija (Ivančan), 315
narodnoe iskusstvo, 1013
Na rozloučení, 883
narrative. *See* epic poetry; oral narrative
Nashville sound, 873
Nastasiia (*bylina* character), 501, 505
Năsturică, Vasile, 834
National Endowment for the Arts, 780
national flags. *See* flag rituals
national identity. *See* identity; nationalism
nationalism. *See also* identity
  assimilation and, 236n2
  laments and, 193–195, 209–210, 213n1–213n3
  laografia and, 194, 213n1
  in Latvia, 439, 443, 450–453, 452f
  in Lithuania, 443, 450–453, 452f
  in modern Greece, 193–195, 213n1–213n3
  romantic (*see* romantic nationalism)
  Slavic supernatural legends and, 690
  Ukrainian nationhood and, 513–514, 519, 535–536, 538
National Songs (Kollár), 645
National Tales and Songs of Slavic Tribes, On the, 644
National Union of Craft Cooperatives, 1041–1043, 1046
naturist belief, in Albania, 225–228, 229f, 237n11–237n16
"Naughty Girl," 928
Naumenko, G. M., 172
Návoj, Ondrej, 636
"Nazad, nazad, mome Kalino," 904
Nazism, 288, 438, 452–453
necromancers, 367
nedeile, 348–349
Ne dirajte mi ravnicu ("Don't Touch My Plain") (Škoro), 94–96
Neizdannye materiialy ekspeditsii B. M. i Iu. Sokolovykh (B. Sokolov & I. Sokolov), 496

Nekliudov, Sergei, 172
Nekliudov, S. Iu., 974
Němcová, Božena, 633–634, 636
"Ne mogu od nje," 931
neo-folk. *See* folk music/instrumentation
neo-Paganism. *See* Paganism
neo-Protestantism. *See* Protestantism
Netsky, Hankus, 774, 780
Neve Roma, 802
"New Age" spirituality, 453, 691
New England Conservatory, 780
New Klezmorim, The: Voices Inside the Revival of Klezmer and Yiddish Music (Kaufman film), 782
newly composed folk music/instrumentation, 91, 104n7
  calendrical cycle and, 301
  Romani, 803
Newman, Zelda Kahan, 744
New York Armory, 210–212, 211f
Nibelungenlied, 485
"Nici nu ninge, nici nu plouă," 834
"Nici tu nici eu," 935–936
Niemis, Augustas, 436
nightmares, 678
Nika, Josif, 223
Nikola Šuhaj loupežník (Olbracht), 884
Nikolić, Sofka, 735
nisam živ, 386
nisiotika, 204–205
Nitsiakos, Vassilis, 344
Nodilo, Natko, 593
Norris, Chuck, 1002
North Russian Lament, The (Efimenkova), 262–263
Nosova, G. A., 250
Novela od Stanca (Držić), 689
noviny, 507–508, 668
Nov pŭt, 802
Novye zapisi bylin na Pechore (Kolpakova), 496
nunta cornilor, 341, 341f, 356n8
nusakh, 772
nymphs. *See* fairies/nymphs

obrabotena muzika, 901, 908
obredna igra, 299, 303

Obrenović, Milan, 848
O Brother, Where Art Thou? (film), 873
obscenity, 616, 671
obstacle ritual, 131, 131f
Occupation of Loss, An (Simon), 210–212, 211f
Od folkloru k world music colloquium, 877
Odyssey (Homer), 555, 579, 593
"Ogre's (Devil's) Heart in the Egg, The," 645–646
"Oh Mother-in-law," 909
oikotypes, 610
okhlupen', 1014
okićenje, 557–559
Olbracht, Ivan, 884
Old Believers, 404, 406–408, 422–423, 424n3, 1019, 1033n2, 1059
"old-time" bluegrass, 882–884
"Oleksii Popovich," 526
Olson, Laura J., 171, 176
omens
    Albanian death rituals and, 224–225, 237n9
    Greek death rituals and, 199
    Ukrainian weddings and, 10, 15–16
Onchukov, N. E., 496
101 sevdalinka (Maglajlić), 723
1001 sevdalinka (Jusufović), 723
Onezhskie byliny (I. Sokolov), 496
Ong, Walter J., 759–760
Onoriu, Ion, 834
ontology, of depicted world and, 713–715
"Opasen," 935–936
Oprișan, Ionel, 414
Orahovac, Sait, 722, 723
oral epic poetry. *See* epic poetry
oral narrative. *See also specific type, e.g.* magic tale
    categories of, 675–676
    composition of, 590–592
    decasyllabic, 577–578, 593
    dual narrator and, 704–706
    epic (*see* epic narrative)
    ethnicity and, 582–583
    ethnography and, 584–585
    fabulates and, 677, 685–688
    folk religion and, 413–415, 425n18
    form of, 632
    gender and, 617–618, 618f
    memorates and, 677, 685–688
    myth and, 592–593
    novelty in, 688–690
    octosyllabic, 577
    ontology of depicted world and, 713–715
    performance of, 676
    Russian folk epics and (*see byliny*)
    Slavic supernatural (*see* Slavic supernatural legends)
    Slovak (*see* Slovak folk tales)
    South Slavic (*see* South Slavic epic songs; South Slavic women's ballads)
    Ukrainian folk epic (*see dumy*)
    urban legend and (*see* Polish urban legend)
    written *vs.*, 552–560, 579–581
Oratnitza, 895–896, 908–909
orko. *See* donkeys
Ormis, Samo, 634, 635f, 638
orphans
    death rites and, 232, 263–265
    dumy and, 534
    Latvian religious folklore and, 434
    Lithuanian religious folklore and, 434
    in Russian wedding songs, 45
    in Serbia, 297
orska igra, 299, 307n5
Orthodox Christianity. *See also* Catholicism; Moldovan folk religion; religion
    in Albania, 221, 225, 236n2, 237n9
    Battle of Kosovo and, 80n9
    calendrical cycle and, 295–297, 301, 307, 336, 339–340, 346, 355n3
    catacomb church and, 404, 424n5
    chapbooks and, 408–409, 415–416, 422–423
    copybooks and, 415–423, 416f, 417f
    Cortorar Romani weddings and, 118, 134n8
    death and, 193–195, 198–199, 206–208, 213n2, 213n3
    death rites and, 240–250, 266n3
    Easter and, 108, 118, 247
    geographic concentrations of, xxiii–xxiv
    in Greece, 193–195, 198–199, 206–208, 213n2, 213n3
    Greek death rituals and, 193–195, 198–199, 206–208, 213n2, 213n3
    in Hungary, 379
    laments and, 198–199

Orthodox Christianity (*cont.*)
  Meatfast Saturday and, 247, 266n3
  in Moldova, 403–409, 414–415, 419–422, 423n2, 424n3, 424n5–424n7, 425n11, 425n15, 425n18, 425n19
  Old Believers and, 404, 406–408, 422–423, 424n3
  Paganism and, 250
  religious paraphernalia in Kosovo and, 62
  in Romania, 336, 339–340, 346, 355n3
  Russian death rituals and, 240–250, 266n3
  seeker culture and, 404, 424n4
  in Serbia, 295–297, 301, 307
  Serbian weddings (Kosovo) and, 74, 76
  South Slavic epic songs and, 541, 548–549
  South Slavic women's ballads and, 581
  tambura music and, 84–85
  Troitsa and, 247, 266n3
  two witnesses and, 414–415, 419, 425n18
  in Ukraine, 460–461, 477
  zavetina and, 307
Osborn, Laurel, 752
Osmani, Remzie, 938
Ossian (MacPherson), 494
ossuary, 198, 198*f*
Ostojić, Ivan K., 722
Ottoman Empire, xxv, 79n5, 80n9
  Albania and, 236n2
  Balkanism and, 897
  Bulgaria and, 901, 910
  Christianity and, 193–194
  esnafi and, 792–793
  foodways (Moldova) and, 1057–1061, 1063
  Greece and, 193–195, 213n1–213n3
  guilds in, 792–793
  Islam and, 193–194
  Janissary Corps and, 793, 864n7
  klezmer music and, 771–772
  makam and, 772
  mehter and, 848, 864n7
  Moldova and, 1057–1061, 1063
  Romani music and, 793–795, 819, 821–822, 846–849, 855–862, 863n2, 864n7
  Serbia and, 299, 846–849, 855–862, 863n2, 864n7
  Serbian Romani music and, 846–849, 855–862, 863n2, 864n7
  sevdalinka and, 721–724
  slavery in, 514, 520–525, 521*f*, 533–534
  South Slavic epic songs and, 541, 548, 561
  tambura music and, 84
Ours Once More: Folklore, Ideology, and the Making of Modern Greece (Herzfeld), 194
Ozhiganova, A. A., 174

Paczolay, Gyula, 987–988, 989–990
Pădureanu, Sava, 823, 825*f*
Paganism, 250
  All Souls Day and, 446–447
  attire and, 448–449
  auseklis and, 451–452, 452*f*
  aušrinė and, 452
  autumnal ancestor veneration and, 446–448
  calendrical cycle and, 281–282, 285–287
  dainas/dainos and, 279, 290n3, 290n4, 432–451, 433*f*, 437*f*, 439*f*, 440*f*, 442*f*, 446*f*, 450*f*
  dance and, 436, 437*f*, 443–444
  Dievturi and, 432, 438–442, 440*f*, 444, 449–451
  geographic concentrations of, xxiii, xxv
  in Hungary, 363–365, 367
  impact of religion on, 438
  inverted ritual behavior and, 397–398
  Jāņi and, 444
  Joninės and, 444
  Kalėdos and, 448–449
  kanklės and, 433
  Kapu svētki and, 447
  kokles and, 433, 440*f*
  Kūčios and, 448
  Kūķa and, 448
  Kūlgrinda and, 441, 448
  in Latvia, 430–453
  Līgo and, 444
  in Lithuania, 430–453
  Marianism and, 438
  "New Age" spirituality and, 453
  perkonskrusts and, 452
  popular culture and, 449–453, 450*f*, 452*f*
  post-communism and, xxix
  puzuri and, 448
  Rasos and, 444
  Romuva and, 432, 433*f*, 438, 440–442, 444, 449

šiaudinis soda and, 448
in South Slavic region, 397–398
sulaužtinis kryžuikas and, 452
summer solstice in, 443–445, 445f, 446f
swastika and, 452–453
symbols and, 450–453, 452f
trinity in, 438
ugunskrusts and, 452
in Ukraine, 460
Vėlinės and, 446–447
Vėlų laiks and, 447
Visuomyė and, 440–441
winter solstice in, 448–449
Ziemassvētki and, 448–449
Zoroastrianism and, 440
"Pak li," 935–937, 929f
Paldum, Hanka, 735
Pamfile, Tudor, 413, 418
Panchenko, Alexandr, 408
Panchenko, Odarka, 24
"pan-Gypsy" music, 838
Pankeev, Ivan, 172
Pann, Anton, 819, 820
Paparrigopoulos, Constantine, 213n3
Papazov, Ivo, 907
parallelism, Estonian runosongs and, 139
paramours, 679
Paraskevi, Lady, 617–618
paremiography, 989
Paris Peace Conference, 275
Paris World's Fair, 823, 824f, 839, 1030
Parry, Milman, xxvii
    South Slavic epic songs and, 542, 543f, 546, 552–560
    South Slavic women's ballads and, 578f, 579, 583–594, 586f, 587f, 589f
participatory presentational forms of dance, 338, 340, 345, 349, 353–355, 356n6, 356n22
Pasternak, Boris, 660
patriarchy/paternalism. *See also* gender
    medical, 174
    Serbian weddings (Kosovo) and, 67, 79
    South Slavic women's ballads and, 577, 581
patriotism. *See* anthems; flag rituals; identity
Paxson, Margaret, 973
Payner music label, 902–904
Pázmány, Péter, 377

Peace (Aristophanes), 609
Pechorskiia byliny (Onchukov), 496
"Pe drumul mănăstiresc," 834
Pelasgos, Stelios, 619
Pelletier, René, 722
Pembe, 857, 858f
Penava, Jozo, 734
penden pes, 112
Pennsylvania, University of, 174
Pennywhistlers, The, 779
Pentecost, 346–348, 418
pentatonic scale, 751, 765n16
Pentikäinen, Juha, 685–686
Perepechai, Motria, 12, 13f
perestroika, 432
performance
    byliny, 492, 497–500, 500f, 503–504, 506–507, 510
    choreography and, 302
    dance and, 302
    dumy, 514–519, 516f–518f
    gender and, 617–618, 618f
    Greek folk tale, 617–619, 618f
    of hospitality, 1070–1081, 1071f, 1073f–1075f, 1077f, 1079f
    klezmer music, 770–779, 781, 783–784
    lament, 31–32, 261–262
    lăutari, 818–821, 823–828, 832–839, 840n2
    oral narrative, 676
    Romani music, 791–812, 818–821, 823–828, 832–839, 840n2, 845–863, 863n2
    Russian wedding song, 31–32
    Serbian Romani music, 845–863, 863n2
    sevdalinka, 732–737, 733f, 737f, 738n17
    "singer's epistemics" and, 588
    South Slavic epic song, 545, 551–552, 555, 557–560
    South Slavic women's ballad, 576–579, 584–585, 588–590, 592–595
    Yiddish folk song, 741–744, 752–754, 756, 759, 761, 763
perkonskrusts, 452
Perlman, Itzhak, 782–783
Perrault, Charles, 610
Peter the Great, 254
Petkov, Boyko, 997
Petković, Jovica, 735

Petőfi, Sándor, 989
Peycheva, Lozanka, 807f
Phanariot rule, 818–820, 840n3
Philhellenes, 193–194
philology of border areas, 547–552, 559–561, 565–566
Pichler, Robert, 64
Pinto, Diana, 781
Pio, Jean, 606, 618
Pittsburgh Symphony, 784
Pius IX (pope), 472
Pjesnarica. See *Mala prostonarodnja slaveno-serbska pjesnarica* (Karadžić)
pjevanje u kolu, 92
"placarding" ethnicity, 63
placism, 467
Plato, 605
Pleiades, 281
ples, 299, 306
Plocek, Jiří, 885–888, 887f
Plutarch, 195
Pobrić, Omer, 723
Pócs, Eva, 368, 370
podvig (feat) of endurance, childbirth and, 180
poetic form, of Estonian runosongs, 139
poetry, epic. *See* epic poetry
"poetskoj prirodi sevdalinke, O" (Krnjević), 722
Pohonia Monastery of the Dormition of the Mother of God, 465, 473, 475
Pohunek, Jan, 877
"point-system of memory," 100, 105n10
poizd, 18–21, 20f
poklad. See Carnival; Lastovo Carnival
pokladari, 312–314, 313f, 316–325, 321f, 329–330, 331n1, 331n6, 332n8, 332n13
Poklad puppet, 312, 316–319, 318f, 322–325, 330, 332n10, 332n12, 332n14
Poland
    Catholicism in, 709, 716n13
    "fast food journalism" and, 710
    Grand Duchy of Lithuania and, 432
    Katyn massacre and, 709, 716n14
    klezmer music and, 771, 782–783
    Lithuania and, 283
    Rzeczpospolita and, 531, 539n6
Polenova, Elena, 1028–1030

Polesitsky, Igor, 784
polianitsa, 490, 501, 504, 506, 509
Polish urban legends, 698–715
    communication context of, 707–708, 716n9
    cultural taboos and, 704
    diction and, 703–704
    dual narrator and, 704–706
    epithets in, 703
    extratextual content of, 700–701, 703
    "fast food journalism" and, 710
    as folklore, 698–699
    form of, 700–703
    function of, 708–710, 713, 716n10–716n13
    humor/satire and, 699, 702, 712–713
    intratextual content of, 700–701, 703
    media and, 699–700, 705, 707, 710, 713
    narrator of, 704–706, 713–715
    ontology of depicted world and, 713–715
    purpose of, 710–713
    scholarship on, 699–700
    sources of, 699
    subject matter of, 708–710, 716n11–716n13
    topics of, 700
    tripartite structure of, 702
    xenophobia and, 710
political jokes, 998–999, 1002
Politis, Nikolaos, 213n1, 609
Politis, Nikolaos G., 607
Polívka, Jiří, 607, 629, 634, 638
Polovina, Himzo, 735, 736–737
Polyidus, tale of, 609
Pompieru, Costache, 821, 840n15
Ponces, Lola, 941
Popescu, Carmen, 1040
pop-folk. *See* Bulgarian popular music
Popov, Veselin, 793
Popović, Pavle, 721–722
Popovschi, Nicolae, 407
popular culture
    bogatyri in, 492, 494f, 506–510, 508f–510f
    Bulgarian (*see* Bulgarian popular music)
    byliny in, 492, 494f, 506–510, 508f–510f
    Greek folk tales in, 619–622, 620f, 621f, 623n13, 623n14
    in Latvia, 449–453, 450f, 452f
    in Lithuania, 449–453, 450f, 452f
    Paganism and, 449–453, 450f, 452f

Porta festivals, 884–885
Porter, James, 588
posidelki, 498
Pospíši, František, 315, 332n8
Po Taslidži pala magla (Šahinpašić), 736
potlach, 884
pottery, 1017–1019, 1018f, 1023–1024, 1024f
poverty, in *dumy*, 531–534
Povodyr (film), 539n7
Povrzanović, Maja, 83, 87
"practice theory" of rituals, 168–169
"Prayers of Saint Basil," 419
"Prayers of Saint Vasile," 422
Pregled srpske književnosti (journal), 721
pregnancy, Estonian runosongs and, 150–155
premarital sex. *See* chastity; sex
"Preševka" (Bakija Bakič ensemble), 849
Presheva, Enis Jr., 930–931, 930f
Preslava, 903
Přiblová, Irena, 877
Přibylová, Irena, 880
Priede, Jānis, 286
Prilog proučavanju ostataka orskih obrednih igaru u Jugoslaviji (Janković & Janković), 298
Primiano, Leonard N., 407, 409, 462, 471, 477–478
"Princess on the Glass Mountain, The," 645
"Princess with the Spindle, The. A Curious Folklore," 611f
prlina, 318–319, 332n10
Pro Band, 938
Problems of Comedy and Laughter (Propp), 659
profanity, 616
"professional informants," 325
professional lamenters, 232–234, 233f
Prohaska, Dragutin, 721
Prokopenko, Oleksii, 28f
Prokopenko, Olena, 28f
propaganda, *chastushki* and, 973–975
Propp, Vladimir, xxvii, 617, 655–660, 656f. *See also* Russian wondertales
  Afanas'ev and, 670, 672
  arrest of, 657
  death of, 660
  family life of, 660
  health of, 658, 670
  Marxism and, 658, 660, 665–667
  military service of, 656
  scholarship of, 661–669, 669f
  siege of Leningrad and, 658
  seminary and, 659
  Soviet Union and, 657–660, 664–672
  university years of, 656–660, 667
Protestantism
  Estonia and, 277–279
  geographic concentrations of, xxiv–xxv
  in Hungary, 366–367
  laments and, 207, 265
  Latvia and, 277–279
  in Ukraine, 460
  white magic and, 366–367
Proverb, The (Taylor), 986
proverbs, 985–994
  anti-, 991–994, 993f
  bible and, 988
  collections of, 989–990
  dictionaries of, 989–990
  of Latin origin, 986–988, 987f
  origins of, 986–989, 987f
  scholarship on, 989–991
provlačenje, 388, 390
Průcha, Jaroslav, 880, 881f
Prussia, Baltic region and, 278, 286, 430, 438, 440–441
prychet, 15, 23
prydane, 23
Przybyła-Dumin, Agnieszka, 700
psalmy, 515, 517–518
"Pseudo-Apocalypse of John the Theologian," 414, 418
psycho-social approach to scholarship, 171–172, 183n5
Ptáček, Ladislav, 880
puberty, Cortorar Romani weddings and, 112, 113f
pub jams, 874, 875f
public domain, Estonian runosongs and, 141–143
Puceanu, Romica, 827, 830, 831f, 834
Puhvel, Jaan, 443
Pumpurs, Andrejs, 437–438
Punjabi MC, 925

puns, 1002–1004
puppet, *Poklad,* 312, 316–319, 318f, 322–325, 330, 332n10, 332n12, 332n14
purification rituals, Russian childbirth folklore and, 175–176, 184n8
Purs, Aldis, 275
Pushkin, Alexander, 509
Puștiu, Liviu, 938
Putin, Vladimir, xxx
puzuri, 448
pyrotechnics, at Croat/Croatian weddings, 97–100, 98f

"Qyqeku," 937–938

Rabinovitch, I., 774
racism, in Lithuania, 440
Radenković, Ljubinko, 386–395, 389f
Radić, Antun, 326, 327, 332n18
Radio Belgrade, 800
Radio Kosovo, 932
Radio Sarajevo, 735
Radio Skopje, 804–805
Rădulescu, Speranța, 820
Ráduly, János, 995
"Radúz and Ľudmila," 644
Rády, Emericus, 373–374
rahvakalender, 279–280
Raim, Ethel, 779–780
Rainis, 438
Rakovnickej Potok, 882–884
Ramadan
　South Slavic epic songs and, 545
　South Slavic women's ballads and, 579
Rambaud, Alfred, 535
Rancāne, Aida, 288
Ranković, Sanja, 63
ransom, 521–522
raqs sharqi, 925
Rasos, 444
Rayko, Stas, 784
Razauskas, Dainius, 443
razbijanje sudova, 392–393
Razumova, I. A., 172
"Realistic Tales," 643
reciprocity, in Cortorar Romani weddings, 114–116

reconciliation, ballads on, 22–23
recordings, of Estonian runosongs, 141
redl, 776–777
Redzhepova, Esma, 805
Reeder, Roberta, 659
Regélő, 994
Reidzāne, Beatrise, 285
reincarnation, snakes as reincarnated spirits and, 228
Reisman, Abigale, 784
Rejhon, Marek, 876
relics, Hungary and, 378
religion. *See also* folk religion; Moldovan folk religion; *specific holidays, e.g.* Easter; *specific religions, e.g.* Christianity
　assimilation and, 236n2
　Baltic region and, 277–279
　butterflies as symbols of resurrection and, 227–228, 237n11
　catacomb church and, 404, 424n5
　Christmas and, 350–353, 352f, 353f, 356n20
　communism and, xxviii–xxx
　as distinct from national boundaries, xxiii–xxv, xxxiiin 3–n5
　Epiphany and, 351–352
　Greek death rituals and, 202–203, 206–208
　in Hungary, 363–365
　icons, Ukrainian weddings and, 17, 23
　impact of, on Paganism, 438
　intersectionality and, 285–287
　inverted ritual behavior and, 390
　in Kosovo, religious paraphernalia and, 62
　"lived religion," 462
　in Moldova, census data on, 1059
　nedeile and, 348–349
　"New Age" spirituality and, 453
　New Year's and, 350–353, 352f, 353f, 356n20
　prohibitions against death rites and, 220–221, 237n7
　psalmy and, 515, 517–518
　religious pluralism in Ukraine, 460–461
　Rusalii and, 346–348
　in Russia, 171–172
　Russian wondertales and, 664–666
　"sacred materiality" and, 470
　saints' days and, 344–345, 348–352, 356n12, 356n13

scholarship in Post–Soviet Russia and, 171
seeker culture and, 404, 424n4
Slavic supernatural legends and, 676–677, 682
snakes as reincarnated spirits and, 228
songs and, 279
trinity and, 438
"vernacular religion," 462
vidpusty and, 515
violence and, 88–89
white magic and, 366–367
"Religious Tales," 643
remembrance, Russian death rituals and, 247–250, 248*f*, 249*f*
"Remnants of Art in the Russian Village" (Bilibin), 1030
repetition
 in *chastushki*, 960
 in Estonian runosongs, 139
 of syntactical features, 32
Repin, Ilia, 493*f*
resentment, Estonian runosongs and, 158–160
responsorium, 374
"return song" type of South Slavic epic songs, 542, 593
Reuss, Ľudovit, 633, 641–642
Reuss, Samuel, 642, 642*f*
Revelation, Book of, 408, 414–415
revivals, lament, 209–212, 211*f*
Revu, 907
Rexhepi, Gazmend, 937
Rėza, Liudvikas, 436
"rhetoric of truth," 678
rhyme
 in *chastushki*, 954–964
 in *dumy*, 513
 in Estonian runosongs, 139
 in laments, 260–261
Riabinin, Trokhim Grigorovich, 496, 499, 500*f*
Riabinin-Andreev (Trokhim Riabinin's son), 496
Riabkov, Varlam, 1028
Ribanje i ribarsko prigovaranje (Hektorović), 580
Rice, Timothy, 898
riddles, xxvii, 985, 994–998
 collections of, 994–996, 995*f*

function of, 997–998
scholarship on, 994–997, 995*f*
subgenres of, 996–997
Ries, Nancy, 180
Rigas ragana (Rainis), 438
Rihtman, Cvjetko, 723
Rihtman-Auguštin, Dunja, 326, 333n20
Rimavský, Janko, 633
Rimskii-Korsakov, Nikolai, 507, 782
"Ripni Kalinke," 907
rites de passage, Les (van Gennep), 168
rites/rituals. *See also specific rite, e.g.* marriage/weddings
 challenges of research on, 169–170, 183n1
 chastushki and, 976–980
 childbirth and, 168–177, 183n1–183n5, 184n8
 death and (*see* death/death rites)
 Esztergom book of rituals and, 377
 flag rituals (*see* flag rituals)
 foodways (Moldova) and, 1059–1060, 1062, 1070–1077, 1071*f*, 1073*f*–1075*f*, 1078–1081, 1079*f*
 gender and, 171, 183n4
 incorporation and, 168
 inverted (*see* inverted ritual behavior)
 Marianism and, 476–478
 modern Russia and, 170–177, 183n2
 multifunctionality of, 168–169
 post-Soviet Russia and, 170–177, 183n2
 "practice theory" of, 168–169
 psycho-social approach to scholarship and, 171–172, 183n5
 purification, 175–176, 184n8
 scholarship on, 168–177, 183n2
 secrecy about, 169–170
 separation and, 168
 Soviet Union and, 170, 183n1
 transition and, 168, 171, 183n3
 Ukrainian Marianism and, 476–478
Ritual Lament in Greek Tradition (Alexiou), 195
rituals. *See* rites/rituals
Ritual v traditsinnoi kul'ture (Baiburin), 171, 183n3
Rivkind, Isaac, 774
Rivkin-Fish, Michele, 174–175
Rizvić, Muhsin, 722

road magic, 12
"Robber Madej," 638
rock music, 907
Ročnik 47 (Daněk), 878
"Rođendan," 934–936, 927f
Rodiny, deti, povitukhi v traditsiiakh narodnoi kul'tury (Belousova & Nekluidov), 172
Roerich, Nikolai, 507
Róheim, Géza, 364
Röhrich, Lutz, 615, 686
Roland (epic hero), 514
Roma, 108–111, 111f. See also Romania; Romani music; Serbian Romani music
   abiav and, 117, 124–132, 125f, 127f, 128f, 131f, 132f
   al Roma and, 109, 133
   Assumption of Mary and, 118, 134n8
   attire and, 110, 111f, 112, 113f, 126–127, 127f
   Bosnian refugees in Croatia and, 83–84, 104n2
   bread ceremony and, 127, 130
   cântecul miresei and, 127–130
   ćef and, 850–851, 851f, 865n17
   chalices and, 110–111, 116–118, 117f, 133n3, 134n7
   chanting and, 126
   chastity and, 109, 112, 116–117, 132, 132f
   childbirth and, 108–109, 113–114, 116–117, 127
   Christmas and, 118
   colax and, 122–124
   commensality and, 113
   dissolution of marriage and, 108–109, 114–116
   dowry and, 113–117, 115f, 134n5, 134n6
   Easter and, 108, 118
   family life and, 109, 110, 112–116
   fertility and, 108–109, 113–114, 116–117, 127
   flag rituals and, 125, 125f
   Gabor, 116, 122, 133n3, 134n4
   Gadge and, 109, 116, 133n1
   gender disparities and, 110, 112–116, 113f, 115f
   gogitul miresei and, 125–130, 127f, 128f
   guilds and, 817
   hair and, 126
   identity and, 109
   înțelegerea and, 118–120, 119f, 134n8
   kafanski orkestri and, 847
   in Kosovo, 61–62
   Latvia and, 449
   lăutari and, 772
   neamo and, 110–111, 134n4
   obstacle ritual and, 131, 131f
   Orthodox Christianity and, 118, 134n8
   private nature of weddings and, 109, 133n1
   puberty and, 112, 113f
   reciprocity in, 114–116
   slavery and, 817–818, 840n1
   social order and, 110, 112–116
   songs and, 127–130
   tocmeala and, 114–115, 118, 119f, 120–122, 124, 125, 134n9
   trousseau and, 113–114, 115f, 134n6
   vici/vitsa and, 134n4
   wealth/material possessions and, 110
   xanamika and, 112, 121
Roman Catholic Church. See Catholicism
Romania. See also Cortorar Romani weddings; Roma; Romanian community celebrations; Romanian folk art
   artizanat and, 1041–1043
   Austria and, 315, 351
   COVID-19 pandemic in, 108
   Culiac brothers and, 403–404, 409–413, 411f, 412f, 415–416, 419–423, 423n1
   history of, 817–820, 840n3
   identity in, 1039–1041
   lăutari in (see *lăutari*)
   media in, 354
   Moldova and, 405–406, 424n6, 424n8, 424n9
   Orthodox Christianity in, 336, 339–340, 346, 355n3
   slavery in, 817–818, 840n1
   under socialism, 1038, 1040–1046
   summer solstice in, 335–336, 336f, 348
   Transylvania region of, 108, 110, 116, 134n4, 134n7
   winter solstice in, 336f
"România, România," 821
Romania Day, 336, 353
Romanian Athenaeum, 824
Romanian community celebrations. See also community
   agrarian festivals and, 343–344, 349–350
   Alesul Oilor and, 349

ardeleana and, 345
attire and, 351–352
brâul bătrân and, 345
căiuți and, 351
calendrical cycle in, 335–355, 336f, 355n3
Căluș and, 346–348, 347f, 351, 353f, 356n16, 356n17
Călușerul Transilvănean and, 351, 353f
capră and, 351, 352f
caroling and, 350
Catholicism in, 336, 340, 342
ceată and, 339
cete and, 350–351
Children's Day and, 336, 354
Christmas and, 350–353, 352f, 353f, 356n20
community celebrations in, 335–355
dance in, 337–352, 341f, 346f, 347f, 352f, 354–355, 356n6, 356n7, 356n13, 356n20, 356n22, 357n23
Epiphany and, 351–352
fairs and, 348–349
Fărșang and, 340–342, 342f, 356n8
Festival of Hearts and, 354
Festivalul datinilor de iarnă and, 351
Flower Saturday and, 343
Focul lui Sumedru and, 350
girl fairs and, 348–349
harvest festivals and, 349–350
hora and, 338, 340–343, 345–346, 348, 349, 354, 356n7
hora de pomană and, 345–346
Hora la Prislop and, 349
house-to-house visits and, 338–340, 343, 347, 350, 355
International Dance Day, 354, 357n23
International Day of the Romanian Blouse and, 354
masked balls and, 342
masks and, 340–342, 342f
nedeile and, 348–349
New Year's and, 350–353, 352f, 353f, 356n20
nunta cornilor and, 341, 341f, 356n8
Orthodox Christianity in, 336, 339–340, 346, 355n3
participatory presentational forms of dance and, 338, 340, 345, 349, 353–355, 356n6, 356n22

Pentecost and, 346–348
Romania Day and, 336, 353
ruga bal and, 345
ruga foeni and, 346f
Rusalii and, 346–348
saints' days and, 344–345, 348–352, 356n12, 356n13
Sâmbra Oilor and, 343–344
sârbă and, 338, 345, 356n7
secular, 353–354, 356n22
Strânsul Oilor and, 349
summer solstice and, 348
supernatural beliefs and, 342, 348
Târgul cepelor and, 349
Târgul de fete and, 349
Union Day and, 354
village life and, 344–345, 346–348, 346f, 347f, 356n12, 356n13, 356n16, 356n17
Romanian folk art, 1036–1052
artizanat and, 1041–1043
"author" museums and, 1045, 1045f
classification of, 1050–1052
collections of, 1037–1038
creativity and, 1046
dwellings and, 1048–1050
ethnography and, 1049
guilds and, 1041–1043
identity and, 1039–1041
museums of, 1043–1050, 1045f, 1047f, 1048f
national interest in, 1039–1041
politics and, 1039–1041
scholarship on, 1036–1039
under socialism, 1038, 1040–1046
Volkskunde and, 1039
Romanian Pavilion of the International Exhibition (Rome), 1040, 1048
Romanian Peasant Museum, 1044–1045
"Romanian Rhapsodies" (Enescu), 824
Romanian Village Museum, 1049
Romani music, 791–812
arii naționale and, 819–826, 822f, 824f, 825f, 840n12, 840n15, 840n16, 841n18, 841n19
in Bulgaria, 791–799, 801–804, 806–809, 811
čalgija orchestras and, 846, 861
cârciumi and, 827, 834
chalga and, 807–808
chalgadzhii and, 793

Romani music (*cont.*)
- *chalgiya* and, 793–796, 799–800, 804–805, 810–811
- *čoček* and, 845, 857–859, 861f, 863n2, 866n27
- collections of, 819–820
- commercialization of, 795–801
- dance and, 832
- *davuldzhii* and, 793
- *esnafi* and, 792–793, 800
- ethnopop and, 807–808
- festivals of, 798f, 807f, 809, 809f, 810f, 849
- gender and, 813n3, 827, 841n23, 846–847
- guilds and, 792–793
- *hora* and, 820–823, 828, 832, 837, 840n11
- identity and, 832–834, 833f
- *kafana* and, 800, 805
- klezmer music and, 825–826
- *lăutari* in (*see lăutari*)
- lyric songs and, 827–832, 831f, 841n23, 842n25, 842n26
- in Macedonia, 791–793, 795–796, 799–801, 804–806, 808–811
- *manele* and, 819, 836–837, 840n8
- marriage/weddings and, 851–855, 853f, 854f, 860f, 861f, 865n18, 865n19, 865n22
- *mehter* and, 848, 864n7
- *mehteri* and, 793
- *mehter-millets* and, 793
- meter and, 854, 857–859, 865n22, 866n27
- *muzica de mahala* and, 834, 842n30
- *muzica lăutărească* and, 819, 826–827, 832–834, 833f, 841n22
- *muzica populară* and, 827
- newly composed, 803
- Ottoman Empire and, 793–795, 819, 821–822, 846–849, 855–862, 863n2, 864n7
- "pan-Gypsy" music and, 838
- performance of, 791–812, 818–821, 823–828, 832–839, 840n2, 845–863, 863n2
- pop folk and, 807–808
- Romfest and, 798f, 807f, 808, 809f, 810f
- *sârbă* and, 821, 823, 840n15
- scholarship on, 793–796
- Serbia and (*see* Serbian Romani music)
- Sobinka and, 845
- under socialism, 801–806
- *surla-goč* and, 847
- *surnadzhii* and, 793
- *svirdzhii* and, 793
- *taraf* and, 820, 827, 837, 840n12
- tonality and, 827–828, 841n25
- trochaic octosyllabic meter and, 829, 842n26
- *tsigani* and, 792
- *tŭpan* and, 795–796, 799, 810–811
- Yugoslavia and, 792, 800, 804–805, 808
- *zurna* and, 793, 794f, 797f
- *zurna-tŭpan* and, 795–796, 799, 810–811

Romano essi, 802
Roman Ritual, 377
romantic nationalism, xxvi
- in Hungary, 363–364
- in Russia, 485–486, 513
- in Serbia, 548
- Slovak folk tales and, 628–629, 631, 634, 639, 641–648

Roma theater, 802
Romfest, 798f, 807f, 808, 809f, 810f
Rommen, Timothy, 91
Romuva, 432, 433f, 438, 440–442, 444, 449
Roots of Vrancea, The (museum), 1045
Rosenberg, Neil, 874–875
Rosenblatt, Elie, 784
Rosenblatt, Jason, 784
Roşioru, Florică, 834
Roskies, David, 759–760
Rosman, Moshe, 744–745
Rostislavichi, 491
Roth, Klaus, 1057
Roussel, Louis, 606
Roustom, Kareem, 784
Roxolana (wife of Suleiman the Magnificent), 520–521
Rožin, Nikola Bonifačić, 316, 332n9
Rozov, Aleksei, 783–784
Rrapaj, Fatos M., 226
rubato, 775
Rubin, Joel, 774, 781, 782
Rudnev, V. A., 250
ruga bal, 345
ruga foeni, 346f
Ruin cycle in *dumy*, 514, 532–535
Rumanian Exhibition: Achievements of the Rumanian People's Republic, 1040

Rumiantsev, Nikolai, 495
runosongs. *See* Estonian runosongs
Rus', *byliny* and, 489, 491
Rusalii, 346–348
rusalki, 41
Rushefsky, Pete, 784
rushnyk, 14–15, 23, 24f, 27, 29n7
Russia. *See also* Russian childbirth folklore; Russian death rituals; Russian folk art; Russian folk epics (*byliny*); Russian weddings; Russian wondertales; Soviet Union
    Baltic region and, 278, 289n3
    baptism and, 175–176, 184n8
    Bolshevik Revolution and, 403, 405
    byliny and (*see byliny*)
    chastushki in (*see chastushki*)
    childbirth in, 168–182, 179f, 180f, 183n1–183n5, 184n8
    COVID-19 pandemic and, 176–177
    epic poetry and, 485
    gender and, 174–177, 181
    gifts and, 175
    Grand Duchy of Lithuania and, 432
    identity and, 1027–1028
    inverted ritual behavior in, 390–391
    klezmer music and, 770–773, 776, 779, 782–783, 785
    Latvia and, 432
    Lithuania and, 432
    media in, 173
    medicalization and, 170, 172, 174–182, 179f, 180f, 184n8
    menopause and, 181
    Moldova and, 404, 408, 410, 422–423, 424n3, 424n5, 424n8, 424n10–425n13, 425n18
    motifs in Yiddish folk songs and, 748t
    religion in, 171–172
    romantic nationalism in, 485–486, 513
    Russian Revolution (1905) and, 405, 408
    Russian Revolution (1917) and, 287, 403, 405
    scholarship in modern, 170–177, 183n2
    scholarship in post-Soviet, 170–177, 183n2
    serfs and, 1028
    under Soviet Union, 250–253, 252f, 256, 266n4
    supernatural beliefs and, 174–177, 184n8
    Ukraine and, 466
Russian Agricultural Feastdays (Propp), 659
Russian childbirth folklore, 168–183. *See also* childbirth
    baptism and, 175–176, 184n8
    endurance and, 180
    evil eye and, 175–177, 184n8
    gender and, 174–177
    gifts and, 175
    medicalization of childbirth and, 170, 172, 174–182, 179f, 180f, 184n8
    menopause and, 180–181
    midwives and, 174–177
    mother as folk hero and, 178–180, 179f, 180f
    purification rituals and, 175–176, 184n8
    religion and, 171–172
    scholarship in modern, 170–177, 183n2
    scholarship in post-Soviet, 170–177, 183n2
    supernatural beliefs and, 174–177, 184n8
    in urban settings, 172–176, 181–182
    verbal charms and, 170, 175
Russian death rituals, 240–266, 245f, 246f. *See also* Russia
    attire and, 240–244, 242f, 243f
    binding and, 240
    "bundle" of death clothes and, 241, 242f
    coffin decoration and, 251, 266n4
    Easter and, 247, 266n3
    gender and, 245, 247, 264–266
    grave goods and, 244, 247–249, 248f, 249f
    grave-markers and, 243, 243f
    howling deceased back to life and, 254
    laments and, 254–266, 255f
    Lent and, 247, 266n3
    market economy and, 253–254
    Meatfast Saturday and, 247, 266n3
    modern, 253–254, 262–263
    Orthodox Christianity and, 240–250, 266n3
    remembrance and, 247–250, 248f, 249f
    scholarship on, 255–256, 262–263
    under Soviet Union, 250–253, 252f, 256, 266n4
    Trinity Saturday and, 247, 266n3
    Troitsa and, 247, 266n3
    Victory Day and, 252, 252f
    village life and, 263–265

Russian death rituals (*cont.*)
   washing and, 240–244
   zaochnoe otpevanie and, 250–251
Russian Fairy Tales (Afanas'ev), 670–671, 671*f*
Russian folk art, 1013–1034
   attire and, 1021–1022, 1022*f*
   books and, 1023
   Christianity and, 1016, 1019, 1025–1026
   design meanings and, 1025–1027, 1027*f*
   dwellings and, 1013–1017, 1015*f*, 1016*f*
   furnishings and, 1013–1017, 1015*f*, 1016*f*, 1028
   heraldry and, 1026–1027, 1027*f*
   identity and, 1027–1028
   ivory and, 1023
   izba and, 1014, 1016, 1031
   krasnyi ugol' and, 1016
   narodnoe iskusstvo and, 1013
   okhlupen' and, 1014
   Old Believers and, 1019, 1033n2
   pottery and, 1017–1019, 1018*f*, 1023–1024, 1024*f*
   regional markets and, 1023–1024
   revival of, 1028–1033
   scholarship on, 1028–1033
   under Soviet Union, 1019, 1030–1033
   specialized crafts and, 1023–1024, 1024*f*, 1025*f*
   tableware and, 1017–1021, 1018*f*, 1020*f*
   textiles and, 1019–1022, 1020*f*
   toys and, 1024, 1025*f*
   utensils and, 1017–1021, 1018*f*, 1020*f*
   woodworking and, 1018*f*, 1019
Russian folk epics. *See byliny*
Russian Folktale, The (Propp), 659, 661, 667–670, 669*f*, 672
Russian Geographical Society, 667, 670
Russian Imperial Geographical Society, 5
Russian Museum (St. Petersburg), 1032
Russian Revolution (1905), 405, 408
Russian Revolution (1917), 287, 403, 405
Russian State University of the Humanities, 172
Russian weddings
  attire and, 32
  bathhouses and, 37
  crowning day and, 30, 39, 43–44, 48–50
  devishnik and, 32
  druzhki and, 30
  fertility and, 31–32, 38, 40–41, 50
  humor/satire and, 50, 54–55
  igritsy and, 50
  journey to the groom's house and, 49–50
  krásota and, 34–39
  post-wedding feast and, 49–50
  songs of (*see* Russian wedding songs)
  supernatural beliefs and, 32
  svakhi and, 30, 38–39
  tysiatskiĭ and, 30
Russian wedding songs, 30–57. *See also* marriage/weddings; Russian weddings
  bathhouses and, 37
  bride as epic hero in, 38–39
  celebratory, 50–55
  chastity in, 31–32, 37–39
  diction and, 31–32
  family life in, 34–35, 45–48, 58n3, 58n5
  green orchard metaphor in, 32–33
  groom as epic hero in, 42
  groom as worthy suitor in, 48–49
  hair and, 37–39, 45
  humor/satire in, 54–55
  hunting in, 39–42, 58n4
  journey to the groom's house and, 49–50
  krásota and, 34–39
  laments of the bride and, 31–39
  laments of the mother and, 34–35, 58n3
  magic tales and, 32
  orphan bride in, 45
  parents of the bride and, 34–35, 45, 58n3
  performance of, 31–32
  post-wedding feast and, 50–55
  sexual innuendo in, 42, 56–57
  supernatural beliefs and, 41
  violence in, 39–42, 58n4
  water as metaphor in, 42–44
  white swan metaphor in, 40–41
  work of the bride in, 44–45
Russian wondertales, xxvii, 655–672. *See also* magic tales
  byliny and, 658–659
  characters in, 661–662, 663*f*–665*f*
  ethnography and, 665–666
  formalism and, 657
  formulaic expression and, 661

functions of, 661
modern, 671–672
obscenity in, 671
religion and, 664–666
under Soviet Union, 657–660, 664–672
Russkie bogatyri (Karnaukhova), 509
Rüütel, Ingrid, 150
Rybnikov, Pavel, 496, 499–500, 511
Ryden, Kent, 469
Ryl's'kyi Institute of Folk Art, Folklore, and Ethnography (Ukrainian Academy of Science), 5
Rylsky Institute of Folk Art, Folklore, and Ethnography, 536
Ryvola, Jiří Wabi, 878
Rzeczpospolita, 531, 539n6

Sabaliauskas, Adolfas, 436
Sabbath, 417, 425n19
Sacra arca benedictionum, 372
sacramentalia, 369
"sacred materiality," 470
Sadan, Dov, 746
Sadko (*bylina* character), 492, 493f, 494f, 497, 507–508, 509f, 511
Sadko (film), 508, 509f
Sadko in the Underwater Kingdom (Repin) (painting), 516
Šahinpašić, Hamdija, 736
Said, Edward, 897
St. Petersburg State University Folklore Archive, 240
saints' days
    Carnival and, 317
    Lastovo Carnival and, 317
    nedeile and, 348–349
    Romanian community celebrations and, 344–345, 348–352, 356n12, 356n13
Sakina, Bronya, 780
Šaknys, Žilvytis, 288
Šaković, Emina, 586–587, 591, 593
Šaković, Hamdija, 586–588
Šaković, Zehra, 577
Salam, Florin, 836
Saliev, Ahmed, 798
Salihović, Selim, 735
Salković, Nedžad, 735

Salmon-Mack, Tamar, 760
Salvator of Horta, 373–374
Sâmbra Oilor, 343–344
Samiilo Kishka (*duma* character), 524
samodivy, 41
sanatur, 318
Sanin, Oles, 539n7
Sanskrit, 436–437
Šantić, Aleksa, 734
Sapoznik, Henry, 780
sârbă
    lăutari and, 821, 823, 840n15
    Romanian community celebrations and, 338, 345, 356n7
"Sârba expoziției," 823
"Sârba lui Pompieru," 821, 840n15
satire. *See* humor/satire
Saturnalian Carnival, 312
Saunier, Guy, 199–201
Savić, Mićo, 543f
Saxons, Transylvanian nobility and, 116, 134n7
saz, 732, 733–736, 734f, 737f
Schaefer, Gregor, 784
Schmidt, Bernard, 606
Schneemelcher, W., 417
Schut, Ralph, 874f
"screaming the dead," 201–202, 200f, 254
"S'dua hiç," 926
secondary burial, 198, 198f
Second Coming. *See* apocalypticism
secular celebrations, 353–354, 356n22
Seeger, Pete, 879–880, 883
seeker culture, 404, 424n4
Seeman, Sonia, 804–805
Sefaja, Vullnet, 918
Selected National Legends and Tales of Other Slavic Branches (Erben), 632
Selected Original Slovak Tales (Dobšinský), 639, 640f
Selection of Individual Original Slovak Tales, A (Dobšinský), 638
Selim II (Ottoman sultan), 846
Selimović, Meša, 683
semiotics, of Greek death rituals, 197–199, 198f
Šemsović, Sead, 727
"Seniai Buvau," 447
separation, rites/rituals and, 168

Sephardim, 752, 765n18, 775
Serbia, 61. *See also* Serbian Romani music;
  Serbian weddings (Kosovo); Slavic
  supernatural legends; South Slavic region
  Albanian *etnopop* and, 920–921
  Borino Vranje and, 856
  Bosnian refugees in Croatia and, 83–84,
    104n2
  Bulgaria and, 795–796, 799–801
  calendrical cycle in, 295–307
  Carnival and, 303
  ćef and, 850–851, 851f, 865n17
  Centre for Folk Dance Research of, 305,
    308n18
  choreography in, 301, 304–305
  COVID-19 pandemic in, 307
  cultural-artistic societies and, 301–302, 304,
    308n11, 308n12, 308n14
  dance in, 295–307
  devils/demons and, 297
  dodole and, 295–298, 302
  ethnochoreology in, 295–307
  First Serbian Uprising and, 548, 560
  gender and, 297–298
  izvorni folklor and, 302
  kafanski orkestri and, 847
  Karadžić and, 548–552
  koledari and, 295–298, 300, 302
  kraljice and, 295–298, 300, 302–303
  laments and, 209
  lazarice and, 295–298, 300, 302, 307n2,
    307n3
  Macedonia and, 795–796, 799–801
  modern, 305–307
  newly composed folk music/
    instrumentation and, 301
  obredna igra and, 299, 303
  orphans in, 297
  Orthodox Christianity in, 295–297, 301, 307
  Ottoman Empire and, 299, 846–849, 855–
    862, 863n2, 864n7
  ples and, 299, 306
  Romani music and, 795–796, 799–801
  romantic nationalism in, 548
  Serbian Empire and, 299
  under Soviet Union, 295–296, 298, 300–304,
    307, 308n11, 308n12, 308n14

Stara Srbija (Old Serbia) and, 73, 80n15
starogradska muzika and, 847
Staro Vranje and, 856
supernatural beliefs and, 297–300, 303
village life in, 295–298, 301–307
Vranje (*see* Serbian Romani music)
Yugoslavia and, 295–296, 298, 300–301,
  303–304, 307, 847, 849, 856
zavetina and, 307
Serbian Academy of Science and Art, 303,
  308n16
Serbian Empire, 299
Serbian Romani music, 845–863. *See also*
  Serbia
  čalgija orchestras and, 846, 861
  čoček and, 845, 857–859, 861f, 863n2, 866n27
  festivals and, 849
  gender and, 846–847
  marriage/weddings and, 851–855, 853f, 854f,
    860f, 861f, 865n18, 865n19, 865n22
  mehter and, 848, 864n7
  meter and, 854, 857–859, 865n22, 866n27
  Ottoman Empire and, 846–849, 855–862,
    863n2, 864n7
  performance of, 845–863, 863n2
  Sobinka and, 845
  surla-goč and, 847
  Vranjski čoček and, 845, 857–859, 863n2
Serbian weddings (Kosovo), 60–79. *See also*
  Kosovo; Serbia
  anthems and, 65, 80n7
  attire and, 64f, 67, 72–75, 73f, 77, 77f, 78f,
    80n13, 80n15
  blaga rakija and, 67
  bošča and, 72, 73f, 74, 80n13
  bride's role in, 76–77, 77f, 78f
  changes in custom practices, 67–68
  činimo žito and, 67
  community and, 66–67, 74
  dever and, 68, 76
  family life and, 76–77
  flag rituals and, 63–64, 64f, 65f, 80n7
  gender and, 67, 79
  identity and, 60–61, 64f, 67, 72–74, 73f,
    74–75, 80n13, 80n15
  kolo and, 63, 65, 67–71, 69f–71f, 73, 75–76,
    80n12

kum and, 67–68
length of festivities surrounding, 67
mothers-in-law and, 65, 67–71, 69f–71f, 73–76, 77f, 78f, 80n12
Orthodox Christianity and, 74, 76
patriarchal nature of, 67, 79
patriarchy/paternalism and, 67, 79
Serb population in post-war Kosovo and, 61–66, 64f, 65f, 79n5, 80n6–80n10
songs at, 65–66, 80n9–80n10
stari svat and, 68
svekrvino kolo and, 65, 67–71, 69f–71f, 73–76, 77f, 78f, 80n12
women in, 66, 74–75
zaigruvanje and, 65, 67, 71–72, 74, 75, 76
zamesuvanje and, 67–68, 72
Šerbo, Ismet Alajbegović, 735
Serbo-Croatian Folk Songs (Bartók & Lord), 588
Serbocroatian Heroic Songs (Parry & Lord), 593
Seremetakis, Nadia, 196–197, 201, 203, 205–206
Serez, 857
serfs, 1028
"Servant Who Took the Place of His Master, The," 616
Šešo, Luka, 681, 683, 691
Seth, Symeon, 609–610
Setleři, 878
Sevdah Bošnjaka (Žero), 723
Sevdah nadahnut životom (Pobrić), 723
sevdalinka, 721–737. *See also* Bosnia-Herzegovina
collections of, 723–727, 727f, 729, 736
courting and, 724–727
development of, 723–727, 727f
"ethno" music shows and, 735–736
gender and, 732, 733f
Islam and, 721–724, 728–729
mahala and, 724–727, 727f
media and, 722
motifs in, 730–732
newly composed folk music/instrumentation and, 733–735
Ottoman Empire and, 721–724
performance of, 732–737, 734f, 737f, 738n17
saz and, 732, 733–736, 734f, 737f
scholarship on, 721–722

starogradska muzika and, 733–734
tepsija and, 732, 733f
Sevdalinka, alhemija duše (Bajtal), 723
Sevdalinke (Žero), 723
Sevdalinke, balade i romanse Bosne i Hercegovine (Orahovac), 723
Sevdalinke 1 i 2 (Gunić), 723
Sevdalinke. Izbor iz bosansko-hercegovačke narodne lirike (Dizdar), 722
Sevdalinke. Narodne biser-pesme za pevanje (Veselinović), 722
sex
benedictions and, 376
Bulgarian popular music and, 903–904
in *byliny*, 504–506
chastity and (*see* chastity)
chastushki and, 953–954
desire and, 158–160
in epic poetry, 504–506
Estonian runosongs and, 155–164
Finland and, 164
genitalia and, 156–157
in Greek folk tales, 617
hunting as metaphor for, 42
obscenity and, 616, 671
resentment and, 158–160
in Russian wedding songs, 56–57
in songs, 504–506
Ukrainian weddings and, 17, 23
sexual orientation, Croat/Croatian weddings and, 90
Shakira, 925
"Shamakhanskaia Tsaritsa" (Pushkin), 509
shamans. *See also* healing
Hungary and, 364, 367
Moldova and, 404
Slavic supernatural legends and, 678
Shening-Parshina, M. M., 182
sher contradance, 772–773, 777
Shibaeva, A. N., 182
sholem-tants, 776
Shrek (film), 510
Shrove Tuesday, 319–323, 320f–322f, 332n14, 332n15
Shtern, Abram, 784
Shtetl Band Amsterdam, 784
Shtreiml, 784

Shukshin, Vasilii, 672
Shut, Andrii, 535
shyshky, 14, 16, 23
šiaudinis soda, 448
Šidlauskas, Domas, 440
Silverman, Carol, 796, 801, 803, 805–806
Simaner, Zekharia, 747, 752
"Šimarik," 925
Siminică, Dona Dumitru, 834
Simon, Taryn, 210
Simonides, Dorota, 699
Simple National Journal IV, 636–637
Simple National Slovak Tales (Dobšinský), 630, 631*f*, 632–634, 636, 638, 641, 643, 647*f*
Singer of Tales, The (D. Imamović album), 736
Singer of Tales, The (Lord), xxviii, 553, 736
singers. *See* performance
Široký, hluboký, 883
Škaljić, Abdulah, 721
Skansen Open-Air Museum, The, 1048
skladka, 11–12
Sklamberg, Lorin, 781
skomorokhi, 497–498, 503
Skoptsy, 407, 425n11
Škoro, Miroslav, 94–96, 99
skotshne, 773, 777
Skovajsa, Honza, 889
skrynia, 15, 28
Skultans, Vieda, 178
Škultéty, August Horislav, 629, 636, 638, 641–643
Slastion, Opanas, 535
Slava, Desi, 903, 938
slavery. *See also* captivity
  galley, 522, 524–525
  in Ottoman Empire, 514, 520–525, 521*f*, 533–534
  in Romania, 817–818, 840n1
Slavic region. *See* Slavic supernatural legend; South Slavic epic songs; South Slavic region; South Slavic women's ballads
Slavic supernatural legends, xxvii, 675–692. *See also* Bosnia-Herzegovina; Croatia; Serbia
  apparitions and, 678, 683
  categories of, 675–676
  characters in, 678–679
  defined, 677–678
  devils/demons and, 677–678
  dog-headed beings and, 678
  donkeys and, 679, 687
  ethnography and, 690–692
  fabulates and, 677, 685–688
  fairies/nymphs and, 678–682, 682*f*, 684, 686–692, 693n7, 693n9
  healing and, 678–679
  Imbrica and, 683, 693n7
  location and, 681–684, 693n7
  Mâli and, 683, 693n7
  memorates and, 677, 685–688
  migration and, 681, 683–685, 687, 693n9
  nationalism and, 690
  nightmares and, 678
  novelty in, 688–690
  paramours and, 679
  religion and, 676–677, 682
  "rhetoric of truth" and, 678
  scholarship on, 677–678, 685–688, 690–692
  shamans and, 678
  under Soviet Union, 690
  succubi and, 678
  unknown world and, 679–680
  vampires and, 678–680, 692, 693n4, 693n5
  "veracity negotiation" and, 678
  werewolves and, 678, 693n4
  witches/witchcraft and, 678, 680, 687, 691
Slavi Trifonov and his Ku-Ku band, 904
"Sleeping Beauty," 611*f*
Slobin, Mark, 749*f*–751*f*, 774
Slovak folk tales. *See also* magic tales
  characteristics of, 628–629
  collections of, 628–648, 630*f*, 631*f*, 635*f*, 637*f*, 640*f*, 642*f*, 647*f*
  devils/demons and, 643, 645–646
  editing of, 628, 632–636, 639, 640*f*, 641–645, 648
  form of oral narrative and, 632
  ideal form of, 636–641, 637*f*, 640*f*
  literary forgery and, 638
  Lutheranism and, 632
  magic and, 628–629, 635*f*, 637*f*, 642*f*, 643–646, 647*f*, 648
  romantic nationalism and, 628–629, 631, 634, 639, 641–648

scholarship on, 628–629, 632, 638
source attributions of, 633–634, 636
Slovakia. *See also* Slovak folk tales
    Habsburg Empire and, 648
    Lutheranism in, 632
    romantic nationalism and, 628–629, 631, 634, 639, 641–648
Slovak Tales (Francisci), 644
Slovak Tales and Legends (Němcová), 633
Slovak Tales: Book I. Tales of Ancient Legendary Times (Dobšinský & Škultéty), 629–630, 630f, 631–634, 636–643
Slovenia, xxiii, xxxiii, 88, 308n9, 364, 562n2, 675, 941
Slovenian scholars influential for study of folklore. *See* Kopitar, Jernej; Murko, Matija
Slovo, 494
Smallman, 907
Smith, Anthony, 470
Smith, Steve, 423
Šmits, Pēteris, 280, 438
snakes as reincarnated spirits, 228
"Snijeg pade na behar na voće," 733
Sobinka, 845
Sochorik, Miko, 633
socialism. *See also* Soviet Union
    Bulgaria under, 801–804, 897–899, 902
    Macedonia under, 804–806
    Romanian folk art under, 1038, 1040–1046
    Romani music under, 801–806
social media
    Albanian *etnopop* and, 919
    healing and, 380
    hungaromeme and, 1003, 1003f
    jokes and, 1001–1004, 1003f
    memes and, 993–994, 993f, 1003, 1003f
social order, Cortorar Romani weddings and, 110, 112–116
Sofia Gypsy Gaydari, 798
Soft Machine, 911
Soimonov, A. D., 497
Sokolov, Boris, 496
Sokolov, Iurii, 496
Sokolova, A. D., 251, 254
Sokolova, Liudmyla, 17, 18f
Sokolova, Serafima Pavlovna, 660

Solon, laments and, 195
Solovei Razboinik (*bylina* character), 490, 503, 509
Solov'ev, Vladimir, 659
"Song of Baghdad, The," 553–554
"Song of Miloš Obilić," 548–549
songs, 30–57. *See also* epic poetry; folk music/instrumentation; oral narrative
    Albanian death rituals and, 217, 230–234, 231f, 233f, 234–236, 237n17
    alliteration and, 139
    anthems (*see* anthems)
    artels and, 498
    ballad (*see* ballads)
    Baltic Germans and, 140–141, 166n3
    bathhouses and, 37
    bećarac and, 91–94, 102
    bride as epic hero in, 38–39
    burdens of motherhood and, 145–147
    byliny (*see byliny*)
    calendrical cycle and, 279, 290n3, 290n4
    cântecul miresei and, 127–130
    caroling and, 350
    celebratory, 50–55
    chastity and, 31–32, 37–39, 159–160
    chastushki (*see chastushki*)
    childbirth and, 150, 153–155
    collections of, 492–496, 514–515, 530–531, 534–537
    community and, 139–141
    Cortorar Romani weddings and, 127–130
    Croat/Croatian weddings and, 86–88, 91–94
    crying with words and, 230–234, 231f, 233f, 237n17
    culture and, 142, 164–165
    dainas/dainos and, 279, 290n3, 290n4, 432–451, 433f, 437f, 439f, 440f, 442f, 446f, 450f
    death and, 144–145
    decasyllabic, 577–578, 593
    desire and, 158–160
    diminutive forms of address in, 257–261
    dirges and, 195
    domoljubne tamburaške pjesme and, 86
    dumy (*see dumy*)
    epic poetry and, 32
    Estonian (*see* Estonian runosongs)
    evil eye and, 155

songs (*cont.*)
    family life and, 34–35, 45–48, 58n3, 58n5, 140, 145–150
    fertility and, 163
    Finland and, 164
    flag rituals and, 87–90, 104n4–104n6
    formula of counting and, 751, 765n17
    gender and, 147–150, 217, 501–506, 509, 774
    genitalia and, 156–157
    green orchard metaphor in, 32–33
    groom as epic hero in, 42
    groom as worthy suitor in, 48–49
    hair and, 37–39, 45
    heroic epic, xxvii
    human sacrifice and, 148
    humor/satire in, 54–55
    hunting in, 39–42, 58n4
    identity and, 139–141, 166n3, 166n4
    illegitimate children and, 148–150
    infanticide and, 147–150
    intonatsia and, 749, 751, 761, 765n15
    journey to the groom's house and, 49–50
    krásota and, 34–39
    of lament (*see* laments)
    lullabies and, 142–145
    lyric (*see* lyric songs)
    magic tales and, 32
    metaphors in, 32–33, 37–45, 257–261
    musical aspects of, 749–753, 749f–751f, 749n15–752n18
    nisiotika and, 204–205
    noviny and, 507–508
    octosyllabic, 577
    okićenje and, 557–559
    orphan bride in, 45
    Paganism and (*see dainas/dainos*)
    parallelism and, 139
    parents of the bride and, 34–35, 45, 58n3
    pentatonic scale and, 751, 765n16
    performance of (*see* performance)
    pjevanje u kolu and, 92
    poetic form of, 139
    posidelki and, 498
    post-traditionality and, 558–560
    post-wedding feast and, 50–55
    pregnancy and, 150–155
    psalmy and, 515, 517–518
    public domain and, 141–143
    recordings of, 141
    religion and, 279
    repetition and, 139
    repetition of syntactical features in, 32
    resentment and, 158–160
    rhyme and, 139, 260–261
    runosongs (*see* Estonian runosongs)
    Russian wedding (*see* Russian wedding songs)
    Serbian weddings (Kosovo) and, 65–66, 80n9–80n10
    sevdalinka (*see sevdalinka*)
    sex in, 155–164, 504–506
    sexual innuendo in, 42, 56–57
    "singer's epistemics" and, 588
    South Slavic (*see* South Slavic women's ballads)
    as spells, 366
    stanzas and, 139
    stariny and, 492, 507
    stichic form in, 32, 139
    supernatural beliefs and, 41, 142, 154–155
    sutartinės, 441
    tonality and, 827–828, 841n25
    traditional expression in, 32
    tramp, 877–878, 884–885
    tripartite structure and, 761, 762f
    trochaic meter and, 139
    trochaic octosyllabic meter and, 829, 842n26
    unfixed song texts and, 139
    unwanted children and, 147–150
    verbal aspects of, 745–749, 748t, 764n10
    verbal charms and, 140, 154
    vernacular, 877–879
    violence in, 39–42, 58n4
    water as metaphor in, 42–44
    white swan metaphor in, 40–41
    work of the bride in, 44–45
    Yiddish folk (*see* Yiddish folk songs)
    zachin and, 495, 501
    zapev and, 495
Soroka, Grigorii, 1028
"Sorrowful Song of the Noble Wife of Hasan Aga, The." *see Hasanaginica*
Sotirov, Atanas, 799

South Africa, 87, 104n5
South Slavic epic songs, 541–562. *See also* South Slavic region; South Slavic women's ballads
  Albania and, 545–546, 561
  border areas and, 541–542, 545–551, 560–561, 565–566
  boundary between oral and written, 552–560
  bugarštica and, 563n11
  Catholicism and, 541, 548
  Christianity and, 541–542, 545, 548–549, 551, 557
  collections of, 542, 543f, 544f, 546–561, 546f, 556f
  cycles of, 543–545
  defining, 541
  deseterac and, 542, 545, 549
  ethnography and, 552
  gender and, 551–552
  gusle and, 544f, 545, 551–552, 561, 579
  Habsburg Empire and, 541
  heroism in, 551–552
  Islam and, 541–542, 544–545, 551, 556–557
  Karadžić and, 548–552, 559–560
  Kosovo cycle in, 544, 548
  lahuta/lahutars and, 545
  loan words and, 545
  Marko Kraljević cycle in, 544
  marriage/weddings and, 542, 549, 557
  "Morlachs" and, 550–551
  myth and, 544
  novelty in, 560
  okićenje and, 557–559
  Orthodox Christianity and, 541, 548–549
  Ottoman Empire and, 541, 548, 561
  performance of, 545, 551–552, 555, 557–560
  philology of border areas and, 547–548, 550–551, 560–561, 565–566
  post-traditionality and, 558–560
  Ramadan and, 545
  "return song" type of, 542, 593
  "tradition of the border" and, 542, 545, 547, 562
  Venetia and, 542, 549
  "Wedding Song" type of, 542

South Slavic region. *See also* Bosnia-Herzegovina; South Slavic epic songs; Yugoslavia; *specific countries, e.g.* Bosnia-Herzegovina
  "anti-behavior" and, 387, 397
  anti-ponašanje and, 386–387
  attire and, 394
  bajalice and, 386, 388
  baptism and, 392
  body gestures and, 385, 394
  childbirth and, 385, 392–394, 397
  čveger and, 385
  death rites and, 392–394
  dever and, 392, 396
  devils/demons and, 388, 391, 395–396
  evil eye and, 392, 395–396
  fairies and, 397
  games and, 394
  Indo-European influence and, 397
  inverted ritual behavior in, 385–398
  marriage/weddings and, 392–394
  naopako ponašanje and, 387, 398n5
  nisam živ and, 386
  Paganism in, 397–398
  provlačenje and, 388, 390
  razbijanje sudova, 392–393
  scholarship on, 386–391, 389f
  spitting and, 385, 394–395
  verbal charms and, 386–391, 389f, 394–397
  violence and, 385, 392–394
  werewolves and, 392
  živ nisam and, 386, 396
South Slavic women's ballads, 576–595, 596n13, 600–602. *See also* South Slavic epic songs
  Catholicism and, 578, 581, 584
  Christianity and, 577, 579, 586f
  collections of, 576, 578f, 579–590, 586f, 587f, 589f, 593–595
  decasyllabic, 577–578, 593
  defined, 576–577
  ethnicity and, 582–583
  ethnography and, 579, 581, 584–585, 591, 594
  gusle and, 579, 584
  Indo-European influence and, 580, 582, 593
  Islam and, 577–581, 584–589 586f, 587f, 589f
  multiformity and, 577–578, 580, 582, 588–591, 593

South Slavic women's ballads (*cont.*)
  musicality of, 578–579
  myth and, 579–580, 582–583, 590–593
  octosyllabic, 577
  oral composition and, 590–592
  oral *vs.* written, 579–581
  Orthodox Christianity and, 581
  patriarchy and, 577, 581
  performance of, 576–579, 584–585, 588–590, 592–595
  Ramadan and, 579
  "singer's epistemics" and, 588
  tragic nature of, 578
Soviet Union. *See also* Russia
  Albania under, 216, 217–221, 218*f*, 236n2, 237n5, 237n6
  Baltic region under, 432, 438–439, 441, 443
  Bolshevik Revolution and, 403, 405
  byliny under, 507–508
  chastushki under, 952–953, 962–977, 980
  Croatia under, 85–86, 316
  Czechoslovakia under, 876, 878, 879–880
  dumy under, 535–536, 539n7
  Estonia under, 164
  glasnost and, 432, 441, 973
  Jewish people/Judaism under, 658
  klezmer music under, 773–774, 780
  Komsomol and, 974
  Kosovo under, 61
  Latvia under, 432, 438, 439
  Lithuania under, 432, 438–439, 441, 443
  Marxism and, 217–219, 262, 658, 660, 665–667
  Moldova under, 403–406, 410, 422, 423n1, 424n5, 424n10
  perestroika and, 432
  Russian folk art under, 1019, 1030–1033
  Russian wondertales under, 657–660, 664–672
  Russia under, 250–253, 252*f*, 256, 266n4
  Serbia under, 295–296, 298, 300–304, 307, 308n11, 308n12, 308n14
  siege of Leningrad and, 658
  Slavic supernatural legends under, 690
  Ukraine under, 5, 10, 17, 27, 28*f*, 459, 535–536, 539n7
Sovremennyi gorodskoi fol'klor (Belousov), 172

Spassov, Teodosii, 907, 908
Speranskyi, Mikhail, 535
spirit, Albanian death rituals and, 224–228, 229*f*, 237n11–237n15
Spirituál kvintet, 880
Spitalul amorului sau Cîntătorul dorului (Pann), 819
spitting, inverted ritual behavior and, 385, 394–395
Spitz, Sheryl Allison, 752
"Sredina i vrijeme nastanka i trajanja sevdalinke" (Maglajlić), 724
Sreznevskyi, Izmail, 534
Srpske narodne pjesme (Karadžić), 548, 581–582
Srpski etnografski zbornik (journal), 690
Srpski rječnik (Karadžić), 386, 398n2
Stahl, Henri, 407
Stalin, Josef, 507, 535–536, 658, 666, 774, 971
Stanevičius, Simonas, 436
Stanković, Borisav, 856
stanzas, Estonian runosongs and, 139
Stara Srbija (Old Serbia), 73, 80n15
stariny, 492, 507. *See also byliny*
stari svat, 68
starogradska, 733
starogradska muzika, 847
Staropražské písničky (Hašler), 877
starosty, 13–14, 18–19, 20*f*, 818
Staro Vranje, 856
"Star Spangled Banner," 88, 104n4
State Literary Museum, Estonia, 277
Stations of the Cross, 471
Statman, Andy, 779, 784, 886
Stavr Godinovich (*bylina* character), 502
Štědroň, Miloš, 885
Sten'ka Razin (*bylina* character), 492
Štěpánek, Libor, 883
"Step-Father, The," 532
stichic form in songs, 32
  Estonian runosongs and, 139
Stimmen der Völker in Liedern (Herder), 548–549, 756
Sting, 925
"Stinge, Doamne, Stelele," 834
Stočević, Arif-bey Rizvanbegović (Hikmet), 729

Storch, Scott, 925
Stories and Folktales. Cinderella. The Prince and the Mermaid. The City of Tritons, 621f
Storm Game (Winograd CD), 785
"Storm on the Black Sea," 525–526
Strânsul Oilor, 349
Strassburger Rätselbuch, 994
Straubergs, Kārlis, 438
Strauss, Deborah, 780
Stroebe, Margaret, 230
Stroebe, Wolfgang, 230
Štúr, Ľudovít, 643
Stutschewsky, Joachim, 774
Subcarpathian Rus, 884
succubi, 379, 678
Sučić, Manda, 689
sulaužtinis kryžiukas, 452–453
Šulek, Juro, 633
Suleyman the Magnificent (Ottoman Sultan), 520–521
summer solstice, 335–336, 336f, 348, 443–445, 445f, 446f
Sumtsov, Mykola, 535
Sunny Side, 873
supernatural beliefs. *See also* fertility; magic; magic tales; myth; *specific beliefs, e.g.* evil eye
    Albanian death rituals and, 224–228, 229f, 237n9, 237n11–237n16
    apparitions and (*see* apparitions)
    calendrical cycle and, 297–300, 303, 348
    Carnival and, 311–312
    childbirth and, 174–177, 184n8
    community and, 6–8, 10, 12
    Croat/Croatian weddings and, 87, 96, 103, 104n9
    curses and (*see* curses)
    dance and, 297–300, 303
    death rites and, 199
    defined, 677–678
    devils and (*see* devils/demons)
    dog-headed beings and, 678
    donkeys and, 679, 687
    Estonian runosongs and, 142, 154–155
    fairies/nymphs and (*see* fairies/nymphs)
    fairy tales and (*see* magic tales)
    Greek death rituals and, 199
    healing and, 678–679
    in Hungary, 363–381
    Imbrica and, 683, 693n7
    inverted ritual behavior and (*see* inverted ritual behavior)
    journey to the groom's house and, 49–50
    location and, 681–684, 693n7
    Mâli and, 683, 693n7
    medicalization and, 174–177, 184n8
    midwives and, 174–177, 184n8, 367
    migration and, 681, 683–685, 687, 693n9
    nightmares and, 678
    paramours and, 679
    religion and, 676–677, 682
    "rhetoric of truth" and, 678
    road magic and, 12
    Romanian community celebrations and, 342, 348
    rusalki and, 41
    Russian childbirth folklore and, 174–177, 184n8
    Russian weddings and, 32
    samodivy and, 41
    scholarship on, 677–678
    Serbia and, 297–300, 303
    Slavic (*see* Slavic supernatural legends)
    succubi and, 379, 678
    summer solstice and, 348
    Ukrainian weddings and, 6–8, 10, 12, 13f, 15–16
    unknown world and, 679–680
    urban legends (*see* Polish urban legends)
    vampires and, 678–680, 692, 693n4, 693n5
    "veracity negotiation" and, 678
    verbal charms and (*see* verbal charms)
    werewolves and, 678, 693n4
    Western Balkan (*see* Slavic supernatural legends)
    witchcraft (*see* witches/witchcraft)
superstitions. *See* inverted ritual behavior; magic; supernatural beliefs; *specific beliefs, e.g.* evil eye
Suprun, Pavlo, 536–537, 537f
Surikova, Domna, 495
surla-goč, 846–849, 861, 864n7
Surý, Petr, 886–887
sutartinės, 441

Šutkafest, 809
Švābe, Arveds, 438
svakhi, 30, 38–39
svashka, 18–19, 21
svatannia, 13–14
svatbarska muzika, 898, 901
svaty, 13–14
svekrvino kolo, 65, 67–71, 69f–71f, 73, 75–76, 80n12, 852–855, 853f, 854f, 865n19, 865n23
Sviatogor (*bylina* character), 486–489, 501, 505
Sviatoslavich, Igor, 492, 494–495
Svigals, Alicia, 781
svirdzhii, 793
svitilka, 18, 21
"Swan Maiden, The," 40–41
swastika, 452–453
sword dance, 312–318, 322–325, 330–331, 331n4, 331n6, 332n8
Sword Dancing in Europe: A History (Corrsin), 314–315
symbols, 450–453, 452f
Székelys, Transylvanian nobility and, 134n7
Szemerkényi, Ágnes, 990
Szendrey, Zsigmond, 994–995
Szmendrovich, Rochus, 378–379

tableware, 1017–1021, 1018f, 1020f
Tacitus, 431
Tairov, Amza, 807f
Tairović, Tea, 937–940, 938f
"Tale of the Stupid Ogre," 643
"Tallava," 933
táltos, 367
tamada, 27
tambura music
  bećarac and, 91–94, 102
  berde and, 84, 84f
  bisernica and, 84, 84f
  Croat/Croatian weddings and, 84–86, 84f, 86f, 89–103, 92f, 93f, 94f, 98f, 104n7, 104n9
  domoljubne tamburaške pjesme and, 86
  hostility towards, 90–91, 100
  humor/satire and, 99
  memory and, 100–104, 105n10
  motor vehicles and, 95–96
  neotraditional, 91, 104n7
  Orthodox Christianity and, 84–85
  Ottoman Empire and, 84
  territoriality and, 100–104, 105n10
  women and, 84
taraf, 820, 827, 837, 840n12
Târgul cepelor, 349
Târgul de fete, 349
Tarkan, 925
Tarkka, Lotte, 164
Tarras, Dave, 777–780, 782–784
Tartari, Aqif, 230
Tartu University, 141
Tătuniștii, 410
Tautumeitas, 450, 450f
"Taxi," 927–928
taxtaja. See chalices
Taylor, Archer, 986
Teagrass, 887–888
Teffi, Nadezhda, 672
Temkina, Anna, 174–175
Tenèze, Marie Louise, 608
Tenisheva, Maria, 1029
tentser, 773
Teodosievski, Stevo, 805
tepsija, 732, 733f
territoriality, *tambura* music and, 100–104, 105n10
textiles, 1019–1022, 1020f
Thagard, Daniel Kunda, 784
theft, community and, 8
Theile-Dohrmann, Klaus, 700
Theogony (Hesiod), 609
Theory and History of Folklore (Liberman), 667
There is Such a People (Bulgarian populist party), 904
Thesmophoria Mystery Cult, 195
Thomas, Deborah, 86
Thomas, Nicholas, 1038
Thompson, Stith, 583, 655. *See also* Aarne-Thompson-Uther Tale-Type Index
Thoms, William, xxv
"Three Brothers by the River Samarka, The," 527
"Three Golden Hairs of the Wise Old Man," 643
"Three Hairs from the Devil's Beard," 643
Three Klezmer Dances (Roustom), 784
"Three Oranges, The," 646

"Three Raven Broths, The," 644
"Three Stolen Princesses, The," 645–646
Tibetan Book of the Dead, The, 236n1
Tichota, Jiří, 880
Timbaland, 925
Time of the Gypsies (Kusturica film), 838
"Ti nuk ekziston," 931
tish nign, 775–776
Tito, Josip Broz, 805, 813n9
tocmeala, 114–115, 118, 119f, 120–122, 124, 125, 134n9
Tolstaya, S. M., 254
Tolstoy, Lev, 1028
tonality, *lăutari* and, 827–828, 841n25
Top Fest (TV show), 933
Topographische Nachrichten von Lief- und Ehstland (Hupel), 286
Toporov, Vladimir, 397, 593
Tormis, Veljo, 150
Toynbee, Jason, 871–872
Tradiční hudba: Hledání kořenů (Tyllner), 877
Traditional Music and Dance, Center for, 784
Traditional Music Study Group on Music and Dance in Southeastern Europe, 812f
"tradition of the border," 542, 545, 547, 562
Tragom srpskohrvatske narodne epike. Putovanja u godinama 1930–1932 (Murko), 584
tramp songs, 877–878, 884–885
trances, 367
transductive attention, 95
transition, rites/rituals and, 168, 171, 183n3
transnational dimensions in music, 743, 920–921
Transylvania, 108, 110, 116, 134n4, 134n7. *See also* Cortorar Romani weddings
trap music, 908
Tráva, Druhá, 873–874, 886
Trento, decrees of, 366
Tri Bogatyri i Shamakhanskaia Tsaritsa, 509, 510f
Trifonov, Slavi, 904
Trinity Saturday, 247, 266n3
Trinkūnas, Jonas, 441–442, 442f
Trinkūnienė, Inija, 441–442, 442f
tripartite structures, 702, 761, 762f
Trischka, Tony, 886

trochaic meter
   Estonian runosongs and, 139
   lyric songs and, 829, 842n26
   octosyllabic, 829, 842n26
Troitsa, 247, 266n3
Tropinin, Vasilii, 1028
trousseau, Cortorar Romani weddings and, 113–114, 115f, 134n6
"Tsar-Maiden, The" (Tsvetaeva), 672
Tsertelev, Mykola, 534
Tsiaris, Alexander, 197
tsigani, 792
Tsishchanka, Ivan, 951
Tsvetaeva, Marina, 672
tsyhanshchyna, 25–26, 26f
Tuda, Shpresa, 221
Tugarin Zmei (*bylina* character), 490–491, 504, 509
Tugar Khan, 490
Tulić, Himzo, 735
Tumėnas, Vytautas, 443, 451
tŭpan, 795–796, 799, 810–811
turbofolk, 925, 933–934
Turco-Greek War (1920–1922), 213n2
Turino, Thomas, 88, 89
Turkey. *See* Ottoman Empire
Turko-Tatar slavery cycle in *dumy*, 514, 520–525, 521f, 533–534
Turner, Victor, 337
"Turski Mekam," 852, 865n18
TV Sarajevo, 735
"Twins or Blood-Brothers, The," 645
"Two Sisters," 637, 631f, 639
two witnesses, 414–415, 419, 425n18
"Tya," 907
Tyllner, Lubomír, 877
tysiatskiĭ, 30

U 2, 911
UCECOM (National Union of Craft Cooperatives), 1041–1043, 1046
Ugljanin, Salih, 546, 546f, 553–554
ugunskrusts, 452
Uguns un nakts (Rainis), 438
Uhde, Milan, 885
Uhlíková, Lucie, 877
Ujváry, Zoltán, 989

Ukraine. *See also* Ukrainian Marianism; Ukrainian weddings
   byliny and, 491, 496, 498, 507
   Catholicism in, 460, 465, 471–472
   chastushki in, 951–955, 962–966, 972, 980
   devils/demons and, 461
   dumy and (*see dumy*)
   epic poetry and, 513–514
   folk religion in, 461–462, 478
   Grand Duchy of Lithuania and, 432
   Hinduism in, 460
   Judaism in, 460
   klezmer music and, 771, 774, 779–781, 783–785
   nationhood of, 513–514, 519, 535–536, 538
   Orthodox Christianity in, 460–461, 477
   Paganism in, 460
   Protestantism in, 460
   religious pluralism in, 460–461
   Russia and, 466
   under Soviet Union, 5, 10, 17, 27, 28*f*, 459, 535–536, 539n7
   war in, xxx
Ukrainian Academy of Science, Ryl's'kyi Institute of Folk Art, Folklore, and Ethnography, 5
Ukrainian ballads, 8–9, 11, 16, 23–24
Ukrainian folk epic. *See dumy*
"Ukrainian Jerusalem," 471, 469*f*, 470*f*
Ukrainian Marianism, 459–479. *See also* Marianism; Ukraine
   apparitions and, 459–460, 462–479, 472*f*, 473*f*, 475*f*, 476*f*
   Bryn apparition and, 463–464, 469–470, 473–478, 476*f*
   "charisma of place" and, 460, 466–467, 478–479
   Dzhubryk apparition and, 464–465
   Malyi Hvizdets apparition and, 464, 466, 468–470, 473, 475–479, 475*f*
   media and, 459, 471
   Pohonia Monastery of the Dormition of the Mother of God and, 465, 473, 475
   rituals and, 476–478
   "Ukrainian Jerusalem" and, 471, 473*f*, 474*f*
   Vybli apparition and, 462–463, 468
   Zarvanytsia apparition and, 465, 470–479, 472*f*, 473*f*

Ukrainian weddings, 5–28. *See also* Ukraine
   attire and, 14–15, 17, 24–26
   ballads and, 8–9, 11, 16, 21–24
   betrothal and, 13–14
   boiary and, 16–17, 19, 22, 29n8
   ceremony and, 17–25, 18*f*–20*f*, 24*f*
   chastity and, 10–11, 24–25
   civil ceremony and, 17
   community and, 6–14
   courting and, 10–11, 14
   courtship and, 10–13, 13*f*
   daughter's relationship with in-laws and, 6–10, 7*f*, 16, 28n2
   divination and, 10
   divych vechir and, 16–17
   domovyny and, 14
   dosvitky and, 10–12, 27
   druzhky and, 16–17, 19, 21–22, 24, 29n8
   family life and, 6–10, 7*f*, 21, 24, 28n2
   fertility and, 15, 17, 29n7
   games and, 10
   hair ceremony and, 24
   hil'tse and, 17
   horilka and, 15, 19, 23
   hromada and, 10
   humor/satire and, 17, 21–23, 25–26, 26*f*
   icons and, 17, 23
   klub and, 17, 19*f*, 27
   korovai and, 14–15, 21, 23, 24*f*, 28
   korovainytsi and, 14–15, 28
   krolevets rushnyk and, 15, 29n7
   modernization and, 27–28, 28*f*
   omens and, 10, 15–16
   poizd and, 18–21, 20*f*
   post–wedding events and, 25–26, 26*f*
   preparations for, 14–17, 29n6–29n8
   prychet and, 15, 23
   prydane and, 23
   reconciliation and, 22–23
   ribaldry at, 17, 23
   rushnyk and, 14–15, 23, 24*f*, 27, 29n7
   shyshky and, 14, 16, 23
   skladka and, 11–12
   skrynia and, 15, 28
   under Soviet Union, 5, 10, 17, 27, 28*f*
   starosty and, 13–14, 18–19, 20*f*
   supernatural beliefs and, 6–8, 10, 12, 13*f*, 15–16

svashka and, 18–19, 21
svatannia and, 13–14
svaty and, 13–14
svitilka and, 18, 21
tamada and, 27
tsyhanshchyna and, 25–26, 26f
ukrains'ke and, 15, 17
in urban settings, 27–28
vechornytsi and, 10–12, 27
voritne and, 19, 21
vulytsia and, 12, 13f, 27
witches/witchcraft and, 6, 12
zmovyny and, 14
Ukrainka, Lesia, 535
ukrains'ke, 15, 17
Ulmanis, Kārlis, 287, 451–452, 452f
Umičević, Dušan, 722
Uncle Dave Macon, 884
Underwater Adventures of Sadko, The (film), 492, 494f
"Under Yankele's Cradle" (Mlotek & Slobin), 749f, 753
Union Day, 354
"Unique," 903
United Nations
    UN administration (Kosovo), 60–62, 72, 79, 921
    UNESCO, 288–289, 327, 348, 441, 1036, 1038
United States
    Albanian *etnopop* and, 922
    Confederacy and, 88, 104n5
    Czech bluegrass and, 871–872, 877–878, 889–890
    klezmer music in, 776–785
    national anthem and, 87–88, 104n4, 104n5
    wild west motifs in Czech bluegrass, 884–885
urban legends. *See* Polish urban legends
urban settings
    calendrical cycle in, 281, 283–285
    Croat/Croatian weddings in, 98–99
    Greek death rituals and, 196–197
    jokes and, 1000–1001
    lăutari in (*see lăutari*)
    Russian childbirth folklore in, 172–176, 181–182
    starogradska muzika and, 847
    Ukrainian weddings in, 27–28

Urdea, Alexandra, 1044–1045
Ushev, Theodore, 906
Uspenski, Boris, 387, 390–391, 397
Uspenskii, Boris, 954
USSR. *See* Soviet Union
U Starého Rebela, 889, 890f
Usual Suspects, 906–907
utensils, 1017–1021, 1018f, 1020f
Uther, Hans-Jörg, 583, 655. *See also* Aarne-Thompson-Uther Tale-Type Index

Vai, Steve, 911
Vaitkevičius, Vykintas, 443, 451
Valdemars, Krišjānis, 435
Valdobrev, Stefan, 906–907
Valéry, Paul, 234
vampires, 678–680, 692, 693n4, 693n5
van Esterik, Penny, 1056
van Gennep, Arnold, 168, 172, 198
Vargha, Katalin, 992
Vas, Bert, 784
Vaseva, Sashka, 900
Vasić, Olivera, 297, 300, 304–305
Vasilii Buslaev (*bylina* character), 492
Vasilisa Nikulichna (*bylina* character), 502
"Vasilisa the Beautiful," 662, 658f–659f
Vasiljević, Miodrag, 736
Vasko the Patch, 997
Vasnetsov, Viktor, 490f, 491f, 507, 1029
Vavro, Mišo, 887
Vázsonyi, Andrew, 685–687
vechornytsi, 10–12, 27
Vėlinės, 446–447
Vėlius, Norbertas, 443
Vėlų laikas, 447
Venetia, 542, 549, 610
Venetsianov, Aleksei, 1028
"veracity negotiation," 678
verbal charms
    "anti-behavior" and, 387, 397
    anti-ponašanje and, 386–387
    bajalice and, 386, 388
    childbirth and, 170, 175
    čveger and, 385
    Estonian runosongs and, 140, 154
    folk religion and, 408–409, 416, 417f, 418–419, 421–423, 426n22

verbal charms (*cont.*)
   in Hungary, 366–371, 374–375, 381
   inverted ritual behavior and, 385–391, 389f, 394–397
   naopako ponašanje and, 387, 398n5
   nisam živ and, 386
   provlačenje and, 388, 390
   Russian childbirth folklore and, 170, 175
   scholarship on, 386–391, 389f
   in South Slavic region, 385–391, 389f, 394–397
   types of, 388–390, 389f
   živ nisam and, 386, 396
Veresai, Ostap, 535
"vernacular religion," 462
vernacular songs, 877–879
Veselinović, Janko, 722
Viaggio in Dalmazia (Fortis), 549, 580
vici/vitsa, 134n4
Victory Day, 252, 252f
vidpusty, 515
Vienna Phonogrammarchiv, 584
Vijelie, Vali, 836, 938
vile. See fairies/nymphs
village life. *See also* community
   Albanian death rituals and, 220, 237n6
   căiuți and, 351
   calendrical cycle and, 295–298, 301–307, 308n11, 308n12, 308n14, 346–348, 347f, 356n16, 356n17
   Căluș and, 346–348, 347f, 351, 353f, 356n16, 356n17
   Călușerul Transilvănean and, 351, 353f
   capră and, 351, 352f
   caroling and, 350
   cete and, 350–351
   "charisma of place" and, 460, 466–467, 478–479
   "chosen places" and, 470
   Christmas and, 350–353, 352f, 353f, 356n20
   "comparative links" and, 470
   cultural–artistic societies and, 301–302, 304, 308n11, 308n12, 308n14
   dance and, 295–298, 301–307, 346–348, 347f, 356n16, 356n17
   Epiphany and, 351–352
   ethnochoreology and, 295–298, 301–307
   fairs and, 348–349
   Festivalul datinilor de iarnă and, 351
   Focul lui Sumedru and, 350
   Hora la Prislop and, 349
   "identity of closeness" and, 470
   izvorni folklor and, 302
   newly composed folk music/instrumentation and, 301
   New Year's and, 350–353, 352f, 353f, 356n20
   placism and, 467
   Romanian community celebrations and, 344–345, 346–348, 346f, 347f, 356n12, 356n13, 356n16, 356n17
   Russian death rituals and, 263–265
   "sacred materiality" and, 470
   in Serbia, 295–298, 301–307
   Târgul cepelor and, 349
   Târgul de fete and, 349
   zavetina and, 307
Village Museum (Bucharest), 1049
Vinogradov, G. S., 240, 245, 256
violence
   anthems and, 88–89
   flag rituals and, 88–90
   Greek death rituals and, 195
   identity and, 88–90
   inverted ritual behavior and, 385, 392–394
   laments and, 195
   marriage/weddings and, 39–42, 58n4, 88–90
   religion and, 88–89
   in Russian wedding songs, 39–42, 58n4
virginity. *See* chastity
Virgin Mary. *See* Marianism
Visendorfs, Henrijs, 290n4
Visions of Grigore Culiac and His Sufferings for the Confession of the Second Coming of Jesus Christ (Culian), 410, 412f, 419–420, 422
Vision That Appeared in the Year 1920, A (A. Culiac), 410, 420, 421
Višnjić, Filip, 559–560
Visuomybė, 440–441
Vitez, Zorica, 98–99
"Vivodan," 65–66, 80n9–80n10
Vizonsky, Nathan, 778

Vladimir, Prince (*bylina* character), 489–490, 495, 498, 502–504
Vladimir I (Russian prince), 489
Vlahovljak, Mumin, 557–559
Vlajka (Ztracenkáři), 877–878
Vlasova, Z., 952
Vlasova, Z. I., 952
Vllasaliu, Sinan, 924f
Voigt, Vilmos, 990, 995
Volkmusik Bosniens und der Herzegovina (Marijić), 722
Volkov, A. D., 973
Volkskalender, 279–280
Volkskunde, Romanian folk art and, 1039
Volkslieder (Herder), 549
Voltron (TV series), 896, 911
von Glasersfeld, Ernst, 236n1
von Sydow, Carl Wilhelm, 685–686
Vöö, Gabriella, 989
voritne, 19, 21
Voronov, Vasilii, 1032
Voyvoda, 907
Vrabac, Avdo, 735
Vranić, Semir, 722
Vrani Volosa, 907
"Vranjanka" (Bakija Bakić ensemble), 849
Vranje, Serbia. *See* Serbian Romani music
Vranjski čoček, 845, 857–859, 861f, 863n2, 866n27
Vrećo, Božo, 736
Vujnović, Nikola, 558, 585, 588
Vukanović, Tatomir, 793, 795–796
Vulpian, Dimitrie, 820
vulytsia, 12, 13f, 27
Vybli apparition, 462–463, 468
Vydūnas, 438
Vytautas the Great, 283

Wald, Gayle, 86
Wałęsa, Lech, 709, 716n12
Waletzky, Joshua, 780
Wang, Iefke, 784
warlocks. *See* witches/witchcraft
Warner, Elizabeth, 263
"Warrior, The" (Dobšinský), 645

Warschauer, Jeffery, 780
washing, Russian death rituals and, 240–244
water as metaphor in Russian wedding songs, 42–44
water nymphs, 615
"Water of Life," 606
wealth. *See* material culture
"Wedding of Banović Stjepan, The," 593
"Wedding of Bećiragić Meho, The," 557–558
weddings. *See* marriage/weddings; Ukrainian weddings
"Wedding Song" type of South Slavic epic songs, 542
Weinreich, Max, 771
Weintraub, Hirsch, 772
Weintraub, Steve, 783
Weisberger, Amit, 784
We Remember, We Love, We Grieve: Mortuary and Memorial Practice in Contemporary Russia (Warner & Adonyeva), 263
werewolves, 285, 392, 678, 693n4
Werthes, Friedrich, 549
Western Balkan supernatural legends. *See* Slavic supernatural legends
We've Come Here to Take Your Jobs Away (Kultur Shock album), 911
"'When Ovaries Retire': Contrasting Women's Experiences with Feminist and Medical Models of Menopause" (Goldstein), 180–181
"Where Have You Been, My Little Daughter?" (Cahan), 762f
"White Goat Comes Along, A" (Mlotek & Slobin), 751f
white magic, 366–367
white swan metaphor in Russian wedding songs, 40–41
"Wide Boy, The," 634
"Widow and Her Three Sons, The," 533
"Wiegeli–Ziegeli," 746
Wilce, James, 209–210
Wilde Flowers, 911
Williams, Patrick, 109
Winograd, Michael, 785
winter solstice, 336f, 448–449
Wirusi (Nexhat Mujova), 926–928, 927f

witches/witchcraft. *See also* magic; supernatural beliefs
   Croat/Croatian weddings and, 103
   Estonian runosongs and, 146
   Hungary and, 365–368, 378
   Latvia and, 285
   táltos and, 367
   Ukrainian weddings and, 6, 12
   witchcraft trials and, 285, 365–368, 378
"With You," 903
"Woman on a horse, Gacko" (image), 578*f*
women. *See* gender; South Slavic women's ballads
woodworking, 1018*f*, 1019
words of magic, 366–367
work of the bride in Russian wedding songs, 44–45
World Trade Center, 1002
Wright-Mills, Charles, 907
Wyatt, Robert, 911

xanamika, 112, 121

"Yana boli belo gŭrlo" (Sofia Gypsy Gaydari), 798
"Ya nour al-ayn," 925
Yermoloff, Alexis, 280
Yiddish folk songs, 741–764
   Ashkenazim (*see* Ashkenazim)
   ballads and, 759–762, 761*f*, 762*f*
   cultural conservatism and, 742, 744–745, 747, 752–754, 760, 763
   Eastern repertoires and, 744–745
   formula of counting and, 751, 765n17
   gender and, 774
   German cultural influence on, 743–749, 753, 756–760, 763
   goats in, 745–747, 748*t*, 749, 751, 763, 764n10
   Holocaust and, 741, 744, 756
   innovative tradition and, 744–745
   inspiration and, 744–745
   intonatsia and, 749, 751, 761, 765n15
   klezmer music and, 742–744, 749, 751, 753, 758–761, 763
   lidir and, 742
   love of God and, 755–756
   lullabies and, 745–753, 748*t*, 749*f*–751*f*, 749n15–752n18, 764n10
   lyric songs and, 51*f*, 753–759, 758*f*
   modality of, 753
   motifs in, 748*t*
   musical aspects of, 749–753, 749*f*–751*f*, 749n15–752n18
   non-ritual, 742–744
   pentatonic scale and, 751, 765n16
   performance of, 741–744, 752–754, 756, 759, 761, 763
   Sephardic sources of, 752, 765n18
   "shtetlspeak" and, 760
   Slavic influence on, 741–743, 745, 747–748, 751–753, 758–760, 763, 764n10
   Talmud and, 744, 751
   Torah and, 747–748, 748*t*
   transnational dimension in song and, 743
   tripartite structure of, 761, 762*f*
   verbal aspects of, 745–749, 748*t*, 764n10
Yiddish Summer Weimar, 783
Yiddish theater, klezmer music and, 778
"Yolumu bulurum," 931
"You're not Around," 903
"Youth Who Wanted to Learn What Fear Is, The," 645
YouTube, 904, 934–939, 941
Ysaÿe, Eugène, 823
"Yugoslav Folk Songs from Sandžak as Sung by Hamdija Šahinpašić from Pljevlje" (Vasilkević), 736
Yugoslavia, 308n9. *See also* South Slavic region
   Albanian *etnopop* and, 920–921, 940–941
   collapse of, 304
   Croatia and, 83, 85–88, 95–96, 103, 316
   dance in, 295–296, 298, 300–301, 303–304, 307
   ethnochoreology in, 295–296, 298, 300–301, 303–304, 307
   Kosovo and, 61, 67
   Lastovo Carnival and, 316
   Romani music and, 792, 800, 804–805, 808
   Serbia and, 295–296, 298, 300–301, 303–304, 307, 847, 849, 856
   Slavic supernatural legends and, 684, 690

Zabava Putiatichna (*bylina* character), 489–490

Zabili, zabili, 885
Zaboravljeno blago. Stotinu bosanskih narodnih pjesama sa notnim zapisima (Vranić & Berbić), 722
zachin, 495, 501
Za gradom jabuka. 200 naljepših sevdalinki (Lovrenović), 723
Zahar, Milutin Popović, 65, 80n9
zaigruvanje, 65, 67, 71–72, 74, 76
Žák, Martín, 876
Zakić, Mirjana, 63
Zālīte, Māra, 437
Zambelios, Spyridon, 213n3
zamesuvanje, 67–68, 72
zaochnoe otpevanie, 250–251
zapev, 495
Zapiski o Iuznoi Rusi (Kulish), 535
Zappa, Frank, 911
Zarvanytsia apparition, 465, 470–479, 472*f*, 473*f*
Zastavniković, Mihajlo, 80n10
zavetina, 307
Zbornik za narodni život i običaje (journal), 690
Zdeněk, 875*f*
Zečaj, Emina, 735
Zečević, Slobodan, 297, 300, 302–304, 305, 308n12, 308n14, 308n16, 308n17
Zelenáči, 884, 886
Zemtsovsky, Izaly, 752–753
Žero, Muhamed, 723

Zguta, Russell, 497–498
Zhemchuzhnikov, Lev, 535
Zhidkova, Elena, 250
Zhirmunsky, Viktor, 657
zhok, 778
"Zidanje Skadra," 582
Ziemassvētki, 448–449
Zipes, Jack, 662
živ nisam, 386, 396
Žižek, Slavoj, 897
Zlotea, Ioan, 404
Zmei Gorynych (*bylina* character), 509, 672
zmovyny, 14
zogekhts, 775
Zog I (King of Albania), 220
Zoroastrianism, 440
Zoshchenko, Mikhail, 658
Zovko, Ivan, 723
Zsigmond, Győző, 999
Ztracenkáři, 877
Zubok, Vladislav, 667
zurna, 793, 794*f*, 797*f*
zurnadzhii, 793
zurna-tŭpan, 795–796, 799, 810–811
Zvizdić, Mukila, 589*f*
Zvizdić, Salih, 587
Zvizdić, Ziba, 589*f*
Zvláštní znamení woodcraft (Ryvola), 878
Çelaj, Mbete, 233
Çelaj, Nazif, 233
Çeta, Anton, 217